the Integration of Technology in the Classroom

Online Tutoring from SmarThinking In partnership with SmarThinking, we offer personalized, online tutoring during typical homework hours. Every new text comes with a one-semester passkey that will allow access to three types of services:

- **Live help** provides access to 20 hours a week of real-time, one-on-one instruction. With Internet access, students may interact live online with an experienced SmarThinking "e-structor" (online tutor) between 9 AM and 1 AM EST, every Sunday through Thursday.
- **Questions anytime** enables students to submit questions 24 hours a day, 7 days a week, for response by an e-structor within 24 hours. Students can even submit spreadsheets for personalized feedback within 24 hours.
- **Independent Study Resources** are available around the clock and provide access to additional educational services, ranging from interactive web sites to Frequently Asked Questions posed to SmarThinking e-structors.

NEW! Introduction to Financial Accounting An interactive multi-media product that provides practical, intuitive instruction on fundamental accounting concepts. This CD-ROM combines video, audio, and text in an interactive simulation. The user learns accounting by recording a series of business transactions for a real-world company. Each transaction is described and recorded in everyday business language and reconciled to financial statements prepared in accordance with Generally Accepted Accounting Principles ("GAAP"). An accounting coach tutors students as they proceed through the program. They are not able to move ahead without correctly completing each transaction, and they receive a performance evaluation at the end of the program. This program is designed to help students:

- Understand fundamental accounting terminology
- Become intelligent readers of financial statements
- Value, record, and classify business transactions
- Assess how business decisions affect profits and liquidity

The Needles Accounting Resource Center at http://accounting.college.hmco.com

For Students

- **NEW! ACE,** an online self-quizzing program, with over 1,000 new questions, that allows students to check their mastery of the topics covered in each chapter
- **Research Activities** based on the material covered in each chapter
- **Toys "R" Us Annual Report Activities** that make use of the latest Toys "R" Us financial statements
- **Links** to the web sites of over 200 real companies and annual reports referenced in the book
- **A List of Business Readings** from leading periodicals
- **Check Figures** for end-of-chapter problems

For Instructors

- **NEW!** A brand new set of **PowerPoint Slides** that will enhance classroom presentation of text material; the new slides are concise, contain lots of examples of transactions, and explain the accounting process in clear, easy-to-follow steps
- **Text previews,** which highlight new features and provide demonstrations of supplements
- **Sample syllabi** from other first-year accounting faculty
- *Accounting Instructors' Report* newsletter, which explores a wide range of contemporary teaching issues
- **Electronic Solutions,** fully functioning Excel spreadsheets for all text exercises, problems, and cases from the printed Instructor's Solutions Manual

Teaching Accounting Online This online training course from Faculty Development Programs provides suggestions for integrating new technologies into accounting education. Available within Blackboard.com, the course includes the following modules: Designing Course Basics; Be the Student; Common Online Tools; Designing Teaching Strategies; Designing Learning Activities; Designing Outcomes Assessment; and Delivering a Course. For more information, contact your Houghton Mifflin sales representative or our Faculty Services Center at (800) 733-1717.

2005e

NINTH EDITION

PRINCIPLES OF ACCOUNTING

VOLUME II: CHAPTERS 13-27

Belverd E. Needles, Jr., Ph.D., C.P.A., C.M.A.
DePaul University

Marian Powers, Ph.D.
Northwestern University

Susan V. Crosson, M.S. Accounting, C.P.A.
Santa Fe Community College, Florida

Houghton Mifflin Company
Boston New York

To Jennifer, Jeffrey, Annabelle, and Abigail
To Bruce, Brent, and Courtney Crosson and in loving memory of Helen and Bryce Van Valkenburgh

Senior Sponsoring Editor: Bonnie Binkert
Senior Development Editor: Margaret M. Kearney
Project Editor: Claudine Bellanton
Editorial Assistants: Lisa Goodman and Rachel Zanders
Senior Production/Design Coordinator: Sarah L. Ambrose
Senior Manufacturing Coordinator: Priscilla J. Bailey
Marketing Manager: Todd Berman

Custom Publishing Editor: Kyle Henderson
Custom Publishing Production Manager: Kathleen McCourt
Project Coordinator: Kim Gavrilles

Photo Credits: page 3, ©Edward Holub/CORBIS; page 5, Courtesy of Intel Corporation; page 45, ©DigitalVision/PictureQuest; page 89, ©Getty Images; page 129, ©Ed Kashi/CORBIS; page 167, ©Getty Images; page 169, Courtesy of Claire's Stores, Inc.; page 213, © Mark Richards/PhotoEdit; page 323, ©Lester Lefkowitz/Getty Images; page 365, ©Bruce Ayres/Getty Images; page 403, © Jose Luis Pelaez, Inc./CORBIS; page 441, ©BananaStock/Picturequest; page 443, Courtesy of J.C. Penney Company, Inc.; page 479, ©Ed Young/CORBIS; page 481, Courtesy of Fermi National Accelerator Laboratory; page 525, ©Getty Images; page 557, ©Arthur Tilley/Getty Images; page 593, ©AP/Wide World Photos; page 629, ©Todd Gipstein/CORBIS; page 669, ©Getty Images, page 709, ©DigitalVision/PictureQuest; page 711, Courtesy of Goodyear Tire & Rubber Company; page 751, ©AP/Wide World Photos; page 793, © AFP/Getty Images; page 795, Courtesy of United Parcel Service; page 835, © Scott Olson/ Getty Images; page 883, ©Don Smetzer/Getty Images; page 925, Courtesy of England , Inc.; page 965, ©Steve Kagan/Getty Images; page 1003, ©Stephen Marks/Getty Images; page 1005, Courtesy of Enterprise Rent-A-Car, page 1049, © Sergio Piumatti; page 1091, ©Ken Redding/CORBIS; page 1093, Courtesy of Harley Davidson, Inc., page 1129, ©David Young-Wolff/Getty Images.

The Toys "R" Us Annual Report (excerpts and complete) for the year ended February 1, 2003, which appears at the end of Chapter 6, pages 267-302, is reprinted by permission.

The 2002 Annual Report from Walgreens, which appears at the end of Chapter 6, pages 303-321, is reprinted with permission of Walgreen Co.

This book is written to provide accurate and authoritative information concerning the covered topics. It is not meant to take the place of professional advice.

This book contains select works from existing Houghton Mifflin Company resources and was produced by Houghton Mifflin Custom Publishing for collegiate use. As such, those adopting and/or contributing to this work are responsible for editorial content, accuracy, continuity and completeness.

Copyright © 2005 by Houghton Mifflin Company. 2005 Impression. All rights reserved.

No part of this work may be reproduced or transmitted in any form or by any means, electronic or mechanical, including photocopying and recording, or by any information storage or retrieval system without the prior written permission of Houghton Mifflin Company unless such copying is expressly permitted by federal copyright law. Address inquiries to College Permissions, Houghton Mifflin Company, 222 Berkeley Street, Boston, MA 02116-3764.

Printed in the United States of America.

ISBN: 0-618-49645-9
N-03357

1 2 3 4 5 6 7 8 9 – CCI – 06 05 04

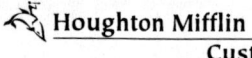

Houghton Mifflin
Custom Publishing

222 Berkeley Street • Boston, MA 02116

Address all correspondence and order information to the above address.

Brief Contents

13 Partnerships 556

14 Contributed Capital 592

15 The Corporate Income Statement and the Statement of Stockholders' Equity 628

16 Long-Term Liabilities 668

17 The Statement of Cash Flows 708

18 Financial Performance Evaluation 750

19 The Changing Business Environment: A Manager's Perspective 792

20 Cost Concepts and Cost Allocation 834

21 Costing Systems: Job Order and Process Costing 882

22 Activity-Based Systems: ABM and JIT 924

23 Cost Behavior Analyses 964

24 The Budgeting Process 1002

25 Standard Costing and Variance Analysis 1048

26 Performance Management and Evaluation 1090

27 Analysis for Decision Making 1128

Appendix A International Accounting 1173

Appendix B Long-Term Investments 1180

Appendix C The Time Value of Money 1187

Appendix D Future Value and Present Value Tables 1200

Appendix E How to Read an Annual Report E1

Contents

13 Partnerships — 556

- DECISION POINT KPMG LLP 556

PARTNERSHIP CHARACTERISTICS 558

Voluntary Association 558

- FOCUS ON INTERNATIONAL BUSINESS
  How Do Partnerships Facilitate International Investment? 559
- FOCUS ON BUSINESS PRACTICE
  Corporations That Look Like Partnerships 559
- FOCUS ON BUSINESS PRACTICE
  How Do Limited Partnerships Help Finance Big Projects? 560

Other Forms of Association 560

- FOCUS ON BUSINESS TECHNOLOGY
  Joint Ventures and the Internet 560

ACCOUNTING FOR PARTNERS' EQUITY 561

DISTRIBUTION OF PARTNERSHIP INCOME AND LOSSES 562

Stated Ratios 562
Capital Balance Ratios 563
Salaries, Interest, and Stated Ratios 564

- FOCUS ON BUSINESS PRACTICE
  What Are the Risks of Being a Partner in an Accounting Firm? 566

DISSOLUTION OF A PARTNERSHIP 567

Admission of a New Partner 567
Withdrawal of a Partner 570

- FOCUS ON BUSINESS PRACTICE
  Can Withdrawal of Partners Harm a Partnership? 570

Death of a Partner 572

LIQUIDATION OF A PARTNERSHIP 572

Gain on Sale of Assets 573
Loss on Sale of Assets 575

Chapter Review 577 Review of Learning Objectives 577 Review of Concepts and Terminology 579 Review Problem 579 Answer to Review Problem 580

Chapter Assignments 581 Questions 581 Short Exercises 582 Exercises 583 Problems 584

Alternate Problems 586

Skills Development Cases 588

Financial Reporting and Analysis Cases 589

14 Contributed Capital — 592

- DECISION POINT Cisco Systems, Inc. 592

MANAGEMENT ISSUES RELATED TO CONTRIBUTED CAPITAL 594

Forming a Corporation 594
Managing Under the Corporate Form of Business 595
Using Equity Financing 597
Determining Dividend Policies 598
Evaluating Performance Using Return on Equity 599
Using Stock Options as Compensation 600

- FOCUS ON BUSINESS PRACTICE
  When Are Stock Options Worthless? Apparently Never! 601

COMPONENTS OF STOCKHOLDERS' EQUITY 601

- FOCUS ON INTERNATIONAL BUSINESS
  Hot New European Stock Markets Have Cooled! 601

DIVIDENDS 602

THE CHARACTERISTICS OF PREFERRED STOCK 603

Preference as to Dividends 603

- FOCUS ON BUSINESS PRACTICE
  Why Did Microsoft Issue Preferred Stock? 604

Preference as to Assets 605
Convertible Preferred Stock 605
Callable Preferred Stock 606

ACCOUNTING FOR STOCK ISSUANCE 606

Par Value Stock 607
No-Par Stock 608
Issuance of Stock for Noncash Assets 608

ACCOUNTING FOR TREASURY STOCK 609

Purchase of Treasury Stock 610
Sale of Treasury Stock 610

- FOCUS ON BUSINESS PRACTICE
  When Are Share Buybacks a Bad Idea? 611

Retirement of Treasury Stock 611

Chapter Review 612 Review of Learning Objectives 612 Review of Concepts and Terminology 613 Review Problem 615 Answer to Review Problem 615

Chapter Assignments 617 Questions 617 Short Exercises 618 Exercises 619 Problems 621 Alternate Problems 622

Skills Development Cases 623

Financial Reporting and Analysis Cases 625

15 The Corporate Income Statement and the Statement of Stockholders' Equity 628

- DECISION POINT AMR Corporation 628

PERFORMANCE MEASUREMENT: QUALITY OF EARNINGS ISSUES 630

The Corporate Income Statement 630

- FOCUS ON BUSINESS PRACTICE
  Why Do Investors Study Quality of Earnings? 630

Choice of Accounting Methods and Estimates 631

Gains and Losses 633

Write-Downs and Restructurings 633

Nature of Nonoperating Items 633

- FOCUS ON BUSINESS ETHICS Whistle-Blowing 634

Effect of Quality of Earnings on Cash Flows and Performance Measures 634

INCOME TAXES EXPENSE 635

Deferred Income Taxes 636

Net of Taxes 637

NONOPERATING ITEMS 638

Discontinued Operations 638

Extraordinary Items 638

Accounting Changes 639

- FOCUS ON INTERNATIONAL BUSINESS
  Were Preussag's Year-End Results Really "Remarkable"? 639

EARNINGS PER SHARE 640

THE STATEMENT OF STOCKHOLDERS' EQUITY 642

Retained Earnings 642

- FOCUS ON INTERNATIONAL BUSINESS
  Why Are Reserves Common in Other Countries? 644

Restriction on Retained Earnings 644

ACCOUNTING FOR STOCK DIVIDENDS AND STOCK SPLITS 644

Stock Dividends 644

Stock Splits 647

- FOCUS ON BUSINESS PRACTICE
  Do Stock Splits Help Increase a Company's Market Price? 647

BOOK VALUE 648

Chapter Review 649 Review of Learning Objectives 649 Review of Concepts and Terminology 651 Review Problem 652 Answer to Review Problem 652

Chapter Assignments 654 Questions 654 Short Exercises 655 Exercises 656 Problems 658 Alternate Problems 661

Skills Development Cases 662

Financial Reporting and Analysis Cases 664

16 Long-Term Liabilities 668

- DECISION POINT AT&T Corporation 668

MANAGEMENT ISSUES RELATED TO ISSUING LONG-TERM DEBT 670

The Decision to Issue Long-Term Debt 670

- FOCUS ON INTERNATIONAL BUSINESS
  Pushed to the Brink of Failure 671

How Much Debt to Carry 671

Types of Long-Term Debt 672

Timing of Long-Term Debt Repayment 672

THE NATURE OF BONDS 673

Secured or Unsecured Bonds 673

Term or Serial Bonds 673

Registered or Coupon Bonds 673

- FOCUS ON INTERNATIONAL BUSINESS
  Choice of Bank Debt Cripples Japanese Firms. 674

USING PRESENT VALUE TO VALUE A BOND 677

AMORTIZATION OF BOND DISCOUNTS AND PREMIUMS 678

Amortizing a Bond Discount 678

Amortizing a Bond Premium 682

- FOCUS ON BUSINESS TECHNOLOGY
  Speed Up the Calculations! 684

OTHER BONDS PAYABLE ISSUES 685

Sale of Bonds Between Interest Dates 685

Year-End Accrual of Bond Interest Expense 686

RETIREMENT OF BONDS 688

Callable Bonds 688

Convertible Bonds 689

OTHER LONG-TERM LIABILITIES 690

Contents vii

ACCOUNTING FOR BONDS PAYABLE 674
Balance Sheet Disclosure of Bonds 674
Bonds Issued at Face Value 674
Face Interest Rate and Market Interest Rate 675

- FOCUS ON BUSINESS PRACTICE
  Check Out Those Bond Prices! 675

Bonds Issued at a Discount 676
Bonds Issued at a Premium 676

- FOCUS ON BUSINESS PRACTICE
  100-Year Bonds Are Not for Everyone. 677

Bond Issue Costs 677

Mortgages Payable 690
Long-Term Leases 690
Pensions 692
Other Postretirement Benefits 693
Chapter Review 693 Review of Learning Objectives 693 Review of Concepts and Terminology 695 Review Problem 696 Answer to Review Problem 697

Chapter Assignments 698 Questions 689 Short Exercises 698 Exercises 699 Problems 701 Alternate Problems 703

Skills Development Cases 704
Financial Reporting and Analysis Cases 705

17 The Statement of Cash Flows 708

- DECISION POINT Marriott International, Inc. 708
- VIDEO CASE Goodyear Tire & Rubber Company 711

OVERVIEW OF THE STATEMENT OF CASH FLOWS 711
Purposes of the Statement of Cash Flows 712
Internal and External Uses of the Statement of Cash Flows 712
Classification of Cash Flows 712

- FOCUS ON INTERNATIONAL BUSINESS
  How Universal Is the Statement of Cash Flows? 714

PREPARING THE STATEMENT OF CASH FLOWS: OPERATING ACTIVITIES 717
Depreciation 720
Gains and Losses 720
Changes in Current Assets 721
Changes in Current Liabilities 721

- FOCUS ON BUSINESS PRACTICE What's Your "Burn Rate"? 722

Schedule of Cash Flows from Operating Activities 722

PREPARING THE STATEMENT OF CASH FLOWS: INVESTING ACTIVITIES 722
Investments 723
Plant Assets 724

Format of the Statement of Cash Flows 714
ANALYZING THE STATEMENT OF CASH FLOWS 714
Cash-Generating Efficiency 714
Free Cash Flow 715

- FOCUS ON BUSINESS PRACTICE What Do You Mean, "Free Cash Flow"? 716
- FOCUS ON BUSINESS PRACTICE Cash Flows Tell All. 716

PREPARING THE STATEMENT OF CASH FLOWS: FINANCING ACTIVITIES 725
Bonds Payable 725
Common Stock 726
Retained Earnings 726
Treasury Stock 726

Chapter Review 728 Review of Learning Objectives 728 Review of Concepts and Terminology 728 Review Problem 729 Answer to Review Problem 731

Chapter Assignments 732 Questions 732 Short Exercises 733 Exercises 734 Problems 737 Alternate Problems 740

Skills Development Cases 743
Financial Reporting and Analysis Cases 746

18 Financial Performance Evaluation 750

- DECISION POINT Sun Microsystems 750

FINANCIAL PERFORMANCE EVALUATION BY INTERNAL AND EXTERNAL USERS 752
Internal Users 752
External Users 752
Financial Reporting Under the Sarbanes-Oxley Act 753

Horizontal Analysis 759
Trend Analysis 760
Vertical Analysis 762
Ratio Analysis 765

COMPREHENSIVE ILLUSTRATION OF RATIO ANALYSIS 765

STANDARDS FOR FINANCIAL STATEMENT ANALYSIS 754
Rule-of-Thumb Measures 754
Past Performance of the Company 754
Industry Norms 754
- FOCUS ON BUSINESS ETHICS
  Take the Numbers with a Grain of Salt. 756

SOURCES OF INFORMATION 756
Reports Published by the Company 756
- FOCUS ON BUSINESS TECHNOLOGY Find It on the Internet. 757

SEC Reports 757
Business Periodicals and Credit and Investment Advisory Services 757

TOOLS AND TECHNIQUES OF FINANCIAL ANALYSIS 759

Evaluating Liquidity 766
Evaluating Profitability 766
- FOCUS ON BUSINESS PRACTICE
  There's More Than One Way to Measure Profitability. 768

Evaluating Long-Term Solvency 768
Evaluating Cash Flow Adequacy 770
Evaluating Market Strength 770
Summary of the Financial Analysis of Sun Microsystems, Inc. 772

Chapter Review 772 Review of Learning Objectives 772 Review of Concepts and Terminology 773 Review Problem 774 Answer to Review Problem 776

Chapter Assignments 777 Questions 777 Short Exercises 778 Exercises 780 Problems 782 Alternate Problems 786

Skills Development Cases 788
Financial Reporting and Analysis Cases 789

19 The Changing Business Environment: A Manager's Perspective 792

- DECISION POINT Honda Motor Company 792

THE ROLE OF MANAGEMENT ACCOUNTING 794
Management Accounting and Financial Accounting: A Comparison 794
- FOCUS ON BUSINESS PRACTICE Why is Managerial Accounting Vitally Important to Excellent Companies? 794

Management Accounting's Support of Value Chain Analysis 802
- FOCUS ON BUSINESS TECHNOLOGY
  How Can the Internet Be Used to Support the Value Chain? 802

MEETING THE DEMANDS OF GLOBAL COMPETITION 804
Management Tools for Continuous Improvement 804
Achieving Continuous Improvement 806
- FOCUS ON INTERNATIONAL BUSINESS
  How Has Ecommerce Changed the Nature of Business? 807

PERFORMANCE MEASURES: A KEY TO ACHIEVING ORGANIZATIONAL OBJECTIVES 807
Use of Performance Measures in the Management Cycle 807
The Balanced Scorecard 808
- FOCUS ON BUSINESS PRACTICE
  Do Many Companies Use the Balanced Scorecard? 808

Management Accounting and the Management Cycle 796

VALUE CHAIN ANALYSIS 800
Primary Processes and Support Services 801
Advantages of Value Chain Analysis 802

Benchmarking 809

ANALYSIS OF NONFINANCIAL DATA IN A SERVICE ORGANIZATION 810

STANDARDS OF ETHICAL CONDUCT 810
- FOCUS ON BUSINESS ETHICS
  What Is Management's Responsibility for the Financial Statements? 812

Chapter Review 814 Review of Learning Objectives 814 Review of Concepts and Terminology 815 Review Problem 816 Answer to Review Problem 817

Chapter Assignments 818 Questions 818 Short Exercises 818 Exercises 820 Problems 824 Alternate Problems 827

Skills Development Cases 829
Managerial Reporting and Analysis Cases 832

20 Cost Concepts and Cost Allocation 834

- DECISION POINT Southwest Airlines 834

COST INFORMATION AND THE MANAGEMENT CYCLE 836
Use of Cost Information in the Management Cycle 836
Cost Information and Organizations 837

COST CLASSIFICATIONS AND THEIR USES 837
Cost Traceability 838
- FOCUS ON BUSINESS PRACTICE
  How Does an Airline Manage Its Fixed Costs? 839

Cost Behavior 839
Value-Adding Versus Nonvalue-Adding Costs 839
Cost Classifications for Financial Reporting 839

ELEMENTS OF PRODUCT COSTS 840
- FOCUS ON BUSINESS TECHNOLOGY
  Has Technology Shifted the Elements of Product Costs? 841

Computing Product Unit Cost 841
Prime Costs and Conversion Costs 843

INVENTORY ACCOUNTS IN MANUFACTURING ORGANIZATIONS 843
Document Flows and Cost Flows Through the Inventory Accounts 844
The Manufacturing Cost Flow 846

FINANCIAL STATEMENTS AND THE REPORTING OF COSTS 847
Statement of Cost of Goods Manufactured 847
Cost of Goods Sold and a Manufacturing Organization's Income Statement 849

Cost Reporting and Accounting for Inventories in Service, Retail, and Manufacturing Organizations 849
- FOCUS ON BUSINESS PRACTICE
  What Candy Company Has the Sweetest Share of the U.S. Market? 849

COST ALLOCATION 851
Allocating the Costs of Manufacturing Overhead 852
The Importance of Good Estimates 854

ALLOCATING MANUFACTURING OVERHEAD: THE TRADITIONAL APPROACH 854

ALLOCATING MANUFACTURING OVERHEAD: THE ABC APPROACH 856
- FOCUS ON BUSINESS ETHICS
  What Can a Company Do to Be Resource-Responsible? 857

Planning Overhead Rates 857
Applying the Overhead Rates 858
- FOCUS ON BUSINESS PRACTICE
  How Costly Is Television Talent? 860

COST ALLOCATION IN SERVICE ORGANIZATIONS 860

Chapter Review 861 Review of Learning Objectives 861 Review of Concepts and Terminology 863 Review Problem 864 Answer to Review Problem 865

Chapter Assignments 866 Questions 866 Short Exercises 866 Exercises 868 Problems 871 Alternate Problems 874

Skills Development Cases 876

Managerial Reporting and Analysis Cases 878

21 Costing Systems: Job Order and Process Costing 882

- DECISION POINT John H. Daniel Company 882

PRODUCT COST INFORMATION AND THE MANAGEMENT CYCLE 884
Planning 884
Executing 885
Reviewing 885
Reporting 885

JOB ORDER VERSUS PROCESS COSTING 885
- FOCUS ON INTERNATIONAL BUSINESS
  Why Does Toyota Use a Hybrid Product Costing System? 887

THE JOB ORDER COSTING SYSTEM 887
Cost Flow in a Job Order Costing System for a Manufacturing Company 887
- FOCUS ON BUSINESS PRACTICE
  How Long Does Production Take? 890

- FOCUS ON BUSINESS ETHICS
  Does a Product's Unit Cost Tell the Whole Story? 892

Costs Flows Through the Work in Process Inventory Accounts 896

COMPUTING EQUIVALENT PRODUCTION 897
Equivalent Production for Direct Materials 897
Equivalent Production for Conversion Costs 898

PREPARING A PROCESS COST REPORT USING THE FIFO COSTING METHOD 899
Accounting for Units 899
Accounting for Costs 901
Assigning Costs 902
Process Costing for Two or More Production Departments 902

USING INFORMATION ABOUT PRODUCT COST TO EVALUATE PERFORMANCE 903

Chapter Review 903 Review of Learning Objectives 903 Review of Concepts and Terminology 905 Review Problem 906 Answer to Review Problem 906

The Job Order Cost Card and Computation of Product Unit Cost 892
Job Order Costing in a Service Organization 892
THE PROCESS COSTING SYSTEM 894
Patterns of Product Flows and Cost Flows 894
- ■ FOCUS ON BUSINESS PRACTICE
  What Kinds of Companies Use Process Costing? 896

Chapter Assignments 907   Questions 907   Short Exercises 908   Exercises 910   Problems 914   Alternate Problems 916
Skills Development Cases 918
Managerial Reporting and Analysis Cases 920

22 Activity-Based Systems: ABM and JIT 924

- ■ DECISION POINT England, Inc. 924

ACTIVITY-BASED SYSTEMS AND MANAGEMENT 926

ACTIVITY-BASED SYSTEMS 926

USING ACTIVITY-BASED COST INFORMATION IN THE MANAGEMENT CYCLE 927

ACTIVITY-BASED MANAGEMENT 928
- ■ FOCUS ON BUSINESS PRACTICE
  How Do Traditional and ABC Reports Differ? 929

Value Chains and Supply Chains 929
- ■ FOCUS ON BUSINESS PRACTICE
  How Can a Changing Business Economy Cause Strategy Shifts in a Company's Value Chain? 929

ABM in a Service Organization 930

VALUE-ADDING AND NONVALUE-ADDING ACTIVITIES AND PROCESS VALUE ANALYSIS 932

Value-Adding and Nonvalue-Adding Activities in a Service Organization 932
- ■ FOCUS ON BUSINESS PRACTICE   What Is VBM? 933

Process Value Analysis 933

BACKFLUSH COSTING 942

COMPARISON OF ABM AND JIT 945

Chapter Review 946   Review of Learning Objectives 946   Review of Concepts and Terminology 947   Review Problem 949   Answer to Review Problem 949

ACTIVITY-BASED COSTING 934
The Cost Hierarchy and the Bill of Activities 934
Activity-Based Costing for Selling and Administrative Activities 937

THE NEW MANUFACTURING ENVIRONMENT AND JIT OPERATIONS 938
Minimum Inventory Levels 939
Pull-Through Production 939
Quick Setup and Flexible Work Cells 939
- ■ FOCUS ON INTERNATIONAL BUSINESS
  Is JIT Right for Every Business? 940

A Multiskilled Work Force 940
High Levels of Product Quality 940
Effective Preventive Maintenance 940
Continuous Improvement of the Work Environment 941

ACCOUNTING FOR PRODUCT COSTS IN THE NEW MANUFACTURING ENVIRONMENT 941
Classifying Costs 941
Assigning Costs 941

Chapter Assignments 951   Questions 951   Short Exercises 951   Exercises 952   Problems 956   Alternate Problems 958
Skills Development Cases 960
Managerial Reporting and Analysis Cases 961

23 Cost Behavior Analysis 964

- DECISION POINT Kraft Foods 964

COST BEHAVIOR AND THE MANAGEMENT CYCLE 966

Planning 966
Executing 966
Reviewing and Reporting 966

- FOCUS ON BUSINESS ETHICS Core Values Guide Kraft Foods 966

THE BEHAVIOR OF COSTS 967

Variable Costs 968
Fixed Costs 971
Mixed Costs 972

- FOCUS ON BUSINESS TECHNOLOGY
  High-Priced vs. Low-Priced Seats 973

COST-VOLUME-PROFIT ANALYSIS 975

- FOCUS ON INTERNATIONAL BUSINESS
  C-V-P Analysis in Grams and Liters 976

BREAKEVEN ANALYSIS 976

Using Contribution Margin to Determine the Breakeven Point 978

- FOCUS ON BUSINESS PRACTICE Supersizing Value Meals 978

The Breakeven Point for Multiple Products 979

USING C-V-P ANALYSIS TO PLAN FUTURE SALES, COSTS, AND PROFITS 980

Applying C-V-P to a Manufacturing Business 980
Applying C-V-P Analysis to a Service Business 984

Chapter Review 986 Review of Learning Objectives 986
Review of Concepts and Terminology 987 Review Problem 987 Answer to Review Problem 988

Chapter Assignments 989 Questions 989 Short Exercises 989 Exercises 990 Problems 994 Alternate Problems 996

Skills Development Cases 997

Managerial Reporting and Analysis Cases 999

24 The Budgeting Process 1002

- DECISION POINT Johnson & Johnson 1002

THE BUDGETING PROCESS 1004

Budgeting and Goals 1004

- FOCUS ON BUSINESS PRACTICE
  What Can Cause the Planning Process to Fail? 1004
- VIDEO CASE Enterprise Rent-A-Car 1005
- FOCUS ON INTERNATIONAL BUSINESS
  Budget Revision Practices in the United Kingdom 1006

The Importance of Participation 1006
Budgeting and the Management Cycle 1006

THE MASTER BUDGET 1008

- FOCUS ON BUSINESS TECHNOLOGY Rolling Budgets Never End 1008

OPERATING BUDGETS 1011

The Sales Budget 1011
The Production Budget 1012
The Direct Materials Purchases Budget 1014
The Direct Labor Budget 1014
The Manufacturing Overhead Budget 1015

The Selling and Administrative Expense Budget 1017
The Cost of Goods Manufactured Budget 1018

FINANCIAL BUDGETS 1018

The Budgeted Income Statement 1018
The Capital Expenditures Budget 1019
The Cash Budget 1020

- FOCUS ON BUSINESS ETHICS
  Does Budgeting Lead to a Breakdown in Corporate Ethics? 1022

The Budgeted Balance Sheet 1022

BUDGET IMPLEMENTATION 1025

Chapter Review 1025 Review of Learning Objectives 1025
Review of Concepts and Terminology 1026 Review Problem 1027 Answer to Review Problem 1028

Chapter Assignments 1029 Questions 1029 Short Exercises 1030 Exercises 1031 Problems 1035 Alternate Problems 1041

Skills Development Cases 1042

Managerial Reporting and Analysis Cases 1046

25 Standard Costing and Variance Analysis 1048

- DECISION POINT Coach, Inc. 1048

STANDARD COSTING 1050

Standard Costs and the Management Cycle 1050

- FOCUS ON BUSINESS PRACTICE
  Why Go on a Factory Tour? 1050

The Relevance of Standard Costing in Today's Business Environment 1051

COMPUTING STANDARD COSTS 1052

Standard Direct Materials Cost 1052
Standard Direct Labor Cost 1052
Standard Manufacturing Overhead Cost 1053
Total Standard Unit Cost 1053

VARIANCE ANALYSIS 1054

The Role of Flexible Budgets in Variance Analysis 1054

- FOCUS ON BUSINESS TECHNOLOGY
  Why Complicate the Flexible Budget? 1055

Using Variance Analysis to Control Costs 1056

COMPUTING AND ANALYZING DIRECT MATERIALS VARIANCES 1058

Computing Direct Materials Variances 1058
Analyzing and Correcting Direct Materials Variances 1059

COMPUTING AND ANALYZING DIRECT LABOR VARIANCES 1060

Computing Direct Labor Variances 1060
Analyzing and Correcting Direct Labor Variances 1061

COMPUTING AND ANALYZING MANUFACTURING OVERHEAD VARIANCES 1062

Using a Flexible Budget to Analyze Manufacturing Overhead Variances 1063
Computing Manufacturing Overhead Variances 1064
Analyzing and Correcting Manufacturing Overhead Variances 1068

- FOCUS ON INTERNATIONAL BUSINESS
  Have You Bought Gold Medal Sneakers Yet? 1068

USING COST VARIANCES TO EVALUATE MANAGERS' PERFORMANCE 1069

- FOCUS ON BUSINESS ETHICS Ethics = Profits 1069

Chapter Review 1071 Review of Learning Objectives 1071 Review of Concepts and Terminology 1072 Review Problem 1073 Answer to Review Problem 1074

Chapter Assignments 1077 Questions 1077 Short Exercises 1078 Exercises 1079 Problems 1081 Alternate Problems 1083

Skills Development Cases 1084

Managerial Reporting and Analysis Cases 1086

26 Performance Management and Evaluation 1090

- DECISION POINT Vail Resorts 1090

ORGANIZATIONAL GOALS AND THE BALANCED SCORECARD 1092

The Balanced Scorecard and the Management Cycle 1092

- VIDEO CASE Harley-Davidson, Inc. 1093
- FOCUS ON BUSINESS PRACTICE
  How Many Stakeholder Groups Has Harley Identified? 1093

PERFORMANCE MEASUREMENT 1096

What to Measure, How to Measure 1096
Other Measurement Issues 1096

- FOCUS ON INTERNATIONAL BUSINESS
  "OLD" Doesn't Mean "Out-of-Date" 1096

RESPONSIBILITY ACCOUNTING 1097

Types of Responsibility Centers 1097
Organizational Structure and Performance Management 1098

- FOCUS ON BUSINESS TECHNOLOGY Keep It Simple! 1098

PERFORMANCE EVALUATION OF COST CENTERS AND PROFIT CENTERS 1100

Evaluating Cost Center Performance Using Flexible Budgeting 1100
Evaluating Profit Center Performance Using Variable Costing 1101

- FOCUS ON BUSINESS ETHICS
  Soundproofing with Blue Jeans 1103

PERFORMANCE EVALUATION OF INVESTMENT CENTERS 1103

Return on Investment 1103
Residual Income 1104
Economic Value Added 1106
The Importance of Multiple Performance Measures 1108

PERFORMANCE INCENTIVES AND GOALS 1108

Linking Goals, Performance Objectives, Measures, and Performance Targets 1108

Performance-Based Pay 1108

The Coordination of Goals 1109

Chapter Review 1110 Review of Learning Objectives 1110 Review of Concepts and Terminology 1111 Review Problem 1112 Answer to Review Problem 1113

Chapter Assignments 1114 Questions 1114 Short Exercises 1115 Exercises 1117 Problems 1120 Alternate Problems 1122

Skills Development Cases 1123

Managerial Reporting and Analysis Cases 1125

27 Analysis for Decision Making 1128

■ DECISION POINT Bank of America 1128

SHORT-RUN DECISION ANALYSIS AND THE MANAGEMENT CYCLE 1130

Planning 1130

Executing 1130

Reviewing 1131

Reporting 1132

INCREMENTAL ANALYSIS FOR SHORT-RUN DECISIONS 1132

Irrelevant Costs and Revenues 1132

■ FOCUS ON BUSINESS TECHNOLOGY
How Much Does It Cost to Process a Check? 1133

Opportunity Costs 1133

APPLICATION OF INCREMENTAL ANALYSIS TO SHORT-RUN DECISIONS 1134

Incremental Analysis for Outsourcing Decisions 1134

Incremental Analysis for Special Order Decisions 1136

Incremental Analysis for Segment Profitability Decisions 1137

■ FOCUS ON BUSINESS PRACTICE
To Drop or Not to Drop a Segment? 1138

■ FOCUS ON INTERNATIONAL BUSINESS
Why Banks Prefer Ebanking 1139

Incremental Analysis for Sales Mix Decisions 1140

Incremental Analysis for Sell or Process-Further Decisions 1142

CAPITAL INVESTMENT DECISIONS 1143

Capital Investment Analysis 1143

Measures Used in Capital Investment Analysis 1144

■ FOCUS ON INTERNATIONAL BUSINESS
Why Look Beyond the Cost of a Capital Investment? 1145

THE TIME VALUE OF MONEY 1146

Interest 1146

Present Value 1147

Present Value of a Single Sum Due in the Future 1147

■ FOCUS ON BUSINESS PRACTICE
How Would You Decide Whether to Buy Rare Dinosaur Bones? 1147

Present Value of an Ordinary Annuity 1148

ANALYZING CAPITAL INVESTMENT PROPOSALS: THE NET PRESENT VALUE METHOD 1149

Advantages of the Net Present Value Method 1149

The Net Present Value Method Illustrated 1150

OTHER METHODS OF CAPITAL INVESTMENT ANALYSIS 1151

The Payback Period Method 1151

The Accounting Rate-of-Return Method 1152

Chapter Review 1153 Review of Learning Objectives 1153 Review of Concepts and Terminology 1155 Review Problem 1156 Answer to Review Problem 1157

Chapter Assignments 1158 Questions 1158 Short Exercises 1158 Exercises 1160 Problems 1163 Alternate Problems 1165

Skills Development Cases 1166

Managerial Reporting and Analysis Cases 1168

Appendix A International Accounting 1173

Appendix B Long-Term Investments 1180

Appendix C The Time Value of Money 1187

Appendix D Future Value and Present Value Tables 1200

Appendix E How to Read an Annual Report E1

Endnotes 1207
Company Name Index 1212
Subject Index 1215

13 Partnerships

Chapter 13 discusses the characteristics of the partnership form of business and examines accounting issues relating to formation, division of income, dissolution, and liquidation of partnerships.

Learning Objectives

LO1 Identify the principal characteristics, advantages, and disadvantages of the partnership form of business.

LO2 Record partners' investments of cash and other assets when a partnership is formed.

LO3 Compute and record the income or losses that partners share, based on stated ratios, capital balance ratios, and partners' salaries and interest.

LO4 Record a person's admission to or withdrawal from a partnership.

LO5 Compute the distribution of assets to partners when they liquidate their partnership.

DECISION POINT
A USER'S FOCUS

KPMG LLP <www.kpmg.com> Many people think of partnerships as relatively small business organizations, and usually they are right. However, some partnerships, among them law firms, investment companies, real estate companies, and accounting firms, are very large. An example is KPMG LLP, which is a member firm in KPMG International, a professional services organization with offices in 150 countries. KPMG LLP provides accounting and auditing services, tax services, and management consulting services. With over 1,500 partners and 98,000 employees, it is one of the largest partnerships in the world. In 2002, the firm was growing rapidly, with revenues of over $10 billion, about half of which came from outside the United States. How does a partnership this large organize to accomplish its objectives?[1]

KPMG LLP is organized as a limited liability partnership. In a normal partnership, the personal financial resources of all partners are subject to risk of loss if the partnership suffers a loss it cannot bear. Accounting firms are at risk of suffering large losses as a result of lawsuits from investors who lose money investing in a company audited by the accounting firm. Because KPMG is organized as a limited liability partnership, the partners are liable to the extent of their partnership interest in the firm, but their personal assets are not subject to risk.

Why did KPMG organize itself as a limited liability partnership?

Financial Highlights		
(in millions of dollars)		
	2002	2001
Annual revenue	$10,720	$10,320

Partnership Characteristics

LO1 Identify the principal characteristics, advantages, and disadvantages of the partnership form of business.

RELATED TEXT ASSIGNMENTS
Q: 1, 2, 3, 4, 5, 6, 7
SE: 1
SD: 1, 3, 4
FRA: 1, 2, 3

KEY POINT: Partnerships and sole proprietorships are not legal entities; corporations are. All three, however, are considered accounting entities.

The Uniform Partnership Act, which has been adopted by most states, defines a **partnership** as "an association of two or more persons to carry on as co-owners of a business for profit." Partnerships are treated as separate entities in accounting, but legally there is no economic separation between them and their owners. They differ in many ways from the other forms of business. Here we describe some of their important characteristics.

Voluntary Association

A partnership is a voluntary association of individuals rather than a legal entity in itself. Therefore, a partner is responsible under the law for his or her partners' actions within the scope of the business. A partner also has unlimited liability for the debts of the partnership. Because of these potential liabilities, a partner must be allowed to choose the people who join the partnership. A person should select as partners individuals who share his or her business objectives.

■ **Partnership Agreement** A partnership is easy to form. Two or more competent people simply agree to be partners in a common business purpose. Their agreement is known as a **partnership agreement**. The partnership agreement does not have to be in writing. However, good business practice calls for a written document that clearly states the details of the arrangement, including the name, location, and purpose of the business; the names of the partners and their respective duties; the investments of each partner; the method of distributing income and losses; and the procedures for the admission and withdrawal of partners, the withdrawal of assets allowed each partner, and the liquidation (termination) of the business.

■ **Limited Life** Because a partnership is formed by an agreement between partners, it has a **limited life**. It may be dissolved when a new partner is admitted; a partner withdraws, goes bankrupt, is incapacitated (to the point that he or she cannot perform as obligated), retires, or dies; or the terms of the partnership agreement are met (e.g., when the project for which the partnership was formed is completed). However, if the partners want the partnership to continue legally, the partnership agreement can be written to cover each of these situations. For example, the partnership agreement can state that if a partner dies, the remaining partner or partners must purchase the deceased partner's capital at book value from the heirs.

■ **Mutual Agency** Each partner is an agent of the partnership within the scope of the business. Because of this **mutual agency**, any partner can bind the partnership to a business agreement as long as he or she acts within the scope of the company's normal operations. For example, a partner in a used-car business can bind the partnership through the purchase or sale of used cars. But this partner cannot bind the partnership to a contract to buy men's clothing or any other goods that are not related to the used-car business. Because of mutual agency, it is very important for an individual to choose business partners who have integrity and who share his or her business objectives.

KEY POINT: Unlimited liability means that potential responsibility for debts is not limited by one's investment, as it is in a corporation. Each person is personally liable for all debts of the partnership, including those arising from contingent liabilities such as lawsuits. Liability can be avoided only by filing for personal bankruptcy.

■ **Unlimited Liability** All partners have **unlimited liability** for their company's debt, which means that each partner is personally liable for all the debts of the partnership. If a partnership cannot pay its debts, creditors must first satisfy their claims from the assets of the business. If these assets are not enough to pay all debts, the creditors can seek payment from the personal assets of each partner. If one partner's personal assets are used up before the debts are paid, the creditors can

Focus on International Business

How Do Partnerships Facilitate International Investment?

American businesses are expanding into emerging markets throughout the world. Many of these markets, such as those of Hungary, Poland, the Czech Republic, India, and China, are in the process of privatizing public entities. This means that operations such as steel mills, cement factories, and utilities that were previously run by the government are being converted into private enterprises. Many countries require that local investors own a substantial proportion of the newly formed businesses. One way of accomplishing this is to form joint ventures, which match a country's need for outside capital and operational know-how with investors' interest in business expansion and profitability. Joint ventures often take the form of partnerships among two or more corporations and other investors. Any income or losses from operations will be divided among the participants according to a predetermined agreement.

◆ **Stop and Think!**
Why is it important for people to form partnerships with people whom they can trust?
Because of mutual agency, unlimited liability, and co-ownership of property, the risks of being a partner are high. This puts a premium on honesty and trust among the partners. Further, goodwill among partners is important in making decisions and distributing income. ■

claim additional assets from the remaining partners who are able to pay. Each partner, then, can be required by law to pay all the debts of the partnership.

■ **Co-ownership of Partnership Property** When individuals invest property in a partnership, they give up the right to their separate use of the property. The property becomes an asset of the partnership and is owned jointly by the partners.

■ **Participation in Partnership Income** Each partner has the right to share in the company's income and the responsibility to share in its losses. The partnership agreement should state the method of distributing income and losses to each partner. If the agreement describes how income should be shared but does not mention losses, losses are distributed in the same way as income. If the agreement does not describe the method of income and loss distribution, the partners must by law share income and losses equally.

KEY POINT: There is no federal income tax on partnerships. However, an informational return must be filed, and partners are taxed at their personal rates. There may be state or local business taxes assessed on a partnership, however. One example of this is the Michigan Single Business Tax.

■ **Advantages and Disadvantages of Partnerships** Partnerships have both advantages and disadvantages. One advantage is that a partnership is easy to form, change, and dissolve. Also, a partnership facilitates the pooling of capital resources and individual talents; it has no corporate tax burden (because a partnership is not a legal entity for tax purposes, it does not have to pay a federal income tax, as do corporations, but must file an informational return); and it gives the partners a certain amount of freedom and flexibility.

On the other hand, partnerships have the following disadvantages: the life of a partnership is limited; one partner can bind the partnership to a contract (mutual agency); the partners have unlimited personal liability; and it is more difficult for a

Focus on Business Practice

Corporations That Look Like Partnerships

Several types of corporations have been created to mimic the characteristics of partnerships in certain ways. *S corporations* are corporations that U.S. tax laws treat in a manner similar to partnerships. S corporations do not pay income taxes like normal corporations. The income or loss of the S corporation is distributed to the stockholders (which are limited to a small number), who report and pay taxes on the income or loss on their personal tax returns. This avoids the problem of double taxation. *Limited liability corporations* are corporations that professional firms such as accounting and consultancy firms mostly use to limit the liability of the partners, who in this form of business are stockholders. *Special-purpose entities (SPEs)*, which have gained notoriety because of the Enron case, are actually quite common. They are separately distinct from the company that forms them and are used by companies to raise money by selling certain assets such as receivables. By meeting certain conditions, the company that sets them up can legitimately avoid including the debt of the SPEs on its balance sheet. Enron used SPEs extensively and fraudulently to hide debt and other commitments of the company.

Focus on Business Practice

How Do Limited Partnerships Help Finance Big Projects?

Limited partnerships are sometimes used in place of the corporate form to raise funds from the public. Because possible investor losses are normally restricted to the amount of the investment, the limited partnership has some characteristics of the corporate form. Limited partnerships are used to obtain financing for many projects, such as locating and drilling oil and gas wells, manufacturing airplanes, and developing real estate (including shopping centers, office buildings, and apartment complexes). For example, Alliance Capital Management Limited Partnership is one of the largest investment advisors, managing more than $90 billion in assets for corporate and individual investors. The company's partnership units, or shares of ownership, sell on the New York Stock Exchange and can be purchased by the individual investor. In 2003, the units were selling at about $28 each and paid an annual dividend of $2.50 per share.[2]

---

partnership to raise large amounts of capital and to transfer ownership interests than it is for a corporation.

OTHER FORMS OF ASSOCIATION

Two other common forms of association that are a type of partnership or similar to a partnership are limited partnerships and joint ventures.

ENRICHMENT NOTE:
Many types of organizations have been created by law. They include S corporations and limited partnerships. Each provides legal (especially tax) advantages and disadvantages.

■ **LIMITED PARTNERSHIPS** A **limited partnership** is a special type of partnership that, like corporations, confines the limited partner's potential loss to the amount of his or her investment. Under this type of partnership the unlimited liability disadvantage of a partnership can be overcome. Usually, the limited partnership has a general partner who has unlimited liability but allows other partners to limit their potential loss. The potential loss of all partners in an ordinary partnership is limited only by personal bankruptcy laws.

■ **JOINT VENTURES** In today's global environment, more companies are looking to form alliances similar to partnerships, called *joint ventures*, with other companies rather than to venture out on their own. A **joint venture** is an association of two or more entities for the purpose of achieving a specific goal, such as the manufacture of a product in a new market. Many joint ventures have an agreed-upon limited life. The entities forming joint ventures usually involve companies but can sometimes involve governments, especially in emerging economies. A joint venture brings together the resources, technical skills, political ties, and other assets of each of the parties for a common goal. Profits and losses are shared on an agreed-upon basis.

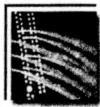

Focus on Business Technology

Joint Ventures and the Internet

The Internet is fostering the formation of many joint ventures by companies that are normally competitors. Among recent developments of this type are the following:
- Eight metals companies, including Allegheny Technologies Inc. and Alcoa Inc. <www.alcoa.com>, have formed a joint venture to establish online service to provide products to businesses in the metals industries.
- Accor <www.accorhotels.com>, Europe's largest hotel chain; Hilton International <www.hilton.com>; and Forte Hotels <www.forte-hotels.com> have launched an Internet joint venture enabling customers to make online bookings at their hotels. This counters a similar effort involving seven other hotel chains including Marriott <www.marriott.com>, Hyatt <www.hyatt.com>, and Holiday Inn <www.holidayinn.com>.
- General Motors Corporation <www.gm.com> and other companies have formed an Internet joint venture to consolidate and coordinate the purchase of parts and supplies in the manufacture of automobiles.

✓ Check out ACE for a Review Quiz at http://accounting.college.hmco.com/students.

ACCOUNTING FOR PARTNERS' EQUITY

LO2 Record partners' investments of cash and other assets when a partnership is formed.

RELATED TEXT ASSIGNMENTS
Q: 8
SE: 2
E: 1
P: 1, 5
SD: 3

Although accounting for a partnership is very similar to accounting for a sole proprietorship, there are differences. One is that the owner's equity in a partnership is called **partners' equity**. In accounting for partners' equity, it is necessary to maintain separate Capital and Withdrawals accounts for each partner and to divide the income and losses of the company among the partners.

The differences in the Capital accounts of a sole proprietorship and a partnership are as follows:

SOLE PROPRIETORSHIP	PARTNERSHIP	
Blake, Capital	Desmond, Capital	Frank, Capital
50,000	30,000	40,000
Blake, Withdrawals	Desmond, Withdrawals	Frank, Withdrawals
12,000	5,000	6,000

In the partners' equity section of the balance sheet, the balance of each partner's Capital account is listed separately:

Liabilities and Partners' Equity

Total liabilities		$28,000
Partners' equity		
Desmond, capital	$25,000	
Frank, capital	34,000	
Total partners' equity		59,000
Total liabilities and partners' equity		$87,000

● **STOP AND THINK!**
When accounts receivable are transferred into a partnership, at what amount should they be recorded?

Accounts receivable should be transferred in at their net realizable value. Thus, the gross amount of accounts receivable should be recorded, and a related contra account Allowance for Uncollected Accounts should also be recorded so that the net amount is the amount that the partnership will realize. ■

Each partner invests cash, other assets, or both in the partnership according to the partnership agreement. Noncash assets should be valued at their fair market value on the date they are transferred to the partnership. The assets invested by a partner are debited to the proper account, and the total amount is credited to the partner's Capital account.

To show how partners' investments are recorded, let's assume that Jerry Adcock and Rose Villa have agreed to combine their capital and equipment in a partnership to operate a jewelry store. According to their partnership agreement, Adcock will invest $28,000 in cash and $37,000 worth of furniture and displays, and Villa will invest $40,000 in cash and $30,000 worth of equipment. Related to the equipment is a note payable for $10,000, which the partnership assumes. The entries to record the partners' initial investments are as follows:

A = L + OE	20x3			
+ +	July 1	Cash	28,000	
+		Furniture and Displays	37,000	
		Jerry Adcock, Capital		65,000
		Initial investment of Jerry		
		Adcock in Adcock and Villa		
A = L + OE				
+ + +	1	Cash	40,000	
+		Equipment	30,000	
		Notes Payable		10,000
		Rose Villa, Capital		60,000
		Initial investment of Rose		
		Villa in Adcock and Villa		

KEY POINT: Old book values from previous entities are irrelevant to the new entity.

KEY POINT: Villa's noncash contribution is equal to the fair market value of the equipment less the amount owed on the equipment.

The values assigned to the assets would be included in the partnership agreement. These values can differ from those carried on the partners' personal books. For example, the equipment that Rose Villa contributed had a value of only $22,000 on her books, but its market value had increased considerably after she purchased it. The book value of Villa's equipment is not important. The fair market value of the equipment at the time of transfer *is* important, however, because that value represents the amount of money Villa has invested in the partnership. Later investments are recorded in the same way.

✓ Check out ACE for a Review Quiz at http://accounting.college.hmco.com/students.

DISTRIBUTION OF PARTNERSHIP INCOME AND LOSSES

LO3 Compute and record the income or losses that partners share, based on stated ratios, capital balance ratios, and partners' salaries and interest.

RELATED TEXT ASSIGNMENTS
Q: 9, 10, 11
SE: 3, 4, 5
E: 2, 3, 4
P: 1, 2, 5, 6
SD: 2
FRA: 1

KEY POINT: The division of income is one area in which a partnership differs from a corporation. In corporations, each common share receives an equal dividend. Partners can use any method they agree on to divide partnership income.

KEY POINT: The computations of each partner's share of net income are relevant to the closing entries in which the Income Summary account is closed to the partners' Capital accounts.

A partnership's income and losses can be distributed according to whatever method the partners specify in the partnership agreement. Income in this form of business normally has three components: return to the partners for the use of their capital (called *interest on partners' capital*), compensation for services the partners have rendered (partners' salaries), and other income for any special contributions individual partners may make to the partnership or risks they may take. The breakdown of total income into its three components helps clarify how much each partner has contributed to the firm.

If all partners contribute equal capital, have similar talents, and spend the same amount of time in the business, then an equal distribution of income and losses would be fair. However, if one partner works full time in the firm and another devotes only a fourth of his or her time, then the distribution of income or losses should reflect the difference. (This concept would apply to any situation in which the partners contribute unequally to the business.)

Distributing income and losses among partners can be accomplished by using stated ratios or capital balance ratios or by paying the partners' salaries and interest on their capital and sharing the remaining income according to stated ratios. *Salaries* and *interest* here are not *salaries expense* or *interest expense* in the ordinary sense of the terms. They do not affect the amount of reported net income. Instead, they refer to ways of determining each partner's share of net income or loss on the basis of time spent and money invested in the partnership.

STATED RATIOS

One method of distributing income and losses is to give each partner a stated ratio of the total income or loss. If each partner is making an equal contribution to the firm, each can assume the same share of income and losses. It is important to understand that an equal contribution to the firm does not necessarily mean an equal capital investment in the firm. One partner may be devoting more time and talent to the firm, whereas another may have made a larger capital investment. And if the partners contribute unequally to the firm, unequal stated ratios can be appropriate.

Let's assume that Adcock and Villa had a net income last year of $30,000. Their partnership agreement states that the percentages of income and losses distributed to Jerry Adcock and Rose Villa should be 60 percent and 40 percent, respectively. The computation of each partner's share of the income and the entry to show the distribution are as follows:

Adcock ($30,000 × .60)	$18,000
Villa ($30,000 × .40)	12,000
Net income	$30,000

A = L + OE	20x4			
−	June 30	Income Summary	30,000	
+		Jerry Adcock, Capital		18,000
+		Rose Villa, Capital		12,000
		Distribution of income for the year to the partners' Capital accounts		

CAPITAL BALANCE RATIOS

If invested capital produces the most income for the partnership, then income and losses may be distributed according to capital balances. The ratio used to distribute income and losses here may be based on each partner's capital balance at the beginning of the year or on the average capital balance of each partner during the year. The partnership agreement must describe the method to be used.

■ **RATIOS BASED ON BEGINNING CAPITAL BALANCES** To show how the first method works, let's look at the beginning capital balances of the partners in Adcock and Villa. At the start of the fiscal year, July 1, 20x3, Jerry Adcock, Capital showed a $65,000 balance and Rose Villa, Capital showed a $60,000 balance. (Actually, these balances reflect the partners' initial investment; the partnership was formed on July 1, 20x3.) The total partners' equity in the firm, then, was $125,000. Each partner's capital balance at the beginning of the year divided by the total partners' equity at the beginning of the year is that partner's beginning capital balance ratio:

	Beginning Capital Balance	Beginning Capital Balance Ratio
Jerry Adcock	$ 65,000	65,000 ÷ 125,000 = .52 = 52%
Rose Villa	60,000	60,000 ÷ 125,000 = .48 = 48%
	$125,000	

The income that each partner should receive when distribution is based on beginning capital balance ratios is determined by multiplying the total income by each partner's capital ratio. If we assume that income for the year was $140,000, Jerry Adcock's share of that income was $72,800, and Rose Villa's share was $67,200.

Jerry Adcock	$140,000 × .52 =	$ 72,800
Rose Villa	140,000 × .48 =	67,200
		$140,000

■ **RATIOS BASED ON AVERAGE CAPITAL BALANCES** If Adcock and Villa use beginning capital balance ratios to determine the distribution of income, they do not consider any investments or withdrawals made during the year. But investments and withdrawals usually change the partners' capital ratios. If the partners believe their capital balances will change dramatically during the year, they can choose average capital balance ratios as a fairer means of distributing income and losses.

The following T accounts show the activity over the year in Adcock and Villa's partners' Capital and Withdrawals accounts:

Jerry Adcock, Capital		Jerry Adcock, Withdrawals	
	7/1/x3 65,000	1/1/x4 10,000	

Rose Villa, Capital		Rose Villa, Withdrawals	
	7/1/x3 60,000	11/1/x3 10,000	
	2/1/x4 8,000		

Jerry Adcock withdrew $10,000 on January 1, 20x4, and Rose Villa withdrew $10,000 on November 1, 20x3, and invested an additional $8,000 of equipment on February 1, 20x4. Again, the income for the year's operation (July 1, 20x3, to June 30, 20x4) was $140,000. The calculations for the average capital balances and the distribution of income are as follows:

Average Capital Balances

Partner	Date	Capital Balance	×	Months Unchanged	=	Total		Average Capital Balance
Adcock	July–Dec.	$65,000	×	6	=	$390,000		
	Jan.–June	55,000	×	6	=	330,000		
				12		$720,000 ÷ 12	=	$ 60,000
Villa	July–Oct.	$60,000	×	4	=	$240,000		
	Nov.–Jan.	50,000	×	3	=	150,000		
	Feb.–June	58,000	×	5	=	290,000		
				12		$680,000 ÷ 12	=	56,667
						Total average capital		$116,667

Average Capital Balance Ratios

$$\text{Adcock} = \frac{\text{Adcock's Average Capital Balance}}{\text{Total Average Capital}} = \frac{\$60,000}{\$116,667} = .514 = 51.4\%$$

$$\text{Villa} = \frac{\text{Villa's Average Capital Balance}}{\text{Total Average Capital}} = \frac{\$56,667}{\$116,667} = .486 = 48.6\%$$

Distribution of Income

Partner	Income	×	Ratio	=	Share of Income
Adcock	$140,000	×	.514	=	$ 71,960
Villa	140,000	×	.486	=	68,040
				Total income	$140,000

Notice that to determine the distribution of income (or loss), you must determine the average capital balances, the average capital balance ratios, and each partner's share of income or loss. To compute each partner's average capital balance, you must examine the changes that have occured during the year in each partner's capital balance, changes that are the product of further investments and withdrawals. The partner's beginning capital is multiplied by the number of months the balance remains unchanged. After the balance changes, the new balance is multiplied by the number of months it remains unchanged. The process continues until the end of the year. The totals of these computations are added, and then they are divided by 12 to determine the average capital balances. Once the average capital balances are determined, the method of figuring capital balance ratios for sharing income and losses is the same as the method used for beginning capital balances.

SALARIES, INTEREST, AND STATED RATIOS

KEY POINT: Partnership income or loss cannot be divided solely on the basis of salaries or interest. An additional component, such as stated ratios, is needed.

Partners' contributions to a firm are usually not equal. To make up for the inequality, a partnership agreement can allow for partners' salaries, interest on partners' capital balances, or both in the distribution of income. Again, salaries and interest of this kind are not deducted as expenses before the partnership income is determined. They represent a method of arriving at an equitable distribution of income or loss.

To illustrate an allowance for partners' salaries, we assume that Adcock and Villa agree to annual salaries of $8,000 and $7,000, respectively, and to divide any

Distribution of Partnership Income and Losses

● **STOP AND THINK!**
What is a disadvantage of receiving a large salary as part of a partner's distribution of income?

If the partnership is not very profitable, partners with the large salaries will see reductions in their respective capital accounts to the extent that the salary distribution exceeds their distributions for income or loss for the year. ■

remaining income equally between them. Each salary is charged to the appropriate partner's Withdrawals account when paid. Assuming the same $140,000 income for the first year, the calculations for Adcock and Villa are as follows:

	Income of Partner — Adcock	Income of Partner — Villa	Income Distributed
Total Income for Distribution			$140,000
Distribution of Salaries			
Adcock	$ 8,000		
Villa		$ 7,000	(15,000)
Remaining Income After Salaries			$125,000
Equal Distribution of Remaining Income			
Adcock ($125,000 × .50)	62,500		
Villa ($125,000 × .50)		62,500	(125,000)
Remaining Income			—
Income of Partners	$70,500	$69,500	$140,000

Salaries allow for differences in the services that partners provide the business. However, they do not take into account differences in invested capital. To allow for capital differences, each partner can receive, in addition to salary, a stated interest on his or her invested capital. Suppose that Jerry Adcock and Rose Villa agree to annual salaries of $8,000 and $7,000, respectively, as well as 10 percent interest on their beginning capital balances, and to share any remaining income equally. The calculations for Adcock and Villa, assuming income of $140,000, are as follows:

CLARIFICATION NOTE: If there is a negative balance after salaries or salaries and interest have been distributed, the terms *Remaining Income After Salaries* and *Remaining Income After Salaries and Interest* become *Negative Balance After Salaries* and *Negative Balance After Salaries and Interest*. The computation proceeds in exactly the same way, regardless of whether the balance is positive or negative.

	Income of Partner — Adcock	Income of Partner — Villa	Income Distributed
Total Income for Distribution			$140,000
Distribution of Salaries			
Adcock	$ 8,000		
Villa		$ 7,000	(15,000)
Remaining Income After Salaries			$125,000
Distribution of Interest			
Adcock ($65,000 × .10)	6,500		
Villa ($60,000 × .10)		6,000	(12,500)
Remaining Income After Salaries and Interest			$112,500
Equal Distribution of Remaining Income			
Adcock ($112,500 × .50)	56,250		
Villa ($112,500 × .50)		56,250	(112,500)
Remaining Income			—
Income of Partners	$70,750	$69,250	$140,000

FOCUS ON BUSINESS PRACTICE

What Are the Risks of Being a Partner in an Accounting Firm?

Partners in large accounting firms can make over $250,000 per year, with top partners drawing over $800,000. However, consideration of those incomes should take into account the risks that partners take and the fact that the incomes of partners in small accounting firms are often much lower.

Partners are not compensated in the same way as managers in corporations. Partners' income is not guaranteed, but rather is based on the performance of the partnership. Also, each partner is required to make a substantial investment of capital in the partnership. This capital remains at risk for as long as the partner chooses to stay in the partnership. For instance, in one notable instance, when a large firm was convicted of destroying evidence in the Enron case, the partners lost their total investments as well as their income when their firm was subjected to lawsuits and other losses. The firm was eventually liquidated.

ENRICHMENT NOTE: When negotiating a partnership agreement, be sure to look at (and negotiate) the impact of both profits (net income) and losses.

If the partnership agreement allows for the distribution of salaries or interest or both, the amounts must be allocated to the partners even if profits are not enough to cover the salaries and interest. In fact, even if the company has a loss, these allocations must still be made. The negative balance, or loss, after the allocation of salaries and interest must be distributed according to the stated ratio in the partnership agreement, or equally if the agreement does not mention a ratio.

For example, let's assume that Adcock and Villa agreed to the following conditions, with much higher annual salaries, for the distribution of income and losses:

	Salaries	Interest	Beginning Capital Balance
Adcock	$70,000	10 percent of beginning	$65,000
Villa	60,000	capital balances	60,000

The computations for the distribution of the income and loss, again assuming income of $140,000, are as follows:

KEY POINT: Using salaries and interest to divide income or loss among partners has no effect on the income statement. They are not expenses. Partners' salaries and interest are used only to allow the equitable division of the partnership's net income.

	Income of Partner		Income
	Adcock	Villa	Distributed
Total Income for Distribution			$140,000
Distribution of Salaries			
Adcock	$70,000		
Villa		$60,000	(130,000)
Remaining Income After Salaries			$ 10,000
Distribution of Interest			
Adcock ($65,000 × .10)	6,500		
Villa ($60,000 × .10)		6,000	(12,500)
Negative Balance After Salaries and Interest			($ 2,500)
Equal Distribution of Negative Balance*			
Adcock ($2,500 × .50)	(1,250)		
Villa ($2,500 × .50)		(1,250)	2,500
Remaining Income			—
Income of Partners	$75,250	$64,750	$140,000

*Notice that the negative balance is distributed equally because the agreement does not indicate how income and losses should be distributed after salaries and interest are paid.

EXHIBIT 1
Partial Income Statement for Adcock and Villa

Adcock and Villa
Partial Income Statement
For the Year Ended June 30, 20x4

Net income		$140,000
Distribution to the partners		
Adcock		
Salary distribution	$70,000	
Interest on beginning capital balance	6,500	
Total	$76,500	
One-half of remaining negative amount	(1,250)	
Share of net income		$ 75,250
Villa		
Salary distribution	$60,000	
Interest on beginning capital balance	6,000	
Total	$66,000	
One-half of remaining negative amount	(1,250)	
Share of net income		64,750
Net income distributed		$140,000

On the income statement for the partnership, the distribution of income or losses is shown below the net income figure. Exhibit 1 shows how this is done.

✓ Check out ACE for a Review Quiz at http://accounting.college.hmco.com/students.

DISSOLUTION OF A PARTNERSHIP

LO4 Record a person's admission to or withdrawal from a partnership.

RELATED TEXT ASSIGNMENTS
Q: 12, 13
SE: 6, 7, 8, 9
E: 5, 6
P: 3, 5, 7
SD: 3, 5

Dissolution of a partnership occurs whenever there is a change in the original association of partners. When a partnership is dissolved, the partners lose their authority to continue the business as a going concern. The fact that the partners lose this authority does not necessarily mean that the business operation is ended or interrupted. However, it does mean—from a legal and accounting standpoint—that the separate entity ceases to exist. The remaining partners can act for the partnership in finishing the affairs of the business or in forming a new partnership that will be a new accounting entity. The dissolution of a partnership takes place through, among other events, the admission of a new partner, the withdrawal of a partner, or the death of a partner.

ADMISSION OF A NEW PARTNER

BUSINESS-WORLD EXAMPLE: Dissolution of a partnership is a legal issue. Consider Ernst & Young, which admits over one hundred partners each year. The entity continues to operate despite the legal changes it must make.

The admission of a new partner dissolves the old partnership because a new association has been formed. Dissolving the old partnership and creating a new one requires the consent of all the original partners and the ratification of a new partnership agreement. When a new partner is admitted, a new partnership agreement should be in place.

An individual can be admitted to a partnership in one of two ways: by purchasing an interest in the partnership from one or more of the original partners or by investing assets in the partnership.

KEY POINT: Admission of a new partner never has an impact on net income. Regardless of the price a new partner pays, there are never any income statement accounts in the entry to admit a new partner.

A = L + OE
      −
      +

■ **PURCHASING AN INTEREST FROM A PARTNER** When a person purchases an interest in a partnership from an original partner, the transaction is a personal one between these two people. However, the interest purchased must be transferred from the Capital account of the selling partner to the Capital account of the new partner.

Suppose that Jerry Adcock decides to sell his interest of $70,000 in Adcock and Villa to Richard Davis for $100,000 on August 31, 20x5, and that Rose Villa agrees to the sale. The entry to record the sale on the partnership books looks like this:

20x5
Aug. 31   Jerry Adcock, Capital   70,000
          Richard Davis, Capital   70,000
          Transfer of Jerry Adcock's equity
          to Richard Davis

KEY POINT: When a partner sells his or her interest directly to a new partner, the partner, not the partnership, realizes the gain or loss. In this case, Adcock has a gain of $30,000, but the assets, liabilities, and total equity of the partnership do not change.

Notice that the entry records the book value of the equity, not the amount Davis pays. The amount Davis pays is a personal matter between Adcock and him. Because the amount paid does not affect the assets or liabilities of the firm, it is not entered in the records.

Here's another example of a purchase: Assume that Richard Davis purchases half of Jerry Adcock's $70,000 interest in the partnership and half of Rose Villa's interest, assumed to be $80,000, by paying a total of $100,000 to the two partners on August 31, 20x5. The entry to record this transaction on the partnership books would be as follows:

A = L + OE
      −
      −
      +

20x5
Aug. 31   Jerry Adcock, Capital   35,000
          Rose Villa, Capital   40,000
             Richard Davis, Capital   75,000
             Transfer of half of Jerry Adcock's
             and Rose Villa's equity to
             Richard Davis

CLARIFICATION NOTE: If the account did not reflect the current value of the assets, the asset accounts (and Capital accounts) would need to be adjusted before admitting the new partner.

■ **INVESTING ASSETS IN A PARTNERSHIP** When a new partner is admitted through an investment in the partnership, both the assets and the partners' equity in the firm increase. The increase occurs because the assets the new partner invests become partnership assets, and as partnership assets increase, partners' equity increases. For example, assume that Jerry Adcock and Rose Villa have agreed to allow Richard Davis to invest $75,000 in return for a one-third interest in their partnership. The Capital accounts of Jerry Adcock and Rose Villa are $70,000 and $80,000, respectively. Davis's $75,000 investment equals a one-third interest in the firm after the investment is added to the previously existing capital of the partnership:

Jerry Adcock, Capital	$ 70,000
Rose Villa, Capital	80,000
Davis's investment	75,000
Total capital after Davis's investment	$225,000
One-third interest = $225,000 ÷ 3 =	$ 75,000

The entry to record Davis's investment is as follows:

A = L + OE
+   +

20x5
Aug. 31   Cash   75,000
          Richard Davis, Capital   75,000
          Admission of Richard Davis for a
          one-third interest in the company

■ **BONUS TO THE OLD PARTNERS** A partnership is sometimes so profitable or otherwise advantageous that a new investor is willing to pay more than the actual

KEY POINT: The original partners receive a bonus because the entity is worth more as a going concern than the fair market value of the net assets would otherwise indicate. That is, the new partner is paying for unrecorded partnership value.

dollar interest he or she receives in the partnership. For instance, suppose an individual pays $100,000 for an $80,000 interest in a partnership. The $20,000 excess of the payment over the interest purchased is a **bonus** to the original partners. The bonus must be distributed to the original partners according to the partnership agreement. When the agreement does not cover the distribution of bonuses, a bonus should be distributed to the original partners in accordance with the method for distributing income and losses.

Assume that the Adcock and Villa Company has operated for several years and that the partners' capital balances and the stated ratios for distribution of income and loss are as follows:

Partners	Capital Balances	Stated Ratios
Adcock	$160,000	55%
Villa	140,000	45
	$300,000	100%

Richard Davis wants to join the firm. He offers to invest $100,000 on December 1 for a one-fifth interest in the business and income. The original partners agree to the offer. This is the computation of the bonus to the original partners:

Partners' equity in the original partnership		$300,000
Cash investment by Richard Davis		100,000
Partners' equity in the new partnership		$400,000
Partners' equity assigned to Richard Davis ($400,000 × 1/5)		$ 80,000
Bonus to the original partners		
Investment by Richard Davis	$100,000	
Less equity assigned to Richard Davis	80,000	$ 20,000
Distribution of bonus to original partners		
Jerry Adcock ($20,000 × .55)	$ 11,000	
Rose Villa ($20,000 × .45)	9,000	$ 20,000

This is the entry that records Davis's admission to the partnership:

A = L + OE
+   +
        +
        +

```
20x5
Dec. 1  Cash                              100,000
            Jerry Adcock, Capital                  11,000
            Rose Villa, Capital                     9,000
            Richard Davis, Capital                 80,000
         Investment by Richard Davis for
         a one-fifth interest in the firm,
         and the bonus distributed to the
         original partners
```

ENRICHMENT NOTE: Human capital plays a large part in the profitability of entities traditionally organized as partnerships (for example, accounting firms, legal firms, and medical practices). When a new partner is admitted, this human capital is recognized in the Capital account of the new partner who receives a bonus.

■ **BONUS TO THE NEW PARTNER** There are several reasons that a partnership might want a new partner. A partnership in financial trouble might need additional cash. Or the partners might want to expand the firm's markets and need more capital for this purpose than they themselves can provide. Also, the partners might know a person who would bring a unique talent to the firm. Under these conditions, a new partner may be admitted to the partnership with the understanding that part of the original partners' capital will be transferred (credited) to the new partner's Capital account as a bonus.

For example, suppose that Jerry Adcock and Rose Villa have invited Richard Davis to join the firm. Davis is going to invest $60,000 on December 1 for a one-fourth interest in the company. The stated ratios for distribution of income or loss

● **STOP AND THINK!**
If the value of a partnership is worth far more than the book value of the assets on the balance sheet, would a new partner entering the partnership be more likely to pay a bonus to the old partners or receive a bonus from the old partners?

The new partner would more likely pay a bonus to the old partners because the value of the incoming partner's share of the partnership would be more than the amounts on the balance sheet. The old partners will want compensation for the value of the proportionate share the new partner is getting. ■

for Adcock and Villa are 55 percent and 45 percent, respectively. If Davis is to receive a one-fourth interest in the firm, the interest of the original partners represents a three-fourths interest in the business. The computation of Davis's bonus is as follows:

Total equity in partnership		
Jerry Adcock, Capital		$160,000
Rose Villa, Capital		140,000
Investment by Richard Davis		60,000
Partners' equity in the new partnership		$360,000
Partners' equity assigned to Richard Davis ($360,000 × ¼)		$ 90,000
Bonus to new partner		
Equity assigned to Richard Davis	$90,000	
Less cash investment by Richard Davis	60,000	$ 30,000
Distribution of bonus from original partners		
Jerry Adcock ($30,000 × .55)	$16,500	
Rose Villa ($30,000 × .45)	13,500	$ 30,000

The entry to record the admission of Richard Davis to the partnership is shown below:

A = L + OE
\+   −
      −
      +

20x5			
Dec. 1	Cash	60,000	
	Jerry Adcock, Capital	16,500	
	Rose Villa, Capital	13,500	
	Richard Davis, Capital		90,000
	To record the investment by		
	Richard Davis of cash and a		
	bonus from Adcock and Villa		

WITHDRAWAL OF A PARTNER

KEY POINT: There is no impact on the income statement of a partnership when a partner withdraws. The only change is on the balance sheet.

Since a partnership is a voluntary association, a partner usually has the right to withdraw at any time. However, to avoid disputes when a partner does decide to withdraw or retire, a partnership agreement should describe the procedures to be followed. The agreement should specify (1) whether an audit will be performed, (2) how the assets will be reappraised, (3) how a bonus will be determined, and (4) by what method the withdrawing partner will be paid.

A partner who wants to withdraw from a partnership can do so in one of several ways. The partner can sell his or her interest to another partner or to an out-

FOCUS ON BUSINESS PRACTICE

Can Withdrawal of Partners Harm a Partnership?

The withdrawal of partners can cause a financial strain on a partnership, as when Goldman, Sachs & Co., the last major Wall Street investment company still organized as a partnership, was scrambling to raise more than $250 million to compensate for the withdrawal of twenty-three partners. The retirements caused a decrease in equity capital of about $400 million, which represented almost 10 percent of the firm's capital. Goldman was looking for private investors to make up for the losses.[3] The majority of Wall Street investment companies, such as Merrill Lynch & Co., Inc., and Salomon Brothers Inc., are organized as corporations. An advantage of this form of organization is that managers who want to leave their jobs can sell their stock to other investors without affecting the firm's capital.

FIGURE 1
Alternative Ways for a Partner to Withdraw

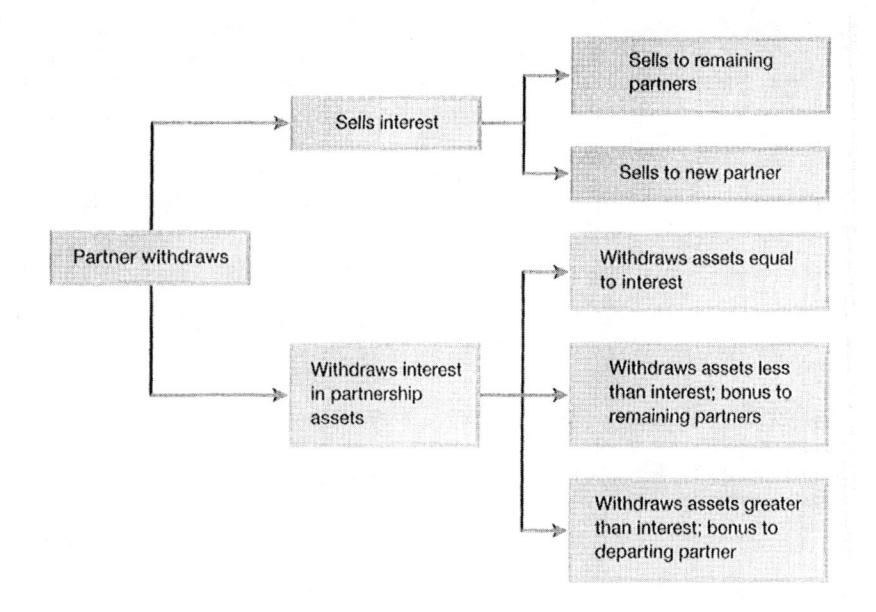

```
                                           ┌─→ Sells to remaining partners
                            ┌─→ Sells interest ─┤
                            │              └─→ Sells to new partner
        Partner withdraws ──┤
                            │                          ┌─→ Withdraws assets equal to interest
                            └─→ Withdraws interest ────┤
                                in partnership assets  ├─→ Withdraws assets less than interest; bonus to remaining partners
                                                       │
                                                       └─→ Withdraws assets greater than interest; bonus to departing partner
```

sider with the consent of the remaining partners, or the partner can withdraw assets equal to his or her capital balance, less than his or her capital balance (in this case, the remaining partners receive a bonus), or greater than his or her capital balance (in this case, the withdrawing partner receives a bonus). These alternatives are illustrated in Figure 1.

KEY POINT: Selling a partnership interest does not affect the assets and liabilities of the partnership. Therefore, total equity remains unchanged. The only effect of a partner's selling his or her interest to the existing partners or to a new partner is the change of names in the partners' equity section of the balance sheet.

■ **WITHDRAWAL BY SELLING INTEREST** When a partner sells his or her interest to another partner or to an outsider with the consent of the other partners, the transaction is personal; it does not change the partnership assets or the partners' equity. For example, let's assume that the capital balances of Adcock, Villa, and Davis are $140,000, $100,000, and $60,000, respectively, for a total of $300,000.

Villa wants to withdraw from the partnership and is reviewing two offers for her interest. The offers are (1) to sell her interest to Davis for $110,000 or (2) to sell her interest to Judy Jones for $120,000. The remaining partners have agreed to either potential transaction. Because Davis and Jones would pay for Villa's interest from their personal assets, the partnership accounting records would show only the transfer of Villa's interest to Davis or Jones. The entries to record these possible transfers are as follows:

1. If Villa's interest is purchased by Davis:

A = L + OE
    −
    +

Rose Villa, Capital	100,000	
Richard Davis, Capital		100,000
Sale of Villa's partnership interest to Davis		

2. If Villa's interest is purchased by Jones:

A = L + OE
    −
    +

Rose Villa, Capital	100,000	
Judy Jones, Capital		100,000
Sale of Villa's partnership interest to Jones		

■ **WITHDRAWAL BY REMOVING ASSETS** A partnership agreement can allow a withdrawing partner to remove assets from the firm equal to his or her capital balance. Assume that Richard Davis decides to withdraw from Adcock, Villa, Davis & Company. Davis's capital balance is $60,000. The partnership agreement states that he can withdraw cash from the firm equal to his capital balance. If there is not enough cash, he must accept a promissory note from the new partnership for the balance. The remaining partners ask that Davis take only $50,000 in cash because of a cash shortage at the time of his withdrawal; he agrees to this request. The following entry records Davis's withdrawal:

A = L + OE
− + −

20x5			
Jan. 21	Richard Davis, Capital	60,000	
	Cash		50,000
	Notes Payable, Richard Davis		10,000
	Withdrawal of Richard Davis from the partnership		

KEY POINT: Even if a bonus was involved, Davis's Capital account would be debited for $60,000 to eliminate it.

When a withdrawing partner removes assets that represent less than his or her capital balance, the equity that the partner leaves in the business is divided among the remaining partners according to their stated ratios. This distribution is considered a bonus to the remaining partners. When a withdrawing partner takes out assets that are greater than his or her capital balance, the excess is treated as a bonus to the withdrawing partner. The remaining partners absorb the bonus according to their stated ratios. Alternative arrangements can be spelled out in the partnership agreement.

DEATH OF A PARTNER

When a partner dies, the partnership is dissolved because the original association has changed. The partnership agreement should state the actions to be taken. Normally, the books are closed, and financial statements are prepared. Those actions are necessary to determine the capital balance of each partner on the date of the death. The agreement may also indicate whether an audit should be conducted, assets appraised, and a bonus recorded, as well as the procedures for settling with the deceased partner's heirs. The remaining partners may purchase the deceased's equity, sell it to outsiders, or deliver specified business assets to the estate. If the firm intends to continue, a new partnership must be formed.

✓ Check out ACE for a Review Quiz at http://accounting.college.hmco.com/students.

LIQUIDATION OF A PARTNERSHIP

LO5 Compute the distribution of assets to partners when they liquidate their partnership.

RELATED TEXT ASSIGNMENTS
Q: 14, 15
SE: 10
E: 7, 8
P: 4, 5, 8

The **liquidation** of a partnership is the process of ending the business, of selling enough assets to pay the partnership's liabilities, and distributing any remaining assets among the partners. Liquidation is a special form of dissolution. When a partnership is liquidated, the business will not continue.

The partnership agreement should indicate the procedures to be followed in the case of liquidation. Usually, the books are adjusted and closed, with the income or loss distributed to the partners. As the assets of the business are sold, any gain or loss should be distributed to the partners according to the stated ratios. As cash becomes available, it must be applied first to outside creditors, then to loans from partners, and finally to the partners' capital balances.

The process of liquidation can have a variety of financial outcomes. We look at two: (1) assets sold for a gain and (2) assets sold for a loss. For both alternatives, we make the assumptions that the books have been closed for Adcock, Villa, Davis & Company and that the following balance sheet exists before liquidation:

STUDY NOTE: Be sure to consider the liquidation procedure step by step. To liquidate a partnership, the partners first must sell the assets and pay the liabilities (or distribute them to the partners). Second, any gains or losses from the sales of assets must be allocated to the partners. Third, when only cash remains, it is paid to the partners. Fourth, when a partner has a negative capital balance, he or she is obligated to pay the deficiency. Otherwise, the remaining partners must absorb the deficiency.

Adcock, Villa, Davis & Company
Balance Sheet
February 2, 20x6

Assets		Liabilities	
Cash	$ 60,000	Accounts payable	$120,000
Accounts receivable	40,000	**Partners' Equity**	
Merchandise inventory	100,000		
Plant assets (net)	200,000	Adcock, Capital	85,000
Total assets	$400,000	Villa, Capital	95,000
		Davis, Capital	100,000
		Total liabilities and partners' equity	$400,000

● **STOP AND THINK!**
When a partnership is dissolved, what is an alternate approach to selling all the assets and distributing the proceeds, and what decisions will have to be made if this approach is taken?

The partners may decide to divide up the assets among themselves. In this case, they will have to decide on the value of the assets and who gets which assets. They will also have to decide how to pay the liabilities. And they will have to settle the capital accounts, just as they would if cash were involved. ■

TERMINOLOGY NOTE:
Notice the proper use of the term *realization* in the February 13 and 14 entries. *Realization* means "conversion into cash."

The stated ratios of Adcock, Villa, and Davis are 3:3:4, or 30, 30, and 40 percent, respectively.

GAIN ON SALE OF ASSETS

Suppose that the following transactions took place in the liquidation of Adcock, Villa, Davis & Company:

1. The accounts receivable were collected for $35,000.
2. The inventory was sold for $110,000.
3. The plant assets were sold for $200,000.
4. The accounts payable of $120,000 were paid.
5. The gain of $5,000 from the realization of the assets was distributed according to the partners' stated ratios.
6. The partners received cash equivalent to the balances of their Capital accounts.

These transactions are summarized in the statement of liquidation in Exhibit 2. The journal entries with their assumed transaction dates are as follows:

Explanation on Statement of Liquidation

A = L + OE	20x6				
+	Feb. 13	Cash		35,000	1
−		Gain or Loss from Realization		5,000	
		Accounts Receivable			40,000
		Collection of accounts receivable			
A = L + OE	14	Cash		110,000	2
+ +		Merchandise Inventory			100,000
−		Gain or Loss from Realization			10,000
		Sale of inventory			

EXHIBIT 2
Statement of Liquidation Showing Gain on Sale of Assets

Adcock, Villa, Davis & Company
Statement of Liquidation
February 2–20, 20x6

Explanation	Cash	Other Assets	Accounts Payable	Adcock, Capital (30%)	Villa, Capital (30%)	Davis, Capital (40%)	Gain (or Loss) from Realization
Balance 2/2/x6	$ 60,000	$340,000	$120,000	$85,000	$95,000	$100,000	
1. Collection of Accounts Receivable	35,000	(40,000)					($ 5,000)
	$ 95,000	$300,000	$120,000	$85,000	$95,000	$100,000	($ 5,000)
2. Sale of Inventory	110,000	(100,000)					10,000
	$205,000	$200,000	$120,000	$85,000	$95,000	$100,000	$ 5,000
3. Sale of Plant Assets	200,000	(200,000)					
	$405,000	—	$120,000	$85,000	$95,000	$100,000	$ 5,000
4. Payment of Liabilities	(120,000)		(120,000)				
	$285,000		—	$85,000	$95,000	$100,000	$ 5,000
5. Distribution of Gain (or Loss) from Realization				1,500	1,500	2,000	(5,000)
	$285,000			$86,500	$96,500	$102,000	—
6. Distribution of Cash to Partners	(285,000)			(86,500)	(96,500)	(102,000)	
	—			—	—	—	

A = L + OE + −	Feb. 16	Cash Plant Assets Sale of plant assets	200,000	200,000	3
A = L + OE − −	16	Accounts Payable Cash Payment of accounts payable	120,000	120,000	4
A = L + OE − + + +	20	Gain or Loss from Realization Jerry Adcock, Capital Rose Villa, Capital Richard Davis, Capital Distribution of the gain on assets ($10,000 gain minus $5,000 loss) to the partners	5,000	1,500 1,500 2,000	5

A = L + OE	Feb. 20	Jerry Adcock, Capital	86,500	
− − −		Rose Villa, Capital	96,500	
		Richard Davis, Capital	102,000	
		Cash		285,000
		Distribution of cash to the partners		

Notice that the cash distributed to the partners is the balance in their respective Capital accounts. Cash is not distributed according to the partners' stated ratios.

LOSS ON SALE OF ASSETS

KEY POINT: The case here is almost the same as the previous one because losses are allocated on the same basis as gains. The only difference is that entry 3 in this case (a loss) and entry 5 in the first case (a gain) switch the debits and credits.

We discuss two cases involving losses on the sale of a company's assets. In the first, the losses are small enough to be absorbed by the partners' capital balances. In the second, one partner's share of the losses is too large for his capital balance to absorb.

When a firm's assets are sold at a loss, the partners share the loss on liquidation according to their stated ratios. For example, assume that during the liquidation of Adcock, Villa, Davis & Company, the total cash received from the collection of accounts receivable and the sale of inventory and plant assets was $140,000. The statement of liquidation appears in Exhibit 3.

EXHIBIT 3
Statement of Liquidation Showing Loss on Sale of Assets

Adcock, Villa, Davis & Company
Statement of Liquidation
February 2–20, 20x6

Explanation	Cash	Other Assets	Accounts Payable	Adcock, Capital (30%)	Villa, Capital (30%)	Davis, Capital (40%)	Gain (or Loss) from Realization
Balance 2/2/x6	$60,000	$340,000	$120,000	$85,000	$95,000	$100,000	
1. Collection of Accounts Receivable and Sale of Inventory and Plant Assets	140,000	(340,000)					($200,000)
	$200,000	—	$120,000	$85,000	$95,000	$100,000	($200,000)
2. Payment of Liabilities	(120,000)		(120,000)				
	$80,000		—	$85,000	$95,000	$100,000	($200,000)
3. Distribution of Gain (or Loss) from Realization				(60,000)	(60,000)	(80,000)	200,000
	$80,000			$25,000	$35,000	$20,000	—
4. Distribution of Cash to Partners	(80,000)			(25,000)	(35,000)	(20,000)	
	—			—	—	—	

The journal entries for the transactions summarized in the statement of liquidation in Exhibit 3 are as follows:

KEY POINT: This example (a loss) uses a compound entry for what was included in entries 1, 2, and 3 in the first example (a gain). If you have difficulty with the concept, here is an opportunity to break the entry down into its three component parts.

				Explanation on Statement of Liquidation	

A = L + OE
+
−
−
−
	20x6
	Feb. 15
		Cash
		Gain or Loss from Realization
		  Accounts Receivable
		  Merchandise Inventory
		  Plant Assets
		    Collection of accounts
		    receivable and the sale of
		    inventory and plant assets
				140,000
				200,000
					40,000
					100,000
					200,000
						1

A = L + OE
− −
	16	Accounts Payable
		  Cash
		    Payment of accounts payable
				120,000	120,000	2

A = L + OE
−
−
−
+
	20	Jerry Adcock, Capital
		Rose Villa, Capital
		Richard Davis, Capital
		  Gain or Loss from Realization
		    Distribution of the loss on
		    assets to the partners
				60,000
				60,000
				80,000
					200,000	3

A = L + OE
−
−
−
	20	Jerry Adcock, Capital
		Rose Villa, Capital
		Richard Davis, Capital
		  Cash
		    Distribution of cash to
		    the partners
				25,000
				35,000
				20,000
					80,000	4

In some liquidations, a partner's share of the loss is greater than his or her capital balance. In such a situation, because partners are subject to unlimited liability, the partner must make up the deficit in his or her Capital account from personal assets. For example, suppose that after the sale of assets and the payment of liabilities, the remaining assets and partners' equity of Adcock, Villa, Davis & Company look like this:

Assets
  Cash $ 30,000

Partners' Equity
  Adcock, Capital $25,000
  Villa, Capital   20,000
  Davis, Capital   (15,000) $ 30,000

Richard Davis must pay $15,000 into the partnership from personal funds to cover his deficit. If he pays cash to the partnership, the following entry would record the cash contribution:

A = L + OE
+   +
	20x6
	Feb. 20
		Cash
		  Richard Davis, Capital
		    Additional investment of
		    Richard Davis to cover the
		    negative balance in his
		    Capital account
				15,000	15,000

After Davis pays $15,000, there is enough cash to pay Adcock and Villa their capital balances and, thus, to complete the liquidation. The transaction is recorded in the following way:

A = L + OE	20x6			
− − −	Feb. 20	Jerry Adcock, Capital	25,000	
		Rose Villa, Capital	20,000	
		Cash		45,000
		Distribution of cash to the partners		

If a partner does not have the cash to cover his or her obligations to the partnership, the remaining partners share the loss according to their established stated ratios. Remember that all partners have unlimited liability. As a result, if Richard Davis cannot pay the $15,000 deficit in his Capital account, Adcock and Villa must share the deficit according to their stated ratios. Each has a 30 percent stated ratio, so each must pay 50 percent of the losses that Davis cannot pay. The new stated ratios are computed as follows:

	Old Ratios	New Ratios	
Adcock	30%	30 ÷ 60 = .50 =	50%
Villa	30	30 ÷ 60 = .50 =	50
	60%		100%

And the entries to record the transactions are as follows:

A = L + OE	20x6			
−	Feb. 20	Jerry Adcock, Capital	7,500	
−		Rose Villa, Capital	7,500	
+		Richard Davis, Capital		15,000
		Transfer of Davis's deficit to Adcock and Villa		
A = L + OE		20 Jerry Adcock, Capital	17,500	
− − −		Rose Villa, Capital	12,500	
		Cash		30,000
		Distribution of cash to the partners		

Davis's inability to meet his obligations at the time of liquidation does not relieve him of his liabilities to Adcock and Villa. If he is able to pay his liabilities at some time in the future, Adcock and Villa can collect the amount of Davis's deficit that they absorbed.

✓ Check out ACE for a Review Quiz at http://accounting.college.hmco.com/students.

Chapter Review

REVIEW OF LEARNING OBJECTIVES

LO1 Identify the principal characteristics, advantages, and disadvantages of the partnership form of business.

A partnership has several major characteristics that distinguish it from the other forms of business. It is a voluntary association of two or more people who combine their talents and resources to carry on a business. Their joint effort should be supported by a partnership agreement that spells out the venture's operating procedures. A partnership is dissolved by a partner's admission, withdrawal, or death, and therefore has a limited life. Each partner acts as an agent of the partnership within the scope of normal operations and is personally liable for the partnership's debts. Property invested in the partnership becomes an asset of the partnership, owned jointly by all the partners. And, finally, each partner has the right to share in the company's income and the responsibility to share in its losses.

The advantages of a partnership are the ease of its formation and dissolution, the opportunity to pool several individuals' talents and resources, the lack of corporate tax burden, and the freedom of action each partner enjoys. The disadvantages are the limited life of a partnership, mutual agency, the unlimited personal liability of the partners, and the difficulty of raising large amounts of capital and transferring partners' interest. Two other common forms of association that are a type of partnership or similar to a partnership are limited partnerships and joint ventures.

LO2 Record partners' investments of cash and other assets when a partnership is formed.

A partnership is formed when the partners contribute cash, other assets, or a combination of both to the business. The details are stated in the partnership agreement. Initial investments are recorded with a debit to Cash or another asset account and a credit to the investing partner's Capital account. The recorded amount of the other assets should be their fair market value on the date of transfer to the partnership. In addition, a partnership can assume an investing partner's liabilities. When this occurs, the partner's Capital account is credited with the difference between the assets invested and the liabilities assumed.

LO3 Compute and record the income or losses that partners share, based on stated ratios, capital balance ratios, and partners' salaries and interest.

The partners must share income and losses in accordance with the partnership agreement. If the agreement says nothing about the distribution of income and losses, the partners share them equally. Common methods used for distributing income and losses include stated ratios, capital balance ratios, and salaries and interest on capital investments. Each method tries to measure the individual partner's contribution to the operations of the business.

Stated ratios usually are based on the partners' relative contributions to the partnership. When capital balance ratios are used, income or losses are divided strictly on the basis of each partner's capital balance. The use of salaries and interest on capital investment takes into account both efforts (salary) and capital investment (interest) in dividing income or losses among the partners.

LO4 Record a person's admission to or withdrawal from a partnership.

An individual is admitted to a partnership by purchasing a partner's interest or by contributing additional assets. When an interest is purchased, the withdrawing partner's capital is transferred to the new partner. When the new partner contributes assets to the partnership, it may be necessary to recognize a bonus shared or borne by the original partners or by the new partner.

A person can withdraw from a partnership by selling his or her interest in the business to the remaining partners or a new partner or by withdrawing company assets. When assets are withdrawn, the amount can be equal to, less than, or greater than the partner's capital interest. When assets that have a value less than or greater than the partner's interest are withdrawn, a bonus is recognized and distributed among the remaining partners or to the departing partner.

LO5 Compute the distribution of assets to partners when they liquidate their partnership.

The liquidation of a partnership entails selling the assets necessary to pay the company's liabilities and then distributing any remaining assets to the partners. Any gain or loss on the sale of the assets is shared by the partners according to their stated ratios. When a partner has a deficit balance in a Capital account, that partner must contribute personal assets equal to the deficit. When a partner does not have personal assets to cover a capital deficit, the deficit must be absorbed by the solvent partners according to their stated ratios.

REVIEW OF CONCEPTS AND TERMINOLOGY

The following concepts and terms were introduced in this chapter:

LO4 **Bonus:** An amount that accrues to the original partners when a new partner pays more to the partnership than the interest received or that accrues to the new partner when the amount paid to the partnership is less than the interest received.

LO4 **Dissolution:** The loss of authority to continue a partnership as a separate entity due to a change in the original association of partners.

LO1 **Joint venture:** An association of two or more entities for the purpose of achieving a specific goal, such as the manufacture of a product in a new market.

LO1 **Limited life:** A characteristic of a partnership; the fact that any event that breaches the partnership agreement—including the admission, withdrawal, or death of a partner—terminates the partnership.

LO1 **Limited partnership:** A form of partnership in which limited partners' liabilities are limited to their investment.

LO5 **Liquidation:** A special form of dissolution in which a business ends by selling assets, paying liabilities, and distributing any remaining assets to the partners.

LO1 **Mutual agency:** A characteristic of a partnership; the authority of each partner to act as an agent of the partnership within the scope of the business's normal operations.

LO2 **Partners' equity:** The owner's equity in a partnership.

LO1 **Partnership:** An association of two or more people to carry on as co-owners of a business for profit.

LO1 **Partnership agreement:** The contractual relationship between partners that identifies the details of their partnership.

LO1 **Unlimited liability:** A characteristic of a partnership; the fact that each partner has personal liability for all the debts of the partnership.

REVIEW PROBLEM

Distribution of Income and Admission of a Partner

LO3
LO4 Jack Holder and Dan Williams reached an agreement in 20x7 to pool their resources and form a partnership to manufacture and sell university T-shirts. In forming the partnership, Holder and Williams contributed $100,000 and $150,000, respectively. They drafted a partnership agreement stating that Holder was to receive an annual salary of $6,000 and Williams was to receive 3 percent interest annually on his original investment of $150,000 in the business. Income and losses after salary and interest were to be shared by Holder and Williams in a 2:3 ratio.

REQUIRED
1. Compute the income or loss that Holder and Williams share, and prepare the required entries in journal form, assuming the partnership made $27,000 income in 20x7 and suffered a $2,000 loss in 20x8 (before salary and interest).
2. Assume that Jean Ratcliffe offers Holder and Williams $60,000 for a 15 percent interest in the partnership on January 1, 20x9. Holder and Williams agree to Ratcliffe's offer because they need her resources to expand the business. On January 1, 20x9, the balance in Holder's Capital account is $113,600, and the balance in Williams's Capital account is $161,400. Record the admission of Ratcliffe to the partnership, assuming that her investment represents a 15 percent interest in the total partners' capital and that a bonus will be distributed to Holder and Williams in the ratio of 2:3.

Answer to Review Problem

1. Compute the income or loss distribution to the partners.

	Income of Partner Holder	Income of Partner Williams	Income Distributed
20x7			
Total Income for Distribution			$27,000
Distribution of Salary			
Holder	$ 6,000		(6,000)
Remaining Income After Salary			$21,000
Distribution of Interest			
Williams ($150,000 × .03)		$ 4,500	(4,500)
Remaining Income After Salary and Interest			$16,500
Distribution of Remaining Income			
Holder ($16,500 × ⅖)	6,600		
Williams ($16,500 × ⅗)		9,900	(16,500)
Remaining Income			—
Income of Partners	$12,600	$14,400	$27,000
20x8			
Total Loss for Distribution			($ 2,000)
Distribution of Salary			
Holder	$ 6,000		(6,000)
Negative Balance After Salary			($ 8,000)
Distribution of Interest			
Williams ($150,000 × .03)		$ 4,500	(4,500)
Negative Balance After Salary and Interest			($12,500)
Distribution of Negative Balance			
Holder ($12,500 × ⅖)	(5,000)		
Williams ($12,500 × ⅗)		(7,500)	12,500
Remaining Loss			—
Income and Loss of Partners	$ 1,000	($ 3,000)	($ 2,000)

Entry in Journal Form—20x7

Income Summary	27,000	
Jack Holder, Capital		12,600
Dan Williams, Capital		14,400
Distribution of income for the year to the partners' Capital accounts		

Entry in Journal Form—20x8

Dan Williams, Capital	3,000	
Income Summary		2,000
Jack Holder, Capital		1,000
Distribution of the loss for the year to the partners' Capital accounts		

2. Record the admission of a new partner.

Capital Balance and Bonus Computation

Ratcliffe, Capital = (Original Partners' Capital + New Partner's Investment) × 15%
= ($113,600 + $161,400 + $60,000) × .15 = $50,250
Bonus = New Partner's Investment − Ratcliffe, Capital
= $60,000 − $50,250
= $9,750

Distribution of Bonus

Holder = $9,750 × 2/5 = $3,900
Williams = $9,750 × 3/5 = 5,850
Total bonus $9,750

Entry in Journal Form

20x9			
Jan. 1	Cash	60,000	
	Jack Holder, Capital		3,900
	Dan Williams, Capital		5,850
	Jean Ratcliffe, Capital		50,250
	Sale of a 15 percent interest in the partnership to Jean Ratcliffe and the bonus paid to the original partners		

Chapter Assignments

BUILDING YOUR KNOWLEDGE FOUNDATION

QUESTIONS

1. Briefly define *partnership*, and list several important characteristics of the partnership form of business.
2. Leon and Jon are partners in a drilling operation. Leon purchased a drilling rig to be used in the partnership's operations. Is Leon's purchase binding on Jon even though Jon was not involved in it? Explain your answer.
3. What is the meaning of unlimited liability when applied to a partnership? Describe a form of partnership that limits investors' liability.
4. The partnership agreement for Anne and Jin-Li does not disclose how they will share income and losses. How would the income and losses be shared in this partnership?
5. What are several key advantages of a partnership? What are some disadvantages?
6. How does a limited partnership overcome a key disadvantage of ordinary partnerships?
7. What form of association is becoming more prevalent in conducting global business? Define it.
8. Charles contributes $10,000 in cash and a building with a book value of $40,000 and fair market value of $50,000 to the Charles and Dean partnership. What is the balance of Charles's Capital account in the partnership?
9. Oscar Perez and Leah Torn are forming a partnership. What are some factors they should consider in deciding how income is to be divided?

10. Sue and Ari share income and losses in their partnership in a 3:2 ratio. The firm's net income for the current year is $80,000. How would the distribution of income be recorded in the journal?

11. Kathy and Roger share income in their partnership in a 2:4 ratio. Kathy and Roger receive salaries of $6,000 and $10,000, respectively. How would they share a net income of $22,000 before salaries?

12. Carol purchases Mary's interest in the Mary and Leo partnership for $62,000. Mary has a $57,000 capital interest in the partnership. How would this transaction be recorded in the partnership books?

13. Dan and Augie each own a $50,000 interest in a partnership. They agree to admit Bea as a partner by selling her a one-third interest for $80,000. How large a bonus will be distributed to Dan and Augie?

14. Describe the ways in which the dissolution of a partnership differs from the liquidation of a partnership.

15. In the liquidation of a partnership, José's Capital account showed a $5,000 debit balance after all the creditors had been paid. What obligation does José have to the partnership?

Short Exercises

SE 1.
LO1 Partnership Characteristics

Indicate whether each statement below is a reflection of (a) voluntary association, (b) a partnership agreement, (c) limited life, (d) mutual agency, or (e) unlimited liability.

1. A partner may be required to pay the debts of the partnership out of personal assets.
2. A partnership must be dissolved when a partner is admitted, withdraws, retires, or dies.
3. Any partner can bind the partnership to a business agreement.
4. A partner does not have to remain a partner if he or she does not want to.
5. Details of the arrangements among partners are specified in a written contract.

SE 2.
LO2 Partnership Formation

Bob contributes cash of $12,000, and Kim contributes office equipment that cost $10,000 but is valued at $8,000 to the formation of a new partnership. Prepare the entry in journal form to form the partnership.

SE 3.
LO3 Distribution of Partnership Income

During the first year, the Bob and Kim partnership (see **SE 2**) earned an income of $5,000. Assume the partners agreed to share income and losses in the ratio of the beginning balances of their capital accounts. How much income should be transferred to each Capital account?

SE 4.
LO3 Distribution of Partnership Income

During the first year, the Bob and Kim partnership (see **SE 2**) earned an income of $5,000. Assume the partners agreed to share income and losses by figuring interest on the beginning capital balances at 10 percent and dividing the remainder equally. How much income should be transferred to each Capital account?

SE 5.
LO3 Distribution of Partnership Income

During the first year, the Bob and Kim partnership (see **SE 2**) earned an income of $5,000. Assume the partners agreed to share income and losses by figuring interest on the beginning capital balances at 10 percent, allowing a salary of $6,000 to Bob, and dividing the remainder equally. How much income (or loss) should be transferred to each Capital account?

SE 6.
LO4 Withdrawal of a Partner and Admission of a Partner

After the partnership has been operating for a year, the Capital accounts of Bob and Kim are $15,000 and $10,000, respectively. Kim withdraws from the partnership by selling her interest in the business to Sonia for $8,000. What will be the Capital account balances of the partners in the new Bob and Sonia partnership? Prepare the journal entry to record the transfer of ownership on the partnership books.

SE 7.
LO4 Admission of a New Partner

After the partnership has been operating for a year, the Capital accounts of Bob and Kim are $15,000 and $10,000, respectively. Sonia buys a one-sixth interest in the partnership by investing cash of $11,000. What will be the Capital account balances of the partners in the new Bob, Kim, and Sonia partnership, assuming a bonus to the old partners, who share income and losses equally? Prepare the entry in journal form to record the transfer of ownership on the partnership books.

SE 8.
LO4 Admission of a New Partner

After the partnership has been operating for a year, the Capital accounts of Bob and Kim are $15,000 and $10,000, respectively. Sonia buys a one-fourth interest in the partnership by investing cash of $5,000. What will be the Capital account balances of the partners in the new Bob, Kim, and Sonia partnership, assuming that the new partner receives a bonus and that Bob and Kim share income and losses equally? Prepare the entry in journal form to record the transfer of ownership on the partnership books.

SE 9.
LO4 Withdrawal of a Partner

After the partnership has been operating for several years, the Capital accounts of Bob, Kim, and Sonia are $25,000, $16,000, and $9,000, respectively. Sonia decides to leave the partnership and is allowed to withdraw $9,000 in cash. Prepare the entry in journal form to record the withdrawal on the partnership books.

SE 10.
LO5 Liquidation of a Partnership

After the partnership has been operating for a year, the Capital accounts of Bob and Kim are $15,000 and $10,000, respectively. The firm has cash of $12,000 and office equipment of $13,000. The partners decide to liquidate the partnership. The office equipment is sold for only $4,000. Assuming the partners share income and losses in the ratio of one-third to Bob and two-thirds to Kim, how much cash will be distributed to each partner in liquidation?

EXERCISES

E 1.
LO2 Partnership Formation

Henri Mikels and Alex Jamison are watch repairmen who want to form a partnership and open a jewelry store. They have an attorney prepare their partnership agreement, which indicates that assets invested in the partnership will be recorded at their fair market value and that liabilities will be assumed at book value.

The assets contributed by each partner and the liabilities assumed by the partnership are as follows:

Assets	Henri Mikels	Alex Jamison	Total
Cash	$40,000	$30,000	$70,000
Accounts receivable	52,000	20,000	72,000
Allowance for uncollectible accounts	4,000	3,000	7,000
Supplies	1,000	500	1,500
Equipment	20,000	10,000	30,000
Liabilities			
Accounts payable	32,000	9,000	41,000

Prepare the entry in journal form necessary to record the original investments of Mikels and Jamison in the partnership.

E 2.
LO3 Distribution of Income

Elijah Samuels and Tony Winslow agreed to form a partnership. Samuels contributed $200,000 in cash, and Winslow contributed assets with a fair market value of $400,000. The partnership, in its initial year, reported net income of $120,000. Calculate the distribution of the first year's income to the partners under each of the following conditions:

1. Samuels and Winslow failed to include stated ratios in the partnership agreement.
2. Samuels and Winslow agreed to share income and losses in a 3:2 ratio.
3. Samuels and Winslow agreed to share income and losses in the ratio of their original investments.
4. Samuels and Winslow agreed to share income and losses by allowing 10 percent interest on original investments and sharing any remainder equally.

E 3.
LO3 Distribution of Income or Losses: Salary and Interest

Assume that the partnership agreement of Samuels and Winslow in E 2 states that Samuels and Winslow are to receive salaries of $20,000 and $24,000, respectively; that Samuels is to receive 6 percent interest on his capital balance at the beginning of the year; and that the remainder of income and losses are to be shared equally. Calculate the distribution of the income or losses under the following conditions:

1. Income totaled $120,000 before deductions for salaries and interest.
2. Income totaled $48,000 before deductions for salaries and interest.
3. There was a loss of $2,000.
4. There was a loss of $40,000.

E 4.
LO3 Distribution of Income: Average Capital Balance

Barbara and Karen operate a furniture rental business. Their capital balances on January 1, 20x7, were $160,000 and $240,000, respectively. Barbara withdrew cash of $32,000 from the business on April 1, 20x7. Karen withdrew $60,000 cash on October 1, 20x7. Barbara and Karen distribute partnership income based on their average capital balances each year. Income for 20x7 was $160,000. Compute the income to be distributed to Barbara and Karen using their average capital balances in 20x7.

E 5.
LO4 Admission of a New Partner: Recording a Bonus

Ernie, Ron, and Denis have equity in a partnership of $40,000, $40,000, and $60,000, respectively, and they share income and losses in a ratio of 1:1:3. The partners have agreed to admit Henry to the partnership. Prepare entries in journal form to record the admission of Henry to the partnership under the following conditions:

1. Henry invests $60,000 for a 20 percent interest in the partnership, and a bonus is recorded for the original partners.
2. Henry invests $60,000 for a 40 percent interest in the partnership, and a bonus is recorded for Henry.

E 6.
LO4 Withdrawal of a Partner

Danny, Steve, and Luis are partners. They share income and losses in the ratio of 3:2:1. Luis's Capital account has a $120,000 balance. Danny and Steve have agreed to let Luis take $160,000 of the company's cash when he retires from the business. What entry in journal form must be made on the partnership's books when Luis retires, assuming that a bonus to Luis is recognized and absorbed by the remaining partners?

E 7.
LO5 Partnership Liquidation

Assume the following assets, liabilities, and partners' equity in the Ming and Demmick partnership on December 31, 20xx:

Assets = Liabilities + Ming, Capital + Demmick, Capital
$160,000 = $10,000 + $90,000 + $60,000

The partnership has no cash. When the partners agree to liquidate the business, the assets are sold for $120,000, and the liabilities are paid. Ming and Demmick share income and losses in a ratio of 3:1.

1. Prepare a statement of liquidation.
2. Prepare entries in journal form for the sale of assets, payment of liabilities, distribution of loss from realization, and final distribution of cash to Ming and Demmick.

E 8.
LO5 Partnership Liquidation

Ariel, Mandy, and Tisha are partners in a tanning salon. The assets, liabilities, and capital balances as of July 1, 20x7, are as follows:

Assets	$480,000
Liabilities	160,000
Ariel, Capital	140,000
Mandy, Capital	40,000
Tisha, Capital	140,000

Because competition is strong, business is declining, and the partnership has no cash, the partners have decided to sell the business. Ariel, Mandy, and Tisha share income and losses in a ratio of 3:1:1, respectively. The assets were sold for $260,000, and the liabilities were paid. Mandy has no other assets and will not be able to cover any deficits in her Capital account. How will the ending cash balance be distributed to the partners?

PROBLEMS

P 1.
LO2 Partnership Formation
LO3 and Distribution of Income

In January 20x3, Edie Rivera and Babs Bacon agreed to produce and sell chocolate candies. Rivera contributed $240,000 in cash to the business. Bacon contributed the building and equipment, valued at $220,000 and $140,000, respectively. The partnership had an income of $84,000 during 20x3 but was less successful during 20x4, when income was only $40,000.

REQUIRED ▶

1. Prepare the entry to record the investment of both partners in the partnership.
2. Determine the share of income for each partner in 20x3 and 20x4 under each of the following conditions: (a) The partners agreed to share income equally. (b) The partners failed to agree on an income-sharing arrangement. (c) The partners agreed to share income according to the ratio of their original investments. (d) The partners agreed to share income by allowing interest of 10 percent on their original investments and dividing the remainder equally. (e) The partners agreed to share income by allowing salaries of $40,000 for Rivera and $28,000 for Bacon, and dividing the remainder equally. (f) The partners agreed to share income by paying salaries of

$40,000 to Rivera and $28,000 to Bacon, allowing interest of 9 percent on their original investments, and dividing the remainder equally.

3. What are some of the factors that need to be considered in choosing the plan of partners' income sharing among the options shown in Part 2?

P 2.
LO3 Distribution of Income: Salary and Interest

Naomi and Petri are partners in a tennis shop. They have agreed that Naomi will operate the store and receive a salary of $104,000 per year. Petri will receive 10 percent interest on his average capital balance during the year of $500,000. The remaining income or losses are to be shared by Naomi and Petri in a 2:3 ratio.

REQUIRED ▶ Determine each partner's share of income and losses under each of the following conditions. In each case, the income or loss is stated before the distribution of salary and interest.

1. Income was $168,000.
2. Income was $88,000.
3. The loss was $25,600.

P 3.
LO4 Admission and Withdrawal of a Partner

Marnie, Stacie, and Samantha are partners in Woodware Company. Their capital balances as of July 31, 20x4, are as follows:

Marnie, Capital	Stacie, Capital	Samantha, Capital
45,000	15,000	30,000

Each partner has agreed to admit Connie to the partnership.

REQUIRED ▶ 1. Prepare the journal entries to record Connie's admission to or Marnie's withdrawal from the partnership under each of the following conditions: (a) Connie pays Marnie $12,500 for 20 percent of Marnie's interest in the partnership. (b) Connie invests $20,000 cash in the partnership and receives an interest equal to her investment. (c) Connie invests $30,000 cash in the partnership for a 20 percent interest in the business. A bonus is to be recorded for the original partners on the basis of their capital balances. (d) Connie invests $30,000 cash in the partnership for a 40 percent interest in the business. The original partners give Connie a bonus according to the ratio of their capital balances on July 31, 20x4. (e) Marnie withdraws from the partnership, taking $52,500. The excess of withdrawn assets over Marnie's partnership interest is distributed according to the balances of the Capital accounts. (f) Marnie withdraws by selling her interest directly to Connie for $60,000.

2. When a new partner enters a partnership, why would the new partner pay a bonus to the old partners, or why would the old partners pay a bonus to the new partner?

P 4.
LO5 Partnership Liquidation

Caruso, Evans, and Weisman are partners in a retail lighting store. They share income and losses in the ratio of 2:2:1, respectively. The partners have agreed to liquidate the partnership. Here is the partnership balance sheet before the liquidation:

Caruso, Evans, and Weisman Partnership
Balance Sheet
August 31, 20x7

Assets		Liabilities	
Cash	$ 280,000	Accounts payable	$ 360,000
Other assets	880,000	**Partners' Equity**	
Total assets	$1,160,000		
		Caruso, Capital	400,000
		Evans, Capital	240,000
		Weisman, Capital	160,000
		Total liabilities and partners' equity	$1,160,000

The other assets were sold on September 1, 20x7, for $720,000. Accounts payable were paid on September 4, 20x7. The remaining cash was distributed to the partners on September 11, 20x7.

REQUIRED
1. Prepare a statement of liquidation.
2. Prepare the following entries in journal form: (a) the sale of the other assets, (b) payment of the accounts payable, (c) the distribution of the loss from realization, and (d) the distribution to the partners of the remaining cash.

P 5.
LO2 Comprehensive Partnership
LO3 Transactions
LO4
LO5

The following events pertain to a partnership formed by Mark Raymond and Stan Bryden to operate a floor-cleaning company:

20x4
Feb. 14 The partnership was formed. Raymond transferred to the partnership $80,000 cash, land worth $80,000, a building worth $480,000, and a mortgage on the building of $240,000. Bryden transferred to the partnership $40,000 cash and equipment worth $160,000.

Dec. 31 During 20x4, the partnership earned income of just $84,000. The partnership agreement specifies that income and losses are to be divided by paying salaries of $40,000 to Raymond and $60,000 to Bryden, allowing 8 percent interest on beginning capital investments, and dividing any remainder equally.

20x5
Jan. 1 To improve the prospects for the company, the partners decided to take in a new partner, Chuck Menzer, who had experience in the floor-cleaning business. Menzer invested $156,000 for a 25 percent interest in the business. A bonus was transferred in equal amounts from the original partners' Capital accounts to Menzer's Capital account.

Dec. 31 During 20x5, the company earned income of $87,200. The new partnership agreement specified that income and losses would be divided by paying salaries of $60,000 to Bryden and $80,000 to Menzer (no salary to Raymond), allowing 8 percent interest on beginning capital balances after Menzer's admission, and dividing the remainder equally.

20x6
Jan. 1 Because it appeared that the business could not support the three partners, the partners decided to liquidate the partnership. The asset and liability accounts of the partnership were as follows: Cash, $407,200; Accounts Receivable (net), $68,000; Land, $80,000; Building (net), $448,000; Equipment (net), $236,000; Accounts Payable, $88,000; and Mortgage Payable, $224,000. The equipment was sold for $200,000. The accounts payable were paid. The loss was distributed equally to the partners' Capital accounts. A statement of liquidation was prepared, and the remaining assets and liabilities were distributed. Raymond agreed to accept cash plus the land and building at book value and the mortgage payable as payment for his share. Bryden accepted cash and the accounts receivable for his share. Menzer was paid in cash.

REQUIRED Prepare entries in journal form to record all of the facts above. Support your computations with schedules, and prepare a statement of liquidation in connection with the January 1, 20x6, entries.

Alternate Problems

P 6.
LO3 Distribution of Income:
Salaries and Interest

Jacob, Deric, and Jason are partners in the South Central Company. The partnership agreement states that Jacob is to receive 8 percent interest on his capital balance at the beginning of the year, Deric is to receive a salary of $100,000 a year, and Jason will be paid interest of 6 percent on his average capital balance during the year. Jacob, Deric, and Jason will share any income or loss after salary and interest in a 5:3:2 ratio. Jacob's capital balance at the beginning of the year was $600,000, and Jason's average capital balance for the year was $720,000.

REQUIRED Determine each partner's share of income and losses under the following conditions. In each case, the income or loss is stated before the distribution of salary and interest.

1. Income was $545,200.
2. Income was $155,600.
3. The loss was $56,800.

P 7.

LO4 Admission and Withdrawal of a Partner

Peter, Mara, and Vanessa are partners in the Image Gallery. As of November 30, 20xx, the balance in Peter's Capital account was $50,000, the balance in Mara's was $60,000, and the balance in Vanessa's was $90,000. Peter, Mara, and Vanessa share income and losses in a ratio of 2:3:5.

REQUIRED

1. Prepare entries in journal form for each of the following independent conditions: (a) Bob pays Vanessa $100,000 for four-fifths of Vanessa's interest. (b) Bob is to be admitted to the partnership with a one-third interest for a $100,000 cash investment. (c) Bob is to be admitted to the partnership with a one-third interest for a $160,000 cash investment. A bonus, based on the partners' ratio for income and losses, is to be distributed to the original partners when Bob is admitted. (d) Bob is to be admitted to the partnership with a one-third interest for an $82,000 cash investment. A bonus is to be given to Bob on admission. (e) Peter withdraws from the partnership, taking $66,000 in cash. (f) Peter withdraws from the partnership by selling his interest directly to Bob for $70,000.
2. In general, when a new partner enters a partnership, why would the new partner pay a bonus to the old partners, or why would the old partners pay a bonus to the new partner?

P 8.

LO5 Partnership Liquidation

The balance sheet of the Rose Partnership as of July 31, 20xx, follows.

Rose Partnership
Balance Sheet
July 31, 20xx

Assets		Liabilities	
Cash	$ 6,000	Accounts payable	$480,000
Accounts receivable	120,000	**Partners' Equity**	
Inventory	264,000		
Equipment (net)	462,000	Gerri, Capital	72,000
Total assets	$852,000	Susi, Capital	180,000
		Mari, Capital	120,000
		Total liabilities and partners' equity	$852,000

The partners—Gerri, Susi, and Mari—share income and losses in the ratio of 5:3:2. Because of a mutual disagreement, Gerri, Susi, and Mari have decided to liquidate the business.

Assume that Gerri cannot contribute any additional personal assets to the company during liquidation and that the following transactions occurred during liquidation: (a) Accounts receivable were sold for 60 percent of their book value. (b) Inventory was sold for $276,000. (c) Equipment was sold for $300,000. (d) Accounts payable were paid in full. (e) Gain or loss from realization was distributed to the partners' Capital accounts. (f) Gerri's deficit was transferred to the remaining partners in their new income and loss ratio. (g) The remaining cash was distributed to Susi and Mari.

REQUIRED

1. Prepare a statement of liquidation.
2. Prepare entries in journal form to liquidate the partnership and distribute any remaining cash.

Skills Development Cases

Conceptual Analysis

SD 1.
LO1 Partnership Agreement

Form a partnership with one or two of your classmates. Assume that the two or three of you are forming a small service business. For example, you might form a company that hires college students to paint houses during the summer or to provide landscaping services.

Working together, draft a partnership agreement for your business. The agreement can be a simple one, with just a sentence or two for each provision. However, it should include the name, location, and purpose of the business; the names of the partners and their respective duties; the investments of each partner; methods for distributing profits and losses; and procedures for dealing with the admission or withdrawal of partners, the withdrawal of assets, the death of a partner, and liquidation of the business. Include a title, date, and signature lines.

Group Activity: Assign groups to prepare partnership agreements.

SD 2.
LO3 Distribution of Partnership Income and Losses

Landow, Donovan, and Hansa, who are forming a partnership to operate an antiques gallery, are discussing how income and losses should be distributed. Among the facts they are considering are the following:

a. Landow will contribute cash for operations of $100,000, Donovan will contribute a collection of antiques that is valued at $300,000, and Hansa will not contribute any assets.
b. Landow and Hansa will handle day-to-day business operations. Hansa will work full time, and Landow will devote about half-time to the partnership. Donovan will not devote time to day-to-day operations. A full-time clerk in a retail store would make about $20,000 in a year, and a full-time manager would receive about $30,000.
c. The current interest rate on long-term bonds is 8 percent.

Landow, Donovan, and Hansa have just hired you as the partnership's accountant. Write a memorandum describing an equitable plan for distributing income and losses. Outline the reasons why you believe this plan is equitable. According to your plan, which partner will gain the most if the partnership is very profitable, and which will lose the most if the partnership has large losses?

Ethical Dilemma

SD 3.
LO1 Death of a Partner
LO2
LO4

South Shore Realty was started 20 years ago when T. S. Tyler, R. C. Strong, and A. J. Hibbert established a partnership to sell real estate near Galveston, Texas. The partnership has been extremely successful. In 20xx, Tyler, the senior partner, who in recent years had not been very active in the partnership, died. Unfortunately, the partnership agreement is vague about how the partnership interest of a partner who dies should be valued. It simply states that "the estate of a deceased partner shall receive compensation for his or her interest in the partnership in a reasonable time after death." The attorney for Tyler's family believes that the estate should receive one-third of the assets of the partnership based on the fair market value of the net assets (total assets less total liabilities). The total assets of the partnership are $10 million in the accounting records, but the assets are worth at least $20 million. Because the firm's total liabilities are $4 million, the attorney is asking for $5.3 million (one-third of $16 million). Strong and Hibbert do not agree, but all parties want to avoid a protracted, expensive lawsuit. They have decided to put the question to an arbitrator, who will make a determination of the settlement.

Here are some other facts that may or may not be relevant. The current balances in the partners' Capital accounts are $1.5 million for Tyler, $2.5 million for Strong, and $2.0 million for Hibbert. Net income in 20xx is to be distributed to the Capital accounts in the ratio of 1:4:3. Before Tyler's semiretirement, the distribution ratio was 3:3:2. Assume you or your group is the arbitrator, and develop what you would consider a fair distribution of assets to Tyler's estate. Defend your solution.

Research Activity

SD 4.
LO1 Basic Research Skills

The limited partnership is a form of business that was particularly important to the U.S. economy in the 1980s. To find the latest developments or to study the practical applications of a particular subject, such as limited partnerships, it is helpful to use periodical indexes in the library to find articles relating to that subject. Three periodical indexes relevant to accounting and business are *The Accountant's Index*, the *Business Periodicals Index*, and *The Wall Street Journal Index*. Use one or more of those periodical indexes in your college or university library to find three articles about limited partnerships. Sometimes the articles are not listed under the heading "Limited Partnerships"; instead, they appear under the uses of limited partnerships. Some examples are real estate, investments, research and development, and cattle or livestock. Write a short summary of each article, relating the content of the article to the content of this chapter or explaining why the limited partnership form of business was important in the situation described in the article.

Decision-Making Practice

SD 5.
LO4 Potential Partnership Purchase

The A-One Fitness Center, owned by Abe Hines and Mario Saconi, has been very successful since its inception five years ago. Hines and Saconi work 10 to 11 hours a day at the business. They have decided to expand by opening up another fitness center in the north part of town. Hines has approached you about becoming a partner in the business. He and Saconi are interested in you because of your experience in operating a small gym. Also, they need additional funds to expand their business. Projected income after the expansion but before partners' salaries for the next five years is as follows:

20x3	20x4	20x5	20x6	20x7
$100,000	$120,000	$130,000	$140,000	$150,000

Currently, Hines and Saconi each draw a $25,000 salary and share remaining profits equally. They are willing to give you an equal share of the business for $142,000. You will receive a $25,000 salary and one-third of the remaining profits. You would work the same hours as Hines and Saconi. Your salary for the next five years where you currently work is expected to be as follows:

20x3	20x4	20x5	20x6	20x7
$34,000	$38,000	$42,000	$45,000	$50,000

Here is financial information for the A-One Fitness Center:

Current Assets	$ 45,000	Long-Term Liabilities	$100,000
Plant and Equipment, net	365,000	Abe Hines, Capital	140,000
Current Liabilities	50,000	Mario Saconi, Capital	120,000

1. Compute your capital balance if you decide to join Hines and Saconi in the fitness center partnership.
2. Analyze your expected income for the next five years.
3. Should you invest in the A-One Fitness Center?
4. Assume that you do not consider Hines and Saconi's offer of partnership to be a good one. Develop a counteroffer that you would be willing to accept (be realistic).

FINANCIAL REPORTING AND ANALYSIS CASES

Interpreting Financial Reports

FRA 1.
LO1 Effects of Lawsuit on
LO3 Partnership

The Springfield Clinic is owned and operated by ten local doctors as a partnership. Recently, a paralyzed patient sued the clinic for malpractice, for a total of $20 million. The clinic carries malpractice liability insurance in the amount of $10 million. There is no provision for the possible loss from this type of lawsuit in the partnership's financial statements. The condensed balance sheet for 20xx is as follows:

Springfield Clinic
Condensed Balance Sheet
December 31, 20xx

Assets

Current assets	$246,000	
Property, plant, and equipment (net)	750,000	
Total assets		$996,000

Liabilities and Partners' Equity

Current liabilities	$180,000	
Long-term debt	675,000	
Total liabilities		$855,000
Partners' equity		141,000
Total liabilities and partners' equity		$996,000

1. How should information about the lawsuit be disclosed in the December 31, 20xx, financial statements of the partnership?
2. Assume that the clinic and its insurance company settle out of court by agreeing to pay a total of $10.1 million, of which $100,000 must be paid by the partnership. What effect will the payment have on the clinic's December 31, 20xx, financial statements? Discuss the effect of the settlement on the Springfield Clinic doctors' personal financial situations.

International Company

FRA 2.
LO1 International Joint Ventures

Nokia <www.nokia.com>, the Finnish telecommunications company, has formed an equally owned joint venture with Capital Corporation, a state-owned Chinese company, to develop a center for the manufacture and development of telecommunications equipment in China, the world's fastest-growing market for this kind of equipment. The main aim of the development is to persuade Nokia's suppliers to move close to the company's main plant. The Chinese government looks favorably on companies that involve local suppliers.[4] What advantages does a joint venture have over a single company in entering a new market in another country? What are the potential disadvantages?

Toys "R" Us Annual Report

This activity is not appropriate for this chapter.

Fingraph® Financial Analysis™

This activity is not appropriate for this chapter.

Comparison Case

This activity is not appropriate for this chapter.

Financial Reporting and Analysis Cases

Internet Case

FRA 3.
LO1 Comparison of Career Opportunities in Partnerships and Corporations

Accounting firms are among the world's largest partnerships and provide a wide range of attractive careers for business and accounting majors. Through the Needles Accounting Resource Center Web Site at http://accounting.college.hmco.com/students, you can explore careers in public accounting by linking to the web site of one of the Big Four accounting firms. The firms are Deloitte & Touche, Ernst & Young, KPMG International, and PricewaterhouseCoopers. Each firm's home page has a career opportunity section. For the firm you choose, compile a list of facts about the firm—size, locations, services, and career opportunities. Do you have the interest and background for a career in public accounting? Why or why not? How do you think working for a large partnership would differ from or be the same as working for a large corporation? Be prepared to discuss your findings in class.

14

Chapter 14 focuses on long-term equity financing, including the types of equity securities and transactions that affect the stockholders' equity section of the balance sheet, such as stock issues, dividends, and treasury stock purchases.

Contributed Capital

Learning Objectives

LO1 Identify and explain the management issues related to contributed capital.
LO2 Identify the components of stockholders' equity.
LO3 Account for cash dividends.
LO4 Identify the characteristics of preferred stock, including the effect on distribution of dividends.
LO5 Account for the issuance of stock for cash and other assets.
LO6 Account for treasury stock.

DECISION POINT A USER'S FOCUS

Cisco Systems, Inc. <www.cisco.com> One way corporations raise new capital is by issuing stock. Cisco Systems, Inc., a major manufacturer of telecommunications equipment, issued almost $3.5 billion of common stock in a recent three-year period, as shown in the Financial Highlights on the opposite page.[1] Why does Cisco Systems' management choose to issue common stock to satisfy some of its needs for new capital? What are some of the advantages and disadvantages of this approach?

Financing with common stock has several advantages. First, it is less risky than financing with bonds because dividends on common stock are not paid unless the board of directors decides to pay them. Cisco Systems does not currently pay any dividends. In contrast, if the interest on bonds is not paid, a company can be forced into bankruptcy. Second, when a company does not pay a cash dividend, the cash generated by profitable operations can be invested in the company's operations. Third, a company may need the proceeds of a common stock issue to maintain or improve the balance between liabilities and stockholders' equity. By issuing common stock in 2001, Cisco Systems offset the impact on stockholders' equity of a $1 billion net loss in 2001. The balance between total liabilities and total equity remains a relatively low 30 percent.

On the other hand, issuing common stock comes with certain disadvantages. Unlike the interest on bonds, dividends paid on stock are not tax-deductible. Furthermore, when it issues more stock, the corpora-

Why does Cisco Systems, Inc. choose to issue common stock to satisfy some of its needs for new capital?

tion dilutes its ownership. This means that the current stockholders must yield some control to the new stockholders. It is important for accountants to understand the nature and characteristics of corporations as well as the process of accounting for a stock issue and other types of stock transactions.

Financial Highlights
(In millions)

	2002	2001	2000
Issuance of common stock	$655	$1,262	$1,564

Management Issues Related to Contributed Capital

LO1 Identify and explain the management issues related to contributed capital.

RELATED TEXT ASSIGNMENTS
Q: 1, 2, 3, 4, 5, 6, 7, 8, 9
SE: 1, 2, 3, 4
E: 1
P: 1, 2, 3, 4, 5, 6, 7, 8
SD: 1, 4, 5, 6
FRA: 1, 4, 5, 6, 7

A **corporation** is defined as a body of persons granted a charter recognizing them as a separate legal entity having its own rights, privileges, and liabilities distinct from those of its members.[2] In other words, a corporation is a legal entity separate and distinct from its owners.

Contributed capital is a critical component in financing a corporation. Important management issues related to this area are managing under the corporate form of business, using equity financing, determining dividend policies, evaluating performance using return on equity, and using stock options as compensation.

Forming a Corporation

To form a corporation, most states require individuals, called incorporators, to sign an application and file it with the proper state official. This application contains the **articles of incorporation**. If approved by the state, these articles become, in effect, a contract, called the company charter, between the state and the incorporators. The company is then authorized to do business. The authority to manage the corporation is delegated by the stockholders to the board of directors and by the board of directors to the corporate officers (see Figure 1). That is, the stockholders elect the board of directors, which sets company policies and chooses the corporate officers, who in turn carry out the corporate policies by managing the business.

■ **STOCKHOLDERS** A unit of ownership in a corporation is called a **share of stock**. The articles of incorporation state the maximum number of shares of stock that the corporation will be allowed, or authorized, to issue. The number of shares held by stockholders is the outstanding capital stock; this is generally less than the number authorized in the articles of incorporation. To invest in a corporation, a stockholder transfers cash or other resources to the corporation. In return, the stockholder receives shares of stock representing a proportionate share of ownership in the corporation. The stockholder may then transfer the shares at will. Corporations may have more than one kind of capital stock, but we will refer only to common stock.

■ **BOARD OF DIRECTORS** As noted, the stockholders elect the board of directors, which in turn decides on the major business policies of the corporation. Among the specific duties of the board are authorizing contracts, setting executive salaries, and arranging major loans with banks. The declaration of dividends is also an important function. Only the board has the authority to declare dividends. **Dividends** are distributions of resources, generally in the form of cash, to the stockholders. Paying dividends is one way of rewarding stockholders for their investment when the corporation has been successful in earning a profit. (The other way is through a rise in the market value of the stock.) There is usually a delay of two or three weeks between the time the board declares a dividend and the date of the actual payment.

The board of directors usually includes several corporate officers and several outsiders. Today, the formation of an **audit committee** with several outside directors is encouraged to ensure that the board will be objective in evaluating management's performance. One function of the audit committee is to engage independent auditors and review their work. Another is to ensure that proper systems safeguard the company's resources and that accounting records are reliable.

■ **MANAGEMENT** The board of directors appoints managers to carry out the corporation's policies and run day-to-day operations. The management consists of the operating officers, generally the president, vice presidents, controller, treasurer, and secretary. Besides being responsible for running the business, management must report the financial results of its administration to the board and stockholders. Though management must make at least one comprehensive annual report, it

FIGURE 1
The Corporate Form of Business

STOCKHOLDERS	→	BOARD OF DIRECTORS	→	MANAGEMENT
Invest in shares of capital stock and elect board of directors		Determines corporate policy, declares dividends, and appoints management		Executes policy and carries out day-to-day operations

generally reports more often. The annual reports of large public corporations are available to the public. Excerpts from many of them appear throughout this book.

MANAGING UNDER THE CORPORATE FORM OF BUSINESS

Although sole proprietorships and partnerships outnumber corporations in the United States, corporations dominate the economy in total dollars of assets and output of goods and services. Corporations are well suited to today's trends toward large organizations, international trade, and professional management. Figure 2 shows the amount and sources of new funds raised by corporations in recent years.

FIGURE 2
Sources of Capital Raised by Corporations in the United States

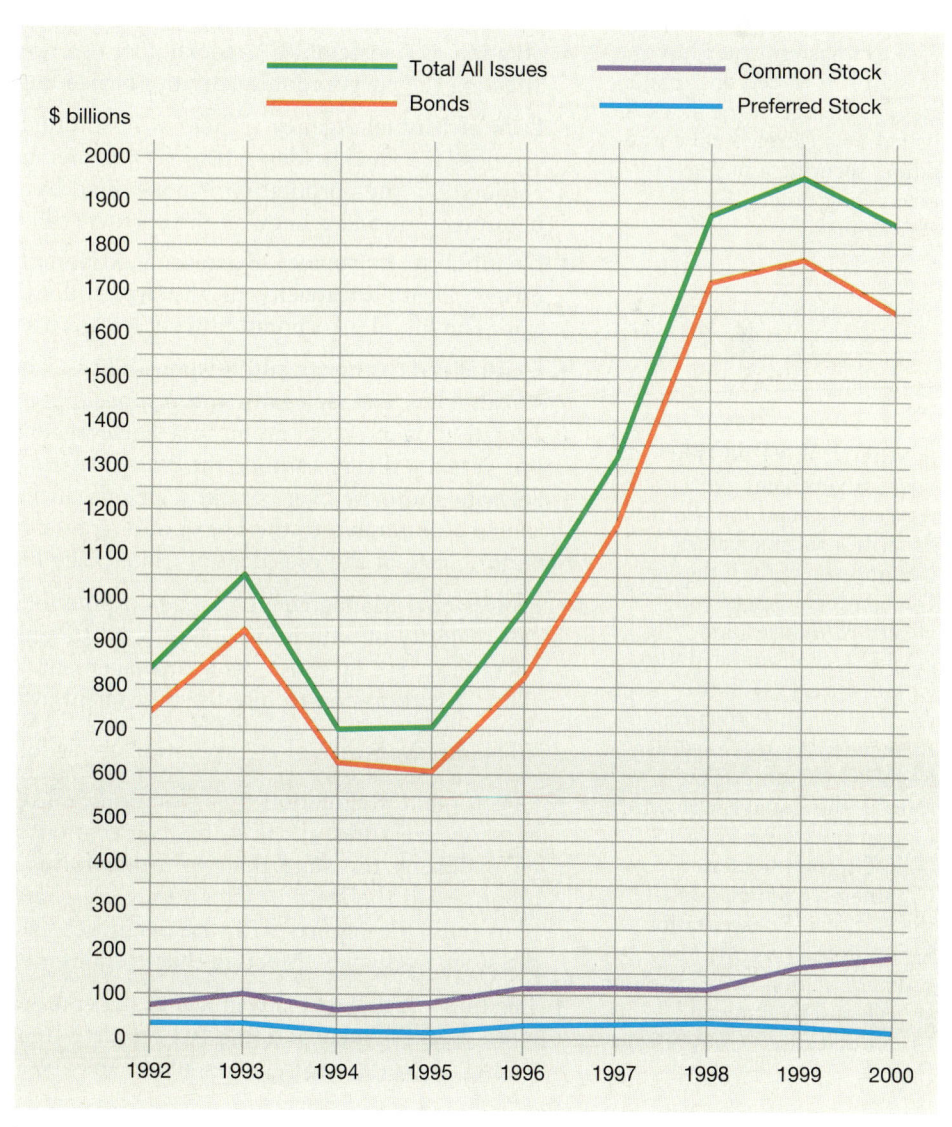

Source: Securities Industry Yearbook 1999–2000 (New York: Securities Industry Association, 1999), p. 895.

The amount raised increased dramatically after 1995. In 2000, the amount of new corporate capital was $1,851.0 billion, of which $1,646.6 billion, or 89 percent, came from new bond issues; $189.1 billion, or 10 percent, came from new common stock issues; and $15.4 billion, or 1 percent, came from preferred stock issues.

In managing a corporation, the advantages and disadvantages of this form of business must be considered. Some of the advantages are as follows:

- **Separate Legal Entity**   A corporation is a separate legal entity. As such, it can buy, sell, or own property; sue and be sued; enter into contracts; hire and fire employees; and be taxed.

- **Limited Liability**   Because a corporation is a separate legal entity, it is responsible for its own actions and liabilities. This means that a corporation's creditors can satisfy their claims only against the assets of the corporation, not against the personal property of the corporation's owners. Because the owners are not responsible for the corporation's debts, their liability is limited to the amount of their investment. The personal property of sole proprietors and partners, however, generally is available to creditors.

- **Ease of Capital Generation**   It is fairly easy for a corporation to raise capital because shares of ownership in the business are available to a great number of potential investors for a small amount of money. As a result, a single corporation can be owned by many people.

- **Ease of Transfer of Ownership**   A share of stock, a unit of ownership in a corporation, is transferable. A stockholder can normally buy and sell shares without affecting the corporation's activities or needing the approval of other owners.

- **Lack of Mutual Agency**   There is no mutual agency in the corporate form of business. If a stockholder, acting as an owner, tries to enter into a contract for the corporation, the corporation is not bound by the contract. But in a partnership, because of mutual agency, all the partners can be bound by one partner's actions.

- **Continuous Existence**   Because a corporation is a separate legal entity, an owner's death, incapacity, or withdrawal does not affect the life of the corporation. The life of a corporation is set by its charter and regulated by state laws.

- **Centralized Authority and Responsibility**   The board of directors represents the stockholders and delegates the responsibility and authority for the day-to-day operation of the corporation to a single person, usually the president. Operating power is not divided among the many owners of the business. The president may delegate authority over certain segments of the business to others, but he or she is held accountable to the board of directors. If the board is dissatisfied with the performance of the president, it can replace him or her.

- **Professional Management**   Large corporations are owned by many people, the vast majority of whom are unequipped to make timely decisions about business operations. So, in most cases, management and ownership are separate. This allows a corporation to hire the best talent available to manage the business.

The disadvantages of a corporation are as follows:

- **Government Regulation**   Corporations must meet the requirements of state laws. As "creatures of the state," corporations are subject to greater control and regulation by the state than are other forms of business. They must file many reports with the state in which they are chartered. Also, publicly held corporations must file reports with the Securities and Exchange Commission and with the stock exchanges. Meeting those requirements is very costly.

- **Taxation**   A major disadvantage of the corporate form of business is **double taxation**. Because a corporation is a separate legal entity, its earnings are subject to federal and state income taxes, which may be as much as 35 percent of corporate

---

STUDY NOTE: Lenders qualify a corporation for a loan as they would a person. If a corporation does not have a credit history or a good credit rating, a loan will not be granted in its name only. Others, such as the corporation's officers, will be required to co-sign the note and will therefore be personally liable.

ENRICHMENT NOTE: It is easy to transfer ownership of a stock if it is traded on a major stock exchange. If the stock is issued by a closely held corporation, securing a buyer can take a long time.

ENRICHMENT NOTE: Some government agencies that regulate corporations are the Securities and Exchange Commission (SEC), the Occupational Safety and Health Administration (OSHA), the Federal Trade Commission (FTC), the Environmental Protection Agency (EPA), the Nuclear Regulatory Commission (NRC), the Equal Employment Opportunity Commission (EEOC), the Interstate Commerce Commission (ICC), the National Transportation Safety Board (NTSB), the Federal Aviation Administration (FAA), and the Federal Communications Commission (FCC).

earnings. If any of the corporation's after-tax earnings are then paid out as dividends, the earnings are taxed again as income to the stockholders. In contrast, the earnings of sole proprietorships and partnerships are taxed only once, as personal income to the owners.

- **Limited Liability** Although limited liability is an advantage of incorporation, it also can be a disadvantage. Limited liability restricts the ability of a small corporation to borrow money. Because creditors can lay claim only to the assets of the corporation, they limit their loans to the level secured by those assets or ask stockholders to guarantee the loans personally.

- **Separation of Ownership and Control** Just as limited liability can be a drawback, so can the separation of ownership and control. Management sometimes makes decisions that are not good for the corporation as a whole. Poor communication can also make it hard for stockholders to exercise control over the corporation or even to recognize that management's decisions are harmful.

USING EQUITY FINANCING

A share of stock is a unit of ownership in a corporation. A **stock certificate** is issued to the owner. It shows the number of shares of the corporation's stock that the stockholder owns. Stockholders can transfer their ownership at will. When they do, they must sign their stock certificate and send it to the corporation's secretary. In large corporations that are listed on the organized stock exchanges, stockholders' records are hard to maintain. Such companies can have millions of shares of stock, thousands of which change ownership every day. Therefore, they often appoint independent registrars and transfer agents (usually banks and trust companies) to help perform the secretary's duties. The outside agents are responsible for transferring the corporation's stock, maintaining stockholders' records, preparing a list of stockholders for stockholders' meetings, and paying dividends.

When a corporation applies for a charter, the articles of incorporation specify the maximum number of shares of stock the corporation is allowed to issue. This number represents **authorized stock**. Most corporations are authorized to issue more shares of stock than are necessary at the time of organization, which allows for future stock issues to raise additional capital. For example, Cisco Systems has 20 billion shares of stock authorized and only 7.3 billion shares issued. If Cisco Systems needs cash to expand in the future, it can sell its unissued shares. If a corporation issues all of its authorized stock, it cannot issue more stock without a change in its state charter.

www.cisco.com

The charter also shows the par value of the stock that has been authorized. **Par value** is an arbitrary amount assigned to each share of stock. It must be recorded in the capital stock accounts and constitutes the legal capital of a corporation. **Legal capital** equals the number of shares issued times the par value; it is the minimum amount that can be reported as contributed capital. Par value usually bears little if any relationship to the market value or book value of the shares. The par value of Cisco Systems' common stock is only $.001 per share, and its legal capital is $7.3 million (7.3 billion shares × $.001). When a corporation is formed, a memorandum entry may be made in the general journal giving the number and description of authorized shares.

KEY POINT: Par value is usually a small amount, $.01 up to $10. The amount is arbitrary and has primarily legal significance.

ENRICHMENT NOTE: In effect, the underwriter buys the stock from the corporation at a set price. The stock price in the secondary markets can be above or below the commitment to the corporation. Thus, the underwriter can gain or lose on the transaction and is exposed to a certain amount of risk.

■ **INITIAL PUBLIC OFFERING** To help with the initial issue of capital stock, called an **initial public offering (IPO)**, a corporation often uses an **underwriter**—an intermediary between the corporation and the investing public. For a fee—usually less than 1 percent of the selling price—the underwriter guarantees the sale of the stock. The corporation records the amount of the net proceeds of the offering—what the public paid less the underwriter's fees, legal and printing expenses, and any other direct costs of the offering—in its capital stock and additional paid-in capital accounts. When Goldman, Sachs, & Co., the renowned 130-year-old investment bank, went public, it had one of the largest IPOs ever recorded, amounting to about $3.6 billion.

■ **START-UP AND ORGANIZATION COSTS** The costs of forming a corporation are called **start-up and organization costs**. Such costs, which are incurred before the corporation begins operations, include state incorporation fees and attorneys' fees for drawing up the articles of incorporation. They also include the cost of printing stock certificates, accountants' fees for services rendered in registering the firm's initial stock, and other expenditures that are necessary for the formation of the corporation.

Theoretically, start-up and organization costs benefit the entire life of the corporation. For that reason, a case can be made for recording them as intangible assets and amortizing them over the years of the life of the corporation. However, the life of a corporation normally is not known, so accountants expense start-up and organization costs as they are incurred.[3]

KEY POINT: Start-up and organization costs are expensed when incurred.

DETERMINING DIVIDEND POLICIES

The board of directors has sole authority to declare dividends, but the dividend policies are influenced by senior managers, who usually serve as members of the board. Receiving dividends from a corporation is one of two ways in which stockholders can earn a return on their investment in the company. The other way is to sell their shares of stock for more than they paid for them.

Investors evaluate the amount of dividends received with the ratio **dividends yield**. Dividends yield measures the current return to an investor in the form of dividends and is computed by dividing the dividends per share by the market price per share. For instance, the dividends yield (shown in Figure 3) for Abbott Laboratories, a large, successful pharmaceutical company, is computed as follows:

www.abbott.com

ENRICHMENT NOTE: Due to the rise in prices of stocks during the 1990s, the average dividends yield has declined and the average P/E ratio has increased.

$$\text{Dividends Yield} = \frac{\text{Dividends per Share}}{\text{Market Price per Share}} = \frac{\$.98}{\$43.22} = 2.3\%$$

Since the yield on corporate bonds exceeds 7 percent, the shareholders of Abbott Labs must expect some of their return to come from increases in the price of the shares.

A measure of investors' confidence in a company's future is the **price/earnings (P/E) ratio**, which is calculated by dividing the market price per share by the earnings per share. The price/earnings ratio will vary as market price per share fluctuates daily and the amount of earnings per share changes. Figure 3 shows a P/E ratio of 25 for Abbott Labs. It was computed using the most recent earnings per share amount available at the time, as follows:

$$\text{Price/Earnings (P/E) Ratio} = \frac{\text{Market Price per Share}}{\text{Earnings per Share}} = \frac{\$43.22}{\$1.73} = 25 \text{ times}$$

Since the market price is 25 times earnings, investors are paying a relatively high price in relation to earnings. They do so in the expectation that this drug company will continue to be successful. Caution must be taken in interpreting high P/E ratios because unusually low earnings can produce a high result.

www.apple.com

Companies usually pay dividends to stockholders only when they have had profitable operations. For example, Apple Computer, Inc., paid a dividend beginning in 1987 but suspended its dividend payments in 1996 to conserve cash after large operating losses in 1995. Factors other than earnings affect the decision to pay dividends. First, a company may change its dividend policy to bring it into line with the prevailing industry policy. For example, despite positive earnings, AT&T Corporation slashed its dividends 83 percent. This action put AT&T's policy more in line with

www.att.com

FIGURE 3
Stock Quotations on the New York Stock Exchange

YTD % CHG	52 WEEKS HI	52 WEEKS LO	STOCK (SYM)	DIV	YLD %	PE	VOL 100S	LAST	NET CHG
5.9	21.50	1.25	AMR **AMR**		...	dd	120058	6.99	0.39
1.7	20.13	8.70	AOL Time **AOL**		...	dd	192018	13.32	0.30
1.7	3.10	1.10	APT Satelt **ATS**	.05e	2.9	...	1614	1.75	0.24
21.2	8.44	3.15	AT&T Wrls **AWE**		...	dd	66961	6.85	0.12
−36.9	29.52	13.45	AT&T **T** s	.75	4.6	dd	62766	16.47	−0.04
6.0	23.60	7.31	AVX Cp **AVX**	.15	1.4	dd	1196	10.39	0.01
13.2	21.97	9.05	♦ AXA ADS **AXA**	.37e	2.4	...	3010	15.22	0.04
−13.5	19.60	8.30	AZZ **AZZ**		...	7	37	10.74	−0.01
14.2	28.49	17.05	AaronRent **RNT**	.04	.2	18	1027	24.98	1.93
− 3.9	27.10	18.80	AaronRent A **RNTA**	.04	.2	16	39	22	0.60
19.5	9.84	1.10	ABB ADS **ABB**		...	dd	666	3.43	−0.02
8.1	52.50	29.80	AbbottLab **ABT**	.98f	2.3	25	33759	43.22	−0.16
51.0	33.65	14.97	Abercrombie A **ANF**		...	16	26051	30.90	0.81
− 9.2	9.63	5.92	Abitibi **ABY**	.40g	...	...	2452	7	−0.02
23.6	9.22	6.77	♦ AcadiaRlty **AKR**	.58f	6.3	12	58	9.17	−0.02
− 7.2	23.08	11.30	Accenture **ACN**		...	19	18982	16.70	−0.15

Source: Stock quotations on the New York Stock Exchange (5/13/03). *Wall Street Journal, Eastern Edition* by Wall Street Journal. Copyright © 2003 by Dow Jones & Co., Inc. Reproduced with permission of Dow Jones & Co., Inc. via Copyright Clearance Center.

the policies of its peers in the telecommunications industry, most of which do not pay dividends.[4] Second, the expected volatility of earnings is a factor. If a company has years of good earnings followed by years of poor earnings, the board may want to keep dividends low to avoid giving a false impression of sustained high earnings. For years, General Motors Corporation followed the practice of having a fairly stable dividend yield and paying a bonus dividend in especially good years. Third, the level of dividends affects cash flows. Some companies may not have the cash to pay higher dividends because operations are not generating cash at the level of earnings or because the companies are investing the cash in future operations. For instance, Abbott Labs pays a dividend of $.98 per share on earnings of $1.79 per share. Management believes a portion of the cash generated by the earnings is better spent for other purposes, such as researching and developing new drugs that will generate revenue in the future. It is partly due to Abbott's investment in new products that stockholders are willing to pay a high price for its stock. In recent years, because the tax rates are more favorable to capital gains made by selling shares than to dividend income, many investors have shown a preference for companies like Cisco Systems that have strong earnings growth but that pay no dividends.

www.gm.com

www.cisco.com

EVALUATING PERFORMANCE USING RETURN ON EQUITY

Return on equity is the most important ratio associated with stockholders' equity because it is a common measure of management's performance. For instance, when *BusinessWeek* and *Forbes* rate companies on their success, return on equity is the major basis of their evaluations. Also, the compensation of top executives is often tied to return on equity benchmarks. This ratio is computed for Abbott Labs from information in the company's 2002 annual report, as follows:[5]

www.abbott.com

$$\text{Return on Equity} = \frac{\text{Net Income}}{\text{Average Stockholders' Equity}}$$

$$= \frac{\$2{,}793{,}703{,}000}{(\$10{,}664{,}553{,}000 + \$9{,}059{,}432{,}000) \div 2}$$

$$= 28.3\%$$

KEY POINT: A company can improve its return on equity by increasing net income or by reducing average stockholders' equity.

Abbott Labs' healthy return on equity of 28.3 percent depends, of course, on the amount of net income the company earns. But it also depends on the level of stockholders' equity, which depends, in turn, on management decisions about the amount of stock the company sells to the public. Management can keep the stockholders' equity at a minimum by financing the business with cash flows from operations and with debt instead of with stock. However, the use of debt to finance the business increases a company's risk because the interest and principal of the debt must be paid in a timely manner. In the case of common stock, dividends may be suspended if there is a cash shortage. Abbott Labs has a debt to equity ratio of 127.5% and thus is taking advantage of the leverage provided by debt.

In addition, management can reduce the number of shares in the hands of the public by buying back the company's shares on the open market. The cost of these shares, which are called *treasury stock*, has the effect of reducing the amount of stockholders' equity and thereby increasing the return on equity. Many companies follow this practice instead of paying or increasing dividends. Their reason for doing so is that it puts money into the hands of stockholders in the form of market price appreciation without creating a commitment to higher dividends in the future. For example, during the three years ended 2002, Abbott Labs purchased its common stock at a cost of $.5 billion.[6] Abbott Labs' stock repurchases improved the company's return on equity, increased its earnings per share, and lowered its price/earnings ratio.

USING STOCK OPTIONS AS COMPENSATION

● **STOP AND THINK!**
Why do companies like to give options as compensation?
Companies do not have to record compensation expense on stock options, which can improve profitability. (There is a proposal to change this rule.) Also, salaries require a cash outflow, but stock options do not. Finally, companies get a tax deduction for the difference between the option price and the market price on the exercise date. Tax deductions decrease taxes owed and increase cash flows. ■

More than 97 percent of public companies encourage the ownership of their common stock through a **stock option plan**, which is an agreement to issue stock to employees according to specified terms.[7] In most cases, the stock option plan gives employees the right to purchase stock in the future at a fixed price. This type of plan, which is usually offered only to management personnel, both compensates and motivates management because the market value of a company's stock is tied to the company's performance. As the market value of the stock goes up, the difference between the option price and the market price grows, which increases management's compensation. Another key benefit of stock options for corporations is a tax deduction for the amount of compensation expense, which lowers income taxes owed.

On the date stock options are granted, the fair value of the options must be estimated, and the amount in excess of the exercise price must be either recorded as compensation expense over the grant period or reported in the notes to the financial statements.[8] If a company chooses to record compensation expense, additional paid-in capital will increase as a result. Almost all companies report the excess of fair value over exercise price in the notes to the financial statements. The notes must include the impact on net income and earnings per share of not recording compensation expense in the income statement.

If note disclosure is the preferred method of reporting compensation costs, then when an option eventually is exercised and the stock is issued, the entry is the same as for issuance of common stock to any outsider. For example, assume that on July 1, 20x4, a company grants its key management personnel the option to purchase 50,000 shares of $10 par value common stock at its then-current market value of $15 per share. Suppose that one of the firm's vice presidents exercises the option to purchase 2,000 shares on March 30, 20x7, when the market price is $25 per share. Although the vice president has a gain of $20,000 (the $50,000 market value less the $30,000 option price), no compensation expense is recorded. Estimation of the fair value of options at the grant date is the subject of more advanced courses.*

---

*Stock options are discussed here in the context of employee compensation. They can also be important features of complex corporate capitalization arrangements.

FOCUS ON BUSINESS PRACTICE

When Are Stock Options Worthless? Apparently Never!

Stock options are supposed to reward employees for good performance. They also act as an incentive for continued good performance, thus aligning the interests of owners and employees. When stock prices rise, the rewards can be handsome; some executives have made staggering sums on stock options. For example, the CEO of Cisco Systems <www.cisco.com> made $156 million in option-related profits in fiscal 2000, dwarfing his salary of about $1.3 million. To keep employees happy when stock prices decline, companies often change the stock-option rules to accommodate them. When their stock prices fell, Amazon <www.amazon.com>, Sprint Corp. <www.sprint.com>, and Real Networks Inc. <www.realnetworks.com> repriced options at a lower value or allowed employees to turn in worthless options to be issued later at a lower price. Yet other companies let employees cancel already exercised options. Actions like these anger owners who believe employees should be held accountable for the company's poor performance and not rewarded for unsatisfactory results.[9]

Check out ACE for a Review Quiz at http://accounting.college.hmco.com/students.

COMPONENTS OF STOCKHOLDERS' EQUITY

LO2 Identify the components of stockholders' equity.

RELATED TEXT ASSIGNMENTS
Q: 16
SE: 5
E: 2, 3, 4
P: 1, 4, 5, 6, 8
SD: 1, 5, 6
FRA: 1, 3, 4, 6

In a corporation's balance sheet, the owners' claims to the business are called *stockholders' equity*. Look at the sample stockholders' equity section of a balance sheet that follows.

Stockholders' Equity

Contributed capital		
Preferred stock, $50 par value, 1,000 shares authorized, issued, and outstanding		$ 50,000
Common stock, $5 par value, 30,000 shares authorized, 20,000 shares issued and outstanding	$100,000	
Paid-in capital in excess of par value, common	50,000	150,000
Total contributed capital		$200,000
Retained earnings		60,000
Total stockholders' equity		$260,000

FOCUS ON INTERNATIONAL BUSINESS

Hot New European Stock Markets Have Cooled!

In 1996, to bring capital to cash-starved growth-stock companies, Europe's stock exchanges began setting up a series of four new exchanges, including France's Nouveau Marche and Germany's Neuer Markt. More than 160 companies went public via this "Euro new market" network. Most owners of these stocks are individual investors, rather than institutional fund managers, as is the case in the United States. The new markets rose quickly, causing a good deal of excitement.[10] However, when they failed to meet expectations, they seemed to fall even faster than they had risen. Case in point, Germany has announced the closing of the Neuer Markt.

Notice that the equity section of the corporate balance sheet is divided into two parts: (1) contributed capital and (2) retained earnings. Contributed capital represents the stockholders' investments in the corporation. Retained earnings are the earnings of the corporation since its inception, less any losses, dividends, or transfers to contributed capital. Retained earnings are not a pool of funds to be distributed to the stockholders; instead, they represent the stockholders' claim to the assets from earnings reinvested in the corporation.

In keeping with the convention of full disclosure, the contributed-capital portion of the stockholders' equity section of the balance sheet gives a great deal

FIGURE 4
Relationship of Authorized, Unissued, Issued, Outstanding, and Treasury Shares

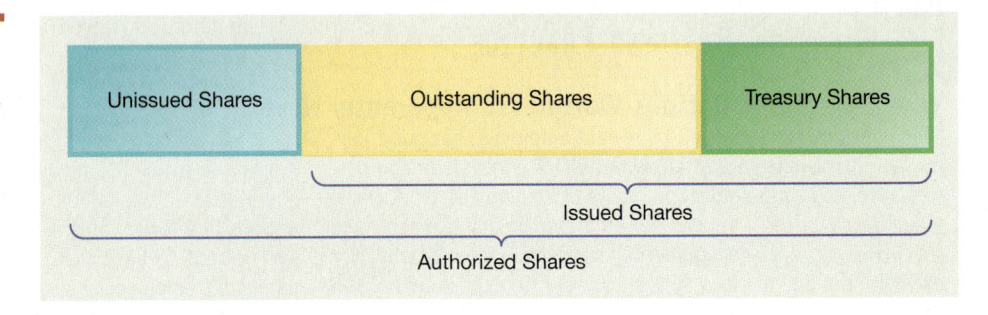

| Unissued Shares | Outstanding Shares | Treasury Shares |

Issued Shares = Outstanding Shares + Treasury Shares
Authorized Shares = Unissued Shares + Outstanding Shares + Treasury Shares

---

of information about the corporation's stock: the kinds of stock; their par value; and the number of shares authorized, issued, and outstanding.

A corporation can issue two basic types of stock: common stock and preferred stock. If only one kind of stock is issued by the corporation, it is called **common stock**. Common stock is the company's **residual equity**. This means that all creditors' and usually preferred stockholders' claims to the company's assets rank ahead of those of the common stockholders in case of liquidation. Because common stock is generally the only stock that carries voting rights, it represents the means of controlling the corporation.

The second kind of stock a company can issue is called **preferred stock**. Preferred stock has preference over common stock in one or more areas. These "preferences" will be described later in the chapter. Both common stock and preferred stock are sold to raise money. But investors in preferred stock and investors in common stock have different investment goals; preferred stock investors place more value on one or more of the preferences attached to the preferred stock.

The **issued stock** of a corporation is the shares sold or otherwise transferred to stockholders. For example, a corporation can be authorized to issue 500,000 shares of stock but may choose to issue only 300,000 shares when the company is organized. The holders of those 300,000 shares own 100 percent of the corporation. The remaining 200,000 shares of stock are unissued shares. No rights or privileges are associated with them until they are issued.

Outstanding stock is stock that has been issued and is still in circulation. A share of stock is not outstanding if the issuing corporation has repurchased it or if a stockholder has given it back to the company that issued it, so a company can have more shares issued than are currently outstanding. Issued shares that are bought back and held by the corporation are called *treasury stock*, which we discuss in detail later in this chapter. The relationship of authorized, issued, unissued, outstanding, and treasury shares is illustrated in Figure 4.

✓ Check out ACE for a Review Quiz at http://accounting.college.hmco.com/students.

> **KEY POINT:** A corporation may have more shares issued than it has outstanding because it has repurchased some shares, which are called *treasury stock*.

> ● **STOP AND THINK!**
> Why are issued shares not the same amount as authorized shares?
> *Authorized shares usually far exceed a corporation's need for immediate capital. Issuing fewer shares than authorized provides a corporation with greater flexibility in raising additional contributed capital in the future.* ■

DIVIDENDS

LO3 Account for cash dividends.
RELATED TEXT ASSIGNMENTS
Q: 10, 11
SE: 6
E: 5, 6
P: 1, 4, 5, 6, 8
SD: 5
FRA: 3, 7

Dividends can be paid quarterly, semiannually, annually, or at other times decided on by the board. Most states do not allow the board to declare a dividend that exceeds retained earnings. When a dividend that exceeds retained earnings is declared, the corporation is, in essence, returning to the stockholders part of their contributed capital. It is called a **liquidating dividend** and is usually paid when a company is going out of business or reducing its operations. Having sufficient retained earnings in itself does not justify the distribution of a dividend. If cash or other readily distributable assets are not available for distribution, the company might have to borrow money to pay a dividend—an action most boards of directors want to avoid.

Three important dates are associated with dividends. In order of occurrence, they are (1) the date of declaration, (2) the date of record, and (3) the date of pay-

ENRICHMENT NOTE:
Some reasons that the board of directors of a corporation with sufficient cash and retained earnings might not declare a dividend include the following: the cash is needed for expansion; the board wants to liquidate debt and improve the overall financial position of the company; major uncertainties threaten the corporation (such as a pending lawsuit or strike); the economy is poor, and the board wants to preserve resources.

A = L + OE
    +   −

🛑 **STOP AND THINK!**
If an investor sells shares after the declaration date but before the date of record, does the seller still receive the dividend?
Yes, but it comes in the form of a higher price for the stock, not in a dividend distribution. After the declaration date, the stock price adjusts upward to include the dividend declared. As a result, the seller receives the dividend even though on the distribution date, the check for the dividend will go to the buyer. ■

A = L + OE
    −   −

ment. The **date of declaration** is the date on which the board of directors formally declares that a dividend is going to be paid. The **date of record** is the date on which ownership of the stock of a company, and therefore of the right to receive a dividend, is determined. Individuals who own the stock on the date of record will receive the dividend. Between that date and the date of payment, the stock is said to be **ex-dividend**. If the owner on the date of record later sells the shares of stock, the right to the cash dividend remains with that person; it does not transfer with the shares to the second owner. The **date of payment** is the date on which the dividend is paid to the stockholders of record.

To illustrate accounting for cash dividends, we assume that the board of directors has decided that sufficient cash is available to pay a $56,000 cash dividend to the common stockholders. The process has two steps. First, the board declares the dividend as of a certain date. Second, the dividend is paid. Assume that the dividend is declared on February 21, 20xx, for stockholders of record on March 1, 20xx, to be paid on March 11, 20xx. Here are the entries to record the declaration and payment of the cash dividend:

Date of Declaration

Feb. 21	Cash Dividends Declared		56,000	
	Cash Dividends Payable			56,000
	Declared cash dividend			
	to common stockholders			

Date of Record

Mar. 1   No entry is required. This date is used simply to determine the owners of the stock who will receive the dividends. After this date (starting March 2), the shares are ex-dividend.

Date of Payment

Mar. 11	Cash Dividends Payable		56,000	
	Cash			56,000
	Paid cash dividends			
	declared on February 21			

Notice that the liability for the dividend is recorded on the date of declaration because the legal obligation to pay the dividend is established on that date. No entry is required on the date of record. The liability is liquidated, or settled, on the date of payment. The Cash Dividends Declared account is a temporary stockholders' equity account that is closed at the end of the accounting period by debiting Retained Earnings and crediting Cash Dividends Declared. Retained Earnings are thereby reduced by the total dividends declared during the period.

✓ Check out ACE for a Review Quiz at http://accounting.college.hmco.com/students.

THE CHARACTERISTICS OF PREFERRED STOCK

LO4 Identify the characteristics of preferred stock, including the effect on distribution of dividends.

RELATED TEXT ASSIGNMENTS
Q: 12, 13
SE: 7
E: 3, 7, 8
P: 2, 4, 5, 7, 8
SD: 2, 5
FRA: 2, 7

Most preferred stock has one or more of the following characteristics: preference as to dividends, preference as to assets of the business in liquidation, convertibility, and a callable option. In fact, a corporation may offer several different classes of preferred stock, each with distinctive characteristics to attract different investors.

PREFERENCE AS TO DIVIDENDS

Preferred stocks ordinarily have a preference over common stock in the receipt of dividends; that is, the holders of preferred shares must receive a certain amount of

KEY POINT: Preferred stock has many different characteristics. They are rarely exactly the same from company to company.

dividends before the holders of common shares can receive dividends. The amount that preferred stockholders must be paid before common stockholders can be paid is usually stated in dollars per share or as a percentage of the par value of the preferred shares. For example, a corporation can issue a preferred stock and pay an annual dividend of $4 per share, or it might issue a preferred stock at $50 par value and pay a yearly dividend of 8 percent of par value, also $4 per share.

Preferred stockholders have no guarantee of ever receiving dividends. The company must have earnings and the board of directors must declare dividends on preferred shares before any liability arises. The consequences of not declaring a dividend to preferred stockholders in the current year vary according to the exact terms under which the shares were issued. In the case of **noncumulative preferred stock**, if the board of directors fails to declare a dividend to preferred stockholders in a given year, the company is under no obligation to make up the missed dividend in future years. In the case of **cumulative preferred stock**, however, the fixed dividend amount per share accumulates from year to year, and the whole amount must be paid before any dividends on common stock can be paid. Dividends not paid in the year they are due are called **dividends in arrears**.

Assume that a corporation has been authorized to issue 10,000 shares of $100 par value, 5 percent cumulative preferred stock and that the shares have been issued and are outstanding. If no dividends were paid in 20x4, at the end of the year there would be preferred dividends of $50,000 (10,000 shares × $100 × .05 = $50,000) in arrears. If dividends are paid in 20x5, the preferred stockholders' dividends in arrears plus the 20x5 preferred dividends must be paid before any dividends on common stock can be paid.

Dividends in arrears are not recognized as liabilities because no liability exists until the board declares a dividend. A corporation cannot be sure it is going to make a profit, so, of course, it cannot promise dividends to stockholders. However, if a company has dividends in arrears, the amount should be reported either in the body of the financial statements or in a note. The following note appeared in a steel company's annual report:

> On January 1, 20xx, the company was in arrears by $37,851,000 ($1.25 per share) on dividends to its preferred stockholders. The company must pay all dividends in arrears to preferred stockholders before paying any dividends to common stockholders.

Suppose that on January 1, 20x4, a corporation issued 10,000 shares of $10 par, 6 percent cumulative preferred stock and 50,000 shares of common stock. The first year's operations resulted in income of only $4,000. The corporation's board of directors declared a $3,000 cash dividend to the preferred stockholders. The dividend picture at the end of 20x4 was as follows:

FOCUS ON BUSINESS PRACTICE

Why Did Microsoft Issue Preferred Stock?

Preferred stock represents a flexible means of achieving goals that cannot be achieved with common stock. For example, Microsoft Corporation <www.microsoft.com> issued almost $1 billion in preferred stock even though the company probably did not need the cash.[11] Since Microsoft does not pay and has no plans to pay a dividend on its common stock, this preferred stock satisfies the desire of investors who want to own Microsoft stock but who want to buy stocks that pay a dividend. The preferred stock pays a fixed dividend and is convertible into common stock or convertible notes. If it is not converted, the company guarantees it can be redeemed at face value for cash in three years. In return for this flexibility and low risk, the company puts a limit of 25 to 30 percent on the gain that can be realized from converting the preferred stock into common stock. As a Microsoft vice president put it, "If you own the preferred, you get a dividend yield and downside protection, but the upside is capped."[12]

20x4 dividends due preferred stockholders ($100,000 × .06)	$6,000
Less 20x4 dividends declared to preferred stockholders	3,000
20x4 preferred stock dividends in arrears	$3,000

Now suppose that in 20x5 the corporation earned income of $30,000 and wanted to pay dividends to both the preferred and the common stockholders. Because the preferred stock is cumulative, the corporation must pay the $3,000 in arrears on the preferred stock, plus the current year's dividends on its preferred stock, before it can distribute a dividend to the common stockholders. For example, assume that the corporation's board of directors declared a $12,000 dividend to be distributed to preferred and common stockholders. It would be distributed as follows:

20x5 declaration of dividends	$12,000
Less 20x4 preferred stock dividends in arrears	3,000
Available for 20x5 dividends	$ 9,000
Less 20x5 dividends due preferred stockholders ($100,000 × .06)	6,000
Remainder available to common stockholders	$ 3,000

This is the entry when the dividend is declared:

A = L + OE
    +   –

Dec. 31	Cash Dividends Declared	12,000	
	Cash Dividends Payable		12,000
	Declared a $9,000 cash dividend to preferred stockholders and a $3,000 cash dividend to common stockholders		

PREFERENCE AS TO ASSETS

ENRICHMENT NOTE: Many companies that liquidate do not have enough assets to pay creditors. Consequently, there is nothing left for shareholders, common or preferred.

Many preferred stocks have preference in terms of the assets of the corporation in the case of liquidation. If the corporation's existence is terminated, the preferred stockholders have a right to receive the par value of their stock or a larger stated liquidation value per share before the common stockholders receive any share of the corporation's assets. This preference can also extend to any dividends in arrears owed to the preferred stockholders.

CONVERTIBLE PREFERRED STOCK

A corporation can make its preferred stock more attractive to investors by adding convertibility. People who hold **convertible preferred stock** can exchange their shares of preferred stock for shares of the company's common stock at a ratio stated in the preferred stock contract. Convertibility appeals to investors for two reasons. First, like all preferred stockholders, owners of convertible preferred stock are more likely to receive regular dividends than are common stockholders. Second, if the market value of a company's common stock rises, the conversion feature allows the preferred stockholders to share in the increase. The rise in value would come either through increases in the value of the preferred stock or through conversion to common stock.

    For example, suppose that a company issues 1,000 shares of 8 percent, $100 par value convertible preferred stock for $100 per share. Each share of stock can be converted into five shares of the company's common stock at any time. The market value of the common stock is now $15 per share. In the past, an owner of the common stock could expect dividends of about $1 per share per year. The owner of one share of preferred stock, on the other hand, now holds an investment that is approaching a value of $100 on the market and is more likely to receive dividends than is the owner of common stock.

Assume that in the next several years, the corporation's earnings increase, and the dividends paid to common stockholders rise to $3 per share. Assume also that the market value of a share of common stock rises from $15 to $30. Preferred stockholders can convert each of their preferred shares into five common shares and increase their dividends from $8 on each preferred share to the equivalent of $15 ($3 on each of five common shares). Further, the market value of each share of preferred stock will be close to the $150 value of the five shares of common stock because each share can be converted into five shares of common stock.

ENRICHMENT NOTE: When a preferred shareholder converts to common stock, he or she gains voting rights but loses the dividend and liquidation preference. Conversion back to preferred stock is not an option.

CALLABLE PREFERRED STOCK

● STOP AND THINK!
Why would a company want to issue callable preferred stock?
Callable preferred stock gives the company greater flexibility. The company can eliminate the related dividends at some future date by redeeming the shares at a specified call price. ■

Most preferred stock is **callable preferred stock**. That is, it can be redeemed or retired at the option of the issuing corporation at a price stated in the preferred stock contract. A stockholder must surrender nonconvertible preferred stock to the corporation when asked to do so. If the preferred stock is convertible, the stockholder can either surrender the stock to the corporation or convert it into common stock when the corporation calls the stock. The *call price*, or redemption price, is usually higher than the par value of the stock. For example, a $100 par value preferred stock might be callable at $103 per share. When preferred stock is called and surrendered, the stockholder is entitled to (1) the par value of the stock, (2) the call premium, (3) any dividends in arrears, and (4) a portion of the current period's dividend, prorated by the proportion of the year to the call date.

A corporation may call its preferred stock for several reasons. First, it may want to force conversion of the preferred stock to common stock because the cash dividend paid on the equivalent common stock is lower than the dividend paid on the preferred shares. Second, it may be able to replace the outstanding preferred stock on the current market with a preferred stock at a lower dividend rate or with long-term debt, which can have a lower after-tax cost. Third, the corporation may simply be profitable enough to retire the preferred stock.

✓ Check out ACE for a Review Quiz at http://accounting.college.hmco.com/students.

ACCOUNTING FOR STOCK ISSUANCE

LO5 Account for the issuance of stock for cash and other assets.
RELATED TEXT ASSIGNMENTS
Q: 14
SE: 8, 9
E: 4, 9, 10
P: 1, 4, 5, 6, 8
SD: 5
FRA: 1, 7

KEY POINT: Legal capital is the minimum amount that can be reported as contributed capital. For the protection of creditors, dividends that would reduce capital below the amount of legal capital cannot be declared.

A share of capital stock may be either par or no-par. The value of par stock is stated in the corporate charter and must be printed on each share of stock. Par value can be $.01, $1, $5, $100, or any other amount established by the organizers of the corporation. The par values of common stocks tend to be lower than those of preferred stocks.

As noted earlier, par value is the amount per share that is entered into a corporation's capital stock accounts and that makes up the legal capital of the corporation. A corporation cannot declare a dividend that would cause stockholders' equity to fall below the firm's legal capital. Par value is thus a minimum cushion of capital that protects the corporation's creditors. Any amount in excess of par value received from the issuance of stock is recorded in the Paid-in Capital in Excess of Par Value account and represents a portion of the company's contributed capital.

No-par stock is capital stock that does not have a par value. There are several reasons for issuing stock without a par value. One is that some investors confuse par value with the market value of stock instead of recognizing it as an arbitrary figure. Another reason is that most states do not allow an original stock issue below par value and thereby limit a corporation's flexibility in obtaining capital.

KEY POINT: When stock is issued with no par and no stated value, all proceeds represent legal capital and are recorded as capital stock. Because stock may be issued at different prices, the legal capital per share varies.

🛑 **STOP AND THINK!**
What relevance does par value or stated value have to a financial ratio, such as return on equity or debt to equity?

Return on equity and debt to equity are computed using total stockholders' equity, which includes par or stated value. Financial analysis does not generally find par or stated value of any relevance. ∎

No-par stock can be issued with or without a stated value. The board of directors of a corporation issuing no-par stock may be required by state law to place a **stated value** on each share of stock or may choose to do so as a matter of convenience. The stated value can be any value set by the board unless the state specifies a minimum amount, which is sometimes the case. The stated value can be set before or after the shares are issued if the state law is not specific.

If a company issues no-par stock without a stated value, all proceeds are recorded in the Capital Stock account. That amount becomes the corporation's legal capital unless a different amount is specified by state law. Because additional shares of the stock can be issued at different prices, the per-share credit to the Capital Stock account will not be uniform. This is a key way in which no-par stock without a stated value differs from par value stock or no-par stock with a stated value.

When no-par stock with a stated value is issued, the shares are recorded in the Capital Stock account at the stated value. Any amount received in excess of the stated value is recorded in the Paid-in Capital in Excess of Stated Value account. The amount in excess of the stated value is part of the corporation's contributed capital. However, the stated value is normally considered to be the legal capital of the corporation.

PAR VALUE STOCK

When par value stock is issued, the appropriate capital stock account (usually Common Stock or Preferred Stock) is credited for the par value regardless of whether the proceeds are more or less than the par value. For example, assume that Bradley Corporation is authorized to issue 20,000 shares of $10 par value common stock and issues 10,000 shares at $10 per share on January 1, 20xx. The entry to record the stock issue at par value would be as follows:

A = L + OE
+   +

Jan. 1	Cash	100,000	
	Common Stock		100,000
	Issued 10,000 shares of $10 par value common stock for $10 per share		

Cash is debited for $100,000 (10,000 shares × $10), and Common Stock is credited for an equal amount because the stock was sold for par value.

When stock is issued for a price greater than par, the proceeds in excess of par are credited to a capital account called Paid-in Capital in Excess of Par Value, Common. For example, assume that the 10,000 shares of Bradley common stock sold for $12 per share on January 1, 20xx. The entry to record the issuance of the stock at the price in excess of par value would be as follows:

TERMINOLOGY NOTE:
Many companies refer to paid-in capital in excess of par value as additional paid-in capital.

A = L + OE
+   +
         +

Jan. 1	Cash	120,000	
	Common Stock		100,000
	Paid-in Capital in Excess of Par Value, Common		20,000
	Issued 10,000 shares of $10 par value common stock for $12 per share		

KEY POINT: Common stock and paid-in capital in excess of par value are separated for legal purposes. Their effect on the company's balance sheet is the same.

Cash is debited for the proceeds of $120,000 (10,000 shares × $12), and Common Stock is credited for the total par value of $100,000 (10,000 shares × $10). Paid-in Capital in Excess of Par Value, Common is credited for the difference of $20,000 (10,000 shares × $2). The amount in excess of par value is part of the corporation's contributed capital and will be included in the stockholders' equity section of the balance sheet. The stockholders' equity section for Bradley Corporation immediately following the stock issue would appear as follows:

Contributed capital
   Common stock, $10 par value, 20,000 shares
     authorized, 10,000 shares issued and outstanding $100,000
   Paid-in capital in excess of par value, common   20,000
    Total contributed capital $120,000
Retained earnings   —
Total stockholders' equity $120,000

If a corporation issues stock for less than par, an account called Discount on Capital Stock is debited for the difference. The issuance of stock at a discount rarely occurs; it is illegal in many states.

No-Par Stock

As mentioned earlier, stock can be issued without a par value. However, most states require that all or part of the proceeds from the issuance of no-par stock be designated as legal capital, which cannot be withdrawn except in liquidation. The purpose of this requirement is to protect the corporation's assets for creditors. Assume that Bradley Corporation's capital stock is no-par common and that 10,000 shares are issued on January 1, 20xx, at $15 per share. The $150,000 (10,000 shares × $15) in proceeds would be recorded as shown in the following entry:

A = L + OE
+   +

Jan. 1 Cash   150,000
        Common Stock   150,000
         Issued 10,000 shares of no-par
         common stock for $15 per share

KEY POINT: When no-par stock has a stated value, the stated value serves the same purpose as par value.

Because the stock does not have a stated or par value, all proceeds of the issue are credited to Common Stock and are part of the company's legal capital.

Most states allow the board of directors to put a stated value on no-par stock, and that value represents the corporation's legal capital. Assume that Bradley's board puts a $10 stated value on its no-par stock. The entry to record the issue of 10,000 shares of no-par common stock with a $10 stated value for $15 per share would appear as follows:

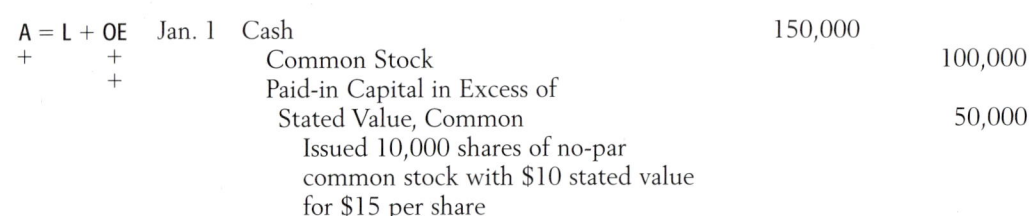

A = L + OE
+   +
    +

Jan. 1 Cash   150,000
        Common Stock   100,000
        Paid-in Capital in Excess of
          Stated Value, Common   50,000
         Issued 10,000 shares of no-par
         common stock with $10 stated value
         for $15 per share

Notice that the legal capital credited to Common Stock is the stated value decided by the board of directors. Notice also that the account Paid-in Capital in Excess of Stated Value, Common is credited for $50,000. The $50,000 is the difference between the proceeds ($150,000) and the total stated value ($100,000). Paid-in Capital in Excess of Stated Value is presented on the balance sheet in the same way as Paid-in Capital in Excess of Par Value.

Issuance of Stock for Noncash Assets

Stock can be issued for assets or services other than cash. The problem is to determine the dollar amount that should be recorded for the exchange. The generally preferred rule is to record the transaction at the fair market value of what the corporation is giving up—in this case, the stock. If the fair market value of the stock cannot be determined, the fair market value of the assets or services received can be used. Transactions of this kind usually involve the use of stock to pay for land or buildings or for the services of attorneys and others who helped organize the company.

KEY POINT: The board of directors may not arbitrarily establish the fair market value of property that is exchanged for stock; it must do so prudently, using all the information at its disposal.

When there is an exchange of stock for noncash assets, the board of directors has the right to determine the fair market value of the property. Suppose that when Bradley Corporation was formed on January 1, 20xx, its attorney agreed to accept 100 shares of its $10 par value common stock for services rendered. At the time the stock was issued, its market value could not be determined. However, for similar services the attorney would have billed the company $1,500. The entry to record the noncash transaction is as follows:

A = L + OE
  +
—   +

Jan. 1	Start-up and Organization Expense	1,500	
	Common Stock		1,000
	Paid-in Capital in Excess of Par Value, Common		500
	Issued 100 shares of $10 par value common stock for attorney's services		

Now suppose that two years later Bradley Corporation exchanged 1,000 shares of its $10 par value common stock for a piece of land. At the time of the exchange, the stock was selling on the market for $16 per share. The following entry records the exchange:

A = L + OE
+   +
        +

Jan. 1	Land	16,000	
	Common Stock		10,000
	Paid-in Capital in Excess of Par Value, Common		6,000
	Issued 1,000 shares of $10 par value common stock with a market value of $16 per share for a piece of land		

✓ Check out ACE for a Review Quiz at http://accounting.college.hmco.com/students.

ACCOUNTING FOR TREASURY STOCK

LO6 Account for treasury stock.

RELATED TEXT ASSIGNMENTS
Q: 15, 16
SE: 10, 11
E: 2, 6, 11, 12
P: 3, 4, 5, 8
SD: 3, 4
FRA: 4, 6, 7

Treasury stock is capital stock, either common or preferred, that the issuing company has reacquired. The company normally gets the stock back by purchasing the shares on the market. It is common for companies to buy and hold their own stock. In a recent year, 410, or 68 percent, of 600 large companies held treasury stock.[13] Although the purchase of treasury stock can be a severe drain on cash, a company may purchase its own stock for several reasons:

1. It may want stock to distribute to employees through stock option plans.
2. It may be trying to maintain a favorable market for its stock.
3. It may want to increase its earnings per share or stock price per share.
4. It may want to have additional shares of stock available for such activities as purchasing other companies.
5. It may want to prevent a hostile takeover.

KEY POINT: Treasury stock is not the same as unissued stock. Treasury stock represents shares that have been issued but are no longer outstanding. Unissued shares, on the other hand, have never been in circulation.

A treasury stock purchase reduces the assets and stockholders' equity of the company. It is not considered a purchase of assets, as the purchase of shares in another company would be. Treasury stock is capital stock that has been issued but is no longer outstanding. Treasury shares can be held for an indefinite period, reissued, or retired. Like unissued stock, treasury stock has no rights until it is reissued. It does not have voting rights, rights to cash dividends and stock dividends, or rights to share in assets during liquidation of the company, and it is not considered to be outstanding in the calculation of book value. However, there is one major difference between unissued shares and treasury shares: A share of stock that originally was issued at par value or greater and fully paid for, and that then was reacquired as treasury stock, can be reissued at less than par value without negative consequences.

PURCHASE OF TREASURY STOCK

When treasury stock is purchased, it is normally recorded at cost. The transaction reduces the firm's assets as well as stockholders' equity. For example, assume that on September 15 Caprock Corporation purchases 1,000 shares of its common stock on the market at a price of $50 per share. The purchase would be recorded as follows:

A = L + OE
−   −

Sept. 15	Treasury Stock, Common	50,000	
	Cash		50,000
	Acquired 1,000 shares of the company's common stock for $50 per share		

The treasury shares are recorded at cost. The par value, stated value, or original issue price of the stock is ignored.

The stockholders' equity section of Caprock's balance sheet shows the cost of the treasury stock as a deduction from the total of contributed capital and retained earnings:

ENRICHMENT NOTE: Since treasury stock reduces stockholders' equity—the denominator of the return on equity ratio—the return on equity will increase when treasury shares are purchased even though there is no increase in earnings.

Contributed capital	
Common stock, $5 par value, 100,000 shares authorized,	
30,000 shares issued, 29,000 shares outstanding	$ 150,000
Paid-in capital in excess of par value, common	30,000
Total contributed capital	$ 180,000
Retained earnings	900,000
Total contributed capital and retained earnings	$1,080,000
Less treasury stock, common (1,000 shares at cost)	50,000
Total stockholders' equity	$1,030,000

Notice that the number of shares issued, and therefore the legal capital, has not changed, although the number of outstanding shares has decreased as a result of the transaction.

SALE OF TREASURY STOCK

Treasury shares can be sold at cost, above cost, or below cost. For example, assume that on November 15, Caprock Corporation sells its 1,000 treasury shares for $50 per share. The following entry records the transaction:

A = L + OE
+   +

Nov. 15	Cash	50,000	
	Treasury Stock, Common		50,000
	Reissued 1,000 shares of treasury stock for $50 per share		

When treasury shares are sold for an amount greater than their cost, the excess of the sales price over cost should be credited to Paid-in Capital, Treasury Stock. No gain should be recorded. For example, suppose that on November 15, Caprock sells its 1,000 treasury shares for $60 per share. The entry for the reissue would be as follows:

A = L + OE
+   +
          +

Nov. 15	Cash	60,000	
	Treasury Stock, Common		50,000
	Paid-in Capital, Treasury Stock		10,000
	Sold 1,000 shares of treasury stock for $60 per share; cost was $50 per share		

If treasury shares are sold below their cost, the difference is deducted from Paid-in Capital, Treasury Stock. When this account does not exist or its balance is

FOCUS ON BUSINESS PRACTICE

When Are Share Buybacks a Bad Idea?

Corporate America set share repurchase records in 2000 of $123 billion. As recently as 1991, share repurchases totaled only $10 billion. Among the companies that spent billions to boost their stock prices were Hewlett-Packard <www.hp.com>, AT&T <www.att.com>, Intel <www.intel.com>, and Microsoft <www.microsoft.com>—all to no avail.

According to renowned investor Warren Buffet, share buybacks are ill-advised when companies buy high and sell low. Such action is the exact opposite of good investment theory (to buy when stocks are cheap and to sell when prices rise).

But in 2000, to avoid increased shares outstanding and the resulting lower earnings per share, companies were buying stock at record high prices and then selling it to employees at much lower prices.

Another bad idea is to borrow money to buy back stock. In 2000, many companies were borrowing money to repurchase stock, thereby increasing their debt to equity ratio. These companies are now suffering credit rating reductions and severe stock price declines.[14]

KEY POINT: Gains and losses on the reissue of treasury stock are never recognized as such. Instead, the accounts Retained Earnings and Paid-in Capital, Treasury Stock are used.

insufficient to cover the excess of cost over the reissue price, Retained Earnings absorbs the excess. No loss is recorded. For example, suppose that on September 15, Caprock bought 1,000 shares of its common stock on the market at a price of $50 per share. The company sold 400 shares on October 15 for $60 per share and the remaining 600 shares on December 15 for $42 per share. The entries for these transactions are as follows:

A = L + OE				
− −	Sept. 15	Treasury Stock, Common	50,000	
		Cash		50,000
		Purchased 1,000 shares of treasury stock at $50 per share		

A = L + OE				
+ +	Oct. 15	Cash	24,000	
+		Treasury Stock, Common		20,000
		Paid-in Capital, Treasury Stock		4,000
		Sold 400 shares of treasury stock for $60 per share; cost was $50 per share		

A = L + OE				
+ −	Dec. 15	Cash	25,200	
+		Paid-in Capital, Treasury Stock	4,000	
		Retained Earnings	800	
		Treasury Stock, Common		30,000
		Sold 600 shares of treasury stock for $42 per share; cost was $50 per share		

STUDY NOTE: Retained Earnings is debited only when the Paid-in Capital, Treasury Stock account has been depleted. In this case, the credit balance of $4,000 is exhausted completely before Retained Earnings absorbs the excess.

In the entry for the December 15 transaction, Retained Earnings is debited for $800 because the 600 shares were sold for $4,800 less than cost. That amount is $800 greater than the $4,000 of paid-in capital generated by the sale of the 400 shares of treasury stock on October 15.

RETIREMENT OF TREASURY STOCK

● **STOP AND THINK!**
Why might a company choose to retire its treasury stock?
A company that does not plan to reissue the shares might decide to retire them. ■

If a company determines that it will not reissue treasury stock, it can, with the approval of its stockholders, retire the stock. When shares of stock are retired, all items related to those shares are removed from the related capital accounts. When treasury stock whose acquisition price is less than the original contributed capital is retired, the difference is recognized in Paid-in Capital, Retirement of Stock. If the acquisition price is more than was received when the stock was first issued, the difference is a reduction in stockholders' equity and is debited to Retained Earnings. For instance, suppose that instead of selling the 1,000 shares of treasury stock it purchased for $50,000, Caprock Corporation decides to retire the shares on November

15. Assuming that the $5 par value common stock was originally issued at $6 per share, this entry records the retirement:

A = L + OE				
–	Nov. 15	Common Stock	5,000	
–		Paid-in Capital in Excess of Par Value, Common	1,000	
–		Retained Earnings	44,000	
+		Treasury Stock, Common		50,000
		Retired 1,000 shares that cost $50 per share and were issued originally at $6 per share		

✓ Check out ACE for a Review Quiz at http://accounting.college.hmco.com/students.

Chapter Review

REVIEW OF LEARNING OBJECTIVES

LO1 Identify and explain the management issues related to contributed capital.

The management of contributed capital is a critical component in corporate financing. The issues faced by management in the area of contributed capital are forming a corporation, managing under the corporate form of business, using equity financing, determining dividend policies, evaluating performance using return on equity, and using stock options as compensation.

LO2 Identify the components of stockholders' equity.

Stockholders' equity consists of contributed capital and retained earnings. Contributed capital includes two basic types of stock: common stock and preferred stock. When only one type of security is issued, it is common stock. Common stockholders have voting rights; they also share in the earnings of the corporation. Preferred stock, like common stock, is sold to raise capital. But the investors in preferred stock have different objectives. To attract such investors, corporations usually give them a preference—in terms of receiving dividends and assets—over common stockholders.

Retained earnings, the other component of stockholders' equity, represents the claim of stockholders to the assets of the company resulting from profitable operations. These are earnings that have been invested in the corporation.

LO3 Account for cash dividends.

The liability for payment of cash dividends arises on the date of declaration by the board of directors. The declaration is recorded with a debit to Cash Dividends Declared and a credit to Cash Dividends Payable. The date of record requires no entry; it is the date on which ownership of the stock, and thus of the right to receive a dividend, is determined. Date of payment is recorded with a debit to Cash Dividends Payable and a credit to Cash.

LO4 Identify the characteristics of preferred stock, including the effect on distribution of dividends.

The dividend on preferred stock is generally figured first; the remainder goes to common stock. If the preferred stock is cumulative and in arrears, the amount in arrears must be allocated to preferred stockholders before any allocation is made to common stockholders. In addition, certain preferred stock is convertible. Preferred stock is often callable at the option of the corporation.

LO5 Account for the issuance of stock for cash and other assets.

A corporation's stock is normally issued for cash and other assets. Most states require that stock be issued at a minimum value called *legal capital*. Legal capital is represented by the par or stated value of the stock.

When stock is issued for cash at par or stated value, Cash is debited and Common Stock or Preferred Stock is credited. When stock is sold at an amount greater than par or stated value, the excess is recorded in Paid-in Capital in Excess of Par or Stated Value.

Stock is sometimes issued for noncash assets. In these cases, the board of directors must decide how to value the stock. The general rule is to record the stock at its mar-

LO6 Account for treasury stock.

ket value. If this value cannot be determined, the fair market value of the asset received is used to record the transaction.

Treasury stock is stock that the issuing company has reacquired. A company may buy its own stock for several reasons, including a desire to create stock option plans, maintain a favorable market for the stock, increase earnings per share, or purchase other companies. Treasury stock is similar to unissued stock in that it does not have rights until it is reissued. However, treasury stock can be resold at less than par value without penalty. The accounting treatment for treasury stock is as follows:

Treasury Stock Transaction	Accounting Treatment
Purchase of treasury stock	Debit Treasury Stock and credit Cash for the cost of the shares.
Sale of treasury stock at the same price as the cost of the shares	Debit Cash and credit Treasury Stock for the cost of the shares.
Sale of treasury stock at an amount greater than the cost of the shares	Debit Cash for the reissue price of the shares, and credit Treasury Stock for the cost of the shares and Paid-in Capital, Treasury Stock for the excess.
Sale of treasury stock at an amount less than the cost of the shares	Debit Cash for the reissue price; debit Paid-in Capital, Treasury Stock for the difference between the reissue price and the cost of the shares; and credit Treasury Stock for the cost of the shares. If Paid-in Capital, Treasury Stock does not exist or its balance is not large enough to cover the difference, Retained Earnings should absorb the difference.
Retirement of treasury stock	Debit Common Stock and Paid-in Capital in Excess of Par Value, Common for the original issue price and Retained Earnings for the remainder to bring the total to the cost of the treasury stock. Credit Treasury Stock for its total cost.

REVIEW OF CONCEPTS AND TERMINOLOGY

The following concepts and terms were introduced in this chapter:

LO1 **Articles of incorporation:** An official document filed with and approved by a state that authorizes the incorporators to do business as a corporation.

LO1 **Audit committee:** A subgroup of the board of directors of a corporation charged with ensuring that the board will be objective in reviewing management's performance; it engages the company's independent auditors and reviews their work.

LO1 **Authorized stock:** The maximum number of shares a corporation can issue without a change in its state charter.

LO4 **Callable preferred stock:** Preferred stock that can be redeemed or retired at a stated price at the option of the issuing corporation.

LO2 **Common stock:** Shares of stock that carry voting rights but that rank below preferred stock in terms of dividends and the distribution of assets.

LO4 **Convertible preferred stock:** Preferred stock that can be exchanged for common stock at the option of the holder.

LO1 **Corporation:** A separate legal entity having its own rights, privileges, and liabilities distinct from those of its owners.

LO4 **Cumulative preferred stock:** Preferred stock on which unpaid dividends accumulate over time and must be satisfied before a dividend can be paid to common stockholders.

LO3 **Date of declaration:** The date on which the board of directors declares a dividend.

LO3 **Date of payment:** The date on which payment of a dividend is made.

LO3 **Date of record:** The date on which ownership of stock for the purpose of receiving a dividend is determined.

LO1 **Dividends:** The distribution of a corporation's assets (usually cash generated by past earnings) to its stockholders.

LO4 **Dividends in arrears:** Past dividends on cumulative preferred stock that remain unpaid.

LO1 **Dividends yield:** Current return to stockholders in the form of dividends; dividends per share divided by market price per share.

LO1 **Double taxation:** Taxation of corporate earnings twice—once as income of the corporation and once again as income to stockholders based on the dividends they receive.

LO3 **Ex-dividend:** A description of capital stock between the date of record and the date of payment, when the right to a dividend already declared on the stock remains with the person who sells the stock and does not transfer to the person who buys it.

LO1 **Initial public offering (IPO):** A company's first issue of capital stock to the public.

LO2 **Issued stock:** The shares of stock sold or otherwise transferred to stockholders.

LO1 **Legal capital:** The number of shares of stock issued times the par value; the minimum amount that can be reported as contributed capital.

LO3 **Liquidating dividend:** A dividend that exceeds retained earnings; usually paid when a corporation goes out of business or reduces its operations.

LO4 **Noncumulative preferred stock:** Preferred stock that does not oblige the issuer to make up a missed dividend in a subsequent year.

LO5 **No-par stock:** Capital stock that does not have a par value.

LO2 **Outstanding stock:** Stock that has been issued and is still in circulation.

LO1 **Par value:** An arbitrary amount assigned to each share of stock; constitutes the legal capital of a corporation.

LO2 **Preferred stock:** Stock that has preference over common stock, usually in terms of dividends and the distribution of assets.

LO1 **Price/earnings (P/E) ratio:** A measure of confidence in a company's future; market price per share divided by earnings per share.

LO2 **Residual equity:** The common stock of a corporation.

LO1 **Return on equity:** A measure of management performance; net income divided by average stockholders' equity.

LO1 **Share of stock:** A unit of ownership in a corporation.

LO1 **Start-up and organization costs:** The costs of forming a corporation.

LO5 **Stated value:** A value assigned by the board of directors of a corporation to no-par stock.

LO1 **Stock certificate:** A document issued to a stockholder indicating the number of shares of stock the stockholder owns.

LO1 **Stock option plan:** An agreement to issue stock to employees according to specified terms.

LO6 **Treasury stock:** Capital stock, either common or preferred, that the issuing company has reacquired but has not subsequently resold or retired.

LO1 **Underwriter:** An intermediary between the corporation and the investing public who facilitates an issue of stock or other securities for a fee.

REVIEW PROBLEM

Stock Entries and Stockholders' Equity

LO1 LO2 LO3 LO4 LO5 LO6 The Beta Corporation was organized in 20x4 in the state of Arizona. Its charter authorized the corporation to issue 1,000,000 shares of $1 par value common stock and an additional 25,000 shares of 4 percent, $20 par value cumulative convertible preferred stock. Here are the transactions related to the company's stock during 20x4:

Feb. 1 Issued 100,000 shares of common stock for $125,000.
      15 Issued 3,000 shares of common stock for accounting and legal services. The services were billed to the company at $3,600.
Mar. 15 Issued 120,000 shares of common stock to Edward Jackson in exchange for a building and land appraised at $100,000 and $25,000, respectively.
Apr. 2 Purchased 20,000 shares of common stock for the treasury at $1.25 per share from a person who changed his mind about investing in the company.
July 1 Issued 25,000 shares of preferred stock for $500,000.
Sept. 30 Sold 10,000 of the shares in the treasury for $1.50 per share.
Dec. 31 The board declared dividends of $24,910 payable on January 15 to stockholders of record on January 8. Dividends included preferred stock cash dividends for one-half year.

For the period ended December 31, 20x4, the company reported net income of $40,000 and earnings per common share of $.14. At December 31, the market price per common share was $1.60.

REQUIRED

1. Record these transactions in journal form. In the explanation for the December 31 entry to record dividends, show dividends payable to each class of stock.
2. Prepare the stockholders' equity section of the Beta Corporation balance sheet as of December 31, 20x4. (**Hint:** Use net income and dividends to calculate retained earnings.)
3. Calculate dividends yield on common stock, price/earnings ratio of common stock, and return on equity.

ANSWER TO REVIEW PROBLEM

1. Entries prepared in journal form:

Feb. 1	Cash		125,000	
	Common Stock			100,000
	Paid-in Capital in Excess of Par Value, Common			25,000
	Issued 100,000 shares of $1 par value common stock for $1.25 per share			
15	Start-up and Organization Expense		3,600	
	Common Stock			3,000
	Paid-in Capital in Excess of Par Value, Common			600
	Issued 3,000 shares of $1 par value common stock for billed accounting and legal services of $3,600			
Mar. 15	Building		100,000	
	Land		25,000	
	Common Stock			120,000
	Paid-in Capital in Excess of Par Value, Common			5,000
	Issued 120,000 shares of $1 par value common stock for a building and land appraised at $100,000 and $25,000, respectively			

Apr. 2	Treasury Stock, Common	25,000	
	Cash		25,000
	Purchased 20,000 shares of common stock for the treasury at $1.25 per share		
July 1	Cash	500,000	
	Preferred Stock		500,000
	Issued 25,000 shares of $20 par value preferred stock for $20 per share		
Sept. 30	Cash	15,000	
	Treasury Stock, Common		12,500
	Paid-in Capital, Treasury Stock		2,500
	Sold 10,000 shares of treasury stock at $1.50 per share; original cost was $1.25 per share		
Dec. 31	Cash Dividends Declared	24,910	
	Cash Dividends Payable		24,910
	Declared a $24,910 cash dividend to preferred and common stockholders		

Total dividend		$24,910
Less preferred stock cash dividend		
$500,000 × .04 × 6/12		10,000
Common stock cash dividend		$14,910

2. Stockholders' equity section of the balance sheet prepared:

Beta Corporation
Balance Sheet
December 31, 20x4

Stockholders' Equity

Contributed capital		
Preferred stock, 4 percent cumulative convertible, $20 par value, 25,000 shares authorized, issued, and outstanding		$500,000
Common stock, $1 par value, 1,000,000 shares authorized, 223,000 shares issued, and 213,000 shares outstanding	$223,000	
Paid-in capital in excess of par value, common	30,600	
Paid-in capital, treasury stock	2,500	256,100
Total contributed capital		$756,100
Retained earnings		15,090*
Total contributed capital and retained earnings		$771,190
Less treasury stock, common (10,000 shares, at cost)		12,500
Total stockholders' equity		$758,690

*Retained Earnings = $40,000 − $24,910 = $15,090.

3. Dividends yield on common stock, price/earnings ratio of common stock, and return on equity calculated:

Dividends per Share = $14,910 Common Stock Dividend ÷ 213,000 Common Shares Outstanding = $.07

$$\text{Dividends Yield} = \frac{\text{Dividends per Share}}{\text{Market Price per Share}} = \frac{\$.07}{\$1.60} = 4.4\%$$

$$\text{Price/Earnings (P/E) Ratio} = \frac{\text{Market Price per Share}}{\text{Earnings per Share}} = \frac{\$1.60}{\$.14} = 11.4 \text{ times}$$

The opening balance of stockholders' equity on February 1, 20x1, was $125,000.

$$\text{Return on Equity} = \frac{\text{Net Income}}{\text{Average Stockholders' Equity}}$$

$$= \frac{\$40,000}{(\$758,690 + \$125,000) \div 2}$$

$$= 9.1\%$$

Chapter Assignments

BUILDING YOUR KNOWLEDGE FOUNDATION

QUESTIONS

1. What management issues are related to contributed capital?
2. Identify and explain several advantages of the corporate form of business.
3. Identify and explain several disadvantages of the corporate form of business.
4. What is dividends yield, and what do investors learn from it?
5. What is the price/earnings (P/E) ratio, and what does it measure?
6. What are the start-up and organization costs of a corporation?
7. What is the proper accounting treatment of start-up and organization costs?
8. What is a stock option plan, and why would a company have one?
9. What is the legal capital of a corporation, and what is its significance?
10. Describe the significance of the following dates as they relate to dividends: (a) date of declaration, (b) date of record, and (c) date of payment.
11. Explain the accounting treatment of cash dividends.
12. What are dividends in arrears, and how should they be disclosed in the financial statements?
13. Define *cumulative*, *convertible*, and *callable* as they apply to preferred stock.
14. How is the value of stock determined when stock is issued for noncash assets?
15. Define *treasury stock* and explain why a company would purchase its own stock.
16. What is the proper classification of the accounts listed below on the balance sheet? Indicate whether stockholders' equity accounts are contributed capital, retained earnings, or contra stockholders' equity.
    a. Common Stock
    b. Treasury Stock
    c. Paid-in Capital, Treasury Stock
    d. Paid-in Capital in Excess of Par Value, Common
    e. Paid-in Capital in Excess of Stated Value, Common
    f. Retained Earnings

1. Record the issuance of the stock in T accounts.
2. Prepare the stockholders' equity section of Wallace Hospital Supply Corporation's balance sheet as it would appear immediately after the company issued the common and preferred stock.

E 5.
LO3 Cash Dividends

Estey Corporation secured authorization from the state for 200,000 shares of $10 par value common stock. It has 160,000 shares issued and 140,000 shares outstanding. On June 5, the board of directors declared a $.50 per share cash dividend to be paid on June 25 to stockholders of record on June 15. Prepare entries in journal form to record these events.

E 6.
LO3 Cash Dividends
LO6

Santori Corporation has 500,000 authorized shares of $1 par value common stock, of which 400,000 are issued, including 40,000 shares of treasury stock. On October 15, the board of directors declared a cash dividend of $.25 per share payable on November 15 to stockholders of record on November 1. Prepare entries in journal form for each of the three dates.

E 7.
LO4 Cash Dividends with Dividends in Arrears

Amsco Corporation has 10,000 shares of its $100 par value, 7 percent cumulative preferred stock outstanding, and 50,000 shares of its $1 par value common stock outstanding. In Amsco's first four years of operation, its board of directors paid cash dividends as follows: 20x3, none; 20x4, $120,000; 20x5, $140,000; 20x6, $140,000. Determine the dividends per share and total cash dividends paid to the preferred and common stockholders during each of the four years.

E 8.
LO4 Cash Dividends on Preferred and Common Stock

Caron Corporation pays dividends at the end of each year. The dividends that it paid for 20x3, 20x4, and 20x5 were $80,000, $60,000, and $180,000, respectively. Calculate the total amount of dividends the Caron Corporation paid in each of these years to its common and preferred stockholders under both of the following capital structures: (1) 20,000 shares of $100 par, 6 percent noncumulative preferred stock and 60,000 shares of $10 par common stock; (2) 10,000 shares of $100 par, 7 percent cumulative preferred stock and 60,000 shares of $10 par common stock. No dividends were in arrears at the beginning of 20x3.

E 9.
LO5 Issuance of Stock

Montana Company is authorized to issue 200,000 shares of common stock. On August 1, the company issued 10,000 shares at $25 per share. Prepare entries in journal form to record the issuance of stock for cash under each of the following alternatives:

1. The stock has a par value of $25.
2. The stock has a par value of $10.
3. The stock has no par value.
4. The stock has a stated value of $1 per share.

E 10.
LO5 Issuance of Stock for Noncash Assets

On July 1, 20xx, Florine, a new corporation, issued 20,000 shares of its common stock to finance a corporate headquarters building. The building has a fair market value of $600,000 and a book value of $400,000. Because Florine is a new corporation, it is not possible to establish a market value for its common stock. Record the issuance of stock for the building, assuming the following conditions: (1) the par value of the stock is $10 per share; (2) the stock is no-par stock; and (3) the stock has a stated value of $4 per share.

E 11.
LO6 Treasury Stock Transactions

Record in T accounts the following stock transactions of Mahtani Company, which represent all the company's treasury stock transactions during 20xx:

May 5 Purchased 400 shares of its own $2 par value common stock for $20 per share, the current market price.
     17 Sold 150 shares of treasury stock purchased on May 5 for $22 per share.
     21 Sold 100 shares of treasury stock purchased on May 5 for $20 per share.
     28 Sold the remaining 150 shares of treasury stock purchased on May 5 for $19 per share.

E 12.
LO6 Treasury Stock Transactions Including Retirement

Record in T accounts the following stock transactions of Theoharis Corporation, which represent all its treasury stock transactions for the year:

June 1 Purchased 2,000 shares of its own $30 par value common stock for $70 per share, the current market price.
     10 Sold 500 shares of treasury stock purchased on June 1 for $80 per share.
     20 Sold 700 shares of treasury stock purchased on June 1 for $58 per share.
     30 Retired the remaining shares purchased on June 1. The original issue price was $42 per share.

Problems

P 1.
LO1 **Start-up and Organization**
LO2 **Costs, Stock and Dividend**
LO3 **Entries Using T Accounts, and**
LO5 **Stockholders' Equity**

On March 1, 20xx, Jung Corporation began operations with a charter from the state that authorized 100,000 shares of $2 par value common stock. Over the next quarter, the firm engaged in the following transactions:

Mar. 1 Issued 30,000 shares of common stock, $100,000.
      2 Paid fees associated with obtaining the charter and starting up and organizing the corporation, $12,000.
Apr. 10 Issued 13,000 shares of common stock, $65,000.
May 31   The board of directors declared a $.10 per share cash dividend to be paid on June 15 to shareholders of record on June 10.

REQUIRED
1. Record the above transactions in T accounts.
2. Prepare the stockholders' equity section of Jung Corporation's balance sheet on May 31, 20xx. Net income earned during the first quarter was $15,000.

P 2.
LO1 **Preferred and Common Stock**
LO4 **Dividends and Dividends Yield**

Taswell Corporation had the following stock outstanding from 20x3 through 20x6:

Preferred stock: $50 par value, 8 percent cumulative, 10,000 shares authorized, issued, and outstanding

Common stock: $5 par value, 200,000 shares authorized, issued, and outstanding

The company paid $30,000, $30,000, $94,000, and $130,000 in dividends during 20x3, 20x4, 20x5, and 20x6, respectively. The market price per common share was $7.25 and $8.00 per share at year end 20x5 and 20x6, respectively.

REQUIRED
1. Determine the dividends per share and the total dividends paid to common stockholders and preferred stockholders in 20x3, 20x4, 20x5, and 20x6.
2. Perform the same computations, with the assumption that the preferred stock was noncumulative.
3. Calculate the 20x5 and 20x6 dividends yield for common stock, using the dividends per share computed in **2**.
4. How are cumulative preferred stock and noncumulative preferred stock similar to long-term bonds? How do they differ from long-term bonds?

P 3.
LO1 **Treasury Stock Transactions**
LO6

Bendix Company was involved in the following treasury stock transactions during 20xx:

Jan. 10 Purchased 52,000 shares of its $2 par value common stock on the market for $40 per share.
     20 Sold 16,000 shares of the treasury stock for $42 per share.
Feb. 8 Sold 12,000 shares of the treasury stock for $38 per share.
     16 Sold 20,000 shares of the treasury stock for $34 per share.
Mar. 14 Purchased an additional 8,000 shares for $36 per share.
     25 Retired all the remaining shares of treasury stock. All shares originally were issued at $16 per share.

REQUIRED
1. Record these transactions in journal form.
2. What effect does the purchase of treasury stock have on return on equity? Why might management prefer to buy treasury stock rather than pay dividends?

P 4.
LO1 **Comprehensive Stockholders'**
LO2 **Equity Transactions and**
LO3 **Financial Ratios**
LO4
LO5
LO6

Arkazian, Inc., was organized and authorized to issue 10,000 shares of $100 par value, 9 percent preferred stock and 100,000 shares of no-par, $10 stated value common stock on July 1, 20xx. Stock-related transactions for Arkazian were as follows:

July 1 Issued 20,000 shares of common stock at $22 per share.
      1 Issued 1,000 shares of common stock at $22 per share for services rendered in connection with the organization of the company.
      2 Issued 4,000 shares of preferred stock at par value for cash.
     10 Issued 5,000 shares of common stock for land on which the asking price was $120,000. Market value of the stock was $24. Management wishes to record the land at full market value of the stock.
Aug. 2 Purchased 3,000 shares of its common stock at $26 per share.
     10 Declared a cash dividend for one month on the outstanding preferred stock and $.04 per share on common stock outstanding, payable on August 22 to stockholders of record on August 12.
     12 Date of record for cash dividends.
     22 Paid cash dividends.

REQUIRED ▶
1. Record the transactions in T accounts.
2. Prepare the stockholders' equity section of the balance sheet as it would appear on August 31, 20xx. Net income for July and August was $50,000.
3. Calculate dividends yield, price/earnings ratio, and return on equity. Assume earnings per common share are $1.97 and market price per common share is $25. For beginning stockholders' equity, use the balance at the close of business on July 1, 20xx.

P 5.

LO1 **Comprehensive Stockholders'**
LO2 **Equity Transactions and**
LO3 **T Accounts**
LO4
LO5
LO6

In January 20xx, Hammond Corporation was organized and authorized to issue 2,000,000 shares of no-par common stock and 50,000 shares of 5 percent, $50 par value, noncumulative preferred stock. The stock-related transactions for the first year's operations were as follows:

Jan. 19 Sold 15,000 shares of the common stock for $31,500. State law requires a minimum of $1 stated value per share.
      21 Issued 5,000 shares of common stock to attorneys and accountants for services valued at $11,000 and provided during the organization of the corporation.
Feb. 7 Issued 30,000 shares of common stock for a building that had an appraised value of $78,000.
Mar. 22 Purchased 10,000 shares of its common stock at $3 per share.
July 15 Issued 5,000 shares of common stock to employees under a stock option plan that allows any employee to buy shares at the current market price, which is now $3 per share.
Aug. 1 Sold 2,500 shares of treasury stock for $4 per share.
Sept. 1 Declared a cash dividend of $.15 per common share to be paid on September 25 to stockholders of record on September 15.
      15 Cash dividends date of record.
      25 Paid cash dividends to stockholders of record on September 15.
Oct. 30 Issued 4,000 shares of common stock for a piece of land. The stock was selling for $3 per share, and the land had a fair market value of $12,000.
Dec. 15 Issued 2,200 shares of preferred stock for $50 per share.

REQUIRED ▶
1. Record the above transactions in T accounts. Prepare T accounts for Cash; Land; Building; Cash Dividends Payable; Preferred Stock; Common Stock; Paid-in Capital in Excess of Stated Value, Common; Paid-in Capital, Treasury Stock; Retained Earnings; Treasury Stock, Common; Cash Dividends Declared; and Start-up and Organization Expense.
2. Prepare the stockholders' equity section of Hammond Corporation's balance sheet as of December 31, 20xx. Net income earned during the year was $100,000.

ALTERNATE PROBLEMS

P 6.

LO1 **Start-up and Organization**
LO2 **Costs, Stock and Dividend**
LO3 **Entries, and Stockholders'**
LO5 **Equity**

Quesnel Corporation began operations on September 1, 20xx. The corporation's charter authorized 300,000 shares of $8 par value common stock. Quesnel Corporation engaged in the following transactions during its first quarter:

Sept. 1 Issued 50,000 shares of common stock, $500,000.
       1 Paid an attorney $32,000 to help start up and organize the corporation and obtain a corporate charter from the state.
Oct. 2 Issued 80,000 shares of common stock, $960,000.
Nov. 30 Declared a cash dividend of $.40 per share to be paid on December 15 to stockholders of record on December 10.

REQUIRED ▶
1. Prepare entries in journal form to record the above transactions.
2. Prepare the stockholders' equity section of Quesnel Corporation's balance sheet on November 30, 20xx. Net income for the quarter was $80,000.

P 7.

LO1 **Preferred and Common Stock**
LO4 **Dividends and Dividends Yield**

DeMarcello Corporation had both common stock and preferred stock outstanding from 20x2 through 20x4. Information about each stock for the three years is as follows:

Type	Par Value	Shares Outstanding	Other
Preferred	$100	40,000	7% cumulative
Common	20	600,000	

The company paid $140,000, $800,000, and $1,100,000 in dividends for 20x2 through 20x4, respectively. The market price per common share was $15 and $17 per share at the end of years 20x3 and 20x4, respectively.

REQUIRED ▶
1. Determine the dividends per share and total dividends paid to the common and preferred stockholders each year.
2. Assuming that the preferred stock was noncumulative, repeat the computations performed in **1**.
3. Calculate the 20x3 and 20x4 dividends yield for common stock using dividends per share computed in **2**.
4. How are cumulative preferred stock and noncumulative preferred stock similar to long-term bonds? How do they differ from long-term bonds?

P 8.
LO1 Comprehensive Stockholders'
LO2 Equity Transactions
LO3
LO4
LO5
LO6

Czerepak, Inc., was organized and authorized to issue 10,000 shares of $100 par value, 9 percent preferred stock and 100,000 shares of no-par, $5 stated value common stock on July 1, 20xx. Stock-related transactions for Czerepak are as follows:

July	1	Issued 20,000 shares of common stock at $11 per share.
	1	Issued 1,000 shares of common stock at $11 per share for services rendered in connection with the organization of the company.
	2	Issued 2,000 shares of preferred stock at par value for cash.
	10	Issued 5,000 shares of common stock for land on which the asking price was $70,000. Market value of the stock was $12. Management wishes to record the land at full market value of the stock.
Aug.	2	Purchased 3,000 shares of its common stock at $13 per share.
	10	Declared a cash dividend for one month on the outstanding preferred stock and $.02 per share on common stock outstanding, payable on August 22 to stockholders of record on August 12.
	12	Date of record for cash dividends.
	22	Paid cash dividends.

REQUIRED ▶
1. Record the transactions in journal form.
2. Prepare the stockholders' equity section of the balance sheet as it would appear on August 31, 20xx. Net income for July and August was $25,000.

SKILLS DEVELOPMENT CASES

Conceptual Analysis

SD 1.
LO1 Reasons for Issuing Common
LO2 Stock

In a recent year, Avaya, Inc. <www.avaya.com>, an East Coast telecommunications company, issued 34,300,000 shares of common stock for a total of $212,000,000.[15] As a growing company, Avaya could have raised this significant amount of money by issuing long-term bonds, but the company's bond rating had recently been lowered. What are some advantages of issuing common stock as opposed to bonds? What are some disadvantages?

SD 2.
LO4 Reasons for Issuing Preferred Stock

Preferred stock is a hybrid security; it has some of the characteristics of stock and some of the characteristics of bonds. Historically, preferred stock has not been a popular means of financing. In the past few years, however, it has become more attractive to companies and individual investors alike, and investors are buying large amounts because of high yields. Large preferred stock issues have been made by such banking firms as Chase <www.chase.com>, Citibank <www.citigroup.com>, HSBC Bank USA <www.us.hsbc.com>, and Wells Fargo <www.wellsfargo.com>, as well as by other companies. The dividends yields on these stocks are over 9 percent, higher than the interest rates on bonds of comparable risk.[16] Especially popular are preferred equity redemption convertible stocks, or PERCs, which are automatically convertible into common stock after three years if the company does not call them first and retire them. What reasons can you give for the popularity of preferred stock, and of PERCs in particular, when the tax-deductible interest on bonds is lower? Discuss from both the company's and the investor's standpoint.

SD 3.
LO6 Purposes of Treasury Stock

Many companies in recent years have bought back their common stock. For example, IBM <www.ibm.com>, with large cash holdings, spent almost $27 billion over five years repurchasing its stock. What are the reasons companies buy back their own shares? What is the effect of common stock buybacks on earnings per share, return on equity, return on assets, debt to equity, and the current ratio?

Ethical Dilemma

SD 4. Compensation of senior management is often tied to earnings per share or return on equity. Treasury stock purchases have a favorable impact on both these measures. In the recent buyback boom, many companies borrowed money to purchase treasury shares, resulting in a higher debt to equity ratio. In some cases, the motivation for the borrowing and repurchase of shares was the desire of executives to secure their year-end cash bonuses. Did these executives act ethically? Were their actions in the best interests of stockholders? Why or why not? How might such behavior be avoided in the future?

LO1 Ethics, Management
LO6 Compensation, and Treasury Stock

Research Activity

SD 5. Select the annual reports of three corporations from sources in your library or from the Fingraph® Financial Analyst™ CD-ROM software that accompanies this text. You can choose them from the same industry or at random, at the direction of your instructor. (Note: You may be asked to use these companies again in the Research Activity cases in later chapters.) Prepare a table with a column for each corporation. Then answer the following questions for each corporation: Does it have preferred stock? If so, what are the preferred stock's par value and dividend, and is the stock cumulative or convertible? Is the common stock par value or no-par? What is its par value or stated value? What cash dividends, if any, did the corporation pay in the past year? What is the dividends yield? From the notes to the financial statements, determine whether the corporation has an employee stock option plan. If so, what are some of its provisions? What is the return on equity? Be prepared to discuss the characteristics of the stocks and dividends of the three corporations in class.

LO1 Comparison of Stockholders'
LO2 Equity Characteristics
LO3
LO4
LO5

Decision-Making Practice

SD 6. Northeast Servotech Corporation, which offers services to the computer industry, has expanded rapidly in recent years. Because of its profitability, the company has been able to grow without obtaining external financing. This fact is reflected in its current balance sheet, which contains no long-term debt. The liabilities and stockholders' equity sections of the balance sheet on March 31, 20xx, appear below.

LO1 Analysis of Alternative
LO2 Financing Methods

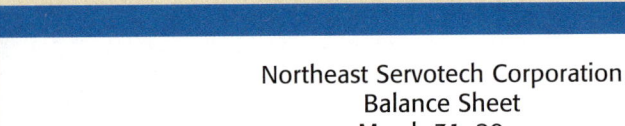

Northeast Servotech Corporation
Balance Sheet
March 31, 20xx

Liabilities

Current liabilities	$ 500,000

Stockholders' Equity

Common stock, $10 par value, 500,000 shares authorized, 100,000 shares issued and outstanding	$1,000,000	
Paid-in capital in excess of par value, common	1,800,000	
Retained earnings	1,700,000	
Total stockholders' equity		4,500,000
Total liabilities and stockholders' equity		$5,000,000

The company now has the opportunity to double its size by purchasing the operations of a rival company for $4,000,000. If the purchase goes through, Northeast Servotech will become one of the top companies in its specialized industry. The problem for management is how to finance the purchase. After much study and discussion with bankers and underwriters, management has prepared the following three financing alternatives to present to the board of directors, which must authorize the purchase and the financing:

Alternative A The company could issue $4,000,000 of long-term debt. Given the company's financial rating and the current market rates, management believes the company will have to pay an interest rate of 12 percent on the debt.

Alternative B The company could issue 40,000 shares of 8 percent, $100 par value preferred stock.

Alternative C The company could issue 100,000 additional shares of $10 par value common stock at $40 per share.

Management explains to the board that the interest on the long-term debt is tax-deductible and that the applicable income tax rate is 40 percent. The board members know that a dividend of $.80 per share of common stock was paid last year, up from $.60 and $.40 per share in the two years before that. The board has had a policy of regular increases in dividends of $.20 per share. It believes each of the three financing alternatives is feasible and now wants to study the financial effects of each one.

1. Prepare a schedule to show how the liabilities and stockholders' equity sections of Northeast Servotech's balance sheet would look under each alternative, and compute the debt to equity ratio (total liabilities ÷ total stockholders' equity) for each.
2. Compute and compare the cash needed to pay the interest or dividends for each kind of new financing, net of income taxes, in the first year.
3. How might the cash needed to pay for the financing change in future years under each alternative?
4. Prepare a memorandum to the board of directors that evaluates the alternatives in order of preference based on cash flow effects, giving arguments for and against each.

Group Activity: Assign the alternatives to different groups to analyze and present to members of the class who act as the board of directors.

FINANCIAL REPORTING AND ANALYSIS CASES

Interpreting Financial Reports

FRA 1. Netscape Communications Corporation <www.netscape.com>, now part of AOL–Time Warner, is a leading provider of software that links people and information over the Internet and intranets. It is one of the great success stories of the Internet age. When Netscape went public with an IPO, it issued stock at $14 per share. In its second year as a public company, it advertised a common stock issue in *The Wall Street Journal*:

LO1 Effect of Stock Issue
LO2
LO5

6,440,000 Shares
NETSCAPE
Common Stock
Price $53¾ a share

If Netscape sold all these shares at the offering price of $53.75, the net proceeds before issue costs would have been $346.15 million. Below is a portion of the stockholders' equity section of the balance sheet adapted from Netscape's annual report, which was issued prior to this stock offering.

Stockholders' Equity
(In thousands)

Common stock, $.0001 par value, 200,000,000 shares authorized, 81,063,158 shares issued and outstanding	$ 8
Additional paid-in capital	196,749
Accumulated deficit	(16,314)

1. Assume the net proceeds from the sale of 6,440,000 shares at $53.75 were $342.6 million after issue costs. Record the stock issuance on Netscape's accounting records in journal form.
2. Prepare the portion of the stockholders' equity section of the balance sheet shown at the bottom of the previous page after the issue of the common stock, based on the information given. Round all answers to the nearest thousand.
3. Based on your answer in **2,** did Netscape have to increase its authorized shares to undertake this stock issue?
4. What amount per share did Netscape receive and how much did Netscape's underwriters receive to help in issuing the stock if investors paid $53.75 per share? What do underwriters do to earn their fee?

FRA 2.
LO4 Effect of Deferring Preferred Dividends

US Airways <www.usairways.com> had indefinitely deferred the quarterly dividend on its $358 million of cumulative convertible 9¼ percent preferred stock.[17] According to a US Airways spokesperson, the company did not want to "continue to pay a dividend while the company is losing money." Others interpreted the action as "an indication of a cash crisis situation."

At the time, Berkshire Hathaway <www.berkshirehathaway.com>, the large company run by Warren Buffett and the owner of the preferred stock, was not happy, but US Airways was able to turn around, become profitable, and return to paying its cumulative dividends on preferred stock. Berkshire Hathaway was able to convert the preferred stock into 9.24 million common shares of US Airways' common stock at $38.74 per share at a time when the market value had risen to $62.[18]

What is cumulative convertible preferred stock? Why is deferring dividends on those shares a drastic action? What is the impact on profitability and liquidity? Why did using preferred stock instead of long-term bonds as a financing method probably save the company from bankruptcy? What was Berkshire Hathaway's gain on its investment at the time of the conversion?

International Company

FRA 3.
LO2 Stockholders' Equity and
LO3 Dividends

Roche Group <www.roche.com> is a giant Swiss pharmaceutical company. Its stockholders' equity shows how little importance common stock, which the Swiss call *share capital,* typically has in the financing of Swiss companies:[19]

	2001	2000
Shareholders' equity (in millions of Swiss francs)		
Share capital	160	160
Retained earnings	32,273	31,614
Total shareholders' equity	32,433	31,774

When Swiss companies need financing, they often rely on debt financing from large Swiss banks and other debt markets. With only 160 million Swiss francs (835 million shares) in share capital, Roche has had few stock issues in its history. In contrast, the company has over 42 billion Swiss francs in liabilities. Roche has been profitable, having built up retained earnings of more than 32 billion Swiss francs over the years. The company also pays a substantial dividend that totaled 981 million Swiss francs in 2001. Calculate the dividends per share and dividends yield assuming a share price of 118.5 Swiss francs. Assuming that dividends and net income were the only factors that affected retained earnings during 2001, how much did Roche earn in 2001 in U.S. dollars (use an exchange rate of 1.7 Swiss francs to the dollar)? What was Roche's return on equity? Comment on Roche's dividend policy and its level of earnings.

Financial Reporting and Analysis Cases

Toys "R" Us Annual Report

FRA 4.

LO1 **Stockholders' Equity**
LO2
LO6

Refer to the Toys "R" Us <www.tru.com> annual report to answer the following questions:

1. What type of capital stock does Toys "R" Us have? What is the par value? How many shares were authorized, issued, and outstanding at the end of fiscal 2002?
2. What is the dividends yield for Toys "R" Us and its relationship to the investors' total return? Does the company rely mostly on stock or on earnings for its stockholders' equity?
3. Does the company have a stock option plan? To whom do the stock options apply? Do employees have significant stock options? Given the market price of the stock shown in the report, do these options represent significant value to the employees?
4. Calculate and discuss the price/earnings ratio and return on equity for 2001 and 2002. The average share price for the fourth quarter was $21.13 and $11.43 for 2001 and 2002, respectively.

Comparison Case: Toys "R" Us and Walgreen Co.

FRA 5.

LO1 **Return on Equity, Treasury Stock, and Dividends Policy**

Refer to the annual report of Toys "R" Us <www.tru.com> and the financial statements and notes of Walgreens <www.walgreens.com> in the Supplement to Chapter 6.

1. Compute the return on equity for both companies for the most recent two years.
2. Did either company purchase treasury stock during these years? How will the purchase of treasury stock affect return on equity and earnings per share?
3. Did either company issue stock during these years? What are the details?
4. Compare the dividend policy of the two companies.

Fingraph® Financial Analyst™

FRA 6.

LO1 **Comparative Analysis of Stockholders' Equity**
LO2
LO6

Select any two companies from the list of Fingraph companies on the Needles Accounting Resource Center Web Site at http://accounting.college.hmco.com/students. Access the Microsoft Excel spreadsheets for the companies you selected.

1. In the Fingraph spreadsheet for each company, identify the equity section of the balance sheet information. Do the companies have more than one kind of capital stock? Do the companies have treasury stock?
2. Using the Fingraph CD-ROM software, prepare a page of text that summarizes the price/earnings ratio and dividends yield for each company.
3. Using the Fingraph CD-ROM software, prepare a page of text that summarizes the financing section of each company's statement of cash flows.
4. Write a one-page summary highlighting the types of capital stock and the significance of treasury stock for these companies. Mention the extent to which they raised cash from recent stock issues or used cash to repurchase capital stock. Describe the impact on total equity. Also compare the price/earnings ratio and dividends yield trends of the two companies. Include your Fingraph pages with your report.

Internet Case

FRA 7.

LO1 **Comparison of Financing of Internet Companies**
LO3
LO4
LO5
LO6

Many Internet start-up companies have gone public in recent years. These companies are generally unprofitable and require a great deal of cash to finance expansion. They also reward their employees with stock options. Choose any two of the following Internet companies: Amazon.com <www.amazon.com>, Yahoo! <www.yahoo.com>, eBay Inc. <www.ebay.com>, or AOL-Time Warner <www.aoltw.com>. Go to the web sites of the two companies you have selected. In their latest annual reports, look at the financing section of the statement of cash flows for the last three years. How have these two companies financed their businesses? Have they issued stock or long-term debt? Have they purchased treasury stock, paid dividends, or issued stock under stock option plans? Are the companies profitable (see net income or earnings at the top of the statement)? Are your findings in line with your expectations about these Internet companies? Find each company's stock price, either on its web site or in a newspaper, and compare it with the average issue price of that company's past stock issues. Summarize your findings.

15

Chapter 15 focuses on the components of the corporate income statement and the statement of stockholders' equity within the context of evaluating quality of earnings. The chapter also covers earnings per share, stock dividends, stock splits, and book value per share.

The Corporate Income Statement and the Statement of Stockholders' Equity

LEARNING OBJECTIVES

LO1 Prepare a corporate income statement and identify the issues related to evaluating the quality of earnings.

LO2 Show the relationships among income taxes expense, deferred income taxes, and net of taxes.

LO3 Describe the disclosure on the income statement of discontinued operations, extraordinary items, and accounting changes.

LO4 Compute earnings per share.

LO5 Prepare a statement of stockholders' equity.

LO6 Account for stock dividends and stock splits.

LO7 Calculate book value per share.

DECISION POINT A USER'S FOCUS

AMR Corporation <www.amrcorp.com> AMR Corporation, American Airlines' parent company, is one of the two largest airline companies in the United States. Its operating results are of interest to many people, but interpreting these results is not always easy. Net earnings per share is the "bottom line" by which many investors judge a company's success or failure. For instance, we know that during 2001 and 2002, the airline industry was adversely affected by the 9/11 attacks and the impending war in Iraq. This is reflected in AMR's basic earnings per share over the past three years, as shown in the Financial Highlights. Net earnings (loss) per share have declined from a positive in 2000 to substantial losses in 2001 and 2002. Note, however, that other factors affect earnings per share. The results in 2002 were also adversely affected by the cumulative effect of an accounting change of $6.35 per share, which made the results appear worse than the company's loss from continuing operations of $16.22. Also, in 2000, the company had discontinued operations and an extraordinary loss.[1] To truly understand a company's "bottom line," it is important to know the various components. In fact, many analysts consider income (loss) from continuing operations to be a better indicator than the "bottom-line" numbers of a company's future operations. In this chapter, we examine the components of the corporate income statement and the statement of stockholders' equity with a view to understanding their impact on a company's future operations.

LO3 Sales Mix Decision

P 7. Dr. Massy, a doctor specializing in internal medicine, wants to analyze his sales mix to find out how the time of his physician assistant, Consuela Ortiz, can be used to generate the highest operating income. Ortiz sees patients in the office, consults with patients over the telephone, and conducts one daily weight-loss support group attended by up to 50 patients. Statistics for the three daily services are:

	Office Visits	Phone Calls	Weight-Loss Support Group
Maximum number of patient billings per day	20	40	50
Minutes per billing	15	6	60
Billing rate	$50	$25	$10
Variable costs	$25	$12	$ 5

Ortiz works seven hours a day.

REQUIRED
1. Determine the best sales mix. Rank the services in order of their profitability.
2. Based on the ranking in **1**, how much time should Ortiz spend on each service in a day? (*Hint:* Remember to consider the maximum number of patient billings per day.) What would be the daily total contribution margin generated by Ortiz?
3. Dr. Massy believes the ranking is incorrect. He knows that the daily 60-minute meeting of the weight-loss support group is attended by 50 patients and should continue to be offered. If the new ranking for the services is (1) weight-loss support group, (2) phone calls, and (3) office visits, how much time should Ortiz spend on each service in a day? What would be the total contribution margin generated by Ortiz, assuming the weight-loss support group has the maximum number of patient billings?
4. Which ranking would you recommend? What additional amount of total contribution margin would be generated if your recommendation is accepted?

LO5 Capital Investment Decision:
LO6 Comprehensive
LO7

P 8. The Arcadia Manufacturing Company, based in Arcadia, Florida, is one of the fastest-growing companies in its industry. According to Ms. Prinze, the company's production vice president, keeping up-to-date with technological changes is what makes the company successful.

Prinze feels that a machine introduced recently would fill an important need. The machine has an estimated useful life of four years, a purchase price of $250,000, and a residual value of $25,000. The company controller has estimated average annual net income of $11,250 and the following cash flows for the new machine:

Year	Cash Inflows	Cash Outflows	Net Cash Inflows
1	$325,000	$250,000	$75,000
2	320,000	250,000	70,000
3	315,000	250,000	65,000
4	310,000	250,000	60,000

Prinze uses a 12 percent minimum rate of return and a three-year payback period for capital investment evaluation purposes.

REQUIRED
1. Analyze the data about the machine and decide if the company should purchase it. Use the following methods in your analysis: (a) the net present value method, (b) the accounting rate-of-return method, and (c) the payback period method. Use Tables 3 and 4 in the appendix on future value and present value tables.
2. Summarize the information generated in **1**, and make a recommendation to Prinze.

SKILLS DEVELOPMENT CASES

Conceptual Analysis

LO1 Management Decision Cycle

SD 1. Two weeks ago your cousin Edna moved from New York City to Houston. She needs a car to drive to work and to run errands but has no experience in selecting a car, and has asked for your help. Using the management cycle presented in this chapter, write her a letter explaining how she can approach making this decision.

packing costs would be $4.30 per 1,000 brochures. Also, the share of general and administrative expenses (fixed costs) to be allocated would be $5.25 per direct labor dollar.

REQUIRED ▶ 1. Prepare an analysis for Crystal management to use in deciding whether to accept or reject Keystone Resorts' offer. What decision should be made?
2. What is the lowest possible price Crystal can charge per thousand and still make a $6,000 profit on the order?

P 4.

LO5 Net Present Value Method
LO6

Sonja and Sons, Inc., owns and operates a group of apartment buildings. Management wants to sell one of its older four-family buildings and buy a new structure. The old building, which was purchased 25 years ago for $100,000, has a 40-year estimated life. The current market value is $80,000, and if it is sold, the cash inflow will be $67,675. Annual net cash inflows from the old building are expected to average $16,000 for the remainder of its estimated useful life.

The new building being considered will cost $300,000. It has an estimated useful life of 25 years. Net cash inflows are expected to be $50,000 annually.

Assume that (1) all cash flows occur at year end, (2) the company uses straight-line depreciation, (3) the buildings will have a residual value equal to 10 percent of their purchase price, and (4) the minimum rate of return is 14 percent. Use Tables 3 and 4 in the appendix on future value and present value tables.

REQUIRED ▶ 1. Compute the net present value of future cash flows from the old building.
2. What will be the net present value of cash flows if the new building is purchased?
3. Should the company keep the old building or purchase the new one?

P 5.

LO7 Accounting Rate-of-Return and Payback Period Methods

The Raab Company is expanding its production facilities to include a new product line: a sporty automotive tire rim. Using new computerized machinery, tire rims can now be produced with little labor cost. The controller has advised management about two such machines. The details about each machine are as follows:

	XJS Machine	HZT Machine
Cost of machine	$500,000	$550,000
Residual value	50,000	55,000
Average annual net income	34,965	40,670
Annual net cash inflows	91,215	90,170

The minimum rate of return is 12 percent. The maximum payback period is six years. (Where necessary, round calculations to the nearest dollar.)

REQUIRED ▶ 1. For each machine, compute the projected accounting rate of return.
2. Compute the payback period for each machine.
3. From the information generated in **1** and **2**, which machine should be purchased? Why?

ALTERNATE PROBLEMS

P 6.

LO3 Outsourcing Decision

The Stainless Refrigerator Company purchases and installs ice makers in its products. The ice makers cost $138 per case, and each case contains 12 ice makers. The supplier recently gave advance notice that the price will rise by 50 percent immediately. Stainless Refrigerator Company has idle equipment that, with only a few minor changes, could be used to produce similar ice makers.

Cost estimates have been prepared under the assumption that the company could make the product itself. Direct materials would cost $100.80 per 12 ice makers. Direct labor required would be 10 minutes per ice maker at a labor rate of $18.00 per hour. Variable manufacturing overhead would be $4.60 per ice maker. Fixed manufacturing overhead, which would be incurred under either decision alternative, would be $32,420 a year for depreciation and $234,000 a year for other costs. Production and usage are estimated at 75,000 ice makers a year. (Assume that any idle equipment cannot be used for any other purpose.)

REQUIRED ▶ 1. Prepare an incremental analysis to determine whether the ice makers should be made within the company or purchased from the outside supplier at the higher price.
2. Compute the unit cost to (1) make one ice maker and (2) buy one ice maker.

Perform an incremental analysis to determine if Bagels, Inc., should process its products further. Explain your findings.

P 2.

LO3 Decision to Discontinue Segment

Seven months ago, Naib Publishing Company published its first book (Book N). Since then, the company has added four more books to its product list (Books S, Q, X, and H). Management is considering proposals for three more new books, but editorial capacity limits the company to producing only seven books annually. Before deciding which of the proposed books to publish, management wants you to evaluate the performance of its existing book list. Recent revenue and cost data appear below.

Naib Publishing Company
Product Profit and Loss Summary
For the Year Ended December 31, 20x8

	Book N	Book S	Book Q	Book X	Book H	Company Totals
Sales	$813,800	$782,000	$634,200	$944,100	$707,000	$3,881,100
Less variable costs						
Materials and binding	$325,520	$312,800	$190,260	$283,230	$212,100	$1,323,910
Editorial services	71,380	88,200	73,420	57,205	80,700	370,905
Author royalties	130,208	125,120	101,472	151,056	113,120	620,976
Sales commissions	162,760	156,400	95,130	141,615	141,400	697,305
Other selling costs	50,682	44,740	21,708	18,334	60,700	196,164
Total variable costs	$740,550	$727,260	$481,990	$651,440	$608,020	$3,209,260
Contribution margin	$ 73,250	$ 54,740	$152,210	$292,660	$ 98,980	$ 671,840
Less total fixed costs	97,250	81,240	89,610	100,460	82,680	451,240
Operating income	($ 24,000)	($ 26,500)	$ 62,600	$192,200	$ 16,300	$ 220,600
Direct fixed costs included in total fixed costs above	$ 51,200	$ 65,100	$ 49,400	$ 69,100	$ 58,800	$ 293,600

Projected data for the proposed new books are Book P, sales, $450,000, contribution margin, $45,000; Book T, sales, $725,000, contribution margin, ($25,200); and Book R, sales, $913,200, contribution margin, $115,500. Projected direct fixed costs are: Book P, $5,000; Book T, $6,000; Book R, $40,000.

REQUIRED

1. Analyze the performance of the five books currently being published.
2. Should the company eliminate any of its present products? If so, which one(s)?
3. Identify the new books you would use to replace those eliminated. Justify your answer.

P 3.

LO3 Special Order Decision

Keystone Resorts, Ltd., has approached Crystal Printers, Inc., with a special order to produce 300,000 two-page brochures. Most of Crystal's work consists of recurring short-run orders. Keystone Resorts is offering a one-time order, and Crystal has the capacity to handle the order over a two-month period.

Keystone's management has stated that the company would be unwilling to pay more than $48 per 1,000 brochures. The following cost data were assembled by Crystal's controller for this decision analysis: Direct materials (paper) would be $26.50 per 1,000 brochures. Direct labor costs would be $6.80 per 1,000 brochures. Direct materials (ink) would be $4.40 per 1,000 brochures. Variable production overhead would be $6.20 per 1,000 brochures. Machine maintenance (fixed cost) is $1.00 per direct labor dollar. Other fixed production overhead amounts to $2.40 per direct labor dollar. Variable

Using the net present value method, prepare an analysis to determine whether the company should purchase the machine. Use Tables 3 and 4 in the appendix on future value and present value tables.

E 11.
LO6 Capital Investment Decision: Net Present Value Method

H and Y Service Station is planning to invest in automatic car wash equipment valued at $250,000. The owner estimates that the equipment will increase annual net cash inflows by $46,000. The equipment is expected to have a ten-year useful life with an estimated residual value of $50,000. The company requires a 14 percent minimum rate of return. Using the net present value method, prepare an analysis to determine whether the company should purchase the equipment. How important is the estimate of residual value to this decision? Use Tables 3 and 4 in the appendix on future value and present value tables.

E 12.
LO6 Capital Investment Decision: Net Present Value Method

Assume the same facts for H and Y Service Station as in **E11,** except that the company requires a 20 percent minimum rate of return. Using the net present value method, prepare an analysis to determine whether the company should purchase the equipment. How important is the estimate of residual value to this decision? Use Tables 3 and 4 in the appendix on future value and present value tables.

E 13.
LO7 Capital Investment Decision: Payback Period Method

Soaking Wet, Inc., a manufacturer of gears for lawn sprinklers, is thinking about adding a new fully automated machine. This machine can produce gears the company currently produces on its third shift. The machine has an estimated useful life of 10 years and will cost $800,000. Gross cash revenue from the machine will be about $520,000 per year, and related operating expenses, including depreciation, should total $500,000. Depreciation is estimated to be $80,000 annually. The payback period should be five years or less.

Use the payback period method to determine whether the company should invest in the new machine. Show your computations to support your answer.

E 14.
LO7 Capital Investment Decision: Accounting Rate-of-Return Method

Perfection Sound, Inc., a manufacturer of stereo speakers, is thinking about adding a new plastic injection molding machine. This machine can produce speaker parts that the company now buys from outsiders. The machine has an estimated useful life of 14 years and will cost $425,000. Residual value of the new machine is $42,500. Gross cash revenue from the machine will be about $400,000 per year, and related cash expenses should total $310,050. Depreciation is estimated to be $30,350 annually. Management has decided that only capital investments that yield at least a 20 percent return will be accepted.

Using the accounting rate-of-return method, decide whether the company should invest in the machine. Show all computations to support your decision.

PROBLEMS

P 1.
LO3 Sell or Process-Further Decision

Bagels, Inc., produces and sells 20 types of bagels by the dozen. Bagels are priced at $6.00 per dozen and cost $.20 per unit to produce. The company is considering further processing the bagels into two products: bagels with cream cheese and bagel sandwiches. It would cost an additional $.50 per unit to produce bagels with cream cheese, and the new selling price would be $2.50 each. It would cost an additional $1.00 per sandwich to produce bagel sandwiches, and the new selling price would be $3.50 each.

REQUIRED ▶
1. Identify the relevant per unit costs and revenues for the alternatives. Are there any sunk costs?
2. Based on the information in **1**, should Bagels, Inc., expand its product offerings?
3. Suppose that Bagels, Inc., did expand its product line to include bagels with cream cheese and bagel sandwiches. Based on customer feedback, the company determined that it could further process those two products into bagels with fruit and cream cheese and bagel sandwiches with cheese. The company's accountant compiled the following information:

Product (per unit)	Sales Revenue if Sold with No Further Processing	Sales Revenue if Processed Further	Additional Processing Costs
Bagels with cream cheese	$2.50	$3.50	Fruit: $1.00
Bagel sandwiches	$3.50	$4.50	Cheese: $.50

1. Compute the most profitable combination of products to be produced in 20x8.
2. Prepare an income statement using the contribution margin format for the product volume computed in **1**.

LO3 Sales Mix Decision

E 6. Grady Enterprises manufactures three computer games. They are called Rising Star, Ghost Master, and Road Warrior. The product line data are as follows:

	Rising Star	Ghost Master	Road Warrior
Current unit sales demand	20,000	30,000	18,000
Machine hours per unit	2	1	2.5
Selling price per unit	$24.00	$18.00	$32.00
Unit variable manufacturing costs	$12.50	$10.00	$18.75
Unit variable selling costs	$6.50	$5.00	$6.25

The current production capacity is 100,000 machine hours.

1. Which computer game should be manufactured first? Which should be manufactured second? Which last?
2. How many of each type of computer game should be manufactured and sold to maximize the company's contribution margin based on the current production activity of 100,000 machine hours? What is the total contribution margin for that combination?

LO3 Sell or Process-Further Decision

E 7. Six Star Pizza manufactures frozen pizzas and calzones and sells them for $4 each. Six Star is currently considering a proposal to manufacture and sell fully prepared products. The following relevant information has been gathered by management:

Product	Sales Revenue with No Additional Processing	Sales Revenue if Processed Further	Additional Processing Costs
Pizza	$4	$ 8	$5
Calzone	$4	$10	$5

Use incremental analysis to determine which products Six Star Pizza should offer.

LO4 Income Taxes and Net Cash Flow

E 8. San Falesco Company has a tax rate of 25 percent on taxable income. It is considering a capital project that will make the following annual contribution to operating income:

Cash revenues	$ 500,000
Cash expenses	(300,000)
Depreciation	(150,000)
Operating income	$ 50,000
Income taxes at 25%	(12,500)
Operating income after income taxes	$ 37,500

1. Determine the net cash inflows for this project in two different ways. Are net cash flows the same under both approaches?
2. What is the impact of income taxes on net cash flows?

LO5 Using the Present Value Tables

E 9. For each of the following situations, identify the correct factor to use from Table 3 or 4 in the appendix on future value and present value tables. Also, compute the appropriate present value.

1. Annual net cash inflows of $22,500 for twelve years, discounted at 14%
2. The following five years of cash inflows, discounted at 10%:

Year 1	$35,000
Year 2	20,000
Year 3	30,000
Year 4	40,000
Year 5	50,000

3. The amount of $70,000 to be received at the beginning of year 7, discounted at 14%

LO6 Capital Investment Decision: Net Present Value Method

E 10. Qen and Associates wants to buy an automated coffee roaster/grinder/brewer. This piece of equipment would have a useful life of six years, would cost $219,500, and would increase annual net cash inflows by $57,000. Assume there is no residual value at the end of six years. The company's minimum rate of return is 14 percent.

Standard unit cost data for 400,000 baseballs
Direct materials	$ .90
Direct labor	.60
Manufacturing overhead	
Variable	.50
Fixed ($100,000 ÷ 400,000)	.25
Packaging per unit	.30
Advertising ($60,000 ÷ 400,000)	.15
Other fixed selling and administrative	
expenses ($120,000 ÷ 400,000)	.30
Product unit cost	$ 3.00
Unit selling price	$ 4.00
Total estimated bulk packaging costs for special order (30,000 baseballs: 500 per box)	$2,500

1. Should Jens Sporting Goods, Inc., accept Leiden's offer?
2. What would be the minimum order price per baseball if Jens would like to earn a profit of $3,000 from the special order?

LO3 Elimination of Unprofitable Segment Decision

E 4. Guld's Glass, Inc., has three divisions: Commercial, Nonprofit, and Residential. The segmented income statement for 20x8 revealed the following:

Guld's Glass, Inc.
Divisional Profit Summary and Decision Analysis

	Commercial Division	Nonprofit Division	Residential Division	Total Company
Sales	$290,000	$533,000	$837,000	$1,660,000
Less variable costs	147,000	435,000	472,000	1,054,000
Contribution margin	$143,000	$ 98,000	$365,000	$ 606,000
Less direct fixed costs	124,000	106,000	139,000	369,000
Segment margin	$ 19,000	($ 8,000)	$226,000	$ 237,000
Less common fixed costs				168,000
Operating income				$ 69,000

1. How will Guld's Glass, Inc., be affected if the Nonprofit Division is dropped?
2. If the Nonprofit Division is dropped, the sales of the Residential Division will decrease by 10 percent. How will Guld's Glass, Inc., be affected if the Nonprofit Division is dropped?

LO3 Sales Mix Decision

E 5. EZ, Inc., manufactures two products that require both machine processing and labor operations. Although there is unlimited demand for both products, EZ could devote all its capacities to a single product. Unit prices, cost data, and processing requirements are:

	Product E	Product Z
Unit selling price	$80	$220
Unit variable costs	$40	$90
Machine hours per unit	.4	1.4
Labor hours per unit	2	6

In 20x8 the company will be limited to 160,000 machine hours and 120,000 labor hours. Fixed costs for 20x8 are $1,000,000.

Chapter 27 Analysis for Decision Making

LO6 Capital Investment Decision: Net Present Value Method

SE 8. Noway Jose Communications, Inc., is considering the purchase of a new piece of computerized data transmission equipment. Estimated annual net cash inflows for the new equipment are $575,000. The equipment costs $2 million, it has a five-year life, and it will have no residual value at the end of the five years. The company has a minimum rate of return of 12 percent. Compute the net present value of the piece of equipment. Should the company purchase it? Use Table 4 in the appendix on future and present value tables.

LO7 Capital Investment Decision: Payback Period Method

SE 9. East-West Cable, Inc., is considering the purchase of new data transmission equipment. Estimated annual cash revenues for the new equipment are $1 million, and operating costs (including depreciation of $400,000) are $825,000. The equipment costs $2 million, it has a five-year life, and it will have no residual value at the end of the five years. Compute the payback period for the piece of equipment. Does this method yield a positive or a negative response to the proposal to buy the equipment, assuming the company sets a maximum payback period of four years?

LO7 Capital Investment Decision: Accounting Rate-of-Return Method

SE 10. Best Cleaners is considering whether to purchase a delivery truck that will cost $29,000, last six years, and have an estimated residual value of $5,000. Average annual net income from the delivery service is estimated to be $4,000. Best Cleaners' owners seek to earn an accounting rate of return of 20 percent. Compute the average investment cost and the accounting rate of return. Should the investment be made?

EXERCISES

LO2 Incremental Analysis

E 1. The managers of Lennox Company must decide which of two mill blade grinders—Y or Z—to buy. The grinders have the same purchase price but different revenues and cost characteristics. The company currently owns Grinder X, which it bought three years ago for $15,000 and which has accumulated depreciation of $9,000 and a book value of $6,000. Grinder X is now obsolete as a result of advances in technology and cannot be sold or traded in.

The accountant has collected the following annual revenue and operating cost estimates for the two new machines:

	Grinder Y	Grinder Z
Increase in revenue	$16,000	$20,000
Increase in annual operating costs		
Direct materials	4,800	4,800
Direct labor	3,000	4,100
Variable manufacturing overhead	2,100	3,000
Fixed manufacturing overhead (depreciation included)	5,000	5,000

1. Identify the relevant data in this problem.
2. Prepare an incremental analysis to aid the managers in their decision.
3. Should the company purchase Grinder Y or Z?

LO3 Outsourcing Decision

E 2. Sunny Hazel, the manager of Cyber Web Services, must decide whether to hire a new employee or to outsource some of the web design work to Ky To, a freelance graphic designer. If she hires a new employee, she will pay $32 per design hour for the employee to work 600 hours and incur service overhead costs of $2 per design hour. If she outsources the work to Ky To, she will pay $36 per design hour for 600 hours of work. She can also redirect the use of a computer and server to generate $4,000 in additional revenue from web page maintenance work. Should Cyber Web Services hire a new designer or outsource the work to Ky To?

LO3 Special Order Decision

E 3. Jens Sporting Goods, Inc., manufactures a complete line of sporting equipment. Leiden Enterprises operates a large chain of discount stores. Leiden has approached Jens with a special order for 30,000 deluxe baseballs. Instead of being packaged separately, the balls are to be bulk packed in boxes containing 500 baseballs each. Leiden is willing to pay $2.45 per baseball. Jens knows that annual expected production is 400,000 baseballs. It also knows that the current year's production is 410,000 baseballs and that the maximum production capacity is 450,000 baseballs. The following additional information is available:

3. Whether competing French restaurants have this entrée on the menu
4. The labor cost of the chef who prepares the chicken
5. The fact that the president of a nearby company, who brings ten guests with him each week, always orders chicken à l'orange.

LO2 Using Incremental Analysis

SE 2. Aries Corporation has assembled the following information related to the purchase of a new automated postage machine.

	Posen Machine	Valuet Machine
Increase in revenue	$43,200	$49,300
Increase in annual operating costs		
Direct materials	12,200	12,200
Direct labor	10,200	10,600
Variable manufacturing overhead	24,500	26,900
Fixed manufacturing overhead (including depreciation)	12,400	12,400

Using incremental analysis and only relevant information, compute the difference in favor of the Valuet machine.

LO3 Outsourcing Decision

SE 3. Marcus Company assembles products from a group of interconnecting parts. Some of the parts are produced by the company, and some are purchased from outside vendors. The vendor for Part X has just increased its price by 35 percent, to $10 per unit for the first 5,000 units and $9 per additional unit ordered each year. The company uses 7,500 units of Part X each year. Unit costs if the company makes the part are:

Direct materials	$3.50
Direct labor	1.75
Variable manufacturing overhead	4.25
Variable selling costs for the assembled product	3.75

Should the company continue to purchase the part, or should it begin making the part?

LO3 Special Order Decision

SE 4. Smith Accounting Services is considering a special order that it received from one of its corporate clients. The special order calls for Smith to prepare the individual tax returns of the corporation's four largest shareholders. The company has idle capacity that could be used to complete the special order. The following data have been gathered about the preparation of individual tax returns:

Materials cost per page	$1
Average hourly labor rate	$60
Standard hours per return	4
Standard pages per return	10
Variable overhead cost per page	$.50
Fixed overhead cost per page	$.50

Smith Accounting Services would be satisfied with a $40 gross profit per return. Compute the minimum bid price for the entire order.

LO3 Sales Mix Decision

SE 5. Snow, Inc., makes three kinds of snowboards, but it has a limited number of machine hours available to make them. Product line data are as follows:

	Wood	Plastic	Graphite
Machine hours per unit	1.25	1.0	1.5
Selling price per unit	$100	$120	$200
Variable manufacturing cost per unit	45	50	100
Variable selling costs per unit	15	26	36

In what order should the snowboard product lines be produced?

LO4 Capital Investment Analysis and Revenue Measures

SE 6. Maize Corp. is analyzing a proposal to switch its factory over to a lights-out operation. To do so, it must acquire a fully automated machine. The machine will be able to produce an entire product line in a single operation. Projected annual net cash inflows from the machine are $180,000, and projected net income is $120,000. Why is projected net income $60,000 less than projected net cash inflows? Identify possible causes.

LO5 Time Value of Money

SE 7. Heidi Layne recently inherited a trust fund from a distant relative. On January 2, the bank managing the trust fund notified Layne that she has the option of receiving a lump-sum check for $175,500 or leaving the money in the trust fund and receiving an annual year-end check for $20,000 for each of the next 20 years. Layne likes to earn at least an 8 percent return on her investments. What should she do?

Chapter Assignments

BUILDING YOUR KNOWLEDGE FOUNDATION

QUESTIONS

1. Briefly describe how each stage of the management cycle applies to short-run decision analysis.
2. List some common types of short-run decisions that can be made during the executing stage of the management cycle.
3. List qualitative factors that will influence a short-run decision.
4. What is incremental analysis? What types of decision analyses depend on the incremental approach?
5. What is an opportunity cost?
6. List the business activities that are likely to be outsourced. What makes them attractive for outsourcing?
7. Which data are relevant to a make-or-buy decision in a manufacturing operation?
8. What are two approaches to making a special order decision?
9. What are the two steps in the analysis for a sales mix decision?
10. What is the role of joint costs in sell or process-further decision analysis?
11. What are capital investments? Give examples of some capital investments.
12. Define *capital investment analysis*.
13. Distinguish between cost savings and net cash inflows.
14. Why is it important to know whether a capital investment will produce equal cash flows or unequal cash flows?
15. "In capital investment analysis, the carrying value of an asset is irrelevant, whereas current and future residual values are relevant." Is this statement valid? Why or why not?
16. In the evaluation of equipment replacement proposals, why is depreciation of the old equipment ignored?
17. How does the relationship between depreciation and income taxes affect capital investment analysis?
18. Discuss the statement, "To treat all future income flows alike ignores the time value of money."
19. Which table in the appendix on future value and present value tables is used to determine the present value of a single sum to be received in the future? Which table is used to determine the present value of a series of payments (ordinary annuity) to be received in the future? How is each table used in the net present value method?
20. What is the role of the average cost of capital when the net present value method is used to evaluate capital investment proposals?
21. Is the payback period method very accurate? Defend your answer.
22. What formula is used to determine the accounting rate-of-return?

SHORT EXERCISES

LO1 Qualitative and Quantitative Information in Short-Run Decision Analysis

SE 1. The owner of Mimi's, a French restaurant, is deciding whether to take chicken à l'orange off the menu. Tell whether each of the following pieces of decision information is qualitative or quantitative. If the information is quantitative, specify whether it is financial or nonfinancial.

1. The time needed to prepare the chicken
2. The daily number of customers who order the chicken

REQUIRED

1. Analyze the performance of the four service lines being reviewed. Should Dale Bandy eliminate any of the service lines? Explain your answer.
2. Why might Bandy want to continue providing unprofitable service lines?
3. Even though some of the unprofitable services can be eliminated, the company still has an operating loss. Identify some possible causes for poor performance by the services. What actions do you recommend?

ANSWER TO REVIEW PROBLEM

1. When deciding whether to eliminate any of the four service lines, Dale Bandy should concentrate on the service lines that have a negative segment margin. If the revenues from a service line are less than the sum of its variable and direct fixed costs, then other service lines must cover some of the losing line's costs while carrying the burden of the common fixed costs.

Home Services, Inc.
Segment Profitability Decision

	Keep Boat Repair and Tile Floor Repair	Drop Boat Repair and Tile Floor Repair	Difference in Favor of Dropping Boat Repair and Tile Floor Repair
Sales	$635,800	$395,100	($240,700)
Less variable costs	548,087	329,050	219,037
Contribution margin	$ 87,713	$ 66,050	($ 21,663)
Less direct fixed costs	81,400	41,000	40,400
Segment margin	$ 6,313	$ 25,050	$ 18,737
Less common fixed costs	32,100	32,100	0
Operating income (loss)	($ 25,787)	($ 7,050)	$ 18,737

By looking at the segmented income statement, Dale Bandy can see that the company will improve its operating income by $18,737 ($6,013 + $12,724) by eliminating the Boat Repair Service and the Tile Floor Repair Service, both of which have a negative segment margin. Bandy's decision can also be supported by the analysis in **2**.

2. Bandy may want to continue offering the unprofitable service lines if their elimination would negatively affect the sale of auto repair or tree trimming services. Bandy may also want to diversify into new markets by offering new services. Bandy should be prepared to suffer some losses initially to enter the new markets.

3. Among the possible causes for poor performance by the company's four services are the following:

   a. Service fees set too low
   b. Inadequate advertising
   c. High direct labor costs
   d. Other variable costs too high
   e. Poor management of fixed costs
   f. Excessive supervision costs

   To improve profitability, the organization can eliminate nonvalue-adding costs, increase service fees, or increase the volume of services provided to customers.

LO3 **Sell or process-further decision:** A decision about whether to sell a joint product at the split-off point or sell it after further processing.

LO1 **Short-run decision analysis:** The systematic examination of any decision whose effects will be most felt over the next year or less.

LO5 **Simple interest:** The interest cost for one or more periods when the amount on which the interest is computed stays the same from period to period.

LO3 **Special order decisions:** Decisions about whether to accept or reject a special order at a price below the normal market price.

LO3 **Split-off point:** A specific point in the production process at which two or more joint products become separate and identifiable. At that point, a company may choose to sell the product as is or process it into another form for sale to a different market.

LO2 **Sunk cost:** A cost that was incurred because of a previous decision and cannot be recovered through the current decision.

LO5 **Time value of money:** The concept that cash flows of equal dollar amounts separated by an interval of time have different present values because of the effect of compound interest.

REVIEW PROBLEM

Short-Run Operating Decision Analysis

LO3 Home Services, Inc., specializes in repair and maintenance services. Recently, its profitability has declined, and Dale Bandy, the company's founder, wants to know which service lines are not meeting the company's profit targets. Once the services have been identified, he will either eliminate them or set higher prices. If higher prices are set, the price structure will cover all variable and fixed operating, selling, and general administrative costs. Four service lines are under serious review. Related data are as follows:

Home Services, Inc.
Segmented Income Statement
For the Year Ended December 31, 20x8

	Auto Repair	Boat Repair	Tile Floor Repair	Tree Trimming	Total Impact
Sales	$297,500	$114,300	$126,400	$97,600	$635,800
Less variable costs					
Direct labor	$119,000	$40,005	$44,240	$34,160	$237,405
Operating supplies	14,875	5,715	6,320	4,880	31,790
Small tools	11,900	4,572	5,056	7,808	29,336
Replacement parts	59,500	22,860	25,280	—	107,640
Truck costs	—	11,430	12,640	14,640	38,710
Selling costs	44,625	17,145	18,960	9,760	90,490
Other variable costs	5,950	2,286	2,528	1,952	12,716
Contribution margin	$ 41,650	$ 10,287	$ 11,376	$24,400	$ 87,713
Less direct fixed costs	35,800	16,300	24,100	5,200	81,400
Segment margin	$ 5,850	($ 6,013)	($ 12,724)	$19,200	$ 6,313
Less common fixed costs					32,100
Operating income (loss)					($ 25,787)

interest increased by $18 ($318 − $300), which exactly equals 6 percent times $300.

PRESENT VALUE

Suppose that you had the choice of receiving $100 either today or one year from today. Intuitively, you would choose to receive the $100 today. Why? You know that if you have the $100 today, you can put it in a savings account to earn interest, so that you will have more than $100 a year from today. Therefore, we can say that an amount to be received in the future (future value) is not worth as much today as the same amount to be received today (present value) because of the cost associated with the passage of time.

Future value and present value are closely related. **Future value** is the amount an investment will be worth at a future date if invested today at compound interest. **Present value** is the amount that must be invested today at a given rate of compound interest to produce a given future value.

For example, assume that Daschel Company needs $1,000 one year from now. How much should the company invest today to achieve that goal if the interest rate is 5 percent? The following equation may be used:

$$\text{Present Value} \times (1.0 + \text{Interest Rate}) = \text{Future Value}$$
$$\text{Present Value} \times 1.05 = \$1,000.00$$
$$\text{Present Value} = \$1,000.00 \div 1.05$$
$$\text{Present Value} = \$952.38$$

● **STOP AND THINK!**
How are present value and future value different?
Present value looks back to determine value in the present, and future value looks forward to determine value at a future time. ■

Thus, to achieve a future value of $1,000.00, a present value of $952.38 must be invested. Interest of 5 percent on $952.38 for one year equals $47.62, and the two amounts added together equal $1,000.00.

PRESENT VALUE OF A SINGLE SUM DUE IN THE FUTURE

When more than one time period is involved, the calculation of present value is more complicated. For example, Reza Company wants to be sure of having $4,000 at the end of three years. How much must the company invest today in a 5 percent savings account to achieve that goal? By adapting the preceding equation, the present value of $4,000 at compound interest of 5 percent for three years in the future may be computed as follows:

Year	Amount at End of Year	Divide by		Present Value at Beginning of Year
3	$4,000.00	÷ 1.05	=	3,809.52
2	3,809.52	÷ 1.05	=	3,628.11
1	3,628.11	÷ 1.05	=	3,455.34

FOCUS ON BUSINESS PRACTICE

How Would You Decide Whether to Buy Rare Dinosaur Bones?

Not-for-profit organizations can also use the techniques of capital investment analysis. For example, the officers of the Field Museum <www.fmnh.org> in Chicago employed these techniques when deciding whether to bid at auction on the most complete skeleton ever found of a *Tyrannosaurus rex*. The museum bought the bones for $8.2 million and spent another $9 million to restore and install the dinosaur, named Sue. The museum projected that Sue would attract 1 million new visitors, who would produce $5 million in admissions and spend several more million dollars on food, gifts, and the like. After deducting operating costs, museum officials used discounted present values to calculate a return on investment of 10.5 percent. Given that the museum's cost of capital was 8.5 percent, Sue's purchase was considered a financial success. Sue has been extremely popular with the public and more than met the museum's attendance goals in the first year after installation.[6]

THE TIME VALUE OF MONEY

LO5 Apply the concept of the time value of money.

RELATED TEXT ASSIGNMENTS
Q: 18, 19
SE: 7
E: 9
P: 4, 8
MRA: 1, 2

An organization has many options for investing capital besides buying fixed assets. Consequently, management expects a fixed asset to yield a reasonable return during its useful life. A key question in capital investment analysis is how to measure the return on a fixed asset. One way is to look at the cash flows the asset will generate during its useful life. When an asset has a long useful life, management will usually analyze those cash flows in terms of the time value of money. The **time value of money** is the concept that cash flows of equal dollar amounts separated by an interval of time have different present values because of the effect of compound interest. The notions of interest, present value, future value, and present value of an ordinary annuity are all related to the time value of money.

INTEREST

KEY POINT: Interest is a cost associated with the passage of time, whether or not there is a stated interest rate.

Interest is the cost associated with the use of money for a specific period of time. Because interest is a cost associated with time and "time is money," interest is an important consideration in any business decision. **Simple interest** is the interest cost for one or more periods when the amount on which the interest is computed stays the same from period to period. **Compound interest** is the interest cost for two or more periods when the amount on which interest is computed changes in each period to include all interest paid in previous periods. In other words, compound interest is interest earned on a principal sum that is increased at the end of each period by the interest for that period.

■ **EXAMPLE: SIMPLE INTEREST** Jo Sanka accepts an 8 percent, $30,000 note due in 90 days. How much will she receive in total when the note comes due? The formula for calculating simple interest is:

$$\text{Interest Expense} = \text{Principal} \times \text{Rate} \times \text{Time}$$
$$= \$30,000 \times 8/100 \times 90/360 = \$600$$

The total that Sanka will receive is computed as follows:

$$\text{Total} = \text{Principal} + \text{Interest}$$
$$= \$30,000 + \$600 = \$30,600$$

If the interest is paid and the note is renewed for an additional 90 days, the interest calculation will remain the same.

■ **EXAMPLE: COMPOUND INTEREST** Andy Clayburn makes a deposit of $5,000 in a savings account that pays 6 percent interest. He expects to leave the principal and accumulated interest in the account for three years. What will be his account total at the end of three years? Assume that the interest is paid at the end of the year, that the interest is added to the principal at that time, and that this total in turn earns interest. The amount at the end of three years is computed as follows:

(1) Year	(2) Principal Amount at Beginning of Year	(3) Annual Amount of Interest (col. 2 × .06)	(4) Accumulated Amount at End of Year (col. 2 + col. 3)
1	$5,000.00	$300.00	$5,300.00
2	5,300.00	318.00	5,618.00
3	5,618.00	337.08	5,955.08

At the end of three years, Clayburn will have $5,955.08 in his savings account. Note that the annual amount of interest increases each year by the interest rate times the interest of the previous year. For example, between year 1 and year 2, the

asset's cost less its residual value, divided by the asset's useful life.) Thus, depreciation expense strongly influences the amount of income taxes a company pays and can lead to significant income tax savings.

Corporate income tax rates vary and can change yearly. To examine how income taxes affect capital investment analysis, assume that a company has a tax rate of 30 percent on taxable income. The company is considering a capital project that will make the following annual contribution to operating income:

Cash revenues	$ 400,000
Cash expenses	(200,000)
Depreciation	(100,000)
Operating income	$ 100,000
Income taxes at 30%	(30,000)
Operating income after income taxes	$ 70,000

The net cash inflows for this project can be determined in two ways:

1. Net cash inflows—receipts and disbursements

Revenues (cash inflows)	$400,000
Cash expenses (outflows)	(200,000)
Income taxes (outflows)	(30,000)
Net cash inflows	$170,000

2. Net cash inflows—income adjustment procedure

Operating income after income taxes	$ 70,000
Add back noncash expenses (depreciation)	100,000
Less noncash revenues	—
Net cash inflows	$170,000

In both computations, the net cash inflows are $170,000, and the total effect of income taxes is to lower the net cash inflows by $30,000.

■ **DISPOSAL OR RESIDUAL VALUES** Proceeds from the sale of an old asset are current cash inflows and are relevant to evaluating a proposed capital investment. Projected disposal or residual values of replacement equipment are also relevant because they represent future cash inflows and usually differ among alternatives. Remember that the residual value, sometimes called the *disposal* or *salvage value*, of an asset will be received at the end of the asset's estimated life.

FOCUS ON INTERNATIONAL BUSINESS

Why Look Beyond the Cost of a Capital Investment?

Because capital investments are made in long-term facilities and projects that require commitments of large amounts of money to be spent in anticipation of profitable future returns, many things in addition to costs should be evaluated. International trade and logistics can also be part of the capital investment decision. A case in point is Koss Corp. <www.koss.com>, located in Milwaukee, Wisconsin, and maker of high-fidelity headphones used for personal stereos, speakerphones, and other audio equipment. Company managers moved much of the production to China, where costs are low. However, that caused a problem with making timely deliveries to customers.[5] The just-in-time inventory philosophy had to be abandoned, and inventories were tripled from $2 million to $6 million to avoid customer backorders and dissatisfaction. Now, finished products are stacked in the Milwaukee factory to insure against dockworker strikes and missed deliveries. Looking beyond the numbers becomes an important consideration in capital investment decisions.

Check out ACE for a Review Quiz at http://accounting.college.hmco.com/students.

> **Stop and Think!**
> How is capital investment analysis part of both the long-term planning and annual budgeting processes?
>
> *Capital investment decisions will affect a company for many years, first as broad estimates used for planning purposes and finally, in the year of the expenditure, as specific investment analyses.* ∎

Every part of the organization participates in this process. Financial analysts supply a target cost of capital or desired rate of return and an estimate of how much money can be spent annually on capital facilities. Marketing specialists predict sales trends and new product demands, which help in determining which operations need expansion or new equipment. Managers at all levels help identify facility needs and often prepare preliminary cost estimates for the desired capital investment. Then they all work together to implement the project selected and to keep the results within revenue and cost estimates.

MEASURES USED IN CAPITAL INVESTMENT ANALYSIS

When evaluating a proposed capital investment, managers must predict how the new asset will perform and how it will benefit the company. Various measures are used to estimate the benefits to be derived from a capital investment.

■ **NET INCOME AND NET CASH INFLOWS** Each capital investment analysis must include a measure of the expected benefit from the investment project. The measure of expected benefit depends on the method of analyzing capital investment alternatives. One possible measure is net income, calculated in the usual way. Managers determine increases in net income resulting from the capital investment for each alternative.

A more widely used measure of expected benefit is projected cash flows. **Net cash inflows** are the balance of increases in projected cash receipts over increases in projected cash payments resulting from a capital investment. In some cases, equipment replacement decisions involve alternatives when revenues are the same among alternatives. In such cases, **cost savings** measure the benefits, such as reduced costs, from proposed capital investments. Either net cash inflows or cost savings can be used as the basis for an evaluation, but one measure should not be confused with the other. If the analysis involves cash receipts, net cash inflows are used. If the analysis involves only cash outlays, cost savings are used. Managers must measure and evaluate all the investment alternatives consistently.

■ **EQUAL VERSUS UNEQUAL CASH FLOWS** Projected cash flows may be the same for each year of an asset's life, or they may vary from year to year. Unequal cash flows are common and must be analyzed for each year of an asset's life. Proposed projects with equal annual cash flows require less detailed analysis. Both a project with equal cash flows and one with unequal cash flows are illustrated and explained later in this chapter.

■ **CARRYING VALUE OF ASSETS** **Carrying value** is the undepreciated portion of the original cost of a fixed asset—that is, the asset's cost less its accumulated depreciation. When a decision to replace an asset is being evaluated, the carrying value of the old asset is irrelevant because it is a past, or historical, cost, and it will therefore not be altered by the decision. Net proceeds from the asset's sale or disposal are relevant, however, because the proceeds affect cash flows and may be different for each alternative.

■ **DEPRECIATION EXPENSE AND INCOME TAXES** The techniques of capital investment analysis in this chapter compare the relative benefits of proposed capital investments by measuring the cash receipts and payments for a facility or project. Income taxes alter the amount and timing of cash flows of projects under consideration by for-profit companies. To assess the benefits of a capital project, a company must include the effects of income taxes in its capital investment analyses. Depreciation expense is deductible when determining income taxes. (You may recall that the annual depreciation expense computation using the straight-line method is the

EXHIBIT 3
Incremental Analysis: Special Order Decision

Home State Bank
Special Order Decision
Incremental Analysis

	Without Order	With Order	Difference in Favor of Accepting Order
Sales	$2,400,000	$2,404,000	$4,000
Less variable costs			
Direct materials	$ 160,000	$ 160,800	($ 800)
Direct labor	80,000	80,400	(400)
Variable overhead	320,000	321,600	(1,600)
Total variable costs	$ 560,000	$ 562,800	($2,800)
Contribution margin	$1,840,000	$1,841,200	$1,200

tions both with and without the special order. Fixed costs are not included because the only costs affected by the order are direct materials, direct labor, and variable overhead. The net result of accepting the special order is a $1,200 increase in contribution margin (and, correspondingly, in operating income). This amount is verified by the following incremental analysis:

Sales (2,000 transactions × 4) × $.50		$4,000
Less variable costs		
Direct materials (8,000 transactions × $.10)	$ 800	
Direct labor (8,000 transactions × $.05)	400	
Variable overhead (8,000 transactions × $.20)	1,600	
Total variable costs		2,800
Contribution margin		$1,200

The analysis reveals that Home State should accept the special order.

Now let us assume that the event sponsor asks Home State what the minimum special order price is. If the incremental costs for the special order are $2,800, the relevant cost per transaction is $.35 ($2,800 ÷ 8,000). The special order price should cover this cost and generate a profit. If Home State would like to earn $800 from the special order, the special order price should be $.45 ($.35 cost per transaction plus $.10 profit per transaction [$800 ÷ 8,000 transactions]).

Of course, the decision that Home State management makes must be consistent with the bank's strategic plan. Qualitative factors that might influence the decision are (1) the impact of the special order on regular customers, (2) the potential of the special order to lead into new sales areas, and (3) the customer's ability to maintain an ongoing relationship that includes good ordering and paying practices. Notice that the sales of $2,400,000 without the special order absorbed all of the fixed costs of overhead, advertising, and selling and administration.

INCREMENTAL ANALYSIS FOR SEGMENT PROFITABILITY DECISIONS

Another type of operating decision that management must face is whether to keep or to drop unprofitable segments, such as product lines, services, sales territories,

and other fixed manufacturing overhead costs are the same for both alternatives; therefore, they are not relevant to the decision. The cost of making the needed cartons is $28,800. The cost of buying 20,000 cartons at the increased purchase price will be $30,000. Since the company would save $1,200 by making the cartons, management will decide to make the cartons.

INCREMENTAL ANALYSIS FOR SPECIAL ORDER DECISIONS

KEY POINT: Special order decisions assume that excess capacity exists to accept the order and that the order, if accepted, will not have an impact on regular sales orders.

Managers are often faced with **special order decisions**, which are decisions about whether to accept or reject special orders at prices below the normal market prices. Special orders usually involve large numbers of similar products that are sold in bulk. Because these orders are not expected, they are not included in annual cost or sales estimates. And because they are one-time events, they should not be included in revenue or cost estimates for subsequent years. Before a firm accepts a special product order, it must be sure that the products involved are sufficiently different from its regular product line to avoid violating federal price discrimination laws and to avoid reducing unit sales from its full-priced regular product line.

The objective of a special order decision is to determine whether a special order should be accepted. A special order should be accepted only if it maximizes operating income, based on the organization's strategic plan and objectives, the relevant costs of the special order, and qualitative factors. One approach to such a decision is to compare the special order price to the relevant costs to produce, package, and ship the order. The relevant costs include the variable costs, variable selling costs, if any, and other costs directly associated with the special order (for example, freight, insurance, packaging, and labeling the product). Another approach is to prepare a special order bid price by calculating a minimum selling price for the special order. The bid price equals the relevant costs plus an estimated profit.

In many situations, sales commission expenses are excluded from a special order decision analysis because the customer approached the company directly. In addition, the fixed costs of existing facilities usually do not change if a company accepts a special order, and therefore they are usually irrelevant to the decision. If additional fixed costs must be incurred to fill the special order, they would be relevant to the decision. Examples of relevant fixed costs are the purchase of additional machinery, an increase in supervisory help, and an increase in insurance premiums required by a specific order.

For example, Home State Bank has been approved to provide and service four ATMs at a special event. The event sponsors want the fee per ATM transaction reduced to $.50 for these machines. At past special events, ATM use has averaged 2,000 transactions per machine. Home State Bank has located four idle ATMs and determined the following additional information:

ATM Cost Data for 400,000 Transactions (Annual Use for One Machine)

Direct materials	$.10
Direct labor	.05
Overhead	
Variable	.20
Fixed ($100,000 ÷ 400,000)	.25
Advertising ($60,000 ÷ 400,000)	.15
Other fixed selling and administrative expenses ($120,000 ÷ 400,000)	.30
Cost per transaction	$1.05
Fee per transaction	$1.50

Should Home State Bank accept the special event offer?

An incremental analysis in the contribution margin reporting format appears in Exhibit 3. The report shows the contribution margin for Home State Bank opera-

BUSINESS WORLD EXAMPLE: Super Bakery, supplier of doughnuts and other baked goods to institutional markets, outsources its selling activities to a network of brokers, its production activities to independent bakeries, and its warehousing and shipping activities to trucking companies.

counts of up to 40 percent off the list price. Outsourcing also enables it to provide additional value-adding services, such as online reviews by customers, personalized recommendations, and discussions and interviews about current products. Banks too are outsourcing to increase their online capabilities, especially in the areas of financial management software and analysis.

In manufacturing companies, a common decision facing managers is whether to make or to buy some or all of the parts used in product assembly. The goal is to select the more profitable choice by identifying the costs of each alternative and their effects on revenues and existing costs. Managers need the following information for this analysis:

Information About Making
Need for additional machinery
Variable costs of making the item
Incremental fixed costs

Information About Outsourcing
Purchase price of item
Rent or net cash flow to be generated from vacated space in the factory
Salvage value of unused machinery

The case of Box Company illustrates an outsourcing decision. For the past five years, the firm has purchased packing cartons from an outside supplier at a cost of $1.25 per carton. The supplier has just informed Box Company that it is raising the price 20 percent, to $1.50 per carton, effective immediately. Box Company has idle machinery that could be adjusted to produce the cartons. Annual production and usage would be 20,000 cartons. The company estimates the cost of direct materials at $.84 per carton. Workers, who will be paid $8.00 per hour, can process 20 cartons per hour ($.40 per carton). The cost of variable manufacturing overhead will be $4 per direct labor hour, and 1,000 direct labor hours will be required. Fixed manufacturing overhead includes $4,000 of depreciation per year and $6,000 of other fixed costs. The company has space and machinery to produce the cartons; the machines are currently idle and will continue to be idle if the part is purchased. Should Box Company continue to outsource the cartons?

Exhibit 2 presents an incremental analysis of the two alternatives. All relevant costs are listed. Because the machinery has already been purchased and neither the machinery nor the required factory space has any other use, the depreciation costs

EXHIBIT 2
Incremental Analysis: Outsourcing Decision

Box Company
Outsourcing Decision
Incremental Analysis

	Make	Outsource	Difference in Favor of Make
Direct materials (20,000 × $.84)	$16,800	—	($16,800)
Direct labor (20,000 × $.40)	8,000	—	(8,000)
Variable manufacturing overhead (1,000 hours × $4)	4,000	—	(4,000)
To purchase completed cartons (20,000 × $1.50)	—	$30,000	30,000
Totals	$28,800	$30,000	$ 1,200

> **STOP AND THINK!**
> When might opportunity costs arise?
> *Opportunity costs arise when the choice of one course of action eliminates the possibility of another course of action.* ■

Consider a plant nursery that has been in business for many years at the intersection of two highways. Suburbs have grown up around the nursery, and a bank has offered the nursery owner a high price for the land. The interest that could be earned from investing the proceeds of the sale is an opportunity cost for the nursery owner. It is revenue that the nursery owner has chosen to forgo to continue operating the nursery in that location.

A bank teller who is deciding whether to go back to school full time to earn a degree in finance also needs to consider opportunity costs. In this case, the opportunity cost is the salary the teller would lose by returning to school. The total cost of the degree includes not only tuition, books, supplies, and living expenses, but also the amount of salary forgone while the teller is a full-time student. This opportunity cost is one reason that many people choose to work full time and attend college part time.

Opportunity costs often come into play when a company is operating at or near capacity and must choose what products or services to offer. For example, assume that The Debit Card Company, which currently services 20,000 cards, has the option of offering 15,000 premium debit cards, a higher-priced product, but it cannot do both. The amount of income from the 20,000 debit cards is an opportunity cost of the premium debit cards.

✓ Check out ACE for a Review Quiz at http://accounting.college.hmco.com/students.

APPLICATION OF INCREMENTAL ANALYSIS TO SHORT-RUN DECISIONS

LO3 Perform incremental analysis for outsourcing decisions, special order decisions, segment profitability decisions, sales mix decisions involving constrained resources, and sell or process-further decisions.

RELATED TEXT ASSIGNMENTS
Q: 6, 7, 8, 9, 10
SE: 3, 4, 5
E: 2, 3, 4, 5, 6, 7
P: 1, 2, 3, 6, 7
SD: 5

In the course of day-to-day operations, managers are called upon to make many decisions that will have an immediate or short-run effect on current or near-term profitability. In this section, we show how incremental analysis can be applied to the following common situations: (1) outsourcing decisions, (2) special order decisions, (3) segment profitability decisions, (4) sales mix decisions involving constrained resources, and (5) sell or process-further decisions.

INCREMENTAL ANALYSIS FOR OUTSOURCING DECISIONS

Outsourcing is the use of suppliers outside the organization to perform services or produce goods that could be performed or produced internally. **Make-or-buy decisions**, which are decisions about whether to make a part internally or buy it from an external supplier, may lead to outsourcing. Or a company may decide to outsource entire operating activities, such as warehousing and distribution, that it traditionally performed in-house.

> **STOP AND THINK!**
> Why are depreciation and other fixed costs considered irrelevant when making an outsourcing decision?
> *Depreciation and other fixed costs do not change, regardless of which alternative is chosen. Only the costs that change—e.g., the cost of direct materials or labor—are included in incremental analysis for outsourcing decisions.* ■

To improve operating income and compete effectively in global markets, many companies are focusing their resources on their core competencies—the activities they perform best. One way to obtain the financial, physical, human, and technological resources needed to emphasize those competencies is to outsource expensive, nonvalue-adding activities. Strong candidates for outsourcing include payroll processing, training, managing fleets of vehicles, sales and marketing, custodial services, and information management. Many such areas involve either relatively low skill levels (such as payroll processing or custodial services) or highly specialized knowledge (such as information management) that could be better acquired from experts outside the company.

Outsourcing production or operating activities can reduce a company's investment in physical assets and human resources, which can improve cash flow. It can also help a company reduce operating costs and improve operating income. Many companies like Bank of America and Amazon.com benefit from outsourcing. For example, Amazon.com outsources the distribution of most of its products and has been able to reduce its storage and distribution costs enough to offer product dis-

www.bankofamerica.com
www.amazon.com

EXHIBIT 1
Incremental Analysis

Home State Bank
Incremental Analysis

	ATM C	ATM W	Difference in Favor of ATM W
Increase in revenue	$16,200	$19,800	$3,600
Increase in operating costs that differ between alternatives			
Direct labor	$ 2,200	$ 4,100	($1,900)
Variable overhead	2,100	3,050	(950)
Total relevant operating costs	$ 4,300	$ 7,150	($2,850)
Resulting change in operating income	$11,900	$12,650	$ 750

KEY POINT: Sunk costs cannot be recovered and are irrelevant in short-run decision making.

cannot be recovered through the current decision. An example of a sunk cost is the book value of ATM B. A manager might be tempted to say that the ATM should not be junked because the company still has $6,000 invested in it. However, the manager would be incorrect because the book value of the old ATM represents money that was spent in the past and so does not affect the decision about whether to replace the old ATM with a new one. The old ATM would be of interest only if it could be sold or traded in, and the amount received for it would be different, depending on which new ATM was chosen. In that case, the amount of the sale or trade-in value would be relevant to the decision because it would affect the future cash flows of the alternatives.

Another look at the financial data for ATMs C and W reveals two other irrelevant costs. The costs of direct materials and fixed overhead (depreciation included) can also be eliminated from the analysis because they are the same under both alternatives.

Once the irrelevant revenues and costs have been identified, the incremental analysis may be prepared using only the differential revenues and costs that will change between the alternative ATMs, as shown in Exhibit 1. The analysis shows that ATM W would produce $750 more in operating income than ATM C. Because the costs of buying the two ATMs are the same, this report would favor the purchase of ATM W.

FOCUS ON BUSINESS TECHNOLOGY

How Much Does It Cost to Process a Check?
The banking industry has found that it has options for processing checks. It can outsource the processing of paper checks, use the quasi-paperless system of ATMs, or process transactions over the Internet. Bank managers have concluded that online banking substantially reduces the cost of processing transactions. According to a study by an international consulting firm, the cost of processing a transaction is 1 cent if completed over the Internet, 27 cents using an ATM, and $1.07 if processed by a teller.[2]

OPPORTUNITY COSTS

Because incremental analysis focuses on only the quantitative differences among the alternatives, it simplifies management's evaluation of a decision and reduces the time needed to choose the best course of action. However, incremental analysis is only one input to the final decision. Management needs to consider other issues. For instance, the manufacturer of ATM C might have a reputation for better quality or service than the manufacturer of ATM W. **Opportunity costs** are the benefits that are forfeited or lost when one alternative is chosen over another.

the bank and the people the bank serves. Depending on what they discover during their review, the managers might consider ways to improve the branch, or they might decide to close the branch location after all.

REPORTING

Managers prepare reports related to short-run decisions throughout the management cycle. They develop budgets that show the estimated costs and revenues related to alternative courses of action. They compile analyses of data that support their decisions. And they issue reports that measure the effect their decisions had on the organization, including its operating income. When deciding whether to continue the branch location, the bank managers would develop budgets showing the costs and revenues they expect the branch to generate. They would also prepare written analyses of the expected costs and revenues and of the qualitative factors mentioned earlier. If the managers decided to continue the branch location, they would evaluate its success by comparing actual financial and nonfinancial results to the results predicted in the budget and initial analyses. They would create reports telling how much operating income the branch has produced and how else the branch has benefited the bank and the people whom the bank serves.

✓ Check out ACE for a Review Quiz at http://accounting.college.hmco.com/students.

INCREMENTAL ANALYSIS FOR SHORT-RUN DECISIONS

LO2 Define *incremental analysis* and describe how it applies to short-run decision analysis.

RELATED TEXT ASSIGNMENTS
Q: 4, 5
SE: 2
E: 1
SD: 4
MRA: 3

ENRICHMENT NOTE:
Incremental analysis is a technique used not only by businesses but also by individuals to solve daily problems.

Once managers have determined that a problem or need is worthy of consideration and have identified alternative courses of action, they must evaluate the effect that each alternative will have on their organization. The method of comparing alternatives by focusing on the differences in their projected revenues and costs is called **incremental analysis**. Incremental analysis is also called *differential analysis* if it ignores revenues or costs that stay the same or do not differ among the alternatives.

IRRELEVANT COSTS AND REVENUES

A cost that changes between alternatives is known as a **differential cost** (also referred to as an *incremental cost*). For example, assume that Home State Bank managers are deciding which of two ATM machines—C or W—to buy. The ATMs have the same purchase price, but they have different revenues and cost characteristics. The company currently owns ATM B, which it bought three years ago for $15,000 and which has accumulated depreciation of $9,000 and a book value of $6,000. ATM B is now obsolete as a result of advances in technology and cannot be sold or traded in.

The accountant has collected the following annual revenue and operating cost estimates for the two new machines:

	ATM C	ATM W
Increase in revenue	$16,200	$19,800
Increase in annual operating costs		
Direct materials	4,800	4,800
Direct labor	2,200	4,100
Variable overhead	2,100	3,050
Fixed overhead (depreciation included)	5,000	5,000

The first step in the incremental analysis is to eliminate any irrelevant revenues and costs. Irrelevant revenues are those that will not differ between the alternatives. Irrelevant costs include sunk costs and costs that will not differ between the alternatives. A **sunk cost** is a cost that was incurred because of a previous decision and

FIGURE 1
Short-Run Decisions in the Management Cycle

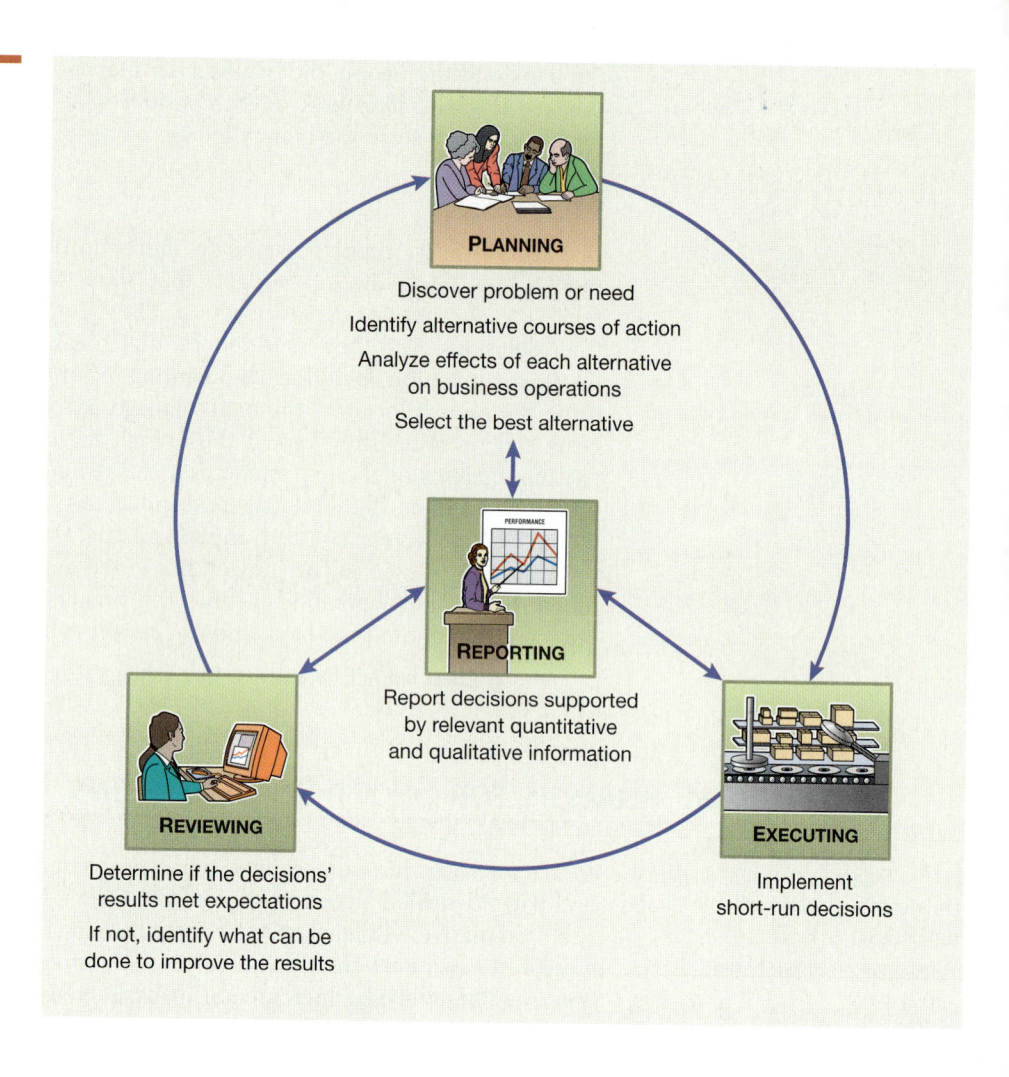

special order, examine the profitability of a segment, select the appropriate product mix given a resource constraint, contract with outside suppliers of goods and services, or sell a product as is or process it further. All of those decisions affect operations in the current operating period.

In the executing stage, the bank's management might eliminate a branch if the costs of the branch exceed the revenues generated by it. However, they may choose to keep the branch because the community expects the organization to provide this service.

REVIEWING

It is in the reviewing stage of the management cycle that managers take the fifth predictable action when performing short-run decision analysis: they evaluate each decision to determine whether it produced the forecast results. They examine how each decision was carried out and how it affected the organization. If results fell short, the managers identify and prescribe corrective action. This resulting post-decision audit supplies feedback about the results of the short-run decision. If the solution is not completely satisfactory or if the problem remains, the management cycle begins again. For example, if the bank decided to keep the branch location, the managers would evaluate the results of their decision in many ways. They would probably consider how successful the branch has been, how many people have benefited from the branch, and how well the branch fits in with the other kinds of services the bank offers. They would be interested in knowing how much operating income the branch has produced and in what other ways the branch has benefited

Short-Run Decision Analysis and the Management Cycle

LO1 Explain how managers make short-run decisions in the management cycle.

RELATED TEXT ASSIGNMENTS
Q: 1, 2, 3
SE: 1
SD: 1

Readers of financial reports are interested in knowing what happened to produce the results that are presented in these reports. The historical information that the reports contain helps answer that question. For planning and control purposes, managers want to know why things happened. They use historical financial and non-financial quantitative information to analyze the results of business actions that will have an effect on their organization's activities in the future. Such information should be relevant, timely, and presented in a format that is easy to use in decision making.

As illustrated in Figure 1, **short-run decision analysis** is the systematic examination of any decision whose effects will be felt over the course of the next year. Although many business problems are unique and cannot be solved by following strict rules, managers frequently take five predictable actions when deciding what to do. The first four actions are taken during the planning stage of the management cycle, and the fifth, and final, action is taken during the reviewing stage.

Planning

In the planning stage of the management cycle, managers take the following four actions when performing short-run decision analysis:

1. Discover a problem or need.
2. Identify all reasonable courses of action that can solve the problem or meet the need.
3. Prepare a thorough analysis of each possible solution, identifying its total costs, savings, and other financial effects.
4. Select the best course of action.

www.bankofamerica.com

As a general rule, the managers of companies like Bank of America make decisions that support the company's strategic plan. For example, the managers of a bank may have to make a decision about keeping or eliminating one of the bank's branch locations. Both quantitative and qualitative factors will influence the decision. The quantitative information includes the costs of operating the branch locations and the fee revenues that the branch generates. Management may also want to know the number of customers serviced each year, the types of services offered, and the number and dollar amount of the branch's accounts.

As the managers perform decision analyses, the following qualitative factors will influence their decision to keep or eliminate the branch:

- Competition (Do our competitors have a branch office located here?)
- Economic conditions (Is the community growing?)
- Social issues (Will our offering of this branch location benefit the community we serve?)
- Product or service quality (Can we attract more business because of the service quality of this branch?)
- Timeliness (Does the branch promote customer service?)

Managers must identify and assess the importance of all such qualitative and quantitative factors when they make short-run decisions.

● **Stop and Think!**
Are qualitative factors important in short-run decision making?
Yes, because qualitative factors such as competition, economic conditions, social issues, quality, and timeliness influence decision making. ■

Executing

For short-run decisions, we focus on the executing stage of the management cycle—the stage in which managers must adapt to changing environments and take advantage of opportunities that will improve their organization's profitability and liquidity in the short run. During the year, managers may have an opportunity to accept a

How can incremental analysis help Bank of America take advantage of the business opportunities offered by banking online?

the bank invest in the latest technology, and if so, how should management evaluate the capital investment alternatives? To analyze these types of questions and make informed decisions, bank managers need useful information and analytic methods that will enable them to determine what could happen under the alternative courses of action.

27

Chapter 27 explains how managers make short-run decisions using incremental analysis and long-term capital investment decisions using the net present value method and other methods of capital investment analysis.

Analysis for Decision Making

LEARNING OBJECTIVES

LO1 Explain how managers make short-run decisions in the management cycle.

LO2 Define *incremental analysis* and describe how it applies to short-run decision analysis.

LO3 Perform incremental analysis for outsourcing decisions, special order decisions, segment profitability decisions, sales mix decisions involving constrained resources, and sell or process-further decisions.

LO4 Identify the types of projected costs and revenues used to evaluate alternatives for capital investment.

LO5 Apply the concept of the time value of money.

LO6 Analyze capital investment proposals using the net present value method.

LO7 Analyze capital investment proposals using the payback period method and the accounting rate-of-return method.

DECISION POINT

A MANAGER'S FOCUS

Bank of America <www.bankofamerica.com>
Bank of America serves banking clients in over 150 countries worldwide. In its quest to find new ways to meet the needs of its commercial, consumer, global corporate, and investment banking customers, it is conducting more and more of its business over the Internet. As of the end of 2002, Bank of America had more than 4.7 million active online customers. Expectations are that by 2006, nearly half of Bank of America's 15 million active checking account customers will do their banking over the Internet.

Bank management believes this trend is good for business. In a survey of its account holders, Bank of America found that its online users were more likely to stay with the bank and maintain higher account balances and were less likely to make customer service calls. John Rosenfeld, senior vice president for ecommerce, believes that besides making money for the bank, online banking "deepens the relationship" and increases customer satisfaction.[1]

As customers become increasingly familiar with handling their finances online, banks will offer more product and service choices over the Internet. As bank managers make decisions about which business alternatives to pursue, they will ask a number of questions—for example: When should bank products and services be outsourced? When should a special order for service be accepted? When is a bank segment profitable? What is the best sales mix when resource constraints exist? When should bank products be sold as is or processed further into different products? Should

Internet Case

MRA 5.
LO6 Top Executive Compensation

Are top executives paid too much? Do the companies run by the most highly paid executives perform better than other companies? Do U.S. executives make more money than their foreign counterparts? These are some of the questions asked routinely in articles and surveys about executive compensation. Use the Internet to locate the top executive salary rankings compiled annually by business publications and other sources. Study the rankings and select several U.S. and foreign companies in the same industry for comparison.

Hint: There are several ways to access this type of information on the Internet. One approach is to do key word searches using search terms like *executive compensation* or *executive salary survey*. Another approach is to access a business publication web site such as <www.forbes.com> and do key word searches of articles. It is also possible to access corporate web sites to view their annual reports. Some corporate web sites are even searchable by key word.

1. In your review of top executive compensation, what types of incentives did you find included in annual compensation?
2. Are the companies with the highest-paid executives the best performers in their industry?
3. Do U.S. executives receive higher pay than their foreign counterparts? If so, do the U.S. companies perform better than their foreign counterparts?

	Worldwide	Europe	Americas	Asia
Cost of capital	9%	10%	8%	12%
Total assets	$210	$70	$70	$70
Current liabilities	80	10	40	30
After-tax operating income	15	5	5	5

1. Compute economic value added for each office and worldwide. What factors affect each office's economic value added? How can an office improve its economic value added?
2. If managers' bonuses are based on economic value added to office performance, what specific actions will managers be motivated to take?
3. Is economic value added the only performance measure needed to evaluate investment centers adequately? Explain your response.

Excel Spreadsheet Analysis

MRA 4.

LO5 Return on Investment and Residual Income

Tina Patel, the manager of the Food and Lodging Division at Winter Wonderland, has hired you as a consultant to help her examine her division's performance under several different circumstances.

1. Type the following format into a spreadsheet to compute the Food and Lodging Division's actual return on investment and residual income. Match your data entry to the rows and columns shown below. Data are from parts 3 and 4 of this chapter's Review Problem. (**Hint:** When entering the formulas, type = in front of the formula in the cell. Then the spreadsheet will know to compute the answer. Remember to format each cell for the type of numbers it holds, such as percentage, currency, or general.)

	A	B	C	D	E	F
1						
2	Investment Center		Food and Lodging Division			
3			Actual Results			
4	Sales		$40,000,000			
5	Operating income		$ 6,450,000			
6	Average assets invested		$10,000,000			
7	Desired ROI		30%			
8						
9	Return on Investment		C5/C6			
10						
11	Profit Margin		C5/C4			
12						
13	Asset Turnover		C4/C6			
14						
15	Residual Income		C5-(C7*C6)			
16						

2. Patel would like to know how the figures would change if Food and Lodging had a desired ROI of 40 percent and average assets invested of $10,000,000. Revise your spreadsheet from 1 to compute the division's return on investment and residual income under those conditions.
3. Patel also wants to know how the figures would change if Food and Lodging had a desired ROI of 30 percent and average assets invested of $12,000,000. Revise your spreadsheet from 1 to compute the division's return on investment and residual income under those conditions.
4. Does the use of formatted spreadsheets simplify the computation of ROI and residual income? Do such spreadsheets make it easier to do "what-if" analyses?

1. Analyze the items listed in the performance report and identify the items Aldo controls and those Yuma controls. In your opinion, what type of responsibility center is Aldo's Tortillas? Explain your response.
2. Prepare a revised performance report for Aldo's Tortillas and an accompanying memo to the president of Yuma Foods that explains why it is important to change the content of the report. Cite some basic principles of responsibility accounting to support your recommendation.

Managerial Reporting and Analysis Cases

Interpreting Management Reports

MRA 1. IT, Inc., has adopted the balanced scorecard approach to motivate the managers of its product divisions to work toward the companywide goal of leading its industry in innovation. The corporation's selected performance measures and scorecard results are as follows:

LO1 Balanced Scorecard Results

| | Division | | | Performance |
Measure	A	B	C	Target
New product ROI	80%	75%	70%	75%
Employees cross-trained in new tasks within 30 days	95	96	94	100
New product's time to market less than one year	85	90	86	80
New product's market share one year after introduction	50	100	80	80

Can you effectively compare the performance of three divisions against the targets? What other measures mentioned in this chapter are needed to evaluate performance effectively?

Formulating Management Reports

MRA 2. Wood4Fun makes wooden playground equipment for the institutional and consumer markets. The company strives for low-cost, high-quality production because it operates in a highly competitive market in which product price is set by the marketplace and is not based on production costs. The company is organized into responsibility centers. The vice president of manufacturing is responsible for three manufacturing plants. The vice president of sales is responsible for four sales regions. Recently, these two vice presidents began to disagree about whether the manufacturing plants are cost centers or profit centers. The vice president of manufacturing views the plants as cost centers because the managers of the plants control only product-related costs. The vice president of sales believes the plants are profit centers because product quality and product cost strongly affect company profits.

LO2 Responsibility Centers
LO3

1. Identify the controllable performance that Wood4Fun values and wants to measure. Give at least three examples of performance measures that Wood4Fun could use to monitor such performance.
2. For the manufacturing plants, what type of responsibility center is most consistent with the controllable performance Wood4Fun wants to measure?
3. For the sales regions, what type of responsibility center is most appropriate?

International Company

MRA 3. Sevilla Consulting offers environmental consulting services worldwide. The managers of branch offices are rewarded for superior performance with bonuses based on the economic value the office adds to the company. Last year's operating results for the entire company and for its three offices, expressed in millions of U.S. dollars, follow.

LO2 Economic Value Added and
LO5 Performance
LO6

the year, corporate headquarters set a targeted return on investment for the store of 20 percent. The upstate store currently averages $140,000 in invested assets (beginning invested assets, $130,000; ending invested assets, $150,000) and is projected to have an operating income of $30,800. Huntington is considering whether to take one or both of the following actions before year end:

- Hold off paying $5,000 in bills owed until the start of the next fiscal year.
- Write down $3,000 in store inventory (nonperishable emergency flood supplies) to zero value because Huntington was unable to sell the items all year.

Currently, Huntington's bonus is based on store profits. Next year, corporate headquarters is changing its performance incentive program so that bonuses will be based on a store's actual return on investment.

1. What effect would each of Huntington's possible actions have on the store's operating income this year? (**Hint:** Use Figure 4 to trace the effects.) In your opinion, is either action unethical?
2. Independent of question 1, if corporate headquarters changes its performance incentive plan for store managers, how will the inventory writedown affect next year's income and return on investment if the items are sold for $4,000 next year? In your opinion, does Huntington have an ethical dilemma?

Research Activity

SD 4. Many large multinational companies have recently taken large one-time write-offs or applied other downsizing or reengineering accounting practices that have affected the measurement of the company's performance in only one year. Conduct a search for the financial statements of a company that has recently taken a sizable reduction in income in just one year. Conduct a keyword search using an Internet search engine. Prepare a one-page description of your findings. Include the name of the company, the reason for the large decrease in income, and the probable effect on the company's ROI. Be prepared to present your findings to your classmates.

LO2 **Earnings Management**
LO4
LO6

Decision-Making Practice

SD 5. Yuma Foods acquired Aldo's Tortillas several years ago. Aldo's has continued to operate as an independent company, except that Yuma Foods has exclusive authority over capital investments, production quantity, and pricing decisions because Yuma has been Aldo's only customer since the acquisition. Yuma uses return on investment to evaluate the performance of Aldo's manager. The most recent performance report is as follows:

LO2 **Types of Responsibility Centers**
LO3
LO4
LO6

Yuma Foods
Performance Report for Aldo's Tortillas
For the Year Ended June 30, 20x8

Sales	$6,000
Variable cost of goods sold	3,000
Variable administrative expenses	1,000
Variable corporate expenses (% of sales)	600
Contribution margin	$1,400
Fixed overhead (includes depreciation of $100)	400
Fixed administrative expenses	500
Operating income	$ 500
Average assets invested	$5,500
Return on investment	9.09%

REQUIRED ▶ 1. Assuming that the theaters are profit centers, prepare a performance report for the Park Theater. Include a flexible budget. Determine the variances between actual results, the flexible budget, and the master budget.
2. Evaluate Burgman's performance as manager of the Park Theater.
3. Assume that the managers are assigned responsibility for capital expenditures and that the theaters are thus investment centers. Park Theater is expected to generate a desired ROI of at least 6 percent on average invested assets of $2,000,000.

   a. Compute the theater's return on investment and residual income.
   b. Using the ROI and residual income, evaluate Burgman's performance as manager.

LO5 Return on Investment and Economic Value Added

P 8. Micanopy Company makes replicas of Indian artifacts. The balance sheet for the Arrowhead Division showed that the company had invested assets of $300,000 at the beginning of the year and $500,000 at the end of the year. During the year, the Arrowhead Division's operating income was $80,000 on sales of $1,200,000.

REQUIRED ▶ 1. Compute the Arrowhead Division's residual income if the desired ROI is 20 percent.
2. Compute the following performance measures for the division:
   a. Profit margin
   b. Asset turnover
   c. Return on investment
3. Compute Micanopy Company's economic value added if total corporate assets are $6,000,000, current liabilities are $800,000, after-tax operating income is $750,000, and the cost of capital is 12 percent.

SKILLS DEVELOPMENT CASES

Conceptual Analysis

SD 1.

LO1 Performance Measures and
LO2 the Balanced Scorecard

Identify several performance measures for a business located near you, and link each measure with a specific stakeholder's perspective from the balanced scorecard. Be sure to select at least one performance measure for each perspective. If you were the manager of the business, how would you set performance targets for each measure? Prepare an email-style report stating the business's name, location, and activities and your linked performance measures and perspectives. Be prepared to discuss your business and performance measures in class.

Group Activity: Have students complete this assignment by working in groups of four to six, with each group member assuming a different stakeholder perspective (add government and community if you want more than four perspectives). The group should become familiar with the background of the business, and interview the business's manager or accountant. Ask the group to discuss all perspectives and to prepare a report summarizing their findings.

SD 2.

LO3 Comparison of Business Types Using Responsibility Accounting

The structure of an organization affects its responsibility accounting system. Accenture <www.accenture.com>, a major management consulting firm, organizes its consultants by industry and location. Target <www.target.com>, formerly Dayton-Hudson Corporation, has a division for each major retail department store chain it owns: Target, Mervyn's, Marshall Field's, Dayton's, and Hudson's. Monsanto <www.monsanto.com>, a manufacturer, structures its organization by products: agricultural, pharmaceutical, and nutritional (the last includes NutraSweet).

What is a responsibility accounting system, what is it based on, and what is the criterion for including an item in a manager's operating report? Discuss the general effects that organizational structure has on the creation of a responsibility reporting system and give an example of a cost center, a profit center, and an investment center at Accenture, Target, and Monsanto.

Ethical Dilemma

SD 3.

LO5 Effects of Manager's Decisions on ROI

Cooper Huntington is the manager of the upstate store of a large farm products retailer. His company is a stable, consistently profitable member of the farming industry. The upstate store is doing fine despite severe drought conditions in the area. At the first of

Chapter 26 Performance Management and Evaluation

REQUIRED
1. Compute the division's profit margin, asset turnover, and return on investment for 20x8 and 20x7. Beginning total assets for 20x7 were $157,900. Round to two decimal places.
2. The desired return on investment for the division has been set at 12 percent. Compute Ornamental Iron's residual income for 20x8 and 20x7.
3. The cost of capital for the division is 8 percent. Compute the division's economic value added for 20x8 and 20x7.
4. Before drawing conclusions on this division's performance, what additional information would you want?

LO5 Return on Investment and Economic Value Added

P 5. The balance sheet for the New Products Division of NuBone Corporation showed invested assets of $200,000 at the beginning of the year and $300,000 at the end of the year. During the year, the division's operating income was $12,500 on sales of $500,000.

REQUIRED
1. Compute the division's residual income if the desired ROI is 6 percent.
2. Compute the following performance measures for the division: (a) profit margin, (b) asset turnover, and (c) return on investment
3. Recompute the division's ROI under each of the following independent assumptions:
   a. Sales increase from $500,000 to $600,000, causing operating income to rise from $12,500 to $30,000.
   b. Invested assets at the beginning of the year are reduced from $200,000 to $100,000.
   c. Operating expenses are reduced, causing operating income to rise from $12,500 to $20,000.
4. Compute NuBone's EVA if total corporate assets are $500,000, current liabilities are $80,000, after-tax operating income is $50,000, and the cost of capital is 8 percent.

ALTERNATE PROBLEMS

LO4 Traditional and Variable Costing Income Statements

P 6. Interior designers often use the deluxe carpet products of Lux Mills, Inc. The Maricopa blend is the company's top product line. In March 20x9, Lux produced and sold 174,900 square yards of Maricopa blend. Factory operating data for the month included variable cost of goods sold of $2,623,500 and fixed manufacturing overhead of $346,875. Other expenses were variable selling expenses, $166,155; fixed selling expenses, $148,665; and fixed general and administrative expenses, $231,500. Total sales revenue equaled $3,935,250. All production took place in March, and there was no work in process at month end. Goods are usually shipped when completed.

REQUIRED
1. Prepare the March 20x9 income statement for Lux Mills, Inc., using the traditional reporting format.
2. Prepare the March 20x9 income statement for Lux Mills, Inc., using the variable costing format.

LO3 Return on Investment and
LO4 Residual Income
LO5

P 7. Portia Carter is the president of a company that owns six multiplex movie theaters. Carter has delegated decision-making authority to the theater managers for all decisions except those relating to capital expenditures and film selection. The theater managers' compensation depends on the profitability of their theaters. Max Burgman, the manager of the Park Theater, had the following master budget and actual results for the month:

	Master Budget	Actual Results
Tickets sold	120,000	110,000
Revenue–tickets	$840,000	$880,000
Revenue–concessions	480,000	330,000
Controllable variable costs		
Concessions	120,000	99,000
Direct labor	420,000	330,000
Variable overhead	540,000	550,000
Contribution margin	$240,000	$231,000
Controllable fixed costs		
Rent	55,000	55,000
Other administrative expenses	45,000	50,000
Theater operating income	$140,000	$126,000

Video Case

Harley-Davidson, Inc.
<www.harley-davidson.com>

Objectives

- To describe the role a performance measurement and evaluation system plays in business today.
- To become familiar with how the balanced scorecard provides a framework for performance management and accountability.
- To show how responsibility accounting is useful in performance evaluation.
- To understand the value of linking organizational goals, objectives, measures, targets, and performance-based pay.

Background for the Case

Harley-Davidson continues to excel at providing motorcyclists and the general public an expanding line of motorcycles and branded products and services. Strong sales of motorcycles, apparel, parts, insurance, product licensing, and financial services have enabled the company to sustain and improve on its success. Harley's journey to success can be charted through its performance management and evaluation system. Performance measures like market share, units shipped, revenue, operating profit, and number of employees illustrate its remarkable turnaround. In the 1980s, Harley rose above near bankruptcy to emerge today as the internationally recognized company that "fulfills dreams through the experience of motorcycling." Like many other companies, Harley-Davidson uses a performance management and evaluation system to identify how well it is doing, where it is going, and what improvements will make it more profitable.

For more information about Harley-Davidson, Inc., visit the company's web site directly or access it through the Needles Accounting Resource Center Web Site at **http://accounting.college.hmco.com/students.**

Required

View the video on Harley-Davidson that accompanies this book. As you are watching the video, take notes related to the following questions:

1. What role does performance measurement and evaluation play in business today?
2. In your own words, describe the balanced scorecard. Who are its stakeholders?
3. Define responsibility accounting. Why is it useful in performance evaluation?
4. Explain how Harley uses Performance Effectiveness Process (PEP) to link performance goals, objectives, measures, and targets. Why does this linking process improve the effectiveness of its performance management and evaluation system?

- **Financial (investors):** hourly lift cost, lift ticket sales in dollars and in units
- **Learning and growth (employees):** number of cross-trained tasks per employee, employee turnover
- **Internal business processes:** number of accident-free days, number and cost of mechanical breakdowns, average lift cycle time (that is, the time between getting in line to ride the ski lift and completing the ski run)
- **Customers:** average number of ski runs per daily lift ticket, number of repeat customers, number of PEAKS points redeemed

Focus on Business Practice

How Many Stakeholder Groups Has Harley Identified?

Harley-Davidson, Inc., <www.harley-davidson.com> has identified not four but six stakeholder groups. In addition to balancing the needs of investors, employees, business processes, and customers, Harley managers also consider the interests of the community at large and government. Taking a broader perspective enables the company to sustain its competitive advantage and implement effective employee reward programs.[2]

Figure 1 summarizes the planning stage of the management cycle: Vail Resorts' managers link their organization's vision and strategy to objectives, then link the objectives to logical performance measures, and, finally, set performance targets. As a result, a ski lift manager will have a variety of performance measures that balance the perspectives and needs of all stakeholders.

■ **EXECUTING** Managers use the mutually agreed-on strategic objectives for the entire organization as the basis for decision making within their individual areas

ORGANIZATIONAL GOALS AND THE BALANCED SCORECARD

LO1 Describe how the balanced scorecard aligns performance with organizational goals, and explain the role of the balanced scorecard in the management cycle.

RELATED TEXT ASSIGNMENTS
Q: 1, 2, 3, 4
SE: 1
E: 1, 2
SD: 1
MRA: 1

The **balanced scorecard**, developed by Robert S. Kaplan and David P. Norton, is a framework that links the perspectives of an organization's four basic stakeholder groups—financial (investors), learning and growth (employees), internal business processes, and customers—with the organization's mission and vision, performance measures, strategic plan, and resources. To succeed, an organization must add value for all groups in both the short and the long terms. Thus, an organization will determine each group's objectives and translate them into performance measures that have specific, quantifiable performance targets. Ideally, managers should be able to see how their actions contribute to the achievement of organizational goals and understand how their compensation is related to their actions. The balanced scorecard assumes that an organization will get only what it measures.

THE BALANCED SCORECARD AND THE MANAGEMENT CYCLE

We will use the Decision Point about the PEAKS card to illustrate the use of the balanced scorecard in the management cycle.

■ **PLANNING** During the planning stage, the balanced scorecard provides a framework that enables managers to translate their organization's vision and strategy into operational terms. Managers evaluate the company vision from the perspective of each stakeholder group and seek to answer one key question for each group:

- **Financial (investors):** To achieve our organization's vision, how should we appear to our shareholders?
- **Learning and growth (employees):** To achieve our organization's vision, how should we sustain our ability to improve and change?
- **Internal business processes:** To succeed, at what business processes must our organization excel?
- **Customers:** To achieve our organization's vision, how should we appear to our customers?

STOP AND THINK!
On which perspective do most businesses focus?
Most businesses focus on the financial perspective. ■

These key questions align the organization's strategy from all perspectives. The answers to the questions result in performance objectives that are mutually beneficial to all stakeholders. Once the organization's objectives are set, managers can select performance measures and set performance targets to translate objectives into an action plan.

For example, if Vail Resorts' collective vision and strategy is customer satisfaction, its managers might establish the following overall objectives:

www.vailresorts.com

Perspective	Objective
Financial (investors)	Customer satisfaction means revenue growth.
Learning and growth (employees)	Customer satisfaction means cross-trained, customer service–oriented employees.
Internal business processes	Customer satisfaction means reliable products and short delivery cycles.
Customers	Customer satisfaction means keeping customer loyalty through repeat visits and redeemed PEAKS points.

KEY POINT: The alignment of an organization's strategy with all the perspectives of the balanced scorecard results in performance objectives that benefit all stakeholders.

These overall objectives are then translated into specific performance objectives and measures for managers. For example, a ski lift manager's performance objectives might be measured in terms of the following:

How do managers at Vail Resorts evaluate for peak performance?

ity to store both financial and nonfinancial data about all aspects of the resorts enables managers to learn about and balance the interests of all the company's stakeholders: financial (investors), learning and growth (employees), internal business processes, and customers. The managers can then use the information to answer traditional financial questions about measuring cost of sales and valuing inventory (such as food ingredients in its restaurants and merchandise in its shops) and to obtain performance information about the resorts' activities, products, services, and customers. In addition, managers and employees receive timely feedback about their performance measures so that they can continuously improve.

26

Chapter 26 discusses performance measurement and describes the role of the balanced scorecard, responsibility accounting, and economic value added as they relate to performance management and evaluation.

Performance Management and Evaluation

LEARNING OBJECTIVES

LO1 Describe how the balanced scorecard aligns performance with organizational goals, and explain the role of the balanced scorecard in the management cycle.

LO2 Discuss performance measurement, and state the issues that affect management's ability to measure performance.

LO3 Define *responsibility accounting,* and describe the role that responsibility centers play in performance management and evaluation.

LO4 Prepare performance reports for cost centers using flexible budgets and for profit centers using variable costing.

LO5 Prepare performance reports for investment centers using traditional measures of return on investment and residual income and the newer measure of economic value added.

LO6 Explain how properly linked performance incentives and measures add value for all stakeholders in performance management and evaluation.

DECISION POINT

A MANAGER'S FOCUS

Vail Resorts <www.vailresorts.com> Vail Resorts PEAKS is an all-in-one card for guests of four Colorado vacation spots: Vail, Breckenridge, Keystone, and Beaver Creek. Guests at all resorts in these areas can use the PEAKS card to pay for lift tickets, skiing and snowboarding lessons, equipment rentals, dining, and more. They like its convenience and its program for earning points toward free or reduced-rate lift tickets, dining, and lodging. They enroll in the PEAKS system by filling out a one-page form that asks for their name, street address, email address, phone number, date of birth, credit card number, and a signed charge privilege authorization. Data for up to eight family members may be linked into one membership account. Each family member receives a bar-coded picture identification card, usually worn on a souvenir cord around the guest's neck, that is scanned each time he or she rides the ski lifts, attends ski school, or charges purchases, dining, or lodging.[1] How can the managers of the Vail Resorts Management Company use the PEAKS card and its integrated database to manage and evaluate the performance of their resorts better?

Managers like PEAKS because it enables them to collect huge amounts of information in a simple way and because the data have so many uses. New data are entered in the system each time a guest's card is scanned. Those data then become part of an integrated management information system that allows managers to measure and control costs, quality, and performance in all four resort areas. The system's abil-

1. Prepare a monthly flexible budget for operating activity at 2,000 machine hours, 2,200 machine hours, and 2,500 machine hours.
2. Develop a flexible budget formula.
3. The company's normal operating capacity is 2,200 machine hours per month. Compute the fixed overhead rate at this level of activity. Then break the rate down into individual rates for each element of fixed overhead.
4. Prepare a detailed comparative cost analysis for October. Include all variable and fixed overhead costs. Format your analysis by using columns for the following five elements: cost category, cost per machine hour, costs applied, actual costs incurred, and variance.
5. Develop a manufacturing overhead variance analysis for October that identifies the variable overhead spending and efficiency variances and the fixed overhead budget and volume variances.
6. Prepare an analysis of the variances. Could a manager control some of the fixed costs? Defend your answer.

Internet Case

MRA 5.
LO1 Resources for Developing Cost Standards

Suppose you have recently taken a job at a company that manufactures parts for automobiles. You have been assigned the task of developing manufacturing cost standards. You want to gather as much background information as you can about these standards. Using a standard search engine, such as Google, search the Internet for web sites that provide information about cost standards, manufacturing, and automobile manufacturers. Visit the sites that look most interesting. List the five sites you think are most useful. Bring your list to class and compare your findings with those of your classmates.

1. Answer the following questions:
    a. Why are you preparing this performance report?
    b. Who will use the report?
    c. What information do you need to develop the report? How will you obtain that information?
    d. When are the performance report and the analysis needed?
2. With the limited information available to you, compute the labor rate variance, the labor efficiency variance, and the variable and fixed overhead variances.
3. Prepare a performance report for the spa for March 20x6. Analyze the report and suggest causes for any problems that you find.

International Company

MRA 3.

LO3 Variance Analysis
LO4
LO5

Ying Zsoa recently became the controller of a joint venture in Hong Kong. He has been using standard costing to plan and control the company's activities. In a meeting with the budget team, which includes managers and employees from purchasing, engineering, and production, Zsoa asked the team members to share any operating problems they had encountered during the last quarter. He explained that his staff would use this information in analyzing the causes of significant cost variances that had occurred in the quarter.

For each of the following situations, identify the direct materials and/or direct labor variance(s) that could be affected and indicate the whether the variances are favorable or unfavorable:

1. The production department used highly skilled, higher-paid workers.
2. Machines were improperly adjusted.
3. Direct labor personnel worked more carefully to manufacture the product.
4. The product design engineer substituted a direct material that was less expensive and of lower quality.
5. The Purchasing Department bought higher-quality materials at a higher price.
6. A major supplier used a less-expensive mode of transportation to deliver the raw materials.
7. Work was halted for two hours because of a power disruption.

Excel Spreadsheet Analysis

MRA 4.

LO3 Developing a Flexible Budget
LO6 and Analyzing Overhead Variances

Ezelda Marva is the controller at FH Industries. She has asked you, her new assistant, to analyze the following data related to projected and actual overhead costs for October 20x8:

	Standard Variable Costs per Machine Hour (MH)	Actual Variable Costs in October
Indirect materials and supplies	$1.10	$ 2,380
Indirect machine setup labor	2.50	5,090
Materials handling	1.40	3,950
Maintenance and repair	1.50	2,980
Utilities	.80	1,490
Miscellaneous	.10	200
Totals	$7.40	$16,090

	Budgeted Fixed Overhead	Actual Fixed Overhead in October
Supervisory salaries	$ 3,630	$ 3,630
Machine depreciation	8,360	8,580
Other	1,210	1,220
Totals	$13,200	$13,430

For October, the number of good units produced was used to compute the 2,100 standard machine hours allowed.

Managerial Reporting and Analysis Cases

Cassen Realtors, Inc.
Performance Report
For the Year Ended December 31, 20x5

	Budgeted*	Actual†	Difference Under (Over) Budget
Total selling fees	$2,052,000	$2,242,200	($190,200)
Less variable costs			
Sales commissions	$1,102,950	$1,205,183	($102,233)
Automobile	36,000	39,560	(3,560)
Advertising	93,600	103,450	(9,850)
Home repairs	77,400	89,240	(11,840)
General overhead	656,100	716,970	(60,870)
	$1,966,050	$2,154,403	($188,353)
Less fixed costs			
general overhead	60,000	62,300	(2,300)
Total costs	$2,026,050	$2,216,703	($190,653)
Operating income	$ 25,950	$ 25,497	$ 453

*Budgeted data are based on 180 units sold.
†Actual data of 200 units sold.

Formulating Management Reports

MRA 2.

LO3 Preparing Performance
LO5 Reports
LO6

Troy Corrente, the president of Forest Valley Spa, is concerned about the spa's operating performance during March 20x6. He budgeted his costs carefully so that he could reduce the 20x6 membership fees. He now needs to evaluate those costs to make sure the spa's profits are at the level he expected.

He has asked you, the spa's controller, to prepare a performance report on labor and overhead costs for March 20x6. He also wants you to analyze the report and suggest possible causes for any problems you find. He wants to attend to any problems quickly, so he has asked you to submit your report as soon as possible. The following information for the month is available to you:

	Budgeted Costs	Actual Costs
Variable costs		
Operating labor	$10,880	$12,150
Utilities	2,880	3,360
Repairs and maintenance	5,760	7,140
Fixed costs		
Depreciation, equipment	2,600	2,680
Rent	3,280	3,280
Other	1,704	1,860
Totals	$27,104	$30,470

Corrente's budget allows for eight employees to work 160 hours each per month. During March, nine employees worked an average of 150 hours each.

Direct labor
  Policy support staff
    3 hours at $12.00 per hour $ 36.00
  Policy salesperson
    8.5 hours at $14.20 per hour   120.70
Operating overhead
  Variable operating overhead
    11.5 hours at $26.00 per hour   299.00
  Fixed operating overhead
    11.5 hours at $18.00 per hour   207.00
Standard unit cost $662.70

Actual costs incurred for the 265 units sold during January were as follows:

Direct labor
  Policy support staff
    848 hours at $12.50 per hour $10,600.00
  Policy salespersons
    2,252.5 hours at $14.00 per hour 31,535.00
Operating overhead
  Variable operating overhead   78,440.00
  Fixed operating overhead   53,400.00

Normal monthly capacity is 260 units, and the budgeted fixed operating overhead for January was $53,820.

1. Compute the standard hours allowed in January for policy support staff and policy salespersons.
2. What should the total standard costs for January have been? What were the total actual costs that the company incurred in January? Compute the total cost variance for the month.
3. Compute the direct labor rate and efficiency variances for policy support staff and policy salespersons.
4. Compute the variable and fixed operating overhead variances for January.
5. Identify possible causes for each variance and suggest possible solutions.

MANAGERIAL REPORTING AND ANALYSIS CASES

Interpreting Management Reports

MRA 1.

LO3 Flexible Budgets and Performance Evaluation

Cassen Realtors, Inc., specializes in the sale of residential properties. It earns its revenue by charging a percentage of the sales price. Commissions for salespersons, listing agents, and listing companies are its main costs. Business has improved steadily over the last ten years. Bonnie Cassen, the managing partner of Cassen Realtors, receives a report summarizing the company's performance each year. The report for the most recent year appears at the top of the facing page.

1. Analyze the performance report. What does it say about the company's performance? Is the performance report reliable? Explain your answer.
2. Calculate the budgeted selling fee and budgeted variable costs per sale.
3. Prepare a performance report using a flexible budget based on the actual number of sales.
4. Analyze the report you prepared in **3**. What does it say about the company's performance? Is the performance report reliable? Explain your answer.
5. What recommendations would you make to improve the company's performance next year?

to evaluate the drivers' performance? How would cost standards for these two service companies be similar, and how would they differ? How do cost standards for service companies differ from those of manufacturing companies?

Ethical Dilemma

SD 3.

LO1 An Ethical Question Involving
LO2 Standard Costs

Taylor Industries, Inc., develops standard costs for all its direct materials, direct labor, and manufacturing overhead costs. It uses these costs for pricing products, costing inventories, and evaluating the performance of purchasing and production managers. It updates standard costs whenever costs, prices, or rates change by 3 percent or more. It also reviews and updates all standard costs each December; this practice provides current standards appropriate for use in valuing year-end inventories on the company's financial statements.

Jody Elgar is in charge of standard costing at Taylor Industries. On November 30, 20x6, she received a memo from the chief financial officer informing her that Taylor Industries was considering purchasing another company and that she and her staff were to postpone adjusting standard costs until late February; they were instead to concentrate on analyzing the proposed purchase.

In the third week of November, prices on over 20 of Taylor Industries' direct materials had been reduced by 10 percent or more, and a new labor union contract had reduced several categories of labor rates. A revision of standard costs in December would have resulted in lower valuations of inventories, higher cost of goods sold due to inventory write-downs, and lower net income for the year. Elgar believed the company was facing an operating loss and that the assignment to evaluate the proposed purchase was designed primarily to keep her staff from revising and lowering standard costs. She questioned the chief financial officer about the assignment and reiterated the need for updating the standard costs but was again told to ignore the update and concentrate on the proposed purchase. Elgar and her staff were relieved of the assignment in early February. The purchase never materialized.

Assess Jody Elgar's actions in this situation. Did this manager follow all ethical paths to solving the problem? What are the consequences of failing to adjust the standard costs?

Research Activity

SD 4.

LO2 Standard Costs and Variance
LO3 Analysis

Domino's Pizza <www.dominos.com> is a major purveyor of home-delivered pizzas. Although customers can pick up their orders at the shops where Domino's makes its pizzas, employees deliver most orders to customers' homes, and they use their own cars to do it.

Specify what standard costing for a Domino's pizza shop would entail. Where would you obtain the information for determining the cost standards? In what ways would the standards help in managing a pizza shop? If necessary to gain a better understanding of the operation, visit a pizzeria. (It does not have to be a Domino's.)

Group Activity: Have students work in groups to complete **SD 4.** Select one person from each group to report the group's findings to the class.

Decision-Making Practice

SD 5.

LO5 Standard Costing in a Service
LO6 Company

Annuity Life Insurance Company (ALIC) markets several types of life insurance policies, but P20A—a permanent, 20-year life annuity policy—is its most popular. This policy sells in $10,000 increments and features variable percentages of whole life insurance and single-payment annuities, depending on the policyholder's needs and age. ALIC devotes an entire department to supporting and marketing the P20A policy. Because both the support staff and salespersons contribute to each P20A policy, ALIC categorizes them as direct labor for purposes of variance analysis, cost control, and performance evaluation. For unit costing, each $10,000 increment is considered one unit; thus, a $90,000 policy is counted as nine units. Standard unit cost information for January is as follows:

as follows: molding, 1.0 hour per batch at an hourly rate of $12; and trimming/packing, 1.2 hours per batch at $10 per hour.

During 20x9, the company produced 48,000 baskets. It used 38,600 grams of liquid plastic at a total cost of $5,404 and 28,950 grams of additive at $2,895. Actual direct labor included 480 hours for molding at a total cost of $5,664 and 560 hours for trimming/packing at $5,656.

REQUIRED
1. Compute the direct materials price and quantity variances for both the liquid plastic and the additive.
2. Compute the direct labor rate and efficiency variances for the molding and trimming/packing processes.

P 8. During 20x6, Biomed Laboratories, Inc., researched and perfected a cure for the common cold. Called Cold-Gone, the product sells for $28.00 per package, each of which contains five tablets. Standard unit costs for this product were developed in late 20x6 for use in 20x7. Per package, the standard unit costs were as follows: chemical ingredients, 6 ounces at $1.00 per ounce; packaging, $1.20; direct labor, .8 hour at $14.00 per hour; standard variable overhead, $4.00 per direct labor hour; and standard fixed overhead, $6.40 per direct labor hour. Normal capacity is 46,875 units per week.

In the first quarter of 20x7, demand for the new product rose well beyond the expectations of management. During those three months, the peak season for colds, the company produced and sold over 500,000 packages of Cold-Gone. During the first week in April, it produced 50,000 packages but used materials for 50,200 packages costing $60,240. It also used 305,000 ounces of chemical ingredients costing $292,800. The total cost of direct labor for the week was $579,600; direct labor hours totaled 40,250. Total variable overhead was $161,100, and total fixed overhead was $242,000. Budgeted fixed overhead for the week was $240,000.

REQUIRED
1. Compute for the first week of April 20x7 (a) all direct materials price variances, (b) all direct materials quantity variances, (c) the direct labor rate variance, (d) the direct labor efficiency variance, (e) the variable overhead spending variance, (f) the variable overhead efficiency variance, (g) the fixed overhead budget variance, and (h) the fixed overhead volume variance.
2. Prepare a performance report based on your variance analysis and suggest possible causes for each significant variance.

SKILLS DEVELOPMENT CASES

Conceptual Analysis

SD 1. Holding down operating costs is an ongoing challenge for managers. The lower the costs a company incurs, the higher its profit will be. But two factors can make a target profit difficult to achieve. First, human error and unexpected machine breakdowns may cause dozens of operating inefficiencies, and each inefficiency will cause costs to rise. Second, a company may control its costs so strictly that it will use cheaper materials or labor, which may cause a decline in the quality of its product or service and in its sales. To control costs and still produce high-quality goods or services, managers must continually assess operating activities by analyzing both financial and nonfinancial data.

Write a one-page paper on how variance analysis helps managers control costs. Focus on both the financial and the nonfinancial data used in standard costing.

SD 2. Both ChemLawn <www.chemlawn.com> and United Parcel Service (UPS) <www.ups.com> use truck drivers to deliver services to clients. ChemLawn's drivers use a hose connected to the tanks on their trucks to spray liquid fertilizers and weed killers on clients' lawns. Drivers of UPS trucks deliver packages to residences and businesses. If you were setting cost standards for ChemLawn and UPS, what standards would you set that apply to the drivers, and what cost components would you use? What measures would you use

and the factory payroll for direct labor for the month was $95,040. Budgeted fixed overhead for August was $9,280. Normal monthly capacity for the year was set at 58,000 doormats.

REQUIRED
1. Compute for August 20x5 the (a) direct materials price variance, (b) direct materials quantity variance, (c) direct labor rate variance, (d) direct labor efficiency variance, (e) variable overhead spending variance, (f) variable overhead efficiency variance, (g) fixed overhead budget variance, and (h) fixed overhead volume variance.
2. Prepare a performance report based on your variance analysis and suggest possible causes for each variance.

P 5.
LO6 Overhead Variances

Celine Corporation's accountant left for vacation before completing the monthly cost variance report. George Celine, the corporation's president, has asked you to complete the report. The following data are available to you (capacities are expressed in machine hours):

Actual machine hours	17,100
Standard machine hours allowed	17,500
Actual variable overhead	a
Standard variable overhead rate	$2.50
Variable overhead spending variance	$ 250 (F)
Variable overhead efficiency variance	b
Actual fixed overhead	c
Budgeted fixed overhead	$153,000
Fixed overhead cost variance	$1,300 (U)
Fixed overhead volume variance	$4,500 (F)
Normal capacity in machine hours	d
Standard fixed overhead rate	e
Fixed overhead applied	f

REQUIRED Analyze the data and fill in the missing amounts. (**Hint:** Use the structure of Figures 5 and 6 in this chapter to guide your analysis.)

ALTERNATE PROBLEMS

P 6.
LO2 Computing Standard Costs for Direct Materials

TickTock, Ltd., assembles clock movements for grandfather clocks. Each movement has four components: the clock facing, the clock hands, the time movement, and the spring assembly. For the current year, 20x5, the company used the following standard costs: clock facing, $15.90; clock hands, $12.70; time movement, $66.10; and spring assembly, $52.50.

Prices of materials are expected to change in 20x6. TickTock will purchase 60 percent of the facings from Company A at $18.50 each and the other 40 percent from Company B at $18.80 each. The clock hands, which are produced for TickTock by Hardware, Inc., will cost $15.50 per set in 20x6. TickTock will purchase 30 percent of the time movements from Company Q at $68.50 each, 20 percent from Company R at $69.50 each, and 50 percent from Company S at $71.90 each. The manufacturer that supplies TickTock with spring assemblies has announced that it will increase its prices by 20 percent in 20x6.

REQUIRED
1. Determine the total standard direct materials cost per unit for 20x6.
2. Suppose that because TickTock has guaranteed Hardware, Inc., that it would purchase 2,500 sets of clock hands in 20x6, the cost of a set of clock hands has been reduced by 20 percent. Find the standard direct materials cost per clock.
3. Suppose that to avoid the increase in the cost of spring assemblies, TickTock purchased substandard ones from a different manufacturer at $50 each; 20 percent of them turned out to be unusable and cannot be returned. Assuming that all other data remain the same, compute the standard direct materials unit cost. Spread the cost of the defective materials over good units produced.

P 7.
LO4 Direct Materials and Direct
LO5 Labor Variances

Fruit Packaging Company makes plastic baskets for food wholesalers. Each basket requires .8 gram of liquid plastic and .6 gram of an additive that includes color and hardening agents. The standard prices are $.15 per gram of liquid plastic and $.09 per gram of additive. Two kinds of direct labor—molding and trimming/packing—are required to make the baskets. The direct labor time and rate standards for a batch of 100 baskets are

Cost Category (Variable Unit Cost)	Budgeted Costs*	Actual Costs	Difference Under (Over) Budget
Direct materials ($.10)	$ 5,000	$ 4,975	$ 25
Direct labor ($.12)	6,000	5,850	150
Manufacturing overhead			
Variable			
Indirect labor ($.03)	1,500	1,290	210
Supplies ($.02)	1,000	960	40
Heat and power ($.03)	1,500	1,325	175
Other ($.05)	2,500	2,340	160
Fixed			
Heat and power	3,500	3,500	—
Depreciation	4,200	4,200	—
Insurance and taxes	1,200	1,200	—
Other	1,600	1,600	—
Totals	$28,000	$27,240	$760

*Based on normal capacity of 50,000 units.

In discussing the report with the controller, Fisher stated, "Profits have been decreasing in recent months, but this report indicates that our production process is operating efficiently."

REQUIRED
1. Prepare a flexible budget for the Beverage Division using production levels of 45,000 units, 50,000 units, and 55,000 units.
2. What is the flexible budget formula?
3. Assume that the Beverage Division produced 46,560 units in April and that all fixed costs remained constant. Prepare a revised performance report similar to the one above, using actual production in units as a basis for the budget column.
4. Which report is more meaningful for performance evaluation, the original one above or the revised one? Why?

P 3.
LO4 Direct Materials and Direct
LO5 Labor Variances

Winners Trophy Company produces a variety of athletic awards, most of them in the form of trophies. Its deluxe trophy stands three feet tall above the base. The company's direct materials standards for the deluxe trophy include one pound of metal and eight ounces of wood for the base. Standard prices for 20x6 were $3.30 per pound of metal and $.45 per ounce of wood. Direct labor standards for the deluxe trophy specify .2 hour of direct labor in the Molding Department and .4 hour in the Trimming/Finishing Department. Standard direct labor rates are $10.75 per hour in the Molding Department and $12.00 per hour in the Trimming/Finishing Department.

During January 20x6, the company made 16,400 deluxe trophies. Actual production data are as follows:

Direct materials
  Metal   16,640 pounds @ $3.25 per pound
  Wood   131,400 ounces @ $.48 per ounce
Direct labor
  Molding   3,400 hours @ $10.60 per hour
  Trimming/Finishing 6,540 hours @ $12.10 per hour

REQUIRED
1. Compute the direct materials price and quantity variances for metal and wood.
2. Compute the direct labor rate and efficiency variances for the Molding and the Trimming/Finishing Departments.

P 4.
LO4 Direct Materials, Direct Labor,
LO5 and Manufacturing Overhead
LO6 Variances

The Doormat Division of Clean Sweep Company produces all-vinyl mats. Each doormat calls for .4 meter of vinyl material; the material should cost $3.10 per meter. Standard direct labor hours and labor cost per doormat are .2 hour and $1.84 (.2 hour × $9.20 per hour), respectively. Currently, the division's standard variable overhead rate is $1.50 per direct labor hour, and its standard fixed overhead rate is $.80 per direct labor hour.

In August 20x5, the division manufactured and sold 60,000 doormats. During the month, it used 25,200 meters of vinyl material; the total cost of the material was $73,080. The total actual manufacturing overhead costs for August were $28,200, of which $18,200 was variable. The total number of direct labor hours worked was 10,800,

hour had been developed based on a budget of 10,000 engineering hours each month. Calculate Engineering Associates' fixed overhead budget and volume variances for the month.

LO6 Manufacturing Overhead Variances

E 13. Cedar Key Company produces handmade clamming buckets and sells them to distributors along the Gulf Coast of Florida. The company incurred $9,400 of actual manufacturing overhead costs ($8,000 variable; $1,400 fixed) in May. Budgeted standard overhead costs for May were $4 of variable overhead costs per direct labor hour and $1,500 of fixed overhead costs. Normal capacity was set at 2,000 direct labor hours per month. In May, the company produced 10,100 clamming buckets by working 1,900 direct labor hours. The time standard is .2 direct labor hour per clamming bucket. Compute (1) the variable overhead spending and efficiency variances and (2) the fixed overhead budget and volume variances for May.

LO6 Manufacturing Overhead Variances

E 14. Suncoast Industries uses standard costing and a flexible budget for cost planning and control. Its monthly budget for overhead costs is $200,000 of fixed costs plus $5.20 per machine hour. Monthly normal capacity of 100,000 machine hours is used to compute the standard fixed overhead rate. During December, employees worked 105,000 machine hours. Only 98,500 standard machine hours were allowed for good units produced during the month. Actual overhead costs incurred during December totaled $441,000 of variable costs and $204,500 of fixed costs. Compute (1) the under- or overapplied overhead during December and (2) the variable overhead spending and efficiency variances and the fixed overhead budget and volume variances.

LO7 Evaluating Managerial Performance

E 15. Ron LaTulip oversees projects for ACE Construction Company. Recently, the company's controller sent him a performance report regarding the construction of the Campus Highlands Apartment Complex, a project that LaTulip supervised. Included in the report was an unfavorable direct labor efficiency variance of $1,900 for roof structures. What types of information does LaTulip need to analyze before he can respond to this report?

PROBLEMS

LO2 Computing and Using Standard Costs

P 1. Prefabricated houses are the specialty of Affordable Homes, Inc., of Corsicana, Texas. Although Affordable Homes produces many models, and customers can even place special orders, the company's best-selling model is the Welcome Home, a three-bedroom, 1,400-square-foot house with an impressive front entrance. In 20x5, the standard costs for the six basic direct materials used in manufacturing the entrance were as follows: wood framing materials, $2,140; deluxe front door, $480; door hardware, $260; exterior siding, $710; electrical materials, $580; and interior finishing materials, $1,520. Three types of direct labor are used to build the entrance: carpenter, 30 hours at $12 per hour; door specialist, 4 hours at $14 per hour; and electrician, 8 hours at $16 per hour. In 20x5, the company used a manufacturing overhead rate of 40 percent of total direct materials cost.

During 20x6, the cost of wood framing materials is expected to increase by 20 percent, and a deluxe front door will cost $496. The cost of the door hardware will increase by 10 percent, and the cost of electrical materials will increase by 20 percent. Exterior siding cost should decrease by $16 per unit. The cost of interior finishing materials is expected to remain the same. The carpenter's wages will increase by $1 per hour, and the door specialist's wages should remain the same. The electrician's wages will increase by $.50 per hour. Finally, the manufacturing overhead rate will decrease to 25 percent of total direct materials cost.

REQUIRED ▶
1. Compute the total standard cost of direct materials per entrance for 20x5.
2. Using your answer to item 1, compute the total standard unit cost per entrance for 20x5.
3. Compute the total standard unit cost per entrance for 20x6.

LO3 Preparing a Flexible Budget and Evaluating Performance

P 2. Home Products Company manufactures a complete line of kitchen glassware. The Beverage Division specializes in 12-ounce drinking glasses. Erin Fisher, the superintendent of the Beverage Division, asked the controller to prepare a report of her division's performance in April 20x4. The following report was handed to her a few days later:

fixed overhead rate. Using these production standards, compute the standard unit cost of one weather balloon.

LO3 Preparing a Flexible Budget

E 4. Keel Company's fixed overhead costs for 20x5 are expected to be as follows: depreciation, $72,000; supervisory salaries, $92,000; property taxes and insurance, $26,000; and other fixed overhead, $14,500. Total fixed overhead is thus expected to be $204,500. Variable costs per unit are expected to be as follows: direct materials, $16.50; direct labor, $8.50; operating supplies, $2.60; indirect labor, $4.10; and other variable overhead costs, $3.20. Prepare a flexible budget for the following levels of production: 18,000 units, 20,000 units, and 22,000 units. What is the flexible budget formula for 20x5?

LO4 Direct Materials Price and Quantity Variances

E 5. SITO Elevator Company manufactures small hydroelectric elevators with a maximum capacity of ten passengers. One of the direct materials used is heavy-duty carpeting for the floor of the elevator. The direct materials quantity standard for April was 8 square yards per elevator. During April, the purchasing agent purchased this carpeting at $11 per square yard; the standard price for the period was $12. Ninety elevators were completed and sold during the month; the Production Department used an average of 8.5 square yards of carpet per elevator. Calculate the company's direct materials price and quantity variances for carpeting for April.

LO4 Direct Materials Variances

E 6. Diekow Productions manufactured and sold 1,000 products at $11,000 each during the past year. At the beginning of the year, production had been set at 1,200 products; direct materials standards had been set at 100 pounds of direct materials at $2 per pound for each product produced. During the year, the company purchased and used 98,000 pounds of direct materials; the cost was $2.04 per pound. Calculate Diekow Production's direct materials price and quantity variances for the year.

LO5 Direct Labor Variances

E 7. At the beginning of last year, Diekow Productions set direct labor standards of 20 hours at $15 per hour for each product produced. During the year, 20,500 direct labor hours were actually worked at an average cost of $16 per hour. Using this information and the applicable information in **E 6**, calculate Diekow Production's direct labor rate and efficiency variances for the year.

LO5 Direct Labor Rate and Efficiency Variances

E 8. NEO Foundry, Inc., manufactures castings that other companies use in the production of machinery. For the past two years, NEO's best-selling product has been a casting for an eight-cylinder engine block. Standard direct labor hours per engine block are 1.8 hours. A labor union contract requires that the company pay all direct labor employees $14 per hour. During June, NEO produced 16,500 engine blocks. Actual direct labor hours and costs for the month were 29,900 hours and $433,550, respectively.

1. Compute the direct labor rate variance for eight-cylinder engine blocks during June.
2. Using the same data, compute the direct labor efficiency variance for eight-cylinder engine blocks during June. Check your answer, assuming that the total direct labor cost variance is $17,750 (U).

LO6 Variable Overhead Variances

E 9. At the beginning of last year, Diekow Productions set standards of 10 machine hours at a variable rate of $10 per hour for each product produced. During the year, 10,800 machine hours were used at a cost of $10.20 per hour. Using this information and the applicable information in **E 6**, calculate Diekow Production's variable overhead spending and efficiency variances for the year.

LO6 Fixed Overhead Variances

E 10. At the beginning of last year, Diekow Productions set budgeted fixed overhead costs at $456,000. During the year, actual fixed overhead costs were $500,000. Using this information and the applicable information in **E 6**, calculate Diekow Production's fixed overhead budget and volume variances for the year.

LO6 Variable Overhead Variances for a Service Business

E 11. Design Architects, LLP, billed clients for 6,000 hours of design work for the month. Actual variable overhead costs for the month were $315,000, and 6,250 hours were worked. At the beginning of the year, a variable overhead standard of $50 per design hour had been developed based on a budget of 5,000 design hours each month. Calculate Design Architect's variable overhead spending and efficiency variances for the month.

LO6 Fixed Overhead Variances for a Service Business

E 12. Engineering Associates billed clients for 11,000 hours of engineering work for the month. Actual fixed overhead costs for the month were $435,000, and 11,850 hours were worked. At the beginning of the year, a fixed overhead standard of $40 per design

Diagram Form:

	Actual Fixed Overhead Costs		Budgeted Fixed Overhead Costs		Standard Rate × Standard Hours
Fixed Overhead	$55,000	Budget Variance	$54,000	Volume Variance	$3.60 × (12,200 × 1.2) = $52,704
		$1,000 (U)	Total Fixed Overhead Variance	$1,296 (U)	
			$2,296 (U)		

Chapter Assignments

BUILDING YOUR KNOWLEDGE FOUNDATION

QUESTIONS

1. What are standard costs?
2. What is a variance?
3. Can a service organization use standard costing? Explain your answer.
4. Explain the following statement: "Standard costing is a total unit cost concept in that standard unit costs are determined for direct materials, direct labor, and manufacturing overhead."
5. What general ledger accounts are affected by a standard costing system?
6. What do a standard overhead manufacturing rate and a predetermined overhead rate have in common? How do they differ?
7. Name the six elements used to compute a standard unit cost.
8. Identify three factors that could affect a direct materials price standard.
9. "Performance is evaluated by comparing what did happen with what should have happened." What does this statement mean? How does it relate to cost control?
10. What is variance analysis?
11. What is a flexible budget? What is its purpose?
12. What are the components of the flexible budget formula? How are they related?
13. How can variances help managers control costs?
14. What is the formula for computing a direct materials price variance?
15. How would you interpret an unfavorable direct materials price variance?
16. Can an unfavorable direct materials quantity variance be caused, at least in part, by a favorable direct materials price variance? Explain your answer.
17. Identify two possible causes of a direct labor rate variance and describe the measures used to track performance in those areas. Then do the same for a direct labor efficiency variance.
18. Distinguish between the fixed overhead budget variance and the fixed overhead volume variance.
19. If standard hours allowed exceed normal hours, will the period's fixed manufacturing overhead volume variance be favorable or unfavorable? Explain your answer.

5. Variable overhead cost variances:
   a. Variable overhead spending variance:

Budgeted variable overhead for actual hours Variable overhead cost ($5.00 per hour × 15,250 labor hours)	$76,250
Less actual variable overhead costs incurred	73,200
Variable overhead spending variance	$ 3,050 (F)

   b. Variable overhead efficiency variance:

Variable overhead applied to good units produced (14,640 hours* × $5.00 per hour)	$73,200
Less budgeted variable overhead for actual hours (15,250 hours × $5.00 per hour)	76,250
Variable overhead efficiency variance	$ 3,050 (U)

   *12,200 units produced × 1.2 hours per unit = 14,640 hours.

   c. Total variable overhead cost variance:

   Total Variable Overhead Cost Variance = Net of Variable Overhead Spending Variance and Variable Overhead Efficiency Variance
   = $3,050 (F) − $3,050 (U)
   = $0

Diagram Form:

	Actual Variable Overhead Costs		Standard Rate × Actual Hours		Standard Rate × Standard Hours
Variable Overhead	$73,200	Spending Variance	$5.00 × 15,250 = $76,250	Efficiency Variance	$5.00 × (12,200 × 1.2) = $73,200
		$3,050 (F)	Total Variable Overhead Cost Variance	$3,050 (U)	
			$0		

6. Fixed overhead cost variances:
   a. Fixed overhead budget variance:

Budgeted fixed overhead	$54,000
Less actual fixed overhead	55,000
Fixed overhead budget variance	$ 1,000 (U)

   b. Fixed overhead volume variance:

Standard fixed overhead applied (14,640 labor hours × $3.60 per hour)	$52,704
Less total budgeted fixed overhead	54,000
Fixed overhead volume variance	$ 1,296 (U)

   c. Total fixed overhead cost variance:

   Total Fixed Overhead Cost Variance = Net of Fixed Overhead Budget Variance and Fixed Overhead Volume Variance
   = $1,000 (U) + $1,296 (U)
   = $2,296 (U)

c. Total Direct Materials Cost Variance:

Total Direct Materials Cost Variance = Net of Direct Materials Price Variance and Direct Materials Quantity Variance
= $3,750 (F) − $11,250 (U)
= $7,500 (U)

Diagram Form:

	Actual Price × Actual Quantity		Standard Price × Actual Quantity		Standard Price × Standard Quantity
Direct Materials	$12.40 × 37,500 = $465,000	Price Variance	$12.50 × 37,500 = $468,750	Quantity Variance	$12.50 × (12,200 × 3) = $457,500
		$3,750 (F)	Total Direct Materials Cost Variance	$11,250 (U)	
			$7,500 (U)		

4. Direct labor cost variances:
   a. Direct labor rate variance:

   Rate difference: Standard labor rate $9.00
   Less actual labor rate 9.20
   Difference $ .20 (U)

   Direct Labor Rate Variance = (Standard Rate − Actual Rate) × Actual Hours
   = $.20 × 15,250 hours
   = $3,050 (U)

   b. Direct labor efficiency variance:

   Difference in hours: Standard hours allowed 14,640 hours*
   Less actual hours 15,250 hours
   Difference 610 hours (U)

   Direct Labor Efficiency Variance = Standard Rate × (Standard Hours Allowed − Actual Hours)
   = $9.00 per hour × 610 hours (U)
   = $5,490 (U)

   *12,200 units produced × 1.2 hours per unit = 14,640 hours.

   c. Total direct labor cost variance:

   Total Direct Labor Cost Variance = Net of Direct Labor Rate Variance and Direct Labor Efficiency Variance
   = $3,050 (U) + $5,490 (U)
   = $8,540 (U)

Diagram Form:

	Actual Rate × Actual Hours		Standard Rate × Actual Hours		Standard Rate × Standard Hours
Direct Labor	$9.20 × 15,250 = $140,300	Rate Variance	$9.00 × 15,250 = $137,250	Efficiency Variance	$9.00 × (12,200 × 1.2) = $131,760
		$3,050 (U)	Total Direct Labor Cost Variance	$5,490 (U)	
			$8,540 (U)		

units, and it purchased and used 37,500 square meters of direct materials; the purchase cost was $12.40 per square meter. The average labor rate was $9.20 per hour, and 15,250 direct labor hours were worked. The company's actual variable overhead costs for the year were $73,200, and its fixed overhead costs were $55,000.

REQUIRED ▶ Using the data given, compute the following using formulas or diagram form:

1. Standard hours allowed for good output
2. Standard fixed overhead rate
3. Direct materials cost variances:
   a. Direct materials price variance
   b. Direct materials quantity variance
   c. Total direct materials cost variance
4. Direct labor cost variances:
   a. Direct labor rate variance
   b. Direct labor efficiency variance
   c. Total direct labor cost variance
5. Variable overhead cost variances:
   a. Variable overhead spending variance
   b. Variable overhead efficiency variance
   c. Total variable overhead cost variance
6. Fixed overhead cost variances:
   a. Fixed overhead budget variance
   b. Fixed overhead volume variance
   c. Total fixed overhead cost variance

ANSWER TO REVIEW PROBLEM

1. Standard Hours Allowed = Good Units Produced × Standard Direct Labor Hours per Unit
   = 12,200 units × 1.2 direct labor hours per unit
   = 14,640 hours

2. Standard Fixed Overhead Rate = $\dfrac{\text{Budgeted Fixed Overhead Cost}}{\text{Normal Capacity}}$

   = $\dfrac{\$54,000}{15,000 \text{ direct labor hours}}$

   = $3.60 per direct labor hour

3. Direct materials cost variances:
   a. Direct materials price variance

Price difference:		
Standard price	$12.50	
Less actual price	12.40	
Difference	$ .10 (F)	

   Direct Materials Price Variance = (Standard Price − Actual Price) × Actual Quantity
   = $.10 × 37,500 sq. meters
   = $3,750 (F)

   b. Direct materials quantity variance

   Quantity difference: Standard quantity
   (12,200 units × 3 sq. meters)   36,600 sq. meters
   Less actual quantity   37,500 sq. meters
   Difference   900 sq. meters (U)

   Direct Materials Quantity Variance = Standard Price × (Standard Quantity − Actual Quantity)
   = $12.50 per sq. meter × 900 sq. meters
   = $11,250 (U)

LO1 **Standard costing:** A method of cost control with three components: a standard, or predetermined, performance level; a measure of actual performance; and a measure of the difference, or variance, between standard and actual performance.

LO1 **Standard costs:** Realistic estimates of costs based on analyses of both past and projected operating costs and conditions.

LO2 **Standard direct labor cost:** The standard wage for direct labor multiplied by the standard hours of direct labor.

LO2 **Standard direct materials cost:** The standard price for direct materials multiplied by the standard quantity for direct materials.

LO2 **Standard fixed overhead rate:** Total budgeted fixed overhead costs divided by an expression of capacity, usually normal capacity in terms of standard hours or units.

LO2 **Standard manufacturing overhead cost:** The sum of the estimates of variable and fixed overhead costs in the next accounting period.

LO2 **Standard variable overhead rate:** Total budgeted variable overhead costs divided by an expression of capacity, such as the expected number of standard machine hours or standard direct labor hours.

LO5 **Total direct labor cost variance:** The difference between the standard direct labor cost for good units produced and actual direct labor costs.

LO4 **Total direct materials cost variance:** The difference between the standard cost and actual cost of direct materials.

LO6 **Total fixed overhead variance:** The difference between actual fixed overhead costs and the standard fixed overhead costs that are applied to good units produced using the standard fixed overhead rate.

LO6 **Total manufacturing overhead variance:** The difference between actual manufacturing overhead costs and standard manufacturing overhead costs.

LO6 **Total variable overhead variance:** The difference between actual variable overhead costs and the standard variable overhead costs that are applied to good units produced using the standard variable overhead rate.

LO6 **Variable overhead efficiency variance:** The difference between the standard direct labor hours allowed for good units produced and the actual hours worked multiplied by the standard variable overhead rate per hour.

LO6 **Variable overhead spending variance:** The difference between actual variable overhead costs and the standard variable overhead rate multiplied by the actual hours used. Also called the *variable overhead rate variance*.

LO1 **Variance:** The difference between a standard cost and an actual cost.

LO3 **Variance analysis:** The process of computing the differences between standard costs and actual costs and identifying the causes of those differences.

REVIEW PROBLEM

Variance Analysis

LO2
LO4
LO5
LO6

Alexa Manufacturing Company has a standard costing system and keeps all its cost standards up to date. The company's main product is copper water pipe, which is made in a single department. The standard variable costs for one unit of finished pipe are as follows:

Direct materials (3 sq. meters @ $12.50 per sq. meter)	$37.50
Direct labor (1.2 hours @ $9.00 per hour)	10.80
Variable overhead (1.2 hours @ $5.00 per direct labor hour)	6.00
Standard variable cost per unit	$54.30

The company's normal capacity is 15,000 direct labor hours. Its budgeted fixed overhead costs for the year were $54,000. During the year, it produced and sold 12,200

the causes of differences between standard direct labor costs and actual direct labor costs.

LO6 Compute and analyze manufacturing overhead variances.

The total manufacturing overhead variance is equal to the amount of under- or overapplied overhead costs for an accounting period. An analysis of the variable and fixed overhead variances will help explain why the amount of overhead applied to units produced differs from the actual overhead costs incurred. The total overhead variance can be broken down into a variable overhead spending variance, a variable overhead efficiency variance, a fixed overhead budget variance, and a fixed overhead volume variance.

LO7 Explain how variances are used to evaluate managers' performance.

How effectively and fairly a manager's performance is evaluated depends on human factors—the people doing the evaluating—as well as on company policies. To ensure that performance evaluation is effective and fair, a company's evaluation policies should be based on input from managers and employees and should be specific about the procedures managers are to follow. The evaluation process becomes more accurate when managerial performance reports include variances from standard costs. A managerial performance report based on standard costs and related variances should identify the causes of each significant variance, as well as the personnel involved, and the corrective actions taken. It should be tailored to the manager's specific areas of responsibility.

REVIEW OF CONCEPTS AND TERMINOLOGY

The following concepts and terms were introduced in this chapter:

LO5 **Direct labor efficiency variance:** The difference between the standard direct labor hours allowed for good units produced and the actual direct labor hours worked multiplied by the standard direct labor rate. Also called *direct labor quantity* or *usage variance*.

LO2 **Direct labor rate standard:** The hourly direct labor rate expected to prevail during the next accounting period for each function or job classification.

LO5 **Direct labor rate variance:** The difference between the standard direct labor rate and the actual direct labor rate multiplied by the actual direct labor hours worked. Also called *direct labor spending variance*.

LO2 **Direct labor time standard:** The expected labor time required for each department, machine, or process to complete the production of one unit or one batch of output.

LO2 **Direct materials price standard:** A careful estimate of the cost of a specific direct material in the next accounting period.

LO4 **Direct materials price variance:** The difference between the standard price and the actual price per unit multiplied by the actual quantity purchased. Also called *direct material spending* or *rate variance*.

LO2 **Direct materials quantity standard:** An estimate of the amount of direct materials, including scrap and waste, that will be used in an accounting period.

LO4 **Direct materials quantity variance:** The difference between the standard quantity allowed and the actual quantity used multiplied by the standard price. Also called *direct material efficiency* or *usage variance*.

LO6 **Fixed overhead budget variance:** The difference between budgeted and actual fixed overhead costs. Also called *budgeted fixed overhead variance*.

LO6 **Fixed overhead volume variance:** The difference between budgeted fixed overhead costs and the overhead costs that are applied to production using the standard fixed overhead rate.

LO3 **Flexible budget:** A summary of expected costs for a range of activity levels. Also called *variable budget*.

LO3 **Flexible budget formula:** An equation that determines the expected, or budgeted, cost for any level of productive output.

Chapter Review

REVIEW OF LEARNING OBJECTIVES

LO1 Define *standard costs* and describe how managers use standard costs in the management cycle.

Standard costs are realistic estimates of costs based on analyses of both past and projected operating costs and conditions. They provide a standard, or predetermined, performance level for use in standard costing, a method of cost control that also includes a measure of actual performance and a measure of the variance between standard and actual performance. In the planning stage of the management cycle, managers use standard costs to develop budgets for direct materials, direct labor, and variable overhead. These estimated costs not only serve as targets for product costing; they are also useful in making decisions about product distribution and pricing. During the executing stage, managers use standard costs to measure expenditures and to control costs as they occur. At the end of an accounting period, they compare actual costs with standard costs and compute the variances. The variances provide measures of performance that can be used to control costs. Managers also use standard costs to report on operations and managerial performance.

LO2 Explain how standard costs are developed and compute a standard unit cost.

A standard unit cost has six elements. The direct materials price standard is based on a careful estimate of all possible price increases, changes in available quantities, and new sources of supply in the next accounting period. The direct materials quantity standard is based on product engineering specifications, the quality of direct materials, the age and productivity of the machines, and the quality and experience of the work force. Labor union contracts or company policies define the direct labor rate standard. Current time and motion studies of workers and machines and records of their past performance provide the data for developing the direct labor time standard. Standard variable and fixed overhead rates are found by dividing total budgeted variable and fixed overhead costs by an appropriate application base.

A total standard unit cost is computed by adding the following costs: direct materials costs (direct materials price standard times direct materials quantity standard), direct labor costs (direct labor rate standard times direct labor time standard), and manufacturing overhead costs (standard variable and standard fixed overhead rate times standard direct labor hours allowed per unit).

LO3 Prepare a flexible budget and describe how variance analysis is used to control costs.

A flexible budget is a summary of anticipated costs for a range of activity levels. It provides forecasted cost data that can be adjusted for changes in level of output. The variable cost per unit and total fixed costs presented in a flexible budget are components of the flexible budget formula, an equation that determines the budgeted cost for any level of output. A flexible budget improves the accuracy of variance analysis, which is a four-step approach to controlling costs. First, managers compute the amount of the variance. If the amount is insignificant, no corrective action is needed. If the amount is significant, managers then analyze the variance to identify its cause. In identifying the cause, they are usually able to pinpoint the activities that need to be monitored. They then select performance measures that will enable them to track those activities, analyze the results, and determine the action needed to correct the problem. Their final step is to take the appropriate corrective action.

LO4 Compute and analyze direct materials variances.

The direct materials price variance is computed by finding the difference between the standard price and the actual price per unit and multiplying it by the actual quantity purchased. The direct materials quantity variance is the difference between the standard quantity that should have been used and the actual quantity used, multiplied by the standard price. An analysis of these variances enables managers to identify what is causing them and to formulate plans for correcting related operating problems.

LO5 Compute and analyze direct labor variances.

The direct labor rate variance is computed by determining the difference between the standard direct labor rate and the actual rate and multiplying it by the actual direct labor hours worked. The direct labor efficiency variance is the difference between the standard hours allowed for the number of good units produced and the actual hours worked multiplied by the standard direct labor rate. Managers analyze these variances to find

Exhibit 5
Managerial Performance Report Using Variance Analysis

Cambria Company
Managerial Performance Report
Bag Assembly Department
For the Month Ended August 31, 20x6

Productivity Summary:

Normal capacity in units	167 bags
Normal capacity in direct labor hours (DLH)	400 DLH
Good units produced	180 bags
Performance level (standard hours allowed for good units produced)	432 DLH

Cost and Variance Analysis:

	Standard Costs	Actual Costs	Total Variance	Variance Breakdown Amount	Variance Breakdown Type
Direct materials	$ 4,320	$ 4,484	$164 (U)	$ 76.00 (F)	Direct materials price variance
				240.00 (U)	Direct materials quantity variance
Direct labor	3,672	4,140	468 (U)	315.00 (U)	Direct labor rate variance
				153.00 (U)	Direct labor efficiency variance
Overhead					
Variable	2,484	2,500	16 (U)	87.50 (F)	Variable overhead spending variance
				103.50 (U)	Variable overhead efficiency variance
Fixed	1,404	1,600	196 (U)	300.00 (U)	Fixed overhead budget variance
				104.00 (F)	Fixed overhead volume variance
Totals	$11,880	$12,724	$844 (U)	$844.00 (U)	

Causes of Variances

Direct materials price variance:
New direct material purchased at reduced price

Direct materials quantity variance:
Poor quality of new direct material

Direct labor rate variance:
Machine operator who had to learn assembly skills

Direct labor efficiency variance:
Machine operator who had to learn assembly skills
Late delivery of parts to assembly floor

Variable overhead spending variance:
Cost savings on purchases

Variable overhead efficiency variance:
Machine operator who had to learn assembly skills on the job

Fixed overhead budget variance:
Large number of factory insurance claims

Fixed overhead volume variance:
High number of orders caused by seasonal demand

Actions Taken

New direct material deemed inappropriate; resumed purchasing material originally specified

New direct material deemed inappropriate; resumed using direct material originally specified

Temporary replacement; no action taken on the job

Temporary replacement; no action taken on the job
Material delivery times and number of delays being tracked

No action necessary

A cross-training program for employees now under consideration

Study of insurance claims being conducted

No action necessary

Check out ACE for a Review Quiz at http://accounting.college.hmco.com/students.

$104 (F) volume variance. The overutilization of capacity was traced to high seasonal demand that pressed the company to use almost all its capacity. Management decided not to do anything about the fixed overhead volume variance because it fell within an anticipated seasonal range.

✓ Check out ACE for a Review Quiz at http://accounting.college.hmco.com/students.

USING COST VARIANCES TO EVALUATE MANAGERS' PERFORMANCE

LO7 Explain how variances are used to evaluate managers' performance.

RELATED TEXT ASSIGNMENTS
Q: 20
SE: 10
E: 15

How effectively and fairly a manager's performance is evaluated depends on human factors—the people doing the evaluating—as well as on company policies. The evaluation process becomes more accurate when managerial performance reports include variances from standard costs.

To ensure that the evaluation of a manager's performance is effective and fair, a company's policies should be based on input from managers and employees and should specify the procedures that managers are to use for

- Preparing operational plans
- Assigning responsibility for carrying out the operational plans
- Communicating the operational plans to key personnel
- Evaluating performance in each area of responsibility
- Identifying the causes of significant variances from the operational plan
- Taking corrective action to eliminate problems

Because variance analysis provides detailed data about differences between standard and actual costs and thus helps identify the causes of those differences, it is usually more effective at pinpointing efficient and inefficient operating areas than are basic comparisons of budgeted and actual data. A managerial performance report based on standard costs and related variances should identify the causes of each significant variance, as well as the personnel involved and the corrective actions taken. It should be tailored to the manager's specific areas of responsibility, explaining clearly and accurately in what way the manager's department met or did not meet operating expectations. Managers should be held accountable only for cost areas under their control.

Exhibit 5 shows a performance report for the manager of Cambria Company's Bag Assembly Department. The report summarizes all cost data and variances for direct materials, direct labor, and manufacturing overhead. In addition, it identifies the causes of the variances and the corrective actions taken. Such a report would enable a supervisor to review a manager's actions and evaluate his or her performance.

● **STOP AND THINK!**
Why should evaluations of managers' performance not follow a set pattern?
Because managers have different responsibilities, evaluations of their performance should be tailored to those responsibilities. ■

A point to remember is that the mere occurrence of a variance does not indicate that a manager has performed poorly. However, if a variance consistently occurs and no cause is identified and no corrective action is taken, it may well indicate poor managerial performance.

The report in Exhibit 5 shows that the causes of the variances have been identified and corrective actions have been taken, indicating that the manager of the Cambria Company's Bag Assembly Department has the operation under control.

FOCUS ON BUSINESS ETHICS

Ethics = Profits

According to a recent five-year study, companies that demonstrate a commitment to ethical practices are more profitable than companies that do not demonstrate such a commitment. Conducted by researchers in the United Kingdom and the United States, the study used financial performance measures, including economic value added and return on capital, and nonfinancial performance measures, such as whether a company was on a list of most admired companies. The study found that in the long run, ethical companies outperformed their less ethical peers.[5]

In some cases, an unfavorable volume variance is in a company's best interest. For example, in a period of slow sales, an unfavorable volume variance would mean the company was not building up excessive inventory that might be subject to obsolescence, weathering, and storage costs. For this reason, a favorable volume variance does not always indicate that a manager has performed well.

■ **SUMMARY OF MANUFACTURING OVERHEAD VARIANCES** If our calculations of variable and fixed overhead variances are correct, the net of these variances should equal the total manufacturing overhead variance. Checking the computations, we find that the variable and fixed overhead variances do equal the total manufacturing overhead variance:

Variable overhead spending variance	$ 87.50 (F)
Variable overhead efficiency variance	103.50 (U)
Fixed overhead budget variance	300.00 (U)
Fixed overhead volume variance	104.00 (F)
Total manufacturing overhead variance	$212.00 (U)

Figures 5 and 6 summarize our analysis of manufacturing overhead variances. The total manufacturing overhead variance is also the amount of overapplied or underapplied overhead. You may recall from an earlier chapter that actual variable and fixed overhead costs are recorded as they occur, that variable and fixed overhead are applied to products as they are produced, and that the overapplied or underapplied overhead is computed and reconciled at the end of each accounting period. By breaking down the total manufacturing overhead variance into variable and fixed variances, managers can more accurately control costs and reconcile their causes. An analysis of these two overhead variances will help explain why the amount of overhead applied to units produced is different from the actual overhead costs incurred.

ANALYZING AND CORRECTING MANUFACTURING OVERHEAD VARIANCES

In analyzing the unfavorable total manufacturing overhead variance of $212, the manager of Cambria Company's Bag Assembly Department found causes for the variances that contributed to it. Although the variable overhead spending variance was favorable ($87.50 less than expected because of savings on purchases), the inefficiency of the machine operator who substituted for an assembly worker created unfavorable variances for both direct labor efficiency and variable overhead efficiency. As a result, the manager is going to consider the feasibility of implementing a program for cross-training employees.

After reviewing the fixed overhead costs, the manager of the Bag Assembly Department concluded that higher than anticipated factory insurance premiums were the reason for the unfavorable fixed overhead budget variance and were the result of an increase in the number of insurance claims filed by employees. To obtain more specific information, the manager will study the insurance claims filed over a three-month period.

Finally, since the 432 standard hours were well above the normal capacity of 400 direct labor hours, fixed overhead was overapplied, and it resulted in a

FOCUS ON INTERNATIONAL BUSINESS

Have You Bought Gold Medal Sneakers Yet?
Founded by Li-Ning, winner of the 1984 Olympic Gold medal for gymnastics, Beijing Li-Ning Sports Goods Company is aiming to become a dominant force in the global market by 2008, when the Olympic games will be held in Beijing. The company's products include athletic shoes and sportswear. Currently, its sneakers are the best-selling ones in China, a market soon to be the second largest in the world. Controlling costs through the use of standard costing is a key to the company's success. Because its prices are up to two-thirds lower than those of its international competitors and because it controls its costs well, Beijing Li-Ning Sports Goods Company is an up-and-coming global contender.[4]

FIGURE 1
Standard Costing, Variance Analysis, and the Management Cycle

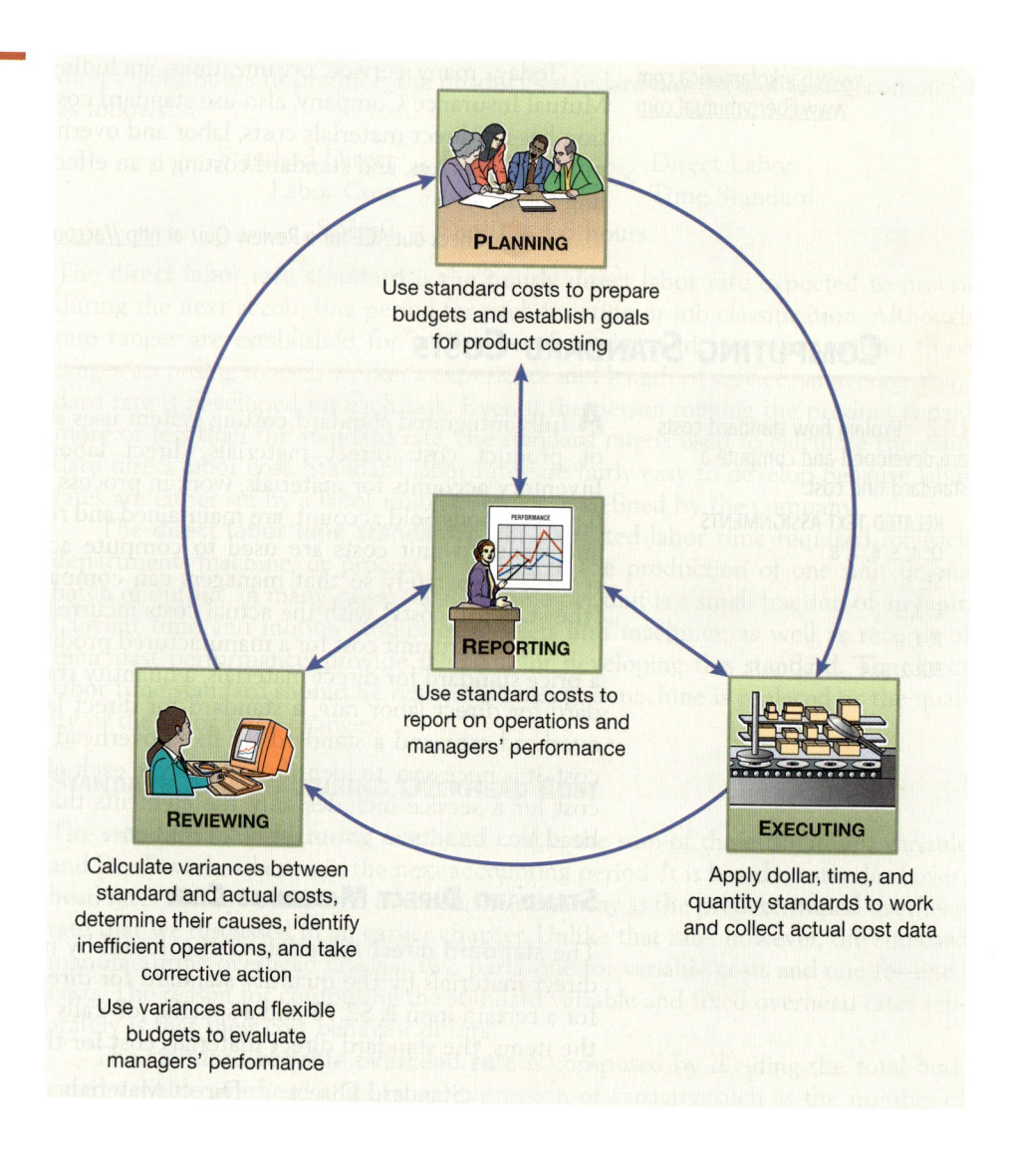

PLANNING
Use standard costs to prepare budgets and establish goals for product costing

REPORTING
Use standard costs to report on operations and managers' performance

EXECUTING
Apply dollar, time, and quantity standards to work and collect actual cost data

REVIEWING
Calculate variances between standard and actual costs, determine their causes, identify inefficient operations, and take corrective action
Use variances and flexible budgets to evaluate managers' performance

◆ **STOP AND THINK!**
Why should managers be interested in changes in the cost of materials?

Information about changes in the cost of materials enables managers to adjust the prices of goods to reflect those changes. ■

www.coach.com
www.kraft.com
www.boeing.com

occurred. Favorable variances may indicate desirable practices that should be implemented elsewhere or a need to revise the existing standards. Both favorable and unfavorable variances from standard costs can be used to evaluate an individual manager's performance.

■ **REPORTING** During the reporting stage, managers use standard costs to report on operations and managerial performance. A variance report tailored to a manager's specific responsibilities provides useful information about how well operations are proceeding and how well the manager is controlling them.

THE RELEVANCE OF STANDARD COSTING IN TODAY'S BUSINESS ENVIRONMENT

In recent years, the increasing automation of manufacturing processes has caused a significant decrease in direct labor costs and a corresponding decline in the importance of labor-related standard costs and variances. As a result, Coach, Kraft Foods, Boeing, and many other manufacturers that once used standard costing for all three elements of product cost now apply this method only to direct materials and manufacturing overhead.

Standard Costing

LO1 Define *standard costs* and describe how managers use standard costs in the management cycle.

RELATED TEXT ASSIGNMENTS
Q: 1, 2, 3
SE: 1, 2
E: 1
SD: 2, 3
MRA: 5

Standard costs are realistic estimates of costs based on analyses of both past and projected operating costs and conditions. They are usually stated in terms of cost per unit. They provide a standard, or predetermined, performance level for use in **standard costing,** a method of cost control that also includes a measure of actual performance and a measure of the difference, or **variance,** between standard and actual performance. This method of measuring and controlling costs differs from the actual and normal costing methods in that it uses estimated costs exclusively to compute all three elements of product cost—direct materials, direct labor, and manufacturing overhead.

Using standard costing can be expensive because the estimated costs are based not just on past costs, but also on engineering estimates, forecasted demand, worker input, time and motion studies, and type and quality of direct materials. However, this method can be used in any type of business. Both manufacturers and service businesses use standard costing in conjunction with a job order costing, process costing, or activity-based costing system.

Standard Costs and the Management Cycle

As shown in Figure 1, standard costs are useful tools throughout the management cycle. Managers use them to develop budgets in the planning stage, to control costs as they occur during the executing stage, and to prepare reports. Because of their usefulness in comparing planned and actual costs, standard costs have usually been most closely associated with the performance evaluation that takes place in the reviewing stage.

KEY POINT: Standard costs are necessary for planning and control. Budgets are developed from standard costs, and performance is measured against them.

■ **PLANNING** During the planning stage, after managers have projected sales and production targets for the next accounting period, standard costs can be used in developing budgets for direct materials, direct labor, and variable manufacturing overhead. These estimated operating costs not only serve as targets for product costing; they are also useful in making decisions about product distribution and pricing.

■ **EXECUTING** During the executing stage, as actual costs are incurred and recorded, managers apply standard costs to the work in process. By using these standards as yardsticks for measuring expenditures, they can control costs as they occur. For example, when the price a vendor offers is higher than the standard cost, a manager may decide to take the company's business elsewhere.

■ **REVIEWING** At the end of an accounting period—whether it is a day, a week, a month, or a quarter—managers compare the actual costs incurred with standard costs and compute the variances. Variances provide measures of performance that can be used to control costs. In reviewing a variance, managers compute its amount, and if the amount is significant, they analyze what is causing it. Their analysis of significant unfavorable variances may reveal operating problems, such as inefficient functions within a department or work cell, which they can then act to correct. Managers also investigate significant favorable variances to determine why and how the positive performance

Focus on Business Practice

Why Go on a Factory Tour?
If you've had some manufacturing experience, you probably understand the importance of standard costing and variance analysis. If you haven't had any manufacturing experience, gain some insight into the importance of cost planning and control by visiting a factory. Consult your local chamber of commerce for factory tours near you. You can also tour factories online. Check out the production of jellybeans at <www.jellybelly.com> or see how crayons are made at <www.crayola.com>.

How do Coach managers control costs by setting performance standards?

25

This chapter describes how standard costs are computed and how managers use the variances between standard and actual costs to evaluate performance and control costs.

Standard Costing and Variance Analysis

LEARNING OBJECTIVES

LO1 Define *standard costs* and describe how managers use standard costs in the management cycle.

LO2 Explain how standard costs are developed and compute a standard unit cost.

LO3 Prepare a flexible budget and describe how variance analysis is used to control costs.

LO4 Compute and analyze direct materials variances.

LO5 Compute and analyze direct labor variances.

LO6 Compute and analyze manufacturing overhead variances.

LO7 Explain how variances are used to evaluate managers' performance.

DECISION POINT

A MANAGER'S FOCUS

Coach, Inc. <www.coach.com> The durability of a well-crafted baseball glove was the inspiration for the high-quality leather goods that Coach began making more than fifty years ago. Now sold worldwide, the company's products include not only leather goods, such as handbags and luggage, but also jewelry, shoes, hats, eyewear, scarves, and home furnishings.

Coach's managers value a by-the-numbers approach to business. They keep Coach highly profitable by using design specifications to set standard costs for the company's product lines.[1] How does setting standard costs help control costs?

Managers base standard costs on realistic estimates of operating costs. They use these figures as performance targets and as benchmarks against which to measure actual spending trends. To keep standard costs realistic, they continuously monitor changes in market prices and operating costs and update the estimated figures as conditions warrant. By analyzing variances between standard and actual costs, they gain insight into the causes of those differences. Once they have identified an operating problem that is causing a cost variance, they can devise a solution to the problem.

Suppose the manager of 3M's Asia-Pacific group is preparing the cash budget for next year's operations. Explain how research and development expenses would affect the cash receipts and cash payments in that cash budget.

Excel Spreadsheet Analysis

MRA 4.
LO3 The Budgeting Process
LO4

Refer to our development of Framecraft Company's master budget for 20x7 in this chapter. Suppose that because of a new customer in Canada, Chase Vittel has decided to increase budgeted sales in the first quarter of 20x7 by 5,000 units. The expenses for this sale will include direct materials, direct labor, variable manufacturing overhead, and variable selling and administrative expenses. The delivery expense for the Canadian customer will be $.18 per unit rather than the regular $.08 per unit. The desired units of beginning finished goods inventory will remain at 1,000 units.

1. Using an Excel spreadsheet, revise Framecraft Company's budgeted income statement and the operating budgets that support it to reflect the changes described above. (Round manufactured cost per unit to three decimals.)
2. What was the change in income from operations? Would you recommend accepting the order from the Canadian customer? If so, why?

Internet Case

MRA 5.
LO1 The Budgeting Process

Some corporate web sites include areas specifically designed for student needs. Search the student area of Johnson & Johnson's web site (www.jnj.com/student_resources/index.htm). What kinds of information does it provide? How does the information apply to the material discussed in this chapter?

MANAGERIAL REPORTING AND ANALYSIS CASES

Interpreting Management Reports

LO1 Policies for Budget
LO2 Development
LO5

MRA 1. Hector Corporation is a manufacturing company with annual sales of $25 million. Its budget committee created a policy that the company uses each year in developing its master budget for the following calendar year. The policy is as follows:

May	The company's controller and corporate officers of the budget committee meet to discuss plans and objectives for next year. The controller conveys all relevant information from this meeting to division managers and department heads.
June	Division managers, department heads, and the controller meet to discuss the corporate plans and objectives for next year. They develop a timetable for developing next year's budget data.
July	Division managers and department heads develop budget data. The vice president of sales provides them with final sales estimates, and they complete monthly sales estimates for each product line.
August	Estimates of next year's monthly production activity and inventory levels are completed. Division managers and department heads communicate these estimates to the controller, who distributes them to other operating areas.
September	All operating areas submit their revised budget data. The controller integrates their labor requirements, direct materials requirements, unit cost estimates, cash requirements, and profit estimates in a preliminary master budget for next year.
October	The budget committee meets to discuss the preliminary master budget and to make any necessary corrections, additions, or deletions. The controller incorporates all authorized changes into a final draft of the master budget.
November	The controller submits the final draft to the corporate officers of the budget committee for approval. If they approve it, it is distributed to all corporate officers, division managers, and department heads.

Comment on this policy. What changes would you recommend?

Formulating Management Reports

LO1 Financial Budgets
LO2
LO4

MRA 2. Suppose you have just signed a partnership agreement with your cousin Eddie to open a bookstore near your college. You believe the store will be able to provide excellent service and undersell the local competition. To fund operations, you and Eddie have applied for a loan from the Small Business Administration. The loan application requires you to submit two financial budgets—a pro forma income statement and a pro forma balance sheet—within six weeks. Because of your expertise in accounting and business, Eddie has asked you to prepare the financial budgets.

1. How do the four *w*'s of preparing an accounting report apply in this situation—that is, *why* are you preparing these financial budgets, *who* needs them, *what* information do you need to prepare for them, and *when* are they due?
2. If you obtain the loan and open the bookstore, how can you and Eddie use the pro forma statements that you prepared?

International Company

LO4 Goals and the Cash Budget

MRA 3. The products of Minnesota Mining and Manufacturing Company (3M) <www.3m.com> range from office supplies, duct tape, and road reflectors to laser imagers for CAT scanners. One of the company's goals is to accelerate sales and product development. Toward that end, it spends over $1 billion a year on research and development and related investment activities. It has also redesigned many of its products to satisfy the needs of its three international operations groups (Asia-Pacific; Europe and Middle East; and Latin American, Africa, and Canada).[7]

Utilities expense: January, $5,450; February, $5,890; March, $6,090
Insurance:
  Fire: January, $3,470
  Liability: March, $3,980
Property taxes: $3,760 due in January
Federal income taxes: 20x6 taxes of $21,000 due in March 20x7
Miscellaneous: January, $2,625; February, $2,800; March, $1,150

Wellness Center's controller anticipates that the beginning cash balance for 20x7 will be $9,840.

REQUIRED ▶ Prepare a cash budget for Wellness Centers, Inc., for the first quarter of 20x7. Use the following column headings:

January	February	March	Quarter

ALTERNATE PROBLEMS

P 6.
LO4 Budgeted Income Statement
LO5

Delft House, Inc., a multinational company based in Amsterdam, organizes and coordinates art shows and auctions throughout the world. Its budgeted and actual costs for last year, 20x4, are as follows:

	Budgeted Cost	Actual Cost
Salaries expense, staging	€ 480,000	€ 512,800
Salaries expense, executive	380,000	447,200
Travel costs	640,000	652,020
Auctioneer services	540,000	449,820
Space rental costs	251,000	246,580
Printing costs	192,000	182,500
Advertising expense	169,000	183,280
Insurance, merchandise	84,800	77,300
Insurance, liability	64,000	67,100
Home office costs	209,200	219,880
Shipping costs	105,000	112,560
Miscellaneous	25,000	25,828
Total expenses	€3,140,000	€3,176,868
Net receipts	€6,200,000	€6,369,200

Delft House has budgeted the following fixed costs for the current year, 20x5: executive salaries, €440,000; advertising expense, €190,000; merchandise insurance, €80,000; and liability insurance, €68,000. Additional information pertaining to the organization's current operations is as follows:

a. Net receipts are estimated at €6,400,000.
b. Salaries expense for staging will increase 20 percent over the actual figures for the previous year.
c. Travel costs are expected to be 11 percent of net receipts.
d. Auctioneer services will be billed at 9.5 percent of net receipts.
e. Space rental costs will be 20 percent higher than the amount budgeted in the previous year.
f. Printing costs are expected to be €190,000.
g. Home office costs are budgeted for €230,000.
h. Shipping costs are expected to be 20 percent higher than the amount budgeted in the previous year.
i. Miscellaneous expenses for the current year will be budgeted at €28,000.

REQUIRED ▶ 1. Prepare the company's budgeted income statement for the current year, 20x5. Since the company sells only services, assume it has expenses only and no cost of sales. (Net receipts equal gross margin.) Use a 34 percent income tax rate.

2. Should the budget committee be worried about the trend in the company's operations? Explain your answer.

information: Projected sales for April are $220,400; for May, $164,220; and for June, $165,980. Direct materials purchases for the period are estimated at $96,840; direct materials usage, at $102,710; direct labor expenses, at $71,460; manufacturing overhead, at $79,940; selling and administrative expenses, at $143,740; capital expenditures, at $125,000 (to be spent on June 29); cost of goods manufactured, at $252,880; and cost of goods sold, at $251,700.

Balance sheet account balances at March 31, 20x7, were as follows: Accounts Receivable, $26,500; Materials Inventory, $23,910; Work in Process Inventory, $31,620; Finished Goods Inventory, $36,220; Prepaid Expenses, $7,200; Plant, Furniture, and Fixtures, $498,600; Accumulated Depreciation, Plant, Furniture, and Fixtures, $141,162; Patents, $90,600; Accounts Payable, $39,600; Notes Payable, $105,500; Common Stock, $250,000; and Retained Earnings, $207,158.

Projected monthly cash balances for the second quarter of 20x7 are as follows: April 30, $20,490; May 31, $35,610; and June 30, $45,400. During the quarter, accounts receivable are expected to increase by 30 percent, patents to go up by $6,500, prepaid expenses to remain constant, and accounts payable to go down by 10 percent (Wishware Products will make a $5,000 payment on a note payable, $4,100 of which is principal reduction).

The federal income tax rate is 34 percent, and the second quarter's tax is paid in July. Depreciation for the quarter will be $6,420, which is included in the manufacturing overhead budget. The company will pay no dividends.

REQUIRED
1. Prepare a budgeted income statement for the quarter ended June 30, 20x7. Round answers to the nearest dollar.
2. Prepare a budgeted balance sheet as of June 30, 20x7.

P 5.
LO4 Comprehensive Cash Budget

Located in Telluride, Colorado, Wellness Centers, Inc., emphasizes the benefits of regular workouts and the importance of physical examinations. The corporation operates three fully equipped fitness centers, as well as a medical center that specializes in preventive medicine. Wellness Center's controller has compiled the following data pertaining to the first quarter of 20x7:

Cash Receipts

Memberships: December 20x6, 870; January 20x7, 880; February, 910; March, 1,030
Membership dues: $90 per month, payable on the 10th of the month (80 percent collected on time; 20 percent collected one month late)
Medical examinations: January, $35,610; February, $41,840; March, $45,610
Special aerobics classes: January, $4,020; February, $5,130; March, $7,130
High-protein food sales: January, $4,890; February, $5,130; March, $6,280

Cash Payments

Salaries and wages:
  Corporate officers: 2 at $12,000 per month
  Physicians: 2 at $7,000 per month
  Nurses: 3 at $2,900 per month
  Clerical staff: 2 at $1,500 per month
  Aerobics instructors: 3 at $1,100 per month
  Clinic staff: 6 at $1,700 per month
  Maintenance staff: 3 at $900 per month
  Health-food servers: 3 at $750 per month
Purchases:
  Muscle-toning machines: January, $14,400; February, $13,800 (no purchases in March)
  Pool supplies: $520 per month
  Health food: January, $3,290; February, $3,460; March, $3,720
  Medical supplies: January, $10,400; February, $11,250; March, $12,640
  Medical uniforms and disposable garments: January, $7,410; February, $3,900; March, $3,450
  Medical equipment: January, $11,200; February, $3,400; March $5,900
Advertising: January, $2,250; February, $1,190; March, $2,450

8. Budgeted income statement:

Bertha's Bathworks
Budgeted Income Statement
For the Year Ended December 31, 20x8

Sales		?
Cost of goods sold		
Finished goods inventory, December 31, 20x7	?	
Cost of goods manufactured	?	
Cost of goods available for sale	?	
Less finished goods inventory, December 31, 20x8	?	
Cost of goods sold		?
Gross margin		?
Selling and administrative expenses		?
Income from operations		?
Income taxes expense (30%)*		?
Net income		?

*The figure in parentheses is the company's income tax rate.

LO4 Basic Cash Budget

P 3. Tex Kinkaid's dream was to develop the biggest produce operation with the widest selection of fresh fruits and vegetables in northern Texas. Within three years of opening Minigarden Produce, Inc., Kincaid accomplished his objective. Kinkaid has asked you to prepare monthly cash budgets for Minigarden Produce for the quarter ended September 30, 20x7.

Credit sales to retailers in the area constitute 80 percent of Minigarden Produce's business; cash sales to customers at the company's retail outlet make up the other 20 percent. Collection records indicate that Minigarden Produce collects payment on 50 percent of all credit sales during the month of sale, 30 percent in the month after the sale, and 20 percent in the second month after the sale.

The company's total sales in May were $66,000; in June, they were $67,500. Anticipated sales in July are $69,500; in August, $76,250; and in September, $84,250. The company's purchases are expected to total $43,700 in July, $48,925 in August, and $55,725 in September. The company pays for all purchases in cash.

Projected monthly costs for the quarter include $1,040 for heat, light, and power; $375 for bank fees; $1,925 for rent; $1,120 for supplies; $1,705 for depreciation of equipment; $1,285 for equipment repairs; and $475 for miscellaneous expenses. Other projected costs for the quarter are salaries and wages of $18,370 in July, $19,200 in August, and $20,300 in September.

The company's cash balance at June 30, 20x7, was $2,745. It has a policy of maintaining a minimum monthly cash balance of $1,500.

REQUIRED
1. Prepare a monthly cash budget for Minigarden Produce, Inc., for the quarter ended September 30, 20x7.
2. Should Minigarden Produce anticipate taking out a loan during the quarter? If so, how much should it borrow, and when?

LO4 Budgeted Income Statement and Budgeted Balance Sheet

P 4. Moontrust Bank has asked the president of Wishware Products, Inc., for a budgeted income statement and budgeted balance sheet for the quarter ended June 30, 20x7. These pro forma statements are needed to support Wishware Product's request for a loan.

Wishware Products routinely prepares a quarterly master budget. The operating budgets prepared for the quarter ending June 30, 20x7, have provided the following

6. Selling and administrative expense budget:

Bertha's Bathworks
Selling and Administrative Expense Budget
For the Year Ended December 31, 20x8

	Quarter 1	Quarter 2	Quarter 3	Quarter 4	Year
Variable selling and administrative expenses					
Delivery expenses ($.10)	$ 400	?	?	?	?
Sales commissions ($.15)	600	?	?	?	?
Accounting ($.05)	200	?	?	?	?
Other administrative expenses ($.20)	800	?	?	?	?
Total variable selling and administrative expenses	$2,000	?	?	?	?
Fixed selling and administrative expenses					
Sales salaries	$5,000	?	?	?	?
Depreciation, office equipment	900	?	?	?	?
Taxes and insurance	1,700	?	?	?	?
Total fixed selling and administrative expenses	$7,600	?	?	?	?
Total selling and administrative expenses	$9,600	?	?	?	?

Note: The figures in parentheses are variable costs per unit.

7. Cost of goods manufactured budget:

Bertha's Bathworks
Cost of Goods Manufactured Budget
For the Year Ended December 31, 20x8

Direct materials used		
Direct materials inventory, December 31, 20x7	?	
Purchases for 20x8	?	
Cost of direct materials available for use	?	
Less direct materials inventory, December 31, 20x8	?	
Cost of direct materials used		?
Direct labor costs		?
Manufacturing overhead costs		?
Total manufacturing costs		?
Work in process inventory, December 31, 20x7*		?
Less work in process inventory, December 31, 20x8*		?
Cost of goods manufactured		?

*It is the company's policy to have no units in process at the end of the year.

4. Direct labor budget:

Bertha's Bathworks
Direct Labor Budget
For the Year Ended December 31, 20x8

	Quarter 1	Quarter 2	Quarter 3	Quarter 4	Year
Total production units	3,900	?	?	?	?
× Direct labor hours per unit	× .1	× ?	× ?	× ?	× ?
Total direct labor hours	390	?	?	?	?
× Direct labor cost per hour	× $7	× ?	× ?	× ?	× ?
Total direct labor cost	$2,730	?	?	?	?

5. Manufacturing overhead budget:

Bertha's Bathworks
Manufacturing Overhead Budget
For the Year Ended December 31, 20x8

	Quarter 1	Quarter 2	Quarter 3	Quarter 4	Year
Variable overhead costs					
Factory supplies ($.05)	$ 195	?	?	?	?
Employee benefits ($.25)	975	?	?	?	?
Inspection ($.10)	390	?	?	?	?
Maintenance and repair ($.15)	585	?	?	?	?
Utilities ($.05)	195	?	?	?	?
Total variable overhead costs	$2,340	?	?	?	?
Fixed overhead costs					
Depreciation, machinery	$ 500	?	?	?	?
Depreciation, building	700	?	?	?	?
Supervision	1,800	?	?	?	?
Maintenance and repair	400	?	?	?	?
Other overhead expenses	600	?	?	?	?
Total fixed overhead costs	$4,000	?	?	?	?
Total manufacturing overhead costs	$6,340	?	?	?	?

Note: The figures in parentheses are variable costs per unit.

2. Production budget:

Bertha's Bathworks
Production Budget
For the Year Ended December 31, 20x8

	Quarter 1	Quarter 2	Quarter 3	Quarter 4	Year
Sales in units	4,000	?	?	?	?
Plus desired units of ending finished goods inventory*	300	?	?	600	600
Desired total units	4,300				
Less desired units of beginning finished goods inventory†	400	?	?	?	400
Total production units	3,900	?	?	?	?

*Desired units of ending finished goods inventory = 10% of next quarter's budgeted sales.
†Desired units of beginning finished goods inventory = 10% of current quarter's budgeted sales.

3. Direct materials purchases budget:

Bertha's Bathworks
Direct Materials Purchases Budget
For the Year Ended December 31, 20x8

	Quarter 1	Quarter 2	Quarter 3	Quarter 4	Year
Total production units	3,900	3,200	5,000	5,100	17,200
× 3 ounces per unit	× 3	× ?	× ?	× ?	× ?
Total production needs in ounces	11,700	?	?	?	?
Plus desired ounces of ending direct materials inventory*	1,920	?	?	3,600	3,600
	13,620				
Less desired ounces of beginning direct materials inventory†	2,340	?	?	?	2,340
Total ounces of direct materials to be purchased	11,280	?	?	?	?
× Cost per ounce	× $.10	× ?	× ?	× ?	× ?
Total cost of direct materials purchases	$ 1,128	?	?	?	?

Note: Budgeted production needs in ounces for the first quarter of 20x9 = 18,000 ounces.
*Desired ounces of ending direct materials inventory = 20% of next quarter's budgeted production needs in ounces.
†Desired ounces of beginning direct materials inventory = 20% of current quarter's budgeted production needs in ounces.

LO3 Production Budget

E 7. Isobel Law, the controller for Aberdeen Lock Company, is preparing a production budget for 20x7. The company's policy is to maintain a finished goods inventory equal to one-half of the following month's sales. Sales of 7,000 locks are budgeted for April. Complete the monthly production budget for the first quarter:

	January	February	March
Sales in units	5,000	4,000	6,000
Add desired units of ending finished goods inventory	2,000	?	?
Desired total units	7,000		
Less desired units of beginning finished goods inventory	2,500	?	?
Total production units	4,500	?	?

LO3 Production Budget

E 8. Santa Fe Corporation produces and sells a single product. Expected sales for September are 12,000 units; for October, 15,000 units; for November, 9,000 units; for December, 10,000 units; and for January, 14,000 units. The company's desired level of ending finished goods inventory at the end of a month is 10 percent of the following month's sales in units. At the end of August, 1,200 units were on hand. How many units need to be produced in the fourth quarter?

LO3 Direct Materials Purchases Budget

E 9. The U-Z Door Company manufactures garage door units. The units include hinges, door panels, and other hardware. Prepare a direct materials purchases budget for the first quarter of 20x7 based on budgeted production of 16,000 garage door units. Sandee Morton, the controller, has provided the following information:

Hinges	4 sets per door	$11.00 per set
Door panels	4 panels per door	$27.00 per panel
Other hardware	1 lock per door	$31.00 per lock
	1 handle per door	$22.50 per handle
	2 roller tracks per door	$16.00 per set of 2 roller tracks
	8 rollers per door	$ 4.00 per roller

Assume no beginning or ending quantities of direct materials inventory.

LO3 Direct Materials Purchases Budget

E 10. Hard Corporation projects sales of $230,000 in May, $250,000 in June, $260,000 in July, and $240,000 in August. The dollar value of the company's cost of goods sold is generally 65 percent of total sales. The dollar value of its desired ending inventory is 25 percent of the following month's cost of goods sold.

Compute the total purchases budgeted for June and the total purchases budgeted for July.

LO3 Direct Labor Budget

E 11. Paige Metals Company has two departments—Cutting and Grinding—and manufactures three products. Budgeted unit production in 20x7 is 21,000 of Product T, 36,000 of Product M, and 30,000 of Product B. The company is currently analyzing direct labor hour requirements for 20x7.

Data for each department are as follows:

	Cutting	Grinding
Estimated hours per unit		
Product T	1.1	.5
Product M	.6	2.9
Product B	3.2	1.0
Hourly labor rate	$9	$7

Prepare a direct labor budget for 20x7 that shows the budgeted direct labor costs for each department and for the company as a whole.

LO3 Manufacturing Overhead Budget

E 12. Carole Dahl is chief financial officer of the Phoenix Division of Dahl Corporation, a multinational company with three operating divisions. As part of the budgeting process, Dahl's staff is developing the manufacturing overhead budget for 20x7. The division estimates that it will manufacture 50,000 units during the year. The budgeted cost information is as follows:

2. "Budgets can include financial or nonfinancial data. In our organization, we plan the number of hours to be worked and the number of customer contacts we want our salespeople to make."
3. "All budgets are complicated. You have to be an expert to prepare one."
4. "Budgets don't need to be highly accurate. No one in our company stays within a budget anyway."

Do you agree or disagree with each comment? Explain.

LO1 Budgeting and Goals

E 3. Effective planning of long- and short-term goals has contributed to the success of Multitasker Calendars, Inc. Described below are the actions the company's management team took during a recent planning meeting. Indicate whether the goals related to those actions are short-term or long-term.

1. In forecasting the next ten-year period, the management team considered economic and industry forecasts, employee-management relationships, and the structure and role of management.
2. Based on the ten-year forecast, the team made decisions about next year's sales and profit targets.

LO1 Budgeting and Goals

E 4. Assume that you work in the accounting department of a small wholesale warehousing company. Inspired by a recent seminar on budgeting, the company's president wants to develop a budgeting system and has asked you to direct it. Identify the points about the initial steps in the budgeting process that you should communicate to the president. Concentrate on principles related to long-term goals and short-term goals.

LO2 Components of a Master
LO3 Budget
LO4

E 5. Identify the order in which the following budgets are prepared. Use the letter *a* to indicate the first budget to be prepared, *b* for the second, and so on.

1. Production budget
2. Direct labor budget
3. Direct materials purchases budget
4. Sales budget
5. Budgeted balance sheet
6. Cash budget
7. Budgeted income statement

LO3 Sales Budget

E 6. Quarterly and annual sales for 20x7 for Steen Manufacturing Company are shown below.

Steen Manufacturing Company
Actual Sales Revenue
For the Year Ended December 31, 20x7

Product Class	January–March	April–June	July–September	October–December	Annual Totals	Estimated 20x8 Percent Increases by Product Class
Marine products	$ 44,500	$ 45,500	$ 48,200	$ 47,900	$ 186,100	10%
Mountain products	36,900	32,600	34,100	37,200	140,800	5%
River products	29,800	29,700	29,100	27,500	116,100	30%
Hiking products	38,800	37,600	36,900	39,700	153,000	15%
Running products	47,700	48,200	49,400	49,900	195,200	25%
Biking products	65,400	65,900	66,600	67,300	265,200	20%
Totals	$263,100	$259,500	$264,300	$269,500	$1,056,400	

Prepare a sales budget for 20x8 for the company. Show both quarterly and annual totals for each product class.

SE 8. **LO4 Estimating Cash Collections**

KD Insurance Company specializes in term life insurance contracts. Cash collection experience shows that 20 percent of billed premiums are collected in the month before they are due, 60 percent are paid in the month they are due, and 16 percent are paid in the month following their due date. Four percent of the billed premiums are paid late (in the second month following their due date) and include a 10 percent penalty payment. Total billing notices in January were $58,000; in February, $62,000; in March, $66,000; in April, $65,000; in May, $60,000; and in June, $62,000. How much cash does the company expect to collect in May?

SE 9. **LO4 Cash Budget**

The projections of direct materials purchases that follow are for the Stromboli Corporation.

	Purchases on Account	Cash Purchases
December 20x6	$40,000	$20,000
January 20x7	60,000	30,000
February 20x7	50,000	25,000
March 20x7	70,000	35,000

The company pays for 60 percent of purchases on account in the month of purchase and 40 percent in the month following the purchase. Prepare a monthly schedule of expected cash payments for direct materials for the first quarter of 20x7.

SE 10. **LO4 Budgeted Balance Sheet**

Wellman Corporation's budgeted balance sheet for the coming year shows total assets of $4,650,000 and total liabilities of $1,900,000. Common stock and retained earnings make up the entire stockholders' equity section of the balance sheet. Common stock remains at its beginning balance of $1,500,000. The projected net income for the year is $349,600. The company pays no cash dividends. What is the balance of retained earnings at the beginning of the budget period?

Exercises

E 1. **LO1 Budgeting and the Management Cycle**

All the activities described below require the use of budget information. Indicate whether each activity is part of the planning stage (P), executing stage (E), reviewing stage (REV), or reporting stage (REP) of the management cycle.

1. Vivian Gentry, manager of a golf and tennis resort, develops a budget to distribute limited resources to the resort's pro shop, maintenance department, golf and tennis operations, hotel operations, and restaurant operations.
2. Gentry challenges employees to increase the volume of customers eating in the restaurant by 10 percent, a goal set forth in the restaurant's budget.
3. Gentry selects the number of golf lessons given each month as a measure of performance for the golf operations.
4. The resort's accountant prepares a performance report for the restaurant.
5. Gentry analyzes the restaurant's performance report and finds that sales volume was 25 percent lower than planned.
6. Gentry meets with restaurant managers and employees to discuss the results from a survey of resort guests. Based on her findings, Gentry decides to expand the number of items offered on the menu, increase advertising for the restaurant, and replace the chef.
7. Edgar Thorn, the manager of golf operations, uses the budgeted number of golf lessons to motivate the golf pros to provide more lessons.
8. At the end of the month, Thorn calculates the variance between the actual number of golf lessons given and the budgeted number of golf lessons. He finds that the number of lessons given was fewer than planned.
9. Thorn prepares a variance report and gives it to the golf pros for review.
10. Thorn selects the number of hours of golf instruction as a new performance measure for the remainder of the year.

E 2. **LO1 Characteristics of Budgets**

You recently attended a workshop on budgeting and overheard the following comments as you walked to the refreshment table:

1. "Budgets are the same regardless of the size of an organization or management's role in the budgeting process."

18. How is the cash budget related to the master budget? What are the purposes of preparing a cash budget?
19. What is the final step in developing a master budget?
20. Who are the people responsible for ensuring that budget implementation is successful? What are their responsibilities?

Short Exercises

LO1 Budgeting and the Management Cycle

SE 1. All the management activities listed below require the use of budget information. Indicate whether each activity is part of the planning stage (P), executing stage (E), reviewing stage (REV), or reporting stage (REP) of the management cycle.
1. Coordinating purchasing, production, sales, and shipping
2. Selecting performance measures to monitor the timeliness of shipping
3. Calculating variances between the planned direct materials and actual direct materials used in production
4. Developing a budget to distribute the organization's resources among its various departments
5. Preparing a report on the performance of the production department over the last three months

LO1 Budgeting in a Retail Organization

SE 2. Sam Zubac is the manager of the shoe department in a discount department store. During a recent meeting, Zubac and his supervisor agreed that Zubac's goal for the next year would be to increase the number of pairs of shoes sold by 20 percent. The department sold 8,000 pairs of shoes last year. Two salespersons currently work for Zubac. What types of budgets should Zubac use to help him achieve his sales goal? What kinds of information should those budgets provide?

LO1 Budgetary Control

SE 3. Toby Andres owns a tree nursery. She analyzes her business's results by comparing actual operating results with figures budgeted at the beginning of the year. When the business generates large profits, she often overlooks the differences between actual and budgeted data. But when profits are low, she spends many hours analyzing the differences. If you owned Andres's business, would you use her approach to budgetary control? If not, what changes would you make?

LO1 Budgeting and Goals

SE 4. The dashboard assembly team at Rockford Automobile Company is participating in the company's budgeting process for the first time. After the team participated in a discussion of the basic principles of budgeting, one team member asked the controller to explain how the company's long-term goals relate to its short-term plan. How should the controller respond?

LO2 LO3 Components of a Master Budget

SE 5. A master budget is a compilation of forecasts for the coming year or operating cycle made by various departments or functions within an organization. What is the most basic forecast made in a master budget? List the reasons for your answer. Which budgets must managers prepare before they can prepare a direct materials purchases budget?

LO3 Preparing an Operating Budget

SE 6. Quester Company expects to sell 50,000 units of its product in the coming year. Each unit sells for $45. Sales brochures and supplies for the year are expected to cost $7,000. Three sales representatives cover the southeast region. Each one's base salary is $20,000, and each earns a sales commission of 5 percent of the selling price of the units he or she sells. The sales representatives supply their own transportation; they are reimbursed for travel at a rate of $.40 per mile. The company estimates that the sales representatives will drive a total of 75,000 miles next year.

From the information provided, calculate Quester Company's budgeted selling expenses for the coming year.

LO3 LO4 Budgeted Gross Margin

SE 7. Operating budgets for the DiPaolo Company reveal the following information: net sales, $450,000; beginning materials inventory, $23,000; materials purchased, $185,000; beginning work in process inventory, $64,700; beginning finished goods inventory, $21,600; direct labor costs, $34,000; manufacturing overhead applied, $67,000; ending work in process inventory, $61,200; ending materials inventory, $18,700; and ending finished goods inventory, $16,300.

Compute DiPaola Company's budgeted gross margin.

VIDEO CASE

Enterprise Rent-A-Car
<www.enterprise.com>

OBJECTIVES

- To become familiar with the budgeting process and budgets
- To understand the relationship between strategic plans and operating budgets
- To describe the role of budgeting in the management cycle

BACKGROUND FOR THE CASE

Because its core business is not the airport market, Enterprise Rent-A-Car does not have the high profile most of its competitors enjoy. However, with over $6.5 billion in annual revenues, more than 4,800 locations worldwide, and offices within 15 miles of 90 percent of the U.S. population, it is the largest car rental company in North America. Founded in 1947 in St. Louis, Missouri, where it operated out of the basement of a car dealership, Enterprise now employs more than 50,000 people. It focuses on two market segments: people who need a replacement vehicle when their own car is unavailable—for instance, when it is undergoing repairs—and people who want a car for a business or leisure trip or for a special occasion.

Enterprise prides itself on providing excellent customer service, including free customer pickup. To accomplish its goals, the company has an incentive plan for employees and a decentralized organization that allows great latitude in decision making. Enterprise's managers prepare budgets to integrate, coordinate, and communicate the operating plans necessary to achieve the company's strategic objectives. The budgeting system includes measurement of performance at each location and for each employee. Good systems and budgeting also facilitate the company's objective of expanding its business in Canada, the United Kingdom, Ireland, and Germany.[3]

REQUIRED

View the video on Enterprise Rent-A-Car that accompanies this book. As you are watching the video, take notes pertaining to the following:

1. In your own words, explain what a budget is and list all the reasons you believe a company like Enterprise would prepare a set of budgets.
2. What is the relationship between Enterprise's strategic plans and its operating budgets?
3. What is the role of budgeting in the management cycle?

ENRICHMENT NOTE: Long-term goals are often expressed in subjective terms, such as increasing market share, becoming the industry leader, or having the best product on the market.

KEY POINT: As plans are formulated for time periods closer to the current date, they become more specific and quantified. The annual budget is a very specific plan of action.

ing is to develop strategies to ensure that the company controls 10 percent of the market in five years and 15 percent by the end of ten years. An organization's strategic plan should include a range of long-term goals and give direction to its efforts to achieve those goals. It should include profit projections and describe new products or services in general terms.

■ **SHORT-TERM GOALS** Annual operating plans involve every part of an enterprise and are much more detailed than long-term strategic plans. To formulate an annual operating plan, an organization must restate its long-term goals in terms of what it needs to accomplish during the next year. The process entails making decisions about sales and profit targets, human resource needs, and the introduction of new products or services. The short-term goals identified in an annual operating plan are the basis of an organization's operating budgets for the year.

Once management has established short-term goals, the organization's controller takes charge of coordinating the budgeting process. This person designs a complete set of budget-development directions, including a timetable complete with deadlines for all parts of the year's operating plan, and assigns clearly defined responsibilities for carrying out each part of the budget's development to specific individuals or management teams.

Depending on organizational practice, a budget may be reviewed and revised during the year. As pointed out in the focus box that follows, there is a growing trend to more frequent budget revisions.

THE BUDGETING PROCESS

LO1 Define *budgeting* and explain its role in the management cycle.

RELATED TEXT ASSIGNMENTS
Q: 1, 2, 3, 4, 5, 6, 7, 8
SE: 1, 2, 3, 4
E: 1, 2, 3, 4
SD: 1, 3, 5
MRA: 1, 2, 5

www.jnj.com
www.merck.com
www.national.unitedway.org
www.unitednations.org

TERMINOLOGY NOTE: For-profit organizations often use the term *profit planning* rather than *budgeting*.

ENRICHMENT NOTE: Any budget, even a poorly prepared one, is probably better than no budget at all. As the budgeting process is refined, the benefits to the organization will increase.

Budgeting is the process of identifying, gathering, summarizing, and communicating financial and nonfinancial information about an organization's future activities. It is an essential part of the continuous planning an organization must do to accomplish its long-term goals. The budgeting process provides managers of all types of organizations—including for-profit organizations, such as Johnson & Johnson and Merck, and not-for-profit organizations, such as the United Way and the United Nations—the opportunity to match organizational goals with the resources necessary to accomplish those goals. As part of the ongoing budgeting process, managers evaluate operational, tactical, value chain, and capacity issues; assess how resources for operating, investing, and financial activities are currently being used and how they can be efficiently used in the future; and develop contingency budgets as business conditions change.

Budgets—plans of action based on forecasted transactions, activities, and events—are synonymous with managing an organization. They are essential to accomplishing the goals articulated in an organization's strategic plan. They are used to communicate information, coordinate activities and resource usage, motivate employees, and evaluate performance. For example, a board of directors may use budgets to determine managers' areas of responsibility and to measure managers' performance in those areas. Budgets are, of course, also used to manage and account for cash. Such budgets establish minimum or targeted levels of cash receipts and limits on the spending of cash for particular purposes.

Budgets come in many forms. For example, a cash budget focuses on financial information; it shows, among other things, how cash resources will be allotted to operating, investing, and financing activities over a future period. A production budget, on the other hand, focuses on nonfinancial information; it shows planned production in units and identifies the activities needed to meet certain requirements or standards established in the planning stage of the management cycle.

To compete successfully in today's fast-paced global market, an organization must ensure that its managers have continuously updated operating data against which to measure performance. Thus, an ongoing budgeting process is especially important in the current business environment.

BUDGETING AND GOALS

■ **LONG-TERM GOALS** **Strategic planning** is the process by which management establishes an organization's long-term goals. These goals define the strategic direction an organization will take over a five- to ten-year period and are the basis for making annual operating plans and preparing budgets. Long-term goals should take into consideration economic and industry forecasts, employee management relations, the structure and role of management, value chain considerations, organizational capacity, and any other operational and tactical issues facing the organization, such as the expected quality of products or services, growth rates, and desired market share.

Long-term goals cannot be vague; they must set specific targets and timetables and assign responsibility for achieving the goals to specific personnel. For example, a long-term goal for a company that currently holds only 4 percent of its product's market share might specify that the vice president of market-

FOCUS ON BUSINESS PRACTICE

What Can Cause the Planning Process to Fail?
When chief financial officers were asked what caused their planning process to fail, the six factors they most commonly cited were as follows:[2]

- An inadequately defined strategy
- No clear link between strategy and the operational budget
- Lack of individual accountability for results
- Lack of meaningful performance measures
- Inadequate pay for performance
- Lack of appropriate data

How is Johnson & Johnson's budgeting process linked to the company's long-term goals and objectives?

prepare cost and expense budgets. Fourth, the company accounting group reviews all budgets from the decentralized companies and analyzes their contents to determine whether they are in accord with the overall strategic plan. Fifth, Johnson & Johnson's controller prepares a complete set of companywide budgeted financial statements.

The budgeting process can be a highly effective way of linking strategic planning to operations, especially when it is coupled with ongoing discussions about a company's activities and direction, as is the case at Johnson & Johnson. Because a budget sets forth a company's objectives in concrete terms, it enables managers and employees to act in ways that will attain those objectives; it also gives them a means of monitoring the results of their actions. At Johnson & Johnson, the budgeting process and ongoing dialogue about strategy foster rapid improvements in productivity and customer service, as well as innovation in product and market development.

24

Chapter 24 describes the budgeting process, identifies the elements of a master budget, and demonstrates the preparation of operating budgets and financial budgets.

The Budgeting Process

LEARNING OBJECTIVES

LO1 Define *budgeting* and explain its role in the management cycle.

LO2 Identify the elements of a master budget in different types of organizations and the guidelines for preparing budgets.

LO3 Prepare the operating budgets that support the financial budgets.

LO4 Prepare a budgeted income statement, a cash budget, and a budgeted balance sheet.

LO5 Describe management's role in budget implementation.

DECISION POINT
A MANAGER'S FOCUS

Johnson & Johnson <www.jnj.com> With products that range from baby powder, Band-Aids, Tylenol, and contact lenses to diagnostic and surgical devices, Johnson & Johnson is the largest and most diversified manufacturer of health care products in the world. It has had affiliated companies operating in Latin America, Europe, Africa, and Australia for more than fifty years. Today, it is a global family of over 200 decentralized companies. Unifying the strategic planning of these companies' management teams are the set of common values and ethical principles expressed in Johnson & Johnson's credo, or mission statement. The strategic direction and major developments of the various companies are discussed at board meetings throughout the year and at meetings between management and board members. This ongoing dialogue provides managers with insight into the activities and direction of the company's businesses and is the basis for Johnson & Johnson's budgeting decisions.[1]

How does Johnson & Johnson's budgeting process work? First, sales and marketing teams from the decentralized companies develop sales budgets by product, geographic territory, and distribution channel. Senior management and staff then review the sales budgets to see that they meet the goals of Johnson & Johnson's strategic plan. Second, scheduling teams prepare production and shipping schedules to coordinate activities at the different manufacturing plants. Third, the managers responsible for functional areas (such as research and development, production, marketing, distribution, and customer service) reported that a new salesperson has just obtained a sales contract with an Australian distributor for 4,500 sets of pottery. The selling price, variable purchases cost per unit, sales commission, and total fixed costs will remain the same, but the variable distribution costs will be €160 per unit.

Using an Excel spreadsheet, complete the following:

1. Calculate the targeted operating income for 20x5.
2. Prepare a budgeted contribution income statement for 20x5 based on the information in **MRA 1** and the adjustments presented in **MRA 2**. Do you agree with Sophia Callas that Datura's projected operating income for 20x5 will be less than the operating income for 20x4? Explain.
3. Calculate the total contribution margin from the Australian sales.
4. Prepare a revised budgeted contribution income statement for 20x5 by combining the information from **2** and **3** above.
5. Does Datura need the Australian sales to achieve its targeted operating income for 20x5?

Internet Case

MRA 5.
LO4 Planning Future Sales and
LO5 Costs

Find a recent annual report on the Internet and read management's letter to the stockholders. This section of an annual report typically discusses initiatives or actions that the company implemented during the year as part of its strategic plan. (1) Identify at least three such initiatives or actions that you believe affected the company's annual sales or costs. (2) Also identify one initiative or action the company is planning for the coming year that you believe will affect revenue or expenses.

Formulating Management Reports

MRA 2.

LO5 C-V-P Analysis Applied

Refer to the information in **MRA 1**. In January 20x5, Sophia Callas, the president and chief executive officer of Datura, Ltd., conducted a strategic planning meeting. During the meeting, Phillipe Mazzeo, vice president of distribution, noted that because of a new contract with an international shipping line, the company's fixed distribution costs for 20x5 would be reduced by 10 percent and its variable distribution costs by 4 percent. Gino Roma, vice president of sales, offered the following information:

> We plan to sell 15,000 sets of pottery again in 20x5, but based on review of the competition, we are going to lower the selling price to €890 per set. To encourage increased sales, we will raise sales commissions to 12 percent of the selling price.

Sophia Callas is concerned that the changes described by Roma and Mazzeo may not improve operating income sufficiently in 20x5. If operating income does not increase by at least 10 percent, she will want to find other ways to reduce the company's costs. She asks you to evaluate the situation in a written report. Because it is already January of 20x5 and changes need to be made quickly, she requests your report within five days.

1. Prepare a budgeted contribution income statement for 20x5. Your report should show the budgeted (estimated) operating income based on the information provided above and in **MRA 1**. Will the changes improve operating income sufficiently? Explain.
2. In preparation for writing your report, answer the following questions:
   a. Why are you preparing the report?
   b. Who needs the report?
   c. What sources of information will you use?
   d. When is the report due?

International Company

MRA 3.

LO3 C-V-P Analysis and Decision Making

The Goslar Corporation cuts granite, marble, and sandstone for use in the construction and restoration of cathedrals throughout Europe. The German-based company has operations in Italy and Switzerland. Gunder Shillar, the controller, recently determined that the breakeven point was €325,000 in sales. In preparation for a quarterly planning meeting, Shillar must provide information for the following six proposals, which will be discussed individually by the planning team:

1. Increase the selling price of marble slabs by 10 percent.
2. Change the sales mix to respond to an increased demand for marble slabs—that is, increase production and sales of marble slabs and decrease the production and sales of sandstone slabs, the least profitable product.
3. Increase fixed production costs by €40,000 annually to cover depreciation on new stone-cutting equipment.
4. Increase variable costs by 1 percent to cover higher export duties on foreign sales.
5. Decrease the sales volume of sandstone slabs because of a reduction in demand in Eastern Europe.
6. Decrease the number of days a customer can defer payment without being charged interest.

1. For each proposal, determine whether cost-volume-profit (C-V-P) analysis would provide useful financial information.
2. Indicate how each proposal that lends itself to C-V-P analysis would affect profit.

Excel Spreadsheet Analysis

MRA 4.

LO5 Planning Future Sales

As noted in **MRA 2**, Datura, Ltd., had targeted sales of 15,000 sets of pottery for 20x5 and was reducing the selling price to €890 per set. It was increasing sales commissions to 12 percent of the selling price and decreasing its fixed distribution costs by 10 percent and its variable distribution costs by 4 percent. Based on analysis of these changes, Sophia Callas has concluded that they would not increase Datura's 20x5 operating income by 10 percent over the previous year's income. Now, however, Gino Roma has

1. Using the high-low method, compute the variable cost rates used last year for each expense. What was the monthly fixed cost for electricity and for repairs and maintenance?
2. Compute the total variable cost and total fixed cost for each expense category for last year.
3. Saud believes that in the coming year, the electricity rate will increase by $.005 and the repairs rate, by $1.20. Usage of all items and their fixed cost amounts will remain constant. Compute the projected total cost for each category. How will those increases in costs affect the club's profits and cash flow?

MANAGERIAL REPORTING AND ANALYSIS CASES

Interpreting Management Reports

LO3 C-V-P Analysis
LO4

MRA 1. Established in 1963 in Datura, Italy, Datura, Ltd., is an international importer-exporter of pottery with distribution centers in the United States, Europe, and Australia. The company was very successful in its early years, but since then, its profitability has steadily declined. As a member of a management team selected to gather information for Datura's next strategic planning meeting, you have been asked to review its most recent contribution income statement, which appears below.

Datura, Ltd.
Contribution Income Statement
For the Year Ended December 31, 20x4

Sales revenue		€13,500,000
Less variable costs		
Purchases	€ 6,000,000	
Distribution	2,115,000	
Sales commissions	1,410,000	
Total variable costs		9,525,000
Contribution margin		€ 3,975,000
Less fixed costs		
Distribution	€ 985,000	
Selling	1,184,000	
General and administrative	871,875	
Total fixed costs		3,040,875
Operating income		€ 934,000

In 20x4, Datura sold 15,000 sets of pottery.

1. For each set of pottery sold in 20x4, calculate the (a) selling price, (b) variable purchases cost, (c) variable distribution cost, (d) variable sales commission, and (e) contribution margin.
2. Calculate the breakeven point in units and in sales euros.
3. Historically, Datura's variable costs have been about 60 percent of sales. What was the ratio of variable costs to sales in 20x4? List three actions Datura could take to correct the difference.
4. How would fixed costs have been affected if Datura had sold only 14,000 sets of pottery in 20x4?

Ethical Dilemma

LO4 Breaking Even and Ethics

SD 3. Lesley Chomski is the supervisor of the New Product Division of MCO Corporation. Her annual bonus is based on the success of new products and is computed on the number of sales that exceed each new product's projected breakeven point. In reviewing the computations supporting her most recent bonus, Chomski found that although an order for 7,500 units of a new product called R56 had been refused by a customer and returned to the company, the order had been included in the calculations. She later discovered that the company's accountant had labeled the return an overhead expense and had charged the entire cost of the returned order to the plantwide Manufacturing Overhead account. The result was that R56 appeared to exceed breakeven by more than 5,000 units and Chomski's bonus from this product amounted to over $800. What actions should Chomski take? Be prepared to discuss your response in class.

Research Activity

LO2 Cost Behavior and
LO4 Contribution Margin

SD 4. Make a trip to a local fast-food restaurant. Observe all aspects of the operation and take notes on the entire process. Describe the procedures used to take, process, and fill an order and deliver the order to the customer. Based on your observations, make a list of the costs incurred by the operation. Identify at least three variable costs and three fixed costs. Can you identify any potential mixed costs? Why is the restaurant willing to sell a large drink for only a few cents more than a medium drink? How is the restaurant able to offer a "value meal" (e.g., sandwich, drink, and fries) for considerably less than those items would cost if they were bought separately? Bring your notes to class and be prepared to discuss your findings.

Decision-Making Practice

LO2 Mixed Costs

SD 5. Officials of the Hidden Hills Golf and Tennis Club are in the process of preparing a budget for the year ending December 31, 20x6. Because Ramon Saud, the club treasurer, has had difficulty with two expense items, the process has been delayed by more than four weeks. The two items are mixed costs—expenses for electricity and for repairs and maintenance—and Saud has been having trouble breaking them down into their variable and fixed components. An accountant friend and golfing partner has suggested that he use the high-low method to divide the costs into their variable and fixed parts. The spending patterns and activity measures related to each cost during the past year are as follows:

Month	Electricity Expense Amount	Kilowatt-Hours	Repairs and Maintenance Amount	Labor Hours
January	$ 7,500	210,000	$ 7,578	220
February	8,255	240,200	7,852	230
March	8,165	236,600	7,304	210
April	8,960	268,400	7,030	200
May	7,520	210,800	7,852	230
June	7,025	191,000	8,126	240
July	6,970	188,800	8,400	250
August	6,990	189,600	8,674	260
September	7,055	192,200	8,948	270
October	7,135	195,400	8,674	260
November	8,560	252,400	8,126	240
December	8,415	246,600	7,852	230
Totals	$92,550	2,622,000	$96,416	2,840

3. Using the original data and sales of 15,000 units, compute the selling price the company must charge to make a profit of $100,000.
4. According to the vice president of marketing, Yvonne Palmer, if the price of the statues is reduced and advertising is increased, the most optimistic annual sales estimate is 25,000 units. How much more can be spent on fixed advertising costs if the selling price is reduced to $28.00 per statue, if the variable costs cannot be reduced, and if the targeted profit for sales of 25,000 statues is $120,000?

P 8.

LO5 Planning Future Sales for a Service Business

Lending Hand Financial Corporation is a subsidiary of Gracey Enterprises. Its main business is processing loan applications. Last year, Bettina Brent, the manager of the corporation's Loan Department, established a policy of charging a $250 fee for every loan application processed. Next year's variable costs have been projected as follows: loan consultant's wages, $15.50 per hour (a loan application takes five hours to process); supplies, $2.40 per application; and other variable costs, $5.60 per application. Annual fixed costs include depreciation of equipment, $8,500; building rental, $14,000; promotional costs, $12,500; and other fixed costs, $8,099.

REQUIRED ▶

1. Using the contribution margin approach, compute the number of loan applications the company must process to (a) break even and (b) earn a profit of $14,476.
2. Using the same approach and assuming promotional costs increase by $5,662, compute the number of applications the company must process to earn a profit of $20,000.
3. Assuming the original information and the processing of 500 applications, compute the loan application fee the company must charge if the targeted profit is $41,651.
4. Brent's staff can handle a maximum of 750 loan applications. How much more can be spent on promotional costs if the highest fee tolerable to the customer is $280, if variable costs cannot be reduced, and if the targeted profit for the loan applications is $50,000?

SKILLS DEVELOPMENT CASES

Conceptual Analysis

SD 1.

LO1 Concept of Cost Behavior
LO2

Gulf Coast Shrimp Company is a small company. It owns an icehouse and processing building, a refrigerated van, and three shrimp boats. Bob Jones inherited the company from his father three months ago. The company employs three boat crews of four people each and five processing workers. Trey Goodfellow of Bayou Accountants, a local accounting firm, has kept the company's financial records for many years. In his last analysis of operations, Goodfellow stated that the company's fixed cost base of $100,000 is satisfactory for its type and size of business. However, variable costs have averaged 70 percent of sales over the last two years, which is too high for the volume of business. Last year, only 30 percent of the sales revenue of $300,000 contributed to covering fixed costs. As a result, the company reported a $10,000 operating loss.

Jones wants to improve the company's net income, but he is confused by Goodfellow's explanation of the fixed and variable costs. Prepare a response to Jones from Goodfellow in which you explain the concept of cost behavior as it relates to Gulf Coast's operations. Include ideas for improving the company's net income based on changes in fixed and variable costs.

SD 2.

LO5 Comparison of Cost Behavior

Allstate Insurance Co. <www.allstate.com> and USAA <www.usaa.com> are two well-known insurers of motorists. Allstate has agents and offices all over the country. USAA sells only through the mail and over the telephone or Internet. In addition to offering collision and liability coverage for automobiles, each company offers life insurance and homeowners' insurance. When a motorist buys auto insurance from Allstate, the agent generally offers life insurance and homeowners' insurance as well—a strategy that helps increase Allstate's profitability. Although USAA usually sells its policies at lower prices than Allstate does, it is a very profitable company.

Identify and discuss the role that fixed costs, sales mix, and contribution margin can play in increasing profitability. Suggest a performance measure that could be used to evaluate agents who sell auto insurance. What is the role of variable costs? What is it about the relationship of USAA's fixed and variable costs that allows the company to sell policies at lower prices than Allstate and yet remain profitable?

3. Unskilled laborers apply a coat of primer.
4. Skilled laborers apply oil-based exterior paint to the entire surface.

On average, skilled laborers work 12 hours per job, and unskilled laborers work 8 hours. The refurbishing process generated the following operating results during 20x5:

Skilled labor	$20.00 per hour
Unskilled labor	$8.00 per hour
Gallons of chlorine used	3,768 gallons at $5.50 per gallon
Paint primer	7,536 gallons at $15.50 per gallon
Paint	6,280 gallons at $16.00 per gallon
Paint spraying equipment	$600.00 per month depreciation
Two leased vans	$800.00 per month total
Rent for storage building	$450.00 per month

Data on utilities for the year are as follows:

Month	Number of Jobs	Cost	Hours Worked
January	42	$ 3,950	840
February	37	3,550	740
March	44	4,090	880
April	49	4,410	980
May	54	4,720	1,080
June	62	5,240	1,240
July	71	5,820	1,420
August	73	5,890	1,460
September	63	5,370	1,260
October	48	4,340	960
November	45	4,210	900
December	40	3,830	800
Totals	628	$55,420	12,560

REQUIRED
1. Classify the costs as variable, fixed, or mixed.
2. Using the high-low method, separate mixed costs into their variable and fixed components. Use total hours worked as the basis.
3. Compute the average cost per job for 20x5. (**Hint**: Divide the total of all costs for 20x5 by the number of jobs completed.)
4. Project the average cost per job in 20x6 if variable costs per job increase 20 percent.

ALTERNATE PROBLEMS

P 6.
LO4 Breakeven Analysis
LO5

At the beginning of each year, the Accounting Department at Moon Glow Lighting, Ltd., must find the point at which projected sales revenue will equal total budgeted variable and fixed costs. The company produces custom-made, low-voltage outdoor lighting systems. Each system sells for an average of $435. Variable costs per unit are $210. Total fixed costs for the year are estimated to be $166,500.

REQUIRED
1. Compute the breakeven point in sales units.
2. Compute the breakeven point in sales dollars.
3. Find the new breakeven point in sales units if the fixed costs go up by $10,125.
4. Using the original figures, compute the breakeven point in sales units if the selling price decreases to $425 per unit, fixed costs go up by $15,200, and variable costs decrease by $15 per unit.

P 7.
LO4 Planning Future Sales:
LO5 Contribution Margin Approach

Garden Marbles manufactures birdbaths, statues, and other decorative items, which it sells to florists and retail home and garden centers. The company's Design Department has proposed a new product, a statue of a frog, that it believes will be popular with home gardeners. Expected variable unit costs are as follows: direct materials, $9.25; direct labor, $4.00; production supplies, $.55; selling costs, $2.40; and other, $3.05. The following are fixed costs: depreciation, building and equipment, $33,000; advertising, $40,000; and other, $6,000. Management plans to sell the product for $29.25.

REQUIRED
1. Using the contribution margin approach, compute the number of statues the company must sell to (a) break even and (b) earn a profit of $50,000.
2. Using the same data, compute the number of statues that must be sold to earn a profit of $70,000 if advertising costs rise by $20,000.

3. Project the same costs for next year, assuming that the anticipated increase in activity will occur and that fixed costs will remain constant.
4. Compute the unit cost per job for next year.
5. Given your answer to 4, should the price remain at $100 per job?

LO4 P 2. Breakeven Analysis
LO5

Luce & Morgan, a law firm in downtown Jefferson City, is considering opening a legal clinic for middle- and low-income clients. The clinic would bill at a rate of $18 per hour. It would employ law students as paraprofessional help and pay them $9 per hour. Other variable costs are anticipated to be $5.40 per hour, and annual fixed costs are expected to total $27,000.

REQUIRED
1. Compute the breakeven point in billable hours.
2. Compute the breakeven point in total billings.
3. Find the new breakeven point in total billings if fixed costs should go up by $2,340.
4. Using the original figures, compute the breakeven point in total billings if the billing rate decreases by $1 per hour, variable costs decrease by $.40 per hour, and fixed costs go down by $3,600.

LO4 P 3. Planning Future Sales:
LO5 Contribution Margin Approach

Icon Industries is considering a new product for its Trophy Division. The product, which would feature an alligator, is expected to have global market appeal and to become the mascot for many high school and university athletic teams. Expected variable unit costs are as follows: direct materials, $18.50; direct labor, $4.25; production supplies, $1.10; selling costs, $2.80; and other, $1.95. Annual fixed costs are depreciation, building and equipment, $36,000; advertising, $45,000; and other, $11,400. Icon Industries plans to sell the product for $55.00.

REQUIRED
1. Using the contribution margin approach, compute the number of units the company must sell to (a) break even and (b) earn a profit of $70,224.
2. Using the same data, compute the number of units that must be sold to earn a profit of $139,520 if advertising costs rise by $40,000.
3. Using the original information and sales of 10,000 units, compute the selling price the company must use to make a profit of $131,600. (**Hint:** Calculate contribution margin per unit first.)
4. According to the vice president of marketing, Albert Flora, the most optimistic annual sales estimate for the product would be 15,000 units, and the highest competitive selling price the company can charge is $52 per unit. How much more can be spent on fixed advertising costs if the selling price is $52, if the variable costs cannot be reduced, and if the targeted profit for 15,000 unit sales is $251,000?

LO4 P 4. Breakeven Analysis and
LO5 Planning Future Sales

Write Company has a maximum capacity of 200,000 units per year. Variable manufacturing costs are $12 per unit. Fixed manufacturing overhead is $600,000 per year. Variable selling and administrative costs are $5 per unit, and fixed selling and administrative costs are $300,000 per year. The current sales price is $23 per unit.

REQUIRED
1. What is the breakeven point in (a) sales units and (b) sales dollars?
2. How many units must Write Company sell to earn a profit of $240,000 per year?
3. A strike at one of the company's major suppliers has caused a shortage of materials, so the current year's production and sales are limited to 160,000 units. To partially offset the effect of the reduced sales on profit, management is planning to reduce fixed costs to $841,000. Variable cost per unit is the same as last year. The company has already sold 30,000 units at the regular selling price of $23 per unit.
    a. What amount of fixed costs was covered by the total contribution margin of the first 30,000 units sold?
    b. What contribution margin per unit will be needed on the remaining 130,000 units to cover the remaining fixed costs and to earn a profit of $210,000 this year?

LO2 P 5. Cost Behavior and Projection
LO5 for a Service Business

Power Brite Painting Company specializes in refurbishing exterior painted surfaces that have been hard hit by humidity and insect debris. It uses a special technique, called pressure cleaning, before priming and painting the surface. The refurbishing process involves the following steps:

1. Unskilled laborers trim all trees and bushes within two feet of the structure.
2. Skilled laborers clean the building with a high-pressure cleaning machine, using about six gallons of chlorine per job.

Chapter 23 Cost Behavior Analysis

LO5 Planning Future Sales

E 13. Short-term automobile rentals are the specialty of ASAP Auto Rentals, Inc. Average variable operating costs have been $12.50 per day per automobile. The company owns 60 cars. Fixed operating costs for the next year are expected to be $145,500. Average daily rental revenue per automobile is expected to be $34.50. Management would like to earn a profit of $47,000 during the year.

1. Calculate the total number of daily rentals the company must have during the year to earn the targeted profit.
2. On the basis of your answer to **1**, determine the average number of days each automobile must be rented.
3. Determine the total revenue needed to achieve the targeted profit of $47,000.
4. What would the total rental revenue be if fixed operating costs could be lowered by $5,180 and the targeted profit increased to $70,000?

LO5 Cost Behavior in a Service Business

E 14. Luke Ricci, CPA, is the owner of a firm that provides tax services. The firm charges $50 per return for the direct professional labor involved in preparing standard short-form tax returns. In January, the firm prepared 850 such returns; in February, 1,000; and in March, 700. Service overhead (telephone and utilities, depreciation on equipment and building, tax forms, office supplies, and wages of clerical personnel) for January was $18,500; for February, $20,000; and for March, $17,000.

1. Determine the variable and fixed cost components of the firm's Service Overhead account.
2. What would the estimated total cost per tax return be if the firm prepares 825 standard short-form tax returns in April?

LO5 C-V-P Analysis in a Service Business

E 15. Flossmoor Inspection Service specializes in inspecting cars that have been returned to automobile leasing companies at the end of their leases. Flossmoor's charge for each inspection is $50; its average cost per inspection is $15. Tony Lomangeno, Flossmoor's owner, wants to expand his business by hiring another employee and purchasing an automobile. The fixed costs of the new employee and automobile would be $3,000 per month. How many inspections per month would the new employee have to perform to earn Lomangeno a profit of $1,200?

Problems

LO2 Cost Behavior and Projection
LO5

P 1. Luster Auto, Inc., specializes in "detailing" automobile exteriors—that is, revitalizing them so the cars look as if they had just rolled off the showroom floor. The company charges $100 for a full exterior detailing. It has just completed its first year of business and has asked its accountants to analyze the operating results. Management wants costs divided into variable, fixed, and mixed components and would like them projected for the coming year. Anticipated volume for next year is 1,100 jobs.

The process used to detail a car's exterior is as follows:

1. One $20-per-hour employee spends 20 minutes cleaning the car's exterior.
2. One can per car of Bugg-Off, a cleaning compound, is used on trouble spots.
3. A chemical compound called Buff Glow is used to remove oxidants from the paint surface and restore the natural oils to the paint.
4. Poly Wax is applied by hand, allowed to sit for 10 minutes, and then buffed off.
5. The final step is an inspection to see that all wax and debris have been removed.

On average, two hours are spent on each car, including cleaning time and drying time for the wax. Operating information for Luster Auto's first year is as follows:

Number of automobiles detailed	840
Labor per auto	2 hours at $20.00 per hour
Containers of Bugg-Off consumed	840 at $3.50 per can
Pounds of Buff Glow consumed	105 pounds at $32.00 per pound
Pounds of Poly Wax consumed	210 pounds at $8.00 per pound
Rent	$1,400.00 per month

During the year, utilities costs ranged from $800 for 40 jobs in March to $1,801 for 110 jobs in August.

REQUIRED
1. Classify the costs as variable, fixed, or mixed.
2. Using the high-low method, separate the mixed costs into their variable and fixed components. Use number of jobs as the basis.

			$240,000
Sales (60,000 units at $4)			
Less cost of goods produced (based on production of 60,000 units)			
Direct materials (variable)		$60,000	
Direct labor (variable)		30,000	
Variable manufacturing costs		45,000	
Fixed manufacturing costs		75,000	
Total cost of goods produced			210,000
Gross margin			$ 30,000
Less selling and administrative expenses			
Selling (fixed)		$24,000	
Administrative (fixed)		36,000	
Total selling and administrative expenses			60,000
Operating income (loss)			($ 30,000)

1. Given the budgeted selling price and cost data, how many units would McLennon have to sell to break even? (**Hint**: Be sure to consider selling and administrative expenses.)
2. Market research indicates that if McLennon were to drop its selling price to $3.80 per unit, it could sell 100,000 units in 20x6. Would you recommend the drop in price? What would the new operating income or loss be?

E 10.
LO4 Breakeven Point for Multiple Products

Saline Aquarium, Inc., manufactures and sells aquariums, water pumps, and air filters. The sales mix is 1:2:2 (i.e., for every one aquarium sold, two water pumps and air filters are sold). Using the contribution margin approach, find the breakeven point in units for each product. The company's fixed costs are $26,000. Other information is as follows:

	Selling Price per Unit	Variable Cost per Unit
Aquariums	$60	$25
Water pumps	20	12
Air filters	10	3

E 11.
LO4 Sales Mix Analysis

Ella Mae Simpson is the owner of a hairdressing salon in Palm Coast, Florida. Her salon provides three basic services: shampoo and set, permanents, and cut and blow dry. The following are its operating results from the past quarter:

Type of Service	Number of Customers	Total Sales	Contribution Margin Dollars
Shampoo and set	1,200	$24,000	$14,700
Permanents	420	21,000	15,120
Cut and blow dry	1,000	15,000	10,000
	2,620	$60,000	$39,820
Total fixed costs			30,000
Profit			$ 9,820

Compute the breakeven point in units based on the weighted average contribution margin for the sales mix.

E 12.
LO4 Contribution Margin and
LO5 Profit Planning

Target Systems, Inc., makes heat-seeking missiles. It has just been offered a government contract from which it may realize a profit. The contract purchase price is $130,000 per missile, but the number of units to be purchased has not yet been decided. The company's fixed costs are budgeted at $3,973,500, and variable costs are $68,500 per unit.

1. Compute the number of units the company should agree to make at the stated contract price to earn a profit of $1,500,000.
2. Using a lighter material, the variable unit cost can be reduced by $1,730, but total fixed overhead will increase by $27,500. How many units must be produced to make $1,500,000 in profit?
3. Given the figures in **2**, how many additional units must be produced to increase profit by $1,264,600?

Chapter 23 Cost Behavior Analysis

LO4 Graphic Breakeven Analysis

E 7. Identify the letter of the point, line segment, or area of the breakeven graph shown below that correctly completes each of the following statements:

1. The maximum possible operating loss is
   a. A.   c. B.
   b. D.   d. F.

2. The breakeven point in sales dollars is
   a. C.   c. A.
   b. D.   d. G.

3. At volume F, total contribution margin is
   a. C.   c. E.
   b. D.   d. G.

4. Net income is represented by area
   a. KDL.   c. BDC.
   b. KCJ.   d. GCJ.

5. At volume J, total fixed costs are represented by
   a. H.   c. I.
   b. G.   d. J.

6. If volume increases from F to J, the change in total costs is
   a. HI minus DE.   c. BC minus DF.
   b. DF minus HJ.   d. AB minus DE.

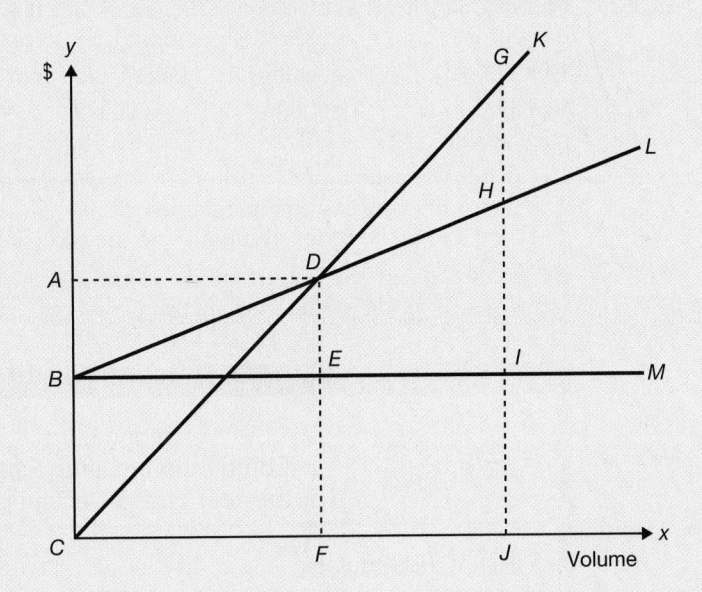

LO4 Breakeven Analysis

E 8. Techno Designs Company produces head covers for golf clubs. The company expects to generate a profit next year. It anticipates fixed manufacturing costs of $126,500 and fixed general and administrative expenses of $82,030 for the year. Variable manufacturing and selling costs per set of head covers will be $4.65 and $2.75, respectively. Each set will sell for $13.40.

1. Compute the breakeven point in sales units.
2. Compute the breakeven point in sales dollars.
3. If the selling price is increased to $14 per unit and fixed general and administrative expenses are cut by $33,465, what will the new breakeven point be in units?
4. Prepare a graph to illustrate the breakeven point computed in 2.

LO4 Breakeven Analysis and
LO5 Pricing

E 9. McLennon Company has a plant capacity of 100,000 units per year, but its budget for 20x6 indicates that only 60,000 units will be produced and sold. The entire budget for 20x6 is as follows:

2. Complete the following sentences by choosing the words that best describe the cost behavior at Zero Time Oil Change:

Cost per unit (increased, decreased, remained constant).
Total variable cost per month (increased, decreased) as the quantity of oil used (increased, decreased).

LO2 Mixed Costs: High-Low Method

E 3. Whitehouse Company manufactures major appliances. Because of increased interest in its refrigerators, it has just had its most successful year. In preparing the budget for next year, Jackson Harper, the company's controller, compiled these data:

Month	Volume in Machine Hours	Electricity Costs
July	6,000	$60,000
August	5,000	53,000
September	4,500	49,500
October	4,000	46,000
November	3,500	42,500
December	3,000	39,000

Using the high-low method, determine (1) the variable electricity cost per machine hour, (2) the monthly fixed electricity cost, and (3) the total variable electricity costs and fixed electricity costs for the six-month period.

LO2 Mixed Costs: High-Low Method

E 4. When Jerome Company's monthly costs were $75,000, sales were $80,000; when its monthly costs were $60,000, sales were $50,000. Use the high-low method to develop a monthly cost formula for Jerome Company's coming year.

LO4 Contribution Margin

E 5. Senora Company manufactures a single product that sells for $110 per unit. The company projects sales of 500 units per month. Projected costs are as follows:

Type of Cost	Manufacturing	Nonmanufacturing
Variable	$10,000	$5,000
Nonvariable	$12,500	$7,500

1. What is the company's contribution margin per unit?
2. What is the contribution margin ratio?
3. What volume, in terms of units, must the company sell to break even?

LO4 Breakeven Point and C-V-P
LO5 Analysis

E 6. Using the data in the contribution income statement for Sedona, Inc., that appears below, calculate (1) selling price, (2) variable costs, and (3) breakeven point in sales.

Sedona, Inc.
Contribution Income Statement
For the Year Ended December 31, 20x7

Sales (10,000 units)		$16,000,000
Less variable costs		
Cost of goods sold	$8,000,000	
Selling, administrative, and general	4,000,000	
Total variable costs		12,000,000
Contribution margin		$ 4,000,000
Less fixed costs		
Overhead	$1,200,000	
Selling, administrative, and general	800,000	
Total fixed costs		2,000,000
Operating Income		$ 2,000,000

LO4 Breakeven Analysis

SE 5. How many units must Braxton Company sell to break even if the selling price per unit is $8.50, variable costs are $4.30 per unit, and fixed costs are $3,780? What is the breakeven point in total dollars of sales?

LO4 Contribution Margin

SE 6. Using the contribution margin approach, find the breakeven point in units for Norcia Consumer Products if the selling price per unit is $11, the variable cost per unit is $6, and the fixed costs are $5,500.

LO4 Contribution Margin Ratio

SE 7. Using the information in **SE 6**, compute the breakeven point in total sales dollars using the contribution margin ratio.

LO4 Breakeven Analysis for Multiple Products

SE 8. Using the contribution margin approach, find the breakeven point in units for Sardinia Company's two products. Product A's selling price per unit is $10, and its variable cost per unit is $4. Product B's selling price per unit is $8, and its variable cost per unit is $5. Fixed costs are $15,000, and the sales mix of Product A to Product B is 2:1.

LO4 Contribution Margin and LO5 Projected Profit

SE 9. If Oui Watches sells 300 watches at $48 per watch and has variable costs of $18 per watch and fixed costs of $4,000, what is the projected profit?

LO5 Cost Behavior in a Service Business

SE 10. Guy Spy, a private investigation firm, has the following costs for December:

Direct labor: $190 per case
Service overhead

Salary for director of investigations	$ 4,800
Telephone	930
Depreciation	8,300
Legal advice	2,300
Supplies	590
Advertising	360
Utilities	1,560
Wages for clerical personnel	2,000
Total service overhead	$20,840

Service overhead for October was $21,150; for November, it was $21,350.

The number of cases investigated during October, November, and December was 93, 97, and 91, respectively. Compute the variable and fixed cost components of service overhead. Then determine the variable and fixed costs per case for December. (Round to nearest dollar where necessary.)

EXERCISES

LO2 Identification of Variable and Fixed Costs

E 1. Indicate whether each of the following costs of productive output is usually variable or fixed: (1) packing materials for stereo components, (2) real estate taxes, (3) gasoline for a delivery truck, (4) property insurance, (5) depreciation expense of buildings (calculated with the straight-line method), (6) supplies, (7) indirect materials, (8) bottles used to package liquids, (9) license fees for company cars, (10) wiring used in radios, (11) machine helper's wages, (12) wood used in bookcases, (13) city operating license, (14) machine depreciation based on machine hours used, (15) machine operator's hourly wages, and (16) cost of required outside inspection of each unit produced.

LO2 Variable Cost Analysis

E 2. Zero Time Oil Change has been in business for six months. The company pays $.50 per quart for the oil it uses in servicing cars, and each job requires an average of four quarts of oil. The company estimates that in the next three months, it will service 240, 288, and 360 cars.

1. Compute the cost of oil for each of the three months and the total cost for all three months.

Month	Cars to Be Serviced	Required Quarts/Car	Cost/Quart	Total Cost/Month
1	240	4	$.50	——
2	288	4	.50	——
3	360	4	.50	——
Three-month total	888			

Chapter Assignments

BUILDING YOUR KNOWLEDGE FOUNDATION

QUESTIONS

1. Define *cost behavior*.
2. Why is an understanding of cost behavior useful to managers?
3. What is the difference between theoretical capacity and practical capacity?
4. Why does a company never operate at theoretical capacity?
5. What is normal capacity? Why is normal capacity considered more relevant and useful than either theoretical or practical capacity?
6. What does *relevant range of activity* mean?
7. What makes variable costs different from fixed costs?
8. "Fixed costs remain constant in total but decrease per unit as productive output increases." Explain this statement.
9. What is a mixed cost? Give an example.
10. What is a scatter diagram?
11. Describe the high-low method of separating mixed costs.
12. Define *cost-volume-profit analysis*.
13. Identify two uses of C-V-P analysis and explain their significance to management.
14. What conditions must be met for C-V-P computations to be accurate?
15. Define *breakeven point*. Why is information about the breakeven point important to managers?
16. Define *contribution margin* and describe its use in breakeven analysis.
17. State the equation that uses fixed costs, targeted profit, and contribution margin per unit to determine targeted sales units.
18. Give examples of the ways in which a service business can use C-V-P analysis.
19. Identify the differences and similarities in breakeven analysis for manufacturing organizations and service organizations.

SHORT EXERCISES

LO1 Concept of Cost Behavior

SE 1. Dapper Hat Makers is in the business of designing and producing specialty hats. The material used for derbies costs $4.50 per unit, and Dapper pays each of its two full-time employees $250 per week. If Employee A makes 15 derbies in one week, what is the variable cost per derby, and what is this worker's fixed cost per derby? If Employee B makes only 12 derbies in one week, what are this worker's variable and fixed costs per derby? (Round to two decimal places where necessary.)

LO2 Identification of Variable, Fixed, and Mixed Costs

SE 2. Identify the following as fixed costs, variable costs, or mixed costs:
1. Direct materials
2. Telephone expense
3. Operating supplies
4. Personnel manager's salary
5. Factory building rent payment

LO2 Mixed Costs: High-Low Method

SE 3. Using the high-low method and the information below, compute the monthly variable cost per telephone hour and total fixed costs for Sadiko Corporation.

Month	Telephone Hours Used	Telephone Expenses
April	96	$4,350
May	93	4,230
June	105	4,710

LO3 C-V-P Analysis

SE 4. DeLuca, Inc., wants to make a profit of $20,000. It has variable costs of $80 per unit and fixed costs of $12,000. How much must it charge per unit if 4,000 units are sold?

REQUIRED
1. Compute the breakeven point in units for 20x5.
2. Olympia sold 6,500 putters in 20x5. How much profit did the company realize?
3. To improve profitability in 20x6, management is considering the four alternative courses of action indicated below. (In performing the required steps, use the figures from item **2** and treat each alternative independently.)
   a. Calculate the number of units Olympia must sell to generate a targeted profit of $95,400. Assume that costs and selling price remain constant.
   b. Calculate the operating income if the company increases the number of units sold by 20 percent and cuts the selling price by $5 per unit.
   c. Determine the number of units that must be sold to break even if advertising costs are increased by $47,700.
   d. Find the number of units that must be sold to generate a targeted profit of $120,000 if variable costs are cut by 10 percent.

ANSWER TO REVIEW PROBLEM

1. Breakeven point in units for 20x5:

$$\text{Breakeven Units} = \frac{FC}{CM \text{ per Unit}} = \frac{\$318,000}{\$95 - \$42} = \frac{\$318,000}{\$53} = 6,000 \text{ Units}$$

2. Profit from sale of 6,500 units:

Units sold	6,500
Units required to break even	6,000
Units over breakeven	500

20x5 profit = $53 per unit × 500 = $26,500

Contribution margin equals sales minus all variable costs. Contribution margin per unit equals the amount left to cover fixed costs and earn a profit after variable costs have been subtracted from sales dollars. If all fixed costs have been absorbed by the time breakeven is reached, the entire contribution margin of each unit sold in excess of breakeven represents profit.

3. a. Number of units that must be sold to generate a targeted profit of $95,400:

$$\text{Targeted Sales Units} = \frac{FC + P}{CM \text{ per Unit}}$$

$$= \frac{\$318,000 + \$95,400}{\$53} = \frac{\$413,400}{\$53} = 7,800 \text{ Units}$$

b. Operating income if unit sales increase 20 percent and unit selling price decreases by $5:

Sales revenue [7,800 (6,500 × 1.20) units at $90 per unit]	$702,000
Less variable costs (7,800 units × $42)	327,600
Contribution margin	$374,400
Less fixed costs	318,000
Operating income	$ 56,400

c. Number of units needed to break even if advertising costs (fixed costs) increase by $47,700:

$$\text{BE Units} = \frac{FC}{CM \text{ per Unit}}$$

$$\frac{\$318,000 + \$47,700}{\$53} = \frac{\$365,700}{\$53} = 6,900 \text{ Units}$$

d. Number of units that must be sold to generate a targeted profit of $120,000 if variable costs decrease by 10 percent:

CM per Unit = $95.00 − ($42.00 × .9) = $95.00 − $37.80 = $57.20

$$\text{Targeted Sales Units} = \frac{FC + P}{CM \text{ per Unit}}$$

$$\frac{\$318,000 + \$120,000}{\$57.20} = \frac{\$438,000}{\$57.20} = 7,658 \text{ Units*}$$

*Note that the answer is rounded up to the next whole unit.

Review of Concepts and Terminology

The following concepts and terms were introduced in this chapter:

LO4 **Breakeven point:** The point at which total revenues equal total costs.

LO4 **Contribution margin:** The amount that remains after all variable costs are subtracted from sales.

LO1 **Cost behavior:** The way costs respond to changes in volume or activity.

LO3 **Cost-volume-profit (C-V-P) analysis:** An examination of the cost behavior patterns that underlie the relationships among cost, volume of output, and profit.

LO2 **Engineering method:** A method that separates costs into their fixed and variable components by performing a step-by-step analysis of the tasks, costs, and processes involved in completing an activity or product.

LO2 **Fixed costs:** Total costs that remain constant within a relevant range of volume or activity.

LO2 **High-low method:** A three-step approach to separating a mixed cost into its variable and fixed components.

LO4 **Margin of safety:** The number of sales units or amount of sales dollars by which actual sales can fall below planned sales without resulting in a loss.

LO2 **Mixed costs:** Costs that have both variable and fixed components.

LO2 **Normal capacity:** The average annual level of operating capacity needed to meet expected sales demand.

LO2 **Operating capacity:** The upper limit of an organization's productive output capability, given its existing resources.

LO2 **Practical capacity:** Theoretical capacity reduced by normal and expected work stoppages.

LO2 **Regression analysis:** A mathematical approach to separating a mixed cost into its variable and fixed components.

LO2 **Relevant range:** The span of activity in which a company expects to operate.

LO4 **Sales mix:** The proportion of each product's unit sales relative to the organization's total unit sales.

LO2 **Scatter diagram:** A chart of plotted points that helps determine whether a linear relationship exists between a cost item and its related activity measure.

LO2 **Theoretical (ideal) capacity:** The maximum productive output for a given period in which all machinery and equipment are operating at optimum speed, without interruption.

LO2 **Variable costs:** Total costs that change in direct proportion to changes in productive output or any other measure of volume.

Review Problem

Breakeven Analysis and Profitability Planning

LO4
LO5 Olympia, Inc., is a major producer of golf clubs. Its oversized putter has a large potential market. The following is a summary of data from the company's operations in 20x5:

Total fixed costs		
Manufacturing overhead		195,000
Advertising		55,000
Administrative expense		68,000
Variable costs per unit		
Direct materials	$	23
Direct labor		8
Manufacturing overhead		6
Selling expense		5
Selling price per unit		95

Chapter Review

REVIEW OF LEARNING OBJECTIVES

LO1 Define *cost behavior* and explain how managers use this concept in the management cycle.

Cost behavior is the way costs respond to changes in volume or activity. In the planning stage of the management cycle, managers use cost behavior to determine how many units of products or services must be sold to generate a targeted amount of profit and how changes in planned activities will affect operating income. In the executing stage, managers must understand and anticipate cost behavior to determine the impact of their decisions on operating income. In the reviewing and reporting stages, managers analyze how changes in cost and sales affect the profitability of product lines, sales territories, customers, departments, and other business segments by preparing reports using variable costing.

LO2 Identify variable, fixed, and mixed costs, and separate mixed costs into their variable and fixed components.

Some costs vary in relation to volume or operating activity; other costs remain fixed as volume changes. Cost behavior depends on whether the focus is total costs or cost per unit. Total costs that change in direct proportion to changes in productive output (or any other volume measure) are called *variable costs*. They include hourly wages, the cost of operating supplies, direct materials costs, and the cost of merchandise. Total *fixed costs* remain constant within a relevant range of volume or activity. They change only when volume or activity exceeds the relevant range—for example, when new equipment or new buildings must be purchased, higher insurance premiums and property taxes must be paid, or additional supervisory personnel must be hired to accommodate increased activity. A *mixed cost*, such as the cost of electricity, has both variable and fixed cost components. For cost planning and control, mixed costs must be separated into their variable and fixed components. To separate them, managers use a variety of methods, including the engineering, scatter diagram, high-low, and statistical methods.

LO3 Define *cost-volume-profit (C-V-P) analysis* and discuss how managers use it as a tool for planning and control.

Cost-volume-profit analysis is an examination of the cost behavior patterns that underlie the relationships among cost, volume of output, and profit. It is a tool for both planning and control. The techniques and problem-solving procedures involved in C-V-P analysis express relationships among revenue, sales mix, cost, volume, and profit. Those relationships provide a general model of financial activity that management can use for short-range planning and for evaluating performance and analyzing alternatives.

LO4 Define *breakeven point* and use contribution margin to determine a company's breakeven point for multiple products.

The *breakeven point* is the point at which total revenues equal total costs—in other words, the point at which net sales equal variable costs plus fixed costs. Once the number of units needed to break even is known, the number can be multiplied by the product's selling price to determine the breakeven point in sales dollars. *Contribution margin* is the amount that remains after all variable costs have been subtracted from sales. A product's contribution margin represents its net contribution to paying off fixed costs and earning a profit. The breakeven point in units can be computed by using the following formula:

$$\text{BE Units} = \frac{\text{FC}}{\text{CM per Unit}}$$

A sales mix is used to calculate the breakeven point for each product when a company sells more than one product.

LO5 Use C-V-P analysis to project the profitability of products and services.

The addition of targeted profit to the breakeven equation makes it possible to plan levels of operation that yield the targeted profit. The formula in terms of contribution margin is

$$\text{Targeted Sales Units} = \frac{\text{FC} + \text{P}}{\text{CM per Unit}}$$

C-V-P analysis, whether used by a manufacturing company or a service organization, enables managers to select several "what if" scenarios and evaluate the outcome of each to determine which will generate the desired amount of profit.

Step 3. *Calculate the total service overhead costs for one month.*

Total Service Overhead Costs = Total Fixed Service Overhead Costs + (Variable Rate × Estimated Number of Appraisals)
= $16,000 + ($41 per Appraisal × Number of Appraisals)

Step 4. *Calculate the total service overhead costs for one month assuming that 100 appraisals will be made.*

Total Overhead Service Costs = $16,000 + ($41 × 100) = $20,100

■ **DETERMINING THE BREAKEVEN POINT** Glenda Haley also wants to know how many appraisals her department must perform each month to cover the fixed and variable appraisal costs. She calculates the breakeven point as follows:

Let x = Number of Appraisals per Month at Breakeven Point
S = VC + FC
$400x = $300x + $16,000
$100x = $16,000
x = 160 Appraisals per Month

The variable rate of $300 per appraisal includes the variable service overhead rate, the direct professional labor, and the county survey map fee ($41 + $160 + $99).

■ **DETERMINING THE EFFECT OF A CHANGE IN OPERATING COSTS** Haley is worried because her department can perform an average of only 100 appraisals each month, but the estimated breakeven point is 160 appraisals per month. Because of strong competition, increasing the appraisal fee is not an option; to make the appraisals profitable, the mortgage company has asked Haley to find ways of reducing costs. In reviewing the situation, Haley has determined that improved scheduling of appraisals will reduce appraisers' travel time. Travel time is included in the current professional labor cost of $160 per appraisal (four hours of an appraiser's time at $40 per hour). By scheduling the jobs according to location, Haley can reduce the appraisers' travel time enough to reduce the total time required by 50 percent, thus cutting the professional labor cost to $80 per appraisal [(.50 × 4 hours) × $40 per hour]. The new scheduling process will increase fixed costs by $200 per month. Given these circumstances, what will the breakeven point be?

Let x = Number of Appraisals per Month at Breakeven Point
S = VC + FC
$400x = $220x + $16,200
$180x = $16,200
x = 90 Appraisals per Month

Variable costs become $220 ($300 − $80) per appraisal due to the reduced labor costs. This change increases the contribution margin by $80 per appraisal. Fixed costs increase from $16,000 to $16,200. The increase in the contribution margin is greater than the increase in the fixed costs, so the breakeven point decreases from 160 appraisals per month to 90 appraisals per month.

■ **ACHIEVING A TARGETED PROFIT** How many appraisals would Glenda Haley's department have to perform each month to achieve a targeted profit of $18,000 per month?

Let x = Targeted Sales in Units
S = VC + FC + P
$400x = $220x + $16,200 + $18,000
$180x = $34,200
x = 190 Units

✓ Check out ACE for a Review Quiz at http://accounting.college.hmco.com/students.

> **STOP AND THINK!**
> Why is the breakeven point important?
> *The breakeven point is important because it is the point at which an organization can begin to earn a profit.* ■

Note that the decrease in variable costs (direct materials) proposed in Alternative 1 increases the contribution margin per unit (from $40 to $43), which reduces the breakeven point. Because fewer sales dollars are required to cover variable costs, the breakeven point is reached sooner than in the original plan—at a sales volume of 466 units rather than at 500 units. In Alternative 2, the increase in fixed costs has no effect on the contribution margin per unit, but it does require the total contribution margin to cover more fixed costs before reaching the breakeven point. Thus, the breakeven point is higher than in the original plan—513 units as opposed to 500. The increase in selling price in Alternative 3 increases the contribution margin per unit, which reduces the breakeven point. Because more sales dollars are available to cover fixed costs, the breakeven point of 400 units is lower than the breakeven point in the original plan.

Which plan should Bryce choose? If he wants the highest operating income, he will choose Alternative 1. If, however, he wants the company to begin generating operating income more quickly, he will choose the plan with the lowest breakeven point, Alternative 3. Remember that the breakeven point provides a rough estimate of the number of units that must be sold to cover the total costs. Additional qualitative information may help Bryce make a better decision. Will customers perceive that the quality of the plant stands is lower if the company uses aluminum rather than iron, as proposed in Alternative 1? Will increased expenditures on advertising yield a 5 percent increase in sales volume, as Alternative 2 postulates? Will the increase in selling price suggested in Alternative 3 create more than a 15 percent decline in unit sales? Quantitative information is essential for planning, but managers must also be sensitive to qualitative factors, such as product quality, reliability and quality of suppliers, and availability of human and technical resources.

APPLYING C-V-P ANALYSIS TO A SERVICE BUSINESS

In this section, we look at how a service business can use C-V-P analysis in planning its operations. Assume that Glenda Haley, the manager of the Appraisal Department at Edmunds Mortgage Company, wants to plan the home appraisal activities that each mortgage loan application requires. She estimates that over the next year, her department will perform an average of 100 appraisals per month and service fee revenue will be $400 per appraisal. Other estimated data for the year are as follows:

Variable costs: direct professional labor, $160 per appraisal; county survey map fee, $99 per appraisal

Mixed costs (monthly service overhead):

Volume	Month	Activity Level	Cost
Highest	March	180 appraisals	$23,380
Lowest	February	98 appraisals	20,018

■ **ESTIMATING SERVICE OVERHEAD COSTS** Haley wants to estimate the total service overhead cost of appraisals for next year. She uses the high-low method to do so:

Step 1. *Calculate the variable service overhead cost per appraisal.*

Variable Service Overhead Cost per Appraisal = (Highest Cost − Lowest Cost) ÷ (Highest Volume − Lowest Volume)
= ($23,380 − $20,018) ÷ (180 − 98)
= $3,362 ÷ 82 Appraisals = $41

Step 2. *Calculate the total fixed service overhead costs.*

Total Fixed Service Overhead Costs = Total Service Overhead Costs − Total Variable Service Overhead Costs

Total Fixed Service Overhead Costs for March = $23,380 − ($41 × 180)
= $16,000

LO3 **Value-adding activity:** An activity that adds value to a product or service as perceived by the customer.

LO2 **Value chain:** A sequence of activities, or primary processes, that add value to a product or service; also includes support services that facilitate these activities.

LO5 **Work cell:** An autonomous production line that can perform all required operations efficiently and continuously.

REVIEW PROBLEM

Activity-Based Costing

LO4 Alvelo Corporation produces more than a dozen types of boat motors. The 240-horsepower motor is the most difficult to produce and the most expensive. The 60-horsepower model, which is the company's leading seller, is the easiest to produce. The other models range from 70 to 220 horsepower, and the difficulty of producing them increases as the horsepower increases. Rodak Company recently ordered 175 of the 80-horsepower model. Because Alvelo Corporation is considering a shift to activity-based costing, its controller, Song Shin, is interested in using this order to compare ABC with traditional costing. Costs directly traceable to the Rodak order are as follows:

Direct materials	$57,290
Purchased parts	$76,410
Direct labor hours	1,320
Average direct labor pay rate per hour	$14.00

With the traditional costing approach, Song Shin applies manufacturing overhead costs at a rate of 320 percent of direct labor costs.

For activity-based costing of the Rodak order, Song Shin uses the following data:

Activity	Cost Driver	Activity Cost Rate	Activity Usage
Product design	Engineering hours	$62 per engineering hour	76 engineering hours
Work cell setup	Number of setups	$90 per setup	16 setups
Parts production	Machine hours	$38 per machine hour	380 machine hours
Assembly	Assembly labor hours	$40 per assembly labor hour	500 assembly labor hours
Product simulation	Testing hours	$90 per testing hour	28 testing hours
Packaging and shipping	Product units	$26 per unit	175 units
Building occupancy	Direct labor cost	125% of direct labor cost	$18,480 direct labor cost

REQUIRED
1. Use the traditional costing approach to compute the total cost and product unit cost of the Rodak order.
2. Using the cost hierarchy for manufacturing companies, classify each activity of the Rodak order according to the level at which it occurs.
3. Prepare a bill of activities for the operating costs.
4. Use ABC to compute the total cost and product unit cost.
5. What is the difference between the product unit cost you computed using the traditional approach and the one you computed using ABC? Does the use of ABC guarantee cost reduction for every order?

ANSWER TO REVIEW PROBLEM

1. Traditional costing approach:

Direct materials	$ 57,290
Purchased parts	76,410
Direct labor	18,480
Manufacturing overhead (320% of direct labor cost)	59,136
Total cost of order	$ 211,316
Product unit cost (total cost ÷ 175 units)	$1,207.52

LO2 **Activity-based management (ABM):** An approach to managing an organization that identifies all major operating activities, determines the resources consumed by each activity and the cause of the resource usage, and categorizes the activities as either adding value to a product or service or not adding value; focuses on reducing or eliminating nonvalue-adding activities.

LO1 **Activity-based systems:** Information systems that provide quantitative information about an organization's activities.

LO7 **Backflush costing:** A product costing approach in which all product costs are first accumulated in the Cost of Goods Sold account and at the end of the period are "flushed back," or worked backward, into the appropriate inventory accounts.

LO4 **Batch-level activities:** Activities performed each time a batch of goods is produced.

LO4 **Bill of activities:** A list of activities and related costs that is used to compute the costs assigned to activities and the product unit cost.

LO6 **Conversion costs:** The sum of the direct labor costs and manufacturing overhead costs incurred by a production department, work cell, or other work center.

LO4 **Cost hierarchy:** A framework for classifying activities according to the level at which their costs are incurred.

LO4 **Facility-level activities:** Activities performed to support a facility's general manufacturing process.

LO1 **Full product cost:** A cost that includes not only the costs of direct materials and direct labor, but also the costs of all production and nonproduction activities required to satisfy the customer.

LO6 **Inspection time:** The time spent looking for product flaws or reworking defective units.

LO5 **Just-in-time (JIT) operating philosophy:** An operating philosophy that requires that all resources—materials, personnel, and facilities—be acquired and used only as needed; focuses on eliminating or reducing waste.

LO6 **Moving time:** The time spent moving a product from one operation or department to another.

LO3 **Nonvalue-adding activity:** An activity that adds cost to a product or service but does not increase its market value.

LO6 **Processing time:** The actual amount of time spent working on a product.

LO3 **Process value analysis (PVA):** A technique that analyzes business processes by relating activities to the events that prompt the activities and to the resources that the activities consume.

LO4 **Product-level activities:** Activities performed to support the diversity of products in a manufacturing plant.

LO5 **Pull-through production:** A production system in which a customer's order triggers the purchase of materials and the scheduling of production for the required products.

LO5 **Push-through method:** A production system in which products are manufactured in long production runs and stored in anticipation of customers' orders.

LO6 **Queue time:** The time a product spends waiting to be worked on once it enters a new operation or department.

LO6 **Storage time:** The time a product spends in materials storage, work in process inventory, or finished goods inventory.

LO2 **Supply chain:** The path that leads from the suppliers of the materials from which a product is made to the final customer.

LO6 **Throughput time:** The time it takes to move a product through the entire production process.

LO4 **Unit-level activities:** Activities performed each time a unit is produced.

LO4 Define *activity-based costing* and explain how a cost hierarchy and a bill of activities are used.

Activity-based costing (ABC) is a method of assigning costs that calculates a more accurate product cost than traditional methods. It does so by categorizing all indirect costs by activity, tracing the indirect costs to those activities, and assigning those costs to products using a cost driver related to the cause of the cost. To implement ABC, managers (1) identify and classify each activity, (2) estimate the cost of resources for each activity, (3) identify a cost driver for each activity and estimate the quantity of each cost driver, (4) calculate an activity cost rate for each activity, and (5) assign costs to cost objects based on the level of activity required to make the product or provide the service.

Two tools—a cost hierarchy and a bill of activities—help in the implementation of ABC. To create a cost hierarchy, managers classify activities into four levels. Unit-level activities are performed each time a unit is produced. Batch-level activities are performed each time a batch of goods is produced. Product-level activities are performed to support the diversity of products in a manufacturing plant. Facility-level activities are performed to support a facility's general manufacturing process. A bill of activities is then used to compute the costs assigned to activities and the product or service unit cost.

LO5 Define the *just-in-time (JIT) operating philosophy* and identify the elements of a JIT operating environment.

The just-in-time (JIT) operating philosophy is a management philosophy that requires that all resources—materials, personnel, and facilities—be acquired and used only as needed. Its objectives are to enhance productivity, eliminate waste, reduce costs, and improve product quality. The elements in a JIT operating environment that are designed to achieve those objectives are minimum inventory levels, pull-through production, quick setup and flexible work cells, a multiskilled work force, high levels of product quality, effective preventive maintenance, and continuous improvement of the work environment.

LO6 Identify the changes in product costing that result when a firm adopts a JIT operating environment.

In product costing under JIT, processing costs are classified as either direct materials costs or conversion costs. The costs associated with inspection time, moving time, queue time, and storage time are reduced or eliminated. With computerized monitoring of the work cells, many costs that are treated as indirect or overhead costs in traditional manufacturing settings, such as the costs of utilities and operating supplies, can be traced directly to work cells. The only costs that remain indirect costs and that must be assigned to the work cells for inclusion in the conversion cost are those associated with building occupancy, insurance, and property taxes.

LO7 Define and apply *backflush costing*, and compare the cost flows in traditional and backflush costing.

In backflush costing, all product costs are first accumulated in the Cost of Goods Sold account, and at the end of the accounting period, they are "flushed back," or worked backward, into the appropriate inventory accounts. Backflush costing is commonly used to account for product costs in a JIT operating environment. It differs from the traditional costing approach, which records the costs of materials purchased in the Materials Inventory account and uses the Work in Process Inventory account to record the costs of direct materials, direct labor, and manufacturing overhead during the production process. The objective of backflush costing is to save recording time, which cuts costs.

LO8 Compare ABM and JIT as activity-based systems.

As activity-based systems, both ABM and JIT seek to eliminate waste and reduce nonvalue-adding activities. However, they differ in their approaches to cost assignment and calculation of product cost. ABM uses ABC to assign indirect costs to products using cost drivers; JIT reorganizes activities so that they are performed within work cells, and the manufacturing overhead costs incurred in a work cell become direct costs of the products made in that cell. ABM uses job order or process costing to calculate product costs, whereas JIT may use backflush costing.

REVIEW OF CONCEPTS AND TERMINOLOGY

The following concepts and terms were introduced in this chapter:

LO4 **Activity-based costing:** A method of assigning costs that calculates a more accurate product cost than traditional methods by categorizing all indirect costs by activity, tracing the indirect costs to those activities, and assigning those costs to products using a cost driver related to the cause of the cost.

TABLE 4. Comparison of ABM and JIT Activity-Based Systems

	ABM	JIT
Primary purpose	To eliminate or reduce nonvalue-adding activities	To eliminate or reduce waste
Cost assignment	Uses ABC to assign manufacturing overhead costs to the product cost by using appropriate cost drivers	Reorganizes activities so that they are performed within work cells; manufacturing overhead costs incurred in the work cell become direct costs of the products made in that cell
Costing method	Integrates ABC with job order or process costing to calculate product costs	May use backflush costing to calculate product costs when the products are completed

waste. To remain competitive in today's fast-changing business environment, many organizations rely on both of these activity-based systems.

Check out ACE for a Review Quiz at http://accounting.college.hmco.com/students.

Chapter Review

REVIEW OF LEARNING OBJECTIVES

LO1 Explain the role of activity-based systems in the management cycle.

Activity-based systems are information systems that provide quantitative information about an organization's activities. They help managers view the organization as a collection of related activities. Activity-based cost information enables managers to improve operating processes and make better pricing decisions. During the planning stage of the management cycle, activity-based systems help managers identify value-adding activities, determine the resources needed for those activities, and estimate product costs. In the executing and reviewing stages, these systems help managers determine the full product or service cost, identify actions that will reduce that cost, and establish whether cost-reduction goals for nonvalue-adding activities were reached. Activity-based systems also help managers report the cost of inventory and determine the degree to which product goals were achieved.

LO2 Define *activity-based management (ABM)* and discuss its relationship to the supply chain and the value chain.

Activity-based management (ABM) is an approach to managing an organization that identifies all major operating activities, determines the resources consumed by each activity and the cause of the resource usage, and categorizes the activities as either adding value to a product or service or not adding value. ABM enables managers to see their organization as a collection of value-creating activities (a value chain) operating as part of a larger system that includes suppliers' and customers' value chains (a supply chain). This perspective helps managers work cooperatively both inside and outside their organizations to reduce costs by eliminating waste and inefficiencies and by redirecting resources toward value-adding activities.

LO3 Distinguish between value-adding and nonvalue-adding activities, and describe process value analysis.

A value-adding activity adds value to a product or service as perceived by the customer. Examples include designing the components of a new car, assembling the car, painting it, and installing seats and airbags. A nonvalue-adding activity adds cost to a product or service but does not increase its market value. Examples include legal services, management accounting, machine repair, materials handling, and building maintenance. PVA is a technique that managers use to identify and link all the activities involved in the value chain. It analyzes business processes by relating activities to the events that prompt the activities and to the resources that the activities consume.

The bottom diagram in Figure 5 shows how backflush costing in a JIT environment would treat the same transactions. The cost of direct materials (Transaction 1) is charged directly to the Cost of Goods Sold account. Transaction 2 in the traditional method is not included because there is no Materials Inventory account when backflush costing is used. The costs of direct labor (Transaction 3) and manufacturing overhead (Transaction 4) are combined in the Conversion Costs account and transferred to the Cost of Goods Sold account. The total in the Cost of Goods Sold account is then $52,000 ($20,000 for direct materials and $32,000 for conversion costs).

Once all product costs for the period have been entered in the Cost of Goods Sold account, the amounts to be transferred back to the inventory accounts are calculated. The amount transferred to the Finished Goods Inventory account is the difference between the cost of units sold (Transaction 6) and the cost of completed units (Transaction 5) ($51,600 − $51,500 = $100). The remaining difference in the Cost of Goods Sold account represents the cost of the work still in production at the end of the period. It is the amount charged to the Cost of Goods Sold account during the period less the actual cost of goods finished during the period (Transaction 5) [($20,000 + $8,000 + $24,000) − $51,600 = $400]; this amount is transferred to the Work in Process Inventory account. Notice that the ending balance in the Cost of Goods Sold account, $51,500, is the same as the ending balance when traditional costing is used. The difference is that backflush costing enabled us to use fewer accounts and to avoid recording several transactions.

● **Stop and Think!**
How is the ending balance in the Finished Goods Inventory account determined when backflush costing is used?
The ending balance in this account is the difference between the cost of goods sold and the cost of goods completed. ■

✓ Check out ACE for a Review Quiz at http://accounting.college.hmco.com/students.

Comparison of ABM and JIT

LO8 Compare ABM and JIT as activity-based systems.
RELATED TEXT ASSIGNMENTS
Q: 20
SE: 10
E: 14, 15

KEY POINT: ABM's primary goal is to calculate product cost accurately. JIT's primary goal is to simplify and standardize business processes.

ABM and JIT have several things in common. As activity-based systems, both analyze processes and identify value-adding and nonvalue-adding activities. Both seek to eliminate waste and reduce nonvalue-adding activities to improve product or service quality, reduce costs, and improve an organization's efficiency and productivity. Both improve the quality of the information managers use to make decisions about bidding, pricing, product lines, and outsourcing. However, the two systems differ in their methods of costing and cost assignment.

ABM's tool, ABC, calculates product cost by using cost drivers to assign the indirect costs of production to cost objects. ABC affects only the assignment of manufacturing overhead costs to the products; the costs of direct materials and direct labor are traced directly to products and are unaffected by ABC. ABC is often a fairly complex accounting method used with job order and process costing systems. Note that the ABC method can also be used to examine nonproduction-related activities, such as marketing and shipping.

JIT reorganizes many activities so that they are performed within work cells. The costs of those activities become direct costs of the work cell and of the products made in that cell. The total production costs within the cell can then be assigned by using simple cost drivers, such as process hours or direct materials cost. Companies that have implemented JIT manufacturing may use backflush costing rather than job order costing or process costing. This approach focuses on the output at the end of the production process and simplifies the accounting system. Table 4 summarizes the characteristics of ABM and JIT.

● **Stop and Think!**
Can a business use both ABM and JIT?
A business can use both of these activity-based systems. ■

A company can use both ABM and JIT. ABM and ABC will improve the accuracy of its product or service costing and help the company reduce or eliminate business activities that do not add value for its customers. It can apply the JIT operating philosophy to simplify processes, use resources effectively, and eliminate

944 Chapter 22 Activity-Based Systems: ABM and JIT

FIGURE 5
Cost Flows Through T Accounts in Traditional and Backflush Costing

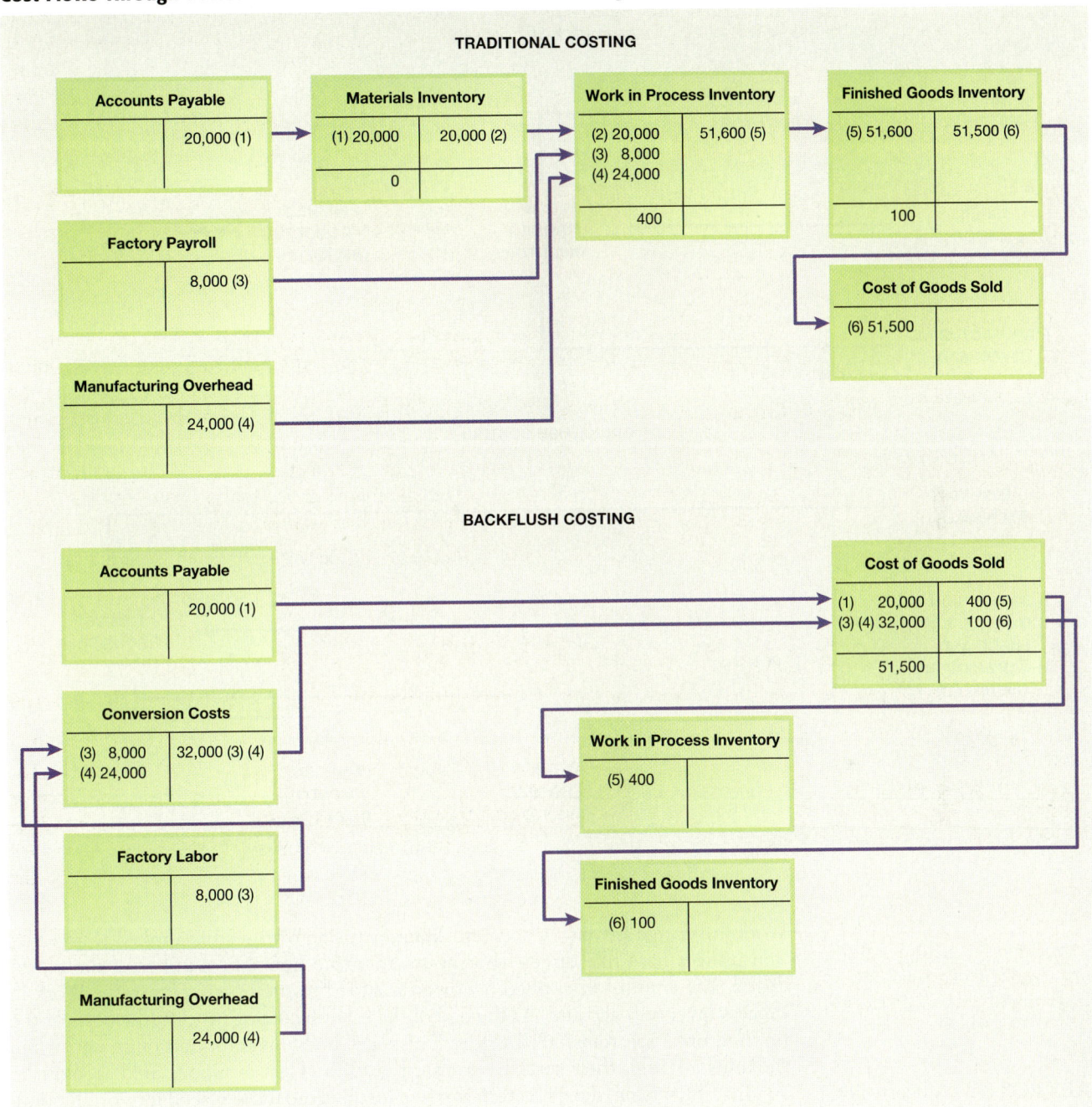

TRADITIONAL COSTING

Accounts Payable		Materials Inventory		Work in Process Inventory		Finished Goods Inventory	
	20,000 (1)	(1) 20,000	20,000 (2)	(2) 20,000	51,600 (5)	(5) 51,600	51,500 (6)
				(3) 8,000			
			0	(4) 24,000			
				400		100	

Factory Payroll: 8,000 (3)

Manufacturing Overhead: 24,000 (4)

Cost of Goods Sold: (6) 51,500

BACKFLUSH COSTING

Accounts Payable: 20,000 (1)

Conversion Costs:
(3) 8,000 | 32,000 (3) (4)
(4) 24,000

Factory Labor: 8,000 (3)

Manufacturing Overhead: 24,000 (4)

Cost of Goods Sold:
(1) 20,000 | 400 (5)
(3) (4) 32,000 | 100 (6)
51,500

Work in Process Inventory: (5) 400

Finished Goods Inventory: (6) 100

---

3. Incurred direct labor costs of $8,000.
4. Applied $24,000 of manufacturing overhead to production.
5. Completed units costing $51,600 during the month.
6. Sold units costing $51,500 during the month.

The top diagram in Figure 5 shows how those transactions would be entered in T accounts when traditional product costing is used. You can trace the flow of each cost by following its transaction number.

FIGURE 4
Comparison of Cost Flows in Traditional and Backflush Costing

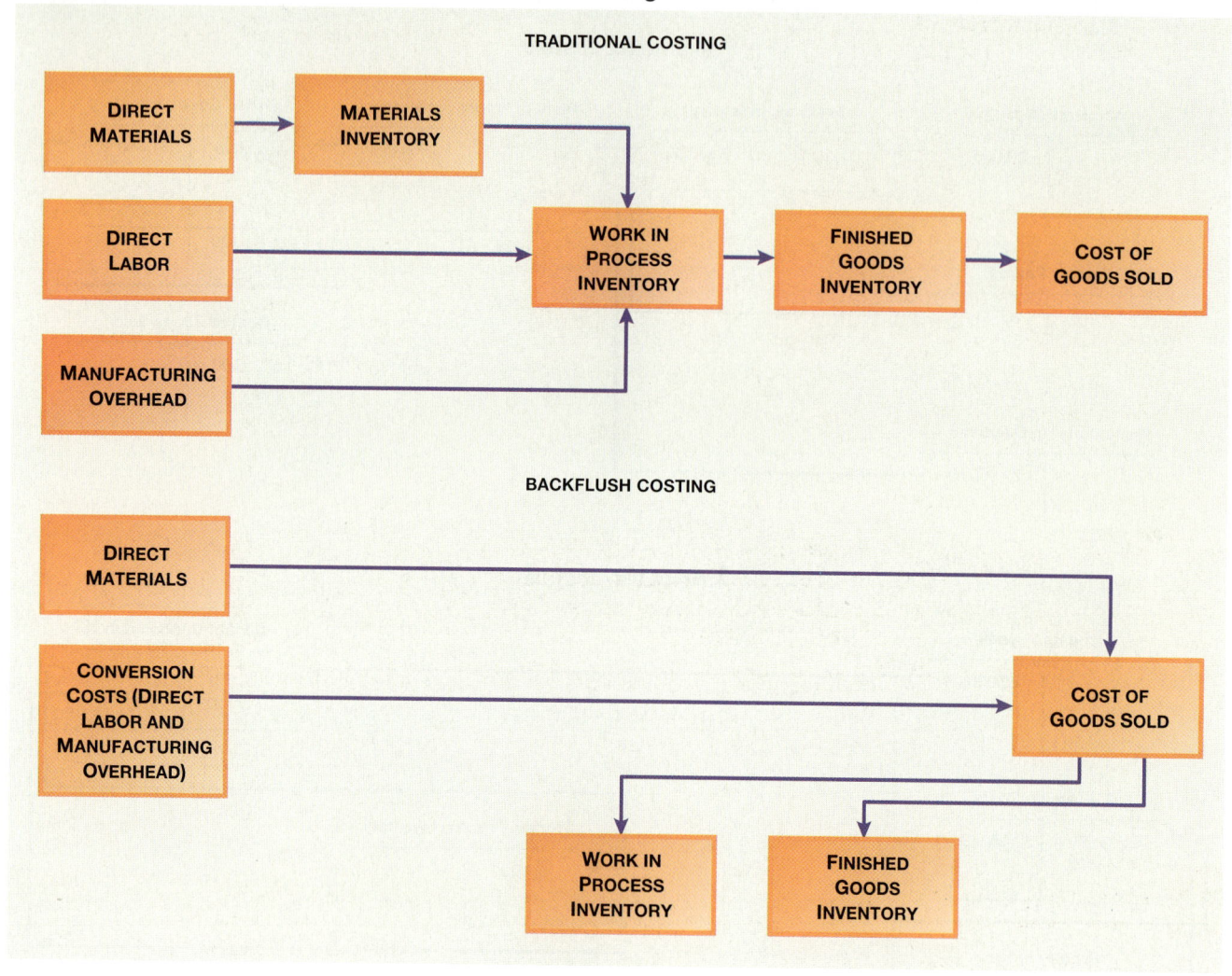

TRADITIONAL COSTING

DIRECT MATERIALS → MATERIALS INVENTORY → WORK IN PROCESS INVENTORY → FINISHED GOODS INVENTORY → COST OF GOODS SOLD

DIRECT LABOR → WORK IN PROCESS INVENTORY

MANUFACTURING OVERHEAD → WORK IN PROCESS INVENTORY

BACKFLUSH COSTING

DIRECT MATERIALS → COST OF GOODS SOLD

CONVERSION COSTS (DIRECT LABOR AND MANUFACTURING OVERHEAD) → COST OF GOODS SOLD

COST OF GOODS SOLD → WORK IN PROCESS INVENTORY

COST OF GOODS SOLD → FINISHED GOODS INVENTORY

KEY POINT: All costs flow directly to the Cost of Goods Sold account during the month.

KEY POINT: In backflush costing, entries to the Work in Process Inventory and Finished Goods Inventory accounts are made at the end of the period.

Work in Process Inventory account. Manufacturing overhead is applied to production using a base like direct labor hours, machine hours, or number of units produced. The amount of applied overhead is added to the other costs in the Work in Process Inventory account. At the end of the manufacturing process, the costs of the finished units are transferred to the Finished Goods Inventory account, and when the units are sold, their costs are transferred to the Cost of Goods Sold account.

In a JIT setting, direct materials arrive just in time to be placed into production. As you can see in Figure 4, when backflush costing is used, the direct materials costs and the conversion costs (direct labor and manufacturing overhead) are immediately charged to the Cost of Goods Sold account. At the end of the period, the costs of goods in work in process inventory and in finished goods inventory are determined, and those costs are flushed back to the Work in Process Inventory account and the Finished Goods Inventory account. Once those costs have been flushed back, the Cost of Goods Sold account contains only the costs of units completed and sold during the period.

To illustrate, assume that the following transactions occurred at Allegro Company last month:

1. Purchased $20,000 of direct materials on account.
2. Used all of the direct materials in production during the month.

TABLE 3. Direct and Indirect Costs in Traditional and JIT Environments

Costs in a Traditional Environment		Costs in a JIT Environment
Direct	Direct materials	Direct
Direct	Direct labor	Direct
Indirect	Repairs and maintenance	Direct to work cell
Indirect	Materials handling	Direct to work cell
Indirect	Operating supplies	Direct to work cell
Indirect	Utilities costs	Direct to work cell
Indirect	Supervision	Direct to work cell
Indirect	Depreciation	Direct to work cell
Indirect	Supporting service functions	Mostly direct to work cell
Indirect	Building occupancy	Indirect
Indirect	Insurance and taxes	Indirect

JIT work cell. Because the products that a work cell manufactures are similar in nature, direct materials and conversion costs should be nearly uniform for each product in a cell. The costs of repairs and maintenance, materials handling, operating supplies, utilities, and supervision can be traced directly to work cells as they are incurred. Depreciation charges are based on units of output, not on time, so depreciation can be charged directly to work cells based on the number of units produced. Building occupancy costs, insurance premiums, and property taxes remain indirect costs and must be assigned to the work cells for inclusion in the conversion cost.

✓ Check out ACE for a Review Quiz at http://accounting.college.hmco.com/students.

BACKFLUSH COSTING

LO7 Define and apply *backflush costing*, and compare the cost flows in traditional and backflush costing.

RELATED TEXT ASSIGNMENTS
Q: 19
SE: 9
E: 12, 13
P: 5, 8

KEY POINT: Backflush costing eliminates the need to make journal entries during the period to track cost flows as the product is made.

Managers in a just-in-time operating environment continuously seek ways of reducing wasted resources and time. So far, we have focused on how they can trim waste from manufacturing operations, but they can reduce waste in other areas as well, including the accounting process. Because a JIT environment reduces labor costs, the accounting system can combine the costs of direct labor and manufacturing overhead into the single category of conversion costs, and because materials arrive just in time to be used in the production process, there is little reason to maintain a separate Materials Inventory account. Thus, by simplifying cost flows through the accounting records, a JIT environment makes it possible to reduce the time it takes to record and account for the costs of the manufacturing process.

A JIT organization can also streamline its accounting process by using backflush costing. In **backflush costing**, all product costs are first accumulated in the Cost of Goods Sold account, and at the end of the accounting period, they are "flushed back," or worked backward, into the appropriate inventory accounts. By having all product costs flow straight to a final destination and working back to determine the proper balances for the inventory accounts at the end of the period, this method saves recording time. As illustrated in Figure 4, it eliminates the need to record several transactions that must be recorded in traditional manufacturing environments.

When direct materials arrive at a factory in which traditional costing methods are used, their costs flow into the Materials Inventory account. Then, when the direct materials are requisitioned into production, their costs flow into the Work in Process Inventory account. When direct labor is used, its costs are added to the

KEY POINT: The JIT operating philosophy must be adopted by everyone in a company before its total benefits can be realized.

CONTINUOUS IMPROVEMENT OF THE WORK ENVIRONMENT

A JIT environment fosters loyalty among workers, who are likely to see themselves as part of a team because they are so deeply involved in the production process. Machine operators must have the skills to run several types of machines, detect defective products, suggest measures to correct problems, and maintain the machinery within their work cells. In addition, each worker is encouraged to suggest improvements to the production process. Companies with a JIT operating environment receive thousands of employee suggestions and implement a high percentage of them, and they reward workers for suggestions that improve the process. Such an environment fosters workers' initiative and benefits the company.

Check out ACE for a Review Quiz at http://accounting.college.hmco.com/students.

ACCOUNTING FOR PRODUCT COSTS IN THE NEW MANUFACTURING ENVIRONMENT

LO6 Identify the changes in product costing that result when a firm adopts a JIT operating environment.

RELATED TEXT ASSIGNMENTS
Q: 18
SE: 8
E: 11
P: 4
SD: 5

When a firm shifts to the new manufacturing environment, the management accounting system must take a new approach to evaluating costs and controlling operations. The changes in the manufacturing operations will affect how costs are determined and what measures are used to monitor performance.

When a company adopts a JIT operating environment, the work cells and goal of reducing or eliminating nonvalue-adding activities change the way costs are classified and assigned. In this section, we examine those changes.

CLASSIFYING COSTS

The traditional production process can be divided into five time frames:

STOP AND THINK!
Which time frame in the production process is value adding?
Processing time is value adding. ■

Processing time	The actual amount of time spent working on a product
Inspection time	The time spent looking for product flaws or reworking defective units
Moving time	The time spent moving a product from one operation or department to another
Queue time	The time a product spends waiting to be worked on once it arrives at the next operation or department
Storage time	The time a product spends in materials storage, work in process inventory, or finished goods inventory

STUDY NOTE: Although separate inspection costs are reduced in a JIT operating environment, some additional time is added to production because the machine operator is now performing the inspection function. The objectives are to reduce *total* costs and to increase quality.

In product costing under JIT, costs associated with processing time are classified as either direct materials costs or conversion costs. **Conversion costs** are the sum of the direct labor costs and manufacturing overhead costs incurred by a production department, work cell, or other work center. According to the JIT philosophy, costs associated with inspection, moving, queue, and storage time should be reduced or eliminated because they do not add value to the product.

ASSIGNING COSTS

In a JIT operating environment, managers focus on **throughput time**, the time it takes to move a product through the entire production process. Measures of product movement, such as machine time, are used to apply conversion costs to products.

Sophisticated computer monitoring of the work cells allows many costs to be traced directly to the cells where products are manufactured. As Table 3 shows, several costs that in a traditional environment are treated as indirect costs and applied to products using a manufacturing overhead rate are treated as the direct costs of a

Focus on International Business

Is JIT Right for Every Business?

For companies whose manufacturing is done mainly in foreign countries where labor is cheap and transportation lag times are long, a JIT production environment may not be right. Koss Corporation <www.koss.com>, a manufacturer of headphones, is one such company. Because retailers expect instant merchandise replenishment and threaten to take their business elsewhere if a supplier does not keep the supply chain filled, Koss concentrates on keeping ample supplies of finished goods in close proximity to the retailers that buy its products. Thus, instead of focusing on *manufacturing* products just in time, Koss and companies like it focus on *delivering* products just in time.[5]

KEY POINT: In the JIT environment, normal operating activities—setup, production, and maintenance—still take place. But the timing of those activities is altered to promote smoother operations and to minimize downtime.

KEY POINT: The fact that inspections are necessary is an admission that problems with quality do occur. Continuous inspection throughout production as opposed to inspection only at the end of the process creates awareness of a problem at the point where it occurs.

The success of JIT has disproved this. By placing machines in more efficient locations, setup time can be minimized. In addition, when workers perform frequent setups, they become more efficient at it.

In a traditional factory layout, similar machines are grouped together, forming functional departments. Products are routed through each department in sequence, so that all necessary operations are completed in order. This process can take several days or weeks, depending on the size and complexity of the job. By changing the factory layout so that all the machines needed for sequential processing are placed together, the JIT operating environment may cut the manufacturing time of a product from days to hours, or from weeks to days. The new cluster of machinery forms a flexible **work cell**, an autonomous production line that can perform all required operations efficiently and continuously. The flexible work cell handles a "family of products"—that is, products of similar shape or size. Product families require minimal setup changes as workers move from one job to the next. The more flexible the work cell is, the greater the potential to minimize total production time.

A Multiskilled Work Force

In the flexible work cells of a JIT environment, one worker may be required to operate several types of machines simultaneously. That worker may have to set up and retool the machines and even perform routine maintenance on them. A JIT operating environment thus requires a multiskilled work force, and multiskilled workers have been very effective in contributing to high levels of productivity.

High Levels of Product Quality

JIT operations result in quality products because high-quality direct materials are used and because inspections are made throughout the production process. According to the JIT philosophy, inspection as a separate step does not add value to a product, so inspection is incorporated into ongoing operations. A JIT machine operator inspects the products as they pass through the manufacturing process. If the operator detects a flaw, he or she shuts down the work cell to prevent the production of similarly flawed products while the cause of the problem is being determined. The operator either fixes the problem or helps the engineer or quality control person find a way to correct it. This integrated inspection procedure, combined with quality raw materials, produces high-quality finished goods.

Effective Preventive Maintenance

When a company rearranges its machinery into flexible work cells, each machine becomes an integral part of its cell. If one machine breaks down, the entire cell stops functioning. Because the product cannot be easily routed to another machine while the malfunctioning machine is being repaired, continuous JIT operations require an effective system of preventive maintenance. Preventing machine breakdowns is considered more important and more cost-effective than keeping machines running continuously. Machine operators are trained to perform minor repairs as they detect problems. Machines are serviced regularly—much as an automobile is—to help guarantee continued operation. The machine operator conducts routine maintenance during periods of downtime between orders. (Remember that in a JIT setting, the work cell does not operate unless there is a customer order for the product. Machine operators take advantage of such downtime to perform routine maintenance.)

Focus on Business Practice

What Is VBM?

Value-based management (VBM) is a long-term strategy that many businesses use to reward managers who create and sustain shareholder wealth and value. In other words, VBM encourages managers to think like business owners. Three elements are essential for a successful VBM program. First, VBM must have the full support of top management. Second, performance and compensation must be linked because "what gets measured and rewarded gets done." Finally, everyone involved must understand the what, why, and how of the program. Since a variety of VBM approaches exist, each company can tailor its VBM performance metrics and implementation strategy to meet its particular needs.[4]

www.westinghouseelectric.com
www.pepsico.com
www.landolakes.com

Process Value Analysis

Process value analysis (PVA) is a technique that managers use to identify and link all the activities involved in the value chain. It analyzes business processes by relating activities to the events that prompt the activities and to the resources that the activities consume. PVA forces managers to look critically at all phases of their operations. Managers who use ABM find it an effective way of reducing nonvalue-adding activities and their costs. PVA improves cost traceability and results in significantly more accurate product costs, which in turn improves management decisions and increases profitability.

By using PVA to identify nonvalue-adding activities, companies can reduce costs and redirect resources to value-adding activities. For example, PVA has enabled companies like Westinghouse Electric, Pepsi-Cola North America, and Land O'Lakes to reduce the processing costs of purchasing and accounts payable. After identifying the nonvalue-adding activities involved in small-dollar purchases (e.g., recording and paying small bills, setting up accounts, and establishing credit with seldom-used suppliers) and their costs, managers of these companies decided to stop performing such activities internally. Instead, they chose the less expensive alternative of using a special credit card known as a procurement (or purchasing)

TABLE 1. Value-Adding Activities for a Service Organization

Western Data Services, Inc.
Value-Adding Activities for the Classic Letter

Value-Adding Activities	How the Activity Adds Value
Designing the letter	Enhances the effectiveness of the communication
Creating a database of customers' names and addresses sorted in ZIP code order	Increases the probability that the client will efficiently and effectively reach the targeted customer group
Verifying the conformity of mailings with USPS requirements	Ensures that the client's mailing will receive the best postal rate
Processing the job: A computer prints a personalized letter A machine folds the letter, inserts it and other information into an envelope, prints the address on the envelope, and seals and meters the envelope.	Creates the client mailing
Delivering the letters to the post office	Begins the delivery process

VALUE-ADDING AND NONVALUE-ADDING ACTIVITIES AND PROCESS VALUE ANALYSIS

LO3 Distinguish between value-adding and nonvalue-adding activities, and describe process value analysis.

RELATED TEXT ASSIGNMENTS
Q: 8, 9
SE: 4
E: 4, 5
P: 1
SD: 2, 5
MRA: 1, 4, 5

KEY POINT: The customer's perspective is what governs whether an activity adds value to a product or service.

An important element of activity-based management is the identification of value-adding and nonvalue-adding activities. A **value-adding activity** adds value to a product or service as perceived by the customer. Examples include designing the components of a new car, assembling the car, painting it, and installing seats and airbags. A **nonvalue-adding activity** adds cost to a product or service but does not increase its market value. ABM focuses on eliminating nonvalue-adding activities that are not essential to an organization and on reducing the costs of those that are essential, such as legal services, management accounting, machine repair, materials handling, and building maintenance. The costs of both value-adding and nonvalue-adding activities are accumulated to measure performance and to determine whether the goal of reducing the cost of nonvalue-adding activities has been achieved.

To minimize costs, managers continuously seek to improve processes and activities. To manage the cost of an activity, they can reduce the activity's frequency or eliminate it. For example, inspection costs can be reduced if an inspector samples one of every three engines received from a supplier rather than inspecting every engine. If the supplier is a reliable source of high-quality engines, such a reduction in inspection activity is appropriate. Another way to reduce costs is to outsource an activity—that is, to have it done by another company that is more competent at the work and can perform it at a lower cost. Many companies outsource purchasing, accounting, and the maintenance of their information systems.

Some activities can be eliminated completely if business processes are changed. For example, when a company adopts a just-in-time operating philosophy, it can eliminate some recordkeeping activities. Because it purchases materials just in time for production and manufactures products just in time for customer delivery, it no longer needs to accumulate costs as the product is made.

VALUE-ADDING AND NONVALUE-ADDING ACTIVITIES IN A SERVICE ORGANIZATION

To illustrate how service organizations deal with value-adding and nonvalue-adding activities, let's suppose Carl Marcus, the owner and manager of WDSI, has examined the activities related to the design, processing, and mailing of his company's Classic Letters and drawn up the list of value-adding activities shown in Table 1. When Marcus's customers ask for database marketing services, these are the activities they pay for. Marcus also identified the following nonvalue-adding activities:

- Preparing a job order form and scheduling the job
- Ordering, receiving, inspecting, and storing paper, envelopes, and other supplies
- Setting up machines to process a specific letter size
- Logging the total number of items processed in a batch
- Billing the client and recording and depositing payments from the client

After reviewing the list of nonvalue-adding activities, Marcus arranged with his suppliers to have paper, envelopes, and other supplies delivered the day a job is performed. This helped reduce WDSI's storage costs. Marcus was also able to reduce the costs of some value-adding activities. For example, he reduced the cost of the labor involved in verifying the conformity of mailings with United States Postal Service (USPS) requirements by purchasing computer software that verifies addresses, determines postage, and automatically sorts the letters.

🛑 **STOP AND THINK!**
Are customers willing to pay for nonvalue-adding activities?
Customers are not willing to pay for such activities, which is why businesses try to minimize or eliminate them. ∎

FIGURE 3
Supply Chain and Value Chain for a Service Organization

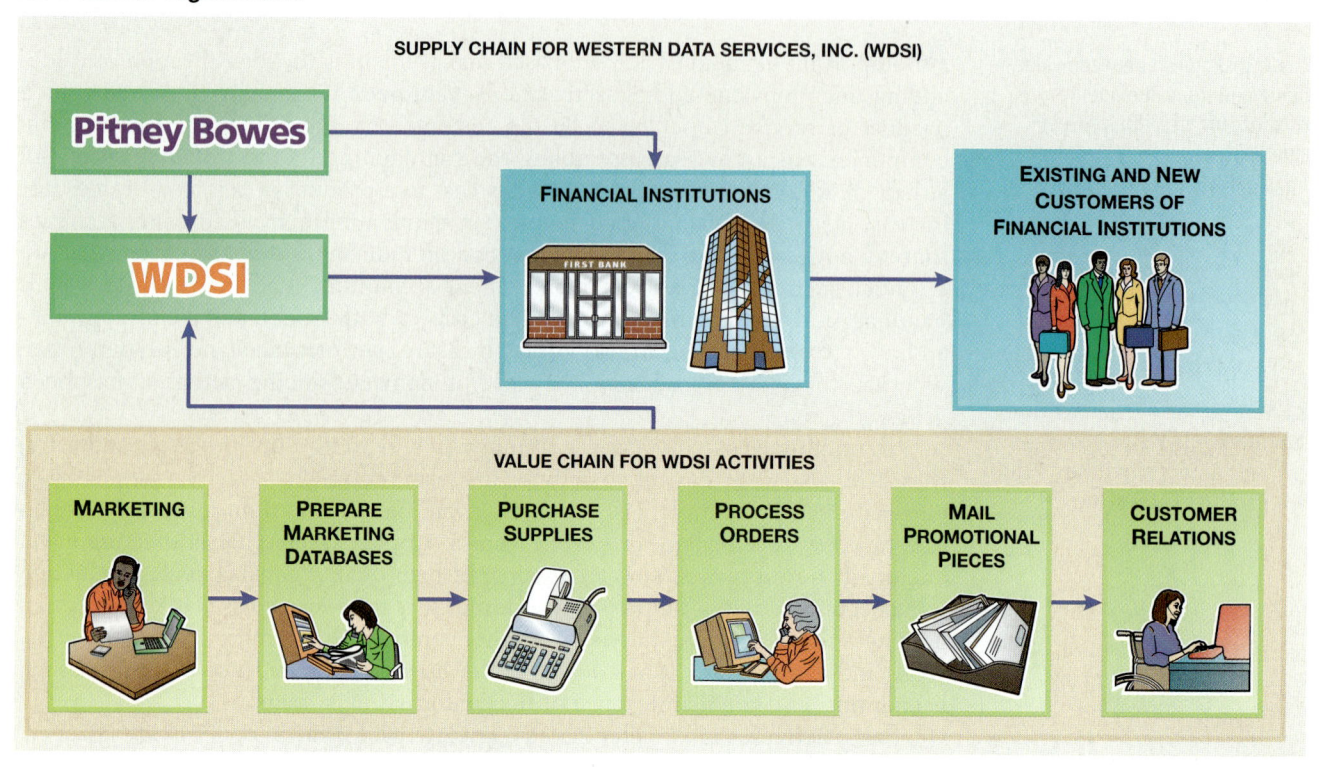

SUPPLY CHAIN FOR WESTERN DATA SERVICES, INC. (WDSI)

Pitney Bowes → WDSI → Financial Institutions → Existing and New Customers of Financial Institutions

VALUE CHAIN FOR WDSI ACTIVITIES

MARKETING → PREPARE MARKETING DATABASES → PURCHASE SUPPLIES → PROCESS ORDERS → MAIL PROMOTIONAL PIECES → CUSTOMER RELATIONS

www.pb.com

creation and maintenance of marketing databases containing information about the client's target group, and a production process that prints a promotional piece and prepares it for mailing. WDSI's primary customers are financial institutions throughout the western states, but the company also serves small businesses and nonprofit organizations.

In preparing WSDI's business plan, Carl Marcus, the owner and manager of WDSI, reviewed the company's supply chain. As Figure 3 shows, this supply chain includes one supplier (Pitney Bowes), WDSI as a service provider, one customer group (financial institutions), and the customer group's customers. WDSI had a number of suppliers, including office supply companies, printers, and computer stores, but Marcus chose to include only Pitney Bowes because of the significant cost savings from using this supplier's equipment to fold, insert, address, seal, and meter mailing pieces. Marcus chose financial institutions as the supply chain's primary customer group because they represent 75 percent of revenues. The customers of the financial institutions are included in the supply chain because those individuals and businesses receive the mailing pieces that WDSI prepares. Based on his review of the supply chain, Marcus concluded that WDSI's strategy to work with Pitney Bowes and the financial institutions to improve WDSI's services was sound.

Marcus also decided to use ABM to manage processes and activities. He developed a value chain of activities for the company so that he could identify all major operating activities, the resources each activity consumes, and the cause of the resource usage. As shown in Figure 3, the activities that add value to WDSI's services are marketing, preparing marketing databases, purchasing supplies, processing orders, mailing promotional pieces, and customer relations.

✓ Check out ACE for a Review Quiz at http://accounting.college.hmco.com/students.

FIGURE 2
Supply Chain and Value Chain for a Manufacturing Company

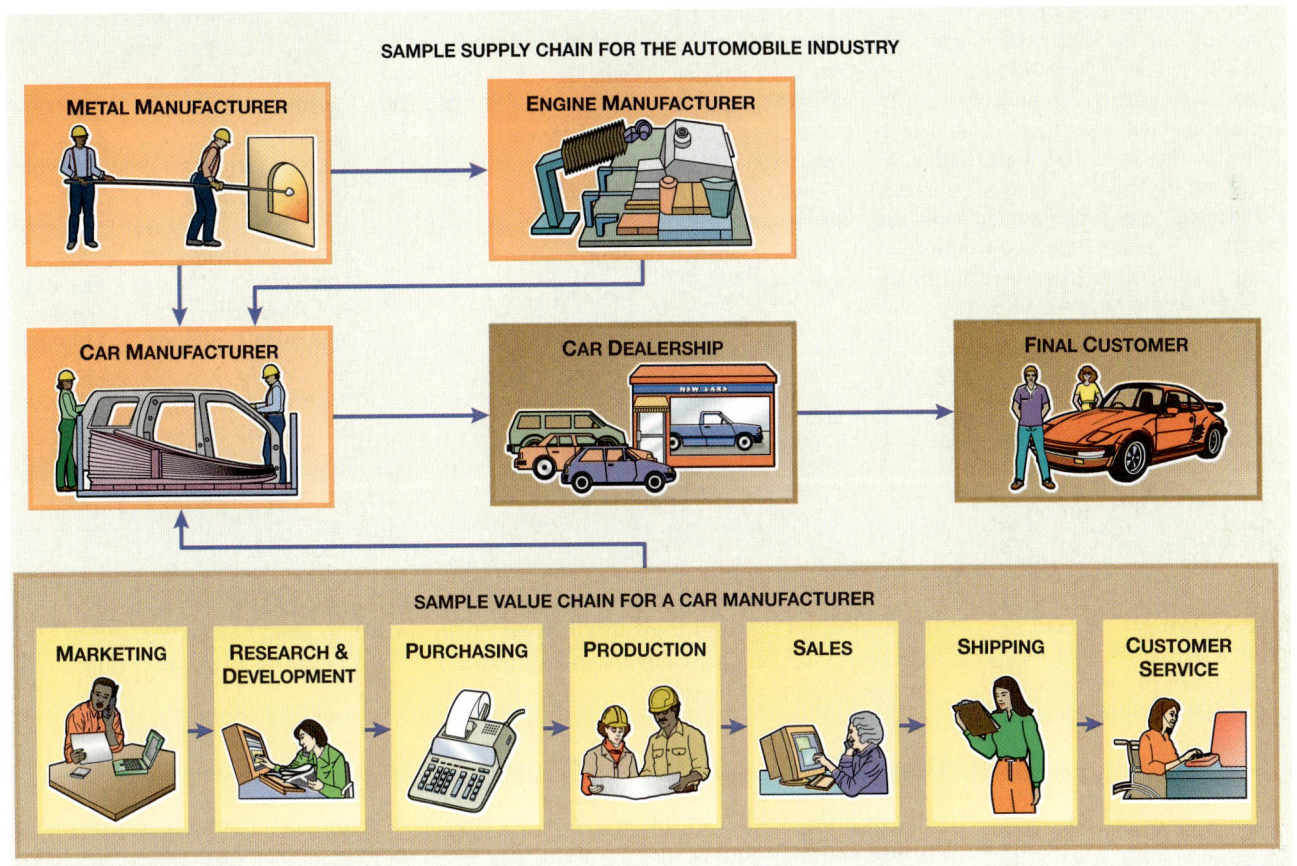

Sample Supply Chain for the Automobile Industry

Metal Manufacturer → Car Manufacturer
Engine Manufacturer → Car Manufacturer
Car Manufacturer → Car Dealership → Final Customer

Sample Value Chain for a Car Manufacturer

Marketing → Research & Development → Purchasing → Production → Sales → Shipping → Customer Service

---

🔸 Stop and Think!

How does the focus of a supply chain differ from that of a value chain?

A supply chain focuses on external relationships, whereas a value chain focuses on internal relationships. ■

www.ford.com

chain and how their company's value-adding activities fit into their suppliers' and customers' value chains can see their company's role in the overall process of creating and delivering products or services. Such an understanding can also make a company more profitable. By working with suppliers and customers across the entire supply chain, managers may be able to reduce the total cost of making a product, even though costs for one activity may increase. For example, assume that Ford Motor Company decided to place computers for online order entry in its car dealerships. The new computers would streamline the processing of orders and make the orders more accurate. In this case, even though Ford would incur the cost of the computers, the total cost of making and delivering a car would decrease because the cost of order processing would decrease. When organizations work cooperatively with others in their supply chain, they can develop new processes that reduce the total costs of their products or services.

ABM IN A SERVICE ORGANIZATION

To illustrate how a service organization can use ABM, let's assume that a firm called Western Data Services, Inc. (WDSI), offers database marketing strategies to help companies increase their sales. WDSI's basic package of services includes the design of a mailing piece (either a Classic Letter with or without inserts or a Self-Mailer),

FOCUS ON BUSINESS PRACTICE

How Do Traditional and ABC Reports Differ?

Many companies are finding that ABC enhances managerial reporting and decision making because it reflects the cause-and-effect relationships between indirect costs and individual processes, products, services, or customers. ABC is not a replacement for traditional general ledger accounting, which collects costs by departments. Rather, it is a practical spreadsheet translation of general ledger data into a format aimed at estimating true cost. The table on the right compares the reports of a department in a health-related company. Identify the report that would be used for financial purposes and the one that would be used for decision making.[2]

Chart of Accounts View	
Salaries	$621,400
Equipment	161,200
Travel Expenses	58,000
Supplies	43,900
Use and Occupancy	30,000
Total	$914,500

Activity-Based Costing View	
Enter claims into system	$ 32,000
Analyze claims	121,000
Suspend claims	32,500
Receive provider inquiries	101,500
Resolve member problems	83,400
Process batches	45,000
Determine eligibility	119,000
Make copies	145,000
Write correspondence	77,100
Attend training	158,000
Total	$914,500

ENRICHMENT NOTE:
Some activities or functions occur before production; their costs are sometimes called *upstream costs*. Other activities or functions occur after production; their costs are called *downstream costs*. In the new operating environment, both upstream and downstream costs are part of a product's total cost.

ing (ABC) is the tool used in an ABM environment to assign activity costs to cost objects. ABC helps managers make better pricing decisions, inventory valuations, and profitability decisions.

VALUE CHAINS AND SUPPLY CHAINS

As we noted earlier in the text, a **value chain** is a sequence of activities, or primary processes, that add value to a company's product or service; the value chain also includes support services, such as management accounting, that facilitate the primary processes. ABM enables managers to see their organization's value chain as part of a larger system that includes the value chains of suppliers and customers. This larger system is the **supply chain**—the path that leads from the suppliers of the materials from which a product is made to the final customer. The supply chain (also called the *supply network*) includes both suppliers and suppliers' suppliers, and customers and customers' customers.

As Figure 2 shows, in the supply chain for automobiles, a metal manufacturer supplies metal to an engine manufacturer, which supplies engines to the car manufacturer. The car manufacturer supplies cars to car dealerships, which supply cars to the final customers. Except for the metal manufacturer, each organization in this supply chain is a customer of an earlier supplier, and each, including the metal manufacturer, has its own value chain. The sequence of primary processes in the value chain varies from company to company depending on a number of factors, including the size of the company and the types of products or services it sells. Figure 2 shows the primary processes that add value for a car manufacturer—marketing, research and development, purchasing, production, sales, shipping, and customer service.

Value chains and supply chains give managers a better grasp of their company's internal and external operations. Managers who understand the supply

FOCUS ON BUSINESS PRACTICE

How Can a Changing Business Economy Cause Strategy Shifts in a Company's Value Chain?

Because of an economic downturn and overcapacity in the technology sector, high-tech companies like Oracle <www.oracle.com>, SAP <www.sap.com>, and PeopleSoft <www.peoplesoft.com> have shifted the emphasis of their value chain from marketing to customer service. Measures once used to gauge the performance of an aggressive sales force, such as sales volume, are no longer relevant and have been replaced by measures of customer satisfaction and retention.[3]

can ensure that the company is offering quality products or services at the lowest cost. With budgeted costs prepared for each activity, they can not only better allocate resources to cost objects (such as product or service lines, customer groups, or sales territories) and estimate product or service unit cost more accurately, but also measure operating performance. If managers assume that resource-consuming activities cause costs and that products and services incur costs by the activities they require, the estimated unit cost will be more accurate.

■ **EXECUTING** In the executing stage, managers want an answer to the question "What is the actual cost of making our product or providing our service?" They want to know what activities are being performed, how well they are being performed, and what resources they are consuming. Although managers focus on the activities that create the most value for customers, they also monitor some nonvalue-adding activities that have been reduced but not completely eliminated. An activity-based accounting information system measures actual quantities of activity (a quantitative nonfinancial measure) and accumulates related activity costs (a quantitative financial measure). Gathering quantitative information at the activity level allows managers the flexibility to create cost pools for different types of cost objects. For example, the costs of the selling activity can be assigned to a customer, a sales territory, or a product or service line.

■ **REVIEWING** In the reviewing stage, managers want answers to the questions "What actions will reduce the full product and service cost?" and "Did we meet our cost-reduction goals for nonvalue-adding activities?" Managers measure an activity's performance by reviewing the difference between its actual and budgeted costs. With this information, they can analyze the variances in activity levels, identify waste and inefficiencies, and take action to improve processes and activities. They can also continue to monitor the costs of nonvalue-adding activities to see if the company met its goals of reducing or eliminating those costs. Careful review and analysis will increase value for the customer by improving product quality and reducing costs and cycle time.

■ **REPORTING** Finally, in the reporting stage of the management cycle, managers prepare reports about the company's performance for internal and external use. Internal reports show the application of the costs of activities to cost objects, which results in a better measurement of profitability, as we discuss later in the chapter. External reports summarize past performance and answer such questions as "Did the company earn a profit?"

✓ Check out ACE for a Review Quiz at http://accounting.college.hmco.com/students.

ACTIVITY-BASED MANAGEMENT

LO2 Define *activity-based management (ABM)* and discuss its relationship to the supply chain and the value chain.

RELATED TEXT ASSIGNMENTS
Q: 6, 7
SE: 2, 3
E: 2, 3
P: 1
SD: 2

As you may recall from an earlier chapter, **activity-based management (ABM)** is an approach to managing an organization that identifies all major operating activities, determines the resources consumed by each activity and the cause of the resource usage, and categorizes the activities as either adding value to a product or service or not adding value. ABM focuses on reducing or eliminating nonvalue-adding activities. Because it provides financial and performance information at the activity level, ABM is useful both for strategic planning and for making operational decisions about business segments, such as product lines, market segments, and customer groups. It also helps managers eliminate waste and inefficiencies and redirect resources to activities that add value to the product or service. Activity-based cost-

KEY POINT: ABM and JIT focus on value-adding activities—not costs—to increase income.

of inventory. Because they were not designed to capture data on activities or to trace the full cost of a product, these systems could not isolate the cost of unnecessary activities, penalize for overproduction, or quantify measures that improved quality or reduced throughput time.

In this chapter, we explore two types of activity-based systems—activity-based management (ABM) and the just-in-time (JIT) operating environment—and consider how they affect product costing. Both systems help organizations manage activities, not costs, but by managing activities, organizations can reduce or eliminate many nonvalue-adding activities, which leads to reduced costs and hence to increased income.

Using Activity-Based Cost Information in the Management Cycle

In this section, we look at the ways in which managers use activity-based cost information to answer basic questions during the management cycle. Figure 1 summarizes those uses.

■ **Planning** In the planning stage, managers want answers to questions like "Which activities add value to a product or service?" "What resources are needed to perform those activities?" and "How much should the product or service cost?" By examining their company's value-adding activities and the related costs, managers

Figure 1
Activity-Based Systems and the Management Cycle

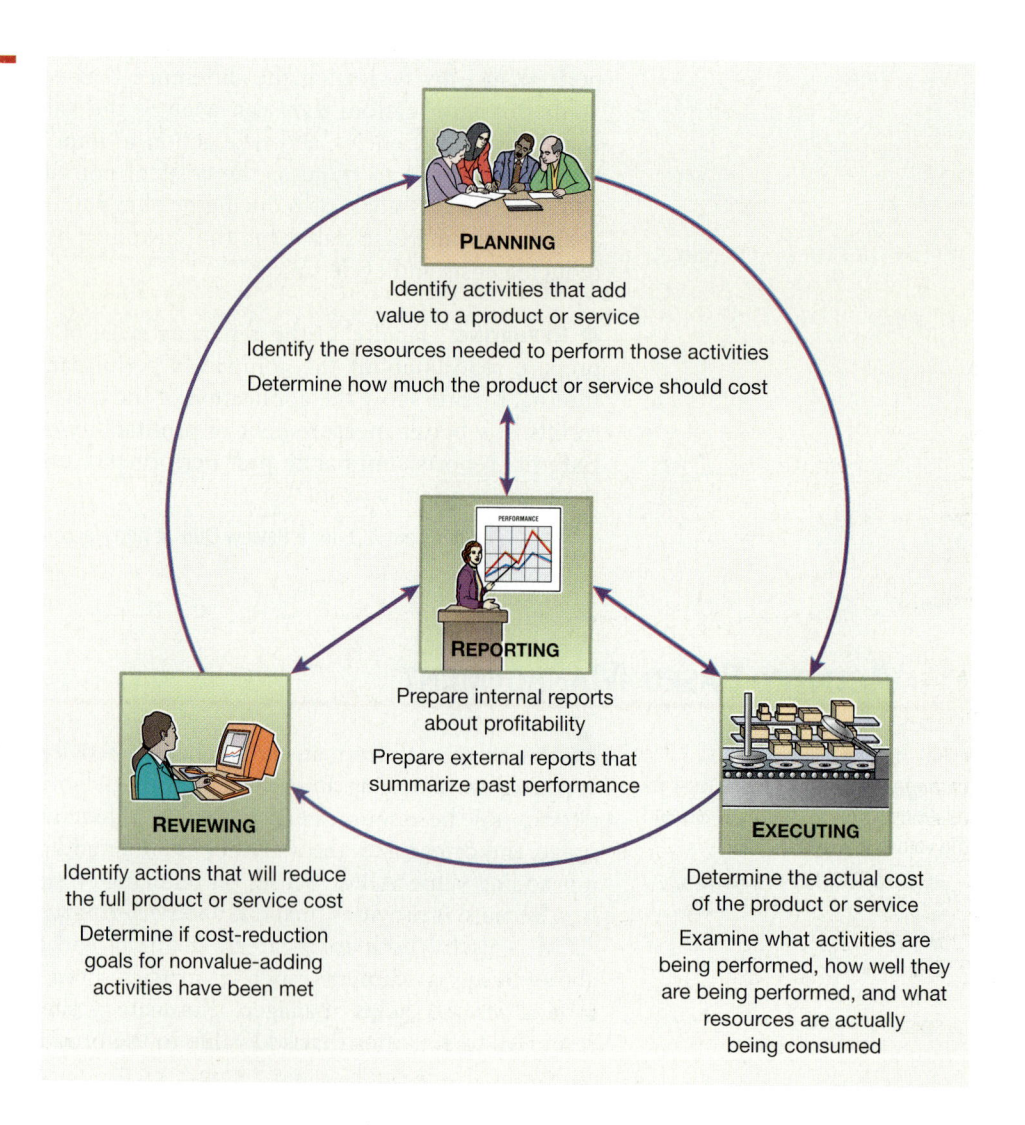

PLANNING
Identify activities that add value to a product or service
Identify the resources needed to perform those activities
Determine how much the product or service should cost

REPORTING
Prepare internal reports about profitability
Prepare external reports that summarize past performance

EXECUTING
Determine the actual cost of the product or service
Examine what activities are being performed, how well they are being performed, and what resources are actually being consumed

REVIEWING
Identify actions that will reduce the full product or service cost
Determine if cost-reduction goals for nonvalue-adding activities have been met

Activity-Based Systems and Management

LO1 Explain the role of activity-based systems in the management cycle.

RELATED TEXT ASSIGNMENTS
Q: 1, 2, 3, 4, 5
SE: 1
E: 1

www.dell.com

Many companies operate in volatile business environments that are strongly influenced by customer demands. Managers know that customers buy value, usually in the form of quality products or services that are delivered on a timely basis for a reasonable price. Companies generate revenue when customers see value and buy their products or services. Thus, companies measure value as revenue (customer value = revenue generated).

Value exists when some characteristic of a product or service satisfies customers' wants or needs. For example, customers who appreciate convenience are an important market segment for Dell Computer Corporation. In response to their needs, Dell creates value and increases revenue by selling customized computer systems that include the latest microprocessor, monitor, graphics card, CD-ROM or DVD drive, sound card, modem, speakers, and preinstalled software products.

Creating value by satisfying customers' needs for quality, reasonable price, and timely delivery requires that managers do the following:

- Work with suppliers and customers.
- View the organization as a collection of value-adding activities.
- Use resources for value-adding activities.
- Reduce or eliminate nonvalue-adding activities.
- Know the total cost of creating value for a customer.

If an organization's business plan focuses on providing products or services that customers esteem, then managers will work with suppliers and customers to find ways of improving quality, reducing costs, and shortening delivery time. Managers will also focus their attention internally to find the best ways of using resources to create and maintain the value of their products or services. This requires matching resources to the operating activities that add value to a product or service. Managers will examine all business activities, including research and development, purchasing, production, storing, selling, shipping, and customer service, so that they can allocate resources effectively. In addition, managers need to know the **full product cost**, which includes not only the costs of direct materials and direct labor, but also the costs of all production and nonproduction activities required to satisfy the customer. For example, the full product cost of a Dell computer system includes the cost of the computer components and software, as well as the costs of taking the sales order, processing the order, packaging and shipping the system, and providing subsequent customer service for warranty work and software upgrades. If the activities are executed well and in agreement with the business plan, and if costs are assigned fairly, the company can improve product pricing and quality, increase productivity, and generate revenues (value) and profits.

Activity-Based Systems

Organizations that focus on customers design their accounting information systems to provide customer-related, activity-based information. **Activity-based systems** are information systems that provide quantitative information about an organization's activities. They create opportunities to improve the cost information supplied to managers. They also help managers view their organization as a collection of activities. Activity-based cost information helps managers improve operating processes and make better pricing decisions.

Activity-based systems developed because traditional accounting systems failed to produce the types of information today's managers need for decision making. Traditional systems focused primarily on measurements needed for financial reporting and auditing, such as the measurement of cost of goods sold and the valuation

● **Stop and Think!**
What is the main focus of an activity-based system?
An activity-based system's main focus is on managing activities rather than costs. ■

How have ABM and JIT helped England, Inc.'s managers to improve production processes and reduce delivery time?

competitive edge. By using ABM and JIT, England has achieved higher productivity than other furniture manufacturers, is able to offer more than 40,000 product variations, and over five years has cut its delivery time by one-half to one-third.[1]

22

Chapter 22 describes activity-based management and the just-in-time operating philosophy, demonstrating how these two activity-based systems help managers improve operating processes and make better pricing decisions.

Activity-Based Systems: ABM and JIT

LEARNING OBJECTIVES

LO1 Explain the role of activity-based systems in the management cycle.

LO2 Define *activity-based management (ABM)* and discuss its relationship to the supply chain and the value chain.

LO3 Distinguish between value-adding and nonvalue-adding activities, and describe process value analysis.

LO4 Define *activity-based costing* and explain how a cost hierarchy and a bill of activities are used.

LO5 Define the *just-in-time (JIT) operating philosophy* and identify the elements of a JIT operating environment.

LO6 Identify the changes in product costing that result when a firm adopts a JIT operating environment.

LO7 Define and apply *backflush costing*, and compare the cost flows in traditional and backflush costing.

LO8 Compare ABM and JIT as activity-based systems.

DECISION POINT

A MANAGER'S FOCUS

England, Inc. England, Inc., is a division of La-Z-Boy, Inc. <www.lazboy.com>. A critical factor in the success of this company is the speed of its value chain. England makes about 11,000 built-to-order sofas and chairs each week in its Tennessee plant, and it generally delivers them less than three weeks after customers have placed their orders with a retailer. This is quite a feat, especially since the company offers 85 styles of sofas and a choice of 550 fabrics. It also gives England, Inc., a competitive advantage. How does the company maintain this advantage?

England's managers use activity-based management (ABM) and a just-in-time (JIT) operating environment to identify and reduce or eliminate activities that do not add value to the company's products. These systems focus on minimizing waste, reducing costs, improving the allocation of resources, and ensuring that suppliers deliver materials just at the time a company needs them. They help managers make better decisions about costing and pricing products, adding or dropping product styles, changing production and delivery systems, and contracting with suppliers. The continuous flow of information that ABM and JIT provide has enabled England's managers to improve production processes; for example, they are able to adjust labor needs each week to meet order requirements. It has also enabled them to schedule timely deliveries from suppliers and thus maintain appropriate inventory levels, as well as to keep track of England's own fleet of delivery trucks.

England's disciplined monitoring of order, production, and delivery activities is the factor that gives it a

they make them, including the manufacturing processes involved. For which products would process costing be most appropriate? For which products would it be inappropriate? Identify differences in the nature of the business conducted by the companies you chose. Do you think those differences have any bearing on the type of product costing system the company uses? Explain your reasoning. Do the companies make any products that might require a costing system other than process costing? Be prepared to present the results of your research in class.

REQUIRED ▶ 1. In preparation for writing your memo, answer the following questions:
   a. For whom are you preparing the memo? Does this affect the length of the memo? Explain.
   b. Why are you preparing the memo?
   c. What actions should you take to gather information for the memo? What information is needed? Is the information that Winslow provided sufficient for analysis and reporting?
   d. When is the memo due? What can be done to provide accurate, reliable, and timely information?

2. Based on your analysis of the information that Winslow provided, where is the main problem in the production process?

3. Prepare an outline of the sections you would want in your memo.

International Company

LO1 Process Costing and Work in
LO4 Process Inventory Accounts

MRA 4. SvenskStål, AB, is a steel-producing company located in Solentuna, Sweden. The company originally produced only specialty steel products that were made to order for customers. A job order product costing system is used for the made-to-order products. This year, after purchasing three continuous processing work cells, the company created a new division that produces three types of sheet steel in continuous rolls. Ingrid Bjorn, the company controller, has redesigned the management accounting system to accommodate these changes and has installed a process costing system for the new division.

At a recent meeting of the company's executive committee, Bjorn explained that the new product costing system uses three new Work in Process Inventory accounts, one for each of the three work cells. Lars Karlsson, the production superintendent, questioned the need to change product costing approaches and did not understand why so many new Work in Process Inventory accounts were necessary.

Why did Bjorn install a process costing system in the new division? Was a new division necessary, or could the three new work cells have been merged with the specialty production facilities? Why were three new Work in Process Inventory accounts required? Could the single Work in Process Inventory account used for the specialty orders have tracked and accumulated the costs incurred in the three new work cells?

Excel Spreadsheet Analysis

LO3 Job Order Costing in a Service Organization

MRA 5. Refer to assignment **P 7** in this chapter. Peruga Engineering Company needs to analyze its jobs in process during the month of January.

1. Using the Chart Wizard and the job order cost cards that you created for Jobs P-12, P-15, and P-19, prepare a bar chart that compares the bid and proposal costs, design costs, and prototype development costs of the jobs. Below is the suggested format to use for the information table necessary to complete the bar chart.

	A	B	C	D
1		P-12	P-15	P-19
2	Bid and proposal			
3	Design			
4	Prototype development			
5	Total job cost			

2. Examine the chart you prepared in **1**. List some reasons for the differences between the costs of the various jobs.

Internet Case

LO4 Comparison of Companies That Use Process Costing Systems

MRA 6. A Focus on Business Practice box in this chapter lists many companies for which process costing systems are appropriate. Access the web sites of at least two of these companies. Find as much information as you can about the products the companies make and how

		Units	Dollars
Equivalent units:	Direct materials costs	84,200	
	Conversion costs	82,800	
Manufacturing costs:	Direct materials		$1,978,700
	Direct labor		800,400
	Manufacturing overhead		1,600,800
Unit cost data:	Direct materials costs		23.50
	Conversion costs		29.00
Work in process inventory:	Beginning (70% complete)	4,200	
	Ending (30% complete)	3,800	

Units started and completed during 20x8 totaled 80,400. Attached to the beginning Work in Process Inventory account were direct materials costs of $123,660 and conversion costs of $57,010. Birdsong found that little spoilage had occurred. The proper cost allowance for spoilage was included in the predetermined overhead rate of $2 per direct labor dollar. The review of direct labor cost revealed, however, that $90,500 had been charged twice to the production account, the second time in error. This resulted in overly high overhead costs being charged to the production account.

So far in 20x9, the radial has sold for $92 per tire. This price was based on the 20x8 unit data plus a 75 percent markup to cover operating costs and profit. During 20x9, Ready Tire's three main competitors have charged about $87 for a tire of comparable quality. The company's process costing system adds all direct materials at the beginning of the process, and conversion costs are incurred uniformly throughout the process.

1. Identify what inaccuracies in costs, inventories, and selling prices result from the company's cost-charging error.
2. Prepare a revised process cost report for 20x8.
3. What should have been the minimum selling price per tire in 20x9?
4. Suggest ways of preventing such errors in the future.

Formulating Management Reports

MRA 3. **LO4 LO5 LO6 LO7 Using the Process Costing System**

You are the production manager for Great Grain Corporation, a manufacturer of four cereal products. The company's best-selling product is Smackaroos, a sugar-coated puffed rice cereal. Yesterday, Clark Winslow, the controller, reported that the production cost for each box of Smackaroos has increased approximately 22 percent in the past four months. Because the company is unable to increase the selling price for a box of Smackaroos, the increased production costs will reduce profits significantly.

Today, you received a memo from Gilbert Rom, the company president, asking you to review your production process to identify inefficiencies or waste that can be eliminated. Once you have completed your analysis, you are to write a memo presenting your findings and suggesting ways to reduce or eliminate the problems. The president will use your information during a meeting with the top management team in ten days.

You are aware of previous problems in the Baking Department and the Packaging Department. At your request, Winslow has provided you with process cost reports for the two departments. He has also given you the following detailed summary of the cost per equivalent unit for a box of Smackaroos cereal:

	April	May	June	July
Baking Department				
Direct materials	$1.25	$1.26	$1.24	$1.25
Direct labor	.50	.61	.85	.90
Manufacturing overhead	.25	.31	.34	.40
Department totals	$2.00	$2.18	$2.43	$2.55
Packaging Department				
Direct materials	$ .35	$ .34	$ .33	$ .33
Direct labor	.05	.05	.04	.06
Manufacturing overhead	.10	.16	.15	.12
Department totals	$ .50	$ .55	$ .52	$ .51
Total cost per equivalent unit	$2.50	$2.73	$2.95	$3.06

product sells for $4.10 per unit; Company B's, for $4.05. All costs are expected to increase by 10 percent in the next three years. Wonder Cola tries to earn a profit of at least 15 percent on the total unit cost.

1. What factors should Wonder Cola, Inc., consider in setting a unit selling price for a case of Zero Cola?
2. Using the FIFO costing approach, compute (a) equivalent units for direct materials, cases of bottles, and conversion costs; (b) the total production cost per unit; and (c) the total cost per unit of Cola Plus for 20x8.
3. What is the expected unit cost of Zero Cola for 20x9?
4. Recommend a unit selling price range for a case of Zero Cola for 20x9, and give the reason(s) for your choice.

MANAGERIAL REPORTING AND ANALYSIS CASES

Interpreting Management Reports

MRA 1. Eagle Manufacturing supplies engine parts to Cherokee Cycle Company, a major U.S. manufacturer of motorcycles. Like all of Cherokee's other suppliers, Eagle has always added a healthy profit margin to its cost when quoting selling prices to Cherokee. Recently, however, several companies have offered to supply engine parts to Cherokee for lower prices than Eagle has been charging.

LO1 Interpreting Nonfinancial
LO7 Data

Because Eagle Manufacturing wants to keep Cherokee Cycle Company's business, a team of Eagle's managers analyzed their company's product costs and decided to make minor changes in the company's manufacturing process. No new equipment was purchased, and no additional labor was required. Instead, the machines were rearranged, and some of the work was reassigned.

To monitor the effectiveness of the changes, Eagle Manufacturing introduced three new performance measures to its information system: inventory levels, lead time (total time required for a part to move through the production process), and productivity (number of parts manufactured per employee per day). The company's goal was to reduce the quantities of the first two performance measures and to increase the quantity of the third.

A section of a recent management report, shown below, summarizes the quantities for each performance measure before and after the changes in the manufacturing process were made.

Measure	Before	After	Improvement
Inventory in dollars	$21,444	$10,772	50%
Lead time in minutes	17	11	35
Productivity (parts per person per day)	515	1,152	124

1. Do you believe Eagle improved the quality of its manufacturing process and the quality of its engine parts? Explain your answer.
2. Can Eagle lower its selling price to Cherokee? Explain your answer.
3. Did the introduction of the new measures affect the design of the product costing system? Explain your answer.
4. Do you believe that the new measures caused a change in Eagle's cost per engine part? If so, how did they cause the change?

MRA 2. Ready Tire Corporation makes several lines of automobile and truck tires. The company operates in a competitive marketplace, so it relies heavily on cost data from its FIFO-based process costing system. It uses that information to set prices for its most competitive tires. The company's radial line has lost some of its market share during each of the past four years. Management believes that price breaks allowed by the company's three biggest competitors are the main reason for the decline in sales.

LO5 Analysis of Product Cost
LO6
LO7

The company controller, Sara Birdsong, has been asked to review the product costing information that supports price decisions on the radial line. In preparing her report, she collected the following data for 20x8, the most recent full year of operations:

Research Activity

LO3 Job Order Costing

SD 4. Many businesses accumulate costs for each job performed. Examples of businesses that use a job order costing system include print shops, car repair shops, health clinics, and kennels.

Visit a local business that uses job order costing, and interview the owner, manager, or accountant about the process and the documents the business uses to accumulate product costs. Write a paper that summarizes the information you obtained. Include the following in your summary:

1. The name of the business and the type of operations performed
2. The name and position of the individual you interviewed
3. A description of the process of starting and completing a job
4. A description of the accounting process and the documents used to track a job
5. Your responses to these questions:

   a. Did the person you interviewed know the actual amount of materials, labor, and overhead charged to a particular job? If the job includes some estimated costs, how are the estimates calculated? Do the costs affect the determination of the selling price of the product or service?

   b. Compare the documents discussed in this chapter with the documents used by the company you visited. How are they similar, and how are they different?

   c. In your opinion, does the business record and accumulate its product costs effectively? Explain your answer.

Group Activity: Group students according to the type of business they selected and ask them to discuss their responses to the questions in **5**.

Decision-Making Practice

LO4 Setting a Selling Price
LO5
LO6
LO7

SD 5. For the past four years, three companies have dominated the soft drink industry, holding a combined 85 percent of market share. Wonder Cola, Inc., ranks second nationally in soft drink sales; it had gross revenues of $27,450,000 last year. Its management is thinking about introducing a new low-calorie drink called Zero Cola.

Wonder soft drinks are processed in a single department. All ingredients are added at the beginning of the process. At the end of the process, the beverage is poured into bottles that cost $.24 per case produced. Direct labor and manufacturing overhead costs are applied uniformly throughout the process.

Corporate controller Adam Daneen believes that costs for the new cola will be very much like those for the company's Cola Plus drink. Last year (20x8), he collected the following data about Cola Plus:

	Units*	Costs
Work in process inventory		
December 31, 20x7†	2,200	
Direct materials costs		$ 2,080
Conversion costs		620
December 31, 20x8‡	2,000	
Direct materials costs		1,880
Conversion costs		600
Units started during 20x8	458,500	
Costs for 20x8		
Liquid materials added		430,990
Direct labor and manufacturing overhead		229,400
Bottles		110,068

*Each unit is a 24-bottle case.
†50% complete.
‡60% complete.

The company's variable general administrative and selling costs are $1.10 per unit. Fixed administrative and selling costs are assigned to products at the rate of $.50 per unit. Each of Wonder Cola's two main competitors is already marketing a diet cola. Company A's

Assume that Good Foods, Inc., experienced no spoilage or evaporation loss during the month of January.

REQUIRED
1. Using the FIFO costing method, prepare a process cost report for the Mixing Department for January.
2. Explain how the analysis for the Cooking Department will differ from the analysis for the Mixing Department.

SKILLS DEVELOPMENT CASES

Conceptual Analysis

LO1 Business Plans

SD 1. In the past 20 years, Fortune 500 companies have eliminated over 5 million jobs, and yet the U.S. economy has grown by almost 30 million jobs. New businesses have created most of the new employment. A key step in starting a new business is a realistic analysis of the people, opportunities, context, risks, and rewards of the venture and the formulation of a business plan. Notice the similarities between the questions accountants answer in the management cycle and the nine questions every great business plan should answer:[4]

- Who is the new company's customer?
- How does the customer make decisions about buying this product or service?
- To what degree is the product or service a compelling purchase for the customer?
- How will the product or service be priced?
- How will the company reach all the identified customer segments?
- How much does it cost (in time and resources) to acquire a customer?
- How much does it cost to produce and deliver the product or service?
- How much does it cost to support a customer?
- How easy is it to retain a customer?

Assume a new business has hired you as a consultant because of your knowledge of the management cycle. Write a memo that discusses how the nine questions fit into the management cycle.

LO4 Concept of Process Costing Systems

SD 2. For more than 60 years, Dow Chemical Company <www.dow.com> has made and sold a tasteless, odorless, and calorie-free substance called Methocel. When heated, this liquid plastic (methyl cellulose) has the unusual characteristic (for plastics) of becoming a gel that resembles cooked egg whites. It is used in over 400 food products, including gravies, soups, and puddings. It was also used as wampa drool in *The Empire Strikes Back* and dinosaur sneeze in *Jurassic Park*. What kind of costing system is most appropriate for the manufacture of Methocel? Why is that system most appropriate? Describe the system; include in the description a general explanation of how costs are determined.

Ethical Dilemma

LO3 Costing Procedures and Ethics

SD 3. Jennifer Martin, the production manager of Fabricated Products Company, entered the office of controller Joe Barnes and asked, "Joe, what gives here? I was charged for 330 direct labor hours on Job AD22, and my records show that we spent only 290 hours on that job. That 40-hour difference caused the total cost of direct labor and manufacturing overhead for the job to increase by over $5,500. Are my records wrong, or was there an error in the direct labor assigned to the job?"

Barnes replied, "Don't worry about it, Jennifer. This job won't be used in your quarterly performance evaluation. Job AD22 was a federal government job, a cost-plus contract, so the more costs we assign to it, the more profit we make. We decided to add a few hours to the job in case there is some follow-up work to do. You know how fussy the feds are."

What should Martin do? Discuss Barnes's costing procedure.

lows: bid and proposal, $18 per hour; design, $22 per hour; and prototype development, $20 per hour. Supplies are treated as direct materials, traceable to each job. Peruga worked on jobs P-12, P-15, and P-19 during January. The following table shows the costs for those jobs:

	P-12	P-15	P-19
Beginning Balances			
Bid and proposal	$2,460	$2,290	$ 940
Design	1,910	460	0
Prototype development	2,410	1,680	0
Costs During January			
Bid and proposal			
Supplies	0	$ 280	$2,300
Labor: hours	12	20	68
dollars	$ 192	$ 320	$1,088
Design			
Supplies	$ 400	$ 460	$ 290
Labor: hours	64	42	26
dollars	$1,280	$ 840	$ 520
Prototype development			
Special materials	$6,744	$7,216	$2,400
Labor: hours	120	130	25
dollars	$2,880	$3,120	$ 600

REQUIRED

1. Using the format shown in Figure 3, create the job order cost card for each of the three jobs.
2. Peruga completed Jobs P-12 and P-15, and the customers approved of the prototype products. Customer A plans to produce 12 special characters using the design and specifications created by Job P-12. Customer B plans to make 18 displays from the design developed by Job P-15. What dollar amount will each customer use as the cost of design for each of those products (i.e., what is the product unit cost for Jobs P-12 and P-15)? Round to the nearest dollar.
3. What is the January ending balance of Peruga's Contract in Process account for the three jobs?
4. Rank the jobs in order of most costly to least costly based on each job's total cost. From the rankings of cost, what observations can you make?
5. Speculate on the price Peruga should charge for such jobs.

LO5 Process Costing: FIFO
LO6 Costing Method

P 8. Canned fruits and vegetables are the main products made by Good Foods, Inc. All direct materials are added at the beginning of the Mixing Department's process. When the ingredients have been mixed, they go to the Cooking Department. There the mixture is heated to 100° Celsius and simmered for 20 minutes. When cooled, the mixture goes to the Canning Department for final processing. Throughout the operations, direct labor and manufacturing overhead costs are incurred uniformly. No direct materials are added in the Cooking Department.

Cost data and other information for the Mixing Department for January 20x8 are as follows:

Production Cost Data	Direct Materials Costs	Conversion Costs
Mixing Department		
Beginning inventory	$ 28,560	$ 5,230
Current period costs	$450,000	$181,200
Work in process inventory		
Beginning inventory		
Mixing Department (40% complete)	5,000 liters	
Ending inventory		
Mixing Department (60% complete)	6,000 liters	
Unit production data		
Units started during January	90,000 liters	
Units transferred out during January	89,000 liters	

inventory. During June, 61,300 pounds of fruit were added: 23,500 pounds of apples costing $20,915, 22,600 pounds of grapes costing $28,153, and 15,200 pounds of bananas costing $22,040. Direct labor for the month totaled $19,760, and overhead costs applied were $31,375. On June 30, 20x6, 3,400 units remained in process. All direct materials for these units had been added, and 50 percent of conversion costs had been incurred.

REQUIRED
1. Using the FIFO costing method, prepare a process cost report for June.
2. From the information in the process cost report, identify the amount that should be transferred out of the Work in Process Inventory account, and state where those dollars should be transferred.

Alternate Problems

P 6. Dori Hatami is the chief financial officer of Gotham Industries, a company that makes special-order printers for personal computers. Her records for February revealed the following information:

Beginning inventory balances	
Materials Inventory	$27,450
Work in Process Inventory	22,900
Finished Goods Inventory	19,200
Direct materials purchased and received	
February 6	$ 7,200
February 12	8,110
February 24	5,890
Direct labor costs	
February 14	$13,750
February 28	13,230
Direct materials requested for production	
February 4	$ 9,080
February 13	5,940
February 25	7,600

Job order cost cards for jobs in process on February 28 had the following totals:

Job No.	Direct Materials	Direct Labor	Manufacturing Overhead
AJ-10	$3,220	$1,810	$2,534
AJ-14	3,880	2,110	2,954
AJ-30	2,980	1,640	2,296
AJ-16	4,690	2,370	3,318

The predetermined manufacturing overhead rate for the month was 140 percent of direct labor costs. Sales for February totaled $152,400, which represented a 70 percent markup over the cost of production.

REQUIRED
1. Using T accounts for Materials Inventory, Work in Process Inventory, Finished Goods Inventory, Manufacturing Overhead, Accounts Receivable, Factory Payroll, Sales, and Cost of Goods Sold, reconstruct the February transactions.
2. Compute the cost of units completed during the month.
3. What was the total cost of units sold during February?
4. Determine the ending balances in the inventory accounts.
5. During the first week of March, Jobs AJ-10 and AJ-14 were completed. No additional direct materials costs were incurred, but Job AJ-10 needed $720 more of direct labor, and Job AJ-14 needed an additional $1,140 of direct labor. Job AJ-10 was 40 units; Job AJ-14, 55 units. Compute the product unit cost for each completed job (round to two decimal places).

P 7. Peruga Engineering Company specializes in designing automated characters and displays for theme parks. It uses cost-plus profit contracts, and its profit factor is 30 percent of total cost. A job order costing system is used to track the costs of developing each job. Costs are accumulated for three primary activities: bid and proposal, design, and prototype development. Current service overhead rates based on engineering hours are as fol-

3. Why should the Manufacturing Overhead account's underapplied or overapplied overhead be transferred to the Cost of Goods Sold account?

LO3 Job Order Cost Flow

P 3. On May 31, the inventory balances of Abbey Designs, a manufacturer of high-quality children's clothing, were as follows: Materials Inventory, $21,360; Work in Process Inventory, $15,112; and Finished Goods Inventory, $17,120. Job order cost cards for jobs in process as of June 30 had these totals:

Job No.	Direct Materials	Direct Labor	Manufacturing Overhead
24-A	$1,596	$1,290	$1,677
24-B	1,492	1,380	1,794
24-C	1,984	1,760	2,288
24-D	1,608	1,540	2,002

The predetermined overhead rate is 130 percent of direct labor cost. Materials purchased and received in June were as follows:

June 4 $33,120
June 16   28,600
June 22   31,920

Direct labor costs for June were as follows:

June 15 payroll $23,680
June 29 payroll   25,960

Direct materials requested by production during June were as follows:

June 6 $37,240
June 23   38,960

During June, Abbey Designs sold finished goods with a 75 percent markup over cost for $320,000.

REQUIRED
1. Using T accounts for Materials Inventory, Work in Process Inventory, Finished Goods Inventory, Manufacturing Overhead, Accounts Receivable, Factory Payroll, Sales, and Cost of Goods Sold, reconstruct the transactions in June.
2. Compute the cost of units completed during the month.
3. What was the total cost of units sold during June?
4. Determine the ending inventory balances.
5. Jobs 24-A and 24-C were completed during the first week of July. No additional materials costs were incurred, but Job 24-A required $960 more of direct labor, and Job 24-C needed an additional $1,610 of direct labor. Job 24-A was composed of 1,200 pairs of trousers; Job 24-C, of 950 shirts. Compute the product unit cost for each job. (Round your answers to two decimal places.)

LO5 Process Costing: FIFO
LO6 Costing Method

P 4. Lightning Industries specializes in making Flash, a low-alkaline wax used to protect and preserve skis. The company began producing a new, improved brand of Flash on January 1, 20x5. Materials A-14 and C-9 and a wax base are introduced at the beginning of the production process. During January, 640 pounds of A-14, 1,860 pounds of C-9, and 12,800 pounds of wax base were used at costs of $15,300, $29,070, and $2,295, respectively. Direct labor of $17,136 and manufacturing overhead costs of $25,704 were incurred uniformly throughout the month. By January 31, 13,600 pounds of Flash had been completed and transferred to the finished goods inventory (one pound of input equals one pound of output). Since no spoilage occurred, the leftover materials remained in production and were 40 percent complete on average.

REQUIRED
1. Using the FIFO costing method, prepare a process cost report for January.
2. From the information in the process cost report, identify the amount that should be transferred out of the Work in Process Inventory account, and state where those dollars should be transferred.

LO5 Process Costing: FIFO
LO6 Costing Method

P 5. Liquid Extracts Company produces a line of fruit extracts for home use in making wine, jams and jellies, pies, and meat sauces. Fruits enter the production process in pounds; the product emerges in quarts (one pound of input equals one quart of output). On May 31, 20x6, 4,250 units were in process. All direct materials had been added, and the units were 70 percent complete for conversion costs. Direct materials costs of $4,607 and conversion costs of $3,535 were attached to the units in beginning work in process

PROBLEMS

LO3 T Account Analysis with Unknowns

P 1. Flagstaff Enterprises makes peripheral equipment for computers. Dana Dona, Flagstaff's new controller, can find only the following partial information for the past two months:

Account/Transaction	May	June
Materials Inventory, Beginning	$ 36,240	$ e
Work in Process Inventory, Beginning	56,480	f
Finished Goods Inventory, Beginning	44,260	g
Materials purchased	a	96,120
Direct materials requested	82,320	h
Direct labor costs	b	72,250
Manufacturing overhead applied	53,200	i
Cost of units completed	c	221,400
Cost of units sold	209,050	j
Materials Inventory, Ending	38,910	41,950
Work in Process Inventory, Ending	d	k
Finished Goods Inventory, Ending	47,940	51,180

The current year's predetermined overhead rate is 80 percent of direct labor cost.

REQUIRED ▶ Using the data provided and T accounts, compute the unknown values.

LO3 Job Order Costing: T Account Analysis

P 2. Par Carts Manufacturing, Inc., produces electric golf carts. The carts are special-order items, so the company uses a job order costing system. Manufacturing overhead is applied at the rate of 90 percent of direct labor cost. The following is a list of transactions for January:

Jan. 1 Purchased direct materials on account, $215,400.
    2 Purchased indirect materials on account, $49,500.
    4 Requested direct materials costing $193,200 (all used on Job X) and indirect materials costing $38,100 for production.
    10 Paid the following manufacturing overhead costs: utilities, $4,400; manufacturing rent, $3,800; and maintenance charges, $3,900.
    15 Recorded the following gross wages and salaries for employees: direct labor, $120,000 (all for Job X) and indirect labor, $60,620.
    15 Applied manufacturing overhead to production.
    19 Purchased indirect materials costing $27,550 and direct materials costing $190,450 on account.
    21 Requested direct materials costing $214,750 (Job X, $178,170; Job Y, $18,170; Job Z, $18,410) and indirect materials costing $31,400 for production.
    31 Recorded the following gross wages and salaries for employees: direct labor, $132,000 (Job X, $118,500; Job Y, $7,000; Job Z, $6,500) and indirect labor, $62,240.
    31 Applied manufacturing overhead to production.
    31 Completed and transferred Job X (375 carts) and Job Y (10 carts) to finished goods inventory; total cost was $855,990.
    31 Shipped Job X to the customer; total production cost was $824,520 and sales invoice totaled $996,800.
    31 Recorded these manufacturing overhead costs (adjusting entries): prepaid insurance expired, $3,700; property taxes (payable at year end), $3,400; and depreciation, machinery, $15,500.

REQUIRED ▶
1. Record the entries for all transactions in January using T accounts for the following: Materials Inventory, Work in Process Inventory, Finished Goods Inventory, Manufacturing Overhead, Cash, Accounts Receivable, Prepaid Insurance, Accumulated Depreciation—Machinery, Accounts Payable, Factory Payroll, Property Taxes Payable, Sales, and Cost of Goods Sold. Use job order cost cards for Job X, Job Y, and Job Z. Determine the partial account balances. Assume no beginning inventory balances.
2. Compute the amount of underapplied or overapplied overhead as of January 31, and transfer it to the Cost of Goods Sold account.

		Total Costs		Direct Materials Costs		Conversion Costs
Step 3: Account for costs.	Beginning inventory	$ 19,900	=	$ 8,100	+	$ 11,800
	Current costs	785,700	=	$202,500	+	$583,200
	Total costs	$805,600				
Step 4: Compute cost per equivalent unit.	Current Costs			$202,500		$583,200
	Equivalent Units			405,000		393,600
	Cost per equivalent unit	$1.98	=	$ .50	+	$ 1.48*
						*Rounded to nearest cent
Step 5: Assign costs to cost of goods manufactured and ending inventory.	Cost of goods manufactured and transferred out:					
	From beginning inventory	$19,900				
	Current costs to complete	7,104	=	0	+	(4,800 × $1.48)
	Units started and completed this period	759,132	=	(383,400 × $.50)	+	(383,400 × $1.48)
	Cost of goods manufactured	$786,808		(Add rounding, $672)		
	Ending inventory	18,792	=	(21,600 × $.50)	+	(5,400 × $1.48)
	Total costs	$805,600				

Work in Process Inventory Account: Cost Recap

Beg. Bal.	$ 19,900	$786,808 (cost of goods manufactured and transferred out)
Direct Materials	$202,500	
Conversion Costs	$583,200	
End. Bal.	$18,792	

Work in Process Inventory Account: Unit Recap

Beg. Bal.	16,000	399,400 (FIFO units transferred out from the 16,000 in beginning inventory plus the 383,400 started and completed)
Direct Materials and Conversion Costs	405,000	
End. Bal.	21,600	

2. The amount of $786,808 should be transferred to the Work in Process Inventory account of the Packaging Department.

Chapter Assignments

BUILDING YOUR KNOWLEDGE FOUNDATION

QUESTIONS

1. How do managers in manufacturing and service organizations use cost information during the planning stage of the management cycle?
2. Managers use cost information to support their decision making during the executing stage of the management cycle. What kinds of decisions do they make at this stage?
3. How do managers use cost information during the reviewing stage of the management cycle?
4. What is a product costing system?
5. What is a job order costing system? Identify the kinds of companies that use such a system.

Review Problem

Process Costing Using the FIFO Costing Method

LO5, LO6, LO7 Pop Chewing Gum Company produces several flavors of bubble gum. Two basic direct materials, gum base and flavored sweetener, are blended at the beginning of the manufacturing process. No materials are lost in the process, so 1 kilogram of materials input produces 1 kilogram of bubble gum. Direct labor and manufacturing overhead costs are incurred uniformly throughout the blending process. On June 30, 20x4, 16,000 units were in process. All direct materials had been added, but the units were only 70 percent complete in regard to conversion costs. Direct materials costs of $8,100 and conversion costs of $11,800 were attached to the beginning inventory. During July, 135,000 kilograms of gum base and 270,000 kilograms of flavored sweetener were used at costs of $122,500 and $80,000, respectively. Direct labor charges were $299,200, and manufacturing overhead costs applied during July were $284,000. The ending work in process inventory was 21,600 kilograms. All direct materials have been added to those units, and 25 percent of the conversion costs have been assigned. Output from the Blending Department is transferred to the Packaging Department.

REQUIRED
1. Prepare a process cost report using the FIFO costing method for the Blending Department for July.
2. Identify the amount that should be transferred out of the Work in Process Inventory account, and state where those dollars should be transferred.

Answer to Review Problem

1. Process cost report using the FIFO costing method:

Pop Chewing Gum Company
Blending Department
Process Cost Report: FIFO Method
For the Month Ended July 31, 20x4

Step 1: Account for physical units.

Beginning inventory (units started last period)	16,000
Units started this period	405,000
Units to be accounted for	421,000

Step 2: Account for equivalent units.

		Direct Materials Costs	% Incurred During Period	Conversion Costs	% Incurred During Period
Beginning inventory (units completed this period)	16,000	0	0%	4,800	30%
Units started and completed this period	383,400	383,400	100%	383,400	100%
Ending inventory (units started but not completed this period)	21,600	21,600	100%	5,400	25%
Units accounted for	421,000	405,000		393,600	

(continued)

processed are the first costs transferred when those materials flow to the next process, department, or work cell. Preparation of a process cost report involves five steps. Steps 1 and 2 account for the physical flow of products and compute the equivalent units of production. Once equivalent production has been determined, the focus of the report shifts to accounting for costs. In Step 3, all direct materials and conversion costs for the current period are added to arrive at total costs. In Step 4, the cost per equivalent unit for both direct materials and conversion costs is found by dividing those costs by their respective equivalent units. In Step 5, costs are assigned to the units completed and transferred out during the period, as well as to the ending work in process inventory. The costs assigned to units completed and transferred out include the costs incurred in the preceding period and the conversion costs needed to complete those units during the current period. That amount is added to the total cost of producing all units started and completed during the period. The result is the total cost transferred out for the units completed during the period. Step 5 also assigns costs to units still in process at the end of the period by multiplying their direct materials and conversion costs by their respective equivalent units. The total equals the balance in the Work in Process Inventory account at the end of the period.

LO7 Evaluate operating performance using information about product cost.

Both the job order and the process costing systems supply information that managers can use to evaluate operating performance. Such an analysis may include consideration of the following: cost trends of a product or product line, units produced per time period, materials usage per unit produced, labor cost per unit produced, special needs of customers, and the cost-effectiveness of changing to a more advanced production process.

REVIEW OF CONCEPTS AND TERMINOLOGY

The following concepts and terms were introduced in this chapter:

- **LO5** **Conversion costs:** The combined total costs of direct labor and manufacturing overhead.

- **LO3** **Cost-plus contracts:** Job contracts that require the customer to pay all costs incurred in performing the job plus a predetermined amount of profit.

- **LO5** **Equivalent production:** A measure that applies a percentage-of-completion factor to partially completed units to compute the equivalent number of whole units produced in an accounting period for each type of input. Also called *equivalent units*.

- **LO4** **FIFO costing method:** A process costing method in which the cost flow follows the actual flow of production, so that the costs assigned to the first materials processed are the first costs transferred out when those materials flow to the next process, department, or work cell.

- **LO2** **Job order:** A customer order for a specific number of specially designed, made-to-order products.

- **LO2** **Job order cost card:** A document on which all costs incurred in the production of a particular job order are recorded; part of the subsidiary ledger for the Work in Process Inventory account.

- **LO2** **Job order costing system:** A product costing system that traces the costs of direct materials, direct labor, and manufacturing overhead to a specific batch of products or a specific job order; used by companies that make large, unique, or special-order products.

- **LO2** **Process costing system:** A product costing system that traces the costs of direct materials, direct labor, and manufacturing overhead to processes, departments, or work cells and then assigns the costs to the products manufactured by those processes, departments, or work cells; used by companies that produce large amounts of similar products or liquid products or that have long, continuous production runs of identical products.

- **LO4** **Process cost report:** A report that managers use to track and analyze costs in a process costing system.

the reviewing stage, they analyze actual and targeted information to evaluate performance and make any necessary adjustments to their planning and decision-making strategies. During the reporting stage, they use unit costs to determine inventory balances and the cost of goods or services sold for the financial statements. They also analyze internal reports that compare the organization's measures of actual and targeted performance to determine whether cost goals for products or services are being achieved.

LO2 Distinguish between the two basic types of product costing systems and identify the information each provides.

A job order costing system is a product costing system used by companies that make large, unique, or special-order products. Such a system traces the costs of direct materials, direct labor, and manufacturing overhead to a specific batch of products or a specific job order. A job order costing system measures the cost of each complete unit and summarizes the cost of all jobs in a single Work in Process Inventory account that is supported by job order cost cards.

A process costing system is a product costing system used by companies that produce large amounts of similar products or liquid products or long, continuous production runs of identical products. Such a system first traces the costs of direct materials, direct labor, and manufacturing overhead to processes, departments, or work cells and then assigns the costs to the products manufactured by those processes, departments, or work cells. A process costing system uses several Work in Process Inventory accounts: one for each department, process, or work cell.

LO3 Explain cost flow in a job order costing system, prepare a job order cost card, and compute product unit cost.

In a manufacturer's job order costing system, the costs of materials are first charged to the Materials Inventory account and to the respective materials accounts in the subsidiary ledger. Labor costs are first accumulated in the Factory Payroll account. The various manufacturing overhead costs are charged to the Manufacturing Overhead account. As products are manufactured, the costs of direct materials and direct labor are transferred to the Work in Process Inventory account and are recorded on the job's job order cost card. Manufacturing overhead costs are applied and charged to the Work in Process Inventory account using a predetermined overhead rate. Those charges are used to reduce the balance in the Manufacturing Overhead account. They too are recorded on the job order cost card. When products and jobs are completed, the costs assigned to them are transferred to the Finished Goods Inventory account. Then, when the products are sold and shipped, their costs are transferred to the Cost of Goods Sold account.

All costs of direct materials, direct labor, and manufacturing overhead for a particular job are accumulated on a job order cost card. When the job has been completed, those costs are totaled. The total is then divided by the number of good units produced to find the product unit cost for that order. The product unit cost is entered on the job order cost card and will be used to value items in inventory.

Job order costing in a service organization differs in that the costs are not associated with a physical product but rather with services, for which the most important cost is labor. Job order cost cards are kept and include the costs for labor, materials and supplies, and service overhead.

LO4 Explain product flow and cost flow in a process costing system.

Process costing is used by companies that produce large amounts of similar products or liquids or that have a continuous production flow. A process costing system accumulates the costs of direct materials, direct labor, and manufacturing overhead for each process, department, or work cell and assigns those costs to the products as they are produced during a particular period. The cost flow follows the logical physical flow of production using the FIFO costing method—that is, the costs assigned to the first materials processed are the first costs transferred out when those materials flow to the next process, department, or work cell.

LO5 Define *equivalent production* and compute equivalent units.

Equivalent production is a measure that applies a percentage-of-completion factor to partially completed units to compute the equivalent number of whole units produced in an accounting period for each type of input. Equivalent units are computed from (1) units in the beginning work in process inventory and their percentage of completion, (2) units started and completed during the period, and (3) units in the ending work in process inventory and their percentage of completion.

LO6 Prepare a process cost report using the FIFO costing method.

In a process cost report that uses the FIFO costing method, the cost flow follows the logical physical flow of production—that is, the costs assigned to the first materials

duction flows to the Packaging Department, the accumulated costs (incurred in the two previous departments) are transferred to that department's Work in Process Inventory account. At the end of the accounting period, a separate process cost report is prepared for each department.

✓ Check out ACE for a Review Quiz at http://accounting.college.hmco.com/students.

Using Information About Product Cost to Evaluate Performance

LO7 Evaluate operating performance using information about product cost.
RELATED TEXT ASSIGNMENTS
Q: 20
SE: 10
E: 15
SD: 5
MRA: 1, 2, 3

🛑 **Stop and Think!**
How can information about product cost help managers evaluate operating performance?
By analyzing the information from a job order or process costing system, managers can compare budgeted and actual costs for a process, department, or work cell. They can also track units produced per time period and monitor labor costs to evaluate operating performance. ∎

A product costing system—whether it's a job order or a process costing system—provides managers with valuable information. As we have noted, managers use the information that such a system provides in determining a product's price and in computing the balances in the Materials Inventory, Work in Process Inventory, and Finished Goods Inventory accounts on the balance sheet and the Cost of Goods Sold account on the income statement. Managers also use product costing information to evaluate operating performance. Such an analysis may include consideration of the following:

- Cost trends of a product or product line
- Units produced per time period
- Materials usage per unit produced
- Labor cost per unit produced
- Special needs of customers
- Cost-effectiveness of changing to a more advanced production process

Cost trends can be developed from product cost data over several time periods. Such trends help managers identify areas of rising costs or areas in which cost-effectiveness has improved. Tracking units produced per time period, a figure easily pulled from a product cost analysis, can help managers evaluate operating efficiency.

Direct materials and labor costs are significant parts of a product's cost and should be monitored constantly. Trends in direct materials usage and labor costs per unit produced can help managers determine optimal resource usage.

Anticipating customers' needs is very important to managers. By tracking the size, cost, and type of products ordered by customers, managers can see which customers are increasing or reducing their orders and take action to improve customer relations.

STUDY NOTE: Performance measures are quantitative tools that help managers assess the performance of a specific process or expected outcome.

Finally, decisions to purchase new machinery and equipment are often based on the savings that the change is expected to produce. Information from a product costing system helps managers make such decisions in that it enables them to estimate unit costs for the new equipment and to compare them with cost trends for the existing equipment.

✓ Check out ACE for a Review Quiz at http://accounting.college.hmco.com/students.

Chapter Review

Review of Learning Objectives

LO1 Discuss the role information about costs plays in the management cycle and explain why unit cost is important.

During the planning stage of the management cycle, information about costs helps managers develop budgets, establish prices, set sales goals, plan production volumes, estimate product or service unit costs, and determine human resource needs. During the executing stage, managers use cost information to make decisions about controlling costs, managing the company's volume of activity, ensuring quality, and negotiating prices. During

Assigning Costs

Step 5 in the preparation of a process costing report uses information from Steps 2 and 4 to assign costs, as shown in Exhibit 2. This final step determines the costs that are transferred out either to the next production process, department, or work cell or to the Finished Goods Inventory account (i.e., the cost of goods manufactured), as well as the costs that remain in the ending balance in the Work in Process Inventory account. The total costs assigned to units completed and transferred out and to ending inventory must equal the total costs in Step 3.

■ **COST OF GOODS MANUFACTURED AND TRANSFERRED OUT** Step 5 of Exhibit 2 shows that the costs transferred to the Finished Goods Inventory account include the $41,540 in direct materials and conversion costs for completing the 6,200 units in beginning inventory. Step 2 in the exhibit shows that 2,480 equivalent units of conversion costs were required to complete these 6,200 units. Because the equivalent unit conversion cost for February is $5.60, the cost to complete the units carried over from January is $13,888 (2,480 units × $5.60).

Each of the 52,500 units started and completed in February cost $8.90 to produce. Their combined cost of $467,250 is added to the $41,540 and $13,888 of costs required to produce the 6,200 units from beginning inventory to arrive at the total of $522,678 that is transferred to the Finished Goods Inventory account.

■ **ENDING INVENTORY** All costs remaining in Soda Products' Work in Process Inventory account after the cost of goods manufactured have been transferred out represent the costs of the drinks still in production at the end of February. As shown in Step 5 of Exhibit 2, the balance of $29,100 in the ending Work in Process Inventory is made up of $16,500 of direct materials costs (5,000 units × $3.30 per unit) and $12,600 of conversion costs (5,000 × 45% × $5.60 per unit).

■ **ROUNDING DIFFERENCES** As you perform Step 5 in any process cost report, remember that the total costs in Steps 3 and 5 must always be the same number. In Exhibit 2, for example, they are both $551,778. If the numbers are not the same, first check for omission of any costs and for calculation errors. If that does not solve the problem, check if any rounding was necessary in computing the costs per equivalent unit in Step 4. If rounding was done in Step 4, rounding differences will occur when assigning costs in Step 5. Adjust the total costs transferred out for any rounding difference so that the total costs in Step 5 equal the total costs in Step 3.

■ **RECAP OF WORK IN PROCESS INVENTORY ACCOUNT** When the process cost report is complete, an account recap may be prepared to show the effects of the report on the Work in Process Inventory account for the period. Two recaps of Soda Products' Work in Process Inventory account for February—one for costs and one for units—appear at the end of Exhibit 2.

PROCESS COSTING FOR TWO OR MORE PRODUCTION DEPARTMENTS

Because Soda Products Company has only one production department, it needs only one Work in Process Inventory account. However, a company that has more than one production department must have a Work in Process Inventory account for each department. For instance, a soft drink maker that has a production department for formulation, another for bottling, and another for packaging needs three Work in Process Inventory accounts. When products flow from the Formulation Department to the Bottling Department, their costs flow from the Formulation Department's Work in Process Inventory account to the Bottling Department's Work in Process Inventory account. The costs transferred into the Bottling Department's Work in Process Inventory account are treated in the same way as the cost of direct materials added at the beginning of the production process. When pro-

---

KEY POINT: All costs must be accounted for, including costs from both beginning inventory and costs incurred during the current period. All costs must be assigned to either ending inventory or the goods transferred out.

STUDY NOTE: Rounding product unit costs to even dollars may lead to a significant difference in total costs, giving the impression that costs have been miscalculated. Carry product unit costs to two decimal places where appropriate.

● **STOP AND THINK!**
How many process cost reports are prepared each period?
One process cost report is prepared for every Work in Process Inventory account. ■

Preparing a Process Cost Report Using the FIFO Costing Method

LO6 Prepare a process cost report using the FIFO costing method.

RELATED TEXT ASSIGNMENTS
Q: 17, 18, 19
SE: 8, 9
E: 9, 10, 11, 12, 13, 14
P: 4, 5, 8
SD: 5
MRA: 2, 3

STUDY NOTE: The FIFO method focuses on the work done in the current period only.

As mentioned earlier, a process cost report is a report that managers use to track and analyze costs for a process, department, or work cell in a process costing system. In a process cost report that uses the FIFO costing method, the cost flow follows the logical physical flow of production—that is, the costs assigned to the first materials processes are the first costs transferred out when those materials flow to the next process, department, or work cell.

As illustrated in Exhibit 2, the preparation of a process cost report has five steps. The first two steps account for the units of product being processed. The next two steps account for the costs of the direct material, direct labor, and manufacturing overhead that are being incurred. The final step assigns costs to products transferring out of the area and to those remaining behind in ending work in process inventory.

Accounting for Units

Managers must account for the physical flow of products through their areas (Step 1) before they can compute equivalent production for the accounting period (Step 2). To continue with the Soda Products example, assume the following facts for the accounting period of February 20x6:

- The beginning work in process inventory consists of 6,200 partially completed units (60 percent processed in the previous period).
- During the period, the 6,200 units in beginning inventory were completed, and 57,500 units were started into production.
- Of the 57,500 units started during the period, 52,500 units were completed. The other 5,000 units remain in ending work in process inventory and are 45 percent complete.

KEY POINT: The process cost report is developed for the purpose of assigning a value to one transaction: the transfer of goods from one department to another or to finished goods inventory. The ending balance in the Work in Process Inventory account represents the costs that remain after this transfer.

In Step 1 of Exhibit 2, Soda Products' department manager computes the total units to be accounted for by adding the 6,200 units in beginning inventory to the 57,500 units started into production in this period. These 63,700 units are the actual physical units that the manager is responsible for during the period. Step 2 continues accounting for physical units. As shown in the "Physical Units" column of Exhibit 2, the 6,200 units in beginning inventory that were completed during the period, the 52,500 units that were started and finished in the period, and the 5,000 units remaining in the department at the end of the period are summed, and the total is listed as "units accounted for." (Notice that the "units accounted for" in Step 2 must equal the "units to be accounted for" in Step 1.) These amounts are used to compute equivalent production for the department's direct materials and conversion costs for the month, as described below.

ENRICHMENT NOTE: The percentage of completion for beginning work in process inventory is the amount of work completed the prior period. Under FIFO, the amount of effort required to complete beginning work in process inventory is the relevant percentage.

■ **Beginning Inventory** Because all direct materials are added at the beginning of the production process, the 6,200 partially completed units that began February as work in process were already 100 percent complete in regard to direct materials. They were 60 percent complete in regard to conversion costs on February 1. The remaining 40 percent of their conversion costs were incurred as they were completed during the month. Thus, as shown in the far right column of Exhibit 2, the equivalent production for their conversion costs is 2,480 units (40% × 6,200).

■ **Units Started and Completed During the Period** All the costs of the 52,500 units started and completed during February were incurred during this accounting

Figure 6
Computation of Equivalent Production

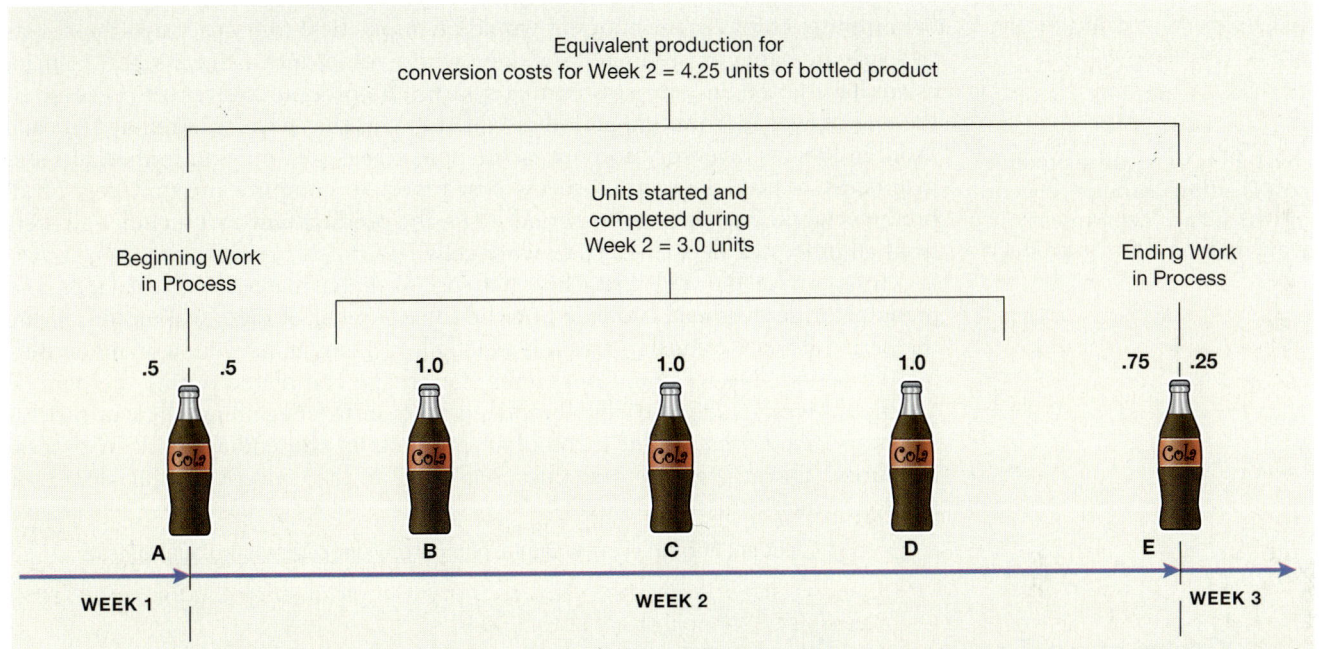

Equivalent production for conversion costs for Week 2 = 4.25 units of bottled product

Beginning Work in Process: .5 | .5 (A)

Units started and completed during Week 2 = 3.0 units: 1.0 (B), 1.0 (C), 1.0 (D)

Ending Work in Process: .75 | .25 (E)

WEEK 1 | WEEK 2 | WEEK 3

Note: Conversion costs (the cost of direct labor and manufacturing overhead) are incurred uniformly as each physical unit of drink moves through production. Equivalent production for Week 2 is 4.25 units for conversion costs. But direct materials costs are all added to production at the beginning of the process. Because four physical units of drinks entered production in Week 2, equivalent production for the week is 4.0 units of effort for direct materials costs.

● STOP AND THINK!
What is an education-based example of equivalent production?

Funding of state-supported universities and colleges is based on the number of full-time equivalents (FTEs) these institutions generate each funding period. One FTE is equal to 12 credit hours of course work—the equivalent whole unit of effort expended on the education process during a period. Since some students take more or less than 12 credit hours, their course loads must be converted into FTEs for funding purposes. ■

During Week 2, Soda Products began work on four new drinks—the three drinks that were completed and the drink that was three-quarters completed at the end of the week. Because all direct materials are added at the beginning of the production process, all four drinks were 100 percent complete in regard to direct materials at the end of Week 2. Thus, for Week 2, the equivalent production for direct materials was 4.0 units. This figure includes direct materials for both the 3.0 units that were started and completed and the 1.0 unit that was three-quarters completed.

EQUIVALENT PRODUCTION FOR CONVERSION COSTS

Because conversion costs at Soda Products are incurred uniformly throughout the production process, the equivalent production for conversion costs during Week 2 consists of three components: the cost to finish the half-completed unit in beginning work in process inventory (0.5), the cost to begin and finish three completed units (3.0), and the cost to begin work on the three-quarters completed unit in ending work in process inventory (0.75). For Week 2, the total equivalent production for conversion costs was 4.25 (0.5 + 3.0 + 0.75) units.

In reality, Soda Products would make many more drinks during an accounting period and would have many more partially completed drinks in its beginning and ending work in process inventories. The number of partially completed drinks would be so great that it would be impractical to take a physical count of them. So, instead of taking a physical count, Soda Products would estimate an average percentage of completion for all drinks in process.

✓ Check out ACE for a Review Quiz at http://accounting.college.hmco.com/students.

KEY POINT: Total product cost is a flow-through concept in which each department's work adds cost to the product.

account. When the packages of cookies are sold, their costs transfer from the Finished Goods Inventory account to the Cost of Goods Sold account.

Because the production of homogeneous products like packaged cookies, paint, or computer chips is continuous, it would be impractical to try to assign their costs to a specific batch of products, as is done with a job order costing system. Instead, as we have noted, in a process costing system, the process cost report prepared at the end of every accounting period assigns the costs that have accumulated in each Work in Process Inventory account to the units transferred out and to the units still in process. Managers use the process cost report to compute the unit cost of all products worked on during the period. Thus, the product unit cost includes all costs from all processes, departments, or work cells.

To compute the unit cost, the total cost of direct materials, direct labor, and manufacturing overhead is divided by the total number of units worked on during the period. Thus, a critical question is exactly how many units were worked on during the period? Do we count only units started and completed during the period? Or should we include partially completed units in the beginning work in process inventory? And what about incomplete products in the ending work in process inventory? The answers to these questions relate to the concept of equivalent production, which is discussed next.

✓ Check out ACE for a Review Quiz at http://accounting.college.hmco.com/students.

COMPUTING EQUIVALENT PRODUCTION

LO5 Define *equivalent production* and compute equivalent units.

RELATED TEXT ASSIGNMENTS
Q: 14, 15, 16
SE: 8
E: 9, 10, 11
P: 4, 5, 8
SD: 5
MRA: 2, 3

STUDY NOTE: The number of units started and completed is not the same as the total number of units completed during the period. Total units completed includes two categories: units in beginning work in process inventory and units started and completed.

ENRICHMENT NOTE: Don't make the mistake of thinking that direct materials are always placed into production at the beginning of the process. In reality, direct materials are often added at different stages of production (e.g., for paint, cans for packaging are added at the end).

A process costing system, because it makes no attempt to associate costs with particular job orders, assigns the costs incurred in a process, department, or work cell to the units worked on during an accounting period by computing an average cost per unit. **Equivalent production** (also called *equivalent units*) is a measure that applies a percentage-of-completion factor to partially completed units to calculate the equivalent number of whole units produced in an accounting period for each type of input (i.e., direct materials, direct labor, and manufacturing overhead). The number of equivalent units produced is the sum of (1) total units started and completed during the period and (2) an amount representing the work done on partially completed products in both the beginning and the ending work in process inventories. Equivalent production must be computed separately for each type of input because of differences in the ways the costs are incurred. Direct materials are usually added to production at the beginning of the process. The costs of direct labor and manufacturing overhead are often incurred uniformly throughout the production process. Thus, it is convenient to combine direct labor and manufacturing overhead when calculating equivalent units. These combined costs are called **conversion costs**.

We will explain the computation of equivalent production by using a simplified example. Soda Products Company makes bottled soft drinks. As illustrated in Figure 6, the company started Week 2 with one half-completed drink in process. During Week 2, it started and completed three drinks, and at the end of Week 2, it had one drink that was three-quarters completed.

EQUIVALENT PRODUCTION FOR DIRECT MATERIALS

At Soda Products, all direct materials, including the liquids and the bottles, are added at the beginning of production. Thus, the drink that was half-completed at the beginning of Week 2 had had all its direct materials added during the previous week. For this reason, no direct materials costs for this drink are included in the computation of Week 2's equivalent units.

Focus on Business Practice

What Kinds of Companies Use Process Costing?

Process costing is appropriate for companies in many types of industries. The following list provides some examples:

Industry	Company
Aluminum	Alcoa, Inc. <www.alcoa.com>
Beverages	Coors <www.coors.com>
Building materials	Owens Corning <www.owenscorning.com>
Chemicals	Engelhard Corporation <www.englehard.com>
Computers	Apple Computer <www.apple.com>
Containers	Crown Cork & Seal <www.crowncork.com>
Electrical equipment	Emerson Electric <www.emersonelectric.com>
Foods	Kellogg Company <www.kelloggs.com>
Machinery	Caterpillar Inc. <www.caterpillar.com>
Manufacturing	Minnesota Mining & Manufacturing <www.3m.com>
Oil and gas	Exxon <www.exxon.com>
Paper products	Boise Cascade <www.boisecascade.com>
Photography	Eastman Kodak <www.eastmankodak.com>
Plastic products	Tupperware <www.tupperware.com>
Soft drinks	Coca-Cola <www.cocacola.com>

Process costing environments can be considerably less complex than the one we have just described, but even in simple process costing environments, production generally involves a number of separate manufacturing processes, departments, or works cells. For example, the separate processes involved in manufacturing sofas include making the frames and cushions, upholstering the frames, and assembling the frames and cushions into finished products.

As products pass through each manufacturing process, department, or work cell, the process costing system accumulates their costs and passes them on to the next process, department, or work cell. At the end of every accounting period, the system generates a report that assigns the costs that have accumulated during the period to the units that have transferred out of the process, department, or work cell and to the units that are still work in process. Managers use this report, called a **process cost report**, to assign costs using the FIFO costing method. In the **FIFO costing method**, the cost flow follows the logical physical flow of production—the costs assigned to the first materials processed are the first costs transferred out when those materials flow to the next process, department, or work cell. Thus, in Figure 5, the costs assigned to the production of the silicon wafers would be the first costs transferred to the fabrication of the chips. How process cost reports are prepared using the FIFO costing method is covered later in this chapter.

● Stop and Think!

How many Work in Process Inventory accounts does a process costing system require?

A process costing system requires a Work in Process Inventory account for each process, department, or work cell in the production process. ■

www.nabisco.com

Costs Flows Through the Work in Process Inventory Accounts

As we pointed out earlier in the chapter, a job order costing system uses a single Work in Process Inventory account, whereas a process costing system has a separate Work in Process Inventory account for each process, department, or work cell. These accounts are the focal point of process costing. As products move from one process, department, or work cell to the next, the costs of the direct materials, direct labor, and manufacturing overhead associated with them flow to the Work in Process Inventory account of that process, department, or work cell. Once the products are completed, packaged, and ready for sale, their costs are transferred to the Finished Goods Inventory account.

To illustrate how costs flow through the Work in Process Inventory accounts in a process costing system, let's consider a company like Nabisco, which makes large quantities of identical cookies in a continuous flow. Such a company would have mixing, baking, and packaging departments. After its Mixing Department has prepared the cookie dough, the costs incurred for direct materials, direct labor, and manufacturing overhead are transferred from that department's Work in Process Inventory account to the Work in Process Inventory account of the Baking Department. When the cookies are baked, the costs of the cookie dough and the baking costs are transferred from the Baking Department's Work in Process Inventory account to the Work in Process Inventory account of the Packaging Department. After the cookies are packaged and ready for sale, all their costs—for dough, baking, and packaging—are transferred to the Finished Goods Inventory

Figure 4
Production Flows for Process Costing

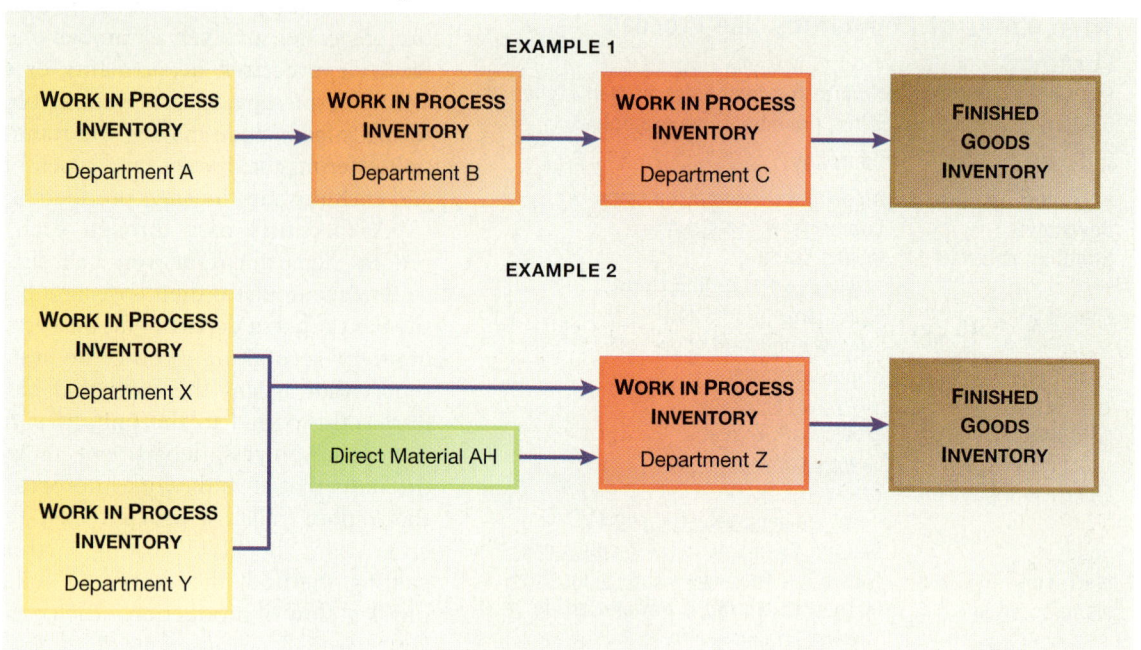

EXAMPLE 1

Work in Process Inventory (Department A) → Work in Process Inventory (Department B) → Work in Process Inventory (Department C) → Finished Goods Inventory

EXAMPLE 2

Work in Process Inventory (Department X) ┐
                                          ├→ Work in Process Inventory (Department Z) → Finished Goods Inventory
Direct Material AH ───────────────────────┤
                                          │
Work in Process Inventory (Department Y) ─┘

---

up each chip on a wafer. Additional direct labor and overhead costs are incurred during fabrication.

- Final testing, assembly, and packaging of the chips: Although the wafers are tested at each step in the fabrication process, each chip on a wafer is tested again when fabrication is complete. Those that pass this test are cut from the wafer, placed in metal or plastic packages, tested once again, and transferred to finished goods inventory in the warehouse. These steps incur additional direct labor, direct materials, and overhead costs.

Figure 5
Product Flows in a Process Costing System for Computer Chip Making

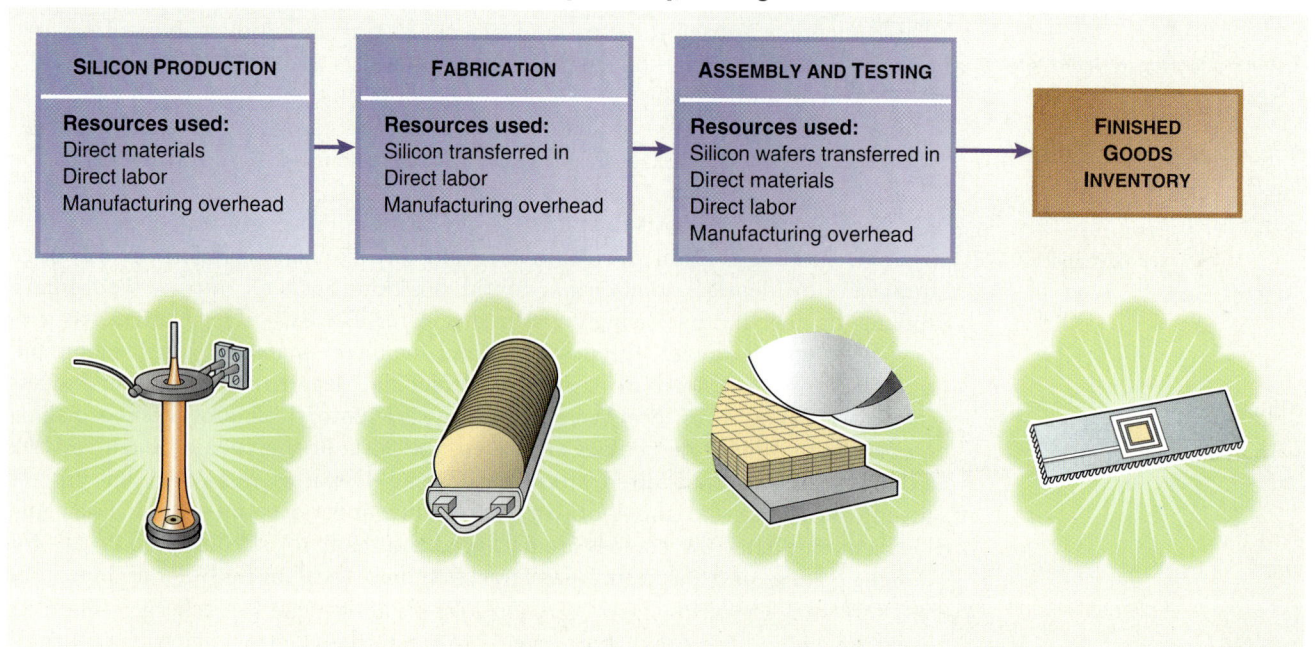

SILICON PRODUCTION
Resources used:
Direct materials
Direct labor
Manufacturing overhead

→

FABRICATION
Resources used:
Silicon transferred in
Direct labor
Manufacturing overhead

→

ASSEMBLY AND TESTING
Resources used:
Silicon wafers transferred in
Direct materials
Direct labor
Manufacturing overhead

→

FINISHED GOODS INVENTORY

installation, and job-site cleanup. Costs have been tracked to the Rico Corporation job throughout its duration, and now that the job is finished, it is time to complete the job order cost card. The service overhead cost for landscape design is 40 percent of design labor cost, and the service overhead cost for landscape installation is 50 percent of installation labor cost. Total costs incurred for this job were $5,400. Gartner's cost-plus contract with Rico has a 15 percent profit guarantee; therefore, $810 of profit margin is added to the total cost to arrive at the total contract revenue of $6,210, which is the amount billed to Rico.

✓ Check out ACE for a Review Quiz at http://accounting.college.hmco.com/students.

THE PROCESS COSTING SYSTEM

LO4 Explain product flow and cost flow in a process costing system.
RELATED TEXT ASSIGNMENTS
Q: 13
SD: 2, 5
MRA: 3, 4, 6

As discussed earlier, a process costing system is used by businesses that produce large amounts of similar products or liquid products or that have long, continuous production runs of identical products. Companies that produce paint, beverages, bricks, canned foods, milk, and paper are typical users of a process costing system. Tracking costs to individual products in a continuous flow environment would be too difficult and too expensive and would not reveal significantly different product costs. One gallon of green paint is identical to the next gallon of green paint; one brick looks just like the next brick. Because the products are alike, they should cost the same amount to produce. A process costing system accumulates the costs of direct materials, direct labor, and manufacturing overhead for each process, department, or work cell and assigns those costs to the products as they are produced during a particular period.

PATTERNS OF PRODUCT FLOWS AND COST FLOWS

In companies that use process costing, the steps in the production process can be combined in hundreds of ways. Two basic production flows are illustrated in Figure 4. Example 1 shows a series of three processing steps, or departments. The completed product from one department becomes the direct materials for the next department. Such a production flow can include from two to a dozen or more departments or processes. The product unit cost is the sum of the cost elements in all departments.

Example 2 in Figure 4 shows a different kind of production flow. Again there are three departments, but the product does not flow through all the departments in a simple 1-2-3 order. Instead, two separate products are developed: one in Department X and the other in Department Y. Both products then go to Department Z, where they are joined with a third direct material, Material AH. The unit cost transferred to the Finished Goods Inventory account when the products are completed includes cost elements from Departments X, Y, and Z.

To further illustrate this linear pattern of production flow, let's consider an example from the computer chip–making industry. The steps below, which describe the production flow during the manufacture of computer chips, are shown in Figure 5.

- Producing the silicon wafer. Silicon, which is extracted from sand and then purified, is the direct material from which computer chips are made. Through a process of crystallization, the refined, molten silicon is converted to a cylindrical ingot. The ingot is then sliced into wafers, and the wafers are polished to meet flatness and thickness specifications. The workers involved in these steps provide direct labor. Overhead includes the costs of the equipment the workers use and the resources necessary to operate and maintain the equipment.
- Fabricating the chips. Fabrication includes photolithography, etching, ion implantation, and all the other steps needed to create the electronic circuits that make

FIGURE 3
Job Order Cost Card—Service Organization

JOB ORDER COST CARD
Gartner Landscaping Services

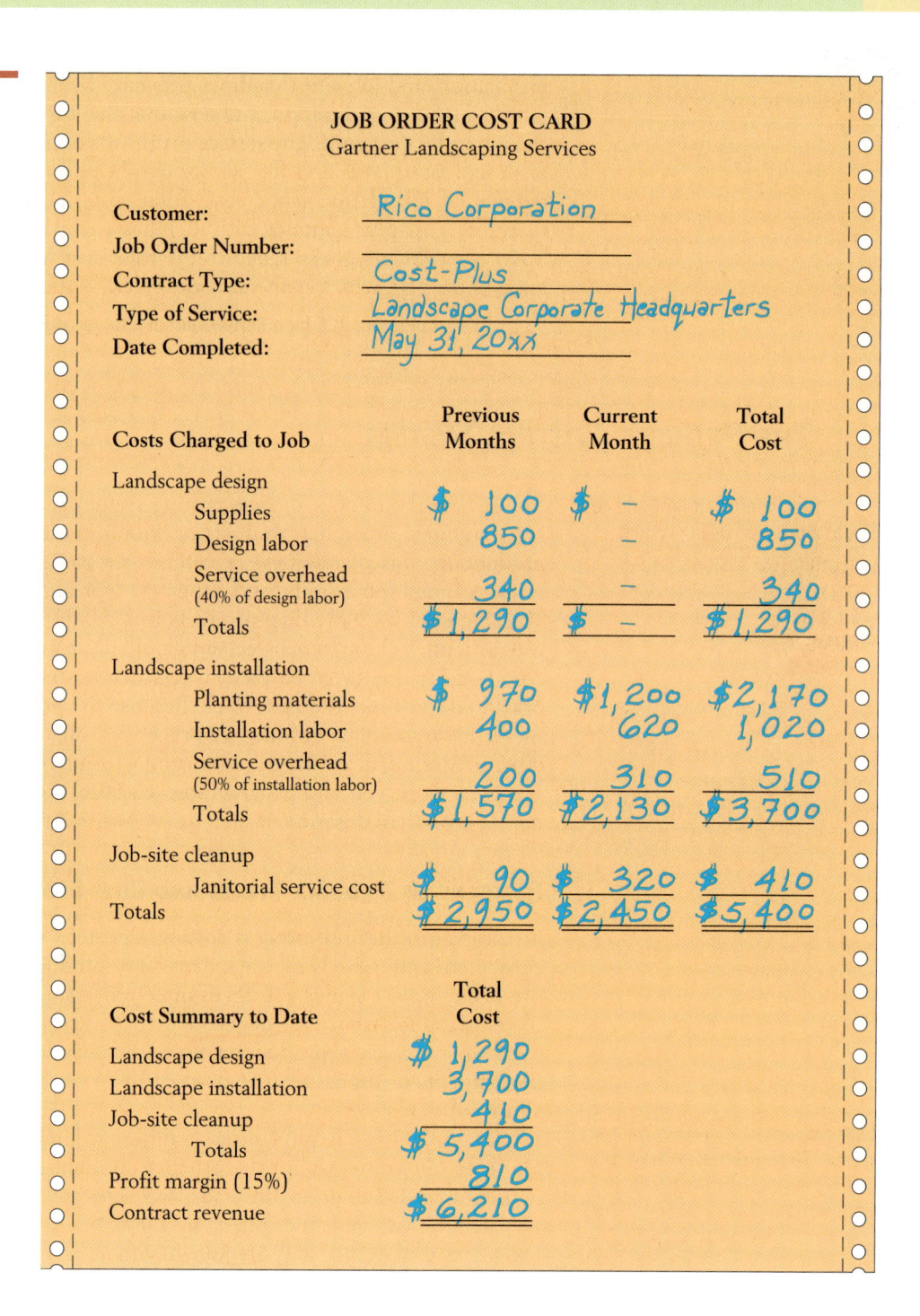

Customer: Rico Corporation
Job Order Number: _____
Contract Type: Cost-Plus
Type of Service: Landscape Corporate Headquarters
Date Completed: May 31, 20xx

Costs Charged to Job	Previous Months	Current Month	Total Cost
Landscape design			
Supplies	$ 100	$ —	$ 100
Design labor	850	—	850
Service overhead (40% of design labor)	340	—	340
Totals	$1,290	$ —	$1,290
Landscape installation			
Planting materials	$ 970	$1,200	$2,170
Installation labor	400	620	1,020
Service overhead (50% of installation labor)	200	310	510
Totals	$1,570	$2,130	$3,700
Job-site cleanup			
Janitorial service cost	$ 90	$ 320	$ 410
Totals	$2,950	$2,450	$5,400

Cost Summary to Date	Total Cost
Landscape design	$ 1,290
Landscape installation	3,700
Job-site cleanup	410
Totals	$ 5,400
Profit margin (15%)	810
Contract revenue	$ 6,210

Such contracts require the customer to pay all costs incurred in performing the job plus a predetermined amount of profit, which is based on the amount of costs incurred. When the job is complete, the costs on the completed job order cost card become the cost of services. The cost of services is adjusted at the end of the accounting period for the difference between the applied service overhead costs and the actual service overhead costs.

To illustrate how a service organization uses a job order costing system, let's assume that a company called Gartner Landscaping Services employs 15 people and serves the San Francisco Bay area. The company earns its revenue by designing and installing landscapes for homes and offices. Figure 3 shows Gartner's job order cost card for the landscaping of Rico Corporation's corporate headquarters. Costs have been categorized into three separate activities: landscape design, landscape

FOCUS ON BUSINESS ETHICS

Does a Product's Unit Cost Tell the Whole Story?

In response to a tip from the fraud hotline maintained by the Department of Defense <www.defenselink.mil>, the Office of the Inspector General <www.oig.hhs.gov>, the watchdog agency for the Pentagon, conducted an audit of The Boeing Company <www.boeing.com>. The audit found several instances in which Boeing had evidently overcharged the government for parts. For example, it had charged $1.24 for each of 31,108 springs previously priced at $.05 and $403 each for 246 actuator sleeves priced earlier at $24.72.

Boeing spokesperson Dick Dalton said, "This is a story that looks a whole lot worse than it is." According to Boeing, the audit cited prices from 15 to 20 years ago, when the Pentagon bought and stored large quantities of products. Today, the Pentagon receives small deliveries of parts on short notice, as needed. The new system saves the Pentagon huge inventory storage costs, but the price per part is higher because of the higher cost of frequent deliveries and on-demand ordering. The inspector general, Eleanor Hill, told the Senate Armed Services Subcommittee, "We found considerable evidence that the Department of Defense had not yet learned how to be an astute buyer in the commercial marketplace."[3]

THE JOB ORDER COST CARD AND COMPUTATION OF PRODUCT UNIT COST

As is evident from the preceding discussion, job order cost cards play a key role in a job order costing system. Because all manufacturing costs are accumulated in one Work in Process Inventory account, a separate accounting procedure is needed to trace those costs to specific jobs. The solution is the subsidiary ledger made up of job order cost cards. Each job being worked on has a job order cost card. As costs are incurred, they are classified by job and recorded on the appropriate card.

As you can see in Figure 2, a manufacturer's job order cost card has space for direct materials, direct labor, and manufacturing overhead costs. It also includes the job order number, product specifications, the name of the customer, the date of the order, the projected completion date, and a cost summary. As a job incurs direct materials and direct labor costs, its job order cost card is updated. Manufacturing overhead is also posted to the job order cost card at the predetermined rate. Job order cost cards for incomplete jobs make up the subsidiary ledger for the Work in Process Inventory account. To ensure correctness, the ending balance in the Work in Process Inventory account is compared with the total of the costs shown on the job order cost cards.

A job order costing system simplifies the calculation of product unit costs. When a job is finished, the costs of direct materials, direct labor, and manufacturing overhead that have been recorded on its job order cost card are totaled. The product unit cost is computed by dividing the total costs for the job by the number of good (i.e., salable) units produced. The product unit cost is entered on the job order cost card and will be used to value items in inventory. The job order cost card in Figure 2 shows the costs for completed Job CC. Two golf carts were produced at a total cost of $3,880, so the product unit cost was $1,940.

KEY POINT: Product unit cost in a job order costing system is the total cost of the job or batch divided by the number of items in the job or batch. This is an average cost for the good units manufactured for that job or batch.

JOB ORDER COSTING IN A SERVICE ORGANIZATION

Many service organizations use a job order costing system to compute the cost of rendering services. As pointed out elsewhere in the text, the costs of service organizations are different from those of a manufacturing organization in that they are not associated with a physical product that can be assembled, stored, and valued as inventory. Because these organizations sell services rather than making products for sale, the costs that they incur for materials are usually negligible. Their most important cost is labor, which is carefully accounted for through the use of time cards.

The cost flow of services is similar to the cost flow of manufactured products. Job order cost cards are used to keep track of the costs incurred for each job. Job costs include labor, materials and supplies, and service overhead. To cover these costs and earn a profit, many service organizations base jobs on **cost-plus contracts.**

KEY POINT: Job order cost cards for service businesses may record costs by activities done for the job. Notice the activity cost includes supplies, labor, and overhead.

> **STOP AND THINK!**
> Why is unit cost important at every stage of the management cycle?
> Unit cost is the primary measure of performance expectations, management control, performance evaluation, and financial reporting.

EXECUTING

During the executing stage, managers make decisions about controlling costs, managing the company's activity volume, ensuring quality, and negotiating prices. They use timely cost and volume information and actual unit costs to support their decision making. In manufacturing companies, managers use information about costs to decide whether to drop a product line, add a production shift, outsource the manufacture of a subassembly to another company, bid on a special order, or negotiate a selling price. In service organizations, managers use cost information to make decisions about bidding on jobs, dropping a current service, outsourcing a task to an independent contractor, adding staff, or negotiating a price. All of these decisions can have far-reaching effects, including possible changes in unit cost or quality.

REVIEWING

During the reviewing stage, managers watch for changes in cost and quality. They compare actual and targeted total and unit costs and monitor relevant price and volume information. They analyze the information to evaluate their performance, and on the basis of this evaluation, they adjust their planning and decision-making strategies. For example, if a product's quality is suffering, managers may study the design, materials purchasing, and manufacturing processes to determine the source of the problem so that they can make changes that will ensure the product's quality. If operating costs in a service business have risen too high, managers may break a unit cost of service down into its many components to analyze where costs can be cut or how the service can be performed more efficiently.

REPORTING

Finally, during the reporting stage, managers prepare financial statements. In manufacturing companies, managers use product unit costs to determine inventory balances for the organization's balance sheet and the cost of goods sold for its income statement. In service organizations, managers use unit costs of services to determine cost of sales for the income statement. During this stage, managers also prepare performance evaluation reports for internal use. These reports compare actual unit costs and targeted costs, as well as actual and targeted nonfinancial measures of performance. Managers in both manufacturing and service organizations analyze the data in the performance evaluation reports to determine whether cost goals for products or services are being achieved.

✓ Check out ACE for a Review Quiz at http://accounting.college.hmco.com/students.

JOB ORDER VERSUS PROCESS COSTING

LO2 Distinguish between the two basic types of product costing systems and identify the information each provides.

RELATED TEXT ASSIGNMENTS
Q: 4, 5, 6, 7
SE: 2, 3
E: 1, 2

For an organization to succeed, its managers must sell its products or services at prices that exceed the costs of creating and delivering them, thus ensuring a profit. To do so, managers need extensive information about such product-related costs as setup, production, and distribution. To meet managers' needs for cost information, it is necessary to have a highly reliable product costing system specifically designed to record and report the organization's operations. A **product costing system** is a set of procedures used to account for an organization's product costs and to provide timely and accurate unit cost information for pricing, cost planning and control, inventory valuation, and financial statement preparation.

The product costing system enables managers to track costs throughout the management cycle. It provides a structure for recording the revenue earned from sales and the costs incurred for direct materials, direct labor, and manufacturing overhead.

Product Cost Information and the Management Cycle

LO1 Discuss the role information about costs plays in the management cycle and explain why unit cost is important.

RELATED TEXT ASSIGNMENTS
Q: 1, 2, 3
SE: 1
SD: 1
MRA: 1, 4

www.toyota.com
www.harley-davidson.com
www.levistrauss.com
www.century21.com
www.hrblock.com
www.orkin.com

Managers depend on relevant and reliable information about costs to manage their organizations. The role of the management accountant is to develop a management information system that provides managers with the cost information they need. Although companies vary in their approaches to gathering, analyzing, and reporting information about costs, managers share the same basic concerns as they move through the management cycle. Figure 1 summarizes the management cycle and the concerns that managers address with relevant and timely information about costs.

Planning

During the planning stage, managers use information about costs to set performance expectations and estimate unit costs. In manufacturing companies, such as Toyota, Harley-Davidson, and Levi Strauss & Co., managers use cost information to develop budgets, establish product prices, and plan production volumes. In service organizations, such as Century 21, H&R Block, and Orkin Exterminating Company, managers use cost information to develop budgets, establish prices, set sales goals, and determine human resource needs. During the planning stage, knowledge of unit costs helps managers of both manufacturing and service companies set reasonable selling prices and estimate the cost of their products or services.

FIGURE 1
Uses of Information about Costs in the Management Cycle

PLANNING
Set performance expectations by developing budgets, establishing prices, setting sales goals, planning production volume, and determining human resource needs
Estimate product or service unit cost

REPORTING
Report inventory balances and cost of goods or services sold information on financial statements
Determine whether goals for product or service costs are being achieved

EXECUTING
Make decisions to control costs, manage activity volume, assure quality, and negotiate prices
Compute unit costs based on actual costs incurred and volume of products manufactured or services provided

REVIEWING
Evaluate performance by analyzing actual and targeted information
Adjust future planning and decision-making strategies

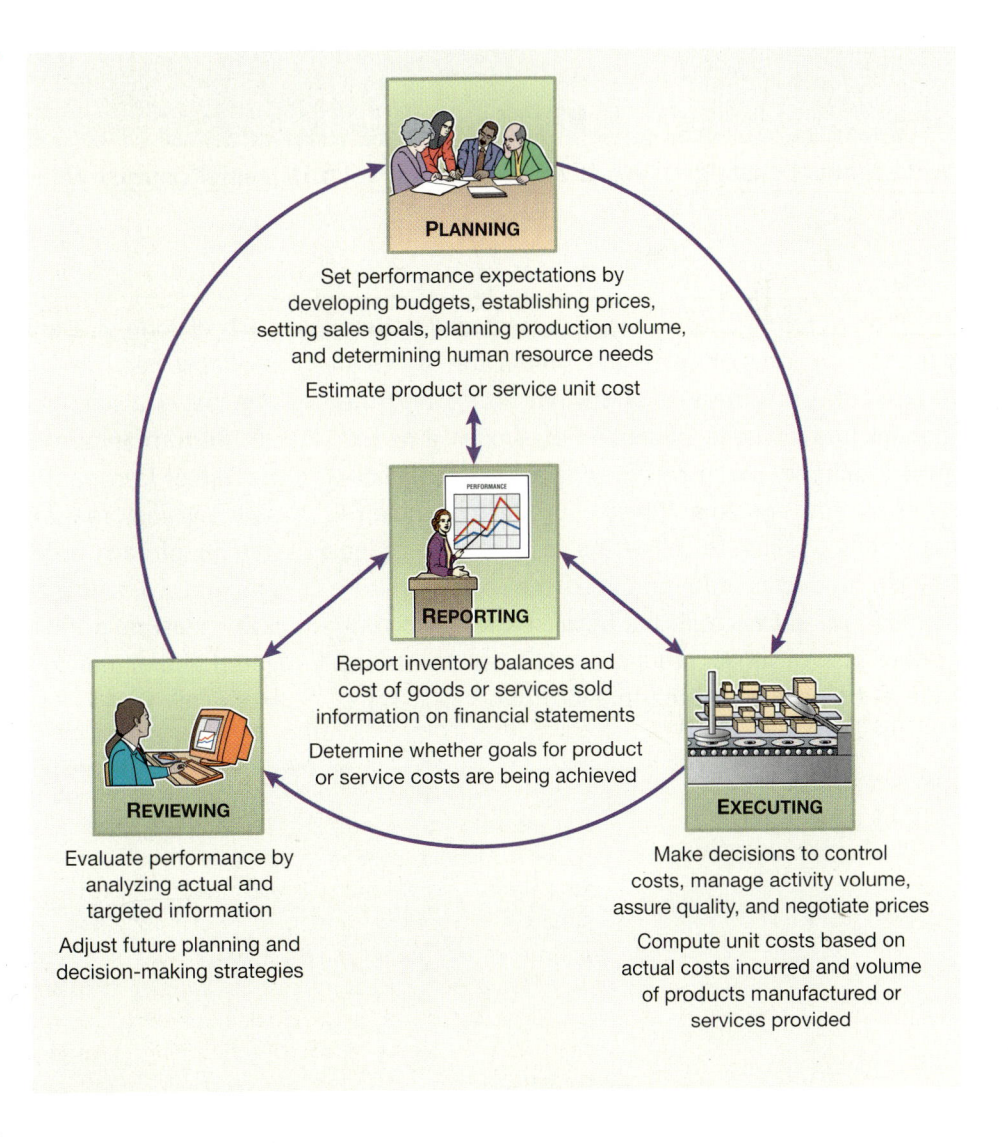

What product costing system is appropriate for John H. Daniel Company?

The appropriateness of a product costing system depends on the nature of the production process. Because the manufacture of custom orders and the manufacture of large quantities of similar products involve different processes, they generally require different costing systems. When a product is custom-made, it is possible to collect the costs of each order. When a product is mass-produced, the costs of a specific unit cannot be collected because there is a continuous flow of similar products; in this case, costs are collected by process, department, or work cell. Thus, each of John H. Daniel Company's two divisions will probably need its own costing system to determine the cost of a suit.

Performance measures will also differ for John H. Daniel Company's two divisions. For the custom suit division, management can measure the profitability of each order by comparing the order's cost and price. For the retail suit division, management will measure performance by comparing the budgeted and actual costs for a process, department, or work cell.

21

Chapter 21 describes the two basic types of product costing systems—job order costing and process costing.

Costing Systems: Job Order and Process Costing

LEARNING OBJECTIVES

LO1 Discuss the role information about costs plays in the management cycle and explain why unit cost is important.

LO2 Distinguish between the two basic types of product costing systems and identify the information each provides.

LO3 Explain cost flow in a job order costing system, prepare a job order cost card, and compute product unit cost.

LO4 Explain product flow and cost flow in a process costing system.

LO5 Define *equivalent production* and compute equivalent units.

LO6 Prepare a process cost report using the FIFO costing method.

LO7 Evaluate operating performance using information about product cost.

DECISION POINT
A MANAGER'S FOCUS

John H. Daniel Company <www.johnhdaniel.com>

Whatever a man's size, John H. Daniel Company has a suit to fit him. In addition to having a division that produces large quantities of ready-to-wear men's suits for retailers, the company has a division that manufactures made-to-order suits for individual customers. The made-to-order process begins when one of over 300 custom tailors from around the United States visits a customer at his home or office to show him the latest fabrics and suit styles. When the customer has made his selections, the tailor takes the measurements to guarantee a proper fit. The tailor then transmits the customer's measurements and choices of fabric, suit model, leg finish, and pocket type to John H. Daniel Company's manufacturing plant in Knoxville, Tennessee. At the factory, workers use state-of-the-art technology to cut the fabric to the order's specifications. A skilled, specialized team sews the pieces together and presses the finished suit. The suit is then shipped to the custom tailor, who delivers it for final fitting and approval at a time convenient for the customer. The whole process generally takes less than five weeks.

Is the product costing system that is used when making a large quantity of ready-to-wear suits appropriate when making suits to an individual customer's specifications? Why might John H. Daniel Company implement a different product costing system for each of its divisions? What performance measures would be most useful in evaluating the results of each division?

overhead from $220,000 to $320,000 for the year, which will increase the assembly activity cost pool from $80,000 to $180,000. The cost driver level for the assembly cost pool will change from 5,000 machine hours to 2,000 machine hours for the Rigger II and from 5,000 machine hours to 8,000 machine hours for the BioScout. The cost driver levels and cost pool amounts for setup, inspection, and engineering activities will remain the same.

1. Use the traditional method of applying overhead costs to
    a. Calculate the overhead rate.
    b. Compute the amount of the total manufacturing overhead costs applied to each product line.
    c. Calculate the product unit cost for each product line.
2. Use the activity-based costing method to
    a. Calculate the manufacturing overhead activity cost rate for each activity pool.
    b. Compute the manufacturing overhead costs applied to each product line by activity pool and in total.
    c. Calculate the product unit cost for each product line.
3. Complete the following table and discuss the differences in the costs assigned to the two product lines resulting from the additional information in this assignment:

Product unit cost	Rigger II	BioScout
Traditional		
Activity-based costing	_____	_____
Difference: decrease (increase)	======	======

Internet Case

MRA 5. Gateway, Inc. <www.gateway.com>, and Dell Computer Corporation <www.dell.com> assemble computers and sell them over the telephone or the Internet. Access the web site of either of these companies. Become familiar with the products of the company you have chosen. For one of these products, such as a desktop or laptop computer, give examples of a direct and indirect cost, a variable and fixed cost, a value-adding and non-value-adding cost, and a product and period cost. Also give examples of the three elements of product cost: direct materials, direct labor, and manufacturing overhead.

LO2 Identification of a
LO3 Manufacturing Company's Costs

include a golf course, a soccer field, jogging and bike paths, and tennis, basketball, and volleyball courts. Maintenance includes gardening (watering, planting, mowing, trimming, removing debris, etc.) and land improvements (e.g., repairing or replacing damaged or worn concrete and gravel areas).

Early in January 20x8, you receive a memo from the president of Latchey requesting information about the cost of operating your department for the last twelve months. She has received a bid from Xeriscape Landscapes, Inc., to perform the gardening activities you now perform. You are to prepare a cost report that will help her decide whether to keep gardening activities within the company or to outsource the work.

1. Before preparing your report, answer the following questions:
   a. What kinds of information do you need about your department?
   b. Why is this information relevant?
   c. Where would you go to obtain this information (sources)?
   d. When would you want to obtain this information?
2. Draft a report showing only headings and line items that best communicate the costs of your department. How would you change your report if the president asked you to reduce the costs of operating your department?
3. One of your department's cost accounts is the Maintenance Expense, Garden Equipment account.
   a. Is this a direct or indirect cost?
   b. Is it a product or period cost?
   c. Is it a variable or fixed cost?
   d. Does the activity add value to the provision of insurance services?
   e. Is it a budgeted or actual cost in your report?

International Company

MRA 3.
LO5 Management Information Needs

The H&W Pharmaceuticals Corporation manufactures most of its three pharmaceutical products in Indonesia. Inventory balances for April 20x8 are as follows:

	April 30	March 31
Materials Inventory	$228,100	$258,400
Work in Process Inventory	127,200	138,800
Finished Goods Inventory	114,100	111,700

During April, purchases of direct materials, which include natural materials, basic organic compounds, catalysts, and suspension agents, totaled $612,600. Direct labor costs were $160,000, and actual manufacturing overhead costs were $303,500. Sales of the company's three products for April totaled $2,188,400. General and administrative expenses were $362,000.

1. Prepare a statement of cost of goods manufactured and an income statement through operating income for the month ended April 30.
2. Why don't the total manufacturing costs equal the cost of goods manufactured?
3. What additional information would you need to determine the profitability of each of the three product lines?
4. Indicate whether each of the following is a product cost or a period cost:
   a. Import duties for suspension agent materials
   b. Shipping expenses to deliver manufactured products to the United States
   c. Rent for manufacturing facilities in Jakarta
   d. Salary of the American production-line manager working at the Indonesian manufacturing facilities
   e. Training costs for an Indonesian accountant

Excel Spreadsheet Analysis

MRA 4.
LO6 LO7 LO8 Allocation of Manufacturing Overhead: Traditional and Activity-Based Costing Methods

Refer to P 8 in this chapter. Assume that Oz Parson, the controller of Sea Scout, Inc., has received some additional information from the production manager, Parvin Hrinda. Hrinda reported that robotic equipment has been installed on the factory floor to increase productivity. As a result, direct labor hours per unit will decrease by 20 percent. Depreciation and other machine costs for the robots will increase total manufacturing

Tarbox Manufacturing Company
Income Statements
For the Years Ended December 31, 20x7 and 20x6

	20x7		20x6	
Sales		$2,942,960		$3,096,220
Cost of goods sold				
Finished goods inventory, beginning	$ 142,640		$ 184,820	
Cost of goods manufactured	2,040,275		1,997,490	
Total cost of finished goods available for sale	$2,182,915		$2,182,310	
Less finished goods inventory, ending	186,630		142,640	
Cost of goods sold		1,996,285		2,039,670
Gross margin		$ 946,675		$1,056,550
Selling and administrative expenses				
Sales salaries and commission expense	$ 394,840		$ 329,480	
Advertising expense	116,110		194,290	
Other selling expenses	82,680		72,930	
Administrative expenses	242,600		195,530	
Total selling and administrative expenses		836,230		792,230
Income from operations		$ 110,445		$ 264,320
Other revenues and expenses				
Interest expense		54,160		56,815
Income before income taxes		$ 56,285		$ 207,505
Income taxes expense		19,137		87,586
Net income		$ 37,148		$ 119,919

You have been asked to comment on why Tarbox's profitability has deteriorated.

1. In preparing your comments, compute the following ratios for each year:
   a. Ratios of cost of direct materials used to total manufacturing costs, direct labor to total manufacturing costs, and total manufacturing overhead to total manufacturing costs. (Round to one decimal place.)
   b. Ratios of sales salaries and commission expense, advertising expense, other selling expenses, administrative expenses, and total selling and administrative expenses to sales. (Round to one decimal place.)
   c. Ratios of gross margin to sales and net income to sales. (Round to one decimal place.)
2. From your evaluation of the ratios computed in 1, state the probable causes of the decline in net income.
3. What other factors or ratios do you believe should be considered in determining the cause of the company's decreased income?

Formulating Management Reports

MRA 2.
LO2 Management Decision About a
LO9 Supporting Service Function

As the manager of grounds maintenance for Latchey, a large insurance company in Missouri, you are responsible for maintaining the grounds surrounding the company's three buildings, the six entrances to the property, and the recreational facilities, which

3. Industry averages for markup rates are as follows:

Equipment	30%	Medications	50%
Doctors' care	50	Medical supplies	50
Special nursing care	40	Room rental	30
Regular nursing care	50	Food and services	25

Using these rates, compute the billing per patient day. (Round answers to the nearest whole dollars.)

4. Based on your findings in **2** and **3**, which billing procedure would you recommend to the hospital's director? Why? Be prepared to discuss your response.

MANAGERIAL REPORTING AND ANALYSIS CASES

Interpreting Management Reports

MRA 1. Tarbox Manufacturing Company makes sheet metal products for heating and air conditioning installations. For the past several years, the company's income has been declining. Its statements of cost of goods manufactured and income statements for 20x7 and 20x6 follow.

LO5 Financial Performance Measures

Tarbox Manufacturing Company
Statements of Cost of Goods Manufactured
For the Years Ended December 31, 20x7 and 20x6

	20x7		20x6	
Direct materials used				
Materials inventory, beginning	$ 91,240		$ 93,560	
Direct materials purchased (net)	987,640		959,940	
Cost of direct materials available for use	$1,078,880		$1,053,500	
Less materials inventory, ending	95,020		91,240	
Cost of direct materials used		$ 983,860		$ 962,260
Direct labor		571,410		579,720
Manufacturing overhead				
Indirect labor	$ 182,660		$ 171,980	
Power	34,990		32,550	
Insurance	22,430		18,530	
Supervision	125,330		120,050	
Depreciation	75,730		72,720	
Other manufacturing costs	41,740		36,280	
Total manufacturing overhead		482,880		452,110
Total manufacturing costs		$2,038,150		$1,994,090
Add work in process inventory, beginning		148,875		152,275
Total cost of work in process during the period		$2,187,025		$2,146,365
Less work in process inventory, ending		146,750		148,875
Cost of goods manufactured		$2,040,275		$1,997,490

Ethical Dilemma

LO9 Preventing Pollution and the Costs of Waste Disposal

SD 3. Lake Weir Power Plant provides power to a metropolitan area of 4 million people. Sundeep Guliani, the plant's controller, has just returned from a conference on the Environmental Protection Agency's regulations concerning pollution prevention. She is meeting with Alton Guy, the president of the company, to discuss the impact of the EPA's regulations on the plant.

"Alton, I'm really concerned. We haven't been monitoring the disposal of the radioactive material we send to the Willis Disposal Plant. If Willis is disposing of our waste material improperly, we could be sued," said Guliani. "We also haven't been recording the costs of the waste as part of our product cost. Ignoring those costs will have a negative impact on our decision about the next rate hike."

"Sundeep, don't worry. I don't think we need to concern ourselves with the waste we send to Willis. We pay them to dispose of it. They take it off of our hands, and it's their responsibility to manage its disposal. As for the cost of waste disposal, I think we would have a hard time justifying a rate increase based on a requirement to record the full cost of waste as a cost of producing power. Let's just forget about waste and its disposal as a component of our power cost. We can get our rate increase without mentioning waste disposal," replied Guy.

What responsibility does Lake Weir Power Plant have to monitor the condition of the waste at the Willis Disposal Plant? Should Guliani take Guy's advice to ignore waste disposal costs in calculating the cost of power? Be prepared to discuss your response.

Research Activity

LO2 Cost Classifications

SD 4. Visit a local fast-food restaurant. Observe all aspects of the operation and take notes on the entire process. Describe the procedures used to take, process, and fill an order and deliver the food to the customer. Based on your observations, make a list of the costs incurred by the owner. Then create a table similar to Table 1 in the text, in which you classify the costs you have identified by their traceability (direct or indirect), cost behavior (variable or fixed), value attribute (value-adding or nonvalue-adding), and implications for financial reporting (product or period costs). Bring your notes and your table to class and be prepared to discuss your findings.

Group Activity: Divide the class into groups and ask them to discuss their findings. Then ask a person from each group to summarize his or her group's discussion.

Decision-Making Practice

LO9 Unit Costs in a Service Business

SD 5. Municipal Hospital relies heavily on cost data to keep its pricing structures in line with those of competitors. The hospital provides a wide range of services, including intensive care, intermediate care, and a neonatal nursery. Joo Young, the hospital's controller, is concerned about the profits generated by the 30-bed intensive care unit (ICU), so she is reviewing current billing procedures for that unit. The focus of her analysis is the hospital's billing per ICU patient day. This billing equals the per diem cost of intensive care plus a 40 percent markup to cover other operating costs and generate a profit. ICU patient costs include the following:

Doctors' care	2 hours per day @ $360 per hour (actual)
Special nursing care	4 hours per day @ $85 per hour (actual)
Regular nursing care	24 hours per day @ $28 per hour (average)
Medications	$237 per day (average)
Medical supplies	$134 per day (average)
Room rental	$350 per day (average)
Food and services	$140 per day (average)

One other significant ICU cost is equipment, which is about $185,000 per room. Young has determined that the cost per patient day for the equipment is $179.

Wiley Dix, the hospital director, has asked Young to compare the current billing procedure with another that uses industry averages to determine the billing per patient day.

1. Compute the cost per patient per day.
2. Compute the billing per patient day using the hospital's existing markup rate. (Round answers to whole dollars.)

Activity Pool	Estimated Manufacturing Overhead Cost
Setup	$ 70,000
Inspection	20,000
Engineering	50,000
Assembly	80,000
Total	$220,000

Cost Driver	Rigger II Cost Driver Level	BioScout Cost Driver Level	Total Cost Driver Level
Number of setups	250	450	700
Number of inspections	150	350	500
Engineering hours	600	1,400	2,000
Machine hours	5,000	5,000	10,000

REQUIRED

1. Use activity-based costing to do the following:
    a. Calculate the activity cost rate for each activity pool.
    b. Compute the overhead costs applied to each product line by activity pool and in total.
    c. Calculate the product unit cost for each product line.
2. What differences in the costs assigned to the two product lines resulted from the shift to activity-based costing?

SKILLS DEVELOPMENT CASES

Conceptual Analysis

SD 1.
LO1 Comparison of Costs in
LO2 Different Types of Businesses

H & R Block <www.hrblock.com> is a service company that prepares tax returns; Borders <www.bordersstores.com> is a retail company that sells books and CDs; Indian Motorcycle Corporation <www.indianmotorcycle.com> is a manufacturing company that makes motorcycles. Show that you understand how these companies differ by giving for each one an example of a direct and indirect cost, a variable and fixed cost, a value-adding and nonvalue-adding cost, and a product and period cost. Discuss the use of cost classifications in these three types of organizations.

SD 2.
LO6 Comparison of Approaches to
LO7 Developing Overhead Rates
LO8

Both Matos Company and Stubee Corporation use predetermined overhead rates for product costing, inventory valuation, and sales quotations. The two businesses are about the same size, and they compete in the corrugated box industry. Because the overhead rate is an estimated measure, Matos Company's management believes that the controller's department should spend little effort in developing it. The company computes the rate annually based on an analysis of the previous year's costs. No one monitors its accuracy during the year. Stubee Corporation takes a different approach. One person in the controller's office is responsible for developing overhead rates on a monthly basis. All cost estimates are checked carefully to make sure they are realistic. Accuracy checks are done routinely at the end of each month, and forecasts of changes in business activity are taken into account.

Assume that Cooke Corporation, an East Coast manufacturer of corrugated boxes, has hired you as a consultant. Asimina Hiona, Cooke's controller, wants you to recommend the best method of developing overhead rates. Based on your knowledge of Matos's and Stubee's practices, write a memo to Hiona that answers the following questions:

1. What are the advantages and disadvantages of Matos's and Stubee's approaches to developing overhead rates?
2. Which company has taken the more cost-effective approach to developing overhead rates? Defend your answer.
3. Is an accurate overhead rate most important for product costing, inventory valuation, or sales quotations? Why?
4. What is activity-based costing (ABC)? Would it be better than the two approaches discussed above? Explain.

4. At what point during 20x6 was the manufacturing overhead rate computed? When was it applied? Finally, when was underapplied or overapplied overhead determined and the Cost of Goods Sold account adjusted to reflect actual costs?

P 7. Fraser Products, Inc., which produces fax machines for wholesale distributors in the Pacific Northwest, has just completed packaging an order from Kent Company for 150 Model 14 fax machines. Fraser recently switched from a traditional system of allocating costs to an activity-based costing system. Before the Kent order is shipped, the controller wants a unit cost analysis comparing the amounts computed under the traditional costing system with those computed under the ABC system. Raw materials, purchased parts, and direct labor costs for the Kent order are as follows:

Cost of direct materials	$17,450.00	Direct labor hours	140
Cost of purchased parts	$14,800.00	Average direct labor pay rate	$16.50

Other operating costs are as follows:

Traditional costing data:
Manufacturing overhead costs were applied at a single, plant-wide overhead rate of 240 percent of direct labor dollars.

Activity-based costing data:

Activity	Cost Driver	Activity Cost Rate	Activity Usage for Kent Order
Engineering systems design	Engineering hours	$28.00 per engineering hour	18 engineering hours
Setup	Number of setups	$42.00 per setup	8 setups
Parts production	Machine hours	$37.50 per machine hour	84 machine hours
Assembly	Assembly hours	$44.00 per assembly hour	36 assembly hours
Packaging	Packaging hours	$28.50 per packaging hour	28 packaging hours
Building occupancy	Machine hours	$10.40 per machine hour	84 machine hours

REQUIRED
1. Using the traditional costing approach, compute the total cost of the Kent order.
2. Using the activity-based costing approach, compute the total cost of the Kent order.
3. What difference in the amount of cost assigned to the Kent order resulted from the shift to activity-based costing? Does the use of activity-based costing guarantee cost reduction for every product?

P 8. Sea Scout, Inc., manufactures two types of underwater vehicles. Oil companies use the vehicle called Rigger II to examine offshore oil rigs, and marine biology research foundations use the BioScout to study coastlines. The company's San Diego factory is not fully automated and requires some direct labor. Using estimated manufacturing overhead costs of $220,000 and an estimated 16,000 hours of direct labor, Oz Parson, the company's controller, calculated a traditional overhead rate of $13.75 per direct labor hour. He used normal costing to calculate the product unit cost for both product lines, as shown in the following summary:

	Rigger II	BioScout
Product costs per unit		
Direct materials	$ 10,000.00	$12,000.00
Direct labor	1,450.00	1,600.00
Applied manufacturing overhead	412.50*	550.00†
Product unit cost	$11,862.50	$14,150.00
Units of production	400	100
Direct labor hours	12,000	4,000

*$13.75 per Direct Labor Hour × 30 Direct Labor Hours per Unit = $412.50
†$13.75 per Direct Labor Hour × 40 Direct Labor Hours per Unit = $550

Parson believes the product unit cost for the BioScout is too low. After carefully observing the production process, he has concluded that the BioScout requires much more attention than the Rigger II. Because of BioScout's more intricate design, it requires more production activities, and fewer subassemblies by suppliers are possible. He has therefore created four overhead activity pools, estimated the manufacturing overhead costs of the activity pools, selected a cost driver for each pool, and estimated the cost driver levels for each product line, as shown in the following summary:

Activity-based costing data:

Activity	Cost Driver	Activity Cost Rate	Activity Usage for Grater Order
Electrical engineering design	Engineering hours	$19.50 per engineering hour	32 engineering hours
Setup	Number of setups	$29.40 per setup	11 setups
Parts production	Machine hours	$26.30 per machine hour	134 machine hours
Product testing	Product testing hours	$32.80 per product testing hour	52 product testing hours
Packaging	Packaging hours	$17.50 per packaging hour	22 packaging hours
Building occupancy	Machine hours	$9.80 per machine hour	134 machine hours

REQUIRED
1. Using the traditional costing method, compute the total cost of the Grater order.
2. Using the activity-based costing method, compute the total cost of the Grater order.
3. What difference in the amount of cost assigned to the Grater order resulted from the shift to activity-based costing? Was Byte Computer Company's shift to activity-based costing a good management decision?

ALTERNATE PROBLEMS

P 6.
LO6 Allocation of Manufacturing
LO7 Overhead

Lund Products, Inc., uses a predetermined manufacturing overhead rate in its production, assembly, and testing departments. One rate is used for the entire company; it is based on machine hours. The rate is determined by analyzing data from the previous two years and projecting figures for the current year, adjusted for expected changes. Lise Jensen is about to compute the rate for 20x6 using the following data:

	20x4	20x5
Machine hours	38,000	41,800
Manufacturing overhead costs		
Indirect materials	$ 44,500	$ 57,850
Indirect labor	21,200	25,440
Supervision	37,800	41,580
Utilities	9,400	11,280
Labor-related costs	8,200	9,020
Depreciation, factory	9,800	10,780
Depreciation, machinery	22,700	27,240
Property taxes	2,400	2,880
Insurance	1,600	1,920
Miscellaneous manufacturing overhead	4,400	4,840
Total manufacturing overhead	$162,000	$192,830

In 20x6, the cost of indirect materials is expected to increase by 30 percent over the previous year. The cost of indirect labor, utilities, machinery depreciation, property taxes, and insurance is expected to increase by 20 percent. All other expenses are expected to increase by 10 percent. Machine hours for 20x6 are estimated at 45,980.

REQUIRED
1. Compute the projected costs and the manufacturing overhead rate for 20x6 using the information about expected cost increases. (Round your answer to three decimal places.)
2. During 20x6, Lund Products completed the following jobs using the machine hours shown:

Job No.	Machine Hours	Job No.	Machine Hours
H–142	7,840	H–201	10,680
H–164	5,260	H–218	12,310
H–175	8,100	H–304	2,460

Determine the amount of manufacturing overhead applied to each job. What was the total manufacturing overhead applied during 20x6? (Round answers to the nearest dollar.)

3. Actual manufacturing overhead costs for 20x6 were $234,485. Was overhead underapplied or overapplied in 20x6? By how much? Should the Cost of Goods Sold account be increased or decreased to reflect actual overhead costs?

2. Assuming that the following information reflects the results of operations for 20x6, calculate the (a) gross margin, (b) cost of goods sold, (c) cost of goods available for sale, and (d) cost of goods manufactured:

Operating income	$138,130
Operating expenses	53,670
Sales	500,000
Finished goods inventory, 12/31/x5	50,900

3. Does Mills Manufacturing use the periodic or perpetual inventory system?

P 4.

LO6 Allocation of Manufacturing
LO7 Overhead

Natural Cosmetics Company applies manufacturing overhead costs on the basis of machine hours. The overhead rate is computed by analyzing data from the previous two years and projecting figures for the current year, adjusted for expected changes. The controller prepared the overhead rate analysis for 20x7 using the following information:

	20x5	20x6
Machine hours	47,800	57,360
Manufacturing overhead costs		
Indirect labor	$ 18,100	$ 23,530
Employee benefits	22,000	28,600
Manufacturing supervision	16,800	18,480
Utilities	10,350	14,490
Factory insurance	6,500	7,800
Janitorial services	11,000	12,100
Depreciation, factory and machinery	17,750	21,300
Miscellaneous manufacturing overhead	5,750	7,475
Total manufacturing overhead	$108,250	$133,775

In 20x7, the cost of utilities is expected to increase by 40 percent over 20x6; the cost of indirect labor, employee benefits, and miscellaneous manufacturing overhead is expected to increase by 30 percent; the cost of insurance and depreciation is expected to increase by 20 percent; and the cost of supervision and janitorial services is expected to increase by 10 percent. Machine hours are expected to total 68,832.

REQUIRED
1. Compute the projected costs and the overhead rate for 20x7 using the information about expected cost increases. (Carry your answer to three decimal places.)
2. Jobs completed during 20x7 and the machine hours used were as follows:

Job No.	Machine Hours
2214	12,300
2215	14,200
2216	9,800
2217	13,600
2218	11,300
2219	8,100

Determine the amount of manufacturing overhead to be applied to each job and to total production during 20x7. (Round answers to whole dollars.)

3. Actual manufacturing overhead costs for 20x7 were $165,845. Was overhead underapplied or overapplied? By how much? Should the Cost of Goods Sold account be increased or decreased to reflect actual overhead costs?

P 5.

LO8 Activities and Activity-Based Costing

Byte Computer Company, a manufacturing organization, has been in operation for ten years. It has just completed an order that Grater, Ltd., placed for 80 computers. Byte recently shifted from a traditional system of allocating costs to an activity-based costing system. Simone Faure, Byte's controller, wants to know the impact that the ABC system had on the Grater order. Raw materials, purchased parts, and direct labor costs for the Grater order are as follows:

Cost of direct materials	$36,750.00	Direct labor hours	220
Cost of purchased parts	$21,300.00	Average direct labor pay rate	$15.25

Other operating costs are as follows:

Traditional costing data:
Manufacturing overhead costs were applied at a single, plant-wide overhead rate of 270 percent of direct labor dollars.

	Department	
	60	61
Direct materials used	$29,440	$3,920
Direct labor	6,800	2,560
Manufacturing overhead	7,360	4,800

REQUIRED
1. Compute the unit cost for each department.
2. Compute the total unit cost for the Milo Company order.
3. The selling price for this order was $14 per unit. Was the selling price adequate? List the assumptions and/or computations upon which you based your answer. What suggestions would you make to Carola Industries' management about the pricing of future orders?
4. Compute the prime costs and conversion costs per unit for each department.

P 2.
LO5 Statement of Cost of Goods Manufactured

Dillo Vineyards, a large winery in Texas, produces a full line of varietal wines. The company, whose fiscal year begins on November 1, has just completed a record-breaking year. Its inventory account balances on October 31, 20x7, were Materials Inventory, $1,803,800; Work in Process Inventory, $2,764,500; and Finished Goods Inventory, $1,883,200. On October 31, 20x6, the inventory account balances were Materials Inventory, $2,156,200; Work in Process Inventory, $3,371,000; and Finished Goods Inventory, $1,596,400.

During the 20x6–20x7 fiscal year, the company's purchases of direct materials totaled $6,750,000. Direct labor hours totaled 142,500, and the average labor rate was $8.20 per hour. The following manufacturing overhead costs were incurred during the year: depreciation, plant and equipment, $685,600; indirect labor, $207,300; property tax, plant and equipment, $94,200; plant maintenance, $83,700; small tools, $42,400; utilities, $96,500; and employee benefits, $76,100.

REQUIRED Prepare a statement of cost of goods manufactured for the fiscal year ended October 31, 20x7.

P 3.
LO5 A Manufacturing Organization's Balance Sheet

The following information is from the balance sheet of Mills Manufacturing Company:

	Debit	Credit
Cash	$ 34,000	
Accounts receivable	27,000	
Materials inventory, 12/31/x6	31,000	
Work in process inventory, 12/31/x6	47,900	
Finished goods inventory, 12/31/x6	54,800	
Production supplies	5,700	
Small tools	9,330	
Land	160,000	
Factory building	575,000	
Accumulated depreciation, factory building		$ 199,000
Factory equipment	310,000	
Accumulated depreciation, factory equipment		137,000
Patents	33,500	
Accounts payable		26,900
Insurance premiums payable		6,700
Income taxes payable		41,500
Mortgage payable		343,000
Common stock		200,000
Retained earnings, 12/31/x6		334,130
	$1,288,230	$1,288,230

REQUIRED
1. Manufacturing organizations use asset accounts that are not needed by merchandising organizations.
   a. List the titles of the asset accounts that are specifically related to manufacturing organizations.
   b. List the titles of the asset, liability, and equity accounts that you would see on the balance sheets of both manufacturing and merchandising organizations.

1. Compute the 20x6 overhead rate. (Carry your answer to three decimal places.)
2. Compute the overhead rate for 20x7. (Carry your answer to three decimal places.)

LO6 **E 12. Computation and Application**
LO7 **of Overhead Rate**

Compumatics specializes in the analysis and reporting of complex inventory costing projects. Materials costs are minimal, consisting entirely of operating supplies (DVDs, inventory sheets, and other recording tools). Labor is the highest single expense, totaling $693,000 for 75,000 hours of work in 20x8. Manufacturing overhead costs for 20x8 were $916,000 and were applied to specific jobs on the basis of labor hours worked. In 20x9, the company anticipates a 25 percent increase in manufacturing overhead costs. Labor costs will increase by $130,000, and the number of hours worked is expected to increase by 20 percent.

1. Determine the total amount of manufacturing overhead anticipated in 20x9.
2. Compute the manufacturing overhead rate for 20x9. (Round your answer to the nearest cent.)
3. During April 20x9, 11,980 labor hours were worked. Calculate the manufacturing overhead amount assigned to April production.

LO6 **E 13. Disposition of Overapplied**
LO7 **Overhead**

At the end of 20x9, Compumatics had compiled a total of 89,920 labor hours worked. The actual manufacturing overhead incurred was $1,143,400.

1. Using the overhead rate computed in **E 12**, determine the total amount of manufacturing overhead applied to operations during 20x9.
2. Compute the amount of overapplied overhead for the year.
3. Will the Cost of Goods Sold account be increased or decreased to correct the overapplication of manufacturing overhead?

LO7 **E 14. Activities and Activity-Based**
LO8 **Costing**

Zone Enterprises produces wireless components used in telecommunications equipment. One of the most important features of the company's new just-in-time production process is quality control. Initially, a traditional allocation method was used to assign the costs of quality control to products; all these costs were included in the plant's overhead cost pool and allocated to products based on direct labor dollars. Recently, the firm implemented an activity-based costing system. The activities, cost drivers, and rates for the quality control function are summarized below, along with cost allocation information from the traditional method. Also shown is information related to one order, Order HL14. Compute the quality control cost that would be assigned to the order under both the traditional method and the activity-based costing method.

Traditional costing method:
Quality control costs were assigned at a rate of 12 percent of direct labor dollars. Order HL14 was charged with $9,350 of direct labor costs.

Activity-based costing method:

Activity	Activity Cost Driver	Activity Usage for Cost Rate	Order HL14
Incoming materials inspection	Types of materials used	$17.50 per type of material used	17 types of materials
In-process inspection	Number of products	$.06 per product	2,400 products
Tool and gauge control	Number of processes per cell	$26.50 per process per cell	11 processes
Product certification	Per order	$94.00 per order	1 order

LO9 **E 15. Unit Costs in a Service Business**

Walden Green provides custom farming services to owners of five-acre wheat fields. In July, he earned $2,400 by cutting, turning, and baling 3,000 bales. In the same month, he incurred the following costs: gas, $150; tractor maintenance, $115; and labor, $600. His annual tractor depreciation was $1,500. What was Green's cost per bale? What was his revenue per bale? Should he increase the amount he charges for his services?

PROBLEMS

LO3 **P 1. Computation of Unit Cost**

Carola Industries, Inc., manufactures discs for several of the leading recording studios in the United States and Europe. Department 60 is responsible for the electronic circuitry within each disc. Department 61 applies the plastic-like surface to the discs and packages them for shipment. Carola recently produced 4,000 discs for the Milo Company. In fulfilling this order, the departments incurred the following costs:

Chapter 20 Cost Concepts and Cost Allocation

6. Sells services
7. Determines the cost of sales
8. Includes the cost of goods manufactured in calculating cost of goods sold
9. Includes the cost of purchases in calculating cost of goods sold

LO5 Missing Amounts— Manufacturing

E 9. Presented below are incomplete inventory and income statement data for Trevor Corporation. Determine the missing amounts.

	Cost of Goods Sold	Cost of Goods Manufactured	Beginning Finished Goods Inventory	Ending Finished Goods Inventory
1.	$ 10,000	$12,000	$ 1,000	?
2.	$140,000	?	$45,000	$60,000
3.	?	$89,000	$23,000	$20,000

LO5 Inventories, Cost of Goods Sold, and Net Income

E 10. The data presented below are for a retail organization and a manufacturing organization.

1. Fill in the missing data for the retail organization:

	First Quarter	Second Quarter	Third Quarter	Fourth Quarter
Sales	$9	$ e	$15	$ k
Gross margin	a	4	5	l
Ending merchandise inventory	5	f	5	m
Beginning merchandise inventory	4	g	h	5
Net cost of purchases	b	7	9	n
Operating income	3	2	i	2
Operating expenses	c	2	2	4
Cost of goods sold	5	6	j	11
Cost of goods available for sale	d	12	15	15

2. Fill in the missing data for the manufacturing organization:

	First Quarter	Second Quarter	Third Quarter	Fourth Quarter
Ending finished goods inventory	$a	$3	$h	$6
Cost of goods sold	6	3	5	l
Operating income	1	3	1	m
Cost of goods available for sale	8	d	10	13
Cost of goods manufactured	5	e	i	8
Gross margin	4	f	j	7
Operating expenses	3	g	5	6
Beginning finished goods inventory	b	2	3	n
Sales	c	10	k	14

LO6 Computation of Overhead Rate
LO7

E 11. The overhead costs that Lucca Industries, Inc., used to compute its overhead rate for 20x6 are as follows:

Indirect materials and supplies	$ 79,200
Repairs and maintenance	14,900
Outside service contracts	17,300
Indirect labor	79,100
Factory supervision	42,900
Depreciation, machinery	85,000
Factory insurance	8,200
Property taxes	6,500
Heat, light, and power	7,700
Miscellaneous manufacturing overhead	5,760
	$346,560

The allocation base for 20x6 was 45,600 total machine hours. In 20x7, all overhead costs except depreciation, property taxes, and miscellaneous manufacturing overhead are expected to increase by 10 percent. Depreciation should increase by 12 percent, and property taxes and miscellaneous manufacturing overhead are expected to increase by 20 percent. Plant capacity in terms of machine hours used will increase by 4,400 hours.

1. Compute the unit cost per bottle for materials, labor, and overhead.
2. How would you advise management regarding the price per bottle of wine?
3. Compute the prime costs per unit and the conversion costs per unit.

LO4 Documentation

E 4. Lisette Company manufactures music boxes. Seventy percent of its products are standard items produced in long production runs. The other 30 percent are special orders with specific requests for tunes. The latter cost from three to six times as much as the standard product because they require additional materials and labor.

Reza Seca, the controller, recently received a complaint memorandum from Iggy Paulo, the production supervisor, about the new network of source documents that was added to the existing cost accounting system. The new documents include a purchase request, a purchase order, a receiving report, and a materials request. Paulo claims that the forms create extra work and interrupt the normal flow of production.

Prepare a written memorandum from Reza Seca to Iggy Paulo that fully explains the purpose of each type of document.

LO4 Cost Flows and Inventory Accounts

E 5. For each of the following activities, identify the inventory account (Materials Inventory, Work in Process Inventory, Finished Goods Inventory), if any, that is affected. If an inventory account is affected, indicate whether the account balance will increase or decrease. (*Example:* Moved completed units to finished goods inventory. *Answer:* Increase Finished Goods Inventory; decrease Work in Process Inventory.) If no inventory account is affected, use "None of these" as your answer.

1. Moved materials requested by production
2. Sold units of product
3. Purchased and received direct materials for production
4. Used direct labor and manufacturing overhead in the production process
5. Received payment from customer
6. Purchased office supplies and paid cash
7. Paid monthly office rent

LO5 Statement of Cost of Goods Manufactured

E 6. During August 31, 20x5, Rao Company's purchases of direct materials totaled $139,000; direct labor for the month was 3,400 hours at $8.75 per hour. Rao also incurred the following manufacturing overhead costs: utilities, $5,870; supervision, $16,600; indirect materials, $6,750; depreciation, $6,200; insurance, $1,830; and miscellaneous, $1,100.

Inventory accounts on July 31 were as follows: Materials Inventory, $48,600; Work in Process Inventory, $54,250; and Finished Goods Inventory, $38,500. Inventory accounts on August 31 were as follows: Materials Inventory, $50,100; Work in Process Inventory, $48,400; and Finished Goods Inventory, $37,450.

From the information given, prepare a statement of cost of goods manufactured.

LO5 Statement of Cost of Goods Manufactured and Cost of Goods Sold

E 7. Treetec Corp. makes irrigation sprinkler systems for tree nurseries. Rama Shih, Treetec's new controller, can find only the following partial information for the past year:

	Oak Division	Loblolly Division	Maple Division	Spruce Division
Direct materials used	$3	$ 7	$ g	$ 8
Total manufacturing costs	6	d	h	14
Manufacturing overhead	1	3	2	j
Direct labor	a	6	4	4
Ending work in process inventory	b	3	2	5
Cost of goods manufactured	7	20	12	k
Beginning work in process inventory	2	e	3	l
Ending finished goods inventory	2	6	i	9
Beginning finished goods inventory	3	f	5	7
Cost of goods sold	c	18	13	9

Using the information given, compute the unknown values. List the accounts in the proper order and show subtotals and totals as appropriate.

LO5 Characteristics of Organizations

E 8. Indicate whether each of the following is typical of a service organization (SER), retail organization (RET), or manufacturing organization (MANF):

1. Maintains only one balance sheet inventory account
2. Maintains no balance sheet inventory accounts
3. Maintains three balance sheet inventory accounts
4. Purchases products ready for resale
5. Designs and makes products for sale

Chapter 20 Cost Concepts and Cost Allocation

LO9 Unit Costs in a Service Business

SE 12. Fickle Picking Services provides inexpensive, high-quality labor for farmers growing vegetable and fruit crops. In September, Fickle Picking Services paid laborers $4,000 to harvest 500 acres of apples. The company incurred overhead costs of $2,400 for apple-picking services in September. This amount included the costs of transporting the laborers to the orchards; of providing facilities, food, and beverages for the laborers; and of scheduling, billing, and collecting from the farmers. Of this amount, 50 percent was related to picking apples. Compute the cost per acre to pick apples.

EXERCISES

LO1 The Management Cycle and Operating Costs

E 1. Indicate whether each of the following activities takes place during the planning (P), executing (E), reviewing (RV), or reporting (RP) stage of the management cycle:
1. Changing regular price to clearance price
2. Communicating results to appropriate personnel
3. Preparing budgets of operating costs
4. Comparing estimated and actual costs to determine variances

LO2 Cost Classifications

E 2. Indicate whether each of the following costs for a bicycle manufacturer is a direct or indirect cost of the bicycle, a variable or fixed cost, a value-adding or nonvalue-adding cost, and a product or period cost:

	Cost Classification			
	Direct or Indirect	Variable or Fixed	Value-adding or Nonvalue-adding	Product or Period
Example: Bicycle tire	Direct	Variable	Value-adding	Product

1. Depreciation on office computer
2. Labor to assemble bicycle
3. Labor to inspect bicycle
4. Internal auditor's salary
5. Lubricant for wheels

LO3 Unit Cost Determination

E 3. The Pattia Winery is one of the finest wineries in the country. One of its famous products is a red wine called Old Vines. Recently, management has become concerned about the increasing cost of making Old Vines and needs to determine if the current selling price of $10 per bottle is adequate. The winery wants to achieve a 25 percent gross profit on the sale of each bottle. The following information is given to you for analysis:

Batch size	10,550 bottles
Costs	
Direct materials	
Olen Millot grapes	$22,155
Chancellor grapes	9,495
Bottles	5,275
Total direct materials costs	$36,925
Direct labor	
Pickers/loaders	2,110
Crusher	422
Processors	8,440
Bottler	$13,293
Total direct labor costs	$24,265
Manufacturing overhead	
Depreciation, equipment	2,743
Depreciation, building	5,275
Utilities	1,055
Indirect labor	6,330
Supervision	7,385
Supplies	9,917
Repairs	1,477
Miscellaneous	633
Total manufacturing overhead costs	$34,815
Total production costs	$96,005

Chapter Assignments

LO3 **SE 3. Computation of Product Unit Cost**

What is the product unit cost for Job 14, which consists of 300 units and has total manufacturing costs of direct materials, $4,500; direct labor, $7,500; and manufacturing overhead, $3,600? What are the prime costs and conversion costs per unit?

LO4 **SE 4. Cost Flow in a Manufacturing Organization**

Given the following information, compute the ending balances of the Materials Inventory, Work in Process Inventory, and Finished Goods Inventory accounts:

Materials Inventory, beginning balance	$ 23,000
Work in Process Inventory, beginning balance	25,750
Finished Goods Inventory, beginning balance	38,000
Direct materials purchased	85,000
Direct materials placed into production	74,000
Direct labor costs	97,000
Manufacturing overhead costs	35,000
Cost of goods completed	123,000
Cost of goods sold	93,375

LO4 **SE 5. Document Flows in a Manufacturing Organization**

Identify the document needed to support each of the following activities in a manufacturing organization:

1. Placing an order for direct materials with a supplier
2. Recording direct labor time at the beginning and end of each work shift
3. Receiving direct materials at the shipping dock
4. Recording the costs of a specific job requiring direct materials, direct labor, and overhead
5. Issuing direct materials into production
6. Billing the customer for a completed order
7. Fulfilling a request from the Production Scheduling Department for the purchase of direct materials

LO5 **SE 6. Income Statement for a Manufacturing Organization**

Using the following information from Hakim Company, prepare an income statement through operating income for 20x6:

Sales	$900,000
Finished goods inventory, December 31, 20x5	45,000
Cost of goods manufactured	585,000
Finished goods inventory, December 31, 20x6	60,000
Operating expenses	275,000

LO5 **SE 7. Comparison of Income Statement Formats**

Indicate whether each of these equations applies to a service organization (SER), retail organization (RET), or manufacturing organization (MANF):

1. Cost of Goods Sold = Beginning Merchandising Inventory + Net Cost of Purchases − Ending Merchandise Inventory
2. Cost of Sales = Net Cost of Services Sold
3. Cost of Goods Sold = Beginning Finished Goods Inventory + Cost of Goods Manufactured − Ending Finished Goods Inventory

LO6 **SE 8. Calculation of Underapplied or Overapplied Overhead**

At year end, records show that actual manufacturing overhead costs incurred were $25,870 and the amount of manufacturing overhead costs applied to production was $27,000. Identify the amount of under- or overapplied manufacturing overhead, and indicate whether the Cost of Goods Sold account should be increased or decreased to reflect actual manufacturing overhead costs.

LO6 **LO7** **SE 9. Computation of Overhead Rate**

Compute the overhead rate per service request for the Maintenance Department if estimated overhead costs are $18,290 and the number of estimated service requests is 3,100.

LO6 **LO7** **SE 10. Allocation of Manufacturing Overhead to Production**

Calculate the amount of manufacturing overhead costs applied to production if the predetermined overhead rate is $4 per direct labor hour and 1,200 direct labor hours were worked.

LO8 **SE 11. Activity-Based Costing and Cost Drivers**

Mazzola Clothiers Company relies on the information from its activity-based costing system when setting prices for its products. Compute ABC rates from the following estimated data for each of the activity centers:

Estimated Activity	Pool Amount	Cost Driver Level
Cutting/Stitching	$5,220,000	145,000 machine hours
Trimming/Packing	998,400	41,600 operator hours
Designing	1,187,500	62,500 designer hours

Chapter Assignments

BUILDING YOUR KNOWLEDGE FOUNDATION

QUESTIONS

1. How do managers use information about costs?
2. Why do managers use different classifications of costs?
3. What is the difference between a direct cost and an indirect cost?
4. What is the difference between a value-adding cost and a nonvalue-adding cost?
5. What are product costs and period costs?
6. What three kinds of costs are included in a product's cost?
7. What characteristics identify a cost as part of manufacturing overhead?
8. What is the difference between actual costing and normal costing?
9. What is the difference between prime costs and conversion costs?
10. Identify and describe the inventory accounts used by a manufacturing company.
11. What does the term *manufacturing cost flow* mean?
12. How do total manufacturing costs differ from the cost of goods manufactured?
13. How do service, retail, and manufacturing organizations differ, and how do these differences affect accounting for inventories?
14. How is the cost of goods manufactured used in computing the cost of goods sold?
15. What is cost allocation?
16. Explain the relationship among cost objects, cost pools, and cost drivers. Give an example of each.
17. List the four steps involved in allocating manufacturing overhead costs. Briefly explain each step.
18. How does traditional overhead allocation differ from ABC overhead allocation?
19. What allocation measure does ABC use to relate an activity pool to a cost object? Explain.
20. "The concept of product costs is not applicable to service organizations." Is this statement correct? Defend your answer.

SHORT EXERCISES

LO2 Cost Classifications

SE 1. Indicate whether each of the following is a direct (D) or indirect (ID) cost and a variable (V) or fixed (F) cost. Also indicate whether each adds value (VA) or does not add value (NVA) to the product and whether each is a product cost (PD), period cost (PER), or neither (N).

1. Production supervisor's salary
2. Sales commission
3. Wages of a production-line worker

LO3 Elements of Manufacturing Costs

SE 2. Daisy Luna, the bookkeeper at Candlelight, Inc., must group the costs of manufacturing candles. Indicate whether each of the following items should be classified as direct materials (DM), direct labor (DL), manufacturing overhead (MO), or none of these (N). Also indicate whether each is a prime cost (PC), conversion cost (CC), or neither (N).

1. Depreciation of the cost of vats to hold melted wax
2. Cost of wax
3. Rent on the factory where candles are made
4. Cost of George's time to dip the wicks into the wax
5. Cost of coloring for candles
6. Cost of Ray's time to design candles for Halloween
7. Sam's commission to sell candles to Candles Plus

Chapter Review

Account	Balance
Plant Supervision	$ 42,500
Factory Insurance	8,100
Utilities, Factory	29,220
Depreciation, Factory Building	46,200
Depreciation, Factory Equipment	62,800
Factory Security	9,460
Factory Repair and Maintenance	14,980
Selling and Administrative Expenses	76,480
Materials Inventory, December 31, 20x5	26,490
Work in Process Inventory, December 31, 20x5	101,640
Finished Goods Inventory, December 31, 20x5	148,290
Materials Inventory, December 31, 20x6	24,910
Work in Process Inventory, December 31, 20x6	100,400
Finished Goods Inventory, December 31, 20x6	141,100

REQUIRED

1. Compute the cost of materials used during the year.
2. Given the cost of materials used, compute the total manufacturing costs for the year.
3. Given the total manufacturing costs for the year, compute the cost of goods manufactured during the year.
4. If 13,397 units were manufactured during the year, what was the actual product unit cost? (Round your answer to two decimal places.)

ANSWER TO REVIEW PROBLEM

1. Cost of materials used:

Materials inventory, December 31, 20x5		$ 26,490
Add direct materials purchased (net)		361,920
Cost of materials available for use		$388,410
Less materials inventory, December 31, 20x6		24,910
Cost of materials used		$363,500

2. Total manufacturing costs:

Cost of materials used		$363,500
Add direct labor costs		99,085
Add total manufacturing overhead costs		
Plant supervision	$ 42,500	
Indirect labor	126,750	
Factory insurance	8,100	
Utilities, factory	29,220	
Depreciation, factory building	46,200	
Depreciation, factory equipment	62,800	
Factory security	9,460	
Factory repair and maintenance	14,980	
Total manufacturing overhead costs		340,010
Total manufacturing costs		$802,595

3. Cost of goods manufactured:

Total manufacturing costs	$802,595
Add work in process inventory, December 31, 20x5	101,640
Total cost of work in process during the year	$904,235
Less work in process inventory, December 31, 20x6	100,400
Cost of goods manufactured	$803,835

4. Actual product unit cost:

$$\frac{\text{Cost of Goods Manufactured}}{\text{Number of Units Manufactured}} = \frac{\$803,835}{13,397} = \$60.00$$

- **LO3 Manufacturing overhead costs:** Production-related costs that cannot be practically or conveniently traced to an end product. Also called *factory overhead, factory burden,* or *indirect manufacturing costs.*

- **LO4 Materials Inventory account:** An inventory account that shows the balance of the cost of unused materials.

- **LO2 Nonvalue-adding cost:** The cost of an activity that adds cost to a product or service but does not increase its market value.

- **LO3 Normal costing:** A method of cost measurement that combines the actual direct costs of materials and labor with estimated manufacturing overhead costs to determine a product unit cost.

- **LO6 Overapplied overhead costs:** The amount that overhead costs applied using the predetermined overhead rate exceed the actual overhead costs for the accounting period.

- **LO2 Period costs:** The costs of resources used during an accounting period and not assigned to products. Also called *noninventoriable costs.*

- **LO6 Predetermined overhead rate:** The rate calculated before an accounting period begins by dividing the cost pool of total estimated overhead costs by the total estimated cost driver for that pool.

- **LO3 Prime costs:** The primary costs of production; the sum of direct materials costs and direct labor costs.

- **LO2 Product costs:** The costs assigned to inventory, which include the costs of direct materials, direct labor, and manufacturing overhead. Also called *inventoriable costs.*

- **LO3 Product unit cost:** The cost of manufacturing a single unit of a product, computed either by dividing the total cost of direct materials, direct labor, and manufacturing overhead by the total number of units produced, or by determining the cost per unit for each element of the product cost and summing those per-unit costs.

- **LO3 Standard costing:** A method of cost measurement that uses the estimated costs of direct materials, direct labor, and manufacturing overhead to calculate a product unit cost.

- **LO5 Statement of cost of goods manufactured:** A formal statement summarizing the flow of all manufacturing costs incurred during an accounting period.

- **LO4 Total manufacturing costs:** The total costs of direct materials, direct labor, and manufacturing overhead incurred and transferred to Work in Process Inventory during an accounting period. Also called *current manufacturing costs.*

- **LO6 Underapplied overhead costs:** The amount that actual overhead costs exceed the overhead costs applied using the predetermined overhead rate for the accounting period.

- **LO2 Value-adding cost:** The cost of an activity that increases the market value of a product or service.

- **LO2 Variable cost:** A cost that changes in direct proportion to a change in productive output (or any other measure of volume).

- **LO4 Work in Process Inventory account:** An inventory account used to record the manufacturing costs incurred and assigned to partially completed units of product.

REVIEW PROBLEM

Calculating Cost of Goods Manufactured: Three Fundamental Steps

LO3
LO4
LO5
Nikita Company requires its controller to prepare not only a year-end balance sheet and income statement, but also a statement of cost of goods manufactured. During 20x6, Nikita purchased $361,920 of direct materials. The company's direct labor costs for the year were $99,085 (10,430 hours at $9.50 per hour); its indirect labor costs totaled $126,750 (20,280 hours at $6.25 per hour). Account balances for 20x6 were as follows:

Indirect monthly overhead costs	
Chief loan officer's salary	$ 4,500
Telephone	750
Depreciation	5,750
Legal advice	2,460
Customer relations	640
Credit check function	1,980
Internal audit function	2,400
Utilities	1,690
Clerical personnel	3,880
Miscellaneous	1,050
Total overhead costs	$25,100

The Loan Department usually processes 100 home-loan applications each month.

The Loan Department performs several other functions in addition to processing home-loan applications. Roughly one-half of the department is involved in loan collection. After determining how many of the processed loans were not home loans, you conclude that only 25 percent of the overhead costs of the Loan Department were applicable to the processing of home-loan applications. The cost of processing one home-loan application can be computed as follows:

Direct professional labor cost:		
$12,000 ÷ 100	$120.00	
Service overhead cost:		
$25,100 × 25% ÷ 100	62.75	
Total processing cost per loan	$182.75	

Finally, you conclude that the chief loan officer was correct; the present fee does not cover the current costs of processing a typical home-loan application. However, doubling the loan fee seems too extreme. To allow for a profit margin, the loan fee could be raised to $225 or $250.

✓ Check out ACE for a Review Quiz at http://accounting.college.hmco.com/students.

Chapter Review

REVIEW OF LEARNING OBJECTIVES

LO1 Describe how managers use information about costs in the management cycle.

During the management cycle, managers in manufacturing, retail, and service organizations use information about operating costs and product or service costs to prepare budgets, make pricing and other decisions, calculate variances between estimated and actual costs, and report results.

LO2 Explain how managers classify costs and how they use these cost classifications.

A single cost can be classified as a direct or indirect cost, a variable or fixed cost, a value-adding or nonvalue-adding cost, and a product or period cost. These cost classifications enable managers to control costs by tracing them to cost objects, to calculate the number of units that must be sold to obtain a certain level of profit, to identify the costs of activities that do and do not add value to a product or service, and to prepare financial statements for parties outside the organization.

LO3 Define and give examples of the three elements of product cost and compute the unit cost of a product.

Direct materials costs are the costs of materials used in making a product that can be conveniently and economically traced to specific product units. Direct labor costs include all labor costs needed to make a product that can be conveniently and economically traced to specific product units. All other production-related costs are classified

Kee presented the following information to Olga Santee:

	Plain	Nut
Product unit cost: Traditional approach with one manufacturing overhead cost pool	$.445	$.520
Product unit cost: ABC with four activity pools	.391	.628
Difference: decrease (increase)	$.054	($.108)

Because ABC assigned more costs to the product line that used more resources, it provided a more accurate estimate of product unit cost. The increased information about the production requirements for the nut candy bar line that went into the ABC calculation of product unit cost also provided valuable insights. Santee found that the nut candy bars cost more to manufacture because the changes in the ingredients require more setups and machine hours and because more inspections are needed to test the candy quality. Because the nut candy bar line requires more production and production-related activities, its product unit cost is higher. Based on this analysis, Santee may want to reconsider some of her decisions about the manufacture and sale of these two product lines.

FOCUS ON BUSINESS PRACTICE

How Costly Is Television Talent?

If salary is measured per unit, your perspective on the cost of television talent may change. Compare the salaries and cost per viewer (salary divided by number of viewers per season) for the following television personalities in 2002. In your opinion, who is the highest paid talent?[5]

	2002 Salary	Season Viewers	Cost per Viewer
Larry King	$7 million	1.3 million	$5.39
Conan O'Brien	$8 million	2.55 million	$3.14
Katie Couric	$13 million	6.1 million	$2.13
David Letterman	$16 million	4.35 million	$3.68

✓ Check out ACE for a Review Quiz at http://accounting.college.hmco.com/students.

COST ALLOCATION IN SERVICE ORGANIZATIONS

LO9 Apply costing concepts to a service organization.

RELATED TEXT ASSIGNMENTS
Q: 20
SE: 12
E: 15
SD: 3, 5
MRA: 2

● **STOP AND THINK!**
How should a manager in a service organization handle materials costs?

Any materials costs in a service organization would be for supplies used in providing services. Because these are indirect materials costs, the manager should include them in service overhead. ■

Processing loans, representing people in courts of law, selling insurance policies, and computing people's income taxes are typical of the services performed by professionals in many service organizations. Like other services, these are labor-intensive processes supported by indirect labor and overhead costs.

Because no products are manufactured in the course of providing services, service organizations have no direct materials costs. As noted, however, they do have both labor and overhead costs, which must be included when computing the cost of providing a service. The most important cost in a service organization is the direct cost of professional labor, and the usual standard is applicable; that is, the direct labor cost must be traceable to the service rendered. The indirect costs incurred in performing a service are similar to those incurred in manufacturing a product. They are classified as service overhead and, along with professional labor costs, are considered service costs rather than period costs. Just as product costs appear on manufacturers' income statements as cost of goods sold, service costs appear on service organizations' income statements as cost of sales.

To illustrate how overhead costs are applied in service organizations, assume that the Loan Department of the Campus Bank wants to determine the total costs incurred in processing a typical loan application. Its policy for the past five years has been to charge a $150 fee for processing a home-loan application. Jerome Hill, the chief loan officer, thinks the fee is far too low. Because of the way operating costs have soared in the past five years, he proposes that the fee be doubled. The bank has asked you to compute the cost of processing a typical home-loan application and has given you the following information about its processing of loan applications:

Direct professional labor

Loan processors' monthly salaries:
4 people at $3,000 each $12,000

TABLE 4. Allocating Manufacturing Overhead Costs and Calculating Product Unit Cost: ABC Approach

Step 1. Calculate activity cost rate for cost pool:

$$\frac{\text{Estimated Total Activity Costs}}{\text{Estimated Total Cost Driver Level}} = \text{Activity Cost Rate for Cost Pool}$$

Activity	Estimated Total Activity Costs	Estimated Total Cost Driver Level	Activity Cost Rate for Cost Pool
Setup	$ 7,000	700 setups	$7,000 ÷ 700 = $10 per setup
Inspection	6,000	500 inspections	$6,000 ÷ 500 = $12 per inspection
Packaging	5,000	2,000 packaging hours	$5,000 ÷ 2,000 = $2.50 per packaging hour
Building	2,000	10,000 machine hours	$2,000 ÷ 10,000 = $.20 per machine hour
	$20,000		

Step 2. Apply predetermined activity cost rates to products:

	Plain Candy Bars	Nut Candy Bars
Activity Pool	Predetermined Overhead Rate × Actual Cost Driver Level = Cost Applied to Production	Predetermined Overhead Rate × Actual Cost Driver Level = Cost Applied to Production
Setup	$10 × 300 = $3,000	$10 × 400 = $4,000
Inspection	$12 × 150 = 1,800	$12 × 350 = 4,200
Packaging	$2.50 × 600 = 1,500	$2.50 × 1,400 = 3,500
Building	$.20 × 4,000 = 800	$.20 × 6,000 = 1,200
Total overhead applied	$7,100	$12,900
Applied overhead cost per unit: Cost Applied ÷ Number of Units	$7,100 ÷ 100,000 = $.071	$12,900 ÷ 50,000 = $.258

Product unit cost using normal costing:

	Plain Candy Bars	Nut Candy Bars
Product costs per unit:		
Direct materials	$.180	$.210
Direct labor	.140	.160
Applied manufacturing overhead	.071	.258
Product unit cost	$.391	$.628

head costs from the four activity pools to the product lines, Kee estimated that total manufacturing overhead costs of $7,100, or $.071 per bar ($7,100 ÷ 100,000 units), should be applied to the plain candy bar line and that $12,900, or $.258 per bar ($12,900 ÷ 50,000 units), should be applied to the nut candy bar line.

Kee also wanted to calculate the unit cost for each product line using normal costing. Her calculations appear at the bottom of Table 4. The product unit cost is $.391 for the plain line and $.628 for the nut line.

FIGURE 9
Using ABC to Assign Manufacturing Overhead Costs to Production

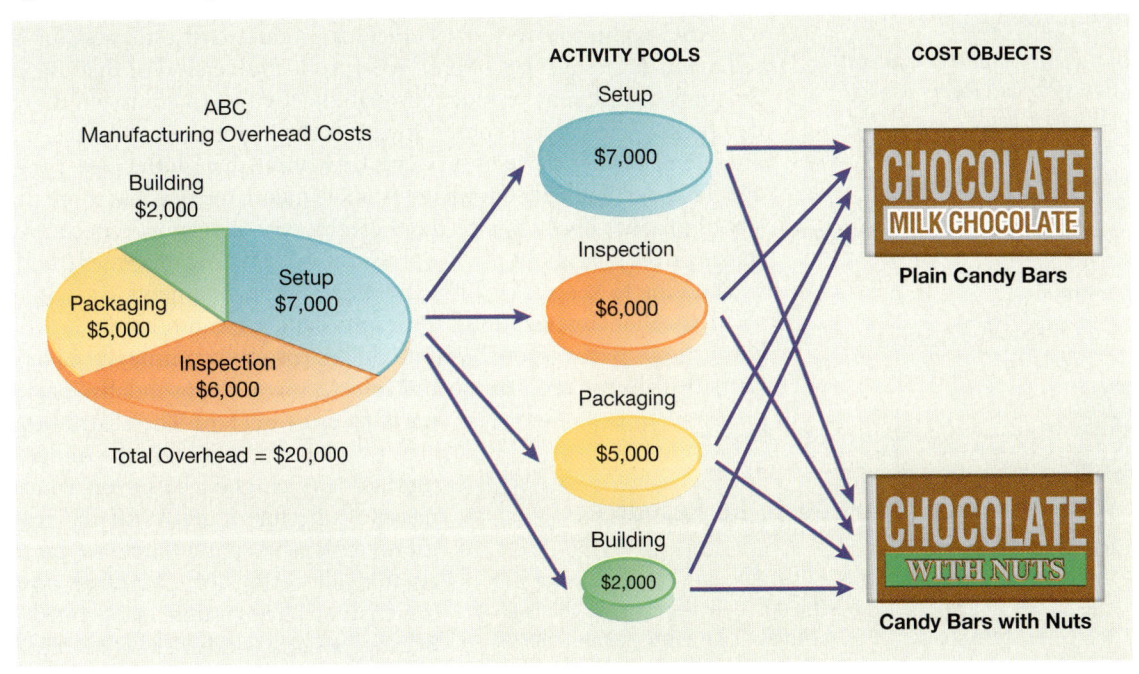

includes estimated total costs of $5,000 for indirect materials, indirect labor, and equipment depreciation. The last activity, building operations, includes estimated total overhead costs of $2,000 for building depreciation, maintenance, janitorial wages, property taxes, insurance, security, and all other costs not related to the first three activities.

After identifying the four activity pools, Kee selected a cost driver and estimated the cost driver level for each activity pool. The following schedule shows those amounts by product line and in total:

	Estimated Cost Driver Level		
Cost Driver	Plain	Nut	Total
Number of setups	300	400	700
Number of inspections	150	350	500
Packaging hours	600	1,400	2,000
Machine hours	4,000	6,000	10,000

KEY POINT: Under ABC, activity pools are allocated to cost objects using multiple cost drivers.

After identifying activity pools, estimated activity pool amounts, cost drivers, and estimated cost driver levels, Kee performed Step 1 of the overhead allocation process by calculating the activity cost rate for each activity pool. The activity cost rate is the estimated activity pool amount divided by the estimated cost driver level. Step 1 of Table 4 shows the activity cost rates to be $10 per setup, $12 per inspection, $2.50 per packaging hour, and $.20 per machine hour.

APPLYING THE OVERHEAD RATES

In Step 2, Kee applied manufacturing overhead to the two product lines using the cost driver level for each cost driver multiplied by the activity cost rate shown in the preceding schedule. Step 2 of Table 4 shows those calculations. For example, Kee applied $3,000 in setup costs ($10 × 300 setups) to the plain candy bar line and $4,000 ($10 × 400 setups) to the nut candy bar line. After applying the over-

● **STOP AND THINK!**
How many overhead cost pools are used in the ABC approach to cost allocation?

In the ABC approach to cost allocation, managers use as many cost pools as are needed for effective and efficient management of overhead costs. ■

www.tacobell.com

benefit of grouping manufacturing overhead costs into several smaller pools to obtain more accurate estimates of product costs is offset by the additional costs of measuring many different cost drivers.

ABC will improve the accuracy of product cost estimates for organizations that sell many different types of products (product diversity) or that use varying, significant amounts of different production-related activities to complete the products (process complexity). To remain competitive in today's global marketplace, many organizations are selling a wider range of products or services than in the past. For example, 20 years ago, Taco Bell had only 6 food items on its menu; today, it has more than 25. This diversity of product lines requires more careful cost allocation, especially when it comes to making decisions about pricing products, outsourcing processes to other organizations, or choosing to keep a food item or drop it from the menu.

For other organizations, some products are more complicated to manufacture, store, move, package, or ship than others (process complexity). For example, an auto parts distributor receives, stores, selects, moves, consolidates, packs, and ships auto parts to auto dealers. The distributor's greatest costs are overhead costs, which under the traditional method are assigned based on what it costs to purchase a part for resale. With the traditional method, more expensive parts, such as car radios, receive a greater allocation of overhead costs than do less expensive parts, such as windshields. However, because a glass windshield is more delicate than a car radio, it costs the distributor more to move, store, pack, and ship. If ABC were used, the cost of the windshield would increase to reflect a fairer allocation of the distributor's overhead costs. Thus, by assigning overhead costs based on the relative use of overhead resources, ABC would provide managers with better information for making decisions, such as pricing car radios, windshields, and other auto parts; choosing to discontinue selling windshields; or reducing the amount of storage space.

FOCUS ON BUSINESS ETHICS

What Can a Company Do to Be Resource-Responsible?

United Parcel Service <www.ups.com> has taken a proactive role in its commitment to efficient and responsible management of resources. UPS recycles computer paper, letter envelopes, and delivery notices, and it records delivery information electronically, which saves an estimated 30,000 trees annually. UPS also helps customers protect the environment by using packaging methods that prevent product damage and minimize waste and by operating a national recycling program for its customer's packaging materials. For example, Ethan Allen, Inc. <www.ethanallen.com>, a furniture maker and retailer, uses UPS's services to retrieve foam-sheet shipping material, which makes money for Ethan Allen in addition to reducing its disposal costs.[4]

PLANNING OVERHEAD RATES

As discussed earlier, Maya Kee, the accountant for Candy Company, Inc., calculated product unit cost by computing one manufacturing overhead rate for one cost pool and applying that rate to the direct labor hours used to manufacture plain candy bars and candy bars with nuts. As we continue with our example, we find that Olga Santee, president of Candy Company, is concerned about the product cost for each type of candy bar. Santee believes that the difference in cost between the plain and nut candy bars should be more than $.075 ($.52 − $.445). She has asked Kee to review her estimate. Kee found no error when she rechecked the calculation of direct materials costs and direct labor costs. However, she believes the traditional approach to assigning manufacturing overhead cost could be misleading, so she wants to use activity-based costing to obtain a more accurate estimate of product cost. Figure 9 illustrates the use of ABC to assign manufacturing overhead costs to two product lines.

Kee analyzed the production-related activities and decided that the estimated $20,000 in manufacturing overhead cost could be grouped into four activity pools. The first activity, setup, includes estimated total costs of $7,000 for indirect labor and indirect materials used in preparing machines for each batch of production. The second activity, inspection, includes $6,000 for salaries and indirect materials costs, indirect labor, and depreciation on testing equipment. The third activity, packaging,

TABLE 3. Allocating Manufacturing Overhead Costs and Calculating Product Unit Cost: Traditional Approach

Step 1. Calculate overhead rate for cost pool:

$$\frac{\text{Estimated Total Overhead Costs}}{\text{Estimated Total Cost Driver Level}} = \frac{\$20,000}{400,000 \text{ (DLH)}} = \$.05 \text{ per DLH}$$

Step 2. Apply predetermined overhead rate to products:

	Plain Candy Bars	Candy Bars with Nuts
	Predetermined Overhead Rate × Actual Cost Driver Level = Cost Applied to Production	Predetermined Overhead Rate × Actual Cost Driver Level = Cost Applied to Production
Manufacturing overhead applied: $.05 per DLH	$.05 × 250,000 DLH = $12,500	$.05 × 150,000 DLH = $7,500
Manufacturing overhead cost per unit: Cost Applied ÷ Number of Units	$12,500 ÷ 100,000 = $.125	$7,500 ÷ 50,000 = $.15

Product unit cost using normal costing:

	Plain Candy Bars	Nut Candy Bars
Product costs per unit:		
Direct materials	$.180	$.21
Direct labor	.140	.16
Applied manufacturing overhead	.125	.15
Product unit cost	$.445	$.52

At the bottom of Table 3 is Kee's calculation of the normal product unit cost for each product line. The nut candy bar's product unit cost ($.52) is higher than the plain candy bar's ($.445) because producing the candy bar with nuts required more expensive materials and more labor time.

✓ Check out ACE for a Review Quiz at http://accounting.college.hmco.com/students.

ALLOCATING MANUFACTURING OVERHEAD: THE ABC APPROACH

LO8 Using activity-based costing to assign manufacturing overhead costs, calculate product unit cost.

RELATED TEXT ASSIGNMENTS
Q: 19
SE: 11
E: 14
P: 5, 7, 8
SD: 2
MRA: 4

Activity-based costing (ABC) is a more accurate method of assigning overhead costs to products than the traditional approach. It categorizes all indirect costs by activity, traces the indirect costs to those activities, and assigns activity costs to products using a cost driver related to the cause of the cost. A company that uses ABC identifies production-related activities and the events and circumstances that cause, or drive, those activities, such as number of inspections or maintenance hours. As a result, many smaller activity pools are created from the single manufacturing overhead cost pool used in the traditional method. This means that managers will calculate an overhead rate, or activity cost rate, for each activity pool and then use that rate and a cost driver amount to determine the portion of manufacturing overhead costs to assign to a product. Managers must select an appropriate number of activity pools for manufacturing overhead, and a system must be designed to capture the actual cost driver amounts. Because each activity pool requires a cost driver, the

Allocating Manufacturing Overhead: The Traditional Approach

FIGURE 8
Using the Traditional Approach to Assign Manufacturing Overhead Costs to Production

COST POOL

Manufacturing Overhead Costs

$20,000

Step 1: Predetermined overhead rate =
$$\frac{\$20,000 \text{ Total Estimated OH}}{\$400,000 \text{ Estimated DLH}} = \$.05$$

COST OBJECTS

Plain Candy Bars

Step 2: Apply predetermined overhead rate to products
$.05 × 250,000 DLH
= $12,500, or
$$\frac{\$12,500}{100,000 \text{ units}} = \$.125 \text{ per unit}$$

Candy Bars with Nuts

Step 2: Apply predetermined overhead rate to products
$.05 × 150,000 DLH
= $7,500, or
$$\frac{\$7,500}{50,000 \text{ units}} = \$.15 \text{ per unit}$$

● **STOP AND THINK!**
How many overhead cost pools are used in the traditional approach to cost allocation?

In the traditional approach to cost allocation, total manufacturing overhead costs constitute one cost pool. ■

STUDY NOTE: Don't make the mistake of thinking that because a cost is not traced directly to a product it is not a product cost. All manufacturing costs, both direct and indirect, are product costs.

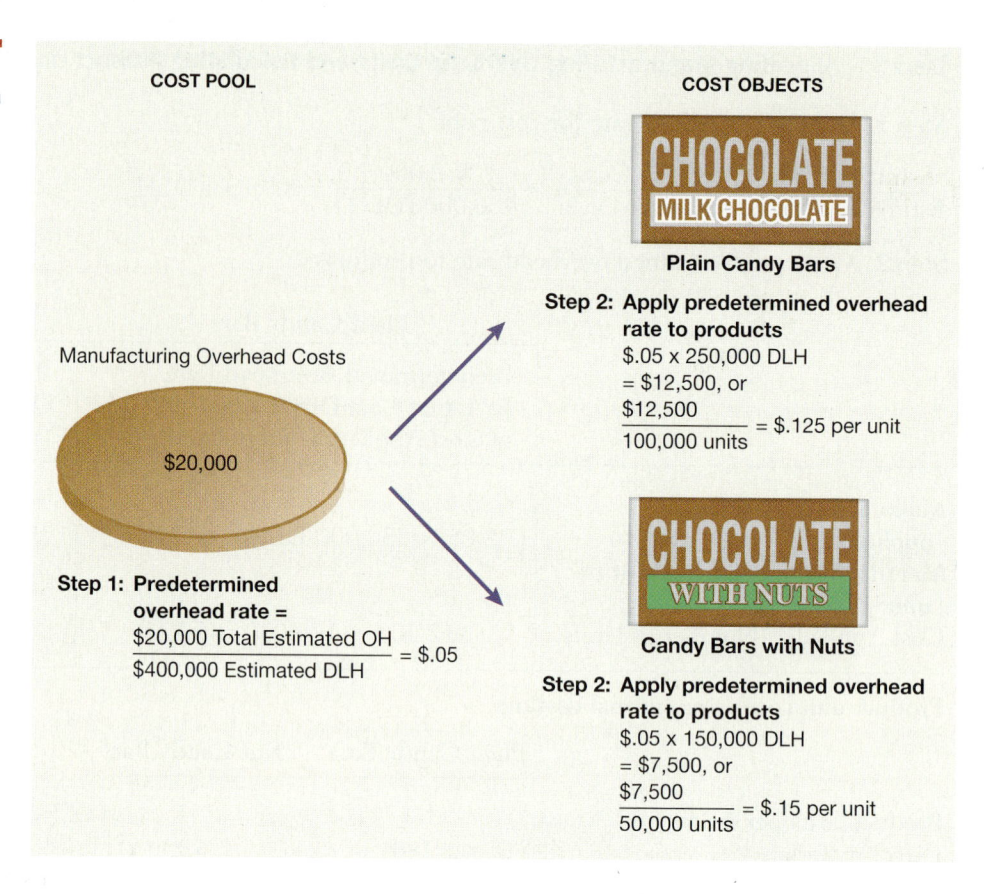

Figure 8 illustrates the application of one cost pool of manufacturing overhead costs to two product lines. As we continue with our example of Candy Company, Inc., let's assume that the company will be selling two product lines in 20x7—plain candy bars and candy bars with nuts—and that Maya Kee chooses direct labor hours as the cost driver. Kee estimates that total manufacturing overhead costs for the next year will be $20,000 and that total direct labor hours (DLH) worked will be 400,000 hours.

Table 3 summarizes the first two steps in the traditional approach to allocating manufacturing overhead costs. In the first step, Kee uses the following formula to compute the rate at which manufacturing overhead costs will be applied:

$$\text{Predetermined Overhead Rate} = \frac{\$20,000}{400,000 \text{ DLH}} = \$.05 \text{ per DLH}$$

In the second step, Kee applies the predetermined overhead rate to the products. During the year, Candy Company used 250,000 direct labor hours to produce 100,000 plain candy bars and 150,000 direct labor hours to produce 50,000 candy bars with nuts. When Kee applies the predetermined overhead rate, the portion of the manufacturing overhead cost applied to the plain candy bars totals $12,500 ($.05 × 250,000 DLH), or $.125 per unit ($12,500 ÷ 100,000 units), and the portion applied to the candy bars with nuts totals $7,500 ($.05 × 150,000 DLH), or $.15 per unit ($7,500 ÷ 50,000 units).

Kee also wanted to calculate the product unit cost for the accounting period using normal costing. She gathered the following data for the two product lines:

	Plain Candy Bars	Candy Bars with Nuts
Actual direct materials cost per unit	$.18	$.21
Actual direct labor cost per unit	.14	.16
Prime cost per unit	$.32	$.37

The Importance of Good Estimates

A predetermined, or estimated, manufacturing overhead rate has two main uses. First, it enables managers to make decisions about pricing products and controlling costs before some of the actual costs are known. The product cost calculated at the end of a period, when all product costs are known, is, of course, more accurate. But when the overhead portion of product cost is estimated in advance, managers can compare actual and estimated costs throughout the year and more quickly correct any problems that may cause the under- or overallocation of overhead costs.

Second, an advance estimate allows managers to apply manufacturing overhead costs to each unit produced in an equitable and timely manner. Actual manufacturing overhead costs fluctuate from month to month as a result of the timing of the costs and the variability of the amounts. For example, some manufacturing overhead costs (such as supervisors' salaries and depreciation on equipment) may be expensed monthly. Others (like payroll taxes) may be paid quarterly, and still others (like property taxes and insurance) may be paid annually. In addition, indirect hourly labor costs (such as the costs of machine maintenance and materials handling) fluctuate with changes in production levels.

The successful allocation of manufacturing overhead costs depends on two factors. One is a careful estimate of the total manufacturing overhead costs. The other is a good forecast of the cost driver level.

An accurate estimate of total manufacturing overhead costs is crucial. If the estimate is wrong, the manufacturing overhead rate will be wrong. This will cause an overstatement or understatement of the product unit cost. If an organization relies on information that overstates product unit cost, it may fail to bid on profitable projects because the costs appear too high. If it relies on information that understates product unit cost, it may accept business that is not as profitable as expected. So, to provide managers with reliable product unit costs, the management accountant must be careful to include all manufacturing overhead items and to forecast the costs of those items accurately.

The budgeting process usually includes estimating manufacturing overhead costs. Managers who use production-related resources will provide cost estimates for direct and indirect production activities. For example, the managers for materials handling and inspection at Candy Company, Inc., estimate the costs related to their departments' activities, and Maya Kee, the accountant, includes their cost estimates in developing total manufacturing overhead costs.

Managers also need to provide accurate estimates of cost driver levels. An understated cost driver level will cause an overstatement of the predetermined manufacturing overhead rate (the cost is spread over a lesser level), and an overstated cost driver level will cause an understatement of the predetermined manufacturing overhead rate (the cost is spread over a greater level).

In the following sections, we present two approaches to allocating manufacturing overhead. We use the first two steps of the four-step overhead allocation process to demonstrate these approaches.

✓ Check out ACE for a Review Quiz at http://accounting.college.hmco.com/students.

Allocating Manufacturing Overhead: The Traditional Approach

LO7 Using the traditional method of allocating manufacturing overhead costs, calculate product unit cost.

RELATED TEXT ASSIGNMENTS
Q: 18
SE: 9, 10
E: 11, 12, 13, 14
P: 4, 6, 8
SD: 2
MRA: 4

The traditional approach to applying manufacturing overhead costs to a product cost is to use a single predetermined overhead rate. This approach is especially useful when companies manufacture only one product or a few very similar products that require the same production processes and production-related activities, such as setup, inspection, and materials handling. The total manufacturing overhead costs constitute one cost pool, and a traditional activity base—such as direct labor hours, direct labor costs, machine hours, or units of production—is the cost driver.

Cost Allocation

FIGURE 7
Allocating Manufacturing Overhead Costs: A Four-Step Process

	Year 20x5 ──────── January 1 ──────── Year 20x6 ──────── December 31			
	Step 1: Planning the Overhead Rate	**Step 2: Applying the Overhead Rate**	**Step 3: Recording Actual Overhead Costs**	**Step 4: Reconciling Applied and Actual Overhead Costs**
Timing and Procedure	Before the accounting period begins, determine cost pools and cost drivers. Calculate the overhead rate by dividing the cost pool of total estimated overhead costs by the total estimated cost driver level.	During the accounting period, as units are produced, apply overhead costs to products by multiplying the predetermined overhead rate for each cost pool by the actual cost driver level for that pool. Record costs.	Record actual manufacturing overhead costs as they are incurred during the accounting period.	At the end of the accounting period, calculate and reconcile the difference between applied and actual manufacturing overhead costs.

Journal Entry	None	Increase Work in Process Inventory account and decrease Manufacturing Overhead account:
		Dr. Work in Process XX
		  Cr. Manufacturing Overhead XX
			Increase Manufacturing Overhead account and decrease asset accounts or increase contra-asset or liability accounts:
			Dr. Manufacturing Overhead XX
			  Cr. Various Accounts XX
				Entry will vary depending on how costs have been applied. If overapplied, increase Manufacturing Overhead and decrease Cost of Goods Sold. If underapplied, increase Cost of Goods Sold and decrease Manufacturing Overhead.

Cost Flow Through the Accounts		Manufacturing Overhead | | Overhead applied using predetermined rate | Work in Process Inventory | Overhead applied using predetermined rate | |	Manufacturing Overhead | Actual overhead costs recorded | | Various Asset and Liability Accounts | | Actual costs recorded |	**Overapplied:** Manufacturing Overhead | Actual overhead costs recorded | Overhead applied using predetermined rate | **Overapplied** Bal. $0 Cost of Goods Sold | Bal. | | | | Overapplied | Actual bal. **Underapplied:** Manufacturing Overhead | Actual overhead costs recorded | Overhead applied using predetermined rate | **Underapplied** Bal. $0 Cost of Goods Sold | Bal. | | **Underapplied** Actual bal.

Allocating the Costs of Manufacturing Overhead

> **Stop and Think!**
> What are the two main uses of a predetermined manufacturing overhead rate?
>
> *A predetermined, or estimated, manufacturing overhead rate enables managers to make timely decisions about pricing products and controlling costs. It also allows them to apply overhead costs to each unit produced in an equitable and timely manner.* ■

Allocating manufacturing overhead costs is a four-step process that corresponds to the four stages of the management cycle. In the first step (the planning stage), managers estimate manufacturing overhead costs and calculate a rate at which they will assign those costs to products. In the second step (the executing stage), this rate is applied to products as manufacturing overhead costs are incurred and recorded during production. In the third step (the reviewing stage), actual manufacturing overhead costs are recorded as they are incurred, and managers calculate the difference between the estimated and actual costs. In the fourth step (the reporting stage), managers report on this difference. Figure 7 summarizes these four steps in terms of their timing, the procedures involved, and the journal entries they require. It also shows how the cost flows in the various steps affect the accounting records.

■ **Planning the Overhead Rate** Before an accounting period begins, managers determine cost pools and cost drivers and calculate a **predetermined overhead rate** by dividing the cost pool of total estimated overhead costs by the total estimated cost driver level. Grouping all estimated overhead costs into one cost pool and using direct labor hours or machine hours as the cost driver results in a single, plantwide overhead rate. By applying this predetermined rate in the same way to all units of production during the period, managers can better estimate product costs. This step requires no journal entry because no business activity has occurred.

■ **Applying the Overhead Rate** As units of the product are manufactured during the accounting period, the estimated manufacturing overhead costs are assigned to the product's costs at the predetermined overhead rate. The overhead rate for each cost pool is multiplied by that pool's actual cost driver level (e.g., the actual number of direct labor hours used to complete the product). The purpose of this calculation is to assign a consistent manufacturing overhead cost to each unit produced during the accounting period. A journal entry records the allocation of overhead to the product as an increase in the Work in Process Inventory account and a decrease in the Manufacturing Overhead account.

■ **Recording Actual Overhead Costs** The actual manufacturing overhead costs are recorded as they are incurred during the accounting period. These costs, which include the costs of indirect materials, indirect labor, depreciation, property taxes, and other production costs, will be part of the actual product cost. The journal entry made for the actual manufacturing overhead costs records an increase in the Manufacturing Overhead account and a decrease in asset accounts or an increase in contra-asset or liability accounts.

■ **Reconciling the Applied and Actual Overhead Amounts** At the end of the accounting period, the difference between the applied and actual manufacturing overhead costs is calculated and reconciled. If the manufacturing overhead costs applied to production during the period are greater than the actual manufacturing overhead costs, the difference in the amounts represents **overapplied overhead costs**. If this difference is immaterial, the Manufacturing Overhead account is increased and the Cost of Goods Sold account is decreased by the difference. If the difference is material, adjustments are made to the accounts affected—that is, the Work in Process Inventory, Finished Goods Inventory, and Cost of Goods Sold accounts. If the manufacturing overhead costs applied to production during the period are less than the actual manufacturing overhead costs, the difference represents **underapplied overhead costs**. The Cost of Goods Sold account is increased and the Manufacturing Overhead account is decreased by this difference, assuming the difference is not material. The adjustment for overapplied or underapplied overhead costs, whether they are immaterial or material, is necessary to reflect the actual manufacturing overhead costs on the income statement.

Finished Goods Inventory accounts. The Materials Inventory account shows the balance of the cost of materials purchased but unused in the production process. During the production process, the costs of manufacturing the product are accumulated in the Work in Process Inventory account; the balance of this account represents the costs of the unfinished product. Once the product is complete and ready for sale, the cost of the goods manufactured is transferred to the Finished Goods Inventory account; the balance in this account is the cost of the unsold completed product. When the product is sold, the manufacturing organization uses the following equation to calculate the cost of goods sold:

$$\text{Cost of Goods Sold} = \text{Beginning Finished Goods Inventory} + \text{Cost of Goods Manufactured} - \text{Ending Finished Goods Inventory}$$

For example, suppose that Candy Company had a balance of $52,000 in its Finished Goods Inventory account on December 31, 20x4. During the next year, the cost of the products that Candy Company manufactured totaled $144,000. On December 31, 20x5, its Finished Goods Inventory balance was $78,000. The cost of goods sold for 20x5 is thus $118,000:

$$\text{Cost of Goods Sold} = \$52,000 + \$144,000 - \$78,000 = \$118,000$$

Remember that all organizations—service, retail, and manufacturing—use the following income statement format:

$$\text{Sales} - \text{Cost of Sales or Cost of Goods Sold} = \text{Gross Margin} - \text{Operating Expenses} = \text{Net Income}$$

Figure 6 compares the financial statements of service, retail, and manufacturing organizations. Note in particular the differences in inventory accounts and cost of goods sold. As pointed out earlier, product costs, or inventoriable costs, appear as finished goods inventory on the balance sheet and as cost of goods sold on the income statement; period costs, or noninventoriable costs, are reflected in the operating expenses on the income statement.

✓ Check out ACE for a Review Quiz at http://accounting.college.hmco.com/students.

COST ALLOCATION

LO6 Define *cost allocation* and explain how cost objects, cost pools, and cost drivers are used to assign manufacturing overhead costs.

RELATED TEXT ASSIGNMENTS
Q: 15, 16, 17
SE: 8, 9, 10
E: 11, 12, 13
P: 4, 6, 8
SD: 2
MRA: 4

ENRICHMENT NOTE:
Because allocation by its very nature is a relatively arbitrary process, a rational allocation scheme is best. Rational allocation approaches help avoid behavior problems for management.

As noted earlier, the costs of direct materials and direct labor can be easily traced to a product, but manufacturing overhead costs are indirect costs that must be collected and allocated in some manner. **Cost allocation** is the process of assigning a collection of indirect costs to a specific **cost object**, such as a product or service, a department, or an operating activity, using an allocation base known as a **cost driver**. A cost driver might be direct labor hours, direct labor costs, units produced, or another activity base that is important to a business. As the cost driver increases in volume, it causes the **cost pool**—the collection of indirect costs assigned to a cost object—to increase in amount. For example, suppose Candy Company has a machine-maintenance cost pool. The cost pool consists of overhead costs for the supplies and labor needed to maintain the machines, the cost object is the product, and the cost driver is machine hours. As more machine hours are used, the amount of the cost pool increases, thus increasing the costs assigned to the product.

For purposes of product costing, cost allocation is defined as the assignment of manufacturing overhead costs to the product (cost object) during an accounting period. It requires (1) the pooling of manufacturing overhead costs that are affected by a common activity (e.g., machine maintenance) and (2) the selection of a cost driver whose activity level causes a change in the cost pool (e.g., machine hours).

FIGURE 6
Financial Statements of Service, Retail, and Manufacturing Organizations

	Service Company	Retail Company	Manufacturing Company
Income Statement	Sales − Cost of sales Gross margin − Operating expenses Net income	Sales − Cost of goods sold* Gross margin − Operating expenses Net income *Cost of goods sold: 　Beginning merchandise inventory + Net cost of purchases 　Cost of goods available for sale − Ending merchandise inventory 　Cost of goods sold	Sales − Cost of goods sold† Gross margin − Operating expenses Net income †Cost of goods sold: 　Beginning finished goods inventory + Cost of goods manufactured 　Cost of goods available for sale − Ending finished goods inventory 　Cost of goods sold
Balance Sheet (current assets section)	No inventory accounts	One inventory account: 　Merchandise Inventory 　(finished product ready for sale)	Three inventory accounts: 　Materials Inventory 　(unused materials) 　Work in Process Inventory 　(unfinished product) 　Finished Goods Inventory 　(finished product ready for sale)
Example with numbers		Income Statement: Beg. merchandise inventory　$ 3,000 Net cost of purchases　　　　 23,000 Cost of goods available for sale $26,000 End. merchandise inventory　　 4,500 Cost of goods sold　　　　　 $21,500 Balance Sheet: Merchandise inventory, ending $ 4,500	Income Statement: Beg. finished goods inventory　$ 52,000 Cost of goods manufactured　　144,000 Cost of goods available for sale $196,000 End. finished goods inventory　 78,000 Cost of goods sold　　　　　$118,000 Balance Sheet: Finished goods inventory, ending $ 78,000

www.walmart.com
www.tru.com

products ready for resale, maintain just one inventory account on the balance sheet. Called the Merchandise Inventory account, it reflects the costs of goods held for resale. Retail organizations include the cost of purchases in the calculation of cost of goods sold, as follows:

$$\text{Cost of Goods Sold} = \text{Beginning Merchandise Inventory} + \text{Net Cost of Purchases} - \text{Ending Merchandise Inventory}$$

Suppose that Sweet Treasures Candy Store had a balance of $3,000 in its Merchandise Inventory account on December 31, 20x4. During the next year, its purchases of candy products totaled $23,000 (adjusted for purchase discounts, returns and allowances, and freight-in). On December 31, 20x5, its Merchandise Inventory balance was $4,500. The cost of goods sold for 20x5 is thus $21,500:

$$\text{Cost of Goods Sold} = \$3,000 + \$23,000 - \$4,500 = \$21,500$$

www.motorola.com
www.sony.com

As we have seen, manufacturing organizations, such as Motorola, Sony, and Candy Company, which make products for sale, maintain three inventory accounts on the balance sheet: the Materials Inventory, Work in Process Inventory, and

ENRICHMENT NOTE: An alternative to the cost of goods manufactured calculation uses the cost flow concept. Current manufacturing costs (direct materials, direct labor, and manufacturing overhead) become the cost of goods manufactured if the Work in Process Inventory balance remains unchanged in the accounting period. Similarly, the cost of goods manufactured becomes the cost of goods sold if the Finished Goods Inventory remains unchanged in the period.

■ **STEP 3** *Determine total cost of goods manufactured for the period.* To do so, add the beginning balance in the Work in Process Inventory account to total manufacturing costs to arrive at the total cost of work in process during the period. From this amount, subtract the ending balance in the Work in Process Inventory account to arrive at the cost of goods manufactured ($450,000 − $150,000 = $300,000).

Total manufacturing costs should not be confused with the cost of goods manufactured. To understand the difference between these two amounts, look again at the computations in Exhibit 1. Total manufacturing costs of $430,000 incurred during the period are added to the $20,000 beginning balance in the Work in Process Inventory account to arrive at the total cost of work in process during the period ($430,000 + $20,000 = $450,000). The costs of products still in process ($150,000) are then subtracted from the total cost of work in process during the year. The remainder, $300,000, is the cost of goods manufactured (completed) during the current year. Note that the costs attached to the ending balance of Work in Process Inventory come from the current period's total manufacturing costs; they will not become part of the cost of goods manufactured until the next period, when the products are completed.

COST OF GOODS SOLD AND A MANUFACTURING ORGANIZATION'S INCOME STATEMENT

STUDY NOTE: It is important not to confuse the cost of goods manufactured with the cost of goods sold.

Exhibit 1 demonstrates the relationship between Candy Company's income statement and its statement of cost of goods manufactured. The total amount of the cost of goods manufactured during the period is carried over to the income statement, where it is used to compute the cost of goods sold. The beginning balance of the Finished Goods Inventory account is added to the cost of goods manufactured to arrive at the total cost of finished goods available for sale during the period ($78,000 + $300,000 = $378,000). The cost of goods sold is then computed by subtracting the ending balance in Finished Goods Inventory (the cost of goods completed but not sold) from the total cost of finished goods available for sale ($378,000 − $138,000 = $240,000). The cost of goods sold is considered an expense in the period in which the goods are sold.

COST REPORTING AND ACCOUNTING FOR INVENTORIES IN SERVICE, RETAIL, AND MANUFACTURING ORGANIZATIONS

www.southwest.com
www.ups.com
www.enterprise.com

Because the operations of service and retail concerns differ from those of manufacturing organizations, the accounts presented in their financial statements differ as well. For example, because service organizations, such as Southwest Airlines, United Parcel Service (UPS), and Enterprise Rent-a-Car, sell services, not products, they maintain no inventories for sale or resale and thus, unlike manufacturing and retail organizations, have no inventory accounts on the balance sheet. When preparing income statements, they calculate the cost of sales rather than the cost of goods sold, using the following equation:

Cost of Sales = Net Cost of Services Sold

FOCUS ON BUSINESS PRACTICE

What Candy Company Has the Sweetest Share of the U.S. Market?
Among the top U.S. candy vendors are Hershey <www.hershey.com>, Mars <www.mars.com>, Wrigley's <www.wrigley.com>, Nestlé <www.nestle.com>, Philip Morris <www.altria.com>, and Russell Stover Candies <www.russellstover.com>. Hershey has the sweetest share of the market, leading with 30 percent. Mars is second with a 17.1 percent market share, and Wrigley's, Nestlé, and Phillip Morris vie for third place, with 6.7 percent, 6.5 percent, and 6.3 percent, respectively.[3]

Suppose, for instance, that Sweet Treasures Candy Store, the retail shop that we used as an example in the last chapter, employs UPS to deliver 50 boxes of candy. The cost of sales for UPS would include the wages and salaries of personnel plus the expense of trucks, planes, supplies, and anything else UPS used to deliver the packages for Sweet Treasures Candy Store.

Retail organizations, such as Wal-Mart, Toys "R" Us, and Sweet Treasures Candy Store, which purchase

EXHIBIT 1
Statement of Cost of Goods Manufactured and Partial Income Statement for a Manufacturing Organization

Candy Company, Inc.
Statement of Cost of Goods Manufactured
For the Year Ended December 31, 20x6

Direct materials used		
Materials inventory, December 31, 20x5	$100,000	
Direct materials purchased	200,000	
Cost of direct materials available for use	$300,000	
Less materials inventory, December 31, 20x6	50,000	
Cost of direct materials used		$250,000
Direct labor		120,000
Manufacturing overhead		60,000
Total manufacturing costs		$430,000
Add work in process inventory, December 31, 20x5		20,000
Total cost of work in process during the year		$450,000
Less work in process inventory, December 31, 20x6		150,000
Cost of goods manufactured		$300,000

Candy Company, Inc.
Income Statement
For the Year Ended December 31, 20x6

Sales		$500,000
Cost of goods sold		
Finished goods inventory, December 31, 20x5	$ 78,000	
Cost of goods manufactured	300,000	
Total cost of finished goods available for sale	$378,000	
Less finished goods inventory, December 31, 20x6	138,000	
Cost of goods sold		240,000
Gross margin		$260,000
Selling and administrative expenses		160,000
Operating income		$100,000

● **STOP AND THINK!**
What inventory accounts accumulate the cost information used in the statement of cost of goods manufactured?
The Materials Inventory and Work in Process Inventory accounts accumulate this information. ■

the cost of direct materials available for use during the accounting period. Next, subtract the ending balance of the Materials Inventory account from the cost of direct materials available for use. The difference is the cost of direct materials used during the period ($300,000 − $50,000 = $250,000).

■ **STEP 2** *Calculate total manufacturing costs for the period.* As shown in Exhibit 1, the costs of direct materials used ($250,000) and direct labor ($120,000) are added to total manufacturing overhead costs incurred during the period ($60,000) to arrive at total manufacturing costs ($430,000).

Financial Statements and the Reporting of Costs

KEY POINT: When costs are transferred from one inventory account to another in a manufacturing company, they remain assets. They are inventoriable product costs and are not expensed until the finished goods are sold.

KEY POINT: Materials Inventory and Work in Process Inventory support the production process, while Finished Goods Inventory supports the sales and distribution functions.

KEY POINT: When a credit sale occurs, Accounts Receivable and Sales are increased by the *revenue* amount. Cost of Goods Sold is increased and Finished Goods Inventory is decreased by the *cost* amount, or inventory carrying value.

The Work in Process Inventory account records the balance of partially completed units of the product. As direct materials and direct labor are used, their costs are added to the Work in Process Inventory account. The cost of manufacturing overhead for the current period is also added. The total costs of direct materials, direct labor, and manufacturing overhead incurred and transferred to work in process inventory during an accounting period are called **total manufacturing costs** (also called *current manufacturing costs*). These costs increase the balance of the Work in Process Inventory account.

The cost of all units completed and moved to finished goods storage during an accounting period is the **cost of goods manufactured**. The cost of goods manufactured for the period decreases the balance of the Work in Process Inventory account. The following formulas show the activity in Candy Company's Work in Process Inventory account during the year:

Total Manufacturing Costs	=	Cost of Direct Materials Used	+	Direct Labor Costs	+	Manufacturing Overhead Costs
$430,000	=	$250,000	+	$120,000	+	$60,000

Work in Process Inventory, Ending Balance	=	Work in Process Inventory, Beginning Balance	+	Total Manufacturing Costs	−	Cost of Goods Manufactured
$150,000	=	$20,000	+	$430,000	−	$300,000

The Finished Goods Inventory account holds the balance of costs assigned to all completed products that a manufacturing company has not yet sold. The cost of goods manufactured increases the balance, and the cost of goods sold decreases the balance. The following formula shows the activity in Candy Company's Finished Goods Inventory account during the year:

Finished Goods Inventory, Ending Balance	=	Finished Goods Inventory, Beginning Balance	+	Cost of Goods Manufactured	−	Cost of Goods Sold
$138,000	=	$78,000	+	$300,000	−	$240,000

✓ Check out ACE for a Review Quiz at http://accounting.college.hmco.com/students.

FINANCIAL STATEMENTS AND THE REPORTING OF COSTS

LO5 Compare how service, retail, and manufacturing organizations report costs on their financial statements and how they account for inventories.

RELATED TEXT ASSIGNMENTS
Q: 13, 14
SE: 6, 7
E: 6, 7, 8, 9, 10
P: 2, 3
MRA: 1, 3

The key to preparing an income statement for a manufacturing organization is to determine the cost of goods manufactured. This dollar amount is calculated on the statement of cost of goods manufactured, a special report based on an analysis of the Work in Process Inventory account.

STATEMENT OF COST OF GOODS MANUFACTURED

At the end of an accounting period, the flow of all manufacturing costs incurred during the period is summarized in the **statement of cost of goods manufactured**. Exhibit 1 shows Candy Company's statement of cost of goods manufactured for the year ended December 31, 20x6. (The company's flow of manufacturing costs for the same period appears in Figure 5.) It is helpful to think of the statement of cost of goods manufactured as being developed in three steps, as described below.

■ **STEP 1** *Compute the cost of direct materials used during the accounting period.* To do so, add the beginning balance in the Materials Inventory account to the direct materials purchased ($100,000 + $200,000). The subtotal ($300,000) represents

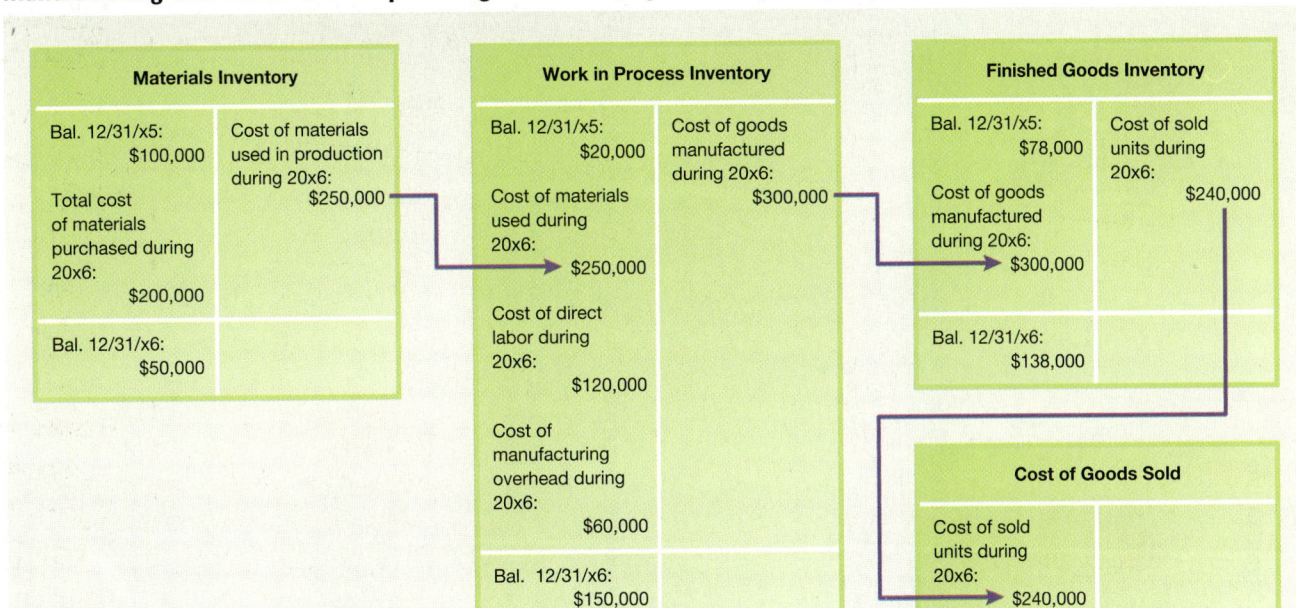

FIGURE 5
Manufacturing Cost Flow: An Example Using Actual Costing for Candy Company, Inc.

Materials Inventory		Work in Process Inventory		Finished Goods Inventory	
Bal. 12/31/x5: $100,000	Cost of materials used in production during 20x6: $250,000	Bal. 12/31/x5: $20,000	Cost of goods manufactured during 20x6: $300,000	Bal. 12/31/x5: $78,000	Cost of sold units during 20x6: $240,000
Total cost of materials purchased during 20x6: $200,000		Cost of materials used during 20x6: $250,000		Cost of goods manufactured during 20x6: $300,000	
Bal. 12/31/x6: $50,000		Cost of direct labor during 20x6: $120,000		Bal. 12/31/x6: $138,000	
		Cost of manufacturing overhead during 20x6: $60,000			
		Bal. 12/31/x6: $150,000			

Cost of Goods Sold	
Cost of sold units during 20x6: $240,000	

balance of the Finished Goods Inventory account and decreases the balance of the Work in Process Inventory account.

When candy bars are sold, a clerk prepares a *sales invoice*, and another employee fills the order by removing the candy bars from the storeroom, packaging them, and shipping them to the customer. A *shipping document* shows the quantity of the products that are shipped and gives a description of them. The cost of the candy bars sold, which is shown on the job order cost card, increases the Cost of Goods Sold account and decreases the balance of the Finished Goods Inventory account.

THE MANUFACTURING COST FLOW

Manufacturing cost flow is the flow of manufacturing costs (direct materials, direct labor, and manufacturing overhead) through the Materials Inventory, Work in Process Inventory, and Finished Goods Inventory accounts into the Cost of Goods Sold account. A defined, structured manufacturing cost flow is the foundation for product costing, inventory valuation, and financial reporting. Figure 5 summarizes the manufacturing cost flow as it relates to the inventory accounts and production activity of Candy Company for the year ended December 31, 20x6. To show the basic flows in this example, we assume that all materials can be traced directly to the candy bars. This means there are no indirect materials in the Materials Inventory account. We also work with the actual amount of manufacturing overhead, rather than an estimated amount.

Because there are no indirect materials in this case, the Materials Inventory account shows the balance of unused direct materials. The cost of direct materials purchased increases the balance of the Materials Inventory account, and the cost of direct materials used by the Production Department decreases it. The following formula may be used to summarize the activity of Candy Company's Materials Inventory account during the year:

Materials Inventory, Ending Balance	=	Materials Inventory, Beginning Balance	+	Cost of Materials Purchased	−	Cost of Materials Used
$50,000	=	$100,000	+	$200,000	−	$250,000

Inventory Accounts in Manufacturing Organizations   845

FIGURE 4
Activities, Documents, and Cost Flows Through the Inventory Accounts of a Manufacturing Organization

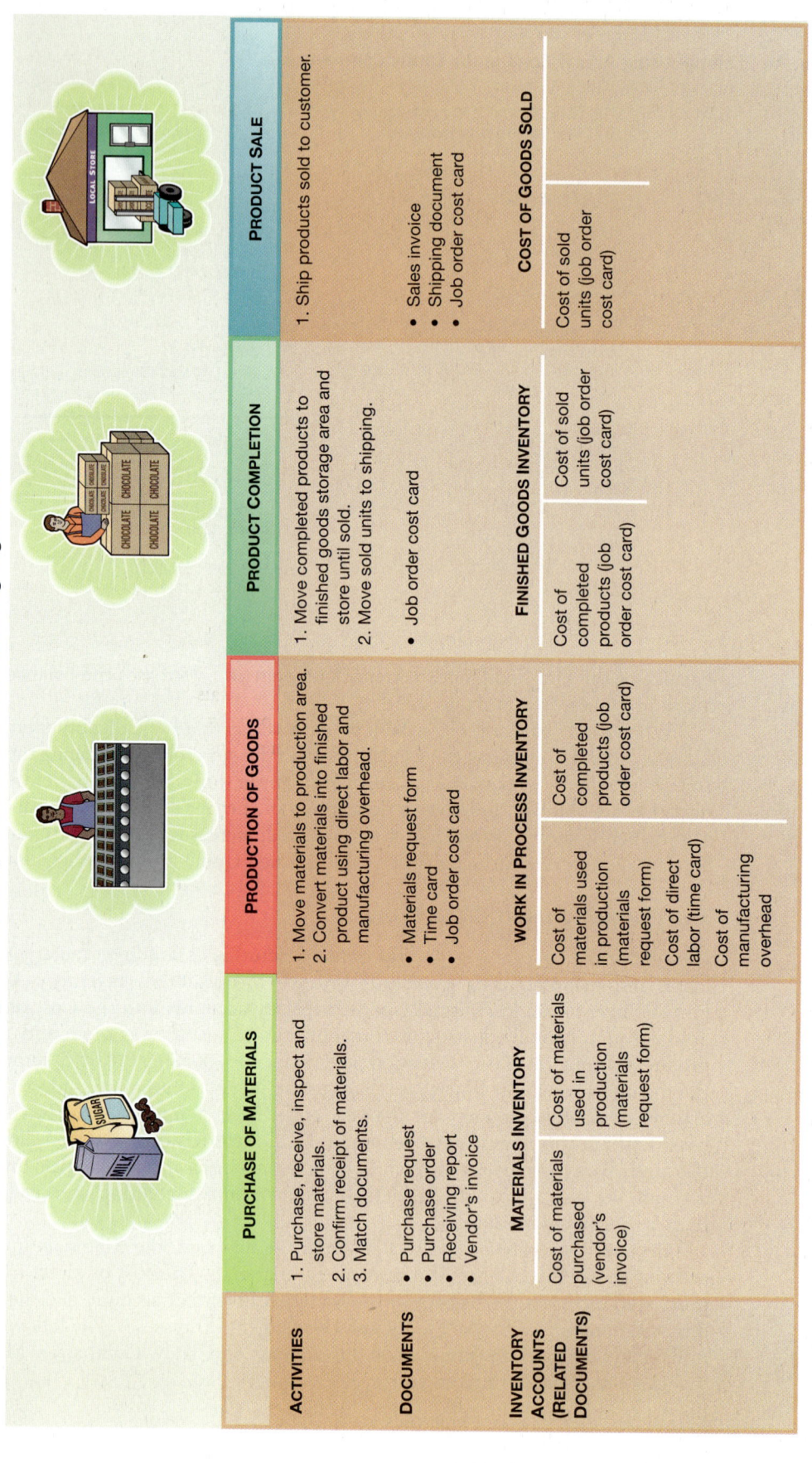

	PURCHASE OF MATERIALS	PRODUCTION OF GOODS	PRODUCT COMPLETION	PRODUCT SALE
ACTIVITIES	1. Purchase, receive, inspect and store materials. 2. Confirm receipt of materials. 3. Match documents.	1. Move materials to production area. 2. Convert materials into finished product using direct labor and manufacturing overhead.	1. Move completed products to finished goods storage area and store until sold. 2. Move sold units to shipping.	1. Ship products sold to customer.
DOCUMENTS	• Purchase request • Purchase order • Receiving report • Vendor's invoice	• Materials request form • Time card • Job order cost card	• Job order cost card	• Sales invoice • Shipping document • Job order cost card
INVENTORY ACCOUNTS (RELATED DOCUMENTS)	**MATERIALS INVENTORY** Cost of materials purchased (vendor's invoice) | Cost of materials used in production (materials request form)	**WORK IN PROCESS INVENTORY** Cost of materials used in production (materials request form) Cost of direct labor (time card) Cost of manufacturing overhead | Cost of completed products (job order cost card)	**FINISHED GOODS INVENTORY** Cost of completed products (job order cost card) | Cost of sold units (job order cost card)	**COST OF GOODS SOLD** Cost of sold units (job order cost card)

account shows the balance of the cost of unused materials, the **Work in Process Inventory account** shows the manufacturing costs that have been incurred and assigned to partially completed units of product, and the **Finished Goods Inventory account** shows the costs assigned to all completed products that have not been sold.

DOCUMENT FLOWS AND COST FLOWS THROUGH THE INVENTORY ACCOUNTS

In many companies, accountants accumulate and report manufacturing costs based on documents pertaining to production and production-related activities. Although paper documents are still used for this purpose, electronic documents have become increasingly common. Looking at how the documents for the three elements of product cost relate to the flow of costs through the three inventory accounts provides insight into when an activity must be recorded in the accounting records. Figure 4 summarizes the relationships among the production activities, the documents for each of the three cost elements, and the inventory accounts affected by the activities.

To illustrate the document flow and changes in inventory balances for production activities, we continue with our example of Candy Company, Inc.

■ **PURCHASE OF MATERIALS**   The same process is used for purchasing both direct and indirect materials. The purchasing process starts with a *purchase request* for specific quantities of materials needed in the manufacturing process but not currently available in the materials storeroom. A qualified manager approves the request. Based on the information in the purchase request, the Purchasing Department sends a *purchase order* to a supplier. When the materials arrive, an employee on the receiving dock counts and examines them and prepares a *receiving report*. Later, an accounting clerk matches the information on the receiving report with the descriptions and quantities listed on the purchase order. A materials handler moves the newly arrived materials from the receiving area to the materials storeroom. Soon, Candy Company receives a *vendor's invoice* from the supplier requesting payment for the purchased materials. The cost of those materials increases the balance of the Materials Inventory account.

■ **PRODUCTION OF GOODS**   When candy bars are scheduled for production, the storeroom clerk receives a *materials request form*. The materials request form is essential for controlling materials. In addition to showing the supervisor's signature of approval, it describes the types and quantities of materials the storeroom clerk is to send to the production area, and it authorizes the release of those materials from the materials inventory into production. If the appropriate manager has approved the materials request form, the storeroom clerk has the materials handler move the materials to the production floor. The cost of the direct materials transferred will increase the balance of the Work in Process Inventory account and decrease the balance of the Materials Inventory account. The cost of the indirect materials transferred will increase the balance of the Manufacturing Overhead account and decrease the balance of the Materials Inventory account. (We discuss overhead in more detail later in this chapter.)

Each of the production employees who make the candy bars prepares a *time card* to record the number of hours he or she has worked on this and other orders each day. The costs of the direct labor and manufacturing overhead used to manufacture the candy bars increase the balance of the Work in Process Inventory account. A *job order cost card* is used to record all costs incurred as the products move through production.

■ **PRODUCT COMPLETION AND SALE**   Employees place completed candy bars in cartons and then move the cartons to the finished goods storeroom, where they are kept until shipped to customers. The cost of the completed candy bars increases the

---

● **STOP AND THINK!**
Are paper documents always used in accounting for manufacturing costs?
Although paper documents have traditionally been used, many companies today use electronic documents. ■

ENRICHMENT NOTE:
Some companies use sophisticated computer programs to match receiving reports to purchase orders.

FIGURE 3
Relationships Among Product Cost Classifications

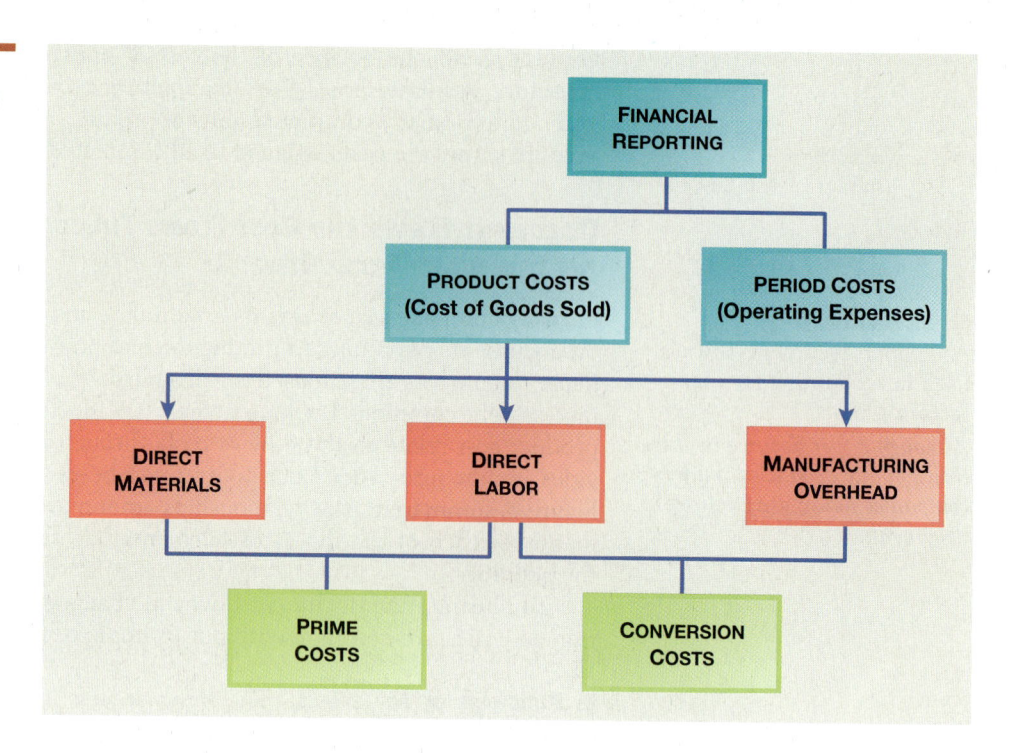

The $.44 product unit cost is useful in determining the cost of the bid, $880 ($.44 × 2,000 candy bars), estimating the gross margin for the job, and deciding the price to bid for the business. We cover standard costing in more detail in another chapter.

PRIME COSTS AND CONVERSION COSTS

The three elements of manufacturing costs can be grouped into prime costs and conversion costs. **Prime costs** are the primary costs of production; they are the sum of the direct materials costs and direct labor costs. **Conversion costs** are the costs of converting direct materials into a finished product; they are the sum of direct labor costs and manufacturing overhead costs. Using the figures for Candy Company's actual unit cost, the per-unit prime costs and conversion costs are as follows:

	Prime Costs	Conversion Costs
Direct materials	$.18	—
Direct labor	.14	$.14
Manufacturing overhead	—	.08
Totals	$.32	$.22

These classifications are important for understanding the costing methods discussed in later chapters. Figure 3 summarizes the relationships among the product cost classifications presented so far.

✓ Check out ACE for a Review Quiz at http://accounting.college.hmco.com/students.

INVENTORY ACCOUNTS IN MANUFACTURING ORGANIZATIONS

LO4 Describe the flow of costs through a manufacturer's inventory accounts.

RELATED TEXT ASSIGNMENTS
Q: 10, 11, 12
SE: 4, 5
E: 4, 5

Transforming materials into finished products ready for sale requires a number of production and production-related activities, including purchasing, receiving, inspecting, storing, and moving materials; converting them into finished products using labor, equipment, and other resources; and moving, storing, and shipping the finished products. A manufacturing organization's accounting system tracks these activities as product costs flowing through the Materials Inventory, Work in Process Inventory, and Finished Goods Inventory accounts. The **Materials Inventory**

KEY POINT: Many management decisions require estimates of future costs. Managers often use actual cost as a basis for estimating future cost.

that Candy Company, Inc., produced 3,000 candy bars on December 28, 20x6, for a corporate customer in Seattle. Maya Kee, the company's accountant, calculated that the actual costs for the Seattle order were direct materials, $540; direct labor, $420; and manufacturing overhead, $240. The actual product unit cost for the order was $.40, calculated as follows:

Direct materials ($540 ÷ 3,000 candy bars)	$.18
Direct labor ($420 ÷ 3,000 candy bars)	.14
Manufacturing overhead ($240 ÷ 3,000 candy bars)	.08
Product cost per candy bar ($1,200 ÷ 3,000 candy bars)	$.40

In this case, the product unit cost was computed after the job was completed and all cost information was known. Sometimes, however, a manufacturer needs to know product unit cost during production, when the actual direct materials costs and direct labor costs are known but the actual manufacturing overhead costs are uncertain. In that case, the computation of product unit cost will include an estimate of the manufacturing overhead, and the normal costing method will be helpful.

■ **NORMAL COSTING METHOD** The **normal costing** method combines actual direct costs of materials and labor with estimated manufacturing overhead costs to determine a product unit cost. The normal costing method is simple and allows a smoother, more even assignment of manufacturing overhead costs to production during an accounting period than is possible with the actual costing method. It also contributes to better pricing decisions and profitability estimates. However, at the end of the accounting period, any difference between the estimated and actual costs must be identified and removed so that the financial statements show only the actual product costs.

Assume that Maya Kee used normal costing to price the Seattle order for 3,000 candy bars and that manufacturing overhead was applied to the product's cost using an estimated rate of 60 percent of direct labor costs. In this case, the costs for the order would include the actual direct materials cost of $540, the actual direct labor cost of $420, and an estimated manufacturing overhead cost of $252 ($420.00 × 60%). The product unit cost would be $.404:

Direct materials ($540.00 ÷ 3,000 candy bars)	$.180
Direct labor ($420.00 ÷ 3,000 candy bars)	.140
Manufacturing overhead ($252.00 ÷ 3,000 candy bars)	.084
Product cost per candy bar ($1,212 ÷ 3,000 candy bars)	$.404

■ **STANDARD COSTING METHOD** Managers sometimes need product cost information before the accounting period begins so that they can control the cost of operating activities or price a proposed product for a customer. In such situations, product unit costs must be estimated, and the **standard costing** method can be helpful. This method uses estimated, or standard, costs of direct materials, direct labor, and manufacturing overhead to calculate the product unit cost.

Assume that Candy Company is placing a bid to manufacture 2,000 candy bars for a new customer. From standard cost information developed at the beginning of the period, Kee estimates the following costs: $.20 per unit for direct materials, $.15 per unit for direct labor, and $.09 per unit for manufacturing overhead (assuming a standard overhead rate of 60 percent of direct labor cost). The standard cost per unit would be $.44:

Direct materials	$.20
Direct labor	.15
Manufacturing overhead ($.15 × 60%)	.09
Product cost per candy bar	$.44

FOCUS ON BUSINESS TECHNOLOGY

Has Technology Shifted the Elements of Product Costs?

New technology and manufacturing processes have produced new patterns of product costs. The three elements of product costs are still direct materials, direct labor, and manufacturing overhead, but the percentage that each contributes to the total cost of a product has changed. From the 1950s through the 1970s, direct labor was the dominant element, making up over 40 percent of total product cost, while direct materials contributed 35 percent and manufacturing overhead, around 25 percent. Thus, 75 percent of total product cost was a direct cost, traceable to the product. Improved production technology caused a dramatic shift in the three product cost elements. Machines replaced people, significantly reducing direct labor costs. Today, only 50 percent of the cost of a product is directly traceable to the product; the other 50 percent is manufacturing overhead, an indirect cost.

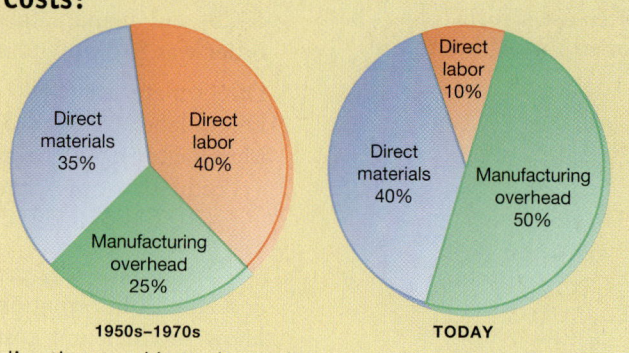

1950s–1970s
- Direct materials 35%
- Direct labor 40%
- Manufacturing overhead 25%

TODAY
- Direct labor 10%
- Direct materials 40%
- Manufacturing overhead 50%

- *Direct labor costs:* costs of labor used in making the candy bar
- *Manufacturing overhead costs:* indirect materials costs, including the costs of salt and flavorings; indirect labor costs, including the costs of labor to move materials to the production area and to inspect the candy bars during production; other indirect overhead costs, including depreciation on the building and equipment, utilities, property taxes, and insurance

COMPUTING PRODUCT UNIT COST

STOP AND THINK!
How do the costing methods used to compute a product's cost per unit affect the three elements of product cost?

The three elements of product cost, direct materials, direct labor, and manufacturing overhead, may differ in amount depending on whether the actual, normal, or standard costing method is used. ■

Product unit cost is the cost of manufacturing a single unit of a product. It is made up of the costs of direct materials, direct labor, and manufacturing overhead. These three cost elements are accumulated as a batch of products is being produced. When the batch has been completed, the product unit cost is computed either by dividing the total cost of direct materials, direct labor, and manufacturing overhead by the total number of units produced, or by determining the cost per unit for each element of the product cost and summing those per-unit costs.

Unit cost information helps managers price products and calculate gross margin and net income. Managers and accountants can calculate product unit cost by using actual costing, normal costing, or standard costing methods. Table 2 summarizes how these three cost-measurement methods use actual and estimated costs.

■ **ACTUAL COSTING METHOD** The **actual costing** method uses the costs of direct materials, direct labor, and manufacturing overhead at the end of an accounting period or when actual costs become known to calculate the product unit cost. The actual product unit cost is assigned to the finished goods inventory on the balance sheet and to the cost of goods sold on the income statement. For example, assume

TERMINOLOGY NOTE:
Estimated costs are also called *projected*, *standard*, *predetermined*, or *budgeted costs*.

TABLE 2. Use of Actual and Estimated Costs in Three Cost-Measurement Methods

Product Cost Elements	Actual Costing	Normal Costing	Standard Costing
Direct materials	Actual costs	Actual costs	Estimated costs
Direct labor	Actual costs	Actual costs	Estimated costs
Manufacturing overhead	Actual costs	Estimated costs	Estimated costs

TABLE 1. Examples of Cost Classifications for a Candy Manufacturer

Cost Examples	Traceability to Product	Cost Behavior	Value Attribute	Financial Reporting
Sugar for candy	Direct	Variable	Value-adding	Product (direct materials)
Labor for mixing	Direct	Variable	Value-adding	Product (direct labor)
Labor for supervision	Indirect	Fixed	Nonvalue-adding	Product (manufacturing overhead)
Depreciation on mixing machine	Indirect	Fixed	Value-adding	Product (manufacturing overhead)
Sales commission	—*	Variable	Value-adding†	Period
Accountant's salary	—*	Fixed	Nonvalue-adding	Period

*Sales commissions and accountants' salaries cannot be directly or indirectly traced to a cost object; they are not product costs.
†Sales commissions can be value-adding because customers' perceptions of the salesperson and the selling experience can strongly affect their perceptions of the product's market value.

STUDY NOTE: Product costs and period costs can be explained using the matching rule. Product costs must be charged to the period in which the product generates revenue, and period costs are charged against the revenue of the current period.

Product costs appear on the income statement as cost of goods sold and on the balance sheet as finished goods inventory. **Period costs**, or *noninventoriable* costs, are costs of resources used during the accounting period and not assigned to products. They appear as operating expenses on the income statement. For example, selling and administrative expenses are period costs.

Table 1 shows how some costs of a candy manufacturer can be classified in terms of traceability, behavior, value attribute, and financial reporting.

✓ Check out ACE for a Review Quiz at http://accounting.college.hmco.com/students.

ELEMENTS OF PRODUCT COSTS

LO3 Define and give examples of the three elements of product cost and compute the unit cost of a product.

RELATED TEXT ASSIGNMENTS
Q: 6, 7, 8, 9
SE: 2, 3
E: 3
P: 1
MRA: 5

KEY POINT: Direct materials and direct labor are costs that can be conveniently and economically traced to the product. This is an application of cost-benefit analysis.

As noted above, product costs include all costs related to the manufacturing process. The three elements of product cost are direct materials costs, direct labor costs, and manufacturing overhead costs, which are indirect costs.

Direct materials costs are the costs of materials used in making a product that can be conveniently and economically traced to specific units of the product. Some examples of direct materials are the iron ore used in making steel, the sheet metal used in making automobiles, and the sugar used in making candy. Direct materials may also include parts purchased from another manufacturer.

Direct labor costs are the costs of the labor needed to make a product that can be conveniently and economically traced to specific units of the product. For example, the wages of production-line workers are direct labor costs.

Manufacturing overhead costs (also called *factory overhead, factory burden,* or *indirect manufacturing costs*) are production-related costs that cannot be practically or conveniently traced directly to an end product. They include **indirect materials costs**, such as the costs of nails, rivets, lubricants, and small tools, and **indirect labor costs**, such as the costs of labor for machinery and tool maintenance, inspection, engineering design, supervision, and materials handling. Other indirect manufacturing costs include the costs of building maintenance, property taxes, property insurance, depreciation on plant and equipment, rent, and utilities. As indirect costs, manufacturing overhead costs are allocated to a product's cost using traditional or activity-based costing methods, which we discuss later in the chapter.

To illustrate product costs and the manufacturing process, we'll refer throughout the chapter to Candy Company, Inc., a manufacturer of chocolate candy bars. Olga Santee, the company's founder and president, has identified the following elements of the product cost of one candy bar:

- *Direct materials costs:* costs of sugar, chocolate, and wrapper

FOCUS ON BUSINESS PRACTICE

How Does an Airline Manage Its Fixed Costs?

One of Southwest Airlines' nonfinancial performance measures is a twenty-minute turnaround time on the ground. This standard helps Southwest <www.southwest.com> efficiently manage the many fixed costs of running an airline. If additional security measures or other circumstances forced Southwest to add even ten minutes to its ground turnaround time, it would result in higher fixed costs because the company would need additional planes to keep to its daily flight schedule. For an airline to be profitable, it needs to maximize its fleet's time in the air and minimize its time on the ground.[2]

COST BEHAVIOR

Managers are also interested in the way costs respond to changes in volume or activity. By analyzing those patterns of behavior, they gain information about how changes in selling prices or operating costs affect the company's net income, and they can then make adjustments so that the company obtains a certain level of profit.

Costs can be separated into variable costs and fixed costs. A **variable cost** is a cost that changes in direct proportion to a change in productive output (or any other measure of volume). A **fixed cost** is a cost that remains constant within a defined range of activity or time period.

All types of organizations have variable and fixed costs. The following are a few examples:

- The variable costs of a landscaping service include the costs of landscaping materials and labor to plant the materials. Fixed costs include the costs of depreciation on trucks and equipment, rent, insurance, and property taxes.

- The variable costs of a used-car dealer include the cost of cars sold and sales commissions. Fixed costs include the costs of building and lot rental, depreciation on office equipment, and receptionist's and accountant's salaries.

- The variable costs of a lawn-mower manufacturer include the costs of direct materials, direct labor, indirect materials (e.g., bolts, nails, lubricants), and indirect labor (e.g., inspection and maintenance labor). Fixed costs include the costs of supervisors' salaries and depreciation on buildings.

As a landscaping service plants more trees, as a used-car dealer sells more cars, or as a lawn-mower manufacturer increases its output of products, its variable costs will increase proportionately. But its fixed costs will remain the same for a specified period; rent, for example, will not change over the term of the lease, and property taxes will remain the same until the next assessment.

VALUE-ADDING VERSUS NONVALUE-ADDING COSTS

A **value-adding cost** is the cost of an activity that increases the market value of a product or service. A **nonvalue-adding cost** is the cost of an activity that adds cost to a product or service but does not increase its market value. For example, the depreciation of a machine that shapes a part used in the final product is a value-adding cost; the depreciation of a car used by the Sales Department is a nonvalue-adding cost. Managers examine the value-adding attributes of their company's operating activities and, wherever possible, reduce or eliminate those that do not directly add value to the company's products or services. Managers also identify which characteristics of their company's products or services customers value and are willing to pay for. This information influences the design of future products or services.

KEY POINT: Product costs remain assets until they are expensed and transferred from the Finished Goods Inventory account to Cost of Goods Sold.

BUSINESS WORLD EXAMPLE: The length of time costs remain in inventory is not a consideration in determining product cost. For example, fast-food operations maintain a direct materials inventory, have a rapid turnover in work in process inventory, and have virtually no finished goods inventory at any given time.

Costs incurred to improve the quality of a product are value-adding costs if the customer is willing to pay more for the higher-quality product; otherwise, they are nonvalue-adding costs because they do not increase the product's market value. The costs of administrative activities, such as accounting and human resource management, are nonvalue-adding costs; they are necessary for the operation of the business, but they do not add value to the product.

COST CLASSIFICATIONS FOR FINANCIAL REPORTING

For purposes of preparing financial statements, managers classify costs as product costs or period costs. **Product costs**, or *inventoriable* costs, are costs assigned to inventory; they include direct materials, direct labor, and manufacturing overhead.

Figure 2
Overview of Cost Classifications

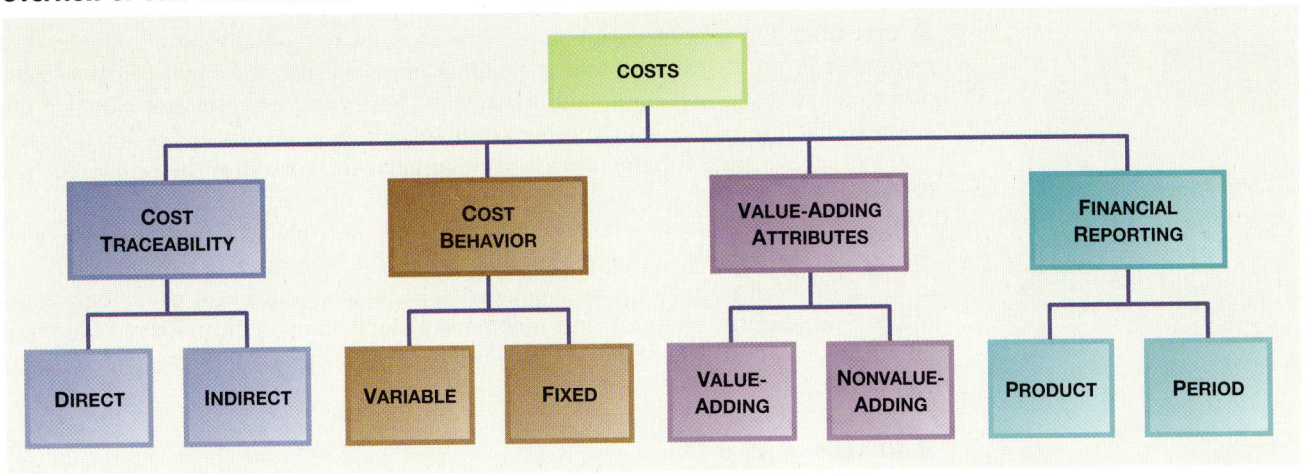

```
                                    COSTS
          ┌──────────────────┬───────────────────┬──────────────────┐
        COST              COST           VALUE-ADDING          FINANCIAL
    TRACEABILITY        BEHAVIOR          ATTRIBUTES           REPORTING
      ┌─────┴─────┐    ┌────┴────┐       ┌────┴─────┐        ┌────┴────┐
    DIRECT    INDIRECT  VARIABLE  FIXED  VALUE-   NONVALUE-  PRODUCT  PERIOD
                                         ADDING    ADDING
```

COST TRACEABILITY

Managers trace costs to cost objects, such as products or services, sales territories, departments, or operating activities, to develop a fairly accurate measurement of costs. They use both direct and indirect measures of costs to support pricing decisions or decisions to reallocate resources to other cost objects.

Direct costs are costs that can be conveniently and economically traced to a cost object. For example, the wages of a Southwest Airlines flight crew can be conveniently traced to a flight because the time worked and the hourly wages are shown on time cards and payroll records. Similarly, jet fuel costs for a flight can be easily traced.

In some cases, even though a material becomes part of a finished product, the expense of tracing its cost is too great. Some examples include the nails used in furniture, the salt used in cookies, and the rivets used in airplanes. Such costs are considered indirect costs of the product. **Indirect costs** are costs that cannot be conveniently and economically traced to a cost object. For the sake of accuracy, however, indirect costs must be included in the cost of a product or service. Because they are difficult to trace, management uses a formula to assign them. For example, Southwest Airlines' insurance costs cannot be conveniently traced to individual flights; management solves the problem by assigning a portion of the insurance costs to each flight flown.

The following examples illustrate cost objects and their direct and indirect costs in service, retail, and manufacturing organizations:

- In a service organization, such as an accounting firm, costs can be traced to a specific service, such as preparation of tax returns. Direct costs for such a service include the costs of government reporting forms, computer usage, and the accountant's labor. Indirect costs include the costs of supplies, office rental, utilities, secretarial labor, telephone usage, and depreciation of office furniture.

- In a retail organization, such as a department store, costs can be traced to a department. For example, the direct costs of the shoe department include the costs of shoes and the wages of employees working in that department. Indirect costs include the costs of utilities, insurance, property taxes, storage, and handling.

- In a manufacturing organization, costs can be traced to the product. Direct costs include the costs of the materials and labor needed to make the product. Indirect costs include the costs of utilities, depreciation of plant and equipment, insurance, property taxes, inspection, supervision, maintenance of machinery, storage, and handling.

---

www.southwest.com

◆ **STOP AND THINK!**
Are the costs of a product always traceable as direct or indirect costs?

Because products are cost objects, their costs can always be classified as direct or indirect. ■

of rendering services to develop budgets, estimate revenues, and manage the organization's work force.

■ **EXECUTING** In the executing stage, managers of manufacturing companies use estimated product costs to predict the gross margin and operating income on sales and to make decisions about such matters as dropping a product line, outsourcing the manufacture of a part to another company, bidding on a special order, or negotiating a selling price. In retail organizations, managers work with the estimated cost of merchandise purchases to predict gross margin, operating income, and value of merchandise sold and to make decisions about such matters as reducing selling prices for clearance sales, lowering selling prices for bulk sales, or dropping a product line. In service organizations, managers find the estimated cost of services helpful in estimating profitability and making decisions about such matters as bidding on future business, lowering or negotiating their fees, or dropping one of their services.

■ **REVIEWING** In the reviewing stage, managers want to know about significant differences between the estimated costs and actual costs of their products, merchandise purchases, or services. The identification of variances between estimated and actual costs helps them determine the causes of cost overruns, which may enable them to make decisions that will avoid such problems in the future.

■ **REPORTING** In the reporting stage, managers expect to see income statements that show the actual costs of operating activities and balance sheets that show the value of inventory. They also expect performance reports that summarize the variance analyses done in the reviewing stage.

COST INFORMATION AND ORGANIZATIONS

Although all organizations use cost information to determine profits and selling prices and to value inventories, different types of organizations have different types of costs. Manufacturing organizations need information about the costs of manufacturing products. Product costs include the costs of direct materials, direct labor, and manufacturing overhead. Retail organizations need information about the costs of purchasing products for resale. These costs include adjustments for freight-in costs, purchase returns and allowances, and purchase discounts. Service organizations need information about the costs of providing services, which include the costs of labor and related overhead. Among the other costs that these organizations incur are the costs of marketing, distributing, installing, and repairing a product or the costs of marketing and supporting the delivery of services. Ultimately, a company is profitable only when its revenues from sales or services rendered exceed all costs.

✓ Check out ACE for a Review Quiz at http://accounting.college.hmco.com/students.

● Stop and Think!
Do managers in all organizations need the same type of cost information?

The type of cost information managers need varies according to the type of organization. Managers in manufacturing organizations need information about the cost of manufacturing a product, those in retail organizations need information about the cost of purchasing a product, and those in service organizations need information about the cost of providing a service. ■

COST CLASSIFICATIONS AND THEIR USES

LO2 Explain how managers classify costs and how they use these cost classifications.

RELATED TEXT ASSIGNMENTS
Q: 2, 3, 4, 5
SE: 1
E: 2
SD: 1, 4
MRA: 2, 5

A single cost can be classified and used in several ways, depending on the purpose of the analysis. Figure 2 provides an overview of commonly used cost classifications. These classifications enable managers to (1) control costs by determining which are traceable to a particular cost object, such as a service or product; (2) calculate the number of units that must be sold to obtain a certain level of profit (cost behavior); (3) identify the costs of activities that do and do not add value to a product or service; and (4) classify costs for the preparation of financial statements. Cost classifications are important in all types of organizations. They help managers select and use relevant information to improve the efficiency of operations, provide quality products or services, and satisfy customer needs.

COST INFORMATION AND THE MANAGEMENT CYCLE

LO1 Describe how managers use information about costs in the management cycle.

RELATED TEXT ASSIGNMENTS
Q: 1
E: 1
SD: 1

One of a company's primary goals is to be profitable. Because owners expect to earn profits, managers have a responsibility to use resources wisely and to generate revenues that will exceed the costs of the company's operating, investing, and financing activities. In this chapter, we focus on costs related to the operating activities of manufacturing, retail, and service organizations. We begin by looking at how managers in these different organizations use information about costs during the management cycle.

USE OF COST INFORMATION IN THE MANAGEMENT CYCLE

During the management cycle, managers use information about operating costs to plan, execute, review, and report the results of operating activities. Figure 1 provides an overview of operating costs and the management cycle.

www.johndeere.com
www.motorola.com
www.gm.com
www.sears.com
www.pepboys.com
www.chicos.com
www.citibank.com
www.humana.com
www.usaa.com

■ **PLANNING** In the planning stage, managers of manufacturing companies, such as John Deere, Motorola, and General Motors, use estimates of product costs to develop budgets for production, materials, labor, and overhead, as well as to determine the selling price or sales level required to cover all costs. In retail companies, such as Sears, Pep Boys, and Chico's, managers work with estimates of the cost of merchandise purchases to develop budgets for purchases and net income, as well as to determine the selling prices or sales units required to cover all costs. In service organizations, like Citibank, Humana, and USAA, managers use the estimated costs

FIGURE 1
Operating Costs and the Management Cycle

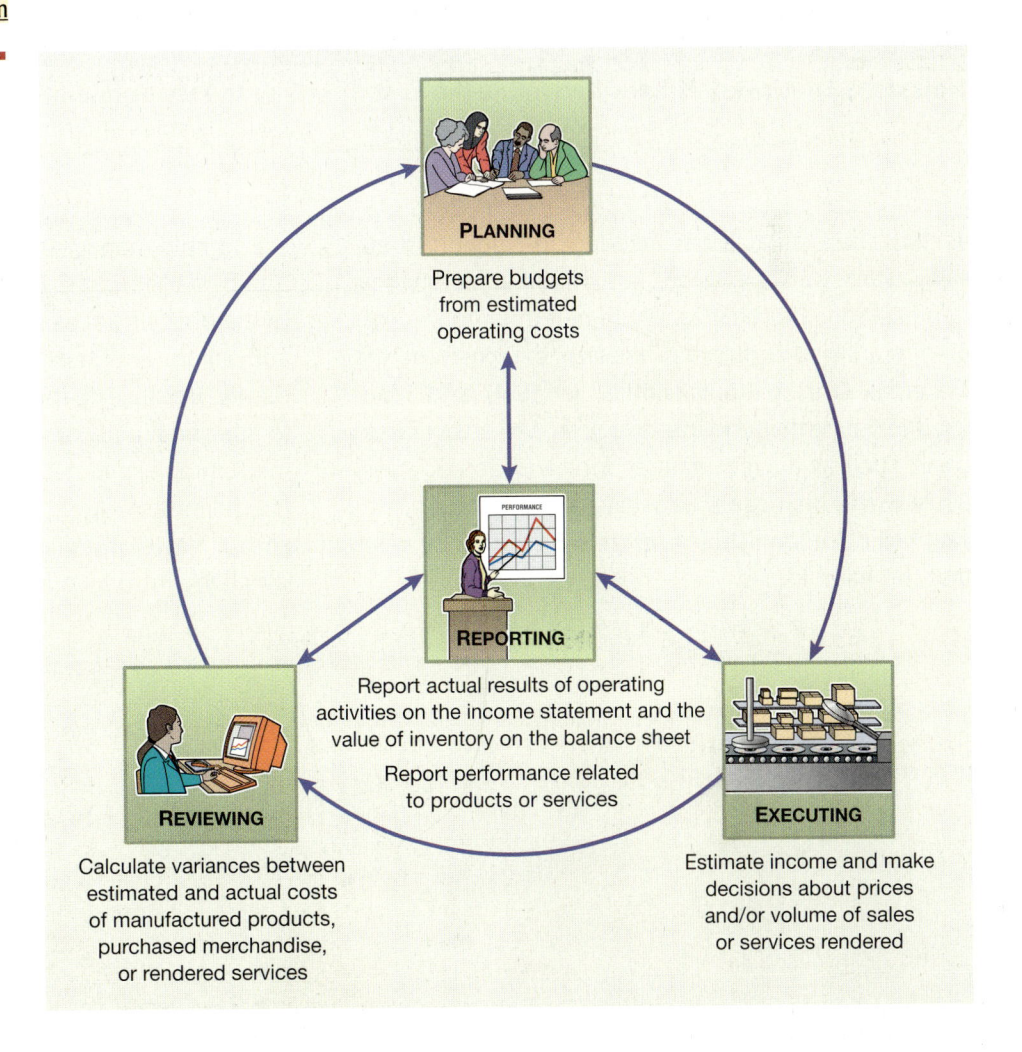

PLANNING
Prepare budgets from estimated operating costs

REPORTING
Report actual results of operating activities on the income statement and the value of inventory on the balance sheet
Report performance related to products or services

EXECUTING
Estimate income and make decisions about prices and/or volume of sales or services rendered

REVIEWING
Calculate variances between estimated and actual costs of manufactured products, purchased merchandise, or rendered services

How does Southwest Airlines determine the cost of selling tickets or operating a flight?

as the costs of activities needed to support these sales, such as supervision, equipment maintenance, depreciation, and utilities. When determining the cost of operating a flight, they analyze the costs of the materials (e.g., peanuts, drinks, jet fuel) and labor used (e.g., flight attendants, pilot), as well as overhead costs, such as aircraft maintenance and depreciation. Southwest's managers also consider any other relevant selling, administrative, or general operating costs that the flight incurs.

To help managers make decisions that will sustain Southwest's profitability, all costs must be analyzed in terms of their traceability and behavior, whether they add value, and how they affect the financial statements. Because many costs cannot be directly traced to specific flights, activities, or departments, management must use a method of allocation to assign them. Possibilities include traditional allocation methods and a newer method called activity-based costing, which we introduce in this chapter.

20

Chapter 20 describes how managers use information about costs, classify costs, compile product unit costs, and allocate costs using the traditional method and the newer activity-based approach.

Cost Concepts and Cost Allocation

LEARNING OBJECTIVES

LO1 Describe how managers use information about costs in the management cycle.

LO2 Explain how managers classify costs and how they use these cost classifications.

LO3 Define and give examples of the three elements of product cost and compute the unit cost of a product.

LO4 Describe the flow of costs through a manufacturer's inventory accounts.

LO5 Compare how service, retail, and manufacturing organizations report costs on their financial statements and how they account for inventories.

LO6 Define *cost allocation* and explain how cost objects, cost pools, and cost drivers are used to assign manufacturing overhead costs.

LO7 Using the traditional method of allocating manufacturing overhead costs, calculate product unit cost.

LO8 Using activity-based costing to assign manufacturing overhead costs, calculate product unit cost.

LO9 Apply costing concepts to a service organization.

DECISION POINT
A MANAGER'S FOCUS

Southwest Airlines <www.southwest.com> With approximately 2,800 flights a day, an average trip length of 715 miles, and an average one-way fare of $82.84, Southwest Airlines is the nation's leading high-frequency, short-haul, low-fare carrier. It is also the only large domestic airline to have remained profitable for more than 30 years. In both 2001 and 2002, the Official Airline Guide <www.oag.com>, an independent provider of travel information, products, and services, named Southwest "Best Low-Cost Airline."

To have achieved such a status and to maintain it, Southwest managers must know the costs the airline is incurring, including the cost of selling tickets and of flight operations. For example, knowing that selling a ticket through a travel agent costs Southwest as much as $6 to $8 whereas selling a ticket through its web site costs the airline just $1 enables managers to offer lower fares to customers who buy tickets online. Online ticket sales at southwest.com generated approximately 46 percent, or $500 million, of the company's passenger revenues for the first quarter of 2002.[1]

Determining the cost of selling tickets online or the cost of operating a flight requires complex analyses of many costs. What are some of these costs, and how do they bear on Southwest's management decisions?

When determining the cost of online ticket sales, Southwest's managers analyze the costs of direct labor and materials (if a paper ticket is issued), as well

financial, (b) quantitative nonfinancial, and (c) qualitative information you will need before you can make a decision.

Group Activity: Divide the class into groups and ask them to discuss this case. Then debrief the entire class by asking one person from each group to summarize his or her group's discussion.

Excel Spreadsheet Analysis

MRA 4.
LO5 Nonfinancial Data Analysis

Refer to assignment **P 2** in this chapter. Lindy Raymond needs to analyze the work performed by each shift in each department during Weeks 1 through 4.

1. For each department, calculate the average labor hours worked per board for each shift during Weeks 1 through 4. Carry your solution to two decimal places. (Note: Hours worked per board = hours worked each week ÷ boards produced each week.)
2. Using the ChartWizard and the information from **1**, prepare a line graph for each department that compares the hours per board worked by the first and second shifts and the estimate for that department during Weeks 1 through 4. The following is the suggested format to use for the information table necessary to complete the line graph for the Molding Department:

Molding Department

	Week 1	Week 2	Week 3	Week 4
First shift	3.50	3.20	3.40	3.80
Second shift	3.60	3.40	3.80	4.20
Estimated	3.40	3.40	3.40	3.40

3. Examine the four graphs that you prepared in **2**. Which shift is more efficient in all four departments? List some reasons for the differences between the shifts.

Internet Case

MRA 5.
LO4 Comparison of Performance Measures

As noted in this chapter's Decision Point, Honda Motor Company <www.honda.com> makes a green car called the Insight. Toyota Motor Company <www.toyota.com> also makes a green car, which it calls the Prius. Search the web sites of both these companies for data concerning the success of their green cars. (**Hint:** Review annual reports and press releases, or use the company's search engine.)

1. List the financial and nonfinancial performance measures that Toyota uses. List the measures used by Honda.
2. Use the data you found to prepare a brief comparison of the two cars. Do the two companies use comparable performance measures? If so, use these measures to evaluate the performance of the Prius and the Insight. If the measures are not comparable, how do they differ?

MANAGERIAL REPORTING AND ANALYSIS CASES

Interpreting Management Reports

MRA 1.

LO1 Management Information

Obtain a copy of a recent annual report of a publicly held organization in which you have a particular interest. (Copies of annual reports are available at your campus library, at a local public library, on the Internet, or by direct request to an organization.) Assume that you have just been appointed to a middle-management position in a division of the organization you have chosen. You are interested in obtaining information that will help you better manage the activities of your division and have decided to study the contents of the annual report in an attempt to learn as much as possible. You particularly want to know about the following:

1. Size of inventory maintained
2. Ability to earn income
3. Reliance on debt financing
4. Types, volume, and prices of products or services sold
5. Type of production process used
6. Management's long-range strategies
7. Success (profitability) of the division's various product lines
8. Efficiency of operations
9. Operating details of your division

1. Write a brief description of the organization and its products or services and activities.
2. Based on a review of the financial statements and the accompanying disclosure notes, prepare a written summary of information pertaining to items 1 through 9 above.
3. Is any of the information in which you are interested in other sections of the annual report? If so, which information, and in which sections of the report is it?
4. The annual report also includes other types of information you may find helpful in your new position. In outline form, summarize this additional information.

Formulating Management Reports

MRA 2.

LO1 Management Information Needs

In **MRA 1**, you examined your new employer's annual report and found some useful information. However, you are interested in knowing whether your division's products or services are competitive, and you were unable to find the necessary information in the annual report.

1. What kinds of information about your competition do you want to find?
2. Why is this information relevant? (Link your response to a particular decision about your organization's products or services. For example, you might seek information to help you determine a new selling price.)
3. From what sources could you obtain the information you need?
4. When would you want to obtain this information?
5. Create a report that will communicate your findings to your superior.

International Company

MRA 3.

LO5 Management Information Needs

McDonald's <www.mcdonalds.com> is a leading competitor in the fast-food restaurant business. One component of McDonald's marketing strategy is to increase sales by expanding its foreign markets. At present, more than 40 percent of McDonald's restaurants are located outside the United States. In making decisions about opening restaurants in foreign markets, the company uses quantitative and qualitative financial and nonfinancial information. For example, the following types of information would be important to such a decision: the cost of a new building (quantitative financial information), the estimated number of hamburgers to be sold in the first year (quantitative nonfinancial information), and site desirability (qualitative information).

You are a member of a management team that must decide whether or not to open a new restaurant in England. Identify at least two examples each of the (a) quantitative

2. Why does the information in a grade report for students' use and in a grade report for instructors' use differ?
3. Visit the registrar's office of your school in person or through your school's web site. Obtain a copy of your grade report and a copy of the form the registrar's office uses to report grades to instructors. Compare the information that these reports supply with the information you listed in **1**. Explain any differences.
4. What can the registrar's office do to make sure that its grade reports are effective in communicating all necessary information to readers?

Decision-Making Practice

SD 6. **LO5 Nonfinancial Data Analysis**

Aviation Products Company is a subcontractor that specializes in producing housings for landing gears on jet airplanes. Its production process begins with Machine 1, which bends pieces of metal into cylinder-shaped housings and trims off the rough edges. Machine 2 welds the seam of the cylinder and pushes the entire piece into a large die to mold the housing into its final shape.

Joe Mee, the production supervisor, believes the current process creates too much scrap (i.e., wasted metal). To verify this, James Kincaid, the company's accountant, began comparing the amounts of scrap generated in the last four weeks with the amounts of scrap the company anticipated for that period. Because of a death in his family, Kincaid could not complete his analysis. His incomplete report appears below. Mee asks you to complete the report and submit a recommendation to him.

Aviation Products Company
Comparison of Actual Scrap and Expected Scrap
Four-Week Period

	Scrap in Pounds		Difference	
	Actual	Expected	Pounds	Percentage
Machine 1				
Week 1	36,720	36,720		
Week 2	54,288	36,288		
Week 3	71,856	35,856		
Week 4	82,440	35,640		
Machine 2				
Week 1	43,200	18,180		
Week 2	39,600	18,054		
Week 3	7,200	18,162		
Week 4	18,000	18,108		

1. Present the information in two ways:
    a. Prepare a table that shows the difference between the actual and the expected scrap in pounds per machine per week. Calculate the difference in pounds and as a percentage (divide the difference in pounds by the expected pounds of scrap for each week). If the actual poundage of scrap is less than the expected poundage, record the difference as a negative. (This means there is less scrap than expected.)
    b. Prepare a line graph for each machine showing the weeks on the X axis and the pounds of scrap on the Y axis.
2. Examine the differences for the four weeks for each machine and determine which machine operation is creating excessive scrap.
3. What could be causing this problem?
4. What could Mee do to encourage early identification of the specific cause of such problems?

1. Answer the following questions:
    a. What standards do you have for assessing your performance?
    b. What processes have you designed for achieving high quality in your performance?
    c. How do you know when you have achieved high quality in your performance?
    d. Once you know you perform well, how easy will it be for you to maintain that level of expertise?
    e. What can you do to ensure that you are continuously improving your performance?
2. If you owned a business, which of the above questions would be important to answer?
3. Answer the questions in 1, assuming you own a business.

LO4 Performance Measures and the Balanced Scorecard

SD 3. General Motors Corporation <www.gm.com> had a plan to revamp the way it makes small cars. Called Project Yellowstone, the plan called for GM to build two U.S. plants that would use modular assembly systems. GM's suppliers would develop and send large chunks of cars, like dashboards, to the two new plants for final assembly. The amount of GM's investment and the number of employees needed to assemble the cars would be greatly reduced. The United Auto Workers union blasted the new approach as an attempt to eliminate union jobs, and GM retreated from the plan.[9]

1. What financial performance measures mentioned in the chapter would have prompted GM to try this new approach?
2. The balanced scorecard uses performance measures that are linked to the perspectives of all stakeholder groups. Who are GM's stakeholders, and what performance measures do they value?
3. Refer to the discussion of Honda Motor Company <www.honda.com> in the Decision Point at the beginning of this chapter. How does Honda's modular assembly plan differ from the one GM proposed?
4. In your opinion, what options does GM have if it wishes to pursue the use of modular assembly systems?

Ethical Dilemma

LO6 Professional Ethics

SD 4. Mark Taylor is the controller for Krohm Corporation. Taylor has been with the company for 17 years and is being considered for the job of chief financial officer (CFO). His boss, the current CFO and former company controller, will be Krohm Corporation's new president. Taylor has just discussed the year-end closing with his boss, who made the following statement during the conversation:

> Mark, why are you being so inflexible? I'm only asking you to postpone the $2,500,000 write-off of obsolete inventory for ten days so that it won't appear on this year's financial statements. Ten days! Do it. Your promotion is coming up, you know. Make sure you keep all the possible outcomes in mind as you complete your year-end work. Oh, and keep this conversation confidential—just between you and me. Okay?

Identify the ethical issue or issues involved and state the appropriate solution to the problem. Be prepared to defend your answer.

Research Activity

LO1 Report Preparation

SD 5. The registrar's office of Polk Community College is responsible for maintaining a record of each student's grades and credits for use by students, instructors, and administrators.

1. Assume you are a manager in the registrar's office and that you recently joined a team of managers to review the grade-reporting process. Explain how you would prepare a report of grades for students' use and the same report for instructors' use by answering the following questions:
    a. Who will read the grade report?
    b. Why is the grade report necessary?
    c. What information should the grade report contain?
    d. When is the grade report due?

LO5 Nonfinancial Data Analysis

P 8. Texas State Bank was founded in 1869. It has had a record of slow, steady growth since its inception. Management has always kept the processing of information as current as technology allows. Leslie Oistins, manager of the Brazas branch, is upgrading the check-sorting equipment in her office. There are ten check-sorting machines in operation. Information on the number of checks sorted by machine during the past eight weeks is as follows:

Machine	One	Two	Three	Four	Five	Six	Seven	Eight
AA	89,260	89,439	89,394	90,288	90,739	90,658	90,676	90,630
AB	91,420	91,237	91,602	91,969	91,950	92,502	92,446	92,816
AC	94,830	95,020	94,972	95,922	96,401	96,315	96,334	96,286
AD	91,970	91,786	92,153	92,522	92,503	93,058	93,002	93,375
AE	87,270	87,445	87,401	88,275	88,716	88,636	88,654	88,610
BA	92,450	92,265	92,634	93,005	92,986	93,544	93,488	93,862
BB	91,910	92,094	92,048	92,968	93,433	93,349	93,368	93,321
BC	90,040	89,860	90,219	90,580	90,562	91,105	91,051	91,415
BD	87,110	87,190	87,210	130,815	132,320	133,560	134,290	135,770
BE	94,330	94,519	94,471	95,416	95,893	95,807	95,826	95,778

The Brazas branch has increased its checking business significantly over the past two years. Oistins must decide whether to purchase additional check-sorting machines or attachments for the existing machines to increase productivity. Five weeks ago the Colonnade Company convinced her to experiment with one such attachment, and it was placed on Machine BD. Oistins is impressed with the attachment but has yet to decide between the two courses of action. Labor costs are not a factor in her decision.

REQUIRED

1. Compute the average weekly output of all machines except BD.
2. Compare the weekly output of Machine BD with the average weekly output of the nine machines without the attachment. Compute the weekly difference in the number of checks and the percentage change (difference divided by the average weekly output of the nine machines).
3. Assume that Colonnade's attachment costs about the same as a new check-sorting machine. Which alternative would you recommend that Oistins choose?
4. Would you change your recommendation if two attachments could be purchased for the price of one check-sorting machine? Does this decision require more data?
5. Assume three attachments could be purchased for the price of one check-sorting machine. What action would you recommend?

SKILLS DEVELOPMENT CASES

Conceptual Analysis

LO2 The Value Chain and Core Competency

SD 1. Medical Products Company (MPC) is known for developing innovative and high-quality products for use in hospitals and medical and dental offices. Its latest product is a nonporous, tough, and very thin disposable glove that will not leak or split and molds tightly to the hand, making it ideal for use in medical and dental procedures. MPC buys the material it uses in making the gloves from another company, which manufactures it according to MPC'S exact specifications and quality standards. MPC makes two models of the glove—one white, and one transparent—in its own plant and sells them through independent agents who represent various manufacturers. When an agent informs MPC of a sale, MPC ships the order directly to the buyer. MPC advertises the gloves in professional journals and gives free samples to physicians and dentists. It provides a product warranty and periodically surveys users about the product's quality.

Briefly explain how MPC accomplishes each of the primary processes of the value chain. What is a core competency? Which one of the primary processes would you say is MPC's core competency? Explain your choice.

LO3 Continuous Improvement

SD 2. Achieving high quality requires high standards of performance. To maintain high standards of quality, individuals and organizations must continuously improve their performance. To illustrate this concept, select your favorite sport or hobby.

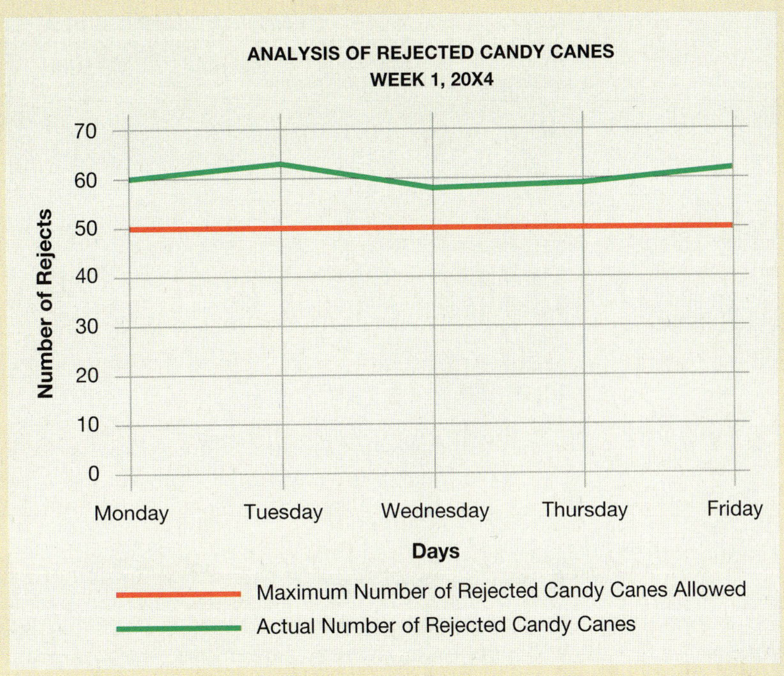

Because the variance was 20.8 percent (52 ÷ 250), Ortes decided to analyze the data further. She found that the rejected candy canes contained too little sugar (ingredients), were not circular in shape (shaping), or were undercooked (cooking time). The number of rejects in each category appears below.

Week 1, 20x4	Reasons for Rejects
Ingredients	40
Shaping	195
Cooking time	67
Total	302

The following week, Ortes reviewed the recipe with the cooks. She trained them to measure ingredients more precisely, to shape the candy more carefully, and to time the cooking process more accurately. Then, in Week 3 of 20x4, she gathered the following information on the actual number of rejected candy canes and reasons for the rejects:

Week 3, 20x4	Actual Number of Rejects
Monday	20
Tuesday	21
Wednesday	22
Thursday	19
Friday	18
Total	100

Week 3, 20x4	Reasons for Rejects
Ingredients	7
Shaping	63
Cooking time	30
Total	100

REQUIRED ▶

1. Analyze the activity in Week 3 of 20x4 by preparing a table showing each day's maximum number of rejected candy canes allowed, actual number of rejected candy canes, and variance under (over) the maximum number allowed. In addition, prepare a graph comparing the maximum and actual numbers for each day of Week 3.
2. Analyze how the reasons for rejecting candy canes changed from Week 1 to Week 3 by preparing a table showing the number of times each reason occurred each week. In addition, prepare a graph comparing the reasons for rejects each week.
3. How successful was Ortes in increasing the quality of Holiday's candy canes? What recommendations, if any, would you make about monitoring candy production in the future?

Passengers Checked by Metal Detectors

Date	Machine 1	Machine 2	Machine 3	Machine 4	Totals
March 6	5,620	5,490	5,436	5,268	21,814
March 7	5,524	5,534	5,442	5,290	21,790
March 8	5,490	5,548	5,489	5,348	21,875
March 9	5,436	5,592	5,536	5,410	21,974
March 10	5,404	5,631	5,568	5,456	22,059
March 11	5,386	5,667	5,594	5,496	22,143
March 12	5,364	5,690	5,638	5,542	22,234
March 13	5,678	6,248	6,180	6,090	24,196
March 14	5,720	6,272	6,232	6,212	24,436
March 15	5,736	6,324	6,372	6,278	24,710

3. Is there anything unusual in the analysis of passenger traffic flow that management should look into? Explain your answer.

ALTERNATE PROBLEMS

LO1 Report Preparation

P 6. Sam Ratha recently purchased Yard & More, Inc., a wholesale distributor of equipment and supplies for lawn and garden care. The organization, headquartered in Baltimore, has four distribution centers that service 14 eastern states. The centers are located in Boston; Rye, New York; Reston, Virginia; and Lawrenceville, New Jersey. Company profits for 20x2, 20x3, and 20x4 were $225,400, $337,980, and $467,200, respectively.

Shortly after purchasing the organization, Ratha appointed people to the following positions: vice president, marketing; vice president, distribution; corporate controller; and vice president, research and development. Ratha has called a meeting of his management group. He wants to create a deluxe retail lawn and garden center that would include a large, fully landscaped plant and tree nursery. The purposes of the retail center would be (1) to test equipment and supplies before selecting them for sales and distribution and (2) to showcase the effects of using the company's products. The retail center must also make a profit on sales.

REQUIRED

1. What types of information will Ratha need before deciding whether to create the retail lawn and garden center?
2. To support his decision, Ratha will need a report from the vice president of research and development analyzing all possible plants and trees that could be planted and their ability to grow in the places where the new retail center might be located. How would each of the four *w*'s pertain to this report?
3. Design a format for the report in **2**.

LO5 Nonfinancial Data Analysis

P 7. Holiday Candy Company, which has recently developed a strategic plan based on total quality management, wants its candy canes to have the highest quality of color, texture, shape, and taste possible. To ensure that quality standards are met, management has chosen many quality performance measures, including the number of rejected candy canes. Working with Luisa Ortes, the production supervisor, management has decided that no more than 50 candy canes should be rejected each day.

Using data on rejections in Week 1 of 20x4, Luisa Ortes prepared the following summary and the graph that appears on the next page.

Week 1, 20x4	Maximum Number of Rejected Candy Canes Allowed	Actual Number of Rejected Candy Canes	Variance Under (Over) Allowed Maximum
Monday	50	60	(10)
Tuesday	50	63	(13)
Wednesday	50	58	(8)
Thursday	50	59	(9)
Friday	50	62	(12)
Total for the week	250	302	(52)
Daily average	50	60.4	

Raymond is concerned about the number of hours her employees are working. The plant has a two-shift labor force. The actual hours worked for the past four weeks are as follows:

Actual Hours Worked—First Shift

Department	Week 1	Week 2	Week 3	Week 4	Totals
Molding	420	432	476	494	1,822
Sanding	60	81	70	91	302
Fiber-Ap	504	540	588	572	2,204
Assembling	768	891	952	832	3,443

Actual Hours Worked—Second Shift

Department	Week 1	Week 2	Week 3	Week 4	Totals
Molding	360	357	437	462	1,616
Sanding	60	84	69	99	312
Fiber-Ap	440	462	529	506	1,937
Assembling	670	714	782	726	2,892

Expected labor hours per product for each operation are Molding, 3.4 hours; Sanding, .5 hour; Fiber-Ap, 4.0 hours; and Assembling, 6.5 hours. Actual units completed are as follows:

Week	First Shift	Second Shift
1	120	100
2	135	105
3	140	115
4	130	110

REQUIRED

1. Prepare an analysis of each week to determine the average actual labor hours worked per board for each phase of the production process and for each shift. Carry your solution to two decimal places.
2. Using the information from 1 and the expected labor hours per board for each department, prepare an analysis showing the differences in each phase of each shift. Identify possible reasons for the differences.

P 5.
LO5 Nonfinancial Data Analysis

The flow of passenger traffic is an important factor in airport management, and over the past year, heightened security measures at Winnebago County Airport in Rockford, Illinois, have slowed passenger flow significantly. The airport uses eight metal detectors to screen passengers for weapons. The facility is open from 6:00 A.M. to 10:00 P.M. daily, and present machinery allows a maximum of 45,000 passengers to be checked each day.

Management has selected four of the metal detectors for special analysis to determine if additional equipment is needed or if a passenger traffic director could solve the problem. The passenger traffic director would be responsible for guiding people to different machines and instructing them on the detection process. Because this solution would be less expensive than acquiring new machines, management decides to assign a suitable person to this function on a trial basis. Management hopes this procedure will speed up the flow of passenger traffic by at least 10 percent. Manufacturers of the machinery have stated that each machine can handle an average of 400 passengers per hour. Data on passenger traffic through the four machines for the past 10 days are shown at the top of the next page.

In the past, passenger flow has favored Machine 1 because of its location. Overflow traffic goes to Machine 2, Machine 3, and Machine 4, in that order.

The passenger traffic director, Lynn Hedlund, began her duties on March 13. If her work results in at least a 10 percent increase in the number of passengers handled, management plans to hire a second traffic director for the other four machines rather than purchasing additional metal detectors.

REQUIRED

1. Calculate the average daily traffic flow for the period March 6–12 and then calculate management's traffic flow goal.
2. Calculate the average traffic flow for the period March 13–15. Did the passenger traffic director's work result in the minimum increase in flow set by management, or should airport officials purchase additional metal directors?

- Distribution costs are already very low, but management will set a target of reducing the cost per unit by 10 percent.
- Customer service is a weakness of the company and has resulted in lost sales. Management therefore proposes increasing the cost per unit of customer service by 50 percent.

REQUIRED

1. Prepare a table showing the current cost per unit of primary processes and the projected cost per unit based on management's proposals for cost reduction.
2. Will management's proposals for cost reduction achieve the targeted total cost per unit? What further steps should management take to reduce costs? Which steps that management is proposing do you believe will be the most difficult to accomplish?
3. What are the company's support services? What role should these services play in the value chain analysis?

P 3.

LO4 The Balanced Scorecard and Benchmarking

Bychowski Associates is an independent insurance agency that sells business, automobile, home, and life insurance. Myra Bychowski, senior partner of the agency, recently attended a workshop at the local university in which the balanced scorecard was presented as a way of focusing all of a company's functions on its mission. After the workshop, she met with her managers in a weekend brainstorming session. The group determined that the agency's mission was to provide high-quality, innovative risk-protection services to individuals and businesses. To ensure that the agency would fulfill this mission, the group established the following objectives:

- To provide a sufficient return on investment by increasing sales and maintaining the liquidity needed to support operations
- To add value to the agency's services by training employees to be knowledgeable and competent
- To retain customers and attract new customers
- To operate an efficient and cost-effective office support system for customer agents

To determine the agency's progress in meeting these objectives, the group established the following performance measures:

- Number of new ideas for customer insurance
- Percentage of customers who rate services as excellent
- Average time for processing insurance applications
- Number of dollars spent on training
- Growth in revenues for each type of insurance
- Average time for processing claims
- Percentage of employees who complete 40 hours of training during the year
- Percentage of new customer leads that result in sales
- Cash flow
- Number of customer complaints
- Return on assets
- Percentage of customers who renew policies
- Percentage of revenue devoted to office support system (information systems, accounting, orders, and claims processing)

REQUIRED

1. Prepare a balanced scorecard for Bychowski Associates by stating the agency's mission and matching its four objectives to the four stakeholder perspectives: the financial, learning and growth, internal business processes, and customer perspectives. Indicate which of the agency's performance measures would be appropriate for each objective.
2. Bychowski Associates is a member of an association of independent insurance agents that provides industry statistics about many aspects of operating an insurance agency. What is benchmarking, and in what ways would the industry statistics assist Bychowski Associates in further developing its balanced scorecard?

P 4.

LO5 Nonfinancial Data Analysis

Action Skateboards, Inc., manufactures state-of-the-art skateboards and related equipment. Lindy Raymond is the manager of the California branch. The production process involves the following departments and tasks: the Molding Department, where the board's base is molded; the Sanding Department, where the base is sanded after being taken out of the mold; the Fiber-Ap Department, where a fiberglass coating is applied; and the Assembling Department, where the wheels are attached and the board is inspected. After the board is molded, all processes are performed by hand.

environmental or social issues? (3) In your opinion, is the company ethically responsible? Select one of the companies you researched and write a brief description of your findings.

PROBLEMS

LO1 Report Preparation

P 1. Classic Industries, Inc., is deciding whether to expand its line of women's clothing called Pants by Olene. Sales in units of this product were 22,500, 28,900, and 36,200 in 20x4, 20x5, and 20x6, respectively. The product has been very profitable, averaging 35 percent profit (above cost) over the three-year period. Classic has ten sales representatives covering seven states in the Northeast. Present production capacity is about 40,000 pants per year. There is adequate plant space for additional equipment, and the labor needed can be easily hired and trained.

The organization's management is made up of four vice presidents: the vice president of marketing, the vice president of production, the vice president of finance, and the vice president of management information systems. Each vice president is directly responsible to the president, Teresa Jefferson.

REQUIRED
1. What types of information will Jefferson need before she can decide whether to expand the Pants by Olene line?
2. Assume that one report needed to support Jefferson's decision is an analysis of sales, broken down by sales representatives, over the past three years. How would each of the four *w*'s pertain to this report?
3. Design a format for the report described in **2**.

LO2 The Value Chain

P 2. Zeigler Electronics is a manufacturer of cell phones, a highly competitive business. Zeigler's phones carry a price of $99, but competition forces the company to offer significant discounts and rebates. As a result, the average price of Zeigler's cell phones has dropped to around $50, and the company is losing money. Management is applying value chain analysis to the company's operations in an effort to reduce costs and improve product quality. A study by the company's management accountant has determined the following per unit costs for primary processes:

Primary Process	Cost per Unit
Research and development	$ 2.50
Design	3.50
Supply	4.50
Production	6.70
Marketing	8.00
Distribution	1.90
Customer service	.50
Total cost	$27.60

To generate a gross margin large enough for the company to cover overhead costs and earn a profit, Zeigler must lower its total cost per unit for primary processes to at least $20. After analyzing operations, management reached the following conclusions with regard to primary processes:

- Research and development and design are critical functions because the market and competition require constant development of new features with "cool" designs at lower cost. Nevertheless, management feels that the cost per unit of these processes must be reduced by 10 percent.
- Six different suppliers currently provide the components for the cell phones. Ordering these components from just two suppliers and negotiating lower prices could result in a savings of 15 percent.
- The cell phones are currently manufactured in Mexico. By shifting production to China, the unit cost of production can be lowered by 20 percent.
- Most cell phones are sold through wireless communication companies that are trying to attract new customers with low-priced cell phones. Management believes these companies should bear more of the marketing costs and that it is feasible to renegotiate its marketing arrangements with them so that they will bear 35 percent of the current marketing costs.

addressing those issues and to present it at the meeting. His report is to include profits generated in each sales territory by the new card line only.

On August 31, Johnson arrived at the meeting late and immediately distributed his report to the strategic planning team. The report consisted of comments made by seven of Johnson's leading sales representatives. The comments were broad in scope and touched only lightly on the success of the new card line. Johnson was pleased that he had met the deadline for distributing the report, but the other team members were disappointed in the information he had provided.

Using the four *w*'s for report presentation, comment on Johnson's effectiveness in preparing his report.

LO1 The Planning Framework

E 4. Edward Ortez has just opened a company that imports fine ceramic gifts from Mexico and sells them over the Internet. In planning his business, Ortez did the following:

1. Listed his expected expenses and revenues for the first six months of operations
2. Decided that he wanted the company to provide him with income for a good lifestyle and funds for retirement
3. Determined that he would keep his expenses low and generate enough revenues during the first two months of operations so that he would have a positive cash flow by the third month
4. Decided to focus his business on providing customers with the finest Mexican ceramics at a favorable price
5. Developed a complete list of goals, objectives, procedures, and policies relating to how he would find, buy, store, sell, and ship goods and collect payment
6. Decided not to have a retail operation but to rely solely on the Internet to market the products

Match each of Ortez's actions to the components of the planning framework: goal, mission, strategic objectives, operating objectives, business plan, and budget.

LO1 The Supply Chain

E 5. In recent years, United Parcel Service (UPS) has been positioning itself as a solver of supply chain issues. Visit its web site at www.ups-scs.com and read one of the case studies related to its supply chain solutions. Explain how UPS helped improve the supply chain of the business featured in the case.

LO2 The Value Chain

E 6. As mentioned in E4, Edward Ortez recently opened his own company. He has been thinking of ways to improve the business. Here is a list of the actions that he will be undertaking:

1. Engaging an accountant to help analyze progress in meeting the objectives of the company
2. Hiring a company to handle payroll records and employee benefits
3. Developing a logo for labeling and packaging the ceramics
4. Making gift packages by placing gourmet food products in ceramic pots and wrapping them in plastic
5. Engaging an attorney to write contracts
6. Traveling to Mexico himself to arrange for purchase and shipment of products back to the company
7. Arranging new ways of taking orders over the Internet and shipping the products
8. Keeping track of the characteristics of customers and the number and types of products they buy
9. Following up with customers to see if they received the products and if they are happy with them
10. Arranging for an outside firm to keep the accounting records
11. Distributing brochures that display the ceramics and refer to the web site

Classify each of Ortez's actions as one of the value chain's primary processes—research and development, design, supply, production, marketing, distribution, or customer service—or as a support service—human resources, legal services, information systems, or management accounting. Of the eleven actions, which are the most likely candidates for outsourcing? Why?

LO3 Management Tools

E 7. Recently, you were dining with four chief financial officers who were attending a seminar on management tools and approaches to improving operations. During dinner, they shared information about their organizations' current operating environments. Excerpts from the dinner conversation appear on the following page. Indicate whether each excerpt describes

3. Low-priced products
4. Improved return on investment
5. Job security
6. Cost-effective production processes

LO5 Analysis of Nonfinancial Data

SE 9. Precision Technologies has been having a problem with the computerized welding operation in its extractor assembly line. The extractors are used to separate metal shavings into piles of individual metals for recycling and scrap sales. The time for each welding operation has been increasing at an erratic rate. Management has asked that the time intervals be analyzed to see if the cause of the problem can be determined. The number of parts welded per shift during the previous week is as follows:

	Machine Number	Monday	Tuesday	Wednesday	Thursday	Friday
First shift:						
Kovacs	1	642	636	625	617	602
Abington	2	732	736	735	729	738
Geisler	3	745	726	717	694	686
Second shift:						
Deragon	1	426	416	410	404	398
Berwager	2	654	656	661	664	670
Grass	3	526	524	510	504	502

What can you deduce from this information that may help management solve the welding operation problem?

LO6 Ethical Conduct

SE 10. Tyler Jones, a management accountant for Pegstone Cosmetics Company, has lunch every day with his friend Joe Blaik, a management accountant for Shepherd Cosmetics, Inc., a competitor of Pegstone. Last week, Jones couldn't decide how to treat some information in a report he was preparing, so he discussed it with Blaik. Is Jones adhering to the ethical standards of management accountants? Defend your answer.

EXERCISES

LO1 Management Accounting Versus Financial Accounting

E 1. Explain this statement: "It is impossible to distinguish the point at which financial accounting ends and management accounting begins."

LO1 The Management Cycle

E 2. Indicate whether each of the following management activities in a community hospital is part of the planning stage (P), the executing stage (E), the reviewing stage (REV), or the reporting stage (REP) of the management cycle:

1. Leasing five ambulances for the current year
2. Comparing the actual number with the planned number of patient days in the hospital for the year
3. Developing a strategic plan for a new pediatric wing
4. Preparing a report showing the past performance of the emergency room
5. Developing standards, or expectations, for performance in the hospital admittance area for next year
6. Preparing and distributing the hospital's balance sheet and income statement to the board of directors
7. Maintaining an inventory of bed linens and bath towels
8. Formulating a corporate policy for the treatment and final disposition of hazardous waste materials
9. Preparing a report of the types and amounts of hazardous waste materials removed from the hospital in the last three months
10. Recording the time taken to deliver food trays to patients

LO1 Report Preparation

E 3. Jeff Johnson is the sales manager for Sunny Days Greeting Cards, Inc. At the beginning of the year, the organization introduced a new line of humorous birthday cards to the U.S. market. Management will hold a strategic planning meeting on August 31 to discuss next year's operating activities. One item on the agenda is to review the success of the new line of cards and decide if there is a need to change the selling price or to stimulate sales volume in the five sales territories. Johnson has been asked to prepare a report

| LO1 | **The Management Cycle** | SE 2. | Indicate whether each of the following management activities in a department store is part of the planning stage (P), the executing stage (E), the reviewing stage (REV), or the reporting stage (REP) of the management cycle:

1. Completing a balance sheet and income statement at the end of the year
2. Training a clerk to complete a cash sale
3. Meeting with department managers to develop performance measures for sales personnel
4. Renting a local warehouse to store excess inventory of clothing
5. Evaluating the performance of the shoe department by examining the significant differences between its actual and planned expenses for the month
6. Preparing an annual budget of anticipated sales for each department and the entire store

| LO1 | **Report Preparation** | SE 3. | Melissa Mertz, president of Mertz Industries, asked controller Rick Caputo to prepare a report on the use of electricity by each of the organization's five divisions. Increases in electricity costs in the divisions ranged from 20 to 35 percent over the past year. What questions should Rick ask before he begins his analysis?

| LO1 LO2 | **The Supply Chain and the Value Chain** | SE 4. | Indicate whether each of the following is part of the supply chain (SC), a primary process (PP) in the value chain, or a support service (SS) in the value chain:

1. Human resources
2. Research and development
3. Supplier
4. Management accounting
5. Customer service
6. Retailer

| LO2 | **The Value Chain** | SE 5. | From the following unit costs, which were determined by dividing total costs of each cost component by the number of products produced, determine the total cost per unit of primary processes and the total cost per unit of support services:

Research and development	$1.25
Human resources	1.35
Design	.15
Supply	1.10
Legal services	.40
Production	4.00
Marketing	.80
Distribution	.90
Customer service	.65
Information systems	.75
Management accounting	.10
Total cost per unit	$11.45

| LO3 | **JIT and Continuous Improvement** | SE 6. | The just-in-time operating environment focuses on reducing or eliminating the waste of resources. Resources include physical assets such as machinery and buildings, labor time, and materials and parts used in the production process. Choose one of those resources and tell how it could be wasted. How can an organization prevent the waste of that resource? How can the concept of continuous improvement be implemented to reduce the waste of that resource?

| LO3 | **ABC and the Assignment of Cost** | SE 7. | Get Away Enterprises offers weeklong Florida vacation packages to student groups. The trip includes meals, lodging, a parasailing excursion, and transportation. The price is $1,400 per couple. Courtney and Chris sign up. What are some ways of assigning the cost of the trip to each of them? Support your answer.

| LO4 | **The Balanced Scorecard: Stakeholder Values** | SE 8. | In the balanced scorecard approach, stakeholder groups with different perspectives value different performance goals. Sometimes, however, they may be interested in the same goal. Indicate which stakeholder groups—financial (F), learning and growth (L), internal business processes (P), and customers (C)—value the following performance goals:

1. High wages
2. Safe products

Chapter Assignments

BUILDING YOUR KNOWLEDGE FOUNDATION

QUESTIONS

1. What is management accounting, and how is it similar to financial accounting?
2. How do management accounting and financial accounting reports differ in terms of format, purpose, and primary users?
3. How do management accounting and financial accounting reports differ in terms of units of measure, nature of information, and frequency of preparation?
4. What are the four stages of the management cycle? Briefly explain each stage.
5. How is management accounting used in the management cycle?
6. What are the six components of the planning framework? Briefly describe each.
7. What is the supply chain?
8. What are the four *w*'s of report preparation? Explain the importance of each.
9. What is the value chain, and what are the primary processes and support services? How do primary processes and support services differ?
10. What are core competencies and outsourcing?
11. What management tools do companies use to deal with expanding global competition?
12. How does the just-in-time operating philosophy affect an organization's operating environment?
13. How does total quality management help managers do their jobs?
14. How does activity-based management affect an organization's operating environment?
15. How does the theory of constraints affect an organization's operating environment?
16. What is the goal of all the management approaches described in this chapter?
17. What are performance measures? Give examples of both financial and nonfinancial performance measures.
18. How does the balanced scorecard help managers evaluate performance?
19. What perspectives are included in the balanced scorecard?
20. Why do ethical standards for management accountants emphasize competence?
21. Why is it so important for management accountants to maintain their integrity?

SHORT EXERCISES

LO1 Management Accounting Versus Financial Accounting

SE 1. Management accounting differs from financial accounting in a number of ways. Indicate whether each of the following characteristics relates to management accounting (MA) or financial accounting (FA):

1. Focuses on various segments of the business entity
2. Demands objectivity
3. Relies on the criterion of usefulness rather than formal guidelines in reporting information
4. Measures units in historical dollars
5. Reports information on a regular basis
6. Uses only monetary measures for reports
7. Adheres to generally accepted accounting principles
8. Prepares reports whenever needed

3. Using the information from 1 and 2, identify which group of painters worked more hours than George Youngdale planned and offer several reasons for the additional hours.

ANSWER TO REVIEW PROBLEM

1.

Interior Painters

Week	Estimated Hours	Actual Hours	Hours Under or (Over) Estimate
1	80	96	(16)
2	80	108	(28)
3	80	116	(36)
4	80	116	(36)
Total	320	436	(116)

Exterior Painters

Week	Projected Hours	Actual Hours	Hours Under or (Over) Estimate
1	120	104	16
2	120	108	12
3	120	116	4
4	120	108	12
Total	480	436	44

2.

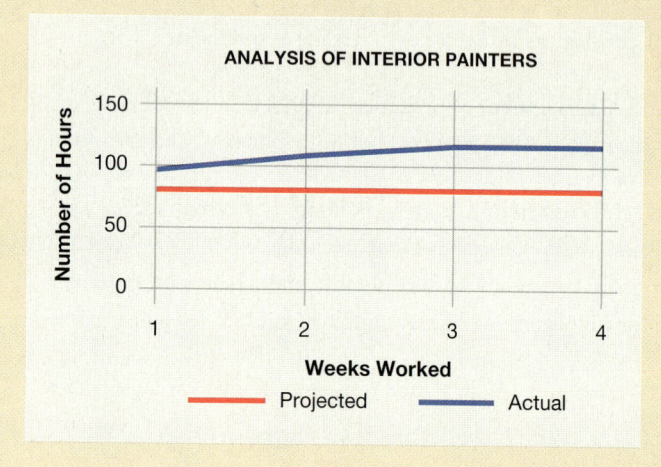

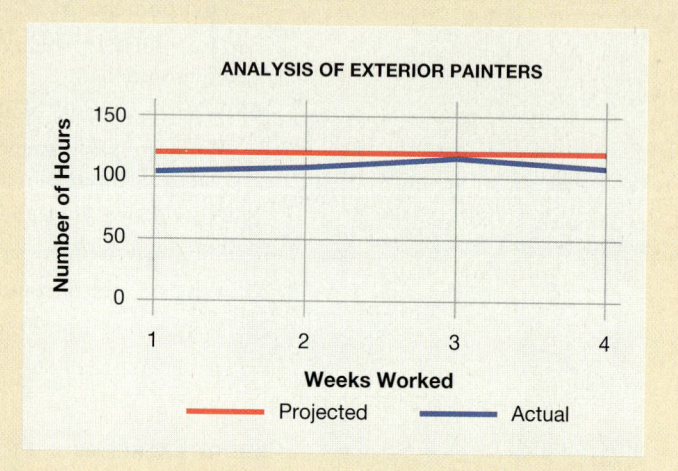

ANALYSIS OF INTERIOR PAINTERS

ANALYSIS OF EXTERIOR PAINTERS

3. The interior painters worked more hours than Youngdale had planned. The following are possible reasons for the additional hours:

   a. The quality of the paint or painting materials may have been poor, which would have required the painters to apply extra coats.
   b. One of the painters may have been recently hired and inexperienced. He would therefore have worked more slowly than anticipated, and the other painter may have taken extra time to train him.
   c. The customer may have requested a change in color or finish after the painting had started, in which case the painters would have had to repaint some areas.
   d. Youngdale may have underestimated the time required for the interior painting.

LO4 Performance measures: Quantitative tools that gauge an organization's performance in relation to a specific goal or expected outcome.

LO2 Primary processes: Components of the value chain that add value to a product or service.

LO1 Strategic objectives: Broad, long-term goals that determine the fundamental nature and direction of a business and that serve as a guide for decision making.

LO1 Supply chain: The path that leads from the suppliers of the materials from which a product is made to the final consumer. Also called the *supply network*.

LO2 Support services: Components of the value chain that facilitate the primary processes but do not add value to a product or service.

LO3 Theory of constraints (TOC): A management theory that contends that limiting factors, or bottlenecks, occur during the production of any product or service, but that once managers identify such a constraint, they can focus attention and resources on it and thus achieve significant improvements.

LO3 Total quality management (TQM): A management tool that requires that all parts of a business work together to build quality into the business's product or service.

LO3 Value-adding activities: Activities that add value to a product or service as perceived by the customer.

LO2 Value chain: A way of defining a business as a set of primary processes and support services that link together to add value to a business's products or services, thus fulfilling the business's mission and objectives.

REVIEW PROBLEM

Analysis of Nonfinancial Data

LO5 Youngdale Painting, Inc., employs painters who specialize in interior walls and exterior trim. George Youngdale, the owner, recently assigned two interior painters and three exterior trim painters to jobs at Yakima High School and Jerome Elementary School. He prepared the following table estimating the number of hours that the painters would work during June:

Estimated Hours to Be Worked

	Week 1	Week 2	Week 3	Week 4	Totals
Interior	80	80	80	80	320
Exterior	120	120	120	120	480

On July 2, Youngdale assembled the following data on the actual number of hours worked:

Actual Hours Worked

	Week 1	Week 2	Week 3	Week 4	Totals
Interior	96	108	116	116	436
Exterior	104	108	116	108	436

Youngdale is concerned about the excess hours worked during June.

REQUIRED ▶
1. For each group of painters (interior and exterior), prepare an analysis that shows the estimated hours, the actual hours worked, and the number of hours under or over the estimates for each week and in total.
2. Using the same information, prepare a line graph for the interior painters and another line graph for the exterior painters. Place the weeks on the X axis and the number of hours on the Y axis.

LO6 Identify the standards of ethical conduct for management accountants.

ing nonfinancial data, it is important to compare performance measures with the objectives that are to be achieved.

Standards of ethical conduct for management accountants emphasize practitioners' responsibilities in the areas of competence, confidentiality, integrity, and objectivity. These standards of conduct help management accountants recognize and avoid situations that could compromise their ability to supply management with accurate and relevant information.

REVIEW OF CONCEPTS AND TERMINOLOGY

The following concepts and terms were introduced in this chapter:

LO3 **Activity-based costing (ABC):** A management accounting practice that identifies all of an organization's major operating activities (both production and nonproduction), traces costs to those activities, and then assigns costs to the products or services that use the resources and services supplied by those activities.

LO3 **Activity-based management (ABM):** An approach to managing an organization that identifies all major operating activities, determines the resources consumed by each of those activities and the cause of the resource usage, categorizes the activities as either adding value to a product or service or not adding value, and seeks to eliminate or reduce nonvalue-adding activities.

LO4 **Balanced scorecard:** A framework that links the perspectives of an organization's stakeholder groups with the organization's mission, objectives, resources, and performance measures.

LO4 **Benchmarking:** A technique for determining a company's competitive advantage by comparing its performance with that of its best competitors.

LO4 **Benchmarks:** Measures of the best practices in an industry.

LO1 **Business plan:** A comprehensive statement of how a company will achieve its objectives.

LO3 **Continuous improvement:** The management concept that one should never be satisfied with what is but should instead constantly seek improved efficiency and lower cost through better methods, products, services, processes, or resources.

LO2 **Core competency:** What a company does best and what gives it an advantage over its competitors.

LO3 **Costs of quality:** Both the costs of achieving quality and the costs of poor quality in the manufacture of a product or the delivery of a service.

LO3 **Just-in-time (JIT) operating philosophy:** A management tool aimed at improving productivity and eliminating waste by requiring that all resources—materials, personnel, and facilities—be acquired and used only as needed.

LO1 **Management accounting:** The process of identifying, measuring, accumulating, analyzing, preparing, interpreting, and communicating information that management uses to plan, evaluate, and control an organization and to ensure that its resources are used and accounted for appropriately.

LO1 **Mission:** A statement of the fundamental way in which a business will achieve its goal of increasing the value of the owners' interest in the business.

LO3 **Nonvalue-adding activities:** Activities that add cost to a product or service but do not increase its market value.

LO1 **Operating objectives:** Short-term goals that outline expectations for the performance of day-to-day operations.

LO2 **Outsourcing:** The engagement of other companies to perform a process or service of the value chain that is not among an organization's core competencies.

Chapter Review

REVIEW OF LEARNING OBJECTIVES

LO1 Distinguish management accounting from financial accounting and explain the role of management accounting in the management cycle.

Management accounting is the process of identifying, measuring, accumulating, analyzing, preparing, interpreting, and communicating information that management uses to plan, evaluate, and control an organization and to ensure that its resources are used and accounted for appropriately. Management accounting reports provide information for planning, control, performance measurement, and decision making to managers and employees when they need such information. These reports follow a flexible format and may present either historical or future-oriented information expressed in dollar amounts or physical measures. In contrast, financial accounting reports provide information about an organization's past performance to owners, lenders, customers, and government agencies on a periodic basis. Financial accounting reports follow strict guidelines defined by generally accepted accounting principles.

Management accounting supports each stage of the management cycle. In the planning stage, managers use the information that management accounting provides to establish strategic and operating objectives that reflect their company's mission and to formulate a comprehensive business plan for achieving those objectives. The plan is usually expressed in financial terms in the form of budgets. In the executing stage, managers use the information in the budgets to implement the plan. In the reviewing stage, they compare actual performance with planned performance and take steps to correct any problems. Reports reflect the results of planning, executing, and reviewing operations and may be prepared for external or internal use.

LO2 Describe the value chain and its usefulness in analyzing a business.

The value chain conceives of each step in the manufacture of a product or the delivery of a service as a link in a chain that adds value to the product or service. These value-adding steps—research and development, design, supply, production, marketing, distribution, and customer service—are known as primary processes. The value chain also includes support services—human resources, legal services, information services, and management accounting. Support services facilitate the primary processes but do not add value to the final product. Value chain analysis enables a company to focus on its core competencies. Parts of the value chain that are not core competencies are frequently outsourced.

LO3 Identify the management tools used for continuous improvement and describe how they work to meet the demands of global competition and how management accounting supports them.

Management tools for continuous improvement include the just-in-time (JIT) operating philosophy, total quality management (TQM), activity-based management (ABM), and the theory of constraints (TOC). These tools are designed to help businesses meet the demands of global competition by reducing resource waste and costs and improving product or service quality, thereby increasing customer satisfaction. Management accounting responds to a JIT operating environment by providing an information system that is sensitive to changes in production processes. In a TQM environment, management accounting provides information about the costs of quality. ABM's assignment of overhead costs to products or services relies on the accounting practice known as activity-based costing (ABC). In businesses that use TOC, management accounting identifies process or product constraints.

LO4 Explain the balanced scorecard and its relationship to performance measures.

The balanced scorecard links the perspectives of an organization's stakeholder groups—financial (investors and owners), learning and growth (employees), internal business processes, and customers—with the organization's mission, objectives, resources, and performance measures. Performance measures are used to assess whether the objectives of each of the four perspectives are being met. Benchmarking is a technique for determining a company's competitive advantage by comparing its performance with that of its industry peers.

LO5 Prepare an analysis of nonfinancial data.

Using management tools like TQM and ABM and comprehensive frameworks like the balanced scorecard requires analysis of both financial and nonfinancial data. In analyz-

- Communicate unfavorable as well as favorable information and professional judgments or opinions.
- Refrain from engaging in or supporting any activity that would discredit the profession.

Objectivity. Practitioners of management accounting and financial management have a responsibility to:

- Communicate information fairly and objectively.
- Disclose fully all relevant information that could reasonably be expected to influence an intended user's understanding of the reports, comments, and recommendations presented.

Resolution of Ethical Conflict. In applying the standards of ethical conduct, practitioners of management accounting and financial management may encounter problems in identifying unethical behavior or in resolving an ethical conflict. When faced with significant ethical issues, practitioners of management accounting and financial management should follow the established policies of the organization bearing on the resolution of such conflict. If these policies do not resolve the ethical conflict, such practitioner should consider the following courses of action:

- Discuss such problems with the immediate superior except when it appears that the superior is involved, in which case the problem should be presented initially to the next higher managerial level. If a satisfactory resolution cannot be achieved when the problem is initially presented, submit the issues to the next higher managerial level.
- If the immediate superior is the chief executive officer, or equivalent, the acceptable reviewing authority may be a group such as the audit committee, executive committee, board of directors, board of trustees, or owners. Contact with levels above the immediate superior should be initiated only with the superior's knowledge, assuming the superior is not involved. Except where legally prescribed, communication of such problems to authorities or individuals not employed or engaged by the organization is not considered appropriate.
- Clarify relevant ethical issues by confidential discussion with an objective advisor (e.g., IMA Ethics Counseling Service) to obtain a better understanding of possible courses of action.
- Consult your own attorney as to legal obligations and rights concerning the ethical conflict.
- If the ethical conflict still exists after exhausting all levels of internal review, there may be no other recourse on significant matters than to resign from the organization and to submit an informative memorandum to an appropriate representative of the organization. After resignation, depending on the nature of the ethical conflict, it may also be appropriate to notify other parties.

Source: From *Standards of Ethical Conduct for Practitioners of Management Accounting and Financial Management.*. Institute of Management Accountants, July 1997. Reprinted by permission.

🛑 STOP AND THINK!

If you encounter financial irregularities in your company, what should your first step be? What is your last recourse?

Your first step should be to discuss the situation with your immediate superior unless he or she is involved, in which case you should discuss the situation with someone at at higher level. You may have to take the matter to the board of directors or to the authorities. If you cannot resolve it, your last resort is to resign. ∎

management could achieve higher profits for the owners by purchasing a less expensive, less effective antipollution device that would not protect the community as well. Such conflicts between external parties can create ethical dilemmas for management and for accountants.

To be viewed credibly by the various parties that rely on the information they provide, management accountants must adhere to the highest standards of performance. To provide guidance, the Institute of Management Accountants has issued standards of ethical conduct for practitioners of management accounting and financial management. Those standards, presented in Exhibit 4, emphasize that management accountants have responsibilities in the areas of competence, confidentiality, integrity, and objectivity.

✓ Check out ACE for a Review Quiz at http://accounting.college.hmco.com/students.

Exhibit 4
Standards of Ethical Conduct for Practitioners of Management Accounting and Financial Management

Practitioners of management accounting and financial management have an obligation to the public, their profession, the organization they serve, and themselves, to maintain the highest standards of ethical conduct. In recognition of this obligation, the Institute of Management Accountants has promulgated the following standards of ethical conduct for practitioners of management accounting and financial management. Adherence to these standards, both domestically and internationally, is integral to achieving the Objectives of Management Accounting. Practitioners of management accounting and financial management shall not commit acts contrary to these standards nor shall they condone the commission of such acts by others within their organizations.

Competence. Practitioners of management accounting and financial management have a responsibility to:

- Maintain an appropriate level of professional competence by ongoing development of their knowledge and skills.
- Perform their professional duties in accordance with relevant laws, regulations, and technical standards.
- Prepare complete and clear reports and recommendations after appropriate analysis of relevant and reliable information.

Confidentiality. Practitioners of management accounting and financial management have a responsibility to:

- Refrain from disclosing confidential information acquired in the course of their work except when authorized, unless legally obligated to do so.
- Inform subordinates as appropriate regarding the confidentiality of information acquired in the course of their work and monitor their activities to assure the maintenance of that confidentiality.
- Refrain from using or appearing to use confidential information acquired in the course of their work for unethical or illegal advantage either personally or through third parties.

Integrity. Practitioners of management accounting and financial management have a responsibility to:

- Avoid actual or apparent conflicts of interest and advise all appropriate parties of any potential conflict.
- Refrain from engaging in any activity that would prejudice their ability to carry out their duties ethically.
- Refuse any gift, favor, or hospitality that would influence or would appear to influence their actions.
- Refrain from either actively or passively subverting the attainment of the organization's legitimate and ethical objectives.
- Recognize and communicate professional limitations or other constraints that would preclude responsible judgment or successful performance of an activity.

Focus on Business Ethics

What Is Management's Responsibility for the Financial Statements?

Top-level managers have not only an ethical responsibility to ensure that the financial statements issued by their companies adhere to the principles of full disclosure and transparency; today, they have a legal responsibility as well. Strong concerns about the integrity of financial reporting created by the collapse of the Enron Corporation <www.enron.com> in 2001 fueled widespread support for accounting reform. An important outcome of the reform efforts was the passage of the Sarbanes-Oxley Act in 2002. Among the provisions of this law is one that directed the Securities and Exchange Commission (SEC) to adopt a rule requiring the chief executive officers and chief financial officers of companies filing reports with the SEC to certify that those reports contain no untrue statements and include all facts needed to ensure that the reports are not misleading. In addition to issuing this rule, the SEC adopted one requiring managers to ensure that the information in reports filed with the SEC "is recorded, processed, summarized and reported on a timely basis."[8]

EXHIBIT 3
Analysis of Nonfinancial Data

King's Beach National Bank
Summary of Number of Customers Served
For the Quarter Ended December 31, 20x5

Part A — Number of Customers Served

Window	October	November	December	Quarter Totals
1	5,428	5,186	5,162	15,776
2	5,280	4,820	4,960	15,060
3	4,593	4,494	4,580	13,667
Totals	15,301	14,500	14,702	44,503

Part B — Number of Customers Served per Hour

Window	October	November	December	Quarter Averages
1	31.93	30.51	30.36	30.93
2	31.06	28.35	29.18	29.53
3	27.02	26.44	26.94	26.80
Totals	90.01	85.30	86.48	87.26
Average per hour per window	30.00	28.43	28.83	26.09

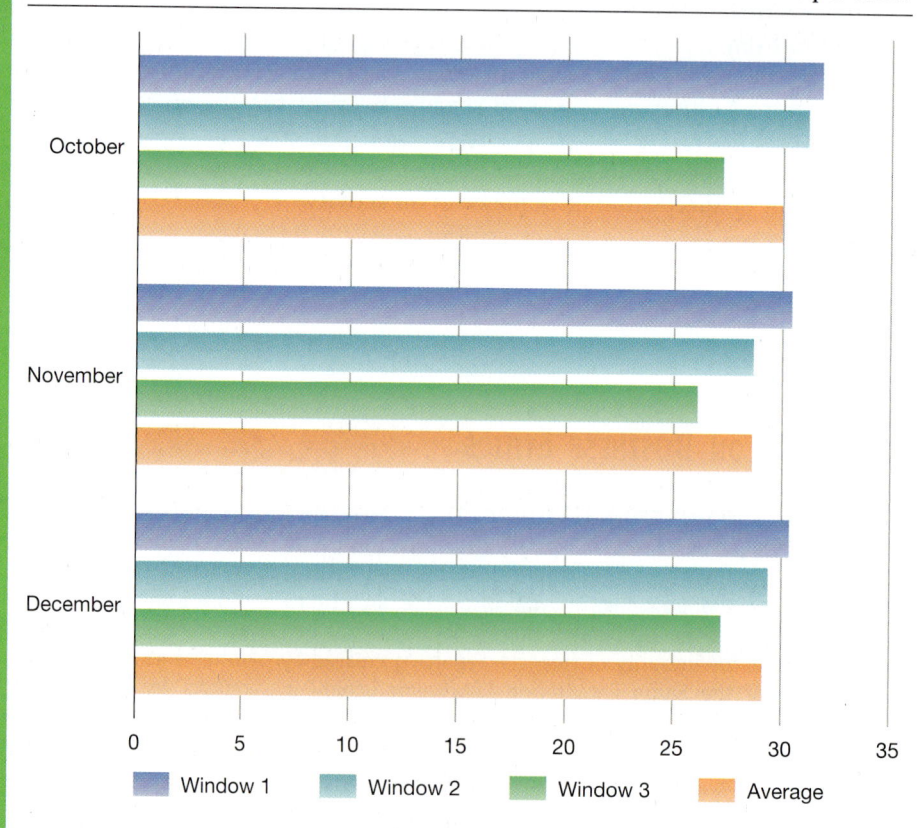

Part C — Graphic Comparison of the Number of Customers Served per Hour

also compare its performance with that of similar companies in the same industry. **Benchmarking** is a technique for determining a company's competitive advantage by comparing its performance with that of its closest competitors. **Benchmarks** are measures of the best practices in an industry. To obtain information about benchmarks in the retail and candy industry, Abbie Wang might join a trade association for small retail shops or candy stores. Information about these benchmarks would be useful to her in setting targets for the performance measures in Sweet Treasures Candy Store's balanced scorecard.

✓ Check out ACE for a Review Quiz at http://accounting.college.hmco.com/students.

ANALYSIS OF NONFINANCIAL DATA IN A SERVICE ORGANIZATION

LO5 Prepare an analysis of nonfinancial data.

RELATED TEXT ASSIGNMENTS
Q: 20
SE: 9
E: 10, 11, 12
P: 4, 5, 7, 8
SD: 6
MRA: 3, 4

As we have noted throughout this chapter, managers use many kinds of nonfinancial measures to determine whether performance targets for internal business processes and customer satisfaction are being met. The following example illustrates how a manager in a service organization uses nonfinancial data in order to analyze changes in employee performance.

Lynda Babb supervises tellers at King's National Bank. The bank has three drive-up windows, each with a full-time teller. In the past, each teller served an average of 30 customers per hour. However, on November 1, 20x5, management implemented a new check-scanning procedure that has reduced the number of customers served per hour.

Data on the number of customers served for the three-month period ended December 31, 20x5, are shown in Part A of Exhibit 3. Each teller works an average of 170 hours per month. Window 1 is always the busiest. Windows 2 and 3 receive progressively less business. Babb is preparing a report for management on the effects of the new procedure. Part B of Exhibit 3 shows her analysis of the number of customers served over the three months at each teller window. She computed the number of customers served per hour by dividing the number of customers served by the monthly average hours worked per teller (170). By averaging the customer service rates for the three tellers, she got 28.43 customers per hour per window for November and 28.83 customers for December. As you can see, the service rate has decreased since October. But December's average is higher than November's, which means the tellers, as a group, are becoming more accustomed to the new procedure. Part C of Exhibit 3 is a graphic comparison of the number of customers served per hour.

🔴 **STOP AND THINK!**
Which is more important to running a company: financial data or nonfinancial data?

Both are important. Nonfinancial data are important for measuring the performance of business processes, but ultimately these data are translated into budgets and financial reports that reflect the financial objectives of the company. ■

✓ Check out ACE for a Review Quiz at http://accounting.college.hmco.com/students.

STANDARDS OF ETHICAL CONDUCT

LO6 Identify the standards of ethical conduct for management accountants.

RELATED TEXT ASSIGNMENTS
Q: 20, 21
SE: 10
E: 13, 14, 15
SD: 4

Managers are responsible to external parties (e.g., owners, creditors, governmental agencies, and the local community) for the proper use of organizational resources and the financial reporting of their actions. Conflicts may arise that require managers to balance the interests of all external parties, and management accountants have a responsibility to help them balance these interests. For example, the community wants a safe living environment, while owners seek to maximize profits. If management decides to purchase an expensive device to extract pollutants from the production process, it will protect the community, but profits will decline. The benefit will be greater for the community than for the owners. On the other hand,

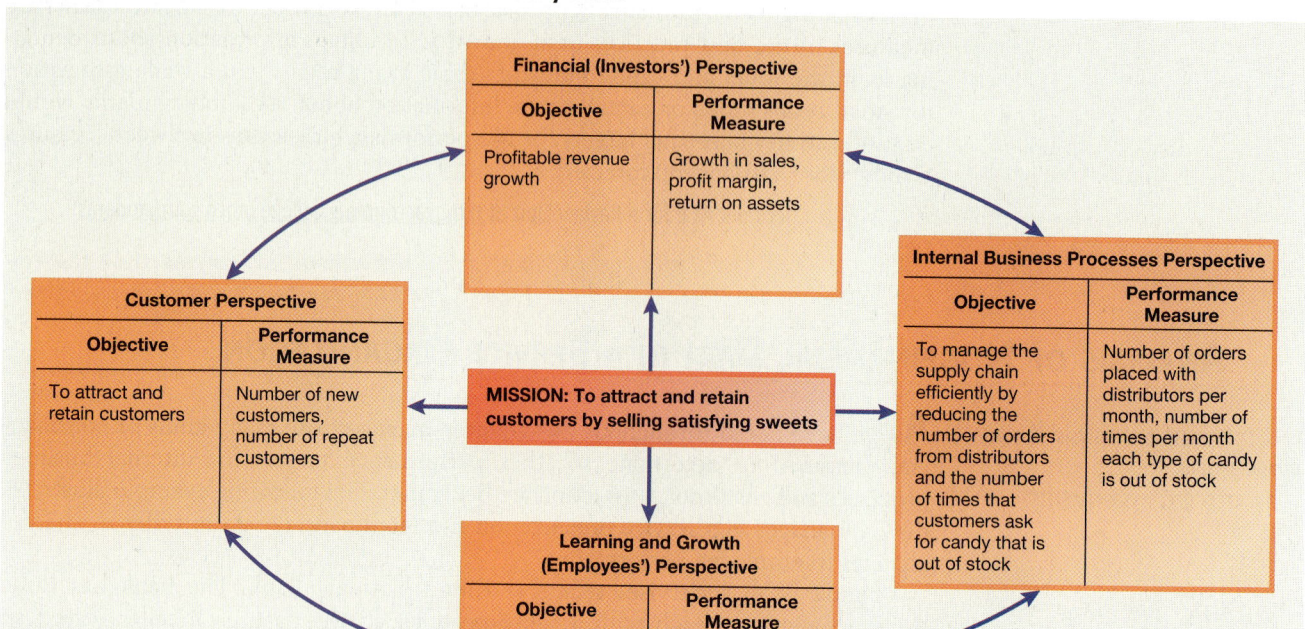

FIGURE 6
The Balanced Scorecard for Sweet Treasures Candy Store

Financial (Investors') Perspective

Objective	Performance Measure
Profitable revenue growth	Growth in sales, profit margin, return on assets

Customer Perspective

Objective	Performance Measure
To attract and retain customers	Number of new customers, number of repeat customers

Internal Business Processes Perspective

Objective	Performance Measure
To manage the supply chain efficiently by reducing the number of orders from distributors and the number of times that customers ask for candy that is out of stock	Number of orders placed with distributors per month, number of times per month each type of candy is out of stock

Learning and Growth (Employees') Perspective

Objective	Performance Measure
To give fast, courteous service	Average time to fill a customer's order, percentage of new employees trained in customer service, number of customer complaints

MISSION: To attract and retain customers by selling satisfying sweets

Source: Adapted from Robert S. Kaplan and David P. Norton, "Using the Balanced Scorecard as a Strategic Management System," *Harvard Business Review,* January-February 1996.

KEY POINT: The balanced scorecard presents a way of linking the management of employees, internal business processes, and customer needs to external financial results.

employees in customer service should result in courteous service, performance related to this objective can be measured in terms of how many employees have received training. The number of customer complaints is another measure of courteous service.

From the perspective of internal business processes, the objective is to help achieve the company's mission by managing the supply chain efficiently, which should contribute to customer satisfaction. Efficiency in the ordering process can be measured by recording the number of orders placed with distributors each month and the number of times per month that customers ask for candy that is not in stock.

If the objectives of the learning and growth and business processes perspectives are met, they should result in attracting customers and retaining them, which is the objective of the customer perspective. Performance related to this objective is measured by tracking the number of new customers and the number of repeat customers. Satisfied customers should help achieve the objective of the financial perspective, which is profitable growth. Profitable growth is measured by growth in sales, profit margin, and return on assets.

BENCHMARKING

The balanced scorecard enables a company to determine whether it is making continuous improvement in its operations. But to ensure its success, a company must

During the executing stage, performance measures guide and motivate the performance of employees and assist in assigning costs to products, departments, or operating activities. Abbie Wang will record the number of customer complaints during the year. She can group the information by type of complaint or the employee involved in the service.

In the reviewing stage, managers use the information that performance measures have provided to analyze significant differences between actual and planned performance and to improvise ways of improving performance. By comparing the actual and planned number of customer complaints, Wang can identify problem areas and develop solutions.

In the reporting stage, performance measurement information is useful in communicating performance evaluations and developing new budgets. If Wang needed formal reports, she could have her accountant prepare performance evaluations based on this information.

THE BALANCED SCORECARD

KEY POINT: The balanced scorecard focuses all perspectives of the business on accomplishing the business's mission.

♦ **STOP AND THINK!**
In what sense is the balanced scorecard "balanced?"
The balanced scorecard is "balanced" in the sense that it weighs the needs of the four perspectives of an organization in a way that achieves the organization's mission. ■

If an organization is to achieve its mission and objectives, it must identify the areas in which it needs to excel and establish measures of performance in these critical areas. As we have indicated, effective performance measurement requires an approach that uses both financial and nonfinancial measures that are tied to a company's mission and objectives. One such approach that has gained wide acceptance is the balanced scorecard. The **balanced scorecard** is a framework that links the perspectives of an organization's four stakeholder groups with the organization's mission, objectives, resources, and performance measures. Stakeholders with a financial perspective (owners, investors, and creditors) value improvements in financial measures, such as net income and return on investment. Stakeholders with a learning and growth perspective (employees) value high wages, job satisfaction, and opportunities to fulfill their potential. Stakeholders who focus on the business's internal processes value the safe and cost-effective production of high-quality products. Holders of the customer perspective value high-quality, low-cost products. Although their perspectives differ, these stakeholder groups may be interested in the same measurable performance goals. For example, holders of both the customer and business processes perspectives are interested in performance that results in high-quality products.

Figure 6 applies the balanced scorecard to Sweet Treasures Candy Store. The company's mission is to be the candy store of choice in the community. It is at the center of the company's balanced scorecard. Surrounding it are the four interrelated perspectives.

At the base of the scorecard is the learning and growth perspective. Here, the objective, or performance goal, is to provide courteous service. Because training

---

FOCUS ON BUSINESS PRACTICE

Do Many Companies Use the Balanced Scorecard?

Research shows that about 50 percent of large companies in the Unites States and about 45 percent of those in Europe use the balanced scorecard. And the number is growing.

One of the most successful companies of the last decade, Dell Computer Corporation <www.dell.com>, uses the balanced scorecard to measure its progress in meeting objectives in the two areas that are most critical to its success: operational efficiency and customer service. Dell's learning and growth measures focus on training, patents, innovations, and sharing of information. Its business process measures focus on defect rates, forecasting accuracy, cash cycle time, and the implementation of innovations. Customer measures focus on customer retention, customer perceptions, and delivery time. Financial measures include cash flows, gross margins, revenue growth, and economic returns.[7]

FOCUS ON INTERNATIONAL BUSINESS

How Has Ecommerce Changed the Nature of Business?

Global ecommerce has radically changed the way in which numerous goods and services, including plane tickets, books, automobiles, and even medical help, are sold. Many products and services are on sale 24 hours a day and can be delivered the day after purchase. These revolutionary changes in the way business is conducted have created a vast array of new opportunities. But they have also forced managers to recognize the important role that performance measures play in keeping a company competitive. Organizations now set performance targets for all areas of their operation—from new-product development to purchasing, marketing, sales, shipping, and customer satisfaction. Such measures are developed and tracked by management accountants. The Business and Industry Executive Committee (formerly the Management Accounting Executive Committee) of the American Institute of Certified Public Accountants has coined the term *new finance* to describe this revolution in management accounting.[6]

🛑 **STOP AND THINK!**

How does a company know whether the quality of its products or services is improving?

Managers must first develop measures that reflect the quality they seek. They must then carefully monitor these measures and report the results on a regular basis. ■

sues continuous improvement by reducing the number of defective products and the time needed to complete a task or provide a service. Activity-based management seeks continuous improvement by emphasizing the ongoing reduction or elimination of nonvalue-adding activities. The theory of constraints helps managers focus resources on efforts that will produce the most effective improvements.

Each of these management tools can be used individually, or parts of them can be combined to create a new operating environment. They are applicable in service businesses, such as banking, as well as in manufacturing and retail businesses. By continuously trying to improve and fine-tune operations, they contribute to the same results in any organization: a reduction in product or service costs and delivery time, an improvement in the quality of the product or service, and an increase in customer satisfaction.

✅ Check out ACE for a Review Quiz at http://accounting.college.hmco.com/students.

PERFORMANCE MEASURES: A KEY TO ACHIEVING ORGANIZATIONAL OBJECTIVES

LO4 Explain the balanced scorecard and its relationship to performance measures.

RELATED TEXT ASSIGNMENTS
Q: 17, 18, 19
SE: 8
E: 9
P: 3
SD: 3
MRA: 5

ENRICHMENT NOTE:
Using nonfinancial measures in an international business environment often eliminates the problems associated with different currencies and different accounting standards.

Performance measures are quantitative tools that gauge an organization's performance in relation to a specific goal or an expected outcome. Performance measures may be financial or nonfinancial. Financial performance measures include return on investment, net income as a percentage of sales, and the costs of poor quality as a percentage of sales. Such measures use monetary information to gauge the performance of a profit-generating organization or its segments—its divisions, departments, product lines, sales territories, or operating activities.

Nonfinancial performance measures include the number of times an activity occurs or the time taken to perform a task. Examples are number of customer complaints, number of orders shipped the same day, hours of inspection, and the time taken to fill an order. Such performance measures are useful in reducing or eliminating waste and inefficiencies in operating activities.

USE OF PERFORMANCE MEASURES IN THE MANAGEMENT CYCLE

Managers use performance measures in all stages of the management cycle. In the planning stage, they establish performance measures that will support the organization's mission and the objectives of its business plan, such as reducing costs and increasing quality, efficiency, timeliness, and customer satisfaction. As you will recall from earlier in the chapter, Abbie Wang selected the number of customer complaints as a performance measure to monitor the quality of service at Sweet Treasures Candy Store.

■ **THEORY OF CONSTRAINTS** According to the **theory of constraints (TOC)**, limiting factors, or bottlenecks, occur during the production of any product or service, but once managers identify such a constraint, they can focus attention and resources on it and achieve significant improvements. TOC thus helps managers set priorities for how they spend their time and resources. In identifying constraints, managers rely on the information that management accounting provides.

To illustrate TOC, suppose a marketing manager wants to increase sales of doughnut-shaped chew toys for dogs. After reviewing management accounting reports, she concludes that potential sales are limited by the production capacity of her company's manufacturing plant. The problem lies in the plant's molding machine, which can shape only 1,000 toys per hour. To overcome this constraint, she persuades the vice president of manufacturing to purchase a second molding machine. The increase in production will enable her to increase sales.

TOC complements JIT, TQM, and ABM by focusing resources on efforts that will yield the most effective improvements.

ACHIEVING CONTINUOUS IMPROVEMENT

JIT, TQM, ABM, and TOC all have perfection by means of continuous improvement as their goal. Figure 5 shows how each approach tries to accomplish this goal. In the just-in-time operating environment, management wages war on wasted time, wasted resources, and wasted space. All employees are encouraged to look for ways of improving processes and saving time. Total quality management focuses on improving the quality of the product or service and the work environment. It pur-

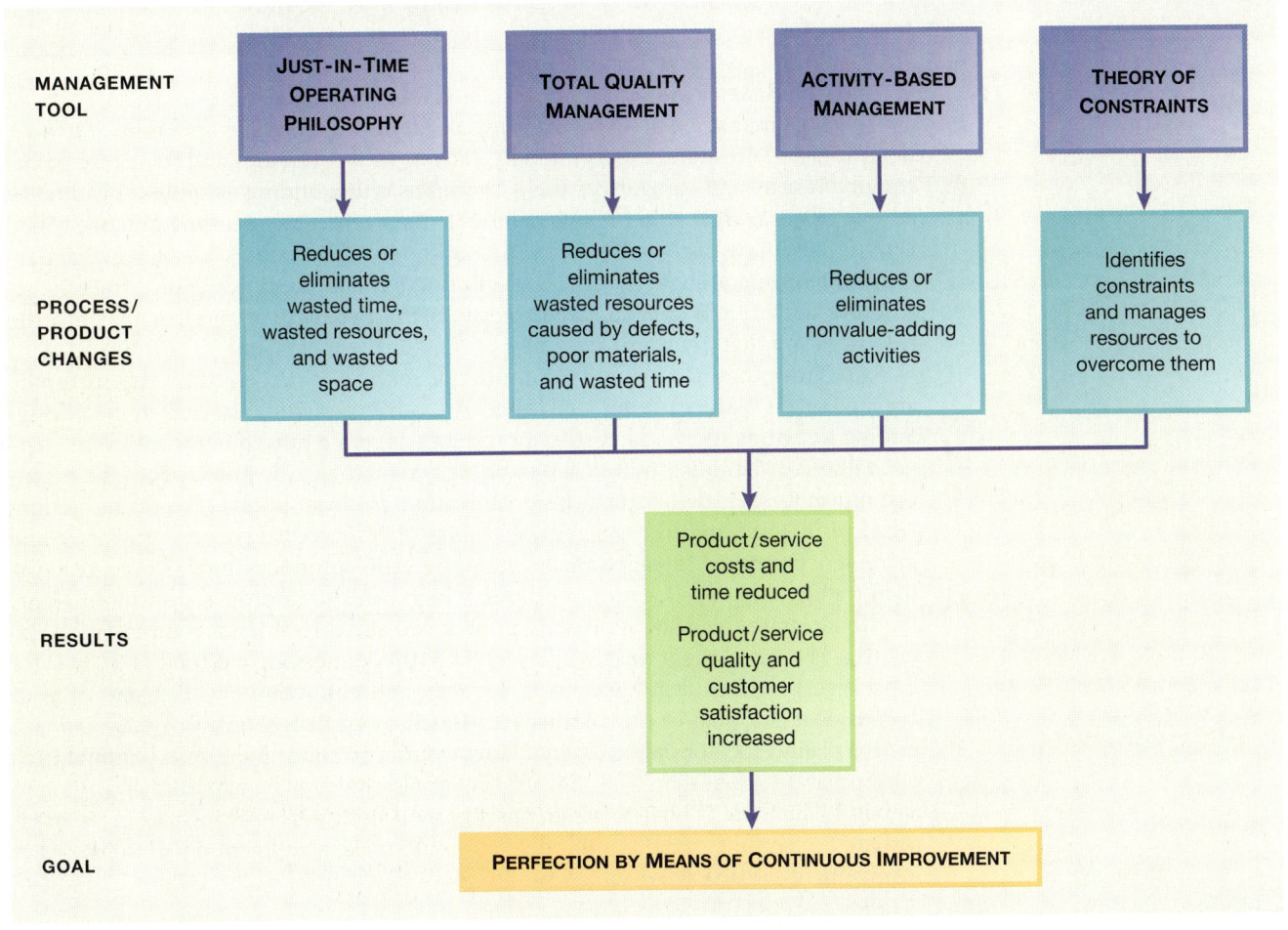

FIGURE 5
The Continuous Improvement Environment

MANAGEMENT TOOL	JUST-IN-TIME OPERATING PHILOSOPHY	TOTAL QUALITY MANAGEMENT	ACTIVITY-BASED MANAGEMENT	THEORY OF CONSTRAINTS
PROCESS/ PRODUCT CHANGES	Reduces or eliminates wasted time, wasted resources, and wasted space	Reduces or eliminates wasted resources caused by defects, poor materials, and wasted time	Reduces or eliminates nonvalue-adding activities	Identifies constraints and manages resources to overcome them
RESULTS		Product/service costs and time reduced Product/service quality and customer satisfaction increased		
GOAL		PERFECTION BY MEANS OF CONTINUOUS IMPROVEMENT		

■ **TOTAL QUALITY MANAGEMENT** **Total quality management (TQM)** requires that all parts of a business work together to build quality into the business's product or service. Improved quality of both the product or service and the work environment is TQM's goal. Workers act as team members and are empowered to make operating decisions that improve quality in both areas.

TQM has many of the characteristics of the JIT operating philosophy. It focuses on improving product or service quality by identifying and reducing or eliminating the causes of waste. The emphasis is on examining current operations to spot possible causes of poor quality and on using resources efficiently and effectively to improve quality and reduce the time needed to complete a task or provide a service. Like JIT, TQM results in reduced waste of materials, higher-quality goods, and lower production costs in manufacturing environments, such as those of Hewlett-Packard and Kodak. It also helps service organizations like USAA and Federal Express realize time savings and provide higher-quality services.

www.hp.com
www.kodak.com
www.usaa.com
www.fedex.com

To determine the impact of poor quality on profits, TQM managers use accounting information about the costs of quality. The **costs of quality** include both the costs of achieving quality (such as training costs and inspection costs) and the costs of poor quality (such as the costs of rework and of handling customer complaints).

www.motorola.com
www.ge.com

Managers at companies like Motorola and General Electric use information about the costs of quality to relate their organization's business plan to daily operating activities, to stimulate improvement by sharing this information with all employees, to identify opportunities for reducing costs and customer dissatisfaction, and to determine the costs of quality relative to net income. For example, Motorola's managers use the information that management accounting supplies about defects per unit and cycle time to ensure that a job is done right the first time and in the shortest amount of time. Motorola uses this approach in everything it does. For retailers like Sweet Treasures Candy Store, TQM results in a quality customer experience before, during, and after the sale.

■ **ACTIVITY-BASED MANAGEMENT** **Activity-based management (ABM)** is an approach to managing an organization that identifies all major operating activities, determines the resources consumed by each of those activities and the cause of the resource usage, and categorizes the activities as either adding value to a product or service or not adding value. ABM includes a management accounting practice called activity-based costing. **Activity-based costing (ABC)** identifies all of an organization's major operating activities (both production and nonproduction), traces costs to those activities, and then assigns costs to the products or services that use the resources supplied by those activities.

Activities that add value to a product or service, as perceived by the customer, are known as **value-adding activities**. All other activities are called **nonvalue-adding activities**; they add cost to a product or service but do not increase its market value. ABM eliminates nonvalue-adding activities that do not support the organization; those that do support the organization are focal points for cost reduction. ABM results in reduced costs, reduced waste of resources, increased efficiency, and increased customer satisfaction. In addition, ABC produces more accurate costs than traditional cost allocation methods, which leads to improved decision making.

To illustrate the ABM approach, suppose you and three friends want to take a skiing trip. The travel agent quotes a flat fee of $400 per person, or a total of $1,600 for a package that includes skiing, food, lodging, and entertainment. But one of your friends does not plan to ski, another eats much more than the rest of you, and two people plan to stay for only two days. How would you allocate the costs? Should each person pay an equal share (i.e., $400)? Or should the costs be allocated according to activity? The issue is how to assign costs fairly if each person is involvd in different activites. According to ABM, each person should make a payment equal to his or her involvement in each activity.

candy. To manufacture candy would require a change in the company's mission and major changes in the way it does business. Second, it is often the best business policy to outsource portions of the value chain that are not part of a business's core competency. Since Sweet Treasures Candy Store does not have a core competency in manufacturing candy, it would not be competitive in this field. Abbie Wang would be better off having an experienced candy manufacturer produce the candy according to her specifications, which she could then sell under her store's label. As Wang's business grows, increased volume may allow her to reconsider undertaking the manufacture of candy.

✓ Check out ACE for a Review Quiz at http://accounting.college.hmco.com/students.

Meeting the Demands of Global Competition

LO3 Identify the management tools used for continuous improvement and describe how they work to meet the demands of global competition and how management accounting supports them.

RELATED TEXT ASSIGNMENTS
Q: 11, 12, 13, 14, 15, 16
SE: 6, 7
E: 7, 8
SD: 2

Today, managers in all parts of the world have ready access to international markets and to current information for informed decision making. As a result, global competition has increased significantly. One of the most valuable lessons gained from this increase in competition is that management cannot afford to become complacent. The concept of **continuous improvement** evolved to avoid such complacency. Organizations that adhere to continuous improvement are never satisfied with what is; they constantly seek improved efficiency and lower cost through better methods, products, services, processes, or resources. Their goal is perfection in everything they do. In response to this concept, several important management tools have emerged. These tools help companies remain competitive by focusing on continuous improvement of business methods.

Management Tools for Continuous Improvement

Among the management tools that companies use to deal with expanding global competition are the just-in-time operating philosophy, total quality management, activity-based management, and the theory of constraints.

■ **Just-in-Time Operating Philosophy** The **just-in-time (JIT) operating philosophy** requires that all resources—materials, personnel, and facilities—be acquired and used only as needed. Its objectives are to improve productivity and eliminate waste. In a JIT environment, production processes are consolidated, and workers are trained to be multiskilled so that they can operate several different machines. Raw materials and parts are scheduled for delivery just at the time they are needed in the production process, which significantly reduces inventories of materials. Goods are produced continuously, so work in process inventories are very small. They are usually put into production only when an order is received and are shipped when completed, which reduces the inventories of finished goods.

Adopting the JIT operating philosophy reduces production time and costs, investment in materials inventory, and materials waste, and it results in higher-quality goods. Funds that are no longer invested in inventory can be redirected according to the goals of the company's business plan. Management accounting responds to a JIT operating environment by providing an information system that is sensitive to changes in production processes. JIT methods help manufacturers like General Motors and Harley-Davidson assign more accurate costs to their products and identify the costs of waste and inefficient operations. JIT methods are also of benefit to service companies like AT&T and retailers like Sweet Treasures Candy Store and Wal-Mart. Wal-Mart, for example, requires vendors to restock inventory often and pays them only when the goods sell. This minimizes the funds invested in inventory and allows the retailer to focus on offering high-demand merchandise at attractive prices.

www.gm.com
www.harley-davidson.com
www.att.com
www.walmart.com

EXHIBIT 2
Value Chain Analysis

Sweet Treasures Candy Store
Projected Costs of New Candy
June 1, 20x5

Primary Process	Initial Costs per Pound	Revised Costs per Pound
Research and development	$ .25	$ .25
Design	.10	.10
Supply	1.10	.60
Production	4.50	3.50
Marketing	.50	.50
Distribution	.90	.90
Customer service	.65	.65
Total cost	$8.00	$6.50

Managers must also make the services that support the primary processes as efficient as possible. These services are essential and cannot be eliminated, but because they do not add value to the final product, they must be implemented as economically as possible. Businesses have been making progress in this area. For example, over the past ten years, the cost of the accounting function in many companies has declined as a percentage of total revenue from 6 percent to 2 percent. Technology has played a big role in making this economy possible.

As a support service, management accounting must be efficient and provide value to managers by developing information useful for decision making. For example, to determine whether manufacturing and selling her own brand of candy will be profitable, Abbie Wang will need accurate information about the cost of the candy. She knows that to be competitive with other candy manufacturers, she cannot sell the candy for more than $10 per pound. Further, she has an idea of how much candy she can sell in the first year. Based on this information, her accountant, Salvador Chavez, analyzes the value chain and projects the initial costs per pound shown in Exhibit 2. The total cost of $8 per pound worries Wang because with a selling price of $10, it leaves only $2, or 20 percent of revenue, to cover all the support services and leave a profit. Wang believes that if the enterprise is to be successful, this percentage, called the *margin*, must be at least 35 percent. Since the selling price is constrained by the competition, she must find a way to reduce costs.

Chavez tells her that the company could achieve a lower total cost per pound by selling a higher volume of candy, but that is not realistic for the new product. He also points out that the largest projected costs in the candy store's value chain are for supply and production. Because Wang plans to order ingredients from a number of suppliers, her orders would not be large enough to qualify for quantity discounts and to save on shipping. By using a single supplier, the supply cost could be reduced by $.50 per unit. A way of reducing the cost of production would be to outsource this process to a candy manufacturer whose high volume of products would allow it to produce the candy at a much lower cost than could be done at Sweet Treasures Candy Store. Outsourcing would reduce the production cost to $3.50 per unit. Thus, the total unit cost would be reduced to $6.50, as shown in Exhibit 2. This per unit cost would enable the company to sell the candy at a competitive $10 per pound and make the targeted margin of 35 percent ($3.50 ÷ $10).

This value chain analysis illustrates two important points. First, Sweet Treasures Candy Store's mission is as a retailer. The company has no experience in making

The services that support the primary processes are as follows:

Human resources: hiring and training employees to carry out all the functions of the business. Wang will need to hire and train personnel to make the new candy.

Legal services: maintaining and monitoring all contracts, agreements, obligations, and other relationships with outside parties. For example, Wang will want legal advice when applying for a trademark for the new candy's name and when signing contracts with suppliers.

Information systems: establishing and maintaining technological means of controlling and communicating within the organization. Wang will want a computerized accounting system that keeps not only financial records, but customer information as well.

Management accounting: provides essential information in any business.

ADVANTAGES OF VALUE CHAIN ANALYSIS

KEY POINT: A company cannot succeed by trying to do everything at the highest level. It has to focus on its core competencies to give customers the best value.
www.sony.com

An advantage of value chain analysis is that it allows a company to focus on its core competencies. A **core competency** is what a company does best. It is what gives a company an advantage over its competitors. For example, Sony Corporation, the company that invented the Walkman, has a reputation for making consumer electronic devices that are ever-smaller in size. Its core competencies are the design and manufacture of these devices.

A common result of value chain analysis is outsourcing, which can also be of benefit to a business. **Outsourcing** is the engagement of other companies to perform a process or service of the value chain that is not among an organization's core competencies. For instance, Nike's core competencies are the design and marketing of athletic shoes. The company does not manufacture any shoes; it outsources manufacturing to companies that specialize in shoe manufacture. Many companies also outsource support services. A main source of IBM's growth in recent years, for instance, has been the operation and maintenance of information systems for other companies.

www.nike.com

www.ibm.com

MANAGEMENT ACCOUNTING'S SUPPORT OF VALUE CHAIN ANALYSIS

www.gm.com
www.honda.com

In today's competitive business environment, analysis of the value chain is critical to most companies' survival. Managers must provide the highest value to customers at the lowest cost, and low cost often equates with the speed at which the primary processes of the value chain are executed. Time to market is very important. For example, General Motors can take up to five years to design and bring a new car to market, whereas Honda may take only three years. Some cars on the General Motors assembly line leave every 60 minutes, whereas Honda can produce a car every 40 minutes. When millions of dollars and thousands of cars are involved, these differences can result in significant competitive advantages for Honda.

FOCUS ON BUSINESS TECHNOLOGY

How Can the Internet Be Used to Support the Value Chain?

The Internet can be a very effective means of supporting the value chain, as Baxter International's use of this technology demonstrates. Baxter <www.baxter.com>, a large pharmaceutical concern, uses an integrated global information system and digital network to support and coordinate human resource management, research and development, supply chain management, manufacturing, and marketing and sales worldwide. Among the benefits the company has realized are savings of $75 million from the outsourcing of parts of the value chain, a reduction in the cost of customer orders from $4.00 to $.80, faster collection of accounts receivable, reduced transportation costs, increased employee productivity, improved customer service, and faster time to market.[5]

FIGURE 4
The Value Chain

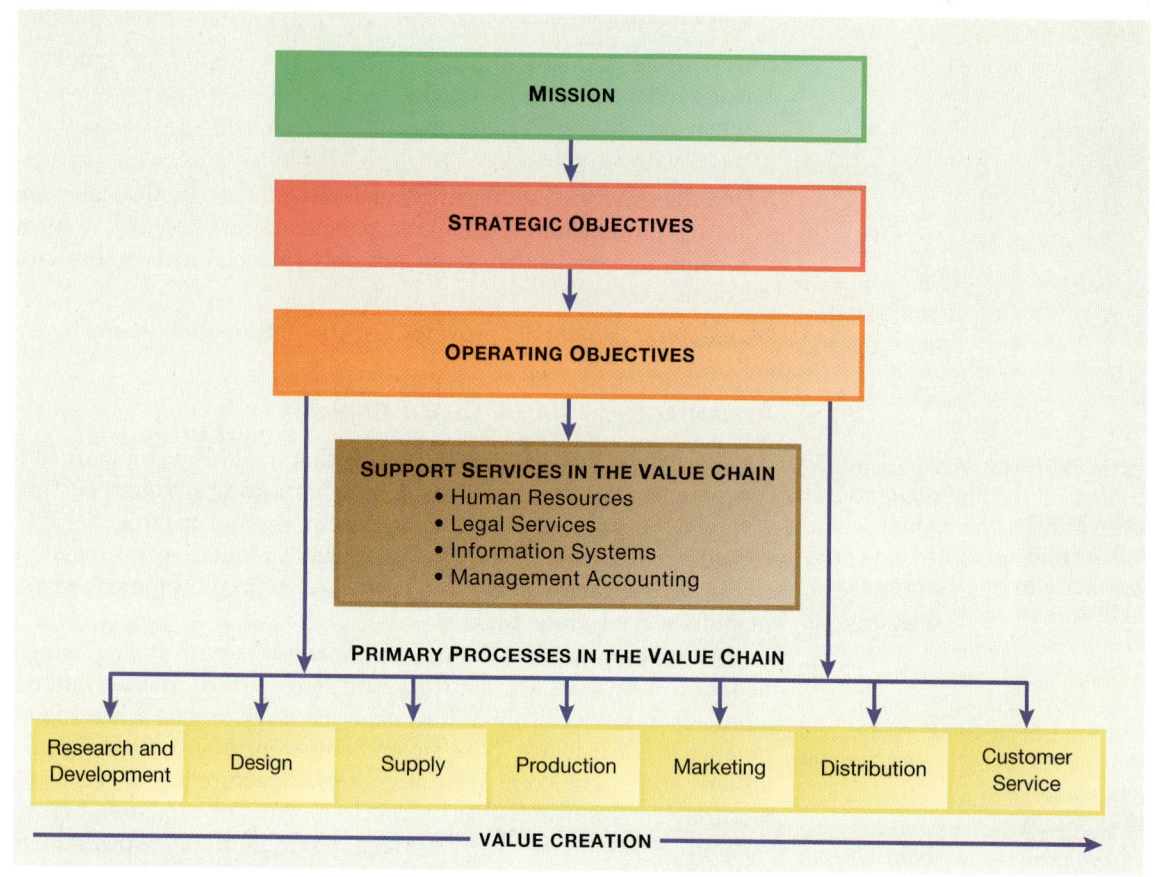

```
                        MISSION
                          ↓
                  STRATEGIC OBJECTIVES
                          ↓
                  OPERATING OBJECTIVES
                          ↓
            SUPPORT SERVICES IN THE VALUE CHAIN
                  • Human Resources
                  • Legal Services
                  • Information Systems
                  • Management Accounting
                          ↓
            PRIMARY PROCESSES IN THE VALUE CHAIN
```

| Research and Development | Design | Supply | Production | Marketing | Distribution | Customer Service |

⟶ **VALUE CREATION** ⟶

PRIMARY PROCESSES AND SUPPORT SERVICES

Let's assume that Sweet Treasures Candy Store has had some success, and Abbie Wang now wants to determine the feasibility of making and selling her own brand of candy. The primary processes that will add value to the new candy are as follows:

Research and development: developing new and better products or services. Wang plans to add value by developing a candy that has less sugar content than similar confections.

Design: creating improved and distinctive shapes, labels, or packages for products. For example, a package that is attractive and that describes the desirable features of Wang's new candy will add value to the product.

Supply: purchasing materials for products or services. Wang will want to purchase high-quality sugar, chocolate, and other ingredients for the candy, as well as high-quality packaging.

Production: manufacturing the product or service. To add value to the new candy, Wang will want to implement efficient manufacturing and packaging processes.

Marketing: communicating information about the products or services and selling them. Attractive advertisements will facilitate sale of the new candy to customers.

Distribution: delivering the product or service to the customer. Courteous and efficient service for in-store customers will add value to the product; Wang may also want to accommodate Internet customers by providing shipping.

Customer service: following up with service after sales or providing warranty service. For example, Wang may offer free replacement of any candy that does not satisfy the customer. She could also use questionnaires to measure customer satisfaction.

🛑 **STOP AND THINK!**

Is it better for a company to have a primary process or a support service as a core competency?

A company needs to be good at both. However, it is more important to have a primary process as a core competency because primary processes add value to the final product, and it is on the basis of primary processes that a company distinguishes itself from its competitors. ■

Exhibit 1
A Management Accounting Report

Memorandum

When:	Today's Date
Who:	To: Abbie Wang, Sweet Treasures Candy Store
	From: Salvador Chavez, Accountant
Why:	Re: Ordering and Shipping Costs—Analysis and Recommendations
What:	As you requested, I have analyzed the ordering and shipping costs of candy that we receive from our distributors. I found that during the past year, the ordering costs of receiving candy were 9 percent of sales, or $36,000.

On average, we are placing about two orders per week, or eight orders per month. Placing each order requires about two and one-half hours of an employee's time. Further, the distributors charge a service fee for each order, and shippers charge high rates for orders as small as ours.

My recommendations are (1) to reduce orders to four per month (the candy's freshness will not be affected if we order at least once a week) and (2) to begin placing orders through the distributors' web sites (our distributors do not charge a service fee for online orders). If we follow these recommendations, I project that the costs of receiving candy will be reduced to 4 percent of sales, or $16,000, annually—a savings of $20,000.

● **STOP AND THINK!**
A financial report often contains estimates and projections. How does the writer of such a report make sure the reader understands the uncertainties involved?

The writer should include a clear statement of the assumptions underlying the report and the conditions under which the estimates and projections were made. This will enable the reader to assess how valid the estimates and projections are. ■

other creditors, and potential investors are the *who*. The *what* consists of disclosures about assets, liabilities, product costs, and sales. The required reporting deadline for the accounting period answers the question of *when*.

Wang will also want periodic internal reports on various aspects of operations. For example, a monthly report may summarize the costs of ordering candy from distributors and the related shipping charges. If the costs in the monthly reports appear too high, she may ask Salvador Chavez to conduct a special study. The results of such a study might result in a memorandum report like the one shown in Exhibit 1.

In summary, management accounting can provide a constant stream of relevant information. Compare Wang's activities and information needs with the management cycle shown in Figure 1. She started with a business plan, executed the plan, and reviewed the results. Accounting information helped her develop her business plan, communicate that plan to her bank and employees, evaluate the performance of employees, and report the results of operations. As you can see, accounting plays a critical role in managing the operations of an organization.

✓ Check out ACE for a Review Quiz at http://accounting.college.hmco.com/students.

VALUE CHAIN ANALYSIS

LO2 Describe the value chain and its usefulness in analyzing a business.

RELATED TEXT ASSIGNMENTS
Q: 9, 10
SE: 4, 5
E: 6
P: 2
SD: 1

Each step in the manufacture of a product or the delivery of a service can be thought of as a link in a chain that adds value to the product or service. This concept of how a business fulfills its mission and objectives is known as the **value chain**. As shown in Figure 4, the steps that add value to a product or service—which range from research and development to customer service—are known as **primary processes**. The value chain also includes **support services**, such as legal services and management accounting. These services facilitate the primary processes but do not add value to the final product or service. Their roles are critical, however, to making the primary processes as efficient and effective as possible.

accounting information about deliveries and sales will help her manage the supply chain.

■ **REVIEWING** In the reviewing stage of the management cycle, managers compare actual performance with the performance levels they established in the planning stage. They earmark any significant variations for further analysis so that they can correct the problems. If the problems result from a change in the organization's operating environment, they may revise the original objectives. Ideally, the adjustments made in the reviewing stage will improve the company's performance.

To evaluate how well Sweet Treasures Candy Store is doing, Abbie Wang will compare the amounts estimated in the budget with information about actual results. If any differences occur, she will analyze why they have occurred. Reasons for these differences may lead Wang to change parts of her original business plan. In addition to reviewing employees' performance in regard to financial goals, such as avoiding waste, Wang will want to review how well her employees served customers. As noted earlier, she decided to monitor service quality by keeping a record of the number and type of complaints about poor customer service. Her review of this record may help her develop new and better business strategies.

KEY POINT: Revenues and expenses accumulated in accounting systems for financial reporting purposes are also used in management accounting to support budgeting of next year's business activities.

■ **REPORTING** Whether accounting reports are prepared for internal or external use, it is essential that they provide accurate information and that they clearly communicate this information to the reader. Internal reports that provide inaccurate information or that present information in such a way that it is unclear to the employee or manager can have a negative effect on a company's operations and ultimately on its profitability. Full disclosure and transparency in financial statements issued to external parties is a fundamental of generally accepted accounting principles, and violation of this precept can now result in stiff penalties. After reporting violations by Enron, WorldCom, and other companies, Congress passed legislation that requires top management of companies that file financial statements with the Securities and Exchange Commission to certify that these statements are accurate; the penalty for issuing false public reports can be loss of compensation, fines, and jail time.

www.enron.com
www.worldcom.com

The key to producing a management accounting report that communicates accurate and useful information in such a way that the meaning is transparent to the reader is to apply the four *w*'s: why, who, what, and when.

- *Why?* Know the purpose of the report. Focus on it as you write.

- *Who?* Identify the audience for your report. Communicate at a level that matches your readers' understanding of the issue and their familiarity with accounting information. A detailed, informal report may be appropriate for your manager, but a more concise summary may be necessary for other audiences, such as the president or board of directors of your organization.

- *What?* What information is needed, and what method of presentation is best? Select relevant information from reliable sources. You may draw information from pertinent documents or from interviews with knowledgeable managers and employees. The information should be not only relevant, but also easy to read and understand. You may need to include visual aids, such as bar charts or graphs, to present the information clearly.

- *When?* Know the due date for the report. Strive to prepare an accurate report on a timely basis. If the report is urgently needed, you may have to sacrifice some accuracy in the interest of timeliness.

The four *w*'s are also applicable to financial accounting reports. Assume that Abbie Wang has hired Salvador Chavez to be her company's accountant. In the financial statements that he prepares, the purpose—or *why*—is to report on the financial health of Sweet Treasures Candy Store. In this case, Wang, her bank and

statement, a forecasted statement of cash flows, and a forecasted balance sheet for both years.

Because Wang does not have a financial background, she will consult a local accounting firm to help her develop the business plan. To provide relevant input for the plan, she will have to determine the types of candy she wants to sell; the volume of sales she anticipates; the selling price for each product; the monthly costs of leasing or purchasing facilities, employing personnel, and maintaining the facilities; and the number of display counters, storage units, and cash registers that she will need.

■ **EXECUTING** Planning alone does not guarantee satisfactory operating results. Management must implement the business plan in ways that make optimal use of available resources. Smooth operations require one or more of the following: hiring and training personnel, matching human and technical resources to the work that must be done, purchasing or leasing facilities, maintaining an inventory of products for sale, and identifying operating activities, or tasks, that minimize waste and improve the quality of the products or services.

Managers execute the business plan by overseeing the daily operations of the organization. In small organizations, managers generally have frequent direct contact with their employees. They supervise them and interact with them to help them learn a task or to improve their performance. In larger, more complex organizations, there is usually less direct contact between managers and employees. Instead of directly observing employees, managers in large companies monitor employees' performance by measuring the time taken to complete an activity (such as the number of inspection hours) or the frequency of an activity (such as the number of inspections).

To illustrate how management accounting provides information to support the executing stage of the management cycle, let's assume that Abbie Wang has obtained the bank loan, and Sweet Treasures Candy Store is now open for business. The budget prepared for the store's first two years of business provides the link between the business plan and executing the plan. Items that relate to the business plan appear in the budget and become authorizations for expenditures. They include such matters as spending on store fixtures, hiring employees, developing advertising campaigns, and pricing items for special sales.

KEY POINT: The supply chain is primarily concerned with logistics and with shortening the cycle time of suppliers to customers.

Critical to managing any retail business is the supply chain. As Figure 3 shows, the **supply chain** (also called the *supply network*) is the path that leads from the suppliers of the materials from which a product is made to the final consumer. In the supply chain for candy, sugar and other ingredients flow from suppliers to manufacturers to distributors to retailers to consumers. Wang's business is toward the end of the supply chain. She buys from distributors and sells to consumers. She must coordinate deliveries from distributors so that she meets the demands of her customers without having too much inventory on hand, which would tie up cash, or being out of stock when a customer asks for a certain type of candy. Management

FIGURE 3
The Supply Chain

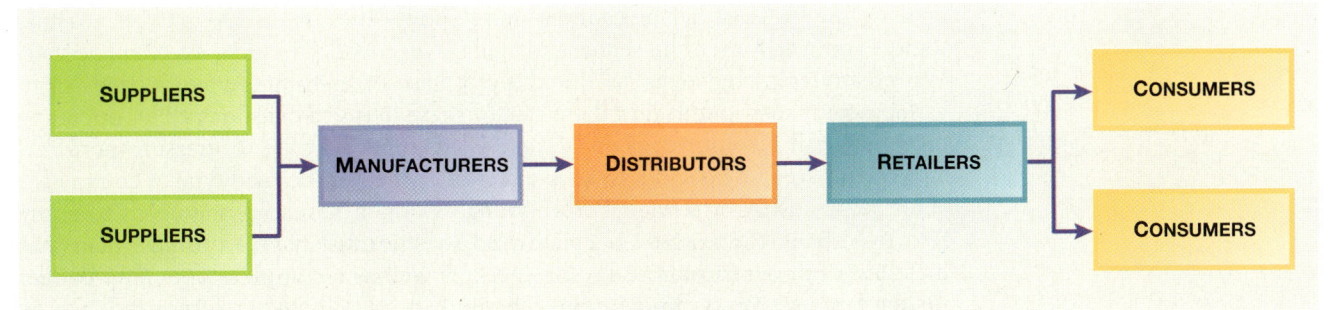

SUPPLIERS → MANUFACTURERS → DISTRIBUTORS → RETAILERS → CONSUMERS
SUPPLIERS ↗   ↘ CONSUMERS

FIGURE 2
Overview of the Planning Framework

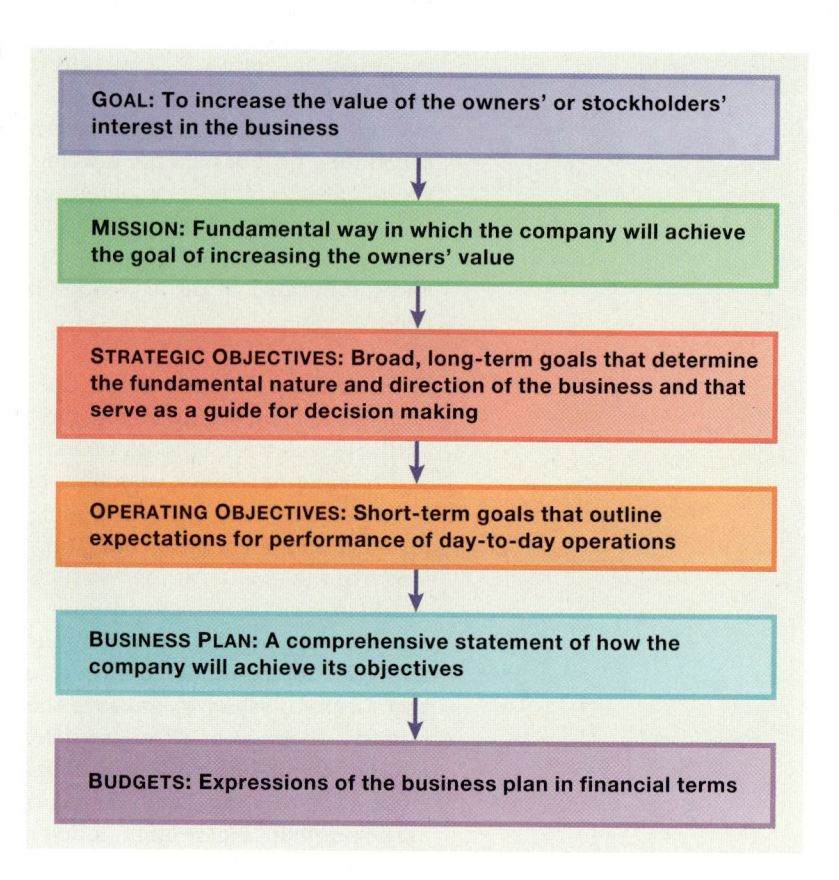

GOAL: To increase the value of the owners' or stockholders' interest in the business

MISSION: Fundamental way in which the company will achieve the goal of increasing the owners' value

STRATEGIC OBJECTIVES: Broad, long-term goals that determine the fundamental nature and direction of the business and that serve as a guide for decision making

OPERATING OBJECTIVES: Short-term goals that outline expectations for performance of day-to-day operations

BUSINESS PLAN: A comprehensive statement of how the company will achieve its objectives

BUDGETS: Expressions of the business plan in financial terms

gic objectives and operating objectives. **Strategic objectives** are broad, long-term goals that determine the fundamental nature and direction of the business and that serve as a guide for decision making. Strategic objectives are established by top management and involve such basic issues as what the company's main products or services will be, who its primary customers will be, and where it will operate. **Operating objectives** are short-term goals that outline expectations for performance of day-to-day operations. The development of strategic and operating objectives requires managers to formulate a business plan, which involves making decisions concerning various alternatives. The **business plan** is a comprehensive statement of how the company will achieve its objectives. It is usually expressed in financial terms in the form of budgets, and it often includes performance goals for individuals, teams, products, or services. Management accounting supports the planning process by providing the information managers need to develop strategic and operating objectives and the comprehensive business plan.

To illustrate the role of management accounting in the planning process, let's suppose that Abbie Wang is about to open her own retail business called Sweet Treasures Candy Store. Wang's goal is to obtain an income from the business and to increase the value of her investment in it. The business's mission is to attract customers and retain them by selling satisfying sweets and providing excellent service. Wang's strategic objectives call for the purchase of high-quality confections from various candy distributors and the resale of these items to consumers. Her operating objectives call for courteous and efficient customer service; to measure performance in this area, she decides to keep a record of the number and type of complaints about poor customer service. Before Wang can open her store, she needs to apply to a local bank for a start-up loan. To do so, she must have a business plan that includes a full description of the business, as well as a complete operating budget for the first two years of operations. The budget must include a forecasted income

historical in nature and measured in monetary terms. Management accounting reports are prepared as often as needed—annually, quarterly, monthly, and even daily if they are needed for special purposes. Financial statements, on the other hand, are prepared and distributed periodically, usually on a quarterly and annual basis.

Management Accounting and the Management Cycle

Management is expected to use resources wisely, operate profitably, pay debts, and abide by laws and regulations. To fulfill these expectations, managers establish the goals, objectives, and strategic plans of the organization and guide and control operating, investing, and financing activities accordingly. Although management actions differ from organization to organization, they generally follow a four-stage cycle. As illustrated in Figure 1, the four stages of the management cycle are (1) planning, (2) executing, (3) reviewing, and (4) reporting. Management accounting supports each stage of the cycle.

■ **Planning** Figure 2 shows the overall framework in which planning takes place. The overriding goal of a business is to increase the value of the owners' interest in the business. For corporations, this means increasing stockholders' value, or the value of the company as represented by the total market value of the shares of stock in the corporation. A company's **mission** is a statement of the fundamental way in which the company will achieve its goal of increasing the owners' value. The mission statement is essential to the planning process, which must consider both strate-

Figure 1
The Management Cycle

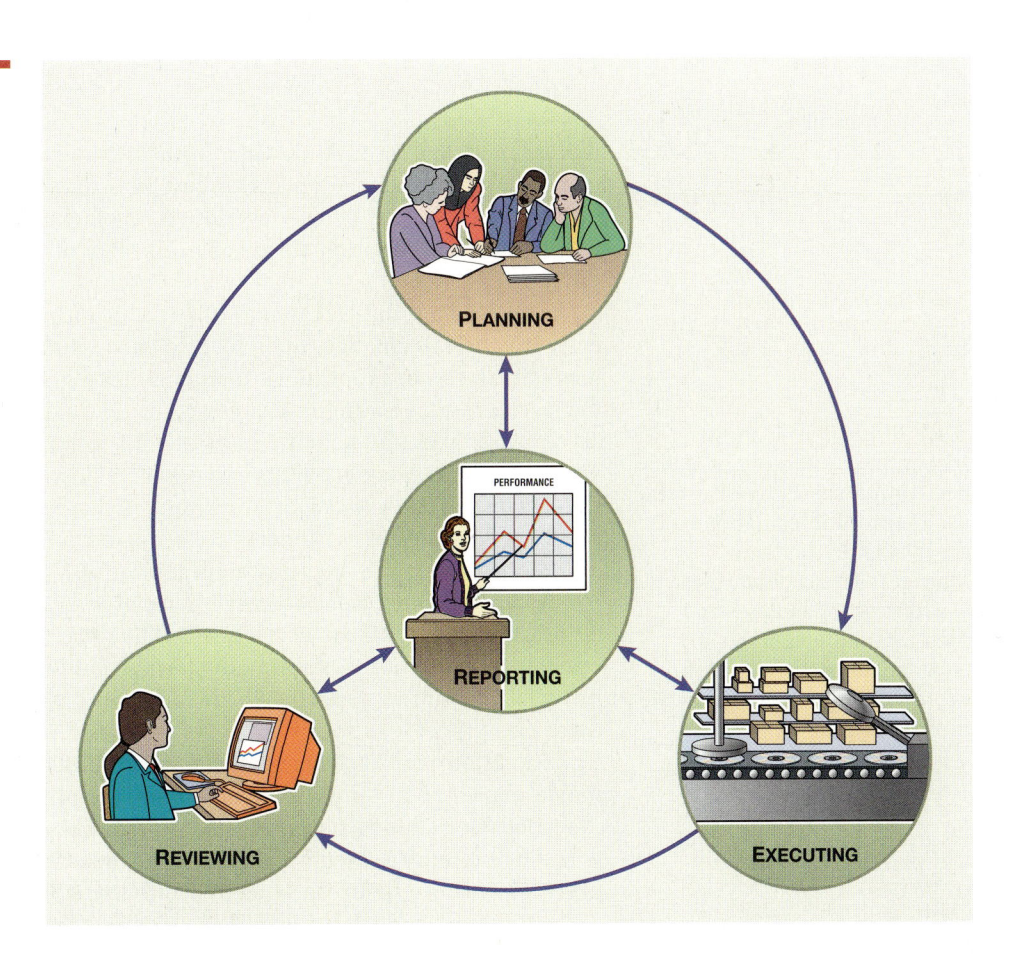

KEY POINT: Management accounting is *not* a subordinate activity to financial accounting. Rather, management accounting is a process that includes financial accounting, tax accounting, information analysis, and other accounting activities.

TABLE 1. Comparison of Management and Financial Accounting

Areas of Comparison	Management Accounting	Financial Accounting
Primary users	Managers, employees	Owners or stockholders, lenders, customers, governmental agencies
Report format	Flexible, driven by user's needs	Based on generally accepted accounting principles
Purpose of reports	Provide information for planning, control, performance measurement, and decision making	Report on past performance
Nature of information	Objective and verifiable for decision making; more subjective for planning (relies on estimates)	Objective and verifiable
Units of measure	Dollars at historical, market, or projected values; physical measures of time or number of objects	Dollars at historical and market values
Frequency of reports	Prepared as needed; may or may not be on a periodic basis	Prepared on a periodic basis

KEY POINT: Financial accounting requires consistency and comparability to ensure the usefulness of information to those outside the firm. Management accounting can use innovative analyses and presentation techniques to enhance information's usefulness to management within the firm.

this information through reports. Both provide managers with key measures of a company's performance and with cost information for valuing inventories on the balance sheet. Despite the overlap in their functions, management accounting and financial accounting differ in a number of ways. Table 1 summarizes these differences.

As we have indicated, management accounting provides managers and employees with the information they need to make informed decisions, to perform their jobs effectively, and to achieve their organization's goals. Thus, the primary users of management accounting information are people inside the organization. Financial accounting takes the actual results of management decisions about operating, investing, and financing activities and prepares financial statements for parties outside the organization—owners or stockholders, lenders, customers, and governmental agencies. Although these reports are prepared primarily for external use, managers also rely on them in evaluating an organization's performance.

Because management accounting reports are for internal use, their format can be flexible, driven by the user's needs. They may report either historical or future-oriented information without any formal guidelines or restrictions. In contrast, financial accounting reports, which focus on past performance, must follow standards and procedures specified by generally accepted accounting principles.

The information in management accounting reports may be objective and verifiable, expressed in terms of dollar amounts or physical measures of time or objects; if needed for planning purposes, the information may be based on estimates, and it will thus be more subjective. In contrast, the statements that financial accounting provides must be based on objective and verifiable information, which is generally

The Role of Management Accounting

LO1 Distinguish management accounting from financial accounting and explain the role of management accounting in the management cycle.

RELATED TEXT ASSIGNMENTS
Q: 1, 2, 3, 4, 5, 6, 7, 8
SE: 1, 2, 3, 4
E: 1, 2, 3, 4, 5
P: 1, 6
SD: 5
MRA: 1, 2

🔶 **Stop and Think!**
A financial report often contains estimates and projections. How does the writer of such a report make sure the reader understands the uncertainties involved?
The writer should include a clear statement of the assumptions underlying the report and the conditions under which the estimates and projections were made. This will enable the reader to assess how valid the estimates and projections are. ∎

To plan and control an organization's operations, to measure its performance, and to make decisions about pricing products or services and many other matters, managers need accurate and timely accounting information. To do their jobs efficiently, employees who handle daily operations, such as managing the flow of materials into a production system, also rely on accurate and timely accounting information. The role of management accounting is to provide an information system that enables persons throughout an organization to make informed decisions, to be more effective at their jobs, and to improve the organization's performance.

The need for management accounting information exists regardless of the type of organization—manufacturing, retail, service, or governmental—or its size. Although multidivisional corporations need more information and more complex accounting systems than small ones, even small businesses need certain types of management accounting information to ensure efficient operating conditions. The precise type of information needed depends on an organization's goals and the nature of its operations.

In 1982, the Institute of Management Accountants (IMA) defined **management accounting** as

> the process of identification, measurement, accumulation, analysis, preparation, interpretation, and communication of financial information used by management to plan, evaluate, and control within the organization and to assure appropriate use of and accountability for its resources.[3]

Since this definition was written, the importance of nonfinancial information has increased significantly. Today, management accounting information includes such nonfinancial data as the time needed to complete one cycle of the production process or to rework production errors, as well as nonfinancial data pertaining to customer satisfaction.

Management Accounting and Financial Accounting: A Comparison

Both management accounting and financial accounting assist decision makers by identifying, measuring, and processing relevant information and communicating

Focus on Business Practice

Why Is Management Accounting Vitally Important to Excellent Companies?

Futura Industries <www.futuraind.com> is not a famous company, but it is one of the best. Based in Utah, it is rated as that state's top privately owned employer. An international company with more than 50 years' experience in aluminum extruding, finishing, fabrication, machining, and design, Futura serves a high-end niche in such diverse markets as floor covering, electronics, transportation, and shower doors.

In achieving its success, Futura has used a management accounting technique called the balanced scorecard. The balanced scorecard focuses on four key dimensions of a company's operations: learning and growth among employees, internal business processes, satisfaction of customers, and financial goals. Using the balanced scorecard, Futura has developed measures of performance in each of these dimensions. For example, employee turnover is a measure of employee learning and growth. Percentage of sales from new products and total production cost per standard hour are measures of how well the company's internal processes are performing, and number of customers' complaints and percentage of materials returned are measures of customer satisfaction. Finally, income and gross margin are among the measures of financial performance. To be truly successful, Futura must excel in all four dimensions.[4]

Management accounting plays an important role in helping companies attain their goals, providing information for making operating decisions, developing budgets, determining costs of products, measuring performance, and evaluating results. Without the interplay of information, decisions, and performance measurement that management accounting facilitates, companies like Futura could not be so successful.

What managment accounting tools does Honda utilize to stay ahead of its competitors?

making decisions about everything from buying materials to developing and implementing new production processes to pricing, marketing, and distributing vehicles. Management accounting also provides Honda's managers with objective data by which they can measure the company's performance in terms of its key success factors. Among the tools of management accounting are budgets, which set daily operating goals for workers and provide targets for evaluating the workers' performance. Performance measures for the production process may include the time to complete one cycle of the process, the number of setups, and the time to rework errors in production. Performance measures of customer satisfaction may include number of customer complaints, number of service change notices, and number of customer referrals. As Honda strives to improve its products and maintain its record of success with vehicles like the Insight, it will continue to rely on the information that management accounting provides.

19

Chapter 19 describes the approaches that businesses have developed to meet the challenges of today's changing business environment and the role that management accounting plays in meeting those challenges.

The Changing Business Environment: A Manager's Perspective

LEARNING OBJECTIVES

LO1 Distinguish management accounting from financial accounting and explain the role of management accounting in the management cycle.

LO2 Describe the value chain and its usefulness in analyzing a business.

LO3 Identify the management tools used for continuous improvement and describe how they work to meet the demands of global competition and how management accounting supports them.

LO4 Explain the balanced scorecard and its relationship to performance measures.

LO5 Prepare an analysis of nonfinancial data.

LO6 Identify the standards of ethical conduct for management accountants.

DECISION POINT

A MANAGER'S FOCUS

Honda Motor Company <www.honda.com> If organizations are to prosper, they must identify the factors that are critical to their success. Key success factors include satisfying customer needs, developing efficient manufacturing processes and advanced technologies, and being a leader in marketing innovative products. Honda Motor Company had all these factors in mind when it introduced a "green car" called the Insight to the U.S. market. Like other green cars, the Insight is a hybrid vehicle, running on both a gasoline engine and an electric motor. Priced at less than $20,000, it gets more than 60 miles to the gallon. The Insight thus meets regulators' demands for vehicles that emit fewer air-polluting fumes and consumers' demands for inexpensive, practical transportation.[1]

Using new technology and innovative design to address both customers' needs and environmental concerns is just part of Honda's strategy to stay agile, flexible, and ahead of its competitors. Equally important to Honda's success is the development of efficient manufacturing operations.[2] The company is standardizing manufacturing tools and eliminating the need to modify its assembly lines. Its model-specific subassembly lines will feed their products to a new and shorter assembly line.

All these innovations demonstrate Honda's resolve to remain an industry leader. What role does management accounting play in this endeavor?

Management accounting provides the information necessary for effective decision making. Honda's managers use management accounting information in

Long-term solvency: debt to equity ratio
Cash flow adequacy: cash flow yield
free cash flow

Evaluate and comment on the relative performance of the two companies with respect to each of the above categories. (**Note:** Accounts Receivable, Inventory, and Accounts Payable for Walgreens in 2000 were (in millions) $614.5, $2,830.8, and $1,364.0, respectively. Total assets for Walgreens in 2000 were $7,103.7 million.)

Fingraph® Financial Analyst™

FRA 5.
LO5 Comprehensive Financial Performance Evaluation

Choose any company from the list of Fingraph companies on the Needles Accounting Resource Center Web Site at http://accounting.college.hmco.com/students. Access the Microsoft Excel spreadsheets for the company you selected.

1. Using the Fingraph CD-ROM software, display and print the following pages for the company you have selected:

    a. Balance Sheet Analysis
    b. Current Assets and Current Liabilities Analysis
    c. Liquidity and Asset Utilization Analysis
    d. Income from Operations Analysis
    e. Statement of Cash Flows: Operating Activities Analysis
    f. Statement of Cash Flows: Investing and Financing Activities Analysis
    g. Market Strength Analysis

2. Prepare an executive summary that describes the company's financial condition and performance over the past two years. Attach the pages you printed in support of your analysis.

Internet Case

FRA 6.
LO2 Using Investors' Services
LO3

Go to the web site for Moody's Investors Service <www.moodys.com>. Click on "ratings," which will show revisions of debt ratings issued by Moody's in the past few days. Choose a rating that has been upgraded or downgraded and read the short press announcement related to it. What reasons does Moody's give for the change in rating? What is Moody's assessment of the future of the company or institution? What financial performance measures are mentioned in the article? Summarize your findings and be prepared to share them in class.

Prepare a trend analysis for Heinz with 1997 as the base year and discuss the results. Identify important trends and state whether the trends are favorable or unfavorable. Discuss significant relationships among the trends.

International Company

FRA 2.
LO5 Comparison of International Companies' Operating Cycles

Ratio analysis enables one to compare the performance of companies whose financial statements are presented in different currencies. Selected data from 2000 for two large pharmaceutical companies—one American, Pfizer, Inc. <www.pfizer.com>, and one Swiss, Roche <www.roche.com>—are presented below (in millions).[12]

	Pfizer, Inc. (U.S.)	Roche (Swiss)
Net Sales	$29,574	SF28,672
Cost of Goods Sold	4,907	9,163
Accounts Receivable	5,489	5,519
Inventories	2,702	5,754
Accounts Payable	1,719	2,215

Accounts receivable in 1999 were $5,368 for Pfizer and SF6,178 for Roche. Inventories in 1999 were $2,588 for Pfizer and SF6,546 for Roche. Accounts payable in 1999 were $1,889 for Pfizer and SF2,378 for Roche.

For each company, calculate the receivable, inventory, and payables turnovers and the respective days associated with each. Then determine the operating cycle for each company and the days of financing required for current operations. Compare the results.

Group Activity: Divide the class into groups to make the calculations. Assign the analysis of Pfizer to half of the groups, and the analysis of Roche to the other half. Have the groups compare results and discuss as a class.

Toys "R" Us Annual Report

FRA 3.
LO5 Comprehensive Ratio Analysis

Using data from the Toys "R" Us <www.tru.com> annual report, conduct a comprehensive ratio analysis that compares the company's performance in 2002 and 2001. If you have computed ratios for Toys "R" Us in previous chapters, you may prepare a table that summarizes the ratios for 2002 and 2001 and show calculations only for the ratios not previously calculated. If this is the first ratio analysis you have done for Toys "R" Us, show all your computations. In either case, after each group of ratios, comment on the performance of Toys "R" Us. Round your calculations to one decimal place. Prepare and comment on the following categories of ratios:

Liquidity analysis: current ratio, quick ratio, receivable turnover, average days' sales uncollected, inventory turnover, average days' inventory on hand, payables turnover, and average days' payable. (Accounts Receivable, Inventory, and Accounts Payable were [in millions] $225, $2,307, and $1,152, respectively, in 2000.)

Profitability analysis: profit margin, asset turnover, return on assets, and return on equity. (Comment on the effect of the restructuring in 2002 on the company's profitability.)

Long-term solvency analysis: debt to equity ratio and interest coverage ratio.

Cash flow adequacy analysis: cash flow yield, cash flows to sales, cash flows to assets, and free cash flow.

Market strength analysis: price/earnings ratio and dividends yield.

Comparison Case: Toys "R" Us and Walgreen Co.

FRA 4.
LO5 Comparison of Key Financial Performance Measures

Refer to the annual report of Toys "R" Us <www.tru.com> and the financial statements for Walgreens <www.walgreens.com> in the Supplement to Chapter 6. Calculate the following key financial performance measures for the two most recent years:

Liquidity: operating cycle
days of financing needed

Profitability: profit margin
asset turnover
return on assets

Decision-Making Practice

SD 6.
LO4 Effect of a One-Time Item on
LO5 a Loan Decision

Apple a Day, Inc., and Unforgettable Edibles, Inc., are food catering businesses that operate in the same metropolitan area. Their customers include *Fortune* 500 companies, regional firms, and individuals. The two firms reported similar profit margins for the current year, and both base bonuses for managers on the achievement of a target profit margin and return on equity. Each firm has submitted a loan request to you, a loan officer for City National Bank. They have provided you with the following information:

	Apple a Day	Unforgettable Edibles
Net sales	$625,348	$717,900
Cost of goods sold	225,125	287,080
Gross margin	$400,223	$430,820
Operating expenses	281,300	371,565
Operating income	$118,923	$ 59,255
Gain on sale of real estate	—	81,923
Interest expense	(9,333)	(15,338)
Income before income taxes	$109,590	$125,840
Income taxes	25,990	29,525
Net income	$83,600	$96,315
Average stockholders' equity	$312,700	$390,560

1. Perform a vertical analysis and prepare a common-size income statement for each firm. Compute profit margin and return on equity.
2. Discuss these results, the bonus plan for management, and loan considerations. Identify the company that is the better loan risk.

FINANCIAL REPORTING AND ANALYSIS CASES

Interpreting Financial Reports

FRA 1.
LO4 Trend Analysis

H. J. Heinz Company <www.heinz.com> is a global company engaged in several lines of business, including food service, infant foods, condiments, pet foods, and weight control food products. Below is a five-year summary of operations and other related data for Heinz.[11] (Dollars are expressed in thousands.)

Five-Year Summary of Operations and Other Related Data
H. J. Heinz Company and Subsidiaries

	2001	2000	1999	1998	1997
Summary of operations					
Sales	$9,430,422	$9,407,949	$9,299,610	$9,209,284	$9,397,007
Cost of products sold	5,883,618	5,788,565	5,944,867	5,711,213	6,385,091
Interest expense	552,957	269,748	258,815	258,616	274,746
Provision for income taxes	178,140	573,123	360,790	453,415	177,193
Net income (before special items)	494,918	890,553	474,341	801,566	301,871
Other related data					
Dividends paid: Common	537,290	513,756	484,817	452,966	416,923
Total assets	9,035,150	8,850,697	8,053,634	8,023,421	8,437,787
Total debt	4,885,687	4,112,401	3,376,413	5,806,905	5,997,366
Shareholders' equity	1,373,727	1,595,856	1,803,004	2,216,516	2,440,921

SKILLS DEVELOPMENT CASES

Conceptual Analysis

SD 1.
LO2 Standards for Financial
LO5 Performance Evaluation

Helene Curtis, a well-known, publicly owned corporation, became a take-over candidate and sold out in the 1990s after years of poor profit performance. As early as 1978, *Forbes* observed, "By almost any standard, Chicago-based Helene Curtis rates as one of America's worst-managed personal care companies. In recent years its return on equity has hovered between 10% and 13%, well below the industry average of 18% to 19%. Net profit margins of 2% to 3% are half that of competitors. . . . As a result, while leading names like Revlon <www.revlon.com> and Avon <www.avon.com> are trading at three and four times book value, Curtis trades at less than two-thirds book value."[9] Considering that many companies in other industries were happy with a return on equity of 10 percent to 13 percent, why is this analysis so critical of Curtis's performance? Assuming that Curtis could have doubled its profit margin, what other information would be necessary to project the resulting return on stockholders' investment? Why did Revlon's and Avon's stocks trade for more than Curtis's? Be prepared to discuss your answers in class.

SD 2.
LO3 Using Segment Information

Refer to Exhibit 1, which shows the segment information of Goodyear Tire & Rubber Company <www.goodyear.com>. In what business segments does Goodyear operate? What is the relative size of its business segments in terms of sales and income in the most recent year shown? Which segment is most profitable in terms of return on assets? In which region of the world is the tires segment largest, and which tire segment is most profitable in terms of return on assets?

SD 3.
LO3 Using Investors' Services

Refer to Exhibit 2, which contains the PepsiCo Inc. <www.pepsi.com> listing from Mergent's *Handbook of Dividend Achievers*. Assume that an investor has asked you to assess PepsiCo's recent history and prospects. Write a memorandum to the investor that addresses the following points:

1. PepsiCo's earnings history. (What has been the general relationship between PepsiCo's return on assets and its return on equity over the last seven years? What does this tell you about the way the company is financed? What figures back up your conclusion?)
2. The trend of PepsiCo's stock price and price/earnings ratio for the seven years shown.
3. PepsiCo's prospects, including developments likely to affect the company's future.

Ethical Dilemma

SD 4.
LO3 Management of Earnings

Management of most companies is very sensitive to the fact that analysts watch key performance measures, such as whether a firm is meeting earnings targets. A slight weakening of analysts' confidence can severely affect the price of a company's stock. The SEC has been cracking down on companies that manipulate earnings to achieve financial goals. For instance, some time ago, the SEC filed a complaint against W. R. Grace & Co. <www.grace.com> for releasing $1.5 million from reserves into earnings in order to meet earnings targets. Grace officials claimed the amount was immaterial and that the company was in accord with accounting rules for booking an immaterial item. (The amount was about 1.5 percent of net income.) The SEC argued that it was a matter of principle: "Does anyone think that it's acceptable to intentionally book an error [false transaction] for the purpose of making earnings targets?" But some think such action on the part of the SEC will harm confidence in business.[10] Do you think it is unethical for a company's management to increase earnings periodically through the use of one-time transactions, such as adjustments of reserves or sale of assets, on which it has a profit?

Research Activity

SD 5.
LO3 Using Investors' Services

Find *Moody's Investors Service* or *Standard & Poor's Industry Guide* in your library. Locate reports on three corporations. You may choose the corporations at random or from the same industry, as directed by your instructor. (If you did a related research activity in a previous chapter, use the same three companies.) Write a summary of what you learned about each company's financial performance, including the performance measures that it uses and its prospects for the future. Be prepared to discuss your findings in class.

Lisle Corporation
Comparative Balance Sheets
December 31, 20x6 and 20x5

	20x6	20x5
Assets		
Cash	$ 40,600	$ 20,400
Accounts receivable (net)	117,800	114,600
Inventory	287,400	297,400
Property, plant, and equipment (net)	375,000	360,000
Total assets	$820,800	$792,400
Liabilities and Stockholders' Equity		
Accounts payable	$133,800	$238,600
Notes payable	100,000	200,000
Bonds payable	200,000	—
Common stock, $5 par value	200,000	200,000
Retained earnings	187,000	153,800
Total liabilities and stockholders' equity	$820,800	$792,400

Additional data for Lisle Corporation in 20x6 and 20x5 are as follows:

	20x6	20x5
Net cash flows from operating activities	$106,500,000	$86,250,000
Net capital expenditures	$22,500,000	$16,000,000
Dividends paid	$22,000,000	$17,200,000
Number of common shares	40,000,000	40,000,000
Market price per share	$9	$15

Selected balances (in thousands) at the end of 20x4 were accounts receivable (net), $103,400; inventory, $273,600; total assets, $732,800; accounts payable $193,300; and stockholders' equity, $320,600. All Lisle Corporation's notes payable were current liabilities. All its bonds payable were long-term liabilities.

REQUIRED ▶ Perform a ratio analysis following the steps outlined below. Round percentages and ratios to one decimal place, and consider changes of .1 or less to be neutral. After making the calculations, indicate whether each ratio had a favorable (F) or unfavorable (U) change from 20x5 to 20x6.

1. Conduct a liquidity analysis by calculating for each year the (a) current ratio, (b) quick ratio, (c) receivable turnover, (d) average days' sales uncollected, (e) inventory turnover, (f) average days' inventory on hand, (g) payables turnover, and (h) average days' payable.
2. Conduct a profitability analysis by calculating for each year the (a) profit margin, (b) asset turnover, (c) return on assets, and (d) return on equity.
3. Conduct a long-term solvency analysis by calculating for each year the (a) debt to equity ratio and (b) interest coverage ratio.
4. Conduct a cash flow adequacy analysis by calculating for each year the (a) cash flow yield, (b) cash flows to sales, (c) cash flows to assets, and (d) free cash flow.
5. Conduct a market strength analysis by calculating for each year the (a) price/earnings ratio and (b) dividends yield.
6. Based on your analysis, assess Lisle's performance in each of the following areas: liquidity, profitability, long-term solvency, and cash flow adequacy. Explain your evaluations.

Alternate Problems

P 5. Mankato Corporation engaged in the transactions listed in the first column of the following table. Opposite each transaction is a ratio and space to indicate the effect of each transaction on the ratio.

		Effect		
Transaction	Ratio	Increase	Decrease	None
a. Sold merchandise on account.	Current ratio			
b. Sold merchandise on account.	Inventory turnover			
c. Collected on accounts receivable.	Quick ratio			
d. Wrote off an uncollectible account.	Receivable turnover			
e. Paid on accounts payable.	Current ratio			
f. Declared cash dividend.	Return on equity			
g. Incurred advertising expense.	Profit margin			
h. Issued stock dividend.	Debt to equity ratio			
i. Issued bonds payable.	Asset turnover			
j. Accrued interest expense.	Current ratio			
k. Paid previously declared cash dividend.	Dividends yield			
l. Purchased treasury stock.	Return on assets			
m. Recorded depreciation expense.	Cash flow yield			

REQUIRED ▶ Place an X in the appropriate column to show whether the transaction increased, decreased, or had no effect on the indicated ratio.

P 6. The condensed comparative income statements and balance sheets of Lisle Corporation follow. All figures are in thousands of dollars, except earnings per share.

Lisle Corporation
Comparative Income Statements
For the Years Ended December 31, 20x6 and 20x5

	20x6	20x5
Net sales	$1,638,400	$1,573,200
Costs and expenses		
Cost of goods sold	$1,044,400	$1,004,200
Selling expenses	238,400	259,000
Administrative expenses	223,600	211,600
Total costs and expenses	$1,506,400	$1,474,800
Income from operations	$ 132,000	$ 98,400
Interest expense	32,800	19,600
Income before income taxes	$ 99,200	$ 78,800
Income taxes	31,200	28,400
Net income	$ 68,000	$ 50,400
Earnings per share	$ 1.70	$ 1.26

	Reynard	Bouche
Assets		
Cash	$ 126,100	$ 514,300
Marketable securities (at cost)	117,500	1,200,000
Accounts receivable (net)	456,700	2,600,000
Inventories	1,880,000	4,956,000
Prepaid expenses	72,600	156,600
Property, plant, and equipment (net)	5,342,200	19,356,000
Intangibles and other assets	217,000	580,000
Total assets	$8,212,100	$29,362,900
Liabilities and Stockholders' Equity		
Accounts payable	$ 517,400	$ 2,342,000
Notes payable	1,000,000	2,000,000
Income taxes payable	85,200	117,900
Bonds payable	2,000,000	15,000,000
Common stock, $1 par value	350,000	1,000,000
Paid-in capital in excess of par value, common	1,747,300	5,433,300
Retained earnings	2,512,200	3,469,700
Total liabilities and stockholders' equity	$8,212,100	$29,362,900

During the year, Reynard paid a total of $140,000 in dividends, and its current price per share is $20. Bouche paid a total of $600,000 in dividends during the year, and its current market price per share is $9. Reynard had net cash flows from operating activities of $771,500 and net capital expenditures of $450,000. Bouche had net cash flows from operating activities of $843,000 and net capital expenditures of $1,550,000.

Information pertaining to these companies' prior years is not readily available. Assume that all their notes payable are current liabilities and that all their bonds payable are long-term liabilities.

REQUIRED ▶ Conduct a comprehensive ratio analysis of Reynard and of Bouche following the steps outlined below. (Round all ratios and percentages except earnings per share to one decimal place.)

1. Prepare a liquidity analysis by calculating for each company the (a) current ratio, (b) quick ratio, (c) receivable turnover, (d) average days' sales uncollected, (e) inventory turnover, (f) average days' inventory on hand, (g) payables turnover, and (h) averages days' payables.
2. Prepare a profitability analysis by calculating for each company the (a) profit margin, (b) asset turnover, (c) return on assets, and (d) return on equity.
3. Prepare a long-term solvency analysis by calculating for each company the (a) debt to equity ratio and (b) interest coverage ratio.
4. Prepare a cash flow adequacy analysis by calculating for each company the (a) cash flow yield, (b) cash flows to sales, (c) cash flows to assets, and (d) free cash flow.
5. Prepare an analysis of market strength by calculating for each company the (a) price/earnings ratio and (b) dividends yield.
6. Compare the two companies by inserting the ratio calculations from 1 through 5 in a table with the following column headings: Ratio Name, Reynard, Bouche, and Company with More Favorable Ratio. Indicate in the last column which company had the more favorable ratio in each case.
7. How could the analysis be improved if information about these companies' prior years were available?

Chapter 18 Financial Performance Evaluation

LO5 Ratio Analysis

P 3. Data for Rochelle Corporation in 20x5 and 20x4 follow. These data should be used in conjunction with the data in **P 1**.

	20x5	20x4
Net cash flows from operating activities	$128,000	$198,000
Net capital expenditures	$238,000	$76,000
Dividends paid	$62,800	$70,000
Number of common shares	60,000	60,000
Market price per share	$40	$60

Selected balances at the end of 20x3 were accounts receivable (net), $105,400; inventory, $198,800; total assets, $1,295,600; accounts payable, $134,400; and stockholders' equity, $753,200. All Rochelle's notes payable were current liabilities; all its bonds payable were long-term liabilities.

REQUIRED ▶ Perform a ratio analysis following the steps outlined below. Round all answers to one decimal place, and consider changes of .1 or less to be neutral. After making the calculations, indicate whether each ratio improved or deteriorated from 20x4 to 20x5 (use F for favorable and U for unfavorable).

1. Prepare a liquidity analysis by calculating for each year the (a) current ratio, (b) quick ratio, (c) receivable turnover, (d) average days' sales uncollected, (e) inventory turnover, (f) average days' inventory on hand, (g) payables turnover, and (h) average days' payable.
2. Prepare a profitability analysis by calculating for each year the (a) profit margin, (b) asset turnover, (c) return on assets, and (d) return on equity.
3. Prepare a long-term solvency analysis by calculating for each year the (a) debt to equity ratio and (b) interest coverage ratio.
4. Prepare a cash flow adequacy analysis by calculating for each year the (a) cash flow yield, (b) cash flows to sales, (c) cash flows to assets, and (d) free cash flow.
5. Prepare a market strength analysis by calculating for each year the (a) price/earnings ratio and (b) dividends yield.
6. Based on your analysis, assess Rochelle's performance in each of the following areas: liquidity, profitability, long-term solvency, and cash flow adequacy. Explain your evaluations.

LO5 Comprehensive Ratio Analysis of Two Companies

P 4. Juanita Maxwell has decided to invest some of her savings in common stock. She feels that the chemical industry has good growth prospects, and she has narrowed her choice to two companies in that industry. As a final step in making the choice, she has decided to perform a comprehensive ratio analysis of the two companies, Reynard and Bouche. Income statement and balance sheet data for these two companies follow.

	Reynard	Bouche
Net sales	$9,486,200	$27,287,300
Costs and expenses		
Cost of goods sold	$5,812,200	$18,372,400
Selling expenses	1,194,000	1,955,700
Administrative expenses	1,217,400	4,126,000
Total costs and expenses	$8,223,600	$24,454,100
Income from operations	$1,262,600	$ 2,833,200
Interest expense	270,000	1,360,000
Income before income taxes	$ 992,600	$ 1,473,200
Income taxes	450,000	600,000
Net income	$ 542,600	$ 873,200
Earnings per share	$ 1.55	$ .87

Rochelle Corporation
Comparative Balance Sheets
December 31, 20x5 and 20x4

	20x5	20x4
Assets		
Cash	$ 62,200	$ 54,400
Accounts receivable (net)	145,000	85,400
Inventory	245,200	215,600
Property, plant, and equipment (net)	1,155,400	1,015,000
Total assets	$1,607,800	$1,370,400
Liabilities and Stockholders' Equity		
Accounts payable	$ 209,400	$ 144,600
Notes payable	100,000	100,000
Bonds payable	400,000	220,000
Common stock, $10 par value	600,000	600,000
Retained earnings	298,400	305,800
Total liabilities and stockholders' equity	$1,607,800	$1,370,400

REQUIRED ▶ Perform the following analyses. (Round all ratios and percentages to one decimal place.)
1. Prepare schedules showing the amount and percentage changes from 20x4 to 20x5 for the comparative income statements and the balance sheets.
2. Prepare common-size income statements and balance sheets for 20x4 and 20x5.
3. Comment on the results in **1** and **2** by identifying favorable and unfavorable changes in the components and composition of the statements.

P 2.
LO5 Effects of Transactions on Ratios

Jamal Corporation, a clothing retailer, engaged in the transactions listed in the first column of the table below. Opposite each transaction is a ratio and space to mark the effect of each transaction on the ratio.

			Effect	
Transaction	Ratio	Increase	Decrease	None
a. Issued common stock for cash.	Asset turnover			
b. Declared cash dividend.	Current ratio			
c. Sold treasury stock.	Return on equity			
d. Borrowed cash by issuing note payable.	Debt to equity ratio			
e. Paid salaries expense.	Inventory turnover			
f. Purchased merchandise for cash.	Current ratio			
g. Sold equipment for cash.	Receivable turnover			
h. Sold merchandise on account.	Quick ratio			
i. Paid current portion of long-term debt.	Return on assets			
j. Gave sales discount.	Profit margin			
k. Purchased marketable securities for cash.	Quick ratio			
l. Declared 5% stock dividend.	Current ratio			
m. Purchased a building.	Free cash flow			

REQUIRED ▶ Place an X in the appropriate column to show whether the transaction increased, decreased, or had no effect on the indicated ratio.

net income of $77,112 on revenues of $1,224,000. In 20x5, the company had net income of $98,952 on revenues of $1,596,000. Compute the profit margin, asset turnover, return on assets, and return on equity for 20x4 and 20x5. Comment on the apparent cause of the increase or decrease in profitability. (Round the percentages and other ratios to one decimal place.)

LO5 Long-Term Solvency and Market Strength Ratios

E 8. An investor is considering investing in the long-term bonds and common stock of Companies M and N. Both companies operate in the same industry. In addition, both companies pay a dividend per share of $4 and have a yield of 10 percent on their long-term bonds. Other data for the two companies are as follows:

	Company M	Company N
Total assets	$2,400,000	$1,080,000
Total liabilities	1,080,000	594,000
Income before income taxes	288,000	129,600
Interest expense	97,200	53,460
Earnings per share	3.20	5.00
Market price of common stock	40	47.50

Compute the debt to equity, interest coverage, price/earnings (P/E), and dividends yield ratios, and comment on the results. (Round computations to one decimal place.)

LO5 Cash Flow Adequacy Analysis

E 9. Using the data below from the financial statements of Cheng, Inc., compute the company's cash flow yield, cash flows to sales, cash flows to assets, and free cash flow. (Round computations to one decimal place.)

Net sales	$6,400,000
Net income	704,000
Net cash flows from operating activities	912,000
Total assets, beginning of year	5,780,000
Total assets, end of year	6,240,000
Cash dividends	240,000
Net capital expenditures	596,000

PROBLEMS

LO4 Horizontal and Vertical Analyses

P 1. The condensed comparative income statements and balance sheets for Rochelle Corporation follow.

Rochelle Corporation
Comparative Income Statements
For the Years Ended December 31, 20x5 and 20x4

	20x5	20x4
Net sales	$1,600,800	$1,485,200
Costs and expenses		
Cost of goods sold	$ 908,200	$ 792,400
Selling expenses	260,200	209,200
Administrative expenses	280,600	231,000
Total costs and expenses	$1,449,000	$1,232,600
Income from operations	$ 151,800	$ 252,600
Interest expense	50,000	40,000
Income before income taxes	$ 101,800	$ 212,600
Income taxes	28,000	70,000
Net income	$ 73,800	$ 142,600
Earnings per share	$ 1.23	$ 2.38

Trumpet Company
Comparative Income Statements
For the Years Ended December 31, 20x6 and 20x5

	20x6	20x5
Net sales	$424,000	$368,000
Cost of goods sold	254,400	239,200
Gross margin	$169,600	$128,800
Selling expenses	$106,000	$ 73,600
General expenses	50,880	36,800
Total operating expenses	$156,880	$110,400
Operating income	$ 12,720	$ 18,400

LO5 Liquidity Analysis

E 5. Partial comparative balance sheet and income statement information for Helig Company is as follows:

	20x4	20x3
Cash	$ 6,800	$ 5,200
Marketable securities	3,600	8,600
Accounts receivable (net)	22,400	17,800
Inventory	27,200	24,800
Total current assets	$ 60,000	$ 56,400
Accounts payable	$ 20,000	$ 14,100
Net sales	$161,280	$110,360
Cost of goods sold	108,800	101,680
Gross margin	$ 52,480	$ 8,680

In 20x2, the year-end balances for Accounts Receivable and Inventory were $16,200 and $25,600, respectively. Accounts Payable was $15,300 in 20x2 and is the only current liability. Compute the current ratio, quick ratio, receivable turnover, average days' sales uncollected, inventory turnover, average days' inventory on hand, payables turnover, and average days' payable for each year. (Round computations to one decimal place.) Comment on the change in the company's liquidity position, including its operating cycle and required days of financing from 20x3 to 20x4.

LO5 Turnover Analysis

E 6. Main Tuxedo Shop has been in business for four years. Because the company has recently had a cash flow problem, management wonders whether there is a problem with receivables or inventories. Here are selected figures from the company's financial statements (in thousands):

	20x4	20x3	20x2	20x1
Net sales	$288	$224	$192	$160
Cost of goods sold	180	144	120	96
Accounts receivable (net)	48	40	32	24
Merchandise inventory	56	44	32	20
Accounts payable	25	20	15	10

Compute the receivable turnover, inventory turnover, and payables turnover for each of the four years, and comment on the results relative to the cash flow problem that Main Tuxedo Shop has been experiencing. Merchandise inventory was $22,000, accounts receivable was $22,000, and accounts payable was $8,000 in 20x0. (Round computations to one decimal place.)

LO5 Profitability Analysis

E 7. D.J. Company had total assets of $640,000 in 20x3, $680,000 in 20x4, and $760,000 in 20x5. Its debt to equity ratio was .67 times in all three years. In 20x4, the company had

SE 10.
LO5 Market Strength Analysis

Using the information for SiteWorks, Inc., in SE 4, SE 5, and SE 9, compute the price/earnings ratio and dividends yield for 20x4 and 20x5. The company had 10,000 shares of common stock outstanding in both years. The price of SiteWorks' common stock was $30 in 20x4 and $20 in 20x5. Comment on the results. (Round computations to one decimal place.)

Exercises

E 1.
LO1 Objectives, Standards, and
LO2 Sources of Information for
LO3 Financial Performance Evaluation

Identify each of the following as (a) an objective of financial statement analysis, (b) a standard for financial statement analysis, or (c) a source of information for financial statement analysis:

1. Average ratios of other companies in the same industry
2. Assessment of the future potential of an investment
3. Interim financial statements
4. Past ratios of the company
5. SEC Form 10-K
6. Assessment of risk
7. A company's annual report

E 2.
LO4 Horizontal Analysis

Compute the amount and percentage changes for the following balance sheets, and comment on the changes from 20x3 to 20x4. (Round the percentage changes to one decimal place.)

Trumpet Company
Comparative Balance Sheets
December 31, 20x4 and 20x3

	20x4	20x3
Assets		
Current assets	$ 37,200	$ 25,600
Property, plant, and equipment (net)	218,928	194,400
Total assets	$256,128	$220,000
Liabilities and Stockholders' Equity		
Current liabilities	$ 22,400	$ 6,400
Long-term liabilities	70,000	80,000
Stockholders' equity	163,728	133,600
Total liabilities and stockholders' equity	$256,128	$220,000

E 3.
LO4 Trend Analysis

Using 20x3 as the base year, prepare a trend analysis of the following data, and tell whether the situation shown by the trends is favorable or unfavorable. (Round your answers to one decimal place.)

	20x7	20x6	20x5	20x4	20x3
Net sales	$25,520	$23,980	$24,200	$22,880	$22,000
Cost of goods sold	17,220	15,400	15,540	14,700	14,000
General and administrative expenses	5,280	5,184	5,088	4,896	4,800
Operating income	3,020	3,396	3,572	3,284	3,200

E 4.
LO4 Vertical Analysis

Express the comparative income statements that follow as common-size statements, and comment on the changes from 20x5 to 20x6. (Round computations to one decimal place.)

SiteWorks, Inc.
Comparative Income Statements
For the Years Ended December 31, 20x5 and 20x4

	20x5	20x4
Net sales	$180,000	$145,000
Cost of goods sold	112,000	88,000
Gross margin	$ 68,000	$ 57,000
Operating expenses	40,000	30,000
Operating income	$ 28,000	$ 27,000
Interest expense	7,000	5,000
Income before income taxes	$ 21,000	$ 22,000
Income taxes	7,000	8,000
Net income	$ 14,000	$ 14,000
Earnings per share	$ 1.40	$ 1.40

SiteWorks, Inc.
Comparative Balance Sheets
December 31, 20x5 and 20x4

	20x5	20x4
Assets		
Current assets	$ 24,000	$ 20,000
Property, plant, and equipment (net)	130,000	100,000
Total assets	$154,000	$120,000
Liabilities and Stockholders' Equity		
Current liabilities	$ 18,000	$ 22,000
Long-term liabilities	90,000	60,000
Stockholders' equity	46,000	38,000
Total liabilities and stockholders' equity	$154,000	$120,000

LO5 Profitability Analysis

SE 7. Using the information for SiteWorks, Inc., in SE 4 and SE 5, compute the profit margin, asset turnover, return on assets, and return on equity for 20x4 and 20x5. In 20x3, total assets were $100,000 and total stockholders' equity was $30,000. Comment on the results. (Round computations to one decimal place.)

LO5 Long-Term Solvency Analysis

SE 8. Using the information for SiteWorks, Inc., in SE 4 and SE 5, compute the debt to equity ratio and the interest coverage ratio for 20x4 and 20x5. Comment on the results. (Round computations to one decimal place.)

LO5 Cash Flow Adequacy Analysis

SE 9. Using the information for SiteWorks, Inc., in SE 4, SE 5, and SE 7, compute the cash flow yield, cash flows to sales, cash flows to assets, and free cash flow for 20x4 and 20x5. Net cash flows from operating activities were $21,000 in 20x4 and $16,000 in 20x5. Net capital expenditures were $30,000 in 20x4 and $40,000 in 20x5. Cash dividends were $6,000 in both years. Comment on the results. (Round computations to one decimal place.)

8. What is the difference between horizontal and vertical analysis?

9. What is the purpose of ratio analysis?

10. In a period of high interest rates, why are receivable turnover and inventory turnover especially important?

11. The following statements were made on page 35 of the November 6, 1978, issue of *Fortune* magazine: "Supermarket executives are beginning to look back with some nostalgia on the days when the standard profit margin was 1 percent of sales. Last year the industry overall margin came to a thin 0.72 percent." How could a supermarket earn a satisfactory return on assets with such a small profit margin?

12. Company A and Company B both have net incomes of $1,000,000. Is it possible to say that these companies are equally successful? Why or why not?

13. Circo Company has a return on assets of 12 percent and a debt to equity ratio of .5. Would you expect return on equity to be more or less than 12 percent?

14. What amount is common to all cash flow adequacy ratios? To what other groups of ratios are the cash flow adequacy ratios most closely related?

15. The market price of Company J's stock is the same as that of Company Q's. How might you determine whether investors are equally confident about the future of these companies?

SHORT EXERCISES

LO1 Objectives and Standards
LO2 of Financial Performance Evaluation

SE 1. Indicate whether each of the following items is (a) an objective or (b) a standard of comparison of financial statement analysis:

1. Industry norms
2. Assessment of a company's past performance
3. The company's past performance
4. Assessment of future potential and related risk
5. Rule-of-thumb measures

LO3 Sources of Information

SE 2. For each piece of information listed below, indicate whether the *best* source would be (a) reports published by the company, (b) SEC reports, (c) business periodicals, or (d) credit and investment advisory services.

1. Current market value of a company's stock
2. Management's analysis of the past year's operations
3. Objective assessment of a company's financial performance
4. Most complete body of financial disclosures
5. Current events affecting the company

LO4 Trend Analysis

SE 3. Using 20x4 as the base year, prepare a trend analysis for the following data, and tell whether the results suggest a favorable or unfavorable trend. (Round your answers to one decimal place.)

	20x6	20x5	20x4
Net sales	$158,000	$136,000	$112,000
Accounts receivable (net)	43,000	32,000	21,000

LO4 Horizontal Analysis

SE 4. The comparative income statements and balance sheets of SiteWorks, Inc., appear on the opposite page. Compute the amount and percentage changes for the income statements, and comment on the changes from 20x4 to 20x5. (Round the percentage changes to one decimal place.)

LO4 Vertical Analysis

SE 5. Express the comparative balance sheets of SiteWorks, Inc., as common-size statements, and comment on the changes from 20x4 to 20x5. (Round computations to one decimal place.)

LO5 Liquidity Analysis

SE 6. Using the information for SiteWorks, Inc., in **SE 4** and **SE 5,** compute the current ratio, quick ratio, receivable turnover, average days' sales uncollected, inventory turnover, average days' inventory on hand, payables turnover, and average days' payable for 20x4 and 20x5. Inventories were $4,000 in 20x3, $5,000 in 20x4, and $7,000 in 20x5. Accounts Receivable were $6,000 in 20x3, $8,000 in 20x4, and $10,000 in 20x5. Accounts Payable were $9,000 in 20x3, $10,000 in 20x4, and $12,000 in 20x5. The company had no marketable securities or prepaid assets. Comment on the results. (Round computations to one decimal place.)

Ratio Name	Quik Burger	Big Steak	6. Company with More Favorable Ratio
b. Interest coverage ratio	$\dfrac{\$3,600 + \$1,400}{\$1,400}$ $= \dfrac{\$5,000}{\$1,400} = 3.6$ times	$\dfrac{\$6,800 + \$3,200}{\$3,200}$ $= \dfrac{\$10,000}{\$3,200} = 3.1$ times	Quik Burger
4. Cash flow adequacy analysis			
a. Cash flow yield	$\dfrac{\$2,200}{\$1,800} = 1.2$ times	$\dfrac{\$3,000}{\$3,400} = .9$ times	Quik Burger
b. Cash flows to sales	$\dfrac{\$2,200}{\$53,000} = 4.2\%$	$\dfrac{\$3,000}{\$86,000} = 3.5\%$	Quik Burger
c. Cash flows to assets	$\dfrac{\$2,200}{\$30,000} = 7.3\%$	$\dfrac{\$3,000}{\$56,000} = 5.4\%$	Quik Burger
d. Free cash flow	$\$2,200 - \$500 - \$2,100$ $= (\$400)$	$\$3,000 - \$600 - \$1,800$ $= \$600$	Big Steak
5. Market strength analysis			
a. Price/earnings ratio	$\dfrac{\$30}{\$1.80} = 16.7$ times	$\dfrac{\$20}{\$1.13} = 17.7$ times	Big Steak
b. Dividends yield	$\dfrac{\$500,000/1,000,000}{\$30} = 1.7\%$	$\dfrac{\$600,000/3,000,000}{\$20} = 1.0\%$	Quik Burger

7. Usefulness of prior years' information
Prior years' information would be helpful in two ways. First, turnover, return, and cash flows to assets ratios could be based on average amounts. Second, a trend analysis could be performed for each company.

Chapter Assignments

BUILDING YOUR KNOWLEDGE FOUNDATION

QUESTIONS

1. How are the objectives of investors and creditors in using financial performance evaluation similar? How do they differ?
2. What role does risk play in making loans and investments?
3. What standards of comparison are commonly used to evaluate financial statements, and what are their relative merits?
4. Why would a financial analyst compare the ratios of Steelco, a steel company, with the ratios of other companies in the steel industry? What factors might invalidate such a comparison?
5. Where can investors find information about a publicly held company in which they are thinking of investing?
6. Why would an investor want to see both horizontal and trend analyses of a company's financial statements?
7. What does the following sentence mean: "Based on 1996 equaling 100, net income increased from 240 in 2002 to 260 in 2003"?

Answer to Review Problem

Ratio Name	Quik Burger	Big Steak	6. Company with More Favorable Ratio*

1. Liquidity analysis

a. Current ratio

$$\frac{\$2{,}000 + \$2{,}000 + \$2{,}000}{\$2{,}500 + \$1{,}500} \qquad \frac{\$4{,}500 + \$6{,}500 + \$5{,}000}{\$3{,}000 + \$4{,}000}$$

$$= \frac{\$6{,}000}{\$4{,}000} = 1.5 \text{ times} \qquad = \frac{\$16{,}000}{\$7{,}000} = 2.3 \text{ times} \qquad \text{Big Steak}$$

b. Quick ratio

$$\frac{\$2{,}000 + \$2{,}000}{\$2{,}500 + \$1{,}500} \qquad \frac{\$4{,}500 + \$6{,}500}{\$3{,}000 + \$4{,}000}$$

$$= \frac{\$4{,}000}{\$4{,}000} = 1.0 \text{ times} \qquad = \frac{\$11{,}000}{\$7{,}000} = 1.6 \text{ times} \qquad \text{Big Steak}$$

c. Receivable turnover

$$\frac{\$53{,}000}{\$2{,}000} = 26.5 \text{ times} \qquad \frac{\$86{,}000}{\$6{,}500} = 13.2 \text{ times} \qquad \text{Quik Burger}$$

d. Average days' sales uncollected

$$\frac{365}{26.5} = 13.8 \text{ days} \qquad \frac{365}{13.2} = 27.7 \text{ days} \qquad \text{Quik Burger}$$

e. Inventory turnover

$$\frac{\$37{,}000}{\$2{,}000} = 18.5 \text{ times} \qquad \frac{\$61{,}000}{\$5{,}000} = 12.2 \text{ times} \qquad \text{Quik Burger}$$

f. Average days' inventory on hand

$$\frac{365}{18.5} = 19.7 \text{ days} \qquad \frac{365}{12.2} = 29.9 \text{ days} \qquad \text{Quik Burger}$$

g. Payables turnover

$$\frac{\$37{,}000 + \$0}{\$2{,}500} = 14.8 \text{ times} \qquad \frac{\$61{,}000 + \$0}{\$3{,}000} = 20.3 \text{ times} \qquad \text{Quik Burger}$$

h. Average days' payable

$$\frac{365}{14.8} = 24.7 \text{ days} \qquad \frac{365}{20.3} = 18.0 \text{ days} \qquad \text{Quik Burger}$$

2. Profitability analysis

a. Profit margin

$$\frac{\$1{,}800}{\$53{,}000} = 3.4\% \qquad \frac{\$3{,}400}{\$86{,}000} = 4.0\% \qquad \text{Big Steak}$$

b. Asset turnover

$$\frac{\$53{,}000}{\$30{,}000} = 1.8 \text{ times} \qquad \frac{\$86{,}000}{\$56{,}000} = 1.5 \text{ times} \qquad \text{Quik Burger}$$

c. Return on assets

$$\frac{\$1{,}800}{\$30{,}000} = 6.0\% \qquad \frac{\$3{,}400}{\$56{,}000} = 6.1\% \qquad \text{Neutral}$$

d. Return on equity

$$\frac{\$1{,}800}{\$1{,}000 + \$9{,}000 + \$6{,}000} \qquad \frac{\$3{,}400}{\$3{,}000 + \$9{,}000 + \$7{,}000}$$

$$= \frac{\$1{,}800}{\$16{,}000} = 11.3\% \qquad = \frac{\$3{,}400}{\$19{,}000} = 17.9\% \qquad \text{Big Steak}$$

3. Long-term solvency analysis

a. Debt to equity ratio

$$\frac{\$2{,}500 + \$1{,}500 + \$10{,}000}{\$1{,}000 + \$9{,}000 + \$6{,}000} \qquad \frac{\$3{,}000 + \$4{,}000 + \$30{,}000}{\$3{,}000 + \$9{,}000 + \$7{,}000}$$

$$= \frac{\$14{,}000}{\$16{,}000} = .9 \text{ times} \qquad = \frac{\$37{,}000}{\$19{,}000} = 1.9 \text{ times} \qquad \text{Quik Burger}$$

*This analysis indicates the company with the apparently more favorable ratio. Class discussion may focus on conditions under which different conclusions may be drawn.

Balance Sheets
December 31, 20xx
(in thousands)

	Quik Burger	Big Steak
Assets		
Cash	$ 2,000	$ 4,500
Accounts receivable (net)	2,000	6,500
Inventory	2,000	5,000
Property, plant, and equipment (net)	20,000	35,000
Other assets	4,000	5,000
Total assets	$30,000	$56,000
Liabilities and Stockholders' Equity		
Accounts payable	$ 2,500	$ 3,000
Notes payable	1,500	4,000
Bonds payable	10,000	30,000
Common stock, $1 par value	1,000	3,000
Paid-in capital in excess of par value, common	9,000	9,000
Retained earnings	6,000	7,000
Total liabilities and stockholders' equity	$30,000	$56,000

Income Statements
For the Year Ended December 31, 20xx
(in thousands, except per share amounts)

	Quik Burger	Big Steak
Net sales	$53,000	$86,000
Costs and expenses		
Cost of goods sold	$37,000	$61,000
Selling expenses	7,000	10,000
Administrative expenses	4,000	5,000
Total costs and expenses	$48,000	$76,000
Income from operations	$ 5,000	$10,000
Interest expense	1,400	3,200
Income before income taxes	$ 3,600	$ 6,800
Income taxes	1,800	3,400
Net income	$ 1,800	$ 3,400
Earnings per share	$ 1.80	$ 1.13

Chapter 18 Financial Performance Evaluation

LO5 **Payables turnover:** Cost of goods sold plus or minus change in inventory divided by average accounts payable; a measure of the relative size of accounts payable.

LO1 **Portfolio:** A group of loans or investments designed to average the returns and risks of a creditor or investor.

LO5 **Price/earnings (P/E) ratio:** Market price per share divided by earnings per share; a measure of investor confidence in a company and a means of comparing stock values.

LO5 **Profit margin:** Net income divided by net sales; a measure that shows the percentage of each revenue dollar that contributes to net income.

LO5 **Quick ratio:** The more liquid current assets—cash, marketable securities or short-term investments, and receivables—divided by current liabilities; a measure of short-term debt-paying ability.

LO4 **Ratio analysis:** A technique of financial performance evaluation that identifies meaningful relationships between the components of the financial statements.

LO5 **Receivable turnover:** Net sales divided by average accounts receivable; a measure of the relative size of accounts receivable and the effectiveness of credit policies.

LO5 **Return on assets:** Net income divided by average total assets; a measure of overall earning power, or profitability, that shows the amount earned on each dollar of assets invested.

LO5 **Return on equity:** Net income divided by average stockholders' equity; a measure of how much income was earned on each dollar invested by stockholders.

LO1 **Sarbanes-Oxley Act:** Legislation passed by the U.S. Congress to improve the financial reporting system.

LO4 **Trend analysis:** A type of horizontal analysis in which percentage changes are calculated for several successive years instead of for two years.

LO4 **Vertical analysis:** A technique for analyzing financial statements that uses percentages to show the relationships of the different parts to a total in a single statement.

REVIEW PROBLEM

Comparative Analysis of Two Companies

LO5 Maggie Washington is considering an investment in one of two fast-food restaurant chains because she believes the trend toward eating out more often will continue. She has narrowed her choices to Quik Burger and Big Steak, whose balance sheets and income statements are presented on the opposite page.

The statements of cash flows show that net cash flows from operating activities were $2,200,000 for Quik Burger and $3,000,000 for Big Steak. Net capital expenditures were $2,100,000 for Quik Burger and $1,800,000 for Big Steak. Dividends of $500,000 were paid by Quik Burger and $600,000 by Big Steak. The market prices of the stocks of Quik Burger and Big Steak were $30 and $20, respectively. Financial information pertaining to prior years is not readily available to Maggie Washington. Assume that all notes payable of these two companies are current liabilities and that all their bonds payable are long-term liabilities.

REQUIRED ▶ Conduct a comprehensive ratio analysis of Quik Burger and Big Steak and compare the results. Perform the analysis by following the steps outlined below. Use end-of-year balances for averages, assume no change in inventory, and round all ratios and percentages to one decimal place.

1. Prepare an analysis of liquidity.
2. Prepare an analysis of profitability.
3. Prepare an analysis of long-term solvency.
4. Prepare an analysis of cash flow adequacy.
5. Prepare an analysis of market strength.
6. Indicate in each analysis the company that apparently had the more favorable ratio. (Consider differences of .1 or less to be neutral.)
7. In what ways would having access to prior years' information aid this analysis?

Review of Concepts and Terminology

The following concepts and terms were introduced in this chapter:

LO5 **Asset turnover:** Net sales divided by average total assets; a measure of how efficiently assets are used to produce sales.

LO5 **Average days' inventory on hand:** Days in the year divided by inventory turnover; a measure that shows the average number of days taken to sell inventory.

LO5 **Average days' payable:** Days in the year divided by payables turnover; a measure that shows the average number of days taken to pay accounts payable.

LO5 **Average days' sales uncollected:** Days in the year divided by receivable turnover; a measure that shows the number of days, on average, that a company must wait to receive payment for credit sales.

LO4 **Base year:** In financial analysis, the first year to be considered in any set of data.

LO5 **Cash flows to assets:** Net cash flows from operating activities divided by average total assets; a measure of the ability of assets to generate operating cash flows.

LO5 **Cash flows to sales:** Net cash flows from operating activities divided by net sales; a measure of the ability of sales to generate operating cash flows.

LO5 **Cash flow yield:** Net cash flows from operating activities divided by net income; a measure of a company's ability to generate operating cash flows in relation to net income.

LO4 **Common-size statement:** A financial statement in which the components of a total figure are stated in terms of percentages of that total.

LO5 **Current ratio:** Current assets divided by current liabilities; a measure of short-term debt-paying ability.

LO5 **Debt to equity ratio:** Total liabilities divided by stockholders' equity; a measure that shows the relationship of debt financing to equity financing, or the extent to which a company is leveraged.

LO2 **Diversified companies:** Companies that operate in more than one industry. Also called *conglomerates*.

LO5 **Dividends yield:** Dividends per share divided by market price per share; a measure of a stock's current return to an investor.

LO1 **Financial performance evaluation:** All the techniques used to show important relationships in financial statements and to relate them to important financial objectives. Also called *financial statement analysis*.

LO5 **Free cash flow:** Net cash flows from operating activities minus dividends minus net capital expenditures; a measure of cash generated or cash deficiency after providing for commitments.

LO4 **Horizontal analysis:** A technique for analyzing financial statements that involves the computation of changes from the previous to the current year in both dollar amounts and percentages.

LO4 **Index number:** In trend analysis, a number that shows changes in related items over time, which is calculated by setting the base year equal to 100 percent.

LO5 **Interest coverage ratio:** Income before income taxes plus interest expense divided by interest expense; a measure of the degree of protection creditors have from default on interest payments.

LO3 **Interim financial statements:** Financial statements issued for a period of less than one year, usually a quarter or a month.

LO5 **Inventory turnover:** The cost of goods sold divided by average inventory; a measure of the relative size of inventory.

LO5 **Operating cycle:** Average days' inventory on hand plus average days' sales uncollected; the time it takes to sell products and collect for them.

The **price/earnings (P/E) ratio**, which measures investor confidence in a company, is the ratio of the market price per share to earnings per share. The P/E ratio is useful in comparing the relative values placed on the earnings of different companies and in comparing the value placed on a company's shares in relation to the overall market. With a lower P/E ratio, the investor obtains more underlying earnings per dollar invested.

Sun Microsystems' P/E ratio decreased from 73.7 times in 2000 to 65.0 times in 2001, which signals that investors have less confidence in the company. The **dividends yield** measures a stock's current return to an investor in the form of dividends. Because Sun Microsystems pays no dividend, it may be concluded that investors expect their return to come from increases in the stock's market value.

SUMMARY OF THE FINANCIAL ANALYSIS OF SUN MICROSYSTEMS, INC.

Our analysis clearly shows that Sun Microsystems' financial condition declined from 2000 to 2001, as measured by its liquidity, profitability, long-term solvency, and cash flow adequacy ratios. This performance resulted in a lower market price per share.

✓ Check out ACE for a Review Quiz at http://accounting.college.hmco.com/students.

Chapter Review

REVIEW OF LEARNING OBJECTIVES

LO1 Describe and discuss financial performance evaluation by internal and external users.

Creditors and investors use financial performance evaluation to judge the past performance and current position of a company, and its future potential with the associated risk. Creditors use the information gained from their analysis to make reliable loans that will be repaid with interest. Investors use the information to make investments that will provide a return worth the risk. The Sarbanes-Oxley Act is intended to improve investor confidence in the financial reporting system.

LO2 Describe and discuss the standards for financial performance evaluation.

Three commonly used standards for financial performance evaluation are rule-of-thumb measures, the company's past performance, and industry norms. Rule-of-thumb measures are weak because of the lack of evidence that they can be widely applied. The past performance of a company can offer a guideline for measuring improvement but is not helpful in judging performance relative to other companies. Although the use of industry norms overcomes this last problem, its disadvantage is that firms are not always comparable, even in the same industry.

LO3 Identify the sources of information for financial performance evaluation.

The main sources of information about publicly held corporations are company-published reports, such as annual reports and interim financial statements; SEC reports; business periodicals; and credit and investment advisory services.

LO4 Apply horizontal analysis, trend analysis, vertical analysis, and ratio analysis to financial statements.

Horizontal analysis involves the computation of changes in both dollar amounts and percentages from year to year. Trend analysis is an extension of horizontal analysis in that it calculates percentage changes for several years. The changes are computed by setting a base year equal to 100 and calculating the results for subsequent years as percentages of that base year. Vertical analysis uses percentages to show the relationship of the component parts to a total in a single statement. The resulting financial statements, which are expressed entirely in percentages, are called common-size statements. Ratio analysis is a technique of financial performance evaluation that identifies meaningful relationships between the components of the financial statements.

LO5 Apply ratio analysis to financial statements in a comprehensive evaluation of a company's financial performance.

A comprehensive ratio analysis includes the evaluation of a company's liquidity, profitability, long-term solvency, cash flow adequacy, and market strength. The ratios for measuring these characteristics are shown in Exhibits 8 to 12.

Exhibit 11
Cash Flow Adequacy Ratios of Sun Microsystems, Inc.

(Dollar amounts in millions)	2001	2000

Cash flow yield: Measure of the ability to generate operating cash flows in relation to net income

$$\frac{\text{Net Cash Flows from Operating Activities}}{\text{Net Income}} \qquad \frac{\$2,089^*}{\$927} = 2.3 \text{ times} \qquad \frac{\$3,754^*}{\$1,854} = 2.0 \text{ times}$$

Cash flows to sales: Measure of the ability of sales to generate operating cash flows

$$\frac{\text{Net Cash Flows from Operating Activities}}{\text{Net Sales}} \qquad \frac{\$2,089^*}{\$18,250} = 11.4\% \qquad \frac{\$3,754^*}{\$15,721} = 23.9\%$$

Cash flows to assets: Measure of the ability of assets to generate operating cash flows

$$\frac{\text{Net Cash Flows from Operating Activities}}{\text{Average Total Assets}} \qquad \frac{\$2,089^*}{(\$18,181 + \$14,152) \div 2} \qquad \frac{\$3,754^*}{(\$14,152 + \$8,499^\dagger) \div 2}$$

$$= \frac{\$2,089}{\$16,167} = 12.9\% \qquad = \frac{\$3,754}{\$11,326} = 33.1\%$$

Free cash flow: Measure of cash generated or cash deficiency after providing for commitments

Net Cash Flows from Operating Activities − Dividends − Net Capital Expenditures

$$\$2,089^* - \$0 - \$1,292^* = \$797 \qquad \$3,754^* - \$0 - \$982^* = \$2,772$$

*These figures are from the statements of cash flows in Sun Microsystems' annual report.
†The 1999 figure is from the 11-year financial history in Sun Microsystems' annual report.
Source: Sun Microsystems, Inc., *Annual Report,* 2001.

Exhibit 12
Market Strength Ratios of Sun Microsystems, Inc.

	2001	2000

Price/earnings (P/E) ratio: Measure of investor confidence in a company

$$\frac{\text{Market Price per Share}}{\text{Earnings per Share}} \qquad \frac{\$18.21^*}{\$.28} = 65.0 \text{ times} \qquad \frac{\$43.47^*}{\$.59} = 73.7 \text{ times}$$

Dividends yield: Measure of a stock's current return to an investor

$$\frac{\text{Dividends per Share}}{\text{Market Price per Share}} \qquad \text{Sun Microsystems does not pay a dividend.}$$

*Market price is from Sun Microsystems' annual report.
Source: Sun Microsystems, Inc., *Annual Report,* 2001.

little long-term debt. It also has ample current assets, as reflected by the current ratio. All these are positive indications of Sun Microsystem's long-term solvency. Management sums up the company's position as follows: "We believe our level of financial resources is a significant competitive factor in our industry and we may choose at any time to raise additional capital through debt or equity financing to strengthen our financial position, facilitate growth, and provide us with additional flexibility to take advantage of business opportunities that may arise."[7]

If debt is risky, why have any? The answer is that the level of debt is a matter of balance. Despite its riskiness, debt is a flexible means of financing certain business operations. Sun Microsystems is using debt to finance a temporary increase in inventory. The interest paid on that debt is deductible for income tax purposes, whereas dividends on stock are not. Because debt usually carries a fixed interest charge, the cost of financing can be limited, and leverage can be used to advantage. If the company is able to earn a return on assets greater than the cost of interest, it makes an overall profit. In addition, there are advantages to being a debtor in periods of inflation because the debt, which is a fixed dollar amount, can be repaid with cheaper dollars. However, the company runs the risk of not earning a return on assets equal to the cost of financing those assets, thereby incurring a loss.

ENRICHMENT NOTE:
Because of innovative financing plans and other means of acquiring assets, a beneficial modern-day ratio is the fixed charges ratio. This ratio includes interest, lease payments, and all other fixed obligations that must be met through earnings.

The **interest coverage ratio** measures the degree of protection creditors have from a default on interest payments. Because of its small amount of long-term debt, Sun Microsystems had interest coverage ratios of 34.0 times in 2000 and 16.8 times in 2001. Interest coverage, though declining, is not a problem for the company.

EVALUATING CASH FLOW ADEQUACY

Because cash flows are needed to pay debts when they are due, cash flow measures are closely related to liquidity and long-term solvency. Sun Microsystems' cash flow adequacy ratios are presented in Exhibit 11. By most measures, the company's ability to generate positive operating cash flows declined from 2000 to 2001. Key to those decreases is that net cash flows from operating activities had a large decrease, from $3,754 million in 2000 to $2,089 million in 2001, while net sales and average total assets increased. **Cash flow yield**, or the relationship of cash flows from operating activities to net income, increased from 2.0 to 2.3 because net income declined faster than net cash flows from operating activities. **Cash flows to sales**, or the ability of sales to generate operating cash flows, decreased from 23.9 to 11.4 percent. **Cash flows to assets**, or the ability of assets to generate operating cash flows, decreased from 33.1 to 12.9 percent.

Free cash flow, the cash generated after providing for commitments, also decreased but remains positive even though capital expenditures increased while net cash flows from operating activities decreased. Another factor is that the company pays no dividends. Management's comment with regard to cash flows in the future is, "We believe that the liquidity provided by existing cash, cash equivalents, and non-strategic investments, along with our borrowing arrangements and cash generated from operations, will provide sufficient capital to meet our requirements for at least the next 12 months."[8]

EVALUATING MARKET STRENGTH

The market price of a company's stock is of interest to the analyst because it represents what investors as a whole think of the company at a point in time. Market price is the price at which the stock is bought and sold. It provides information about how investors view the potential return and risk connected with owning the company's stock. Market price by itself is not very informative for this purpose, however. Companies differ in number of outstanding shares and amount of underlying earnings and dividends. Thus, market price must be related to earnings by considering the price/earnings ratio and the dividends yield. Those ratios for Sun Microsystems appear in Exhibit 12 and have been computed using the market prices for Sun Microsystems' stock at the end of 2000 and 2001.

EXHIBIT 9
Profitability Ratios of Sun Microsystems, Inc.

(Dollar amounts in millions)	2001	2000

Profit margin: Measure of net income produced by each dollar of sales

$$\frac{\text{Net Income}}{\text{Net Sales}} \qquad \frac{\$927}{\$18,250} = 5.1\% \qquad \frac{\$1,854}{\$15,721} = 11.8\%$$

Asset turnover: Measure of how efficiently assets are used to produce sales

$$\frac{\text{Net Sales}}{\text{Average Total Assets}} \qquad \frac{\$18,250}{(\$18,181 + \$14,152) \div 2} \qquad \frac{\$15,721}{(\$14,152 + \$8,499^*) \div 2}$$

$$= \frac{\$18,250}{\$16,167} = 1.1 \text{ times} \qquad = \frac{\$15,721}{\$11,326} = 1.4 \text{ times}$$

Return on assets: Measure of overall earning power or profitability

$$\frac{\text{Net Income}}{\text{Average Total Assets}} \qquad \frac{\$927}{\$16,167} = 5.7\% \qquad \frac{\$1,854}{\$11,326} = 16.4\%$$

Return on equity: Measure of the profitability of stockholders' investments

$$\frac{\text{Net Income}}{\text{Average Stockholders' Equity}} \qquad \frac{\$927}{(\$10,586 + \$7,309) \div 2} \qquad \frac{\$1,854}{(\$7,309 + \$4,867^*) \div 2}$$

$$= \frac{\$927}{\$8,948} = 10.4\% \qquad = \frac{\$1,854}{\$6,088} = 30.5\%$$

*1999 figures are from the 11-year financial history and the statement of stockholders' equity in Sun Microsystems' annual report.
Source: Sun Microsystems, Inc., *Annual Report,* 2001.

EXHIBIT 10
Long-Term Solvency Ratios of Sun Microsystems, Inc.

(Dollar amounts in millions)	2001	2000

Debt to equity ratio: Measure of capital structure and leverage

$$\frac{\text{Total Liabilities}}{\text{Stockholders' Equity}} \qquad \frac{\$7,595}{\$10,586} = .7 \text{ times} \qquad \frac{\$6,843}{\$7,309} = .9 \text{ times}$$

Interest coverage ratio: Measure of creditors' protection from default on interest payments

$$\frac{\text{Income Before Income Taxes} + \text{Interest Expense}}{\text{Interest Expense}} \qquad \frac{\$1,584 + \$100}{\$100} \qquad \frac{\$2,771 + \$84}{\$84}$$

$$= 16.8 \text{ times} \qquad = 34.0 \text{ times}$$

Source: Sun Microsystems, Inc., *Annual Report,* 2001.

Focus on Business Practice

There's More Than One Way to Measure Profitability.

Efforts to link management compensation to the company's performance measures and to the creation of shareholder wealth are increasing. One such measure compares the company's return on assets with the cost of debt and equity capital. If the return on assets exceeds the cost of financing the assets with debt and equity, then management is indeed creating value for the shareholders. This measure is referred to in various ways. The originators refer to it as *Economic Value Added*, or *EVA*®. Coca-Cola <www.coca-cola.com>, which uses this measure to evaluate management performance, calls it by its more generic name, *economic profit*. In its annual report, Coca-Cola reports economic profit along with other key financial measures, such as free cash flow and return on equity.

ENRICHMENT NOTE: In both asset turnover and return on assets, the analysis is improved if only productive assets are used in the calculations. For example, unfinished new plant construction or investments in obsolete or non-operating plants could be removed from the asset base to give a better picture of the productivity of assets.

cash flow. For this reason, evaluating profitability is important to both investors and creditors. The profitability ratios of Sun Microsystems, Inc., are shown in Exhibit 9.

Profit margin, which measures the net income produced by each dollar of sales, decreased from 11.8 to 5.1 percent. **Asset turnover**, which measures how efficiently assets are used to produce sales, decreased from 1.4 to 1.1 times. The result is a decrease in the company's earning power, or **return on assets**, from 16.4 percent in 2000 to 5.7 percent in 2001. These computations show the relationships:

	Profit Margin		Asset Turnover		Return on Assets
	$\dfrac{\text{Net Income}}{\text{Net Sales}}$	×	$\dfrac{\text{Net Sales}}{\text{Average Total Assets}}$	=	$\dfrac{\text{Net Income}}{\text{Average Total Assets}}$
2000	11.8%	×	1.4	=	16.5%
2001	5.1%	×	1.1	=	5.6%

KEY POINT: Profit often is expressed in different ways in accounting literature. Examples are income before income taxes, income after income taxes, and net operating income. Being aware of the content of net income data in profitability ratios enables analysts to draw appropriate conclusions about the results of ratio computations.

(The small difference in the two sets of return on assets figures results from the rounding of the ratios.) The profitability of stockholders' investments, or **return on equity**, also declined, from 30.5 percent in 2000 to 10.4 percent in 2001.

Although we have used net income in computing profitability ratios for Sun Microsystems, net income is not always a good indicator of a company's sustainable earnings. For instance, if a company has discontinued operations, then income from continuing operations may be a better measure of sustainable earnings. For a company that has one-time items on the income statement, such as restructurings, gains, or losses, income from operations before these items may be a better measure. Some analysts like to use earnings before interest and taxes, or EBIT, for the earnings measure because it excludes the effects of the company's borrowings and the tax rates from the analysis. Whatever figure one uses for earnings, it is important to try to determine the effects of various components on future operations.

EVALUATING LONG-TERM SOLVENCY

KEY POINT: Liquidity is a firm's ability to meet its current obligations, whereas solvency is a firm's ability to meet its maturing obligations as they come due, without losing the ability to continue operations.

Long-term solvency has to do with a company's ability to survive for many years. The aim of long-term solvency analysis is to detect early signs that a company is headed for financial difficulty. Studies have indicated that accounting ratios can show as much as five years in advance that a company may fail.[6] Declining profitability and liquidity ratios are key indicators of possible business failure. Two other ratios that analysts often consider when assessing long-term solvency are debt to equity and interest coverage, which are shown in Exhibit 10.

Increasing amounts of debt in a company's capital structure mean the company is becoming more heavily leveraged. Because of increasing legal obligations to pay interest periodically and the principal at maturity, this condition negatively affects long-term solvency. Failure to make those payments can result in bankruptcy. The **debt to equity ratio** measures capital structure and leverage by showing the amount of assets provided by creditors in relation to the amount provided by stockholders. Sun Microsystems' debt to equity ratio was only .9 times in 2000 and .7 times in 2001. Recall from Exhibit 3 that the company has primarily short-term debt and

EXHIBIT 8
Liquidity Ratios of Sun Microsystems, Inc.

(Dollar amounts in millions)	2001	2000

Current ratio: Measure of short-term debt-paying ability

$$\frac{\text{Current Assets}}{\text{Current Liabilities}} \qquad \frac{\$7,934}{\$5,146} = 1.5 \text{ times} \qquad \frac{\$6,877}{\$4,546} = 1.5 \text{ times}$$

Quick ratio: Measure of short-term debt-paying ability

$$\frac{\text{Cash + Marketable Securities + Receivables}}{\text{Current Liabilities}} \qquad \frac{\$1,472 + \$387 + \$2,955}{\$5,146} \qquad \frac{\$1,849 + \$626 + \$2,690}{\$4,546}$$

$$= \frac{\$4,814}{\$5,146} = .9 \text{ times} \qquad = \frac{\$5,165}{\$4,546} = 1.1 \text{ times}$$

Receivable turnover: Measure of relative size of accounts receivable and effectiveness of credit policies

$$\frac{\text{Net Sales}}{\text{Average Accounts Receivable}} \qquad \frac{\$18,250}{(\$2,955 + \$2,690) \div 2} \qquad \frac{\$15,721}{\$2,690 + \$2,287^* \div 2}$$

$$= \frac{\$18,250}{\$2,823} = 6.5 \text{ times} \qquad = \frac{\$15,721}{\$2,489} = 6.3 \text{ times}$$

Average days' sales uncollected: Measure of average days taken to collect receivables

$$\frac{\text{Days in Year}}{\text{Receivable Turnover}} \qquad \frac{365 \text{ days}}{6.5 \text{ times}} = 56.2 \text{ days} \qquad = \frac{365 \text{ days}}{6.3 \text{ times}} = 57.9 \text{ days}$$

Inventory turnover: Measure of relative size of inventory

$$\frac{\text{Costs of Goods Sold}}{\text{Average Inventory}} \qquad \frac{\$10,041}{(\$1,049 + \$557) \div 2} \qquad \frac{\$7,549}{\$557 + \$308^* \div 2}$$

$$= \frac{\$10,041}{\$803} = 12.5 \text{ times} \qquad = \frac{\$7,549}{\$433} = 17.4 \text{ times}$$

Average days' inventory on hand: Measure of average days taken to sell inventory

$$\frac{\text{Days in Year}}{\text{Inventory Turnover}} \qquad \frac{365 \text{ days}}{12.5 \text{ times}} = 29.2 \text{ days} \qquad = \frac{365 \text{ days}}{17.4 \text{ times}} = 21.0 \text{ days}$$

Payables turnover: Measure of relative size of accounts payable

$$\frac{\text{Costs of Goods Sold} +/- \text{ Change in Inventory}}{\text{Average Accounts Payable}} \qquad \frac{\$10,041 + \$492}{(\$1,050 + \$924) \div 2} \qquad \frac{\$7,549 + \$249^*}{(\$924 + \$754^*) \div 2}$$

$$= \frac{\$10,533}{\$987} = 10.7 \text{ times} \qquad = \frac{\$7,798}{\$839} = 9.3 \text{ times}$$

Average days' payable: Measure of average days taken to pay accounts payable

$$\frac{\text{Days in Year}}{\text{Payables Turnover}} \qquad = \frac{365 \text{ days}}{10.7 \text{ times}} = 34.1 \text{ days} \qquad = \frac{365 \text{ days}}{9.3 \text{ times}} = 39.2 \text{ days}$$

*1999 figures are derived from the statement of cash flows in Sun Microsystems' annual report.
Source: Sun Microsystems, Inc., *Annual Report,* 2001.

KEY POINT: When examining ratios in published sources, be aware that publishers often redefine the content of the ratios provided by companies. While the general content is similar, variations occur. Be sure to evaluate exactly what information a published source says it uses to calculate its ratios.

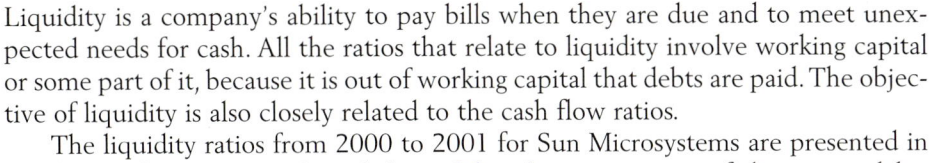

● **STOP AND THINK!**
Why does a decrease in receivable turnover or inventory turnover create the need for cash from operating activities?

When receivable turnover or inventory turnover decreases, it means that the company has more average days' sales uncollected or more average days' inventory on hand to finance. Consequently, the company needs more cash to pay for the increase in receivables or inventory. ■

EVALUATING LIQUIDITY

Liquidity is a company's ability to pay bills when they are due and to meet unexpected needs for cash. All the ratios that relate to liquidity involve working capital or some part of it, because it is out of working capital that debts are paid. The objective of liquidity is also closely related to the cash flow ratios.

The liquidity ratios from 2000 to 2001 for Sun Microsystems are presented in Exhibit 8. The **current ratio** and the **quick ratio** are measures of short-term debt-paying ability. The principal difference between the two is that the numerator of the current ratio includes inventories and prepaid expenses. Inventories take longer to convert to cash than do the current assets included in the numerator of the quick ratio. The quick ratio was 1.1 times in 2000 and 0.9 times in 2001. The current ratio was 1.5 times in both years primarily because current assets and current liabilities grew at similar rates. However, the composition of current assets shows a decline in quick ratio assets offset by increases in the remaining current assets.

Two major components of current assets, receivables and inventories, show improving trends. The relative size of the accounts receivable and the effectiveness of credit policies are measured by the **receivable turnover**, which rose from 6.3 times in 2000 to 6.5 times in 2001. The related ratio of **average days' sales uncollected** decreased by about one day, from 57.9 days in 2000 to 56.2 days in 2001. The major change in this category of ratios is in the inventory turnover. The **inventory turnover**, which measures the relative size of inventories, worsened. Inventory turnover decreased from 17.4 times in 2000 to 12.5 times in 2001. This results in an unfavorable increase in **average days' inventory on hand**, from 21.0 days in 2000 to 29.2 days in 2001. When taken together this means that Sun Microsystems' **operating cycle**, or the time it takes to sell products and collect for them, increased from 78.9 days in 2000 (57.9 days + 21.0 days or the average days' sales uncollected plus the average days' inventory on hand) to 85.4 days in 2001 (56.2 days + 29.2 days). Related to the operating cycle is the number of days the company takes to pay its accounts payable. The **payables turnover** increased from 9.3 times in 2000 to 10.7 times in 2001. This results in average days' payable of 39.2 days in 2000 and 34.1 days in 2001. Thus, if the **average days' payable** is subtracted from the operating cycle, the financing period, or days of financing required, are 39.7 days in 2000 and 51.3 days in 2001, a significant decline (see Figure 4). Overall, Sun Microsystems' liquidity declined.

EVALUATING PROFITABILITY

Profitability relates to a company's ability to earn a satisfactory income so that investors and stockholders will continue to provide capital to the company. Profitability is also closely linked to liquidity because earnings ultimately produce

FIGURE 4
Financing Period for Sun Microsystems, 2001

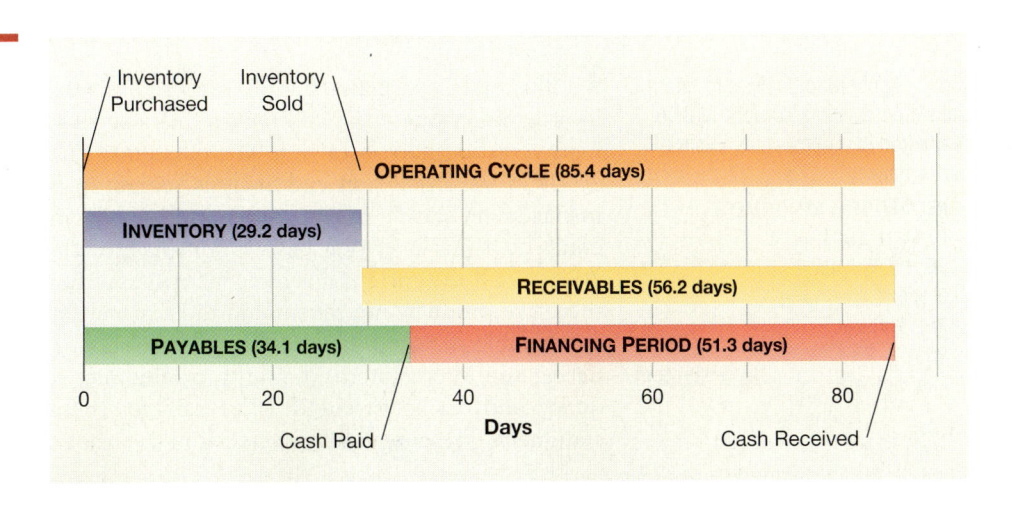

- OPERATING CYCLE (85.4 days)
- INVENTORY (29.2 days)
- RECEIVABLES (56.2 days)
- PAYABLES (34.1 days)
- FINANCING PERIOD (51.3 days)

Inventory Purchased — Inventory Sold — Cash Paid — Cash Received

Days: 0, 20, 40, 60, 80

KEY POINT: It is important to discern what base amount is used when a percentage describes an item. For example, inventory may be 50 percent of *total current assets* but only 10 percent of *total assets.*

PARENTHETICAL NOTE: Common-size statements can be used to compare characteristics of firms reporting in different currencies.

Microsystems' assets shifted from current assets and long-term investments toward goodwill, while current liabilities decreased and stockholders' equity increased. The main conclusions to be drawn from this analysis are that current assets and current liabilities make up a large portion of Sun Microsystems' financial structure and that the company has few long-term liabilities. The graphs in Figure 2 and the common-size balance sheets in Exhibit 6 show that the composition of assets at Sun Microsystems shifted from long-term investments and current assets toward goodwill. In the relationship of liabilities and stockholders' equity, there was a shift from total liabilities to stockholders' equity.

The common-size income statements in Exhibit 7, illustrated in Figure 3, show that Sun Microsystems reduced its selling, general, and administrative expenses from 2000 to 2001 by 1.0 percent of revenues (25.9% − 24.9%). This reduction was offset by an increase in goodwill amortization of 1.0 percent (1.4% − 0.4%).

Common-size statements are often used to make comparisons between companies. They allow an analyst to compare the operating and financing characteristics of two companies of different size in the same industry. For example, the analyst might want to compare Sun Microsystems with other companies in terms of percentage of total assets financed by debt or in terms of selling, general, and administrative expenses as a percentage of net revenues. Common-size statements would show those and other relationships.

RATIO ANALYSIS

Ratio analysis is a technique of financial performance evaluation that identifies meaningful relationships between the components of the financial statements. To be most meaningful, the interpretation of ratios must include a study of the underlying data. Ratios are useful guides or shortcuts in evaluating a company's financial position and operations and in comparing financial data for several years or for several companies. The primary purpose of ratios is to point out areas needing further investigation. To interpret ratios correctly, an analyst must have a general understanding of the company and its environment. Ratios may be expressed in several ways. For example, a ratio of net income of $100,000 to sales of $1,000,000 may be stated as:

1. Net income is 1/10 or 10 percent of sales.
2. The ratio of sales to net income is 10 to 1 (10:1), or sales are 10 times net income.
3. For every dollar of sales, the company has an average net income of 10 cents.

Check out ACE for a Review Quiz at http://accounting.college.hmco.com/students.

COMPREHENSIVE ILLUSTRATION OF RATIO ANALYSIS

LO5 Apply ratio analysis to financial statements in a comprehensive evaluation of a company's financial performance.

RELATED TEXT ASSIGNMENTS
Q: 10, 11, 12, 13, 14, 15
SE: 6, 7, 8, 9, 10
E: 5, 6, 7, 8, 9
P: 2, 3, 4, 5, 6
SD: 1, 6
FRA: 2, 3, 4, 5

www.sun.com

To illustrate how analysts apply ratio analysis to a company's financial statements in order to evaluate the company's financial situation, we will perform a comprehensive ratio analysis of Sun Microsystems' financial performance for 2000 and 2001. In the discussion and analysis section in Sun Microsystems' annual report, management states: "While we reported significant growth in our products net revenues on a year-over-year basis, all of this growth occurred in the first half of fiscal 2001. . . . If the current macro economic conditions persist, we expect demand, and therefore products net revenue in the first half of fiscal 2002, will be less than the comparable period in fiscal 2001."[5] These statements provide the context for evaluating Sun Microsystems' liquidity, profitability, long-term solvency, cash flow adequacy, and market strength. Most data for the analyses come from the financial statements presented in Exhibits 3 and 4. Other data are presented as needed.

FIGURE 3
Common-Size Income Statements Presented Graphically

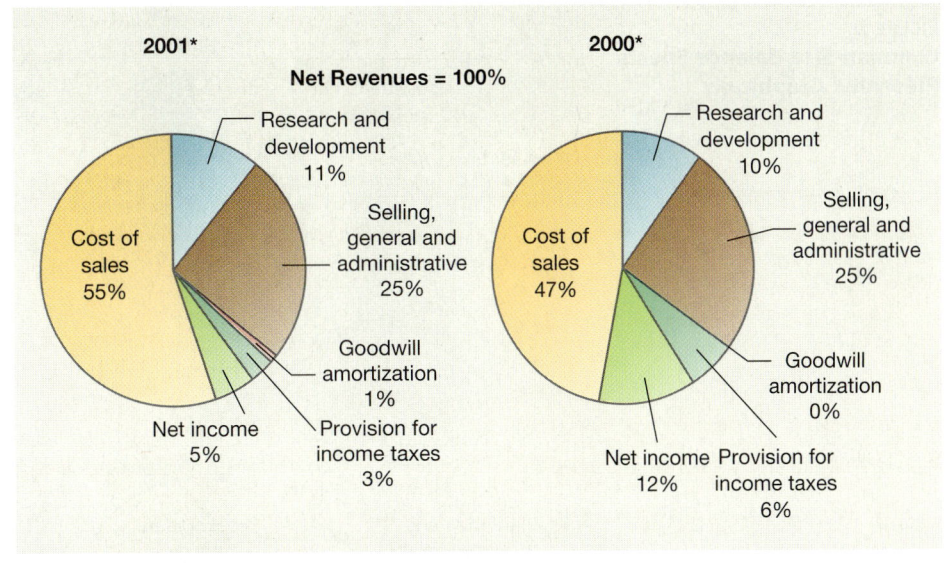

2001*

Net Revenues = 100%

- Cost of sales 55%
- Research and development 11%
- Selling, general and administrative 25%
- Goodwill amortization 1%
- Provision for income taxes 3%
- Net income 5%

2000*

- Cost of sales 47%
- Research and development 10%
- Selling, general and administrative 25%
- Goodwill amortization 0%
- Provision for income taxes 6%
- Net income 12%

*Rounding causes some additions not to total precisely.
Note: Not all items are presented.

EXHIBIT 7
Common-Size Income Statements

Sun Microsystems, Inc.
Common-Size Income Statements
For the Years Ended June 30, 2001 and 2000

	2001*	2000*
Net revenues	100.0%	100.0%
Cost of sales	55.0	48.0
Gross margin	45.0%	52.0%
Operating expenses:		
Research and development	11.0%	10.4%
Selling, general, and administrative	24.9	25.9
Goodwill amortization	1.4	0.4
Purchased in-process R&D	0.4	0.1
Total operating expenses	37.8%	36.8%
Operating income	7.2%	15.2%
Other income (expense)	1.5	2.4
Income before income taxes	8.7%	17.6%
Provision for income taxes	3.3	5.8
Income before cumulative effect of change in accounting principle	5.4%	11.8%
Cumulative effect of change in accounting principle	(0.3)	—
Net income	5.1%	11.8%

*Rounding causes some additions and subtractions not to total precisely.
Source: Sun Microsystems, Inc., *Annual Report*, 2001.

FIGURE 2
Common-Size Balance Sheets Presented Graphically

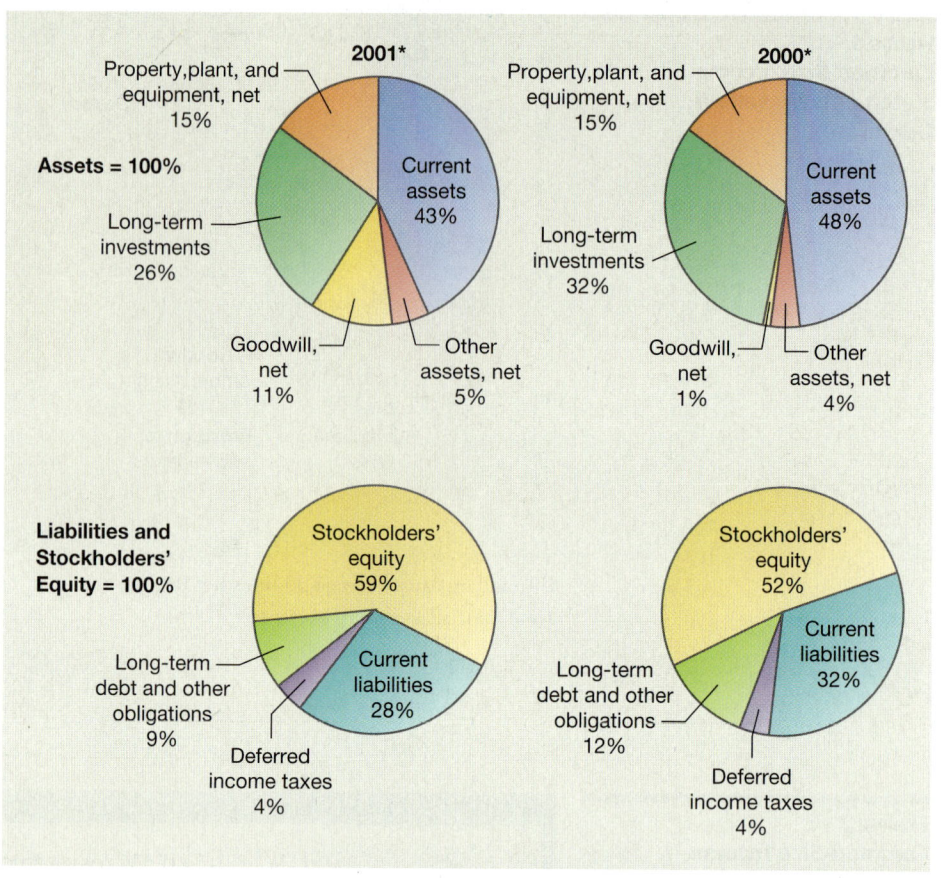

2001*
Assets = 100%
- Property, plant, and equipment, net 15%
- Long-term investments 26%
- Goodwill, net 11%
- Other assets, net 5%
- Current assets 43%

2000*
- Property, plant, and equipment, net 15%
- Long-term investments 32%
- Goodwill, net 1%
- Other assets, net 4%
- Current assets 48%

Liabilities and Stockholders' Equity = 100%

2001*
- Stockholders' equity 59%
- Long-term debt and other obligations 9%
- Deferred income taxes 4%
- Current liabilities 28%

2000*
- Stockholders' equity 52%
- Long-term debt and other obligations 12%
- Deferred income taxes 4%
- Current liabilities 32%

* Rounding causes some additions not to total precisely.

EXHIBIT 6
Common-Size Balance Sheets

Sun Microsystems, Inc.
Common-Size Balance Sheets
June 30, 2001 and 2000

	2001*	2000*
Assets		
Current assets	43.6%	48.6%
Property, plant and equipment, net	14.8	14.8
Long-term investments	25.7	31.8
Goodwill, net	11.2	1.2
Other assets, net	4.6	3.7
Total assets	100.0%	100.0%
Liabilities and Stockholders' Equity		
Current liabilities	28.3%	32.1%
Deferred income taxes	4.1	4.1
Long-term debt and other obligations	9.4	12.2
Stockholders' equity	58.2	51.6
Total liabilities and stockholders' equity	100.0%	100.0%

*Amounts do not precisely total 100 percent in all cases due to rounding.
Source: Sun Microsystems, Inc., *Annual Report,* 2001.

762 Chapter 18 Financial Performance Evaluation

EXHIBIT 5
Trend Analysis

ENRICHMENT NOTE:
Trend analysis is usually done for a five-year period to reflect the general five-year economic cycle that affects the U.S. economy. Cycles of other lengths exist and are tracked by the National Bureau of Economic Research. Trend analysis needs to use the appropriate cycle time to cover the complete cycle's impact on the business being studied.

Sun Microsystems, Inc.
Net Revenues and Operating Income
Trend Analysis

	2001	2000	1999	1998	1997
Dollar values (in millions)					
Net revenues	$18,250	$15,721	$11,806	$9,862	$8,661
Operating income	1,311	2,393	1,520	1,114	1,033
Trend analysis (in percentages)					
Net revenues	210.7	181.5	136.3	113.9	100.0
Operating income	126.9	231.7	147.1	107.8	100.0

Source: Sun Microsystems, Inc., *Annual Report,* 2001.

The trend analysis in Exhibit 5 shows that net revenues at Sun Microsystems increased over the five-year period, as did operating income in every year except 2001, when it declined dramatically. Figure 1 illustrates these trends.

VERTICAL ANALYSIS

In **vertical analysis**, percentages are used to show the relationship of the different parts to a total in a single statement. The analyst sets a total figure in the statement equal to 100 percent and computes each component's percentage of that total. (The figure would be total assets or total liabilities and stockholders' equity on the balance sheet, and net revenues or net sales on the income statement.) The resulting statement of percentages is called a **common-size statement**. Common-size balance sheets and common-size income statements for Sun Microsystems are shown in pie-chart form in Figures 2 and 3, and in financial statement form in Exhibits 6 and 7.

Vertical analysis is useful for comparing the importance of specific components in the operation of a business. Also, comparative common-size statements can be used to identify important changes in the components from one year to the next. As shown in Figure 2 and Exhibit 6, from 2000 to 2001 the composition of Sun

FIGURE 1
Graph of Trend Analysis Shown in Exhibit 5

🛑 **STOP AND THINK!**
In a five-year trend analysis, why do the dollar values remain the same for their respective years while the percentages usually change when a new five-year period is chosen?

In a five-year trend analysis for a new five-year period, the base year changes. Unless two successive base years have exactly the same dollar values, the trend analysis percentages will be different each year. ■

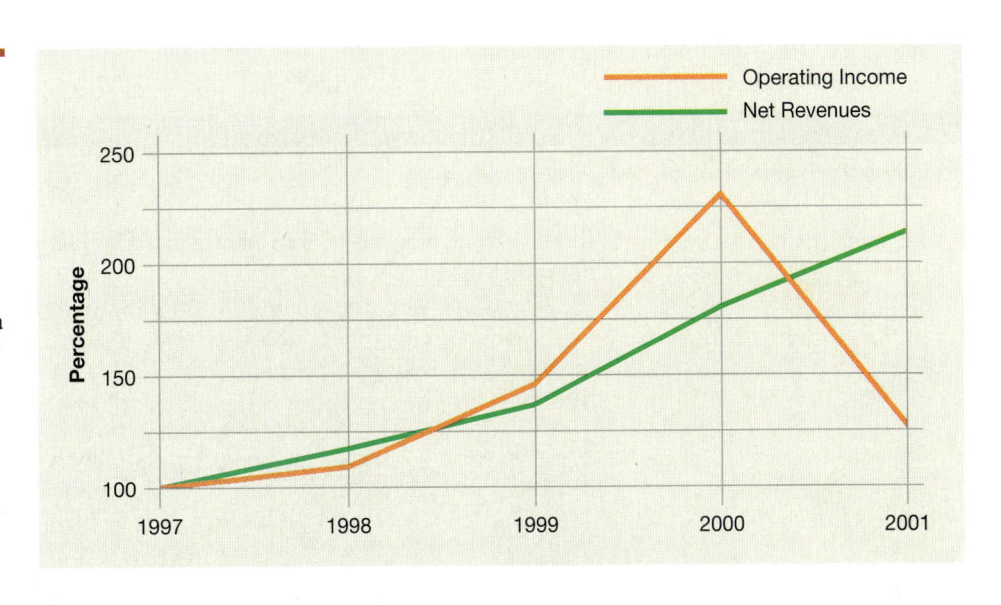

EXHIBIT 4
Comparative Income Statements with Horizontal Analysis

Sun Microsystems, Inc.
Consolidated Income Statements
For the Years Ended June 30, 2001 and 2000

(Dollar amounts in millions, except per share amounts)	2001	2000	Increase (Decrease) Amount	Percentage
Net revenues	$18,250	$15,721	$ 2,529	16.1
Cost of sales	10,041	7,549	2,492	33.0
Gross margin	$ 8,209	$ 8,172	37	0.5
Operating expenses				
Research and development	$ 2,016	$ 1,630	$ 386	23.7
Selling, general and administrative	4,544	4,072	472	11.6
Goodwill amortization	261	65	196	301.5
Purchased in-process R&D	77	12	65	541.7
Total operating expenses	$ 6,898	$ 5,779	$ 1,119	19.4
Operating income	$ 1,311	$ 2,393	($ 1,082)	(45.2)
Gain (loss) on investments	(90)	208	(298)	(143.3)
Interest income	463	254	209	82.3
Interest expense	(100)	(84)	(16)	19.0
Income before income taxes	$ 1,584	$ 2,771	($ 1,187)	(42.8)
Provision for income taxes	603	917	(314)	(34.2)
Income before cumulative effect of change in accounting principle	$ 981	$ 1,854	$ (873)	(47.1)
Cumulative effect of change in accounting principle	(54)	—	(54)	NA
Net income	$ 927	$ 1,854	($ 927)	(50.0)
Net income per common share—basic	$0.28	$0.59	($0.31)	(52.2)
Net income per common share—diluted	$0.27	$0.55	($0.28)	(50.9)
Shares used in calculation of net income per common share—basic	3,234	3,151	83	2.6
Shares used in calculation of net income per common share—diluted	3,417	3,379	38	1.1

Source: Sun Microsystems, Inc., *Annual Report,* 2001

shows a trend analysis of Sun Microsystems' five-year summary of net revenues and operating income.

Trend analysis uses an **index number** to show changes in related items over time. For index numbers, the base year is equal to 100 percent. Other years are measured in relation to that amount. For example, the 2001 index for Sun Microsystems' net revenues is figured as follows (dollar amounts in millions):

$$\text{Index} = 100 \times \left(\frac{\text{Index Year Amount}}{\text{Base Year Amount}}\right)$$

$$= 100 \times \left(\frac{\$18,250}{\$8,661}\right) = 210.7\%$$

EXHIBIT 3
Comparative Balance Sheets with Horizontal Analysis

Sun Microsystems, Inc.
Consolidated Balance Sheets
June 30, 2001 and 2000

(Dollar amounts in millions)	2001	2000	Increase (Decrease) Amount	Percentage
Assets				
Current assets:				
Cash and cash equivalents	$ 1,472	$ 1,849	($377)	(20.4)
Short-term investments	387	626	(239)	(38.2)
Accounts receivable, net of allowances of $410 in 2001 and $534 in 2000	2,955	2,690	265	9.9
Inventories	1,049	557	492	88.3
Deferred tax assets	1,102	673	429	63.7
Prepaids and other current assets	969	482	487	101.0
Total current assets	$ 7,934	$ 6,877	$1,057	15.4
Property, plant and equipment, net	2,697	2,095	602	28.7
Long-term investments	4,677	4,496	181	4.0
Goodwill, net of accumulated amortization of $349 in 2001 and $88 in 2000	2,041	163	1,878	1,152.1
Other assets, net	832	521	311	59.7
Total assets	$18,181	$14,152	$4,029	28.5
Liabilities and Stockholders' Equity				
Current liabilities:				
Short-term borrowings	$ 3	$ 7	$ (4)	(57.1)
Accounts payable	1,050	924	126	13.6
Accrued payroll-related liabilities	488	751	(263)	(35.0)
Accrued liabilities and other	1,374	1,155	219	19.0
Deferred revenues and customer deposits	1,827	1,289	538	41.7
Warranty reserve	314	211	103	48.8
Income taxes payable	90	209	(119)	(56.9)
Total current liabilities	$ 5,146	$ 4,546	$ 600	13.2
Deferred income taxes	744	577	167	28.9
Long-term debt and other obligations	1,705	1,720	(15)	(0.9)
Stockholders' equity	10,586	7,309	3,277	44.8
Total liabilities and stockholders' equity	$18,181	$14,152	$4,029	28.5

Source: Sun Microsystems, Inc., *Annual Report,* 2001.

TREND ANALYSIS

A variation of horizontal analysis is **trend analysis**, in which percentage changes are calculated for several successive years instead of for two years. Trend analysis, with its long-run view, is important because it may point to basic changes in the nature of a business. In addition to presenting comparative financial statements, most companies present a summary of key data for five or more years. Exhibit 5 (page 762)

TOOLS AND TECHNIQUES OF FINANCIAL ANALYSIS

LO4 Apply horizontal analysis, trend analysis, vertical analysis, and ratio analysis to financial statements.

RELATED TEXT ASSIGNMENTS
Q: 6, 7, 8, 9
SE: 3, 4, 5
E: 2, 3, 4
P: 1
SD: 6
FRA: 1

www.sun.com

Few numbers are very significant when looked at individually. It is their relationship to other numbers or their change from one period to another that is important. The tools of financial analysis are intended to show relationships and changes. Among the more widely used tools are horizontal analysis, trend analysis, vertical analysis, and ratio analysis. To illustrate how these tools are used, we devote the rest of this chapter to a comprehensive financial analysis of Sun Microsystems, Inc. Sun Microsystems was formed in 1982 and, as noted in this chapter's Decision Point, it has emerged as a global leader in network computing. It developed many of the networking technologies that are the basis of the Internet and corporate intranets, including the widely adopted Java technology.

HORIZONTAL ANALYSIS

Generally accepted accounting principles require the presentation of comparative financial statements that give financial information for the current year and the previous year. A common starting point for studying such statements is **horizontal analysis**, which computes changes from the previous year to the current year in both dollar amounts and percentages. The percentage change relates the size of the change to the size of the dollar amounts involved.

Exhibits 3 and 4 present the comparative balance sheets and income statements of Sun Microsystems and show both the dollar and percentage changes. The percentage change is computed as follows:

$$\text{Percentage Change} = 100 \times \left(\frac{\text{Amount of Change}}{\text{Base Year Amount}} \right)$$

The **base year** in any set of data is always the first year to be considered. For example, when studying data from 2000 and 2001, 2000 is the base year. As the balance sheets in Exhibit 3 show, between 2000 and 2001, Sun Microsystems' total current assets increased by $1,057 million, from $6,877 million to $7,934 million, or by 15.4 percent. This is computed as follows:

$$\text{Percentage Change} = 100 \times \left(\frac{\$1{,}057 \text{ million}}{\$6{,}877 \text{ million}} \right) = 15.4\%$$

The company's total current liabilities also increased—by $600 million, or 13.2 percent—in this two-year period. When examining such changes, it is important to consider both the dollar amount of the change as well as the percentage change in each component. For example, the difference between the percentage increase in warranty reserve (48.8 percent) and deferred revenues and customer deposits (41.7 percent) is not great. However, the dollar increase in deferred revenues and customer deposits is more than five times the dollar increase in warranty reserve ($538 million versus $103 million).

Sun Microsystems' balance sheets for this period also show an increase in total assets of $4,029 million, or 28.5 percent, which included an increase of $602 million, or 28.7 percent, in property, plant, and equipment, net. In addition, they show that stockholders' equity increased by $3,277 million, or 44.8 percent. All of this indicates that Sun Microsystems is a rapidly growing company.

The most important findings from the income statements in Exhibit 4 are that net revenues increased by $2,529 million, or 16.1 percent; operating income decreased by $1,082 million, or 45.2 percent; and net income decreased by $927 million, or 50.0 percent. These extremely negative results occurred in part because net revenues grew at a slower rate (16.1 percent) than cost of sales (33.0 percent) and operating expenses (19.4 percent).

ENRICHMENT NOTE:
Traditional horizontal analysis presents trends in terms of nominal dollars. Advanced analysis might adjust data over several time periods to remove any inflation effect or price-level changes.

EXHIBIT 2
Listing from Mergent's *Handbook of Dividend Achievers*

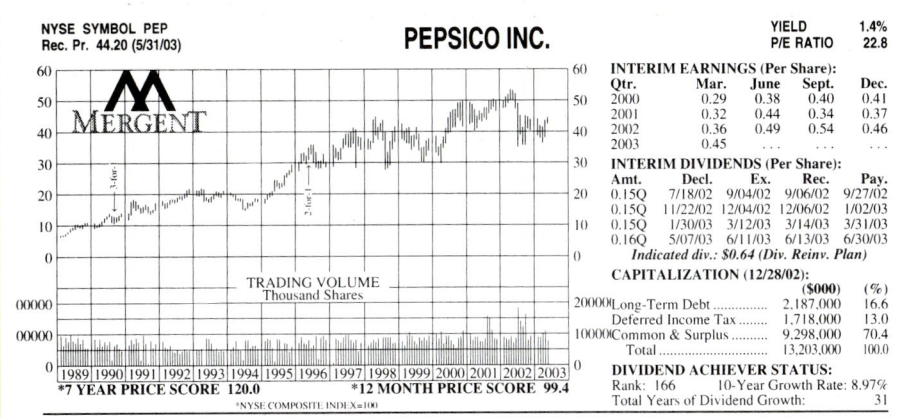

NYSE SYMBOL PEP
Rec. Pr. 44.20 (5/31/03)

PEPSICO INC.

YIELD 1.4%
P/E RATIO 22.8

INTERIM EARNINGS (Per Share):

Qtr.	Mar.	June	Sept.	Dec.
2000	0.29	0.38	0.40	0.41
2001	0.32	0.44	0.34	0.37
2002	0.36	0.49	0.54	0.46
2003	0.45	...	...	...

INTERIM DIVIDENDS (Per Share):

Amt.	Decl.	Ex.	Rec.	Pay.
0.15Q	7/18/02	9/04/02	9/06/02	9/27/02
0.15Q	11/22/02	12/04/02	12/06/02	1/02/03
0.15Q	1/30/03	3/12/03	3/14/03	3/31/03
0.16Q	5/07/03	6/11/03	6/13/03	6/30/03

Indicated div.: $0.64 (Div. Reinv. Plan)

CAPITALIZATION (12/28/02):

	($000)	(%)
Long-Term Debt	2,187,000	16.6
Deferred Income Tax	1,718,000	13.0
Common & Surplus	9,298,000	70.4
Total	13,203,000	100.0

*7 YEAR PRICE SCORE 120.0 *12 MONTH PRICE SCORE 99.4
*NYSE COMPOSITE INDEX=100

DIVIDEND ACHIEVER STATUS:
Rank: 166   10-Year Growth Rate: 8.97%
Total Years of Dividend Growth: 31

RECENT DEVELOPMENTS: For the 12 weeks ended 3/22/03, net income was $777.0 million versus $689.0 million in the same period a year earlier. Results for 2003 and 2002 included pre-tax merger-related costs of $11.0 million and $36.0 million, respectively. Results for 2003 also included an after-tax gain of $16.0 million on Quaker's Mission pasta business. Net sales grew 4.1% to $5.53 billion, and operating profit rose 13.5% to $1.14 billion.

PROSPECTS: PEP's solid near-term outlook is supported by the roll-out of new products and market programs designed to fuel growth over the balance of 2003. They include the introduction of MOUNTAIN DEW LIVEWIRE, an orange-flavored version of MOUNTAIN DEW that is expected to be available from Memorial Day through Labor Day; new packaging and re-designed graphics for PEPSI; and a number of new Quaker products.

BUSINESS

PEPSICO INC. is a worldwide consumer products company. Worldwide snacks (57.1% of 2002 division net sales and 56.4% of operating profit) manufactures, markets, sells and distributes primarily salty, sweet and grain-based snacks including such brands as LAY'S, DORITOS, CHEETOS, ROLD GOLD, SABRITAS and WALKERS. Worldwide beverages (36.9%, 34.6%) includes such brands as PEPSI, DIET PEPSI, MOUNTAIN DEW, MUG, AQUAFINA, SOBE, TROPICANA PURE PREMIUM, GATORADE and MIRINDA and 7-UP internationally. Quaker Foods North America (6.0%, 9.0%) manufactures, markets and sells a variety of food products. PEP also has various ownership interests in a number of bottling concerns. In August 2001, PEP acquired The Quaker Oats Company.

ANNUAL FINANCIAL DATA

	12/28/02	12/29/01	12/30/00	12/25/99	12/26/98	12/27/97	12/28/96
Earnings Per Share	[2] 1.85	[6] 1.47	1.48	[4] 1.37	[5] 1.31	[1] 0.95	[2] 0.72
Cash Flow Per Share	2.47	2.07	2.13	2.06	2.12	1.65	1.79
Tang. Book Val. Per Share	2.37	2.17	1.91	1.47	...	0.72	...
Dividends Per Share	0.59	0.57	0.55	0.53	0.51	0.48	0.43
Dividend Payout %	31.9	38.8	37.2	38.7	38.9	50.5	59.7

INCOME STATEMENT (IN MILLIONS):

Total Revenues	25,112.0	26,935.0	20,438.0	20,367.0	22,348.0	20,917.0	31,645.0
Costs & Expenses	19,270.0	21,832.0	16,253.0	16,517.0	18,530.0	17,149.0	27,380.0
Depreciation & Amort.	1,112.0	1,082.0	960.0	1,032.0	1,234.0	1,106.0	1,719.0
Operating Income	4,730.0	4,021.0	3,225.0	2,818.0	2,584.0	2,662.0	2,546.0
Net Interest Inc./(Exp.)	d142.0	d152.0	d145.0	d245.0	d321.0	d353.0	d499.0
Income Before Income Taxes	4,868.0	4,029.0	3,210.0	3,656.0	2,263.0	2,309.0	2,047.0
Income Taxes	1,555.0	1,367.0	1,027.0	1,606.0	270.0	818.0	898.0
Net Income	[7] 3,313.0	[6] 2,662.0	2,183.0	[4] 2,050.0	[3] 1,993.0	[1] 1,491.0	[2] 1,149.0
Cash Flow	4,421.0	3,740.0	3,143.0	3,082.0	3,227.0	2,597.0	2,868.0
Average Shs. Outstg. (000)	1,789,000	1,807,000	1,475,000	1,496,000	1,519,000	1,570,000	1,606,000

BALANCE SHEET (IN MILLIONS):

Cash & Cash Equivalents	1,845.0	1,649.0	1,330.0	1,056.0	394.0	2,883.0	786.0
Total Current Assets	6,413.0	5,853.0	4,604.0	4,173.0	4,362.0	6,251.0	5,139.0
Net Property	7,390.0	6,876.0	5,438.0	5,266.0	7,318.0	6,261.0	10,191.0
Total Assets	23,474.0	21,695.0	18,339.0	17,551.0	22,660.0	20,101.0	24,512.0
Total Current Liabilities	6,052.0	4,998.0	3,935.0	3,788.0	7,914.0	4,257.0	5,139.0
Long-Term Obligations	2,187.0	2,651.0	2,346.0	2,812.0	4,028.0	4,946.0	8,439.0
Net Stockholders' Equity	9,298.0	8,648.0	7,249.0	6,881.0	6,401.0	6,936.0	6,623.0
Net Working Capital	361.0	855.0	669.0	385.0	d3,552.0	1,994.0	...
Year-end Shs. Outstg. (000)	1,722,000	1,756,000	1,446,000	1,455,000	1,471,000	1,502,000	1,545,000

STATISTICAL RECORD:

Operating Profit Margin %	18.8	14.9	15.8	13.8	11.6	12.7	8.0
Net Profit Margin %	13.2	9.9	10.7	10.1	8.9	7.1	3.6
Return on Equity %	35.6	30.8	30.1	29.8	31.1	21.5	17.3
Return on Assets %	14.1	12.3	11.9	11.7	8.8	7.4	4.7
Debt/Total Assets %	9.3	12.2	12.8	16.0	17.8	24.6	34.4
Price Range	53.50-35.01	50.46-40.25	49.94-29.69	42.56-30.13	44.81-27.56	41.31-28.25	35.88-27.25
P/E Ratio	28.9-18.9	34.3-27.4	33.7-20.1	31.1-22.0	34.2-21.0	43.5-29.7	49.8-37.8
Average Yield %	1.3	1.3	1.4	1.5	1.4	1.4	1.4

Statistics are as originally reported. [1] Incl. non-recurr. chrgs. of $290.0 mill.; bef. disc. oper. gain of $651.0 mill. [2] Incl. non-recurr. chrgs. of $716.0 mill. [3] Incl. non-recurr. chrg. of $288.0 mill. [4] Incl. non-recurr. chrg. of $65.0 mill. [5] Incl. after-tax merger-rel. chrgs. of $322.0 mill. and oth. asset impairmnt. & restruct. chrgs. of $19.0 mill. [6] Refl. 10/6/97 spin-off of TRICON Global Restaurants. [7] Incl. merger-rel. chrgs. of $224.0 mill.

OFFICERS:
S. S. Reinemund, Chmn., C.E.O.
I. K. Nooyi, Pres., C.F.O.
D. R. Andrews, Sr. V.P., Sec., Gen. Couns.

INVESTOR CONTACT: Kathleen Luke, V.P., Inv. Rel., (914) 253-3691

PRINCIPAL OFFICE: 700 Anderson Hill Road, Purchase, NY 10577-1444

TELEPHONE NUMBER: (914) 253-2000
FAX: (914) 253-2070
WEB: www.pepsico.com
NO. OF EMPLOYEES: 142,000 (approx.)
SHAREHOLDERS: 220,000 (approx.)
ANNUAL MEETING: In May
INCORPORATED: DE, Sept., 1919; reincorp.. NC, Dec., 1986

INSTITUTIONAL HOLDINGS:
No. of Institutions: 1,072
Shares Held: 1,123,709,222
% Held: 65.4

INDUSTRY: Bottled and canned soft drinks (SIC: 2086)

TRANSFER AGENT(S): The Bank of New York, Newark, NJ

Source: Sample listing from *Handbook of Dividend Achievers, 2002.* Reprinted by permission of Mergent, Inc.

✓ Check out ACE for a Review Quiz at http://accounting.college.hmco.com/students.

Focus on Business Technology

Find It on the Internet.

Performance reports and other financial information, including stock quotes, reference data, and news about companies and markets, are available instantaneously through such Internet services as CompuServe <www.compuserve.com>, America Online, <www.aol.com>, Yahoo <www.yahoo.com>, and Wall Street Journal Interactive Edition <http://online.wsj.com>. With access to these online services and those of brokers like Charles Schwab & Co., Inc. <www.schwab.com>, which allow customers to use their own computers to buy and sell stock and other securities, individuals today can avail themselves of resources equivalent to those used by many professional analysts.

🔴 **STOP AND THINK!**

Why would ratios that include one balance sheet account and one income statement or statement of cash flows account, such as receivable turnover or return on assets, be questionable if they came from quarterly or other interim financial reports?

On quarterly financial statements, all numbers on the income statement and statement of cash flows are for less than one year, whereas the balance sheet figures are full values similar to those at year end. Thus, any ratios that use data from the income statement or statement of cash flows as their basis will be less than they might be on a full-year basis. ■

www.moodys.com
www.standardpoor.com
www.dunandbradstreet.com

www.rmahq.com

www.pepsi.com

SEC REPORTS

Publicly held corporations in the United States must file annual reports, quarterly reports, and current reports with the Securities and Exchange Commission (SEC). If they have more than $10 million in assets and more than 500 shareholders, they must file these reports electronically at www.sec.gov/edgar.shtml, where anyone can access them free of charge.

The Securities and Exchange Commission requires companies to use a standard form, called Form 10-K, for the annual report. Form 10-K contains more information than the annual reports published by companies. For that reason, it is a valuable source of information.

Companies file their quarterly reports with the SEC on Form 10-Q. This report presents important facts about interim financial performance. The current report, filed on Form 8-K must be submitted to the SEC within a few days of the date of certain significant events, such as the sale or purchase of a division of the company or a change in the company's auditors. The current report is often the first indicator of important changes that may affect a company's financial performance in the future.

BUSINESS PERIODICALS AND CREDIT AND INVESTMENT ADVISORY SERVICES

Financial analysts must keep up with current events in the financial world. Probably the best source of financial news is *The Wall Street Journal*, which is published every business day and is the most complete financial newspaper in the United States. Some helpful magazines, published every week or every two weeks, are *Forbes, Barron's, Fortune,* and the *Financial Times.*

For further details about the financial history of companies, the publications of such services as Moody's Investors Service, Inc., and Standard & Poor's are useful. Data on industry norms, average ratios and relationships, and credit ratings are available from such agencies as The Dun & Bradstreet Corp. In its publication entitled *Industry Norms and Key Business Ratios,* Dun & Bradstreet offers an annual analysis of 14 ratios for each of 125 industry groups, classified as retailing, wholesaling, manufacturing, and construction. *Annual Statement Studies,* published by the Risk Management Association (formerly Robert Morris Associates), presents many facts and ratios for 223 different industries. A number of private services are also available for a yearly fee.

An example of specialized financial reporting readily available to the public is Mergent's *Handbook of Dividend Achievers,* which profiles companies that have increased their dividends consistently over the past ten years. A listing from that publication—for PepsiCo Inc.—is shown in Exhibit 2. A wealth of information about the company is summarized on one page, including the market action of its stock; its business operations, recent developments, and prospects; earnings and dividend data; and annual financial data for the past ten years. The kind of data in these profiles is used in many of the analyses and ratios explained in this chapter.

FOCUS ON BUSINESS ETHICS

Take the Numbers with a Grain of Salt.

Traditionally, pro-forma statements presented financial statements as they would appear after certain agreed-upon transactions, such as mergers or acquisitions, took place. In recent years, pro-forma statements have become more widely used as a way for companies to present a better picture of their operations than would be the case under GAAP. According to a survey by the National Investor Relations Institute, 57 percent of companies across a range of industries use pro-forma reporting.[2] In one quarter, Amazon.com <www.amazon.com> reported a "pro-forma operating" loss of $49 million and a "pro-forma net" loss of $76 million; had the company used GAAP, it would have reported a net loss of $234 million. Among many other examples, JDS Uniphase <www.jdsu.com> reported a "pro-forma" gain of $.14 per share, when, in fact, its net loss using GAAP was $1.13 per share. Pro-forma statements, which are unaudited, have come to mean whatever a company's management wants them to mean. Thus, the analyst should rely exclusively on financial statements that are prepared using GAAP and that are audited by an independent CPA.[3]

---

www.goodyear.com

a partial solution to this problem. It states that diversified companies must report profit or loss, certain revenue and expense items, and assets for each of their segments. Depending on how the company is organized for assessing performance, segment information may be reported for operations in different industries or different geographical areas, or for major customers.[4]

Exhibit 1 on page 755 shows an example of segment reporting. Goodyear Tire & Rubber Co., well known as a tire manufacturer, also has significant engineered and chemical products divisions. The data on sales, income, and assets for these segments, shown in Exhibit 1, allow the analyst to compute important profitability performance measures, such as profit margin, asset turnover, and return on assets, for each segment and to compare them with the appropriate industry norms.

The third limitation of industry norms is that companies in the same industry with similar operations may use different acceptable accounting procedures. That is, they may use different methods to value inventories and different methods to depreciate assets. Even so, if little information about a company's past performance is available, industry norms probably offer the best available standards for judging current performance—as long as they are used with care.

✓ Check out ACE for a Review Quiz at http://accounting.college.hmco.com/students.

SOURCES OF INFORMATION

LO3 Identify the sources of information for financial performance evaluation.

RELATED TEXT ASSIGNMENTS
Q: 5
SE: 2
E: 1
SD: 2, 3, 4, 5
FRA: 6

The external analyst is often limited to using publicly available information about a company. The major sources of information about publicly held corporations are reports published by the company, SEC reports, business periodicals, and credit and investment advisory services.

REPORTS PUBLISHED BY THE COMPANY

A publicly held corporation's annual report is an important source of financial information. From a financial analyst's perspective, its main parts are management's analysis of the past year's operations; the financial statements; the notes to the financial statements, which include a summary of significant accounting policies; the auditors' report; and financial highlights for a five- or ten-year period.

Most publicly held companies also publish **interim financial statements** each quarter. Those reports present limited information in the form of condensed financial statements, which need not be subjected to a full audit by the independent auditor. The financial community watches the interim statements closely for early signs of important changes in a company's earnings trend.

uation is most useful. Creditors and investors use financial performance evaluation in two general ways: to judge past performance and current position, and to judge future potential and the risk connected with that potential.

KEY POINT: Past performance is a measure of certainty, whereas trends and projections entail varying degrees of risk and uncertainty.

■ **ASSESSMENT OF PAST PERFORMANCE AND CURRENT POSITION** Past performance is often a good indicator of future performance. Therefore, an investor or creditor looks at the trends of past sales, expenses, net income, cash flow, and return on investment not only as means of judging management's past performance but also as possible indicators of future performance. In addition, an evaluation of current position will tell, for example, what assets the business owns and what liabilities it must pay. It will also tell what the company's cash position is, how much debt it has in relation to equity, and what levels of inventories and receivables exist. Knowing a company's past performance and current position is often important in judging future potential and the related risk.

■ **ASSESSMENT OF FUTURE POTENTIAL AND RELATED RISK** Information about the past and present is useful only insofar as it bears on decisions about the future. An investor evaluates a company's potential earning ability because that ability will affect the market price of the company's stock and the amount of dividends the company will pay. A creditor evaluates the company's potential debt-paying ability.

The riskiness of an investment or loan depends on how easy it is to predict future profitability or liquidity. If an investor can predict with confidence that a company's earnings per share will be between $2.50 and $2.60 in the next year, the investment is less risky than if the earnings per share are expected to fall between $2.00 and $3.00. For example, the potential associated with an investment in an established and stable electric utility, or a loan to it, is relatively easy to predict on the basis of the company's past performance and current position. The potential associated with investment in a small Internet firm, on the other hand, may be much harder to predict. For this reason, the investment in or loan to the electric utility carries less risk than the investment in or loan to the small Internet company.

Often, in return for taking a greater risk, an investor in the small Internet company will demand a higher expected return (increase in market price plus dividends) than will an investor in the established utility company. Also, a creditor of the Internet company will demand a higher interest rate and possibly more assurance of repayment (a secured loan, for instance) than a creditor of the utility company. The higher interest rate reimburses the creditor for assuming a higher risk.

FINANCIAL REPORTING UNDER THE SARBANES-OXLEY ACT

www.enron.com
www.worldcom.com

In response to the financial reporting issues raised by the cases of Enron, WorldCom, and others, the U.S. Congress passed broad legislation, referred to as the **Sarbanes-Oxley Act**, in an attempt to rectify the problems. This act includes numerous provisions designed to improve investor confidence in the financial reporting system as it applies to publicly traded companies, including the following:

- Establishes a Public Oversight Board for the accounting profession, which will establish auditing standards and oversee other regulations involving auditors.
- Requires the chief executor officer and chief financial officer to take responsibility for the accuracy of annual and quarterly financial statements under criminal penalties.
- Requires the audit committee of public corporations to be made up of independent (nonofficer) board members, some of whom must have financial expertise.
- Requires that the audit committee appoint the company's auditor and that the auditor not be allowed to do any consulting for the company.

The Sarbanes-Oxley Act does not apply to private (nonpublic) companies.

Check out ACE for a Review Quiz at http://accounting.college.hmco.com/students.

Financial Performance Evaluation by Internal and External Users

LO1 Describe and discuss financial performance evaluation by internal and external users.

RELATED TEXT ASSIGNMENTS
Q: 1, 2
SE: 1
E: 1

Financial performance evaluation, also called *financial statement analysis*, comprises all the techniques users of financial statements employ to show important relationships in a firm's financial statements and to relate them to important financial objectives. Users of financial statements who evaluate financial performance fall into two categories: internal users and external users. Both groups have a strong interest in financial performance. Internal users include top managers, who set and strive to achieve financial performance objectives; middle-level managers of business processes; and employee stockholders. External users are creditors and investors who want to assess management's accomplishment of financial objectives, as well as customers who have cooperative agreements with the company.

Internal Users

■ **Stop and Think!**
Why is it essential that management compensation, including bonuses, be linked to financial goals and strategies that achieve shareholder value?

If the overall financial plan is expected to increase the owners' wealth, then aligning managers' compensation and bonuses with achieving or exceeding these financial targets encourages managers to act in their own and the owners' best interests. ■

Setting financial performance objectives is a major function of management's plan to achieve the company's strategic goals. All strategic and operating plans established by management must eventually be stated in terms of financial objectives. A primary objective of management is to increase the wealth of the owners or stockholders of the business, but this objective must be divided into categories. A complete financial plan should have balanced financial performance objectives in all the following categories:

Business Objectives	Links to Financial Performance
Liquidity	Ability to pay bills when due and to meet unexpected needs for cash
Profitability	Ability to earn a satisfactory net income
Long-term solvency	Ability to survive for many years
Cash flow adequacy	Ability to generate sufficient cash through operating, investing, and financing activities
Market strength	Ability to increase the wealth of owners

Management's main responsibility is to put into action and to carry out its plan to achieve the financial performance objectives. Management must constantly monitor key financial performance measures, determine the cause of any deviations in the measures, and propose corrective actions. Annual measures provide data for long-term trend analysis. Management develops monthly, quarterly, and annual reports that compare actual performance with objectives for key financial measures in each of the above categories. These reports should be formatted to highlight key performance measures.

External Users

Creditors make loans in the form of trade accounts, notes, or bonds. They expect them to be repaid according to specified terms and to receive interest on the notes and bonds payable. Investors buy capital stock, from which they hope to receive dividends and an increase in value. Both groups face risks. The creditor faces the risk that the debtor will fail to pay back the loan. The investor faces the risks that dividends will be reduced or not paid and that the market price of the stock will drop. For both groups, the goal is to achieve a return that makes up for the risk. In general, the greater the risk taken, the greater the return required as compensation.

Any one loan or any one investment can turn out badly. As a result, most creditors and investors put their funds into a **portfolio**, which is a group of loans or investments. The portfolio is designed to average the returns and the risks. Nevertheless, individual decisions about the loans or stock in the portfolio must still be made. It is in making those individual decisions that financial performance eval-

How is financial performance tied to the annual incentive bonuses that executives at Sun hope to receive?

performance is an important factor in management compensation. Managers who work in such an environment must understand the comprehensive framework that internal and external users of financial statements commonly employ to evaluate a company's results. This chapter presents that framework.

Financial Highlights
(In millions except earnings per share)

	2001	2000	1999
Net revenues	$18,250	$15,721	$11,806
Net income	927	1,854	1,030
Earnings per share—basic	0.28	0.59	0.33

18

Chapter 18 focuses on financial performance evaluation by internal and external users. The chapter describes the tools and techniques of financial analysis and ratio analysis.

Financial Performance Evaluation

LEARNING OBJECTIVES

LO1 Describe and discuss financial performance evaluation by internal and external users.

LO2 Describe and discuss the standards for financial performance evaluation.

LO3 Identify the sources of information for financial performance evaluation.

LO4 Apply horizontal analysis, trend analysis, vertical analysis, and ratio analysis to financial statements.

LO5 Apply ratio analysis to financial statements in a comprehensive evaluation of a company's financial performance.

DECISION POINT
A USER'S FOCUS

Sun Microsystems <www.sun.com> Sun Microsystems is a global leader in providing products and services for computer networking. A committee of its board of directors has developed a compensation package for top management that is linked to, among other things, financial performance measures, some of which are presented in the Financial Highlights. These measures are, in turn, linked to creating shareholder value. How does Sun Microsystems make these links?

The company's executive compensation package consists primarily of the following three components:

- Base salary
- Long-term incentives
- Annual incentive bonus

Executives' base salaries are competitive within the industry, and long-term incentives are tied to stock options that will become more valuable if the stock price goes up, thereby creating shareholder value. Of the three components, the annual incentive bonus is most closely linked to financial performance in any given year. Although the company was profitable and its revenues increased in 2001, no annual incentive bonuses were awarded because growth in revenues and in earnings per share was below the company's plan. These results contrast sharply with those in 2000, when financial performance was outstanding and several executives received bonuses in excess of $1 million.[1]

Thus, at Sun Microsystems, as at many other companies that demand outstanding results, financial

FRA 6.
LO2 Follow-up Analysis of Cash Flows

Internet Case

Go to Marriott International's web site <www.marriott.com> and find the statement of cash flows in the company's latest annual report. Compare it with the 2002 statement at the beginning of this chapter by (1) identifying major changes in operating, investing, and financing activities; (2) reading management's financial review of cash flows; and (3) calculating the cash flow ratios (cash flow yield, cash flows to sales, cash flows to assets) and free cash flow for the most recent year. How does Marriott's cash flow performance differ between these two years? Be prepared to discuss your conclusions in class.

Which company is most efficient in generating cash flow? Which company has the best year-to-year trend? Which company do you think will most probably need external financing?

Toys "R" Us Annual Report

FRA 3. Refer to the statement of cash flows in the Toys "R" Us <www.tru.com> annual report to answer the following questions:

LO1 **Analysis of the Statement of**
LO2 **Cash Flows**
LO3
LO4
LO5

1. Does Toys "R" Us use the indirect method of reporting cash flows from operating activities? Other than net earnings, what are the most important factors affecting the company's cash flows from operating activities? Explain the trend of each of these factors.
2. Based on the cash flows from investing activities, would you say that Toys "R" Us is a contracting or an expanding company? Explain.
3. Has Toys "R" Us used external financing? If so, where did it come from?

Comparison Case: Toys "R" Us and Walgreen Co.

FRA 4. Refer to the annual report of Toys "R" Us <www.tru.com> and the financial statements of Walgreens <www.walgreens.com> in the Supplement to Chapter 6. Calculate for two years each company's cash flow yield, cash flows to sales ratio, cash flows to assets ratio, and free cash flows. In 2000, Walgreens' total assets were $7,103,700,000. Discuss and compare the trends of the cash-generating ability of both Toys "R" Us and Walgreens. Comment on each company's change in cash and cash equivalents over the two-year period.

LO2 **Cash Flows Analysis**

Fingraph® Financial Analyst™

FRA 5. Choose any two companies in the same industry from the list of Fingraph companies on the Needles Accounting Resource Center Web Site at http://accounting.college.hmco.com/students. Access the Microsoft Excel spreadsheets for the companies you selected. Click on the URL at the top of each company's spreadsheet for a link to the company's web site and annual report.

LO2 **Cash Flow Analysis**
LO3
LO4
LO5

1. In the annual reports of the companies you have selected, find the statement of cash flows. Do the companies use the direct or indirect method of preparing the statement?
2. Using the Fingraph CD-ROM software, display and print in tabular and graphic form the Statement of Cash Flows: Operating Activities Analysis page. Prepare a table that compares the cash flow yield, cash flows to sales, and cash flows to assets ratios for both companies for two years. Are the ratios moving in the same direction or opposite ones? Study the operating activities sections of the statements to determine the main causes of differences between the net income and cash flows from operations. How do the companies compare?
3. Using the Fingraph CD-ROM software, display and print in tabular and graphic form the Statement of Cash Flows: Investing and Financing Activities Analysis page. Prepare a table that compares the free cash flow for both companies for two years. How do the companies compare? Are the companies growing or contracting? Study the investing and financing activities sections of the statements to determine the main causes of differences between the companies.
4. Find and read references to cash flows in the liquidity analysis section of management's discussion and analysis in each annual report.
5. Write a one-page executive summary that reports your findings from parts **1–4**, including your assessment of the companies' comparative liquidity. Include the Fingraph pages and your tables with your report.

Enron Corporation
Statement of Cash Flows
For the Nine Months Ending September 30, 2001 and 2002

	2001	2000
	(In millions)	
Cash Flows from Operating Activities		
Reconciliation of net income to net cash provided by operating activities		
Net income	$ 225	$ 797
Cumulative effect of accounting changes, net of tax	(19)	0
Depreciation, depletion and amortization	746	617
Deferred income taxes	(134)	8
Gains on sales of non-trading assets	(49)	(135)
Investment losses	768	0
Changes in components of working capital		
Receivables	987	(3,363)
Inventories	1	339
Payables	(1,764)	2,899
Other	464	(455)
Trading investments		
Net margin deposit activity	(2,349)	541
Other trading activities	173	(555)
Other, net	198	(566)
Net Cash Provided by (Used in) Operating Activities	$ (753)	$ 127
Cash Flows from Investing Activities		
Capital expenditures	(1,584)	(1,539)
Equity investments	(1,172)	(858)
Proceeds from sales of non-trading investments	1,711	222
Acquisition of subsidiary stock	0	(485)
Business acquisitions, net of cash acquired	(82)	(773)
Other investing activities	(239)	(147)
Net Cash Used in Investing Activities	$(1,366)	$(3,580)
Cash Flows from Financing Activities		
Issuance of long-term debt	4,060	2,725
Repayment of long-term debt	(3,903)	(579)
Net increase in short-term borrowings	2,365	1,694
Issuance of common stock	199	182
Net redemption of company-obligated preferred securities of subsidiaries	0	(95)
Dividends paid	(394)	(396)
Net (acquisition) disposition of treasury stock	(398)	354
Other financing activities	(49)	(12)
Net Cash Provided by Financing Activities	$ 1,880	$ 3,873
Increase (Decrease) in Cash and Cash Equivalents	$ (239)	$ 420
Cash and Cash Equivalents, Beginning of Period	1,240	333
Cash and Cash Equivalents, End of Period	$ 1,001	$ 753

Source: Adapted from Enron Corporation, SEC filings, 2001.

1. To what statement is Klein referring? From the information given, prepare the additional statement using the indirect method.
2. Hashimi Print Gallery, Inc., has a cash problem despite profitable operations. Why is this the case?

FINANCIAL REPORTING AND ANALYSIS CASES

Interpreting Financial Reports

FRA 1. On October 16, 2001, Kenneth Lay, chairman and CEO of Enron Corporation <www.enron.com>, announced the company's earnings for the first nine months of 2001 as follows:

> Our 26 percent increase in recurring earnings per diluted share shows the very strong results of our core wholesale and retail energy businesses and our natural gas pipelines. The continued excellent prospects in these businesses and Enron's leading market position make us very confident in our strong earnings outlook.[12]

Less than six months later, the company filed for the biggest bankruptcy in U.S. history. Its stock dropped to less than $1 per share, and a major financial scandal was underway. Presented on the opposite page is Enron's statement of cash flows for the first nine months of 2001 and 2000 (restated to correct the previous accounting errors). Assume you report to an investment analyst who has asked you to analyze this statement for clues as to why the company went under.

1. For the two time periods shown, compute the cash-generating efficiency ratios of cash flow yield, cash flows to sales (Enron's revenues were $133,762 million in 2001 and $55,494 million in 2000), and cash flows to assets (use total assets of $61,783 million for 2001 and $64,926 million for 2000). Also compute free cash flows for the two years.
2. Prepare a memorandum to the investment analyst that assesses Enron's cash-generating efficiency in light of the chairman's remarks and that evaluates its available free cash flow, taking into account its financing activities. Identify significant changes in operating items and any special operating items that should be considered. Include your computations as an attachment.

International Company

FRA 2. The following data pertain to two of Japan's best-known and most successful companies, Sony Corporation <www.sony.com> and Canon, Inc. <www.canon.com>.[13] (Numbers are in billions of yen.)

	Sony Corporation 2000	Sony Corporation 1999	Canon, Inc. 2000	Canon, Inc. 1999
Net sales	¥6,238	¥6,415	¥2,781	¥2,622
Net income	122	179	134	70
Average total assets	6,579	6,351	2,711	2,658
Net cash flows from operating activities	597	663	347	309
Dividends	21	25	15	15
Net capital expenditures	374	340	165	194

Calculate the ratios of cash flow yield, cash flows to sales, and cash flows to assets, as well as free cash flow, for the two years for both Sony Corporation and Canon, Inc.

Hashimi Print Gallery, Inc.
Income Statement
For the Year Ended December 31, 20x4

Net sales	$884,000
Cost of goods sold	508,000
Gross margin	$376,000
Operating expenses (including depreciation expense of $20,000)	204,000
Operating income	$172,000
Interest expense	24,000
Income before income taxes	$148,000
Income taxes	28,000
Net income	$120,000

After examining the statement, Hashimi said to Klein, "Lou, the statement seems to be well done, but what I need to know is why I don't have enough cash to pay my bills this month. You show that I earned $120,000 in 20x4, but I have only $24,000 in the bank. I know I bought a building on a mortgage and paid a cash dividend of $48,000, but what else is going on?" Klein replied, "To answer your question, we have to look at comparative balance sheets and prepare another type of statement. Take a look at these balance sheets." The statement handed to Hashimi follows.

Hashimi Print Gallery, Inc.
Comparative Balance Sheets
December 31, 20x4 and 20x3

	20x4	20x3
Assets		
Cash	$ 24,000	$ 40,000
Accounts receivable (net)	178,000	146,000
Inventory	240,000	180,000
Prepaid expenses	10,000	14,000
Building	400,000	—
Accumulated depreciation	(20,000)	—
Total assets	$832,000	$380,000
Liabilities and Stockholders' Equity		
Accounts payable	$ 74,000	$ 96,000
Income taxes payable	6,000	4,000
Mortgage payable	400,000	—
Common stock	200,000	200,000
Retained earnings	152,000	80,000
Total liabilities and stockholders' equity	$832,000	$380,000

Ethical Dilemma

SD 2. Chemical Waste Treatment, Inc., a fast-growing company that disposes of chemical wastes, has an $800,000 line of credit at its bank. One section in the credit agreement says that the ratio of cash flows from operations to interest expense must exceed 3.0. If this ratio falls below 3.0, the company must reduce the balance outstanding on its line of credit to one-half the total line if the funds borrowed against the line of credit exceed one-half of the total line.

After the end of the fiscal year, the company's controller informs the president: "We will not meet the ratio requirements on our line of credit in 20x5 because interest expense was $1.2 million and cash flows from operations were $3.2 million. Also, we have borrowed 100 percent of our line of credit. We do not have the cash to reduce the credit line by $400,000." The president says, "This is a serious situation. To pay our ongoing bills, we need our bank to increase our line of credit, not decrease it. What can we do?" "Do you recall the $500,000 two-year note payable for equipment?" replied the controller. "It is now classified as 'Proceeds from Notes Payable' in cash flows provided from financing activities in the statement of cash flows. If we move it to cash flows from operations and call it 'Increase in Payables,' it would increase cash flows from operations to $3.7 million and put us over the limit." "Well, do it," ordered the president. "It surely doesn't make any difference where it is on the statement. It is an increase in both places. It would be much worse for our company in the long term if we failed to meet this ratio requirement."

What is your opinion of the president's reasoning? Is the president's order ethical? Who benefits and who is harmed if the controller follows the president's order? What are management's alternatives? What would you do?

Group Activity. Assign in-class groups to develop a position in support of or against the president's reasoning and have them defend that position in a debate.

Research Activity

SD 3. Find the statement of cash flows in the annual reports of three corporations, using sources in your library or the Fingraph® Financial Analyst™ CD-ROM software that accompanies this text. You may choose corporations from the same industry or at random, at the direction of your instructor. (If you did a Research Activity in a previous chapter, use the same three companies.)

For any year covered by these companies' statements of cash flows, answer the following questions: Does the company use the direct or the indirect method? Is its net income more or less than its net cash flows from operating activities? What are the major causes of differences between net income and net cash flows from operating activities? Compute cash flow efficiency ratios and free cash flow for each company. Does the dividend appear secure? Did the company make significant capital expenditures during the year? How did the company finance the expenditures? Do you notice anything unusual about the investing and financing activities of these three companies? Do the investing and financing activities provide any insights into management's plan for each company? If so, what are they?

Be prepared to discuss your findings in class.

Decision-Making Practice

SD 4. Lou Klein, certified public accountant, has just given his employer May Hashimi, the president of Hashimi Print Gallery, Inc., the income statement that appears at the top of the next page.

Fernandez Fashions, Inc.
Comparative Balance Sheets
December 31, 20x6 and 20x5

	20x6	20x5
Assets		
Cash	$174,120	$ 54,720
Accounts receivable (net)	204,860	150,860
Inventory	225,780	275,780
Prepaid expenses	—	40,000
Land	50,000	—
Building	274,000	—
Accumulated depreciation, building	(30,000)	—
Equipment	66,000	68,000
Accumulated depreciation, equipment	(29,000)	(48,000)
Patents	8,000	12,000
Total assets	$943,760	$553,360
Liabilities and Stockholders' Equity		
Accounts payable	$ 21,500	$ 73,500
Notes payable	20,000	—
Accrued liabilities (current)	—	24,600
Mortgage payable	324,000	—
Common stock, $20 par value	370,000	310,000
Paid-in capital in excess of par value, common	114,400	74,400
Retained earnings	118,860	80,860
Treasury stock	(25,000)	(10,000)
Total liabilities and stockholders' equity	$943,760	$553,360

REQUIRED

1. Using the indirect method, prepare a statement of cash flows for Fernandez Fashions, Inc.
2. Why did Fernandez Fashions have an increase in cash of $119,400 when it recorded net income of $56,000? Discuss and interpret.
3. Compute and assess cash flow yield and free cash flow for 20x6.

SKILLS DEVELOPMENT CASES

Conceptual Analysis

SD 1.
LO1 EBITDA and the Statement of
LO3 Cash Flows

When Fleetwood Enterprises, Inc. <www.fleetwood.com>, a large producer of recreational vehicles and manufactured housing, warned that it might not be able to generate enough cash to satisfy debt requirements and avoid default of a loan agreement, its cash flow, defined in the financial press as "EBITDA" (earnings before interest, taxes, depreciation, and amortization), was a negative $2.7 million. The company would have had to generate $17.7 million in the next accounting period to comply with the loan terms.[11] To what section of the statement of cash flows does EBITDA most closely relate? Is EBITDA a good approximation for this section of the statement of cash flows?

How would your response change if the president of your company asked you to help make a decision about acquiring a fleet of cars for use by sales personnel?

LO4 **Factors in Capital Investment Decisions**

SD 2. PPG Industries <www.ppg.com>, founded in 1883, was the first commercially successful plate glass manufacturer in the United States. Today it is a global supplier of coatings, chemicals, and glass. Every year, its management approves capital spending for modernization and productivity improvements, expansion of existing businesses, and environmental control projects.

Because PPG Industries' management receives many proposals for capital investment projects, it must set an appropriate acceptance-rejection standard. What factors should management consider in setting this standard? If more proposed projects meet the minimum standard than can be funded, what other factors should mangement consider, and what should management do?

Ethical Dilemma

LO4 **LO6** **Ethics, Capital Investment Decisions, and the New Globally Competitive Business Environment**

SD 3. Marika Jonssen is the controller of Bramer Corporation, a globally competitive producer of standard and custom-designed window units for the housing industry. As part of the corporation's move to become automated, Jonssen was asked to prepare a capital investment analysis for a robot-guided aluminum extruding and stamping machine. This machine would automate the entire window-casing manufacturing line.

Jonssen had recently returned from an international seminar on the subject of qualitative inputs into the capital investment decision process, and she was eager to incorporate what she had learned into the analysis. In addition to the normal net present value analysis (which produced a significant negative result) Jonssen factored in figures for customer satisfaction, scrap reduction, reduced inventory needs, and reputation for quality. With the additional information included, the analysis produced a positive response to the decision question.

When the chief financial officer finished reviewing Jonssen's work, he threw the papers on the floor and said, "What kind of garbage is this! You know it's impossible to quantify such things as customer satisfaction and reputation for quality. How do you expect me to go to the board of directors and explain your work? I want you to redo the entire analysis and follow only the traditional approach to net present value. Get it back to me in two hours!"

What is Jonssen's dilemma? What ethical courses of action are available to her?

Research Activity

LO2 **Identifying Relevant Decision Information**

SD 4. Assume you want to take a two-week vacation. Select two destinations for your vacation, and gather information about them from brochures, magazines, travel agents, the Internet, and people you know. Then list the relevant quantitative and qualitative information in its order of importance to your decision. Analyze the information, and select a destination. What factors were the most important to your decision? Why? What factors were the least important to your decision? Why? How would the process of identifying relevant decision information differ if you were asked by the president of your company to prepare a budget for the next training meeting, to be held at a location of your choice?

Group Activity: Divide the class into groups, and ask them to discuss this skills development case. Then debrief the entire class by asking one person from each group to summarize his or her group's findings.

Decision-Making Practice

LO3 **Decision to Add a New Department**

SD 5. Management at Transco Company is considering a proposal to install a third production department within its factory building. With the company's existing production setup, direct materials are processed through the Mixing Department to produce Materials A and B in equal proportions. Material A is then processed through the Shaping Department to yield Product C. Material B is sold as is at $20.25 per pound. Product C has a selling price of $100 per pound.

There is a proposal to add a Baking Department to process Material B into Product D. It is expected that any quantity of Product D can be sold for $30 per pound. Costs per pound under this proposal are as follows:

	Mixing Department (Materials A & B)	Shaping Department (Product C)	Baking Department (Product D)
Cost from Mixing Department	—	$33.00	$13.20
Direct materials	$20.00	—	—
Direct labor	6.00	9.00	3.50
Variable manufacturing overhead	4.00	8.00	4.00
Fixed manufacturing overhead			
Traceable (direct, avoidable)	2.25	2.25	1.80
Allocated (common, unavoidable)	.75	.75	.75
	$33.00	$53.00	$23.25

1. If (a) sales and production levels are expected to remain constant in the foreseeable future and (b) there are no foreseeable alternative uses for the factory space, should Transco Company add a Baking Department and produce Product D, if 100,000 pounds of D can be sold? Show calculations of incremental revenues and costs to support your answer.
2. List at least two qualitative reasons that Transco Company may not want to install a Baking Department and produce Product D, even if it appears that this decision is profitable.
3. List at least two qualitative reasons why Transco Company may want to install a Baking Department and produce Product D, even if it appears that this decision is unprofitable.

(CMA adapted)

Managerial Reporting and Analysis Cases

Interpreting Management Reports

MRA 1.

LO5 Capital Investment Analysis

Automated teller machines (ATMs) have become common in the banking industry. San Angelo Federal Bank is planning to replace some old teller machines and has decided to use the York Machine. Nola Chavez, the controller, has prepared the analysis shown at the top of the facing page. She has recommended the purchase of the machine based on the positive net present value shown in the analysis.

The York Machine has an estimated useful life of five years and an expected residual value of $35,000. Its purchase price is $385,000. Two existing ATMs, each having a carrying value of $25,000, can be sold to a neighboring bank for a total of $50,000. Annual operating cash inflows are expected to increase as follows:

Year 1	$79,900
Year 2	76,600
Year 3	79,900
Year 4	83,200
Year 5	86,500

The bank uses straight-line depreciation. The minimum rate of return is 12 percent.

1. Analyze Chavez's work. What changes need to be made in her capital investment analysis?
2. What would be your recommendation to bank management about the purchase of the York Machine?

San Angelo Federal Bank
Capital Investment Analysis
Net Present Value Method
March 2, 20x7

Year	Net Cash Inflows	Present-Value Factors	Present Value
1	$ 85,000	.909	$ 77,265
2	80,000	.826	66,080
3	85,000	.751	63,835
4	90,000	.683	61,470
5	95,000	.621	58,995
5 (residual value)	35,000	.621	21,735

Total present value $349,380
Initial investment $385,000
Less proceeds from the sale of
  existing ATMs 50,000

Net capital investment (335,000)

Net present value $ 14,380

Formulating Management Reports

LO4 Evaluating a Capital
LO5 Investment Proposal
LO6
LO7

MRA 2. Quality work and timely output are the distinguishing characteristics of Smile Photo, Inc. Smile Photo is a nationally franchised company with over 50 outlets located in the southern states. Part of the franchise agreement promises a centralized photo developing process with overnight delivery to the outlets.

Because of the tremendous increase in demand for its photo processing, Emma DuBarry, the corporation's president, is considering the purchase of a new, deluxe photo processing machine by the end of this month. DuBarry wants you to formulate a memo showing your evaluation of this purchase. Your memo will be presented at the board of directors' meeting next week.

According to your research, the new machine will cost $320,000. It will function for an estimated five years and should have a $32,000 residual value. All capital investments are expected to produce a 20 percent minimum rate of return, and the investment should be recovered in three years or less. All fixed assets are depreciated using the straight-line method. The forecast increases in operating results for the new machine are as follows:

	Cash Flow Estimates	
Year	Cash Inflows	Cash Outflows
1	$310,000	$210,000
2	325,000	220,000
3	340,000	230,000
4	300,000	210,000
5	260,000	180,000

1. In preparation for writing your memo, answer the following questions.
   a. What kinds of information do you need to prepare this memo?
   b. Why is the information relevant?
   c. Where would you find the information?
   d. When would you want to obtain the information?

2. Analyze the purchase of the machine, and decide if the company should purchase it. Use (a) the net present value method, (b) the accounting rate-of-return method, and (c) the payback period method.

International Company

MRA 3. Gourmet Burgers is a competitor in the fast-food restaurant business. One component of the company's marketing strategy is to increase sales by expanding in foreign markets. The company uses both financial and nonfinancial quantitative and qualitative information when deciding whether to open restaurants in foreign markets.

Gourmet Burgers decided to open a restaurant in Prague (Czech Republic) five years ago. The following information helped the managers in making that decision.

Financial Quantitative Information

Operating information

Estimated food, labor, and other operating costs (for example, taxes, insurance, utilities, and supplies)
Estimated selling price for each food item

Capital investment information

Cost of land, building, equipment, and furniture
Financing options and amounts

Nonfinancial Quantitative Information

Estimated daily number of customers, hamburgers to be sold, employees to work
High-traffic time periods
Income of people living in the area
Ratio of population to number of restaurants in the market area
Traffic counts in front of similar restaurants in the area

Qualitative Information

Government regulations, taxes, duties, tariffs, political involvement in business operations
Property ownership restrictions
Site visibility
Accessibility of store location
Training process for local managers
Hiring process for employees
Local customs and practices

Gourmet Burgers has hired you as a consultant and has given you an income statement comparing the operating incomes of its five restaurants in Eastern Europe. You have noticed that the Prague location is operating at a loss (including unallocated fixed costs) and must decide whether to recommend closing that restaurant.

Review the information used in making the decision to open the restaurant. Identify the types of information that would also be relevant in deciding whether to close the restaurant. What period or periods of time should be reviewed in making your decision? What additional information would be relevant in making your decision?

Excel Spreadsheet Analysis

MRA 4. Marketeers, Inc., has developed a promotional program for a large shopping center in Sunset Living, Arizona. After investing $360,000 in developing the original promotion campaign, the firm is ready to present its client with an add-on contract offer that includes the original promotion areas of (1) TV advertising campaign, (2) a series of brochures for mass mailing, and (3) a special rotating BIG SALE schedule for 10 of the 28 tenants in the shopping center. Following are the revenue terms from the original contract with the shopping center and the offer for an add-on contract, which extends the original contract terms.

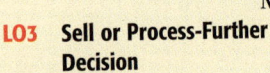

	Contract Terms	
	Original Contract Terms	Extended Contract Including Add-On Terms
TV advertising campaign	$520,000	$ 580,000
Brochure series	210,000	230,000
Rotating BIG SALE schedule	170,000	190,000
Totals	$900,000	$1,000,000

Marketeers estimates that the following additional costs will be incurred by extending the contract:

	TV Campaign	Brochures	BIG SALE Schedule
Direct labor	$30,000	$ 9,000	$7,000
Variable overhead costs	22,000	14,000	6,000
Fixed overhead costs*	12,000	4,000	2,000

*80 percent are direct fixed costs applied to this contract.

1. Using an Excel spreadsheet, compute the costs that will be incurred for each part of the add-on portion of the contract.
2. Should Marketeers, Inc., offer the add-on contract, or should it ask for a final settlement check based on the original contract only? Defend your answer.
3. If management of the shopping center indicated the terms of the add-on contract were negotiable, how should Marketeers respond?

Internet Case

MRA 5.
LO4 Comparison of Capital Investment Disclosures by Two Large Companies

Companies vary in the amount of information they disclose about their criteria for selecting capital investments. Access the web sites for two companies—for example, Coca-Cola <www.coca-cola.com> and International Paper <www.internationalpaper.com>. Find management's discussion and analysis (also called the financial review), which precedes the presentation of the financial statements. In that section, find the discussion of capital investments. Which company provides the more in-depth discussion? Does either disclose its criteria for making capital investment decisions? Also look at the investing activities listed in the statement of cash flows for each company. What is the extent of capital expenditures for each company? Compare each company's capital investments with the amount of total assets on the balance sheet. Which company is more of a growth company? Explain.

Appendix A
International Accounting

As businesses grow, they naturally look for new sources of supply and new markets in other countries. Today, it is common for businesses to operate in more than one country, and many of these so-called *multinational* or *transnational corporations* operate throughout the world.

The extent of a company's international operations can be found in its annual report in the segment information note to the financial statements. The annual report will also contain a description of the company's international operations.

www.pepsico.com

For example, the Frito Lay segment of PepsiCo, Inc., obtains more than one-third of its $13 billion in revenues from countries outside the United States. PepsiCo's annual report contains the following description of this division's international operations:

> Frito-Lay International manufactures, markets, sells and distributes salty and sweet snacks. Products include Walkers brand snack foods in the United Kingdom, Smith's brand snack foods in Australia, Sabritas brand snack foods and Alegro and Gamesa brand sweet snacks in Mexico. Many of our U.S. brands have been introduced internationally such as Lay's and Ruffles brand potato chips, Doritos and Tostitos brand tortilla chips, Fritos brand corn chips and Cheetos brand cheese-flavored snacks. Principal international snack markets include Mexico, the United Kingdom, Brazil, Spain, the Netherlands, Australia and South Africa.[1]

www.ibm.com

Table 1 shows the extent of the foreign revenues of five large U.S. corporations. IBM, for example, has operations in 80 countries and receives almost 60 percent of its sales from outside the United States. Other industrial countries, such as Switzerland, France, Germany, Great Britain, the Netherlands, and Japan, have also given rise to numerous worldwide corporations. Nestlé, the large Swiss food company, makes 98 percent of its sales outside Switzerland. Other companies that make more than half their sales outside their home countries include Michelin, the French tire maker; Unilever, the British/Netherlands consumer products company; and Sony, the Japanese electronics company. More than five hundred companies are listed on at least one stock exchange outside their home countries.

www.nestle.com

www.michelin.com
www.unilever.com
www.sony.com

Sophisticated investors no longer restrict their investment activities to domestic securities markets. Many Americans invest in foreign securities markets, and

TABLE 1. Extent of Foreign Revenues for Selected U.S. Companies

Company	Foreign Revenues (millions)	Total Revenues (millions)	Foreign Revenues (percentage)
Exxon Mobil <www.exxonmobil.com>	$158,403	$228,439	69.3
IBM <www.ibm.com>	50,377	87,548	57.5
Ford <www.ford.com>	51,691	170,064	30.4
General Motors <www.gm.com>	48,233	184,632	26.1
PepsiCo <www.pepsico.com>	7,259	20,438	35.5

Source: Form 10-K of each company.

FIGURE 1
Value of Securities Traded on the World's Stock Markets

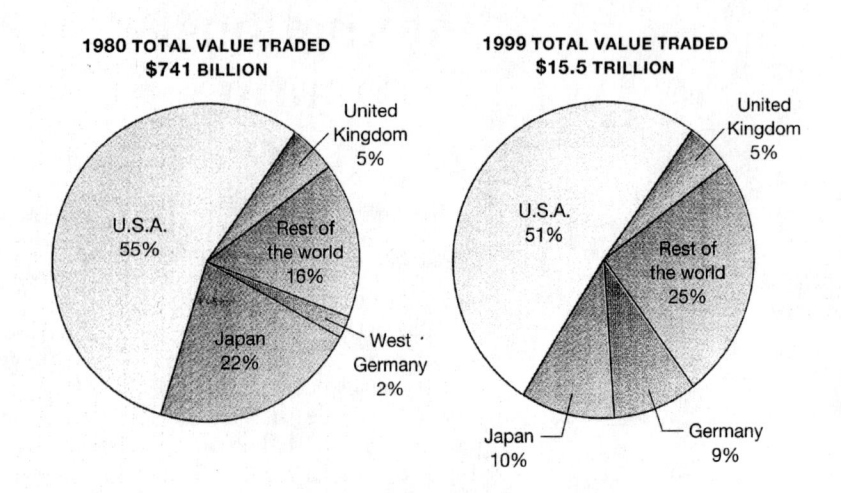

1980 TOTAL VALUE TRADED $741 BILLION
- U.S.A. 55%
- United Kingdom 5%
- Rest of the world 16%
- West Germany 2%
- Japan 22%

1999 TOTAL VALUE TRADED $15.5 TRILLION
- U.S.A. 51%
- United Kingdom 5%
- Rest of the world 25%
- Germany 9%
- Japan 10%

Source: International Finance Corporation, *Emerging Stock Markets Factbook,* © 2000.

non-Americans invest heavily in the stock market in the United States. Figure 1 shows that from 1980 to 1999, the total value of securities traded on the world's stock markets increased over twentyfold, with the U.S. share of the pie declining from 55 to 51 percent.

EFFECTS OF FOREIGN BUSINESS TRANSACTIONS

Foreign business transactions have two major effects on accounting. First, most sales or purchases of goods and services in other countries involve different currencies. Thus, one currency needs to be translated into another, using exchange rates.* An *exchange rate* is the value of one currency stated in terms of another. For example, an English company purchasing goods from a U.S. company and paying in U.S. dollars must exchange British pounds for U.S. dollars before making payment. In effect, currencies are goods that can be bought and sold. Table 2 lists the exchange rates of several currencies in terms of dollars. It shows the exchange rate for the British pound as $1.61. Like the price of any good or service, these prices change daily according to supply and demand. Accounting for these price changes in recording foreign transactions and preparing financial statements for foreign subsidiaries are discussed in the next two sections.

The second major effect of international business on accounting is that financial standards differ from country to country, which makes it difficult to compare companies from different countries. The obstacles to achieving comparability and some of the progress in solving the problem are discussed later in this appendix.

TABLE 2. Partial Listing of Foreign Exchange Rates

Country	Price in $ U.S.	Country	Price in $ U.S.
Britain (pound)	1.61	Hong Kong (dollar)	0.128
Canada (dollar)	0.704	Japan (yen)	0.008
Europe (euro)	1.12	Mexico (peso)	0.10

Source: The Wall Street Journal, May 5, 2003.

*At the time this chapter was written, exchange rates were fluctuating rapidly. The examples, exercises, and probems in this book use exchange rates in the general range for the countries involved.

ACCOUNTING FOR TRANSACTIONS IN FOREIGN CURRENCIES

A U.S. manufacturer may expand by selling its product to foreign customers, or it may lower its product cost by buying a less expensive part from a source in another country. In previous chapters of the text, all purchases and sales were recorded in dollars, and it was assumed that the dollar is a uniform measure in the same way that the inch and the centimeter are. But in the international marketplace, a transaction may take place in Japanese yen, British pounds, or some other currency. The values of these currencies in relation to the dollar rise and fall daily. Thus, if there is a delay between the date of sale or purchase and the date of receipt or payment, the amount of cash involved may differ from that originally agreed upon.

■ **FOREIGN SALES** When a domestic company sells merchandise abroad, it may bill either in its own country's currency or in the foreign currency. If the billing and payment are both in the domestic currency, no accounting problem arises. For example, assume that a U.S. maker of precision tools sells $160,000 worth of its products to a British company and bills the British company in dollars. The entry to record the sale and receipt of payment is familiar:

Date of Sale

A = L + OE   Accounts Receivable, British company   160,000
+   +   Sales   160,000

Date of Receipt

A = L + OE   Cash   160,000
+   Accounts Receivable, British company   160,000
−

However, if the U.S. company bills the British company in British pounds and accepts payment in pounds, the U.S. company may incur an *exchange gain or loss*. A gain or loss will occur if the exchange rate between dollars and pounds changes between the date of sale and the date of receipt. Since gains and losses tend to offset one another, a single account is used during the year to accumulate the activity. The net exchange gain or loss is reported on the income statement. For example, assume that the sale of $160,000 above was billed at £100,000, reflecting an exchange rate of 1.60 (that is, $1.60 per pound) on the sale date. Now assume that by the date of receipt, the exchange rate has fallen to 1.50. The entries to record the transactions follow:

Date of Sale

A = L + OE   Accounts Receivable, British company   160,000
+   +   Sales   160,000
               £100,000 × $1.60 = $160,000

Date of Receipt

A = L + OE   Cash   150,000
+   −   Exchange Gain or Loss   10,000
−   Accounts Receivable, British company   160,000
               £100,000 × $1.50 = $150,000

The U.S. company has incurred an exchange loss of $10,000 because it agreed to accept a fixed number of British pounds in payment for its products, and the value of each pound dropped before the payment was made. Had the value of the pound in relation to the dollar increased, the U.S. company would have made an exchange gain.

■ **FOREIGN PURCHASES** The same logic applies to purchases as to sales, except that the relationship of exchange gains and losses to changes in exchange rates is reversed. For example, assume that the U.S. toolmaker purchases parts from a Japanese supplier for $15,000. If the purchase and payment are made in U.S. dollars, no accounting problem arises.

Date of Purchase

A = L + OE	Purchases	15,000	
+ −	Accounts Payable, Japanese company		15,000

Date of Payment

A = L + OE	Accounts Payable, Japanese company	15,000	
− −	Cash		15,000

However, the Japanese company may bill the U.S. company in yen and be paid in yen. If so, the U.S. company will incur an exchange gain or loss if the exchange rate changes between the date of purchase and the date of payment. For example, assume that the transaction is for ¥2,500,000 and that the exchange rates on the dates of purchase and payment are $.0090 and $.0085 per yen, respectively. The entries are as follows:

Date of Purchase

A = L + OE	Purchases	22,500	
+ −	Accounts Payable, Japanese company		22,500
	¥2,500,000 × $.0090 = $22,500		

Date of Payment

A = L + OE	Accounts Payable, Japanese company	22,500	
− − +	Exchange Gain or Loss		1,250
	Cash		21,250
	¥2,500,000 × $.0085 = $21,250		

In this case, the U.S. company received an exchange gain of $1,250 because it agreed to pay a fixed ¥2,500,000, and between the dates of purchase and payment, the exchange value of the yen decreased in relation to the dollar.

■ **REALIZED VERSUS UNREALIZED EXCHANGE GAIN OR LOSS** The preceding illustrations dealt with completed transactions (in the sense that payment was made). In each case, the exchange gain or loss was recognized on the date of receipt or payment. If financial statements are prepared between the sale or purchase and the receipt or payment and exchange rates have changed, there will be unrealized gains or losses. The Financial Accounting Standards Board's *Statement No. 52* requires that exchange gains and losses "be included in determining net income for the period in which the exchange rate changes."[2] The requirement includes interim (quarterly) statements and applies whether or not a transaction is complete.

This ruling has caused much debate. Critics charge that it gives too much weight to fleeting changes in exchange rates, causing random changes in earnings that hide long-run trends. Others believe that the use of current exchange rates to value receivables and payables as of the balance sheet date is a major step toward economic reality (current values). To illustrate, we use the preceding case, in which a U.S. company buys parts from a Japanese supplier. We assume that the transaction has not been completed by the balance sheet date, when the exchange rate is $.0080 per yen:

	Date	Exchange Rate ($ per Yen)
Date of purchase	Dec. 1	.0090
Balance sheet date	Dec. 31	.0080
Date of payment	Feb. 1	.0085

The accounting effects of the unrealized gain are as follows:

	Dec. 1	Dec. 31	Feb. 1
Purchase recorded in U.S. dollars (billed as ¥2,500,000)	$22,500	$22,500	$22,500
Dollars to be paid to equal ¥2,500,000 (¥2,500,000 × exchange rate)	22,500	20,000	21,250
Unrealized gain (or loss)	—	$ 2,500	
Realized gain (or loss)			$ 1,250

A = L + OE + −	Dec. 1	Purchases Accounts Payable, Japanese company	22,500	22,500
A = L + OE − +	Dec. 31	Accounts Payable, Japanese company Exchange Gain or Loss	2,500	2,500
A = L + OE − − −	Feb. 1	Accounts Payable, Japanese company Exchange Gain or Loss Cash	20,000 1,250	21,250

In this case, the original sale was billed in yen by the Japanese company. Following the rules of *Statement No. 52*, an exchange gain of $2,500 is recorded on December 31, and an exchange loss of $1,250 is recorded on February 1. Even though these large fluctuations do not affect the net exchange gain of $1,250 for the whole transaction, the effect on each year's income statements may be important.

RESTATEMENT OF FOREIGN SUBSIDIARY FINANCIAL STATEMENTS

Companies often expand by establishing or buying foreign subsidiaries. If a company owns more than 50 percent of a foreign subsidiary and thus exercises control, then the foreign subsidiary should be included in the consolidated financial statements. The reporting of foreign subsidiaries is covered by FASB *Statement No. 52*. The consolidation procedure is the same as the one we described for domestic subsidiaries, except that the statements of the foreign subsidiary must be restated in the reporting currency before consolidation takes place. The *reporting currency* is the currency in which the consolidated financial statements are presented, which for U.S. companies is usually the U.S. dollar. Clearly, it makes no sense to combine the assets of a Mexican subsidiary stated in pesos with the assets of the U.S. parent company stated in dollars. Thus, *restatement* in the currency of the parent company is necessary.

The method of restatement depends on the foreign subsidiary's *functional currency*, which is the currency of the place where the subsidiary carries on most of its business. Generally, it is the currency in which a company earns and spends its cash. The functional currency used depends on the kind of foreign operation in which the subsidiary takes part.

There are two broad types of foreign operation. Type I includes those that are fairly self-contained and integrated within a certain country or economy. Type II includes those that are mainly a direct and integral part or extension of the parent company's operations. As a rule, Type I subsidiaries use the currency of the country in which they are located, and Type II subsidiaries use the currency of the parent company. If the parent is a U.S. company, the functional currency of a Type I subsidiary will be the currency of the country where the subsidiary carries on its business, and the functional currency of a Type II subsidiary will be the U.S. dollar. *Statement No. 52* makes an exception when a Type I subsidiary operates in a country where there is hyperinflation (as a rule of thumb, more than 100 percent cumulative inflation over three years), such as Brazil or Argentina. In such a case, the subsidiary is treated as a Type II subsidiary, with the functional currency being the U.S. dollar. Restatements in these situations do not affect cash flows because they are done simply for the convenience of preparing consolidated statements.

INTERNATIONAL ACCOUNTING STANDARDS

International investors need to compare the financial position and results of operations of companies from different countries. At present, however, few standards of accounting are recognized worldwide.[3] For example, LIFO is the most popular method of valuing inventory in the United States, but it is not acceptable in most European countries. Historical cost is strictly followed in Germany, replacement cost is used by some companies in the Netherlands, and a mixed system, allowing lower of cost or market in some cases, is used in the United States and Britain. Even the formats of financial statements differ from country to country. In Britain and France, for example, the order of the balance sheets is almost the reverse of that in the United States. In those countries, property, plant, and equipment is the first listing in the assets section.

A number of major problems stand in the way of setting international standards. One is that accountants and users of accounting information have not been able to agree on the goals of financial statements. Differences in the way the accounting profession has developed in various countries, in the laws regulating companies, and in governmental and other requirements present other hurdles. Further difficulties are created by differences among countries in the basic economic factors affecting financial reporting, inconsistencies in practices recommended by the accounting profession in different countries, and the influence of tax laws on financial reporting.

Probably the best hopes for finding areas of agreement among different countries are the International Accounting Standards Board (IASB) and the International Federation of Accountants (IFAC).

The role of the IASB is to contribute to the development and adoption of accounting principles that are relevant, balanced, and comparable throughout the world by formulating and publicizing accounting standards and encouraging their observance in the presentation of financial statements.[4] The standards issued by the IASB are generally followed by large multinational companies that are clients of international accounting firms. The IASB has been especially helpful to companies in developing economies that do not have the financial history or resources to develop accounting standards. The IASB is currently engaged in a major project to improve financial reporting worldwide by introducing a set of international accounting standards that will be acceptable to the world's securities regulators, such as the SEC in the United States. If successful, the effort should make it easier for companies to raise equity capital and list their stocks in other countries.

The IFAC, formed in 1977, also includes most of the world's accountancy organizations. It fully supports the work of the IASB and recognizes the IASB as the sole body with responsibility and authority to issue pronouncements on international accounting standards. The IFAC's principal role is to assure quality audits and financial statements prepared in accordance with international accounting standards. It attempts to accomplish this objective by issuing international auditing standards and monitoring the practice of international firms.

PROBLEMS

P 1.
Recording International Transactions: Fluctuating Exchange Rate

Part A: Wooster Corporation purchased a special-purpose machine from Konigsberg Corporation on credit for E 50,000. At the date of purchase, the exchange rate was $.90 per euro. On the date of the payment, which was made in euros, the value of the euro was $.95. Prepare entries in journal form to record the purchase and payment in Wooster Corporation's accounting records.

Part B: U.S. Corporation made a sale on account to U.K. Company on November 15 in the amount of £300,000. Payment was to be made in British pounds on February 15. U.S. Corporation's fiscal year is the same as the calendar year. The British pound was worth $1.70 on November 15, $1.58 on December 31, and $1.78 on February 15. Prepare entries in journal form to record the sale, year-end adjustment, and collection on U.S. Corporation's books.

P 2.
International Transactions

Dolfsky Import/Export Company, whose year end is October 31, engaged in the following transactions (exchange rates in parentheses):

Aug. 12 Sold goods to a Mexican firm for $20,000; terms n/30 in U.S. dollars (peso = $.131).

24 Purchased goods from a Japanese firm for $40,000; terms n/20 in yen (yen = $.0080).

Sept. 2 Sold goods to a British firm for $48,000; terms n/30 in pounds (pound = $1.60).

11 Received payment in full for August 12 sale (peso = $.128).

13 Paid for the goods purchased on August 24 (yen = $.0088).

21 Purchased goods from an Italian firm for $28,000; terms n/10 in U.S. dollars (euro = $.90).

30 Purchased goods from a Japanese firm for $35,200; terms n/60 in yen (yen = $.0088).

Oct. 2 Paid for the goods purchased on September 21 (euro = $.85).

3 Received payment in full for the goods sold on September 2 (pound = $1.50).

8 Sold goods to a French firm for $66,000; terms n/30 in euros (euro = $.88).

19 Purchased goods from a Mexican firm for $37,000; terms n/30 in U.S. dollars (peso = $.135).

31 Made year-end adjusting entries for incomplete foreign exchange transactions (euro = $.85; peso = $.130; pound = $1.40; yen = $.0100).

Nov. 9 Received payment for the goods sold on October 8 (euro = $.87).

18 Paid for the goods purchased on October 19 (peso = $.132).

28 Paid for the goods purchased on September 30 (yen = $.0090).

REQUIRED ▶ Prepare entries in journal form for these transactions.

Appendix B
Long-Term Investments

www.pepsico.com

Companies make long-term investments for a variety of reasons. For instance, PepsiCo makes investments in operations critical to the distribution of its products, such as its investments in PepsiCo Bottling Company. It also makes investments to expand its markets, as in its purchases of Tropicana, South Beach Beverage, and Quaker Oats. These are stock investments, but a company can also make long-term investments in bonds. Investments in bonds can be a way of ensuring that an affiliate company has sufficient long-term capital, or it can simply be a way of making a relatively secure investment. The following sections discuss the classifications of bonds and stocks and the methods used to account for such investments.

Long-Term Investments in Bonds

Like all investments, investments in bonds are recorded at cost, which, in this case, is the price of the bonds plus the broker's commission. When bonds are purchased between interest payment dates, the purchaser must also pay an amount equal to the interest that has accrued on the bonds since the last interest payment date. Then, on the next interest payment date, the purchaser receives an interest payment for the whole period. The payment for accrued interest should be recorded as a debit to Interest Income, which will be offset by a credit to Interest Income when the semiannual interest is received.

Subsequent accounting for a corporation's long-term bond investments depends on the classification of the bonds. If the company plans at some point to sell the bonds, they are classified as *available-for-sale securities*. If the company plans to hold the bonds until they are paid off on their maturity date, they are considered *held-to-maturity securities*. Except in industries like insurance and banking, it is unusual for companies to buy the bonds of other companies with the express purpose of holding them until they mature, which can be in 10 to 30 years. Thus, most long-term bond investments are available-for-sale securities. Such bonds are accounted for at fair value, much as equity or stock investments are; fair value is usually the market value. When bonds are intended to be held to maturity, they are accounted for not at fair value but at cost, adjusted for the amortization of their discount or premium. The procedure is similar to accounting for long-term bond liabilities, except that separate accounts for discounts and premiums are not used.

KEY POINT: The fair value of bonds is closely related to interest rates. An increase in interest rates lowers the fair value of bonds, and vice versa.

Long-Term Investments in Stocks

All long-term investments in stocks are recorded at cost, in accordance with generally accepted accounting principles. The treatment of the investment in the accounting records after the initial purchase depends on the extent to which the investing company can exercise *significant influence* or *control* over the operating and financial policies of the other company. The Accounting Principles Board (APB) defined these important terms in its *Opinion No. 18*.

Significant influence is an investing firm's ability to affect the operating and financial policies of the company whose shares it owns, even though it holds 50 percent or less of the voting stock. Indications of significant influence include representation on the board of directors, participation in policymaking, and material

KEY POINT: Influence and control are related specifically to equity holdings, not debt holdings.

TABLE 1. Accounting Treatments of Long-Term Investments in Stocks

Level of Ownership	Percentage of Ownership	Accounting Treatment
Noninfluential and noncontrolling	Less than 20%	Cost initially; investment adjusted subsequent to purchase for changes in market value
Influential but noncontrolling	Between 20% and 50%	Equity method; investment valued subsequently at cost plus investor's share of income (or minus investor's share of loss) minus dividends received
Controlling	More than 50%	Financial statements consolidated

transactions, exchange of managerial personnel, and technological dependency between the two companies. For the sake of uniformity, the APB decided that without proof to the contrary, ownership of 20 percent or more of the voting stock should be presumed to confer significant influence.* Ownership of less than 20 percent of the voting stock does not confer significant influence.

Control is an investing firm's ability to decide the operating and financial policies of the other company. Control exists when the investor owns more than 50 percent of the voting stock of the company in which it has invested.

Thus, in the absence of information to the contrary, a noninfluential and noncontrolling investment would be less than 20 percent ownership. An influential but noncontrolling investment would be 20 to 50 percent ownership. And a controlling investment would be more than 50 percent ownership. The accounting treatment differs for each kind of investment. Table 1 summarizes these treatments.

■ **NONINFLUENTIAL AND NONCONTROLLING INVESTMENT** Available-for-sale securities are debt or equity securities that are not classified as trading or held-to-maturity securities. When equity securities are involved, a further criterion is that they be noninfluential and noncontrolling investments of less than 20 percent of the voting stock. The Financial Accounting Standards Board requires a *cost-adjusted-to market method* for accounting for available-for-sale securities. Under this method, available-for-sale securities must be recorded initially at cost and thereafter adjusted periodically through the use of an allowance account to reflect changes in the market value.[1]

Available-for-sale securities are classified as long term if management intends to hold them for more than one year. When accounting for long-term available-for-sale

---

*The Financial Accounting Standards Board pointed out in its *Interpretation No. 35* (May 1981) that this rule is not a rigid one. All relevant facts and circumstances should be examined to determine whether significant influence exists. The FASB noted five circumstances that may negate significant influence: (1) The company files a lawsuit against the investor or a complaint with a government agency; (2) the investor tries but fails to become a director; (3) the investor agrees not to increase its holdings; (4) the company is operated by a small group that ignores the investor's wishes; (5) the investor tries but fails to obtain company information that is not available to other stockholders.

securities, the unrealized gain or loss resulting from the adjustment is not reported on the income statement. Instead, the gain or loss is reported as a special item in the stockholders' equity section of the balance sheet and in comprehensive income disclosure.

At the end of each accounting period, the total cost and the total market value of these long-term stock investments must be determined. If the total market value is less than the total cost, the difference must be credited to a contra-asset account called Allowance to Adjust Long-Term Investments to Market. Because of the long-term nature of the investment, the debit part of the entry, which represents a decrease in value below cost, is treated as a temporary decrease and does not appear as a loss on the income statement. It is shown in a contra-stockholders' equity account called Unrealized Loss on Long-Term Investments.* Thus, both of these accounts are balance sheet accounts. If the market value exceeds the cost, the allowance account is added to Long-Term Investments, and the unrealized gain appears as an addition to stockholders' equity.

When long-term investments in stock are sold, the difference between the sale price and the cost of the stock is recorded and reported as a realized gain or loss on the income statement. Dividend income from such investments is recorded by a debit to Cash and a credit to Dividend Income. For example, assume the following facts about the long-term stock investments of Coleman Corporation:

June 1, 20x3   Paid cash for the following long-term investments: 10,000 shares of Durbin Corporation common stock (representing 2 percent of outstanding stock) at $25 per share; 5,000 shares of Kotes Corporation common stock (representing 3 percent of outstanding stock) at $15 per share.

Dec. 31, 20x3   Quoted market prices at year end: Durbin common stock, $21; Kotes common stock, $17.

KEY POINT: On April 1, 20x4, a *change in policy* requires the sale. This points out that intent is often the only difference between long-term investments and short-term investments.

Apr. 1, 20x4   Change in policy required sale of 2,000 shares of Durbin common stock at $23.

July 1, 20x4   Received cash dividend from Kotes equal to $.20 per share.

Dec. 31, 20x4   Quoted market prices at year end: Durbin common stock, $24; Kotes common stock, $13.

Entries to record these transactions are as follows:

Investment

A = L + OE
+
—

20x3			
June 1	Long-Term Investments	325,000	
	Cash		325,000
	Investments in Durbin common stock (10,000 shares × $25 = $250,000) and Kotes common stock (5,000 shares × $15 = $75,000)		

Year-End Adjustment

A = L + OE
—   —

20x3			
Dec. 31	Unrealized Loss on Long-Term Investments	30,000	
	Allowance to Adjust Long-Term Investments to Market		30,000
	To record reduction of long-term investment to market		

---

*If the decrease in market value of the long-term investment is deemed permanent, a different procedure is followed to record the decline. A loss account on the income statement is debited instead of the Unrealized Loss account.

Long-Term Investments in Stocks

Company	Shares	Market Price	Total Market	Total Cost
Durbin	10,000	$21	$210,000	$250,000
Kotes	5,000	17	85,000	75,000
			$295,000	$325,000

Total Cost − Total Market Value = $325,000 − $295,000 = $30,000

Sale

A = L + OE	20x4			
+	Apr. 1	Cash	46,000	
−		Loss on Sale of Investments	4,000	
		Long-Term Investments		50,000
		Sale of 2,000 shares of Durbin		
		common stock		
		2,000 × $23 = $46,000		
		2,000 × $25 = 50,000		
		Loss $ 4,000		

Dividend Received

A = L + OE	20x4			
+	July 1	Cash	1,000	
+		Dividend Income		1,000
		Receipt of cash dividend from Kotes stock		
		5,000 × $.20 = $1,000		

Year-End Adjustment

A = L + OE	20x4			
+	Dec. 31	Allowance to Adjust Long-Term		
+		Investments to Market	12,000	
		Unrealized Loss on Long-Term		
		Investments		12,000
		To record the adjustment in long-		
		term investment so it is reported		
		at market		

The adjustment equals the previous balance ($30,000 from the December 31, 20x3, entry) minus the new balance ($18,000), or $12,000. The new balance of $18,000 is the difference at the present time between the total market value and the total cost of all investments. It is figured as follows:

Company	Shares	Market Price	Total Market	Total Cost
Durbin	8,000	$24	$192,000	$200,000
Kotes	5,000	13	65,000	75,000
			$257,000	$275,000

Total Cost − Total Market Value = $275,000 − $257,000 = $18,000

The Allowance to Adjust Long-Term Investments to Market and the Unrealized Loss on Long-Term Investments are reciprocal contra accounts, each with the same dollar balance, as shown by the effects of these transactions on the T accounts:

Contra-Asset Account   **Contra-Stockholders' Equity Account**

Allowance to Adjust   Unrealized Loss on
Long-Term Investments to Market   Long-Term Investment

20x4	12,000	20x3	30,000	20x3	30,000	20x4	12,000
		Bal. 20x4	18,000	Bal. 20x4	18,000		

The Allowance account reduces long-term investments by the amount by which the cost of the investments exceeds market; the Unrealized Loss account reduces stockholders' equity by a similar amount. The opposite effects will exist if market value exceeds cost, resulting in an unrealized gain.

■ **INFLUENTIAL BUT NONCONTROLLING INVESTMENT** As we have noted, ownership of 20 percent or more of a company's voting stock is considered sufficient to influence the company's operations. When this is the case, the stock investment should be accounted for using the *equity method*. The equity method presumes that an investment of 20 percent or more is not a passive investment and that the investor should therefore share proportionately in the success or failure of the company. The three main features of this method are as follows:

1. The investor records the original purchase of the stock at cost.
2. The investor records its share of the company's periodic net income as an increase in the Investment account, with a corresponding credit to an income account. Similarly, it records its share of a periodic loss as a decrease in the Investment account, with a corresponding debit to a loss account.
3. When the investor receives a cash dividend, the asset account Cash is increased, and the Investment account is decreased.

To illustrate the equity method of accounting, we assume the following facts about an investment by Vassor Corporation: On January 1 of the current year, Vassor acquired 40 percent of the voting common stock of Block Corporation for $180,000. With this share of ownership, Vassor can exert significant influence over Block's operations. During the year, Block reported net income of $80,000 and paid cash dividends of $20,000. Vassor recorded these transactions as follows:

Investment

A = L + OE	Investment in Block Corporation	180,000	
+ −	Cash		180,000
	Investment in Block Corporation common stock		

Recognition of Income

A = L + OE	Investment in Block Corporation	32,000	
+ +	Income, Block Corporation Investment		32,000
	Recognition of 40% of income reported by Block Corporation 40% × $80,000 = $32,000		

Receipt of Cash Dividend

A = L + OE	Cash	8,000	
+ −	Investment in Block Corporation		8,000
	Cash dividend from Block Corporation 40% × $20,000 = $8,000		

The balance of the Investment in Block Corporation account after these transactions is $204,000, as shown here:

Investment in Block Corporation

Investment	180,000	Dividend received	8,000
Share of Income	32,000		
Balance	204,000		

STUDY POINT: Under the equity method, dividends received are credited to the Investment account because the dividends represent a return from or a decrease in the investment in Block Corporation.

■ **CONTROLLING INVESTMENT** Some investing firms that own less than 50 percent of the voting stock of a company exercise such powerful influence that for all practical purposes, they control the policies of the other company. Nevertheless, ownership of more than 50 percent of the voting stock is required for accounting recognition of control. When a firm has a controlling interest, a parent-subsidiary relationship is said to exist. The investing company is known as the *parent company*; the other company is a *subsidiary*. Because the two corporations are separate legal entities, each prepares separate financial statements. However, owing to their special relationship, they are viewed for public financial reporting purposes as a single economic entity. For this reason, they must combine their financial statements into a single set of statements called *consolidated financial statements*.

Accounting for consolidated financial statements is complex and is usually the subject of an advanced accounting course. However, most large public corporations have subsidiaries and must prepare consolidated financial statements. It is therefore important to have some understanding of accounting for consolidations.

ENRICHMENT NOTE:
Parents and subsidiaries are separate legal entities even though they combine their financial reports at year end.

PROBLEMS

P 1.
Methods of Accounting for Long-Term Investments

Diversified Corporation has the following long-term investments:

1. 60 percent of the common stock of Down Corporation
2. 13 percent of the common stock of West Lake, Inc.
3. 50 percent of the nonvoting preferred stock of Invole Corporation
4. 100 percent of the common stock of its financing subsidiary, DCF, Inc.
5. 35 percent of the common stock of the French company Maison de Boutaine
6. 70 percent of the common stock of the Canadian company Alberta Mining Company

For each of these investments, tell which of the following methods should be used for external financial reporting, and why.

a. Cost adjusted to market method
b. Equity method
c. Consolidation of parent and subsidiary financial statements

P 2.
Long-Term Investment Transactions

Red Bud Corporation made the following transactions in its Long-Term Investments account over a two-year period:

20x4
Apr. 1 Purchased with cash 20,000 shares of Season Company stock for $152 per share.
June 1 Purchased with cash 15,000 shares of Abbado Corporation stock for $72 per share.
Sept. 1 Received a $1 per share dividend from Season Company.
Nov. 1 Purchased with cash 25,000 shares of Frankel Corporation stock for $110 per share.
Dec. 31 Market values per share of shares held in the Long-Term Investments account were as follows: Season Company, $140; Abbado Corporation, $32; and Frankel Corporation, $122.

20x4
Feb. 1 Because of unfavorable prospects for Abbado Corporation, Abbado stock was sold for cash at $40 per share.
May 1 Purchased with cash 10,000 shares of Schulian Corporation for $224 per share.
Sept. 1 Received $2 per share dividend from Season Company.
Dec. 31 Market values per share of shares held in the Long-Term Investments account were as follows: Season Company, $160; Frankel Corporation, $140; and Schulian Corporation, $200.

REQUIRED ▶ Prepare entries to record these transactions in the Red Bud Corporation records. Assume that all investments represent less than 20 percent of the voting stock of the company whose stock was acquired.

Long-Term Investments: Equity Method

P 3. The Modi Company owns 40 percent of the voting stock of the Vivanco Company. The Investment account for this company on the Modi Company's balance sheet had a balance of $600,000 on January 1, 20xx. During 20xx, the Vivanco Company reported the following quarterly earnings and dividends paid:

Quarter	Earnings	Dividends Paid
1	$ 80,000	$ 40,000
2	60,000	40,000
3	160,000	40,000
4	(40,000)	40,000
	$260,000	$160,000

The Modi Company exercises a significant influence over the operations of the Vivanco Company and therefore uses the equity method to account for its investment.

REQUIRED ▶
1. Prepare the entries in journal form that the Modi Company must make each quarter in accounting for its investment in the Vivanco Company.
2. Prepare a T account for the investment in common stock of the Vivanco Company. Enter the beginning balance, relevant portions of the entries made in **1**, and the ending balance.

Appendix C

The Time Value of Money

SIMPLE INTEREST AND COMPOUND INTEREST

Interest is the cost associated with the use of money for a specific period of time. Because interest is a cost associated with time, and "time is money," it is also an important consideration in any business decision. *Simple interest* is the interest cost for one or more periods, under the assumption that the amount on which the interest is computed stays the same from period to period. *Compound interest* is the interest cost for two or more periods, under the assumption that after each period the interest of that period is added to the amount on which interest is computed in future periods. In other words, compound interest is interest earned on a principal sum that is increased at the end of each period by the interest for that period.

EXAMPLE—SIMPLE INTEREST Joe Sanchez accepts an 8 percent, $30,000 note due in ninety days. How much will he receive in total at that time? Remember that the formula for calculating simple interest is as follows:

$$\begin{aligned}\text{Interest} &= \text{Principal} \times \text{Rate} \times \text{Time} \\ &= \$30{,}000 \times 8/100 \times 90/360 \\ &= \$600\end{aligned}$$

Therefore, the total that Sanchez will receive is calculated as follows:

$$\begin{aligned}\text{Total} &= \text{Principal} + \text{Interest} \\ &= \$30{,}000 + \$600 \\ &= \$30{,}600\end{aligned}$$

EXAMPLE—COMPOUND INTEREST Ann Clary deposits $5,000 in a savings account that pays 6 percent interest. She expects to leave the principal and accumulated interest in the account for three years. How much will her account total at the end of three years? Assume that the interest is paid at the end of the year and is added to the principal at that time, and that this total in turn earns interest. The amount at the end of three years is computed as follows:

(1) Year	(2) Principal Amount at Beginning of Year	(3) Annual Amount of Interest (Col. 2 × 6%)	(4) Accumulated Amount at End of Year (Col. 2 + Col. 3)
1	$5,000.00	$300.00	$5,300.00
2	5,300.00	318.00	5,618.00
3	5,618.00	337.08	5,955.08

At the end of three years, Clary will have $5,955.08 in her savings account. Note that the annual amount of interest increases each year by the interest rate times the interest of the previous year. For example, between year 1 and year 2, the interest increased by $18 ($318 − $300), which exactly equals 6 percent times $300.

FUTURE VALUE OF A SINGLE INVESTED SUM AT COMPOUND INTEREST

Another way to ask the question in the example of compound interest above is, What is the future value of a single sum ($5,000) at compound interest (6 percent) for three years? *Future value* is the amount that an investment will be worth at a future date if invested at compound interest. A businessperson often wants to know future value, but the method of computing the future value illustrated above is too time-consuming in practice. Imagine how tedious the calculation would be if the example were ten years instead of three. Fortunately, there are tables that simplify solving problems involving compound interest. Table 1, showing the future value of $1 after a given number of time periods, is an example. It is actually part of a larger table, Table 1 in the appendix on future value and present value tables. Suppose that we want to solve the problem of Clary's savings account above. We simply look down the 6 percent column in Table 1 until we reach the line for three periods and find the factor 1.191. This factor, when multiplied by $1, gives the future value of that $1 at compound interest of 6 percent for three periods (years in this case). Thus, we solve the problem as follows:

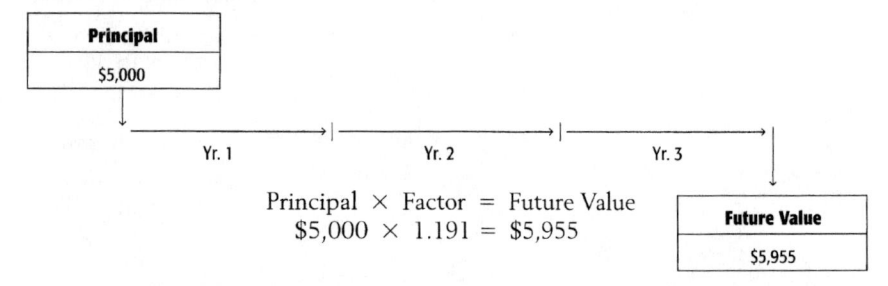

Principal × Factor = Future Value
$5,000 × 1.191 = $5,955

Except for a rounding difference of $.08, the answer is exactly the same as that calculated earlier.

TABLE 1. Future Value of $1 after a Given Number of Time Periods

Periods	1%	2%	3%	4%	5%	6%	7%	8%	9%	10%	12%	14%	15%
1	1.010	1.020	1.030	1.040	1.050	1.060	1.070	1.080	1.090	1.100	1.120	1.140	1.150
2	1.020	1.040	1.061	1.082	1.103	1.124	1.145	1.166	1.188	1.210	1.254	1.300	1.323
3	1.030	1.061	1.093	1.125	1.158	1.191	1.225	1.260	1.295	1.331	1.405	1.482	1.521
4	1.041	1.082	1.126	1.170	1.216	1.262	1.311	1.360	1.412	1.464	1.574	1.689	1.749
5	1.051	1.104	1.159	1.217	1.276	1.338	1.403	1.469	1.539	1.611	1.762	1.925	2.011
6	1.062	1.126	1.194	1.265	1.340	1.419	1.501	1.587	1.677	1.772	1.974	2.195	2.313
7	1.072	1.149	1.230	1.316	1.407	1.504	1.606	1.714	1.828	1.949	2.211	2.502	2.660
8	1.083	1.172	1.267	1.369	1.477	1.594	1.718	1.851	1.993	2.144	2.476	2.853	3.059
9	1.094	1.195	1.305	1.423	1.551	1.689	1.838	1.999	2.172	2.358	2.773	3.252	3.518
10	1.105	1.219	1.344	1.480	1.629	1.791	1.967	2.159	2.367	2.594	3.106	3.707	4.046

Source: Excerpt from Table 1 in the appendix on future value and present value tables.

FUTURE VALUE OF AN ORDINARY ANNUITY

Another common problem involves an *ordinary annuity*, which is a series of equal payments made at the end of equal intervals of time, with compound interest on these payments.

The following example shows how to find the future value of an ordinary annuity. Assume that Ben Katz makes a $200 payment at the end of each of the next three years into a savings account that pays 5 percent interest. How much money will he have in his account at the end of the three years? One way of computing the amount is shown in the following table.

(1) Year	(2) Beginning Balance	(3) Interest Earned (5% × Col. 2)	(4) Periodic Payment	(5) Accumulated at End of Period (Col. 2 + Col. 3 + Col. 4)
1	—	—	$200	$200.00
2	$200.00	$10.00	200	410.00
3	410.00	20.50	200	630.50

Katz would have $630.50 in his account at the end of three years, consisting of $600.00 in periodic payments and $30.50 in interest.

This calculation can also be simplified by using Table 2. We look down the 5 percent column until we reach three periods and find the factor 3.153. This factor, when multiplied by $1, gives the future value of a series of three $1 payments at compound interest of 5 percent. Thus, we solve the problem as follows:

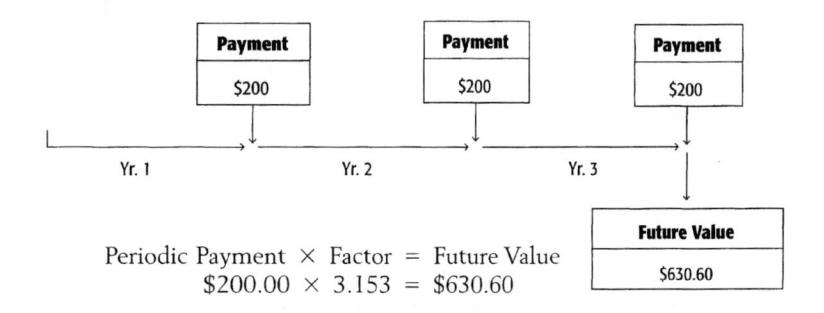

Periodic Payment × Factor = Future Value
$200.00 × 3.153 = $630.60

Except for a rounding difference of $.10, this result is the same as our earlier one.

PRESENT VALUE

Suppose that you had the choice of receiving $100 today or one year from today. Intuitively, you would choose to receive the $100 today. Why? You know that if you have the $100 today, you can put it in a savings account to earn interest, so that you will have more than $100 a year from today. Therefore, we can say that an amount to be received in the future (future value) is not worth as much today as an amount to be received today (present value) because of the cost associated with the passage of time. In fact, present value and future value are closely related. *Present value* is the amount that must be invested now at a given rate of interest to produce a given future value. For example, assume that Sue Dapper needs $1,000 one year from now. How much should she invest today to achieve that goal if the interest rate is 5 percent? From earlier examples, the following equation may be established.

$$\text{Present Value} \times (1.0 + \text{Interest Rate}) = \text{Future Value}$$
$$\text{Present Value} \times 1.05 = \$1,000.00$$
$$\text{Present Value} = \$1,000.00 \div 1.05$$
$$\text{Present Value} = \$952.38$$

Thus, to achieve a future value of $1,000.00, a present value of $952.38 must be invested. Interest of 5 percent on $952.38 for one year equals $47.62, and these two amounts added together equal $1,000.00.

■ **PRESENT VALUE OF A SINGLE SUM DUE IN THE FUTURE** When more than one time period is involved, the calculation of present value is more complicated. Consider the following example. Don Riley wants to be sure of having $4,000 at the end of three years. How much must he invest today in a 5 percent savings account to achieve this goal? Adapting the above equation, we compute the present value of $4,000 at compound interest of 5 percent for three years in the future.

Year	Amount at End of Year	Divide by	Present Value at Beginning of Year
3	$4,000.00	÷ 1.05 =	$3,809.52
2	3,809.52	÷ 1.05 =	3,628.11
1	3,628.11	÷ 1.05 =	3,455.34

Riley must invest a present value of $3,455.34 to achieve a future value of $4,000.00 in three years.

This calculation is again made much easier by using the appropriate table. In Table 3, we look down the 5 percent column until we reach three periods and find the factor .864. This factor, when multiplied by $1, gives the present value of $1 to be received three years from now at 5 percent interest. Thus, we solve the problem as shown on the next page.

TABLE 2. Future Value of an Ordinary Annuity of $1 Paid in Each Period for a Given Number of Time Periods

Periods	1%	2%	3%	4%	5%	6%	7%	8%	9%	10%	12%	14%	15%
1	1.000	1.000	1.000	1.000	1.000	1.000	1.000	1.000	1.000	1.000	1.000	1.000	1.000
2	2.010	2.020	2.030	2.040	2.050	2.060	2.070	2.080	2.090	2.100	2.120	2.140	2.150
3	3.030	3.060	3.091	3.122	3.153	3.184	3.215	3.246	3.278	3.310	3.374	3.440	3.473
4	4.060	4.122	4.184	4.246	4.310	4.375	4.440	4.506	4.573	4.641	4.779	4.921	4.993
5	5.101	5.204	5.309	5.416	5.526	5.637	5.751	5.867	5.985	6.105	6.353	6.610	6.742
6	6.152	6.308	6.468	6.633	6.802	6.975	7.153	7.336	7.523	7.716	8.115	8.536	8.754
7	7.214	7.434	7.662	7.898	8.142	8.394	8.654	8.923	9.200	9.487	10.09	10.73	11.07
8	8.286	8.583	8.892	9.214	9.549	9.897	10.26	10.64	11.03	11.44	12.30	13.23	13.73
9	9.369	9.755	10.16	10.58	11.03	11.49	11.98	12.49	13.02	13.58	14.78	16.09	16.79
10	10.46	10.95	11.46	12.01	12.58	13.18	13.82	14.49	15.19	15.94	17.55	19.34	20.30

Source: Excerpt from Table 2 in the appendix on future value and present value tables.

TABLE 3. Present Value of $1 to Be Received at the End of a Given Number of Time Periods

Periods	1%	2%	3%	4%	5%	6%	7%	8%	9%	10%
1	0.990	0.980	0.971	0.962	0.952	0.943	0.935	0.926	0.917	0.909
2	0.980	0.961	0.943	0.925	0.907	0.890	0.873	0.857	0.842	0.826
3	0.971	0.942	0.915	0.889	0.864	0.840	0.816	0.794	0.772	0.751
4	0.961	0.924	0.888	0.855	0.823	0.792	0.763	0.735	0.708	0.683
5	0.951	0.906	0.863	0.822	0.784	0.747	0.713	0.681	0.650	0.621
6	0.942	0.888	0.837	0.790	0.746	0.705	0.666	0.630	0.596	0.564
7	0.933	0.871	0.813	0.760	0.711	0.665	0.623	0.583	0.547	0.513
8	0.923	0.853	0.789	0.731	0.677	0.627	0.582	0.540	0.502	0.467
9	0.914	0.837	0.766	0.703	0.645	0.592	0.544	0.500	0.460	0.424
10	0.905	0.820	0.744	0.676	0.614	0.558	0.508	0.463	0.422	0.386

Source: Excerpt from Table 3 in the appendix on future value and present value tables.

Future Value
$4,000

Present Value
$3,456

Future Value × Factor = Present Value
$4,000 × .864 = $3,456

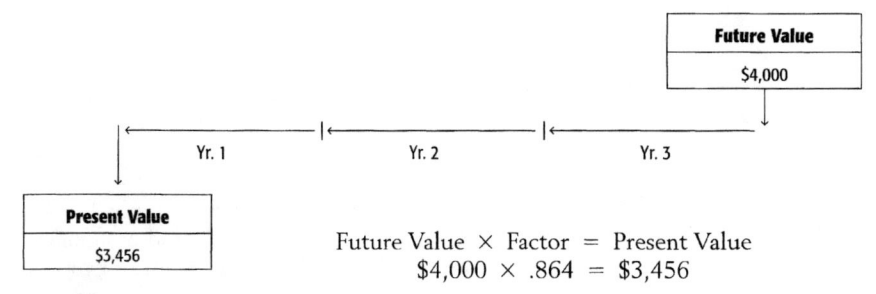

Except for a rounding difference of $.66, this result is the same as the one above.

■ **PRESENT VALUE OF AN ORDINARY ANNUITY** It is often necessary to compute the present value of a series of receipts or payments. When we calculate the present value of equal amounts equally spaced over a period of time, we are computing the present value of an ordinary annuity.

For example, assume that Kathy Foster has sold a piece of property and is to receive $15,000 in three equal annual payments of $5,000, beginning one year from today. What is the present value of this sale, assuming a current interest rate of 5 percent? This present value may be computed by calculating a separate present value for each of the three payments (using Table 3) and summing the results, as shown in the table below.

Future Receipts (Annuity)			Present Value Factor at 5 Percent (from Table 3)	Present Value
Year 1	Year 2	Year 3		
$5,000			× .952 =	$ 4,760
	$5,000		× .907 =	4,535
		$5,000	× .864 =	4,320
Total Present Value				$13,615

The present value of this sale is $13,615. Thus, there is an implied interest cost (given the 5 percent rate) of $1,385 associated with the payment plan that allows the purchaser to pay in three installments.

We can make this calculation more easily by using Table 4. We look down the 5 percent column until we reach three periods and find the factor 2.723. This factor, when multiplied by $1, gives the present value of a series of three $1 payments (spaced one year apart) at compound interest of 5 percent. Thus, we solve the problem as shown below.

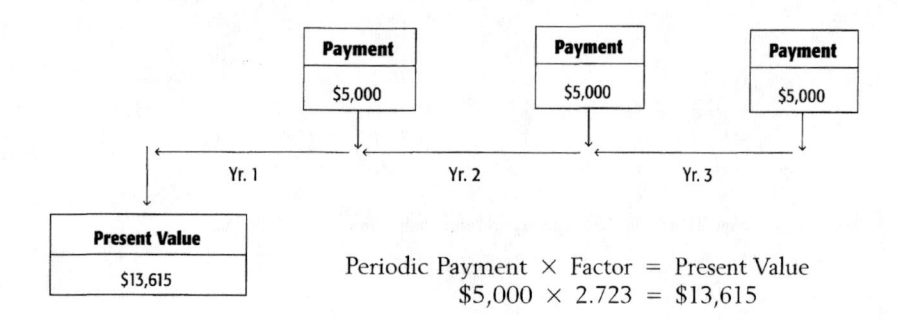

	Payment	Payment	Payment
	$5,000	$5,000	$5,000
	Yr. 1	Yr. 2	Yr. 3

Present Value
$13,615

Periodic Payment × Factor = Present Value
$5,000 × 2.723 = $13,615

This result is the same as the one computed earlier.

TIME PERIODS

In all of the previous examples, and in most other cases, the compounding period is one year, and the interest rate is stated on an annual basis. However, in each of the four tables, the left-hand column refers not to years but to periods. This wording is intended to accommodate compounding periods of less than one year. Savings accounts that record interest quarterly and bonds that pay interest semiannually are cases in which the compounding period is less than one year. To use the tables in such cases, it is necessary to (1) divide the annual interest rate by the number of periods in the year, and (2) multiply the number of periods in one year by the number of years.

For example, assume that a $6,000 note is to be paid in two years and carries an annual interest rate of 8 percent. Compute the maturity (future) value of the note, assuming that the compounding period is semiannual. Before using the table, it is

TABLE 4. Present Value of an Ordinary Annuity of $1 Received Each Period for a Given Number of Time Periods

Periods	1%	2%	3%	4%	5%	6%	7%	8%	9%	10%
1	0.990	0.980	0.971	0.962	0.952	0.943	0.935	0.926	0.917	0.909
2	1.970	1.942	1.913	1.886	1.859	1.833	1.808	1.783	1.759	1.736
3	2.941	2.884	2.829	2.775	2.723	2.673	2.624	2.577	2.531	2.487
4	3.902	3.808	3.717	3.630	3.546	3.465	3.387	3.312	3.240	3.170
5	4.853	4.713	4.580	4.452	4.329	4.212	4.100	3.993	3.890	3.791
6	5.795	5.601	5.417	5.242	5.076	4.917	4.767	4.623	4.486	4.355
7	6.728	6.472	6.230	6.002	5.786	5.582	5.389	5.206	5.033	4.868
8	7.652	7.325	7.020	6.733	6.463	6.210	5.971	5.747	5.535	5.335
9	8.566	8.162	7.786	7.435	7.108	6.802	6.515	6.247	5.995	5.759
10	9.471	8.983	8.530	8.111	7.722	7.360	7.024	6.710	6.418	6.145

Source: Excerpt from Table 4 in the appendix on future value and present value tables.

necessary to compute the interest rate that applies to each compounding period and the total number of compounding periods. First, the interest rate to use is 4 percent (8% annual rate ÷ 2 periods per year). Second, the total number of compounding periods is 4 (2 periods per year × 2 years). From Table 1, therefore, the maturity value of the note is computed as follows:

$$\text{Principal} \times \text{Factor} = \text{Future Value}$$
$$\$6{,}000 \times 1.170 = \$7{,}020$$

The note will be worth $7,020 in two years.

This procedure for determining the interest rate and the number of periods when the compounding period is less than one year may be used with all four tables.

APPLICATIONS OF PRESENT VALUE TO ACCOUNTING

The concept of present value is widely applicable in the discipline of accounting. Here, the purpose is to demonstrate its usefulness in some simple applications. In-depth study of present value is deferred to more advanced courses.

■ **IMPUTING INTEREST ON NON-INTEREST-BEARING NOTES** Clearly there is no such thing as an interest-free debt, regardless of whether the interest rate is explicitly stated. The Accounting Principles Board has declared that when a long-term note does not explicitly state an interest rate (or if the interest rate is unreasonably low), a rate based on the normal interest cost of the company in question should be assigned, or imputed.[1]

The following example applies this principle. On January 1, 20x0, Gato purchased merchandise from Haines by issuing an $8,000 non-interest-bearing note due in two years. Gato can borrow money from the bank at 9 percent interest. Gato paid the note in full after two years.

Note that the $8,000 note represents partly a payment for merchandise and partly a payment of interest for two years. In recording the purchase and sale, it is necessary to use Table 3 to determine the present value of the note. The calculation follows.

$$\text{Future Payment} \times \text{Present Value Factor (9\%, 2 years)} = \text{Present Value}$$
$$\$8{,}000 \quad \times \quad .842 \quad = \quad \$6{,}736$$

The imputed interest cost is $1,264 ($8,000 − $6,736) and is recorded as a discount on notes payable in Gato's records and as a discount on notes receivable in Haines's records.

The entries necessary to record the purchase in the Gato records and the sale in the Haines records are as follows:

	Gato Journal			Haines Journal			
A = L + OE	Purchases	6,736		Notes Receivable	8,000		A = L + OE
− −	Discount on			Discount on			+ +
+	Notes Payable	1,264		Notes Receivable		1,264	−
	Notes Payable		8,000	Sales		6,736	

On December 31, 20x0, the adjustments to recognize the interest expense and interest income are as follows:

	Gato Journal			Haines Journal			
A = L + OE	Interest Expense	606.24		Discount on			A = L + OE
+ −	Discount on			Notes Receivable	606.24		+ +
	Notes Payable		606.24	Interest Income		606.24	

The interest is calculated by multiplying the amount of the original purchase by the interest rate for one year ($6,736.00 × .09 = $606.24). When payment is made on December 31, 20x0, the following entries are made in the respective journals.

	Gato Journal			Haines Journal		
A = L + OE	Interest Expense	657.76		Discount on		A = L + OE
− + −	Notes Payable	8,000.00		Notes Receivable	657.76	+ +
−	Discount on			Cash	8,000.00	+
	Notes Payable		657.76	Interest Income	657.76	−
	Cash		8,000.00	Notes Receivable	8,000.00	

The interest entries represent the remaining interest to be expensed or realized ($1,264 − $606.24 = $657.76). This amount approximates (because of rounding differences in the table) the interest for one year on the purchase plus last year's interest [($6,736 + $606.24) × .09 = $660.80].

■ **VALUING AN ASSET** An asset is recorded because it will provide future benefits to the company that owns it. These future benefits are the basis for the definition of an asset. Usually, the purchase price of the asset represents the present value of these future benefits. It is possible to evaluate a proposed purchase price for an asset by comparing that price with the present value of the asset to the company.

For example, Sam Hurst is thinking of buying a new machine that will reduce his annual labor cost by $700 per year. The machine will last eight years. The interest rate that Hurst assumes for making managerial decisions is 10 percent. What is the maximum amount (present value) that Hurst should pay for the machine?

The present value of the machine to Hurst is equal to the present value of an ordinary annuity of $700 per year for eight years at compound interest of 10 percent. Using the factor from Table 4, we compute the value as follows:

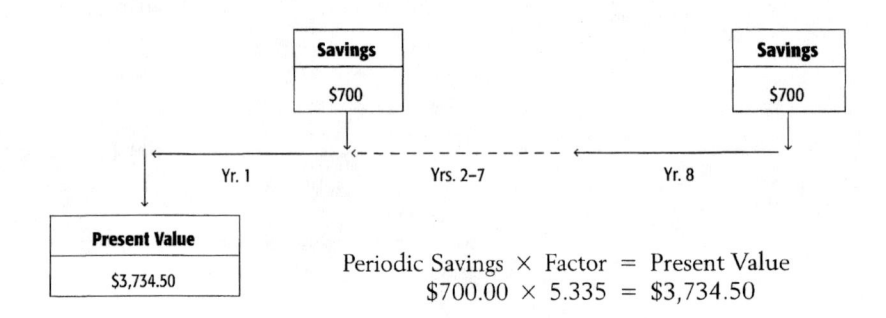

Periodic Savings × Factor = Present Value
$700.00 × 5.335 = $3,734.50

Hurst should not pay more than $3,734.50 for the new machine because this amount equals the present value of the benefits that will be received from owning the machine.

■ **DEFERRED PAYMENT** A seller will sometimes agree to defer payment for a sale in order to encourage the buyer to make the purchase. This practice is common, for example, in the farm implement industry, where the farmer needs the equipment in the spring but cannot pay for it until the fall crop is in. Assume that Plains Implement Corporation sells a tractor to Dana Washington for $50,000 on February 1, agreeing to take payment ten months later, on December 1. When this type of agreement is made, the future payment includes not only the sales price of the tractor but also an implied (imputed) interest cost. If the prevailing annual interest rate for such transactions is 12 percent compounded monthly, the actual sale (purchase) price of the tractor would be the present value of the future payment, computed using the factor from Table 3 (10 periods, 1 percent), as follows:

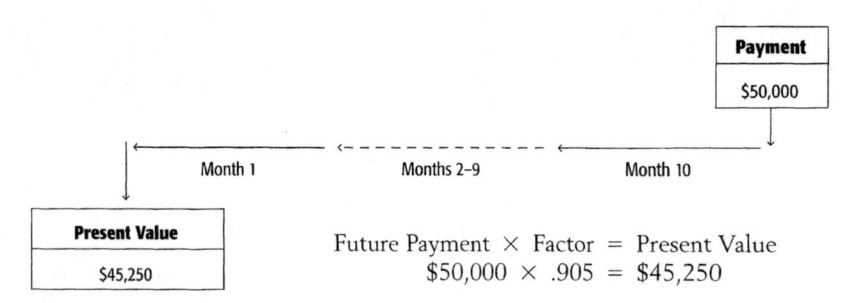

	Month 1	Months 2–9	Month 10

Payment: $50,000

Present Value: $45,250

Future Payment × Factor = Present Value
$50,000 × .905 = $45,250

The present value, $45,250, is recorded in Washington's purchase records and in Plains's sale records. The balance consists of interest income. Washington records the purchase and Plains records the sale using the following entries:

	Washington Journal			Plains Journal		

A = L + OE
+   +
	Feb. 1 Tractor
	    Accounts Payable
	    Purchased tractor
		45,250	45,250	Accounts Receivable
				    Sales
				    Sold tractor
					45,250	45,250	A = L + OE
							+ +

When Washington pays for the tractor, the entries are as follows:

	Washington Journal			Plains Journal		

A = L + OE
− − −
	Dec. 1 Accounts Payable
	    Interest Expense
	    Cash
	        Paid on account,
	        including imputed
	        interest expense
		45,250
		4,750
			50,000	Cash
				    Accounts Receivable
				    Interest Income
				        Received on account
				        from Washington,
				        including imputed
				        interest earned
					50,000	45,250
						4,750
							A = L + OE
							− +
							+

■ **INVESTMENT OF IDLE CASH** Childware Corporation, a toy manufacturer, has just completed a successful selling season and has $10,000,000 in cash to invest for six months. The company places the cash in a money market account expected to pay 12 percent annual interest. Interest is compounded and credited to the company's account monthly. How much cash will the company have at the end of six months, and what entries will be made to record the investment and the monthly interest? The future value factor from Table 1 is based on six monthly periods of 1 percent (12 percent divided by 12 months), and the future value is computed as follows:

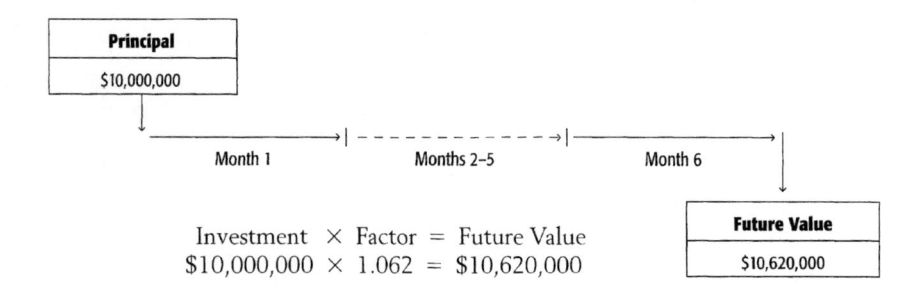

Principal: $10,000,000

	Month 1	Months 2–5	Month 6

Investment × Factor = Future Value
$10,000,000 × 1.062 = $10,620,000

Future Value: $10,620,000

When the investment is made, the following entry is made:

A = L + OE   Short-Term Investments   10,000,000
+   Cash   10,000,000
−   Made investment of cash

After the first month, the interest is recorded by increasing the Short-Term Investments account.

A = L + OE   Short-Term Investments   100,000
+   +   Interest Income   100,000
               Earned one month's interest income
               $10,000,000 × .01 = $100,000

After the second month, the interest is earned on the new balance of the Short-Term Investments account.

A = L + OE   Short-Term Investments   101,000
+   +   Interest Income   101,000
               Earned one month's interest income
               $10,100,000 × .01 = $101,000

Entries would continue in a similar manner for four more months, at which time the balance of Short-Term Investments would be about $10,620,000. The actual amount accumulated may vary from this total because the interest rate paid on money market accounts can vary over time as a result of changes in market conditions.

■ **ACCUMULATION OF A FUND** When a company owes a large fixed amount due in several years, management would be wise to accumulate a fund with which to pay off the debt at maturity. Sometimes creditors, when they agree to provide a loan, require that such a fund be established. In establishing the fund, management must determine how much cash to set aside each period in order to pay the debt. The amount will depend on the estimated rate of interest the investments will earn. Assume that Vason Corporation agrees with a creditor to set aside cash at the end of each year to accumulate enough to pay off a $100,000 note due in five years. Since the first contribution to the fund will be made in one year, five annual contributions will be made by the time the note is due. Assume also that the fund is projected to earn 8 percent, compounded annually. The amount of each annual payment is calculated using Table 2 (5 periods, 8 percent), as follows:

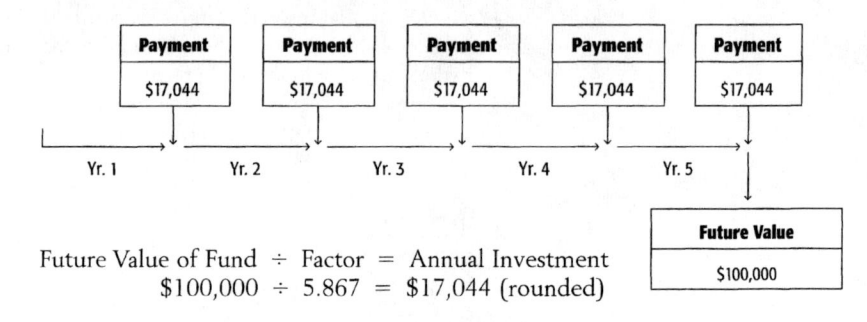

Payment	Payment	Payment	Payment	Payment
$17,044	$17,044	$17,044	$17,044	$17,044
Yr. 1	Yr. 2	Yr. 3	Yr. 4	Yr. 5

Future Value
$100,000

Future Value of Fund ÷ Factor = Annual Investment
$100,000 ÷ 5.867 = $17,044 (rounded)

Each year's contribution to the fund is $17,044, which is recorded as follows:

A = L + OE   Loan Repayment Fund   17,044
+   Cash   17,044
−   Recorded annual contribution to loan repayment fund

■ **OTHER ACCOUNTING APPLICATIONS** There are many other applications of present value in accounting, including accounting for installment notes, valuing a bond, and recording lease obligations. Present value is also applied in such areas as pension obligations; premium and discount on debt; depreciation of property, plant, and equipment; capital expenditure decisions; and generally any problem in which time is a factor.

EXERCISES

Tables 1 to 4 in the appendix on future value and present value tables may be used where appropriate to solve these exercises.

Future Value Calculations

E 1. Wieland receives a one-year note for $3,000 that carries a 12 percent annual interest rate for the sale of a used car.

Compute the maturity value under each of the following assumptions: (1) The interest is simple interest. (2) The interest is compounded semiannually. (3) The interest is compounded quarterly. (4) The interest is compounded monthly.

Future Value Calculations

E 2. Find the future value of (1) a single payment of $20,000 at 7 percent for ten years, (2) ten annual payments of $2,000 at 7 percent, (3) a single payment of $6,000 at 9 percent for seven years, and (4) seven annual payments of $6,000 at 9 percent.

Future Value Calculations

E 3. Assume that $40,000 is invested today. Compute the amount that would accumulate at the end of seven years when the interest rate is (1) 8 percent compounded annually, (2) 8 percent compounded semiannually, and (3) 8 percent compounded quarterly.

Future Value Calculations

E 4. Calculate the accumulation of periodic payments of $1,000 made at the end of each of four years, assuming (1) 10 percent annual interest compounded annually, (2) 10 percent annual interest compounded semiannually, (3) 4 percent annual interest compounded annually, and (4) 16 percent annual interest compounded quarterly.

Future Value Applications

E 5. a. Two parents have $20,000 to invest for their child's college tuition, which they estimate will cost $40,000 when the child enters college twelve years from now.

Calculate the approximate rate of annual interest that the investment must earn to reach the $40,000 goal in twelve years. (**Hint:** Make a calculation; then use Table 1 in the appendix on future value and present value tables.)

b. Ted Pruitt is saving to purchase a summer home that will cost about $64,000. He has $40,000 now, on which he can earn 7 percent annual interest.

Calculate the approximate length of time he will have to wait to purchase the summer home. (**Hint:** Make a calculation; then use Table 1 in the appendix on future value and present value tables.)

Working Backward from a Future Value

E 6. Gloria Faraquez has a debt of $90,000 due in four years. She wants to save enough money to pay it off by making annual deposits in an investment account that earns 8 percent annual interest.

Calculate the amount she must deposit each year to reach her goal. (**Hint:** Use Table 2 in the appendix on future value and present value tables; then make a calculation.)

Determining an Advance Payment

E 7. Ellen Saber is contemplating paying five years' rent in advance. Her annual rent is $9,600.

Calculate the single sum that would have to be paid now for the advance rent, if we assume compound interest of 8 percent.

Appendix C The Time Value of Money

Present Value Calculations

E 8. Find the present value of (1) a single payment of $24,000 at 6 percent for twelve years, (2) twelve annual payments of $2,000 at 6 percent, (3) a single payment of $5,000 at 9 percent for five years, and (4) five annual payments of $5,000 at 9 percent.

Present Value of a Lump-Sum Contract

E 9. A contract calls for a lump-sum payment of $60,000. Find the present value of the contract, assuming that (1) the payment is due in five years, and the current interest rate is 9 percent; (2) the payment is due in ten years, and the current interest rate is 9 percent; (3) the payment is due in five years, and the current interest rate is 5 percent; and (4) the payment is due in ten years, and the current interest rate is 5 percent.

Present Value of an Annuity Contract

E 10. A contract calls for annual payments of $1,200. Find the present value of the contract, assuming that (1) the number of payments is seven, and the current interest rate is 6 percent; (2) the number of payments is fourteen, and the current interest rate is 6 percent; (3) the number of payments is seven, and the current interest rate is 8 percent; and (4) the number of payments is fourteen, and the current interest rate is 8 percent.

Non-Interest-Bearing Note

E 11. On January 1, 20x0, Pendleton purchased a machine from Leyland by signing a two-year, non-interest-bearing $32,000 note. Pendleton currently pays 12 percent interest to borrow money at the bank.

Prepare entries in Pendleton's and Leyland's journals to (1) record the purchase and the note, (2) adjust the accounts after one year, and (3) record payment of the note after two years (on December 31, 20x2).

Valuing an Asset for the Purpose of Making a Purchasing Decision

E 12. Oscaro owns a service station and has the opportunity to purchase a car wash machine for $30,000. After carefully studying projected costs and revenues, Oscaro estimates that the car wash machine will produce a net cash flow of $5,200 annually and will last for eight years. Oscaro believes that an interest rate of 14 percent is adequate for his business.

Calculate the present value of the machine to Oscaro. Does the purchase appear to be a correct business decision?

Deferred Payment

E 13. Johnson Equipment Corporation sold a precision tool machine with computer controls to Borst Corporation for $800,000 on January 1, agreeing to take payment nine months later, on October 1. Assuming that the prevailing annual interest rate for such a transaction is 16 percent compounded quarterly, what is the actual sale (purchase) price of the machine tool, and what journal entries will be made at the time of the purchase (sale) and at the time of the payment (receipt) on the records of both Borst and Johnson?

Investment of Idle Cash

E 14. Scientific Publishing Company, a publisher of college books, has just completed a successful fall selling season and has $5,000,000 in cash to invest for nine months, beginning on January 1. The company placed the cash in a money market account that is expected to pay 12 percent annual interest compounded monthly. Interest is credited to the company's account each month. How much cash will the company have at the end of nine months, and what entries are made to record the investment and the first two monthly (February 1 and March 1) interest amounts?

Accumulation of a Fund

E 15. Laferia Corporation borrowed $3,000,000 from an insurance company on a five-year note. Management agreed to set aside enough cash at the end of each year to accumulate the amount needed to pay off the note at maturity. Since the first contribution to the fund will be made in one year, four annual contributions are needed. Assuming that the fund will earn 10 percent compounded annually, how much will the annual contribution to the fund be (round to nearest dollar), and what will be the journal entry for the first contribution?

E 16.
Negotiating the Sale of a Business

Horace Raftson is attempting to sell his business to Ernando Ruiz. The company has assets of $900,000, liabilities of $800,000, and owner's equity of $100,000. Both parties agree that the proper rate of return to expect is 12 percent; however, they differ on other assumptions. Raftson believes that the business will generate at least $100,000 per year of cash flows for twenty years. Ruiz thinks that $80,000 in cash flows per year is more reasonable and that only ten years in the future should be considered. Using Table 4 in the appendix on future value and present value tables, determine the range for negotiation by computing the present value of Raftson's offer to sell and of Ruiz's offer to buy.

Appendix D
Future Value and Present Value Tables

Table 1 provides the multipliers necessary to compute the future value of a *single* cash deposit made at the *beginning* of year 1. Three factors must be known before the future value can be computed: (1) the time period in years, (2) the stated annual rate of interest to be earned, and (3) the dollar amount invested or deposited.

■ **EXAMPLE—TABLE 1** Determine the future value of $5,000 deposited now that will earn 9 percent interest compounded annually for five years. From Table 1, the necessary multiplier for five years at 9 percent is 1.539, and the answer is

$$\$5,000 \times 1.539 = \$7,695$$

TABLE 1. Future Value of $1 After a Given Number of Time Periods

Periods	1%	2%	3%	4%	5%	6%	7%	8%	9%	10%	12%	14%	15%
1	1.010	1.020	1.030	1.040	1.050	1.060	1.070	1.080	1.090	1.100	1.120	1.140	1.150
2	1.020	1.040	1.061	1.082	1.103	1.124	1.145	1.166	1.188	1.210	1.254	1.300	1.323
3	1.030	1.061	1.093	1.125	1.158	1.191	1.225	1.260	1.295	1.331	1.405	1.482	1.521
4	1.041	1.082	1.126	1.170	1.216	1.262	1.311	1.360	1.412	1.464	1.574	1.689	1.749
5	1.051	1.104	1.159	1.217	1.276	1.338	1.403	1.469	1.539	1.611	1.762	1.925	2.011
6	1.062	1.126	1.194	1.265	1.340	1.419	1.501	1.587	1.677	1.772	1.974	2.195	2.313
7	1.072	1.149	1.230	1.316	1.407	1.504	1.606	1.714	1.828	1.949	2.211	2.502	2.660
8	1.083	1.172	1.267	1.369	1.477	1.594	1.718	1.851	1.993	2.144	2.476	2.853	3.059
9	1.094	1.195	1.305	1.423	1.551	1.689	1.838	1.999	2.172	2.358	2.773	3.252	3.518
10	1.105	1.219	1.344	1.480	1.629	1.791	1.967	2.159	2.367	2.594	3.106	3.707	4.046
11	1.116	1.243	1.384	1.539	1.710	1.898	2.105	2.332	2.580	2.853	3.479	4.226	4.652
12	1.127	1.268	1.426	1.601	1.796	2.012	2.252	2.518	2.813	3.138	3.896	4.818	5.350
13	1.138	1.294	1.469	1.665	1.886	2.133	2.410	2.720	3.066	3.452	4.363	5.492	6.153
14	1.149	1.319	1.513	1.732	1.980	2.261	2.579	2.937	3.342	3.798	4.887	6.261	7.076
15	1.161	1.346	1.558	1.801	2.079	2.397	2.759	3.172	3.642	4.177	5.474	7.138	8.137
16	1.173	1.373	1.605	1.873	2.183	2.540	2.952	3.426	3.970	4.595	6.130	8.137	9.358
17	1.184	1.400	1.653	1.948	2.292	2.693	3.159	3.700	4.328	5.054	6.866	9.276	10.760
18	1.196	1.428	1.702	2.026	2.407	2.854	3.380	3.996	4.717	5.560	7.690	10.580	12.380
19	1.208	1.457	1.754	2.107	2.527	3.026	3.617	4.316	5.142	6.116	8.613	12.060	14.230
20	1.220	1.486	1.806	2.191	2.653	3.207	3.870	4.661	5.604	6.728	9.646	13.740	16.370
21	1.232	1.516	1.860	2.279	2.786	3.400	4.141	5.034	6.109	7.400	10.800	15.670	18.820
22	1.245	1.546	1.916	2.370	2.925	3.604	4.430	5.437	6.659	8.140	12.100	17.860	21.640
23	1.257	1.577	1.974	2.465	3.072	3.820	4.741	5.871	7.258	8.954	13.550	20.360	24.890
24	1.270	1.608	2.033	2.563	3.225	4.049	5.072	6.341	7.911	9.850	15.180	23.210	28.630
25	1.282	1.641	2.094	2.666	3.386	4.292	5.427	6.848	8.623	10.830	17.000	26.460	32.920
26	1.295	1.673	2.157	2.772	3.556	4.549	5.807	7.396	9.399	11.920	19.040	30.170	37.860
27	1.308	1.707	2.221	2.883	3.733	4.822	6.214	7.988	10.250	13.110	21.320	34.390	43.540
28	1.321	1.741	2.288	2.999	3.920	5.112	6.649	8.627	11.170	14.420	23.880	39.200	50.070
29	1.335	1.776	2.357	3.119	4.116	5.418	7.114	9.317	12.170	15.860	26.750	44.690	57.580
30	1.348	1.811	2.427	3.243	4.322	5.743	7.612	10.060	13.270	17.450	29.960	50.950	66.210
40	1.489	2.208	3.262	4.801	7.040	10.290	14.970	21.720	31.410	45.260	93.050	188.900	267.900
50	1.645	2.692	4.384	7.107	11.470	18.420	29.460	46.900	74.360	117.400	289.000	700.200	1,084.000

Where r is the interest rate and n is the number of periods, the factor values for Table 1 are

$$\text{FV Factor} = (1 + r)^n$$

Situations requiring the use of Table 2 are similar to those requiring Table 1 except that Table 2 is used to compute the future value of a *series* of *equal* annual deposits at the end of each period.

■ **EXAMPLE—TABLE 2** What will be the future value at the end of 30 years if $1,000 is deposited each year on January 1, beginning in one year, assuming 12 percent interest compounded annually? The required multiplier from Table 2 is 241.3, and the answer is

$$\$1,000 \times 241.3 = \$241,300$$

The factor values for Table 2 are

$$\text{FVa Factor} = \frac{(1 + r)^n - 1}{r}$$

TABLE 2. Future Value of $1 Paid in Each Period for a Given Number of Time Periods

Periods	1%	2%	3%	4%	5%	6%	7%	8%	9%	10%	12%	14%	15%
1	1.000	1.000	1.000	1.000	1.000	1.000	1.000	1.000	1.000	1.000	1.000	1.000	1.000
2	2.010	2.020	2.030	2.040	2.050	2.060	2.070	2.080	2.090	2.100	2.120	2.140	2.150
3	3.030	3.060	3.091	3.122	3.153	3.184	3.215	3.246	3.278	3.310	3.374	3.440	3.473
4	4.060	4.122	4.184	4.246	4.310	4.375	4.440	4.506	4.573	4.641	4.779	4.921	4.993
5	5.101	5.204	5.309	5.416	5.526	5.637	5.751	5.867	5.985	6.105	6.353	6.610	6.742
6	6.152	6.308	6.468	6.633	6.802	6.975	7.153	7.336	7.523	7.716	8.115	8.536	8.754
7	7.214	7.434	7.662	7.898	8.142	8.394	8.654	8.923	9.200	9.487	10.090	10.730	11.070
8	8.286	8.583	8.892	9.214	9.549	9.897	10.260	10.640	11.030	11.440	12.300	13.230	13.730
9	9.369	9.755	10.160	10.580	11.030	11.490	11.980	12.490	13.020	13.580	14.780	16.090	16.790
10	10.460	10.950	11.460	12.010	12.580	13.180	13.820	14.490	15.190	15.940	17.550	19.340	20.300
11	11.570	12.170	12.810	13.490	14.210	14.970	15.780	16.650	17.560	18.530	20.650	23.040	24.350
12	12.680	13.410	14.190	15.030	15.920	16.870	17.890	18.980	20.140	21.380	24.130	27.270	29.000
13	13.810	14.680	15.620	16.630	17.710	18.880	20.140	21.500	22.950	24.520	28.030	32.090	34.350
14	14.950	15.970	17.090	18.290	19.600	21.020	22.550	24.210	26.020	27.980	32.390	37.580	40.500
15	16.100	17.290	18.600	20.020	21.580	23.280	25.130	27.150	29.360	31.770	37.280	43.840	47.580
16	17.260	18.640	20.160	21.820	23.660	25.670	27.890	30.320	33.000	35.950	42.750	50.980	55.720
17	18.430	20.010	21.760	23.700	25.840	28.210	30.840	33.750	36.970	40.540	48.880	59.120	65.080
18	19.610	21.410	23.410	25.650	28.130	30.910	34.000	37.450	41.300	45.600	55.750	68.390	75.840
19	20.810	22.840	25.120	27.670	30.540	33.760	37.380	41.450	46.020	51.160	63.440	78.970	88.210
20	22.020	24.300	26.870	29.780	33.070	36.790	41.000	45.760	51.160	57.280	72.050	91.020	102.400
21	23.240	25.780	28.680	31.970	35.720	39.990	44.870	50.420	56.760	64.000	81.700	104.800	118.800
22	24.470	27.300	30.540	34.250	38.510	43.390	49.010	55.460	62.870	71.400	92.500	120.400	137.600
23	25.720	28.850	32.450	36.620	41.430	47.000	53.440	60.890	69.530	79.540	104.600	138.300	159.300
24	26.970	30.420	34.430	39.080	44.500	50.820	58.180	66.760	76.790	88.500	118.200	158.700	184.200
25	28.240	32.030	36.460	41.650	47.730	54.860	63.250	73.110	84.700	98.350	133.300	181.900	212.800
26	29.530	33.670	38.550	44.310	51.110	59.160	68.680	79.950	93.320	109.200	150.300	208.300	245.700
27	30.820	35.340	40.710	47.080	54.670	63.710	74.480	87.350	102.700	121.100	169.400	238.500	283.600
28	32.130	37.050	42.930	49.970	58.400	68.530	80.700	95.340	113.000	134.200	190.700	272.900	327.100
29	33.450	38.790	45.220	52.970	62.320	73.640	87.350	104.000	124.100	148.600	214.600	312.100	377.200
30	34.780	40.570	47.580	56.080	66.440	79.060	94.460	113.300	136.300	164.500	241.300	356.800	434.700
40	48.890	60.400	75.400	95.030	120.800	154.800	199.600	259.100	337.900	442.600	767.100	1,342.000	1,779.000
50	64.460	84.580	112.800	152.700	209.300	290.300	406.500	573.800	815.100	1,164.000	2,400.000	4,995.000	7,218.000

Table 3. Present Value of $1 to Be Received at the End of a Given Number of Time Periods

Periods	1%	2%	3%	4%	5%	6%	7%	8%	9%	10%	12%
1	0.990	0.980	0.971	0.962	0.952	0.943	0.935	0.926	0.917	0.909	0.893
2	0.980	0.961	0.943	0.925	0.907	0.890	0.873	0.857	0.842	0.826	0.797
3	0.971	0.942	0.915	0.889	0.864	0.840	0.816	0.794	0.772	0.751	0.712
4	0.961	0.924	0.888	0.855	0.823	0.792	0.763	0.735	0.708	0.683	0.636
5	0.951	0.906	0.883	0.822	0.784	0.747	0.713	0.681	0.650	0.621	0.567
6	0.942	0.888	0.837	0.790	0.746	0.705	0.666	0.630	0.596	0.564	0.507
7	0.933	0.871	0.813	0.760	0.711	0.665	0.623	0.583	0.547	0.513	0.452
8	0.923	0.853	0.789	0.731	0.677	0.627	0.582	0.540	0.502	0.467	0.404
9	0.914	0.837	0.766	0.703	0.645	0.592	0.544	0.500	0.460	0.424	0.361
10	0.905	0.820	0.744	0.676	0.614	0.558	0.508	0.463	0.422	0.386	0.322
11	0.896	0.804	0.722	0.650	0.585	0.527	0.475	0.429	0.388	0.350	0.287
12	0.887	0.788	0.701	0.625	0.557	0.497	0.444	0.397	0.356	0.319	0.257
13	0.879	0.773	0.681	0.601	0.530	0.469	0.415	0.368	0.326	0.290	0.229
14	0.870	0.758	0.661	0.577	0.505	0.442	0.388	0.340	0.299	0.263	0.205
15	0.861	0.743	0.642	0.555	0.481	0.417	0.362	0.315	0.275	0.239	0.183
16	0.853	0.728	0.623	0.534	0.458	0.394	0.339	0.292	0.252	0.218	0.163
17	0.844	0.714	0.605	0.513	0.436	0.371	0.317	0.270	0.231	0.198	0.146
18	0.836	0.700	0.587	0.494	0.416	0.350	0.296	0.250	0.212	0.180	0.130
19	0.828	0.686	0.570	0.475	0.396	0.331	0.277	0.232	0.194	0.164	0.116
20	0.820	0.673	0.554	0.456	0.377	0.312	0.258	0.215	0.178	0.149	0.104
21	0.811	0.660	0.538	0.439	0.359	0.294	0.242	0.199	0.164	0.135	0.093
22	0.803	0.647	0.522	0.422	0.342	0.278	0.226	0.184	0.150	0.123	0.083
23	0.795	0.634	0.507	0.406	0.326	0.262	0.211	0.170	0.138	0.112	0.074
24	0.788	0.622	0.492	0.390	0.310	0.247	0.197	0.158	0.126	0.102	0.066
25	0.780	0.610	0.478	0.375	0.295	0.233	0.184	0.146	0.116	0.092	0.059
26	0.772	0.598	0.464	0.361	0.281	0.220	0.172	0.135	0.106	0.084	0.053
27	0.764	0.586	0.450	0.347	0.268	0.207	0.161	0.125	0.098	0.076	0.047
28	0.757	0.574	0.437	0.333	0.255	0.196	0.150	0.116	0.090	0.069	0.042
29	0.749	0.563	0.424	0.321	0.243	0.185	0.141	0.107	0.082	0.063	0.037
30	0.742	0.552	0.412	0.308	0.231	0.174	0.131	0.099	0.075	0.057	0.033
40	0.672	0.453	0.307	0.208	0.142	0.097	0.067	0.046	0.032	0.022	0.011
50	0.608	0.372	0.228	0.141	0.087	0.054	0.034	0.021	0.013	0.009	0.003

Table 3 is used to compute the value today of a single amount of cash to be received sometime in the future. To use Table 3, you must first know: (1) the time period in years until funds will be received, (2) the stated annual rate of interest, and (3) the dollar amount to be received at the end of the time period.

■ **EXAMPLE—TABLE 3** What is the present value of $30,000 to be received 25 years from now, assuming a 14 percent interest rate? From Table 3, the required multiplier is .038, and the answer is

$$\$30,000 \times .038 = \$1,140$$

Present Value of $1 to Be Received

14%	15%	16%	18%	20%	25%	30%	35%	40%	45%	50%	Periods
0.877	0.870	0.862	0.847	0.833	0.800	0.769	0.741	0.714	0.690	0.667	1
0.769	0.756	0.743	0.718	0.694	0.640	0.592	0.549	0.510	0.476	0.444	2
0.675	0.658	0.641	0.609	0.579	0.512	0.455	0.406	0.364	0.328	0.296	3
0.592	0.572	0.552	0.516	0.482	0.410	0.350	0.301	0.260	0.226	0.198	4
0.519	0.497	0.476	0.437	0.402	0.328	0.269	0.223	0.186	0.156	0.132	5
0.456	0.432	0.410	0.370	0.335	0.262	0.207	0.165	0.133	0.108	0.088	6
0.400	0.376	0.354	0.314	0.279	0.210	0.159	0.122	0.095	0.074	0.059	7
0.351	0.327	0.305	0.266	0.233	0.168	0.123	0.091	0.068	0.051	0.039	8
0.308	0.284	0.263	0.225	0.194	0.134	0.094	0.067	0.048	0.035	0.026	9
0.270	0.247	0.227	0.191	0.162	0.107	0.073	0.050	0.035	0.024	0.017	10
0.237	0.215	0.195	0.162	0.135	0.086	0.056	0.037	0.025	0.017	0.012	11
0.208	0.187	0.168	0.137	0.112	0.069	0.043	0.027	0.018	0.012	0.008	12
0.182	0.163	0.145	0.116	0.093	0.055	0.033	0.020	0.013	0.008	0.005	13
0.160	0.141	0.125	0.099	0.078	0.044	0.025	0.015	0.009	0.006	0.003	14
0.140	0.123	0.108	0.084	0.065	0.035	0.020	0.011	0.006	0.004	0.002	15
0.123	0.107	0.093	0.071	0.054	0.028	0.015	0.008	0.005	0.003	0.002	16
0.108	0.093	0.080	0.060	0.045	0.023	0.012	0.006	0.003	0.002	0.001	17
0.095	0.081	0.069	0.051	0.038	0.018	0.009	0.005	0.002	0.001	0.001	18
0.083	0.070	0.060	0.043	0.031	0.014	0.007	0.003	0.002	0.001		19
0.073	0.061	0.051	0.037	0.026	0.012	0.005	0.002	0.001	0.001		20
0.064	0.053	0.044	0.031	0.022	0.009	0.004	0.002	0.001			21
0.056	0.046	0.038	0.026	0.018	0.007	0.003	0.001	0.001			22
0.049	0.040	0.033	0.022	0.015	0.006	0.002	0.001				23
0.043	0.035	0.028	0.019	0.013	0.005	0.002	0.001				24
0.038	0.030	0.024	0.016	0.010	0.004	0.001	0.001				25
0.033	0.026	0.021	0.014	0.009	0.003	0.001					26
0.029	0.023	0.018	0.011	0.007	0.002	0.001					27
0.026	0.020	0.016	0.010	0.006	0.002	0.001					28
0.022	0.017	0.014	0.008	0.005	0.002						29
0.020	0.015	0.012	0.007	0.004	0.001						30
0.005	0.004	0.003	0.001	0.001							40
0.001	0.001	0.001									50

The factor values for Table 3 are

$$\text{PV Factor} = (1 + r)^{-n}$$

Table 3 is the reciprocal of Table 1.

Table 4. Present Value of $1 Received Each Period for a Given Number of Time Periods

Periods	1%	2%	3%	4%	5%	6%	7%	8%	9%	10%	12%
1	0.990	0.980	0.971	0.962	0.952	0.943	0.935	0.926	0.917	0.909	0.893
2	1.970	1.942	1.913	1.886	1.859	1.833	1.808	1.783	1.759	1.736	1.690
3	2.941	2.884	2.829	2.775	2.723	2.673	2.624	2.577	2.531	2.487	2.402
4	3.902	3.808	3.717	3.630	3.546	3.465	3.387	3.312	3.240	3.170	3.037
5	4.853	4.713	4.580	4.452	4.329	4.212	4.100	3.993	3.890	3.791	3.605
6	5.795	5.601	5.417	5.242	5.076	4.917	4.767	4.623	4.486	4.355	4.111
7	6.728	6.472	6.230	6.002	5.786	5.582	5.389	5.206	5.033	4.868	4.564
8	7.652	7.325	7.020	6.733	6.463	6.210	5.971	5.747	5.535	5.335	4.968
9	8.566	8.162	7.786	7.435	7.108	6.802	6.515	6.247	5.995	5.759	5.328
10	9.471	8.983	8.530	8.111	7.722	7.360	7.024	6.710	6.418	6.145	5.650
11	10.368	9.787	9.253	8.760	8.306	7.887	7.499	7.139	6.805	6.495	5.938
12	11.255	10.575	9.954	9.385	8.863	8.384	7.943	7.536	7.161	6.814	6.194
13	12.134	11.348	10.635	9.986	9.394	8.853	8.358	7.904	7.487	7.103	6.424
14	13.004	12.106	11.296	10.563	9.899	9.295	8.745	8.244	7.786	7.367	6.628
15	13.865	12.849	11.938	11.118	10.380	9.712	9.108	8.559	8.061	7.606	6.811
16	14.718	13.578	12.561	11.652	10.838	10.106	9.447	8.851	8.313	7.824	6.974
17	15.562	14.292	13.166	12.166	11.274	10.477	9.763	9.122	8.544	8.022	7.120
18	16.398	14.992	13.754	12.659	11.690	10.828	10.059	9.372	8.756	8.201	7.250
19	17.226	15.678	14.324	13.134	12.085	11.158	10.336	9.604	8.950	8.365	7.366
20	18.046	16.351	14.878	13.590	12.462	11.470	10.594	9.818	9.129	8.514	7.469
21	18.857	17.011	15.415	14.029	12.821	11.764	10.836	10.017	9.292	8.649	7.562
22	19.660	17.658	15.937	14.451	13.163	12.042	11.061	10.201	9.442	8.772	7.645
23	20.456	18.292	16.444	14.857	13.489	12.303	11.272	10.371	9.580	8.883	7.718
24	21.243	18.914	16.936	15.247	13.799	12.550	11.469	10.529	9.707	8.985	7.784
25	22.023	19.523	17.413	15.622	14.094	12.783	11.654	10.675	9.823	9.077	7.843
26	22.795	20.121	17.877	15.983	14.375	13.003	11.826	10.810	9.929	9.161	7.896
27	23.560	20.707	18.327	16.330	14.643	13.211	11.987	10.935	10.027	9.237	7.943
28	24.316	21.281	18.764	16.663	14.898	13.406	12.137	11.051	10.116	9.307	7.984
29	25.066	21.844	19.189	16.984	15.141	13.591	12.278	11.158	10.198	9.370	8.022
30	25.808	22.396	19.600	17.292	15.373	13.765	12.409	11.258	10.274	9.427	8.055
40	32.835	27.355	23.115	19.793	17.159	15.046	13.332	11.925	10.757	9.779	8.244
50	39.196	31.424	25.730	21.482	18.256	15.762	13.801	12.234	10.962	9.915	8.305

Table 4 is used to compute the present value of a *series* of *equal* annual cash flows.

■ **EXAMPLE—TABLE 4** Arthur Howard won a contest on January 1, 2002, in which the prize was $30,000, the money was payable in 15 annual installments of $2,000 every December 31, beginning in 2002. Assuming a 9 percent interest rate, what is the present value of Mr. Howard's prize on January 1, 2002? From Table 4, the required multiplier is 8.061, and the answer is:

$$\$2,000 \times 8.061 = \$16,122$$

The factor values for Table 4 are

$$\text{PVa Factor} = \frac{1 - (1 + r)^{-n}}{r}$$

Table 4 is the columnar sum of Table 3. Table 4 applies to *ordinary annuities*, in which the first cash flow occurs one time period beyond the date for which the present value is to be computed.

14%	15%	16%	18%	20%	25%	30%	35%	40%	45%	50%	Periods
0.877	0.870	0.862	0.847	0.833	0.800	0.769	0.741	0.714	0.690	0.667	1
1.647	1.626	1.605	1.566	1.528	1.440	1.361	1.289	1.224	1.165	1.111	2
2.322	2.283	2.246	2.174	2.106	1.952	1.816	1.696	1.589	1.493	1.407	3
2.914	2.855	2.798	2.690	2.589	2.362	2.166	1.997	1.849	1.720	1.605	4
3.433	3.352	3.274	3.127	2.991	2.689	2.436	2.220	2.035	1.876	1.737	5
3.889	3.784	3.685	3.498	3.326	2.951	2.643	2.385	2.168	1.983	1.824	6
4.288	4.160	4.039	3.812	3.605	3.161	2.802	2.508	2.263	2.057	1.883	7
4.639	4.487	4.344	4.078	3.837	3.329	2.925	2.598	2.331	2.109	1.922	8
4.946	4.772	4.607	4.303	4.031	3.463	3.019	2.665	2.379	2.144	1.948	9
5.216	5.019	4.833	4.494	4.192	3.571	3.092	2.715	2.414	2.168	1.965	10
5.453	5.234	5.029	4.656	4.327	3.656	3.147	2.752	2.438	2.185	1.977	11
5.660	5.421	5.197	4.793	4.439	3.725	3.190	2.779	2.456	2.197	1.985	12
5.842	5.583	5.342	4.910	4.533	3.780	3.223	2.799	2.469	2.204	1.990	13
6.002	5.724	5.468	5.008	4.611	3.824	3.249	2.814	2.478	2.210	1.993	14
6.142	5.847	5.575	5.092	4.675	3.859	3.268	2.825	2.484	2.214	1.995	15
6.265	5.954	5.669	5.162	4.730	3.887	3.283	2.834	2.489	2.216	1.997	16
6.373	6.047	5.749	5.222	4.775	3.910	3.295	2.840	2.492	2.218	1.998	17
6.467	6.128	5.818	5.273	4.812	3.928	3.304	2.844	2.494	2.219	1.999	18
6.550	6.198	5.877	5.316	4.844	3.942	3.311	2.848	2.496	2.220	1.999	19
6.623	6.259	5.929	5.353	4.870	3.954	3.316	2.850	2.497	2.221	1.999	20
6.687	6.312	5.973	5.384	4.891	3.963	3.320	2.852	2.498	2.221	2.000	21
6.743	6.359	6.011	5.410	4.909	3.970	3.323	2.853	2.498	2.222	2.000	22
6.792	6.399	6.044	5.432	4.925	3.976	3.325	2.854	2.499	2.222	2.000	23
6.835	6.434	6.073	5.451	4.937	3.981	3.327	2.855	2.499	2.222	2.000	24
6.873	6.464	6.097	5.467	4.948	3.985	3.329	2.856	2.499	2.222	2.000	25
6.906	6.491	6.118	5.480	4.956	3.988	3.330	2.856	2.500	2.222	2.000	26
6.935	6.514	6.136	5.492	4.964	3.990	3.331	2.856	2.500	2.222	2.000	27
6.961	6.534	6.152	5.502	4.970	3.992	3.331	2.857	2.500	2.222	2.000	28
6.983	6.551	6.166	5.510	4.975	3.994	3.332	2.857	2.500	2.222	2.000	29
7.003	6.566	6.177	5.517	4.979	3.995	3.332	2.857	2.500	2.222	2.000	30
7.105	6.642	6.234	5.548	4.997	3.999	3.333	2.857	2.500	2.222	2.000	40
7.133	6.661	6.246	5.554	4.999	4.000	3.333	2.857	2.500	2.222	2.000	50

An *annuity due* is a series of equal cash flows for N time periods, but the first payment occurs immediately. The present value of the first payment equals the face value of the cash flow; Table 4 then is used to measure the present value of $N - 1$ remaining cash flows.

■ **EXAMPLE—TABLE 4** Determine the present value on January 1, 2002, of 20 lease payments; each payment of $10,000 is due on January 1, beginning in 2002. Assume an interest rate of 8 percent.

$$\text{Present Value} = \text{Immediate Payment} + \begin{cases} \text{Present Value of 19 Subsequent} \\ \text{Payments at 8\%} \end{cases}$$

$$= \$10,000 + (\$10,000 \times 9.604) = \$106,040$$

Appendix E
How to Read an Annual Report

More than 4 million corporations are chartered in the United States. Most of these are small, family-owned businesses. They are called *private* or *closely held corporations* because their common stock is held by only a few people and is not available for sale to the public. Larger companies usually find it desirable to raise investment funds from many investors by issuing common stock to the public. These companies are called *public companies*. Although they are fewer in number than private companies, their total economic impact is much greater.

Public companies must register their common stock with the Securities and Exchange Commission (SEC), which regulates the issuance and subsequent trading of the stock of public companies. One important responsibility of the management of public companies under SEC rules is to report each year to the company's stockholders on the financial performance of the company. This report, called an *annual report*, contains the annual financial statements and other information about the company. Annual reports, which are a primary source of financial information about public companies, are distributed to all the company's stockholders and filed with the SEC. When filed with the SEC, the annual report is called the 10-K because a Form 10-K is used to file the report. The general public may obtain an annual report by calling or writing the company or accessing it online at the company's web site. If a company has filed its 10-K electronically with the SEC, it may be accessed at **http://www.sec.gov/edgar.shtml**. Many libraries also maintain files of annual reports or have them available on electronic media, such as *Compact Disclosure*.

This supplement describes the major sections of the typical annual report and contains the annual report of one of the most successful retailers of this generation, Toys "R" Us, Inc. In addition to operating stores that sell toys and other items for children, the company has a chain of stores that sell children's clothes, called Kids "R" Us and a chain of stores devoted exclusively to babies, called Babies "R" Us. The Toys "R" Us annual report should be referred to in completing the case assignments related to the company in each chapter. For purposes of comparison, the supplement also includes the financial statements and notes to the financial statements of Walgreens, one of the largest drugstore chains in the United States.

THE COMPONENTS OF AN ANNUAL REPORT

In addition to listing the corporation's directors and officers, an annual report contains a letter to the stockholders, a multiyear summary of financial highlights, a description of the company, management's discussion of operating results and financial conditions, the financial statements, notes to the financial statements, a report of management's responsibilities, the auditors' report, and supplementary information notes.

LETTER TO THE STOCKHOLDERS

Traditionally, an annual report begins with a letter in which the top officers of the corporation tell stockholders about the performance and prospects of the company. In its 2002 annual report, the president and chief executive officer of Toys "R" Us wrote to the stockholders about the highlights of the past year, the key priorities for the new year, store format and redeployment plans, corporate citizenship, and other aspects of the business. He reported on results as follows:

> 2002 was a year of encouraging progress, but a time of disappointments as well. Three divisions in our portfolio of businesses—Babies "R" Us, Toys "R" Us International, and Toysrus.com—enjoyed the best performances in their history. Those results, coupled with improved expense discipline, resulted in a 19% gain in net earnings, before restructuring and other charges in 2001, for Toys "R" Us, Inc. However, weaker results in Toys "R" Us U.S. and Kids "R" Us were very disappointing, despite progress in strategic execution in both divisions. . . .
>
> Nonetheless, we were encouraged by the progress we made in the execution of our strategy, which we believe further strengthened our ability to improve our performance in 2003 and beyond.

FINANCIAL HIGHLIGHTS

The financial highlights section of an annual report presents key statistics for a ten-year period and is often accompanied by graphs. The Toys "R" Us annual report, for example, gives key figures for operations, financial position, and number of stores at year end. Note that the financial highlights section often includes nonfinancial data, such as the number of stores.

DESCRIPTION OF THE COMPANY

An annual report contains a detailed description of the products and divisions of the company. Some analysts tend to scoff at this section of the annual report because it often contains glossy photographs and other image-building material, but it should not be overlooked because it may provide useful information about past results and future plans.

MANAGEMENT'S DISCUSSION AND ANALYSIS

Management also presents a discussion and analysis of financial condition and results of operations. In this section, management explains the difference from one year to the next. For example, the management of Toys "R" Us describes the company's net sales in the following way:

> *Comparison of Fiscal Year 2002 to 2001*
> We reported consolidated net sales of $11.3 billion for the 52-week fiscal year ended February 1, 2003 versus $11.0 billion for the 52-week fiscal year ended February 2, 2002, or a 3% increase in consolidated net sales. Our consolidated net sales were $11.2 billion for 2002, after excluding the impact of foreign currency translation, representing a 1% increase over 2001 net sales.

Its management of cash flows is described as follows:

> The seasonal nature of our business typically causes cash balances to decline from the beginning of the year through October as inventory increases for the holiday selling season and funds are used for construction of new stores, remodeling and other initiatives that normally occur in this period. The fourth quarter, including the holiday season, accounts for more than 40% of our net sales and substantially all of our operating earnings.

FINANCIAL STATEMENTS

All companies present four basic financial statements in their annual reports. As you can see in the annual report included with this supplement, Toys "R" Us presents statements of earnings (income statements), balance sheets, statements of cash flows, and statements of stockholders' equity (retained earnings).

The headings of all Toys "R" Us financial statements are preceded by the word *consolidated*. A corporation issues *consolidated* financial statements when it consists of more than one company and has combined their data for reporting purposes. For example, Toys "R" Us has combined the financial data of Kids "R" Us and Babies "R" Us with those of the Toys "R" Us stores.

Toys "R" Us provides several years of data for each financial statement: two years for the balance sheet and three years for the others. Financial statements presented in this fashion are called *comparative financial statements*. Such statements are in accordance with generally accepted accounting principles and help readers assess the company's performance over several years.

You may notice that the fiscal year for Toys "R" Us ends on the Saturday nearest the end of January, rather than on the same date each year. The reason is that Toys "R" Us is a retail company. It is common for retailers to end their fiscal years at a slow period after the busiest time of year.

In a note at the bottom of each page of the financial statements, Toys "R" Us reminds the reader that the accompanying notes are an integral part of the statements and must be consulted in interpreting the data.

■ **STATEMENTS OF EARNINGS** Toys "R" Us uses a multistep form of the income statement that shows gross margin as the difference between net sales and cost of sales (goods sold). Total operating expenses are deducted from gross margin to arrive at operating earnings (income). Interest expense is shown separately, and income taxes are deducted in another step. *Net earnings* is an alternative name for *net income*. The company also discloses the earnings per share, which is the net earnings divided by the weighted average number of shares of common stock held by stockholders during the year.

■ **BALANCE SHEETS** Toys "R" Us has a typical balance sheet for a merchandising company. In the assets and liabilities sections, the company separates out the current assets and the current liabilities. Current assets will become available as cash or be used up in the next year; current liabilities will have to be paid or satisfied in the next year. These groupings help in understanding the company's liquidity.

Several items in the stockholders' equity section need additional explanation. Common stock represents the number of shares outstanding at par value. Additional paid-in capital represents amounts invested by stockholders in excess of the par value of the common stock. Treasury shares is a deduction from stockholders' equity that represents the cost of previously issued shares that have been bought back and held by the company.

■ **STATEMENTS OF CASH FLOWS** Whereas the income statement reflects a company's profitability, the statement of cash flows reflects its liquidity. This statement provides information about a company's cash receipts, cash payments, and investing and financing activities during an accounting period.

Refer to the consolidated statements of cash flows in the Toys "R" Us annual report. The first major section shows cash flows from operating activities. It begins with the net earnings (income) from the consolidated statements of earnings and adjusts that figure to a figure that represents the net cash from operating activities. Among the adjustments are increases for depreciation and amortization, which are expenses that do not require the use of cash, and increases and decreases for the changes in the working capital accounts. In the year ended February 1, 2003, Toys "R" Us had net earnings of $229,000,000, and its net cash from operating activities was $574,000,000. Added to net income are such expenses as depreciation and amortization. Two small negative items were more than offset by a positive amount associated with deferred income taxes. Accounts and other receivables showed little change. Increases in merchandise inventories, prepaid expenses, and other operating assets contributed to declines in cash, as did a decrease in income taxes payable. An increase of $112,000,000 in accounts payable, accrued expenses, and other liabilities was a significant source of cash.

The second major section of the consolidated statements of cash flows is cash flows from investing activities. The main item in this category is capital expenditures, net, of $388,000,000. This figure demonstrates that Toys "R" Us is a growing company.

The third major section of the consolidated statements of cash flows is cash flows from financing activities. You can see here that the sources of cash from financing are long-term borrowings of $548,000,000 and issuance of stock of $266,000,000, which were helpful in making debt repayments of $141,000,000. In total, the company generated $613,000,000 in cash from financing activities during the year.

At the bottom of the consolidated statements of cash flows, the net effect of the operating, investing, and financing activities on the cash balance may be seen. Toys "R" Us had an increase in cash and cash equivalents during the year of $740,000,000 and ended the year with $1,023,000,000 of cash and cash equivalents on hand.

The supplemental disclosures of cash flow information show income tax and interest payments for the last three years.

■ **STATEMENTS OF STOCKHOLDERS' EQUITY** Instead of a simple statement of retained earnings, Toys "R" Us presents a *statement of stockholders' equity*. This statement explains the changes in five components of stockholders' equity.

NOTES TO THE FINANCIAL STATEMENTS

To meet the requirements of full disclosure, a company must add *notes to the financial statements* to help users interpret some of the more complex items. The notes are considered an integral part of the financial statements. In recent years, the need for explanation and further details has become so great that the notes often take more space than the statements themselves. The notes to the financial statements include a summary of significant accounting policies and explanatory notes.

■ **SUMMARY OF SIGNIFICANT ACCOUNTING POLICIES** Generally accepted accounting principles require that the financial statements include a *Summary of Significant Accounting Policies*. In most cases, this summary is presented in the first note to the financial statements or as a separate section just before the notes. In this summary, the company tells which generally accepted accounting principles it has followed in preparing the statements. For example, in the Toys "R" Us report, the company states the principles followed for property and equipment:

> Property and equipment are recorded at cost. Leasehold improvements represent capital improvements made to leased locations. Depreciation and amortization are provided using the straight-line method over the estimated useful lives of the assets or, where applicable, the terms of the respective leases, whichever is shorter.

Other important accounting policies listed by Toys "R" Us deal with fiscal year; reclassification; principles of consolidation; use of estimates; revenue recognition; advertising costs; cash and cash equivalents; merchandise inventories; credits and allowances received from vendors; cost of sales and selling, general, and administrative expenses; costs of computer software; financial instruments; and stock options.

■ **EXPLANATORY NOTES** Other notes explain some of the items in the financial statements. For example, Toys "R" Us showed the details of its Property and Equipment account, which is reproduced below.

Property and Equipment

	Useful Life (in years)	February 1, 2003	February 2, 2002
Land		$ 825	$ 811
Buildings	45–50	2,009	1,980
Furniture and equipment	5–20	1,786	1,800
Leasehold improvements	12½–35	1,726	1,542
Costs of computer software	5	192	127
Construction in progress		33	41
Leased property and equipment under capital lease		53	53
		6,624	6,354
Less accumulated depreciation and amortization		1,861	1,810
		$4,763	$4,544

Other notes had to do with restricted cash, merchandise inventories, goodwill, investment in Toys–Japan, seasonal financing and long-term debt, derivative instruments and hedging activities, issuance of common stock and equity security units, stockholders' equity, earnings per share, stock purchase warrants, leases, taxes on income, stock options, replacement of certain stock option grants with restricted stock, profit-sharing plan, Toysrus.com, segments, restructuring and other charges, gain from initial public offering of Toys–Japan, subsequent events, and other matters.

REPORT OF MANAGEMENT'S RESPONSIBILITIES

A statement of management's responsibility for the financial statements and the internal control structure may accompany the financial statements. The management report of Toys "R" Us acknowledges management's responsibility for the integrity and objectivity of the financial information and for the system of internal controls. It mentions the company's internal audit program and its distribution of company policies to employees. It also mentions the Audit Committee of the Board of Directors and states that the company's financial statements have been audited.

REPORT OF CERTIFIED PUBLIC ACCOUNTANTS

The *independent auditors' report* deals with the credibility of the financial statements. This report by independent certified public accountants gives the accountants' opinion about how fairly these statements have been presented. Using financial statements prepared by managers without an independent audit would be like having a judge hear a case in which he or she was personally involved. Management, through its internal accounting system, is logically responsible for recordkeeping because it needs similar information for its own use in operating the business. The

FIGURE 11
Auditors' Report for Toys "R" Us, Inc.

REPORT OF INDEPENDENT AUDITORS

To the Board of Directors and Stockholders
Toys"R"Us, Inc.

(1) We have audited the accompanying consolidated balance sheets of Toys"R"Us, Inc. and subsidiaries as of February 1, 2003 and February 2, 2002, and the related consolidated statements of earnings, stockholders' equity and cash flows for each of the three years in the period ended February 1, 2003. These financial statements are the responsibility of the company's management. Our responsibility is to express an opinion on these financial statements based on our audits.

(2) We conducted our audits in accordance with auditing standards generally accepted in the United States. Those standards require that we plan and perform the audit to obtain reasonable assurance about whether the financial statements are free of material misstatement. An audit includes examining, on a test basis, evidence supporting the amounts and disclosures in the financial statements. An audit also includes assessing the accounting principles used and significant estimates made by management, as well as evaluating the overall financial statement presentation. We believe that our audits provide a reasonable basis for our opinion.

(3) In our opinion, the financial statements referred to above present fairly, in all material respects, the consolidated financial position of Toys"R"Us, Inc. and subsidiaries at February 1, 2003 and February 2, 2002, and the consolidated results of their operations and their cash flows for each of the three years in the period ended February 1, 2003, in conformity with accounting principles generally accepted in the United States.

(4) As discussed in the note entitled "Goodwill," the company adopted SFAS No. 142, Goodwill and Other Intangible Assets, effective February 3, 2002.

Ernst & Young LLP

Ernst & Young LLP
New York, New York
March 5, 2003

Source: Reprinted by permission of Toys "R" Us. The notes to the financial statement, which are an integral part of the report, are not included.

certified public accountants, acting independently, add the necessary credibility to management's figures for interested third parties. They report to the board of directors and the stockholders rather than to management.

In form and language, most auditors' reports are like the one shown in Figure 11. Usually such a report is short, but its language is very important. The report is usually divided into three parts, but it can have a fourth part if there is a need for further explanation.

1. The first paragraph identifies the financial statements subject to the auditors' report. This paragraph also identifies responsibilities. Company management is responsible for the financial statements, and the auditor is responsible for expressing an opinion on the financial statements based on the audit.

2. The second paragraph, or *scope section*, states that the examination was made in accordance with generally accepted auditing standards. These standards call for an acceptable level of quality in ten areas established by the American Institute of Certified Public Accountants. This paragraph also contains a brief description of the objectives and nature of the audit.

3. The third paragraph, or *opinion section*, states the results of the auditors' examination. The use of the word *opinion* is very important because the auditor does not certify or guarantee that the statements are absolutely correct. To do so would go beyond the truth, since many items, such as depreciation, are based on estimates. Instead, the auditors simply give an opinion about whether, overall, the financial statements "present fairly," in all material respects, the financial position, results of operations, and cash flows. This means that the statements are

prepared in accordance with generally accepted accounting principles. If, in the auditors' opinion, the statements do not meet accepted standards, the auditors must explain why and to what extent.

4. The optional fourth paragraph mentions the adoption of a new accounting standard.

SUPPLEMENTARY INFORMATION NOTES

In recent years, the FASB and the SEC have ruled that certain supplemental information must be presented with financial statements. Examples are the quarterly reports that most companies present to their stockholders and to the SEC. These quarterly reports, called *interim financial statements*, are in most cases reviewed but not audited by the company's independent CPA firm. In its annual report, Toys "R" Us presents unaudited quarterly financial data from its 2002 quarterly statements, which are shown in the following table (for the year ended February 1, 2003; dollars in millions, except per share amounts):

	First Quarter	Second Quarter	Third Quarter	Fourth Quarter
Year Ended February 1, 2003				
Net Sales	$2,095	$2,070	$2,271	$4,869
Gross Margin	682	670	722	1,432
Net (Loss)/Earnings	(4)	(17)	(28)	278
Basic (Loss)/ Earnings per Share	$(0.02)	$(0.08)	$(0.13)	$ 1.31
Diluted (Loss)/ Earnings per Share	$(0.02)	$(0.08)	$(0.13)	$ 1.30

Interim data are presented for the prior year as well. Toys "R" Us also provides supplemental information on the market price of its common stock during the years and data on its store locations.

The Annual Report Project

Many instructors assign a term project that requires reading and analyzing a real annual report. The Annual Report Project described here has proved successful in the authors' classes. It may be used with the annual report of any company, including the Toys "R" Us annual report and the financial statements from the Walgreen Co. annual report that are provided with this supplement.

The extent to which financial analysis is required depends on the point in the course at which the Annual Report Project is assigned. Several options are provided in Instruction 3E, below.

INSTRUCTIONS:

1. Select any company from the list of Fingraph companies on the Needles Accounting Resource Center Web Site at **http://accounting.college.hmco.com/students**. Click on the company to access the Microsoft Excel spreadsheet for that company. Then click on the URL in the heading of the spreadsheet for a link to the company's web site and annual report. You may also obtain the annual report of a company of your own choice and access the company's annual report online or obtain it through your library or another source.

2. Library and Internet Research

   Go to the library or the Needles Accounting Resource Center Web Site (**http://accounting.college.hmco.com/students**) to learn about the company you have chosen and the industry in which it operates. Find at least two articles or other references to the industry and the company and summarize your findings.

   Also, access the company's Internet home page directly or through the Needles Accounting Resource Center. Review the company's products and services and find its financial information. Summarize what you have learned.

3. Your term project should consist of five or six double-spaced pages organized according to the following outline:

   A. **Introduction**

   Identify your company by writing a summary that includes the following elements:
   - Name of the chief executive officer
   - Location of the home office
   - Ending date of latest fiscal year
   - Description of the principal products or services that the company provides
   - Main geographic area of activity
   - Name of the company's independent accountants (auditors). In your own words, explain what the accountants said about the company's financial statements.
   - The most recent price of the company's stock and its dividend per share. Be sure to provide the date for this information.

   B. **Industry Situation and Company Plans**

   Describe the industry and its outlook; then summarize the company's future plans based on your library research and on reading the annual report. Be sure to read the letter to the stockholders. Include relevant information about the company's plans from that discussion.

C. **Financial Statements**

Income Statement: Is the format more like a single-step or multistep format? Determine gross profit, income from operations, and net income for the last two years; comment on the increases or decreases in these amounts.

Balance Sheet: Show that Assets = Liabilities + Stockholders' Equity for the past two years.

Statement of Cash Flows: Are cash flows from operations more or less than net income for the past two years? Is the company expanding through investing activities? What is the company's most important source of financing? Overall, has cash increased or decreased over the past two years?

D. **Accounting Policies**

What are the significant accounting policies, if any, relating to revenue recognition, cash, short-term investments, merchandise inventories, and property and equipment?

What are the topics of the notes to the financial statements?

E. **Financial Analysis**

For the past two years, calculate and discuss the significance of the following ratios:

Option (a): Basic (After Completing Chapters 1–6)

Liquidity Ratios
   Working capital
   Current ratio

Profitability Ratios
   Profit margin
   Asset turnover
   Return on assets
   Debt to equity ratio
   Return on equity

Option (b): Basic with Enhanced Liquidity Analysis (After Completing Chapters 1–10)

Liquidity Ratios
   Working capital
   Current ratio
   Receivable turnover
   Average days' sales uncollected
   Inventory turnover
   Average days' inventory on hand
   Operating cycle

Profitability Ratios
   Profit margin
   Asset turnover
   Return on assets
   Debt to equity ratio
   Return on equity

Option (c): Comprehensive (After Completing Chapters 1–18)

Liquidity Ratios
   Working capital
   Current ratio
   Receivable turnover
   Average days' sales uncollected
   Inventory turnover

　　　　　　　　Average days' inventory on hand
　　　　　　　　Payables turnover
　　　　　　　　Average days' payable
　　　　　　　　Operating cycle
　　　　　　　　Financing period
　　　　Profitability Ratios
　　　　　　　　Profit margin
　　　　　　　　Asset turnover
　　　　　　　　Return on assets
　　　　　　　　Return on equity
　　　　Long-Term Solvency Ratios
　　　　　　　　Debt to equity ratio
　　　　　　　　Interest coverage
　　　　Cash Flow Adequacy
　　　　　　　　Cash flow yield
　　　　　　　　Cash flows to sales
　　　　　　　　Cash flows to assets
　　　　　　　　Free cash flow
　　　　Market Strength Ratios
　　　　　　　　Price/earnings per share
　　　　　　　　Dividends yield

Option (d): Comprehensive Using Fingraph® Financial Analyst™ Software on the CD-ROM That Accompanies This Text

Toys "R" Us Annual Report E11

TOYS R US
Annual Report
2002

Shaping
our future and
our brands

This annual report is for the year ended February 1, 2003. Pages 1–5 and 20–48 reprinted by permission of Toys "R" Us, Inc.

Company Profile

We are one of the world's leading retailers of toys, children's apparel and baby products based on our consolidated net sales in 2002. As of February 1, 2003, we operated 1,595 "R"Us retail stores worldwide. These consist of 1,051 United States locations comprised of 681 toy stores under the name "Toys"R"Us," 183 infant-toddler stores under the name "Babies"R"Us," 146 children's clothing stores under the name "Kids"R"Us," 37 educational specialty stores under the name "Imaginarium" and 4 "Geoffrey" stores that include products from Toys"R"Us, Kids"R"Us and Babies"R"Us as well as many interactive events. Internationally, as of February 1, 2003, we operated 544 stores, including licensed and franchised stores, under the "R"Us name. We also sell merchandise through Internet sites at www.toysrus.com, www.babiesrus.com, www.imaginarium.com and www.giftsrus.com. Toys"R"Us, Inc. is incorporated in the state of Delaware.

Our History

Toys"R"Us got its start in 1948 when founder Charles Lazarus opened a baby furniture store, Children's Bargain Town, in Washington D.C. Lazarus quickly realized the potential of fulfilling customer's requests for baby toys and toys for older children.

In 1957, Lazarus introduced a "supermarket environment." That same year, the Toys"R"Us name made its debut, complete with a backwards "R". By 1966, Lazarus had four stores with approximately $12 million in annual sales. Around this time, Lazarus sold his stores to retail conglomerate Interstate Stores. He maintained responsibility for running Toys"R"Us, which continued to grow profitably. Interstate, however, faced major difficulties and was forced to declare bankruptcy. During this critical period, Lazarus led and restructured the company. In 1978, when Interstate emerged from bankruptcy it was renamed Toys"R"Us, Inc.

The 1980s were a time of major expansion for Toys"R"Us, Inc. In 1983, the company had 169 toy stores in 26 states and had added four stores under its new Kids"R"Us brand. The company opened its first international stores in Singapore and Canada in 1984. Just 10 years later, the company completed its 1993 fiscal year with 581 U.S. toy stores, 217 Kids"R"Us stores and 234 stores in international locations. In 2001, Toys"R"Us opened its flagship store in Times Square.

In 1996, the company opened its first Babies"R"Us store. The acquisition of Baby Superstore in 1997 added 76 locations and helped Babies"R"Us become the undisputed leader in the juvenile market. Imaginarium was acquired in 1998 to bring the learning and educational toy categories to the "R"Us family of retail stores. Between 2000 and 2002, Imaginarium boutiques were added to U.S. toy stores as part of the division's Mission Possible renovation. In addition, Imaginarium also operates 37 freestanding locations.

Geoffrey the Giraffe was first introduced in 1960. However, he didn't receive his name until 1970 when a contest was held among company associates to name him. In 2000, Geoffrey was reintroduced, in his current animatronic form, as the company's lovable wisecracking "spokesanimal." Today he's one of the world's most recognized icons by kids and grown-ups alike, representative of a worldwide chain of stores that has forever changed the way the world shops for toys.

financial highlights

Toys"R"Us, Inc. and Subsidiaries

(Dollars in millions, except per share data)   Fiscal Year Ended

	Feb. 1, 2003	Feb. 2, 2002	Feb. 3, 2001	Jan. 29, 2000	Jan. 30, 1999	Jan. 31, 1998	Feb. 1, 1997	Feb. 3, 1996	Jan. 28, 1995	Jan. 29, 1994
Operations										
Total Enterprise Sales*	**$13,067**	$12,630	$12,774	$12,118	$11,459	$11,315	$10,113	$9,498	$8,819	$8,018
Net Sales	**11,305**	11,019	11,332	11,862	11,170	11,038	9,932	9,427	8,746	7,946
Net Earnings/(Loss)	**229**	67	404	279	(132)	490	427	148	532	483
Basic Earnings/(Loss) Per Share	**1.10**	0.34	1.92	1.14	(0.50)	1.72	1.56	0.54	1.88	1.66
Diluted Earnings/(Loss) Per Share	**1.09**	0.33	1.88	1.14	(0.50)	1.70	1.54	0.53	1.85	1.63
Financial Position at Year End										
Working Capital	**$ 1,182**	$ 657	$ 575	$ 35	$ 106	$ 579	$ 619	$ 326	$ 484	$ 633
Real Estate - Net	**2,398**	2,313	2,348	2,342	2,354	2,435	2,411	2,336	2,271	2,036
Total Assets	**9,397**	8,076	8,003	8,353	7,899	7,963	8,023	6,738	6,571	6,150
Long-Term Debt	**2,139**	1,816	1,567	1,230	1,222	851	909	827	785	724
Stockholders' Equity	**4,030**	3,414	3,418	3,680	3,624	4,428	4,191	3,432	3,429	3,148
Common Shares Outstanding	**212.5**	196.7	197.5	239.3	250.6	282.4	287.8	273.1	279.8	289.5
Number of Stores at Year End										
Toys"R"Us – U.S.	**681**	701	710	710	704	700	682	653	618	581
Toys"R"Us – International**	**544**	507	491	462	452	441	396	337	293	234
Babies"R"Us – U.S.	**183**	165	145	131	113	98	82	–	–	–
Kids"R"Us – U.S.	**146**	184	198	205	212	215	212	213	204	217
Imaginarium – U.S.	**37**	42	37	40	–	–	–	–	–	–
Geoffrey – U.S.	**4**	–	–	–	–	–	–	–	–	–
Total Stores	**1,595**	1,599	1,581	1,548	1,481	1,454	1,372	1,203	1,115	1,032

*Total enterprise sales consist of all Toys"R"Us branded net sales, which include net sales from all the company's stores and from the company's internet businesses, in addition to net sales from licensed and franchised stores.

**Includes licensed and franchised stores.

contents

Financial Highlights . . . . page 1

Letter to Our Shareholders . . . . page 3

Divisional Highlights . . . . page 7

Corporate Philanthropy and Corporate Responsibility . . . . page 19

Management's Discussion and Analysis
of Results of Operations and Financial Condition . . . . . . page 22

Financial Statements . . . . page 31

Report of Management and
Report of Independent Auditors . . . . page 45

Directors and Officers . . . . page 46

Quarterly Financial Data and Market Information . . . . . . page 48

Store Locations, Corporate Data
and Stockholder Information . . . . page 49

Toys "R" Us Annual Report

Building
our portfolio of
brands

TOYS R US   KIDS R US   BABIES US

Toys "R" Us Annual Report E15

letter to our shareholders

Performance and Progress

A year in review

2002 was a year of encouraging progress, but a time of disappointments as well. Three divisions in our portfolio of businesses – Babies"R"Us, Toys"R"Us International and Toysrus.com – enjoyed the best performances in their history. Those results, coupled with improved expense discipline resulted in a 19% gain in net earnings, before restructuring and other charges in 2001, for Toys"R"Us, Inc. However, weaker results in Toys"R"Us U.S. and Kids"R"Us were very disappointing, despite progress in strategic execution in both divisions.

The performance of our U.S. toy stores did not meet our expectations. Our comparable store sales declined 1% for the year and, in a difficult retail environment, our operating earnings declined as well.

Nonetheless, we were encouraged by the progress we made in the execution of our strategy; which we believe further strengthened our ability to improve our performance in 2003 and beyond. For example, by working closely with our vendors last year, we gained market share in core toy, defined as the Boys and Girls, Learning (i.e. Imaginarium) and Preschool categories. Our core toy sales outpaced toy industry performance, as reported by the Toy Industry Association, by 4% for the year.

John Eyler
Chairman and Chief Executive Officer

We continued to improve our in-stock position, content, presentation and service levels. In addition, we experienced significant improvements in customer satisfaction scores related to pricing and value perception. Both messages were effectively reinforced through our award-winning television commercials featuring our charismatic "spokesanimal," Geoffrey the Giraffe.

We enjoyed historically high levels of success in several of our divisions in 2002. Babies"R"Us and Toys"R"Us International both turned in record-setting operating earnings for the fourth quarter and full year of 2002. In addition, Toysrus.com achieved operating profitability in the fourth quarter – a full year ahead of schedule. Our Kids"R"Us division has been struggling in its stand-alone stores for some time now, but we have seen positive results from sourcing apparel through Kids"R"Us for our Babies"R"Us stores as well as our Toys"R"Us/Kids"R"Us combo stores. Currently, our total apparel business represents approximately $900 million in sales per year, at above company average profit margins, and we expect continued growth. Approximately 65% of these sales come from exclusive products that generate higher margins than nationally branded items. We'll talk about these divisions in greater detail in this report.

Geoffrey the Giraffe helped boost consumer awareness for Toys"R"Us in 2002.

maginarium   TOYS"R"US.COM   Geoffrey

letter to our shareholders

We worked diligently in 2002 to improve our productivity, reduce expenses and enhance our financial strength.

We took steps to strengthen our balance sheet and improve our liquidity. As a result, we had substantial excess liquidity in early November during our seasonal borrowing peak, and ended the fiscal year with more than $1 billion in cash.

We reduced capital spending significantly in 2002. Net capital expenditures were $398 million in 2002 as compared to $705 million in 2001.

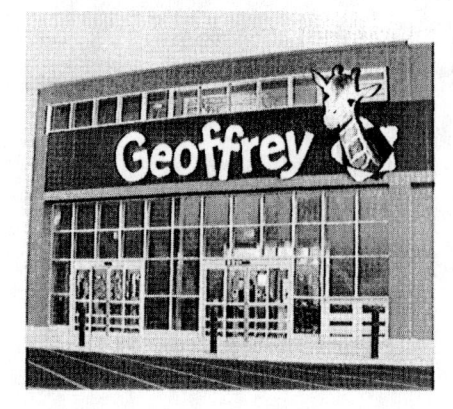

We made solid progress on our commitment to reduce selling, general and administrative (SG&A) expenses by 200 basis points by 2005. We were able to achieve a reduction of 70 basis points in 2002, so we're approximately a third of the way to achieving our four-year objectives in the first year.

We will also continue to find ways to strengthen and expand our portfolio, and, in fact, made progress in the development of new businesses for the future in 2002. Our test of Toys"R"Us ToyBox, our store concept within grocery stores which first opened in the summer of 2001, is generating positive results. By the end of the year, we expanded our initial test to more than 30 stores, and we are currently evaluating further expansion opportunities for 2003.

The customer response to our recently launched Geoffrey stores has been positive.

We also launched Geoffrey, which is a combination Toys"R"Us, Kids"R"Us and Babies"R"Us store, in four smaller markets in 2002. The customer response has been positive, and we've already derived some key learnings from Geoffrey that may be applicable to our other divisions. We plan to move forward carefully with this concept, but we are encouraged by the results we've seen.

Challenges for 2003

We are committed to doing all it takes to turn the U.S. toy stores around and to expand further on the successes that we've seen. This progress clearly indicates that we are on the right track with our strategies. Our challenge and our commitment is to build on what we've accomplished. We will accelerate execution of our merchandising, presentation, customer service, pricing and advertising efforts designed to drive traffic and increase profitable sales. Knowing that we also need the support of our vendor community to succeed, we continue to work in partnership with them to build excitement for their brands and to re-energize underperforming product categories.

We will accelerate execution of our strategies in 2003.

letter to our shareholders

We will also continue to improve our cost effectiveness to reduce our SG&A even further in 2003. In March, we reduced our national headquarters staff by approximately 200 positions, or 10%. We also announced that we would combine our Kids"R"Us and Babies"R"Us management teams into one group. This will help Kids"R"Us reduce its operating costs. In addition, we will ensure that our balance sheet remains strong and that we have ample liquidity now and into the future.

I think it truly says something about the strength of our portfolio that even in a year where we did not see the kind of success we expected in the largest division of our company, we were still able to announce a meaningful earnings increase. As we look to the future, I'm very proud of the steps that we've taken to manage the business in an undeniably difficult operating environment.

Babies"R"Us registers more expectant parents than any other retailer in the U.S.

Conclusion

As I write this letter, our associates from all divisions and all disciplines are working with tremendous commitment to make ours a more profitable organization. They share my absolute conviction that in 2003 we will seize upon every opportunity to drive sales and profits across every division. Given the solid improvement in our earnings in 2002, despite very difficult and uncertain economic and world environments, we believe we have ample evidence that we're on the right track. We will build on that progress, and we will not stop until we can deliver a better value for your investment and repay your faith in our company.

John H. Eyler, Jr.
Chairman, President and Chief Executive Officer
March 29, 2003

E18 Toys "R" Us Annual Report

Responding
to our
World

corporate responsibility

The Demand for Corporate **Responsibility**

Corporate Governance

Corporate governance is a joint responsibility requiring the involvement of and interaction between the Board of Directors and the senior management of the company.

Toys"R"Us, Inc. is fortunate to have a talented Board of Directors committed to the success of the company. For example, during fiscal year 2002, 11 Board meetings and 34 additional Board committee meetings were held. At several of the Board meetings, the Board met in executive session, outside the presence of senior management, to further discuss and examine issues of importance to the company.

After many months of careful research, investigation and thought, the Board adopted Corporate Governance Guidelines of the company in March 2002 to reflect the Board's commitment to monitor the effectiveness of policy and decision-making, both at the Board and management level, and to enhance stockholder value over the long term. Those Guidelines covered such issues as conflicts of interest, the compensation of the company's Chief Executive Officer and other Board members, the process and criteria for selecting Board members and the requirements that the Audit, Compensation and former Corporate Governance Committees be comprised solely of independent Board members and that independent Board members constitute a substantial majority of the Board.

In the past year, the Board has adopted Amended and Restated Corporate Governance Guidelines of the company that further address those issues and cover such issues as director orientation and continuing education and the Board's retention of independent advisors, as well as the requirement that the new Corporate Governance and Nominating Committee be comprised solely of independent Board members. The current Guidelines and committee charters are published in the company's proxy materials filed with the SEC in 2003.

The Toys"R"Us Board of Directors is fully engaged in and focused on the strategic issues facing our business. Each year, the Board devotes one meeting to develop, discuss and refine the company's long-range operating plan and overall corporate strategy. Following the Board's annual strategic meeting, the Board reviews the progress of one or more strategic initiatives at each scheduled meeting. Through the established procedures, the Board, consistent with good corporate governance, encourages the long-term success of the company by exercising sound and independent business judgment on the strategic issues that are important to the company's business.

Code of Conduct for Suppliers

There is growing concern in the global community about working conditions in many nations, including the United States, which may fall below the basic standards of fair and humane treatment. In an effort to source products in a manner that is both socially responsible and profitable, Toys"R"Us, Inc. developed its Code of Conduct for Suppliers program in 1997.

Implementation of the Code and the use of SA8000®, an independent monitoring and factory certification program, enable the company and its business partners to continually improve their performance in relation to workers' rights, labor standards and other human rights issues integral to the manufacturing process.

Developed by Social Accountability International (SAI) in 1998 and currently in use by businesses and governments around the world, SA8000® assessments are widely recognized by trade unions and non-governmental organizations as a powerful tool for creating environments where both workers and management benefit. Facilities in more than 20 nations and 15 industries have been SA8000® certified.

Participation in the Toys"R"Us Code of Conduct program and compliance with all of its provisions is mandatory for all suppliers who sell products, for the purpose of resale, to any Toys"R"Us, Inc. division. The company will terminate its business relationship with any supplier that elects not to participate in the Code of Conduct program or fails to abide by any of its stated provisions.

The Toys"R"Us Code of Conduct includes provisions covering the following issues: Child Labor, Forced Labor, Worker Environment, Working Conditions, Discrimination, Wages & Hours, and Freedom of Association.

Suppliers must post copies of the Toys"R"Us Code of Conduct for all workers to view. The company also encourages suppliers to implement their own Code of Conduct that meets or exceeds the provisions of the Toys"R"Us, Inc. program.

Inquiries about the Toys"R"Us Code of Conduct can be directed to: Vice President of Product Development, Safety Assurance & Imports, Toys"R"Us, Inc., 461 From Road, Paramus, NJ 07652.

Management's Discussion and Analysis
of Results of Operations and Financial Condition

RESULTS OF OPERATIONS

Comparison of Fiscal Year 2002 to 2001

We reported consolidated net sales of $11.3 billion for the 52-week fiscal year ended February 1, 2003 versus $11.0 billion for the 52-week fiscal year ended February 2, 2002, or a 3% increase in consolidated net sales. Our consolidated net sales were $11.2 billion for 2002, after excluding the impact of foreign currency translation, representing a 1% increase over 2001 net sales.

Total enterprise sales consist of all Toys"R"Us branded net sales from all of our stores and from our internet businesses, and the net sales from international licensed and franchised stores. We believe that enterprise sales are useful in analyzing the worldwide strength of our family of brands:

(In billions)	2002	2001	2000
Consolidated net sales	$ 11.3	$ 11.0	$ 11.3
Licensed and franchised net sales	1.8	1.6	1.5
Total enterprise sales	$ 13.1	$ 12.6	$ 12.8

Our consolidated comparable store sales, in local currencies, were flat for the fourth quarter and the fiscal year. Comparable store sales for our U.S. toy store division declined 1% for both the fourth quarter and the full year. Video game sales, which include sales of video hardware, software and accessories, were the primary factor contributing to these decreases. The video game category posted an 18% decline for the fourth quarter and a 13% decline for the year. The introduction of three video platforms (X-Box, Gamecube and Gameboy Advance) drove strong video sales in 2001. The performance of the video game category was also negatively impacted by significant reductions in the retail prices of video game platforms this year, such as the reduction in retail price from $299 to $199 for X-Box and PlayStation 2, and a reduction in retail price from $199 to $149 for Gamecube. Video game sales accounted for approximately 19% of our total U.S. toy store sales, excluding apparel sales, in the fourth quarter of 2002, down from 22% in 2001. Juvenile product sales in our U.S. toy stores declined 8% for the full year, mainly due to a shift of some sales to Babies"R"Us stores in the same markets. However, our core toy sales, which include boys and girls, learning and preschool toy categories, increased 3% in 2002.

Our International division reported comparable toy store sales increases, in local currencies, of 5% for the fourth quarter and 6% for the full year. These increases were primarily driven by the strong performance of our toy stores in the United Kingdom and Spain. We continued to expand the presence of in-store shops, such as Universe of Imagination (learning and educational products), Animal Alley (plush), Teentronics (electronic entertainment products) and Babies"R"Us (newborn and infant products). In addition, the penetration of exclusive products in the International division continues to grow, and, as a result, contributed to the improvement of our gross margin in this division.

Our Babies"R"Us division reported 12% net sales growth for the full year, primarily driven by the opening of 19 new Babies"R"Us stores in the United States this year. This division reported a 2% increase in comparable store sales for the fourth quarter and a 3% increase for the full year. A variety of initiatives helped to drive sales and guest traffic, including the rollout of extended apparel sizing to all stores and the addition of in-store photo studios in 21 Babies"R"Us stores.

Toysrus.com reported a net sales increase of 11% for the fourth quarter and 23% for the full year. Growth in the on-line toy business and the Babiesrus.com (baby products), Imaginarium.com (learning products) and the new Giftsrus.com (personalized gifts) on-line stores were factors in the sales performance of Toysrus.com.

We record the costs associated with operating our distribution network as a part of selling, general and administrative expenses (SG&A), including those costs that primarily relate to moving merchandise from distribution centers to stores. Therefore, our consolidated gross margin may not be comparable to some other retailers which include similar costs in their cost of sales. Our consolidated gross margin, as a percentage of sales, increased by 0.4% for the fourth quarter and was flat at 31.0% for the full year. Our consolidated gross margin for the fourth quarter of 2001 included $27 million of store closing markdowns, which were recorded as part of the restructuring and other charges announced in January 2002. Credits and allowances from vendors, which are netted against our cost of sales, have a positive impact on our consolidated gross margin. These credits and allowances increased our consolidated gross margin by 0.4% for the year, primarily in support of our increased promotional activities. Our U.S. toy store division reported a 0.7% decline in gross margin for the fourth quarter and a 0.8% decline for the full year. These declines were primarily attributed to the impact of increased promotional activity, such as our "Low Price Super Stars" pricing campaign, as well as the impact of higher markdowns recorded to keep our inventories fresh. Our International toy store division reported a 0.3% increase in gross margin to 32.2% for the year, primarily due to our continued emphasis on exclusive products which carry higher margins. Our Babies"R"Us division reported a 1.0% improvement in gross margin to 36.0%, primarily due to a shift in sales mix to higher margin import product. Gross margin for Toysrus.com improved 2.7% to 24.8%, reflecting an ongoing mix shift toward higher margin juvenile and learning products, as well as lower markdowns due to decreased inventory levels this year.

Our consolidated SG&A, as a percentage of net sales, increased 0.3% to 18.3% for the fourth quarter of 2002. This increase was primarily due to an increase in net advertising expense as a result of our decision to defer certain of our advertising activities to this year's fourth quarter. Our consolidated SG&A, as a percentage of sales, decreased 0.7% to 24.0% for the full year, primarily as a result of our continued focus on expense control. During 2002, we implemented shared services in a variety of functional groups, which, along with other efforts, helped us to achieve the overall reduction in SG&A as a percentage of sales. Advertising allowances, which are netted against

management's discussion and analysis

SG&A and have a positive impact on our SG&A, did not significantly vary year over year. SG&A for our U.S. toy store division decreased in absolute dollars, however it remained flat as a percentage of sales at 22.6% for the year. SG&A for the Babies"R"Us division decreased 0.2% to 23.6% for the year, primarily as a function of expense control coupled with higher sales productivity. SG&A for our International toy store business was reduced by 0.2% to 22.6% for the year. SG&A for Toysrus.com decreased for the year, due to lower fulfillment costs associated with product bundling, and a reduction in net advertising costs. The SG&A decrease, as well as an increase in Toysrus.com's net sales for the year, contributed to the overall reduction in consolidated SG&A, as a percentage of sales.

Depreciation and amortization increased by $9 million to $317 million for the year. Depreciation and amortization for 2001 included $13 million related to the amortization of goodwill. We ceased amortizing this goodwill on February 3, 2002 when we adopted the provisions of Statement of Financial Accounting Standard No. 142, "Goodwill and Other Intangible Assets,"(SFAS No. 142) (see the section "Recent Accounting Pronouncements"). Therefore, excluding the 2001 goodwill amortization, depreciation and amortization increased by $22 million for the year. This increase was primarily due to our Mission Possible store remodeling program, new store openings, and strategic investments to improve our management information systems. These increases were partially offset by the impact of closed stores. As part of the restructuring initiatives announced in January 2002, we closed 37 Kids"R"Us stores and 27 Toys"R"Us stores in the United States.

Interest expense, net of interest income, increased by $4 million to $23 million for the fourth quarter of 2002 and increased by $1 million to $110 million for the full year. These increases in net interest expense are mainly attributable to increased long-term borrowings, partly offset by increased cash investments, lower short-term borrowings and a decrease in interest rates.

Our effective tax rate was 36.5% versus 26.9% in the prior year. Our 2001 effective tax rate was impacted by the reversal of prior years' charges included in restructuring and other charges recorded in 2001.

Foreign currency translation had a 3% favorable impact on our consolidated net earnings for the fourth quarter of 2002 and a 4% favorable impact on our consolidated net earnings for the full year of 2002. Inflation did not have a significant impact on our full year consolidated net earnings for 2002.

Fourth Quarter Results

Our business is highly seasonal, with net sales and net earnings typically highest in the fourth quarter due to the inclusion of the holiday selling season. Fourth quarter 2002 net earnings were $278 million compared with $158 million in 2001. Diluted earnings per share were $1.30 for the fourth quarter of 2002 compared with $0.78 in 2001. Total consolidated comparable store sales, in local currencies, were flat in the fourth quarter of 2002 compared with an increase of 2% in 2001. Our results for 2001 included restructuring and other charges of $213 million ($126 million, net of taxes). Excluding the impact of these charges, net earnings were $284 million and diluted earnings per share were $1.39 for the fourth quarter of 2001.

Fourth Quarter Net Sales by Segment

(In millions)	2002	2001	2000
Toys"R"Us – U.S.	**$3,114**	$3,202	$3,270
Toys"R"Us – International	**1,069**	915	907
Babies"R"Us	**381**	342	335
Toysrus.com[1]	**193**	174	140
Other[2]	**112**	126	147
Total	**$4,869**	$4,759	$4,799

Fourth Quarter Operating Earnings by Segment

(In millions)	2002	2001	2000
Toys"R"Us – U.S.[3]	**$ 271**	$ 331	$ 335
Toys"R"Us – International	**157**	131	128
Babies"R"Us	**40**	29	29
Toysrus.com, net of minority interest[4]	**3**	(17)	(54)
Other[3], [5]	**(9)**	(35)	(13)
Restructuring and other charges	**–**	(186)	–
Total	**$ 462**	$ 253	$ 425

(1) Includes the sales of Toysrus.com – Japan.

(2) Includes the sales of the Kids"R"Us and Geoffrey divisions.

(3) Includes markdowns related to the store closings announced as part of the restructuring in 2001.

(4) Includes the operations of Toysrus.com – Japan, net of minority interest.

(5) Includes corporate expenses, the operating results of the Kids"R"Us and Geoffrey divisions and the equity in net earnings of Toys"R"Us – Japan, Ltd. (Toys – Japan).

Comparison of Fiscal Year 2001 to 2000

We reported consolidated net sales of $11.0 billion for the 52-week fiscal year ended February 2, 2002 versus $11.3 billion for the 53-week fiscal year ended February 3, 2001. Net sales of Toys – Japan, which has been accounted for on the "equity method" since its initial public offering, are included in our consolidated net sales in the first quarter of 2000 and excluded from our net sales thereafter. Our consolidated net sales were $11.0 billion for both years, after excluding sales of Toys – Japan. Currency translation did not have a significant impact on our consolidated net sales in 2001.

Total enterprise sales, which consist of all Toys"R"Us branded net sales from all of our stores and from our internet businesses, and the net sales from international licensed and franchised stores, were $12.6 billion in 2001 versus $12.8 billion in 2000.

Our consolidated comparable store sales, in local currencies, declined 1%. Comparable store sales for our U.S. toy store division increased 2% for the fourth quarter and declined 1% for the fiscal year. Video game sales were the primary drivers of the fourth quarter increase due to the introduction of X-Box, Gamecube and Gameboy Advance in the latter half of the year. Video game sales accounted for approximately 22% of our total U.S. toy store sales, excluding apparel sales, in the fourth quarter of 2001 as compared to 18% in the fourth quarter of the prior year. We had 433 stores in the Mission Possible format by the start of the 2001 holiday season, which also contributed to the comparable store sales increase in the fourth quarter. This gain partially offset the negative impact of 268 stores under construction during the first nine months of 2001 that were retrofitted to the Mission Possible format, as well as the negative impact resulting from the events of the September 11th terrorist attacks. Our International division reported comparable toy store sales increases of 5%, in local currencies, primarily driven by the performance of our toy stores in the United Kingdom, which reported double-digit comparable store sales growth. Our Babies"R"Us division reported 8% net sales growth, primarily driven by the opening of 20 new Babies"R"Us stores in the United States this year, as well as a 2% comparable store sales increase. Toysrus.com reported a net sales increase of 24% for the fourth quarter and 54% for the full year, which continued to reflect increases in its market share and the impact of the Toysrus.com alliance with Amazon.com that began in 2000.

Our consolidated gross margin, as a percentage of net sales, remained flat at 31.0%. Our consolidated margin for 2001 included $27 million of store closing markdowns, which were recorded as part of the restructuring and other charges announced in January 2002, and our consolidated margin for 2000 included $10 million of markdowns resulting from the alliance between Toysrus.com and Amazon.com. Excluding the impact of these items, our consolidated gross margin would have increased from 31.0% to 31.2%. Credits and allowances from our vendors, which are netted against our gross margin and have a positive impact on our cost of sales, did not vary significantly. Gross margin for the U.S. toy store division decreased 0.2% to 30.1% due to the impact of $15 million in store closing markdowns, that we recorded with the 2001 restructuring and other charges. The Babies"R"Us division reported a 1.2% improvement in gross margin to 35.0%, primarily due to a favorable sales shift to higher margin juvenile import and proprietary product. Our International toy store business reported a 0.2% increase in gross margin to 31.9%, primarily due to our continued emphasis on exclusive products.

Our consolidated SG&A, as a percentage of net sales, remained flat at 24.7% for the full year. Our consolidated SG&A for 2000 included $85 million of non-recurring charges related to the alliance between Toysrus.com and Amazon.com. Excluding these charges, our 2000 consolidated SG&A would have been 24.0% of sales. A reduction in advertising allowances, which are netted against SG&A and have a positive impact on SG&A, accounted for 0.3% of the increase in consolidated SG&A. SG&A for our U.S. toy store division increased 1.1% to 22.6%, reflecting the strategic investments we made in our business, including the renovation of our U.S. toy stores to the Mission Possible format and certain guest focused initiatives, both of which accounted for approximately 1.0% of this increase. Additional SG&A expenses resulting from the September 11th events accounted for approximately 0.1% of this increase. SG&A for our International toy store business increased 0.1% to 22.8%. SG&A for the Babies"R"Us division increased 0.4% to 23.8%, primarily attributable to increased payroll costs to support our emphasis on guest focused initiatives.

Depreciation and amortization increased by $18 million, primarily due to the Mission Possible store remodeling program, continued new store expansion and strategic investments to improve our management information systems.

Interest expense decreased by $10 million, primarily due to lower interest rates, partially offset by the impact of higher average total debt outstanding during the year. Interest and other income decreased by $15 million, primarily due to lower average investments outstanding, as well as lower interest rates.

Our effective tax rate declined to 26.9% from 36.5%. The reduction in our effective tax rate was due to the impact of the restructuring and other charges recorded in 2001.

Neither foreign currency exchange nor inflation had a significant impact on our consolidated net earnings in 2001.

Restructuring and Other Charges

In January 2002, we announced plans to reposition our business and, as part of this plan, we closed 27 non-Mission Possible format Toys"R"Us stores and 37 Kids"R"Us stores. In conjunction with the Kids"R"Us store closings in most all of these locations, we converted the nearest Toys"R"Us store into a Toys"R"Us/Kids"R"Us combo store.

As part of this plan, we eliminated approximately 1,700 staff positions in our stores and our headquarters. In addition, these plans included the costs of consolidating five of our store support center facilities into our new headquarters in Wayne, New Jersey, in 2003.

The costs associated with the facilities' consolidation, elimination of positions, and other actions designed to improve efficiency in support functions were $79 million, of which $15 million related to severance. The costs associated with store closings were $73 million for Kids"R"Us and $85 million for Toys"R"Us, of which $27 million was recorded in

management's discussion and analysis

cost of sales. The fair value of the facilities to be consolidated and stores identified for closure were obtained from third party appraisals. We also reversed $24 million of previously accrued charges ($11 million from the 1998 charge and $13 million from the 1995 charge) that we determined to be no longer needed. Accordingly, based on these actions, we recorded $213 million of pre-tax ($126 million after-tax) restructuring and other charges in the fourth quarter of the fiscal year ending February 2, 2002. Details on the components of the charges are as follows:

Description (in millions)	Initial charge	Utilized in 2001	Reserve balance at 2/02/02	Utilized in 2002	Adjustments to charge in 2002	Reserve balance at 2/01/03
Store closing:						
Lease commitments	$ 52	$ —	$ 52	$ (11)	$ —	$ 41
Severance	4	—	4	(4)	—	—
Write-down of property and equipment	75	(75)	—	—	—	—
Markdowns	27	—	27	(27)	—	—
Store support center consolidation:						
Lease commitments	28	—	28	—	11*	39
Write-down of property and equipment	29	(29)	—	—	—	—
Severance	15	—	15	(9)	(1)	5
Other	7	(7)	—	—	—	—
Total restructuring and other charges	$237	$(111)	$126	$ (51)	$ 10	$ 85

*In the fourth quarter of 2002, we determined that the reserve for lease costs for the disposition of one of our store support center facilities needed to be increased and, accordingly, recorded an additional charge of $11 million.

In 2000, Toysrus.com, our internet subsidiary, recorded $118 million in non-recurring charges as a result of the transition to its co-branded on-line store with Amazon.com, of which $10 million was included in cost of sales and $108 million was included in SG&A. These costs and charges related primarily to the closure of three distribution centers, as well as web-site asset write-offs and other costs. We had remaining lease commitment reserves of $3 million at February 1, 2003, that will be utilized in 2003 and thereafter.

We previously announced strategic initiatives to reposition our worldwide business and recorded related restructuring and other charges of $698 million in 1998 and $396 million in 1995 to complete these initiatives. As of February 1, 2003, we substantially completed all announced initiatives. We reversed reserves of $10 million in the fourth quarter of 2002 that were determined to no longer be needed. We also reversed reserves of $29 million in 2001, $24 million of which were reversed in the fourth quarter of 2001 and is discussed above, and $11 million in 2000 that were determined to no longer be needed. We had $42 million of reserves remaining at February 1, 2003, primarily for long-term lease commitments that will be utilized in 2003 and thereafter.

We believe that the remaining reserves at February 1, 2003 are reasonable estimates of what is required to complete all remaining initiatives.

Liquidity and Capital Resources

Our contractual obligations mainly consist of operating leases related to real estate used in the operation of our business and long-term debt. The table below shows the amounts we are obligated to pay for operating leases and principal amounts due under long-term debt issuances by fiscal period:

Contractual Obligations at February 1, 2003 (in millions)

	Amounts due in Fiscal 2003	Amounts due in Fiscal 2004 and Fiscal 2005	Amounts due in Fiscal 2006 and Fiscal 2007	Amounts due subsequent to 2007	Total
Operating leases*	$ 317	$ 615	$ 552	$ 1,786	$ 3,270
Sub-leases to third parties	17	26	20	40	103
Net operating lease obligations	300	589	532	1,746	3,167
Capital lease obligations	6	9	2	1	18
Long-term debt	367	541	697**	723	2,328
Minimum royalty obligations	14	7	—	—	21
Other obligations	2	4	—	—	6
Total contractual obligations	$ 689	$ 1,150	$ 1,231	$ 2,470	$ 5,540

*Includes synthetic lease obligation for our new headquarters facility in Wayne, New Jersey as described in the section "Critical Accounting Policies" and the note to our consolidated financial statements entitled "LEASES."

**Includes $390 million of equity security units, due 2007, which we are obligated to remarket in 2005. See the section "Financing Activities" and the note to our consolidated financial statements entitled "ISSUANCE OF COMMON STOCK AND EQUITY UNITS."

We are in compliance with all covenants associated with the above contractual obligations. The covenants include, among other things, requirements to provide financial information and public filings, and to comply with specified financial ratios. Non-compliance with associated covenants could give rise to accelerated payments, requirements to provide collateral, or changes in terms contained in the respective agreements.

At February 1, 2003, we had available over $1 billion of cash and cash equivalents. Our current portion of long-term debt of $379 million at February 1, 2003 includes a 475 million Swiss Franc note, due on January 28, 2004. In addition, our long-term debt at February 1, 2003 includes a 500 million Euro bond, due on February 13, 2004. See the section "Other Matters" and the note to our consolidated financial statements entitled "SUBSEQUENT EVENTS" for a discussion regarding the registration of $800 million of debt securities in March 2003 and the sale and issuance of $400 million of notes in April 2003.

We have $985 million in unsecured committed revolving credit facilities from a syndicate of financial institutions. These credit facilities are available for seasonal borrowings. There were no outstanding balances under these credit facilities at the end of fiscal 2002, 2001 or 2000. Additionally, we have lines of credit with various banks to meet certain of the short-term financing needs of our foreign subsidiaries. The following table shows our commercial commitments with their related expirations and availability:

25

management's discussion and analysis

Commercial Commitments at February 1, 2003 (in millions)

	Total amounts committed	Fiscal 2003	Fiscal 2004 and Fiscal 2005	Fiscal 2006 and Fiscal 2007	Fiscal 2008 and subsequent	Amounts available at February 1, 2003
Unsecured revolving credit facilities:						
Facility expiring in September 2006	$ 685	$ –	$ –	$ 685	$ –	$ 685
364-day facility expiring August 25, 2003	300	300	–	–	–	300
Total unsecured revolving credit facilities	$ 985	$ 300	$ –	$ 685	$ –	$ 985

Cash requirements for operating and investing activities will be met primarily through use of our exisiting cash and cash equivalents, cash flows from operating activities, and utilization of our unsecured committed revolving credit facilities. At February 1, 2003, we had in place stand-by letters of credit of $360 million, primarily as a guarantee for a debt obligation and $75 million of outstanding letters of credit related to import merchandise.

Credit Ratings

	Moody's	Standard & Poor's
Long-term debt	Baa3	BBB-
Commercial paper	P-3	A-3
Outlook	Negative	Stable
Date of last rating update	March 19, 2003	March 5, 2003

Our debt instruments do not contain provisions requiring acceleration of payment upon a debt rating downgrade. We continue to be confident in our ability to refinance maturing debt. Other credit ratings for our debt are available; however we disclosed above only ratings of the two largest nationally recognized statistical rating organizations because we believe these are the most relevant to our business.

The seasonal nature of our business typically causes cash balances to decline from the beginning of the year through October as inventory increases for the holiday selling season and funds are used for construction of new stores, remodeling and other initiatives that normally occur in this period. The fourth quarter, including the holiday season, accounts for more than 40% of our net sales and substantially all of our operating earnings.

Operating Activities

Our net cash inflows from operating activities increased to $574 million in 2002 from net cash inflows of $504 million in 2001 and net cash outflows of $151 in 2000. Net earnings, as adjusted for non-cash items, of $600 million in 2002 and $425 million in 2001 were the primary drivers of the net cash inflows from operations in those years. The net cash outflows from operations in 2000 were primarily driven by an increase in merchandise inventories of $486 million, and a net decrease in accounts payable, accrued expenses and other liabilities of $178 million, and was partially offset by net earnings, as adjusted for non-cash items, of $444 million for that year.

Investing Activities

Capital expenditures, net of dispositions, were $398 million in 2002, $705 million in 2001 and $402 million in 2000. Capital expenditures during these periods include investments to: open 55 new Babies"R"Us stores in the United States; open 18 new Toys"R"Us stores internationally; reformat our existing Toys"R"Us store base in the United States to our Mission Possible format and remodel 41 existing Kids"R"Us stores to our R-Generation store format; convert 286 existing Toys"R"Us stores into Toys"R"Us/Kids"R"Us combo stores; improve and enhance our management information systems.

During 2003, we plan to reduce our capital expenditures for our business to less than $350 million. We plan to open approximately 20 new Babies"R"Us stores in the United States and approximately five new international Toys"R"Us stores, and we also plan to continue to improve and enhance our management information systems in 2003.

Financing Activities

Net cash inflows from financing activities were $613 million in 2002, primarily driven by net long-term borrowings of $407 million, as well as proceeds received from the issuance of our common stock and contracts to purchase common stock totaling $266 million. In May 2002, we issued 14,950,000 shares of our common stock at a price of $17.65 per share and received net proceeds of $253 million. On the same date, we issued 8,050,000 equity security units with a stated amount of $50 per unit and received net proceeds of $390 million. Each security unit consists of a contract to purchase, for $50, a specified number of shares of Toys"R"Us common stock in August 2005, and a senior note due in 2007 with a principal amount of $50. The fair value of the contract to purchase shares of Toys"R"Us common stock was estimated at $1.77 per equity security unit. The fair value of the senior note was estimated at $48.23 per equity security unit. Interest on the senior notes is payable quarterly at an initial rate of 6.25%. We are obligated to remarket the notes in May 2005 at the then prevailing interest rate for similar notes. If the remarketing were not to be successful, we would be entitled to take possession of the senior notes, and the holder's obligation under the contracts to purchase shares of our common stock would be deemed to have been satisfied. The net proceeds from these public offerings were used to refinance short-term borrowings and for other general corporate purposes.

Net cash inflows from financing activities were $191 million in 2001, primarily as a result of net borrowings of $216 million during the year. In July 2001, we issued and sold $750 million of notes, comprised of $500 million of notes bearing interest at 7.625% per annum, maturing in 2011, and $250 million of notes bearing interest at 6.875% per annum, maturing in 2006. The proceeds from these notes were used to reduce outstanding commercial paper obligations. Simultaneously with the sale of the notes, we entered into interest rate swap agreements. As a result of the interest rate swap agreements, interest on the $500 million notes accrues at an effective rate of LIBOR plus 1.5120% and interest on the $250 million notes accrues at an effective rate of LIBOR plus 1.1515%. In October 2002, we terminated a portion of the interest rate swap agreeements and received a payment of $27 million, which is being amortized over the remaining lives of the related notes. Concurrently, we entered into new interest rate swap agreements. Of the $500 million notes, $200 million accrues interest at an effective rate of LIBOR plus 3.06%, and $125 million of the $250 million notes accrues interest at an effective rate of LIBOR plus 3.54%. Interest is payable on both notes semi-annually on February 1 and August 1 of each year. In February 2001, we borrowed 500 million EURO through the public issuance of a EURO bond bearing interest at 6.375% per annum. The obligation was swapped into a $466 million fixed rate obligation with an effective rate of 7.43% per annum with interest payments due annually and principal due February 13, 2004.

Net cash outflows from financing activities were $2 million for 2000. Net borrowings for 2000 were $521 million and were used primarily to repurchase 42 million shares of our common stock, to fund increased inventory levels, and to fund our Toysrus.com internet subsidiary. In 2000, we received a total of $97 million from SOFTBANK Venture Capital and affiliates representing their 20% minority interest investment in Toysrus.com.

Other Matters

On March 24, 2003, we filed a "shelf" registration statement with the Securities and Exchange Commission giving us the capability to sell up to $800 million of debt securities that would be used to repay outstanding debt and for general corporate purposes. In April 2003, we sold and issued $400 million in notes bearing interest at a coupon rate of 7.875%, maturing on April 15, 2013. The notes were sold at a price of 98.305%, resulting in an effective yield of 8.125%. Simultaneously with the sale of the notes, we entered into interest rate swap agreements. As a result of these swap agreements, interest will accrue at the effective rate of LIBOR plus 3.622%. Interest is payable semi-annually commencing on October 15, 2003. We plan to use the proceeds from these notes for the repayment of indebtedness maturing in the 2004 calendar year, and pending such repayment, for working capital needs and other general corporate purposes.

In August 2000, eleven purported class action lawsuits were filed (six in the United States District Court for the District of New Jersey, three in the United States District Court for the Northern District of California, one in the United States District Court for the Western District of Texas and one in the Superior Court of the State of California, County of San Bernardino), against us and our affiliates Toysrus.com, Inc. and Toysrus.com, LLC. In September 2000, three additional purported class action lawsuits were filed (two in the United States District Court for the District of New Jersey and one in the United States District Court for the Western District of Texas). These actions generally purport to bring claims under federal privacy and computer fraud statutes, as well as under state statutory and common law, on behalf of all persons who have visited one or more of our websites and either made an online purchase or allegedly had information about them unlawfully "intercepted," "monitored," "transmitted," or "used." All the suits (except one filed in the United States District Court for the District of New Jersey) also named Coremetrics, Inc. (Coremetrics) as a defendant. Coremetrics is an internet marketing company with whom we have an agreement. These suits seek damages in unspecified amounts and other relief under state and federal law.

With Coremetrics, we filed a joint application with the Multidistrict litigation panel which resulted in all of the federal actions being consolidated and transferred to the United States District Court for the Northern District of California. Plaintiffs voluntarily dismissed the action in the Superior Court of the State of California, County of San Bernardino without prejudice. On October 16, 2001, plaintiffs filed an amended complaint in the United States District Court for the Northern District of California. We believe that we have substantial defenses to all of these claims. On November 13, 2002, we entered into a settlement agreement with plaintiffs in connection with all causes of action. This settlement agreement is subject to the court's review and approval and will not have a material impact on our consolidated financial statements.

We are party to certain other litigation, which, in our judgment, based in part on the opinion of legal counsel, will not have a material adverse effect on our consolidated financial statements.

In August 2000, Toysrus.com entered into a 10-year strategic alliance with Amazon.com to operate a co-branded toy and video game on-line store, which was launched in the third quarter of 2000. In addition, a co-branded baby products on-line store was launched in May 2001 and a co-branded creative and learning products on-line store was launched in July 2001. Under this alliance, Toysrus.com and Amazon.com are responsible for specific aspects of the on-line stores. Toysrus.com is responsible for merchandising, marketing and content for the co-branded store. Toysrus.com also identifies, buys, owns and manages the inventory. Amazon.com handles web-site development, order fulfillment, guest service, and the housing of Toysrus.com's inventory in Amazon.com's U.S. distribution centers. Also in August 2000, Amazon.com was granted a warrant entitling it to acquire up to 5% (subject to dilution under certain circumstances) of the capital of Toysrus.com at the then market value. This warrant has not been exercised.

We recorded a non-operating gain of $315 million ($200 million net of taxes) resulting from the initial public offering of shares of Toys – Japan, which was completed in April 2000. Of this gain, $91 million resulted from an adjustment to the basis of our investment in Toys – Japan, and $224 million was related to the sale of a portion of company-owned common stock of Toys – Japan, for which we received net cash proceeds of $267 million. In connection with this transaction, we recorded a provision for current income taxes of $82 million and a provision for deferred income taxes of $33 million. As a result of this transaction, our ownership percentage in the common stock of Toys – Japan was reduced from 80% to 48%. Toys – Japan is a licensee of our company.

Quantitative and Qualitative Disclosures About Market Risks

We are exposed to market risk from potential changes in interest rates and foreign exchange rates. The countries in which we own assets and operate stores are politically stable, and we regularly evaluate these risks and have taken the following measures to mitigate these risks: our foreign exchange risk management objectives are to stabilize cash flow from the effects of foreign currency fluctuations; we do not participate in speculative hedges; and we will, whenever practical, offset local investments in foreign currencies with liabilities denominated in the same currencies. We also enter into derivative financial instruments to hedge a variety of risk exposures, including interest rate and currency risks.

Our foreign currency exposure is primarily concentrated in the United Kingdom, Europe, Canada, Australia and Japan. We face currency exposures that arise from translating the results of our worldwide operations into U.S. dollars from exchange rates that have fluctuated from the beginning of the period. We also face transactional currency exposures relating to merchandise that we purchase in foreign currencies. We enter into forward exchange contracts to minimize and manage the currency risks associated with these transactions. The counter-parties to these contracts are highly rated financial institutions and we do not have significant exposure to any one counter-party. Gains or losses on these derivative instruments are largely offset by the gains or losses on the underlying hedged transactions. For foreign currency derivative instruments, market risk is determined by calculating the impact on fair value of an assumed one-time change in foreign rates relative to the U.S. dollar. Fair values were estimated based on market prices, where available, or dealer quotes. With respect to derivative instruments outstanding at February 1, 2003, a 10% appreciation of the U.S. dollar would have increased pre-tax earnings in 2002 by $39 million, while a 10% depreciation of the U.S. dollar would have decreased pre-tax earnings in 2002 by $42 million. Comparatively, considering our derivative instruments outstanding at February 2, 2002, a 10% appreciation of the U.S. dollar would have increased pre-tax earnings in 2001 by $13 million, while a 10% depreciation of the U.S. dollar would have decreased pre-tax earnings in 2001 by $13 million.

We are faced with interest rate risks resulting from interest rate fluctuations. We have a variety of fixed and variable rate debt instruments. In an effort to manage interest rate exposures, we strive to achieve an acceptable balance between fixed and variable rate debt and have entered into interest rate swaps to maintain that balance. For interest rate derivative instruments, market risk is determined by calculating the impact to fair value of an assumed one-time change in interest rates across all maturities. Fair values were estimated based on market prices, where available, or dealer quotes. A change in interest rates on variable rate debt is assumed to impact earnings and cash flow, but not the fair value of debt. A change in interest rates on fixed rate debt is assumed to impact the fair value of debt, but not earnings and cash flow. Based on our overall interest rate exposure at February 1, 2003 and February 2, 2002, a 1% increase in interest rates would have decreased pre-tax earnings by $15 million in 2002 and $11 million in 2001, respectively. A 1% decrease in interest rates would have increased pre-tax earnings by $15 million in 2002 and $11 million in 2001. A 1% increase in interest rates would decrease the fair value of our long-term debt at February 1, 2003 and February 2, 2002 by approximately $90 million and $79 million, respectively. A 1% decrease in interest rates would increase the fair value of our long-term debt at February 1, 2003 and February 2, 2002 by approximately $98 million and $87 million, respectively.

See notes to our consolidated financial statements for additional discussion of our outstanding derivative financial instruments at February 1, 2003.

Critical Accounting Policies

Our consolidated financial statements have been prepared in accordance with accounting principles generally accepted in the United States. The preparation of these financial statements requires us to make certain estimates and assumptions that affect the reported amounts of assets, liabilities, revenues and expenses, and the related disclosure of contingent assets and liabilities as of the date of the financial statements and during the applicable periods. We base these estimates on historical experience and on other various assumptions that we believe to be reasonable under the circumstances. Actual results may differ materially from these estimates under different assumptions or conditions and could have a material impact on our consolidated financial statements.

We believe the following are some of the critical accounting policies that include significant judgments and estimates used in the preparation of our consolidated financial statements.

Inventories and Vendor Allowances:

Merchandise inventories for the U.S. toy store division, which represent approximately 60% of total merchandise inventories, are stated at the lower of LIFO (last-in, first-out) cost or market value, as determined by the retail inventory method. All other merchandise inventories are stated at the lower of FIFO (first-in, first-out) cost or market value, as determined by the retail inventory method.

We receive various types of merchandise and other types of allowances from our vendors, which are based on negotiated terms. We use estimates at interim periods to record our provisions for inventory shortage and to record vendor funded merchandise allowances. These estimates are based on available data and other factors and are adjusted to actual amounts at the completion of our physical inventories and finalization of all vendor allowances.

management's discussion and analysis

Deferred Tax Assets:
As part of the process of preparing our consolidated financial statements, we are required to estimate our income taxes in each of the jurisdictions in which we operate. This process involves estimating our actual current tax exposure, together with assessing temporary differences resulting from differing treatment of items for tax and accounting purposes. These differences result in deferred tax assets and liabilities, which are included within our consolidated balance sheet. The measurement of deferred tax assets is adjusted by a valuation allowance to recognize the extent to which, more likely than not, the future tax benefits will be recognized.

At February 1, 2003, we recorded deferred tax assets, net of valuation allowances, of $317 million. We believe it is more likely than not that we will be able to realize these assets through the reduction of future taxable income. We base this belief upon the levels of taxable income historically generated by our businesses, as well as projections of future taxable income. If future levels of taxable income are not consistent with our expectations, we may be required to record an additional valuation allowance, which could reduce our net earnings by a material amount.

Derivatives and Hedging Activities:
We enter into derivative financial arrangements to hedge a variety of risk exposures, including interest rate and currency risks associated with our long-term debt, as well as foreign currency risk relating to import merchandise purchases. We account for these hedges in accordance with SFAS No. 133, "Accounting for Derivative Instruments and Hedging Activities," and we record the fair value of these instruments within our consolidated balance sheet. Gains and losses from derivative financial instruments are largely offset by gains and losses on the underlying transactions. At February 1, 2003, we increased the carrying amount of our long-term debt by $172 million, representing the fair value of debt in excess of the carrying amount on that date. Also at February 1, 2003, we recorded derivative assets of $158 million and derivative liabilities of $10 million. While we intend to continue to meet the conditions for hedge accounting, if hedges were not to be highly effective in offsetting cash flows attributable to the hedged risk, the changes in the fair value of the derivatives used as hedges could have a material effect on our consolidated financial statements.

Insurance Risks:
We insure a substantial portion of our general liability and workers' compensation risks through a wholly-owned insurance subsidiary, in addition to third party insurance coverage. Provisions for losses related to self-insured risks are based upon independent actuarially determined estimates. While we believe these provisions for losses to be adequate, the ultimate liabilities may be in excess of, or less than, the amounts recorded.

Stock Options:
We account for stock options under Accounting Principles Board Opinion No. 25, "Accounting for Stock Issued to Employees", which does not require compensation costs related to stock options to be recorded in net income, as all options granted under the various stock option plans had an exercise price equal to the market value of the underlying common stock at grant date. SFAS No. 148 "Accounting for Stock-Based Compensation – Transition and Disclosure – an amendment of SFAS No. 123," provides guidance on acceptable approaches to the implementation of SFAS No. 123, and requires more prominent disclosures of pro forma net earnings and earnings per share determined as if the fair value method of accounting for stock options had been applied in measuring compensation cost. Stock options are further detailed in the note to our consolidated financial statements entitled "STOCK OPTIONS."

Synthetic Lease:
Our new corporate headquarters facility, located in Wayne, New Jersey, is financed under a lease arrangement commonly referred to as a "synthetic lease." Under this lease, unrelated third parties, arranged by Wachovia Development Corporation, a multi-purpose real estate investment company, will fund up to $125 million for the acquisition and construction of the facility. Upon completion of the construction, which is expected to be in 2003, we will begin to pay rent on the facility until the lease expires in 2011. The rent will be based on a mix of fixed and variable interest rates, which will be applied against the final amount funded. Upon expiration of the lease, we would expect to either: renew the lease arrangement; purchase the facility from the lessor; or remarket the property on behalf of the owner. The lease agreement provides the lessor with a residual value guarantee equal to the funding for the acquisition and construction of the facility. Under accounting principles generally accepted in the United States, this arrangement is required to be treated as an operating lease for accounting purposes and as a financing for tax purposes.

Recent Accounting Pronouncements

In 2002, the FASB Emerging Issues Task Force issued EITF issue No. 02-16, "Accounting by a Reseller for Cash Consideration Received from a Vendor" (EITF 02-16). EITF 02-16 considers vendor allowances as a reduction in the price of a vendor's product that should be recognized as a reduction of cost of sales. Advertising allowances that are received for specific, identifiable and incremental costs are considered a reduction of advertising expenses and should be recognized as a reduction of SG&A. The provisions of EITF 02-16 are effective for all new arrangements, or modifications to existing arrangements, beginning after December 31, 2002. We are currently evaluating the potential impact of the provisions of EITF 02-16 on our consolidated financial statements for 2003.

In January 2003, the Financial Accounting Standards Board (FASB) issued Interpretation No. 46, "Consolidation of Variable Interest Entities" (FIN 46), which will require the consolidation of entities that are controlled by a company through interests other than voting interests. Under the requirements of this interpretation, an entity that maintains a majority of the risks or rewards associated with Variable Interest Entities (VIEs), commonly known as special purpose entities, is effectively in the same position as the parent in a parent-subsidiary relationship. Disclosure requirements of VIEs are effective in all financial statements issued after January 31, 2003. The consolidation requirements apply to all VIEs created after January 31, 2003. FIN 46 requires public companies to apply the consolidation requirements to VIEs that existed prior to February 1, 2003 and remained in existence as of the beginning of annual or interim periods beginning after June 15, 2003. Our new corporate headquarters facility, located in Wayne, New Jersey, is leased from unrelated third parties, arranged by a multi-purpose real estate investment company that we do not control. In addition, we do not have the majority of the associated risks or rewards. Accordingly, we believe that FIN 46 will have no impact on the accounting for this synthetic lease. The synthetic lease is discussed above and in the note to our consolidated financial statements entitled "LEASES." We believe that FIN 46 will not have a material impact on our consolidated financial statements.

In November 2002, the FASB issued Interpretation No. 45, "Guarantor's Accounting and Disclosure Requirements for Guarantees, Including Indirect Guarantees of Indebtedness of Others" (FIN 45), which imposes new disclosure and liability-recognition requirements for financial guarantees, performance guarantees, indemnifications and indirect guarantees of the indebtedness of others. FIN 45 requires certain guarantees to be recorded at fair value. This is different from previous practice, where a liability would typically be recorded only when a loss is probable and reasonably estimable. The initial recognition and initial measurement provisions are applicable on a prospective basis to guarantees issued or modified after December 31, 2002. FIN 45 also requires new disclosures, even when the likelihood of making any payments under the guarantee is remote. The disclosure requirements are effective for interim and annual periods ending after December 15, 2002. We have procedures to identify guarantees contained in the various legal documents and agreements that have been executed, and those to be executed in the future, that fall within the scope of FIN 45. We expect that FIN 45 will not have a material impact on our consolidated financial statements.

In July 2002, the FASB issued SFAS No. 146, "Accounting for Costs Associated with Exit or Disposal Activities" (SFAS No. 146), which addresses the recognition, measurement, and reporting of costs associated with exit or disposal activities and supercedes Emerging Issues Task Force issue No. 94-3, "Liability Recognition for Certain Employee Termination Benefits and Other Costs to Exit an Activity (including Certain Costs Incurred in a Restructuring)," (EITF No. 94-3). The fundamental difference between SFAS No. 146 and EITF No. 94-3 is the requirement that a liability for a cost associated with an exit or disposal activity be recognized when the liability is incurred rather than at the date an entity commits to an exit plan. A fundamental conclusion of SFAS No. 146 is that an entity's commitment to a plan, by itself, does not create an obligation that meets the definition of a liability. SFAS No. 146 also establishes that the initial measurement of a liability recognized be recorded at fair value. The provisions of this statement are effective for exit or disposal activities that are initiated after December 31, 2002, with early application encouraged. We believe that the adoption of this pronouncement will not have a significant effect on our consolidated financial statements.

In August 2001, the FASB issued SFAS No. 144, "Accounting for the Impairment or Disposal of Long-Lived Assets" (SFAS No. 144), which addresses financial accounting and reporting for the impairment or disposal of long-lived assets and supersedes SFAS No. 121, "Accounting for the Impairment of Long-Lived Assets and for Long-Lived Assets to be Disposed Of." We adopted SFAS No. 144 as of February 3, 2002 and the adoption did not have a significant effect on our consolidated financial statements.

In July 2001, the FASB issued SFAS No. 142, "Goodwill and Other Intangible Assets" (SFAS No. 142), which is effective for fiscal years beginning after December 15, 2001. SFAS No. 142 changes the accounting for goodwill from an amortization method to an impairment only approach. We adopted this pronouncement on February 3, 2002. As a result of this adoption, amortization of $348 million of goodwill, which was to be amortized ratably through 2037, ceased. Based on the historical and projected operating results of the reporting units to which the goodwill relates, we determined that no impairment of this goodwill exists. Application of the non-amortization provisions of SFAS No. 142 resulted in an increase in net earnings of $2 million for the fourth quarter of 2002 and $8 million for the 2002 fiscal year.

Forward Looking Statements

This annual report contains "forward looking" statements within the meaning of Section 27A of the Securities Act of 1933, as amended, and Section 21E of the Securities Exchange Act of 1934, which are intended to be covered by the safe harbors created thereby. All statements that are not historical facts, including statements about our beliefs or expectations, are forward-looking statements. We generally identify these statements by words or phrases such as "anticipate," "estimate," "plan," "expect," "believe," "intend," "foresee," "will," "may," and similar words or phrases. These statements discuss, among other things, our strategy, store openings and renovations, future performance and anticipated cost savings, results of our restructuring, anticipated international development and other goals and targets. Such statements involve risks and uncertainties that exist in our operations and business environment that could render actual outcomes and results materially different than predicted. Our forward-looking statements are based on assumptions about many factors, including, but not limited to, ongoing competitive pressures in the retail industry, changes in consumer spending and consumer preferences, general economic conditions in the United States and other jurisdictions in which we conduct our business (such as interest rates, currency exchange rates and consumer confidence) and normal business uncertainty. While we believe that our assumptions are reasonable at the time forward-looking statements were made, we caution that it is impossible to predict the actual outcome of numerous factors and, therefore, readers should not place undue reliance on such statements. Forward-looking statements speak only as of the date they are made, and we undertake no obligation to update such statements in light of new information or future events that involve inherent risks and uncertainties. Actual results may differ materially from those contained in any forward-looking statement.

consolidated financial statements

Consolidated Statements of Earnings
Toys"R"Us, Inc. and Subsidiaries

			Year Ended
(in millions, except per share data)	**February 1, 2003**	February 2, 2002	February 3, 2001
Net sales	**$ 11,305**	$ 11,019	$ 11,332
Cost of sales	**7,799**	7,604	7,815
Gross margin	**3,506**	3,415	3,517
Selling, general and administrative expenses	**2,718**	2,721	2,801
Depreciation and amortization	**317**	308	290
Restructuring and other charges	**–**	186	–
Total operating expenses	**3,035**	3,215	3,091
Operating earnings	**471**	200	426
Other (expense) income:			
Interest expense	**(119)**	(117)	(127)
Interest and other income	**9**	8	23
Gain from IPO of Toys – Japan	**–**	–	315
Earnings before income taxes	**361**	91	637
Income taxes	**132**	24	233
Net earnings	**$ 229**	$ 67	$ 404
Basic earnings per share	**$ 1.10**	$ 0.34	$ 1.92
Diluted earnings per share	**$ 1.09**	$ 0.33	$ 1.88

See notes to consolidated financial statements.

Consolidated Balance Sheets
Toys"R"Us, Inc. and Subsidiaries

(In millions)	February 1, 2003	February 2, 2002
Assets		
Current Assets:		
Cash and cash equivalents	$ 1,023	$ 283
Restricted cash	60	–
Accounts and other receivables	202	210
Merchandise inventories	2,190	2,041
Prepaid expenses and other current assets	85	97
Total current assets	3,560	2,631
Property and Equipment:		
Real estate, net	2,398	2,313
Other, net	2,365	2,231
Total property and equipment	4,763	4,544
Goodwill, net	348	348
Derivative assets	158	42
Other assets	568	511
	$ 9,397	$ 8,076
Liabilities and Stockholders' Equity		
Current Liabilities:		
Short-term borrowings	$ –	$ –
Accounts payable	896	878
Accrued expenses and other current liabilities	824	738
Income taxes payable	279	319
Current portion of long-term debt	379	39
Total current liabilities	2,378	1,974
Long-term debt	2,139	1,816
Deferred income taxes	545	447
Derivative liabilities	10	122
Other liabilities	282	276
Minority interest in Toysrus.com	13	27
Stockholders' Equity:		
Common stock	30	30
Additional paid-in capital	414	444
Retained earnings	5,457	5,228
Accumulated other comprehensive loss	(149)	(267)
Treasury shares, at cost	(1,722)	(2,021)
Total stockholders' equity	4,030	3,414
	$ 9,397	$ 8,076

See notes to consolidated financial statements.

consolidated financial statements

Consolidated Statements of Cash Flows
Toys"R"Us, Inc. and Subsidiaries

			Year Ended	
(In millions)		February 1, 2003	February 2, 2002	February 3, 2001
Cash Flows from Operating Activities				
Net earnings		$ 229	$ 67	$ 404
Adjustments to reconcile net earnings to net cash from operating activities:				
Depreciation and amortization		317	308	290
Deferred income taxes		99	(6)	67
Minority interest in Toysrus.com		(14)	(24)	(52)
Other non-cash items		(31)	(29)	50
Restructuring and other charges		–	109	–
Gain from initial public offering of Toys – Japan		–	–	(315)
Changes in operating assets and liabilities:				
Accounts and other receivables		8	15	(69)
Merchandise inventories		(100)	217	(486)
Prepaid expenses and other operating assets		(18)	36	(54)
Accounts payable, accrued expenses and other liabilities		112	(241)	(178)
Income taxes payable		(28)	52	192
Net cash from operating activities		574	504	(151)
Cash Flows from Investing Activities				
Capital expenditures, net		(398)	(705)	(402)
Net proceeds from sale of Toys – Japan common stock		–	–	267
Reduction in cash due to deconsolidation of Toys – Japan		–	–	(15)
Net cash from investing activities		(398)	(705)	(150)
Cash Flows from Financing Activities				
Short-term borrowings, net		–	(588)	419
Long-term borrowings		548	1,214	147
Long-term debt repayment		(141)	(410)	(45)
Proceeds from issuance of stock and contracts to purchase stock		266	–	–
Increase in restricted cash		(60)	–	–
Exercise of stock options		–	19	2
Proceeds received from investors in Toysrus.com		–	–	97
Share repurchase program		–	(44)	(632)
Issuance of stock warrants		–	–	10
Net cash from financing activities		613	191	(2)
Effect of exchange rate changes on cash and cash equivalents		(49)	18	(6)
Cash and Cash Equivalents				
Increase/(decrease) during year		740	8	(309)
Beginning of year		283	275	584
End of year		$ 1,023	$ 283	$ 275
Supplemental Disclosures of Cash Flow Information				
Income tax payments (refunds), net		$ 32	$ (22)	$ (2)
Interest payments		$ 93	$ 85	$ 128

See notes to consolidated financial statements.

Consolidated Statements of Stockholders' Equity
Toys"R"Us, Inc. and Subsidiaries

(In millions)	Common Stock Issued Shares	Common Stock Issued Amount	Common Stock In Treasury Shares	Common Stock In Treasury Amount	Additional paid-in capital	Accumulated other comprehensive loss	Retained earnings	Total stockholders' equity
Balance, January 29, 2000	300.4	$ 30	(61.1)	$ (1,423)	$ 453	$ (137)	$ 4,757	$ 3,680
Net earnings for the year	–	–	–	–	–	–	404	404
Foreign currency translation adjustments	–	–	–	–	–	(74)	–	(74)
Comprehensive income								330
Share repurchase program	–	–	(42.1)	(632)	–	–	–	(632)
Issuance of restricted stock, net	–	–	–	50	(21)	–	–	29
Exercise of stock options, net	–	–	0.3	4	(3)	–	–	1
Issuance of stock warrants	–	–	–	–	10	–	–	10
Balance, February 3, 2001	300.4	$ 30	(102.9)	$ (2,001)	$ 439	$ (211)	$ 5,161	$ 3,418
Net earnings for the year	–	–	–	–	–	–	67	67
Foreign currency translation adjustments	–	–	–	–	–	(55)	–	(55)
Unrealized loss on hedged transactions	–	–	–	–	–	(1)	–	(1)
Comprehensive income								11
Share repurchase program	–	–	(2.1)	(44)	–	–	–	(44)
Issuance of restricted stock, net	–	–	0.5	5	4	–	–	9
Exercise of stock options, net	–	–	0.8	19	1	–	–	20
Balance, February 2, 2002	300.4	$ 30	(103.7)	$ (2,021)	$ 444	$ (267)	$ 5,228	$ 3,414
Net earnings for the year	–	–	–	–	–	–	229	229
Foreign currency translation adjustments	–	–	–	–	–	127	–	127
Unrealized loss on hedged transactions	–	–	–	–	–	(9)	–	(9)
Comprehensive income								347
Common stock equity offering	–	–	14.9	301	(35)	–	–	266
Issuance of restricted stock, net	–	–	0.9	(2)	5	–	–	3
Balance, February 1, 2003	**300.4**	**$ 30**	**(87.9)**	**$(1,722)**	**$ 414**	**$ (149)**	**$ 5,457**	**$ 4,030**

See notes to consolidated financial statements.

Notes to Consolidated Financial Statements

Toys"R"Us, Inc. and Subsidiaries

(Amounts in millions, except per share data)
SUMMARY OF SIGNIFICANT ACCOUNTING POLICIES

Fiscal Year
The company's fiscal year ends on the Saturday nearest to January 31. References to 2002, 2001, and 2000 are for the 52 weeks ended February 1, 2003 and February 2, 2002 and the 53 weeks ended February 3, 2001.

Reclassification
Certain reclassifications have been made to prior periods to conform to current presentations.

Principles of Consolidation
The consolidated financial statements include the accounts for the company and its subsidiaries. All material intercompany balances and transactions have been eliminated. Assets and liabilities of foreign operations are translated at current rates of exchange at the balance sheet date while results of operations are translated at average rates in effect for the period. Unrealized translation gains or losses are shown as a component of accumulated other comprehensive loss within stockholders' equity.

Use of Estimates
The preparation of financial statements in conformity with accounting principles generally accepted in the United States requires management to make estimates and assumptions that affect the amounts reported in the consolidated financial statements and accompanying notes. Actual results could differ from those estimates.

Revenue Recognition
The company recognizes sales revenue at the time the guest takes possession of merchandise or at the point of sale in our stores, or at the time of delivery for products purchased from our web-sites. Layaway transactions are recognized as revenue when the guest satisfies all payment obligations and takes possession of the merchandise. Revenues from the sale of gift cards and issuance of store credits are recognized as they are redeemed.

Advertising Costs
Net advertising costs are included in selling, general and administrative expenses and are expensed at the point of first broadcast or distribution. Net advertising costs were $147, $160, and $135 for 2002, 2001 and 2000, respectively.

Cash and Cash Equivalents
The company considers its highly liquid investments with original maturities of less than three months to be cash equivalents.

Merchandise Inventories
Merchandise inventories for the U.S. toy store division, which represent approximately 60% of total inventories, are stated at the lower of LIFO (last-in, first-out) cost or market, as determined by the retail inventory method. All other merchandise inventories are stated at the lower of FIFO (first-in, first-out) cost or market, as determined by the retail inventory method.

Credits and Allowances Received from Vendors
Credits and allowances are received from vendors and are related to formal agreements negotiated with such vendors. These credits and allowances are predominantly for cooperative advertising, promotions, and volume related purchases. These credits and allowances, excluding advertising allowances, are netted against cost of sales. The company's policy is to recognize credits, that are related directly to inventory purchases, as the related inventory is sold. Cooperative advertising allowances offset the cost of cooperative advertising that is agreed to by the company and its vendors, and are netted against advertising expenses included in selling, general and administrative expenses. The company's policy is to recognize cooperative advertising allowances in the period that the related advertising media is run.

Cost of Sales and Selling, General and Administrative Expenses
The significant components of the line item "Cost of sales" include the cost to acquire merchandise from vendors; freight in; markdowns; provision for inventory shortages; and discounts and allowances related to merchandise inventories.

The significant components of the line item "Selling, general and administrative expenses" include store payroll and related payroll benefits; rent and other store operating expenses; net advertising expenses; costs associated with operating the company's distribution network that primarily relate to moving merchandise from distribution centers to stores; and other corporate-related expenses.

Property and Equipment
Property and equipment are recorded at cost. Leasehold improvements represent capital improvements made to leased locations. Depreciation and amortization are provided using the straight-line method over the estimated useful lives of the assets or, where applicable, the terms of the respective leases, whichever is shorter. Accelerated depreciation methods are used for income tax reporting purposes with recognition of deferred income taxes for the resulting temporary differences. The company periodically evaluates the need to recognize impairment losses relating to long-lived assets. If indications of impairment exist and if the value of the assets are impaired, an impairment loss would be recognized.

Costs of Computer Software
The company capitalizes certain costs associated with computer software developed or obtained for internal use in accordance with the provisions of Statement Of Position No. 98-1, "Accounting for the Costs of Computer Software Developed or Obtained for Internal Use," issued by the American Institute of Certified Public Accountants. The company's policy provides for the capitalization of costs from the acquisition of external materials and services associated with developing or obtaining internal use computer software. Certain payroll costs for employees that are directly associated with internal use computer software projects are capitalized once specific criteria are met. The amount of payroll costs capitalized is limited to the time directly

spent on computer software projects. Costs associated with preliminary stage activities, training, maintenance and all other post-implementation stage activities are expensed as incurred. All costs capitalized in connection with internal use computer software projects are amortized on a straight-line basis over a useful life of five years.

Financial Instruments

The company adopted the provisions of Statement of Financial Accounting Standards No. 133, "Accounting for Derivative Instruments and Hedging Activities" (SFAS No. 133), as amended, effective February 4, 2001, as discussed in the footnote entitled "DERIVATIVE INSTRUMENTS AND HEDGING ACTIVITIES." This statement requires that all derivatives be recorded on the balance sheet at fair value and that changes in fair value be recognized currently in earnings unless specific hedge accounting criteria is met.

The company enters into forward foreign exchange contracts to minimize the risk associated with currency movement relating to its short-term intercompany loan program with foreign subsidiaries. Gains and losses, which offset the movement in the underlying transactions, are recognized as part of such transactions. Gross deferred unrealized losses on the forward contracts were not material at either February 1, 2003 or at February 2, 2002. The related receivable, payable and deferred gain or loss are included on a net basis in the balance sheet. The company had $205 and $108 of short-term outstanding forward contracts at February 1, 2003 and February 2, 2002, maturing in 2003 and 2002, respectively. These contracts are entered into with counter-parties that have high credit ratings and with which the company has the contractual right to net forward currency settlements.

Stock Options

The company accounts for stock options in accordance with the provisions of Accounting Principles Board Opinion No. 25, "Accounting for Stock Options Issued to Employees" (APB 25). The company has adopted the disclosure only provisions of SFAS No. 123 "Accounting for Stock Based Compensation" (FAS 123), issued in 1995.

In accordance with the provisions of SFAS No. 123, the company applies APB Opinion No. 25 and related interpretations in accounting for its stock option plans and, accordingly, does not recognize compensation cost. If the company had elected to recognize compensation cost based on the fair value of the options granted at grant date as prescribed by SFAS No. 123, net earnings and earnings per share would have been reduced to the pro forma amounts indicated in the following table:

	2002	2001	2000
Net earnings – as reported	$ 229	$ 67	$ 404
Net earnings – pro forma	190	28	385
Basic earnings per share – as reported	1.10	0.34	1.92
Basic earnings per share – pro forma	0.92	0.14	1.83
Diluted earnings per share – as reported	1.09	0.33	1.88
Diluted earnings per share – pro forma	0.91	0.14	1.79

The weighted-average fair value at the date of grant for options granted in 2002, 2001, 2000 was $6.42, $9.16 and $5.88, respectively. The fair value of each option grant is estimated on the date of grant using the Black-Scholes option pricing model. As there were a number of options granted during the years of 2000 through 2002, a range of assumptions are provided below:

	2002	2001	2000
Expected stock price volatility	.407 –.507	.407 –.567	.434 –.585
Risk-free interest rate	2.6% – 5.0%	3.6% – 5.1%	5.0% – 6.8%
Weighted average expected life of options	5 years	5 years	5 years

The effects of applying SFAS No. 123 and the results obtained through the use of the Black-Scholes option pricing model are not necessarily indicative of future values.

RESTRICTED CASH

The company had restricted cash of $60 at February 1, 2003. Included in this amount is $45 being used as support for a letter of credit in exchange for reduced letter of credit fees. This letter of credit partially supports the company's 475 Swiss Franc note, due January 28, 2004. The remaining $15 relates to a pending real estate transaction that is expected to close in 2003.

MERCHANDISE INVENTORIES

Merchandise inventories for the U.S. toy store division are stated at the lower of LIFO (last-in, first-out) cost or market. If inventories had been valued at the lower of FIFO (first-in, first-out) cost or market, inventories would show no change at February 1, 2003 or February 2, 2002.

	February 1, 2003	February 2, 2002
Toys"R"Us – U.S.	$ 1,387	$ 1,328
Toys"R"Us – International	362	278
Babies"R"Us	287	282
Toysrus.com	34	52
Other	120	101
	$ 2,190	$ 2,041

PROPERTY AND EQUIPMENT

	Useful life (in years)	February 1, 2003	February 2, 2002
Land		$ 825	$ 811
Buildings	45-50	2,009	1,980
Furniture and equipment	5-20	1,786	1,800
Leasehold improvements	12½-35	1,726	1,542
Costs of computer software	5	192	127
Construction in progress		33	41
Leased property and equipment under capital lease		53	53
		6,624	6,354
Less accumulated depreciation and amortization		1,861	1,810
		$ 4,763	$ 4,544

GOODWILL

In July 2001, the Financial Accounting Standards Board ("FASB") issued SFAS No. 142, "Goodwill and Other Intangible Assets" (SFAS No. 142), which is effective for fiscal years beginning after December 15, 2001. SFAS No. 142 changes the accounting for goodwill from an amortization method to an impairment only approach. The company adopted this pronouncement on February 3, 2002. As a result of this adoption, amortization of $348 of goodwill, which was to be amortized ratably through 2037, ceased. The carrying amount of goodwill at February 1, 2003 relates to the acquisition of Baby Super Stores, Inc. in 1997 ($319), which is now part of the Babies"R"Us division, and the acquisition of Imaginarium Toy Centers, Inc. in 1999 ($29), which is part of the Toys"R"Us – U.S. division. Based on the estimated fair market values (calculated using historical operating results of the reporting units to which the goodwill relates and relative industry multiples) of these divisions compared with the related book values, the company has determined that no impairment of this goodwill exists. Application of the non-amortization provisions of SFAS No. 142 resulted in an increase in net earnings of $8 for 2002. Had the non-amortization provisions of SFAS No. 142 been applied for 2001 and 2000, the company would have reported net earnings of $75 and $412, respectively, and diluted earnings per share of $0.36 and $1.92, respectively.

INVESTMENT IN TOYS – JAPAN

The company is accounting for its 48% ownership investment in the common stock of Toys – Japan on the "equity method" of accounting since the initial public offering in April 2000. Toys – Japan operates as a licensee of the company. As part of the initial public offering, Toys – Japan issued 1.3 shares of common stock to the public at a price of 12,000 yen or $113.95 per share. In November 2001, the common stock of Toys - Japan split 3 for 1. The company's accounting policy for the sales of subsidiaries' stock is to recognize gains or losses for value received in excess of or less than its basis in such subsidiary. No similar issuances of subsidiaries' stock are contemplated at this time. The carrying value of the investment is reflected on the consolidated balance sheets as part of "Other Assets" and was $140 and $123 at February 1, 2003 and February 2, 2002, respectively. At February 1, 2003, the quoted market value of the company's investment was $188, which exceeds the carrying value of the investment. The valuation represents a mathematical calculation based on the closing quotation published by the Tokyo over-the-counter market and is not necessarily indicative of the amount that could be realized upon sale. The company is a guarantor of 80% of a 10 billion yen ($84) loan from third parties in Japan with an annual rate of 6.47%, due in 2012, for which Toys – Japan is the borrower.

SEASONAL FINANCING AND LONG-TERM DEBT

	February 1, 2003	February 2, 2002
7.625% notes, due fiscal 2011	$ 554	$ 505
6.875% notes, due fiscal 2006	267	254
500 Euro bond, due February 13, 2004	538	431
475 Swiss Franc note, due January 28, 2004[a]	348	277
Equity Security Units	408	–
8¾% debentures, due fiscal 2021, net of expenses[b]	198	198
Note at an effective cost of 2.32% due in semi-annual installments through fiscal 2005[c]	158	126
Industrial revenue bonds, net of expenses	21	34
Obligation under capital leases	18	21
Mortgage notes at annual interest rates from 10.16% to 11.00%	8	9
	2,518	1,855
Less current portion	379	39
	$ 2,139	$ 1,816

Long-term debt balances as of February 1, 2003 and February 2, 2002 have been impacted by certain interest rate and currency swaps that have been designated as fair value and cash flow hedges, as discussed in the note entitled, "DERIVATIVE INSTRUMENTS AND HEDGING ACTIVITIES."

(a) Supported by a 475 Swiss Franc bank letter of credit. This note has been converted by an interest rate and currency swap to a floating rate, U.S. dollar obligation at 3 month LIBOR.

(b) Fair value was $192 and $204 at February 1, 2003 and February 2, 2002, respectively. The fair value was estimated using quoted market rates for publicly traded debt and estimated interest rates for non-public debt.

(c) Amortizing note secured by the expected future yen cash flows from license fees due from Toys – Japan.

On May 28, 2002, the company completed public offerings of Toys"R"Us common stock and equity security units, as described in the note entitled "ISSUANCE OF COMMON STOCK AND EQUITY SECURITY UNITS."

In February 2001, the company issued and sold 500 EURO through the public issuance of a EURO bond bearing interest at 6.375% per annum. Through the use of derivative instruments, this obligation was swapped into a $466 fixed rate obligation at an effective rate of 7.43% per annum with interest payments due annually and principal due on February 13, 2004.

In July 2001, the company issued and sold $750 of notes comprised of $500 of notes bearing interest at 7.625% per annum, maturing in August 2011, and $250 of notes bearing interest at 6.875% per annum, maturing in August 2006. Simultaneously with the issuance of these notes, the company entered into interest rate swap agreements. As a result of the interest rate swap agreements, interest on the $500 notes will accrue at the rate of LIBOR plus 1.5120% per annum and interest on the $250 notes accrues at the rate of LIBOR plus 1.1515% per annum. Interest is payable on both notes semi-annually on February 1 and August 1, commencing on February 1, 2002. In October 2002, the company terminated a portion of the interest rate swap agreements and received a payment of $27, which is being amortized over the lives of the related notes. Concurrently, the company entered into new interest rate swap agreements. Of the $500 notes, $200 accrues interest at the rate of LIBOR plus 3.06%, and $125 of the $250 notes accrues interest at the rate of LIBOR plus 3.54%.

As of February 1, 2003, the company had $985 in unsecured committed revolving credit facilities from a syndicate of financial institutions. These credit facilities consist of a $685 facility expiring September 2006 and a $300 facility expiring on August 25, 2003. The facilities are used for seasonal borrowings and to support the company's domestic commercial paper borrowings. As of February 1, 2003, all of the $685 facility expiring September 2006 and all of the $300 facility expiring on August 25, 2003 were available.

The annual maturities of long-term debt at February 1, 2003 are as follows:

	Annual maturities	Fair value hedging adjustment	Annual maturities, including fair value hedging adjustment
2003	$ 373	$ 6	$ 379
2004	499	75	574
2005	51	–	51
2006	279	17	296
2007	420*	19	439
2008 and subsequent	724	55	779
	$ 2,346	$ 172	$ 2,518

Long-term debt balances as of February 1, 2003 have been impacted by certain interest rate and currency swaps that have been designated as fair value and cash flow hedges, as discussed in the note entitled, "DERIVATIVE INSTRUMENTS AND HEDGING ACTIVITIES."

*Includes $390 of equity security units, due 2007, which the company is obligated to remarket in 2005. See the note entitled "ISSUANCE OF COMMON STOCK AND EQUITY SECURITY UNITS."

DERIVATIVE INSTRUMENTS AND HEDGING ACTIVITIES

The company is exposed to market risk from potential changes in interest rates and foreign exchange rates. The company continues to regularly evaluate these risks and continues to take measures to mitigate these risks, including, among other measures, entering into derivative financial instruments to hedge a variety of risk exposures including interest rate and currency risks. The company enters into forward exchange contracts to minimize and manage the currency risks related to its import merchandise purchase program. The company enters into interest rate swaps to manage interest rate risk and strives to achieve what it believes is an acceptable balance between fixed and variable rate debt.

The company purchases forward exchange contracts to minimize and manage the foreign currency risks related to its import merchandise purchase program. The counter-parties to these contracts are highly rated financial institutions and the company does not have significant exposure to any one counter-party. These forward exchange contracts are designated as cash flow hedges, as defined by SFAS No. 133, and are effective as hedges. Accordingly, changes in the effective portion of the fair value of these forward exchange contracts are included in other comprehensive income. Once the hedged transactions are completed, or when merchandise is sold, the unrealized gains and losses on the forward contracts are reclassified from accumulated other comprehensive income and recognized in earnings. The unrealized losses related to the import merchandise purchase program contracts, that were recorded in other comprehensive income, were not material at February 1, 2003 or February 2, 2002.

The company is faced with interest rate risks resulting from interest rate fluctuations. The company has a variety of fixed and variable rate debt instruments. In an effort to manage interest rate exposures, the company strives to achieve an acceptable balance between fixed and variable rate debt and has entered into interest rate swaps to maintain that balance.

On May 28, 2002, the company entered into an interest rate swap agreement on its Equity-Linked Securities. Under the agreement, the company will pay interest at a variable rate in exchange for fixed rate payments, effectively transforming these debentures to floating rate obligations. This swap is designated as a highly effective fair value hedge, as defined by SFAS No. 133. Changes in the fair value of the interest rate swap offset changes in the fair value of the fixed rate debt due to changes in market interest rates with some ineffectiveness present. The amount of ineffectiveness did not have a material effect on earnings.

On March 19, 2002, the company refinanced a note payable originally due in 2005 and increased the amount outstanding to $160 from $100. This borrowing is repayable in semi-annual installments of principal and interest, with the final installment due on February 20, 2008. The effective cost of this borrowing is 2.23% and is secured by expected future cash flows from license fees due from Toys – Japan. The company also entered into a contract to swap yen to U.S. dollars, within exact terms of the loan. This cross currency swap has been designated as a foreign currency cash flow hedge, as defined by SFAS No. 133, and is effective as a hedge.

In July 2001, the company entered into interest rate swap agreements on its 7.625% $500 notes, due August 1, 2011, and its 6.875% $250 notes, due August 1, 2006. Under these agreements, the company will pay interest at a variable rate in exchange for fixed rate payments, effectively transforming the debentures to floating rate obligations. These swaps are designated as highly effective fair value hedges, as defined by SFAS No. 133. Changes in the fair value of the interest rate swaps perfectly offset changes in the fair value of the fixed rate debt due to changes in market interest rates. As such, there were no ineffective hedge portions recognized in earnings during 2001.

notes to consolidated financial statements

In February 2001, the company issued and sold 500 EURO through the public issuance of a EURO bond bearing interest at 6.375% per annum. The obligation was swapped into a $466 fixed rate obligation with an effective rate of 7.43% per annum with interest payments due annually and principal due February 13, 2004. This cross currency swap is designated as a cash flow hedge, as defined by SFAS No. 133, and is effective as a hedge. The portion of the fair value of the swap attributable to changes in the spot rate is matched in earnings against changes in the fair value of debt.

The company entered into a Swiss Franc floating rate loan with a financial institution in January 1999, due January, 28 2004. The company also entered into a contract to swap U.S. dollars to Swiss Francs, within exact terms of the loan. This cross currency swap has been designated as a foreign currency fair value hedge, as defined by SFAS No. 133, and is effective as a hedge.

The company increased the carrying amount of its long-term debt by $172 at February 1, 2003, representing the fair value of debt in excess of the carrying amount on that date. Also at February 1, 2003, the company recorded derivative assets of $158 and derivative liabilities of $10, representing the fair value of these derivatives at that date.

ISSUANCE OF COMMON STOCK AND EQUITY SECURITY UNITS

On May 28, 2002, the company completed public offerings of Toys"R"Us common stock and equity security units. On that date, the company issued 15.0 shares of its common stock at a price of $17.65 per share and received net proceeds of $253. Also on that date, the company issued 8.0 equity security units with a stated amount of $50 per unit and received net proceeds of $390. Each security unit consists of a contract to purchase, for $50, a specified number of shares of Toys"R"Us common stock in August 2005, and a senior note due in 2007 with a principal amount of $50. The fair value of the contract to purchase shares of Toys"R"Us common stock was estimated at $1.77 per equity security unit. The fair value of the senior note was estimated at $48.23 per equity security unit. Interest on the senior notes is payable quarterly at an initial rate of 6.25%, which commenced in August 2002. The company is obligated to remarket the notes in May 2005 at the then prevailing market interest rate for similar notes. If the remarketing were not to be successful, the company would be entitled to take possession of the senior notes, and the holder's obligation under the contracts to purchase shares of Toys"R"Us common stock would be deemed to have been satisfied. The proceeds allocated to the purchase contracts were recorded in stockholders' equity on the consolidated balance sheet. The fair value of the senior notes is reflected as long-term debt on the consolidated balance sheet. The net proceeds from the public offerings were used to refinance short-term borrowings and for other general corporate purposes. As a result of the interest rate swap agreements, interest on the senior notes will accrue at the rate of LIBOR plus 3.43% per annum. Interest is payable quarterly each year, beginning in August 2002.

STOCKHOLDERS' EQUITY

The common shares of the company, par value $0.10 per share, were as follows:

	February 1, 2003	February 2, 2002
Authorized shares	650.0	650.0
Issued shares	300.4	300.4
Treasury shares	87.9	103.7
Issued and outstanding shares	212.5	196.7

EARNINGS PER SHARE

The following table sets forth the computation of basic and diluted earnings per share:

	2002	2001	2000
Numerator:			
Net earnings available to common stockholders	$ 229	$ 67	$ 404
Denominator for basic earnings per share – weighted average shares	207.6	197.6	210.9
Impact of dilutive securities	2.0	8.4	4.1
Denominator for diluted earnings per share – weighted average shares	209.6	206.0	215.0
Basic earnings per share	$ 1.10	$ 0.34	$ 1.92
Diluted earnings per share	$ 1.09	$ 0.33	$ 1.88

Options to purchase approximately 32.5, 10.3 and 3.0 shares of common stock were outstanding during 2002, 2001 and 2000, respectively, but were not included in the computation of diluted earnings per share because the option exercise prices were greater than the average market price of the common shares.

STOCK PURCHASE WARRANTS

The company issued 1.2 stock purchase warrants to SOFTBANK Venture Capital and affiliates ("SOFTBANK") for $8.33 per warrant. Each warrant gives the holder thereof the right to purchase one share of Toys"R"Us common stock at an exercise price of $13 per share, until the expiration date of February 24, 2010. In addition, the company granted a warrant on August 9, 2000 entitling Amazon.com to acquire up to 5% (subject to dilution under certain circumstances) of the capital of Toysrus.com at the then market value. As of February 1, 2003, none of these warrants have been exercised.

notes to consolidated financial statements

LEASES

The company leases a portion of the real estate used in its operations. Most leases require the company to pay real estate taxes and other expenses; some require additional amounts based on percentages of sales.

Minimum rental commitments under noncancelable operating leases having a term of more than one year as of February 1, 2003 are as follows:

	Gross minimum rentals	Sublease income	Net minimum rentals
2003	$ 317	$ 17	$ 300
2004	314	14	300
2005	301	12	289
2006	285	11	274
2007	267	9	258
2008 and subsequent	1,786	40	1,746
	$ 3,270	$ 103	$ 3,167

Total rent expense, net of sublease income, was $267, $261 and $291 in 2002, 2001 and 2000, respectively. The company remains contingently liable for lease payments related to the sub-lease of locations to third parties. To the extent that sub-lessees fail to perform, the company's total net rent expense would be increased.

The company's new corporate headquarters facility, located in Wayne, New Jersey, is financed under a lease arrangement commonly referred to as a "synthetic lease." Under this lease, unrelated third parties, arranged by Wachovia Development Corporation, a multi-purpose real estate investment company, will fund up to $125 for the acquisition and construction of the facility. Upon completion of the construction, which is expected to be in 2003, the company will begin to pay rent on the facility until the lease expires in 2011. The rent will be based on a mix of fixed and variable interest rates that will be applied against the final amount funded. Upon expiration of the lease, the company would expect to either: renew the lease arrangement; purchase the facility from the lessor; or remarket the property on behalf of the owner. The lease agreement provides the lessor with a residual value guarantee equal to the funding for the acquisition and construction of the facility. Under accounting principles generally accepted in the United States, this arrangement is required to be treated as an operating lease for accounting purposes and as a financing for tax purposes.

TAXES ON INCOME

The provisions for income taxes consist of the following:

	2002	2001	2000
Current:			
Federal	$ 4	$ 63	$ 120
Foreign	31	10	36
State	(2)	9	10
	$ 33	$ 82	$ 166
Deferred:			
Federal	62	(61)	50
Foreign	23	16	13
State	14	(13)	4
	99	(58)	67
Total tax provision	$ 132	$ 24	$ 233

At February 1, 2003 and February 2, 2002, the company had gross deferred tax assets, before valuation allowances, of $612 and $576, respectively, and gross deferred tax liabilities of $600 and $484, respectively. Deferred tax assets of $32 and $45 were included in "Prepaid Expenses and Other Current Assets" at February 1, 2003 and February 2, 2002, respectively. Deferred tax assets, net of valuation allowances, of $285 and $245 were included in "Other Assets" at February 1, 2003 and February 2, 2002, respectively. Deferred tax liabilities of $55 and $36 were included in "Accrued Expenses and Other Current Liabilities" at February 1, 2003 and February 2, 2002, respectively. The tax effects of temporary differences and carryforwards that give rise to significant portions of deferred tax assets and liabilities consist of the following:

	February 1, 2003	February 2, 2002
Deferred tax assets:		
Foreign loss carryforwards	$ 305	$ 296
Restructuring	116	131
Other	143	115
Depreciation and amortization	30	22
Derivative instruments and hedging activities	11	–
LIFO reserves	7	12
Valuation allowances, related to foreign loss carryforwards	(295)	(287)
	$ 317	$ 289
Deferred tax liabilities:		
Depreciation and amortization	$ (404)	$ (344)
Other	(169)	(131)
LIFO reserves	(27)	(9)
	$ (600)	$ (484)
Net deferred liabilities	$ (283)	$ (195)

On February 1, 2003, the company had foreign loss carryforwards available to reduce future taxable income of certain foreign subsidiaries. The foreign loss carryforwards, as well as the related tax benefits associated with the foreign loss carryforwards, will expire as follows:

Expiration	Net operating loss carryforwards	Tax benefit
1 – 5 years	$ 208	$ 71
6 – 7 years	9	4
Indefinitely	572	230
	$ 789	$ 305

At February 1, 2003, the company had valuation allowances of $295 against the tax benefit of foreign loss carryforwards of $305.

A reconciliation of the federal statutory tax rate with the effective tax rate follows:

	2002	2001	2000
Statutory tax rate	35.0%	35.0%	35.0%
State income taxes, net of federal income tax benefit	1.4	1.8	1.4
Foreign taxes, net of valuation allowance	(2.4)	(9.4)	1.1
Reversal of deferred tax asset	–	(6.5)	–
Subpart F income	1.5	5.4	0.6
Amortization of goodwill	–	3.5	0.5
Other, net	1.0	(2.9)	(2.1)
Effective tax rate	36.5%	26.9%	36.5%

40

notes to consolidated financial statements

Deferred income taxes are not provided on un-remitted earnings of foreign subsidiaries that are intended to be indefinitely invested. Exclusive of amounts that, if remitted, would result in little or no tax under current U.S. tax laws, unremitted earnings were approximately $607 at February 1, 2003. Net income taxes of approximately $120 would be due if these earnings were remitted.

STOCK OPTIONS

The company has stock option plans (the "Plans") that provide for the granting of options to purchase the company's common stock. The Plans cover employees and directors of the company and provide for the issuance of non-qualified options, incentive stock options, performance share options, performance units, stock appreciation rights, restricted shares, restricted units and unrestricted shares. The Plans provide for a variety of vesting dates with the majority of the options vesting approximately three years from the date of grant, 50% over the first two years and the remaining 50% over three years. Options granted to directors are exercisable one-third on a cumulative basis commencing on the third, fourth and fifth anniversaries from the date of the grant.

The exercise price per share of all options granted has been the average of the high and low market price of the company's common stock on the date of grant. All options must be exercised within ten years from the date of grant.

At February 1, 2003, an aggregate of 47.7 shares of authorized common stock were reserved for all of the Plans noted above, including 1.6 shares reserved for the future issuance of restricted shares, restricted units, performance units, unrestricted shares and 2 shares reserved for the restricted shares of units granted but not yet vested. Of these amounts, 11.5 were available for future grants. All outstanding options expire at dates ranging from February 17, 2003 to December 30, 2012.

Stock option transactions are summarized as follows:

	Shares	Exercise price per share	Weighted-average exercise price
Outstanding at January 29, 2000	39.8	$11.69 – $40.94	$24.59
Granted	7.5	10.25 – 26.25	15.29
Exercised	(0.4)	14.78 – 22.06	18.96
Canceled	(22.2)	14.63 – 40.94	28.60
Outstanding at February 3, 2001	24.7	$10.25 – $40.94	$18.36
Granted	8.6	15.53 – 38.36	28.03
Exercised	(1.1)	14.63 – 25.44	16.21
Canceled	(1.6)	11.50 – 39.88	24.26
Outstanding at February 2, 2002	30.6	$10.25 – $40.94	$20.39
Granted	6.0	9.83 – 20.41	20.08
Exercised	0.0	0.00 – 0.00	0.00
Canceled	(4.0)	10.25 – 38.19	19.62
Outstanding at February 1, 2003	**32.6**	**$ 9.83 – $40.94**	**$20.43**

The following table summarizes information about stock options outstanding at February 1, 2003:

Range of exercise prices	Outstanding Number of options	Weighted average remaining years of contractual life	Weighted average exercise price	Exercisable (Vested) Number of options	Weighted average exercise price
$ 9.83 – $14.99	2.0	6	$12.83	1.9	$12.84
$15.00 – $19.99	15.2	6	$17.60	12.6	$17.81
$20.00 – $24.99	7.3	8	$21.00	3.4	$21.47
$25.00 – $29.99	7.1	7	$25.85	3.7	$26.08
$30.00 – $40.94	1.0	4	$35.57	1.0	$35.57
Outstanding at February 1, 2003	32.6	7	$20.43	22.6	$20.07

Options exercisable and the weighted-average exercise prices were 11.3 and $19.60 at February 3, 2001; 16.1 and $20.74 at February 2, 2002; and 22.6 and $20.07 at February 1, 2003, respectively.

At February 1, 2003 and February 2, 2002, Toysrus.com, the company's internet subsidiary, had approximately 11.3 stock options outstanding to both employees and non-employees of the company. This represents approximately 11% of the authorized common stock of Toysrus.com at February 1, 2003 and February 2, 2002. These outstanding options, with exercise prices ranging between $0.30 and $2.25 per share, entitle each option holder the right to purchase one share of the common stock of Toysrus.com.

The company utilizes a restoration feature to encourage the early exercise of certain options and retention of shares, thereby promoting increased employee ownership. This feature provides for the grant of new options when previously owned shares of company stock are used to exercise existing options. Restoration option grants are non-dilutive, as they do not increase the combined number of shares of company stock and options held by an employee prior to exercise. The new options are granted at a price equal to the fair market value on the date of the new grant and generally expire on the same date as the original options that were exercised.

REPLACEMENT OF CERTAIN STOCK OPTION GRANTS WITH RESTRICTED STOCK

In 2000, the company authorized the exchange of certain stock options having an exercise price above $22 per share for an economically equivalent grant of restricted stock. The exchange, which was voluntary, replaced approximately 14.4 options with approximately 1.7 restricted shares. Shares of restricted stock resulting from the exchange vest over a period of three years. One-half of the grant vested on April 1, 2002 and the remainder vests on April 1, 2003. Accordingly, the company recognizes compensation expense throughout the vesting period of the restricted stock. The company recorded $3 in compensation expense related to this restricted stock in 2002 and $8 in both 2001 and 2000.

PROFIT SHARING PLAN

The company has a profit sharing plan with a 401(k) salary deferral feature for eligible domestic employees. The terms of the plan call for annual contributions by the company as determined by the Board of Directors, subject to certain limitations. The profit sharing plan may be terminated at the company's discretion. Provisions of $34, $46 and $50 have been charged to earnings in 2002, 2001 and 2000, respectively.

TOYSRUS.COM

Toysrus.com operates a co-branded toy and video game on-line store (Toysrus.com), a co-branded baby products on-line store (Babiesrus.com), and a co-branded learning products and information on-line store (Imaginarium.com) under a strategic alliance with Amazon.com.

The Toysrus.com strategic alliance with Amazon.com was launched in the third quarter of 2000 and expires in 2010. Under this alliance, each company is responsible for specific aspects of the on-line stores. Toysrus.com is responsible for merchandising, marketing and content for the co-branded stores. Toysrus.com also identifies, buys, owns and manages the inventory. Amazon.com handles web-site development, order fulfillment, customer service, and the housing of Toysrus.com's inventory in Amazon.com's U.S. distribution centers. The company recognizes revenue for Toysrus.com at the point in time when merchandise is shipped to customers, in accordance with the shipping terms (FOB shipping point) that exist under the agreement with Amazon.com.

Toysrus.com also opened a personalized gifts for all ages on-line store (Giftsrus.com) in November 2002. Visitors can choose from hundreds of products, ranging from exclusive stuffed animals, toys, clothing, home décor, and keepsakes, have them personalized with messages, monogrammed, hand-painted or engraved, gift wrapped, and then delivered. Giftsrus.com does not operate as part of the strategic alliance with Amazon.com.

In February 2000, the company entered into an agreement with SOFTBANK that included an investment of $60 by SOFTBANK in Toysrus.com. Accordingly, the company records a 20% minority interest in the net losses of Toysrus.com in selling, general and administrative expenses. Toysrus.com received additional capital contributions of $37 from SOFTBANK, representing its proportionate share of funding required for the operations of Toysrus.com.

SEGMENTS

The company's reportable segments are Toys"R"Us – U.S., which operates toy stores in 49 states and Puerto Rico; Toys"R"Us – International, which operates, licenses or franchises toy stores in 29 countries outside the United States; Babies"R"Us, which operates stores in 35 states; and Toysrus.com, the company's internet subsidiary.

Information on segments and reconciliation to earnings before income taxes, are as follows:

	February 1, 2003	February 2, 2002	February 3, 2001
Net sales			
Toys"R"Us – U.S.	$ 6,743	$ 6,877	$ 7,073
Toys"R"Us – International	2,161	1,889	1,872
Babies"R"Us	1,595	1,421	1,310
Toysrus.com[1]	340	277	180
Other[2]	466	555	897
Total	$11,305	$11,019	$11,332
Operating earnings			
Toys"R"Us – U.S.[3]	$ 280	$ 308	$ 431
Toys"R"Us – International	160	131	124
Babies"R"Us	174	138	120
Toysrus.com, net of minority interest[4]	(37)	(76)	(212)
Other[3],[5]	(106)	(115)	(37)
Restructuring and other charges	–	(186)	–
Operating earnings	$ 471	$ 200	$ 426
Interest expense, net	(110)	(109)	(104)
Gain from IPO of Toys – Japan	–	–	315
Earning before income taxes	$ 361	$ 91	$ 637
Identifiable assets			
Toys"R"Us – U.S.	$ 5,513	$ 5,412	$ 5,384
Toys"R"Us – International	1,430	1,146	1,235
Babies"R"Us	758	574	486
Toysrus.com	58	84	141
Other[6]	1,638	860	757
Total	$ 9,397	$ 8,076	$ 8,003
Depreciation and amortization			
Toys"R"Us – U.S.	$ 176	$ 166	$ 143
Toys"R"Us – International	49	41	42
Babies"R"Us	24	29	26
Toysrus.com	4	6	6
Other[6]	64	66	73
Total	$ 317	$ 308	$ 290

(1) Includes the net sales of Toysrus.com – Japan.
(2) Includes the net sales of the Kids"R"Us and Geoffrey divisions, and the net sales of the Toys – Japan division prior to its initial public offering on April 24, 2000.
(3) Includes markdowns related to the store closings announced as part of the restructuring in 2001.
(4) Includes the operations of Toysrus.com – Japan, net of minority interest.
(5) Includes corporate expenses, the operating results of the Kids"R"Us and Geoffrey divisions, and the equity in net earnings of Toys – Japan.
(6) Includes the Kids"R"Us and Geoffrey divisions, as well as corporate assets and related depreciation.

RESTRUCTURING AND OTHER CHARGES

In January 2002, the company announced plans to reposition its business, and as part of this plan, the company closed 27 non-Mission Possible format Toys"R"Us stores and closed 37 Kids"R"Us stores. In conjuction with the Kids"R"Us store closings in most of these locations, the company converted the nearest Toys"R"Us store into a Toys"R"Us/Kids"R"Us combo store.

notes to consolidated financial statements

As part of this plan, the company eliminated approximately 1,700 staff positions in its stores and its headquarters. In addition, these plans include the cost of consolidating five of the company's store support center facilities into its new headquarters in Wayne, New Jersey in 2003.

The costs associated with the facilities consolidation, elimination of positions, and other actions designed to improve efficiency in support functions were $79, of which $15 related to severance. The costs associated with store closings were $73 for Kids"R"Us and $85 for Toys"R"Us, of which $27 was recorded in cost of sales. The fair value of the facilities to be consolidated and store closings were obtained from third party appraisals. The company also reversed $24 of previously accrued charges ($11 from the 1998 charge and $13 from the 1995 charge) that the company determined to be no longer needed. Accordingly, based on these actions, the company recorded $213 million of pre-tax ($126 after-tax) restructuring and other charges in the fourth quarter of its fiscal year ending February 2, 2002. Details on the components of the charges are as follows:

Description	Initial charge	Utilized in 2001	Reserve balance at 2/02/02	Utilized in 2002	Adjustments to charge in 2002	Reserve balance at 2/01/03
Store closing:						
Lease commitments	$ 52	$ –	$ 52	$ (11)	$ –	$ 41
Severance	4	–	4	(4)	–	–
Write-down of property and equipment	75	(75)	–	–	–	–
Markdowns	27	–	27	(27)	–	–
Store support center consolidation:						
Lease commitments	28	–	28	–	11*	39
Write-down of property and equipment	29	(29)	–	–	–	–
Severance	15	–	15	(9)	(1)	5
Other	7	(7)	–	–	–	–
Total restructuring and other charges	**$237**	**$(111)**	**$126**	**$ (51)**	**$ 10**	**$ 85**

*In the fourth quarter of 2002, we determined that a reserve for lease costs for the disposition of one of our store support center facilities was no longer adequate and, accordingly, recorded an additional charge of $11 million.

In 2000, Toysrus.com the company's internet subsidiary, recorded $118 in non-recurring charges as a result of the transition to its co-branded on-line store with Amazon.com, of which $10 were included in cost of sales and $108 were included in selling, general and administrative expenses. These costs and charges related primarily to the closure of three distribution centers, as well as web-site asset write-offs and other costs. The company had remaining lease commitment reserves of $3 at February 1, 2003, that will be utilized in 2003 and thereafter.

The company previously announced strategic initiatives to reposition its worldwide business and recorded related restructuring and other charges of $698 in 1998 and $396 in 1995 to complete these initiatives. As of February 1, 2003, the company had substantially completed all announced initiatives. The company reversed unused reserves of $10 in the fourth quarter of 2002, and also reversed unused reserves of $29 in 2001, $24 of which were reversed in the fourth quarter of 2001 and are discussed above, and $11 in 2000, as these reserves were concluded to be no longer necessary. The company had $42 of reserves remaining at February 1, 2003, primarily for long-term lease commitments that will be utilized in 2003 and thereafter. The company believes that remaining reserves at February 1, 2003 are reasonable estimates of what is required to complete all remaining initiatives.

GAIN FROM INITIAL PUBLIC OFFERING OF TOYS – JAPAN

The company recorded a pre-tax non-operating gain of $315 ($200 net of taxes) in the first quarter of fiscal 2000 resulting from the initial public offering of shares of Toys – Japan. Of this gain, $91 resulted from an adjustment to the basis of the company's investment in Toys – Japan and $224 was related to the sale of a portion of the company-owned common stock of Toys – Japan, for which the company received net cash proceeds of $267. In connection with this transaction, the company recorded a provision for current income taxes of $82 and a provision for deferred income taxes of $33, respectively. As a result of this transaction, the company's ownership percentage in the common stock of Toys – Japan was reduced from 80% to 48%. Toys – Japan is a licensee of the company.

SUBSEQUENT EVENTS

On March 24, 2003, the company filed a "shelf" registration statement with the Securities and Exchange Commission, giving the company the capability to sell up to $800 of debt securities that would be used to repay outstanding debt and for general corporate purposes. In April 2003, the company sold and issued $400 million in notes bearing interest at a coupon rate of 7.875%, maturing on April 15, 2013. The notes were sold at a price of 98.305%, resulting in an effective yield of 8.125%. Simultaneously with the sale of the notes, we entered into interest rate swap agreements. As a result of these swap agreements, interest will accrue at the rate of LIBOR plus 3.622%. Interest is payable semi-annually commencing on October 15, 2003. The company plans to use the proceeds from these notes for the repayment of indebtedness maturing in the 2004 calendar year, and pending such repayment, for working capital needs and other general corporate purposes.

On March 5, 2003 the company announced that it would be eliminating approximately 200 positions in its store support facilities in 2003, representing approximately 10% of total headquarters staff.

OTHER MATTERS

In August 2000, eleven purported class action lawsuits were filed (six in the United States District Court for the District of New Jersey, three in the United States District Court for the Northern District of California, one in the United States District Court for the Western District of Texas and one in the Superior Court of the State of California, County of San Bernardino), against the company and our affiliates Toysrus.com, Inc. and Toysrus.com, LLC. In September 2000, three additional purported class action lawsuits were filed (two in the United

States District Court for the District of New Jersey and one in the United States District Court for the Western District of Texas). These actions generally purport to bring claims under federal privacy and computer fraud statutes, as well as under state statutory and common law, on behalf of all persons who have visited one or more of the company's web sites and either made an online purchase or allegedly had information about them unlawfully "intercepted," "monitored," "transmitted," or "used." All the suits (except one filed in the United States District Court for the District of New Jersey) also named Coremetrics, Inc. ("Coremetrics"), as a defendant. Coremetrics is an internet marketing company with whom the company has an agreement. These suits seek damages in unspecified amounts and other relief under state and federal law.

With Coremetrics the company filed a joint application with the Multidistrict litigation panel which resulted in all of the federal actions being consolidated and transferred to the United States District Court for the Northern District of California. Plaintiffs voluntarily dismissed the action in the Superior Court of the State of California, County of San Bernardino without prejudice. On October 16, 2001, plaintiffs filed an amended complaint in the United States District Court for the Northern District of California. The company believes that it has substantial defenses to all of these claims. On November 13, 2002, the company entered into a settlement agreement with plaintiffs in connection with all causes of action. This settlement agreement is subject to the court's review and approval and will not have a material impact on the company's consolidated financial statements.

RECENT ACCOUNTING PRONOUNCEMENTS

In 2002, the FASB Emerging Issues Task Force issued EITF issue No. 02-16, "Accounting by a Reseller for Cash Consideration Received from a Vendor" (EITF 02-16). EITF 02-16 considers vendor allowances as a reduction in the price of a vendor's product that should be recognized as a reduction of cost of sales. Advertising allowances that are received for specific, identifiable and incremental costs are considered a reduction of advertising expenses and should be recognized as a reduction of SG&A. The provisions of EITF 02-16 are effective for all new arrangements, or modifications to existing arrangements, beginning after December 31, 2002. The company is currently evaluating the potential impact of the provisions of EITF 02-16 on its consolidated financial statements for 2003.

In January 2003, the FASB issued Interpretation No. 46, "Consolidation of Variable Interest Entities" (FIN 46), which will require the consolidation of entities that are controlled by a company through interests other than voting interests. Under the requirements of this interpretation, an entity that maintains a majority of the risks or rewards associated with Variable Interest Entities ("VIEs"), commonly known as special purpose entities, is effectively in the same position as the parent in a parent-subsidiary relationship. Disclosure requirements of VIEs are effective in all financial statements issued after January 31, 2003. The consolidation requirements apply to all VIEs created after January 31, 2003. FIN 46 requires public companies to apply the consolidation requirements to VIEs that existed prior to February 1, 2003 and remained in existence as of the beginning of annual or interim periods beginning after June 15, 2003. The company's new corporate headquarters facility, located in Wayne, New Jersey, is leased from unrelated third parties, arranged by a multi-purpose real estate investment company that the company does not control. In addition the company does not have the majority of the associated risks or rewards. Accordingly, the company believes that FIN 46 will have no impact on the accounting for the synthetic lease for such facility. The synthetic lease is discussed in the note entitled "LEASES." The company believes that FIN 46 will not have a material impact on its consolidated financial statements.

In November 2002, the FASB issued Interpretation No. 45, "Guarantor's Accounting and Disclosure Requirements for Guarantees, Including Indirect Guarantees of Indebtedness of Others" (FIN 45), which imposes new disclosure and liability-recognition requirements for financial guarantees, performance guarantees, indemnifications and indirect guarantees of the indebtedness of others. FIN 45 requires certain guarantees to be recorded at fair value. This is different from previous practice, where a liability would typically be recorded only when a loss was probable and reasonably estimable. The initial recognition and initial measurements provisions are applicable on a prospective basis to guarantees issued or modified after December 31, 2002. FIN 45 also requires additional disclosures, even when the likelihood of making any payments under the guarantee is remote. The disclosure requirements are effective for interim and annual periods ending after December 15, 2002. The company instituted procedures to identify guarantees contained in the various legal documents and agreements, already executed and those to be executed in the future that fall within the scope of FIN 45. The company expects that FIN 45 will not have a material impact on its consolidated financial statements.

In July 2002, the FASB issued SFAS No. 146 "Accounting for Costs Associated with Exit or Disposal Activities" (SFAS No. 146), which addresses the recognition, measurement, and reporting of costs associated with exit or disposal activities and supercedes Emerging Issues Task Force Issue No. 94-3, "Liability Recognition for Certain Employee Termination Benefits and Other Costs to Exit an Activity (including Certain Costs Incurred in a Restructuring)" (EITF No. 94.3). The fundamental difference between SFAS No. 146 and EITF No. 94-3 is the requirement that a liability for a cost associated with an exit or disposal activity be recognized when the liability is incurred rather than at the date an entity commits to an exit plan. A fundamental conclusion of SFAS No. 146 is that an entity's commitment to a plan, by itself, does not create an obligation that meets the definition of a liability. SFAS No. 146 also establishes that the initial measurement of a liability recognized be recorded at fair value. The provisions of this statement are effective for exit or disposal activities that are initiated after December 31, 2002, with early application encouraged. The company believes that adoption of this pronouncement will not have a significant effect on the company's consolidated financial statements.

In August 2001, the FASB issued SFAS No. 144, "Accounting for the Impairment or Disposal of Long-Lived Assets" (SFAS No. 144), which addresses financial accounting and reporting for the impairment or disposal of long-lived assets and supersedes SFAS No. 121, "Accounting for the Impairment of Long-Lived Assets and for Long-Lived Assets to be Disposed Of." The company adopted SFAS No. 144 as of February 3, 2002. The adoption did not have a significant effect on the company's consolidated financial statements.

reports

Report of Management

Responsibility for the integrity and objectivity of the financial information presented in this Annual Report resides with the management of Toys"R"Us. The accompanying financial statements have been prepared from accounting records which management believes fairly and accurately reflect the operations and financial position of the company.

Management has established a system of internal controls to provide reasonable assurance that assets are maintained and accounted for in accordance with its policies and that transactions are recorded accurately on the company's books and records. The company's disclosure controls provide reasonable assurance that appropriate information is accumulated and communicated to senior management to allow decisions regarding accurate, complete and timely financial disclosures.

The company's comprehensive internal audit program provides for constant evaluation of the adequacy of the adherence to management's established policies and procedures. The company has distributed to key employees its policies for conducting business affairs in a lawful and ethical manner.

The Audit Committee of the Board of Directors, which is comprised solely of outside directors, provides oversight of the financial reporting process through periodic meetings with our independent auditors, internal auditors, and management.

The financial statements of the company have been audited by Ernst & Young LLP, the company's independent auditors, in accordance with auditing standards generally accepted in the United States, including a review of financial reporting matters and internal controls to the extent necessary to express an opinion on the consolidated financial statements.

John H. Eyler, Jr.
Chairman, President and
Chief Executive Officer
March 5, 2003

Louis Lipschitz
Executive Vice President
and Chief Financial Officer

Report of Independent Auditors

The Board of Directors and Stockholders
Toys"R"Us, Inc.

We have audited the accompanying consolidated balance sheets of Toys"R"Us, Inc. and subsidiaries as of February 1, 2003 and February 2, 2002, and the related consolidated statements of earnings, stockholders' equity and cash flows for each of the three years in the period ended February 1, 2003. These financial statements are the responsibility of the company's management. Our responsibility is to express an opinion on these financial statements based on our audits.

We conducted our audits in accordance with auditing standards generally accepted in the United States. Those standards require that we plan and perform the audit to obtain reasonable assurance about whether the financial statements are free of material misstatement. An audit includes examining, on a test basis, evidence supporting the amounts and disclosures in the financial statements. An audit also includes assessing the accounting principles used and significant estimates made by management, as well as evaluating the overall financial statement presentation. We believe that our audits provide a reasonable basis for our opinion.

In our opinion, the financial statements referred to above present fairly, in all material respects, the consolidated financial position of Toys"R"Us, Inc. and subsidiaries at February 1, 2003 and February 2, 2002, and the consolidated results of their operations and their cash flows for each of the three years in the period ended February 1, 2003, in conformity with accounting principles generally accepted in the United States.

As discussed in the note entitled "Goodwill", the company adopted SFAS No. 142, Goodwill and Other Intangible Assets, effective February 3, 2002.

Ernst & Young LLP
New York, New York
March 5, 2003

board of directors

The Board of Directors

Charles Lazarus
Chairman Emeritus and founder
Toys"R"Us, Inc.
Board member since 1969

Charles Lazarus, founder of Toys"R"Us, Inc., is a pioneer of off-price specialty retailing. He opened his first retail establishment totally dedicated to children's needs in 1948 in Washington D.C. Mr. Lazarus continued to lead Toys"R"Us, Inc. as Chairman of the Board and Chief Executive Officer until 1994. Under his leadership, the company expanded internationally and launched its Kids"R"Us and Babies"R"Us brands. Mr. Lazarus remained Chairman of the Board from 1994 until 1998 when he became Chairman Emeritus.

Mr. Lazarus is a Director of Loral Space Systems and has served on the boards of Wal-Mart and Automatic Data Processing. He also served on the Advisory Board for Trade Policy under both President George Bush and President Bill Clinton. He is a member of the Toy Industry Hall of Fame.

John H. Eyler, Jr. [1]
Chairman, President and
Chief Executive Officer
Toys"R"Us, Inc.
Board member since 2000

John H. Eyler Jr. joined Toys"R"Us, Inc. as President and Chief Executive Officer in January 2000. He was named Chairman of the Board in 2001. Prior to joining the company, Mr. Eyler was Chairman and Chief Executive Officer of FAO Schwarz in New York, where he had been employed since 1992.

Mr. Eyler's previous positions include Chief Executive Officer of Chicago's Hartmarx retail subsidiary, and Chairman and Chief Executive Officer of MainStreet, a division of Federated Department Stores, Inc.

He serves on the Board of Directors for the National Retail Federation and The Andre Agassi Charitable Foundation. Mr. Eyler is also on the Board of NYC 2012, an effort to bring the 2012 Olympic Games to New York City. He holds a degree in Finance from the University of Washington and an M.B.A. from Harvard Business School.

RoAnn Costin [2]
President
Reservoir Capital Management, Inc.
Board member since 1996

RoAnn Costin is the President of Reservoir Capital Management, Inc., an investment advisory firm. She has worked in investment management since 1981, holding the position of Senior Vice President, Investment Manager for The Putnam Companies and Portfolio Manager for State Street Research and Management, Inc.

Ms. Costin holds an M.B.A. from the Stanford University Graduate School of Business and a B.A. in Government from Harvard University. In addition to Toys"R"Us, Inc., she serves on the Board of Directors for the Paul Taylor Dance Company in New York and on the Board of Trustees for The Boston Conservatory.

Roger N. Farah [1,4]
President and Chief Operating Officer
Polo Ralph Lauren
Board member since 2001

Roger N. Farah, has been President and Chief Operating Officer of Polo Ralph Lauren and a member of its Board of Directors since 2000.

From 1994 to 2000, Mr. Farah was Chairman of the Board and Chief Executive Officer of Venator Group, Inc. Prior to that, he held positions as President and Chief Operating Officer of Macy's Inc., Chairman and Chief Executive Officer of Federated Merchandising Services, and Chairman and Chief Executive Officer of Rich's Department Stores. From 1998 until 2000, he served on the Board of Directors at Liz Claiborne, Inc.

Mr. Farah received his B.S. in Economics from the University of Pennsylvania, Wharton School. He currently serves on the Wharton School's Board of Directors.

Peter A. Georgescu [2,4]
Chairman Emeritus
Young & Rubicam, Inc.
Board member since 2001

Peter A. Georgescu is Chairman Emeritus of Young & Rubicam, Inc. where he served as the company's Chairman and CEO from 1994 until 2000. He also served as President of Young and Rubicam Advertising and President of the company's former International division. Under Mr. Georgescu's tenure, Young & Rubicam transformed from a private to a publicly-held company and built an extensive database for global branding.

Mr. Georgescu also serves on the Board of Directors for EMI Group PLC, International Flavors & Fragrances Inc. and Levi Strauss & Co. He is Vice Chairman/Director of New York Presbyterian Hospital and a Director of A Better Chance. He received his B.A. from Princeton and an M.B.A. from the Stanford Business School. He was elected to the Advertising Hall of Fame in 2001.

Michael Goldstein [1]
Chairman, The Toys"R"Us
Children's Fund, Inc.
Board member since 1989

Michael Goldstein is Chairman of The Toys"R"Us Children's Fund, Inc. and Toys"R"Us.com, Inc. He has spent 19 years with Toys"R"Us, Inc. serving as both Chairman of the Board and Chief Executive Officer. Prior to 1983, Mr. Goldstein held positions as Sr. Executive Vice President-Operations & Finance with Lerner Stores Corporation and as a Partner with Ernst & Young.

Mr. Goldstein is a Director of Finlay Enterprises, Inc., United Retail Group, 4 Kids Entertainment, Inc. and Columbia House. He is President-elect of the 92nd Street Y, a Director of The Special Contributions Fund of the NAACP, and serves on the Advisory Boards of the For All Kids Foundation, USA Tennis Foundation and the New York Restoration Project. Mr. Goldstein is President and Director of the Northside Center for Child Development. He serves on the Board and Executive Committee of Reading is Fundamental and on the Board and Executive Committee of the Queens College Foundation. He is an inductee into the Toy Industry Hall of Fame and was appointed by President George W. Bush to serve on the Advisory Committee for Trade Policy and Negotiation. He is a graduate of Queens College with a B.S. in Economics.

Calvin Hill [3]
Consultant
Board member since 1997

Calvin Hill is a consultant to The Dallas Cowboys Football Club, Mental Health Management, Inc., Fleet Financial Services and Alexander & Associates, Inc. Mr. Hill was Vice President with the Baltimore Orioles from 1987 to 1994, also serving on its Board of Directors. From 1993 to 2000, he served on President Bill Clinton's Council on Physical Fitness.

Mr. Hill currently serves on the Boards of the Rand Corporation Drug Policy and Research Center, the NCAA Foundation, Duke Divinity School, and International Special Olympics. He launched his professional athletic career with the Dallas Cowboys in 1969 and has played professional football in both the World Football League and the NFL. He is a graduate of Yale University.

Nancy Karch [2,4]
Senior Partner (retired)
McKinsey & Company
Board member since 2000

Nancy Karch is a retired Director of the international consulting firm McKinsey & Company and a member of the McKinsey Advisory Council, comprised of former partners who provide advice to the firm. During 26 years with McKinsey, she held several leadership positions, including Managing Partner of the Retail and Consumer Industries Sector, and Managing Partner of McKinsey Southeast United States.

Ms. Karch is a recognized expert in the field of general merchandise retailing and an active speaker in the retailing and consumer goods fields. She also serves on the Board of Directors of Liz Claiborne, Inc., Gillette, and the Corporate Executive Board, a business research firm. Ms. Karch holds a B.A. in mathematics from Cornell University, an M.S. in mathematics from Northeastern University, and an M.B.A. from Harvard Business School.

company officers

Norman S. Matthews [1,3,4]
Consultant
Board member since 1996

Norman S. Matthews has worked in consulting and venture capital since 1989. Prior to that he held various executive positions with Federated Department stores, including President, Vice Chairman and Executive Vice President. He was also Chairman of Federated's Gold Circle Stores Division.

In addition to Toys"R"Us, Inc., Mr. Matthews serves on the Board of Directors for The Progressive Corporation, Sunoco, Eye Care Centers of America, Finlay Enterprises, Inc., Galyan's Trading Company, and Henry Schein, Inc. He holds a B.A. degree from Princeton University and an M.B.A. from Harvard Business School.

Arthur B. Newman [1,2,3]
Senior Managing Director,
The Blackstone Group, L.P.
Board member since 1997

Arthur B. Newman has been a Senior Managing Director and head of The Restructuring Group of The Blackstone Group, L.P., a private investment bank, since 1991. Previously, Mr. Newman was a Managing Director and head of the Restructuring and Reorganization Group of Chemical Bank and a senior partner at Ernst & Young. Mr. Newman has been an advisor in many of this country's largest reorganizations, including AMF Bowling, Arch Wireless, The Charter Company, Chiquita Banana, Dow Corning Corporation, Eastern Airlines, Exide Technologies, Global Crossing, Iridium, LTV Corporation, Levitz Furniture, Macy's, Manville Corporation, Mobile Media Corporation, Montgomery Ward, Texaco, Inc., White Motor Corporation and the Wickes Corporation.

Mr. Newman is a member of the America College of Bankruptcy and was the recipient of the 1990 award by the Bankruptcy & Reorganization Group, Lawyers Division of UJA-Federation. Mr. Newman holds a B.S. degree in economics and an M.B.A. from Rutgers University. He is a certified public accountant in New York.

[1] Executive Committee
[2] Audit Committee
[3] Compensation & Organizational Development Committee
[4] Corporate Governance and Nominating Committee

Corporate and Administrative Officers

John H. Eyler, Jr.
Chairman, President and Chief Executive Officer

Francesca L. Brockett
Executive Vice President – Strategic Planning & Business Development

Michael D'Ambrose
Executive Vice President – Human Resources

Karen Duvall
Executive Vice President – Supply Chain

John Holohan
Executive Vice President – Chief Information Officer

Christopher K. Kay
Executive Vice President – Operations & General Counsel, Corporate Secretary

Warren F. Kornblum
Executive Vice President – Chief Marketing Officer

Louis Lipschitz
Executive Vice President – Chief Financial Officer

Jon W. Kimmins
Sr. Vice President – Treasurer

Dorvin D. Lively
Sr. Vice President – Corporate Controller

Peter W. Weiss
Sr. Vice President – Taxes

Rebecca A. Caruso
Vice President – Corporate Communications

Ursula H. Moran
Vice President – Investor Relations

Divisional Officers

Richard L. Markee
Executive Vice President and President – Specialty Businesses and International Operations

Raymond L. Arthur
President – Toysrus.com

John Barbour
Executive Vice President and President – Toys"R"Us International

James E. Feldt
Executive Vice President and President – Merchandising and Marketing, Toys"R"Us U.S.

Elliott Wahle
President – Babies"R"Us & Kids"R"Us

Joan W. Donovan
Sr. Vice President – General Merchandise Manager, Toys"R"Us International

Jonathan M. Friedman
Sr. Vice President – Chief Financial Officer, Toys"R"Us U.S.

Andrew R. Gatto
Sr. Vice President – Product Development, Toys"R"Us U.S.

Steven J. Krajewski
Sr. Vice President – Operations, Toys"R"Us U.S.

James G. Parros
Sr. Vice President – Stores & Distributions Center Operations, Kids"R"Us

David Schoenbeck
Sr. Vice President – Operations, Babies"R"Us

Pamela B. Wallack
Sr. Vice President – General Merchandise Manager, Babies"R"Us & Kids"R"Us

International Country Presidents and Managing Directors

David Rurka
Managing Director – Toys"R"Us U.K.

Jacques LeFoll
President – Toys"R"Us France

Monika Merz
President – Toys"R"Us Canada

John Schryver
Managing Director – Toys"R"Us Australia

Michael C. Taylor
Managing Director – Toys"R"Us Central Europe

Antonio Urcelay
Managing Director – Toys"R"Us Iberia

A Heartfelt Tribute

After decades of much appreciated leadership and service, Charles Lazarus and Michael Goldstein will be leaving the Board at the end of this year's (2002-2003) term. Charles and Mike have both served many years as Chief Executive Officer and as Chairman of the Board of Directors of Toys"R"Us, Inc., where they both played significant roles in the growth of the company. Thereafter, they served the company with distinction as members of the Board of Directors. We are extremely grateful for their leadership, their inspiration, their compassion and their commitment to the Toys"R"Us family of stockholders, colleagues and guests.

Quarterly Financial Data and Market Information
Toys"R"Us, Inc. and Subsidiaries

Quarterly Financial Data
(In millions except per share data)

The following table sets forth certain unaudited quarterly financial information:

	First Quarter	Second Quarter	Third Quarter	Fourth Quarter
Year Ended February 1, 2003				
Net Sales	$ 2,095	$ 2,070	$ 2,271	$ 4,869
Gross Margin	682	670	722	1,432
Net (Loss)/Earnings	(4)	(17)	(28)	278
Basic (Loss)/ Earnings per Share	$ (0.02)	$ (0.08)	$ (0.13)	$ 1.31
Diluted (Loss)/ Earnings per Share	$ (0.02)	$ (0.08)	$ (0.13)	$ 1.30

	First Quarter	Second Quarter	Third Quarter	Fourth Quarter[a]
Year Ended February 2, 2002				
Net Sales	$ 2,061	$ 2,021	$ 2,178	$ 4,759
Gross Margin	665	661	710	1,379
Net (Loss)/Earnings	(18)	(29)	(44)	158
Basic (Loss)/ Earnings per Share	$ (0.09)	$ (0.15)	$ (0.22)	$ 0.80
Diluted (Loss)/ Earnings per Share	$ (0.09)	$ (0.15)	$ (0.22)	$ 0.78

(a) Includes restructuring and other charges of $213 ($126 net of tax, or $0.61 per share).

Market Information

The company's common stock is listed on the New York Stock Exchange. The following table reflects the high and low prices (rounded to the nearest hundredth) based on New York Stock Exchange trading since February 3, 2001.

The company has not paid any cash dividends, however, the Board of Directors of the company periodically reviews this policy.

The company had approximately 30,736 Stockholders of Record on March 12, 2003.

		High	Low
2001	1st Quarter	$ 26.52	$ 23.00
	2nd Quarter	31.00	22.30
	3rd Quarter	25.10	16.81
	4th Quarter	24.00	18.25
2002	1st Quarter	$ 20.31	$ 16.18
	2nd Quarter	18.28	12.58
	3rd Quarter	14.09	8.70
	4th Quarter	13.81	9.04

Why Walgreens?

2002 ANNUAL REPORT

Financial Highlights
For the Years Ended August 31, 2002 and 2001

(In Millions, except per share data)	2002	2001	Increase
Net Sales	$28,681.1	$24,623.0	16.5%
Net Earnings	$ 1,019.2	$ 885.6	15.1%
Net Earnings per Common Share (diluted)	$ .99	$ .86	15.1%
Shareholders' Equity	$ 6,230.2	$ 5,207.2	19.6%
Return on Average Shareholders' Equity	17.8%	18.8%	
Closing Stock Price per Common Share	$ 34.75	$ 34.35	
Total Market Value of Common Stock	$ 35,616	$ 35,017	1.7%
Dividends Declared per Common Share	$ .145	$ .140	3.6%
Average Shares Outstanding (diluted)	1,032.3	1,028.9	0.3%

Questions and Answers for Our Shareholders
November 18, 2002

Chairman L. Daniel Jorndt (left) with president and chief executive officer David W. Bernauer.

"Beautifully boring" – that was the description of Walgreens and other companies who made *Bloomberg Personal Finance's* "Profit Champ" list this fall. Each of the 51 firms recognized has achieved increased earnings per share for at least 10 consecutive years. In Walgreens case, the streak is approaching three decades.

During this past rocky year, when the bears ruled the stock market and economic news turned morning coffee bitter, we completed our 28th consecutive record year – and first billion-dollar earnings year – while opening 471 stores and investing nearly $1 billion in new stores, distribution centers and technology improvements. And in a world where cash is now king, we ended 2002 with over $400 million in the bank, nearly $3 billion in owned real estate, virtually no debt and the wherewithal to self-finance accelerating growth and customer service innovations. As one analyst commented recently: "Profits are opinion, but cash is a fact."

It was a record year, but fourth quarter earnings came in a penny light of expectations. Why?
Dave Bernauer: Pure and simple, this was a sales problem. Prescriptions were excellent – up 20 percent for the quarter and more than 21 percent for the year. But fourth quarter front-end – non-pharmacy – sales were anemic, particularly for promotional and summer seasonal merchandise. Those weak sales held our profit below Wall Street's expectations. A company with our stock market valuation isn't allowed a toe-stub, and our stock took a hit.

Why the weak sales?
Dan Jorndt: The easiest culprit is the economy, but we're not taking that bait. One of the beauties of our admittedly "boring" business is its staying power – we sell everyday, consumable items that people *need* more than *want*. Some times are tougher than others, but since the mid-1970s – through recessions and boom times – we've never had a down year. So when sales are tight, we look in the mirror…and adjust. We've made lots of corrections, especially in our advertising, to ensure that fall and holiday sales are more "Walgreen-like," that is, good, strong front-end sales.

Quite frankly, we got out of balance this summer. We were less promotion-oriented, which helped increase our gross profits, but hurt the top sales line. Advertising is always a delicate balance and we're moving the pendulum a little more in favor of traffic building. But we're seeking middle ground. Walgreens is not a retailer that sacrifices all to drive sales. We will get the top line moving…sensibly.

Walgreens keeps adding stores despite the economic slowdown. Is this smart?
Bernauer: There's never been a better time for us to expand. We have the sites, the cash, the people…and America has the need. The only retail segment where sales are outpacing store growth is drugstores. In 2001, the number of retail prescriptions climbed 5 percent, while drugstore outlets grew only 1 percent. Although we're the largest prescription provider in the nation, we still fill only 12 percent of the total, which gives us outstanding growth opportunity.

What about Wal*Mart?
Bernauer: What about *any* competitor? Any store that sells what we sell is on our radar screen. Our strategy has always been to define our segment – convenient healthcare and basic need retailing – and do it better than anyone else. We've seriously – and successfully – competed head-on with Wal*Mart for a quarter century now. They're not new competition. They *are* excellent, respected competition…and they're also one of the few retailers expanding at the same pace we are. Top competitors like Wal*Mart make us better. We watch them… they watch us.

Inventory was high going into fiscal 2002. How did you end up?
Bernauer: A chunk of our positive cash position is due to a big improvement in inventory levels. We had a bad case of indigestion last year, but ended 2002 with inventories up just 5 percent, despite a 16.5 percent sales increase and opening a record 363 net new stores plus new distribution centers in Jupiter, Florida, and Waxahachie, Texas. More importantly, we didn't just blow out product with severe price cuts. We used our systems to attack overages on an orderly basis without hurting gross profit margins and in-stock conditions.

Short-term borrowings of $441 million were completely repaid during the year. For my money, the beauty of our 2002 balance sheet rivals Monet, showing a positive cash swing from borrowing to investing of nearly $900 million.

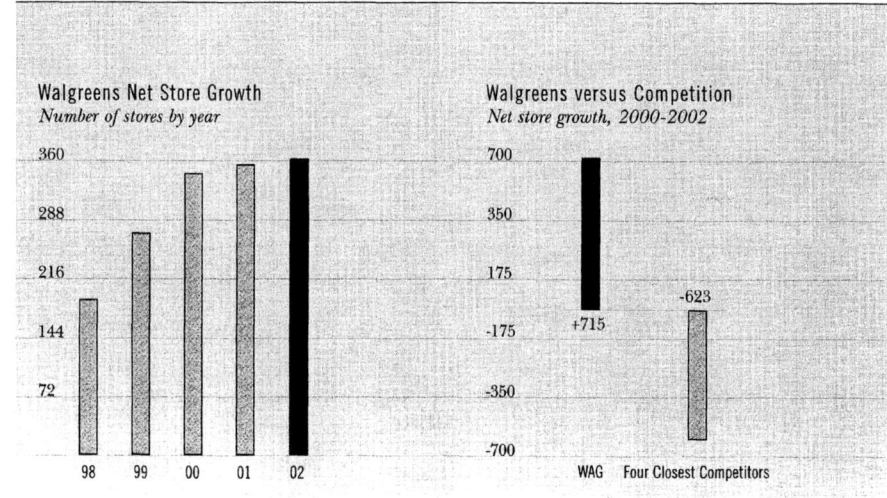

Walgreens Net Store Growth
Number of stores by year

Walgreens versus Competition
Net store growth, 2000-2002

WAG: +715
Four Closest Competitors: -623

Source: Published company reports

3,883 AND GROWING
Walgreens is the most "national" – and fastest growing – drugstore chain in America. In 2002, we filled 361 million prescriptions – 12 percent of the U.S. retail market and more per store than all major competitors. Our stores average $7.1 million or $654 per square foot in annual sales. Looking ahead, in 2003 we plan to open 450 new stores (approximately 360 net), add 12,000 new jobs and open our third new distribution center in just two years.

Dan Jorndt retires in January after 40 years with Walgreens. Since 1990 he's served as president, CEO and then chairman, leading this company through its period of greatest expansion and innovation. Dan Jorndt's two favorite words are "thank you." On behalf of all shareholders, we thank him for his leadership, honesty, retail savvy, tough decisions, long days and nights, sense of humor and the example he's set. Quite simply, he's made all of those whose lives he's touched a little richer. We wish him and his wife, Pat, the best — and most active — of retirements.

What was the impact of generic drug introductions last year?

Jorndt: Very positive. Generics save money for patients and their providers, both private insurance companies and state Medicaid plans. For Walgreens, while the higher mix of generics to brands slowed our top-line sales growth trend slightly last year, it had a healthy impact on the bottom line. The most important metric in pharmacy is the number of prescriptions. We filled 361 million in 2002, up almost 12 percent from the previous year, and more than double the national increase.

Is there still a pharmacist shortage?

Bernauer: There is a shortage...a big one. But aside from a few markets, we're in good shape. At the end of fiscal 2002, we had 1,600 more pharmacists working for us than a year ago. We're meeting ongoing needs and staffing over 360 net new drugstores a year. We also have the pharmacists to cover 900 24-hour stores. That's more than half of *all* 24-hour pharmacies in America.

If you could stress just one thing to shareholders this year, what would it be?

Jorndt: The quality of our earnings. Warren Buffet has a good quote: "It's only when the tide goes out that you learn who's been swimming naked." A lot of skinny-dippers have surfaced in the past year, bringing down high-flying companies and millions of shareholders. Believe me, we at Walgreens have our swimsuits on, and they're those scratchy knee-to-neck getups beach lovers wore in the 1920s. More boring than bikinis and thongs? You'd better believe it. But accounting works best when it's boring.

Our earnings are all about quality. Our financial statements are straightforward...what you see is what you get. We pay as we go and, other than store leases, everything is on our balance sheet. With no one-time charges and virtually no debt, WAG made the "Top 10" on a recent Merrill Lynch list of firms with quality earnings.

What worries you?

Bernauer: Mostly, stuff that's difficult to control. That includes the current economy as well as government actions. As our population ages, healthcare costs are going up, up, up. This will require government at all levels to make some very tough decisions about resource allocation. We believe it's our job to invest, create jobs, serve customer needs and get a return for these efforts, a return on which we pay significant taxes. It's the government's job to provide social

WHAT ARE WE WORTH?

As of August 31, 2002, Walgreens market capitalization was $35.6 billion. That ranks us third among U.S. retailers and third in the world. In terms of sales volume, we rank No. 78 in the *Fortune 100*. Walgreens has paid dividends in every quarter since 1933 and has raised them for 27 consecutive years. Since 1980, we've had seven two-for-one stock splits.

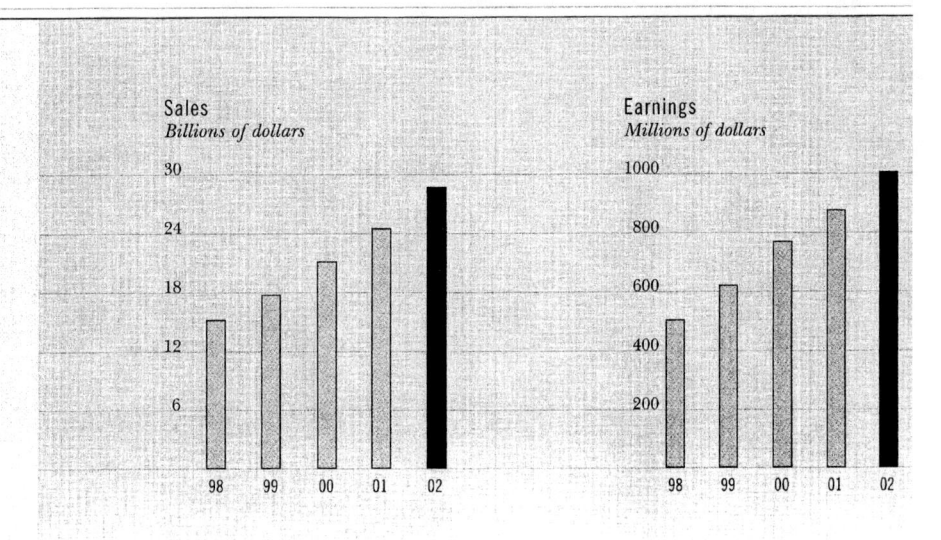

Sales
Billions of dollars

Earnings
Millions of dollars

4 2002 WALGREENS ANNUAL REPORT

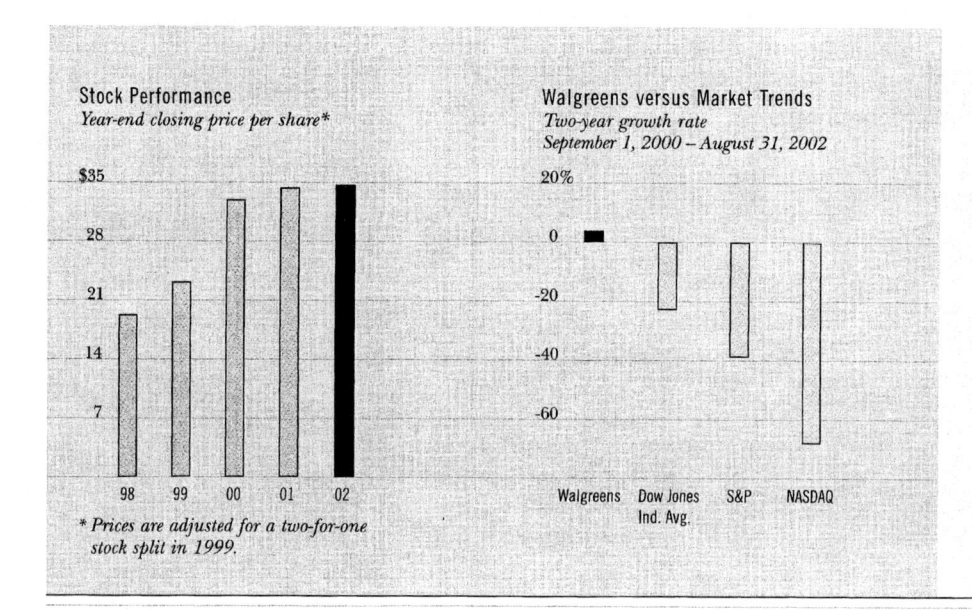

Stock Performance
Year-end closing price per share*

Year	
98	~$14
99	~$21
00	~$31
01	~$32
02	~$34

* Prices are adjusted for a two-for-one stock split in 1999.

Walgreens versus Market Trends
Two-year growth rate
September 1, 2000 – August 31, 2002

Walgreens	~0%
Dow Jones Ind. Avg.	~-25%
S&P	~-35%
NASDAQ	~-65%

WALGREENS STOCK PERFORMANCE

10 YEARS

On August 31, 1992, 100 shares of Walgreen stock sold for $3,838. Ten years later, on August 31, 2002, those 100 shares, having split three times, were 800 shares worth $27,800, for a gain of 624 percent.

20 YEARS

On August 31, 1982, 100 shares of Walgreen stock sold for $3,600. Twenty years later, those 100 shares, having split six times, were 6,400 shares worth $222,400, for a gain of 6,078 percent.

---

services. Although pharmacy consumes only 10 percent of the nation's healthcare bill and is the most cost-effective form of treatment, there have been moves recently to slash state Medicaid reimbursement to levels below the filling cost. We and other community pharmacies cannot accept plans – public or private – on which we lose money.

January marks a new era, as Dan Jorndt retires and Dave Bernauer adds "chairman" to his CEO position. What will change?

Jorndt: I've had a great 40-year run with this company, but it's time for new blood. Same core strategy, same execution...someone else calling the shots. These moves are part of our long-term succession plan. We're blessed in not having to go outside for CEOs. Dave Bernauer and our new president, Jeff Rein, are both pharmacists who started in the stores and have spent long careers here. They, and what I call the "new generation" of Walgreen leaders behind them, are among the top retailers in the country. These men and women know drugstores inside out and bring amazing energy and relentless character to their work. It will be a pleasure to watch their progress.

IN A TOUGH BUSINESS ENVIRONMENT, where confidence in corporate America has plummeted, we feel compelled to say, "No, Chicken Little, the sky isn't falling." We read volumes about the failures...while the thousands of successful companies receive little press. We can't solve the world's ills, but we can promise you, our shareholders and employees, that we'll do our level best to restore faith in what's good about American business. At Walgreens, we know who we are and what we're about. We have a competitive format and clearly defined strategy...a growing demand for our products and services...healthy cash and inventory positions...superior real estate and technology...and motivated, seasoned people at every level. Thanks for your faith in our long-term future...it's a solid one.

Jeffrey A. Rein will become president and chief operating officer in January 2003.

L. Daniel Jorndt
Chairman

David W. Bernauer
President and Chief Executive Officer

Eleven-Year Summary of Selected Consolidated Financial Data

Walgreen Co. and Subsidiaries (Dollars in Millions, except per share data)

Fiscal Year		2002	2001	2000
Net Sales		$28,681.1	$24,623.0	$21,206.9
Costs and Deductions	Cost of sales	21,076.1	18,048.9	15,465.9
	Selling, occupancy and administration	5,980.8	5,175.8	4,516.9
	Other (income) expense *(1)*	(13.1)	(24.4)	(39.2)
	Total Costs and Deductions	27,043.8	23,200.3	19,943.6
Earnings	Earnings before income tax provision and cumulative effect of accounting changes	1,637.3	1,422.7	1,263.3
	Income tax provision	618.1	537.1	486.4
	Earnings before cumulative effect of accounting changes	1,019.2	885.6	776.9
	Cumulative effect of accounting changes *(2)*	—	—	—
	Net Earnings	$ 1,019.2	$ 885.6	$ 776.9
Per Common Share *(3)*	Net earnings *(2)*			
	Basic	$ 1.00	$ .87	$ .77
	Diluted	.99	.86	.76
	Dividends declared	.15	.14	.14
	Book value	6.08	5.11	4.19
Non-Current Liabilities	Long-term debt	$ 11.2	$ 20.8	$ 18.2
	Deferred income taxes	176.5	137.0	101.6
	Other non-current liabilities	505.7	457.2	446.2
Assets and Equity	Total assets	$ 9,878.8	$ 8,833.8	$ 7,103.7
	Shareholders' equity	6,230.2	5,207.2	4,234.0
	Return on average shareholders' equity	17.8%	18.8%	20.1%
Drugstore Units	Year-end: Units *(4)*	3,883	3,520	3,165

(1) Fiscal 2002, 2001 and 2000 include pre-tax income of $6.2 million ($.004 per share), $22.1 million ($.01 per share) and $33.5 million ($.02 per share), respectively, from the partial payments of the brand name prescription drugs litigation settlement. Fiscal 1998 includes a pre-tax gain of $37.4 million ($.02 per share) from the sale of the company's long-term care pharmacy business.

(2) Fiscal 1998 includes the after-tax $26.4 million ($.03 per share) charge from the cumulative effect of accounting change for system development costs. Fiscal 1993 includes the after-tax $23.6 million ($.02 per share) costs from the cumulative effect of accounting changes for postretirement benefits and income taxes.

(3) Per share data have been adjusted for two-for-one stock splits in 1999, 1997 and 1995.

(4) Units include mail service facilities.

1999	1998	1997	1996	1995	1994	1993	1992
$17,838.8	$15,306.6	$13,363.0	$11,778.4	$10,395.1	$9,235.0	$8,294.8	$7,475.0
12,978.6	11,139.4	9,681.8	8,514.9	7,482.3	6,614.4	5,959.0	5,377.7
3,844.8	3,332.0	2,972.5	2,659.5	2,392.7	2,164.9	1,929.6	1,738.8
(11.9)	(41.9)	(3.9)	(2.9)	(3.6)	(2.7)	6.5	5.5
16,811.5	14,429.5	12,650.4	11,171.5	9,871.4	8,776.6	7,895.1	7,122.0
1,027.3	877.1	712.6	606.9	523.7	458.4	399.7	353.0
403.2	339.9	276.1	235.2	202.9	176.5	154.4	132.4
624.1	537.2	436.5	371.7	320.8	281.9	245.3	220.6
—	(26.4)	—	—	—	—	(23.6)	—
$ 624.1	$ 510.8	$ 436.5	$ 371.7	$ 320.8	$ 281.9	$ 221.7	$ 220.6
$ .62	$ .51	$ .44	$ .38	$ .33	$ .29	$ .23	$ .22
.62	.51	.44	.37	.32	.29	.23	.22
.13	.13	.12	.11	.11	.09	.08	.07
3.47	2.86	2.40	2.08	1.82	1.60	1.40	1.25
$ 18.0	$ 13.6	$ 3.3	$ 3.4	$ 2.4	$ 1.8	$ 6.2	$ 18.7
74.8	89.1	112.8	145.2	142.3	137.7	144.2	171.8
405.8	369.9	279.2	259.9	237.6	213.8	176.2	103.8
$ 5,906.7	$ 4,901.6	$ 4,207.1	$ 3,633.6	$ 3,252.6	$2,872.8	$2,506.0	$2,346.9
3,484.3	2,848.9	2,373.3	2,043.1	1,792.6	1,573.6	1,378.8	1,233.3
19.7%	19.6%	19.8%	19.4%	19.1%	19.1%	18.8%	19.1%
2,821	2,549	2,358	2,193	2,085	1,968	1,836	1,736

Management's Discussion and Analysis of Results of Operations and Financial Condition

Results of Operations

Fiscal 2002 was the 28th consecutive year of record sales and earnings. Net earnings were $1.019 billion or $.99 per share (diluted), an increase of 15.1% from last year's earnings of $885.6 million or $.86 per share. Included in this year's results was a $6.2 million pre-tax gain ($.004 per share) for a partial payment of the company's share of the brand name prescription drugs antitrust litigation settlement. Last year's results included a $22.1 million ($.01 per share) comparable payment. Excluding these gains, fiscal year earnings rose 16.5%.

Total net sales increased by 16.5% to $28.7 billion in fiscal 2002 compared to increases of 16.1% in 2001 and 18.9% in 2000. Drugstore sales increases resulted from sales gains in existing stores and added sales from new stores, each of which include an indeterminate amount of market-driven price changes. Comparable drugstore (those open at least one year) sales were up 10.5% in 2002, 10.5% in 2001 and 11.7% in 2000. New store openings accounted for 9.6% of the sales gains in 2002, 11.3% in 2001 and 10.6% in 2000. The company operated 3,883 drugstores as of August 31, 2002, compared to 3,520 a year earlier.

Prescription sales increased 21.2% in 2002, 20.9% in 2001 and 25.3% in 2000. Comparable drugstore prescription sales were up 16.3% in 2002, 17.6% in 2001 and 19.0% in 2000. Prescription sales were 59.8% of total sales for fiscal 2002 compared to 57.5% in 2001 and 55.2% in 2000. Third party sales, where reimbursement is received from managed care organizations and government and private insurance, were 89.8% of pharmacy sales in 2002, 88.4% in 2001 and 86.1% in 2000. Pharmacy sales trends are expected to continue primarily because of increased penetration in existing markets, availability of new drugs and demographic changes such as the aging population.

Gross margins as a percent of total sales were 26.5% in 2002, 26.7% in 2001 and 27.1% in 2000. The decrease in gross margin was caused by a number of factors. Non-pharmacy margins declined as a result of more aggressive advertising and in-store promotions. Although prescription margins increased, due in part to the shift to more generic medications, the trend in sales mix continued toward pharmacy, which carries lower margins than the rest of the store. Within the pharmacy, third party sales, which typically have lower profit margins than cash prescriptions, continue to become a larger portion of prescription sales.

The company uses the last-in, first-out (LIFO) method of inventory valuation. The effective LIFO inflation rates were 1.42% in 2002, 1.93% in 2001 and 1.36% in 2000, which resulted in charges to cost of sales of $55.9 million in 2002, $62.8 million in 2001 and $38.8 million in 2000. Inflation on prescription inventory was 4.3% in 2002, 4.9% in 2001 and 3.5% in 2000.

Selling, occupancy and administration expenses were 20.9% of sales in fiscal 2002, 21.0% of sales in fiscal 2001 and 21.3% of sales in fiscal 2000. The decrease in fiscal 2002, as a percent to sales, was caused by lower store direct expenses, which were partially offset by higher occupancy costs. The decline in fiscal 2001 resulted from lower advertising and headquarters expense. Fixed costs continue to be spread over a larger base of stores.

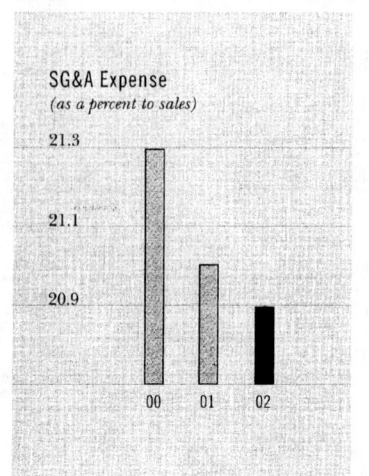

Interest income net of interest expense increased in 2002 principally due to higher investment levels. Average net investment levels were approximately $162 million in 2002, $31 million in 2001 and $64 million in 2000.

The fiscal 2002 and 2001 effective income tax rates were 37.75% compared to 38.50% in 2000. The decrease in rates compared to 2000 was principally the result of lower state income taxes and the settlement of various IRS matters.

Critical Accounting Policies

The consolidated financial statements are prepared in accordance with accounting principles generally accepted in the United States of America and include amounts based on management's prudent judgments and estimates. Actual results may differ from these estimates. Management believes that any reasonable deviation from those judgments and estimates would not have a material impact on the company's consolidated financial position or results of operations. However, to the extent that the estimates used differ from actual results, adjustments to the statement of earnings and corresponding balance sheet accounts would be necessary. Some of the more significant estimates include liability for closed locations, liability for insurance reserves, vendor allowances, allowance for doubtful accounts, and cost of sales. The company uses the following techniques to determine estimates:

Liability for closed locations – The present value of future rent obligations and other related costs to the first lease option date or estimated sublease date.

Liability for insurance reserves – Incurred losses by policy year extended by historical growth factors to derive ultimate losses.

Vendor allowances – Vendor allowances are principally received as a result of meeting defined purchase levels or promoting vendors' products. Those received as a result of purchase levels are accrued as a reduction of merchandise purchase prices over the incentive period based on estimates. Those received for promoting vendors' products are offset against advertising expense and result in a reduction of selling, occupancy and administration expense.

Allowance for doubtful accounts – Based on both specific receivables and historic write-off percents.

Cost of sales – Based primarily on point-of-sale scanning information with an estimate for shrinkage and adjusted based on periodic inventories.

Financial Condition

Cash and cash equivalents were $449.9 million at August 31, 2002, compared to $16.9 million at August 31, 2001. Short-term investment objectives are to minimize risk, maintain liquidity and maximize after-tax yields. To attain these objectives, investment limits are placed on the amount, type and issuer of securities. Investments are principally in top-tier money market funds, tax exempt bonds and commercial paper.

Net cash provided by operating activities for fiscal 2002 was $1.5 billion compared to $719.2 million a year ago. The change between periods was principally due to tighter control over inventory levels. The company's profitability is the principal source for providing funds for expansion and remodeling programs, dividends to shareholders and funding for various technological improvements.

Net cash used for investing activities was $551.9 million in fiscal 2002 and $1.1 billion in 2001. Additions to property and equipment were $934.4 million compared to $1.2 billion last year. During the year, 471 new or relocated drugstores were opened. This compares to 474 new or relocated drugstores opened in the same period last year. New stores are owned or leased. There were 150 owned locations opened during the year or under construction at August 31, 2002, versus 245 for the same period last year. During the year, two new distribution centers opened, one in West Palm Beach (Jupiter), Florida, and the other in the Dallas metropolitan area.

During fiscal 2002, the company entered into two sale-leaseback transactions. These transactions involved 86 drugstore locations and resulted in proceeds of $302 million.

Capital expenditures for fiscal 2003 are expected to exceed $1 billion. The company expects to open more than 450 new stores in fiscal 2003 and have a total of 7,000 drugstores by the year 2010. The company is continuing to relocate stores to more convenient and profitable freestanding locations. In addition to new stores, a significant portion of the expenditures will be made for technology and distribution centers. A new distribution center is under construction in Ohio. Another is planned in Southern California.

Net cash used for financing activities was $488.9 million compared to $419.4 million provided a year ago. The change was principally due to payments of short-term borrowings this year versus proceeds from borrowings last year. There were no short-term borrowings at August 31, 2002, compared to $440.7 million at August 31, 2001. Borrowings were needed during each year to support working capital needs and store and distribution center growth, which included purchases of new store property, equipment and inventory. At August 31, 2002, the company had a syndicated bank line of credit facility of $600 million to support the company's short-term commercial paper program. On July 2, 2002, the company deregistered the remaining $100 million of unissued authorized debt securities, previously filed with the Securities and Exchange Commission.

Recent Accounting Pronouncements

During the first quarter of 2002, the company adopted Statement of Financial Accounting Standards (SFAS) No. 142, "Goodwill and Other Intangible Assets." Under this pronouncement, goodwill is no longer amortized but periodically tested for impairment. No significant impact to the consolidated financial position or results of operations occurred as a result of adopting this standard.

The adoption of SFAS No. 144, "Accounting for the Impairment or Disposal of Long-Lived Assets," resulted in additional disclosures which can be found under "Impaired Assets and Liabilities for Store Closings" in the Summary of Major Accounting Policies.

During the fourth quarter of 2002, the company early adopted SFAS No. 146, "Accounting for Costs Associated with Exit or Disposal Activity." As a result, beginning in June 2002, the remaining lease obligations for closed locations were no longer recognized at the time management made the decision to close the location but were recognized at the time of closing. The adoption of this pronouncement did not have a material impact in the fourth quarter and is not expected to have a material impact on the company's consolidated financial position or results of operations in the future.

Cautionary Note Regarding Forward-Looking Statements

Certain statements and projections of future results made in this report constitute forward-looking information that is based on current market, competitive and regulatory expectations that involve risks and uncertainties. Those risks and uncertainties include changes in economic conditions generally or in the markets served by the company; consumer preferences and spending patterns; changes in state or federal legislation or regulations; the availability and cost of real estate and construction; competition; and risks of new business areas. Please see Walgreen Co.'s Form 10-K for the period ended August 31, 2002, for a discussion of certain other important factors as they relate to forward-looking statements. Actual results could differ materially.

Capital Expenditures Fiscal Year 2003
We plan to spend $1.021 billion.

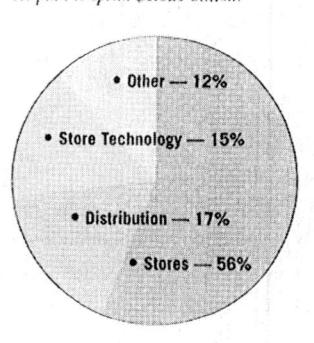

- Other — 12%
- Store Technology — 15%
- Distribution — 17%
- Stores — 56%

Consolidated Statements of Earnings and Shareholders' Equity

Walgreen Co. and Subsidiaries for the Years Ended August 31, 2002, 2001 and 2000 (Dollars in Millions, except per share data)

	Earnings	2002	2001	2000
Net Sales		$28,681.1	$24,623.0	$21,206.9
Costs and Deductions	Cost of sales	21,076.1	18,048.9	15,465.9
	Selling, occupancy and administration	5,980.8	5,175.8	4,516.9
		27,056.9	23,224.7	19,982.8
Other (Income) Expense	Interest income	(6.9)	(5.4)	(6.1)
	Interest expense	—	3.1	.4
	Other income	(6.2)	(22.1)	(33.5)
		(13.1)	(24.4)	(39.2)
Earnings	Earnings before income tax provision	1,637.3	1,422.7	1,263.3
	Income tax provision	618.1	537.1	486.4
	Net Earnings	$ 1,019.2	$ 885.6	$ 776.9
Net Earnings per Common Share	Basic	$ 1.00	$ .87	$ .77
	Diluted	.99	.86	.76
	Average shares outstanding	1,022,554,460	1,016,197,785	1,007,393,572
	Dilutive effect of stock options	9,716,486	12,748,828	12,495,236
	Average shares outstanding assuming dilution	1,032,270,946	1,028,946,613	1,019,888,808

Shareholders' Equity	Common Stock Shares	Amount	Paid-in Capital	Retained Earnings
Balance, August 31, 1999	1,004,022,258	$78.4	$258.9	$3,147.0
Net earnings	—	—	—	776.9
Cash dividends declared ($.135 per share)	—	—	—	(136.1)
Employee stock purchase and option plans	6,796,632	.6	108.3	—
Balance, August 31, 2000	1,010,818,890	79.0	367.2	3,787.8
Net earnings	—	—	—	885.6
Cash dividends declared ($.14 per share)	—	—	—	(142.5)
Employee stock purchase and option plans	8,606,162	.6	229.5	—
Balance, August 31, 2001	1,019,425,052	79.6	596.7	4,530.9
Net earnings	—	—	—	1,019.2
Cash dividends declared ($.145 per share)	—	—	—	(148.4)
Employee stock purchase and option plans	5,483,224	.5	151.7	—
Balance, August 31, 2002	1,024,908,276	$80.1	$748.4	$5,401.7

The accompanying Summary of Major Accounting Policies and the Notes to Consolidated Financial Statements are integral parts of these statements.

Consolidated Balance Sheets

Walgreen Co. and Subsidiaries at August 31, 2002 and 2001 (Dollars in Millions)

	Assets	2002	2001
Current Assets	Cash and cash equivalents	$ 449.9	$ 16.9
	Accounts receivable, net	954.8	798.3
	Inventories	3,645.2	3,482.4
	Other current assets	116.6	96.3
	Total Current Assets	5,166.5	4,393.9
Non-Current Assets	Property and equipment, at cost, less accumulated depreciation and amortization	4,591.4	4,345.3
	Other non-current assets	120.9	94.6
	Total Assets	$9,878.8	$8,833.8

	Liabilities and Shareholders' Equity		
Current Liabilities	Short-term borrowings	$ —	$ 440.7
	Trade accounts payable	1,836.4	1,546.8
	Accrued expenses and other liabilities	1,017.9	937.5
	Income taxes	100.9	86.6
	Total Current Liabilities	2,955.2	3,011.6
Non-Current Liabilities	Deferred income taxes	176.5	137.0
	Other non-current liabilities	516.9	478.0
	Total Non-Current Liabilities	693.4	615.0
Shareholders' Equity	Preferred stock, $.0625 par value; authorized 32 million shares; none issued	—	—
	Common stock, $.078125 par value; authorized 3.2 billion shares; issued and outstanding 1,024,908,276 in 2002 and 1,019,425,052 in 2001	80.1	79.6
	Paid-in capital	748.4	596.7
	Retained earnings	5,401.7	4,530.9
	Total Shareholders' Equity	6,230.2	5,207.2
	Total Liabilities and Shareholders' Equity	$9,878.8	$8,833.8

The accompanying Summary of Major Accounting Policies and the Notes to Consolidated Financial Statements are integral parts of these statements.

Consolidated Statements of Cash Flows

Walgreen Co. and Subsidiaries for the Years Ended August 31, 2002, 2001 and 2000 (In Millions)

Fiscal Year		2002	2001	2000
Cash Flows from Operating Activities	Net earnings	$1,019.2	$ 885.6	$ 776.9
	Adjustments to reconcile net earnings to net cash provided by operating activities –			
	Depreciation and amortization	307.3	269.2	230.1
	Deferred income taxes	22.9	46.9	21.0
	Income tax savings from employee stock plans	56.8	67.3	38.5
	Other	(8.6)	2.1	13.6
	Changes in operating assets and liabilities –			
	Inventories	(162.8)	(651.6)	(368.2)
	Trade accounts payable	289.6	182.8	233.7
	Accounts receivable, net	(170.6)	(177.3)	(135.4)
	Accrued expenses and other liabilities	75.0	82.2	101.2
	Income taxes	14.3	(5.4)	28.6
	Other	30.7	17.4	31.7
	Net cash provided by operating activities	1,473.8	719.2	971.7
Cash Flows from Investing Activities	Additions to property and equipment	(934.4)	(1,237.0)	(1,119.1)
	Disposition of property and equipment	368.1	43.5	22.9
	Net proceeds from corporate-owned life insurance	14.4	59.0	58.8
	Net cash used for investing activities	(551.9)	(1,134.5)	(1,037.4)
Cash Flows from Financing Activities	(Payments of) proceeds from short-term borrowings	(440.7)	440.7	—
	Cash dividends paid	(147.0)	(140.9)	(134.6)
	Proceeds from employee stock plans	111.1	126.1	79.2
	Other	(12.3)	(6.5)	(7.9)
	Net cash (used for) provided by financing activities	(488.9)	419.4	(63.3)
Changes in Cash and Cash Equivalents	Net increase (decrease) in cash and cash equivalents	433.0	4.1	(129.0)
	Cash and cash equivalents at beginning of year	16.9	12.8	141.8
	Cash and cash equivalents at end of year	$ 449.9	$ 16.9	$ 12.8

The accompanying Summary of Major Accounting Policies and the Notes to Consolidated Financial Statements are integral parts of these statements.

Summary of Major Accounting Policies

Description of Business
The company is principally in the retail drugstore business and its operations are within one reportable segment. Stores are located in 43 states and Puerto Rico. At August 31, 2002, there were 3,880 retail drugstores and 3 mail service facilities. Prescription sales were 59.8% of total sales for fiscal 2002 compared to 57.5% in 2001 and 55.2% in 2000.

Basis of Presentation
The consolidated statements include the accounts of the company and its subsidiaries. All significant intercompany transactions have been eliminated. The consolidated financial statements are prepared in accordance with accounting principles generally accepted in the United States of America and include amounts based on management's prudent judgments and estimates. While actual results may differ from these estimates, management does not expect the differences, if any, to have a material effect on the consolidated financial statements.

Cash and Cash Equivalents
Cash and cash equivalents include cash on hand and all highly liquid investments with an original maturity of three months or less. The company's cash management policy provides for the bank disbursement accounts to be reimbursed on a daily basis. Checks issued but not presented to the banks for payment of $317 million and $233 million at August 31, 2002 and 2001, respectively, are included in cash and cash equivalents as reductions of other cash balances.

Financial Instruments
The company had approximately $37 million and $53 million of outstanding letters of credit at August 31, 2002 and 2001, respectively, which guaranteed foreign trade purchases. Additional outstanding letters of credit of $84 million and $71 million at August 31, 2002 and 2001, respectively, guaranteed payments of casualty claims. The casualty claim letters of credit are annually renewable and will remain in place until the casualty claims are paid in full. The company pays a nominal facility fee to the financing bank to keep this line of credit facility active. The company also had purchase commitments of approximately $70 million and $162 million at August 31, 2002 and 2001, respectively, related to the purchase of store locations. There were no investments in derivative financial instruments during fiscal 2002 and 2001.

Inventories
Inventories are valued on a lower of last-in, first-out (LIFO) cost or market basis. At August 31, 2002 and 2001, inventories would have been greater by $693.5 million and $637.6 million, respectively, if they had been valued on a lower of first-in, first-out (FIFO) cost or market basis. Included in inventory are product cost and in-bound freight. Cost of sales is primarily derived based upon point-of-sale scanning information with an estimate for shrinkage and adjusted based on periodic inventories. At August 31, 2001 and 2000, the company experienced lower inventory levels in certain LIFO pools compared with the previous year-end inventory levels which caused a liquidation of LIFO inventories which were carried at lower costs prevailing in prior years. The effect of this liquidation was a reduction in cost of sales of $4.2 million in fiscal 2001 and $3.1 million in fiscal 2000.

Vendor Allowances
The company receives vendor allowances principally as a result of meeting defined purchase levels or promoting vendors' products. Those received as a result of purchase levels are accrued as a reduction of merchandise purchase price over the incentive period and result in a reduction of cost of sales. Those received for promoting vendors' products are offset against advertising expense and result in a reduction of selling, occupancy and administration expense.

Property and Equipment
Depreciation is provided on a straight-line basis over the estimated useful lives of owned assets. Leasehold improvements and leased properties under capital leases are amortized over the estimated physical life of the property or over the term of the lease, whichever is shorter. Estimated useful lives range from 12½ to 39 years for land improvements, buildings and building improvements and 5 to 12½ years for equipment. Major repairs, which extend the useful life of an asset, are capitalized in the property and equipment accounts. Routine maintenance and repairs are charged against earnings. The composite method of depreciation is used for equipment; therefore, gains and losses on retirement or other disposition of such assets are included in earnings only when an operating location is closed, completely remodeled or impaired. Fully depreciated property and equipment are removed from the cost and related accumulated depreciation and amortization accounts.

Property and equipment consists of *(In Millions)*:

	2002	2001
Land and land improvements		
Owned stores	**$1,080.4**	$1,109.2
Distribution centers	**57.8**	38.7
Other locations	**9.3**	18.6
Buildings and building improvements		
Owned stores	**1,185.9**	1,156.6
Leased stores (leasehold improvements only)	**425.6**	411.1
Distribution centers	**364.9**	309.1
Other locations	**58.2**	70.6
Equipment		
Stores	**1,609.6**	1,440.3
Distribution centers	**499.4**	350.2
Other locations	**464.9**	462.7
Capitalized system development costs	**144.1**	117.4
Capital lease properties	**17.8**	18.8
	5,917.9	5,503.3
Less: accumulated depreciation and amortization	**1,326.5**	1,158.0
	$4,591.4	$4,345.3

The company capitalizes application stage development costs for significant internally developed software projects, including "SIMS Plus," an inventory management system, and "Basic Department Management," a marketing system. These costs are amortized over a five-year period. Amortization of these costs was $19.5 million in 2002, $17.3 million in 2001 and $13.1 million in 2000. Unamortized costs as of August 31, 2002 and 2001, were $73.2 million and $66.1 million, respectively.

Revenue Recognition
For all sales other than third party pharmacy sales, the company recognizes revenue at the time of the sale. For third party sales, revenue is recognized at the time the prescription is filled, adjusted by an estimate for those that will be unclaimed by customers. Customer returns are immaterial.

Impaired Assets and Liabilities for Store Closings
The company tests long-lived assets for impairment whenever events or circumstances indicate. Store locations that have been open at least five years are periodically reviewed for impairment indicators. Once identified, the amount of the impairment is computed by comparing the carrying value of the assets to the fair value, which is based on the discounted estimated future cash flows. Included in selling, occupancy and administration expense were impairment charges of $8.4 million in 2002, $9.7 million in 2001, and $15.1 million in 2000.

Summary of Major Accounting Policies
(continued)

During the fourth quarter of fiscal 2002, the company implemented SFAS No. 146, "Accounting for Costs Associated with Exit or Disposal Activities." Since implementation, the present value of expected future lease costs are charged against earnings when the location is closed. Prior to this, the liability was recognized at the time management made the decision to relocate or close the store.

Insurance
The company obtains insurance coverage for catastrophic exposures as well as those risks required to be insured by law. It is the company's policy to retain a significant portion of certain losses related to worker's compensation, property losses, business interruptions relating from such losses and comprehensive general, pharmacist and vehicle liability. Provisions for these losses are recorded based upon the company's estimates for claims incurred. The provisions are estimated in part by considering historical claims experience, demographic factors and other actuarial assumptions.

Pre-Opening Expenses
Non-capital expenditures incurred prior to the opening of a new or remodeled store are charged against earnings as incurred.

Advertising Costs
Advertising costs, which are reduced by the portion funded by vendors, are expensed as incurred. Net advertising expenses which are included in selling, occupancy and administration expense were $64.5 million in 2002, $54.1 million in 2001 and $76.7 million in 2000.

Stock-Based Compensation Plans
As permitted by SFAS No. 123, the company applies Accounting Principles Board (APB) Opinion No. 25 and related interpretations in accounting for its plans. Under APB 25, compensation expense is recognized for stock option grants if the exercise price is below the fair value of the underlying stock at the date of grant. The company complies with the disclosure provisions of SFAS No. 123, which requires presentation of pro forma information applying the fair-value based method of accounting.

Income Taxes
The company provides for federal and state income taxes on items included in the Consolidated Statements of Earnings regardless of the period when such taxes are payable. Deferred taxes are recognized for temporary differences between financial and income tax reporting based on enacted tax laws and rates.

Earnings Per Share
In fiscal year 2002 and 2001, the diluted earnings per share calculation excluded certain stock options, because the options' exercise price was greater than the average market price of the common shares for the year. If they were included, anti-dilution would have resulted. At August 31, 2002 and August 31, 2001, options to purchase 3,186,227 and 3,316,906 common shares granted at a price ranging from $35.90 to $45.625 and $36.875 to $45.625 per share were excluded from the fiscal year 2002 and 2001 calculations, respectively.

Notes to Consolidated Financial Statements

Interest Expense
The company capitalized $8.5 million, $15.6 million and $4.0 million of interest expense as part of significant construction projects during fiscal 2002, 2001 and 2000, respectively. Interest paid, net of amounts capitalized, was $.3 million in 2002, $3.4 million in 2001 and $.2 million in 2000.

Other Income
In fiscal 2002, 2001 and 2000, the company received partial payments of the brand name prescription drug antitrust litigation settlement for pre-tax income of $6.2 million ($.004 per share), $22.1 million ($.01 per share) and $33.5 million ($.02 per share), respectively. These payments, which are now concluded, were a result of a pharmacy class action against drug manufacturers, which resulted in a $700 million settlement for all recipients.

Leases
Although some locations are owned, the company generally operates in leased premises. Original non-cancelable lease terms typically are 20-25 years and may contain escalation clauses, along with options that permit renewals for additional periods. The total amount of the minimum rent is expensed on a straight-line basis over the term of the lease. In addition to minimum fixed rentals, most leases provide for contingent rentals based upon sales.

Minimum rental commitments at August 31, 2002, under all leases having an initial or remaining non-cancelable term of more than one year are shown below *(In Millions)*:

2003	$ 897.9
2004	943.3
2005	933.4
2006	914.0
2007	895.0
Later	10,659.2
Total minimum lease payments	$15,242.8

The above minimum lease payments include minimum rental commitments related to capital leases amounting to $10.7 million at August 31, 2002. Total minimum lease payments have not been reduced by minimum sublease rentals of approximately $49.1 million on leases due in the future under non-cancelable subleases.

During fiscal 2002, the company entered into two sale-leaseback transactions. The properties were sold at net book value and resulted in proceeds of $302 million. The related leases are accounted for as operating leases.

Rental expense was as follows *(In Millions)*:

	2002	2001	2000
Minimum rentals	**$873.0**	$730.1	$605.7
Contingent rentals	**23.6**	26.2	31.4
Less: Sublease rental income	**(11.1)**	(10.4)	(7.6)
	$885.5	$745.9	$629.5

26 2002 WALGREENS ANNUAL REPORT

Notes to Consolidated Financial Statements
(continued)

Income Taxes

The provision for income taxes consists of the following *(In Millions)*:

	2002	2001	2000
Current provision –			
Federal	**$510.2**	$417.1	$400.9
State	**85.0**	73.1	64.5
	595.2	490.2	465.4
Deferred provision –			
Federal	**24.0**	47.1	17.7
State	**(1.1)**	(.2)	3.3
	22.9	46.9	21.0
	$618.1	$537.1	$486.4

The deferred tax assets and liabilities included in the Consolidated Balance Sheets consist of the following *(In Millions)*:

	2002	2001
Deferred tax assets –		
Employee benefit plans	**$106.2**	$146.3
Accrued rent	**56.5**	52.7
Insurance	**82.7**	68.3
Inventory	**35.6**	28.1
Other	**95.3**	39.0
	376.3	334.4
Deferred tax liabilities –		
Accelerated depreciation	**401.9**	341.7
Inventory	**98.9**	92.9
Other	**14.7**	16.1
	515.5	450.7
Net deferred tax liabilities	**$139.2**	$116.3

Income taxes paid were $528.0 million, $432.1 million and $398.4 million during the fiscal years ended August 31, 2002, 2001 and 2000, respectively. The difference between the statutory income tax rate and the effective tax rate is principally due to state income tax provisions.

Short-Term Borrowings

The company obtained funds through the placement of commercial paper, as follows *(Dollars in Millions)*:

	2002	2001	2000
Average outstanding during the year	**$250.2**	$304.9	$14.0
Largest month-end balance	**689.0**	461.2	98.0
	(Nov)	(Nov)	(Nov)
Weighted-average interest rate	**2.3%**	5.2%	5.9%

At August 31, 2002, the company had a syndicated bank line of credit facility of $600 million to support the company's short-term commercial paper program. On July 2, 2002, the company deregistered the remaining $100 million of unissued authorized debt securities, previously filed with the Securities and Exchange Commission.

Contingencies

The company is involved in various legal proceedings incidental to the normal course of business. Company management is of the opinion, based upon the advice of General Counsel, that although the outcome of such litigation cannot be forecast with certainty, the final disposition should not have a material adverse effect on the company's consolidated financial position or results of operations.

Capital Stock

The company's common stock is subject to a Rights Agreement under which each share has attached to it a Right to purchase one one-hundredth of a share of a new series of Preferred Stock, at a price of $37.50 per Right. In the event an entity acquires or attempts to acquire 15% of the then outstanding shares, each Right, except those of an acquiring entity, would entitle the holder to purchase a number of shares of common stock pursuant to a formula contained in the Agreement. These non-voting Rights will expire on August 21, 2006, but may be redeemed at a price of $.0025 per Right at any time prior to a public announcement that the above event has occurred.

As of August 31, 2002, 102,738,392 shares of common stock were reserved for future stock issuances under the company's various employee benefit plans. Preferred stock of 10,249,083 shares has been reserved for issuance upon the exercise of Preferred Share Purchase Rights.

Stock Compensation Plans

The Walgreen Co. Executive Stock Option Plan provides to key employees the granting of options to purchase company common stock over a 10-year period, at a price not less than the fair market value on the date of the grant. Under this Plan, options may be granted until October 9, 2006, for an aggregate of 38,400,000 shares of common stock of the company. Compensation expense related to the plan was less than $1 million in fiscal 2002, $1.4 million in fiscal 2001 and less than $1 million in fiscal 2000. The options granted during fiscal 2002, 2001 and 2000 have a minimum three-year holding period.

The Walgreen Co. Stock Purchase/Option Plan (Share Walgreens) provides for the granting of options to purchase company common stock over a period of 10 years to eligible employees upon the purchase of company shares subject to certain restrictions. Under the terms of the Plan, the option price cannot be less than 85% of the fair market value at the date of grant. Compensation expense related to the Plan was $10.9 million in fiscal 2002, $9.6 million in fiscal 2001 and less than $1 million in fiscal 2000. Options may be granted under this Plan until September 30, 2012, for an aggregate of 42,000,000 shares of common stock of the company. The options granted during fiscal 2002, 2001 and 2000 have a two-year holding period.

The Walgreen Co. Restricted Performance Share Plan provides for the granting of up to 32,000,000 shares of common stock to certain key employees, subject to restrictions as to continuous employment except in the case of death, normal retirement or total and permanent disability. Restrictions generally lapse over a four-year period from the date of grant. Compensation expense is recognized in the year of grant. Compensation expense related to the Plan was $5.4 million in fiscal 2002, $3.6 million in fiscal 2001 and $5.1 million in fiscal 2000. The number of shares granted was 81,416 in 2002, 61,136 in 2001 and 84,746 in 2000.

Under the Walgreen Co. 1982 Employees Stock Purchase Plan, eligible employees may purchase company stock at 90% of the fair market value at the date of purchase. Employees may purchase shares through cash purchases, loans or payroll deductions up to certain limits. The aggregate number of shares for which all participants have the right to purchase under this Plan is 64,000,000.

On May 11, 2000, substantially all employees, in conjunction with opening the company's 3,000th store, were granted a stock option award to purchase from 75 to 500 shares, based on years of service. The stock option award, issued at fair market value on the date of the grant, represents a total of 14,859,275 shares of Walgreen Co. common stock. The options vest after three years and are exercisable up to 10 years after the grant date.

The Walgreen Co. Broad Based Employee Stock Option Plan provides for the granting of options to eligible employees to purchase common stock over a 10-year period, at a price not less than the fair market value on the date of the grant, in connection with the achievement of store opening milestones. Options may be granted for an aggregate of 15,000,000 shares of company common stock until all options have either been exercised or have expired. There is a holding period of three years for options granted under this plan.

Notes to Consolidated Financial Statements
(continued)

A summary of information relative to the company's stock option plans follows:

	Options Outstanding		Options Exercisable	
	Shares	Weighted-Average Exercise Price	Shares	Weighted-Average Exercise Price
August 31, 1999	28,479,238	$ 7.89		
Granted	17,040,383	28.43		
Exercised	(5,055,842)	5.59		
Canceled/Forfeited	(1,086,118)	27.39		
August 31, 2000	39,377,661	$16.55	19,267,211	$6.45
Granted	5,354,388	36.68		
Exercised	(5,532,895)	5.75		
Canceled/Forfeited	(2,943,030)	28.02		
August 31, 2001	36,256,124	$20.24	14,824,227	$7.40
Granted	2,886,365	34.05		
Exercised	(3,525,955)	7.28		
Canceled/Forfeited	(1,315,499)	30.32		
August 31, 2002	34,301,035	$22.35	13,786,657	$9.71

Net options granted as a percentage of outstanding shares at fiscal year-end were 0.2% in fiscal 2002, 0.2% in fiscal 2001 and 1.6% in fiscal 2000.

The following table summarizes information concerning currently outstanding and exercisable options:

Range of Exercise Prices	Options Outstanding			Options Exercisable	
	Number Outstanding at 8/31/02	Weighted-Average Remaining Contractual Life	Weighted-Average Exercise Price	Number Exercisable at 8/31/02	Weighted-Average Exercise Price
$ 4 to 14	11,511,707	3.13 yrs.	$ 7.64	11,511,707	$ 7.64
15 to 30	14,869,487	7.31	26.65	2,212,570	19.81
31 to 46	7,919,841	8.48	35.67	62,380	34.17
$ 4 to 46	34,301,035	6.18 yrs.	$22.35	13,786,657	$ 9.71

The company applies Accounting Principles Board (APB) Opinion No. 25 and related interpretations in accounting for its plans. Accordingly, no compensation expense has been recognized based on the fair value of its grants under these plans. Had compensation costs been determined consistent with the method of SFAS No. 123 for options granted in fiscal 2002, 2001 and 2000, pro forma net earnings and net earnings per common share would have been as follows (In Millions, except per share data):

	2002	2001	2000
Net earnings			
As reported	$1,019.2	$885.6	$776.9
Pro forma	958.7	833.3	754.3
Net earnings per common share – Basic			
As reported	1.00	.87	.77
Pro forma	.94	.82	.75
Net earnings per common share – Diluted			
As reported	.99	.86	.76
Pro forma	.93	.81	.74

The weighted-average fair value and exercise price of options granted for fiscal 2002, 2001 and 2000 were as follows:

	2002	2001	2000
Granted at market price –			
Weighted-average fair value	$13.60	$14.28	$12.17
Weighted-average exercise price	34.40	32.88	28.44
Granted below market price –			
Weighted-average fair value	11.86	20.78	10.56
Weighted-average exercise price	33.21	38.78	24.12

The fair value of each option grant used in the pro forma net earnings and net earnings per share was determined using the Black-Scholes option pricing model with weighted-average assumptions used for grants in fiscal 2002, 2001 and 2000:

	2002	2001	2000
Risk-free interest rate	4.56%	6.16%	6.64%
Average life of option (years)	7	7	7
Volatility	27.58%	25.95%	25.86%
Dividend yield	.22%	.16%	.27%

Retirement Benefits

The principal retirement plan for employees is the Walgreen Profit-Sharing Retirement Trust to which both the company and the employees contribute. The company's contribution, which is determined annually at the discretion of the Board of Directors, has historically related to pre-tax income. The profit-sharing provision was $145.7 million in 2002, $126.6 million in 2001 and $112.4 million in 2000.

The company provides certain health and life insurance benefits for retired employees who meet eligibility requirements, including age and years of service. The costs of these benefits are accrued over the period earned. The company's postretirement health and life benefit plans currently are not funded.

Components of net periodic benefit costs (In Millions):

	2002	2001	2000
Service cost	$ 6.0	$ 4.8	$ 4.7
Interest cost	10.5	8.7	7.7
Amortization of actuarial loss	1.4	.3	—
Amortization of prior service cost	(0.4)	—	—
Total postretirement benefit cost	$17.5	$13.8	$12.4

Change in benefit obligation (In Millions):

	2002	2001
Benefit obligation at September 1	$142.7	$118.6
Service cost	6.0	4.8
Interest cost	10.5	8.7
Amendments	—	(7.1)
Actuarial loss	72.6	23.1
Benefit payments	(6.6)	(6.3)
Participants contributions	1.2	.9
Benefit obligation at August 31	$226.4	$142.7

Notes to Consolidated Financial Statements
(continued)

Change in plan assets *(In Millions)*:

	2002	2001
Plan assets at fair value at September 1	$ —	$ —
Plan participants contributions	1.2	.9
Employer contributions	5.4	5.4
Benefits paid	(6.6)	(6.3)
Plan assets at fair value at August 31	$ —	$ —

Funded status *(In Millions)*:

	2002	2001
Funded status	$(226.4)	$(142.7)
Unrecognized actuarial loss	99.1	27.9
Unrecognized prior service cost	(6.7)	(7.1)
Accrued benefit cost at August 31	$(134.0)	$(121.9)

The discount rate assumptions used to compute the postretirement benefit obligation at year-end were 7.0% for 2002 and 7.5% for 2001.

Future benefit costs were estimated assuming medical costs would increase at a 9% annual rate decreasing to 5.25% over the next seven years and then remaining at a 5.25% annual growth rate thereafter. A one percentage point change in the assumed medical cost trend rate would have the following effects *(In Millions)*:

	1% Increase	1% Decrease
Effect on service and interest cost	$ 4.0	$ (3.0)
Effect on postretirement obligation	49.0	(37.8)

Supplementary Financial Information

Included in the Consolidated Balance Sheets captions are the following assets and liabilities *(In Millions)*:

	2002	2001
Accounts receivable –		
Accounts receivable	$ 974.9	$819.2
Allowances for doubtful accounts	(20.1)	(20.9)
	$ 954.8	$798.3
Accrued expenses and other liabilities –		
Accrued salaries	$ 323.8	$272.7
Taxes other than income taxes	179.9	155.5
Profit sharing	143.3	122.1
Other	370.9	387.2
	$1,017.9	$937.5

Summary of Quarterly Results *(Unaudited)*
(Dollars in Millions, except per share data)

		November	February	May	August	Fiscal Year
Fiscal 2002	Net sales	$6,559.4	$7,488.5	$7,397.9	$7,235.3	$28,681.1
	Gross profit	1,697.9	2,033.9	1,937.2	1,936.0	7,605.0
	Net earnings	185.9	326.6	259.0	247.7	1,019.2
	Per Common Share – Basic	$ .18	$ .32	$ .25	$ .25	$ 1.00
	Diluted	.18	.32	.25	.24	.99
Fiscal 2001	Net sales	$5,614.2	$6,429.0	$6,296.2	$6,283.6	$24,623.0
	Gross profit	1,488.1	1,770.8	1,651.6	1,663.6	6,574.1
	Net earnings	158.4	296.9	213.4	216.9	885.6
	Per Common Share – Basic	$ .16	$ .29	$ .21	$ .21	$ .87
	Diluted	.15	.29	.21	.21	.86

Comments on Quarterly Results: In further explanation of and supplemental to the quarterly results, the 2002 fourth quarter LIFO adjustment was a credit of $9.9 million compared to a 2001 charge of $2.8 million. If the 2002 interim results were adjusted to reflect the actual inventory inflation rates and inventory levels as computed at August 31, 2002, earnings per share would have increased in the first quarter by $.01 and decreased in the fourth quarter by $.01. Similar adjustments in 2001 would have increased earnings per share in the second quarter by $.01 and decreased earnings per share in the fourth quarter by $.01.

The quarter ended November 30, 2001, includes the pre-tax income of $5.5 million (less than $.01 per share) from the partial payment of the brand name prescription drugs antitrust litigation settlement. The quarter ended August 31, 2002, includes the pre-tax income of $.7 million (less than $.01 per share). The quarter ended February 28, 2001, includes the pre-tax income of $22.1 million ($.01 per share) from the second partial payment.

Common Stock Prices
Below is the New York Stock Exchange high and low sales price for each quarter of fiscal 2002 and 2001.

		November	February	May	August	Fiscal Year
Fiscal 2002	High	$36.00	$40.70	$40.29	$39.49	$40.70
	Low	28.70	30.72	36.10	30.20	28.70
Fiscal 2001	High	$45.75	$45.00	$45.29	$42.40	$45.75
	Low	32.75	35.38	37.13	31.00	31.00

Reports of Independent Public Accountants

To the Board of Directors and Shareholders of Walgreen Co.:

We have audited the accompanying consolidated balance sheet of Walgreen Co. and subsidiaries (the "Company") as of August 31, 2002, and the related consolidated statements of earnings, shareholders' equity, and cash flows for the year then ended. These consolidated financial statements are the responsibility of the Company's management. Our responsibility is to express an opinion on these consolidated financial statements based on our audit. The consolidated financial statements of the Company for the years ended August 31, 2001 and 2000 were audited by other auditors who have ceased operations. Those auditors expressed in their report dated September 28, 2001 an unqualified opinion on those statements.

We conducted our audit in accordance with auditing standards generally accepted in the United States of America. Those standards require that we plan and perform the audit to obtain reasonable assurance about whether the consolidated financial statements are free of material misstatement. An audit includes examining, on a test basis, evidence supporting the amounts and disclosures in the financial statements. An audit also includes assessing the accounting principles used and significant estimates made by management, as well as evaluating the overall financial statement presentation. We believe that our audit provides a reasonable basis for our opinion.

In our opinion, such consolidated financial statements present fairly, in all material respects, the financial position of Walgreen Co. and subsidiaries as of August 31, 2002, and the results of their operations and their cash flows for the year then ended, in conformity with accounting principles generally accepted in the United States of America.

Deloitte & Touche LLP
Chicago, Illinois
September 27, 2002

To the Board of Directors and Shareholders of Walgreen Co.:

We have audited the accompanying consolidated balance sheets of Walgreen Co. (an Illinois corporation) and Subsidiaries as of August 31, 2001 and 2000, and the related consolidated statements of earnings, shareholders' equity and cash flows for each of the three years in the period ended August 31, 2001. These financial statements are the responsibility of the company's management. Our responsibility is to express an opinion on these financial statements based on our audits.

We conducted our audits in accordance with auditing standards generally accepted in the United States. Those standards require that we plan and perform the audit to obtain reasonable assurance about whether the financial statements are free of material misstatement. An audit includes examining, on a test basis, evidence supporting the amounts and disclosures in the financial statements. An audit also includes assessing the accounting principles used and significant estimates made by management, as well as evaluating the overall financial statement presentation. We believe that our audits provide a reasonable basis for our opinion.

In our opinion, the financial statements referred to above present fairly, in all material respects, the financial position of Walgreen Co. and Subsidiaries as of August 31, 2001 and 2000 and the results of their operations and their cash flows for each of the three years in the period ended August 31, 2001 in conformity with accounting principles generally accepted in the United States.

Arthur Andersen LLP (1)
Chicago, Illinois
September 28, 2001

(1) This report is a copy of the previously issued report covering fiscal years 2001 and 2000. The predecessor auditor has not reissued their report.

Management's Report

The primary responsibility for the integrity and objectivity of the consolidated financial statements and related financial data rests with the management of Walgreen Co. The financial statements were prepared in conformity with accounting principles generally accepted in the United States of America appropriate in the circumstances and included amounts that were based on management's most prudent judgments and estimates relating to matters not concluded by fiscal year-end. Management believes that all material uncertainties have been either appropriately accounted for or disclosed. All other financial information included in this annual report is consistent with the financial statements.

The firm of Deloitte & Touche LLP, independent public accountants, was engaged to render a professional opinion on Walgreen Co.'s consolidated financial statements as of August 31, 2002. Their report contains an opinion based on their audit, which was made in accordance with auditing standards generally accepted in the United States of America and procedures, which they believed were sufficient to provide reasonable assurance that the consolidated financial statements, considered in their entirety, are not misleading and do not contain material errors. The financial statements for the years ended August 31, 2001 and 2000 were audited by other auditors whose report expressed an unqualified opinion on those statements.

Four outside members of the Board of Directors constitute the company's Audit Committee, which meets at least quarterly and is responsible for reviewing and monitoring the company's financial and accounting practices. Deloitte & Touche LLP and the company's General Auditor meet alone with the Audit Committee, which also meets with the company's management to discuss financial matters, auditing and internal accounting controls.

The company's systems are designed to provide an effective system of internal accounting controls to obtain reasonable assurance at reasonable cost that assets are safeguarded from material loss or unauthorized use and transactions are executed in accordance with management's authorization and properly recorded. To this end, management maintains an internal control environment which is shaped by established operating policies and procedures, an appropriate division of responsibility at all organizational levels, and a corporate ethics policy which is monitored annually. The company also has an Internal Control Evaluation Committee, composed primarily of senior management from the Accounting and Auditing Departments, which oversees the evaluation of internal controls on a company-wide basis. Management believes it has appropriately responded to the internal auditors' and independent public accountants' recommendations concerning the company's internal control system.

David W. Bernauer
*President
and Chief Executive Officer*

William M. Rudolphsen
*Controller
and Chief Accounting Officer*

Roger L. Polark
*Senior Vice President
and Chief Financial Officer*

Board of Directors
As of November 18, 2002

Directors

L. Daniel Jorndt*
Chairman
Elected 1990

David W. Bernauer*
President and
Chief Executive Officer
Elected 1999

William C. Foote
Chairman of the Board,
Chief Executive Officer
and President
USG Corporation
Elected 1997

James J. Howard
Chairman Emeritus
Xcel Energy, Inc.
Elected 1986

Alan G. McNally
Chairman
Harris Bankcorp Inc.
Elected 1999

Cordell Reed
Former Senior Vice President
Commonwealth Edison Co.
Elected 1994

David Y. Schwartz
Former Partner
Arthur Andersen LLP
Elected 2000

John B. Schwemm
Former Chairman and
Chief Executive Officer
R.R. Donnelley & Sons Co.
Elected 1985

Marilou M. von Ferstel
Former Executive Vice President
and General Manager
Ogilvy Adams & Rinehart
Elected 1987

Charles R. Walgreen III
Chairman Emeritus
Elected 1963

* L. Daniel Jorndt will retire in January 2003. David W. Bernauer will become chairman and chief executive officer. Jeffrey A. Rein will become president and chief operating officer. George J. Riedl will become senior vice president–Marketing.

Committees

Audit Committee
John B. Schwemm,
  Chairman
William C. Foote
David Y. Schwartz
Marilou M. von Ferstel

Compensation Committee
Cordell Reed,
  Chairman
James J. Howard
John B. Schwemm

Finance Committee
David Y. Schwartz,
  Chairman
David W. Bernauer
L. Daniel Jorndt
Alan G. McNally
Cordell Reed
Charles R. Walgreen III

Nominating and Governance Committee
William C. Foote,
  Chairman
James J. Howard
Alan G. McNally
John B. Schwemm
Marilou M. von Ferstel

Officers
As of November 18, 2002

Corporate

Chairman
L. Daniel Jorndt*

President
David W. Bernauer*
  Chief Executive Officer

Executive Vice Presidents
Jerome B. Karlin
  Store Operations
Jeffrey A. Rein*
  Marketing

Senior Vice Presidents
R. Bruce Bryant
  Western Store Operations
George C. Eilers
  Eastern Store Operations
J. Randolph Lewis
  Distribution & Logistics
Julian A. Oettinger
  General Counsel and
  Corporate Secretary
Roger L. Polark
  Chief Financial Officer
William A. Shiel
  Facilities Development
Trent E. Taylor
  Chief Information Officer
Mark A. Wagner
  Central Store Operations

Vice Presidents
John W. Gleeson
  Corporate Strategy and Treasurer
Dana I. Green
  Human Resources
Dennis R. O'Dell
  Health Services
Gregory D. Wasson
  President
  Walgreens Health Initiatives

Operational and Divisional

Store Operations Vice Presidents
James F. Cnota
Kermit R. Crawford
George C. Eilers Jr.
Debra M. Ferguson
John J. Foley
David L. Gloudemans
John W. Grant
Frank C. Grilli
William M. Handal
Patrick E. Hanifen
Barry L. Markl
Richard Robinson
Michael D. Tovian
Kevin P. Walgreen
Christine D. Whelan
Bruce C. Zarkowsky
Barry W. Zins

Divisional Vice Presidents
Thomas L. Bergseth
  Facilities Planning and Design
Donald A. Churchill
  Construction and Facilities
Thomas J. Connolly
  Real Estate
Robert M. Kral
  Operations/Merchandising
  Development
Laurie L. Meyer
  Corporate Communications
Allan M. Resnick
  Law
George J. Riedl*
  Purchasing
Robert E. Rogan
  Distribution Centers
Jerry A. Rubin
  Real Estate
William M. Rudolphsen
  Controller
James M. Schultz
  Performance Development
Craig M. Sinclair
  Advertising
Patrick W. Tupa
  Real Estate
Terry R. Watkins
  Distribution Centers
Kenneth R. Weigand
  Employee Relations
Denise K. Wong
  Supply Chain Systems
Chester G. Young
  General Auditor
Robert G. Zimmerman
  Vice President – Administration
  Walgreens Health Initiatives

Endnotes

Chapter 1
1. Walgreen Co., *Annual Report*, 2002.
2. *Statement of Financial Accounting Concepts No. 1*, "Objectives of Financial Reporting by Business Enterprises" (Norwalk, Conn.: Financial Accounting Standards Board, 1978), par. 9.
3. Ibid.
4. Christopher D. Ittner, David F. Larcker, and Madhav V. Rajan, "The Choice of Performance Measures in Annual Bonus Contracts," *The Accounting Review*, April 1997.
5. Walgreen Co., *Annual Report*, 2002.
6. Kathy Williams and James Hart, "Microsoft: Tooling the Information Age," *Management Accounting*, May 1996, p. 42.
7. *Statement of the Accounting Principles Board No. 4*, "Basic Concepts and Accounting Principles Underlying Financial Statements of Business Enterprises" (New York: American Institute of Certified Public Accountants, 1970), par. 138.
8. Touche Ross & Co., "Ethics in American Business" (New York: Touche Ross & Co., 1988), p. 7.
9. "Global Ethics Codes Gain Importance as a Tool to Avoid Litigation and Fines," *The Wall Street Journal*, August 19, 1999.
10. *Statement Number IC*, "Standards of Ethical Conduct for Management Accountants" (Montvale, N.J.: Institute of Management Accountants, 1983, revised 1997).
11. J.C. Penney Company, Inc., *Annual Report*, 1995.
12. Nikhil Deogun, "Coca-Cola Reports 27% Drop in Profits Hurt by Weakness in Foreign Markets," *The Wall Street Journal*, January 27, 1999.
13. Southwest Airlines Co., *Annual Report*, 1996.
14. Queen Sook Kim, "Lechters Inc. Files for Chapter 11, Arranges Financing," *The Wall Street Journal*, May 22, 2001.
15. Charles Schwab Corporation, *Annual Report*, 2001.
16. Robert Frank, "Facing a Loss, Lego Narrates a Sad Toy Story," *The Wall Street Journal*, January 22, 1999.

Chapter 2
1. "Boeing Scores a Deal to Sell 15 Planes for Long-Haul Routes," *The Wall Street Journal*, October 5, 2000.
2. The Boeing Co., *Annual Report*, 1994.
3. Craig S. Smith, "China Halts New Purchases of Jets," *The Wall Street Journal*, February 9, 1999.
4. The Boeing Co., *Annual Report*, 2000.
5. Patricia Kranz, "Rubles? Who Needs Rubles?" *BusinessWeek*, April 13, 1998; Andrew Higgins, "Lacking Money to Pay, Russian Firms Survive on Deft Barter System," *The Wall Street Journal*, August 27, 1998.
6. Intel Corp., *Annual Report*, 2002.
7. Shawn Young, "Lucent Revises Its Revenue Downward," *The Wall Street Journal*, December 22, 2000.
8. Nike, Inc., *Annual Report*, 2002.
9. Mellon Bank, *Annual Report*, 2000.
10. Ajinomoto Company, *Annual Report*, 2000.

Chapter 3
1. Kelly Services, *Annual Report*, 2002.
2. *Statement of Financial Accounting Concepts No. 1*, "Objectives of Financial Reporting by Business Enterprises" (Norwalk, Conn.: Financial Accounting Standards Board, 1978), par. 44.
3. Thomas J. Phillips Jr., Michael S. Luehlfing, and Cynthia M. Daily, "The Right Way to Recognize Revenue," *Journal of Accountancy*, June 2001.
4. "Revenue Recognition in Financial Statements," *Staff Accounting Bulletin No. 10* (Securities and Exchange Commission, 1999).
5. Michael Schroeder and Elizabeth MacDonald, "SEC Expects More Big Cases on Accounting," *The Wall Street Journal*, December 24, 1998.
6. PricewaterhouseCoopers presentation, 1999.
7. Lyric Opera of Chicago, *Annual Report*, 2001.
8. The Walt Disney Company, *Annual Report*, 2001.
9. H. J. Heinz Company, *Annual Report*, 2001.
10. Takashimaya Company, Limited, *Annual Report*, 2000.

Chapter 4
1. Dell Compter Corporation, *Annual Report*, 2002.
2. Adapted from H & R Block, Inc., *Annual Report*, 2002.
3. Nestlé S.A., *Annual Report*, 2000.

Chapter 5
1. Target, *Annual Report*, 2002.
2. Ibid.
3. "Shop Online—Pickup at the Store," *BusinessWeek*, June 12, 2000; Nick Wingfield, "As Web Sales Grow Mail-Order Sellers Are Benefiting the Most," *The Wall Street Journal*, May 2, 2001.
4. Joel Millman, "Here's What Happens to Many Lovely Gifts After Santa Rides Off," *The Wall Street Journal*, December 26, 2001.
5. Matthew Rose, "Magazine Revenue at Newsstands Falls in Worst Year Ever," *The Wall Street Journal*, May 15, 2001.
6. Matthew Schifrin, "The Big Squeeze," *Forbes*, March 11, 1996.
7. Wal-Mart Stores, Inc., *Annual Report*, 2000; Kmart Corp., *Annual Report*, 2000.

Chapter 6
1. General Mills, Inc., *Annual Report*, 2001.
2. "Objectives of Financial Reporting by Business Enterprises," *Statement of Financial Accounting Concepts No. 1* (Norwalk, Conn.: Financial Accounting Standards Board, 1978), pars. 32–54.
3. "Qualitative Characteristics of Accounting Information," *Statement of Financial Accounting Concepts No. 1* (Norwalk, Conn.: Financial Accounting Standards Board, 1980), par. 20.
4. Accounting Principles Board, "Accounting Changes," *Opinion No. 20* (New York: American Institute of Certified Public Accountants, 1971), par. 17.
5. Securities and Exchange Commission, *Staff Accounting Bulletin No. 99*, 1999.
6. Reynolds Metals Company, *Annual Report*, 1998.
7. Ray J. Groves, "Here's the Annual Report. Got a Few Hours?" *The Wall Street Journal Europe*, August 26–27, 1994.
8. Roger Lowenstein, "Investors Will Fish for Footnotes in 'Abbreviated' Annual Reports," *The Wall Street Journal*, September 14, 1995.
9. General Mills, *Annual Report*, 2001.
10. Ibid.
11. National Commission on Fraudulent Financial Reporting, *Report of the National Commission on Fraudulent Financial Reporting* (Washington, D.C., 1987), p. 2.
12. Arthur Levitt, "The Numbers Game," NYU Center for Law and Business, September 28, 1998.
13. "Ex-Chairman of Cendant Is Indicted," *The Wall Street Journal*, March 1, 2001; "SEC Sues Former Sunbeam Executive," *Chicago Tribune*, May 16, 2001; "Enron: A Wake-up Call," *The Wall Street*

Journal, December 4, 2001; "SEC List of Accounting-Fraud Probes Grows," *The Wall Street Journal*, July 6, 2001.
14. *Accounting Research and Terminology Bulletin*, final edition (New York: American Institute of Certified Public Accountants, 1961), p. 20.
15. "Debt vs. Equity: Whose Call Counts," *BusinessWeek*, July 19, 1999.
16. Roger Lowenstein, "The '20% Club' No Longer Is Exclusive," *The Wall Street Journal*, May 4, 1995.
17. "SEC Probes Lucent Accounting Practices," *The Wall Street Journal*, February 9, 2001.
18. Albertson's Inc., *Annual Report*, 2001; Great Atlantic & Pacific Tea Company, *Annual Report*, 2001.
19. GlaxoSmithKline PLC, *Annual Report*, 2000.
20. Toys "R" Us, *Annual Report*, 1987.

Chapter 7
1. Lee Copeland, "Donnelley Goes Dutch in Software Conversion," *Chicago Tribune*, June 3, 2002.
2. News item, *Crain's Chicago Business*, October 2001.
3. AICPA Press Release, Jan. 2, 2003
4. News item, *The Wall Street Journal*, July 29, 1999.
5. Michael Totty, "The Next Phase," *The Wall Street Journal*, May 21, 2001.
6. Frank Potter, "Event-to-Knowledge: A New Metric for Finance Department Efficiency," *Strategic Finance*, July 2001.
7. Walgreens, *Annual Report*, 1993.
8. Anthony Bianco, "Virtual Bookstores to Get Real," *BusinessWeek*, October 27,1997.

Chapter 8
1. Ron Winslow and George Anders, "How New Technology Was Oxford's Nemesis," *The Wall Street Journal*, December 11, 1997.
2. Circuit City Stores, *Annual Report*, 2001.
3. *Professional Standards*, vol. 1 (New York: American Institute of Certified Public Accountants, June 1, 1999), Sec. AU 322.07.
4. "1998 Fraud Survey," KPMG Peat Marwick, 1998.
5. *Professional Standards*, vol. 1, Sec. AU 325.16.
6. Lynette Khalfani, "Information-Destruction Finds Lucrative Business in Going to Waste," *The Wall Street Journal*, December 6, 1996.
7. "B-to-B Communities," *Business 2.0*, December 1999.
8. Amy Merrick, "Starbucks Accuses Employee, Husband of Embezzling $3.7 Million from Firm," *The Wall Street Journal*, November 20, 2000.

Chapter 9
1. Pioneer Corporation, *Annual Report*, 2001.
2. "So Much for Detroit's Cash Cushion," *BusinessWeek*, November 5, 2001.
3. Michael Selz, "Big Customers' Late Bills Choke Small Suppliers," *The Wall Street Journal*, June 22, 1994.
4. Pioneer Corporation, *Annual Report*, 2001.
5. Circuit City Stores, Inc., *Annual Report*, 2001.
6. Pioneer Corporation, *Annual Report*, 2001.
7. *Accounting Trends & Techniques* (New York: American Institute of CPAs, 2000), p. 130.
8. *Statement of Financial Accounting Standards No. 115*, "Accounting for Certain Investments in Debt and Equity Securities" (Norwalk, Conn.: Financial Accounting Standards Board, 1993).
9. Pioneer Corporation, *Annual Report*, 2001.
10. "Bad Loans Rattle Telecom Vendors," *BusinessWeek*, February 19, 2001.
11. Craig S. Smith, "Chinese Companies Writing Off Old Debt," *The Wall Street Journal*, December 28, 1995.
12. Information based on promotional brochures of Mitsubishi Electric Corp.

13. Elizabeth McDonald, "Unhatched Chickens," *Forbes*, February 19, 2001.
14. Philips Electronics N.V., *Annual Report*, 2001; Heineken N.V., *Annual Report*, 2001.

Chapter 10
1. J.C. Penney Company, Inc., *Annual Report*, 2002.
2. Illinois Tool Works, Inc., *Annual Report*, 2002.
3. American Institute of Certified Public Accountants, *Accounting Research Bulletin No. 43* (New York: AICPA, 1953), ch. 4.
4. Gary McWilliams, "Whirlwind on the Web," *BusinessWeek*, April 7, 1997.
5. Karen Lundebaard, "Bumpy Ride," *The Wall Street Journal*, May 21, 2001.
6. American Institute of Certified Public Accountants, *Accounting Research Bulletin No. 43* (New York: AICPA, 1953), ch. 4.
7. Micah Frankel and Robert Trezevant, "The Year-End LIFO Inventory Purchasing Decision: An Empirical Test," *The Accounting Review*, April 1994.
8. American Institute of Certified Public Accountants, *Accounting Trends & Techniques* (New York: AICPA, 2002).
9. "As Rite Aid Grew, CEO Seemed Unable to Manage His Empire," *The Wall Street Journal*, October 20, 1999; "RentWay Details Improper Bookkeeping," *The Wall Street Journal*, June 8, 2001.
10. International Paper Company, *Annual Report*, 2001.
11. American Institute of Certified Public Accountants, *Accounting Trends & Techniques* (New York: AICPA, 2002).
12. "Cisco's Numbers Confound Some," *International Herald Tribune*, April 19, 2001; "Kmart Posts $67 Million Loss Due to Markdowns," *The Wall Street Journal*, November 10, 2000.
13. American Institute of Certified Public Accountants, *Accounting Trends & Techniques* (New York: AICPA, 2002).
14. Exxon Mobil, *Annual Report*, 2000.
15. Adapted from Hershey Foods Corp., *Annual Report*, 2000.
16. "SEC Case Judge Rules Crazy Eddie Principals Must Pay $72.7 Million," *The Wall Street Journal*, May 11, 2000.
17. Crane Company, *Annual Report*, 2000.
18. Pioneer Corporation, *Annual Report*, 2001; Yamaha Motor Co., Ltd., *Annual Report*, 2001.

Chapter 11
1. H. J. Heinz Company, *Annual Report*, 2002.
2. *Statement of Financial Accounting Standards No. 144*, "Accounting for the Impairment or Disposal of Long-Lived Assets" (Norwalk, Conn.: Financial Accounting Standards Board, 2001).
3. David Henry, "The Numbers Game," *BusinessWeek*, May 14, 2001.
4. H. J. Heinz Company, *Annual Report*, 2002.
5. Ford Motor Company, *Annual Report*, 2002.
6. *Statement of Position No. 98-1*, "Accounting for the Costs of Computer Software Developed or Planned for Internal Use" (New York: American Institute of Certified Public Accountants, 1996).
7. *Statement of Financial Accounting Standards No. 34*, "Capitalization of Interest Cost" (Norwalk, Conn.: Financial Accounting Standards Board, 1979), par. 9–11.
8. Jared Sandberg, Deborah Solomon, and Rebecca Blumenstein, "Inside WorldCom's Unearthing of a Vast Accounting Scandal," *The Wall Street Journal*, June 27, 2002.
9. *Financial Accounting Standards: Original Pronouncements as of July 1, 1977* (Norwalk, Conn.: Financial Accounting Standards Board, 1977), ARB No. 43, Ch. 9, Sec. C, par. 5.
10. Accounting Principles Board, *Opinion No. 29*, "Accounting for Nonmonetary Transactions" (New York: American Institute of Certified Public Accountants, 1973); Emerging Issues Task Force, *EITF Issue Summary 86-29*, "Nonmonetary Transactions: Magnitude of Boot and the Exceptions to the Use of Fair Value" (Norwalk, Conn.: Financial Accounting Standards Board, 1986).
11. *Statement of Financial Accounting Standards No. 25*, "Suspension of Certain Accounting Requirements for Oil and Gas Producing

Companies" (Norwalk, Conn.: Financial Accounting Standards Board, 1979).
12. Adapted from Accounting Principles Board, *Opinion No. 17*, "Intangible Assets" (New York: American Institute of Certified Public Accountants, 1970), par. 2.
13. "What's in a Name?" *Time*, May 3, 1993.
14. General Motors, *Annual Report*, 2000.
15. Abbott Laboratories, *Annual Report*, 2000; Roche Group, *Annual Report*, 2000.
16. Allan B. Afterman, *International Accounting, Financial Reporting and Analysis* (New York: Warren, Gorham & Lamont, 1995).
17. *Statement of Financial Accounting Standards No. 2*, "Accounting for Research and Development Costs" (Norwalk, Conn.: Financial Accounting Standards Board, 1974), par. 12.
18. *Statement of Financial Accounting Standards No. 86*, "Accounting for the Costs of Computer Software to be Sold, Leased, or Otherwise Marketed" (Norwalk, Conn.: Financial Accounting Standards Board, 1985).
19. *Accounting Trends & Techniques*, 2002.
20. General Mills, *Annual Report*, 2002; Sara Lee Corporation, *Annual Report*, 2002; Tribune Company, *Annual Report*, 2002.
21. *Statement of Financial Accounting Standards No. 144*, "Accounting for the Impairment or Disposal of Long-Lived Assets" (Norwalk, Conn.: Financial Accounting Standards Board, 2001).
22. Edward P. McTague, "Accounting for Trade-Ins of Operational Assets," *National Public Accountant* (January 1986), p. 39.
23. General Motors Corp., *Annual Report*, 1987.
24. Polaroid Corporation, *Annual Report*, 1997.
25. Hilton Hotels Corporation, *Annual Report*, 2000; Marriott International, *Annual Report*, 2000.
26. "Stock Gives Case the Funds He Needs to Buy New Technology," *BusinessWeek*, April 15, 1996.
27. Roche Group, *Annual Report*, 2000; Baxter International, Inc., *Annual Report*, 2000.

Chapter 12
1. US Airways, Inc., *Annual Report*, 2001.
2. RadioShack Corporation, *Annual Report*, 2002.
3. Pamela L. Moore, "How Xerox Ran Short of Black Ink," *BusinessWeek*, October 30, 2000.
4. Goodyear Tire & Rubber Company, *Annual Report*, 2002.
5. US Airways, Inc., *Annual Report*, 2002.
6. Andersen Enterprise Group, cited in *Crain's Chicago Business*, July 5, 1999.
7. Raju Narisetti, "P&G Ad Chief Plots Demise of the Coupon," *The Wall Street Journal*, April 17, 1996; Renae Merle, "Slowdown Is Business Boon for Coupon Seller Valassis," *The Wall Street Journal*, May 1, 2001.
8. Scott McCartney, "Free Airline Miles Become a Potent Tool for Selling Everything," *The Wall Street Journal*, April 16, 1996; "You've Got Miles," *BusinessWeek*, March 6, 2000.
9. *Statement of Financial Accounting Standards No. 5*, "Accounting for Contingencies" (Norwalk, Conn.: Financial Accounting Standards Board, 1975).
10. American Institute of Certified Public Accountants, *Accounting Trends & Techniques*, 2002.
11. General Motors Corp., *Annual Report*, 2000.
12. American Institute of Certified Public Accountants, *Accounting Trends & Techniques*, 2002.
13. US Airways, Inc., *Annual Report*, 2000.
14. General Motors Corp., *Annual Report*, 2002.
15. Sun Micosystems Inc., *Annual Report*, 2001; Cisco Systems, *Annual Report*, 2001.
16. Texaco, Inc., *Annual Report*, 1986.
17. Man Nutzfahrzeuge Aktiengesellschaft, *Annual Report*, 1997.

Chapter 13
1. KPMG International, Internet site www.kpmg.com, February 10, 2002. KPMG has announced plans to separate its consulting practice as a corporation.
2. Information excerpted from the 1990 and 2002 annual reports of Alliance Capital Management Limited Partnership; *The Wall Street Journal*, February 10, 2003.
3. Anita Raghavan, "Goldman Scrambles to Find $250 Million in Equity Capital from Private Investors," *The Wall Street Journal*, September 15, 1994.
4. "Nokia Unveils Plans for Chinese Centre," *Financial Times London*, May 9, 2000.

Chapter 14
1. Cisco Systems, Inc., *Annual Report*, 2002.
2. Copyright © 2000 by Houghton Mifflin Company. Reproduced by permission from *The American Heritage Dictionary of the English Language, Fourth Edition*.
3. *Statement of Position No. 98-5*, "Report on the Costs of Start up Activities" (New York: American Institute of Certified Public Accountants, 1998).
4. Deborah Solomon, "AT&T Slashes Dividends 83%, Cuts Forecasts," *The Wall Street Journal*, December 21, 2002.
5. Abbott Laboratories, *Annual Report*, 2002.
6. Ibid.
7. American Institute of Certified Public Accountants, *Accounting Trends & Techniques* (New York: AICPA, 2001).
8. *Statement of Accounting Standards No. 123*, "Accounting for Stock-Based Compensation" (Norwalk, Conn.: Financial Accounting Standards Board, 1995).
9. Ruth Simon and Ianthe Jeanne Dugan, "Options Overdose," *The Wall Street Journal*, June 4, 2001.
10. Suzanne McGee, "Europe's New Markets for IPOs of Growth Start-Ups Fly High," *The Wall Street Journal*, February 22, 1999.
11. Microsoft Corporation, Inc., *Annual Report*, 1997.
12. G. Christian Hill, "Microsoft Plans Preferred Issue of $750 Million," *The Wall Street Journal*, December 3, 1996.
13. American Institute of Certified Public Accountants, *Accounting Trends & Techniques* (New York: AICPA, 2001).
14. Robert McGough, Suzanne McGee, and Cassell Bryan-Low, "Buyback Binge Now Creates Big Hangover," *The Wall Street Journal*, December 18, 2000.
15. "Avaya Prices Public Offering of Common Stock" and "Avaya Completes Sale of Approximately $200 Million Common Stock," *The Wall Street Journal Online*, March 22, 2002.
16. Tom Herman, "Preferreds' Rich Yields Blind Some Investors to Risks," *The Wall Street Journal*, March 24, 1992.
17. Stanley Ziemba, "USAir Defers Dividends on Preferred Stock," *Chicago Tribune*, September 30, 1994.
18. Susan Carey, "US Airways to Redeem Preferred Owned by Berkshire Hathaway," *The Wall Street Journal*, February 4, 1998.
19. Roche Group, *Annual Report*, 2001.

Chapter 15
1. AMR Corporation, *Annual Report*, 2002.
2. *Statement of Financial Accounting Standards No. 130*, "Reporting Comprehensive Income" (Norwalk, Conn.: Financial Accounting Standards Board, 1997).
3. American Institute of Certified Public Accountants, *Accounting Trends & Techniques* (New York: American Institute of Certified Public Accountants, 2002).
4. Cited in *The Week in Review* (Deloitte Haskins & Sells), February 28, 1985.
5. "Up to the Minute, Down to the Wire," *Twentieth Century Mutual Funds Newsletter*, 1996.

6. American Institute of Certified Public Accountants, *Accounting Trends & Techniques* (New York: American Institute of Certified Public Accountants, 2001).
7. Robert Manor and Melita Marie Garza, "Company's Accounting May Prove Hard to Criminalize," *Chicago Tribune*, January 11, 2002.
8. Sears, Roebuck and Co., *Annual Report*, 1997.
9. *Statement of Financial Accounting Standards No. 109*, "Accounting for Income Taxes" (Norwalk, Conn.: Financial Accounting Standards Board, 1992).
10. American Institute of Certified Public Accountants, *Accounting Trends & Techniques* (New York: American Institute of Certified Public Accountants, 2002).
11. Accounting Principles Board, *Opinion No. 30*, "Reporting the Results of Operations" (New York: American Institute of Certified Public Accountants, 1973), par. 20.
12. Ibid.
13. American Institute of Certified Public Accountants, *Accounting Trends & Techniques* (New York: American Institute of Certified Public Accountants, 2002).
14. Accounting Principles Board, *Opinion No. 20*, "Accounting Changes" (New York: American Institute of Certified Public Accountants, 1971), par. 20.
15. David Cairns International, *IAS Survey Update*, July 2001.
16. American Institute of Certified Public Accountants, *Accounting Trends & Techniques* (New York: American Institute of Certified Public Accountants, 2002).
17. Accounting Principles Board, *Opinion No. 15*, "Earnings per Share" (New York: American Institute of Certified Public Accountants, 1969), par. 12.
18. Minnesota Mining and Manufacturing Company, *Annual Report*, 2000.
19. *Statement of Financial Accounting Standards No. 128*, "Earnings per Share and the Disclosure of Information About Capital Structure" (Norwalk, Conn.: Financial Accounting Standards Board, 1997).
20. Tribune Company, *Annual Report*, 2002.
21. Skandia Group, *Annual Report*, 2000.
22. *Accounting Research Bulletin No. 43* (New York: American Institute of Certified Public Accountants, 1953), chap. 7, sec. B, par. 10.
23. Ibid., par. 13.
24. Robert O'Brien, "Techs' Chill Fails to Stem Stock Splits," *The Wall Street Journal*, June 8, 2000.
25. Rebecca Buckman, "Microsoft Posts Hefty 18% Revenue Rise," *The Wall Street Journal*, January 18, 2002; William M. Bulkeley, "IBM Reports 13% Decline in Net Income," *The Wall Street Journal*, January 18, 2002.
26. "Technology Firms Post Strong Earnings but Stock Prices Decline Sharply," *The Wall Street Journal*, January 21, 1988; Donald R. Seace, "Industrials Plunge 57.2 Points—Technology Stocks' Woes Cited," *The Wall Street Journal*, January 21, 1988.
27. The Washington Post Company, *Annual Report*, 2000.
28. Yamaha Motor Company, Ltd., *Annual Report*, 2001.

Chapter 16
1. AT&T Corporation, *Annual Report*, 2002.
2. "Canadian Airline's Demise Adds to Industry Woes," *The Washington Post*, November 16, 2001; "A Striking End for Air Afrique," British Broadcasting Company, November 26, 2001; "Small Airlines Adapting Quicker," Associated Press, November 22, 2001; "Swiss Air Rescue Hopes Brighten," British Broadcasting Company, November 21, 2001.
3. AT&T Corporation, *Annual Report*, 2002.
4. Ibid.
5. Quentin Hardy, "Japanese Companies Need to Raise Cash, but First a Bond Market Must Be Built," *The Wall Street Journal*, October 20, 1992.
6. Bill Barnhart, "Bond Bellwether," *Chicago Tribune*, December 4, 1996.
7. Accounting Principles Board, *Opinion No. 21*, "Interest on Receivables and Payables" (New York: American Institute of Certified Public Accountants, 1971), par. 15.
8. *Statement of Financial Accounting Standards No. 13*, "Accounting for Leases" (Norwalk, Conn.: Financial Accounting Standards Board, 1976), par. 10.
9. Philip Morris Companies, Inc., *Annual Report*, 2000.
10. *Statement of Financial Accounting Standards No. 87*, "Employers' Accounting for Pensions" (Norwalk, Conn.: Financial Accounting Standards Board, 1985).
11. *Statement of Financial Accounting Standards No. 106*, "Employers' Accounting for Postretirement Benefits Other than Pensions" (Norwalk, Conn.: Financial Accounting Standards Board, 1990).
12. Stanley Ziemba, "TWA, American Revise O'Hare Gate Agreement," *The Wall Street Journal*, May 13, 1992.
13. FedEx Corporation, *Annual Report*, 2001.
14. "More Hotels Won't Be Able to Pay Debt from Operations, Study Says," *The Wall Street Journal*, October 30, 2001.
15. Amazon.com, Press Release, January 28, 1999.
16. NEC Corporation, *Annual Report*, 2001; Sanyo Electric Co., *Annual Report*, 2001.

Chapter 17
1. Marriott International, Inc., *Annual Report*, 2002, adapted.
2. *Statement of Financial Accounting Standards No. 95*, "Statement of Cash Flows" (Norwalk, Conn.: Financial Accounting Standards Board, 1987); *Statement of Financial Accounting Concepts No. 1*, "Objectives of Financial Reporting for Business Enterprises" (Norwalk, Conn.: Financial Accounting Standards Board, 1978), par. 37–39.
3. Marriott International, Inc., *Annual Report*, 2002.
4. Gary Slutsker, "Look at the Birdie and Say: 'Cash Flow,'" *Forbes*, October 25, 1993.
5. Jonathan Clements, "Yacktman Fund Is Bloodied but Unbowed," *The Wall Street Journal*, November 8, 1993.
6. Jeffrey Laderman, "Earnings, Schmearnings—Look at the Cash," *BusinessWeek*, July 24, 1989.
7. "Deadweight on the Markets," *BusinessWeek*, February 19, 2001.
8. Marriott International, Inc., *Annual Report*, 2002.
9. American Institute of Certified Public Accountants, *Accounting Trends & Techniques* (New York: AICPA, 2001).
10. Pallavi Gogoi, "Cash-Rich, So?" *BusinessWeek*, March 19, 2001.
11. "Cash Flow Shortfall in Quarter May Lead to Default on Loan," *The Wall Street Journal*, September 4, 2001.
12. Enron Corporation, *Press Release*, October 16, 2001.
13. Sony Corporation, *Annual Report*, 2000; Canon, Inc., *Annual Report*, 2000.

Chapter 18
1. Sun Microsystems, *Proxy Statement*, 2001.
2. Phyllis Plitch, "Firms Embrace Pro Forma Way on Earnings," *The Wall Street Journal*, January 22, 2002.
3. David Henry, "The Numbers Game," *BusinessWeek*, May 14, 2001.
4. *Statement of Financial Accounting Standards No. 131*, "Segment Disclosures" (Norwalk, Conn.: Financial Accounting Standards Board, 1997).
5. Sun Microsystems, Inc. *Annual Report*, 2001.
6. William H. Beaver, "Alternative Accounting Measures as Indicators of Failure," *Accounting Review*, January 1968; Edward Altman, "Financial Ratios, Discriminant Analysis and the Prediction of Corporate Bankruptcy," *Journal of Finance*, September 1968.
7. Sun Microsystems, Inc., "Management's Discussion and Analysis," *Annual Report*, 2001.
8. Ibid.
9. *Forbes*, November 13, 1978, p. 154.
10. Elizabeth MacDonald, "Firms Say SEC Earnings Scrutiny Goes Too Far," *The Wall Street Journal*, February 1, 1999.
11. H. J. Heinz Company, *Annual Report*, 2001.
12. Pfizer, Inc., *Annual Report*, 2000; Roche Group, *Annual Report*, 2000.

Endnotes

Chapter 19
1. Frederic M. Biddle, "A Little Gas Fuels Hope for a New Type of Electric Car," *The Wall Street Journal*, July 9, 1999.
2. Northiko Shirouzu, "Honda Bucks Industry Wisdom, Aiming to Be Small and Efficient," *The Wall Street Journal*, July 9, 1999.
3. *Statement No. 1A* (New York: Institute of Management Accountants, 1982).
4. Andra Gumbus and Susan D. Johnson, "The Balanced Scorecard at Futura Industries," *Strategic Finance*, July 2003.
5. Presentation by management of Baxter International, October 2001.
6. American Institute of Certified Public Accountants, "The New Finance," www.aicpa.org.
7. Peter Brewer, "Putting Strategy into the Balanced Scorecard," *Strategic Finance*, January 2002.
8. American Institute of Certified Public Accountants, "Summary of Sarbanes-Oxley Act of 2002," www.aicpa.org/info/sarbanes_oxley_summary.htm; Securities and Exchange Commission, "Final Rule: Certification of Disclosure in Companies' Quarterly and Annual Reports," August 28, 2002, www.sec.gov/rules/final/33-8124.htm.
9. Gregory L. White, "GM Appears to Step Back from Proposal," *The Wall Street Journal*, March 30, 1999.

Chapter 20
1. Southwest Airlines, "Fact Sheet," www.southwest.com.
2. Melanie Trottman, "Vaunted Southwest Slips in On-Time Performance," *The Wall Street Journal*, September 25, 2002.
3. Robert Frank and Sarah Ellison, "Meltdown in Chocolatetown," *The Wall Street Journal*, September 19, 2002.
4. United Parcel Service, "About UPS," www.ups.com.
5. Lisa de Moraes, "Conan the Cost: NBC's Thrifty Numbers Game," *The Washington Post*, February 8, 2002.

Chapter 21
1. Robert L. Simison, "Toyota Finds Way to Make Custom Car in 5 Days," *The Wall Street Journal*, August 6, 1999.
2. John M. Parkinson, "Equivalent Units in Process Costing" (paper presented at the meeting of the American Accounting Association, August 2002).
3. Associated Press, "$75 Screws? The Pentagon Pays It," *The Gainesville Sun*, March 19, 1998.
4. William A. Sahlman, "How to Write a Great Business Plan," *Harvard Business Review*, July–August 1997.

Chapter 22
1. Dan Morse, "Tennessee Producer Tries New Tactic in Sofas: Speed," *The Wall Street Journal*, November 19, 2002.
2. Gary Cokins, "Learning to Love ABC," *Journal of Accountancy*, August 1999.
3. Mylene Mangalindan, "Oracle Puts Priority on Customer Service," *The Wall Street Journal*, January 21, 2003.
4. Lance Thompson, "Examining Methods of VBM," *Strategic Finance*, December 2002.
5. Paulette Thomas, "Electronics Firm Ends Practice Just in Time," *The Wall Street Journal*, October 29, 2002.
6. Gina Imperato, "Time for Zero Time," *Net Company*, Fall 1999.
7. Sally Beatty, "Levi's Strive to Keep a Hip Image," *The Wall Street Journal*, January 23, 2003.

Chapter 23
1. Kraft Foods, "Profile," www.kraft.com.
2. Kraft Foods, "Inside Kraft: A Company Overview," http://164.109.16.145/investors/overview.html.

Chapter 24
1. Johnson & Johnson, "Our Company," www.jnj.com.
2. Omar Aguilar, "How Strategic Performance Management Is Helping Companies Create Business Value," *Strategic Finance*, January 2003.
3. Enterprise Rent-a-Car, "Overview," "Facts," "History," www.enterprise.com.
4. Richard Barrett, "From Fast Close to Fast Forward," *Strategic Finance*, January 2003.
5. Jeremy Hope and Robin Fraser, "Who Needs Budgets?" *Harvard Business Review*, February 2003.
6. Ibid.
7. Minnesota Mining and Manufacturing Company, "About 3M," www.3m.com.

Chapter 25
1. Erin White, "How Stogy Turned Stylish," *The Wall Street Journal*, May 3, 2002.
2. Katy McLaughlin, "Factory Tours," *The Wall Street Journal*, October 29, 2002.
3. David E. Keys and Anton Van Der Merwe, "Gaining Effective Organizational Control with RCA," *Strategic Finance*, May 2002.
4. Gabriel Kahn, "Still Going for Gold," *The Wall Street Journal*, January 28, 2003.
5. Curtis C. Verschoor, "Ethical Corporations Are Still More Profitable," *Strategic Finance*, June 2003.

Chapter 26
1. PEAKS Resorts, www.peakscard.com.
2. Rich Teerlink, "Harley's Leadership U-Turn," *Harvard Business Review*, July–August 2000.
3. Marc J. Epstein and Jean-François Manzoni, "The Balanced Scorecard and Tableau de Bord: Translating Strategy into Action," *Management Accounting*, August 1997.
4. Jill Rosenfeld, "Information as if Understanding Mattered," *Fast Company*, March 2000.
5. "Blue Jeans to Help Keep Cars Quiet: Who Thinks This Stuff Up?" *Fast Company*, May 2000.
6. Ans Kolk, "Green Reporting," *Harvard Business Review*, January–February 2000.
7. Russ Banham, "Better Budgets," *Journal of Accountancy*, February 2000.
8. Julia Flynn, "Use of Performance-Based Pay Spreads Across Continental Europe, Survey Says," *The Wall Street Journal*, November 17, 1999.

Chapter 27
1. Stephanie Miles, "What's a Check?" *Wall Street Journal*, October 21, 2002, p. R5.
2. Miles, p. R5.
3. Michael Liedtke, "Keeping the Books," *The Gainesville Sun*, August 22, 2002.
4. Alan Fuhrman, "Your e-Banking Future," *Strategic Finance*, April, 2002.
5. Paulette Thomas, "Case Study: Electronics Firm Ends Practice Just in Time," *The Wall Street Journal*, October 29, 2002.
6. From a speech by Jim Croft, vice president of finance and administration of the Field Museum, Chicago, November 14, 2000.

Appendix A
1. PepsiCo., Inc., *Annual Report*, 2000.
2. *Statement of Financial Accounting Standards No. 52*, "Foreign Currency Translation" (Norwalk, Conn.: Financial Accounting Standards Board, 1981), par. 15.
3. *Financial Reporting: An International Survey* (New York: Price Waterhouse, May 1995).
4. "International Accounting Standards Committee Objectives and Procedures," *Professional Standards* (New York: American Institute of Certified Public Accountants, 1988), vol. B, sec. 9000, par. 24–27.

Appendix B
1. *Statement of Financial Accounting Standards No. 115*, "Accounting for Certain Investments in Debt and Equity Securities" (Norwalk, Conn.: Financial Accounting Standards Board, 1993).

Appendix C
1. Accounting Principles Board, *Opinion No. 21*, "Interest on Receivables and Payables" (New York: American Institute of Certified Public Accountants, 1971), par. 13.

Company Name Index

Abbott Laboratories, 500, 598, 599–600
Accenture, 363, 1123
Accor, 560
Ace Hardware, 11
Air Afrique, 671
Ajinomoto Company, 85–86
Albertson's Inc., 252
Alcoa Inc., 560, 647, 896
Allegheny Technologies Inc., 560
Alliance Capital Management Limited Partnership, 560
Allstate Insurance Co., 997
Amazon.com, 84, 104, 232, 362, 481, 601, 627, 705–706, 756, 1134–1135
American Airlines, Inc., 537, 628–629, 704
American Century Services Corp., 630
American Express, 632
America Online (AOL), 93, 180, 519, 537, 625, 627, 757
Ameritech Corp., 405
AMR Corporation, 628–629, 638
Amtrak, 1009
AOL Time Warner Inc., 93, 180, 519, 537, 625, 627, 757
Apple Computer, Inc., 598, 647, 896, 1097
Association for Investment Management and Research, 630
AT&T Corporation, 598–599, 611, 654, 668–669, 671–672, 674, 675, 804
AutoLiv, Inc., 446
Avaya, Inc., 623
Avon, 788

Babies "R" Us, 257
Bank of America, 409, 632, 1052, 1128–1129, 1130, 1134, 1143
BankOne, 409
Barnes & Noble, 211, 362, 450
Baxter International, 521, 802
Beijing Li-Ning Sports Goods Company, 1068
Bell South, 677
Berkshire Hathaway, 626
Blockbuster Entertainment Corporation, 450, 966
The Boeing Company, 44–45, 46, 222, 488, 892, 1051

Boise Cascade, 896
Borders, 362, 876
BP Corporation, 411–412
Brinker International, Inc., 1098, 1099(table)
Bristol-Myers Squibb, 139, 1108

Caesars World Inc., 91
Canon, Inc., 746, 748
Caterpillar Inc., 139, 896
Century 21, 884
Charles Schwab & Co., Inc., 41–42, 757
Chase Manhattan, 623, 647
ChemLawn, 1084–1085
Chico's, 836
Chili's Grill and Bar, 1098, 1099(table)
Circuit City Stores, Inc., 177, 366, 401, 407–408
Cisco Systems, Inc., 330, 415, 458, 481, 554, 592–593, 597, 599, 601
Citibank, 409, 623, 836–837
Claire's Stores, Inc., 169
Coach, Inc., 1048–1049, 1051
Coca-Cola Company, 23(table), 39, 235, 677, 768, 896, 1104, 1171
Coleman, 209
Columbia HCA Healthcare, 677
CompuCredit, 438
CompuServe, 757
Continental Airlines, Inc., 44–45, 46, 670, 973
Coors, 896
Costco Wholesale Corporation, 176
Crane Company, 476
Crate & Barrel, 401
Crazy Eddie, Inc., 476
Crown Cork & Seal, 896

DaimlerChrysler Corp., 405, 887, 966, 1097, 1098, 1108–1109
Dayton-Hudson Corporation, 1123
Daytons Stores, 1123
Defense Department, U.S., 892
Dell Computer Corporation, 128–129, 132, 164, 224–225, 225(exh.), 226(fig.), 228(exh.), 228–229, 229(fig.), 236(fig.), 237, 253, 255, 444, 473, 808, 881, 926
Deloitte & Touche, 23(table)

Delta Airlines, 488, 973
Department of Defense, 892
Department of Energy, U.S., 481
Dillard Dept. Stores, Inc., 169–170, 406
Disney, 91, 125, 235, 677
DocuShred, Inc., 374
Domino's Pizza, 1085
Dow Chemical Company, 139, 918
Dun & Bradstreet Corp., 536, 754, 757
Du Pont, 23(table)

Eastman Kodak, 805, 896
eBay Inc., 627
Eclipsys, 93
Eddie Bauer Inc., 401
Emerson Electric, 896
Energy, U.S. Department of, 481
Engelhard Corporation, 896
England, Inc., 924–925
Enron Corporation, 25, 219, 220, 374, 559, 634, 746, 747, 753, 799, 812
Enterprise Rent-a-Car, 849, 1005, 1009
Ernst & Young, 23(table), 218
Ethan Allen, Inc., 857
ExxonMobil, 14, 23(table), 410–412, 473, 896, 1173(table)

Federal Express Corporation (FedEx), 704, 805, 967
Fermi National Accelerator Laboratory (Fermilab), 481
Field Museum of Chicago, 1147
Financial Executives Research Foundation, 693
Fleetwood Enterprises, Inc., 91, 743–744
FMCC (Ford Motor Credit Co.), 407
Forbes, 1127
Ford Motor Company, 23(table), 405, 407, 437, 483, 522, 929, 1103, 1173(table)
Ford Motor Credit Co. (FMCC), 407
Forte Hotels, 560
Fruit of the Loom, 209

The Gap, 7
Gateway, Inc., 881

1212

Company Name Index

General Electric, 23(table), 805, 1104
General Mills, Inc., 5, 212–213, 219, 502
General Motors Acceptance Corp. (GMAC), 407
General Motors Corporation, 23(table), 405, 407, 500, 518, 538, 552–553, 560, 599, 802, 804, 830, 836, 886, 887, 1104, 1173(table)
Getty Oil, 554
Gillette Company, 139, 647
GlaxoSmithKline PLC, 253–255
GMAC (General Motors Acceptance Corp.), 407
Goldman, Sachs & Co., 570, 598
Goodyear Tire & Rubber Company, 529, 711, 756, 788, 968
Great Atlantic & Pacific Tea Company (A&P), 252

Harley-Davidson, Inc., 804, 884, 1093, 1098
Harrods, 210
Heineken N.V., 438
Helene Curtis Corp., 788
Hershey Foods Corp., 322, 475–476, 849
Hertz, 1098
Hewlett-Packard, 611, 805
Hilton Hotels Corp., 5, 518–519
Hilton International, 560
H.J. Heinz Company, 91, 125–126, 478–479, 498, 789–790
Holiday Inn, 560
The Home Depot, Inc., 404–405, 450
Honda Motor Company, 792–793, 802, 833
H&R Block, Inc., 163, 876, 884, 1043
HSBC Bank USA, 623
Hudsons Stores, 1123
Humana, 836–837
Hyatt, 560

IBM (International Business Machines), 23(table), 437, 623, 662–663, 677, 802, 1173, 1173(table)
Illinois Tool Works, Inc., 442
Indian Motorcycle Corporation, 876
Inspector General, U.S. Office of the, 892
Intel Corporation, 5, 43, 48, 611, 647, 663, 1008–1009, 1097
International Business Machines (IBM), 23(table), 437, 623, 662–663, 677, 802, 1173, 1173(table)

International Paper Co., 457, 1171
Intuit Corporation, 361, 1138

J.C. Penney Company, Inc., 39, 329, 413, 439, 440–441, 442, 443, 444–445, 473
JDS Uniphase, 756
Jiffy Lube, 1098, 1099(table)
John Deere, 836, 1008–1009
John H. Daniel Company, 882–883, 886
Johnson & Johnson, 1002–1003, 1004
J.P. Morgan Investment Management Inc., 41
Juniper Networks, 647

Kellogg Company, 896
Kelly Services, 88–89, 91
Kids "R" Us, 257
Kinko's, 1098, 1099(table)
Kmart, 210, 211, 458
KnowledgeWare, 93
Kodak, 805, 896
Koss Corporation, 940, 1145
KPMG LLP, 23(table), 556–557
Kraft Foods, 964–965, 966, 975, 1051, 1097

Land O'Lakes, 933
Land Rover, 968
Lands' End, 177, 211
La-Z-Boy, Inc., 924
Lechters, Inc., 41
Lego Group, 42
Lehman Brothers Inc., 232
Levi Strauss & Co., 884, 963
Liberty Mutual Insurance Company, 1052
The Limited, 443
L.L. Bean, 177
Lowe's, 1009
Lucent Technologies, Inc., 56, 93, 251, 415, 481
Lyric Opera of Chicago, 124

Macy's, 406, 443
Man Nutzfahrzeuge Aktiengesellschaft, 554–555
Marriott International, Inc., 518–519, 560, 708–710, 714–717, 749
Mars, 849
Marshall Field's, 406, 1123
May SWS Securities, 421
Maytag Corporation, 477
McDonald's, 23(table), 231, 437, 832–833, 978
Mellon Bank, 85
Merck, 1004
Mergent, Inc., 757, 758(exh.), 788

Merrill Lynch Lynch & Co., Inc., 570
Mervyn's, 1123
MGM-UA Communications Co., 91
Michelin, 1173
Microsoft Corporation, 10, 43, 604, 611, 662
Midway Airlines, 670, 671
Minnesota Mining and Manufacturing Company (3M), 640, 896, 1046–1047
Mitsubishi Corp., 436, 1043
Montgomery Ward, 325
Monsanto, 1097, 1123
Moody's Investor Services, Inc., 757, 788, 790–791
Motorola, 415, 805, 836, 850–851

Nabisco, 654, 896
NCH Promotional Services, 536
NEC Corporation, 706
Neiman Marcus, 176
Nestlé S.A., 163, 849, 1173
Netscape Communications Corporation, 625–626
Neuer Markt, 601
Newark Morning Ledger Co., 500
Nike, Inc., 83–84, 229–230, 230(exh.), 802
Nokia, 590
Nordstrom, 406, 1009, 1098
Nortel Networks, 415
Nouveau Marche, 601
Nvidia, 647

Office Depot, 177
Office of the Inspector General, U.S., 892
Official Airline Guide, 834
Oracle Corporation, 86–87, 324, 929
Orkin Exterminating Company, 884
Owens Corning, 896
Oxford Health Plans, Inc., 364–365, 371

Peachtree Software, 361
Pennzoil Company, 554
PeopleSoft, 324, 363, 929
Pep Boys, 836
PepsiCo Bottling Company, 1180
PepsiCo Inc., 757, 758(exh.), 788, 1173, 1173(table), 1180
Pepsi Cola North America, 933
Pfizer, Inc., 790
Philip Morris Companies, Inc., 555, 692, 849
Philips Electronics N.V., 438
Phillips Petroleum, 139
Piedmont Airlines, 488
Pillsbury, 212

Company Name Index

Pioneer Corporation, 402–403, 406, 408, 412, 476–477
Pitney Bowes, 931
Polaroid Corporation, 518
PPG Industries, 1167
Preussag, 639
PricewaterhouseCoopers, 23(table), 363
Procter & Gamble, 23(table)

Quaker Oats, 1180
Qualcomm, 415

RadioShack Corporation, 526–527
Rambus Inc., 647
Real Networks Inc., 601
Reebok International Ltd., 5
RentWay, Inc., 456
Revlon, 788
Reynolds Metals Company, 217
Risk Management Association, 757
Rite Aid Corp., 456
RJR Nabisco, 555
Robert Morris Associates, 757
Roche Group, 500, 521, 626, 790
Royal Dutch/Shell, 1108
RR Donnelley, 322–323, 324, 325
Rubbermaid, 209
Russell Stover Candies, 849

Safeway Inc., 329, 704
Salomon Brothers Inc., 570
Sam's Clubs, 176
Sanyo Electric Co., 706
SAP, 324, 929
Sara Lee Corporation, 502
Sears, Roebuck and Co., 401, 407, 413, 439, 443, 634, 836
Sears Roebuck Acceptance Corp. (SRAC), 407
Shanghai Industrial Sewing Machine, 416
Shanghai Steel Tube, 416
Simon & Schuster, 180
Skandia Group, 644
Sony Corporation, 5, 746, 748, 802, 850–851, 975, 1173
South Beach Beverage, 1180
Southwest Airlines Co., 5, 39, 834–835, 838, 839, 849, 973

Sprint Corp., 601, 966
SRAC (Sears Roebuck Acceptance Corp.), 407
Standard & Poor's, 706, 757, 788
Starbucks Corporation, 399
Sunbeam Corporation, 209, 220
Sun Microsystems, Inc., 86–87, 554, 750–751, 759–772, 760–764(exh.), 762–764(fig.), 766(fig.), 767(exh.), 769(exh.), 771(exh.)
Swiss Air, 670, 671

Taco Bell, 857
Takashimaya Company, Ltd., 126
Talbots, 1009
Tandy Corporation, 401
Target, 166–167, 170, 329, 443, 1123
Texaco Inc., 410–412, 554, 555
3M (Minnesota Mining and Manufacturing Company), 640, 896, 1046–1047
Tiffany & Co., 176, 647
Toyota Motor Company, 5–6, 833, 884, 886, 887
Toys "R" Us, 42–43, 86, 91, 126, 163–164, 211, 255, 257–263, 262(fig.), 264, 362, 401, 438–439, 442, 477, 521, 522, 555, 627, 632, 666, 706, 748, 790–791, 849–850, 1043
Trans World Airlines (TWA), 670, 671, 704
Travelocity.com, 104
Tribune Company, 502, 641–642
Tropicana, 1180
Tupperware, 896
TWA (Trans World Airlines), 670, 671, 704
Twentieth Century Mutual Funds, 630

Unilever, 1138, 1173
United Nations, 1004
United Parcel Service (UPS), 444, 849, 857, 967, 1009, 1084–1085, 1104
U.S. Department of Defense, 892
U.S. Department of Energy, 481

U.S. Office of the Inspector General, 892
U.S. Postal Service (USPS), 932, 973
United Way, 1004, 1098
UPS (United Parcel Service), 444, 849, 857, 967, 1009, 1084–1085, 1104
USAA, 805, 836–837, 997
US Airways, Inc., 488, 524–525, 526, 528, 529–530, 537, 538, 626, 671
USPS (U.S. Postal Service), 932, 973

Vail Resorts, 1090–1091, 1092–1095, 1094(fig.), 1095(fig.)
Vanguard Airlines, 488
Verizon, 966
Vicorp Restaurants, 1099

Walgreen Co., 2–3, 7, 42–43, 86, 126, 164, 211, 255, 264, 331, 439, 477, 522, 555, 627, 666, 706, 748, 790–791
Wall Street Journal, 757
Wal-Mart Stores, Inc., 209, 210, 211, 235, 409, 450, 804, 849–850, 963, 968, 1098, 1099(table)
The Walt Disney Company, 91, 125, 235, 677
Washington Post Company, 665–666
Waste Management, Inc., 555
Webvan Group, Inc., 722
Wells Fargo, 623, 968
Wendy's International Inc., 5
Western Airlines, 488
Westinghouse Electric, 933
WorldCom, 219, 220, 487, 753, 799, 1022
W.R. Grace & Co., 788
Wrigley's, 849

Xerox Corporation, 23(table), 528

Yahoo!, 627, 757
Yamaha Motor Company, Ltd., 476–477, 666

Subject Index

Note: **Boldface** type indicates key terms.

ABC, *see* Activity-based costing (ABC)
ABM, *see* Activity-based management (ABM)
Abnormal balance, 62
Absorption costing income statement, profit center performance evaluation using, 1101–1103, 1102(exh.)
Accelerated methods, 490, 490–491, 492, 492(fig.)
Account(s), 16
  accumulated depreciation, 99(fig.), 99–100
  adjusting, 93(exh.), 93–94
  balance of, 52
  chart of, 48, 49–50(exh.)
  clearing, 890
  after closing, 136, 137–138(exh.)
  contra, 99–100
  controlling (control), 332
  owner's equity, 50, 51(fig.)
  permanent (real), 130
  temporary (nominal), 130
  titles of, 50–51
  uncollectible, *see* Uncollectible accounts
  see also specific accounts
Account balance, 52
Accounting, 4
  development of, 8
  as information system, 4(fig.), 4–8
Accounting cycle, 130
Accounting equation, 14, 14–19
  transactions' effects on, 16–19
Accounting information
  processing, 7–8
  users of, 8(fig.), 8–10
  see also Financial statement(s); Report(s); *specific financial statements*
Accounting information systems, 322–348, 324
  computerized accounting systems and, *see* Computerized accounting systems
  design principles for, 324–325
  Internet and, *see* Internet
  special-purpose journals in, *see* Special-purpose journals; *specific journals*

Accounting period issue, 91
Accounting policies, 46
Accounting practices
  adoption in emerging economies, 416
  changes in, cumulative effect of, 639
  operating decisions and, 455
  quality of earnings and, 631–633
Accounting Principles Board (APB)
  on amortization of bond discount, 680
  on depreciation, 503
  on earnings per share, 640
  on extraordinary items, 638–639
  on imputing interest on noninterest-bearing notes, 1193
  on influence and control, 1180
  on intangible assets, 498, 500
  Opinion No. 9 of, 503
  Opinion No. 10 of, 1180
  Opinion No. 17 of, 498
  Opinion No. 20 of, 503
  Opinion No. 30 of, 638–639
Accounting rate-of-return method, 1152, 1152–1153
Accounting standards
  international accounting and, 1174, 1178–1179
  international comparability of, 500
Accounts payable, 15, 529
Accounts Payable account, 18, 19, 385
  expense recognition and, 93
  under periodic inventory system, 183
Accounts receivable, 15, 413, 413(fig.), 413–420
  collection of, 18
  installment, 413
  job order costing system and, 891
  uncollectible, *see* Uncollectible accounts
Accounts Receivable account, 18, 90
  under periodic inventory system, 184
  revenue recognition and, 93
  in subsidiary ledgers, 332
Accounts receivable aging method, 416, 416–419, 417(exh.), 418(fig.)
Accrual(s), 95

adjusting entries for accrued expenses and, 100–101, 101(fig.)
adjusting entries for accrued revenues and, 103(fig.), 103–104
year-end, of bond interest expense, 686–688
Accrual accounting, 92, 92–95
  adjustments and, *see* Adjusting entries; Adjustments
  cash flows and, 107
  performance measures and, 94–95
  recognition of revenues and expenses and, 93
Accrued expenses, 100
  adjusting entries for, 100–101, 101(fig.)
Accrued liabilities, 88, 89, 531
Accrued revenues, adjusting entries for, 103(fig.), 103–104
Accumulated depreciation accounts, 99, 99(fig.), 99–100, 724
Activity-based costing (ABC), 805, 856, 856–860, **934,** 934–938
  cost hierarchy and bill of activities and, 934–937
  reports and, 929
  for selling and administrative activities, 937–938, 938(exh.)
Activity-based management (ABM), 805, 928, 928–938
  just-in-time operating philosophy compared with, 945–946, 946(table)
  in service organizations, 930–931, 931(fig.)
Activity-based systems, 926, 926–927
  management cycle and, 927(fig.), 927–928
  see also Activity-based management (ABM); Just-in-time (JIT) *entries*
Actual costing, 841, 841–842
Additions, 504
Adjusted trial balance, 104, 104–105, 105(exh.), 106(exh.)
  merchandising business and, 185
Adjusting entries, 95, 95(fig.), 95–104
  for accrued expenses, 100–101, 101(fig.)

for accrued revenues, 103(fig.), 103–104
for deferred expenses, 96–100
for deferred revenues, 101–102, 102(fig.)
for merchandising business using periodic inventory system, 185
for merchandising business using perpetual inventory system, 187
for promissory notes, 423
on work sheet, 144, 144(exh.)
Adjustments, 93(exh.), 93–104
Aging of accounts receivable, 416
AICPA, *see* American Institute of Certified Public Accountants (AICPA)
Airline industry
bankruptcies in, 671
debt financing in, 670–671
fixed costs in, 839
frequent-flier miles and, 537
pricing in, 973
Allowance for Doubtful Accounts account, 415
Allowance for Uncollectible Accounts account, 414, 414–415, 417, 420
Allowance method, 414, 414–415
Allowance to Adjust Long-Term Investments to Market account, 1182, 1183–1184
American Institute of Certified Public Accountants (AICPA), 24
on consistency, 217
on depreciation, 487
on inventory cost, 446
Amortization, 482(fig.)
of bond discounts, 678–682
of bond premium, 682–685
Annual reports
accounting policies summary in, 46
components of, 257–263
Annual Statement Studies, 757
Annuities, ordinary, 1148–1149, 1189, 1190(table)
Annuities due, 1205
APB, *see* Accounting Principles Board (APB)
Arithmetica, Geometrica, Proportioni et Proportionalita, 8
Articles of incorporation, 594
Asset(s), 15
carrying value of, 1144
cash flows to, 715, 770, 771(exh.)
on classified balance sheet, 220, 222–223
current, 220, 222, 721
depreciation of, *see* Depreciation

intangible, 223, 498, 498(fig.), 499(table), 500–502
investing in partnership, 568
long-term, *see* Long-term assets; Plant assets
net, 15
noncash, issuance of stock for, 608–609
other, 220
plant (fixed; long-lived; operating; tangible), *see* Plant assets
preference as to, 605
purchase by incurring liabilities, 17
purchase with cash, 16
removal from partnership, 571–572
return on, 768, 769(exh.)
short-term, *see* Short-term financial assets
valuing, 1194
Asset impairment, 480
Asset turnover, 232, 768, 769(exh.), **1104**
ATMs (automated teller machines), 409
Audit committees, 594
Audit trail, 380
Authorization, as control activity, 367
Authorized stock, 597
Automated teller machines (ATMs), 409
Available-for-sale securities, 412, 1180, 1181
Average-cost method, 448, 448–449
Average days' inventory on hand, 445, 766, 767(exh.)
Average days' payable, 526, 527, 527(fig.), **766,** 767(exh.)
Average days' sales uncollected, 405, 406, **766,** 767(exh.)
Avoidable costs, 1138

Backflush costing, 942, 942–945, 943(fig.), 944(fig.)
Bad debts, *see* Uncollectible accounts
Bad Debts Expense account, 415
Balance(s), 52
abnormal, 62
compensating, 408
normal, 61
trial, *see* Trial balance
Balanced scorecard, 808, 808–809, 809(fig.), **1092,** 1092–1095
management cycle and, 1092–1095
Balance sheet, 21(exh.), **22**
in annual report, 259
budgeted, 1022, 1024(exh.)

classified, 220, 221(exh.), 222–225
disclosure of bonds on, 674
reading and graphing, 224–225, 225(exh.), 226(fig.)
Balance Sheet column, merchandising business and, 186–187, 188–189
Bank loans, 529–530
Bank reconciliations, 375, 375–378
illustration of, 376–377, 377(exh.)
recording transactions after, 377–378
Bank statement, 373(fig.)
Bar codes, 172
Barron's, 757
Base year, 759
Basic earnings per share, 640, 640–642
Batch-level activities, 934, 934–935
Batch posting, 328
Beginning inventory, 181
Benchmarking, 809–810, **810**
Bennett, Steve, 1138
Betterments, 504
"Big baths," 633
Bill of activities, **935,** 936(exh.), 937
Boards of directors, 594
Bond(s), 673, 673–789, 1180
balance sheet disclosure of, 674
callable, 688
convertible, 689
costs of issuing, 677
coupon, 674
interest rates on, 675–676
issued at discount, 676
issued at face value, 674–675
issued at premium, 676–677
100-year, 677
prices of, 675
registered, 673–674
retirement of, 688–689
sale between interest dates, 685–686, 687(fig.)
secured, 673
serial, 673
statement of cash flows and, 725
term, 673
unsecured, 673
year-end accrual of interest expense for, 686–688
zero coupon, 679
Bond certificates, 673
Bond discounts, amortizing, 678–682
Bond indentures, 673
Bonding, 368
Bond issues, 673
Bond premium, amortization of, 682–685

Bonds Payable account, bonds issued at discount and, 676
Bonuses, 569
  to new partners, 569–570
  to old partners, 568–569
Bookkeeping, 8, 51–54
  T account and, 51–52
  transaction analysis and processing in, 52–54, 53(fig.)
Book of original entry, *see* Journal *entries*
Book value, 100, 480, **648,** 648–649, 1144
  in capital investment analysis, 1144
Book value per share, 648
Brand names, 499(table)
Breakeven analysis, 976–980, 977(fig.)
Breakeven point, 976
  contribution margin to determine, 978–979
  for multiple products, 979(fig.), 979–980
Budget(s), 1004
  capital expenditures, 1019–1020
  cash, 1020(table), 1020–1022, 1021–1023(exh.)
  cost of goods manufactured, 1018, 1018(exh.)
  direct labor, 1014–1015, 1016(exh.)
  direct materials purchases, 1014, 1015(exh.)
  financial, 1008, 1018–1022
  implementation of, 1025
  manufacturing overhead, 1015, 1016(exh.), 1017
  master, *see* Master budget
  operating, 170–171, 171(exh.), 1008, 1011–1018
  production, 1012–1013, 1013(exh.)
  sales, 1011–1012, 1013(exh.)
  selling and administrative expense, 1017, 1017(exh.)
Budget committee, 1025
Budgeted balance sheet, 1022, 1024(exh.)
Budgeted income statement, 1018, 1018–1019, 1019(exh.)
Budgeting, 1002–1027, **1004**
  goals and, 1004–1005
  management cycle and, 1006–1008, 1007(fig.)
  participative, 1006
Buildings
  acquisition cost of, 486
  see also Plant assets
Business, 4

goals and activities of, 4–6, 6(fig.)
international, *see* International business
performance measures for, 6–7
Business organization forms, 12–14, 13(table)
see also specific forms
Business periodicals
  as information source for financial statement analysis, 757
  as users of accounting information, 10
Business plans, 797
Business transactions, 11
  analysis and processing in bookkeeping, 52–54, 53(fig.)
  analysis of, illustration of, 54–61, 602
  classification of, 331
  document-less, 330
  effects on accounting equation, 16–19
  in foreign currencies, 1175–1177
  see also International accounting
  measurement of, *see* Measurement
  merchandising, internal control over, 368–375
  not recorded in special-purpose journals, 343, 343(exh.)
  recording after bank reconciliation, 377–378
  recording of, as control activity, 367
Buyers, big, power of, 405

Callable bonds, 688
Callable preferred stock, 606
Call price, 606, 688
Candy industry, market share in, 849
Capital
  contributed (paid-in), 224
  cost of, 1106–1107, 1149
  legal, 597
  working, 230–231
  see also Owner's equity
Capital account, 17, 18–19, 19, 50
  closing Income Summary account balance to, 135–136, 136(exh.)
  dissolution of partnership and, 568
  distribution of partnership income/losses and, 563
  dividends and, 224
  partners' equity and, 561
  under periodic inventory system, 191
Capital balance ratios, 563–564
Capital budgeting, 1143–1144
Capital expenditures, 485

Capital expenditures budget, 1019, 1019–1020
Capital investment analysis, 1143, 1143–1144, 1147
Capital investment decisions, 1143, 1143–1153
  accounting rate-of-return method for, 1152–1153
  capital investment analysis and, 1143–1144
  measures used in, 1144–1145
  net present value method for, 1149–1151
  payback period method for, 1151–1152
  time value of money and, 1146–1149
Capital leases, 691
Capital Stock account, 607
Capital structure, 641
Carrying value, 100, 480, 648–649, **1144**
  in capital investment analysis, 1144
Cash, 408, 408–409, **711**
  "burn rate" for, 722
  idle, investment of, 1195–1196
  plant assets sold for, 493–494
  purchase of assets with, 16
  receipts of, control of, 370–371
  see also Petty cash *entries*
Cash account, 17, 18–19, 19, 711, 712
  bonds issued at discount and, 676
  job order costing system and, 891
  under periodic inventory system, 184
Cash basis of accounting, 92
Cash budget, 1020, 1020(table), 1020–1022, 1021–1023(exh.)
Cash disbursements, control of, 371–373(fig.), 374–375
Cash disbursements journal, 340, 341(exh.), 342–343
Cash equivalents, 408, 711
Cash flow(s), 22
  from accrual-based information, 107
  in capital investment analysis, 1144
  classification of, 712–714, 713(fig.)
  evaluating adequacy of, 770, 771(exh.)
  free, 715–717, 770, 771(exh.)
  inventory measurement and, 457
  liquidity and, 526–527, 527(fig.)
  quality of earnings and, 634–635
Cash flow management, 168, 168(fig.), 168–170, 169(fig.)

Cash flows to assets, 715, 770, 771(exh.)
Cash flows to sales, 715, 770, 771(exh.)
Cash flow yield(s), 715, 770, 771(exh.)
Cash gap, 168–170, 169(fig.)
Cash-generating efficiency, 714, 714–715
Cash inflows, net, 1144
Cash payments journal, 340, 341(exh.), 342–343
Cash receipts journal, 338, 339(exh.), 340
Cash reserves, 405
Cash sales receipts, control of, 370–371
Cash Short or Over account, 379
Category killers, 450
Certified public accountants (CPAs), 23, reports of, 23–24
CFOs (chief financial officers), functions of, 10
Chart of accounts, 48, 49–50(exh.)
Check(s), 373(fig.), 374, 374–375
  processing time for, 1133
  voucher, 381
Check authorization, 373(fig.), 374
Checkmarks, in general journal, 64
Check registers, 382, 382–383
Chief financial officers (CFOs), functions of, 10
Classification, 48, 56
Classified financial statements, 220, 230–237
  liquidity evaluation using, 230–231
  profitability evaluation using, 231–237
Clearing accounts, 890
Closely held corporations, 257
Closing entries, 130, 132(fig.), 132–239
  accounts after closing and, 136, 137–138(exh.)
  for merchandising business using periodic inventory system, 190(exh.), 190–191
  for merchandising business using perpetual inventory system, 187, 187(exh.)
  required, 132–136, 133(exh.)
  on work sheet, 145
CM (contribution margin), 978–979
Codes of professional conduct, 25–26
Collection, of accounts receivable, 18
Commas, in financial reports, 66
Commercial paper, 530

Commitments, 538
Common-size statements, 762, 763(exh.), 763(fig.), 764(exh.), 764(fig.), 765
Common stock, 602
  statement of cash flows and, 726
Common Stock account, 607, 608, 646
Common Stock Distributable account, 646
Comparability, 216
Comparability principle, 325
Compensating balances, 408
Complex capital structure, 641
Compound entries, 63
Compound interest, 1146, 1146–1147, 1187–1188, 1188(table)
Comprehensive income, 630
Computer(s), 8
  networking, 326
  software costs and, 501
Computerized accounting systems, 325–328
  adjustments using, 104
  general ledger systems, 326, 327(fig.), 328, 328(fig.)
  interest and amortization tables and, 684
  spreadsheet software and, 325–326
  trial balance and, 62
  value of, 325
Condensed financial statements, 226
Confidentiality, 342
Conglomerate companies, 755–756
Connors, John, 10
Conservatism, 217, 217–218
Consignments, 447
Consistency, 216
Consolidated financial statements, 1185
Consumers, as users of accounting information, 10
Contingent liabilities, 407, 538
Continuing operations, income from, 630
Continuity issue, 91, 91–92
Continuous improvement, 804, 804–807
  achieving, 806(fig.), 806–807
  activity-based management and, 805
  just-in-time operating philosophy and, 804
  theory of constraints and, 806
  total quality management and, 805
Contra accounts, 99, 99–100

Allowance to Adjust Long-Term Investments to Market account, 1182, 1183–1184
  Purchases Discounts account, 192
  Sales Returns and Allowances account, 174, 180–181
  Unamortized Bond Discount account, 676
  Unrealized Loss on Long-Term Investments account, 1182, 1183–1184
Contributed capital, 224
Contribution margin (CM), 978, 978–979
Control
  internal, see Internal control(s)
  long-term investment in stock and, 1180, 1181
Control activities, 366
Control environment, 366
Controllable costs and revenues, 1098
Controlling (control) accounts, 332
Controlling interest, 1181, 1181(table), 1185
Control principle, 324
Conventions, 216
  for interpreting accounting information, 216–219
Conversion costs, 843, 843(fig.), 897, 941
  equivalent production for, 898
Conversion Costs account, backflush costing and, 945
Convertible bonds, 689
Convertible preferred stock, 605, 605–606
Copyrights, 499(table)
Core competencies, 802
Core values, 966
Corporations, 13, 13(table), 13–14, 14(fig.), 594, 594–614
  advantages of, 596
  disadvantages of, 596–597
  dividends and, see Dividend(s)
  equity financing and, 597–598
  formation of, 594–595, 595(fig.)
  limited liability, 559
  management of, 594–597, 595(fig.)
  owner's equity in, 224
  private (closely held), 257
  resembling partnerships, 559
  S corporations, 559
  size of, 13, 14
  stockholders' equity and, 601–602, 602(fig.)
  stock of, see Common stock; Dividend(s); Preferred stock; Stock entries

Subject Index

stock options and, 600, 601
Cost(s), 47
  of acquisition of plant assets, 485–487
  assigning in new manufacturing environment, 941–942, 942(table)
  avoidable, 1138
  behavior of, 839
  classification in new manufacturing environment, 941
  classifications of, 837–840, 838(fig.)
  of computer software, 501
  controllable, 1098
  controlling using variance analysis, 1056, 1057(fig.), 1058
  conversion, 843, 843(fig.), 897, 898, 941
  depreciable, 488
  development and exploration, in oil and gas industry, 497–498
  differential (incremental), 1132
  direct, 838
  of doing business, *see* Expenses
  expired, 91
  fixed, 839, 971–972, 972(fig.)
  indirect, 838
  mixed, 972(fig.), 972–975
  net, of purchases, 181
  opportunity, 1133–1134
  original (historical), 47
  overhead, *see* Manufacturing overhead costs
  period (noninventoriable), 840
  prime, 843, 843(fig.)
  product (inventoriable), *see* Product cost(s)
  research and development, 500–501
  of sales, 174–175
  standard, 1050–1051
  start-up and organization, 598
  sunk, 1132–1133
  of television talent, 860
  traceability of, 838
  value-adding and nonvalue-adding, 839
  variable, 968–970, 969(fig.)
Cost allocation, 851, 851–861
  ABC approach for, 856–860
  estimates and, 854
  of manufacturing overhead costs, 852, 853(fig.), 854–860, 855(fig.)
  for service organizations, 860–861
  traditional approach for, 854–856, 855(fig.), 856
Cost behavior, 964–987, **966**

breakeven analysis and, 976–980, 977(fig.)
cost-volume-profit analysis and, *see* Cost-volume-profit (CVP) analysis
  of fixed costs, 971–972, 972(fig.)
  management cycle and, 966–967, 967(fig.)
  of mixed costs, 972(fig.), 972–975
  of variable costs, 968–970, 969(fig.)
Cost-benefit convention, 218, 218–219
Cost-benefit principle, 324
Cost centers, 1097, 1097–1098, 1099(table)
  discretionary, 1097–1098, 1099(table)
  evaluating performance using flexible budgeting, 1100–1101, 1101(exh.)
Cost drivers, 851
Cost flows, 447
  of manufacturing costs, 846(fig.), 846–847
  process costing system and, 894–896, 895(fig.)
Cost hierarchy, 934, 934–935, 935(table)
Cost information
  management cycle and, 836(fig.), 836–837
  organizations and, 837
Costing
  activity-based, *see* Activity-based costing (ABC)
  backflush, 942–945, 943(fig.), 944(fig.)
  job order, *see* Job order costing systems
  process, *see* Process costing systems
  product, *see* Product costing systems
  standard, 1050–1052
    see also Variance analysis
  variable (full), profit center performance evaluation using, 1101–1103, 1102(exh.)
Cost objects, 851
Cost of capital, 1106, 1106–1107, **1149**
Cost of goods manufactured, 847
Cost of goods manufactured budget, 1018, 1018(exh.)
Cost of goods sold, 174, 174–175, 181
  income statement and, 849
Cost of Goods Sold account, 184, 846, 852

backflush costing and, 943, 945
closing, 187, 187(exh.)
job order costing system and, 891
under periodic inventory system, 180–181
under perpetual inventory system, 172, 173, 179, 180, 185
process costing system and, 897
Cost-plus contracts, 892, 892–893
Cost pools, 851
Cost principle, 47
  alternatives to, 48
Cost savings, 1144
Costs of quality, 805
Cost-volume-profit (CVP) analysis, 975, 975–976
  for manufacturing businesses, 980–984, 983(exh.)
  for service businesses, 984–985
Coupon(s), 536
Coupon bonds, 674
Couric, Katie, 860
CPAs (certified public accountants), reports of, 23–24
Credit, 52
Credit analysts, 232
Credit cards, 170, 178, 933–934
Creditors
  statement of cash flows and, 712
  as users of accounting information, 9–10
  as users of financial performance evaluation, 752–753
Credit policies, 405–406, 406(fig.), 407(fig.)
Credit services, as information source for financial statement analysis, 757
Crossfooting, 142, 340
Cumulative effect of accounting changes, 639
Cumulative preferred stock, 604
Current assets, 220, 222
  changes in, statement of cash flows and, 721
Current liabilities, 223, 528, 528–545
  changes in, statement of cash flows and, 721–722
  contingent, 538
  definitely determinable, 529–535
  estimated, 535–537
  payroll accounting and, *see* Payroll accounting
Current manufacturing costs, 847
Current position, assessment of, 753
Current ratio, 231, 231(fig.), **766,** 767(exh.)
Customer lists, 499(table)
Customer numbers, 330

Customer service, technology and, 331
CVP, *see* Cost-volume-profit (CVP) analysis

Dalton, Dick, 892
Dashboard system, 1096
Data processing, 324
   electronic, *see* Computerized accounting systems; Technology manual, 330
Date(s)
   for bonds, 420–421, 603
   for promissory notes, 420–421
Date of declaration, 603
Date of payment, 603
Date of record, 603
Death, of partner, 572
Debentures, 672
Debit, 52
Debit cards, 170, 409
Debt(s)
   bad, *see* Uncollectible accounts
   early extinguishment of, 688
   long-term, *see* Bond *entries*; Long-term liabilities
Debt to equity ratio, 234, 234–235, 235(fig.), **768,** 769(exh.), 770
Decimal points, in financial reports, 66
Decision makers, 8(fig.), 8–10
Decision making, 1128–1156
   capital investment decisions and, *see* Capital investment decisions
   incremental analysis for, *see* Incremental analysis
   management cycle and, 1130–1132, 1131(fig.)
   short-run decision analysis and, 1130–1132, 1131(fig.)
Declining-balance method, 490, 490–491
Deferrals, 95
   adjusting entries for deferred expenses and, 96–100
   adjusting entries for deferred revenues and, 101–102, 102(fig.)
Deferred Income Taxes account, 636, 636–637
Deferred payment, 1194–1195
Deficit, 642
Defined benefit plans, 692
Defined contribution plans, 692
Definitely determinable liabilities, 529, 529–535
Delivery Expense account, 176
   under perpetual inventory system, 180
Depletion, 482(fig.), 496–497

Depreciable cost, 488
Depreciation, 98, 482(fig.), 487–491, 502–505
   accumulated, 99(fig.), 99–100
   adjusting entries for, 98–100
   in capital investment analysis, 1144–1145
   of closely related plant assets, 497
   comparison of methods for computing, 491, 491(fig.)
   cost recovery for income tax purposes and, 505
   declining-balance method for computing, 490–491
   disposal of depreciable assets and, 492–496
   factors affecting computation of, 488–489
   group, 504
   for partial years, 502–503
   production method for computing, 489–490
   revision of depreciation rates and, 503
   of special types of capital expenditures, 504–505
   statement of cash flows and, 720
   straight-line method for computing, 489
Development costs, in oil and gas industry, 497–498
Differential analysis, *see* Incremental analysis
Differential costs, 1132
Diluted earnings per share, 641, 641–642
Direct charge-off method, 413–414, **414**
Direct costs, 838
Direct labor budget, 1014, 1014–1015, 1016(exh.)
Direct labor costs, 840
   standard costs for, 1052–1053
Direct labor efficiency variance, 1061
Direct labor rate standard, 1053
Direct labor rate variance, 1061
Direct labor time standard, 1053
Direct labor variances, 1060–1062
Direct materials costs, 840
   equivalent production for, 897–898
   standard costs for, 1052
Direct materials price standard, 1052
Direct materials price variance, 1058, 1058–1059
Direct materials purchases budget, 1014, 1015(exh.)

Direct materials quantity standard, 1052
Direct materials quantity variance, 1059
Direct materials variances, 1058–1060, 1060(fig.)
Direct method, 717
Disclosure
   of bonds on balance sheet, 674
   of liabilities, 529
Discontinued operations, 638
Discount(s), 675
   on bonds, 675–676
   sales, 177, 191
   trade, 176
Discounting, 408
Discount on Common Stock account, 608
Discretionary cost centers, 1097, 1097–1098, 1099(table)
Dishonored notes, 423
Disposal, of depreciable assets, 492–496
Disposal value, 488
   in capital investment analysis, 1145
Dissolution (of partnership), **567,** 567–572
   by admission of new partner, 567–570
   by death of partner, 572
   by withdrawal of partner, 570–572, 571(fig.)
Diversified companies, 755, 755–756
Dividend(s), 224
   liquidating, 602
   policies for, 598
   preference as to, 603–605
   stock, 644–647
Dividend income, 412
Dividends in arrears, 604
Dividends payable, 531
Dividends yield, 598, 771(exh.), **772**
Documents, internal control and, 367
Dollar amounts, in financial reports, 66
Dollar signs, in financial statements, 66
Double-declining-balance method, 490
Double-entry bookkeeping, 8, 51–54
   T account and, 51–52
   transaction analysis and processing in, 52–54, 53(fig.)
Double taxation, 596, 596–597
Drawing account, *see* Withdrawals account

Duality, principle of, 51
Due care, 25
Dun & Bradstreet Corp., 757
Duration of note, 421, 421–422

Early extinguishment of debt, 688
Earned Capital account, 224
Earnings before interest and taxes (EBT), 768
Earnings per share, 640–642
Ebanking, 1139
Ebbers, Bernard, 1022
EBT (earnings before interest and taxes), 768
Ecommerce, *see* Electronic commerce (ecommerce)
Economic planners, as users of accounting information, 10
Economic profit, 768
Economic value added (EVA), 768, **1106,** 1106(exh.), 1106–1107, 1107(fig.)
Economy, value chains and, 929
Edgar, 329
EDI (electronic data interchange), 329
Effective interest method, 680
for amortization of bond discount, 680–682, 681(table), 682(fig.)
for amortization of bond premium, 683–684, 684(table), 685(fig.)
Effective interest rate, 675, 679
EFT (electronic funds transfer), 409
E2K (event-to-knowledge) management, 330
Electronic commerce (ecommerce), 104, **329**
global, 807
voucher systems and, 380
Electronic data interchange (EDI), 329
Electronic funds transfer (EFT), 409
Electronic work sheets, 146
Emerging economies, accounting practices in, 416
Employee earnings record, 541–542
Employee's Withholding Exemption Certificate, 539
Ending inventory, 181
Engineering method, 973
Enterprise resource planning (ERP) systems, 324
Equipment, acquisition cost of, 486
Equities, 14
Equity
  owner's, 15
  residual, 15, 602
  return on, 235–236, 236(fig.), 599–600, 768, 769(exh.)

stockholders,' components of, 601–602, 602(fig.)
trading on, 670
Equity financing, 597–598
Equity method, for accounting for stock investments, 1184
Equivalent production, 897, 897–898, 898(fig.)
for conversion costs, 898
for direct materials, 897–898
ERP (enterprise resource planning) systems, 324
Estimated liabilities, 535, 535–637
Estimated useful life, 488, 488–489
Estimation
inventory valuation by, 459–460
of overhead rate, 854
quality of earnings and, 631–633
of uncollectible accounts expense, 415
Ethics, 25, 25–26
accounting misstatements and, 220
budgeting and, 1022
confidentiality and, 342
core values and, 966
deceptive use of accounting principles and, 93
of decision between long-term assets and expenses, 487
of electronic funds transfer, 409
financial reporting and, 219–220
frauds and, 367
inventory overstatement and, 456
management's responsibility for financial statements and, 812
professional, 25–26
profits and, 1069
pro-forma statements and, 756
recycling and, 1103
standards of ethical conduct and, 810, 812–813(exh.), 813
truthfulness of financial statements and, 56
unit costs and, 892
whistle-blowing and, 634
European Community, accounting standards and, 1179
EVA (economic value added), 768, 1106(exh.), 1106–1107, 1107(fig.)
Event-to-knowledge (E2K) management, 330
Exchange, of plant assets, 494–496
Exchange gains/losses, 1175
realized versus unrealized, 1176–1177
Exchange rates, 12, 1174, 1174(table)
Ex-dividend stock, 603

Executing stage of management cycle
activity-based cost information and, 928
balanced scorecard and, 1093–1094
budgeting and, 1007
cost behavior and, 966
cost information and, 837
management accounting and, 798(fig.), 798–799
product cost information and, 885
short-run decision analysis and, 1130–1131
standard costs and, 1050
Expenditure(s), 485
Expenses, 16, 18–19, **90,** 90–91
accrued, 100–101, 101(fig.)
deferred, 96–100
income taxes, 635(table), 635–638
long-term assets versus, 487
operating, 176
other, 226
prepaid, 96–98, 97(fig.)
recognition of, 93
Expired costs, 91
Explanatory notes, in annual report, 261
Exploration costs, in oil and gas industry, 497–498
Extensible Business Reporting Language (XBRL), 329
Extraordinary items, 638, 638–639
Extraordinary repairs, 504

Face interest rate, 675
Face value, bonds issued at, 674–675
Facility-level activities, 935
Factor(s), 407
Factoring, 407
Factory burden, 840
Factory overhead, 840
  see also Manufacturing overhead costs
Factory Payroll account, 890
Factory tours, 1050
FASB, *see* Financial Accounting Standards Board (FASB)
Fast-food restaurants, supersizing meals in, 978
Federal Reserve Board, 10
Federal Unemployment Insurance tax, 534
FICA tax, 534
FIFO costing method, 896
for preparing process cost report, 899, 900(exh.), 901–903
FIFO (first-in, first-out) method, 449

Subject Index

Financial accounting, 7
  management accounting compared with, 794, 795(table), 796
Financial Accounting Standards Board (FASB), 24
  on available-for-sale securities accounting, 1181
  on comprehensive income, 630
  on conglomerates, 755–756
  on cost-benefit convention, 218–219
  on exchange gains and losses, 1176, 1177
  on full disclosure, 218
  on goodwill, 501–502
  on long-term leases, 691
  on noncash investing and financing transactions, 713–714
  on objectives of financial reporting, 214
  on other postretirement benefits, **693**
  on pension expense, 693
  on qualitative characteristics of accounting information, 215
  on reporting of foreign subsidiaries, 1177, 1178
  on short-term investments, 409
  Statement No. 13 of, 691
  Statement No. 52 of, 1176, 1177, 1178
  Statement No. 87 of, 693
  Statement No. 131 of, 755–756
Financial advisors and analysts, as users of accounting information, 10
Financial budgets, 1008, 1018–1022
Financial highlights, in annual report, 258
Financial information
  conventions for interpretation of, 216–219
  qualitative characteristics of, 214–216, 215(fig.)
Financial leverage, 670
Financial performance evaluation, 750–774, **752**
  external users of, 752–753
  horizontal analysis for, 759, 760(exh.), 761(exh.)
  information sources for, 756–757
  internal users of, 752
  ratio analysis for, 765–772
  Sarbanes-Oxley Act and, 753
  standards for, 754–756
  trend analysis for, 760–762, 762(exh.), 762(fig.)
  vertical analysis for, 762, 763(exh.), 763(fig.), 764(exh.), 764(fig.), 765

Financial position, 14
Financial press
  as information source for financial statement analysis, 757
  as user of accounting information, 10
Financial statement(s), 7
  adjusted trial balance in preparation of, 104–105, 105(exh.), 106(exh.)
  in annual report, 258–260
  classified, *see* Classified financial statements
  common-size, 762, 763(exh.), 763(fig.), 764(exh.), 764(fig.), 765
  condensed, 226
  consolidated, 1185
  cost classifications for, 839–840, 840(table)
  dollar signs in, 66
  of foreign subsidiaries, restatement of, 1177–1178
  GAAP and, 23
  interim, 128, 263, 756
  inventory systems and, 454, 454(fig.)
  notes to, in annual report, 260–261
  preparing using work sheet, 145(exh.), 145–146, 146(exh.)
  pro forma, 756, 1008
  relationships among, 19, 21(exh.), 22–23
  truthfulness of, 56
  see also specific statements
Financial statement analysis, *see* Financial performance evaluation
Financial Times, 757
Financing
  equity, 597–598
  of long-term assets, 483
Financing activities, 6, 712, 712–713
  statement of cash flows preparation and, 725–727
Financing period, 168, 168–170, 169(fig.)
Finished Goods Inventory account, 844, 846, 847, 851, 852
  backflush costing and, 943, 945
  job order costing system and, 890–891
  process costing system and, 896–897, 902
First-in, first-out (FIFO) method, 449
Fiscal year, 91
Fixed assets, *see* Long-term assets; Plant assets
Fixed costs, 839, 971, 971–972, 972(fig.)

  in airline industry, 839
Fixed overhead budget variance, 1066
Fixed overhead volume variance, 1066, 1066–1068
Flexibility principle, 325
Flexible budget(s), 1055
  analyzing manufacturing overhead variances using, 1063(exh.), 1063–1064
  cost center performance evaluation using, 1100–1101, 1101(exh.)
  in variance analysis, 1054–1056, 1055–1057(exh.)
Flexible budget formula, 1055, 1055–1056
FOB destination, 177
FOB shipping point, 177
Folio column, *see* Post. Ref. column
Footings, 52
Forbes, 757
Form 8-K, 757
Form 10-K, 257, 757
Form 10-Q, 757
Form W-4, 539
Fortune, 757
Franchises, 499(table)
Fraud, 367
  payroll, 542
Fraudulent financial reporting, 219, 219–220
Free cash flow, 715–717, **770,** 771(exh.)
Freight In account, under periodic inventory system, 183, 190–191
Freight Out Expense account, 176
  under perpetual inventory system, 180
Frequent-flier miles, 537
Full-costing method, 497, 497–498
  profit center performance evaluation using, 1101–1103, 1102(exh.)
Full disclosure, 218
Full product cost, 926
Functional currency, 1177
Fund accumulation, 1196
FUTA tax, 534
Future potential, assessment of, 753
Future value, 1147, 1188–1189
  of ordinary annuity, 1189, 1190(table)
  of single sum at compound interest, 1188, 1188(table)
  tables of, 1200, 1200(table)–1201(table)

GAAP, *see* Generally accepted accounting principles (GAAP)

Gains
　exchange, 1175, 1176–1177
　on exchange of assets, 495–496
　from extraordinary items, 639
　quality of earnings and, 633
　on sale of partnership assets, 573–575, 574(exh.)
　statement of cash flows and, 720–721
GASB (Governmental Accounting Standards Board), 24
Gas industry, development and exploration costs in, 497–498
General journal, 63, 63–64
General ledger, 48, 64–66
　ledger account form in, 64(exh.), 64–65
　posting to, 65(exh.), 65–66
General Ledger Software, 326
General ledger systems, 326, 327(fig.), 328, 328(fig.)
　structure of, 326, 328, 328f
Generally accepted accounting principles (GAAP), 23, 23–24
　financial statements and, 23–24
　independent CPAs' reports and, 23
　organizations influencing, 24
Global business, *see* International business
Goals
　budgeting and, 1004–1005
　coordination of, 1109
　linking to objectives and targets, 1108
Goethe, 51
Going concern, 92
Goods available for sale, 181
Goods flow, 447
Good units, 1060
Goodwill, 499(table), 501–502
Governmental Accounting Standards Board (GASB), 24
Governmental organizations, 10
Graphical user interfaces (GUIs), 326
Gross margin, 175, 175–176
Gross margin method, 460, 460(table)
Gross profit, 175–176
Gross profit method, 460, 460(table)
Gross sales, 174
Group depreciation, 504
Group purchases, 487
GUIs (graphical user interfaces), 326

Handbook of Dividend Achievers, 757, 758
Held-to-maturity securities, 410, 1180

High-low method, 974, 974–975
Hill, Eleanor, 892
Historical cost, 47
Horizontal analysis, 759, 760(exh.), 761(exh.)

IASB (International Accounting Standards Board), 1178
Ideal capacity, 968
IFAC (International Federation of Accountants), 1178
IMA, *see* Institute of Management Accountants (IMA)
Impairment reviews, 501–502
Imprest system, 378
In balance, defined, 62
Income, 88–113
　comprehensive, 630
　dividend, 412
　interest, 412
　measurement issues and, 91–92
　net, *see* Net income
　operating, 975
　residual, 1104–1105, 1106(exh.)
　taxable, 635
Income from continuing operations, 630
Income from operations, 226
Income statement, 21(exh.), 22, 226–230, 227(exh.)
　absorption costing, profit center performance evaluation using, 1101–1103, 1102(exh.)
　budgeted, 1018–1019, 1019(exh.)
　cost of goods sold and, 849
　for merchandising businesses, 173–176, 174(fig.), 175(exh.)
　quality of earnings and, 630–631, 631(exh.)
　reading and graphing data from, 228(exh.), 228–230, 229(fig.), 230(exh.)
Income statement column, merchandising business and, 186–187, 188–189
Income Summary account, 130
　closing process and, 130, 132(fig.), 132–139
　under periodic inventory system, 188, 190, 191
Income tax(es), 535–638, 635(table)
　in capital investment analysis, 1145
　of corporations, 596–597
　cost recovery and, 505
　deferred, 636–637
　inventory systems and, 454–455
　net of taxes and, 637–638
　payroll accounting and, 534
Income tax allocation, 636
Income taxes payable, 531–532

Incremental analysis, 1132, 1132–1143
　irrelevant costs and revenues and, 1132–1133, 1133(exh.)
　opportunity costs and, 1133–1134
　for outsourcing decisions, 1134–1136, 1135(exh.)
　for sales mix decisions, 1140–1141, 1141(exh.)
　for segment probability decisions, 1137–1140, 1139(exh.)
　for sell or process-further decisions, 1142–1143, 1143(exh.)
　for special order decisions, 1136–1137, 1137(exh.)
Incremental costs, 1132
Independence, 25
Independent auditors' report, in annual report, 261–263, 262(fig.)
Independent verification, for internal control, 367–368
Index numbers, 761
Indirect costs, 838
Indirect labor costs, 840
Indirect manufacturing costs, 840
Indirect material costs, 840
Indirect method, 717
　for preparing statement of cash flows, 717–718, 717–720, 719f, 720(exh.)
Industry norms, for financial statement analysis, 754–756, 755(exh.)
Industry Norms and Key Business Ratios, 754, 757
Influential but noncontrolling interest, 1180–1181, 1181(table), 1184
Information and communication, 366
Initial public offerings (IPOs), 597, 597–598
Inspection time, 941
Installment accounts receivable, 413
Institute of Management Accountants (IMA), 25
　Code of Professional Conduct for Management Accountants of, 25–26, 812–813(exh.)
　definition of management accounting, 794
Intangible assets, 223, 498, 498(fig.), 499(table), 500–502
Intangible resources, 482(fig.)
Integrated programs, 326
Integrity, 25
Interest, 422, 1146, 1187–1188
　imputing on noninterest-bearing notes, 1193–1194

on partners' capital, 562
on promissory notes, 422
Interest (in company)
controlling, 1181, 1181(table), 1185
influential but noncontrolling, 1180–1181, 1181(table), 1184
noninfluential and noncontrolling, 1180–1181, 1181(table)
Interest (in partnership), 564–567, 567(exh.)
purchase of, 568
sale of, 571
Interest coverage ratio, 671, 769(exh.), 770
Interest expense, for bonds, year-end accrual of, 686–688
Interest income, 412
Interest rates
on bonds, 675–676
on promissory notes, 422
Interim financial statements, 128, 756
in annual report, 263
Internal control(s), 172, 172–173, 364–389, 366
activities of, 367–368
bank reconciliations for, 375–378
components of, 366–367
limitations of, 368
management goals and, 369
management's responsibility for, 366
over merchandising transactions, 368–375
petty cash procedures for, 378–379
voucher systems for, 380–385
Internal Revenue Service (IRS), 24
International accounting, 1173(table), 1173–1179, 1174(fig.)
accounting standards for, 500, 1174, 1178–1179
exchange rates and, 1174, 1174(table)
foreign purchases and, 1176
foreign sales and, 1175
realized versus unrealized exchange gain or loss and, 1176–1177
restatement of foreign subsidiary financial statements and, 1177–1178
International Accounting Standards (IASs), 500
International Accounting Standards Board (IASB), 1178
International business
accounting changes and, 639

accounting practices in emerging economies and, 416
airline bankruptcies and, 671
budgeting and, 1006
capital investment and, 1145
closing and, 139
comparability of accounting standards and, 500
continuous improvement to address global competition and, see Continuous improvement
cost-volume-profit analysis and, 976
dashboard system and, 1096
ebanking and, 1139
ecommerce and, 807
European stock markets and, 601
hybrid costing systems and, 887
just-in-time operating philosophy and, 940
partnerships and, 559
privatization and, 99
reserves and, 644
standard costing and, 1068
statement of cash flows and, 714
valuation of transactions in, 47
International Federation of Accountants (IFAC), 1178
Internet, 328, 328–330
financial reports on, 757
joint ventures and, 560
support of value chain, 802
uses of, 329–330
Internet retailing, 177
Inventoriable costs, see Product cost(s)
Inventory
beginning, 181
ending, 181
under just-in-time operating philosophy, 939
in manufacturing businesses, accounts for, 843–847
in merchandising businesses, see Merchandise inventory
physical, 172–173
see also Merchandise inventory; specific inventory accounts
Inventory cost, 446, 446–447
goods flow versus cost flow and, 447
merchandise in transit and, 446(fig.), 446–447
merchandise on hand not included in inventory and, 447
Inventory systems
financial statements and, 454, 454(fig.)
income taxes and, 454–455
perpetual, 171–172

see also Periodic inventory system; Perpetual inventory system
Inventory turnover, 444, 444–446, 445(fig.), **766,** 767(exh.)
Inventory valuation
by estimation, 459–460
at lower of cost or market, 457–458
under periodic inventory system, 447–450
under perpetual inventory system, 451–453, 453(fig.)
Investing activities, 6, 712
statement of cash flows preparation and, 722–725
Investment(s), 222
capital, see Capital investment entries
of idle cash, 1195–1196
long-term, 409, 1180–1185
owner's, 15, 16
in partnership, 568
short-term, see Short-term investments
statement of cash flows and, 723
Investment advisory services, as information source for financial statement analysis, 757
Investment centers, 1098, 1099(table), 1103–1108
economic value added and, 1106(exh.), 1106–1107, 1107(fig.)
multiple performance measures for, 1108
residual income and, 1104–1105, 1106(exh.)
return on investment and, 1103(exh.), 1103–1104, 1105(fig.)
Investors
statement of cash flows and, 712
as users of accounting information, 9
as users of financial performance evaluation, 752–753
Invoice, 373(fig.), **374**
IPOs (initial public offerings), 597–598
IRS (Internal Revenue Service), 24
Issued stock, 602
Item-by-item method, 458
Item column, in general ledger, 64–65

JIT, see Just-in-time (JIT) entries
Job order(s), 886
Job order cost cards, 844, 886
for manufacturing businesses, 892

Job order costing systems, 886, 887–894
 job order cost cards and, 892
 in manufacturing businesses, 887–891, 888–889(exh.)
 in service organizations, 892–894, 893(fig.)
Joint products, 1142
Joint ventures, 560
Journal(s), 63
 general, 63–64
 special-purpose, *see* Special-purpose journals
Journal entries, 63
 adjusting, *see* Adjusting entries
 closing, *see* Closing entries
 compound, 63
 reversing, 140–141
Journal form, 54
Journalizing, 63
Just-in-time (JIT) operating environment, 446
Just-in-time (JIT) operating philosophy, 804, 938, 938–946
 activity-based management compared with, 945–946, 946(table)
 backflush costing and, 942–945, 943(fig.), 944(fig.)
 continuous improvement of work environment and, 941
 minimum inventory levels and, 939
 multiskilled work force and, 940
 preventive maintenance and, 940
 product costs in, 941–942
 product quality and, 940
 pull-through production and, 939
 quick setup and flexible work cells and, 939–940

Kaplan, Robert S., 1092
King, Larry, 860

Land, acquisition cost of, 486
Land improvements, acquisition cost of, 486
Last-in, first-out (LIFO) method, 449, 449–450, 450(fig.), 452
LCM (lower-of-cost-or-market) rule, 457–458
Lease(s)
 capital, 691
 long-term, 690–692, 691(table)
 operating, 690
Leasehold(s), 499(table)
Leasehold improvements, 499(table), 501
Ledger(s), 48
 subsidiary, 332

Ledger account form, 64, 64(exh.), 64–65
Legal capital, 597
Letterman, David, 860
Letter to stockholders, 257–258
Liabilities, 15, 524–545
 accrued, 88, 89, 531
 classification of, 528
 on classified balance sheet, 223
 contingent, 407, 538
 current, *see* Current liabilities
 disclosure of, 529
 estimated, 535–537
 long-term, 223, 528
 managing liquidity and cash flows and, 526–527, 527(fig.)
 payment of, 17
 payroll, 532, 533(fig.), 534–535
 purchase of assets by incurring, 17
 recognition of, 528
 valuation of, 528
Liability, unlimited, 558–559
Licenses, 499(table)
Life
 limited, 558
 useful, estimated, 488–489
LIFO liquidation, 455
LIFO method, *see* Last-in, first-out (LIFO) method
Limited liability corporations, 559
Limited life, 558
Limited partnerships, 560
Linear approximation, 970
Lines of credit, 529, 529–530
Li-Ning, 1068
Liquidating dividends, 602
Liquidation (of partnership), **572,** 572–577
 gain on sale of assets and, 573–575, 574(exh.)
 loss on sale of assets and, 575(exh.), 575–577
Liquidity, 5, 5–6, **230,** 526–527, 527(fig.), 528
 evaluation of, 230–231, 766, 766(fig.), 767(exh.)
Loans, from banks, 529–530
Long-lived assets, *see* Plant assets
Long-term assets, 478–509, 480
 decision to acquire, 481–483
 depreciation of, *see* Depreciation
 expenses versus, 487
 financing, 483
 intangible, 498, 498(fig.), 499(table), 500–502
 matching rule applied to, 484, 484(fig.)
 natural resources, 496–498
 see also Plant assets

Long-term debt, current portions of, 532
Long-term investments, 409, 1180–1185
 in bonds, 1180
 in stocks, 1180–1185, 1181(table)
Long-term leases, 690–692, 691(table)
Long-term liabilities, 223, 528, 668–696
 amount of debt to carry and, 671(fig.), 671–672
 bonds, *see* Bond *entries*
 decision to issue long-term debt and, 670
 leases, 690–692, 691(table)
 mortgages payable, 690
 other postretirement benefits, 693
 pensions, 692–693
 types of debt and, 672
Losses
 exchange, 1175, 1176–1177
 on exchange of assets, 495
 from extraordinary items, 639
 net, 16, 90
 quality of earnings and, 633
 on sale of partnership assets, 575(exh.), 575–577
 statement of cash flows and, 720–721
Lower-of-cost-or-market (LCM) rule, 457, 457–458
LP column, *see* Post. Ref. column

MACRS (modified accelerated cost recovery system), 505
Mail, cash received through, control of, 370
Major category method, 458, 459(table)
Make-or-buy decisions, 1134
Management, 9
 basic functions of, 9
 goals of, internal control and, 369
 responsibility for financial statements, 812
 statement of cash flows and, 712
 as users of accounting information, 9
 as users of financial performance evaluation, 752
Management accounting, 7, 794, 794–800
 financial accounting compared with, 794, 795(table), 796
 management cycle and, 796(fig.), 796–800
 support of value chain analysis, 802–804, 803(exh.)

Management information systems (MISs), 8
Management's discussion and analysis, in annual report, 258
Managers, cost variances for evaluating performance of, 1069, 1070(exh.)
Manual data processing, 330
Manufacturing businesses
 cost reporting and inventory accounting in, 849, 850(fig.), 850–851
 cost-volume-profit analysis for, 980–984, 983(exh.)
 job order costing system for, 887–891, 888–889(exh.)
 tours of, 1050
Manufacturing cost flow, 846, 846(fig.), 846–847
Manufacturing Overhead account, 844, 852
 job order costing system and, 890, 891
 Manufacturing overhead budget, 1015, 1016(exh.), 1017
 Manufacturing overhead costs, 840
 allocating, 852, 853(fig.), 854–860, 855(fig.)
 over- and underapplied, 852
Manufacturing overhead variances, 1062–1069
 analyzing using flexible budgets, 1063(exh.), 1063–1064
Margin(s), 803
 gross, 175–176
 segment, 1138
Margin of safety, 976
Marketable securities, 409
 see also Short-term investments
Market interest rate, 675, 679
Market price, of companies, stock splits and, 647
Market share, in candy industry, 849
Market strength, evaluating, 770, 771(exh.), 772
Market value, 458
Master budget, 1008, 1008–1011, 1009–1011(fig.)
Matching rule, 92
 applying to inventories, 442–443
 long-term assets and, 484, 484(fig.)
Materiality, 217
Materials Inventory account, 843–844, 846, 850–851
 backflush costing and, 942
 job order costing system and, 889–890
Materials request form, 844

Maturity date, 420, 420–421
Maturity value, 422
 of promissory notes, 422
Measurement, 11–12, 44–68
 accounts and, 48, 49–50, 50–51
 clarification issue and, 48
 double-entry system and, 51–54
 of income, *see* Income
 of inventory, *see* Inventory cost; Inventory systems; Inventory valuation
 money measure and, 11–12
 object of, 11
 of profitability, 90–91
 recognition issue and, 46–47
 recording and posting transactions and, 63–66
 separate entity concept and, 12
 transaction analysis illustration and, 54–61, 60(exh.)
 trial balance and, 61(exh.), 61–63, 62(table)
 valuation issue and, 47–48
Medical insurance, payroll accounting and, 534
Medicare tax, 534
Merchandise in transit, cost of, 446(fig.), 446–447
Merchandise inventory, 168, 440–466, **442**
 cost of, *see* Inventory cost
 evaluating level of, 444–446, 445(fig.)
 impact of inventory decisions and, 443, 444(fig.)
 loss of, 458
 matching rule applied to, 442–443
 overstatement of, 456
 valuation of, *see* Inventory valuation
 see also Inventory systems; *specific inventory systems*
Merchandise Inventory account, 850
 under periodic inventory system, 180–181, 182–183, 184, 188
 under perpetual inventory system, 172, 173, 178, 179, 180, 185
Merchandising businesses, 166–195, 168
 adjusting entries for, 187
 cash flow management and, 168(fig.), 168–170, 169(fig.)
 closing entries for, 187, 187(exh.), 190(exh.), 190–191
 control of, 172–173
 income statement for, 173–176, 174(fig.), 175(exh.)
 inventory systems for, 171–172
 see also Inventory systems; *specific inventory systems*

 profitability management and, 170–171, 171(exh.)
 purchases discounts and, 191–192
 sales discounts and, 191
 terms of sale and, 176–178
 work sheet for, 185–187, 186(exh.), 188–191, 189(exh.)
Merchandising transactions, internal control over, 368–375
Mergent's, 757
MISs (management information systems), 8
Mission, 796, 796–797
Misstatements, inventory measurement and, 455–457
Mixed costs, 972, 972(fig.), 972–975
 engineering method of separating, 973
 high-low method for, 974–975
 scatter diagram method for, 973–974, 974(fig.)
 statistical methods for, 975
Modified accelerated cost recovery system (MACRS), 505
Money, time value of, *see* Time value of money
Money measure, 11, 11–12
Monitoring, 367
Moody's Investors Service, Inc., 757
Mortgages(s), 690
Mouse, 326
Moving time, 941
Multistep form (of income statement), **226,** 226–227, 227(exh.)
Mutual agency, 558

Natural resources, 482(fig.), 496–498
 depletion of, 496–497
 depreciation of closely related plant assets and, 497
 development and exploration costs in oil and gas industry and, 497–498
Net assets, 15
Net cash inflows, 1144
Net cost of purchases, 181
Net income, 16, 90, 176
 in capital investment analysis, 1144
Net losses, 16, 90
Net of taxes, 637, 637–638
Net present value method, 1149, 1149–1151
 advantages of, 1149–1150
 illustration of, 1150–1151
Net purchases, 181
Net sales, 174

Subject Index

Net worth, *see* Owner's equity
Neuer Markt, 601
New manufacturing environment, *see* Just-in-time (JIT) operating philosophy
New York Stock Exchange (NYSE), 7
Nominal accounts, 130
Noncash investing and financing transactions, 713, 713–714
Noncompete covenants, 499(table)
Noncumulative preferred stock, 604
Nonfinancial measures, in service organizations, 810, 811(exh.)
Noninfluential and noncontrolling interest, 1180–1181, 1181(table)
Noninventoriable costs, 840
Nonoperating items, 638–640
  accounting changes, 639–640
  discontinued operations, 638
  extraordinary items, 638–639
  quality of earnings and, 633–634
Nonvalue-adding activities, 805, 932
  process value analysis and, 933–934
  in service organizations, 932
Nonvalue-adding costs, 839
No-par stock, 606, 608
Normal balance, 61
Normal capacity, 968
Normal costing, 842
Norton, David P., 1092
Notes payable, 420, 530(fig.), 530–531
Notes receivable, 420
  see also Promissory notes
Notes Receivable account, 90
Notes to the financial statements, in annual report, 260–261
Not-for-profit organizations, 10
  capital investment analysis for, 1147
Nouveau Marche, 601
NYSE (New York Stock Exchange), 7

Objectives, linking of goals to, 1108
Objectivity, 25
O'Brien, Conan, 860
Obsolescence, 488
Oil industry, development and exploration costs in, 497–498
100-year bonds, 677
Operating activities, 6, 712
  statement of cash flows preparation and, 717–722, 718–720(exh.), 719(fig.)
Operating assets, 222–223

Operating budgets, 170, 170–171, 171(exh.), **1008**
Operating capacity, 968, 968–969
Operating cycle, 168, 168(fig.), **766**
Operating decisions, accounting methods and, 455
Operating expenses, 176
Operating income, 975
Operating leases, 690
Operating objectives, 797
Operations
  discontinued, 638
  income from, 226
Opinion section, of auditors' report, 262(fig.), 262–263
Opportunity costs, 1133, 1133–1134
Ordinary annuities, 1148, 1148–1149
Ordinary repairs, 504
Organization charts, 1098, 1098–1100, 1100(fig.)
Original cost, 47
Other assets, 220
Other postretirement benefits, 693
Other revenues and expenses, 226
Outsourcing, 802, 1134, 1134–1136, 1135(exh.)
Outstanding stock, 602
Overapplied overhead costs, 852
Overhead rates
  applying, 858–860
  estimation of, 854
  planning, 857–858, 858(fig.), 859(table)
  predetermined, 852
Owner's equity, 15
  business form and, 223–224
  on classified balance sheet, 223–224
Owner's investments, 15, 16
Owner's withdrawals, 15, 19

Pacioli, Fra Luca, 8, 51
Paid-in Capital in Excess of Par Value account, 646
Paid-in Capital in Excess of Stated Value account, 607, 608
Paid-in Capital, Retirement of Stock account, 611
Paid-in Capital, Treasury Stock account, 610–611
Parent company, 1185
Participative budgeting, 1006
Partner(s), in accounting firms, risks of being, 566
Partners' equity, 223
Partners' equity, 561, 561–562
Partnership(s), 13, 13(table), 14(fig.), 556–579, **558**

  advantages and disadvantages of, 559
  characteristics of, 558–560
  corporations resembling, 559
  dissolution of, 567–572
  distribution of income and losses of, 562–567
  international investment and, 559
  limited, 560
  liquidation of, 572–577
  owner's equity in, 223
  partners' equity and, 561–562
Partnership agreement, 558
Partnership income/losses
  distribution of, 562–567
  participation in, 559
Par value, 597
Par value stock, 607–608
Past performance
  assessment of, 753
  as standard for financial statement analysis, 754
Patents, 499(table)
Payables turnover, 526, 527, 527(fig.), **766,** 767(exh.)
Payback period method, 1151, 1151–1152
Payment
  deferred, 1194–1195
  of liabilities, 17
  of long-term debt, timing of, 672
  of payroll and payroll taxes, 542–543
Payroll accounting, 538–543
  computation of take-home pay and, 538–539, 540(fig.)
  employee earnings record and, 541–542
  fraud and, 542
  payment of payroll and payroll taxes and, 542–543
  payroll register and, 540(exh.), 540–541, 541(exh.)
  recording payroll and, 541
  recording payroll taxes and, 542
Payroll Bank Account account, 542
Payroll liabilities, 532, 533(fig.), 534–535
Payroll register, 540, 540(exh.), 540–541, 541(exh.)
Payroll taxes
  payment of, 542–543
  recording, 542
Peachtree Complete Accounting, 326, 327(fig.)
Pension(s), 692–693
Pension contributions, payroll accounting and, 534
Pension funds, 692
Pension plans, 692

Subject Index

P/E (price/earnings) ratio, 598, 771(exh.), 772
Percentage of net sales method, 415, 415–416, 418(fig.), 418–419
Performance-based pay, 1108, 1108–1109
Performance evaluation
   for managers, cost variances for, 1069, 1070(exh.)
   product cost information for, 903
Performance management and evaluation systems, 1096
Performance measure(s), 6, 6–7, **807,** 807–810
   balanced scorecard and, 808–809, 809(fig.)
   benchmarking and, 809–810
   in management cycle, 807–808
Performance measurement, 1090–1112, **1096**
   incentives and goals and, 1108–1109
   multiple measures for, 1108
   object of, 1096
   quality of earnings and, 634–635
   responsibility accounting for, *see* Investment centers; Responsibility accounting
Period costs, 840
Periodic inventory system, 82(exh.), 181–185, 183(fig.)
   pricing inventory under, 447–450
   work sheet for merchandising business using, 188–191, 189(exh.)
Periodicity, 91
Permanent accounts, 130
Perpetual inventory system, 171, 171–172, 178–181
   merchandise purchase transactions under, 178–179
   merchandise sales transactions under, 179–181
   pricing inventory under, 451–453, 453(fig.)
   work sheet for merchandising business using, 185–187, 186(exh.)
Personal account, *see* Withdrawals account
Personnel procedures, internal control and, 368
Petty Cash account, 379
Petty cash fund, 378, 378–379
   establishing, 378
   making disbursements from, 378–379
   reimbursing, 379

Petty cash vouchers, 378, 378–379, 379(exh.)
Physical controls, 367
Physical deterioration, 488
Physical inventory, 172, 172–173
Planning
   activity-based cost information and, 927–928
   balanced scorecard and, 1092–1093, 1094(fig.)
   budgeting and, 1007
   cost behavior and, 966
   cost information and, 836–837
   management accounting and, 796–798, 797(fig.)
   product cost information and, 884
   short-run decision analysis and, 1130
   standard costs and, 1050
   strategic, 1004
Plant assets, 222–223
   acquisition cost of, 485–487
   closely related to natural resources, depreciation of, 497
   depreciation of, *see* Depreciation
   discarding, 492–493
   exchanges of, 494–496
   sale of, 492–494
   statement of cash flows and, 724–725
Plant Assets account, 724
Portfolio, 752
Post. Ref. column
   in cash payments journal, 342
   in cash receipts journal, 338, 340
   in general journal, 64
   in general ledger, 65, 66
   in purchases journal, 337
   in sales journal, 334, 335
Post-closing trial balance, 139, 139(exh.)
Posting, 65. 65(exh.), 65–66
   batch, 328
   real-time, 328
Potentially dilutive securities, 641
Practical capacity, 968
Predetermined overhead rate, 852
Preferred stock, 602, 603–606
   callable, 606
   convertible, 605–606
   cumulative, 604
   noncumulative, 604
   preference as to assets, 605
   preference as to dividends, 603–605
Preferred Stock account, 607
Premiums, 676
   on bonds, 676–677
Prepaid expenses, 96

   adjusting entries for, 96–98, 97(fig.)
Present value, 1147, 1147–1149, 1189–1192
   of ordinary annuity, 1148–1149, 1191–1192, 1192(table)
   of single sum due in future, 1147–1148, 1190–1191, 1191(table)
   tables of, 1201(table)–1205(table), 1201–1205
   valuing bonds using, 677–678
President's Council of Economic Advisers, 10
Preventive maintenance, in just-in-time operating philosophy, 940
Price(s)
   of bonds, 675
   call (redemption), 606, 688
Price/earnings (P/E) ratio, 598, 771(exh.), **772**
Primary processes, 800
   in value chain analysis, 801–802
Prime costs, 843, 843(fig.)
Principle of duality, 51
Private corporations, 257
Process costing systems, 886, 894–897
   cost flows through Work in Process Inventory accounts and, 896–897
   FIFO costing method for preparing report and, 899, 900(exh.), 901–903
   patterns of product flows and cost flows and, 894–896, 895(fig.)
   for two or more production departments, 902–903
Process cost report, 896
   FIFO costing method for preparing, 899, 900(exh.), 901–903
Processing time, 941
Process value analysis (PVA), 933, 933–934
Procurement cards, 933–934
Product(s)
   joint, 1142
   quality of, *see* Continuous improvement; Quality
Product cost(s), 839, 839–840, 840(table), 840–843
   computation of product unit cost and, 841(table), 841–843
   management cycle and, 884(fig.), 884–885
   performance evaluation and, 903
   prime cost and conversion cost and, 843, 843(fig.)

shifting patterns of, 841
Product costing systems, 882–906, **885,** 885–887
  hybrid, 887
  job order, *see* Job order costing systems
  process, *see* Process costing systems
Product flows, process costing system and, 894–896, 895(fig.)
Production, time required for, 890
Production budget, **1012,** 1012–1013, 1013(exh.)
Production method, 489, 489–490
Product-level activities, 935
Product quality, in just-in-time operating philosophy, 940
Product unit cost, 841, 841(table), 841–843
Product warranty liability, 536–537
Professional ethics, 25, 25–26
Profit, 90, 975
  economic, 768
  ethics and, 1069
  gross, 175–176
  see also Cost-volume-profit (CVP) analysis
  see also Net income
Profitability, 5, 5–6, **231**
  desirable level of, 235
  evaluation of, 231–237, 766, 768, 769(exh.)
  in fast-food industry, 978
  measurement of, 90–91
  of segments, incremental analysis for decisions about, 1137–1140, 1139(exh.)
Profitability management, 170, 170–171, 171(exh.)
Profit centers, 1098, 1099(table)
  evaluating performance using flexible budgeting, 1101–1103, 1102(exh.)
Profit margin, 232, 768, 769(exh.), **1104**
Pro forma statements, 756, **1008**
Promissory notes, 420
  accounting entries for, 422–423
  computations for, 420–422
  dishonored, 423
Property, plant, and equipment, 222, 222–223
  see also Plant assets
Property taxes, 536
Proprietorship, *see* Owner's equity
Public companies, 257
Pull-through production, 939
Purchase(s)
  of assets by incurring liabilities, 17
  of assets with cash, 16

control of, 371–373(fig.), 374–375
foreign, 1176
group, 487
of interest from partners, 568
of materials, 844
net, 181
net cost of, 181
under perpetual inventory system, 178–179
of treasury stock, 610
Purchase order, 373(fig.), **374,** 844
Purchase request, 844
Purchase requisition, 373(fig.), **374**
Purchases account, 183
  under periodic inventory system, 190–191
Purchases discounts, 191, 191–192
Purchases Discounts account, 192
Purchases journal, 335, 335–338, 336(exh.), 337(exh.)
Purchases Returns and Allowances account, 184
  under periodic inventory system, 183
Push-through method, 939
PVA (process value analysis), 933–934

Qualitative characteristics, 214–216, **215,** 215(fig.)
Quality
  costs of, 805
  in just-in-time operating philosophy, 940
  see also Continuous improvement
Quality of earnings, 630, 630–635
  accounting method and estimate choices and, 631–633
  corporate income statement and, 630–631, 631(exh.)
  effect on cash flows and performance measures, 634–635
  gains and losses and, 633
  nonoperating items and, 633–634
  reasons to study, 630
  write-downs and restructurings and, 633
Queue time, 941
QuickBooks, 326
Quick ratio, 402, 766, 767(exh.)

Ratio analysis, 765, 765–772
  of cash flow adequacy, 770, 771(exh.)
  of cash-generating efficiency, 714–715
  of liquidity, 766, 766f, 767(exh.)
  of long-term solvency, 768, 769(exh.), 770

of market strength, 770, 771(exh.), 772
of profitability, 231–237, 766, 768, 769(exh.)
Real accounts, 130
Realizable value, 458
Real-time posting, 328
Receivable turnover, 405, 406, **766,** 767(exh.)
Receiving report, 373(fig.), **374,** 844
Recognition, 46, 46–47, 56
  of expenses, 93
  of liabilities, 528
  of revenues, 93
Recognition point, 46
Records, internal control and, 367
Recourse, factoring and, 407
Redemption price, 606, 688
Registered bonds, 673, 673–674
Regression analysis, 975
Regulatory agencies, as users of accounting information, 10
Relevance, 215
Relevant range, 970
Reliability, 216
Report(s)
  activity-based costing, 929
  of CPAs, in annual report, 261–263, 262(fig.)
  fraudulent, 219–220
  of independent CPAs, 23–24
  objectives of, 214
  presentation of, 66
  process cost, FIFO method for preparing, 899, 900(exh.), 901–903
  see also Financial statement(s); *specific financial statements*
Reporting currency, 1177
Reporting stage of management cycle
  activity-based cost information and, 928
  balanced scorecard and, 1095, 1095(fig.)
  budgeting and, 1008
  cost behavior and, 966–967
  cost information and, 837
  management accounting and, 799–800, 800(exh.)
  product cost information and, 885
  short-run decision analysis and, 1132
  standard costs and, 1051
Report of management's responsibilities, in annual report, 261
Research and development costs, 500–501
Reserve(s)

cash, 405
  international business and, 644
Reserve for Bad Debts account, 415
Residual equity, 15, 602
Residual income (RI), 1104, 1104–1105, 1106(exh.)
Residual value, 488
  in capital investment analysis, 1145
Responsibility accounting, 1097, 1097–1108
  responsibility centers and, 1097–1098
    see also Cost centers; Investment centers; Profit centers; Revenue centers
Responsibility centers, 1097, 1097–1098
  see also Cost centers; Investment centers; Profit centers; Revenue centers
Restatement, of foreign subsidiary financial statements, 1177–1178
Restriction on retained earnings, 644
Restructurings, 633
  Retail businesses, cost reporting and inventory accounting in, 849–850, 850(fig.)
Retail method, 459, 459–460, 460(table)
Retained earnings, 642, 644
  restrictions on, 644
  statement of cash flows and, 726
Retained Earnings account, 224, 611
Retirement
  of bonds, 688–689
  of treasury stock, 611–612
Return on assets, 232, 232–234, 233(fig.), 234(fig.), 768, 769(exh.)
Return on equity, 235, 235–236, 236(fig.), 599, 599–600, 768, 769(exh.)
Return on investment (ROI), 1103, 1103(exh.), 1103–1104, 1105(fig.)
Revenue(s), 16, 17, 90
  accrued, 103(fig.), 103–104
  controllable, 1098
  deferred, 101–102, 102(fig.)
  other, 226
  unearned, 102, 535
Revenue centers, 1098, 1099(table)
Revenue expenditures, 485
Revenue recognition, 93
Reversing entries, 140, 140–141
Reviewing stage of management cycle

activity-based cost information and, 928
balanced scorecard and, 1094–1095
budgeting and, 1008
cost behavior and, 966–967
cost information and, 837
management accounting and, 799
product cost information and, 885
short-run decision analysis and, 1131–1132
standard costs and, 1050–1051
RI (residual income), 1104–1105, 1106(exh.)
Risk assessment, 366, 753
Risk Management Association, 757
Robert Morris Associates, 757
ROI (return on investment), 1103(exh.), 1103–1104, 1105(fig.)
Rolling forecasts, 1008
Rule-of-thumb measures, for financial statement analysis, 754

Salaries, 532
  of partners, 564–567, 567(exh.)
Sales, 174
  of bonds between interest dates, 685–686, 687(fig.)
  cash flows to, 715, 770, 771(exh.)
  collecting on, 415
  cost of, 174–175
  foreign, 1175
  gross, 174
  of interest in partnership, 571
  net, 174
  of partnership assets, 573–577, 574(exh.), 575(exh.)
  under perpetual inventory system, 179–181
  of plant assets, 492–494
  terms of, 176–178
  of treasury stock, 610–611
Sales account
  job order costing system and, 891
  under periodic inventory system, 191
Sales budget, 1011, 1011–1012, 1013(exh.)
Sales discounts, 177, 191
Sales Discounts account, 191
Sales forecasts, 1012
Sales invoice, 846
Sales journal, 333, 333–335, 333–335(exh.)
Sales mix, 979, 979(fig.)
Sales mix decisions, 1140
  incremental analysis for, 1140–1141, 1141(exh.)
Sales returns, 180

Sales Returns and Allowances account, 174, 180
  under periodic inventory system, 180–181, 185, 190–191
Sales taxes payable, 531–532
Salvage value, 488
Sarbanes-Oxley Act, 219–220, 753, 812
Scatter diagrams, 973, 973–974, 974(fig.)
Scope section, of auditors' report, 262, 262(fig.)
S corporations, 559
Seasonal cycle, managing cash needs during, 404(fig.), 404–405
Secured bonds, 673
Securities and Exchange Commission (SEC), 24
  on accrual accounting, 94
  on cost-benefit convention, 218–219
  deceptive use of accounting principles and, 93
  Edgar and, 329
  Form 10-K of, 257
  on full disclosure, 218
  materiality and, 217
  reports filed with, 757, 799, 812
  stock registration with, 257
  as user of accounting information, 10
Securitization, 407, 407–408
Segment(s), 638
  decision to drop, 1138
Segment margins, 1138
Segment probability decisions, incremental analysis for, 1137–1140, 1139(exh.)
Seiberling, Frank, 711
Selling and administrative activities, activity-based costing for, 937–938, 938(exh.)
Selling and administrative expense budget, 1017, 1017(exh.)
Sell or process-further decisions, 1142
  incremental analysis for, 1142–1143, 1143(exh.)
Separate entity, 12
Separation of duties, 368
Servers, 326
Service businesses, 168
  activity-based management in, 930–931, 931(fig.)
  cost allocation in, 860–861
  cost reporting in, 849, 850(fig.)
  cost-volume-profit analysis for, 984–985
  job order costing in, 892–894, 893(fig.)

Subject Index

nonfinancial data in, 810, 811(exh.)
value-adding and nonvalue-adding activities in, 932, 933(table)
Share buybacks, 611
Shares of stock, 594
Shipping documents, 846
Shoplifting, 173
Short-run decision(s), incremental analysis for, *see* Incremental analysis
Short-run decision analysis, 1130, 1130–1132, 1131
Short-term financial assets, 402, 402–427
  accounts receivable and, *see* Accounts receivable
  cash and cash equivalents and, 408–409
  credit policies and, 405–406, 406(fig.), 407(fig.)
  financing receivables and, 407–408
  investments as, 409–412
  managing cash needs during seasonal cycles and, 404(fig.), 404–405
  notes receivable, *see* Promissory notes
Short-term investments, 409, 409–512
  available-for-sale securities, 412
  dividend and interest income and, 412
  held-to-maturity securities, 410
  trading securities, 410–412
Significant influence, 1180–1181
Simple capital structure, 641
Simple interest, 1146, 1187
Single-step form (of income statement), 117(exh.), **227,** 227–228
Social security tax, 534
Software costs, 501
Sole proprietorships, 13, 13(table), 14(fig.), 223
Source documents, 54, 326, 328
Special order decisions, 1136
  incremental analysis for, 1136–1137, 1137(exh.)
Special-purpose entities (SPEs), 559
Special-purpose journals, 330, 330–343
  cash payments journal, 34(fig.)(exh.), 340, 342–343
  cash receipts journal, 338, 339(exh.), 340
  flexibility of, 343
  purchases journal, 335–338, 336(exh.), 337(exh.)

sales journal, 333–335, 333–335(exh.)
transactions not recorded in, 343, 343(exh.)
Specific identification method, 448
SPEs (special-purpose entities), 559
Split-off point, 1142
Spoilage, 173
Spreadsheets, 325, 325–326
Stakeholders, 1093
Standard cost(s), 1050, 1050–1051
  computing, 1052–1054
  management cycle and, 1050–1051, 1051(fig.)
  total standard unit cost, 1053–1054
Standard costing, 842, 842–843, **1050,** 1050–1052
  relevance in today's business environment, 1051–1052
  see also Variance analysis
Standard direct labor cost, 1052, 1052–1053
Standard direct materials cost, 1052
Standard fixed overhead rate, 1053
Standard manufacturing overhead cost, 1053
Standard & Poor's, 757
Standard variable overhead rate, 1053
Start-up and organization costs, 598
Stated ratios, 562–563, 564–567, 567(exh.)
Stated value, 607
Statement of cash flows, 21(exh.), **22,** 22–23, 708–729, **711**
  in annual report, 259–260
  cash-generating efficiency and, 714–715
  classification of cash flows and, 712–714, 713(fig.)
  financing activities and, 725–727
  format of, 714
  free cash flow and, 715–717
  international use of, 714
  investing activities and, 722–725
  operating activities and, 717–722, 718–720(exh.), 719(fig.)
  purposes of, 712
  uses of, 712
Statement of changes in stockholders' equity, *see* Statement of stockholders' equity
Statement of cost of goods manufactured, 847, 847–849, 848(exh.)
Statement of earnings, in annual report, 259

Statement of owner's equity, 21(exh.), **22**
Statement of stockholders' equity, **642,** 643(exh.), 644
  in annual report, 260
Statements of Financial Accounting Standards, 24
State unemployment insurance tax, 534
Stock
  authorized, 597
  book value of, 648–649
  common, *see* Common stock
  earnings per share and, 640–642
  ex-dividend, 603
  Initial public offerings of, 597–598
  issued, 602
  long-term investments in, 1180–1185, 1181(table)
  outstanding, 602
  par value, 597
  preferred, *see* Preferred stock
  share buybacks and, 611
  shares of, 594
  treasury, *see* Treasury stock
Stock certificates, 597
Stock dividends, 644, 644–647
Stock Dividends Declared account, 646
Stockholders, 7, 594
Stockholders' equity, components of, 601–602, 602(fig.)
Stock issuance, 606–609
  for noncash assets, 608–609
  of no-par stock, 608
  of par value stock, 607–608
Stock markets, 7
  European, 601
Stock option plans, 600, 601
Stock splits, 647, 647–648
Storage time, 941
Straight-line method, 489, 679
  for amortization of bond discount, 679–680
  for amortization of bond premium, 683
  for depreciation, 489
Strategic objectives, 797
Strategic planning, 1004
Subscriber lists, 500
Subsidiaries, 1185
Subsidiary ledgers, 332
Successful efforts method, 497
Summary of Significant Accounting Policies, 46
  in annual report, 260
Sunk costs, 1132, 1132–1133
Supplementary information notes, in annual report, 263

Supply chain (network), **798,** 798–799, **929,** 929–930, 930(fig.)
Supply-chain management, 329, 446
Support services, 800
  in value chain analysis, 801–802

T accounts, 51–52, **52**
Tangible assets, 482(fig.)
  see also Plant assets
Targets, linking of goals to, 1108
Taxable income, 635
Tax authorities, as users of accounting information, 10
Technology, 499(table)
  airline industry pricing and, 973
  bar codes and, 172
  challenges faced by businesses and, 329
  check processing and, 1133
  computer networks and, 326
  credit versus debit cards and, 170
  customer numbers and, 330
  customer service and, 331
  ecommerce and, 104, 329
  electronic work sheets and, 146
  flexible budget and, 1055
  interest and amortization tables and, 684
  internal control and, 370
  Internet retailing, 177
  inventory turnover and, 444
  LIFO inventory valuation and, 452
  product costs and, 841
  rolling forecasts and, 1008
  simplicity and, 1098
  time savings and, 330
  see also Computerized accounting systems; Internet
Telecommunications industry, cash flows in, 716
Television talent, cost of, 860
Temporary accounts, 130
Terms of sale, 176–178
Theft, of inventory, 173
Theoretical capacity, 968
Theory of constraints (TOC), 806
Throughput time, 941
Time
  for check processing, 1133
  in new manufacturing environment, 941
Time and motion studies, 973
Time cards, 844
Time periods, for compounding interest, 1192–1193
Time value of money, 1146, 1146–1149, 1187–1197

  accounting applications of, 1193–1197
  future value and, 1188(table), 1188–1189, 1190(table)
  interest and, 1146–1147, 1187–1188
  present value and, 1147–1149, 1189–1192, 1191(table), 1192(table)
  time periods and, 1192–1193
TOC (theory of constraints), 806
Total direct labor cost variance, 1060, 1060–1061, 1062(fig.)
Total direct materials cost variance, 1058
Total fixed overhead variance, 1066
Total manufacturing costs, 847
Total manufacturing overhead variance, 1064
Total quality management (TQM), 805
Total variable overhead variance, 1064, 1064–1065, 1065(fig.)
TQM (total quality management), 805
Trackballs, 326
Trade credit, 413
Trade discounts, 176
Trademarks, 499(table)
Trading on the equity, 670
Trading securities, 410, 410–412
Treasury stock, 600, 609, 609–612
  purchase of, 610
  retirement of, 611–612
  sale of, 610–611
  statement of cash flows and, 726–727, 727(exh.)
Trend analysis, 760, 760–762, 762(exh.), 762(fig.)
Trial balance, 61, 61(exh.), 61–63, 62(table)
  adjusted, 104–105, 105(exh.), 106(exh.), 185
  post-closing, 139

Unamortized Bond Discount account, 676
Uncollectible accounts, 413, 413–420
  allowance method for, 414–415
  direct charge-off method for, 413–414
  estimating expense of, 415–419
  recovery of written off accounts receivable and, 419–420
  writing off, 419
Uncollectible Accounts Expense account, 414
Underapplied overhead costs, 852
Understandability, 215

Underwriters, 597
Unearned revenues, 102, 535
Unemployment insurance tax, 534
Uniform Partnership Act, 558
Unit-level activities, 934
Universal product codes (UPCs), 172
Unlimited liability, 558, 558–559
Unrealized Loss on Long-Term Investments account, 1182, 1183–1184
Unsecured bonds, 673
UPCs (universal product codes), 172
Useful life, estimated, 488–489
Usefulness, 215

Vacation pay liability, 537
Valuation, 47, 47–48, 56
  of assets, 1194
  of bonds, using present value, 677–678
  of liabilities, 528
Value, 47
  carrying (book), 100, 480, 648–649, 1144
  disposal, in capital investment analysis, 1145
  face, bonds issued at, 674–675
  future, *see* Future value
  market, 458
  maturity, of promissory notes, 422
  par, 597
  present, *see* Present value
  realizable, 458
  residual (disposal; salvage), 488
  residual, in capital investment analysis, 1145
  stated, 607
  time, of money, *see* Time value of money
Value added, economic, 1106(exh.), 1106–1107, 1107(fig.)
Value-adding activities, 805, 932
  process value analysis and, 933–934
  in service organizations, 932, 933(table)
Value-adding costs, 839
Value-based management (VBM), 933
Value chain, 800
  Internet support of, 802
Value chain(s), 929, 929–930
Value chain analysis, 800–804, 801(fig.)
  advantages of, 802
  management's support of, 802–804, 803(exh.)
  primary processes and support services and, 801–802

Values, core, 966
Variable budgets, in variance analysis, 1054–1056, 1055–1057(exh.)
Variable cost(s), 839, 968, 968–970, 969(fig.)
  linear relationships and relevant range and, 969–970, 970(fig.), 971(fig.)
  operating capacity and, 968–969
Variable costing, 1101
  profit center performance evaluation using, 1101–1103, 1102(exh.)
Variable overhead efficiency variance, 1065, 1065–1066
Variable overhead spending variance, 1065
Variance(s), 1050
Variance analysis, 1054, 1054–1069
  controlling costs using, 1056, 1057(fig.), 1058
  direct labor variances and, 1060–1062
  direct materials variances and, 1058–1060
  evaluating managers' performances using cost variances and, 1069, 1070(exh.)
  flexible budgets in, 1054–1056, 1055–1057(exh.)
  manufacturing overhead variances and, 1062–1069
VBM (value-based management), 933
Vendor's invoice, 844

Vertical analysis, 762, 763(exh.), 763(fig.), 764(exh.), 764(fig.), 765
Voucher(s), 380, 380–381, 381(fig.)
  petty cash, 378–379, 379(exh.)
Voucher checks, 381
Voucher registers, 381, 381–382, 382(exh.)
Vouchers Payable account, 385, 542
Voucher systems, 380, 380–385
  components of, 380–383
  operations of, 383–385, 384(exh.), 385(exh.)

Wages, 532
Wages Payable account, 18–19
Wall Street Journal, 757
Whistle-blowing, 634
Windows compatibility, 326
Withdrawal, of partner, 570–572, 571(fig.)
Withdrawals, owner's, 15, 19
Withdrawals account, 50
  closing, 130, 136, 136(exh.)
  distribution of partnership income/losses and, 563
  partners' equity and, 561
  under periodic inventory system, 191
Work cells, 940
Work environment, in just-in-time operating philosophy, 941
Work force, in just-in-time operating philosophy, 940
Working capital, 230, 230–231
Working papers, 141

Work in Process Inventory account, 844, 846, 847, 850–851, 852
  backflush costing and, 942–943
  job order costing system and, 890
  process costing system and, 896–897, 901, 902–903
Work sheet, 141, 141–146
  adjusting entries on, 144, 144(exh.)
  closing entries on, 145
  electronic, 146
  financial statement preparation using, 145(exh.), 145–146, 146(exh.)
  for merchandising business using periodic inventory system, 188–191, 189(exh.)
  for merchandising business using perpetual inventory system, 185–187, 186(exh.)
  preparing, 142–143
Write-downs, 633
Write-offs, 633
Writing off uncollectible accounts, 419–420
Wurman, Richard Saul, 1098

XBRL (Extensible Business Reporting Language), 329

Years
  base, 759
  fiscal, 90
  partial, depreciation for, 502–503
Yield, cash flow, 715, 770, 771(exh.)

Zero coupon bonds, 679

Print and Electronic Supplements for Instructors

NEW! Eduspace® Powered by Blackboard™ Houghton Mifflin's homework system, Eduspace, enables students to complete text assignments online. After students complete each text problem, they are asked a series of questions to test their understanding of the problem. They submit their answers online and receive immediate feedback on right and wrong answers. Assignments are automatically graded and entered into a grade book, saving instructors a great deal of time. Eduspace also offers a wealth of other instructor resources, including HMTesting (the computerized test bank), brand new PowerPoint slide presentations, and a complete course manual.

Instructor's Solutions Manual. Contains answers to all text exercises, problems, and cases.

Electronic Solutions. Contains solutions from the printed Instructor's Solutions Manual, allows instructors to manipulate the numbers in the classroom or to distribute solutions electronically.

Solutions Transparencies. More than 1,200 transparencies provide solutions for every exercise, problem, and case in the text, including the appendixes.

Course Manual. Available on the HMClassPrep with HMTesting Instructor CD-ROM. Filled with practical advice and teaching tips, it contains a planning matrix and time/difficulty chart for every chapter and chapter-by-chapter instructional materials and review quizzes.

NEW! PowerPoint Slides. A brand new set of PowerPoint slides is available on the HMClassPrep with HMTesting Instructor CD-ROM. The slides can also be downloaded from the Needles Accounting Resource Center Web Site at http://accounting.college.hmco.com/instructors. The new slides are concise, contain lots of examples of transactions, and explain the accounting process in clear, easy-to-follow steps.

Video Cases. The following video cases are available on the HMClassPrep with HMTesting Instructor CD-ROM: Intel (Chapter 1), **NEW!** Claire's Stores (Chapter 5), **NEW!** J. C. Penney (Chapter 10), Fermi National Accelerator Laboratory (Chapter 11), Goodyear Tire & Rubber Company (Chapter 17), Enterprise Rent-A-Car, and Harley-Davidson, Inc. A corresponding text case relates each video to the themes of the chapter.

Test Bank with Achievement Test Masters and Answers. This printed test bank provides more than 3,000 true-false, multiple choice, short essay, and critical-thinking questions, as well as exercises and problems.

NEW! HMClassPrep with HMTesting CD-ROM. This CD contains the computerized version of the Test Bank. It allows instructors to select, edit, and add questions, or generate randomly selected questions to produce a test master for easy duplication. The 2005 edition allows tests to be compiled from learning objectives or key words from the text. Online Testing and Gradebook functions allow instructors to administer tests via their local area network or the Web, set up classes, record grades from tests or assignments, analyze grades, and compile class and individual statistics. The instructor CD also contains the Solutions Manual, the complete Course Manual, PowerPoint slides, Video Cases, check figures for end-of-chapter problems, and Web links to the Needles Accounting Resource Center Web Site.

Needles Accounting Resource Center Instructor Web Site (http://accounting.college.hmco.com/instructors). Includes downloadable PowerPoint slides of text presentation materials and text illustrations, electronic solutions, PowerPoint slides, check figures for the end-of-chapter problems, and links to other valuable text resources. In addition, the Instructor Web site includes sample syllabi from other first-year accounting faculty and the *Accounting Instructors' Report* newsletter, which covers a wide range of contemporary teaching issues.

Blackboard Course Cartridges. These cartridges provide flexible, efficient, and creative ways to present learning materials and manage distance learning courses. Specific resources include chapter overviews, check figures for in-text problems, practice quizzes, PowerPoint slides, and Excel Solutions. In addition to course management benefits, instructors may make use of an electronic grade book, receive papers from students enrolled in the course via the Internet, and track student use of the communication and collaboration functions.

WebCT e-Packs. These e-packs provide instructors with a flexible, Internet-based education platform. The WebCT e-packs come with a full array of features to enrich the online learning experience, including online quizzes, bulletin board, chat tool, whiteboard, and other functionality. The e-packs contain text-specific resources, including chapter overviews, check figures, practice quizzes, PowerPoint slides, and Excel Solutions.

Is American Airlines' income from operations a better measure than its "bottom-line" numbers?

Financial Highlights

Earnings (Loss) per Share: Basic	2002	2001	2000
Income (loss) from continuing operations	$(16.22)	$(11.43)	$ 5.20
Discontinued operations	—	—	0.30
Extraordinary loss	—	—	(0.07)
Cumulative effect of accounting change	(6.35)	—	—
Net earnings (loss)	$(22.57)	$(11.43)	$ 5.43

PERFORMANCE MEASUREMENT: QUALITY OF EARNINGS ISSUES

LO1 Prepare a corporate income statement and identify the issues related to evaluating the quality of earnings.

RELATED TEXT ASSIGNMENTS
Q: 1, 2, 3, 4, 5
SE: 1, 2
E: 1, 2, 3
P: 1, 2, 3, 6
SD: 1, 2, 4
FRA: 1, 4, 6, 7

The Financial Accounting Standards Board (FASB) has taken the position that income for a period should be all-inclusive, comprehensive income, which is different from net income.[2] **Comprehensive income** is the change in a company's equity from sources other than owners during a period; it includes net income, changes in unrealized investment gains and losses, and other items affecting equity. Companies are reporting comprehensive income and its components as a separate financial statement or as a part of another financial statement.

In a recent survey of 600 large companies, 519 reported comprehensive income. Of these, 81 percent reported comprehensive income on the statement of stockholders' equity, 13 percent reported it on a separate statement, and only 6 percent reported it on the income statement.[3] In the illustration of comprehensive income later in this chapter, we follow the most common practice and show it as a part of the statement of stockholders' equity.

THE CORPORATE INCOME STATEMENT

www.aimr.org

Net income is the most commonly used measure of earnings because current and expected earnings are important factors in evaluating a company's performance and analyzing its prospects. In fact, a survey of 2,000 members of the Association for Investment Management and Research indicated that the two most important economic measures in evaluating common stocks were expected changes in earnings per share and expected return on equity;[4] net income is a key component of both measures. The corporate income statement is the statement that shows how a company's net income is derived.

KEY POINT: It is important to know which items included in earnings are recurring and which are one-time items. Income from continuing operations before nonoperating items gives a clear signal about future results. In assessing the company's future earnings potential, nonoperating items are excluded because they are not expected to continue.

Net income or loss for a period includes all revenues, expenses, gains, and losses over the period, with the exception of prior period adjustments. Thus, the corporate income statement may consist of several components, as illustrated in Exhibit 1. When a company has both continuing and discontinued operations, the operating income section is called **income from continuing operations**. Income from continuing operations before income taxes is affected by choices of accounting methods and estimates and may contain such items as gains and losses, write-downs, and restructurings. The income taxes expense section of the statement is also subject to special accounting rules. The lower part of the statement may contain such nonoperating items as discontinued operations, extraordinary gains and losses, and effects of accounting changes. Another item that may appear in this section is the write-off of goodwill when its value has been impaired. Finally, earnings per share information appears at the bottom of the statement. We discuss these components of the corporate income statement in more detail later in the chapter.

Because of the importance of net income, or the "bottom line," in measuring a company's prospects, there is significant interest in evaluating the quality of the net income figure, or the **quality of earnings**. The quality of a company's earnings refers to the substance of earnings and their sustainability into future accounting periods. For example, if earnings increase because of a gain on the sale of an asset, analysts may not view this portion of earnings as sustainable. The quality of earnings may be affected by the accounting methods and estimates the company's management chooses and by the gains and losses, the write-downs and restructurings, and the nature of the nonoperating items reported on the income statement. Since management has choices in the content and positioning of these income-

FOCUS ON BUSINESS PRACTICE

Why Do Investors Study Quality of Earnings?
Analysts for Twentieth Century Mutual Funds, a major investment company, now merged with American Century Services Corp. <www.americancentury.com>, make adjustments to a company's reported financial performance to create a more accurate picture of the company's ongoing operations. Assume a paper company reports earnings of $1.30 per share, which makes year-to-year comparisons unusually strong. Upon further investigation, however, it is found that the per share number includes a one-time gain on the sale of assets of $.25 per share. Twentieth Century would list the company in its data base as earning only $1.05 per share. "These kinds of adjustments help assure long-term decisions aren't based on one-time events."[5]

EXHIBIT 1
Corporate Income Statement

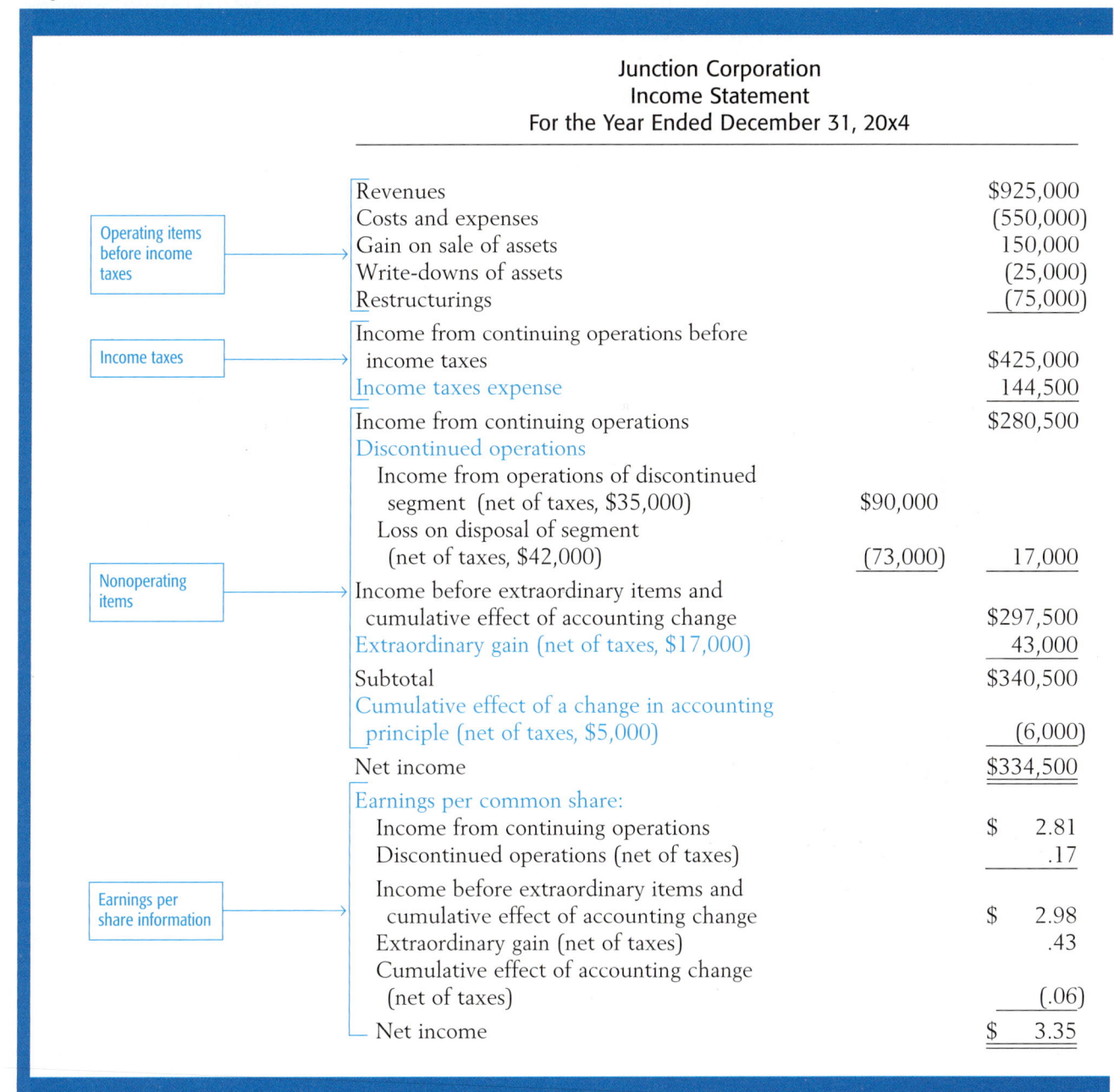

<table>
<tr><td colspan="4" align="center">Junction Corporation
Income Statement
For the Year Ended December 31, 20x4</td></tr>
<tr><td>Operating items before income taxes →</td><td>Revenues
Costs and expenses
Gain on sale of assets
Write-downs of assets
Restructurings</td><td></td><td>$925,000
(550,000)
150,000
(25,000)
(75,000)</td></tr>
<tr><td>Income taxes →</td><td>Income from continuing operations before
  income taxes
Income taxes expense</td><td></td><td>$425,000
144,500</td></tr>
<tr><td rowspan="3">Nonoperating items →</td><td>Income from continuing operations
Discontinued operations
  Income from operations of discontinued
    segment (net of taxes, $35,000)
  Loss on disposal of segment
    (net of taxes, $42,000)</td><td>

$90,000

(73,000)</td><td>$280,500

17,000</td></tr>
<tr><td>Income before extraordinary items and
  cumulative effect of accounting change
Extraordinary gain (net of taxes, $17,000)
Subtotal
Cumulative effect of a change in accounting
  principle (net of taxes, $5,000)
Net income</td><td></td><td>$297,500
43,000
$340,500

(6,000)
$334,500</td></tr>
<tr><td></td><td></td><td></td></tr>
<tr><td>Earnings per share information →</td><td>Earnings per common share:
  Income from continuing operations
  Discontinued operations (net of taxes)
  Income before extraordinary items and
    cumulative effect of accounting change
  Extraordinary gain (net of taxes)
  Cumulative effect of accounting change
    (net of taxes)
  Net income</td><td></td><td>$ 2.81
.17

$ 2.98
.43

(.06)
$ 3.35</td></tr>
</table>

ENRICHMENT NOTE: Management is responsible for the content of financial statements. Financial statements report on the performance of management. When a group is responsible for reporting on its own activity, usually the best or most favorable position will be reported.

statement categories, there is the potential for managing earnings to achieve specific income targets. Thus, users of income statements must understand these factors and take them into consideration when evaluating a company's performance.

CHOICE OF ACCOUNTING METHODS AND ESTIMATES

Choices of accounting methods and estimates affect a firm's operating income. To assure proper matching of revenues and expenses, accounting requires cost allocations and estimates of data that will not be known with certainty until some future date. For example, accountants estimate the useful life of assets when they are acquired. However, technological obsolescence could shorten the expected useful life, and excellent maintenance and repairs could lengthen it. The actual useful life will not be known with certainty until some future date. The estimate affects both current and future operating income.

Because there is considerable latitude in assumptions underlying estimates, management and other financial statement users must be aware of the impact of accounting estimates on reported operating income. Estimates include percentage of uncollectible accounts receivable, sales returns, useful life, residual or salvage value, total units of production, total recoverable units of natural resources, amortization period, expected warranty claims, and expected environmental cleanup costs.

These estimates are not equally important to all firms. Their relative importance depends on the industry in which a firm operates. For example, the estimate of uncollectible receivables for a credit card firm, such as American Express, or a financial services firm, such as Bank of America, can have a material impact on earnings, but the estimate of useful life may be less important because depreciable assets represent only a small percentage of total assets. Toys "R" Us has very few receivables, but it has substantial investment in depreciable assets; thus, estimates of useful life and residual value are much more important than the estimate of uncollectible accounts receivable.

www.americanexpress.com
www.bankofamerica.com

www.tru.com

The choice of methods also affects a firm's operating income. Generally accepted accounting methods include uncollectible receivable methods (percentage of net sales and aging of accounts receivable), inventory methods (last-in, first-out [LIFO]; first-in, first-out [FIFO]; and average-cost), depreciation methods (accelerated, production, and straight-line), and revenue recognition methods. These methods are designed to match revenues and expenses. Costs are allocated based on a determination of the benefits to the current period (expenses) versus the benefits to future periods (assets). The expenses are estimates, and the period or periods benefited cannot be demonstrated conclusively. The estimates are also subjective, because in practice it is hard to justify one method of estimation over another.

KEY POINT: Two companies in the same industry may have comparable earnings quantity but not comparable earnings quality. To assess the quality of reported earnings, one must know the methods and estimates used to compute income. GAAP allow several methods and estimates, all yielding different results.

For these reasons, management, the accountant, and the financial statement user need to understand the possible effects of different accounting procedures on net income and financial position. Some methods and estimates are more conservative than others because they tend to produce a lower net income in the current period. For example, suppose that two companies have similar operations, but one uses FIFO for inventory costing and straight-line (SL) for computing depreciation, whereas the other uses LIFO for inventory costing and double-declining-balance (DDB) for computing depreciation. The income statements of the two companies might appear as follows:

	FIFO and SL	LIFO and DDB
Net sales	$875,000	$875,000
Goods available for sale	$400,000	$400,000
Less ending inventory	60,000	50,000
Cost of goods sold	$340,000	$350,000
Gross margin	$535,000	$525,000
Less depreciation expense	$ 40,000	$ 80,000
Less other expenses	170,000	170,000
Total operating expenses	$210,000	$250,000
Income from continuing operations before income taxes	$325,000	$275,000

The income from continuing operations before income taxes (operating income) for the firm using LIFO and DDB is lower because in periods of rising prices, the LIFO inventory costing method produces a higher cost of goods sold, and, in the early years of an asset's useful life, accelerated depreciation yields a higher depreciation expense. The result is lower operating income. However, future operating income is expected to be higher. It is also important that the choice of accounting method does not affect cash flows except for possible differences in income taxes caused by the use of one method instead of another.

The $50,000 difference in operating income stems only from the differences in accounting methods. Differences in the estimated lives and residual values of the plant assets could lead to an even greater variation. In practice, of course, differences in net income occur for many reasons, but the user must be aware of the discrepancies that can occur as a result of the accounting methods chosen by management. In general, an accounting method or estimate that results in lower current earnings is considered to produce a better quality of operating income.

The existence of such alternatives could cause problems in the interpretation of financial statements were it not for the conventions of full disclosure and consistency. As noted in an earlier chapter, full disclosure requires that management explain the significant accounting policies used in preparing the financial statements in a note to the statements. Consistency requires that the same accounting procedures be followed from year to year. If a change in procedure is made, the nature of the change and its monetary effect must be explained in a note.

GAINS AND LOSSES

When a company sells or otherwise disposes of operating assets or marketable securities, a gain or loss generally results. These gains or losses appear in the operating portion of the income statement, but they usually represent one-time events. They are not sustainable, ongoing operations, and management often has some choice as to their timing. Thus, from an analyst's point of view, they should be ignored when considering operating income.

WRITE-DOWNS AND RESTRUCTURINGS

Management has considerable latitude in deciding when an asset is no longer of value to the company. If the value of an asset is impaired, management may decide to record a write-down. A **write-down**, also referred to as a *write-off*, is the recording of a decrease in the value of an asset below the carrying value on the balance sheet and the reduction of income in the current period by the amount of the decrease. If operations have changed, management may decide to record a restructuring. A **restructuring** is the estimated cost associated with a change in a company's operations, usually involving the closing of facilities and the laying off of personnel. Both write-downs and restructurings reduce current operating income and boost future income by shifting future costs to the current accounting period.

Write-downs and restructurings are important to consider because they often are an indication of bad management decisions in the past, such as paying too much for the assets of another company or making operational changes that do not work out. Companies sometimes take all possible losses in the current year so that future years will be "clean" of these costs. Such "big baths," as they are called, commonly occur when a company is having a bad year. They also often occur in years when there is a change in management. The new management takes a "big bath" in the current year so it can show improved results in future years.

Write-downs and restructurings are common. In a recent year, 27 percent of 600 large companies had write-downs, and 26 percent had restructurings. Another 24 percent had write-downs or charges involving intangible assets.[6] As discussed in the chapter on long-term assets, goodwill is subject to an annual impairment test to determine if its current fair value is below cost.

NATURE OF NONOPERATING ITEMS

The nonoperating items that appear on the income statement, such as discontinued operations, extraordinary gains and losses, and effects of accounting changes, can also significantly affect the bottom line, or net income. In fact, in Exhibit 1, earnings

● **STOP AND THINK!**
Is it unethical for new management to take a "big bath" in order to enhance future performance?

It is not unethical as long as new management stays within the accounting rules and properly discloses its actions. An investor or analyst must be aware of these actions and take them into consideration when evaluating the company's performance. ■

Focus on Business Ethics

Whistle-Blowing

External users of financial statements depend on management's honesty and openness in disclosing factual information about a company. In the vast majority of cases, management's reports are reliable, but there are exceptions. Whistle-blowers—employees who step forward to disclose such exceptions and other types of wrongdoing they observe in their companies—run various risks, including losing their jobs, with no assurance that their actions will have any effect. In the recent Enron case, the largest bankruptcy in U.S. history, the whistle-blower was a company accountant who, well before the firm's collapse, informed her CEO and the firm's external auditors of Enron's questionable accounting practices. Although her warnings were ignored then, they made headlines during the SEC and congressional investigations, as well as the criminal prosecutions that followed the collapse.[7]

ENRICHMENT NOTE: Discontinued operations, extraordinary items, and cumulative effects of a change in accounting principle are more likely to occur in large, public corporations. A knowledge of these items is important when analyzing the financial results of such companies. These items do not occur as frequently in small, private corporations.

www.sears.com

per common share for income from continuing operations are $2.81, but net income per share is $3.35 when all the nonoperating items are taken into consideration.

For practical reasons, the calculations of trends and ratios are based on the assumption that net income and other components are comparable from year to year and from company to company. However, in making interpretations, the astute analyst will always look beyond the ratios to the quality of the components. For example, write-downs, restructurings, and nonoperating items, if the charges are large enough, can have a significant effect on a company's return on equity.

A company may boost income by including one-time gains. For example, Sears, Roebuck and Co. used a gain from the change of an accounting principle to bolster its net income by $136 million or by $.35 per share. Without the gain, earnings per share (EPS) would have decreased from $3.12 to $2.92, not increased as Sears reported.[8] The quality of Sears's earnings is, in fact, lower than it might appear on the surface. Unless analysts are prepared to go beyond the "bottom line" in analyzing and interpreting financial reports, they can come to the wrong conclusions.

Effect of Quality of Earnings on Cash Flows and Performance Measures

The reason for considering quality of earnings issues is to assess their effects on cash flows and performance measures. Generally speaking, except for possible income tax effects, none of the gains and losses, asset write-downs, restructurings, and nonoperating items has any effect on cash flows. The cash expenditures for these items were made previously. For this reason, the focus of analysis is on sustainable earnings, which generally have a relationship to future cash flows.

Since management's performance and compensation are often linked to return on assets or return on equity, it is important to understand the nature of both the numerator and denominator of these performance measures. Most commonly, the numerator in these ratios is net income. However, when a company has a complex income statement with items that affect quality of earnings, such as those discussed above, it is important not to take net income at face value. Consider the example of Junction Corporation in Exhibit 1. The reported net income is $334,500, whereas income from continuing operations is $280,500. Even the latter amount is a questionable measure of sustainable earnings because of the gain, write-down, and restructuring, which collectively added $50,000 to income from continuing operations before income taxes. With a tax rate of 34 percent, the sustainable earnings after income taxes are probably close to $247,500 [$280,500 − ($50,000 × .66)].

It also pays to examine how quality of earnings issues affect the denominator of the return on assets and return on equity ratios. If a company has a write-down or restructuring of assets, in addition to a reduction in net income, there is also a reduction in assets and in stockholders' equity, which tends to improve these ratios in both current and future years. This contributes to the motivation to take "big-bath" write-offs in years that are poor anyway so that it will be easier to show improvement in future ratios.

✓ Check out ACE for a Review Quiz at http://accounting.college.hmco.com/students.

INCOME TAXES EXPENSE

LO2 Show the relationships among income taxes expense, deferred income taxes, and net of taxes.

RELATED TEXT ASSIGNMENTS
Q: 6, 7
SE: 3
E: 3, 4, 5
P: 2, 3, 6
SD: 4
FRA: 2

Corporations determine their taxable income (the amount on which taxes are paid) by subtracting allowable business deductions from includable gross income. The federal tax laws determine which business expenses may be deducted and which cannot be deducted from taxable gross income. (Rules for calculating and reporting taxable income in specialized industries, such as banking, insurance, mutual funds, and cooperatives, are highly technical and may vary significantly from the ones we discuss in this chapter.)

Table 1 shows the tax rates that apply to a corporation's taxable income. A corporation with taxable income of $70,000 would have a federal income tax liability of $12,500: $7,500 (the tax on the first $50,000 of taxable income) plus $5,000 (25 percent of the $20,000 earned in excess of $50,000).

Income taxes expense is the expense recognized in the accounting records on an accrual basis that applies to income from continuing operations. This expense may or may not equal the amount of taxes actually paid by the corporation and recorded as income taxes payable in the current period. The amount payable is determined from taxable income, which is measured according to the rules and regulations of the income tax code.

For the sake of convenience, most small businesses keep their accounting records on the same basis as their tax records, so that the income taxes expense on the income statement equals the income taxes liability to be paid to the U.S. Treasury. This practice is acceptable when there is no material difference between the income on an accounting basis and the income on an income tax basis. However, the purpose of accounting is to determine net income in accordance with generally accepted accounting principles, not to determine taxable income and tax liability.

Management has an incentive to use methods that minimize the firm's tax liability, but accountants, who are bound by accrual accounting and the materiality concept, cannot let tax procedures dictate their method of preparing financial statements if the result would be misleading. As a consequence, there can be a material

ENRICHMENT NOTE: Most people think it is illegal to keep accounting records on a different basis from income tax records. However, the Internal Revenue Code and GAAP often do not agree. To work with two conflicting sets of guidelines, the accountant must keep two sets of records.

ENRICHMENT NOTE: The federal income tax is progressive. That is, the rate increases as taxable income increases.

TABLE 1. Tax Rate Schedule for Corporations, 2002

Taxable Income		Tax Liability	
Over	But Not Over		Of the Amount Over
—	$ 50,000	0 + 15%	—
$ 50,000	75,000	$ 7,500 + 25%	$ 50,000
75,000	100,000	13,750 + 34%	75,000
100,000	335,000	22,250 + 39%	100,000
335,000	10,000,000	113,900 + 34%	335,000
10,000,000	15,000,000	3,400,000 + 35%	10,000,000
15,000,000	18,333,333	5,150,000 + 38%	15,000,000
18,333,333	—	6,416,667 + 35%	18,333,333

Note: Tax rates are subject to change by Congress.

difference between accounting income and taxable income, especially in larger businesses. This discrepancy can result from differences in the timing of the recognition of revenues and expenses under the two accounting methods. Some possible variations are shown below.

	Accounting Method	Tax Method
Expense recognition	Accrual or deferral	At time of expenditure
Accounts receivable	Allowance	Direct charge-off
Inventories	Average-cost	FIFO
Depreciation	Straight-line	Modified Accelerated Cost Recovery System

Deferred Income Taxes

KEY POINT: The discrepancy between GAAP-based tax expense and Internal Revenue Code-based tax liability produces the need for the Deferred Income Taxes account.

The accounting method used to accrue income taxes expense on the basis of accounting income whenever there are differences between accounting and taxable income is called **income tax allocation**. The account used to record the difference between the income taxes expense and income taxes payable is called **Deferred Income Taxes**. For example, Junction Corporation shows income taxes expense of $144,500 on its income statement in Exhibit 1, but it has actual income taxes payable to the U.S. Treasury of $92,000. The following entry records the estimated income taxes expense applicable to income from continuing operations using the income tax allocation procedure:

A = L + OE
    +   −
        +

Dec. 31	Income Taxes Expense	144,500	
	Income Taxes Payable		92,000
	Deferred Income Taxes		52,500
	To record estimated current and deferred income taxes		

● **Stop and Think!**
What is an argument against the recording of deferred income taxes?
Because the recording of deferred income taxes depends on future actions of management, which may or may not happen, critics of deferred taxes argue that the income taxes for a particular year should simply be the amount of income taxes paid. Thus, each year is allowed to stand on its own. ■

In other years, it is possible for Income Taxes Payable to exceed Income Taxes Expense, in which case the same entry is made except that Deferred Income Taxes is debited.

The Financial Accounting Standards Board has issued specific rules for recording, measuring, and classifying deferred income taxes.[9] Deferred income taxes are recognized for the estimated future tax effects resulting from temporary differences in the valuation of assets, liabilities, equity, revenues, expenses, gains, and losses for tax and financial reporting purposes. Temporary differences include revenues and expenses or gains and losses that are included in taxable income before or after they are included in financial income. In other words, the recognition point for revenues, expenses, gains, and losses is not the same for tax and financial reporting. For example, advance payments for goods and services, such as magazine subscriptions, are not recognized in financial income until the product is shipped, but for tax purposes they are usually recognized as revenue when cash is received. The result is that taxes paid exceed taxes expense, which creates a deferred income taxes asset (or prepaid taxes).

STUDY NOTE: Deferred Income Taxes is classified as a liability when it has a credit balance and as an asset when it has a debit balance. It is further classified as either current or long-term depending on when it is expected to reverse.

Classification of deferred income taxes as current or noncurrent depends on the classification of the related asset or liability that created the temporary difference. For example, the deferred income taxes asset mentioned above would be classified as current if unearned subscription revenue is classified as a current liability. On the other hand, the temporary difference arising from depreciation is related to a long-term depreciable asset. Therefore, the resulting deferred income taxes would be classified as long-term. However, if a temporary difference is not related to an asset or liability, then it is classified as current or noncurrent based on its expected date of reversal. Temporary differences and the classification of deferred income taxes that results are covered in depth in more advanced courses.

Each year, the balance of the Deferred Income Taxes account is evaluated to determine whether it still accurately represents the expected asset or liability in light of legislated changes in income tax laws and regulations. If changes have occurred, an adjusting entry to bring the account balance into line with current laws is required. For example, a decrease in corporate income tax rates, like the one that occurred in 1987, means that a company with a deferred income taxes liability will pay less in taxes in future years than the amount indicated by the credit balance of its Deferred Income Taxes account. As a result, the company would debit Deferred Income Taxes to reduce the liability and credit Gain from Reduction in Income Tax Rates. This credit increases the reported income on the income statement. If the tax rate increases in future years, a loss would be recorded and the deferred income taxes liability would be increased.

In any given year, the amount a company pays in income taxes is determined by subtracting (or adding, as the case may be) the deferred income taxes for that year, as reported in the notes to the financial statements, from (or to) income taxes expense, which is reported in the financial statements. In subsequent years, the amount of deferred income taxes can vary based on changes in tax laws and rates.

Some understanding of the importance of deferred income taxes to financial reporting can be gained from studying a survey of the financial statements of 600 large companies. About 65 percent reported deferred income taxes with a credit balance in the long-term liability section of the balance sheet.[10]

NET OF TAXES

The phrase **net of taxes**, as used in Exhibit 1, means that the effect of applicable taxes (usually income taxes) has been considered in determining the overall effect of an item on the financial statements. The phrase is used on the corporate income statement when a company has items that must be disclosed in a separate section. Each such item should be reported net of the applicable income taxes to avoid distorting the income taxes expense associated with ongoing operations and the resulting net operating income. For example, assume that a corporation with operating income before income taxes of $120,000 has a total tax expense of $66,000 and that the total income includes a gain of $100,000 on which a tax of $30,000 is due. Also assume that the gain is not part of normal operations and must be disclosed separately on the income statement as an extraordinary item (explained later). This is how the income taxes expense would be reported on the income statement:

Operating income before income taxes	$120,000
Income taxes expense	36,000
Income before extraordinary item	$ 84,000
Extraordinary gain (net of taxes, $30,000)	70,000
Net income	$154,000

If all the income taxes expense were deducted from operating income before income taxes, both the income before extraordinary item and the extraordinary gain would be distorted.

A company follows the same procedure in the case of an extraordinary loss. For example, assume the same facts as before except that the total income taxes expense is only $6,000 because of a $100,000 extraordinary loss. The result is a $30,000 tax savings, shown as follows:

Operating income before income taxes	$120,000
Income taxes expense	36,000
Income before extraordinary item	$ 84,000
Extraordinary loss (net of taxes, $30,000)	(70,000)
Net income	$ 14,000

In Exhibit 1, the total of the income tax items for Junction Corporation is $149,500. That amount is allocated among five statement components, as follows:

Income taxes expense on income from continuing operations	$144,500
Income taxes on income from a discontinued segment	35,000
Income tax savings on the loss on the disposal of the segment	(42,000)
Income taxes on the extraordinary gain	17,000
Income tax savings on the cumulative effect of a change in accounting principle	(5,000)
Total income taxes expense	$149,500

✓ Check out ACE for a Review Quiz at http://accounting.college.hmco.com/students.

NONOPERATING ITEMS

LO3 Describe the disclosure on the income statement of discontinued operations, extraordinary items, and accounting changes.

RELATED TEXT ASSIGNMENTS
Q: 8, 9, 10
E: 3
P: 2, 3, 6
SD: 2, 4
FRA: 4, 6

Nonoperating items are items not related to the company's normal operations. They appear in a separate section of the income statement because they are considered one-time items that will not affect future results. There are three principal kinds of nonoperating items: discontinued operations, extraordinary items, and accounting changes.

DISCONTINUED OPERATIONS

Large companies in the United States usually have many **segments**. A segment may be a separate major line of business or serve a separate class of customer. For example, a company that makes heavy drilling equipment may also have another line of business, such as the manufacture of mobile homes. A large company may discontinue or otherwise dispose of certain segments of its business that do not fit its future plans or are not profitable. **Discontinued operations** are segments of a business that are no longer part of its ongoing operations. Generally accepted accounting principles require that gains and losses from discontinued operations be reported separately on the income statement. Such separation makes it easier to evaluate the ongoing activities of the business. For example, the Financial Highlights in the Decision Point in this chapter show that AMR's discontinued operations are a significant factor in its "bottom-line" earnings per share. The discontinued operations are AMR's Sabre reservation services, one of the steadiest and most profitable parts of the company's business, which it is divesting to the shareholders of the company. For the analyst, this important piece of information means that in the future, the company is going to be more dependent on the volatile airline business.

www.amrcorp.com

🛑 **STOP AND THINK!**
Why is it useful to disclose discontinued operations separately on the income statement?
Users of financial statements want to assess the effects of past performance on the future performance of a company. Separating discontinued operations on the income statement helps accomplish that objective. ∎

In Exhibit 1, the disclosure of discontinued operations has two parts. One part shows that after the decision to discontinue, the income from operations of the disposed segment was $90,000 (net of $35,000 taxes). The other part shows that the loss from the disposal of the segment was $73,000 (net of $42,000 tax savings). Computation of the gains or losses is covered in more advanced accounting courses. We have described the disclosure to give a complete view of the corporate income statement.

EXTRAORDINARY ITEMS

In its *Opinion No. 30*, the Accounting Principles Board defines **extraordinary items** as "events or transactions that are distinguished by their unusual nature *and* by the infrequency of their occurrence."[11] Unusual and infrequent occurrences are explained in the opinion as follows:

> Unusual Nature—the underlying event or transaction should possess a high degree of abnormality and be of a type clearly unrelated to, or only incidentally related to, the ordinary and typical activities of the entity, taking into account the environment in which the entity operates.

KEY POINT: To qualify as extraordinary, an event must be unusual (not in the ordinary course of business) and must not be expected to occur again in the foreseeable future. Occasionally, it is not clear whether an event meets these two criteria, and the decision then becomes a matter of judgment.

Infrequency of Occurrence—the underlying event or transaction should be of a type that would not reasonably be expected to recur in the foreseeable future, taking into account the environment in which the entity operates.[12]

If an item is both unusual and infrequent (and material in amount), it should be reported separately from continuing operations on the income statement. The disclosure allows readers to identify gains or losses in income that would not be expected to happen again soon. Items usually treated as extraordinary include (1) an uninsured loss from flood, earthquake, fire, or theft; (2) a gain or loss resulting from the passage of a new law; and (3) the expropriation (taking) of property by a foreign government.

Gains or losses from extraordinary items should be reported on the income statement after discontinued operations. And they should be shown net of applicable taxes. In a recent year, 78 (13 percent) of 600 large companies reported extraordinary items on their income statements.[13] In Exhibit 1, the extraordinary gain was $43,000 after applicable taxes of $17,000.

ACCOUNTING CHANGES

ENRICHMENT NOTE: A change in accounting method (principle) violates the convention of consistency. Such a change is allowed, however, when it can be demonstrated that the new method will produce more useful financial statements. The effect of the change is disclosed just above net income on the income statement.

ETHICAL CONSIDERATION: Some accounting changes can produce a significant increase in net income without an accompanying improvement in performance. The user of financial statements should be aware that some businesses implement an accounting change solely for the increase in net income that results.

In a departure from the consistency convention, a company is allowed to make accounting changes if current procedures are incorrect or inappropriate. For example, a change from the FIFO to the LIFO inventory method can be made if there is adequate justification for the change. Adequate justification usually means that if the change occurs, the financial statements will better show the financial activities of the company. A company's desire to lower the amount of income taxes it pays is not considered adequate justification for an accounting change. If justification does exist and an accounting change is made, generally accepted accounting principles require the disclosure of the change in the financial statements.

The **cumulative effect of an accounting change** is the effect that the new accounting principle would have had on net income in prior periods if it had been applied instead of the old principle. This effect is shown on the income statement immediately after extraordinary items.[14] For example, assume that in the five years prior to 20x4, Junction Corporation had used the straight-line method to depreciate its machinery. This year, the company retroactively changed to the double-declining-balance method of depreciation. The controller computed the cumulative effect of the change in depreciation charges (net of taxes) as $6,000, as follows:

Cumulative, five-year double-declining-balance depreciation	$29,000
Less cumulative, five-year straight-line depreciation	18,000
Before tax effect	$11,000
Income tax savings	5,000
Cumulative effect of accounting change	$ 6,000

FOCUS ON INTERNATIONAL BUSINESS

Were Preussag's Year-End Results Really "Remarkable"?

The big German travel company Preussag <www.preussag.com> reported that the year 2000 was "a remarkable year" in which the company achieved "all-time high" results and "profit rose by 16.5 percent." The financial reports reveal that profits would not have been so remarkable if the effects of four voluntary accounting changes had not been taken into account. Profits would have increased by only 6.7 percent if Preussag had not made these changes. The company began recognizing revenue from holiday packages at the beginning of the holiday instead of at the stage of completion, but it began deferring the cost of brochures over future tourist seasons. In addition, the cost of "empty-leg flights" at the beginning and the end of each tourist season are now amortized over the season. Finally the inventory method was changed from LIFO to the average-cost method. None of these cosmetic changes affect future cash flows or change the company's operations for the better.[15]

Relevant information about the accounting change is shown in the notes to the financial statements. The change results in $11,000 of depreciation expense for prior years being deducted in the current year, in addition to the current year's depreciation costs included in the $550,000 costs and expenses section of the income statement. This expense must be shown in the current year's income statement as a reduction in income (see Exhibit 1). In a recent year, over 90 percent of 600 large companies reported changes in accounting procedures, mostly in order to conform to new FASB pronouncements.[16] Further study of accounting changes is left to more advanced accounting courses.

✓ Check out ACE for a Review Quiz at http://accounting.college.hmco.com/students.

EARNINGS PER SHARE

LO4 Compute earnings per share.
RELATED TEXT ASSIGNMENTS
Q: 11, 12, 13
SE: 4
E: 3, 6
P: 2, 3, 6
FRA: 6, 7

Readers of financial statements use earnings per share information to judge a company's performance and to compare it with the performance of other companies. Because such information is so important, the Accounting Principles Board concluded that earnings per share of common stock should be presented on the face of the income statement.[17] As shown in Exhibit 1, the information is usually disclosed just below the net income.

An earnings per share amount is always shown for (1) income from continuing operations, (2) income before extraordinary items and cumulative effect of accounting change, (3) cumulative effect of accounting change, and (4) net income. If the statement shows a gain or loss from discontinued operations or a gain or loss on extraordinary items, earnings per share amounts can also be presented for them.

The following per share data from the income statement of Minnesota Mining and Manufacturing Company (3M) show why it is a good idea to study the components of earnings per share:[18]

www.3m.com

ENRICHMENT NOTE:
Earnings per share is a measure of a corporation's profitability. It is one of the most closely watched financial statement ratios in the business world. Its disclosure on the income statement is required.

Financial Highlights

	2000	1999	1998
Earnings per share—basic			
Income before extraordinary loss and cumulative effect of accounting change	$ 4.69	$ 4.39	$ 3.01
Extraordinary loss	—	—	(.10)
Cumulative effect of accounting change	(.19)	—	—
Net income	$ 4.50	$ 4.39	$ 2.91

Note that net income was influenced by special items in 1998 and 2000: An extraordinary loss decreased income from continuing operations by $.10 per share in 1998, and the cumulative effect of an accounting change decreased earnings by $.19 in 2000. In 1999, the company had no special items; thus, 100 percent of 3M's basic earnings per share were attributable to continuing operations.

Basic earnings per share is net income applicable to common stock divided by the weighted-average number of common shares outstanding. To compute this figure, one must determine if the number of common shares outstanding changed during the year, and if the company paid preferred stock dividends.

When a company has only common stock and has the same number of shares outstanding throughout the year, the earnings per share computation is simple. From Exhibit 1, we know that Junction Corporation reported net income of $334,500.

● **STOP AND THINK!**
What is one action a company can take to improve its earnings per share without improving its earnings or net income?

Many companies attempt to improve their earnings per share by reducing the number of shares outstanding through buybacks of their own stock. ■

Assume that the company had 100,000 shares of common stock outstanding for the entire year. The earnings per share of common stock is computed as follows:

$$\text{Earnings per Share} = \frac{\$334,500}{100,000} = \$3.35 \text{ per share}$$

If the number of shares outstanding changes during the year, it is necessary to figure the weighted-average number of shares outstanding for the year. Suppose that during various periods of the year, Junction Corporation had the following amounts of common shares outstanding: January–March, 100,000 shares; April–September, 120,000 shares; and October–December, 130,000 shares. The weighted-average number of common shares outstanding and basic earnings per share would be calculated this way:

100,000 shares × 3/12 year	25,000
120,000 shares × 6/12 year	60,000
130,000 shares × 3/12 year	32,500
Weighted-average common shares outstanding	117,500

$$\text{Basic Earnings per Share} = \frac{\text{Net Income}}{\text{Weighted-Average Common Shares Outstanding}}$$

$$= \frac{\$334,500}{117,500 \text{ shares}} = \$2.85 \text{ per share}$$

If a company has nonconvertible preferred stock outstanding, the dividend for that stock must be subtracted from net income before earnings per share for common stock are computed. Suppose that Junction Corporation has preferred stock on which the annual dividend is $23,500. Earnings per share on common stock would be $2.65 [($334,500 − $23,500) ÷ 117,500 shares].

Companies with a capital structure in which there are no bonds, stocks, or stock options that can be converted into common stock are said to have a **simple capital structure**. The earnings per share for these companies is computed as shown above. Some companies, however, have a **complex capital structure**, which includes exercisable stock options or convertible preferred stocks and bonds. Those convertible securities have the potential of diluting the earnings per share of common stock. *Potential dilution* means that a stockholder's proportionate share of ownership in a company could be reduced through the conversion of stocks or bonds or the exercise of stock options, which would increase the total number of shares the company has outstanding.

For example, suppose that a person owns 10,000 shares of a company, which equals 2 percent of the outstanding shares of 500,000. Now suppose that holders of convertible bonds convert the bonds into 100,000 shares of stock. The person's 10,000 shares would then equal only 1.67 percent (10,000 ÷ 600,000) of the outstanding shares. In addition, the added shares outstanding would lower earnings per share and would most likely lower market price per share.

Because stock options and convertible preferred stocks or bonds have the potential to dilute earnings per share, they are referred to as **potentially dilutive securities**. When a company has a complex capital structure, it must report two earnings per share figures: basic earnings per share and diluted earnings per share.[19] **Diluted earnings per share** are calculated by adding all potentially dilutive securities to the denominator of the basic earnings per share calculation. This figure shows stockholders the maximum potential effect of dilution on their ownership position in the company.

The difference between basic and diluted earnings per share can be significant. For example, consider the results reported by Tribune Company:

KEY POINT: A company with potentially dilutive securities (such as convertible preferred stock or bonds) has a complex capital structure and must present two earnings per share figures—basic and diluted. The latter figure is the more conservative of the two.

www.amrcorp.com

Financial Highlights

	2002	2001	2000
Basic earnings per share	$1.38	$.28	$.74
Diluted earnings per share	1.30	.28	.70

Note that in 2000 and 2002, diluted earnings per share are about 5-6 percent less than basic earnings per share.[20] The basic earnings per share is used in various ratios, including the price/earnings ratio.

The computation of diluted earnings per share is a complex process and is reserved for more advanced courses.

✓ Check out ACE for a Review Quiz at http://accounting.college.hmco.com/students.

THE STATEMENT OF STOCKHOLDERS' EQUITY

LO5 Prepare a statement of stockholders' equity.

RELATED TEXT ASSIGNMENTS
Q: 14, 15, 16
SE: 5, 6, 7
E: 7, 8
P: 4, 5, 7, 8
SD: 4, 5
FRA: 1, 3, 4, 6, 7

The **statement of stockholders' equity**, also called the *statement of changes in stockholders' equity*, summarizes the changes in the components of the stockholders' equity section of the balance sheet. More and more companies are using this statement in place of the statement of retained earnings because it reveals much more about the year's stockholders' equity transactions. In the statement of stockholders' equity in Exhibit 2, for example, the first line shows the beginning balance of each account in the stockholders' equity section. Each subsequent line discloses the effects of transactions on those accounts. Tri-State earned net income of $270,000 and had a foreign currency translation loss of $10,000, reported as accumulated other comprehensive income. These two items together resulted in comprehensive income of $260,000. The statement also shows that during 20x4 Tri-State Corporation issued 5,000 shares of common stock for $250,000, had a conversion of $100,000 of preferred stock into common stock, declared and issued a 10 percent stock dividend on common stock, had a net purchase of treasury shares of $24,000, and paid cash dividends on both preferred and common stock. The ending balances of the accounts are presented at the bottom of the statement. Those accounts and balances make up the stockholders' equity section of Tri-State's balance sheet on December 31, 20x4, as shown in Exhibit 3.

● **STOP AND THINK!**
In Exhibit 2, what is the total amount of comprehensive income?

The total amount of comprehensive income includes all changes in stockholders' equity not involving the owners. In Exhibit 2, it is the net income of $270,000 and accumulated other comprehensive income (foreign currency translation adjustment) of ($10,000), or $260,000. ■

RETAINED EARNINGS

Notice that in Exhibit 2 the Retained Earnings column has the same components as the statement of retained earnings. The **retained earnings** of a company are the part of stockholders' equity that represents stockholders' claims to assets arising from the earnings of the business. Retained earnings equal a company's profits since the date of its inception, less any losses, dividends to stockholders, or transfers to contributed capital.

It is important to remember that retained earnings are not the assets themselves. The existence of retained earnings means that assets generated by profitable operations have been kept in the company to help it grow or meet other business needs. A credit balance in Retained Earnings is *not* directly associated with a specific amount of cash or designated assets. Rather, such a balance means that assets as a whole have been increased.

KEY POINT: In accounting, a deficit is a negative (debit) balance in Retained Earnings. It is not the same thing as a net loss, which reflects the performance in just one accounting period.

Retained Earnings can carry a debit balance. Generally, this happens when a company's dividends and subsequent losses are greater than its accumulated profits from operations. In such a case, the firm is said to have a **deficit** (debit balance) in Retained Earnings. A deficit is shown in the stockholders' equity section of the balance sheet as a deduction from contributed capital.

EXHIBIT 2
Statement of Stockholders' Equity

Tri-State Corporation
Statement of Stockholders' Equity
For the Year Ended December 31, 20x4

	Preferred Stock $100 Par Value 8% Convertible	Common Stock $10 Par Value	Paid-in Capital in Excess of Par Value, Common	Retained Earnings	Treasury Stock	Accumulated Other Comprehensive Income	Total
Balance, December 31, 20x3	$400,000	$300,000	$300,000	$600,000	—		$1,600,000
Net income				270,000			270,000
Foreign currency translation adjustment						($10,000)	(10,000)
Issuance of 5,000 shares of common stock		50,000	200,000				250,000
Conversion of 1,000 shares of preferred stock to 3,000 shares of common stock	(100,000)	30,000	70,000				—
10 percent stock dividend on common stock, 3,800 shares		38,000	152,000	(190,000)			—
Purchase of 500 shares of treasury stock					($24,000)		(24,000)
Cash dividends							
Preferred stock				(24,000)			(24,000)
Common stock				(47,600)			(47,600)
Balance, December 31, 20x4	$300,000	$418,000	$722,000	$608,400	($24,000)	($10,000)	$2,014,400

EXHIBIT 3
Stockholders' Equity Section of a Balance Sheet

KEY POINT: The ending balances on the statement of stockholders' equity are transferred to the stockholders' equity section of the balance sheet.

Tri-State Corporation
Stockholders' Equity
December 31, 20x4

Contributed capital			
Preferred stock, $100 par value, 8 percent convertible, 10,000 shares authorized, 3,000 shares issued and outstanding			$ 300,000
Common stock, $10 par value, 100,000 shares authorized, 41,800 shares issued, 41,300 shares outstanding		$418,000	
Paid-in capital in excess of par value, common		722,000	1,140,000
Total contributed capital			$1,440,000
Retained earnings			608,400
Total contributed capital and retained earnings			$2,048,400
Less: Treasury stock, common (500 shares, at cost)		$ 24,000	
Foreign currency translation adjustment		10,000	34,000
Total stockholders' equity			$2,014,400

FOCUS ON INTERNATIONAL BUSINESS

Why Are Reserves Common in Other Countries?

Restrictions on retained earnings, called *reserves*, are much more common in some foreign countries than in the United States. In Sweden, for instance, reserves are used to respond to fluctuations in the economy. The Swedish tax code allows companies to set up contingency reserves for the purpose of maintaining financial stability. Appropriations to those reserves reduce taxable income and income taxes. The reserves become taxable when they are reversed, but they are available to absorb losses should they occur. For example, Skandia Group <www.skandia.com>, a large Swedish insurance company, reported a net income of only SK2,826 million in 2000, considerably less than the SK3,456 million in 1999. An examination of its statement of stockholders' equity shows restricted reserves in 2000 of SK10.2 billion. Skandia also increased its dividends in 2000 to SK512 million and still had SK9.5 billion in unrestricted reserves.[21]

RESTRICTION ON RETAINED EARNINGS

A corporation may be required or may want to restrict all or a portion of its retained earnings. A **restriction on retained earnings** means that dividends can be declared only to the extent of the *unrestricted* retained earnings. The following are reasons a company might restrict retained earnings:

1. *A contractual agreement.* For example, bond indentures may place a limitation on the dividends the company can pay.
2. *State law.* Many states do not allow a corporation to distribute dividends or purchase treasury stock if doing so reduces equity to a level that would impair the legal capital of the company.
3. *Voluntary action by the board of directors.* Often, a board decides to retain assets in the business for future needs. For example, the company may want to limit dividends to save enough money for a new building or to offset a possible future loss of assets resulting from a lawsuit.

A restriction on retained earnings does not change the total retained earnings or stockholders' equity of the company. It simply divides retained earnings into two parts: restricted and unrestricted. The unrestricted amount represents earnings kept in the business that the company can use for dividends and other purposes. Also, the restriction of retained earnings does not restrict cash or other assets in any way. It simply explains to the readers of the financial statements that a certain amount of assets generated by earnings will remain in the business for the purpose stated. It is still management's job to make sure enough cash or assets are on hand to fulfill the purpose. The removal of a restriction does not necessarily mean that the board of directors can then declare a dividend.

The most common way to disclose restricted retained earnings is by reference to a note to the financial statements. For example:

Retained earnings (Note 15) $900,000

Note 15:
Because of plans to expand the capacity of the company's clothing division, the board of directors has restricted retained earnings available for dividends by $300,000.

✓ Check out ACE for a Review Quiz at http://accounting.college.hmco.com/students.

ACCOUNTING FOR STOCK DIVIDENDS AND STOCK SPLITS

LO6 Account for stock dividends and stock splits.

RELATED TEXT ASSIGNMENTS
Q: 17, 18
SE: 6, 8, 9
E: 9, 10, 11
P: 4, 5, 7, 8
SD: 3, 4, 5
FRA: 6

Two common transactions that can modify the content of stockholders' equity are stock dividends and stock splits.

STOCK DIVIDENDS

A **stock dividend** is a proportional distribution of shares among a corporation's stockholders. Unlike a cash dividend, it involves no distribution of assets, so it has no effect on a firm's assets and liabilities. A board of directors may declare a stock dividend for several reasons:

1. It may want to give stockholders some evidence of the company's success without paying a cash dividend, which would affect working capital.

2. It may want to reduce the stock's market price by increasing the number of shares outstanding. (This goal is, however, more often met by a stock split.)
3. It may want to make a nontaxable distribution to stockholders. Stock dividends that meet certain conditions are not considered income, so they are not taxed.
4. It may wish to increase the company's permanent capital by transferring an amount from retained earnings to contributed capital.

The total stockholders' equity is not affected by a stock dividend. The effect of a stock dividend is to transfer a dollar amount from retained earnings to contributed capital on the date of declaration. The amount transferred is the fair market value (usually, the market price) of the additional shares to be issued. The laws of most states specify the minimum value of each share transferred under a stock dividend, which is normally the minimum legal capital (par or stated value). However, generally accepted accounting principles state that market value reflects the economic effect of small stock distributions (less than 20 to 25 percent of a company's outstanding common stock) better than par or stated value does. For this reason, market price should be used to account for small stock dividends.[22]

To illustrate how to account for a stock dividend, let us assume that Caprock Corporation has the following stockholders' equity structure:

Contributed capital
Common stock, $5 par value, 100,000 shares
authorized, 30,000 shares issued and outstanding $ 150,000
Paid-in capital in excess of par value, common   30,000
Total contributed capital $ 180,000
Retained earnings   900,000
Total stockholders' equity $1,080,000

Suppose that the board of directors declares a 10 percent stock dividend on February 24, distributable on March 31 to stockholders of record on March 15, and that the market price of the stock on February 24 is $20 per share. The entries to record the declaration and distribution of the stock dividend are as follows:

Date of Declaration

A = L + OE   Feb. 24   Stock Dividends Declared   60,000
 −   Common Stock Distributable   15,000
 +   Paid-in Capital in Excess of Par
 +   Value, Common   45,000
                          Declared a 10 percent stock dividend
                          on common stock, distributable on
                          March 31 to stockholders of record
                          on March 15:
                          30,000 shares × .10 = 3,000 shares
                          3,000 shares × $20/share = $60,000
                          3,000 shares × $5/share = $15,000

KEY POINT: For a small stock dividend, the portion of retained earnings transferred is determined by multiplying the number of shares to be distributed by the stock's market price on the date of declaration.

Date of Record

Mar. 15   No entry required.

Date of Distribution

A = L + OE   Mar. 31   Common Stock Distributable   15,000
 −   Common Stock   15,000
 +   Distributed a stock dividend of
                          3,000 shares

The effect of this stock dividend is to permanently transfer the market value of the stock, $60,000, from retained earnings to contributed capital and to increase the

KEY POINT: The declaration of a stock dividend results in a reshuffling of stockholders' equity. That is, a portion of retained earnings is converted into contributed capital (by closing the Stock Dividends Declared account). Total stockholders' equity is not affected. Retained earnings are transferred at the time of the recording (date of declaration) and not at the closing of the Stock Dividends Declared account.

KEY POINT: Common Stock Distributable is a contributed capital (stockholders' equity) account, not a liability. When the shares are issued, this account is converted to the Common Stock account.

● **STOP AND THINK!**
The receipt of additional shares of stock resulting from a stock dividend has no effect on a stockholder's income. Why not? *Although the stockholder receives additional shares of stock, that stockholder's share of ownership remains unchanged because all other stockholders receive the same proportionate increase in the number of shares owned. The company's net worth remains unchanged since net assets have not increased or decreased. Therefore, the stockholder still owns the same percentage of the company's unchanged net worth.* ■

number of shares outstanding by 3,000. The Stock Dividends Declared account is used to record the total amount of the stock dividend. Retained Earnings is reduced by the amount of the stock dividend when the Stock Dividends Declared account is closed to Retained Earnings at the end of the accounting period. Common Stock Distributable is credited for the par value of the stock to be distributed (3,000 × $5 = $15,000).

In addition, when the market value is greater than the par value of the stock, Paid-in Capital in Excess of Par Value, Common must be credited for the amount by which the market value exceeds the par value. In this case, the total market value of the stock dividend ($60,000) exceeds the total par value ($15,000) by $45,000. No entry is required on the date of record. On the distribution date, the common stock is issued by debiting Common Stock Distributable and crediting Common Stock for the par value of the stock ($15,000).

Common Stock Distributable is not a liability account because there is no obligation to distribute cash or other assets. The obligation is to distribute additional shares of capital stock. If financial statements are prepared between the date of declaration and the date of distribution, Common Stock Distributable should be reported as part of contributed capital:

Contributed capital
Common stock, $5 par value, 100,000 shares
   authorized, 30,000 shares issued and outstanding $ 150,000
  Common stock distributable, 3,000 shares   15,000
  Paid-in capital in excess of par value, common   75,000
  Total contributed capital $ 240,000
Retained earnings   840,000
Total stockholders' equity $1,080,000

Three points can be made from this example. First, the total stockholders' equity is the same before and after the stock dividend. Second, the assets of the corporation are not reduced as they are with a cash dividend. Third, the proportionate ownership in the corporation of any individual stockholder is the same before and after the stock dividend. To illustrate these points, assume that a stockholder owns 1,000 shares before the stock dividend. After the 10 percent stock dividend is distributed, this stockholder would own 1,100 shares, as illustrated below.

Stockholders' Equity	Before Dividend	After Dividend
Common stock	$ 150,000	$ 165,000
Paid-in capital in excess of par value, common	30,000	75,000
Total contributed capital	$ 180,000	$ 240,000
Retained earnings	900,000	840,000
Total stockholders' equity	$1,080,000	$1,080,000
Shares outstanding	30,000	33,000
Stockholders' equity per share	$ 36.00	$ 32.73

Stockholders' Investment

Shares owned	1,000	1,100
Shares outstanding	30,000	33,000
Percentage of ownership	3⅓%	3⅓%
Proportionate investment ($1,080,000 × .03⅓)	$36,000	$36,000

Both before and after the stock dividend, the stockholders' equity totals $1,080,000 and the stockholder owns 3⅓ percent of the company. The proportionate investment (stockholders' equity times percentage ownership) remains at $36,000.

KEY POINT: When a large (greater than 20 to 25 percent) stock dividend is declared, the transfer from retained earnings is based on the stock's par or stated value, not on its market value.

All stock dividends have an effect on the market price of a company's stock. But some stock dividends are so large that they have a material effect. For example, a 50 percent stock dividend would cause the market price of the stock to drop about 33 percent because the increase is now one-third of shares outstanding. The AICPA has decided that large stock dividends, those greater than 20 to 25 percent, should be accounted for by transferring the par or stated value of the stock on the date of declaration from retained earnings to contributed capital.[23]

STOCK SPLITS

A **stock split** occurs when a corporation increases the number of issued shares of stock and reduces the par or stated value proportionally. A company may plan a stock split when it wants to lower the stock's market value per share and increase the demand for the stock at this lower price. This action may be necessary if the market value per share has become so high that it hinders the trading of the stock or if the company wants to signal to the market its success in achieving its operating goals. The Gillette Company achieved these strategic objectives in a recent year by declaring a 2-for-1 stock split and raising its cash dividend. The market viewed these actions positively, pushing Gillette's share price from $77 to $106. After the stock split, the number of shares outstanding doubled, thereby cutting the share price in half and also the dividend per share. Most important, each stockholder's total wealth was unchanged as a result of the stock split.

KEY POINT: Stock splits and stock dividends reduce earnings per share because they increase the number of shares issued and outstanding. Cash dividends have no effect on earnings per share.

www.gillette.com

To illustrate a stock split, suppose that Caprock Corporation has 30,000 shares of $5.00 par value stock outstanding. The market value is $70.00 per share. The corporation plans a 2-for-1 split. This split will lower the par value to $2.50 and increase the number of shares outstanding to 60,000. A stockholder who previously owned 400 shares of the $5.00 par value stock would own 800 shares of the $2.50 par value stock after the split. When a stock split occurs, the market value tends to fall in proportion to the increase in outstanding shares of stock. For example, a 2-for-1 stock split would cause the price of the stock to drop by approximately 50 percent, to about $35.00. It would also halve earnings per share and cash dividends per share (if the board does not increase the dividend). The lower price and the increase in shares tend to promote the buying and selling of shares.

ENRICHMENT NOTE: Stock splits greater than 2 for 1 are unusual. Splits such as 3 for 2 or 4 for 3 are far more common. On occasion, companies whose stock sells for a very low price will perform a reverse stock split, which reduces the number of shares and increases the market price.

A stock split does not increase the number of shares authorized. Nor does it change the balances in the stockholders' equity section of the balance sheet. It simply changes the par value and number of shares issued, both shares outstanding and treasury stock. Thus, an entry is unnecessary. However, it is appropriate to document the change with a memorandum entry in the general journal. For example:

July 15   The 30,000 shares of $5 par value common stock issued and outstanding were split 2 for 1, resulting in 60,000 shares of $2.50 par value common stock issued and outstanding.

FOCUS ON BUSINESS PRACTICE

Do Stock Splits Help Increase a Company's Market Price?

Stock splits tend to follow the market. When the market went up dramatically in 1998, 1999, and 2000, there were record numbers of stock splits—more than 1,000 per year. At the height of the market in early 2000, stock splitters included such diverse companies as Alcoa <www.alcoa.com>, Apple Computer <www.apple.com>, Chase Manhattan <www.chase.com>, Intel <www.intel.com>, Nvidia <www.nvidia.com>, Juniper Networks <www.juniper.net>, and Tiffany & Co. <www.tiffany.com>. Some analysts liken stock splits to the air a pastry chef whips into a mousse: it doesn't make it any sweeter, just frothier. There is no fundamental reason a stock should go up because of a stock split. When Rambus Inc. <www.rambus.com>, a developer of high-speed memory technology, announced a four-for-one split on March 10, 2000, its stock rose more than 50 percent, to $471 per share.[24] But when the market deflated in 2001, its stock dropped to less than $10 per share. Research shows that stock splits have no long-term effect on stock prices.

The change for the Caprock Corporation is as follows:

Before Stock Split

Contributed capital		
Common stock, $5 par value, 100,000 shares authorized, 30,000 shares issued and outstanding		$ 150,000
Paid-in capital in excess of par value, common		30,000
Total contributed capital		$ 180,000
Retained earnings		900,000
Total stockholders' equity		$1,080,000

After Stock Split

Contributed capital		
Common stock, $2.50 par value, 100,000 shares authorized, 60,000 shares issued and outstanding		$ 150,000
Paid-in capital in excess of par value, common		30,000
Total contributed capital		$ 180,000
Retained earnings		900,000
Total stockholders' equity		$1,080,000

KEY POINT: A stock split affects only the common stock calculation. In this case, there are twice as many shares after the split, but par value is now half of what it was.

KEY POINT: As long as the newly outstanding shares do not exceed the previously authorized shares, permission from the state is not needed for a stock split.

Although the amount of stockholders' equity per share is half as much, each stockholder's proportionate interest in the company remains the same.

If the number of split shares will exceed the number of authorized shares, the board of directors must secure state and stockholders' approval before it can issue additional shares.

✓ Check out ACE for a Review Quiz at http://accounting.college.hmco.com/students.

BOOK VALUE

LO7 Calculate book value per share.

RELATED TEXT ASSIGNMENTS
Q: 19
SE: 10
E: 12
P: 4, 5, 7, 8
SD: 4, 5
FRA: 5, 6

KEY POINT: Book value per share represents the equity of one share of stock in the net assets (assets minus liabilities) of a corporation. It can apply to both common and preferred stock.

The word *value* is associated with shares of stock in several ways. Par value or stated value is set when the stock is authorized and establishes the legal capital of a company. Neither par value nor stated value has any relationship to a stock's book value or market value. The **book value** of a company's stock represents the total assets of the company less its liabilities. It is simply the stockholders' equity of the company or, to look at it another way, the company's net assets. The **book value per share** therefore represents the equity of the owner of one share of stock in the net assets of the corporation. That value, of course, does not necessarily equal the amount the shareholder would receive if the company were sold or liquidated. It differs in most cases because assets are usually recorded at historical cost, not at the current value at which they could be sold.

When a company has only common stock outstanding, book value per share is calculated by dividing the total stockholders' equity by the total common shares outstanding. In computing the shares outstanding, common stock distributable is included. Treasury stock (shares previously issued and now held by the company), however, is not included. For example, suppose that Caprock Corporation has total stockholders' equity of $1,030,000 and 29,000 shares outstanding after recording the purchase of treasury shares. The book value per share of Caprock's common stock is $35.52 ($1,030,000 ÷ 29,000 shares).

If a company has both preferred and common stock, the determination of book value per share is not so simple. The general rule is that the call value (or par value, if a call value is not specified) of the preferred stock plus any dividends in arrears is subtracted from total stockholders' equity to determine the equity pertaining to common stock. As an illustration, refer to the stockholders' equity section of Tri-

> **STOP AND THINK!**
> What is the effect of a stock dividend or a stock split on book value per share?
>
> Both a stock dividend and a stock split reduce the book value per share because they increase the number of shares outstanding without changing the total of stockholders' equity. ∎

State Corporation's balance sheet in Exhibit 3. Assuming that no dividends are in arrears and that the preferred stock is callable at $105, the equity pertaining to common stock is calculated as follows:

Total stockholders' equity	$2,014,400
Less equity allocated to preferred shareholders (3,000 shares × $105)	315,000
Equity pertaining to common shareholders	**$1,699,400**

There are 41,300 shares of common stock outstanding (41,800 shares issued less 500 shares of treasury stock). The book values per share are computed as follows:

Preferred Stock: $315,000 ÷ 3,000 shares = $105 per share
Common Stock: $1,699,400 ÷ 41,300 shares = $41.15 per share

If we assume the same facts except that the preferred stock is 8 percent cumulative and that one year of dividends is in arrears, the stockholders' equity would be allocated as follows:

Total stockholders' equity		$2,014,400
Less: Call value of outstanding preferred shares	$315,000	
Dividends in arrears ($300,000 × .08)	24,000	
Equity allocated to preferred shareholders		339,000
Equity pertaining to common shareholders		**$1,675,400**

The book values per share are then as follows:

Preferred Stock: $339,000 ÷ 3,000 shares = $113 per share
Common Stock: $1,675,400 ÷ 41,300 shares = $40.57 per share

Undeclared preferred dividends fall into arrears on the last day of the fiscal year (the date shown on the financial statements). Also, dividends in arrears do not apply to unissued preferred stock.

✓ Check out ACE for a Review Quiz at http://accounting.college.hmco.com/students.

Chapter Review

REVIEW OF LEARNING OBJECTIVES

LO1 Prepare a corporate income statement and identify the issues related to evaluating the quality of earnings.

The operating income section on the income statement of a corporation with both continuing and discontinued operations is called income from continuing operations. Income from continuing operations before income taxes is affected by choices of accounting methods and estimates and may contain such items as gains and losses, write-downs, and restructurings. The income taxes expense section of the statement is also subject to special accounting rules. The lower part of the statement may contain such nonoperating items as discontinued operations, extraordinary gains and losses, and effects of accounting changes. Earnings per share information appears at the bottom of the statement. The quality of a company's earnings refers to the substance of earnings and their sustainability into future accounting periods. The quality of earnings may be affected by the accounting methods and estimates the company's management chooses and by the gains and losses, the write-downs and restructurings, and the nature of the nonoperating items reported on the income statement. The reason for considering quality of earnings issues is to assess their effects on cash flows and performance measures. Generally speaking, except for possible income tax effects, none of the gains and losses, asset write-downs, restructurings, and nonoperating items has any effect on cash flows. Quality of earnings issues can affect key performance ratios like return on assets and return on equity.

LO2 Show the relationships among income taxes expense, deferred income taxes, and net of taxes.

Income taxes expense is the taxes applicable to income from operations on an accrual basis. Income tax allocation is necessary when differences between accrual-based accounting income and taxable income cause a material difference between income taxes expense as shown on the income statement and actual income tax liability. The difference between income taxes expense and income taxes payable is debited or credited to an account called Deferred Income Taxes. *Net of taxes* is a phrase used to indicate that the effect of income taxes has been considered when showing an item on the income statement.

LO3 Describe the disclosure on the income statement of discontinued operations, extraordinary items, and accounting changes.

Because of their unusual nature, a gain or loss on discontinued operations and on extraordinary items and the cumulative effect of accounting changes must be disclosed on the income statement separately from continuing operations and net of income taxes. Relevant information about any accounting change is shown in the notes to the financial statements.

LO4 Compute earnings per share.

Stockholders and other readers of financial statements use earnings per share data to evaluate a company's performance and to compare it with the performance of other companies. Therefore, earnings per share data are presented on the face of the income statement. The amounts are computed by dividing the income applicable to common stock by the number of common shares outstanding for the year. If the number of shares outstanding has varied during the year, then the weighted-average number of common shares outstanding should be used in the computation. When the company has a complex capital structure, both basic and diluted earnings per share must be disclosed on the face of the income statement.

LO5 Prepare a statement of stockholders' equity.

A statement of stockholders' equity shows changes over the period in each component of the stockholders' equity section of the balance sheet. This statement reveals much more about the transactions that affect stockholders' equity than does the statement of retained earnings.

LO6 Account for stock dividends and stock splits.

A stock dividend is a proportional distribution of shares among a corporation's stockholders. Here is a summary of the key dates and accounting treatment of stock dividends:

Key Date	Stock Dividend
Date of declaration	Debit Stock Dividends Declared for the market value of the stock to be distributed (if it is a small stock dividend), and credit Common Stock Distributable for the stock's par value and Paid-in Capital in Excess of Par Value, Common for the excess of the market value over the stock's par value.
Date of record	No entry.
Date of distribution	Debit Common Stock Distributable and credit Common Stock for the par value of the stock that has been distributed.

A stock split is usually undertaken to reduce the market value of a company's stock and improve the demand for the stock. Because there is normally a decrease in the par value of the stock in proportion to the number of additional shares issued, a stock split has no effect on the dollar amounts in the stockholders' equity accounts. The split should be recorded in the general journal by a memorandum entry only.

LO7 Calculate book value per share.

Book value per share is the stockholders' equity per share. It is calculated by dividing stockholders' equity by the number of common shares outstanding plus shares distributable. When a company has both preferred and common stock, the call or par value of the preferred stock plus any dividends in arrears is deducted from total stockholders' equity before dividing by the common shares outstanding.

Review of Concepts and Terminology

The following concepts and terms were introduced in this chapter:

LO4 **Basic earnings per share:** The net income applicable to common stock divided by the weighted-average number of common shares outstanding.

LO7 **Book value:** The total assets of a company less its liabilities; stockholders' equity or net assets.

LO7 **Book value per share:** The equity of the owner of one share of stock in the net assets of the corporation.

LO4 **Complex capital structure:** A capital structure that includes exercisable stock options or convertible preferred stocks and bonds.

LO1 **Comprehensive income:** The change in a company's equity from sources other than owners during a period; it includes net income, changes in unrealized investment gains and losses, and other items affecting equity.

LO3 **Cumulative effect of an accounting change:** The effect that a different accounting principle would have had on the net income of prior periods if it had been used instead of the old principle.

LO2 **Deferred Income Taxes:** The account used to record the difference between the Income Taxes Expense and Income Taxes Payable accounts.

LO5 **Deficit:** A debit balance in the Retained Earnings account.

LO4 **Diluted earnings per share:** The net income applicable to common stock divided by the sum of the weighted-average number of common shares outstanding plus potentially dilutive securities.

LO3 **Discontinued operations:** Segments of a business that are no longer part of its ongoing operations.

LO3 **Extraordinary items:** Events or transactions that are both unusual in nature and infrequent in occurrence.

LO1 **Income from continuing operations:** The operating income section of the income statement when a company has both continuing and discontinued operations.

LO2 **Income tax allocation:** An accounting method used to accrue income taxes expense on the basis of accounting income whenever there are differences between accounting and taxable income.

LO2 **Net of taxes:** A phrase indicating that the effect of applicable taxes (most often, income taxes) has been considered in determining the overall effect of an item on the financial statements.

LO4 **Potentially dilutive securities:** Stock options and convertible preferred stocks or bonds, which have the potential to dilute earnings per share.

LO1 **Quality of earnings:** The substance of earnings and their sustainability into future accounting periods.

LO5 **Restriction on retained earnings:** The required or voluntary identification of a portion of retained earnings that cannot be used to declare dividends.

LO1 **Restructuring:** The estimated cost associated with a change in a company's operations, usually involving the closing of facilities and the laying off of personnel.

LO5 **Retained earnings:** Stockholders' claims to assets arising from the earnings of the business; the accumulated earnings of a corporation from its inception, minus any losses, dividends, or transfers to contributed capital.

LO3 **Segments:** Distinct parts of business operations, such as a line of business or a class of customer.

LO4 **Simple capital structure:** A capital structure in which there are no stocks, bonds, or stock options that can be converted into common stock.

Chapter 15 The Corporate Income Statement and the Statement of Stockholders' Equity

LO5 **Statement of stockholders' equity:** A financial statement that summarizes changes in the components of the stockholders' equity section of the balance sheet. Also called *statement of changes in stockholders' equity*.

LO6 **Stock dividend:** A proportional distribution of shares among a corporation's stockholders.

LO6 **Stock split:** An increase in the number of outstanding shares of stock accompanied by a proportionate reduction in the par or stated value.

LO1 **Write-down:** The recording of a decrease in the value of an asset below the carrying value on the balance sheet and the reduction of income in the current period by the amount of the decrease. Also called *write-off*.

REVIEW PROBLEM

Comprehensive Stockholders' Equity Transactions

LO5
LO6
LO7

The stockholders' equity of Szatkowski Company on June 30, 20x4, was as follows:

Contributed capital		
Common stock, no par value, $6 stated value, 1,000,000 shares authorized, 250,000 shares issued and outstanding	$1,500,000	
Paid-in capital in excess of stated value, common	820,000	
Total contributed capital		$2,320,000
Retained earnings		970,000
Total stockholders' equity		$3,290,000

Stockholders' equity transactions for the next fiscal year were as follows:

a. The board of directors declared a 2-for-1 stock split.
b. The board of directors obtained authorization to issue 50,000 shares of $100 par value, 6 percent noncumulative preferred stock, callable at $104.
c. Issued 12,000 shares of common stock for a building appraised at $96,000.
d. Purchased 8,000 shares of the company's common stock for $64,000.
e. Issued 20,000 shares of preferred stock for $100 per share.
f. Sold 5,000 shares of treasury stock for $35,000.
g. Declared cash dividends of $6 per share on preferred stock and $.20 per share on common stock.
h. Declared a 10 percent stock dividend on common stock. The market value was $10 per share. The stock dividend is distributable after the end of the fiscal year.
i. Closed Net Income for the year, $340,000.
j. Closed the Cash Dividends Declared and Stock Dividends Declared accounts to Retained Earnings.

Because of a loan agreement, the company is not allowed to reduce retained earnings below $100,000. The board of directors determined that this restriction should be disclosed in the notes to the financial statements.

REQUIRED ▶
1. Record the stockholders' equity components of the preceding transactions in T accounts. Indicate when there is no entry.
2. Prepare the stockholders' equity section of the company's balance sheet on June 30, 20x5, including appropriate disclosure of the restriction on retained earnings.
3. Compute the book values per share of common stock on June 30, 20x4 and 20x5, and of preferred stock on June 30, 20x5, using end-of-year shares outstanding.

ANSWER TO REVIEW PROBLEM

1. Entries in T accounts:
   a. No entry: memorandum in journal
   b. No entry: memorandum in journal

Preferred Stock			Common Stock		
	e.	2,000,000		Beg. bal.	1,500,000
				c.	36,000
				End. Bal	1,536,000

Common Stock Distributable			Paid-in Capital in Excess of Stated Value, Common		
	h.	152,700		Beg. bal.	820,000
				c.	60,000
				h.	356,300
				End. Bal.	1,236,300

Retained Earnings					Treasury Stock, Common			
f.	5,000	Beg. bal.	970,000	d.	64,000	f.	40,000
j.	730,800	i.	340,000	End. Bal.	24,000		
		End. bal.	574,200				

Cash Dividends Declared				Stock Dividend Declared			
g.	221,800*	j.	221,800	h.	509,000**	j.	509,000

* 20,000 × $6 = $120,000
509,000 × $.20 = $101,800
Total = $221,800

**509,000 shares × .10 × $10 = $509,000

2. Stockholders' equity section of the balance sheet:

Szatkowski Company
Stockholders' Equity
June 30, 20x5

Contributed capital		
Preferred stock, $100 par value, 6 percent noncumulative, 50,000 shares authorized, 20,000 shares issued and outstanding		$2,000,000
Common stock, no par value, $3 stated value, 1,000,000 shares authorized, 512,000 shares issued, 509,000 shares outstanding	$1,536,000	
Common stock distributable, 50,900 shares	152,700	
Paid-in capital in excess of stated value, common	1,236,300	2,925,000
Total contributed capital		$4,925,000
Retained earnings (Note x)		574,200
Total contributed capital and retained earnings		$5,499,200
Less treasury stock, common (3,000 shares, at cost)		24,000
Total stockholders' equity		$5,475,200

Note x: The board of directors has restricted retained earnings available for dividends by the amount of $100,000 as required under a loan agreement.

3. Book values:
    June 30, 20x4
        Common Stock: $3,290,000 ÷ 250,000 shares = $13.16 per share

June 30, 20x5
Preferred Stock: Call price of $104 per share equals book value per share
Common Stock:
($5,475,200 − $2,080,000) ÷ (509,000 shares + 50,900 shares) =
$3,395,200 ÷ 559,900 shares = $6.06 per share

Chapter Assignments

BUILDING YOUR KNOWLEDGE FOUNDATION

QUESTIONS

1. What is comprehensive income? How does it differ from net income?
2. What is quality of earnings, and what are four ways in which quality of earnings may be affected?
3. Why would the reader of financial statements be interested in management's choice of accounting methods and estimates? Give an example.
4. What is the difference between a write-down and a restructuring, and where do they appear on the corporate income statement?
5. In the first quarter of 1994, AT&T, the giant telecommunications company, reported a net loss because it reduced its income by $1.3 billion, or $.96 per share, as a result of changing its method of accounting for disability and severance payments. Without this charge, the company would have earned $1.15 billion, or $.85 per share. Where on the corporate income statement do you find the effects of changes in accounting principles? As an analyst, how would you treat this accounting change?
6. "Accounting income should be geared to the concept of taxable income because the public understands that concept." Comment on this statement, and tell why income tax allocation is necessary.
7. Nabisco had about $1.3 billion of deferred income taxes in 1996, equal to about 11 percent of total liabilities. This percentage had risen or remained steady for many years. Given management's desire to put off the payment of taxes for as long as possible, the long-term growth of the economy and inflation, and the definition of a liability (probable future sacrifice of economic benefits arising from present obligations), make an argument for not accounting for deferred income taxes.
8. Why should a gain or loss on discontinued operations be disclosed separately on the income statement?
9. Explain the two major criteria for extraordinary items. How should extraordinary items be disclosed in the financial statements?
10. When an accounting change occurs, what disclosures must be made in the financial statements?
11. How are earnings per share disclosed in the financial statements?
12. When does a company have a simple capital structure? A complex capital structure?
13. What is the difference between basic and diluted earnings per share?
14. What is the difference between the statement of stockholders' equity and the stockholders' equity section of the balance sheet?
15. When does a company have a deficit in retained earnings?
16. What is the purpose of a restriction on retained earnings? Why might a company have restrictions on its retained earnings?
17. Explain how the accounting treatment of stock dividends differs from that of cash dividends.
18. What is the difference between a stock dividend and a stock split? What is the effect of each on the capital structure of the corporation?

19. Would you expect a corporation's book value per share to equal its market value per share? Why or why not?

Short Exercises

LO1 Quality of Earnings

SE 1. Each of the items listed below is a quality of earnings issue. Indicate whether the item is (a) an accounting method, (b) an accounting estimate, or (c) a nonoperating item. For any item for which the answer is (a) or (b), indicate which alternative is usually the more conservative choice.

1. LIFO versus FIFO
2. Extraordinary loss
3. 10-year useful life versus 15-year useful life
4. Effect of change in accounting principle
5. Straight-line versus accelerated method
6. Discontinued operations
7. Immediate write-off versus amortization
8. Increase versus decrease in percentage of uncollectible accounts

LO1 Corporate Income Statement

SE 2. Assume that Bedard Company's chief financial officer gave you the following information: Net Sales, $720,000; Cost of Goods Sold, $350,000; Loss from Discontinued Operations (net of income tax benefit of $70,000), $200,000; Loss on Disposal of Discontinued Operations (net of income tax benefit of $16,000), $50,000; Operating Expenses, $130,000; Income Taxes Expense on Continuing Operations, $80,000. From this information, prepare the company's income statement for the year ended June 30, 20xx. (Ignore earnings per share information.)

LO2 Corporate Income Tax Rate Schedule

SE 3. Using the corporate tax rate schedule in Table 1, compute the income tax liability for taxable income of (1) $400,000 and (2) $20,000,000.

LO4 Earnings per Share

SE 4. During 20x4, Halmut Corporation reported a net income of $669,200. On January 1, Halmut had 360,000 shares of common stock outstanding. The company issued an additional 240,000 shares of common stock on August 1. In 20x4, the company had a simple capital structure. During 20x5, there were no transactions involving common stock, and the company reported net income of $870,000. Determine the weighted-average number of common shares outstanding for 20x4 and 20x5. Also, compute earnings per share for 20x4 and 20x5.

LO5 Statement of Stockholders' Equity

SE 5. Refer to the statement of stockholders' equity for Tri-State Corporation in Exhibit 2 to answer the following questions: (1) At what price per share were the 5,000 shares of common stock sold? (2) What was the conversion price per share of the common stock? (3) At what price was the common stock selling on the date of the stock dividend? (4) At what price per share was the treasury stock purchased?

LO5 LO6 Effects of Stockholders' Equity Actions

SE 6. Tell whether each of the following actions will increase, decrease, or have no effect on total assets, total liabilities, and total stockholders' equity:

1. Declaration of a stock dividend
2. Declaration of a cash dividend
3. Stock split
4. Restriction of retained earnings
5. Purchase of treasury stock

LO5 Restriction of Retained Earnings

SE 7. Jasmine Company has a lawsuit filed against it. The board took action to restrict retained earnings in the amount of $2,500,000 on May 31, 20x4, pending the outcome of the suit. On May 31, the company had retained earnings of $3,725,000. Show how the restriction on retained earnings would be disclosed as a note to the financial statements.

LO6 Stock Dividends

SE 8. On February 15, Purple Mountain Corporation's board of directors declared a 2 percent stock dividend applicable to the outstanding shares of its $10 par value common stock, of which 200,000 shares are authorized, 130,000 are issued, and 20,000 are held in the treasury. The stock dividend was distributable on March 15 to stockholders of record on March 1. On February 15, the market value of the common stock was $15 per share. On March 30, the board of directors declared a $.50 per share cash dividend. No other stock transactions have occurred. Record, as necessary, the transactions of February 15, March 1, March 15, and March 30.

LO6 Stock Split

SE 9. On August 10, the board of directors of Torrinni International declared a 3-for-1 stock split of its $9 par value common stock, of which 800,000 shares were authorized and 250,000 were issued and outstanding. The market value on that date was $60 per share. On the same date, the balance of paid-in capital in excess of par value, common was $6,000,000, and the balance of retained earnings was $6,500,000. Prepare the stockholders' equity section of the company's balance sheet after the stock split. What entry, if any, is needed to record the stock split?

LO7 Book Value for Preferred and Common Stock

SE 10. Using data from the stockholders' equity section of Gerhardt Corporation's balance sheet shown below, compute the book value per share for both the preferred and the common stock.

Contributed capital		
Preferred stock, $100 par value, 8 percent cumulative, 10,000 shares authorized, 500 shares issued and outstanding*		$ 50,000
Common stock, $10 par value, 100,000 shares authorized, 40,000 shares issued and outstanding	$400,000	
Paid-in capital in excess of par value, common	516,000	916,000
Total contributed capital		$ 966,000
Retained earnings		275,000
Total stockholders' equity		$1,241,000

*The preferred stock is callable at $104 per share, and one year's dividends are in arrears.

EXERCISES

LO1 Effect of Alternative Accounting Methods

E 1. At the end of its first year of operations, a company calculated its ending merchandise inventory according to three different accounting methods, as follows: FIFO, $95,000; average-cost, $90,000; LIFO, $86,000. If the company used the average-cost method, its net income for the year would be $34,000.

1. Determine net income if the company used the FIFO method.
2. Determine net income if the company used the LIFO method.
3. Which method is more conservative?
4. Will the consistency convention be violated if the company chooses to use the LIFO method?
5. Does the full-disclosure convention require disclosure of the inventory method used in the financial statements?

LO1 Corporate Income Statement

E 2. Assume that the Sedgeway Furniture Company's chief financial officer gave you the following information: net sales, $1,900,000; cost of goods sold, $1,050,000; extraordinary gain (net of income taxes of $3,500), $12,500; loss from discontinued operations (net of income tax benefit of $30,000), $50,000; loss on disposal of discontinued operations (net of income tax benefit of $13,000), $35,000; selling expenses, $50,000; administrative expenses, $40,000; income taxes expense on continuing operations, $300,000. From this information, prepare the company's income statement for the year ended June 30, 20xx. (Ignore earnings per share information.)

LO1 LO2 LO3 LO4 Corporate Income Statement

E 3. The following items are components of Asheville Corporation's income statement for the year ended December 31, 20x4:

Sales	$555,000
Cost of goods sold	(275,000)
Operating expenses	(112,500)
Restructuring	(55,000)
Total income taxes expense for period	(82,350)
Income from operations of a discontinued segment	80,000
Gain on disposal of segment	70,000
Extraordinary gain	36,000
Cumulative effect of a change in accounting principle	(24,000)
Net income	$192,150
Earnings per share	$.96

Recast the income statement in proper multistep form, including allocating income taxes to appropriate items (assume a 30 percent income tax rate) and showing earnings per share figures (200,000 shares outstanding).

LO2 Corporate Income Tax Rate Schedule

E 4. Using the corporate tax rate schedule in Table 1, compute the income tax liability for the following situations:

Situation	Taxable Income
A	$ 70,000
B	85,000
C	320,000

LO2 Income Tax Allocation

E 5. Ft. Worth Corporation reported the following accounting income before income taxes, income taxes expense, and net income for 20x2 and 20x3:

	20x2	20x3
Income before income taxes	$280,000	$280,000
Income taxes expense	88,300	88,300
Net income	$191,700	$191,700

On the balance sheet, deferred income taxes liability increased by $38,400 in 20x2 and decreased by $18,800 in 20x3.

1. How much did Ft. Worth Corporation actually pay in income taxes for 20x2 and 20x3?
2. Prepare entries in journal form to record income taxes expense for 20x2 and 20x3.

LO4 Earnings per Share

E 6. During 20x3, Portland Corporation reported a net income of $1,529,500. On January 1, Portland had 700,000 shares of common stock outstanding. The company issued an additional 420,000 shares of common stock on October 1. In 20x3, the company had a simple capital structure. During 20x4, there were no transactions involving common stock, and the company reported net income of $2,016,000.

1. Determine the weighted-average number of common shares outstanding each year.
2. Compute earnings per share for each year.

LO5 Restriction of Retained Earnings

E 7. The board of directors of the Sunset Company has approved plans to acquire another company during the coming year. The acquisition should cost approximately $550,000. The board took action to restrict retained earnings of the company in the amount of $550,000 on July 17, 20x4. On July 31, the company had retained earnings of $975,000. Show how the restriction on retained earnings would be disclosed in a note to the financial statements.

LO5 Statement of Stockholders' Equity

E 8. The stockholders' equity section of Mallory Corporation's balance sheet on December 31, 20x4, appears as follows:

Contributed capital
  Common stock, $2 par value, 500,000 shares
    authorized, 400,000 shares issued and outstanding $ 800,000
  Paid-in capital in excess of par value, common   1,200,000
  Total contributed capital $2,000,000
Retained earnings   4,200,000
Total stockholders' equity $6,200,000

Prepare a statement of stockholders' equity for the year ended December 31, 20x5, assuming the following transactions occurred in sequence during 20x5:

a. Issued 10,000 shares of $100 par value, 9 percent cumulative preferred stock at par after obtaining authorization from the state.
b. Issued 40,000 shares of common stock in connection with the conversion of bonds having a carrying value of $600,000.
c. Declared and issued a 2 percent common stock dividend. The market value on the date of declaration was $14 per share.
d. Purchased 10,000 shares of common stock for the treasury at a cost of $16 per share.
e. Earned net income of $460,000.
f. Declared and paid the full year's dividend on preferred stock and a dividend of $.40 per share on common stock outstanding at the end of the year.
g. Had foreign currency translation adjustment of minus $100,000.

Chapter 15 The Corporate Income Statement and the Statement of Stockholders' Equity

LO6 Journal Entries: Stock Dividends

E 9. Perfect Rest Company has 30,000 shares of its $1 par value common stock outstanding. Record in journal form the following transactions as they relate to the company's common stock:

July 17 Declared a 10 percent stock dividend on common stock to be distributed on August 10 to stockholders of record on July 31. Market value of the stock was $5 per share on this date.
31 Record date.
Aug. 10 Distributed the stock dividend declared on July 17.
Sept. 1 Declared a $.50 per share cash dividend on common stock to be paid on September 16 to stockholders of record on September 10.

LO6 Stock Split

E 10. Teuong Company currently has 500,000 shares of $1 par value common stock authorized with 200,000 shares outstanding. The board of directors declared a 2-for-1 split on May 15, when the market value of the common stock was $2.50 per share. The retained earnings balance on May 15 was $700,000. Paid-in capital in excess of par value, common on this date was $20,000. Prepare the stockholders' equity section of the company's balance sheet before and after the stock split. What entry, if any, would be necessary to record the stock split?

LO6 Stock Split

E 11. On January 15, the board of directors of Exavier International declared a 3-for-1 stock split of its $12 par value common stock, of which 800,000 shares were authorized and 200,000 were issued and outstanding. The market value on that date was $45 per share. On the same date, the balance of paid-in capital in excess of par value, common was $4,000,000, and the balance of retained earnings was $8,000,000. Prepare the stockholders' equity section of the company's balance sheet before and after the stock split. What entry, if any, is needed to record the stock split?

LO7 Book Value for Preferred and Common Stock

E 12. Below is the stockholders' equity section of Village Corporation's balance sheet. Determine the book value per share for both the preferred and the common stock.

Contributed capital
Preferred stock, $100 per share, 6 percent
  cumulative, 10,000 shares authorized, 200
  shares issued and outstanding* $ 20,000
Common stock, $5 par value, 100,000 shares
  authorized, 10,000 shares issued, 9,000 shares
  outstanding $50,000
Paid-in capital in excess of par value, common   28,000   78,000
Total contributed capital $ 98,000
Retained earnings   95,000
Total contributed capital and retained earnings $193,000
Less treasury stock, common (1,000 shares at cost)   15,000
Total stockholders' equity $178,000

*The preferred stock is callable at $105 per share, and one year's dividends are in arrears.

PROBLEMS

LO1 Effect of Alternative Accounting Methods

P 1. Carsey Company began operations in 20xx. At the beginning of the year, the company purchased plant assets of $450,000, with an estimated useful life of ten years and no salvage value. During the year, the company had net sales of $650,000, salaries expense of $100,000, and other expenses of $40,000, excluding depreciation. In addition, Carsey Company purchased inventory as follows:

Jan. 15	400 units at $200	$ 80,000
Mar. 20	200 units at $204	40,800
June 15	800 units at $208	166,400
Sept. 18	600 units at $206	123,600
Dec. 9	300 units at $210	63,000
Total	2,300 units	$473,800

At the end of the year, a physical inventory disclosed 500 units still on hand. The managers of Carsey Company know they have a choice of accounting methods, but they are unsure how those methods will affect net income. They have heard of the FIFO and LIFO inventory methods and the straight-line and double-declining-balance depreciation methods.

REQUIRED
1. Prepare two income statements for Carsey Company, one using the FIFO and straight-line methods and the other using the LIFO and double-declining-balance methods. Ignore income taxes.
2. Prepare a schedule accounting for the difference in the two net income figures obtained in **1**.
3. What effect does the choice of accounting method have on Carsey's inventory turnover? What conclusions can you draw?
4. How does the choice of accounting methods affect Carsey's return on assets? Assume the company's only assets are cash of $40,000, inventory, and plant assets. Use year-end balances to compute the ratios. Is your evaluation of Carsey's profitability affected by the choice of accounting methods?

P 2. **Corporate Income Statement**
LO1 LO2 LO3 LO4

Income statement information for Dimsum Corporation during 20x3 is as follows:
a. Administrative expenses, $110,000.
b. Cost of goods sold, $440,000.
c. Restructuring charge, $125,000.
d. Cumulative effect of a change in inventory methods that decreased income (net of taxes, $28,000), $60,000.
e. Extraordinary loss from a storm (net of taxes, $10,000), $20,000.
f. Income taxes expense, continuing operations, $42,000.
g. Net sales, $1,015,000.
h. Selling expenses, $190,000.

REQUIRED
1. Prepare Dimsum Corporation's income statement for 20x3, including earnings per share, assuming a weighted average of 200,000 shares of common stock outstanding for 20x3.
2. What is a restructuring charge, and why is it deducted before income from operations before income taxes?

P 3. **Corporate Income Statement and Evaluation of Business Operations**
LO1 LO2 LO3 LO4

During 20x3, Burston Corporation engaged in a number of complex transactions to improve the business—selling off a division, retiring bonds, and changing accounting methods. The company has always issued a simple single-step income statement, and the accountant has accordingly prepared the December 31 year-end income statements for 20x2 and 20x3, as shown below.

Burston Corporation
Income Statements
For the Years Ended December 31, 20x3 and 20x2

	20x3	20x2
Net sales	$3,500,000	$4,200,000
Cost of goods sold	(1,925,000)	(2,100,000)
Operating expenses	(787,500)	(525,000)
Income taxes expense	(576,450)	(472,500)
Income from operations of a discontinued segment	560,000	
Gain on disposal of discontinued segment	490,000	
Extraordinary gain	252,000	
Cumulative effect of a change in accounting principle	(168,000)	
Net income	$1,345,050	$1,102,500
Earnings per share	$ 6.73	$ 5.51

Theodore Burston, the president of Burston Corporation, is pleased to see that both net income and earnings per share increased by 22 percent from 20x2 to 20x3 and intends to announce to the company's stockholders that the plan to improve the business has been successful.

REQUIRED
1. Recast the 20x3 and 20x2 income statements in proper multistep form, including allocating income taxes to appropriate items (assume a 30 percent income tax rate) and showing earnings per share figures (200,000 shares outstanding).
2. What is your assessment of Burston Corporation's plan and business operations in 20x3?

P 4. The stockholders' equity section of Montpelior Linen Mills, Inc., as of December 31, 20x2, was as follows:

LO5 Dividends, Stock Splits, and
LO6 Stockholders' Equity
LO7

Contributed capital		
Common stock, $6 par value, 500,000 shares authorized, 80,000 shares issued and outstanding		$ 480,000
Paid-in capital in excess of par value, common		150,000
Total contributed capital		$ 630,000
Retained earnings		480,000
Total stockholders' equity		$1,110,000

A review of the stockholders' equity records of Montpelior Linen Mills, Inc., disclosed the following transactions during 20x3:

Mar. 25 The board of directors declared a 5 percent stock dividend to stockholders of record on April 20 to be distributed on May 1. The market value of the common stock was $11 per share.
Apr. 20 Date of record for the stock dividend.
May 1 Distributed the stock dividend.
Sept. 10 Declared a 3-for-1 stock split.
Dec. 15 Declared a 10 percent stock dividend to stockholders of record on January 15 to be distributed on February 15. The market price on this date is $3.50 per share.

REQUIRED
1. Record the stockholders' equity components of the transactions for Montpelior Linen Mills, Inc., in T accounts.
2. Prepare the stockholders' equity section of the company's balance sheet as of December 31, 20x3. Assume net income for 20x3 is $47,000.
3. Calculate book value per share before and after the above transactions.

P 5. The balance sheet of O'Malley Woolen Company disclosed the following stockholders' equity as of September 30, 20x3:

LO5 Dividends, Stock Splits, and
LO6 Stockholders' Equity
LO7

Contributed capital		
Common stock, $2 par value, 1,000,000 shares authorized, 300,000 shares issued and outstanding		$ 600,000
Paid-in capital in excess of par value, common		370,000
Total contributed capital		$ 970,000
Retained earnings		350,000
Total stockholders' equity		$1,320,000

The following stockholders' equity transactions were completed during the next fiscal year in the order presented:

20x3
Dec. 17 Declared a 10 percent stock dividend to be distributed January 20 to stockholders of record on January 1. The market value per share on the date of declaration was $4.

20x4
Jan. 1 Date of record.
    20 Distributed the stock dividend.
Apr. 14 Declared a $.25 per share cash dividend. The cash dividend is payable May 15 to stockholders of record on May 1.

May   1 Date of record.
     15 Paid the cash dividend.
June 17 Split its stock 2 for 1.
Sept. 15 Declared a cash dividend of $.10 per share payable October 10 to stockholders of record on October 1.

On September 14, the board of directors restricted retained earnings for plant expansion in the amount of $175,000. The restriction should be shown in the notes to the financial statements.

REQUIRED ▶

1. Record the above transactions in journal form.
2. Prepare the stockholders' equity section of the company's balance sheet as of September 30, 20x4, with an appropriate disclosure of the restriction of retained earnings. Assume net income for the year is $150,000.
3. Calculate book value per share before and after the transactions.

ALTERNATE PROBLEMS

P 6.
LO1 Corporate Income Statement
LO2
LO3
LO4

Information concerning operations of MacFarland Weather Gear Corporation during 20xx is as follows:

a. Administrative expenses, $90,000.
b. Cost of goods sold, $420,000.
c. Write-down of assets, $75,000.
d. Cumulative effect of an accounting change in depreciation methods that increased income (net of taxes, $20,000), $42,000.
e. Extraordinary loss from an earthquake (net of taxes, $36,000), $60,000.
f. Sales (net), $975,000.
g. Selling expenses, $80,000.
h. Income taxes expense applicable to continuing operations, $105,000.

REQUIRED ▶

1. Prepare the corporation's income statement for the year ended December 31, 20xx, including earnings per share information. Assume a weighted average of 100,000 common shares outstanding during the year.
2. What is a write-down, and why is it deducted before income from operations?

P 7.
LO5 Dividends, Stock Splits, and
LO6 Stockholders' Equity
LO7

The stockholders' equity section of the balance sheet of Boysan Corporation as of December 31, 20x4, was as follows:

Contributed capital	
Common stock, $4 par value, 500,000 shares authorized, 200,000 shares issued and outstanding	$ 800,000
Paid-in capital in excess of par value, common	1,000,000
Total contributed capital	$1,800,000
Retained earnings	1,200,000
Total stockholders' equity	$3,000,000

The following transactions occurred in 20x5 for Boysan Corporation:

Feb. 28 The board of directors declared a 10 percent stock dividend to stockholders of record on March 25 to be distributed on April 5. The market value on this date is $16.
Mar. 25 Date of record for stock dividend.
Apr. 5 Distributed the stock dividend.
Aug. 3 Declared a 2-for-1 stock split.
Nov. 20 Purchased 18,000 shares of the company's common stock at $8 per share for the treasury.
Dec. 31 Declared a 5 percent stock dividend to stockholders of record on January 25 to be distributed on February 5. The market value per share was $9.

REQUIRED ▶

1. Record the stockholders' equity components of the transactions for Boysan Corporation in T accounts.
2. Prepare the stockholders' equity section of the company's balance sheet as of December 31, 20x5. Assume net income for 20x5 is $108,000.
3. Calculate book value per share before and after the above transactions.

P 8.
LO5 Dividends, Stock Splits, and
LO6 Stockholders' Equity
LO7

The stockholders' equity section of Blue Ridge Furniture Restoration Company's balance sheet as of December 31, 20x2, was as follows:

Contributed capital	
Common stock, $1 par value, 3,000,000 shares authorized, 500,000 shares issued and outstanding	$ 500,000
Paid-in capital in excess of par value, common	200,000
Total contributed capital	$ 700,000
Retained earnings	540,000
Total stockholders' equity	$1,240,000

The company engaged in the following stockholders' equity transactions during 20x3:

Mar. 5 Declared a $.20 per share cash dividend to be paid on April 6 to stockholders of record on March 20.
  20 Date of record.
Apr. 6 Paid the cash dividend.
June 17 Declared a 10 percent stock dividend to be distributed August 17 to stockholders of record on August 5. The market value of the stock was $7 per share.
Aug. 5 Date of record.
  17 Distributed the stock dividend.
Oct. 2 Split its stock 3 for 1.
Dec. 27 Declared a cash dividend of $.05 payable January 27, 20x4, to stockholders of record on January 14, 20x4.

On December 9, the board of directors restricted retained earnings for a pending lawsuit in the amount of $100,000. The restriction should be shown in the notes to the firm's financial statements.

REQUIRED
1. Record the 20x3 transactions in journal form.
2. Prepare the stockholders' equity section of the company's balance sheet as of December 31, 20x3, with an appropriate disclosure of the restriction on retained earnings. Assume net income for the year is $200,000.
3. Calculate book value per share before and after the above transactions.

SKILLS DEVELOPMENT CASES

Conceptual Analysis

SD 1.
LO1 Interpretation of Earnings Reports

In a recent year, analysts expected International Business Machines (IBM) <www.ibm.com> to earn $1.32 per share. The company actually earned $1.33. Microsoft Corporation <www.microsoft.com> was expected to earn $.43 per share, but it earned only $.41. The corporate income statements of these companies show that Microsoft had a special charge (with corresponding liability) of $660 million, or $.06 per share, based on settlement of a class-action law suit filed on behalf of consumers, whereas IBM had no such a charge.[25] Who did better, Microsoft or IBM? Use quality of earnings to support your answer. Also, what is the effect of Microsoft's special charge on current and future cash flows?

SD 2.
LO1 Classic Quality of Earnings
LO3

On Tuesday, January 19, 1988, IBM <www.ibm.com> reported greatly increased earnings for the fourth quarter of 1987. Despite this reported gain in earnings, the price of IBM's stock on the New York Stock Exchange declined by $6 per share to $111.75. In sympathy with this move, most other technology stocks also declined.[26]

IBM's fourth-quarter net earnings rose from $1.39 billion, or $2.28 a share, to $2.08 billion, or $3.47 a share, an increase of 49.6 percent and 52.2 percent over the same period a year earlier. Management declared that these results demonstrated the effectiveness of IBM's efforts to become more competitive and that, despite the economic uncertainties of 1988, the company was planning for growth.

The apparent cause of the stock price decline was that the huge increase in income could be traced to nonrecurring gains. Investment analysts pointed out that IBM's high earnings stemmed primarily from such factors as a lower tax rate. Despite most analysts' expectations of a tax rate between 40 and 42 percent, IBM's was a low 36.4 percent, down from the previous year's 45.3 percent. Analysts were also disappointed in IBM's revenue growth. Revenues within the United States were down, and much of the company's growth in revenues came through favorable currency translations, increases that might not be repeated. In fact, some estimates of IBM's fourth-quarter earnings attributed $.50 per share to currency translations and another $.25 to tax-rate changes.

Other factors contributing to IBM's rise in earnings were one-time transactions, such as the sale of Intel Corporation stock and bond redemptions, along with a corporate stock buyback program that reduced the amount of stock outstanding in the fourth quarter by 7.4 million shares.

The analysts were concerned about the quality of IBM's earnings. Identify four quality of earnings issues reported in the case and the analysts' concern about each. In percentage terms, what is the impact of the currency changes on fourth-quarter earnings? Comment on management's assessment of IBM's performance. Do you agree with management? (Optional question: What has IBM's subsequent performance been?) Be prepared to discuss your answers in class.

Ethical Dilemma

SD 3.
LO6 Ethics and Stock Dividends

For 20 years Bass Products Corporation, a public corporation, has followed the practice of paying a cash dividend every quarter and has promoted itself to investors as a stable, reliable company. Recent competition from Asian companies has negatively affected its earnings and cash flows. As a result, Sandra Bass, president of the company, is proposing that the board of directors declare a stock dividend of 5 percent this year instead of a cash dividend. She says, "This will maintain our consecutive dividend record and will not require any cash outflow." What is the difference between a cash dividend and a stock dividend? Why does a corporation usually distribute either kind of dividend, and how does each affect the financial statements? Is the action that Sandra Bass has proposed ethical?

Research Activity

SD 4.
LO1 Corporate Income Statement,
LO2 Statement of Stockholders'
LO3 Equity, and Book Value per
LO5 Share
LO6
LO7

Select the annual reports of three corporations, using one or more of the following sources: your library, the Internet, or the Needles Accounting Resource Center Web Site at http://accounting.college.hmco.com/students. You may choose companies from the same industry or at random, at the direction of your instructor. (If you completed the related research activity in the chapter on contributed capital, use the same three companies.) Prepare a table with a column for each corporation. Then, for any year covered by the balance sheet, the statement of stockholders' equity, and the income statement, answer the following questions: Does the company own treasury stock? Did it buy or retire any treasury stock? Did it declare a stock dividend or a stock split? What other transactions appear in the statement of stockholders' equity? Has the company deferred any income taxes? Were there any discontinued operations, extraordinary items, or accounting changes? Compute the book value per common share for the company. In *The Wall Street Journal* or the financial section of another daily newspaper, find the current market price of each company's common stock and compare it with the book value you computed. Should there be any relationship between the two values? Be prepared to discuss your answers in class.

Decision-Making Practice

SD 5.
LO5 Analyzing Effects of
LO6 Stockholders' Equity
LO7 Transactions

Metzger Steel Corporation (MSC) is a small specialty steel manufacturer located in northern Alabama. It has been owned by the Metzger family for several generations. Arnold Metzger is a major shareholder in MSC by virtue of his having inherited 200,000 shares of common stock in the company. Metzger has not shown much interest in the business because of his enthusiasm for archaeology, which takes him to far parts of the world. However, when he received the minutes of the last board of directors meeting, he questioned a number of transactions involving stockholders' equity. He asks you, as a person with a knowledge of accounting, to help him interpret the effect of these transactions on his interest in MSC.

You begin by examining the stockholders' equity section of MSC's December 31, 20x4, balance sheet:

Metzger Steel Corporation
Stockholders' Equity
December 31, 20x4

Contributed capital	
Common stock, $10 par value, 5,000,000 shares authorized, 1,000,000 shares issued and outstanding	$10,000,000
Paid-in capital in excess of par value, common	25,000,000
Total contributed capital	$35,000,000
Retained earnings	20,000,000
Total stockholders' equity	$55,000,000

Then you read the relevant parts of the minutes of the board of directors meeting on December 15, 20x5:

Item A The president reported the following transactions involving the company's stock during the last quarter:

October 15. Sold 500,000 shares of authorized common stock through the investment banking firm of T.R. Kendall at a net price of $50 per share.

November 1. Purchased 100,000 shares for the corporate treasury from Lucy Metzger at a price of $55 per share.

Item B The board declared a 2-for-1 stock split (accomplished by halving the par value and doubling each stockholder's shares), followed by a 10 percent stock dividend. The board then declared a cash dividend of $2 per share on the resulting shares. Cash dividends are declared on outstanding shares and shares distributable. All these transactions are applicable to stockholders of record on December 20 and are payable on January 10. The market value of MSC stock on the board meeting date after the stock split was estimated to be $30.

Item C The chief financial officer stated that he expected the company to report net income for the year of $4,000,000.

1. Prepare a stockholders' equity section of MSC's balance sheet as of December 31, 20x5, that reflects the above transactions. (**Hint:** Use T accounts to analyze the transactions. Also use a T account to keep track of the shares of common stock outstanding.)
2. Write a memorandum to Arnold Metzger that shows the book value per share and Metzger's percentage of ownership at the beginning and end of the year. Explain the difference and state whether Metzger's position has improved during the year. Tell why or why not and state how Metzger may be able to maintain his percentage of ownership.

FINANCIAL REPORTING AND ANALYSIS CASES

Interpreting Financial Reports

FRA 1. The consolidated statement of stockholders' equity for Jackson Electronics, Inc., a manufacturer of a broad line of electrical components, is presented at the top of the next page.

LO1 Interpretation of Statement
LO5 of Stockholders' Equity

This statement has nine summary transactions. (1) Show that you understand it by preparing an entry in journal form with an explanation for each entry. In each case,

Jackson Electronics, Inc.
Consolidated Statement of Stockholders' Equity
(In thousands)

	Preferred Stock $100 Par Value	Common Stock $1 Par Value	Paid-in Capital in Excess of Par Value, Common	Retained Earnings	Treasury Stock, Common	Accumulated Other Comprehensive Income	Total
Balance at September 30, 20x4	$2,756	$3,902	$14,149	$119,312	($942)		$139,177
Net income	—	—	—	18,753	—		18,753
Unrealized gain on available for sale securities						$12,000	12,000
Redemption and retirement of preferred stock (27,560 shares)	(2,756)	—	—	—	—		(2,756)
Stock options exercised (89,000 shares)	—	89	847	—	—		936
Purchases of common stock for treasury (501,412 shares)	—	—	—	—	(12,552)		(12,552)
Issuance of common stock (148,000 shares) in exchange for convertible subordinated debentures	—	148	3,635	—	—		3,783
Issuance of common stock (715,000 shares) for cash	—	715	24,535	—	—		25,250
Issuance of 500,000 shares of common stock in exchange for investment in Electrix Company shares	—	500	17,263	—	—		17,763
Cash dividends—common stock ($.80 per share)				(3,086)			(3,086)
Balance at September 30, 20x5	$—	$5,354	$60,429	$134,979	($13,494)	$12,000	$199,268

if applicable, determine the average price per common share. At times, you will have to make assumptions about an offsetting part of the entry. For example, assume debentures (long-term bonds) are recorded at face value and that employees pay cash for stock purchased under company incentive plans. (2) Define comprehensive income and determine the amount for Jackson Electronics.

Group Activity: Assign each transaction to a different group to develop the entry and present the explanation to the class.

FRA 2.
LO2 Analysis of Income Taxes from Annual Report

In its 2000 annual report, The Washington Post Company <www.washingtonpost.com>, a newspaper publishing and television broadcasting company based in Washington, D.C., provided the following data about its current and deferred income tax provisions (in millions):[27]

	2000	
	Current	Deferred
U.S. federal	$ 77.5	$ 4.9
Foreign	1.0	—
State	22.6	(12.7)
	$101.1	($7.8)

1. What was the 2000 income taxes expense? Record in journal form the overall income tax liability for 2000, using income tax allocation procedures.
2. In the long-term liability section of its balance sheet, The Washington Post Company shows deferred income taxes of $117.7 million in 2000 versus $114.0 million in 1999. This shows an increase in the amount of deferred income taxes. How do such deferred income taxes arise? What would cause deferred income taxes to increase? Give an example of this process. Given the definition of a liability, do you see a potential problem with the company's classifying deferred income taxes as a liability?

International Company

FRA 3.
LO5 Restriction of Retained Earnings

In some countries, including Japan, the availability of retained earnings for the payment of dividends is restricted. The following disclosure appeared in the annual report of Yamaha Motor Company, Ltd. <www.yamaha.com>, the Japanese motorcycle manufacturer:[28]

> The Commercial Code of Japan provides that an amount not less than 10 percent of the total of cash dividends and bonuses [paid] to directors and corporate auditors be appropriated as a legal reserve until such reserve equals 25 percent of stated capital. The legal reserve may be used to reduce a deficit or may be transferred to stated capital, but is not available as dividends.

"Stated capital" is equivalent to common stock. For Yamaha, this legal reserve amounted to ¥34.4 billion, or $290 million. How does this practice differ from that in the United States? Why do you think it is government policy in Japan? Do you think it is a good idea?

Toys "R" Us Annual Report

FRA 4.
LO1 Corporate Income Statement,
LO3 Statement of Stockholders'
LO5 Equity, and Book Value per Share

Refer to the Toys "R" Us <www.tru.com> annual report to answer the following questions:

1. Does Toys "R" Us have discontinued operations, extraordinary items, or cumulative effects from accounting changes? Would you say the income statement for Toys "R" Us is relatively simple or relatively complex?
2. What transactions most commonly affect the stockholders' equity section of the balance sheet of Toys "R" Us? Examine the statements of stockholders' equity.

Comparison Case: Toys "R" Us and Walgreen Co.

FRA 5.
LO7 Book Value and Market Value

Refer to the annual report for Toys "R" Us <www.tru.com> and the financial statements for Walgreens <www.walgreens.com> in the Supplement to Chapter 6. Compute the 2002 and 2001 book value per share for both companies and compare the results to the average stock price of each in the fourth quarter of 2002 as shown in the notes to the financial statements. How do you explain the differences in book value per share, and how do you interpret their relationship to market prices?

Fingraph® Financial Analyst™

FRA 6.
LO1 Stockholders' Equity Analysis
LO3
LO4
LO5
LO6
LO7

Choose any two companies in the same industry from the list of Fingraph companies on the Needles Accounting Resource Center Student Web Site at http://accounting.college.hmco.com/students. Access the Microsoft Excel spreadsheets for the companies you selected. Click on the URL at the top of each company's spreadsheet for a link to the company's web site and annual report.

1. In the annual reports of the companies you have selected, find the corporate income statement and summary of significant accounting policies (usually the first note to the financial statements). Did the companies report any discontinued operations, extraordinary items, or accounting changes? What percentage impact did these items have on earnings per share? Summarize the methods and estimates each company

uses in a table. If the company changed its accounting methods, was the change the result of a new accounting standard or a voluntary choice by management? Evaluate the quality of earnings for each company.

2. Did the companies provide a statement of stockholders' equity or summarize changes in stockholders' equity in the notes only? Did the companies declare any stock dividends or stock splits? Calculate book value per common share.
3. Find in the financial section of your local paper the current market prices of the companies' common stock. Discuss the difference between market price per share and book value per share.
4. Find and read references to earnings per share in management's discussion and analysis in each annual report.
5. Write a one-page executive summary that highlights the quality of earnings for these companies, the relationship of book value and market value, and the existence or absence of stock splits or dividends, including reference to management's assessment. Include your table with your report.

Internet Case

FRA 7.

LO1 **Comparison of Comprehensive**
LO4 **Income Disclosures**
LO5

When the FASB ruled that public companies should report comprehensive income, it did not issue specific guidelines for how this amount and its components should be disclosed. Choose two companies in the same industry from the Needles Accounting Resource Center Web Site at http://accounting.college.hmco.com/students. Using web links, go to the annual reports on the web sites of the two companies you have selected. In the latest annual report, look at the financial statements. How have your two companies reported comprehensive income—as a part of the income statement, a part of stockholders' equity, or a separate statement? What items create a difference between net income and comprehensive income? Is comprehensive income greater or less than net income? Is comprehensive income more volatile than net income? Which measure of income is used to compute basic earnings per share?

16 Long-Term Liabilities

Chapter 16 covers the management issues related to sources of long-term financing, with an emphasis on bond liabilities.

LEARNING OBJECTIVES

LO1 Identify the management issues related to issuing long-term debt.

LO2 Identify and contrast the major characteristics of bonds.

LO3 Record the issuance of bonds at face value and at a discount or premium.

LO4 Use present values to determine the value of bonds.

LO5 Amortize bond discounts and bond premiums using the straight-line and effective interest methods.

LO6 Record bonds issued between interest dates and year-end adjustments.

SUPPLEMENTAL OBJECTIVES

SO7 Account for the retirement of bonds and the conversion of bonds into stock.

SO8 Explain the basic features of mortgages payable, long-term leases, and pensions and other postretirement benefits as long-term liabilities.

DECISION POINT
A USER'S FOCUS

AT&T Corporation <www.att.com> During 2002, AT&T Corporation reduced its debt financing. How much to borrow and how much debt should be financed long term are two questions management must consider. What is the impact of AT&T's lower debt level on its capital structure and its interest-paying ability?

Decisions related to the issuance of long-term debt are among the most important that management has to make because, next to the success or failure of a company's operations, how the company finances its operations is the most important factor in the company's long-term viability. Long-term liabilities, or long-term debt, are obligations of a business that are due to be paid after one year or beyond the operating cycle, whichever is longer. Even after reducing its debt, AT&T's capital structure includes a large amount of long-term debt, as shown by the figures for 2002 in the Financial Highlights.[1] Total liabilities are greater than stockholders' equity, and the debt to equity ratio is 3.5 ($42,960 ÷ $12,312). What factors might have influenced AT&T's management to incur a large amount of debt?

In the past, AT&T was the nation's largest long-distance telephone company. The investments in power lines, transformers, computers, and other types of property, plant, and equipment required for this business are enormous. These are mostly long-term assets, and the most sensible way to finance them is through long-term financing. When the business was protected from competition, management could reasonably predict sufficient earnings and cash flow to

Now that AT&T is facing competition for its markets, why must management reassess the company's long-term liabilities?

meet the debt and interest obligations. Now that AT&T is facing open competition for its markets, the company must reassess not only the kind of business it is but also the amount and kinds of debt it carries. The amount and type of debt a company incurs depends on many factors, including the nature of the business, its competitive environment, the state of the financial markets, and the predictability of its earnings.

Financial Highlights: Capital Structure
(In millions)

Liabilities	
Total current liabilities	$12,024
Long-term debt	$18,812
Long-term benefit-related liabilities	4,001
Deferred income taxes	4,739
Other long-term liabilities and deferred credits	3,384
Total long-term liabilities	$30,936
Total liabilities	$42,960
Stockholders' equity	12,312
Total liabilities and stockholders' equity	$55,272

Management Issues Related to Issuing Long-Term Debt

LO1 Identify the management issues related to issuing long-term debt.

RELATED TEXT ASSIGNMENTS
Q: 1
SE: 1
E: 1
SD: 6
FRA: 1, 3, 4, 5, 6

Profitable operations and short-term credit seldom provide sufficient cash for a growing business. Growth often requires investment in long-term assets and in research and development and other activities that will produce income in future years. To finance such assets and activities, the company requires funds that will be available for longer periods. Two key sources of long-term funds are the issuance of capital stock and the issuance of long-term debt in the form of bonds, notes, mortgages, and leases. The management issues related to issuing long-term debt are (1) whether to take on long-term debt, (2) how much long-term debt to carry, (3) what types of long-term debt to incur, and (4) how to handle debt repayment.

The Decision to Issue Long-Term Debt

A key decision for management is whether to rely solely on stockholders' equity—capital stock issued and retained earnings—for long-term funds for the business or to rely partially on long-term debt for those funds. Since long-term debts represent financial commitments that must be paid at maturity and interest or other payments that must be paid periodically, common stock would seem to have two advantages over long-term debt: it does not have to be paid back, and dividends on common stock are usually paid only if the company earns sufficient income. Long-term debt does, however, have the following advantages over common stock:

KEY POINT: Although carrying a lot of debt is risky, there are some advantages to issuing bonds instead of stock. First, bond interest expense is tax-deductible for the issuing corporation, whereas dividends paid on stock are not. Second, issuing bonds is a way to raise capital without diluting ownership of the corporation. The challenge is to determine the optimal balance between stocks and bonds so that the advantages of each can be enjoyed.

1. **Stockholder control.** Since bondholders and other creditors do not have voting rights, common stockholders do not relinquish any control of the company.

2. **Tax effects.** The interest on debt is tax-deductible, whereas dividends on common stock are not. For example, if a corporation pays $100,000 in interest and the income tax rate is 30 percent, the net cost to the corporation is $70,000 because it will save $30,000 on its income taxes. To pay $100,000 in dividends, the company would have to earn $142,857 before taxes ($100,000 ÷ .70).

3. **Financial leverage.** If a corporation is able to earn more on its assets than it pays in interest on debt, the excess will increase its earnings for stockholders. This concept is called *financial leverage* or *trading on the equity*. For example, if a company is able to earn 12 percent, or $120,000, on a $1,000,000 investment financed by long-term 10 percent notes, it will earn $20,000 before taxes ($120,000 − $100,000). Financial leverage makes heavily debt-financed investments in office buildings and shopping centers attractive to investors, who hope to earn a return that exceeds the cost of the interest on the underlying debt. The debt to equity ratio is considered an overall measure of the financial leverage of a company.

www.continental.com

Despite these advantages, using debt financing is not always in a company's best interest. First, since cash is required to make periodic interest payments and to pay back the principal amount of the debt at the maturity date, a company whose plans for earnings do not pan out, whose operations are subject to ups and downs, or whose cash flow is weak can be in danger. If the company fails to meet its obligations, it can be forced into bankruptcy by creditors. In other words, a company may become overcommitted. Consider, for example, the heavily debt-financed airline industry. Both TWA and Continental Airlines filed for bankruptcy protection because they could not make payments on their long-term debt and other liabilities. (While in bankruptcy both firms restructured their debt and interest payments, but only Continental survived.) And Swiss Air and Midway Airlines shut down all operations because of insufficient cash to pay creditors and employees. Second, financial leverage can work against a company if the earnings from its investments do not exceed its interest payments. This happened during the savings and loan crisis when long-term debt was used to finance the construction of office buildings that subsequently could not be leased for enough money to cover interest payments.

Focus on International Business

Pushed to the Brink of Failure

Due to recent declines in passenger revenue, a record number of airlines are shutting down operations, operating under bankruptcy protection, seeking purchase by another airline, or relying on government loan guarantees for their short-term survival. Air Afrique, Canada 3000, Swiss Air, and Midway Airlines have been among those hardest hit.[2] Subsequently, TWA and US Airways joined the group as the largest airline bankruptcies. In a weak economy, the large amount of debt financing that airlines use to fund operations and purchases of aircraft adds to their troubles. With lower cash flows, the airlines find it harder to make payments of interest and principal on debt, thereby increasing the risk of default.

How Much Debt to Carry

The amount of total debt that companies carry varies widely. Many companies carry less than 100 percent of their stockholders' equity. However, as can be seen from Figure 1, the average debt to equity for these selected industries exceeds 100 percent of stockholders' equity. The range is from about 105 percent to 200 percent of equity. Clearly the use of debt financing varies widely across industries. Firms that own a high percentage of long-term assets would be looking to long-term financing as an option. We saw previously that AT&T has a debt to equity ratio of 3.5 times. Financial leverage makes it advantageous to have long-term debt so long as the company earns a satisfactory income and is able to make interest payments and repay the debt at maturity. Since failure to make timely interest payments could force a company into bankruptcy, it is important for companies to assess the risk of default or nonpayment of interest or principal.

www.att.com

A common measure of how much risk a company is undertaking with its debt is the **interest coverage ratio**. It measures the degree of protection a company has from default on interest payments. For AT&T, which in 2002 had income before taxes and special items of $2,836 million and interest expense of $1,448 million, this ratio is computed as follows:

$$\text{Interest Coverage Ratio} = \frac{\text{Income Before Taxes} + \text{Interest Expense}}{\text{Interest Expense}}$$

$$= \frac{\$2,836,000,000 + \$1,448,000,000}{\$1,448,000,000}$$

$$= 3.0 \text{ times}$$

This ratio shows that the interest expense for AT&T was covered 3.0 times in 2002. AT&T's interest coverage ratio was much higher in 2001 (6.1 times). Its income

FIGURE 1
Average Debt to Equity for Selected Industries

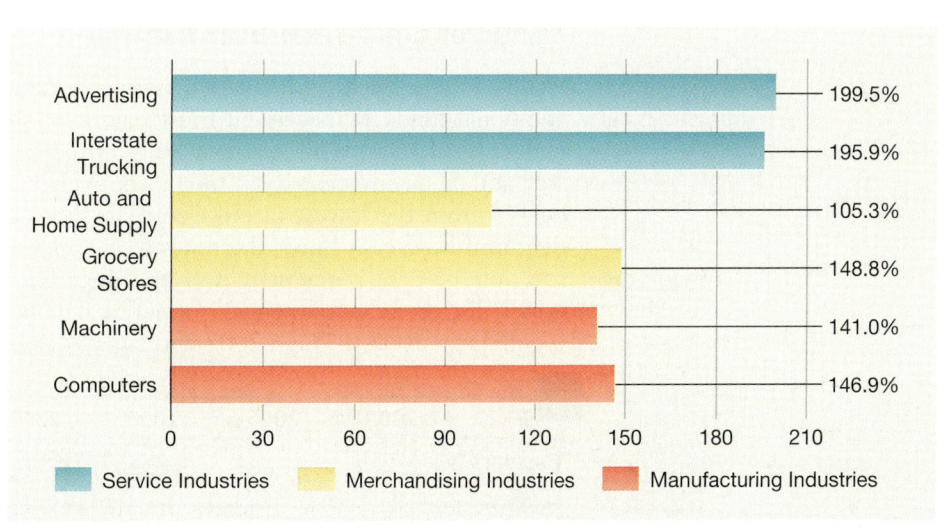

Industry	Percentage
Advertising	199.5%
Interstate Trucking	195.9%
Auto and Home Supply	105.3%
Grocery Stores	148.8%
Machinery	141.0%
Computers	146.9%

Service Industries — Merchandising Industries — Manufacturing Industries

Source: Data from Dun & Bradstreet, *Industry Norms and Key Business Ratios*, 2000–2001.

> **STOP AND THINK!**
> How does a lender assess the risk that a borrower may default—that is, not pay interest and principal when due?
>
> *The lender reviews the enterprise's current earnings and cash flows as well as its debt to equity and interest coverage ratios. The analysis may also include a historical comparison that reflects both good and poor economic times. The lender can then judge how well the company has met its past debt obligations.* ∎

before taxes in 2002 was 63 percent lower, and its interest expense was about the same, resulting in the dramatic decline in interest coverage. The risk for lenders increased substantially, and a lower debt rating is likely if earnings before taxes do not return to levels of previous years.

TYPES OF LONG-TERM DEBT

Long-term bonds (most of which are also called debentures) are the most common type of long-term debt. They can have many different characteristics, including the time until repayment, amount of interest, whether the company can elect to repay early, and whether they can be converted into common stock or other securities. But there are many other types of long-term debt, such as long-term notes, mortgages, and long-term leases. AT&T, for example, has a mixture of long-term obligations, as shown by the following excerpt from its 2002 annual report:[3]

www.att.com

Financial Highlights: Long-Term Obligations
(This table shows the outstanding long-term debt obligations, in millions, at December 31.)

Interest Rates (b)	Maturities	2002
Debentures and Notes		
4.59%–6.00%	2004–2009	$ 1,455
6.06%–6.50%	2004–2029	6,678
6.75%–7.50%	2004–2006	2,449
7.75%–8.85%	2003–2031	6,796
9.90%–19.95%	2004–2004	13
Variable rate	2003–2054	3,012
Total debentures and notes		20,403
Other		105
Less: Unamortized discount—net		(115)
Total long-term obligations		20,393
Less: Currently maturing long-term debt		1,581
Net long-term obligations		$18,812

To structure long-term financing to the best advantage of their companies, managers must know the characteristics of the various types of long-term debt.

TIMING OF LONG-TERM DEBT REPAYMENT

Ability to repay debt influences a company's debt rating and the cost of borrowing additional funds. Management must plan its cash flows carefully to ensure that it will have sufficient funds to repay long-term debt when it comes due. If this is done well and on a consistent basis, then a company can achieve the best debt rating and benefit from the lowest interest cost. To show the potential effects of long-term debt on future cash flows, the notes to a company's financial statements provide a schedule of debt repayment over the next five years. For example, in its notes, AT&T disclosed the following information detailing cash payments totaling $20,393 required for 2003 through 2007 and later:[4]

www.att.com

2003	2004	2005	2006	2007	Later years
$1,581	$2,437	$1,185	$4,328	$296	$10,566

Check out ACE for a Review Quiz at http://accounting.college.hmco.com/students.

THE NATURE OF BONDS

LO2 Identify and contrast the major characteristics of bonds.
RELATED TEXT ASSIGNMENTS
Q: 2, 3
SD: 4, 6
FRA: 6, 7

● **STOP AND THINK!**
If a company with a high debt to equity ratio wants to increase its debt when the economy is weak, what kind of bond might it issue?

It would most likely issue a secured bond because, rather than being issued on the company's general credit, certain assets are pledged as a guarantee of repayment. ■

TERMINOLOGY NOTE:
Do not confuse the terms *indenture* and *debenture*. They sound alike, but an indenture is a bond contract, whereas a debenture is an unsecured bond.

STUDY NOTE: A debenture of a solid company actually might be a less risky investment than a secured bond of an unstable company.

STUDY NOTE: An advantage of issuing serial bonds is that the organization retires the bonds over a period of years, rather than all at once.

A **bond** is a security, usually long term, representing money that a corporation or other entity borrows from the investing public. (Bonds are also issued by the U.S. government, state and local governments, and foreign countries to raise money.) A bond must be repaid at a specified time and requires periodic payments of interest.* Interest is usually paid semiannually (twice a year). Bonds must not be confused with stocks. Because stocks are shares of ownership, stockholders are owners. Bondholders are creditors. Bonds are promises to repay the amount borrowed, called the *principal*, and interest at a specified rate on specified future dates.

Often, a bondholder receives a **bond certificate** as evidence of the organization's debt. In most cases, the face value (denomination) of the bond is $1,000 or some multiple of $1,000. A **bond issue** is the total value of bonds issued at one time. For example, a $1,000,000 bond issue could consist of a thousand $1,000 bonds. Because a bond issue can be bought and held by many investors, the organization usually enters into a supplementary agreement called a **bond indenture**. The bond indenture defines the rights, privileges, and limitations of the bondholders. It generally describes such things as the maturity date of the bonds, interest payment dates, and interest rate. It may also cover repayment plans and restrictions.

The prices of bonds are stated in terms of a percentage of face value. A bond issue quoted at 103½ means that a $1,000 bond costs $1,035 ($1,000 × 1.035). When a bond sells at exactly 100, it is said to sell at face or par value. When it sells above 100, it is said to sell at a premium; below 100, at a discount. A $1,000 bond quoted at 87.62 would be selling at a discount and would cost the buyer $876.20.

A bond indenture can be written to fit the financing needs of an individual organization. As a result, the bonds being issued in today's financial markets have many different features. Several of the more important ones are described in the following paragraphs.

SECURED OR UNSECURED BONDS

Bonds can be either secured or unsecured. If issued on the general credit of the organization, they are **unsecured bonds** (also called *debenture bonds*). **Secured bonds** give the bondholders a pledge of certain assets as a guarantee of repayment. The security identified by a secured bond can be any specific asset of the organization or a general category of asset, such as property, plant, or equipment.

TERM OR SERIAL BONDS

When all the bonds of an issue mature at the same time, they are called **term bonds**. For instance, an organization may decide to issue $1,000,000 worth of bonds, all due 20 years from the date of issue. When the bonds in an issue mature on different dates, the bonds are called **serial bonds**. An example of serial bonds would be a $1,000,000 issue that calls for retiring $200,000 of the principal every five years. This arrangement means that after the first $200,000 payment is made, $800,000 of the bonds would remain outstanding for the next five years. In other words, $1,000,000 is outstanding for the first five years, $800,000 for the second five years, and so on. An organization may issue serial bonds to ease the task of retiring its debt.

REGISTERED OR COUPON BONDS

Most bonds issued today are **registered bonds**. The names and addresses of the owners of such bonds must be recorded with the issuing organization. The organization keeps a register of the owners and pays interest by check to the bondholders

---

*At the time this chapter was written, the market interest rates on corporate bonds were volatile. We therefore use a variety of interest rates to demonstrate the concepts.

Focus on International Business

Choice of Bank Debt Cripples Japanese Firms.

When U.S. companies need cash, one ready source is a bond issue, but this source of funds is not available in many other countries. For instance, surprising as it may seem, Japan, with one of the world's largest economies and financial systems, has only a fledgling corporate bond market. Whereas corporate bonds account for 31 percent of U.S. corporate debt, only 57 of the 2,500 publicly listed companies in Japan have any domestic bonds outstanding. Japanese companies have traditionally relied on loans from big Japanese banks when they need cash. Reliance on bank debt has caused problems for Japanese companies because, as a result of the collapse of the real estate industry in Japan, Japanese banks do not have the funds to lend them.[5] Similar problems have occurred recently in other Asian countries.

---

of record on the interest payment date. **Coupon bonds** generally are not registered with the organization; instead, they bear interest coupons stating the amount of interest due and the payment date. The bondholder removes the coupons from the bonds on the interest payment dates and presents them at a bank for collection.

✓ Check out ACE for a Review Quiz at http://accounting.college.hmco.com/students.

ACCOUNTING FOR BONDS PAYABLE

LO3 Record the issuance of bonds at face value and at a discount or premium.

RELATED TEXT ASSIGNMENTS
Q: 4, 5
SE: 2, 3, 5, 7
E: 2, 3, 4, 5, 10, 12
P: 1, 2, 3, 4, 5, 6, 7, 8
SD: 1, 5

When the board of directors of a public corporation decides to issue bonds, the company must submit the appropriate legal documents to the Securities and Exchange Commission for permission to borrow the funds. The SEC reviews the corporation's financial health and the specific terms of the bond agreement. Once approved, the company has a limited time in which to issue the authorized bonds. It is not necessary to make an entry for the bond authorization, but most companies prepare a memorandum in the Bonds Payable account describing the issue. This note lists the number and value of bonds authorized, the interest rate, the interest payment dates, and the life of the bonds.

Once the bonds are issued, the corporation must pay interest to the bondholders over the life of the bonds (in most cases, semiannually) and the principal of the bonds at maturity.

BALANCE SHEET DISCLOSURE OF BONDS

KEY POINT: Bonds payable are presented on the balance sheet as either a current or a long-term liability, depending on the maturity date and method of retiring the bonds.

www.att.com

Bonds payable and unamortized discounts or premiums (which we explain later) are typically shown on a company's balance sheet as long-term liabilities. However, if the maturity date of the bond issue is one year or less and the bonds will be retired using current assets, bonds payable should be listed as a current liability. If the issue is to be paid with segregated assets or replaced by another bond issue, the bonds should still be shown as a long-term liability.

Important provisions of the bond indenture are reported in the notes to the financial statements, as illustrated by the Financial Highlights excerpted from the AT&T annual report. Often reported with them is a list of all bond issues, the kinds of bonds, any securities connected with the bonds, interest payment dates, maturity dates, and interest rates.

BONDS ISSUED AT FACE VALUE

Suppose that the Vason Corporation has authorized the issuance of $100,000 of 9 percent, five-year bonds on January 1, 20x4. According to the bond indenture, interest is to be paid on January 1 and July 1 of each year. Assume that the bonds are sold on January 1, 20x4, for their face value. The entry to record the issuance is as follows:

Accounting for Bonds Payable

	20x4		
A = L + OE + +	Jan. 1	Cash	100,000
		Bonds Payable		100,000
		Sold $100,000 of 9%, 5-year bonds at face value		

STUDY NOTE: When calculating semiannual interest, do not use the annual rate (9 percent in this case) by mistake. Rather, use half the annual rate.

As stated above, interest is paid on January 1 and July 1 of each year. Therefore, the corporation would owe the bondholders $4,500 interest on July 1, 20x4:

$$\text{Interest} = \text{Principal} \times \text{Rate} \times \text{Time}$$

$$= \$100{,}000 \times .09 \times \frac{6}{12} \text{ year}$$

$$= \$4{,}500$$

The interest paid to the bondholders on each semiannual interest payment date (January 1 or July 1) would be recorded as follows:

A* = L + OE − −	Bond Interest Expense	4,500	
*assumes cash paid	Cash (or Interest Payable)		4,500
	Paid (or accrued) semiannual interest to bondholders of 9%, 5-year bonds		

FACE INTEREST RATE AND MARKET INTEREST RATE

KEY POINT: A bond sells at face value when the face interest rate of the bond is identical to the market interest rate for similar bonds on the date of issue.

KEY POINT: When bonds with an interest rate different from the market rate are issued, they sell at a discount or premium. The discount or premium acts as an equalizing factor.

When issuing bonds, most organizations try to set the face interest rate as close as possible to the market interest rate. The **face interest rate** is the rate of interest paid to bondholders based on the face value, or principal, of the bonds. The rate and amount are fixed over the life of the bond. An organization must decide in advance what the face interest rate will be to allow time to file with regulatory bodies, publicize the issue, and print the certificates.

The **market interest rate** is the rate of interest paid in the market on bonds of similar risk. It is also referred to as the *effective interest rate*. The market interest rate fluctuates daily. Because an organization has no control over the market interest rate, it often differs from the face interest rate on the issue date. As a result, the issue price of the bonds does not always equal their face value. If the market interest rate is higher than the face interest rate, the issue price will be less than the face value and the bonds are said to be issued at a **discount**. The discount equals the excess of the face value over the issue price. On the other hand, if the market interest rate is

FOCUS ON BUSINESS PRACTICE

Check Out Those Bond Prices!

The price of many bonds can be found daily in business publications like *The Wall Street Journal*. For instance, shown to the right are the quotations for a number of AT&T <www.att.com> bonds. The first is a bond with a face interest rate of 6¾ percent that is due in 2004. The current yield is 6.5 percent based on the closing price of 103. The volume of $1,000 bonds traded was 70, and the last sale was up by .22 point from the previous day's last sales.

Corporation bond price/change (5/30/03), from *Wall Street Journal*. Copyright 2003 by Dow Jones & Co. Inc. Reproduced with permission of Dow Jones & Co. Inc. in the format textbook via Copyright Clearance Center.

Bonds	Cur Yld	Vol	Close	Net Chg
ATT 6¾04	6.5	70	103	0.22
ATT 5⅝04	5.5	15	102.06	...
ATT 7½04	7.2	37	103.59	0.06
ATT 7½06	6.8	362	111.13	1.13
ATT 7¾07	6.9	25	111.75	...
ATT 6s09	5.8	1136	103.63	0.13
ATT 6½13	6.2	86	105.25	0.38
ATT 8⅛22	7.9	200	102.75	0.25
ATT 8⅛24	7.9	190	103.25	...
ATT 8.35s25	7.9	101	105.13	0.63
ATT 6½29	6.7	263	97.50	0.75
ATT 8⅝31	8.3	41	104.25	0.63

lower than the face interest rate, the issue price will be more than the face value and the bonds are said to be issued at a **premium**. The premium equals the excess of the issue price over the face value.

BONDS ISSUED AT A DISCOUNT

Suppose that the Vason Corporation issues $100,000 of 9 percent, five-year bonds at 96.149 on January 1, 20x4, when the market interest rate is 10 percent. In this case, the bonds are being issued at a discount because the market interest rate exceeds the face interest rate. The following entry records the issuance of the bonds at a discount:

A = L + OE
+   +
     −

20x4
Jan. 1 Cash   96,149
          Unamortized Bond Discount   3,851
            Bonds Payable   100,000
            Sold $100,000 of 9%, 5-year
              bonds at 96.149

Face amount of bonds	$100,000
Less purchase price of bonds ($100,000 × .96149)	96,149
Unamortized bond discount	$ 3,851

KEY POINT: The carrying amount is always the face value of the bonds plus the unamortized premium or less the unamortized discount. The carrying amount always approaches the face value over the life of the bond.

In the entry, Cash is debited for the amount received ($96,149), Bonds Payable is credited for the face amount ($100,000) of the bond liability, and the difference ($3,851) is debited to Unamortized Bond Discount. If a balance sheet is prepared right after the bonds are issued at a discount, the liability for bonds payable is reported as follows:

Long-term liabilities
  9% bonds payable, due 1/1/x9 $100,000
  Less unamortized bond discount   3,851 $96,149

KEY POINT: The unamortized bond discount is subtracted from bonds payable on the balance sheet. The carrying value will be below the face value until the maturity date.

Unamortized bond discount is a contra-liability account: its balance is deducted from the face amount of the bonds to arrive at the carrying value, or present value, of the bonds. The bond discount is described as unamortized because it will be amortized (written off) over the life of the bonds.

BONDS ISSUED AT A PREMIUM

🛑 **STOP AND THINK!**
What determines whether bonds are issued at a discount, premium, or face value?
The relationship between the prevailing market interest rate and the face interest rate on the issue date is the determinant. ■

When bonds have a face interest rate above the market interest rate for similar investments, they are issued at a price above the face value, or at a premium. For example, assume that the Vason Corporation issues $100,000 of 9 percent, five-year bonds for $104,100 on January 1, 20x4, when the market interest rate is 8 percent. This means that investors will purchase the bonds at 104.1 percent of their face value. The issuance would be recorded as follows:

A = L + OE
+   +
     +

20x4
Jan. 1 Cash   104,100
            Unamortized Bond Premium   4,100
            Bonds Payable   100,000
            Sold $100,000 of 9%, 5-year bonds
              at 104.1 ($100,000 × 1.041)

KEY POINT: The unamortized bond premium is *added* to bonds payable on the balance sheet. The carrying value will be above the face value until the maturity date.

Right after this entry is made, bonds payable would be presented on the balance sheet as follows:

Long-term liabilities
  9% bonds payable, due 1/1/x9 $100,000
  Unamortized bond premium   4,100 $104,100

Focus on Business Practice

100-Year Bonds Are Not for Everyone.

In 1993, interest rates on long-term debt were at historically low levels, which induced some companies to attempt to lock in those low costs for long periods. One of the most aggressive companies in that regard was The Walt Disney Company <www.disney.go.com>, which issued $150 million of 100-year bonds at a yield of only 7.5 percent. It was the first time since 1954 that 100-year bonds had been issued. Among the others that followed Walt Disney's lead by issuing 100-year bonds were the Coca-Cola Company <www.coca-cola.com>, Columbia HCA Healthcare <www.hcahealthcare.com>, Bell South <www.bellsouth.com>, IBM <www.ibm.com>, and even the People's Republic of China. Some analysts wondered if even Mickey Mouse could survive 100 years. Investors who purchase such bonds take a financial risk because if interest rates rise, which would seem likely, then the market value of the bonds will decrease.[6]

The carrying value of the bonds payable is $104,100, which equals the face value of the bonds plus the unamortized bond premium. The cash received from the bond issue is also $104,100. This means that the purchasers were willing to pay a premium of $4,100 to buy these bonds because their face interest rate was higher than the market interest rate.

Bond Issue Costs

KEY POINT: A separate Bond Issue Costs account is usually established and amortized over the life of the issue.

Most bonds are sold through underwriters, who receive a fee for taking care of the details of marketing the issue or for taking a chance on receiving the selling price. Such costs are connected with the issuance of bonds. Because bond issue costs benefit the whole life of a bond issue, it makes sense to spread the costs over that period. It is generally accepted practice to establish a separate account for bond issue costs and to amortize them over the life of the bonds. However, issue costs decrease the amount of money a company receives from a bond issue. They have the effect, then, of raising the discount or lowering the premium on the issue. As a result, bond issue costs can be spread over the life of the bonds through the amortization of a discount or premium. Because this method simplifies recordkeeping, we assume in the text and problems of this book that all bond issue costs increase the discounts or decrease the premiums of bond issues.

✓ Check out ACE for a Review Quiz at http://accounting.college.hmco.com/students.

Using Present Value to Value a Bond

LO4 Use present values to determine the value of bonds.
RELATED TEXT ASSIGNMENTS
SE: 4
E: 6, 7, 8, 13

Present value is relevant to the study of bonds because the value of a bond is based on the present value of two components of cash flow: (1) a series of fixed interest payments and (2) a single payment at maturity. The amount of interest a bond pays is fixed over its life. However, the market interest rate varies from day to day. Thus, the amount investors are willing to pay for a bond changes as well.

Assume, for example, that a bond has a face value of $10,000 and pays fixed interest of $450 every six months (a 9 percent annual rate). The bond is due in five years. If the market interest rate today is 14 percent, what is the present value of the bond?

To determine the present value of the bond, we use Table 4 in the appendix on future value and present value tables to calculate the present value of the periodic interest payments of $450, and we use Table 3 in the same appendix to calculate the present value of the single payment of $10,000 at maturity. Since interest payments are made every six months, the compounding period is half a year. Because of this, it is necessary to convert the annual rate to a semiannual rate of 7 percent (14 percent divided by two six-month periods per year) and to use ten periods (five

STUDY NOTE: The amount buyers are willing to pay for an investment is normally based on what they expect to receive in return, taken at present value. In the case of a bond, the theoretical value equals the present value of the periodic interest payments plus the present value of the maturity value. The discount rate is set at the market rate (what investors are looking for), not at the face rate.

years multiplied by two six-month periods per year). Using this information, we compute the present value of the bond as follows:

Present value of 10 periodic payments at 7% (from Table 4 in the appendix on future value and present value tables): $450 × 7.024	$3,160.80
Present value of a single payment at the end of 10 periods at 7% (from Table 3 in the appendix on future value and present value tables): $10,000 × .508	5,080.00
Present value of $10,000 bond	$8,240.80

The market interest rate has increased so much since the bond was issued (from 9 percent to 14 percent) that the value of the bond is only $8,240.80 today. That amount is all investors would be willing to pay at this time for a bond that provides income of $450 every six months and a return of the $10,000 principal in five years.

If the market interest rate falls below the face interest rate, say to 8 percent (4 percent semiannually), the present value of the bond will be greater than the face value of $10,000:

● **STOP AND THINK!**
Why do bond prices vary over time?
Bond price is the present value of the principal and interest cash flows at the market interest rate; therefore, as the market interest rate changes over time, bond prices will change. ■

Present value of 10 periodic payments at 4% (from Table 4 in the appendix on future value and present value tables): $450 × 8.111	$ 3,649.95
Present value of a single payment at the end of 10 periods at 4% (from Table 3 in the appendix on future value and present value tables): $10,000 × .676	6,760.00
Present value of $10,000 bond	$10,409.95

✓ Check out ACE for a Review Quiz at http://accounting.college.hmco.com/students.

AMORTIZATION OF BOND DISCOUNTS AND PREMIUMS

LO5 Amortize bond discounts and bond premiums using the straight-line and effective interest methods.

RELATED TEXT ASSIGNMENTS
Q: 6, 7
SE: 2, 3, 7
E: 2, 3, 4, 5, 9, 12
P: 1, 2, 3, 4, 5, 6, 7, 8
SD: 2

A bond discount or premium represents the amount by which the total interest cost is higher or lower than the total interest payments. To record interest expense properly and ensure that at maturity the carrying value of bonds payable equals its face value, systematic reduction of the bond discount or premium over the bond term is required. That is, the discount or premium has to be amortized over the life of the bonds. This is accomplished by using either the straight-line method or the effective interest method.

AMORTIZING A BOND DISCOUNT

In one of the examples on page 676, Vason Corporation issued $100,000 of five-year bonds at a discount because the market interest rate of 10 percent exceeded the face interest rate of 9 percent. The bonds were sold for $96,149, resulting in an unamortized bond discount of $3,851. Because this discount affects interest expense in each year of the bond issue, the bond discount should be amortized (reduced gradually) over the life of the issue. This means that the unamortized bond discount will decrease gradually over time, and that the carrying value of the bond issue (face value less unamortized discount) will increase gradually. By the maturity date of the bond, the carrying value of the issue will equal its face value, and the unamortized bond discount will be zero. In the following sections, the total interest cost is calculated, and the bond discount is amortized using the straight-line and the effective interest methods.

Amortization of Bond Discounts and Premiums

KEY POINT: A bond discount is considered a component of total interest cost because a bond discount represents the amount in excess of the issue price that the corporation must pay on the maturity date.

■ **CALCULATION OF TOTAL INTEREST COST** When bonds are issued at a discount, the effective (or market) interest rate paid by the company is greater than the face interest rate on the bonds. The reason is that the interest cost to the company is the stated interest payments *plus* the amount of the bond discount. That is, although the company does not receive the full face value of the bonds on issue, it still must pay back the full face value at maturity. The difference between the issue price and the face value must be added to the total interest payments to arrive at the actual interest expense. The full cost to the corporation of issuing the bonds at a discount is as follows:

Cash to be paid to bondholders	
Face value at maturity	$100,000
Interest payments ($100,000 × .09 × 5 years)	45,000
Total cash paid to bondholders	$145,000
Less cash received from bondholders	96,149
Total interest cost	$ 48,851

Or, alternatively:

Interest payments ($100,000 × .09 × 5 years)	$ 45,000
Bond discount	3,851
Total interest cost	$ 48,851

The total interest cost of $48,851 is made up of $45,000 in interest payments and the $3,851 bond discount, so the bond discount increases the interest paid on the bonds from the face interest rate to the market interest rate. The *market (effective) interest rate* is the real interest cost of the bond over its life.

For each year's interest expense to reflect the market interest rate, the discount must be allocated over the remaining life of the bonds as an increase in the interest expense each period. The process of allocation is called *amortization of the bond discount*. Thus, interest expense for each period will exceed the actual payment of interest by the amount of the bond discount amortized over the period.

KEY POINT: The discount on a zero coupon bond represents the interest that will be paid (in its entirety) on the maturity date.

Some companies and governmental units issue bonds that do not require periodic interest payments. These bonds, called **zero coupon bonds**, are simply a promise to pay a fixed amount at the maturity date. They are issued at a large discount because the only interest earned by the buyer or paid by the issuer is the discount. For example, a five-year, $100,000 zero coupon bond issued at a time when the market rate is 14 percent, compounded semiannually, would sell for only $50,800. That amount is the present value of a single payment of $100,000 at the end of five years. The discount of $49,200 ($100,000 − $50,800) is the total interest cost; it is amortized over the life of the bond.

■ **STRAIGHT-LINE METHOD** The **straight-line method** assumes equal amortization of the bond discount for each interest period. Suppose that the interest payment dates for the Vason Corporation bond issue are January 1 and July 1. The amount of the bond discount amortized and the interest expense for each semiannual period are calculated in four steps:

1. Total Interest Payments = Interest Payments per Year × Life of Bonds
   = 2 × 5 = 10

2. Amortization of Bond Discount per Interest Period = $\dfrac{\text{Bond Discount}}{\text{Total Interest Payments}}$

   = $\dfrac{\$3,851}{10}$ = $385*

*Rounded.

3. Cash Interest Payment = Face Value × Face Interest Rate × Time
   = $100,000 × .09 × 6/12 = $4,500

4. Interest Expense per Interest Period = Interest Payment + Amortization of Bond Discount
   = $4,500 + $385 = $4,885

On July 1, 20x4, the first semiannual interest date, the entry would be as follows:

20x4
July 1 Bond Interest Expense   4,885
            Unamortized Bond Discount   385
            Cash (or Interest Payable)   4,500
        Paid (or accrued) semiannual interest
        to bondholders and amortized the
        discount on 9%, 5-year bonds

A* = L + OE
 −   +   −
*assumes cash paid

Notice that the bond interest expense is $4,885, but the amount paid to the bondholders is the $4,500 face interest payment. The difference of $385 is the credit to Unamortized Bond Discount. This lowers the debit balance of Unamortized Bond Discount and raises the carrying value of the bonds payable by $385 each interest period. Assuming that no changes occur in the bond issue, this entry will be made every six months for the life of the bonds. When the bond issue matures, there will be no balance in the Unamortized Bond Discount account, and the carrying value of the bonds will be $100,000—exactly equal to the amount due the bondholders.

The straight-line method has long been used, but it has a certain weakness. Because the carrying value goes up each period and the bond interest expense stays the same, the rate of interest falls over time. Conversely, when the straight-line method is used to amortize a premium, the rate of interest rises over time. Therefore, the Accounting Principles Board has ruled that the straight-line method can be used only when it does not lead to a material difference from the effective interest method.[7] An amount is material if it affects a decision on the evaluation of the company.

> **STOP AND THINK!**
> When is it acceptable to use the straight-line method to amortize a bond discount or premium?
> It is acceptable only when it does not produce a result materially different from that produced by the effective interest method. ∎

■ **EFFECTIVE INTEREST METHOD** To compute the interest and amortization of a bond discount for each interest period under the **effective interest method**, a constant interest rate is applied to the carrying value of the bonds at the beginning of the interest period. This constant rate equals the market rate, or effective rate, at the time the bonds were issued. The amount to be amortized each period is the difference between the interest computed by using the market rate and the actual interest paid to bondholders. As an example, we use the same facts presented earlier—a $100,000 bond issue at 9 percent, with a five-year maturity and interest to be paid twice a year. The market, or effective, interest rate at the time the bonds were issued was 10 percent. The bonds were sold for $96,149, a discount of $3,851. The interest and amortization of the bond discount are shown in Table 1.

The amounts in the table (using period 1) were computed as follows:

Column A: The carrying value of the bonds is their face value less the unamortized bond discount ($100,000 − $3,851 = $96,149).

Column B: The interest expense to be recorded is the effective interest. It is found by multiplying the carrying value of the bonds by the effective (market) interest rate for one-half year ($96,149 × .10 × 6/12 = $4,807).

Column C: The interest paid in the period is a constant amount computed by multiplying the face value of the bonds by their face interest rate by the interest time period ($100,000 × .09 × 6/12 = $4,500).

Column D: The discount amortized is the difference between the effective interest expense to be recorded and the interest to be paid on the interest payment date ($4,807 − $4,500 = $307).

Amortization of Bond Discounts and Premiums

TABLE 1. Interest and Amortization of a Bond Discount: Effective Interest Method

Semiannual Interest Period	A Carrying Value at Beginning of Period	B Semiannual Interest Expense at 10% to Be Recorded* (5% × A)	C Semiannual Interest Payment to Bondholders (4½% × $100,000)	D Amortization of Bond Discount (B − C)	E Unamortized Bond Discount at End of Period (E − D)	F Carrying Value at End of Period (A + D)
0					$3,851	$ 96,149
1	$96,149	$4,807	$4,500	$307	3,544	96,456
2	96,456	4,823	4,500	323	3,221	96,779
3	96,779	4,839	4,500	339	2,882	97,118
4	97,118	4,856	4,500	356	2,526	97,474
5	97,474	4,874	4,500	374	2,152	97,848
6	97,848	4,892	4,500	392	1,760	98,240
7	98,240	4,912	4,500	412	1,348	98,652
8	98,652	4,933	4,500	433	915	99,085
9	99,085	4,954	4,500	454	461	99,539
10	99,539	4,961†	4,500	461	—	100,000

*Rounded to the nearest dollar.
†Last period's interest expense equals $4,961 ($4,500 + $461); it does not equal $4,977 ($99,539 × .05) because of the cumulative effect of rounding.

Column E: The unamortized bond discount is the balance of the bond discount at the beginning of the period less the current period amortization of the discount ($3,851 − $307 = $3,544). The unamortized discount decreases each interest payment period because it is amortized as a portion of interest expense.

Column F: The carrying value of the bonds at the end of the period is the carrying value at the beginning of the period plus the amortization during the period ($96,149 + $307 = $96,456). Notice that the sum of the carrying value and the unamortized discount (Column F + Column E) always equals the face value of the bonds ($96,456 + $3,544 = $100,000).

The entry to record the interest expense is like the one used with the straight-line method, but the amounts debited and credited to the various accounts differ. With the effective interest method, the entry for July 1, 20x4, would be as follows:

A* = L + OE
−   +   −
*assumes cash paid

20x4			
July 1	Bond Interest Expense	4,807	
	Unamortized Bond Discount		307
	Cash (or Interest Payable)		4,500
	Paid (or accrued) semiannual		
	interest to bondholders and		
	amortized the discount on 9%,		
	5-year bonds		

KEY POINT: The bond interest expense recorded exceeds the amount of interest paid because of the amortization of the bond discount. The matching rule dictates that the discount be amortized over the life of the bond.

Notice that it is not necessary to prepare an interest and amortization table to determine the amortization of a discount for any one interest payment period. It is necessary only to multiply the carrying value by the effective interest rate and subtract the interest payment from the result. For example, the amount of discount to be amortized in the seventh interest payment period is $412, calculated as follows: ($98,240 × .05) − $4,500.

■ **VISUAL SUMMARY OF THE EFFECTIVE INTEREST METHOD** The effect on carrying value and interest expense of the amortization of a bond discount using the effective

FIGURE 2
Carrying Value and Interest Expense—Bonds Issued at a Discount

KEY POINT: The bond interest expense *increases* each period because the carrying value of the bonds (the principal on which the interest is calculated) increases each period.

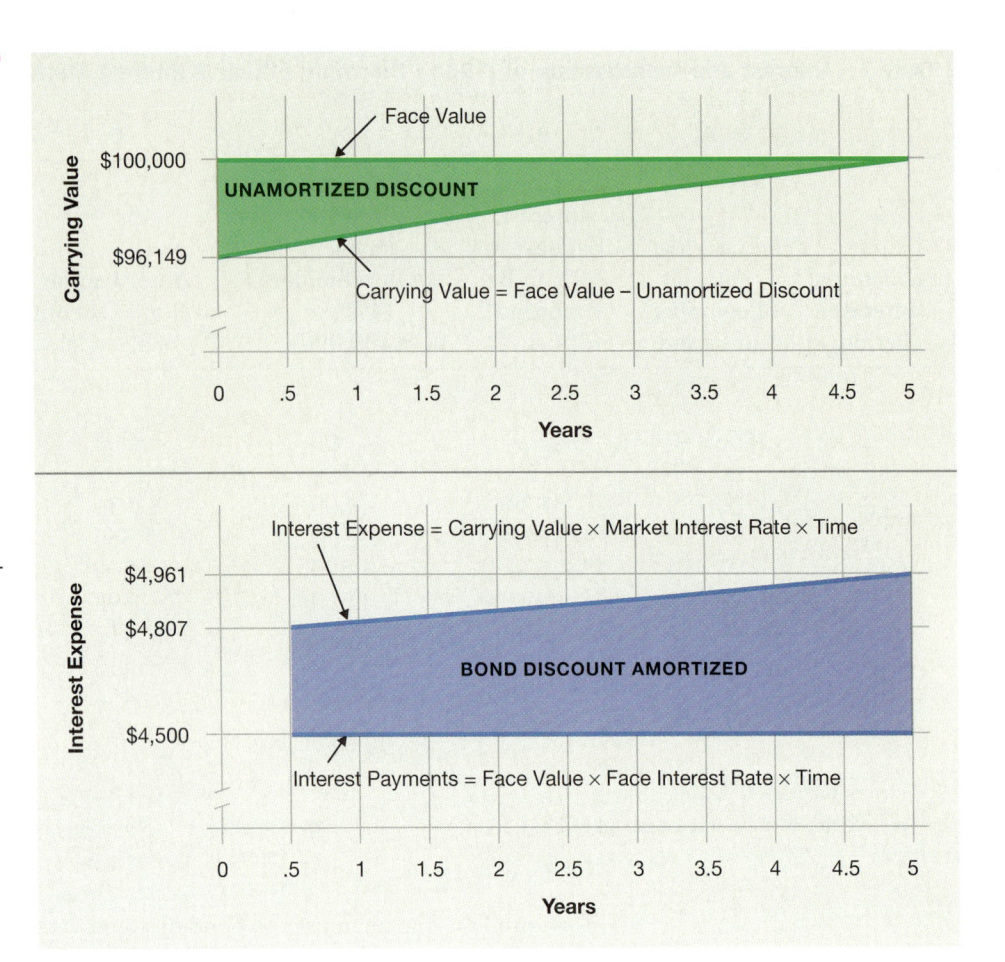

interest method can be seen in Figure 2 (which is based on the data from Table 1). Notice that initially the carrying value (the issue price) is less than the face value, but that it gradually increases toward the face value over the life of the bond issue. Notice also that interest expense exceeds interest payments by the amount of the bond discount amortized. Interest expense increases gradually over the life of the bond because it is based on the gradually increasing carrying value (multiplied by the market interest rate).

AMORTIZING A BOND PREMIUM

In our example of bonds issued at a premium, Vason Corporation issued $100,000 of five-year bonds at a premium because the market interest rate of 8 percent was less than the face interest rate of 9 percent. The bonds were sold for $104,100, which resulted in an unamortized bond premium of $4,100. Like a discount, a premium must be amortized over the life of the bonds so that it can be matched to its effects on interest expense during that period. In the following sections, the total interest cost is calculated, and the bond premium is amortized using the straight-line and the effective interest methods.

■ **CALCULATION OF TOTAL INTEREST COST** Because the bondholders paid more than face value for the bonds, the premium of $4,100 ($104,100 − $100,000) represents an amount that the bondholders will not receive at maturity. The premium is in effect a reduction, in advance, of the total interest paid on the bonds over the life of the bond issue. The total interest cost over the issue's life can be computed as follows:

KEY POINT: The bond interest expense recorded is less than the amount of the interest paid because of the amortization of the bond premium. The matching rule dictates that the premium be amortized over the life of the bond.

KEY POINT: A bond premium is deducted from interest payments in calculating total interest cost because a bond premium represents an amount over the face value of a bond that the corporation never has to return to the bondholders. In effect, it reduces the higher-than-market interest the corporation is paying on the bond.

A* = L + OE
– – –
*assumes cash paid

STUDY NOTE: Whether a bond is sold at a discount or a premium, its carrying value will equal its face value on the maturity date.

Cash to be paid to bondholders
  Face value at maturity $100,000
  Interest payments ($100,000 × .09 × 5 years) 45,000
Total cash paid to bondholders $145,000
Less cash received from bondholders 104,100
Total interest cost .... $ 40,900

Or, alternatively:

Interest payments ($100,000 × .09 × 5 years) .... $ 45,000
Less bond premium 4,100
Total interest cost .... $ 40,900

Notice that the total interest payments of $45,000 exceed the total interest cost of $40,900 by $4,100, the amount of the bond premium.

■ **STRAIGHT-LINE METHOD** Under the straight-line method, the bond premium is spread evenly over the life of the bond issue. As with bond discounts, the amount of the bond premium amortized and the interest expense for each semiannual period are computed in four steps:

1. Total Interest Payments = Interest Payments per Year × Life of Bonds
   = 2 × 5 = 10

2. Amortization of Bond Premium per Interest Period = $\frac{\text{Bond Premium}}{\text{Total Interest Payments}}$
   = $\frac{\$4,100}{10}$ = $410

3. Cash Interest Payment = Face Value × Face Interest Rate × Time
   = $100,000 × .09 × 6/12 = $4,500

4. Interest Expense per Interest Period = Interest Payment − Amortization of Bond Premium
   = $4,500 − $410 = $4,090

On July 1, 20x4, the first semiannual interest date, the entry would be as follows:

20x4
July 1 Bond Interest Expense   4,090
        Unamortized Bond Premium   410
          Cash (or Interest Payable)   4,500
          Paid (or accrued) semiannual interest
          to bondholders and amortized the
          premium on 9%, 5-year bonds

Notice that the bond interest expense is $4,090, but the amount received by the bondholders is the $4,500 face interest payment. The difference of $410 is the debit to Unamortized Bond Premium. This lowers the credit balance of the Unamortized Bond Premium account and the carrying value of the bonds payable by $410 each interest period. Assuming that the bond issue remains unchanged, the same entry will be made on every semiannual interest date over the life of the bond issue. When the bond issue matures, there will be no balance in the Unamortized Bond Premium account, and the carrying value of the bonds payable will be $100,000, exactly equal to the amount due the bondholders.

As noted earlier, the straight-line method should be used only when it does not lead to a material difference from the effective interest method.

■ **EFFECTIVE INTEREST METHOD** Under the straight-line method, the effective interest rate changes constantly, even though the interest expense is fixed, because

TABLE 2. Interest and Amortization of a Bond Premium: Effective Interest Method

	A	B	C	D	E	F
Semiannual Interest Period	Carrying Value at Beginning of Period	Semiannual Interest Expense at 8% to Be Recorded* (4% × A)	Semiannual Interest Payment to Bondholders (4½% × $100,000)	Amortization of Bond Premium (C − B)	Unamortized Bond Premium at End of Period (E − D)	Carrying Value at End of Period (A − D)
0					$4,100	$104,100
1	$104,100	$4,164	$4,500	$336	3,764	103,764
2	103,764	4,151	4,500	349	3,415	103,415
3	103,415	4,137	4,500	363	3,052	103,052
4	103,052	4,122	4,500	378	2,674	102,674
5	102,674	4,107	4,500	393	2,281	102,281
6	102,281	4,091	4,500	409	1,872	101,872
7	101,872	4,075	4,500	425	1,447	101,447
8	101,447	4,058	4,500	442	1,005	101,005
9	101,005	4,040	4,500	460	545	100,545
10	100,545	3,955†	4,500	545	—	100,000

*Rounded to the nearest dollar.
†Last period's interest expense equals $3,955 ($4,500 − $545); it does not equal $4,022 ($100,545 × .04) because of the cumulative effect of rounding.

the effective interest rate is determined by comparing the fixed interest expense with a carrying value that changes as a result of amortizing the discount or premium. To apply a fixed interest rate over the life of the bonds based on the actual market rate at the time of the bond issue requires the use of the effective interest method. Under this method, the interest expense decreases slightly each period (see Table 2, Column B) because the amount of the bond premium amortized increases slightly (Column D). This occurs because a fixed rate is applied each period to the gradually decreasing carrying value (Column A).

The first interest payment is recorded as follows:

A* = L + OE

*assumes cash paid

20x4			
July 1	Bond Interest Expense	4,164	
	Unamortized Bond Premium	336	
	Cash (or Interest Payable)		4,500
	Paid (or accrued) semiannual interest to bondholders and amortized the premium on 9%, 5-year bonds		

FOCUS ON BUSINESS TECHNOLOGY

Speed Up the Calculations!
Interest and amortization tables like those in Tables 1 and 2 are ideal applications for computer spreadsheet software, such as Lotus and Microsoft Excel. Once the tables have been set up with the proper formula in each cell, only five variables must be entered to produce the entire table. These variables are the face value of the bonds, selling price, life of the bonds, face interest rate, and market interest rate.

Notice that the unamortized bond premium (Column E) decreases gradually to zero as the carrying value decreases to the face value (Column F). To find the amount of premium amortized in any one interest payment period, subtract the effective interest expense (the carrying value times the effective interest rate, Column B) from the interest payment (Column C). In semiannual interest period 5, for example, the amortization of premium is $393, which is calculated in the following manner: $4,500 − ($102,674 × .04).

FIGURE 3
Carrying Value and Interest Expense—Bonds Issued at a Premium

KEY POINT: Over the life of a bond, the premium or discount amortized increases each period.

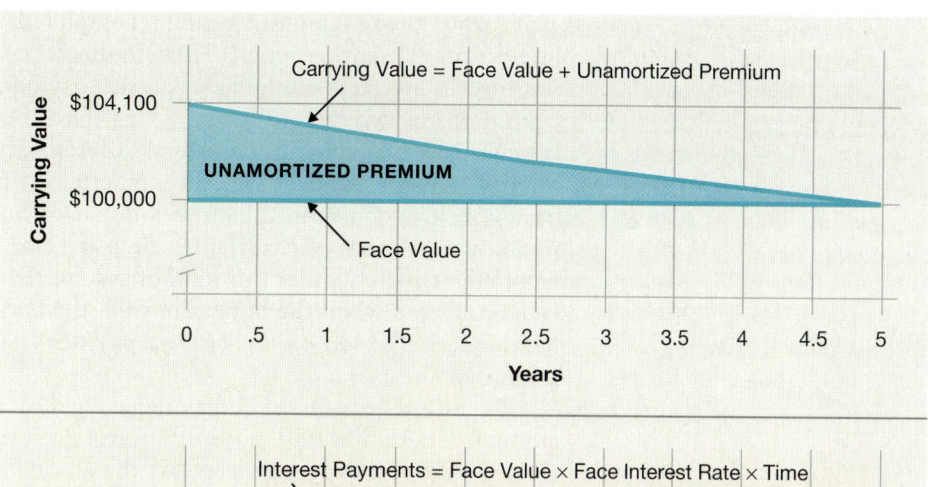

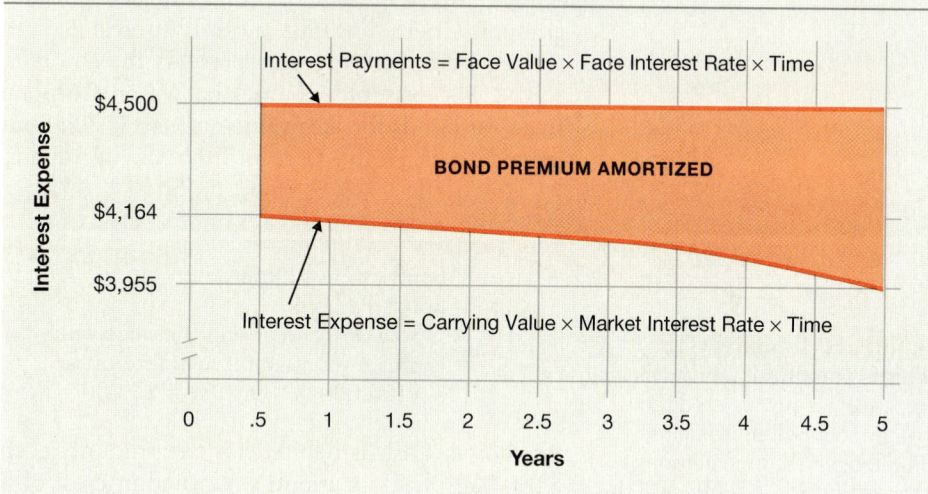

Figure 3 (top panel): Carrying Value vs. Years (0 to 5)
- Carrying Value = Face Value + Unamortized Premium
- $104,100 at year 0, declining to $100,000 (Face Value) at year 5
- UNAMORTIZED PREMIUM shown as the area between carrying value and face value

Figure 3 (bottom panel): Interest Expense vs. Years (0 to 5)
- Interest Payments = Face Value × Face Interest Rate × Time ($4,500)
- Interest Expense = Carrying Value × Market Interest Rate × Time (starts at $4,164, declines to $3,955)
- BOND PREMIUM AMORTIZED shown as the area between interest payments and interest expense

■ **VISUAL SUMMARY OF THE EFFECTIVE INTEREST METHOD** The effect on carrying value and interest expense of the amortization of a bond premium using the effective interest method can be seen in Figure 3 (which is based on data from Table 2). Notice that initially the carrying value (issue price) is greater than the face value, but that it gradually decreases toward the face value over the life of the bond issue. Notice also that interest payments exceed interest expense by the amount of the premium amortized and that interest expense decreases gradually over the life of the bond because it is based on the gradually decreasing carrying value (multiplied by the market interest rate).

✓ Check out ACE for a Review Quiz at http://accounting.college.hmco.com/students.

OTHER BONDS PAYABLE ISSUES

LO6 Record bonds issued between interest dates and year-end adjustments.

RELATED TEXT ASSIGNMENTS
Q: 8
SE: 3, 5, 6, 7
E: 4, 5, 9, 10, 11, 12
P: 1, 2, 3, 5, 6, 7, 8

Several other issues arise in accounting for bonds payable. Among them are the sale of bonds between interest payment dates and the year-end accrual of bond interest expense.

SALE OF BONDS BETWEEN INTEREST DATES

Bonds may be issued on an interest payment date, as in the previous examples, but they are often issued between interest payment dates. The generally accepted method of handling bonds issued in this manner is to collect from investors the interest that would have accrued for the partial period preceding the issue date.

Then, when the first interest period is completed, the corporation pays investors the interest for the entire period. Thus, the interest collected when bonds are sold is returned to investors on the next interest payment date.

There are two reasons for following this procedure. The first is a practical one. If a company issued bonds on several different days and did not collect the accrued interest, records would have to be maintained for each bondholder and date of purchase. In such a case, the interest due each bondholder would have to be computed on the basis of a different time period. Clearly, large bookkeeping costs would be incurred under this kind of system. On the other hand, if accrued interest is collected when the bonds are sold, the corporation can pay the interest due for the entire period on the interest payment date, eliminating the extra computations and costs.

The second reason for collecting accrued interest in advance is that when that amount is netted against the full interest paid on the interest payment date, the resulting interest expense represents the amount for the time the money was borrowed. For example, assume that Vason Corporation sold $100,000 of 9 percent, five-year bonds for face value on May 1, 20x4, rather than on January 1, 20x4, the issue date. The entry to record the sale of the bonds is as follows:

A = L + OE
+   +   +

```
20x4
May 1   Cash                                          103,000
            Bond Interest Expense                                  3,000
            Bonds Payable                                         100,000
          Sold 9%, 5-year bonds at face value
          plus 4 months' accrued interest
          $100,000 × .09 × 4/12 = $3,000
```

ENRICHMENT NOTE:
This is one of the few times an expense account is credited (other than when it is closed). The ledger account demonstrates that the net effect is the recording of two months' interest (May and June).

As shown, Cash is debited for the amount received, $103,000 (the face value of $100,000 plus four months' accrued interest of $3,000). Bond Interest Expense is credited for the $3,000 of accrued interest, and Bonds Payable is credited for the face value of $100,000.

When the first semiannual interest payment date arrives, this entry is made:

A* = L + OE
−   −

*assumes cash paid

```
20x4
July 1   Bond Interest Expense                         4,500
            Cash (or Interest Payable)                           4,500
          Paid (or accrued) semiannual interest
          $100,000 × .09 × 6/12 = $4,500
```

Notice that the entire half-year interest is both debited to Bond Interest Expense and credited to Cash because the corporation pays bond interest only once every six months, in full six-month amounts. This process is illustrated in Figure 4. The actual interest expense for the two months that the bonds were outstanding is $1,500. This amount is the net balance of the $4,500 debit to Bond Interest Expense on July 1 less the $3,000 credit to Bond Interest Expense on May 1. You can see these steps clearly in the following T account:

Bond Interest Expense			
Bal.	0	May 1	3,000
July 1	4,500		
Bal.	1,500		

YEAR-END ACCRUAL OF BOND INTEREST EXPENSE

Bond interest payment dates rarely correspond with a company's fiscal year. Therefore, an adjustment must be made at the end of the accounting period to

FIGURE 4
Effect on Bond Interest Expense When Bonds Are Issued Between Interest Dates

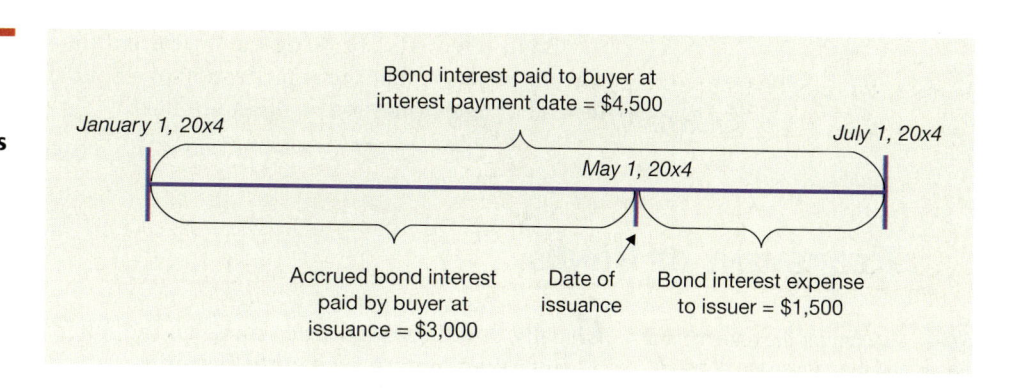

```
January 1, 20x4                                                                July 1, 20x4
    |                          Bond interest paid to buyer at
    |                          interest payment date = $4,500
    |--------------------------------------------------------------|
                                       May 1, 20x4
                                            ↑
         Accrued bond interest         Date of      Bond interest expense
         paid by buyer at              issuance     to issuer = $1,500
         issuance = $3,000
```

accrue the interest expense on the bonds from the last payment date to the end of the fiscal year. Further, if there is any discount or premium on the bonds, it must also be amortized for the fractional period.

Remember that in the example of bonds issued at a premium, Vason Corporation issued $100,000 in bonds on January 1, 20x4, at 104.1 percent of face value. Suppose the company's fiscal year ends on September 30, 20x4. In the period since the interest payment and amortization of the premium on July 1, three months' worth of interest has accrued, and the following adjusting entry under the effective interest method must be made:

KEY POINT: Remember that adjusting entries never affect cash.

A = L + OE
−   −
    +

20x0			
Sept. 30	Bond Interest Expense	2,075.50	
	Unamortized Bond Premium	174.50	
	Interest Payable		2,250.00
	To record accrual of interest on		
	9% bonds payable for 3 months and		
	amortization of one-half of the		
	premium for the second interest		
	payment period		

CLARIFICATION NOTE: The matching rule dictates that both the accrued interest and the amortization of a premium or discount be recorded at year end.

This entry covers one-half of the second interest period. Unamortized Bond Premium is debited for $174.50, which is one-half of $349, the amortization of the premium for the second period from Table 2. Interest Payable is credited for $2,250, three months' interest on the face value of the bonds ($100,000 × .09 × 3/12). The net debit figure of $2,075.50 ($2,250.00 − $174.50) is the bond interest expense for the three-month period.

When the January 1, 20x5, payment date arrives, the entry to pay the bondholders and amortize the premium is as follows:

A = L + OE
−   −   −

20x1			
Jan. 1	Bond Interest Expense	2,075.50	
	Interest Payable	2,250.00	
	Unamortized Bond Premium	174.50	
	Cash		4,500.00
	Paid semiannual interest, including		
	interest previously accrued, and		
	amortized the premium for the		
	period since the end of the fiscal		
	year		

● **STOP AND THINK!**
Why must the accrual of bond interest expense be recorded?
Bond interest expense must be accrued at the close of each accounting period to ensure proper matching of all the borrowing costs associated with bonds payable. Interest payment dates rarely coincide with the end of the accounting period. ■

As shown here, one-half ($2,250) of the amount paid ($4,500) was accrued on September 30. Unamortized Bond Premium is debited for $174.50, the remaining amount to be amortized for the period ($349.00 − $174.50). The resulting bond interest expense is the amount that applies to the three-month period from October 1 to December 31.

Retirement of Bonds

S07 Account for the retirement of bonds and the conversion of bonds into stock.

RELATED TEXT ASSIGNMENTS
Q: 9, 10
SE: 8, 9
E: 13, 14, 15
P: 4, 5
FRA: 2

ENRICHMENT NOTE: When interest rates drop, corporations frequently refinance their bonds at the lower rate, much like homeowners who refinance their mortgage loans when interest rates go down. Even though a call premium is usually paid to extinguish the bonds, the interest saved makes the refinancing cost-effective in the long run.

Usually, bonds are paid when due—on the stated maturity date. However, it can be advantageous not to wait until maturity, as is sometimes the case with callable bonds and convertible bonds.

Callable Bonds

Callable bonds give the issuer the right to buy back and retire the bonds at a specified **call price**, usually above face value, before maturity. Such bonds give the company flexibility in financing its operations. For example, if bond interest rates drop, the company can call its bonds and reissue debt at a lower interest rate. A company might also call its bonds if it has earned enough to pay off the debt, if the reason for having the debt no longer exists, or if it wants to restructure its debt to equity ratio. The bond indenture states the time period and the prices at which the bonds can be redeemed. The retirement of a bond issue before its maturity date is called **early extinguishment of debt**.

Let's assume that Vason Corporation can call or retire at 105 the $100,000 of bonds it issued at a premium (104.1) and that it decides to do so on July 1, 20x7. (To simplify the example, the retirement is made on an interest payment date.) Because the bonds were issued on January 1, 20x4, the retirement takes place on the seventh interest payment date. Assume that the entry for the required interest payment and the amortization of the premium has been made. The entry to retire the bonds is as follows:

A = L + OE
− − −
−

20x7			
July 1	Bonds Payable	100,000	
	Unamortized Bond Premium	1,447	
	Loss on Retirement of Bonds	3,553	
	Cash		105,000
	Retired 9% bonds at 105		

In this entry, the cash paid is the face value times the call price ($100,000 × 1.05 = $105,000). The unamortized bond premium can be found in Column E of Table 2. The loss on retirement of bonds occurs because the call price of the bonds is greater than the carrying value ($105,000 − $101,447 = $3,553).

Sometimes, a rise in the market interest rate can cause the market value of bonds to fall considerably below their face value. If it has the cash to do so, the company may find it advantageous to purchase the bonds on the open market and retire them, rather than wait and pay them off at face value. A gain is recognized for the difference between the purchase price of the bonds and the carrying value of the retired bonds. For example, assume that because of a rise in interest rates, Vason Corporation is able to purchase the $100,000 bond issue on the open market at 85. The entry would be as follows:

STUDY NOTE: The goal is to eliminate from the books any reference to the bonds being retired.

A = L + OE
− − +
−

20x7			
July 1	Bonds Payable	100,000	
	Unamortized Bond Premium	1,447	
	Cash		85,000
	Gain on Retirement of Bonds		16,447
	Purchased and retired 9% bonds at 85		

CONVERTIBLE BONDS

Bonds that can be exchanged for common stock or other securities of the corporation are called **convertible bonds**. Convertibility enables an investor to make more money if the market price of the common stock rises, because the value of the bonds then rises. However, if the common stock price does not rise, the investor still holds the bonds and receives both the periodic interest payments and the principal at the maturity date.

Several factors related to the issuance of convertible bonds are favorable to the company. First, the interest rate is usually less than the company would have to offer if the bonds were not convertible. An investor is willing to give up some current interest for the prospect that the value of the stock will increase and therefore the value of the bonds will also increase. Another advantage is that management will not have to give up any current control of the company. Unlike stockholders, bondholders do not have voting rights. A third benefit is tax savings. Interest paid on bonds is fully deductible for income tax purposes, whereas cash dividends on common stock are not. Fourth, the company's income will be affected favorably if the company earns a return that exceeds the interest cost of the bonds. Finally, the convertible feature offers financial flexibility. If the market value of the stock rises to a level at which the bond is worth more than face value, management can avoid repaying the bonds by calling them for redemption, thereby forcing the bondholders to convert their bonds into common stock. The bondholders will agree to convert because no gain or loss results from the transaction.

One major disadvantage of bonds is that interest must be paid semiannually. Inability to make an interest payment could force the company into bankruptcy. Common stock dividends are declared and paid only when the board of directors decides to do so. Another disadvantage of bonds is that when the bonds are converted, they become new outstanding common stock. These new shares give the bondholders stockholders' rights and reduce the proportional ownership of the existing stockholders.

When a bondholder wishes to convert bonds into common stock, the common stock is recorded at the carrying value of the bonds. The bond liability and the associated unamortized discount or premium are written off the books. For this reason, no gain or loss on the transaction is recorded. For example, suppose that Vason Corporation's bonds are not called on July 1, 20x7. Instead, the corporation's bondholders decide to convert all the bonds to $8 par value common stock under a convertible provision of 40 shares of common stock for each $1,000 bond. The entry would be as follows:

A = L + OE
    − +
    − +

20x7			
July 1	Bonds Payable	100,000	
	Unamortized Bond Premium	1,447	
	Common Stock		32,000
	Paid-in Capital in Excess of Par Value, Common		69,447
	Converted 9% bonds payable into $8 par value common stock at a rate of 40 shares for each $1,000 bond		

STUDY POINT: The credits to the contributed capital accounts are based on the carrying value of the bonds converted. As a result, no gain or loss is recognized. If only a portion of the bonds had been converted, proportionate shares of the balances in Bonds Payable and Unamortized Bond Premium would be eliminated.

The unamortized bond premium is found in Column E of Table 2. At a rate of 40 shares for each $1,000 bond, 4,000 shares will be issued, with a total par value of $32,000 (4,000 × $8). The Common Stock account is credited for the amount of the par value of the stock issued. In addition, Paid-in Capital in Excess of Par Value, Common is credited for the difference between the carrying value of the bonds and the par value of the stock issued ($101,447 − $32,000 = $69,447). No gain or loss is recorded.

Check out ACE for a Review Quiz at http://accounting.college.hmco.com/students.

OTHER LONG-TERM LIABILITIES

SO8 Explain the basic features of mortgages payable, long-term leases, and pensions and other post-retirement benefits as long-term liabilities.

RELATED TEXT ASSIGNMENTS
Q: 11, 12, 13, 14, 15
SE: 10
E: 16, 17
SD: 3, 6
FRA: 4, 6

A company may have other long-term liabilities besides bonds. The most common are mortgages payable, long-term leases, and pensions and other postretirement benefits.

MORTGAGES PAYABLE

A **mortgage** is a long-term debt secured by real property. It is usually paid in equal monthly installments. Each monthly payment includes interest on the debt and a reduction in the debt. Table 3 shows the first three monthly payments on a $50,000, 12 percent mortgage. The mortgage was obtained on June 1, and the monthly payments are $800. According to the table, the entry to record the July 1 payment would be as follows:

A = L + OE
    –   –   –

July 1	Mortgage Payable	300	
	Mortgage Interest Expense	500	
	Cash		800
	Made monthly mortgage payment		

Notice from the entry and from Table 3 that the July 1 payment represents interest expense of $500 ($50,000 × .12 × 1/12) and a reduction in the debt of $300 ($800 – $500). Therefore, the unpaid balance is reduced to $49,700 by the July payment. August's interest expense is slightly less than July's because of the decrease in the debt.

LONG-TERM LEASES

A company can obtain new operating assets in several ways. One way is to borrow money and buy the asset. Another is to rent the equipment on a short-term lease. A third way is to obtain the equipment on a long-term lease. The first two methods do not create accounting problems. In the first case, the asset and liability are recorded at the amount paid, and the asset is subject to periodic depreciation. In the second case, the lease is short term in relation to the useful life of the asset, and the risks of ownership remain with the lessor. This type of agreement is called an **operating lease**. It is proper accounting procedure to treat operating lease payments as an expense and to debit the amount of each monthly payment to Rent Expense.

The third alternative, a long-term lease, is one of the fastest-growing ways of financing operating equipment in the United States today. It has several advantages.

TABLE 3. Monthly Payment Schedule on a $50,000, 12 Percent Mortgage

	A	B	C	D	E
Payment Date	Unpaid Balance at Beginning of Period	Monthly Payment	Interest for 1 Month at 1% on Unpaid Balance* (1% × A)	Reduction in Debt (B – C)	Unpaid Balance at End of Period (A – D)
June 1					$50,000
July 1	$50,000	$800	$500	$300	49,700
Aug. 1	49,700	800	497	303	49,397
Sept. 1	49,397	800	494	306	49,091

*Rounded to the nearest dollar.

Other Long-Term Liabilities

TABLE 4. Payment Schedule on a 16 Percent Capital Lease

Year	A Lease Payment	B Interest (16%) on Unpaid Obligation* (D × 16%)	C Reduction of Lease Obligation (A − B)	D Balance of Lease Obligation (D − C)
Beginning				$14,740
1	$ 4,000	$2,358	$ 1,642	13,098
2	4,000	2,096	1,904	11,194
3	4,000	1,791	2,209	8,985
4	4,000	1,438	2,562	6,423
5	4,000	1,028	2,972	3,451
6	4,000	549†	3,451	—
	$24,000	$9,260	$14,740	

*Computations are rounded to the nearest dollar.
†The last year's interest equals $549 ($4,000 − $3,451); it does not exactly equal $552 ($3,451 × .16) because of the cumulative effect of rounding.

TERMINOLOGY NOTE: From the lessee's point of view, a lease is treated as either an operating lease or a capital lease. An operating lease is a true lease and is treated as such. A capital lease, however, is in substance an installment purchase, and the leased asset and related liability must be recognized at their present value.

KEY POINT: Under a capital lease, the lessee must record depreciation, using any allowable method. Depreciation is *not* recorded under an operating lease, however, because the leased asset is not recognized on the lessee's books.

For instance, a long-term lease requires no immediate cash payment, the rental payment is deducted in full for tax purposes, and it costs less than a short-term lease. Acquiring the use of plant assets under long-term leases does create several accounting challenges, however. Often, such leases cannot be canceled. Also, their duration may be about the same as the useful life of the asset. Finally, they stipulate that the lessee has the option to buy the asset at a nominal price at the end of the lease. The lease is much like an installment purchase because the risks of ownership are transferred to the lessee. Both the lessee's available assets and its legal obligations (liabilities) increase because the lessee must make a number of payments over the life of the asset.

The Financial Accounting Standards Board has described this kind of long-term lease as a **capital lease**. The term reflects the provisions of such a lease, which make the transaction more like a purchase or sale on installment. The FASB has ruled that in the case of a capital lease, the lessee must record an asset and a long-term liability equal to the present value of the total lease payments during the lease term. In doing so, the lessee must use the present value at the beginning of the lease.[8] Much like a mortgage payment, each lease payment consists partly of interest expense and partly of repayment of debt. Further, depreciation expense is figured on the asset and entered on the records of the lessee.

Suppose, for example, that Isaacs Company enters into a long-term lease for a machine used in its manufacturing operations. The lease terms call for an annual payment of $4,000 for six years, which approximates the useful life of the machine (see Table 4). At the end of the lease period, the title to the machine passes to Isaacs. This lease is clearly a capital lease and should be recorded as an asset and a liability according to FASB *Statement No. 13*.

A lease is a contract that provides for a periodic payment for the right to use an asset or assets. Present value techniques can be used to place a value on the asset and on the corresponding liability associated with a capital lease. If Isaacs's interest cost is 16 percent, the present value of the lease payments can be computed as follows:

Periodic Payment × Factor (Table 4 in the appendix on future value and present value tables: 16%, 6 periods) = Present Value

$4,000 × 3.685 = $14,740

The entry to record the lease contract is as follows:

A = L + OE
+   +

Capital Lease Equipment	14,740	
Capital Lease Obligations		14,740
To record capital lease on machinery		

Capital Lease Equipment is classified as a long-term asset; Capital Lease Obligations is classified as a long-term liability. Each year, Isaacs must record depreciation on the leased asset. Using straight-line depreciation, a six-year life, and no salvage value, the following entry would record the depreciation:

A = L + OE
−   −

Depreciation Expense, Capital Lease Equipment	2,457	
Accumulated Depreciation, Capital Lease Equipment		2,457
To record depreciation expense on capital lease		

The interest expense for each year is computed by multiplying the interest rate (16 percent) by the amount of the remaining lease obligation. Table 4 shows these calculations. Using the data in the table, the first lease payment would be recorded as follows:

A = L + OE
− −   −

Interest Expense (Column B)	2,358	
Capital Lease Obligations (Column C)	1,642	
Cash		4,000
Made payment on capital lease		

PENSIONS

Most employees who work for medium-sized and large companies are covered by some sort of pension plan. A **pension plan** is a contract between a company and its employees in which the company agrees to pay benefits to the employees after they retire. Many companies pay the full cost of the pension, but frequently the employees also contribute part of their salary or wages. The contributions from both parties are typically paid into a **pension fund**, from which benefits are paid to retirees. In most cases, pension benefits consist of monthly payments to retired employees and other payments upon disability or death.

There are two kinds of pension plans. Under a *defined contribution plan*, the employer is required to contribute an annual amount specified by an agreement between the company and its employees or by a resolution of the board of directors. Retirement payments depend on the amount of pension payments the accumulated contributions can support. Under a *defined benefit plan*, the employer's annual contribution is the amount required to fund pension liabilities arising from employment in the current year, but the exact amount will not be determined until the retirement and death of the current employees. Under a defined benefit plan, the amount of future benefits is fixed, but the annual contributions vary depending on assumptions about how much the pension fund will earn. Under a defined contribution plan, each year's contribution is fixed, but the benefits vary depending on how much the pension fund earns.

Accounting for annual pension expense under a defined contribution plan is simple. After the required contribution is determined, Pension Expense is debited and a liability (or Cash) is credited. Accounting for annual expense under a defined benefit plan is, however, one of the most complex topics in accounting; thus, the intricacies are reserved for advanced courses. In concept, though, the procedure is simple. First, the amount of pension expense is determined. Then, if the amount of cash contributed to the fund is less than the pension expense, a liability results, which is reported on the balance sheet. If the amount of cash paid to the pension plan exceeds the pension expense, a prepaid expense arises and appears on the asset side of the balance sheet. For example, the annual report for Philip Morris Companies, Inc., includes among assets on the balance sheet a prepaid pension of $628 million.[9]

ENRICHMENT NOTE:
Companies prefer defined contribution plans because the employees assume the risk that their pension assets will earn a sufficient return to meet their retirement needs.

www.philipmorris.com

ENRICHMENT NOTE: Accounting for a defined benefit plan is far more complex than accounting for a defined contribution plan. Fortunately, accountants can rely on the calculations of professional actuaries, whose expertise includes the mathematics of pension plans.

In accordance with the FASB's *Statement No. 87*, all companies should use the same actuarial method to compute pension expense.[10] However, because actuarial methods require the estimation of many factors, such as the average remaining service life of active employees, the long-run return on pension plan assets, and future salary increases, the computation of pension expense is not simple. In addition, terminology further complicates pension accounting. In nontechnical terms, the pension expense for the year includes not only the cost of the benefits earned by people working during the year but also interest costs on the total pension obligation (which are calculated on the present value of future benefits to be paid) and other adjustments. Those costs are reduced by the expected return on the pension fund assets.

Since 1989, all employers whose pension plans do not have sufficient assets to cover the present value of their pension benefit obligations (on a termination basis) must record the amount of the shortfall as a liability on their balance sheets. Thus, investors don't have to read the notes to the financial statements to learn whether the pension plan is fully funded. If a pension plan does have sufficient assets to cover its obligations, no balance sheet reporting is required or permitted.

OTHER POSTRETIREMENT BENEFITS

KEY POINT: Other postretirement benefits should be expensed when earned by the employee, not when received after retirement. This practice conforms to the matching rule.

Many companies provide retired employees not only with pensions but also with health care and other benefits. In the past, these **other postretirement benefits** were accounted for on a cash basis; that is, they were expensed when the benefits were paid, after an employee had retired. The FASB has concluded, however, that those benefits are earned by the employee and that, in accordance with the matching rule, they should be estimated and accrued during the period of time the employee is working.[11]

The estimates must take into account assumptions about retirement age, mortality, and, most significantly, future trends in health care benefits. Like pension benefits, such future benefits should be discounted to the current period. A field test conducted by the Financial Executives Research Foundation determined that the change to accrual accounting increased postretirement benefits by two to seven times the amount recognized on a cash basis.

✓ Check out ACE for a Review Quiz at http://accounting.college.hmco.com/students.

Chapter Review

REVIEW OF LEARNING OBJECTIVES

LO1 Identify the management issues related to issuing long-term debt.

Long-term debt is used to finance long-term assets and business activities that have long-term earnings potential, such as property, plant, and equipment and research and development. In issuing long-term debt, management must decide (1) whether to take on long-term debt, (2) how much long-term debt to carry, (3) what types of long-term debt to incur, and (4) how to handle debt repayment. Among the advantages of long-term debt financing are that (1) common stockholders do not relinquish any control, (2) interest on debt is tax deductible, and (3) financial leverage may increase earnings. Disadvantages of long-term financing are that (1) interest and principal must be repaid on schedule, and (2) financial leverage can work against a company if an investment is not successful.

LO2 Identify and contrast the major characteristics of bonds.

A bond is a security that represents money borrowed from the investing public. When a corporation issues bonds, it enters into a contract, called a bond indenture, with the bondholders. The bond indenture identifies the major conditions of the bonds. A corporation can issue several types of bonds, each having different characteristics. For example, a bond issue may or may not require security (secured versus unsecured

Chapter 16 Long-Term Liabilities

bonds). It may be payable at a single time (term bonds) or at several times (serial bonds). And the holder may receive interest automatically (registered bonds) or may have to return coupons to receive interest payable (coupon bonds).

LO3 Record the issuance of bonds at face value and at a discount or premium.

When bonds are issued, the bondholders pay an amount equal to, less than, or greater than the bonds' face value. Bondholders pay face value for bonds when the interest rate on the bonds approximates the market rate for similar investments. The issuing corporation records the bond issue at face value as a long-term liability in the Bonds Payable account.

Bonds are issued at an amount less than face value when their face interest rate is lower than the market rate for similar investments. The difference between the face value and the issue price is called a discount and is debited to Unamortized Bond Discount.

When the face interest rate on bonds is greater than the market interest rate on similar investments, investors are willing to pay more than face value for the bonds. The difference between the issue price and the face value is called a premium and is credited to Unamortized Bond Premium.

LO4 Use present values to determine the value of bonds.

The value of a bond is determined by summing the present values of (1) the series of fixed interest payments of the bond issue and (2) the single payment of the face value at maturity. Tables 3 and 4 in the appendix on future value and present value tables should be used in making these computations.

LO5 Amortize bond discounts and bond premiums using the straight-line and effective interest methods.

When bonds are sold at a discount or a premium, the interest rate is adjusted from the face rate to an effective rate that is close to the market rate when the bonds were issued. Therefore, bond discounts or premiums have the effect of increasing or decreasing the interest expense on the bonds over their life. Under these conditions, it is necessary to amortize the discount or premium over the life of the bonds by using either the straight-line method or the effective interest method.

The straight-line method allocates a fixed portion of the bond discount or premium each interest period to adjust the interest payment to interest expense. The effective interest method, which is used when the effects of amortization are material, results in a constant rate of interest on the carrying value of the bonds. To find interest and the amortization of discounts or premiums, the effective interest rate is applied to the carrying value of the bonds (face value minus the discount or plus the premium) at the beginning of the interest period. The amount of the discount or premium to be amortized is the difference between the interest figured by using the effective rate and that obtained by using the face rate. The results of using the effective interest method on bonds issued at a discount or a premium are summarized below and compared with issuance at face value.

	Bonds Issued At		
	Face Value	Discount	Premium
Trend in carrying value over bond term	Constant	Increasing	Decreasing
Trend in interest expense over bond term	Constant	Increasing	Decreasing
Interest expense versus interest payments	Interest expense = interest payments	Interest expense > interest payments	Interest expense < interest payments
Classification of bond discount or premium	Not applicable	Contra-liability (deducted from Bonds Payable)	Liability (added to Bonds Payable)

Chapter Review

LO6 Record bonds issued between interest dates and year-end adjustments.

When bonds are sold on dates between the interest payment dates, the issuing corporation collects from investors the interest that has accrued since the last interest payment date. When the next interest payment date arrives, the corporation pays the bondholders interest for the entire interest period.

When the end of a corporation's fiscal year does not fall on an interest payment date, the corporation must accrue bond interest expense from the last interest payment date to the end of the company's fiscal year. This accrual results in the inclusion of the interest expense in the year incurred.

Supplemental Objectives

SO7 Account for the retirement of bonds and the conversion of bonds into stock.

Callable bonds can be retired before maturity at the option of the issuing corporation. The call price is usually an amount greater than the face value of the bonds, in which case the corporation recognizes a loss on the retirement of the bonds. A gain can be recognized on the early extinguishment of debt when a company purchases its bonds on the open market at a price below carrying value. This happens when a rise in the market interest rate causes the market value of the bonds to fall below face value.

Convertible bonds allow the bondholder to convert bonds to common stock in the issuing corporation. In this case, the common stock issued is recorded at the carrying value of the bonds being converted. No gain or loss is recognized.

SO8 Explain the basic features of mortgages payable, long-term leases, and pensions and other postretirement benefits as long-term liabilities.

A mortgage is a long-term debt secured by real property. It usually is paid in equal monthly installments. Each payment is partly interest expense and partly debt repayment. If a long-term lease is a capital lease, the risks of ownership lie with the lessee. Like a mortgage payment, each lease payment is partly interest and partly a reduction of debt. For a capital lease, both an asset and a long-term liability should be recorded. The liability should be equal to the present value at the beginning of the lease of the total lease payments over the lease term. The recorded asset is subject to depreciation. Pension expense must be recorded in the current period. Other postretirement benefits should be estimated and accrued while the employee is still working.

Review of Concepts and Terminology

The following concepts and terms were introduced in this chapter:

LO2 **Bond:** A security, usually long term, representing money that a corporation or other entity borrows from the investing public.

LO2 **Bond certificate:** Evidence of an organization's debt to a bondholder.

LO2 **Bond indenture:** A supplementary agreement to a bond issue that defines the rights, privileges, and limitations of bondholders.

LO2 **Bond issue:** The total value of bonds issued at one time.

SO7 **Callable bonds:** Bonds that an organization can buy back and retire at a call price before maturity.

SO7 **Call price:** A specified price, usually above face value, at which a corporation may buy back and retire bonds before maturity.

SO8 **Capital lease:** A long-term lease in which the risk of ownership lies with the lessee and whose terms resemble those of a purchase or sale on installment.

SO7 **Convertible bonds:** Bonds that can be exchanged for common stock or other securities of the corporation.

LO2 **Coupon bonds:** Bonds that are usually not registered with the issuing organization but instead bear interest coupons stating the amount of interest due and the payment date.

LO3 **Discount:** The amount by which the face value of a bond exceeds the issue price, which occurs when the market interest rate is higher than the face interest rate.

SO7 **Early extinguishment of debt:** The retirement of a bond issue before its maturity date.

- **LO5** **Effective interest method:** A method of amortizing bond discounts or premiums that applies a constant interest rate (the market rate at the time the bonds were issued) to the carrying value of the bonds at the beginning of each interest period.
- **LO3** **Face interest rate:** The rate of interest paid to bondholders based on the face value of the bonds.
- **LO1** **Financial leverage:** The ability to increase earnings for stockholders by earning more on assets than is paid in interest on debt incurred to finance the assets. Also called *trading on the equity*.
- **LO1** **Interest coverage ratio:** A measure of the degree of protection a company has from default on interest payments; income before taxes plus interest expense divided by interest expense.
- **LO3** **Market interest rate:** The rate of interest paid in the market on bonds of similar risk. Also called *effective interest rate*.
- **SO8** **Mortgage:** A long-term debt secured by real property.
- **SO8** **Operating lease:** A short-term lease in which the risks of ownership remain with the lessor and whose payments are recorded as rent expense.
- **SO8** **Other postretirement benefits:** Health care and other nonpension benefits paid to a worker after retirement but earned while the employee is still working.
- **SO8** **Pension fund:** A fund established through contributions by an employer, and often by employees, from which payments are made to employees after retirement or on disability or death.
- **SO8** **Pension plan:** A contract between a company and its employees under which the company agrees to pay benefits to the employees after they retire.
- **LO3** **Premium:** The amount by which the issue price of a bond exceeds its face value, which occurs when the market interest rate is lower than the face interest rate.
- **LO2** **Registered bonds:** Bonds for which the names and addresses of bondholders are recorded with the issuing organization.
- **LO2** **Secured bonds:** Bonds that give the bondholders a pledge of certain assets as a guarantee of repayment.
- **LO2** **Serial bonds:** Bonds in an issue that mature on different dates.
- **LO5** **Straight-line method:** A method of amortizing bond discounts or premiums that allocates the discount or premium equally over each interest period of the life of a bond.
- **LO2** **Term bonds:** Bonds in an issue that mature at the same time.
- **LO2** **Unsecured bonds:** Bonds issued on the general credit of an organization. Also called *debenture bonds*.
- **LO5** **Zero coupon bonds:** Bonds that do not pay periodic interest but that promise to pay a fixed amount on the maturity date.

REVIEW PROBLEM

Interest and Amortization of a Bond Discount, Bond Retirement, and Bond Conversion

LO3
LO5
SO7

When Merrill Manufacturing Company was expanding its metal window division, it did not have enough capital to finance the expansion. So, management sought and received approval from the board of directors to issue bonds. The company planned to issue $5,000,000 of 8 percent, five-year bonds in 20x4. Interest would be paid on June 30 and December 31 of each year. The bonds would be callable at 104, and each $1,000 bond would be convertible into 30 shares of $10 par value common stock.

On January 1, 20x4, the bonds were sold at 96 because the market rate of interest for similar investments was 9 percent. The company decided to amortize the bond discount by using the effective interest method. On July 1, 20x6, management called and retired half the bonds, and investors converted the other half into common stock.

REQUIRED
1. Prepare an interest and amortization schedule for the first five interest periods.
2. Prepare entries in journal form to record the sale of the bonds, the first two interest payments, the bond retirement, and the bond conversion.

ANSWER TO REVIEW PROBLEM

1. Schedule prepared for the first five interest periods:

Interest and Amortization of Bond Discount

Semiannual Interest Payment Date	Carrying Value at Beginning of Period	Semiannual Interest Expense* (9% × ½)	Semiannual Interest Payment (8% × ½)	Amortization of Discount	Unamortized Bond Discount at End of Period	Carrying Value at End of Period
Jan. 1, 20x4					$200,000	$4,800,000
June 30, 20x4	$4,800,000	$216,000	$200,000	$16,000	184,000	4,816,000
Dec. 31, 20x4	4,816,000	216,720	200,000	16,720	167,280	4,832,720
June 30, 20x5	4,832,720	217,472	200,000	17,472	149,808	4,850,192
Dec. 31, 20x5	4,850,192	218,259	200,000	18,259	131,549	4,868,451
June 30, 20x6	4,868,451	219,080	200,000	19,080	112,469	4,887,531

*Rounded to the nearest dollar.

2. Entries made in journal form:

20x4
Jan. 1 Cash   4,800,000
    Unamortized Bond Discount   200,000
        Bonds Payable   5,000,000
        Sold $5,000,000 of 8%,
        5-year bonds at 96

June 30 Bond Interest Expense   216,000
        Unamortized Bond Discount   16,000
        Cash   200,000
        Paid semiannual interest and
        amortized the discount on 8%,
        5-year bonds

Dec. 31 Bond Interest Expense   216,720
        Unamortized Bond Discount   16,720
        Cash   200,000
        Paid semiannual interest and
        amortized the discount on 8%,
        5-year bonds

20x6
July 1 Bonds Payable   2,500,000
    Loss on Retirement of Bonds   156,235
        Unamortized Bond Discount   56,235
        Cash   2,600,000
        Called $2,500,000 of 8% bonds and
        retired them at 104
        $112,469 × ½ = $56,235*

1 Bonds Payable   2,500,000
        Unamortized Bond Discount   56,234
        Common Stock   750,000
        Paid-in Capital in Excess of Par
            Value, Common   1,693,766
        Converted $2,500,000 of 8% bonds into
        common stock:
        2,500 × 30 shares = 75,000 shares
        75,000 shares × $10 = $750,000
        $112,469 − $56,235 = $56,234
        $2,500,000 − ($56,234 + $750,000) =
        $1,693,766

*Rounded.

Chapter Assignments

BUILDING YOUR KNOWLEDGE FOUNDATION

QUESTIONS

1. What are the advantages and disadvantages of issuing long-term debt?
2. What are a bond certificate, a bond issue, and a bond indenture? What information is in a bond indenture?
3. What are the essential differences between (a) secured and debenture bonds, (b) term and serial bonds, and (c) registered and coupon bonds?
4. Napier Corporation sold $500,000 of 5 percent $1,000 bonds on the interest payment date. What would the proceeds from the sale be if the bonds were issued at 95, at 100, and at 102?
5. If you were about to buy bonds on which the face interest rate was less than the market interest rate, would you expect to pay more or less than par value for the bonds?
6. Why does the amortization of a bond discount increase interest expense to an amount greater than interest paid? Why does the amortization of a premium have the opposite effect?
7. When the effective interest method of amortizing a bond discount or premium is used, why does the amount of interest expense change from period to period?
8. When bonds are issued between interest dates, why is it necessary for the issuer to collect an amount equal to accrued interest from the buyer?
9. Why would a company want to exercise the call provision of a bond when it can wait to pay off the debt?
10. What are the advantages of convertible bonds to the company issuing them and to the investor?
11. What are the two components of a uniform monthly mortgage payment?
12. What is a capital lease? Why should an accountant record both an asset and a liability in connection with this type of lease? What items should appear on the income statement as the result of a capital lease?
13. What is a pension plan? What is a pension fund?
14. What is the difference between a defined contribution plan and a defined benefit plan? In general, how is expense determined under each plan? What assumptions must be made to account for the expenses of a defined benefit plan?
15. What are other postretirement benefits, and how is the matching rule applied?

SHORT EXERCISES

SE 1.
LO1 Bond Versus Common Stock Financing

Indicate whether each of the following is an advantage or a disadvantage of using long-term bond financing rather than issuing common stock:

1. Interest paid on bonds is tax deductible.
2. Investments are sometimes not as successful as planned.
3. Financial leverage can have a negative effect when investments do not earn as much as the interest payments on the related debt.
4. Bondholders do not have voting rights in a corporation.
5. Positive financial leverage may be achieved.

SE 2.
LO3 Entries for Interest Using
LO5 the Straight-Line Method

On April 1, 20x4, Agaki Corporation issued $4,000,000 in 8.5 percent, five-year bonds at 98. The semiannual interest payment dates are April 1 and October 1. Prepare entries in journal form for the issue of the bonds by Agaki on April 1, 20x4, and the first two interest payments on October 1, 20x4, and April 1, 20x5. Use the straight-line method and ignore year-end accruals.

Chapter Assignments

LO3 **SE 3.** On March 1, 20xx, Westward Freight Company sold $100,000 of its 9.5 percent, 20-year bonds at 106. The semiannual interest payment dates are March 1 and September 1. The market interest rate is about 8.9 percent. The company's fiscal year ends August 31. Prepare entries in journal form to record the sale of the bonds on March 1, the accrual of interest and amortization of premium on August 31, and the first interest payment on September 1. Use the effective interest method to amortize the premium.
LO5 **Entries for Interest Using the Effective Interest Method**
LO6

LO4 **SE 4.** Cap Art, Inc., is considering the sale of two bond issues. Choice A is a $400,000 bond issue that pays semiannual interest of $32,000 and is due in 20 years. Choice B is a $400,000 bond issue that pays semiannual interest of $30,000 and is due in 15 years. Assume that the market interest rate for each bond is 12 percent. Calculate the amount that Cap Art will receive if both bond issues occur. (Calculate the present value of each bond issue and sum.)
Valuing Bonds Using Present Value

LO3 **SE 5.** League Company is authorized to issue $900,000 in bonds on June 1. The bonds carry a face interest rate of 8 percent, with interest to be paid on June 1 and December 1. Prepare entries in journal form for the issue of the bonds under the independent assumptions that (a) the bonds are issued on September 1 at 100 and (b) the bonds are issued on June 1 at 103.
LO6 **Entries for Bond Issues**

LO6 **SE 6.** Eisley Corporation sold $200,000 of 9 percent, ten-year bonds for face value on September 1, 20xx. The issue date of the bonds was May 1, 20xx. The company's fiscal year ends on December 31, and this is its only bond issue. Record the sale of the bonds on September 1 and the first semiannual interest payment on November 1, 20xx. What is the bond interest expense for the year ended December 31, 20xx?
Sale of Bonds Between Interest Dates

LO3 **SE 7.** On October 1, 20x4, Knight Corporation issued $500,000 of 9 percent bonds at 96. The bonds are dated October 1 and pay interest semiannually. The market rate of interest is 10 percent, and the company's year end is December 31. Prepare the entries to record the issuance of the bonds, the accrual of the interest on December 31, 20x4, and the payment of the first semiannual interest on April 1, 20x5. Assume that the company does not use reversing entries and uses the effective interest method to amortize the bond discount.
LO5 **Year-End Accrual of Bond Interest**
LO6

SO7 **SE 8.** Ross Corporation has outstanding $800,000 of 8 percent bonds callable at 104. On December 1, immediately after the payment of the semiannual interest and the amortization of the bond discount were recorded, the unamortized bond discount equaled $21,000. On that date, $480,000 of the bonds were called and retired. Prepare the entry to record the retirement of the bonds on December 1.
Entry for Bond Retirement

SO7 **SE 9.** Hui Corporation has $1,000,000 of 6 percent bonds outstanding. There is $20,000 of unamortized discount remaining on the bonds after the March 1, 20x5, semiannual interest payment. The bonds are convertible at the rate of 20 shares of $10 par value common stock for each $1,000 bond. On March 1, 20x5, bondholders presented $600,000 of the bonds for conversion. Prepare the entry to record the conversion of the bonds.
Entry for Bond Conversion

SO8 **SE 10.** Sedaka Corporation purchased a building by signing a $300,000 long-term mortgage with monthly payments of $2,400. The mortgage carries an interest rate of 8 percent. Prepare a monthly payment schedule showing the monthly payment, the interest for the month, the reduction in debt, and the unpaid balance for the first three months. (Round to the nearest dollar.)
Mortgage Payable

EXERCISES

LO1 **E 1.** Compute the interest coverage ratios for 20x4 and 20x5 from the partial income statements of Ivy Wall Company that appear below. State whether the ratio improved or worsened over time.
Interest Coverage Ratio

	20x5	20x4
Income from operations	$23,890	$18,460
Interest expense	5,800	3,300
Income before income taxes	$18,090	$15,160
Income taxes	5,400	4,500
Net income	$12,690	$10,660

Chapter 16 Long-Term Liabilities

LO3 **Entries for Interest Using the**
LO5 **Straight-Line Method**

E 2. Agga Corporation issued $4,000,000 in 10.5 percent, ten-year bonds on February 1, 20x4, at 104. The semiannual interest payment dates are February 1 and August 1. Prepare entries in journal form for the issue of bonds by Agga on February 1, 20x4, and the first two interest payments on August 1, 20x4, and February 1, 20x5. Use the straight-line method and ignore year-end accruals.

LO3 **Entries for Interest Using**
LO5 **the Straight-Line Method**

E 3. Famina Corporation issued $8,000,000 in 8.5 percent, five-year bonds on March 1, 20x5, at 96. The semiannual interest payment dates are March 1 and September 1. Prepare entries in journal form for the issue of the bonds by Famina on March 1, 20x5, and the first two interest payments on September 1, 20x5, and March 1, 20x6. Use the straight-line method and ignore year-end accruals.

LO3 **Entries for Interest Using the**
LO5 **Effective Interest Method**
LO6

E 4. Whistle Toy Company sold $500,000 of 9.5 percent, 20-year bonds on April 1, 20xx, at 106. The semiannual interest payment dates are April 1 and October 1. The market interest rate is 8.9 percent. The company's fiscal year ends September 30. Prepare entries in journal form to record the sale of the bonds on April 1, the accrual of interest and amortization of premium on September 30, and the first interest payment on October 1. Use the effective interest method to amortize the premium.

LO3 **Entries for Interest Using**
LO5 **the Effective Interest Method**
LO6

E 5. On March 1, 20x4, Eddy Corporation issued $1,200,000 of 10 percent, five-year bonds. The semiannual interest payment dates are March 1 and September 1. Because the market rate for similar investments was 11 percent, the bonds had to be issued at a discount. The discount on the issuance of the bonds was $48,670. The company's fiscal year ends February 28. Prepare entries in journal form to record the bond issue on March 1, 20x4; the payment of interest and the amortization of the discount on September 1, 20x4; the accrual of interest and the amortization of the discount on February 28, 20x5; and the payment of interest on March 1, 20x5. Use the effective interest method. (Round answers to the nearest dollar.)

LO4 **Valuing Bonds Using Present**
Value

E 6. Octogon, Inc., is considering the sale of two bond issues. Choice A is an $800,000 bond issue that pays semiannual interest of $64,000 and is due in 20 years. Choice B is an $800,000 bond issue that pays semiannual interest of $60,000 and is due in 15 years. Assume that the market interest rate for each bond is 12 percent. Calculate the amount that Octogon, Inc., will receive if both bond issues are made. (**Hint:** Calculate the present value of each bond issue and sum.)

LO4 **Valuing Bonds Using Present**
Value

E 7. Use the present value tables in the appendix on future value and present value tables to calculate the issue price of a $1,200,000 bond issue in each of the following independent cases, assuming that interest is paid semiannually:

a. A ten-year, 8 percent bond issue; the market interest rate is 10 percent.
b. A ten-year, 8 percent bond issue; the market interest rate is 6 percent.
c. A ten-year, 10 percent bond issue; the market interest rate is 8 percent.
d. A 20-year, 10 percent bond issue; the market interest rate is 12 percent.
e. A 20-year, 10 percent bond issue; the market interest rate is 6 percent.

LO4 **Zero Coupon Bonds**

E 8. The state of Idaho needs to raise $100,000,000 for highway repairs. Officials are considering issuing zero coupon bonds, which do not require periodic interest payments. The current market interest rate for the bonds is 10 percent. What face value of bonds must be issued to raise the needed funds, assuming the bonds will be due in 30 years and compounded annually? How would your answer change if the bonds were due in 50 years? How would both answers change if the market interest rate were 8 percent instead of 10 percent?

LO5 **Entries for Interest Payments**
LO6 **Using the Effective Interest**
Method

E 9. The long-term debt section of the Sanchos Corporation's balance sheet at the end of its fiscal year, December 31, 2005, was as follows:

Long-term liabilities
  Bonds payable—8%, interest payable
    1/1 and 7/1, due 12/31/13 $1,000,000
    Less unamortized bond discount   80,000 $920,000

Prepare entries in journal form relevant to the interest payments on July 1, 2006, December 31, 2006, and January 1, 2007. Use the effective interest rate method and assume a market interest rate of 10 percent.

LO3 **Entries for Bond Issue**
LO6

E 10. Water Symphonics, Inc., is authorized to issue $1,800,000 in bonds on June 1. The bonds carry a face interest rate of 9 percent, which is to be paid on June 1 and December 1. Prepare entries in journal form for the issue of the bonds by Water Symphonics, Inc., under the assumptions that (a) the bonds are issued on September 1 at 100 and (b) the bonds are issued on June 1 at 105.

LO6 Sale of Bonds Between Interest Dates

E 11. Margi Corporation sold $400,000 of 12 percent, ten-year bonds at face value on September 1, 20xx. The issue date of the bonds was May 1, 20xx.

1. Record the sale of the bonds on September 1 and the first semiannual interest payment on November 1, 20xx.
2. The company's fiscal year ends on December 31, and this is its only bond issue. What is the bond interest expense for the year ended December 31, 20xx?

LO3 Year-End Accrual of Bond
LO5 Interest
LO6

E 12. Lon Corporation issued $1,000,000 of 9 percent bonds on October 1, 20x3, at 96. The bonds are dated October 1 and pay interest semiannually. The market interest rate is 10 percent, and Lon's fiscal year ends on December 31. Prepare the entries to record the issuance of the bonds, the accrual of the interest on December 31, 20x3, and the first semiannual interest payment on April 1, 20x4. Assume the company does not use reversing entries and uses the effective interest method to amortize the bond discount.

LO4 Time Value of Money and
SO7 Early Extinguishment of Debt

E 13. Brown, Inc., has a $1,400,000, 8 percent bond issue that was issued a number of years ago at face value. There are now ten years left on the bond issue, and the market interest rate is 16 percent. Interest is paid semiannually.

1. Using present value tables, figure the current market value of the bond issue.
2. Record the retirement of the bonds, assuming the company purchases the bonds on the open market at the calculated value.

SO7 Entry for Bond Retirement

E 14. The Pucinski Corporation has outstanding $1,600,000 of 8 percent bonds callable at 104. On September 1, immediately after recording the payment of the semiannual interest and the amortization of the discount, the unamortized bond discount equaled $42,000. On that date, $960,000 of the bonds were called and retired. Prepare the entry to record the retirement of the bonds on September 1.

SO7 Entry for Bond Conversion

E 15. The Daglar Corporation has $400,000 of 6 percent bonds outstanding. There is $20,000 of unamortized discount remaining on these bonds after the July 1, 20x8, semiannual interest payment. The bonds are convertible at the rate of 40 shares of $5 par value common stock for each $1,000 bond. On July 1, 20x8, bondholders presented $300,000 of the bonds for conversion. Prepare the entry to record the conversion of the bonds.

SO8 Mortgage Payable

E 16. Fiery Corporation purchased a building by signing a $150,000 long-term mortgage with monthly payments of $2,000. The mortgage carries an interest rate of 12 percent.

1. Prepare a monthly payment schedule showing the monthly payment, the interest for the month, the reduction in debt, and the unpaid balance for the first three months. (Round to the nearest dollar.)
2. Prepare entries in journal form to record the purchase and the first two monthly payments.

SO8 Recording Lease Obligations

E 17. Foxx Corporation has leased a piece of equipment that has a useful life of 12 years. The terms of the lease are $43,000 per year for 12 years. Foxx currently is able to borrow money at a long-term interest rate of 15 percent. Round answers to the nearest dollar.)

1. Calculate the present value of the lease.
2. Prepare the entry to record the lease agreement.
3. Prepare the entry to record depreciation of the equipment for the first year using the straight-line method.
4. Prepare the entries to record the lease payments for the first two years.

PROBLEMS

LO3 Bond Transactions—Straight-
LO5 Line Method
LO6

REQUIRED ▶

P 1. Gala Corporation has $30,000,000 of 10.5 percent, 20-year bonds dated June 1, with interest payment dates of May 31 and November 30. The company's fiscal year ends on December 31. It uses the straight-line method to amortize bond premiums or discounts.

1. Assume the bonds are issued at 103 on June 1. Prepare entries in journal form for June 1, November 30, and December 31.
2. Assume the bonds are issued at 97 on June 1. Prepare entries in journal form for June 1, November 30, and December 31.
3. Assume the bonds are issued at face value plus accrued interest on August 1. Prepare entries in journal form for August 1, November 30, and December 31.

issuing common stock directly? Are there any disadvantages to this approach? If the price of the company's common stock returns to $200 per share, what would be the total theoretical value of the notes? If the holders of the notes were to elect to convert the notes into common stock, what would be the effect on the company's debt to equity ratio, and what would be the effect on the percentage ownership of the company by other stockholders?

International Company

FRA 3.
LO1 Comparison of Interest Coverage

Japanese companies have historically relied more on debt financing and are more highly leveraged than U.S. companies. For instance, NEC Corporation <www.nec.com> and Sanyo Electric Co. <www.sanyo.com>, two large Japanese electronics companies, had debt to equity ratios of about 4.3 and 3.5, respectively, in 2001. From the selected data from the companies' annual reports shown below (in millions of yen), compute the interest coverage ratios for the two companies for the two years. Comment on the riskiness of the companies and on the trends they show.[16]

	NEC 2001	NEC 2000	Sanyo 2001	Sanyo 2000
Interest expense	63,873	70,211	26,427	27,914
Income before income taxes	92,323	30,183	73,484	36,953

Group Activity: Assign the two companies to different groups to calculate the ratios and discuss the results. Debrief by discussing the advantages and disadvantages of a debt-laden capital structure.

Toys "R" Us Annual Report

FRA 4.
LO1 Business Practice, Long-Term
SO8 Debt, and Leases

Refer to the financial statements and the notes to the financial statements in the Toys "R" Us <www.tru.com> annual report to answer the following questions:
1. Is it the practice of Toys "R" Us to own or lease most of its property and equipment?
2. Does Toys "R" Us lease property predominantly under capital leases or under operating leases? How much was rental expense for operating leases in 2002?

Comparison Case: Toys "R" Us and Walgreen Co.

FRA 5.
LO1 Use of Debt Financing

Refer to the annual report of Toys "R" Us <www.tru.com> and the financial statements of Walgreens <www.walgreens.com> in the Supplement to Chapter 6. Calculate the debt to equity ratio and the interest coverage ratio for both companies' most recent two years. Evaluate and comment on the relative performance of the two companies with regard to debt financing. Which company has more risk of not being able to meet its interest obligations? Explain.

FRA 6.
LO1 Long-Term Liabilities
LO2
SO8

Fingraph® Financial Analyst™

Select any two companies from the same industry from the list of Fingraph companies on the Needles Accounting Resource Center Web Site at http://accounting.college.hmco.com/students. Access the Microsoft Excel spreadsheets for the companies you selected. For parts 1, 3, and 4, click on the URL at the top of each company's spreadsheet for a link to the company's web site and annual report.
1. In the annual reports of the companies you have selected, identify the long-term liabilities on the balance sheet and read any reference to long-term liabilities in the summary of significant accounting policies or notes to the financial statements. There is likely to be a separate note for each type of long-term liability. What are the most important long-term liabilities for each company?
2. Using the Fingraph CD-ROM software, display and print in tabular and graphic form the Balance Sheet Analysis page. Prepare a table that compares the debt to equity and interest coverage ratios for both companies for two years.
3. Read the statements of cash flows in both annual reports. Have the companies been increasing or decreasing their long-term debt? If increasing, what were each com-

pany's most important sources of long-term financing over the past two years? If decreasing, which liabilities are being decreased?

4. Find and read references to long-term liabilities in management's discussion and analysis in each annual report.

5. Write a one-page executive summary that highlights the most important types of long-term liabilities for these companies, identifies their accounting policies for specific long-term liabilities, and compares their debt to equity and interest coverage trends. The summary should refer to management's assessment. Include the Fingraph page and your table with your report.

Internet Case

LO2 Bond Rating Changes

FRA 7. Go to the Needles Accounting Resource Center Web Site at http://accounting.college.hmco.com/students. Under Web Links, select Standard & Poor's or access their web site directly at <www.standardandpoors.com>. In times of economic or industry recessions, it is common to see downward revisions of bond ratings. From the Standard & Poor's list of companies with lowered bond ratings, identify three whose names you recognize. For each company, give reasons that you believe contributed to the ratings downgrade.

17

Chapter 17 presents the statement of cash flows and explains the changes in cash flows from operating, investing, and financing activities. The chapter also focuses on how to analyze the statement of cash flows to determine a company's cash-generating ability and its free cash flow.

The Statement of Cash Flows

LEARNING OBJECTIVES

LO1 State the principal purposes and uses of the statement of cash flows, and identify its components.

LO2 Analyze the statement of cash flows.

LO3 Use the indirect method to determine cash flows from operating activities.

LO4 Determine cash flows from investing activities.

LO5 Determine cash flows from financing activities.

DECISION POINT A USER'S FOCUS

Marriott International, Inc. <www.marriott.com> Marriott International, Inc., is a world leader in lodging and contract hotel services. The balance sheet, income statement, and statement of stockholders' equity presented in Marriott's annual report give an excellent picture of the company's philosophy and performance.

Although these three financial statements are essential to the evaluation of any company, they do not tell the entire story. A fourth statement, the statement of cash flows, contains some additional information, as shown in the Financial Highlights on page 710.[1] This statement shows how much cash the company's operations generated during the past three years and how much cash investing and financing activities used or provided.

Marriott feels that maintaining adequate cash flows is important to the future of the company. In fact, Marriott's emphasis on cash flows is reflected in its compensation plan for top executives. A review of the plan indicates that cash flows, at the firm or business group level, are the financial measure given the greatest weight in determining compensation. Why would Marriott emphasize cash flows to such an extent?

Strong cash flows are essential to management's key goal of liquidity. If cash flows exceed the amount needed for operations and expansion, the company will not have to borrow additional funds. The excess cash flows will be available to reduce the company's debt and improve its financial position by lowering its debt to equity ratio. Another reason for the emphasis

What does Marriott's statement of cash flows reveal about the company's success in providing top-notch lodging and hotel services?

on cash flows may be the belief that strong cash flows from operations generate shareholder value and increase the market value of the company's stock.

The statement of cash flows demonstrates management's commitments in ways that are not readily apparent in the other financial statements. For example, it can show whether management's focus is on the short term or the long term. This statement, which is required by the FASB,[2] satisfies the board's long-held position that a primary objective of financial statements is to provide investors and creditors with information about a company's cash flows.

Financial Highlights: Consolidated Statement of Cash Flows
Marriott International, Inc., and Subsidiaries
(In millions)

	2002	2001	2000
OPERATING ACTIVITIES			
Net income	$ 448	$ 236	$ 479
Adjustments to reconcile to cash provided by operations:			
Depreciation and amortization	187	222	195
Income taxes	(105)	9	133
Timeshare activity, net	(63)	(358)	(195)
Loss on discontinued operations	(171)	—	—
Other	223	278	54
Working capital changes:			
Accounts receivable	(31)	57	(53)
Other current assets	60	(20)	24
Accounts payable and accruals	(32)	(21)	219
Cash provided by operations	516	403	856
INVESTING ACTIVITIES			
Capital expenditures	(292)	(560)	(1,095)
Dispositions	729	554	742
Loan advances	(237)	(367)	(389)
Loan collections and sales	124	71	93
Other	(7)	(179)	(377)
Cash used in investing activities	317	(481)	(1,026)
FINANCING ACTIVITIES			
Commercial paper, net	102	(827)	46
Issuance of long-term debt	26	1,329	338
Repayment of long-term debt	(946)	(123)	(26)
Redemption of convertible subordinated debt	(347)	405	—
Issuance of Class A common stock	35	76	58
Dividends paid	(65)	(61)	(55)
Purchase of treasury stock	(252)	(235)	(340)
Cash provided by financing activities	(1,447)	564	21
(DECREASE) INCREASE IN CASH AND EQUIVALENTS	(614)	486	(149)
CASH AND EQUIVALENTS, beginning of year	812	326	475
CASH AND EQUIVALENTS, end of year	$ 198	$ 812	$ 326

VIDEO CASE

Goodyear Tire & Rubber Company
<www.goodyear.com>

OBJECTIVES

- To state the purposes of the statement of cash flows
- To identify the three components of the statement of cash flows
- To identify the reasons why cash flows from operating activities usually differ from net income
- To understand the importance of cash flows from investing and financing activities

BACKGROUND FOR THE CASE

Goodyear was founded in 1898 by Frank Seiberling, who borrowed $3,500 to start a bicycle tire factory and subsequently began making tires for horseless carriages. Today, Goodyear is the world's largest tire and rubber company, with factories in 28 countries and more than 100,000 employees. In a recent year, sales exceeded $14 billion. In addition to producing Goodyear tires, the company makes Dunlop, Kelly, Fulda, Lee, Sava, and Debica tires and rubber products for the automotive and industrial markets.

Goodyear's goal is to be ranked by all measures as the best tire and rubber company in the world. It intends to accomplish this by doing the following:

- having fast and profitable growth in all core businesses.
- achieving a number one or two market position.
- making strategic acquisitions and expansions.
- being the lowest cost producer.

To achieve these objectives, especially "fast and profitable growth" and "strategic acquisitions and expansions," Goodyear will need adequate funding. Management expects the funding to come from strong cash flows; divestiture of underperforming, nonstrategic assets; and debt issues. Within this framework, management must maintain the company's financial health and a strong balance sheet, with a debt to debt plus equity ratio of 25 to 30 percent.

Understanding Goodyear's performance in meeting the challenge of achieving adequate funding requires an ability to read and understand the statement of cash flows.

For more information about Goodyear Tire & Rubber Company, visit the company's web site through the Needles Accounting Resource Center Web Site at http://accounting.college.hmco.com/students.

REQUIRED

1. What are the purposes and three main components of the statement of cash flows?
2. What is the most important amount in the statement of cash flows? Why is it the most important?
3. What is the relationship of cash flows from operating activities to net income for Goodyear, and how do you account for the difference?
4. What are Goodyear's principal investing and financing activities?

OVERVIEW OF THE STATEMENT OF CASH FLOWS

LO1 State the principal purposes and uses of the statement of cash flows, and identify its components.

RELATED TEXT ASSIGNMENTS
Q: 1, 2, 3, 4, 5, 6
SE: 1, 8
E: 1
P: 1, 5
SD: 1, 2, 3
FRA: 3

The **statement of cash flows** shows how a company's operating, investing, and financing activities have affected cash during an accounting period. It explains the net increase (or decrease) in cash during the period. For purposes of preparing this statement, **cash** is defined as including both cash and cash equivalents. The FASB defines **cash equivalents** as short-term, highly liquid investments, including money market accounts, commercial paper, and U.S. Treasury bills. A company maintains cash equivalents to earn interest on cash that would otherwise remain unused temporarily. Suppose, for example, that a company has $1,000,000 that it will not need for 30 days. To earn a return on this amount, the company may place the cash in an account that earns interest (such as a money market account), it may lend the cash to another corporation by purchasing that corporation's short-term notes (commercial paper), or it may purchase a short-term obligation of the U.S. government (Treasury bills). In this context, short-term refers to original maturities of 90 days or less. Since cash and cash equivalents are considered the same, transfers between the Cash account and cash equivalents are not treated as cash receipts or cash payments. In effect, cash equivalents are combined with the Cash account on the statement of cash flows.

KEY POINT: Money market accounts, commercial paper (short-term notes), and U.S. Treasury bills are considered cash equivalents because they are highly liquid, temporary (90 days or less) holding places for cash not currently needed to operate the business. They can be quickly converted into cash if the need arises.

🛑 **STOP AND THINK!**
Which statement is more useful—the income statement or the statement of cash flows?

The statements are equally useful. The income statement relates most directly to the goal of profitability, whereas the statement of cash flows is more closely tied to the goal of liquidity. ■

KEY POINT: Management uses the statement of cash flows to make various investing and financing decisions. Investors and creditors, on the other hand, use the statement primarily to assess cash flow prospects.

KEY POINT: Operating activities arise from the day-to-day sale of goods and services, investing activities involve long-term assets and investments, and financing activities deal with stockholders' equity accounts and debt (borrowing).

Cash equivalents should not be confused with short-term investments or marketable securities, which are not combined with the Cash account on the statement of cash flows. Purchases of marketable securities are treated as cash outflows and sales of marketable securities as cash inflows on the statement of cash flows. In this chapter, we assume that cash includes cash and cash equivalents.

PURPOSES OF THE STATEMENT OF CASH FLOWS

The primary purpose of the statement of cash flows is to provide information about a company's cash receipts and cash payments during an accounting period. A secondary purpose of the statement is to provide information about a company's operating, investing, and financing activities during the accounting period. Some information about those activities may be inferred from other financial statements, but it is on the statement of cash flows that all the transactions affecting cash are summarized.

INTERNAL AND EXTERNAL USES OF THE STATEMENT OF CASH FLOWS

The statement of cash flows is useful internally to management and externally to investors and creditors. Management uses the statement to assess liquidity, to determine dividend policy, and to evaluate the effects of major policy decisions involving investments and financing. In other words, management may use the statement to determine if short-term financing is needed to pay current liabilities, to decide whether to raise or lower dividends, and to plan for investing and financing needs.

Investors and creditors find the statement useful in assessing the company's ability to manage cash flows, to generate positive future cash flows, to pay its liabilities, to pay dividends and interest, and to anticipate its need for additional financing. Also, they may use the statement to explain the differences between net income on the income statement and the net cash flows generated from operations. In addition, the statement shows both the cash and the noncash effects of investing and financing activities during the accounting period.

CLASSIFICATION OF CASH FLOWS

The statement of cash flows classifies cash receipts and cash payments into the categories of operating, investing, and financing activities. The components of these activities are illustrated in Figure 1 and summarized below.

1. **Operating activities** include the cash effects of transactions and other events that enter into the determination of net income. Included in this category as cash inflows are cash receipts from customers for goods and services, interest and dividends received on loans and investments, and sales of trading securities. Included as cash outflows are cash payments for wages, inventory, expenses, interest, taxes, and purchases of trading securities. In effect, the income statement is changed from an accrual to a cash basis.

2. **Investing activities** include the acquisition and sale of long-term assets and marketable securities, other than trading securities or cash equivalents, and the making and collecting of loans. Cash inflows include the cash received from selling long-term assets and marketable securities and from collecting loans. Cash outflows include the cash expended for purchases of long-term assets and marketable securities and the cash lent to borrowers.

3. **Financing activities** include obtaining resources from stockholders and providing them with a return on their investments, and obtaining resources from creditors and repaying the amounts borrowed or otherwise settling the obligations. Cash inflows include the proceeds from issues of stocks and from short-term and long-term borrowing. Cash outflows include the repayments of loans (excluding interest) and payments to owners, including cash dividends. Treasury stock transactions are also considered financing activities. Repayments of

Figure 1
Classification of Cash Inflows and Cash Outflows

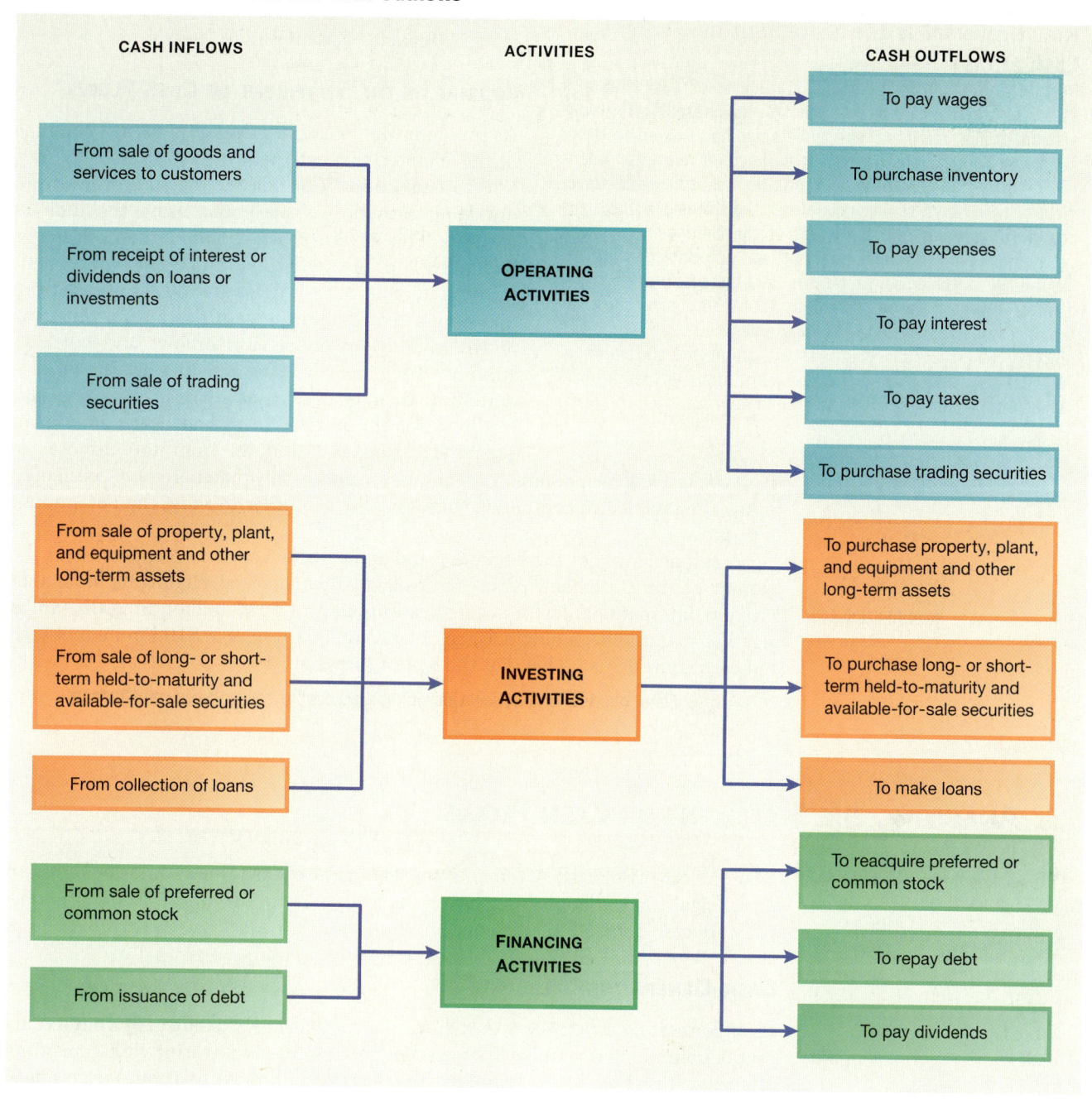

CASH INFLOWS	ACTIVITIES	CASH OUTFLOWS
From sale of goods and services to customers	**OPERATING ACTIVITIES**	To pay wages
From receipt of interest or dividends on loans or investments		To purchase inventory
From sale of trading securities		To pay expenses
		To pay interest
		To pay taxes
		To purchase trading securities
From sale of property, plant, and equipment and other long-term assets	**INVESTING ACTIVITIES**	To purchase property, plant, and equipment and other long-term assets
From sale of long- or short-term held-to-maturity and available-for-sale securities		To purchase long- or short-term held-to-maturity and available-for-sale securities
From collection of loans		To make loans
From sale of preferred or common stock	**FINANCING ACTIVITIES**	To reacquire preferred or common stock
From issuance of debt		To repay debt
		To pay dividends

accounts payable or accrued liabilities are not considered repayments of loans under financing activities; they are classified as cash outflows under operating activities.

Companies occasionally engage in significant **noncash investing and financing transactions** involving only long-term assets, long-term liabilities, or stockholders' equity. For instance, a company might exchange a long-term asset for a long-term liability, settle a debt by issuing capital stock, or take out a long-term mortgage for the purchase of land and a building. Such transactions represent significant investing and financing activities, but they would not be reflected on the statement of cash flows because they do not involve either cash inflows or outflows. However, because such transactions will affect future cash flows, the FASB has determined

FOCUS ON INTERNATIONAL BUSINESS

How Universal Is the Statement of Cash Flows?

Despite the importance of the statement of cash flows in assessing the liquidity of companies in the United States, considerable variation in its use and format has existed in other countries. For example, the principal directives related to financial reporting for the European Union do not address the statement of cash flows. In many countries, the statement shows the change in working capital instead of the change in cash and cash equivalents. However, international accounting standards require the statement of cash flows, and international financial markets expect it to be presented. As a result, most multinational companies include the statement in their financial reports. Most European countries will adopt the statement of cash flows by 2006, when the European Union will require the use of international accounting standards.

that they should be disclosed in a separate schedule as part of the statement of cash flows. In this way, the reader of the statement can see the company's investing and financing activities more clearly.

FORMAT OF THE STATEMENT OF CASH FLOWS

As shown in the Financial Highlights at the beginning of this chapter, the statement of cash flows is divided into three sections. The first section, cash flows from operating activities, is presented using the indirect method. This is the most common method and is explained later in the chapter. The other two sections of the statement of cash flows are the cash flows from investing activities and the cash flows from financing activities. The individual cash inflows and outflows from investing and financing activities are shown separately in their respective categories. Normally, cash outflows for the purchase of plant assets are shown separately from cash inflows from the disposal of plant assets. However, because the inflows are not usually material, some companies follow the practice of combining these two lines in order to show the net amount of outflow.

A reconciliation of the beginning and ending balances of cash appears near the bottom of the statement. Again referring to the Financial Highlights, note that Marriott International had a net decrease in cash of $614 million in 2002, which together with the beginning balance of $812 million results in $198 million of cash and cash equivalents on hand at the end of the year.

www.marriott.com

✓ Check out ACE for a Review Quiz at http://accounting.college.hmco.com/students.

ANALYZING THE STATEMENT OF CASH FLOWS

LO2 Analyze the statement of cash flows.

RELATED TEXT ASSIGNMENTS
Q: 7, 8
SE: 2, 3
E: 2
P: 2, 3, 4, 6, 7
SD: 3, 4
FRA: 1, 2, 3, 4, 5, 6

www.marriott.com

Like the other financial statements, the statement of cash flows can be analyzed to reveal significant relationships. Two areas analysts examine when studying a company are cash-generating efficiency and free cash flow.

CASH-GENERATING EFFICIENCY

Cash-generating efficiency is the ability of a company to generate cash from its current or continuing operations. Three ratios are helpful in measuring cash-generating efficiency: cash flow yield, cash flows to sales, and cash flows to assets. We compute these ratios for Marriott International in 2002 using data from the Financial Highlights at the beginning of this chapter and those presented below.[3] All dollar amounts are stated in millions.

Financial Highlights for Marriott International
(In millions of dollars)

	2002	2001	2000
Net Sales	$8,441	$7,786	$7,911
Total Assets	8,296	9,107	8,237

ENRICHMENT NOTE: The cash flow yield enables users to assess whether sufficient cash flows underlie earnings. Serious questions would be raised if cash flow yield was less than 1.0. For example, receivables and inventories might be growing too fast, perhaps signaling a slowdown in sales growth or a problem in managing receivables collection or inventory levels.

Cash flow yield is the ratio of net cash flows from operating activities to net income, computed as follows:

$$\text{Cash Flow Yield} = \frac{\text{Net Cash Flows from Operating Activities}}{\text{Net Income}}$$

$$= \frac{\$516}{\$448}$$

$$= 1.2 \text{ times}$$

Marriott International has a good cash flow yield of 1.2 times; that is, the corporation's operating activities are generating about 20 percent more cash flow than net income. If special items, such as discontinued operations, appear on the income statement and are material, income from continuing operations should be used as the denominator.

Cash flows to sales is the ratio of net cash flows from operating activities to sales, computed as follows:

$$\text{Cash Flows to Sales} = \frac{\text{Net Cash Flows from Operating Activities}}{\text{Net Sales}}$$

$$= \frac{\$516}{\$8,441}$$

$$= 6.1\%$$

Marriott generates cash flows to sales of 6.1 percent. The company generated a positive but relatively small percentage of net cash from sales.

Cash flows to assets is the ratio of net cash flows from operating activities to average total assets, computed as follows:

$$\text{Cash Flows to Assets} = \frac{\text{Net Cash Flows from Operating Activities}}{\text{Average Total Assets}}$$

$$= \frac{\$516}{(\$8,296 + \$9,107) \div 2}$$

$$= 5.9\%$$

> **STOP AND THINK!**
> If cash flow yield is less than 1.0, would cash flows to sales and cash flows to assets be greater or less than profit margin and return on assets, respectively?
>
> Cash flows to sales and cash flows to assets would be less than profit margin and return on assets, respectively, because a cash flow yield of less than 1.0 means that cash flows from operations are less than net income. Both are numerators in ratios that have the same denominators. ■

The cash flows to assets ratio is slightly less than the cash flows to sales ratio because Marriott International has a good asset turnover ratio (sales ÷ average total assets) of approximately .97 times (5.9% ÷ 6.1%). Cash flows to sales and cash flows to assets are closely related to the profitability measures of profit margin and return on assets. They exceed those measures by the amount of the cash flow yield ratio because cash flow yield is the ratio of net cash flows from operating activities to net income.

Although Marriott's cash flow yield and cash flows to assets are relatively good, its efficiency at generating cash flows from operating activities, as measured by cash flows to sales, could be improved.

FREE CASH FLOW

www.marriott.com

In 2002, Marriott had a net cash outflow of $317 million for investing activities, which could indicate that the company was expanding. However, that figure mixes capital expenditures for plant assets, which reflect management's expansion of operations, with loan advances and collections. Cash flows from financing activities used $1,447 million, but that figure combines financing activities associated with long-term debt and stocks with dividends paid to stockholders. While something can be learned by looking at those broad categories, many analysts

Focus on Business Practice

What Do You Mean, "Free Cash Flow"?

Because the statement of cash flows has been around for less than 20 years, no generally accepted analyses have yet been developed. For example, the term *free cash flow* is commonly used in the business press, but there is no agreement on its definition. An article in *Forbes* defines *free cash flow* as "cash available after paying out capital expenditures and dividends, *but before taxes and interest*"[4] [emphasis added]. An article in *The Wall Street Journal* defines it as "operating income less maintenance-level capital expenditures."[5] The definition with which we are most in agreement is the one used in *Business Week*: free cash flow is net cash flows from operating activities less net capital expenditures and dividends. This "measures truly discretionary funds—company money that an owner could pocket without harming the business."[6]

KEY POINT: Free cash flow should be interpreted in light of the company's overall need for cash. For instance, the purchase of treasury stock will reduce the amount of cash that is free for operating uses.

find it more informative to go beyond them to focus on a computation called free cash flow.

Free cash flow is the amount of cash that remains after deducting the funds a company must commit to continue operating at its planned level. The commitments must cover current or continuing operations, interest, income taxes, dividends, and net capital expenditures. Cash requirements for current or continuing operations, interest, and income taxes must be paid or the company's creditors and the government can take legal action. Although the payment of dividends is not strictly required, dividends normally represent a commitment to stockholders. If these payments are reduced or eliminated, stockholders will be unhappy and the price of the company's stock will fall. Net capital expenditures represent management's plans for the future.

If free cash flow is positive, it means that the company has met all its planned cash commitments and has cash available to reduce debt or to expand. A negative free cash flow means that the company will have to sell investments, borrow money, or issue stock in the short term to continue at its planned level. If free cash flow remains negative for several years, a company may not be able to raise cash by issuing stock or bonds.

Since cash commitments for current or continuing operations, interest, and income taxes are incorporated in cash flows from current operations, free cash flow for Marriott is computed as follows (in millions):

$$\text{Free Cash Flow} = \text{Net Cash Flows from Operating Activities} - \text{Dividends} - \text{Purchases of Plant Assets} + \text{Sales of Plant Assets}$$

$$= \$516 - \$65 - \$292 + \$729$$

$$= \$888$$

Focus on Business Practice

Cash Flows Tell All.

In early 2001, the telecommunications industry began one of the biggest market crashes in history. Could it have been predicted? The telecommunications industry depends on heavy capital expenditures in equipment, such as cable lines and computers. When the cash flows from sales of 41 telecommunications companies are compared with their capital expenditures (a negative component of free cash flow) over the six years preceding the crash, an interesting pattern emerges. In the first three years, both cash flows from sales and capital expenditures were about 20 percent of sales. In other words, free cash flows were neutral, with operations generating enough cash flows to cover capital expenditures. In the next three years, these measures diverged. Cash flows to sales stayed at about 20 percent of sales, but the companies increased capital expenditures dramatically, to 35 percent of sales. Thus, free cash flows turned very negative, and almost half of capital expenditures had to be financed by debt instead of operations, making these companies more vulnerable to the downturn in the economy that occurred in 2001.[7]

Purchases and sales of plant assets appear in the investing activities section of the statement of cash flows; Marriott reported both capital expenditures and dispositions of property and equipment. Dividends are in the financing activities section. Marriott had positive free cash flow of $888 million due mainly to its strong operating cash flow of $516 million and $729 million cash received on disposal of property and equipment. The cash used by financing activities was the largest in three years, $1,447 million, because Marriott repaid long-term debt of $946 million and convertible subordinated debt of $347 million. Marriott also issued common stock in the amount of $35 million and purchased treasury stock for $252 million.

Cash flows can vary from year to year, so it is best to look at trends in cash flow measures over several years when analyzing a company's cash flows. Marriott's cash flow yield was less in 2002 than in 2001 and thus should be watched in 2003. Management summed this up in the company's annual report:

> **Liquidity and Capital Resources**
> We consider [our credit] resources, together with cash we expect to generate from operations, adequate to meet our short-term and long-term liquidity requirements.[8]

✓ Check out ACE for a Review Quiz at http://accounting.college.hmco.com/students.

PREPARING THE STATEMENT OF CASH FLOWS: OPERATING ACTIVITIES

LO3 Use the indirect method to determine cash flows from operating activities.

RELATED TEXT ASSIGNMENTS
Q: 9, 10, 11, 12
SE: 4, 5, 8
E: 3, 4, 5, 9
P: 2, 3, 4, 6, 7
SD: 1, 4
FRA: 3, 5

To demonstrate the preparation of the statement of cash flows, we will work through an example step by step. The data for this example are presented in Exhibits 1 and 2, which show Ryan Corporation's balance sheets for December 31, 20x5 and 20x4, and its 20x5 income statement. Exhibit 1 shows the balance sheet accounts that we use for analysis and whether the change in each account is an increase or a decrease. Exhibit 2 contains data about transactions that affected noncurrent accounts. The company's accountants would identify those transactions from the records.

The first step in preparing the statement of cash flows is to determine cash flows from operating activities. The income statement indicates a business's success or failure in earning an income from its operating activities. However, because the income statement is prepared on an accrual basis, it does not reflect the inflow and outflow of cash from those activities. Revenues are recorded even though the cash for them may not have been received, and expenses are recorded even though the cash for them may not have been expended. Thus, to arrive at cash flows from operations, the figures on the income statement must be converted from an accrual basis to a cash basis. There are two methods of accomplishing this: the direct method and the indirect method. Under the **direct method**, each item on the income statement is adjusted from the accrual basis to the cash basis. The result is a statement that begins with cash receipts from sales and interest and deducts cash payments for purchases, operating expenses, interest payments, and income taxes to arrive at net cash flows from operating activities. The **indirect method** does not require the individual adjustment of each item on the income statement; it lists only the adjustments necessary to convert net income to cash flows from operations.

KEY POINT: The direct and indirect methods relate only to the operating activities section of the statement of cash flows. They are both acceptable for financial reporting purposes.

The direct and indirect methods always produce the same net figure. The direct method is more easily understood by the average reader because it results in a more straightforward presentation of operating cash flows than does the indirect method. However, the indirect method is the overwhelming choice of most companies and accountants. A survey of large companies shows that 99 percent use this method.[9] The indirect method is superior to the direct method from the analysts' perspective because its format begins with net income and derives cash flows from operations.

Exhibit 1
Comparative Balance Sheets with Changes in Accounts Indicated

Ryan Corporation
Comparative Balance Sheets
December 31, 20x5 and 20x4

	20x5	20x4	Change	Increase or Decrease
Assets				
Current assets				
Cash	$ 46,000	$ 15,000	$ 31,000	Increase
Accounts receivable (net)	47,000	55,000	(8,000)	Decrease
Inventory	144,000	110,000	34,000	Increase
Prepaid expenses	1,000	5,000	(4,000)	Decrease
Total current assets	$238,000	$185,000	$ 53,000	
Investments available for sale	$115,000	$127,000	($ 12,000)	Decrease
Plant assets				
Plant assets	$715,000	$505,000	$210,000	Increase
Accumulated depreciation	(103,000)	(68,000)	(35,000)	Increase
Total plant assets	$612,000	$437,000	$175,000	
Total assets	$965,000	$749,000	$216,000	
Liabilities				
Current liabilities				
Accounts payable	$ 50,000	$ 43,000	$ 7,000	Increase
Accrued liabilities	12,000	9,000	3,000	Increase
Income taxes payable	3,000	5,000	(2,000)	Decrease
Total current liabilities	$ 65,000	$ 57,000	$ 8,000	
Long-term liabilities				
Bonds payable	295,000	245,000	50,000	Increase
Total liabilities	$360,000	$302,000	$ 58,000	
Stockholders' Equity				
Common stock, $5 par value	$276,000	$200,000	$ 76,000	Increase
Paid-in capital in excess of par value, common	214,000	115,000	99,000	Increase
Retained earnings	140,000	132,000	8,000	Increase
Treasury stock	(25,000)	0	(25,000)	Increase
Total stockholders' equity	$605,000	$447,000	$158,000	
Total liabilities and stockholders' equity	$965,000	$749,000	$216,000	

KEY POINT: The indirect method begins with net income and adjusts up or down to produce net cash flows from operating activities.

The analyst can readily identify the factors that cause cash flows from operations. Further, from the company's standpoint, the indirect method is easier and less expensive to prepare. For these reasons, we use the indirect method in this book.

As illustrated in Figure 2, the indirect method focuses on items from the income statement that must be adjusted to reconcile net income to net cash flows

EXHIBIT 2
Income Statement and Other Information on Noncurrent Accounts

Ryan Corporation
Income Statement
For the Year Ended December 31, 20x5

Net sales		$698,000
Cost of goods sold		520,000
Gross margin		$178,000
Operating expenses (including depreciation expense of $37,000)		147,000
Operating income		$ 31,000
Other income (expenses)		
Interest expense	($23,000)	
Interest income	6,000	
Gain on sale of investments	12,000	
Loss on sale of plant assets	(3,000)	(8,000)
Income before income taxes		$ 23,000
Income taxes		7,000
Net income		$ 16,000

Other transactions affecting noncurrent accounts during 20x5:

1. Purchased investments in the amount of $78,000.
2. Sold investments that cost $90,000 for $102,000.
3. Purchased plant assets in the amount of $120,000.
4. Sold plant assets that cost $10,000 with accumulated depreciation of $2,000 for $5,000.
5. Issued $100,000 of bonds at face value in a noncash exchange for plant assets.
6. Repaid $50,000 of bonds at face value at maturity.
7. Issued 15,200 shares of $5 par value common stock for $175,000.
8. Purchased treasury stock in the amount of $25,000.
9. Paid cash dividends in the amount of $8,000.

from operating activities. The items that require adjustment are those that affect net income but not net cash flows from operating activities. They include depreciation and amortization, gains and losses, and changes in the balances of current asset and current liability accounts. The reconciliation of Ryan Corporation's net income to net cash flows from operating activities is shown in Exhibit 3. Each adjustment is discussed in the sections that follow.

FIGURE 2
Indirect Method of Determining Net Cash Flows from Operating Activities

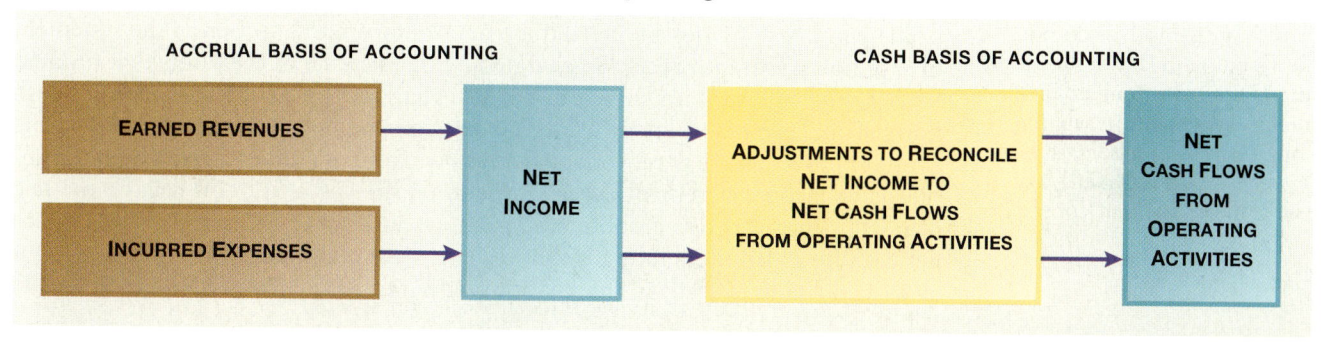

ACCRUAL BASIS OF ACCOUNTING → EARNED REVENUES / INCURRED EXPENSES → **NET INCOME** → **CASH BASIS OF ACCOUNTING** → ADJUSTMENTS TO RECONCILE NET INCOME TO NET CASH FLOWS FROM OPERATING ACTIVITIES → NET CASH FLOWS FROM OPERATING ACTIVITIES

EXHIBIT 3
Schedule of Cash Flows from Operating Activities: Indirect Method

Ryan Corporation
Schedule of Cash Flows from Operating Activities
For the Year Ended December 31, 20x5

Cash flows from operating activities		
Net income		$16,000
Adjustments to reconcile net income to net cash flows from operating activities		
Depreciation expense	$37,000	
Gain on sale of investments	(12,000)	
Loss on sale of plant assets	3,000	
Changes in current assets and current liabilities		
Decrease in accounts receivable	8,000	
Increase in inventory	(34,000)	
Decrease in prepaid expenses	4,000	
Increase in accounts payable	7,000	
Increase in accrued liabilities	3,000	
Decrease in income taxes payable	(2,000)	14,000
Net cash flows from operating activities		$30,000

● **STOP AND THINK!**
If a company has positive earnings, can cash flows from operating activities ever be negative?

If a company has large gains, large increases in current assets, or decreases in current liabilities, the results could overwhelm the earnings and create negative cash flows from operating activities. ■

DEPRECIATION

Cash payments for plant assets, intangibles, and natural resources occur when the assets are purchased and are reflected as investing activities on the statement of cash flows at that time. When depreciation expense, amortization expense, and depletion expense appear on the income statement, they simply indicate allocations of the costs of the original purchases to the current accounting period; they do not affect net cash flows in the current period. The amount of such expenses can usually be found by referring to the income statement or a note to the financial statements. For Ryan Corporation, the income statement reveals depreciation expense of $37,000, which would have been recorded as follows:

KEY POINT: Operating expenses on the income statement include depreciation expense, which does not require a cash outlay.

$A = L + OE$
$- \quad -$

Depreciation Expense	37,000	
Accumulated Depreciation		37,000
To record annual depreciation on plant assets		

The recording of depreciation involved no outlay of cash even though depreciation expense appears on the income statement. Thus, to derive cash flows from operations, an adjustment for depreciation is needed to increase net income by the amount of depreciation recorded.

GAINS AND LOSSES

STUDY NOTE: Gains and losses by themselves do not represent cash flows; they are merely bookkeeping adjustments. For example, when a long-term asset is sold, it is the *proceeds* (cash received), not the gain or loss, that constitute cash flow.

Gains and losses that appear on the income statement also do not affect cash flows from operating activities and need to be removed from this section of the statement of cash flows. The cash receipts generated by the disposal of the assets that resulted in the gains or losses are shown in the investing section of the statement of cash flows. Thus, gains and losses are removed from net income (preventing double counting) to reconcile net income to cash flows from operating activities. For example, on its income statement, Ryan Corporation showed a $12,000 gain on the sale of investments, and this is subtracted from net income to reconcile net income to net cash flows from operating activities. The reason for this is that the $12,000 is already included (added) in the investing activities section as part of the $102,000 cash from the sale of the investment. Because the gain is included in the calculation of net income, the $12,000 gain needs to be subtracted to prevent double counting. Also, Ryan Corporation showed a $3,000 loss on the sale of plant assets. Following the same logic, the $3,000 loss is already reflected in the $5,000 sale of plant assets in the investing activities section. Thus, the $3,000 is added to net income to reconcile net income to net cash flows from operating activities.

CHANGES IN CURRENT ASSETS

Decreases in current assets other than cash have positive effects on cash flows, and increases in current assets have negative effects on cash flows. A decrease in a current asset frees up invested cash, thereby increasing cash flow. An increase in a current asset consumes cash, thereby decreasing cash flow. For example, refer to the balance sheets and income statement for Ryan Corporation in Exhibits 1 and 2. Note that net sales in 20x5 were $698,000 and that Accounts Receivable decreased by $8,000. Thus, cash received from sales was $706,000, calculated as follows:

$$\$706,000 = \$698,000 + \$8,000$$

Collections were $8,000 more than sales recorded for the year. This relationship may be illustrated as follows:

Accounts Receivable

Sales to Customers →	Beg. Bal. 55,000	706,000 →	Cash Receipts from Customers
	698,000		
	End. Bal. 47,000		

Thus, to reconcile net income to net cash flows from operating activities, the $8,000 decrease in Accounts Receivable is added to net income.

Inventory may be analyzed in the same way. For example, Exhibit 1 shows that Inventory increased by $34,000 from 20x4 to 20x5. This means that Ryan Corporation expended $34,000 more in cash for purchases than was included in cost of goods sold on the income statement. As a result of this expenditure, net income is higher than the net cash flows from operating activities, so $34,000 must be deducted from net income. Using the same logic, the decrease of $4,000 in Prepaid Expenses is added to net income to reconcile net income to net cash flows from operating activities.

CHANGES IN CURRENT LIABILITIES

Changes in current liabilities have the opposite effects on cash flows from those of changes in current assets. Increases in current liabilities are added to net income, and decreases in current liabilities are deducted from net income to reconcile net income to net cash flows from operating activities. An increase in a current liability represents a postponement of a cash payment, which frees up cash and increases cash flow in the current period. A decrease in current liabilities consumes cash, thereby decreasing cash flow. For example, Exhibit 1 shows that Ryan Corporation had a $7,000 increase in accounts payable from 20x4 to 20x5. This means that Ryan Corporation paid $7,000 less to creditors than the amount of purchases indicates in cost of goods sold on the income statement. This relationship may be visualized as follows:

Accounts Payable

Cash Payments to Suppliers ←	547,000	Beg. Bal. 43,000	
		554,000* ←	Purchases
		End. Bal. 50,000	

*Purchases = Cost of Goods Sold ($520,000) + Increase in Inventory ($34,000).

FOCUS ON BUSINESS PRACTICE

What's Your "Burn Rate"?

Why would a company have a total market value less than the amount of cash it has on hand? The answer is "burn rate." Burn rate is the pace at which companies use cash in their operations. A major contributor to the market crash of the stocks of dot-com companies was the difficulty these firms had in generating enough revenue to produce positive cash flows from operations. For example, when investors thought Webvan Group, Inc., the Internet grocer, would be the delivery service model of the future, the company was valued as high as $11.4 billion. However, as Webvan's burn rate reached $55 million a month, its market value dropped to a mere $132 million, even though the company had $212 million in cash.[10] The company was never able to generate sufficient revenues and soon declared bankruptcy.

As a result, $7,000 is added to net income to reconcile net income to net cash flows from operating activities. By the same logic, the increase of $3,000 in accrued liabilities is added to net income, and the decrease of $2,000 in income taxes payable is deducted from net income.

SCHEDULE OF CASH FLOWS FROM OPERATING ACTIVITIES

In summary, Exhibit 3 shows that by using the indirect method, net income of $16,000 has been adjusted by reconciling items totaling $14,000 to arrive at net cash flows from operating activities of $30,000. This means that although net income was $16,000, Ryan actually had net cash flows of $30,000 available from operating activities to use for purchasing assets, reducing debts, or paying dividends.

The effects of items on the income statement that do not affect cash flows may be summarized as follows:

	Add to or Deduct from Net Income
Depreciation expense	Add
Amortization expense	Add
Depletion expense	Add
Losses	Add
Gains	Deduct

The adjustments for increases and decreases in current assets and current liabilities may be summarized as follows:

	Add to Net Income	Deduct from Net Income
Current assets		
Accounts receivable (net)	Decrease	Increase
Inventory	Decrease	Increase
Prepaid expenses	Decrease	Increase
Current liabilities		
Accounts payable	Increase	Decrease
Accrued liabilities	Increase	Decrease
Income taxes payable	Increase	Decrease

✓ Check out ACE for a Review Quiz at http://accounting.college.hmco.com/students.

PREPARING THE STATEMENT OF CASH FLOWS: INVESTING ACTIVITIES

LO4 Determine cash flows from investing activities.

RELATED TEXT ASSIGNMENTS
Q: 13
SE: 6, 8
E: 6, 7, 8, 9
P: 2, 3, 4, 6, 7
SD: 4
FRA: 3, 5

To determine cash flows from investing activities, accounts involving cash receipts and cash payments from investing activities are examined individually. The objective is to explain the change in each account balance from one year to the next.

Investing activities center on the long-term assets shown on the balance sheet, but they also include transactions affecting short-term investments from the current assets section of the balance sheet and investment gains and losses from the income statement. The balance sheets in Exhibit 1 show that Ryan Corporation had long-term assets of investments and plant assets, but no short-term investments. The income statement in Exhibit 2 shows that Ryan had investment-related items in the form of a gain on the sale of investments and a loss on the sale of plant assets.

KEY POINT: Investing activities involve long-term assets and short- or long-term investments. Both inflows and outflows of cash are shown in the investing activities section of the statement of cash flows.

The schedule at the bottom of Exhibit 2 lists the following five items pertaining to investing activities in 20x5:

1. Purchased investments in the amount of $78,000.
2. Sold investments that cost $90,000 for $102,000.
3. Purchased plant assets in the amount of $120,000.
4. Sold plant assets that cost $10,000 with accumulated depreciation of $2,000 for $5,000.
5. Issued $100,000 of bonds at face value in a noncash exchange for plant assets.

The following sections analyze the accounts related to investing activities to determine their effects on Ryan Corporation's cash flows.

INVESTMENTS

The objective here is to explain Ryan Corporation's $12,000 decrease in investments, all of which are classified as available-for-sale securities. This is accomplished by analyzing the increases and decreases in the Investments account to determine the effects on the Cash account. Purchases increase investments, and sales decrease investments.

Item **1** in Ryan's list of investing activities shows purchases of $78,000 during 20x5. This transaction is recorded as follows:

A = L + OE
 +
 −

Investments	78,000	
Cash		78,000
Purchase of investments		

The entry shows that the effect of this transaction is a $78,000 decrease in cash flows.

Item **2** in the list shows that Ryan sold investments that cost $90,000 for $102,000, resulting in a gain of $12,000. This transaction is recorded as follows:

A = L + OE
 +   +
 −

Cash	102,000	
Investments		90,000
Gain on Sale of Investments		12,000
Sale of investments for a gain		

KEY POINT: The $102,000 price obtained, not the $12,000 gain, constitutes the cash flow here.

The effect of this transaction is a $102,000 increase in cash flows. Note that the gain on sale of investments is included in the $102,000. This is why we excluded it in computing cash flows from operations. If it had been included in that section, it would have been counted twice.

The $12,000 decrease in the Investments account (unrelated to the $12,000 gain above) during 20x5 has now been explained, as seen in the following T account:

Investments

Beg. Bal.	127,000	Sales	90,000
Purchases	78,000		
End. Bal.	115,000		

● **STOP AND THINK!**
Which adjustments to net income in the operating activities section of the statement of cash flows are directly related to cash flows reported in other sections?

Gains and losses from operating activities are directly related to the cash flows from the sale of assets reported in the investing activities section. ■

The cash flow effects from these transactions are shown in the investing activities section on the statement of cash flows as follows:

Purchase of investments	($ 78,000)
Sale of investments	102,000

Notice that purchases and sales are listed separately as cash outflows and inflows to give readers of the statement a complete view of investing activity. Some companies prefer to combine them into a single net amount.

If Ryan Corporation had short-term investments or marketable securities, the analysis of cash flows would be the same.

PLANT ASSETS

In the case of plant assets, it is necessary to explain the changes in both the Plant Assets account and the related Accumulated Depreciation account. According to Exhibit 1, Ryan Corporation's plant assets increased by $210,000, and accumulated depreciation increased by $35,000. Purchases increase plant assets, and sales decrease plant assets. Accumulated depreciation is increased by the amount of depreciation expense and decreased by the removal of the accumulated depreciation associated with plant assets that are sold. Three items listed in Exhibit 2 affect plant assets. Item 3 in the list indicates that Ryan Corporation purchased plant assets totaling $120,000 during 20x5, as shown by the following entry:

A = L + OE			
+	Plant Assets	120,000	
–	Cash		120,000
	Purchase of plant assets		

This transaction results in a cash outflow of $120,000.

Item 4 states that Ryan Corporation sold for $5,000 plant assets that cost $10,000 and had accumulated depreciation of $2,000, which resulted in a loss of $3,000. The entry to record this transaction is as follows:

A = L + OE			
+	Cash	5,000	
–	Accumulated Depreciation	2,000	
+	Loss on Sale of Plant Assets	3,000	
–	Plant Assets		10,000
	Sale of plant assets at a loss		

KEY POINT: Even though Ryan had a loss on the sale, it realized a positive cash flow of $5,000, which will be reported in the investing activities section of the statement of cash flows. When the indirect approach is used, the loss is eliminated with an "add-back" to net income.

Note that in this transaction the positive cash flow is equal to the amount of cash received, or $5,000. The loss on the sale of plant assets is included here, and excluded from the operating activities section (see page 721), by adjusting net income for the amount of the loss. The amount of a loss or gain on the sale of an asset is determined by the amount of cash received and does not represent a cash outflow or inflow.

The disclosure of these two transactions in the investing activities section of the statement of cash flows is as follows:

Purchase of plant assets   ($120,000)
Sale of plant assets   5,000

Cash outflows and cash inflows are listed separately here, though companies sometimes combine them into a single net amount, as they do the purchase and sale of investments.

Item 5 in Exhibit 2 is a noncash exchange that affects two long-term accounts, Plant Assets and Bonds Payable. It is recorded as follows:

A = L + OE			
+ +	Plant Assets	100,000	
	Bonds Payable		100,000
	Issued bonds at face value for plant assets		

Although this transaction does not involve an inflow or outflow of cash, it is a significant transaction involving both an investing activity (the purchase of plant assets) and a financing activity (the issue of bonds payable). Because one purpose of the statement of cash flows is to show important investing and financing activities, the transaction is listed in a separate schedule, either at the bottom of the statement of cash flows or accompanying the statement, as follows:

Schedule of Noncash Investing and Financing Transactions
Issue of bonds payable for plant assets $100,000

Through our analysis of the preceding transactions and the depreciation expense for plant assets, we have now accounted for all the changes in the Plant Assets accounts, as shown in the following T accounts:

Plant Assets

Beg. Bal.	505,000	Sale	10,000
Cash Purchase	120,000		
Noncash Purchase	100,000		
End. Bal.	715,000		

Accumulated Depreciation

Sale	2,000	Beg. Bal.	68,000
		Dep. Expense	37,000
		End. Bal.	103,000

Had the balance sheet included specific plant asset accounts (e.g., Buildings and Equipment and related accumulated depreciation accounts) or other long-term asset accounts (e.g., Intangibles), the analysis would have been the same.

✓ Check out ACE for a Review Quiz at http://accounting.college.hmco.com/students.

PREPARING THE STATEMENT OF CASH FLOWS: FINANCING ACTIVITIES

LO5 Determine cash flows from financing activities.

RELATED TEXT ASSIGNMENTS
Q: 14
SE: 7, 8
E: 8, 9
P: 2, 3, 4, 6, 7
SD: 4
FRA: 3, 5

KEY POINT: Financing activities involve stockholders' equity accounts and short- and long-term borrowings. Because dividends paid involve retained earnings, they are appropriately included in this category.

The procedure for determining cash flows from financing activities is like the analysis of investing activities, including treatment of related gains or losses, but the accounts analyzed are short-term borrowings, long-term liabilities, and stockholders' equity accounts. Cash dividends from the statement of stockholders' equity must also be considered. Since Ryan Corporation does not have short-term borrowings, we deal only with long-term liabilities and stockholders' equity accounts.

These items from Exhibit 2 pertain to Ryan's financing activities in 20x5:

5. Issued $100,000 of bonds at face value in a noncash exchange for plant assets.
6. Repaid $50,000 of bonds at face value at maturity.
7. Issued 15,200 shares of $5 par value common stock for $175,000.
8. Purchased treasury stock for $25,000.
9. Paid cash dividends in the amount of $8,000.

BONDS PAYABLE

Exhibit 1 shows that Bonds Payable increased by $50,000 in 20x5. This account is affected by items **5** and **6**. Item **5** was analyzed in connection with plant assets. As noted above, it is reported on the schedule of noncash investing and financing transactions, but it must be remembered here in preparing the T account for Bonds Payable. Item **6** results in a cash outflow, which is recorded as follows:

A = L + OE
− −

Bonds Payable	50,000	
Cash		50,000
Repayment of bonds at face value at maturity		

This appears in the financing activities section of the statement of cash flows as:

Repayment of bonds   ($50,000)

The following T account explains the change in Bonds Payable:

Bonds Payable

Repayment	50,000	Beg. Bal.	245,000
		Noncash Issue	100,000
		End. Bal.	295,000

If Ryan Corporation had any notes payable, the analysis would be the same.

COMMON STOCK

Like the Plant Asset account and its related accounts, related stockholders' equity accounts should be analyzed together. For example, Paid-in Capital in Excess of Par Value, Common should be examined with Common Stock. In 20x5, Ryan Corporation's Common Stock account increased by $76,000, and Paid-in Capital in Excess of Par Value, Common increased by $99,000. Those increases are explained by item 7 in the list in Exhibit 2, which states that Ryan issued 15,200 shares of $5 par value common stock for $175,000. The entry to record the cash inflow is as follows:

A = L + OE
+   +
         +

Cash	175,000	
Common Stock		76,000
Paid-in Capital in Excess of Par Value, Common		99,000
Issued 15,200 shares of $5 par value common stock		

STUDY NOTE: The purchase of treasury stock would also qualify as a financing activity, but would appear as a cash outflow.

This appears in the financing activities section of the statement of cash flows as:

Issue of common stock $175,000

The following analysis of this transaction is all that is needed to explain the changes in the two accounts during 20x5:

Common Stock		Paid-in Capital in Excess of Par Value, Common	
	Beg. Bal. 200,000		Beg. Bal. 115,000
	Issue 76,000		Issue 99,000
	End. Bal. 276,000		End. Bal. 214,000

RETAINED EARNINGS

At this point, we have dealt with several items that affect retained earnings. For instance, we used Ryan's net income in the analysis of cash flows from operating activities. The only other item affecting Ryan's retained earnings is the payment of $8,000 in cash dividends (item 9 in Exhibit 2), which is recorded as follows:

A = L + OE
–   –

Retained Earnings	8,000	
Cash		8,000
Cash dividends for 20x5		

Ryan Corporation would have declared the dividend before paying it and therefore would have debited the Cash Dividends Declared account instead of Retained Earnings, but after paying the dividend and closing the Cash Dividends Declared account to Retained Earnings, the effect is as shown. Cash dividends are displayed in the financing activities section of the statement of cash flows as follows:

KEY POINT: It is dividends paid, not dividends declared, that appear on the statement of cash flows.

Payment of dividends   ($8,000)

The following T account shows the change in the Retained Earnings account:

Retained Earnings			
Dividends	8,000	Beg. Bal.	132,000
		Net Income	16,000
		End. Bal.	140,000

TREASURY STOCK

As noted in the chapter on contributed capital, many companies buy back their own stock on the open market. These buybacks use cash, as this entry shows:

A = L + OE
–   –

Treasury Stock	25,000	
Cash		25,000

This use of cash is classified in the statement of cash flows as a financing activity:

> **STOP AND THINK!**
> In computing free cash flow, what is an argument for treating purchases of treasury stock like dividend payments?
>
> *Both purchases of treasury stock and dividend payments represent payments to stockholders. Each diverts cash from productive use in the business (as assets), and thus each reduces free cash flow.* ∎

Purchase of treasury stock   ($25,000)

The T account for this transaction is as follows:

Treasury Stock	
Purchase 25,000	

We have now analyzed all Ryan's income statement items, explained all balance sheet changes, and taken all additional data into account. The resulting information can now be assembled into the statement of cash flows shown in Exhibit 4.

EXHIBIT 4
Statement of Cash Flows: Indirect Method

Ryan Corporation
Statement of Cash Flows
For the Year Ended December 31, 20x5

Cash flows from operating activities		
Net income		$ 16,000
Adjustments to reconcile net income to net cash flows from operating activities		
Depreciation expense	$ 37,000	
Gain on sale of investments	(12,000)	
Loss on sale of plant assets	3,000	
Changes in current assets and current liabilities		
Decrease in accounts receivable	8,000	
Increase in inventory	(34,000)	
Decrease in prepaid expenses	4,000	
Increase in accounts payable	7,000	
Increase in accrued liabilities	3,000	
Decrease in income taxes payable	(2,000)	14,000
Net cash flows from operating activities		$ 30,000
Cash flows from investing activities		
Purchase of investments	($ 78,000)	
Sale of investments	102,000	
Purchase of plant assets	(120,000)	
Sale of plant assets	5,000	
Net cash flows from investing activities		(91,000)
Cash flows from financing activities		
Repayment of bonds	($ 50,000)	
Issue of common stock	175,000	
Payment of dividends	(8,000)	
Purchase of treasury stock	(25,000)	
Net cash flows from financing activities		92,000
Net increase (decrease) in cash		$ 31,000
Cash at beginning of year		15,000
Cash at end of year		$ 46,000

Schedule of Noncash Investing and Financing Transactions

Issue of bonds payable for plant assets	$100,000

✓ Check out ACE for a Review Quiz at http://accounting.college.hmco.com/students.

Chapter Review

REVIEW OF LEARNING OBJECTIVES

LO1 State the principal purposes and uses of the statement of cash flows, and identify its components.

The statement of cash flows explains the changes in cash and cash equivalents from one accounting period to the next by showing cash inflows and outflows from the operating, investing, and financing activities of a company for an accounting period. For the statement of cash flows, *cash* is defined as including both cash and cash equivalents. The primary purpose of the statement is to provide information about a firm's cash receipts and cash payments during an accounting period. A secondary purpose is to provide information about a firm's operating, investing, and financing activities.

Cash flows may be classified as stemming from (1) operating activities, which include the cash effects of transactions and other events that enter into the determination of net income; (2) investing activities, which include the acquisition and sale of marketable securities and property, plant, and equipment, and the making and collecting of loans, excluding interest; or (3) financing activities, which include obtaining resources from stockholders and creditors and providing the former with a return on their investments and the latter with repayment. Noncash investing and financing transactions are also important because they affect future cash flows; these exchanges of long-term assets or liabilities are of interest to potential investors and creditors.

LO2 Analyze the statement of cash flows.

In analyzing a firm's statement of cash flows, analysts tend to focus on cash-generating efficiency and free cash flow. Cash-generating efficiency is a firm's ability to generate cash from its current or continuing operations. Three ratios used in measuring cash-generating efficiency are cash flow yield, cash flows to sales, and cash flows to assets. Free cash flow is the cash that remains after deducting the funds a firm must commit to continue operating at its planned level. Such commitments must cover current or continuing operations, interest, income taxes, dividends, and net capital expenditures.

LO3 Use the indirect method to determine cash flows from operating activities.

The indirect method adjusts net income for all noncash effects and for items that need to be converted from an accrual to a cash basis to arrive at a cash flow basis, as follows:

Cash flows from operating activities		
Net income		xxx
Adjustments to reconcile net income to net cash flows from operating activities (list of individual items)	xxx	xxx
Net cash flows from operating activities		xxx

LO4 Determine cash flows from investing activities.

Cash flows from investing activities are determined by identifying the cash flow effects of the transactions that affect each account relevant to investing activities. Such accounts include all long-term assets and short-term marketable securities.

LO5 Determine cash flows from financing activities.

The procedure for determining cash flows from financing activities is almost identical to that for investing activities. The difference is that the accounts involved are short-term borrowings, long-term liabilities, and stockholders' equity. The effects of gains and losses reported on the income statement must also be considered. After the changes in the balance sheet accounts from one accounting period to the next have been explained, all the cash flow effects should have been identified.

REVIEW OF CONCEPTS AND TERMINOLOGY

The following concepts and terms were introduced in this chapter:

LO1 **Cash:** For purposes of the statement of cash flows, both cash and cash equivalents.

LO1 **Cash equivalents:** Short-term (90 days or less), highly liquid investments, including money market accounts, commercial paper, and U.S. Treasury bills.

LO2 **Cash flows to assets:** The ratio of net cash flows from operating activities to average total assets.

LO2 **Cash flows to sales:** The ratio of net cash flows from operating activities to sales.

LO2 **Cash flow yield:** The ratio of net cash flows from operating activities to net income.

LO2 **Cash-generating efficiency:** The ability of a company to generate cash from its current or continuing operations.

LO3 **Direct method:** The procedure for converting the income statement from an accrual basis to a cash basis by separately adjusting each item on the income statement.

LO1 **Financing activities:** Business activities that involve obtaining resources from stockholders and creditors and providing the former with a return on their investments and the latter with repayment.

LO2 **Free cash flow:** The amount of cash that remains after deducting the funds a company must commit to continue operating at its planned level; net cash flows from operating activities minus dividends paid minus net capital expenditures.

LO3 **Indirect method:** The procedure for converting the income statement from an accrual basis to a cash basis by adjusting net income for items that do not affect cash flows, including depreciation, amortization, depletion, gains, losses, and changes in current assets and current liabilities.

LO1 **Investing activities:** Business activities that involve the acquisition and sale of long-term assets and marketable securities, other than trading securities or cash equivalents, and the making and collecting of loans.

LO1 **Noncash investing and financing transactions:** Significant investing and financing transactions involving only long-term assets, long-term liabilities, or stockholders' equity that do not affect current cash inflows or outflows.

LO1 **Operating activities:** Business activities that involve the cash effects of transactions and other events that enter into the determination of net income.

LO1 **Statement of cash flows:** A financial statement that shows how a company's operating, investing, and financing activities have affected cash during an accounting period.

REVIEW PROBLEM

The Statement of Cash Flows

LO2
LO3
LO4
LO5

Northwest Corporation's 20x5 income statement appears below. Its comparative balance sheets for 20x5 and 20x4 are presented on the next page.

Northwest Corporation
Income Statement
For the Year Ended December 31, 20x5

Net sales		$1,650,000
Cost of goods sold		920,000
Gross margin		$ 730,000
Operating expenses (including depreciation expense of $12,000 on buildings and $23,100 on equipment, and amortization expense of $4,800)		470,000
Operating income		$ 260,000
Other income (expenses)		
Interest expense	($ 55,000)	
Dividend income	3,400	
Gain on sale of investments	12,500	
Loss on disposal of equipment	(2,300)	(41,400)
Income before income taxes		$ 218,600
Income taxes		52,200
Net income		$ 166,400

Northwest Corporation
Comparative Balance Sheets
December 31, 20x5 and 20x4

	20x5	20x4	Change	Increase or Decrease
Assets				
Cash	$ 105,850	$ 121,850	($16,000)	Decrease
Accounts receivable (net)	296,000	314,500	(18,500)	Decrease
Inventory	322,000	301,000	21,000	Increase
Prepaid expenses	7,800	5,800	2,000	Increase
Long-term investments	36,000	86,000	(50,000)	Decrease
Land	150,000	125,000	25,000	Increase
Buildings	462,000	462,000	—	—
Accumulated depreciation, buildings	(91,000)	(79,000)	(12,000)	Increase
Equipment	159,730	167,230	(7,500)	Decrease
Accumulated depreciation, equipment	(43,400)	(45,600)	2,200	Decrease
Intangible assets	19,200	24,000	(4,800)	Decrease
Total assets	$1,424,180	$1,482,780	($58,600)	
Liabilities and Stockholders' Equity				
Accounts payable	$ 133,750	$ 233,750	($100,000)	Decrease
Notes payable (current)	75,700	145,700	(70,000)	Decrease
Accrued liabilities	5,000	—	5,000	Increase
Income taxes payable	20,000	—	20,000	Increase
Bonds payable	210,000	310,000	(100,000)	Decrease
Mortgage payable	330,000	350,000	(20,000)	Decrease
Common stock, $10 par value	400,000	340,000	60,000	Increase
Paid-in capital in excess of par value, common	90,000	50,000	40,000	Increase
Retained earnings	209,730	93,330	116,400	Increase
Treasury stock	(50,000)	(40,000)	(10,000)	Increase
Total liabilities and stockholders' equity	$1,424,180	$1,482,780	($ 58,600)	

The company's records for 20x5 provide the following additional information:

a. Long-term investments (available-for-sale securities) that cost $70,000 were sold at a gain of $12,500; additional long-term investments were made in the amount of $20,000.
b. Five acres of land to build a parking lot were purchased for $25,000.
c. Equipment that cost $37,500 with accumulated depreciation of $25,300 was sold at a loss of $2,300; new equipment costing $30,000 was purchased.
d. Notes payable in the amount of $100,000 were repaid; an additional $30,000 was borrowed by signing notes payable.
e. Bonds payable in the amount of $100,000 were converted into 6,000 shares of common stock.
f. The Mortgage Payable account was reduced by $20,000.
g. Cash dividends declared and paid were $50,000.
h. Treasury stock was purchased for $10,000.

REQUIRED
1. Prepare a statement of cash flows using the indirect method.
2. Compute cash flow yield, cash flows to sales, cash flows to assets, and free cash flow for 20x5.

Answer to Review Problem

1. Statement of cash flows using the indirect method:

Northwest Corporation
Statement of Cash Flows
For the Year Ended December 31, 20x5

Cash flows from operating activities

Net income		$166,400
Adjustments to reconcile net income to net cash flows from operating activities		
Depreciation expense, buildings	$ 12,000	
Depreciation expense, equipment	23,100	
Amortization expense, intangible assets	4,800	
Gain on sale of investments	(12,500)	
Loss on disposal of equipment	2,300	
Changes in current assets and current liabilities		
Decrease in accounts receivable	18,500	
Increase in inventory	(21,000)	
Increase in prepaid expenses	(2,000)	
Decrease in accounts payable	(100,000)	
Increase in accrued liabilities	5,000	
Increase in income taxes payable	20,000	(49,800)
Net cash flows from operating activities		$116,600

Cash flows from investing activities

Sale of long-term investments	$ 82,500[a]	
Purchase of long-term investments	(20,000)	
Purchase of land	(25,000)	
Sale of equipment	9,900[b]	
Purchase of equipment	(30,000)	
Net cash flows from investing activities		17,400

Cash flows from financing activities

Repayment of notes payable	($100,000)	
Issuance of notes payable	30,000	
Reduction in mortgage	(20,000)	
Payment of dividends	(50,000)	
Purchase of treasury stock	(10,000)	
Net cash flows from financing activities		(150,000)

Net increase (decrease) in cash		($ 16,000)
Cash at beginning of year		121,850
Cash at end of year		$105,850

Schedule of Noncash Investing and Financing Transactions

Conversion of bonds payable into common stock	$100,000

[a] $70,000 + $12,500 (gain) = $82,500
[b] $37,500 − $25,300 = $12,200 (book value) − $2,300 (loss) = $9,900

2. Cash flow yield, cash flows to sales, cash flows to assets, and free cash flow for 20x5:

$$\text{Cash Flow Yield} = \frac{\$116{,}600}{\$166{,}400} = .7 \text{ times}$$

$$\text{Cash Flows to Sales} = \frac{\$116{,}600}{\$1{,}650{,}000} = 7.1\%$$

$$\text{Cash Flows to Assets} = \frac{\$116{,}600}{(\$1{,}424{,}180 + \$1{,}482{,}780) \div 2} = 8.0\%$$

$$\text{Free Cash Flow} = \$116{,}600 - \$50{,}000 - \$25{,}000 - \$30{,}000 + \$9{,}900$$
$$= \$21{,}500$$

Chapter Assignments

BUILDING YOUR KNOWLEDGE FOUNDATION

QUESTIONS

1. In the statement of cash flows, what does cash include?
2. To earn a return on cash on hand during 20x3, Sallas Corporation transferred $45,000 from its checking account to a money market account, purchased a $25,000 Treasury bill, and invested $35,000 in common stocks. How will each of these transactions affect the statement of cash flows?
3. What are the purposes of the statement of cash flows?
4. Why is the statement of cash flows needed when most of the information in it is available from a company's comparative balance sheets and income statement?
5. What are the three classifications of cash flows? Give some examples of each.
6. Why is it important to disclose certain noncash transactions? How should they be disclosed?
7. Define *cash-generating efficiency* and identify three ratios that measure it.
8. Define *free cash flow* and identify its components. What do *positive* and *negative* free cash flows mean?
9. What is the basic difference between the direct method and the indirect method of determining cash flows from operations?
10. In determining net cash flows from operating activities (assuming the indirect method is used), what are the effects on cash generated by the following items: (a) an increase in accounts receivable, (b) a decrease in inventory, (c) an increase in accounts payable, (d) a decrease in wages payable, (e) depreciation expense, and (f) amortization of patents?
11. In 20x1, Cell-Borne Corporation had a net loss of $12,000 but positive cash flows from operations of $9,000. What conditions might have caused this situation?
12. Glen Corporation has the following other income and expense items: interest expense, $12,000; interest income, $3,000; dividend income, $5,000; and loss on the retirement of bonds, $6,000. Where does each of these items appear on the statement of cash flows, or how does the item affect the statement?
13. What is the proper treatment on the statement of cash flows of a transaction in which a building that cost $50,000 with accumulated depreciation of $32,000 was sold at a loss of $5,000?
14. What is the proper treatment on the statement of cash flows of (a) a transaction in which buildings and land were purchased by the issuance of a mortgage for

$234,000 and (b) a conversion of $50,000 in bonds payable into 2,500 shares of $6 par value common stock?

Short Exercises

LO1 SE 1. Classification of Cash Flow Transactions

Stahl Corporation engaged in the transactions listed below. Identify each as (a) an operating activity, (b) an investing activity, (c) a financing activity, (d) a noncash transaction, or (e) none of the above.

1. Sold land.
2. Declared and paid a cash dividend.
3. Paid interest.
4. Issued common stock for plant assets.
5. Issued preferred stock.
6. Borrowed cash on a bank loan.

LO2 SE 2. Cash-Generating Efficiency Ratios and Free Cash Flow

In 20x5, Portillo Corporation had year-end assets of $550,000, net sales of $790,000, net income of $90,000, net cash flows from operating activities of $180,000, purchases of plant assets of $120,000, and sales of plant assets of $20,000, and it paid dividends of $40,000. In 20x4, year-end assets were $500,000. Calculate the cash-generating efficiency ratios of cash flow yield, cash flows to sales, and cash flows to assets. Also calculate free cash flow.

LO2 SE 3. Cash-Generating Efficiency Ratios and Free Cash Flow

Examine the cash flow measures in part 2 of the review problem in this chapter. Discuss the meaning of these ratios.

LO3 SE 4. Computing Cash Flows from Operating Activities: Indirect Method

Global Market Corporation had a net income of $33,000 during 20x4. During the year, the company had depreciation expense of $14,000. Accounts Receivable increased by $11,000, and Accounts Payable increased by $5,000. Those were the company's only current assets and current liabilities. Use the indirect method to determine net cash flows from operating activities.

LO3 SE 5. Computing Cash Flows from Operating Activities: Indirect Method

During 20x4, Cheng Corporation had a net income of $72,000. Included on its income statement were depreciation expense of $8,000 and amortization expense of $900. During the year, Accounts Receivable decreased by $4,100, Inventories increased by $2,700, Prepaid Expenses decreased by $500, Accounts Payable decreased by $7,000, and Accrued Liabilities decreased by $850. Use the indirect method to determine net cash flows from operating activities.

LO4 SE 6. Cash Flows from Investing Activities and Noncash Transactions

During 20x5, Okee Company purchased land for $750,000. It paid $250,000 in cash and signed a $500,000 mortgage for the rest. The company also sold a building that originally cost $180,000, on which it had $140,000 of accumulated depreciation, for $190,000 cash, making a gain of $150,000. Prepare the cash flows from investing activities and schedule of noncash investing and financing transactions sections of the statement of cash flows.

LO5 SE 7. Cash Flows from Financing Activities

During 20x4, Dakota Company issued $1,000,000 in long-term bonds at 96, repaid $150,000 of bonds at face value, paid interest of $80,000, and paid dividends of $50,000. Prepare the cash flows from the financing activities section of the statement of cash flows.

LO1 LO3 LO4 LO5 SE 8. Identifying Components of the Statement of Cash Flows

Assuming the indirect method is used to prepare the statement of cash flows, tell whether each of the following items would appear (a) in cash flows from operating activities, (b) in cash flows from investing activities, (c) in cash flows from financing activities, (d) in the schedule of noncash investing and financing transactions, or (e) not on the statement of cash flows at all:

1. Dividends paid
2. Cash receipts from sales
3. Decrease in accounts receivable
4. Sale of plant assets
5. Gain on sale of investment
6. Issue of stock for plant assets
7. Issue of common stock
8. Net income

Exercises

E 1.
LO1 Classification of Cash Flow Transactions

Trout Corporation engaged in the transactions listed below. Identify each transaction as (a) an operating activity, (b) an investing activity, (c) a financing activity, (d) a noncash transaction, or (e) not on the statement of cash flows. (Assume the indirect method is used.)

1. Declared and paid a cash dividend.
2. Purchased a long-term investment.
3. Increased accounts receivable.
4. Paid interest.
5. Sold equipment at a loss.
6. Issued long-term bonds for plant assets.
7. Increased dividends receivable on securities held.
8. Issued common stock.
9. Declared and issued a stock dividend.
10. Repaid notes payable.
11. Decreased wages payable.
12. Purchased a 60-day Treasury bill.
13. Purchased land.

E 2.
LO2 Cash-Generating Efficiency Ratios and Free Cash Flow

In 20x5, Ignatz Corporation had year-end assets of $4,800,000, net sales of $6,600,000, net income of $560,000, net cash flows from operating activities of $780,000, dividends of $240,000, and net capital expenditures of $820,000. In 20x4, year-end assets were $4,200,000.

Calculate the cash-generating efficiency ratios of cash flow yield, cash flows to sales, and cash flows to assets. Also calculate free cash flow.

E 3.
LO3 Cash Flows from Operating Activities: Indirect Method

The condensed single-step income statement for the year ended December 31, 20x4, of Gro-More Chem Company, a distributor of farm fertilizers and herbicides, appears as follows:

Sales		$6,500,000
Less: Cost of goods sold	$3,800,000	
Operating expenses (including depreciation of $410,000)	1,900,000	
Income taxes	200,000	5,900,000
Net income		$ 600,000

Selected accounts from Gro-More Chem Company's balance sheets for 20x4 and 20x3 are as follows:

	20x4	20x3
Accounts receivable, net	$1,200,000	$850,000
Inventory	420,000	510,000
Prepaid expenses	130,000	90,000
Accounts payable	480,000	360,000
Accrued liabilities	30,000	50,000
Income taxes payable	70,000	60,000

Present in good form a schedule of cash flows from operating activities using the indirect method.

E 4.
LO3 Computing Cash Flows from Operating Activities: Indirect Method

During 20x5, Germaine Corporation had net income of $41,000. Included on its income statement were depreciation expense of $2,300 and amortization expense of $300. During the year, Accounts Receivable increased by $3,400, Inventories decreased by $1,900, Prepaid Expenses decreased by $200, Accounts Payable increased by $5,000, and Accrued Liabilities decreased by $450. Determine net cash flows from operating activities using the indirect method.

E 5.
LO3 Preparing a Schedule of Cash Flows from Operating Activities: Indirect Method

For the year ended June 30, 20xx, net income for Pine Corporation was $7,400. Depreciation expense was $2,000. During the year, Accounts Receivable increased by $4,400, Inventories increased by $7,000, Prepaid Rent decreased by $1,400, Accounts Payable increased by $14,000, Salaries Payable increased by $1,000, and Income Taxes Payable decreased by $600. Use the indirect method to prepare a schedule of cash flows from operating activities.

E 6.

LO4 Computing Cash Flows from Investing Activities: Investments

FBR Company's T account for long-term available-for-sale investments at the end of 20x3 is as follows:

Investments			
Beg. Bal.	38,000	Sales	39,000
Purchases	58,000		
End Bal.	57,000		

In addition, FBR's income statement shows a loss on the sale of investments of $6,500. Compute the amounts to be shown as cash flows from investing activities and show how they are to appear in the statement of cash flows.

E 7.

LO4 Computing Cash Flows from Investing Activities: Plant Assets

The T accounts for plant assets and accumulated depreciation for FBR Company at the end of 20x3 are as follows:

Plant Assets				Accumulated Depreciation			
Beg. Bal.	65,000	Disposals	23,000	Disposals	14,700	Beg. Bal.	34,500
Purchases	33,600					Depreciation	10,200
End. Bal.	75,600					End. Bal.	30,000

In addition, FBR Company's income statement shows a gain on sale of plant assets of $4,400. Compute the amounts to be shown as cash flows from investing activities and show how they are to appear on the statement of cash flows.

E 8.

LO4 Determining Cash Flows from
LO5 Investing and Financing Activities

All transactions involving Notes Payable and related accounts of Wix Company during 20x4 are as follows:

```
Cash                                          18,000
   Notes Payable                                      18,000
       Bank loan
Patent                                        30,000
   Notes Payable                                      30,000
       Purchase of patent by issuing note payable
Notes Payable                                  5,000
Interest Expense                                 500
   Cash                                                5,500
       Repayment of note payable at maturity
```

Determine the amounts of the transactions affecting financing activities and show how they are to appear on the statement of cash flows for 20x4.

E 9.

LO3 Preparing the Statement of
LO4 Cash Flows: Indirect Method
LO5

Margol Corporation's 20x5 income statement appears below. Its comparative balance sheets for June 30, 20x5 and 20x4 are on the next page.

Margol Corporation
Income Statement
For the Year Ended June 30, 20x5

Sales		$468,000
Cost of goods sold		312,000
Gross margin		$156,000
Operating expenses		90,000
Operating income		$ 66,000
Interest expense		5,600
Income before income taxes		$ 60,400
Income taxes		24,600
Net income		$ 35,800

Margol Corporation
Comparative Balance Sheets
June 30, 20x5 and 20x4

	20x5	20x4
Assets		
Cash	$139,800	$ 25,000
Accounts receivable (net)	42,000	52,000
Inventory	86,800	96,800
Prepaid expenses	6,400	5,200
Furniture	110,000	120,000
Accumulated depreciation, furniture	(18,000)	(10,000)
Total assets	$367,000	$289,000
Liabilities and Stockholders' Equity		
Accounts payable	$ 26,000	$ 28,000
Income taxes payable	2,400	3,600
Notes payable (long-term)	74,000	70,000
Common stock, $10 par value	230,000	180,000
Retained earnings	34,600	7,400
Total liabilities and stockholders' equity	$367,000	$289,000

The following information is also available: The company issued a $44,000 note payable for purchase of furniture; sold furniture that cost $54,000 with accumulated depreciation of $30,600 at carrying value; recorded depreciation on the furniture during the year, $38,600; repaid a note in the amount of $40,000; issued $50,000 of common stock at par value; and declared and paid dividends of $8,600.

Prepare Margol Corporation's statement of cash flows for the year 20x5 using the indirect method.

Problems

LO1 Classification of Cash Flow Transactions

P 1. Analyze each transaction listed in the table that follows and place X's in the appropriate columns to indicate the transaction's classification and its effect on cash flows using the indirect method.

Transaction	Operating Activity	Investing Activity	Financing Activity	Noncash Transaction	Increase	Decrease	No Effect
1. Incurred a net loss.							
2. Declared and issued a stock dividend.							
3. Paid a cash dividend.							
4. Decreased accounts receivable.							
5. Increased inventory.							
6. Retired long-term debt with cash.							
7. Sold available-for-sale securities at a loss.							
8. Issued stock for equipment.							
9. Decreased prepaid insurance.							
10. Purchased treasury stock with cash.							
11. Retired a fully depreciated truck (no gain or loss).							
12. Increased interest payable.							
13. Decreased dividends receivable on investment.							
14. Sold treasury stock.							
15. Increased income taxes payable.							
16. Transferred cash to money market account.							
17. Purchased land and building with a mortgage.							

LO2 Statement of Cash Flows:
LO3 Indirect Method
LO4
LO5

P 2. Maron Corporation's comparative balance sheets as of December 31, 20x5 and 20x4 and its income statement for the year ended December 31, 20x5 are presented on the next page.

During 20x5, Maron Corporation sold furniture and fixtures that cost $35,600, on which it had accumulated depreciation of $28,800, at a gain of $7,000. The corporation also purchased furniture and fixtures in the amount of $39,600; paid a $20,000 note payable and borrowed $40,000 on a new note; converted bonds payable in the amount of $100,000 into 2,000 shares of common stock; and declared and paid $6,000 in cash dividends.

REQUIRED

1. Using the indirect method, prepare a statement of cash flows for Maron Corporation. Include a supporting schedule of noncash investing and financing transactions.

Maron Corporation
Comparative Balance Sheets
December 31, 20x5 and 20x4

	20x5	20x4
Assets		
Cash	$164,800	$ 50,000
Accounts receivable (net)	165,200	200,000
Merchandise inventory	350,000	450,000
Prepaid rent	2,000	3,000
Furniture and fixtures	148,000	144,000
Accumulated depreciation, furniture and fixtures	(42,000)	(24,000)
Total assets	$788,000	$823,000
Liabilities and Stockholders' Equity		
Accounts payable	$143,400	$200,400
Income taxes payable	1,400	4,400
Notes payable (long-term)	40,000	20,000
Bonds payable	100,000	200,000
Common stock, $20 par value	240,000	200,000
Paid-in capital in excess of par value, common	181,440	121,440
Retained earnings	81,760	76,760
Total liabilities and stockholders' equity	$788,000	$823,000

Maron Corporation
Income Statement
For the Year Ended December 31, 20x5

Net sales		$1,609,000
Cost of goods sold		1,127,800
Gross margin		$ 481,200
Operating expenses (including depreciation expense of $46,800)		449,400
Income from operations		$ 31,800
Other income (expenses)		
Gain on sale of furniture and fixtures	$ 7,000	
Interest expense	(23,200)	(16,200)
Income before income taxes		$ 15,600
Income taxes		4,600
Net income		$ 11,000

2. What are the primary reasons for Maron Corporation's large increase in cash from 20x4 to 20x5, despite its low net income?
3. Compute and assess cash flow yield and free cash flow for 20x5.

P 3. The comparative balance sheets for Pierre Fabrics, Inc., for December 31, 20x5, and 20x4 appear below.

LO2 Statement of Cash Flows:
LO3 Indirect Method
LO4
LO5

Pierre Fabrics, Inc.
Comparative Balance Sheets
December 31, 20x5 and 20x4

	20x5	20x4
Assets		
Cash	$ 38,560	$ 27,360
Accounts receivable (net)	102,430	75,430
Inventory	112,890	137,890
Prepaid expenses	—	20,000
Land	25,000	—
Building	137,000	—
Accumulated depreciation, building	(15,000)	—
Equipment	33,000	34,000
Accumulated depreciation, equipment	(14,500)	(24,000)
Patents	4,000	6,000
Total assets	$423,380	$276,680
Liabilities and Stockholders' Equity		
Accounts payable	$ 10,750	$ 36,750
Notes payable (current)	10,000	—
Accrued liabilities	—	12,300
Mortgage payable	162,000	—
Common stock, $10 par value	180,000	150,000
Paid-in capital in excess of par value, common	57,200	37,200
Retained earnings	3,430	40,430
Total liabilities and stockholders' equity	$423,380	$276,680

Additional information about Pierre Fabrics' operations during 20x5 is as follows: net loss, $28,000; building and equipment depreciation expense amounts, $15,000 and $3,000, respectively; equipment that cost $13,500 with accumulated depreciation of $12,500 sold for a gain of $5,300; equipment purchases, $12,500; patent amortization, $3,000; purchase of patent, $1,000; funds borrowed by issuing notes payable, $25,000; notes payable repaid, $15,000; land and building purchased for $162,000 by signing a mortgage for the total cost; 3,000 shares of $10 par value common stock issued for a total of $50,000; and cash dividend paid, $9,000.

REQUIRED
1. Using the indirect method, prepare a statement of cash flows for Pierre Fabrics, Inc.
2. Why did Pierre Fabrics have an increase in cash in a year in which it recorded a net loss of $28,000? Discuss and interpret.
3. Compute and assess cash flow yield and free cash flow for 20x5.

P 4. The comparative balance sheets for Maggio Masonry, Inc., for December 31, 20x5 and 20x4 are presented on the next page. During 20x5, the company had net income of $96,000 and building and equipment depreciation expenses of $80,000 and $60,000, respectively. It amortized intangible assets in the amount of $20,000; purchased

LO2 Statement of Cash Flows:
LO3 Indirect Method
LO4
LO5

Maggio Masonry, Inc.
Comparative Balance Sheets
December 31, 20x5 and 20x4

	20x5	20x4
Assets		
Cash	$ 257,600	$ 305,600
Accounts receivable (net)	738,800	758,800
Inventory	960,000	800,000
Prepaid expenses	14,800	26,800
Long-term investments	440,000	440,000
Land	361,200	321,200
Building	1,200,000	920,000
Accumulated depreciation, building	(240,000)	(160,000)
Equipment	480,000	480,000
Accumulated depreciation, equipment	(116,000)	(56,000)
Intangible assets	20,000	40,000
Total assets	$4,116,400	$3,876,400
Liabilities and Stockholders' Equity		
Accounts payable	$ 470,800	$ 660,800
Notes payable (current)	40,000	160,000
Accrued liabilities	10,800	20,800
Mortgage payable	1,080,000	800,000
Bonds payable	1,000,000	760,000
Common stock	1,300,000	1,300,000
Paid-in capital in excess of par value, common	80,000	80,000
Retained earnings	254,800	194,800
Treasury stock	(120,000)	(100,000)
Total liabilities and stockholders' equity	$4,116,400	$3,876,400

investments for $116,000; sold investments for $150,000, on which it recorded a gain of $34,000; issued $240,000 of long-term bonds at face value; purchased a warehouse and land through a $320,000 mortgage; paid $40,000 to reduce the mortgage; borrowed $60,000 by issuing notes payable; repaid notes payable in the amount of $180,000; declared and paid cash dividends in the amount of $36,000; and purchased treasury stock in the amount of $20,000.

REQUIRED

1. Using the indirect method, prepare a statement of cash flows for Maggio Masonry, Inc.
2. Why did Maggio Masonry experience a decrease in cash in a year in which it had a net income of $96,000? Discuss and interpret.
3. Compute and assess cash flow yield and free cash flow for 20x5.

ALTERNATE PROBLEMS

P 5. Analyze each transaction listed in the table that follows and place X's in the appropriate columns to indicate the transaction's classification and its effect on cash flows using the indirect method.

LO1 Classification of Cash Flow Transactions

	Cash Flow Classification				Effect on Cash Flows		
Transaction	Operating Activity	Investing Activity	Financing Activity	Noncash Transaction	Increase	Decrease	No Effect
1. Earned a net income.							
2. Declared and paid a cash dividend.							
3. Issued stock for cash.							
4. Retired long-term debt by issuing stock.							
5. Increased accounts payable.							
6. Decreased inventory.							
7. Increased prepaid insurance.							
8. Purchased a long-term investment with cash.							
9. Sold trading securities at a gain.							
10. Sold a machine at a loss.							
11. Retired fully depreciated equipment.							
12. Decreased interest payable.							
13. Purchased available-for-sale securities (long-term).							
14. Decreased dividends receivable.							
15. Decreased accounts receivable.							
16. Converted bonds to common stock.							
17. Purchased 90-day Treasury bill.							

P 6. Sulyat Corporation's income statement for 20x7 appears below.

LO2 **Statement of Cash Flows:**
LO3 **Indirect Method**
LO4
LO5

Sulyat Corporation
Income Statement
For the Year Ended June 30, 20x7

Net sales		$1,040,900
Cost of goods sold		656,300
Gross margin		$ 384,600
Operating expenses (including depreciation expense of $60,000)		189,200
Income from operations		$ 195,400
Other income (expenses)		
Loss on sale of equipment	($ 4,000)	
Interest expense	(37,600)	(41,600)
Income before income taxes		$ 153,800
Income taxes		34,200
Net income		$ 119,600

Sulyat Corporation's comparative balance sheets as of June 30, 20x7 and 20x6 are as follows:

Sulyat Corporation
Comparative Balance Sheets
June 30, 20x7 and 20x6

	20x7	20x6
Assets		
Cash	$167,000	$ 20,000
Accounts receivable (net)	100,000	120,000
Inventory	180,000	220,000
Prepaid expenses	600	1,000
Property, plant, and equipment	628,000	552,000
Accumulated depreciation, property, plant, and equipment	(183,000)	(140,000)
Total assets	$892,600	$773,000
Liabilities and Stockholders' Equity		
Accounts payable	$ 64,000	$ 42,000
Notes payable (due in 90 days)	30,000	80,000
Income taxes payable	26,000	18,000
Mortgage payable	360,000	280,000
Common stock, $5 par value	200,000	200,000
Retained earnings	212,600	153,000
Total liabilities and stockholders' equity	$892,600	$773,000

During 20x7, Sulyat Corporation sold equipment that cost $24,000, on which it had accumulated depreciation of $17,000, at a loss of $4,000. The corporation also purchased land and a building for $100,000 through an increase of $100,000 in Mortgage Payable; made a $20,000 payment on the mortgage; repaid notes of $80,000 but borrowed an additional $30,000 through the issuance of a new note payable; and declared and paid a $60,000 cash dividend.

REQUIRED
1. Using the indirect method, prepare a statement of cash flows. Include a supporting schedule of noncash investing and financing transactions.
2. What are the primary reasons for Sulyat Corporation's large increase in cash from 20x6 to 20x7?
3. Compute and assess cash flow yield and free cash flow for 20x7.

P 7. The comparative balance sheets for Fernandez Fashions, Inc., for December 31, 20x6 and 20x5 appear on the next page. Additional information about Fernandez Fashions' operations during 20x6 is as follows: net income, $56,000; building and equipment depreciation expense amounts, $30,000 and $6,000, respectively; equipment that cost $27,000 with accumulated depreciation of $25,000 sold at a gain of $10,600; equipment purchases, $25,000; patent amortization, $6,000; purchase of patent, $2,000; funds borrowed by issuing notes payable, $50,000; notes payable repaid, $30,000; land and building purchased for $324,000 by signing a mortgage for the total cost; 3,000 shares of $20 par value common stock issued for a total of $100,000; cash dividend paid $18,000; and treasury stock purchased, $15,000.

LO2 **Statement of Cash Flows:**
LO3 **Indirect Method**
LO4
LO5